Out of Many

Sixth Edition

VOLUME II

Out of Many

Sixth Edition

A History of the American People

John Mack Faragher
YALE UNIVERSITY

Mari Jo Buhle
BROWN UNIVERSITY

Daniel Czitrom
MOUNT HOLYOKE COLLEGE

Susan H. Armitage
WASHINGTON STATE UNIVERSITY

PEARSON

Prentice
Hall

Upper Saddle River, NJ 07458

Library of Congress Cataloging-in-Publication Data

Out of many: a history of the American people/John Mack Faragher . . . [et al].–6th ed.

   p. cm.

Includes bibliographical references and index.

ISBN 0-13-614955-3 (combined volume)—ISBN 0-13-614956-1 (v. 1)—ISBN 0-13-614957-X (v. 2)

   1. United States–History–Textbooks.   I. Faragher, John Mack

E178.1.O935 2009

973–dc22   2007048426

To Our Students,
Our Sisters,
And Our Brothers

Publisher: Charlyce Jones Owen
Senior Assistant: Maureen Diana
Senior Managing Editor: Mary Carnis
Production Liaison: Louise Rothman
Senior Operations Supervisor: MaryAnn Gloriande
Operations Specialist: Maura Zaldivar
Director of Marketing: Brandy Dawson
Pegasus Program Manager: Mayda Bosco
Lead Media Project Manager: Tina Rudowski
Multimedia Specialist: Alison Lorber
Director, Image Resource Center: Melinda Reo
Manager, Rights & Permissions: Zina Arabia
Manager, Visual Research: Beth Brenzel
Manager, Cover Visual Research & Permissions: Karen Sanatar
Photo Researcher: Diane Austin
Image Permission Coordinator: Michelina Viscusi
Art Manager: Mirella Signoretto

Cartographer: International Mapping Associates
Design Development Art Director: Blair Brown
Cover and Interior Designer: Blair Brown
Cover Images: Portrait of Machito, Jose Mangual, Carlos Vidal(?), and Graciella Grillo, Glen Island Casino, New York, N.Y., ca. July 1947. Courtesy of the Library of Congress; Suffragette Trixie Friganza, descending steps, New York. Courtesy of the Library of Congress; Piegan Indian, Mountain Chief, having his voice recorded by ethnologist Frances Densmore. Courtesy of the Library of Congress; Mining: Gold: Head of Auburn Ravine, 1852. California State Library; New York workers, angered by the Mayor's apparent anti-Vietnam-War sympathies, wave American flags as they march in demonstration near City Hall in New York City, 1905. The Granger Collection.
Composition and Full Service Project Management: Prepare/Emilcomp
Printer/Binder: Quebecor/Dubuque
Cover Printer: Phoenix Color Corporation

Credits and acknowledgments borrowed from other sources and reproduced, with permission, in this textbook appear on appropriate page within text (or on pages C1–C4).

Pearson Education LTD.
Pearson Education Australia PTY, Limited
Pearson Education Singapore, Pte. Ltd
Pearson Education North Asia Ltd

Pearson Education, Canada, Ltd
Pearson Educación de Mexico, S.A. de C.V.
Pearson Education–Japan
Pearson Education Malaysia, Pte. Ltd

10 9 8 7 6 5 4 3 2

ISBN-13: 978-0-13-614957-6
ISBN-10:   0-13-614957-X

BRIEF CONTENTS

CONTENTS

CHAPTER 1

A CONTINENT OF VILLAGES,
to 1500 xlviii

MAPS

CHARTS, GRAPHS & TABLES

OVERVIEW TABLES

PREFACE

Out of Many: A History of the American People, sixth edition, offers a distinctive and timely approach to American history, highlighting the experiences of diverse communities of Americans in the unfolding story of our country. The stories of these communities offer a way of examining the complex historical forces shaping people's lives at various moments in our past. The debates and conflicts surrounding the most momentous issues in our national life—independence, emerging democracy, slavery, westward settlement, imperial expansion, economic depression, war, technological change—were largely worked out in the context of local communities. Through communities we focus on the persistent tensions between everyday life and those larger decisions and events that continually reshape the circumstances of local life. Each chapter opens with a description of a representative community. Some of these portraits feature American communities struggling with one another: African slaves and English masters on the rice plantations of colonial Georgia, or *Tejanos* and Americans during the Texas war of independence. Other chapters feature portraits of communities facing social change: the feminists of Seneca Falls, New York, in 1848, or the African Americans of Montgomery, Alabama, in 1955. As the story unfolds we find communities growing to include ever larger groups of Americans: the soldiers from every colony who forged the Continental Army into a patriotic national force at Valley Forge during the American Revolution, or the moviegoers who aspired to a collective dream of material prosperity and upward mobility during the 1920s.

Out of Many is also the only American history text with a truly continental perspective. With community vignettes from New England to the South, the Midwest to the far West, we encourage students to appreciate the great expanse of our nation. For example, a vignette of seventeenth-century Santa Fé, New Mexico, illustrates the founding of the first European settlements in the New World. We present territorial expansion into the American West from the viewpoint of the Mandan villagers of the upper Missouri River of North Dakota. We introduce the policies of the Reconstruction era through the experience of African Americans in Hale County, Alabama. A continental perspective drives home to students that American history has never been the preserve of any particular region.

Out of Many includes extensive coverage of our diverse heritage. Our country is appropriately known as "a nation of immigrants," and the history of immigration to America, from the seventeenth to the twenty-first centuries, is fully integrated into the text. There is sustained and close attention to our place in the world, with special emphasis on our relations with the nations of the Western Hemisphere, especially our near neighbors, Canada and Mexico. The statistical data in the final chapter has been completely updated with the results of the 2000 census.

In these ways *Out of Many* breaks new ground, but without compromising its coverage of the traditional turning points that we believe are critically important to an understanding of the American past. Among these watershed events are the Revolution and the struggle over the Constitution, the Civil War and Reconstruction, and the Great Depression and World War II. In *Out of Many*, however, we seek to integrate the narrative of national history with the story of the nation's many diverse communities. The Revolutionary and Constitutional period tested the ability of local communities to forge a new unity, and success depended on their ability to build a nation without compromising local identity. The Civil War and Reconstruction formed a second great test of the balance between the national ideas of the Revolution and the power of local and sectional communities. The depression and the New Deal demonstrated the importance of local communities and the growing power of national institutions during the greatest economic challenge in our history. *Out of Many* also looks back in a new and comprehensive way—from the vantage point of the beginning of a new century and the end of the Cold War—at the salient events of the last fifty years and their impact on American communities. The community focus of *Out of Many* weaves the stories of the people and the nation into a single compelling narrative.

Out of Many, sixth edition, is completely updated with the most recent scholarship on the history of America and the United States. All the chapters have been extensively reviewed, revised, and rewritten. The final chapter details the tumultuous events of the new century, including a completely new section on the "war on terror," and concluding with the national election of 2004. Throughout the book the text and graphics are presented in a stunning new design. Moreover, this edition incorporates two important new features. The sixth edition offers two new features in each chapter designed to bring history vividly alive for students: *Communities in Conflict*, featuring two primary sources that offer opposing voices on a controversial historical issue and *Seeing History*, carefully chosen images that show how visual sources can illuminate their understanding of American history.

SPECIAL FEATURES

With each edition of *Out of Many* we have sought to strengthen its unique integration of the best of traditional American history with its innovative community-based focus and strong continental perspective. This new version is no exception. A wealth of special features and pedagogical aids reinforces our narrative and helps students grasp key issues.

- **Community and Diversity.** This special introductory essay begins students' journey into the narrative history that unfolds in *Out of Many*. The essay acquaints students with the major themes of the book and provides them with a framework for understanding American History. (pp. xliii–xlvi)
- **Communities in Conflict.** *NEW* to this edition, this special feature highlights two primary sources that offer opposing voices on a controversial historical issue. With introductory source notes and critical thinking questions, "Communities in Conflict" offers students and instructors the opportunity to discuss how Americans have struggled to resolve their differences at every point in our past.
- **Seeing History.** *NEW* to this edition, this new feature helps students use visual culture for making sense of the past. These carefully chosen images, with critical thinking questions for interpretation, include a broad array of fine art, drawings, political cartoons, advertisements, and photographs. Encouraged to look at the image with an analytical eye, students will think critically about how visual sources can illuminate their understanding of American history and the important role visuals play in our knowledge of the past.
- **Map Explorations.** *NEW* to this edition—the entire map program has been re-designed. The new attractive design provides more pedagogical support for analyzing and interpreting the information maps provide to the study of history. As in previous editions, selected maps in each chapter can be explored interactively. They provide interactive exploration of key geographical, chronological, and thematic concepts to reinforce the content contained in the maps and the text. Each interactive map is accessible via the url for each individual interactive map and on the new *MyHistoryLab* website available with the text.
- **Overview tables.** Overview tables provide students with a summary of complex issues. Interactive versions are included on the new *MyHistoryLab* website as a review resource.

- **Photos and Illustrations.** The abundant illustrations in *Out of Many* include extensive captions that treat the images as visual primary source documents from the American past, describing their source and explaining their significance. In addition, each chapter includes the new Seeing History feature that highlights a stunning visual and introduces students to the importance of visual documents in the study of history.
- **Chronologies.** A chronology at the end of each chapter helps students build a framework of key events.
- **Review Questions.** Review questions at the end of chapters help students review, reinforce, and retain the material in each chapter and encourage them to relate the material to broader issues in American history.
- **Recommended Readings.** The works in the short, annotated Recommended Reading list at the end of each chapter have been selected with the interested introductory student in mind.

SUPPLEMENTARY MATERIAL

Out of Many is supported by an extensive supplements package for instructors and students that gives flexibility to the process of learning. A full description of the supplements available with the text is provided on page xlii.

ACKNOWLEDGMENTS

In the years it has taken to bring *Out of Many* from idea to reality and to improve it in successive editions, we have often been reminded that although writing history sometimes feels like isolated work, it actually involves a collective effort. We want to thank the dozens of people whose efforts have made the publication of this book possible.

We wish to thank our many friends at Prentice Hall for their efforts in creating the sixth edition of *Out of Many*: Yolanda de Rooy, President; Charlyce Jones Owen, Publisher; Jeannine Cilotta and James Miller, Development Editors; Rochelle Diogenes, Editor-in-Chief, Development, Kate Mitchell, Senior Marketing Manager, Brandy Dawson, Director of Marketing, Louise Rothman, Production Liaison; Mary Carnis, Managing Editor, Blair Brown, Interior and Cover Designer, Rosaria Cassinese, Production Editor, and Donna Mulder, Copyeditor.

Although we share joint responsibility for the entire book, the chapters were individually authored: John Mack Faragher wrote chapters 1–8; Susan Armitage wrote chapters 9–16; Mari Jo Buhle wrote chapters 18–20, 25–26, 29; and Daniel Czitrom wrote chapters 17, 21–24, 27–28. (For this edition Buhle and Czitrom co-authored Chapters 30–31.

Each of us depended on a great deal of support and assistance with the research and writing that went into this book. We want to thank: Kathryn Abbott, Nan Boyd, Krista Comer, Jennifer Cote, Crista DeLuzio, Keith Edgerton, Carol Frost, Jesse Hoffnung Garskof, Pailin Gaither, Jane Gerhard, Todd Gernes, Mark Krasovic, Melani McAlister, Cristi, Rebecca McKenna, and Mitchell, J. C. Mutchler, Keith Peterson, Alan Pinkham, Tricia Rose, Gina Rourke, Jessica Shubow, Gordon P. Utz Jr., Maura Young, Teresa Bill, Gill Frank, and Naoko Shibusawa.

Our families and close friends have been supportive and ever so patient over the many years we have devoted to this project. But we want especially to thank Paul Buhle, Meryl Fingrutd, Bob Greene, and Michele Hoffnung.

REVIEWERS AND CONSULTANTS

Historians around the country greatly assisted us by reading and commenting on chapters for this and previous editions. Their many insightful suggestions, encouragement, and dedication have been a tremendous help to us and to the textbook. We want to thank each of them for the commitment of their valuable time and for sharing their experience and ideas.

Jeffrey. S. Adler, *University of Florida*

Jennifer L. Altenhofel, *Taft College*

Lee Annis, *Montgomery College*

Caroline Barton, *Holmes Community College*

Jon S. Blackman, *University of Oklahoma*

James Bradford, *Texas A&M University*

Fran Campbell, *College of Southern Nevada*

Frank Chartrand, *Los Angeles Pierce College*

Robert E. Cray, *Montclair State University*

Lawrence Culver, *Utah State University*

Amy Curry, *Montgomery College*

Alan Downs, *Georgia Southern University*

John T. Duke, *Alvin Community College*

Keith Edgerton, *Montana State University, Billings*

Greg Ference, *Salisbury University*

Kate Foss-Mollan, *University of Wisconsin, Milwaukee*

Jennifer Fry, *King's College*

Michael Gabriel, *Kutztown University*

Jessica Gerard, *Ozarks Technical College*

George Gerdow, *Northeastern Illinois University*

Jerry Gershenhorn, *North Carolina Central University*

Jolyon P. Girard, *Cabrini College*

Wendy Gordon, *SUNY Plattsburgh*

Kathleen Gorman, *Minnesota State University, Mankato*

W. Scott Haine, *College of San Mateo*

Gordon Harvey, *The University of Louisiana, Monroe*

Leslie Heaphy, *Kent State University*

Rebecca Hill, *CUNY, Borough of Manhattan Community College*

Don Jacobson, *Oakton Community College*

Jeff Janowick, *Lansing Community College*

Hasan Jeffries, *Ohio State University*

Jeanette Keith, *Bloomsburg University*

Kathleen Kennedy, *Western Washington University*

William Kerrigan, *Muskingum College*

Jonathan Mercantini, *Canisius College*

Peter Messer, *Mississippi State University*

James Mills, *University of Texas, Brownsville*

Joseph P. Moore III, *University of Vermont*

James Owens, *Oakton Community College*

Ken Poston, *Beaumont Independent School District*

G. David Price, *University of Florida*

Caroline Pruden, *North Carolina State University*

Carol Quirke, *SUNY Old Westbury*

Kathleen L. Riley, *Ohio Dominican University*

James R. Rohrer, *University of Nebraska, Kearney*

Joshua P. Schier, *Western Michigan University*

Melissane Schrems, *St. Lawrence University*

Jeffrey Shepherd, *University of Texas, El Paso*

Jean Stuntz, *West Texas A&M*

Karen R. Utz, *University of Alabama, Birmingham*

James Williams, *Middle Tennessee State University*

Larry Wilson, *San Jacinto College*

James Wolfinger, *DePaul University*

Jason Young, *SUNY Buffalo*

Charles A. Zappia, *San Diego Mesa College*

ABOUT THE AUTHORS

John Mack Faragher

John Mack Faragher is Arthur Unobskey Professor of American History and director of the Howard R. Lamar Center for the Study of Frontiers and Borders at Yale University. Born in Arizona and raised in southern California, he received his B.A. at the University of California, Riverside, and his Ph.D. at Yale University. He is the author of *Women and Men on the Overland Trail* (1979), *Sugar Creek: Life on the Illinois Prairie* (1986), *Daniel Boone: The Life and Legend of an American Pioneer* (1992), *The American West: A New Interpretive History* (2000), and *A Great and Noble Scheme: The Tragic Story of the Expulsion of the French Acadians from their American Homeland* (2005).

Daniel Czitrom

Daniel Czitrom is Professor of History at Mount Holyoke College. Born and raised in New York City, he received his B.A. from the State University of New York at Binghamton and his M.A. and Ph.D. from the University of Wisconsin, Madison. He is the author of *Media and the American Mind: From Morse to McLuhan* (1982), which won the First Books Award of the American Historical Association and has been translated into Spanish and Chinese. He is co-author of *Rediscovering Jacob Riis: Exposure Journalism and Photography in Turn of the Century New York* (2007). He has served as a historical consultant and featured on-camera commentator for several documentary film projects, including the PBS productions *New York: A Documentary Film; American Photography: A Century of Images*; and *The Great Transatlantic Cable*. He currently serves on the Executive Board of the Organization of American Historians.

Mari Jo Buhle

Mari Jo Buhle is William R. Kenan Jr. University Professor and Professor of American Civilization and History at Brown University, specializing in American women's history. She received her B.A. from the University of Illinois, Urbana–Champaign, and her Ph.D. from the University of Wisconsin, Madison. She is the author of *Women and American Socialism, 1870–1920* (1981) and *Feminism and Its Discontents: A Century of Struggle with Psychoanalysis* (1998). She is also coeditor of *Encyclopedia of the American Left*, second edition (1998). Professor Buhle held a fellowship (1991–1996) from the John D. and Catherine T. MacArthur Foundation.

Susan H. Armitage

Susan H. Armitage is Claudius O. and Mary R. Johnson Distinguished Professor of History at Washington State University. She earned her Ph.D. from the London School of Economics and Political Science. Among her many publications on western women's history are three coedited books, *The Women's West* (1987), *So Much To Be Done: Women on the Mining and Ranching Frontier* (1991), and *Writing the Range: Race, Class, and Culture in the Women's West* (1997). She currently serves as an editor of a series of books on women and American history for the University of Illinois Press.

Out of Many

Dear Reader,

Out of Many grew out of our years of experience teaching the American history survey course. When we were young professors, the old narrative of strict political history was in the process of being supplemented with a new narrative of social history. But the two remained mostly unconnected. New textbooks sequestered these two narratives in separate chapters. Isn't there a way, we wondered, to write a new, unified narrative of American history, in which political and social history might be combined? This was the inspiration behind *Out of Many*, one of the most successful American History textbooks of this generation. Organized around the theme of American communities, the text offers a single, engaging narrative of American social, economic, and political history.

We began working on this book twenty years ago. It has been a long and rewarding journey. We are proud to have been the first American history college text to put the diversity of America's peoples at the center of our historical experience. Our narrative weaves the distinct experiences and voices of northerners, southerners, and westerners, of African Americans, Latinos, and immigrants, of women and men, throughout each chapter. Coming ourselves from different backgrounds and from different regions of the country, we developed a continental approach to the American past, demonstrating how each region has been closely linked to the broader currents of global development. It is our hope that *Out of Many* will best help students understand the history that has produced the increasingly complex America of the twenty-first century.

Out of Many provides truly integrated coverage of American social and political history. The authors weave the everyday stories of individuals and communities and the major events of the nation's history into a single compelling narrative that both enlightens and inspires students.

PACIFIC
OCEAN

Gulf of Mex

MAP 5.2 Growing Use of the Horse by Plains Indians In the seventeenth and eighteenth centuries, Spanish settlers introduced horses into their New Mexican colony. Through trading and raiding, horses spread northward in streams both west and east of the Rocky Mountains. The horse, whose genetic ancestor had been native to the American continent in pre-Archaic times, offered the Indian peoples of the Great Plains the opportunity to create a distinctive hunting and warrior culture.

north. With Portolá were Franciscan missionaries led by Junípero Serra, president of the missions in Baja. At the harbor of San Diego their company, composed of some 200 men, founded the first mission and presidio in present-day California. Portolá then proceeded overland, becoming the first European to explore the interior valleys and mountains, and in 1770 he and Serra established their headquarters at Monterey Bay on the central coast. In 1774 Captain Juan Bautista de Anza and a small party of soldiers blazed an overland route across the deserts connecting Arizona to California, and two years later he chose the sites for the presidio and mission of San Francisco. Over the next fifty years the number of California settlements grew to include twenty-one missions and a half-dozen presidios and pueblos (towns), including Los Angeles, founded in 1781 by a group of mestizo pio-

neers. By the end of the century Los Angeles, with a population of only 300, was California's largest settlement.

The Spanish plan for California called for converting the natives to Catholicism, subjecting them to the rule of the crown, and putting them to work raising the subsistence necessary for a small civil and military establishment that would hold the province against colonial rivals. The first contacts between Franciscans and natives were not encouraging. "What is it you seek here," a chief and his entourage of warriors shouted at the missionaries. "Get out of our country!" But numerous native families were attracted by offerings of food and clothing, by new tools and crafts, and by fascination with the spiritual power of the newcomers. Gradually the Spanish built a flourishing local economy based on irrigated farming

Out of Many's **richly detailed narrative** offers an in-depth social history of the nation's diverse communities as well as coverage of the key events that make up America's political history. This integrated approach to history offers students the best possible insight into the American experience.

. . .through an integrated social and political narrative.

secret fraternal societies open o[...] tants who pledged never to vote for a Ca[...] grounds that all Catholics took their orders straight from the pope in Rome. When questioned about their beliefs, [...]nt into northern [...]ery) wings. Soon after [...] had voted for the Know-[...]pport to another new party, one [...]any characteristics of the Whigs with a westward-looking, expansionist, free-soil policy. This was the Republican Party, founded in 1854.

SEEING HISTORY

Brooks Beats Sumner

SOUTHERN CHIVALRY — ARGUMENT versus CLUB'S.

In a violent episode on the floor of the U.S. Senate in 1856, Senator Charles Sumner of Massachusetts suffered permanent injury in a vicious attack by Congressman Preston Brooks of South Carolina. Trapped at his desk, Sumner was helpless as Brooks beat him so hard with his cane that it broke. A few days earlier, Sumner had given an insulting antislavery speech. Using the abusive, accusatory style favored by abolitionists, he had singled out for ridicule Senator Andrew Butler of South Carolina, charging him with choosing "the harlot, slavery" as his mistress. Senator Butler was Preston Brooks's uncle; in Brooks's mind, he was simply avenging an intolerable affront to his uncle's honor.

So far had the behavioral codes of North and South diverged that each man found his own action perfectly justifiable and the action of the other outrageous. Their attitudes were mirrored in their respective sections. Protest rallies were held in most northern cities; Sumner himself received sympathy letters from hundreds of strangers, all expressing indignation, as one writer put it, over "the most foul, most damnable and dastardly attack," and sympathetic illustrations like this one appeared in northern papers. In contrast, southern newspapers almost unanimously supported Brooks, regarding it as a well-deserved whipping for an intolerable insult. A group of Charleston merchants even bought Brooks a new cane inscribed: "Hit him again."

What would a southern version of this episode look like? Which version is "true"?

New *Seeing History* features offer in-depth analysis of an image or series of images from a particular historical period. These visually engaging features help students to understand how various individuals and events have been depicted throughout American history and underscore the important role images and illustrations play in understanding and interpreting the past.

Out of Many, you experience America's history...

The history of America lies in the stories of the nation's diverse communities—from African Americans to Latinos to Native Americans, from New England fisherman to ranchers of the Great Plains. *Out of Many* is among the first textbooks to focus on the history of the many ethnic and multicultural communities that have played a vital role in the evolution of the United States.

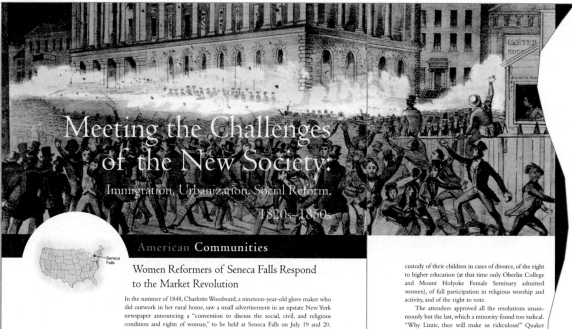

Meeting the Challenges of the New Society:
Immigration, Urbanization, Social Reform, 1820s–1850s

American **Communities**

Women Reformers of Seneca Falls Respond to the Market Revolution

In the summer of 1848, Charlotte Woodward, a nineteen-year-old glove maker who did outwork in her rural home, saw a small advertisement in an upstate New York newspaper announcing a "convention to discuss the social, civil, and religious condition and rights of woman," to be held at Seneca Falls on July 19 and 20. Woodward persuaded six friends to join her in the forty-mile journey to the convention. "At first we travelled quite alone," she recalled. "But before we had gone many miles we came on other wagon-loads of women, bound in the same direction. As we reached different crossroads we saw wagons coming from every part of the country, and long before we reached Seneca Falls we were a procession."

To the surprise of the convention organizers, almost 300 people—men as well as women—attended the two-day meeting, which focused on the Declaration of Sentiments, a petition for women's rights modeled on the Declaration of Independence. "We hold these truths to be self-evident," it announced: "That all men and women are created equal." As the Declaration of Independence detailed the oppressions King George III had imposed on the colonists, the Declaration of Sentiments detailed, in a series of resolutions, the oppressions men had imposed on women. Men had deprived women of legal rights, of the right to own their own property, of

custody of their children in cases of divorce, of the right to higher education (at that time only Oberlin College and Mount Holyoke Female Seminary admitted women), of full participation in religious worship and activity, and of the right to vote.

The attendees approved all the resolutions unanimously but the last, which a minority found too radical. "Why Lizzie, thee will make us ridiculous!" Quaker Lucretia Mott had exclaimed when Elizabeth Cady Stanton proposed the voting rights measure. Indeed the newspapers reporting on the convention thought the demand for the vote was ridiculously unfeminine. Undeterred, and buoyed by the success of this first women's rights convention, the group promptly planned another convention to reach new supporters and develop strategies to implement their resolutions.

The struggle for women's rights was only one of many reform movements that emerged in the United States in the wake of the economic and social disruptions of the market revolution that deeply affected regions like Seneca Falls. A farming frontier in ➤

Each chapter begins with an ***American Community*** feature that shows how the events discussed in the chapter affected a particular community. These snapshots of life add up to a well-rounded understanding of the American story.

...through a focus on the nation's diverse communities.

COMMUNITIES *in* CONFLICT

Two Sides of Anti-Imperialism

Industrialist Andrew Carnegie (1835–1919) gave generously to help finance the Anti-Imperialist League from its formation until his death. He also served as a vice president of the league. His position on American expansion was complex, arising out of his opinion that some peoples were incapable of assimilation into a democratic society. For example, Carnegie reluctantly agreed with the annexation of Hawai'i, in part because the islands were only thinly settled and, therefore, could absorb more advanced "races," including American immigrants. Strongly opposed to acquiring the Philippines, he made an offer to President McKinley to purchase the islands from the United States, after which he would restore governance to the Filipinos. McKinley rejected this offer, ensuring Carnegie's

alliance with the anti-imperialists. His statement was originally published in August 1898, when U.S. forces were invading the Philippines and Americans were debating what to do with the Spanish colonies.

The widow of a prominent businessman and throughout her life a committed reformer, Josephine Shaw Lowell (1843–1905) also opposed the Spanish-American War. Like Carnegie, she denounced the annexation of the Philippines and likewise was a leader of the Anti-Imperialist League, serving as a vice president from 1901 to 1905. Lowell wrote her impassioned protest after the outbreak of Filipino resistance against American rule but before the U.S. Army completed its bloody subjugation of the islands.

Are these two arguments contradictory or complementary?
Is there more to Carnegie's objection to imperialism than racism? And is Lowell correct in arguing
that some wars can be not only just but also morally elevating?

Andrew Carnegie, Anti-Imperialist:
America Cannot Absorb Alien Populations
(August 1898)

Is the Republic, the apostle of Triumphant Democracy, of the rule of the people, to abandon her political creed and endeavor to establish in other lands the rule of the foreigner over the people, Triumphant Despotism?

Is the Republic to remain one homogeneous whole, one united people, or to become a scattered and disjointed aggregate of widely separated and alien races?

Is she to continue the task of developing her vast continent until it holds a population as great as that of Europe, all Americans, or to abandon that destiny to annex, and to attempt to govern, other far distant parts of the world as outlying possessions, which can never be integral parts of the Republic? . . .

There are two kinds of national possessions, one colonies, the other dependencies. In the former we establish and reproduce our own race. Thus Britain has peopled Canada and Australia with English-speaking people, who have naturally adopted our ideas of self-government.

With dependencies it is otherwise. The most grievous burden which Britain has upon her shoulders is that of India, for there it is impossible for our race to grow. The child of English-speaking parents must be removed and reared in Britain. The

British Indian official must have long respites in his native land. India means death to our race. The characteristic feature of a dependency is that the acquiring power cannot reproduce its own race there.

If we could establish colonies of Americans, and grow Americans in any part of the world now unpopulated and unclaimed by any of the great powers, and thus follow the example of Britain, heart and mind might tell us that we should have to think twice, yea, thrice, before deciding adversely. Even then our decision should be adverse; but there is at present no such question before us. What we have to face is the question whether we should embark upon the difficult and dangerous policy of undertaking the government of alien races in lands where it is impossible for our own race to be produced . . . .

I am no "Little" American, afraid of growth, either in population or territory, provided always that the new territory be American, and that it will produce Americans, and not foreign races bound in time to be false to the Republic in order to be true to themselves . . . . The Philippines have about seven and a half millions of people, composed of races bitterly hostile to one another, alien races, ignorant of our language and institutions. Americans cannot be grown there . . . .

SOURCE: Andrew Carnegie, "Distant Possessions: The Parting of the Ways," in *The Gospel of Wealth* (New York: Century Company, 1901), p. 151. Originally published in the *North American Review* (August. 1898).

> "[T]he question [is] whether we should embark upon the difficult and dangerous policy of undertaking the government of alien races . . . ."

Josephine Shaw Lowell, Anti-Imperialist:
America Must Not Wage Unjust
Wars (ca. 1900)

I cannot speak on this subject without making a distinction between different kinds of wars.

A war which requires personal sacrifice, a war which makes a whole people place patriotism and public duty above private comfort and ease, which forces men and women out of self-indulgence, devotion to material wealth—such a war does not as a whole cause moral deterioration—but on the contrary, moral development in a nation.

Such a war was the Civil War in this country, forty years ago . . . .

The history of the introduction of the United States to the Philippine Islands is a disgraceful one . . . In December, 1898 . . . the President of the United States proclaimed sovereignty over the Philippine Archipelago, this naturally aroused the anger of the Filipinos, who had been treasuring for six months or more the hope that the United States intended to help and protect their young republic against the attacks of other nations, and the feelings became more and more bitter, and finally culminated in a fight between the outposts of the two armies on February 4, 1899; and from that time, the United States devoted itself to the task of crushing out what was called the insurrection of the Filipinos.

That is, th[...]
foreign country [...]
those inhabitants [...]
and try to defend [...]
all resistance. The [...]
saying, as did Patr[...]
liberty or give me [...]
un-American, such [...]
gradually more and[...]

It is incredible [...]
so ignorant and so [...]
has been done in th[...]
we are beginning [...]
of the United Stat[...]
Filipino people, f[...]
come the tyrant[...]
backs so compl[...]
country a wor[...]
of all governm[...]
twenty-five y[...]
our moral de[...]
so hardened [...]
that, we sh[...]

SOURCE: "M[...]
*Philanthropic[...]
of Her Life, c[...]
Co., 1911), [...]

New to the Sixth Edition, ***Communities in Conflict*** features reveal how conflicts amongst individuals and groups have changed the course of history. These sections present a primary source passage from each side of a specific event or issue, helping students to see how controversy and discussion have shaped America.

Out of Many, you experience America's history...

Every new copy of *Out of Many*, Sixth Edition includes the *Primary Source: Documents in U.S. History* CD-ROM. This versatile resource offers 400 primary source documents—in accessible PDF format—and over 350 images and maps. It also provides a number of features that help students work with documents, including headnotes, focus questions, highlighting and note-taking tools, and a key terms for certain documents.

Primary Source
Documents in U.S. History

View Tutorial | Help | Exit

| Chapter | Theme | Author | Timeline | Recent Documents |

▶ **Chapter 1: A CONTINENT OF VILLAGES TO 1500**

▶ **Chapter 2: WHEN WORLDS COLLIDE 1492-1590**

▶ **Chapter 3: PLANTING COLONIES IN NORTH AMERICA 1588-1701**

▶ **Chapter 4: SLAVERY AND EMPIRE 1441-1770**

▶ **Chapter 5: THE CULTURES OF COLONIAL NORTH AMERICA 1700-1780**

▶ **Chapter 6: FROM EMPIRE TO INDEPENDENCE 1750-1776**

▶ **Chapter 7: THE AMERICAN REVOLUTION 1776-1786**

▶ **Chapter 8: THE NEW NATION 1786-1800**

▶ **Chapter 9: AN AGRARIAN REPUBLIC 1790-1824**

▶ **Chapter 10: THE SOUTH AND SLAVERY 1790s-1850s**

▶ **Chapter 11: THE GROWTH OF DEMOCRACY 1824-1840**

▶ **Chapter 12: INDUSTRY AND THE NORTH 1790s-1840s**

▶ **Chapter 13: COMING TO TERMS WITH THE NEW AGE 1820s-1850s**

▶ **Chapter 14: THE TERRITORIAL EXPANSION OF THE UNITED STATES 1830s-1850s**

An **easy navigation function** allows students to search for documents by chapter, theme, author, or timeline.

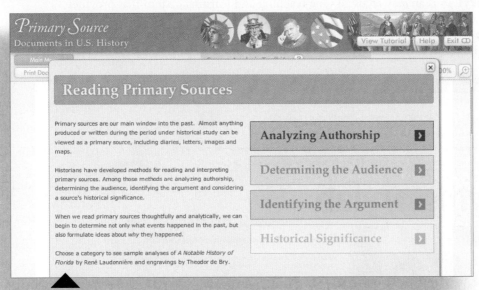

An **interactive tutorial** offers strategies for reading, analyzing, and writing about various types of documents.

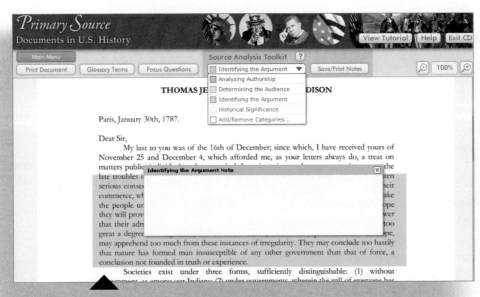

An accessible *Source Analysis Toolkit* helps students easily utilize reading, analyzing, and writing tools.

MyHistoryLab is an easy to use online teaching and learning system that provides helpful tools to both students and instructors. In addition to numerous instructor and student resources, it includes a complete e-book version of *Out of Many*, making the text available to students online.

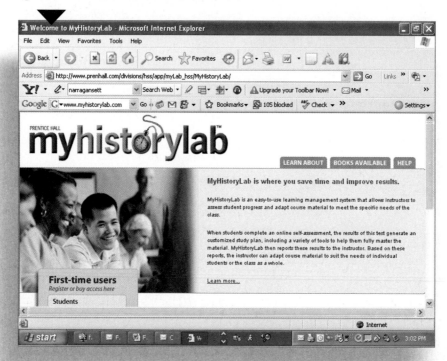

For students

MyHistoryLab is packed with **readings that expand upon the material** found in the text. These include over 300 primary source documents with questions for analysis as well as classic works such as Thomas Paine's *Common Sense*.

...with MyHistoryLab.

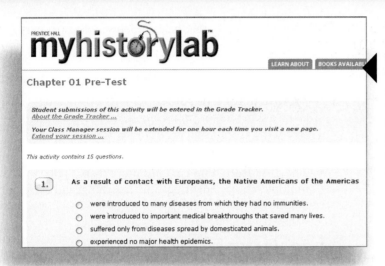

MyHistoryLab offers students various **review and assessment tools** in one convenient online platform. Self-study quizzes with targeted feedback help students assess their progress. A study guide, PowerPoint™ presentations, and key terms flashcards help students master the material in preparation for exams.

MyHistoryLab interactive activities and exercises let students explore materials from the text in an engaging fashion. MyHistoryLab brings U.S. history to life via *Exploring America* interactive learning activities, map explorations, animation, and audio and video clips.

For instructors

MyHistoryLab is a one-stop collection of instructional material for teaching from *Out of Many*, including the instructor's manual, the test item file, images, maps, charts, and graphs from the text, video and audio clips, and PowerPoint™ lecture presentations. In addition, MyHistoryLab provides instructor access to all student resources.

For more information, visit www.myhistorylab.com and click Prentice Hall.

Prentice Hall is proud to offer a number of resources that help students and instructors get the most from *Out of Many*.

For students

- A robust **Study Guide** provides practice tests, essay questions, chronologies, an expanded map skills section, and *Interpreting the Past* activities for each chapter.
  For **Volume I**: 978-0-13-602836-9
  For **Volume II**: 978-0-13-602835-2

- A full-color **Atlas of United States History** offers maps and charts depicting crucial times and events in American History. An index lists historically important places, areas, events, and geographical features.
  978-0-13-603349-3

- **VangoNotes** downloadable audio study guides are ideal for both concept review and exam preparation. The content is tied, chapter-by-chapter, to *Out of Many* and includes *Big Ideas* overviews, practice tests, audio flashcards of key terms, and *Rapid Review* quick drill sessions for each chapter.
  www.vangonotes.com

- The print version of **Primary Source: Documents in U.S. History** presents a collection of more than 300 primary source documents that directly relate to the themes and content of the text.
  For **Volume I**: 978-0-13-605198-5
  For **Volume II**: 978-0-13-605199-2

For instructors

- The **Instructor's Resource Manual** contains everything instructors need for developing and preparing lecture presentations, including chapter outlines and overviews, lecture topics, discussion questions, and information about audio-visual resources. It also includes a new section on teaching American history.
  978-0-13-602837-6

- An **Instructor's Resource CD-ROM** includes all of the instructor supplements, multimedia resources, images, and art from the text.
  978-0-13-602840-6

- The **Test Item File** contains more than 3,000 multiple-choice, identification, matching, and essay questions.
  978-0-13-602838-3

- **Test Generator**—a computerized test management program available for Windows and Macintosh environments—allows instructors to design their own exams by selecting items from the Test Item File. Instructors may download the Test Gen from the Pearson Instructor Resource Center.
  www.prenhall.com/irc

- The **Transparencies Set** offers over 150 full-color transparency acetates of all the maps, charts, and graphs in the text for easy classroom presentation.
  978-0-13-602839-0

- A customized **Retrieving the American Past reader** may be created to accompany *Out of Many*. Instructors can select from a database of 300 primary source documents on key topics in American history to create a reader ideally suited to their course.
  http://www.pearsoncustom.com/database/rtap.html

- The two-volume **American Stories: Biographies in United States History, Third Edition** presents sixty-two biographies of key figures in American history with introductions, pre-reading questions, suggested readings, and a special prologue about the role of biography in the study of American history.
  For **Volumes I**: 978-0-13-182654-0
  For **Volume II**: 978-0-13-182653-3

- The Prentice Hall **Package a Penguin program** provides instructors an opportunity to receive significant discounts on Penguin American history titles when ordered with *Out of Many*.

COMMUNITY & DIVERSITY

One of the most characteristic features of our country is its astounding variety. The American people include the descendants of native Indians, colonial Europeans of British, French, and Spanish background, Africans, and migrants from virtually every country and continent. Indeed, at the beginning of the new century the United States is absorbing a flood of immigrants from Latin America and Asia that rivals the great tide of people from eastern and southern Europe one hundred years before. What's more, our country is one of the world's most spacious, sprawling across than 3.6 million square miles of territory. The struggle to meld a single nation out of our many far-flung communities is what much of American history is all about. That is the story told in this book.

Every human society is made up of communities. A community is a set of relationships linking men, women, and their families to a coherent social whole that is more than the sum of its parts. In a community people develop the capacity for unified action. In a community people learn, often through trial and error, how to transform and adapt to their environment. The sentiment that binds the members of a community together is the mother of group consciousness and ethnic identity. In the making of history, communities are far more important than even the greatest of leaders, for the community is the institution most capable of passing a distinctive historical tradition to future generations.

William Sidney Mount (1807–1868) *California News* 1850. Oil on canvas. The Long Island Museum of American Art, History and Carriages.

Gift of Mr. and Mrs. Ward Melville, 1955.

Harvey Dinnerstein, *Underground, Together* 1996, oil on canvas, 90" × 107".

Photograph courtesy of Gerold Wunderlich & Co., New York, NY.

Communities bind people together in multiple ways. They can be as small as local neighborhoods, in which people maintain face-to-face relations, or as large as the nation itself. This book examines American history from the perspective of community life—an ever-widening frame that has included larger and larger groups of Americans.

Networks of kinship and friendship, and connections across generations and among families, establish the bonds essential to community life. Shared feelings about values and history establish the basis for common identity. In communities, people find the power to act collectively in their own interest. But American communities frequently took shape as a result of serious conflicts among groups, and within communities there was often significant fighting among competing groups or classes. Thus the term *community*, as we use it here, includes conflict and discord as well as harmony and agreement.

For decades Americans have complained about the "loss of community." But community has not disappeared—it has been continuously reinvented. Until the late eighteenth century, community was defined primarily by space

and local geography. But in the nineteenth century communities were reshaped by new and powerful historical forces such as the marketplace, industrialization, the corporation, mass immigration, mass media, and the growth of the nation-state. In the twentieth century, Americans struggled to balance commitments to multiple communities. These were defined not simply by local spatial arrangements, but by categories as varied as race and ethnicity, occupation, political affiliation, and consumer preference.

The "American Communities" vignettes that open each chapter reflect these transformations. Most of the vignettes in the pre–Civil War chapters focus on geographically defined communities, such as the ancient Indian city at Cahokia, or the experiment in industrial urban planning in early nineteenth-century Lowell, Massachusetts. Post–Civil War chapters explore different and more modern kinds of communities. In the 1920s, movies and radio offered communities of identification with dreams of freedom, material success, upward mobility, youth and beauty. In the 1950s, rock 'n' roll music helped germinate a new national community of teenagers, with profound effects on the culture of the entire country in the second half of the twentieth century. In the late 1970s, fear of nuclear accidents like the one at Three Mile Island brought concerned citizens together in communities around the country and encouraged a national movement opposing nuclear power.

The title for our book was suggested by the Latin phrase selected by John Adams, Benjamin Franklin, and Thomas Jefferson for the Great Seal of the United States: *E Pluribus Unum*—"Out of Many Comes Unity." These men understood that unity could not be imposed by a powerful central authority but had to develop out of mutual respect among Americans of different backgrounds. The revolutionary leadership expressed the hope that such respect could grow on the basis of a remarkable proposition: "We hold these truths to be self-evident, that all men are created equal; that they are endowed by their Creator with certain unalienable rights; that among these are life, liberty, and the pursuit of happiness." The national government of the United States would preserve local and state authority but would guarantee individual rights. The nation would be strengthened by guarantees of difference.

"Out of Many" comes strength. That is the promise of America and the premise of this book. The underlying dialectic of American history, we believe, is that as a people we must locate our national unity in the celebration of the differences that exist among us; these differences can be our strength, as long as we affirm the promise of the Declaration. Protecting the "right to be different," in other words, is absolutely fundamental to the continued existence of democracy, and that right is best protected by the existence of strong and vital communities. We are bound together as a nation by the ideal of local and cultural differences protected by our common commitment to the values of the American Revolution.

Today those values are endangered by those who use the tactics of mass terror. In the wake of the September 11, 2001 attack on the United States, and with the continuing threat of biological, chemical, or even nuclear assaults, Americans can not afford to lose faith in our historic vision. The thousands of victims buried in the smoking ruins of the World Trade Center included people from dozens of different ethnic and national groups. The United States is a multicultural and transnational society. We must rededicate ourselves to the protection and defense of the promise of diversity and unity.

Our history demonstrates that the promise has always been problematic. Centrifugal forces have been powerful

Thomas Satterwhite Noble, *Last Sale of Slaves on the Courthouse Steps*, 1860, oil on canvas, Missouri Historical Society.

in the American past, and at times the country seemed about to fracture into its component parts. Our transformation from a collection of groups and regions into a nation was marked by painful and often violent struggles. Our past is filled with conflicts between Indians and colonists, masters and slaves, Patriots and Loyalists, Northerners and Southerners, Easterners and Westerners, capitalists and workers, and sometimes the government and the people. War can bring out our best, but it can also bring out our worst. During World War II thousands of Japanese American citizens were deprived of their rights and locked up in isolated detention centers because of their ethnic background. Americans often appear to be little more than a contentious collection of peoples with conflicting interests, divided by region and background, race and class.

Our most influential leaders have also sometimes suffered a crisis of faith in the American project of "liberty and justice for all." Thomas Jefferson not only believed in the inferiority of African Americans but feared that immigrants from outside the Anglo-American tradition might "warp and bias" the development of the nation "and render it a heterogeneous, incoherent, distracted mass." We have not always lived up to the American promise and there is a dark side to our history. It took the bloodiest war in American history to secure the human rights of African Americans, and the struggle for full equality for all our citizens has yet to be won. During the great influx of immigrants in the early twentieth century, fears much like Jefferson's led to movements to Americanize the foreign born by forcing them, in the words of one leader, "to give up the languages, customs, and methods of life which they have brought with them across the ocean, and adopt instead the language, habits, and customs of this country, and the general standards and ways of American living." Similar thinking motivated Congress at various times to bar the immigration of Africans, Asians, and other people of color into the country, and to force assimilation on American Indians by denying them the freedom to practice their religion or even to speak their own language. Such calls for restrictive unity resound in our own day.

But other Americans have argued for a more fulsome version of Americanization. "What is the American, this new man?" asked the French immigrant Michel Crévecoeur in 1782. "A strange mixture of blood which you will find in no other country." In America, he wrote, "individuals of all nations are melted into a new race of men." A century later Crévecoeur was echoed by historian Frederick Jackson Turner, who believed that "in the crucible of the frontier, the immigrants were Americanized, liberated, and fused into a mixed race, English in neither nationality nor characteristics. The process has gone on from the early days to our own."

The process by which diverse communities have come to share a set of common American values is one of the most fundamental aspects of our history. It did not occur, however, because of compulsory Americanization programs, but because of free public education, popular participation in democratic politics, and the impact of popular culture. Contemporary America does have a common culture: We share a commitment to freedom of thought and expression, we join in the aspirations to own our own homes and send our children to college, we laugh at the same television programs or video clips on You Tube.

To a degree that too few Americans appreciate, this common culture resulted from a complicated process of mutual discovery that took place when different ethnic and regional groups encountered one another. Consider just one small and unique aspect of our culture: the barbecue. Americans have been barbecuing since before the beginning of written history. Early settlers adopted this technique of cooking from the Indians—the word itself comes from a native term for a framework of sticks over a fire on which meat was slowly cooked. Colonists typically barbecued pork, fed on Indian corn. African slaves lent their own touch by introducing the use of spicy sauces. The ritual that is a part of nearly every American family's Fourth of July silently celebrates the heritage of diversity that went into making our common culture.

The American educator John Dewey recognized this diversity early in the last century. "The genuine American, the typical American, is himself a hyphenated character," he declared, "international and interracial in his make-up." It was up to all Americans, Dewey argued, "is to see to it that the hyphen connects instead of separates." We, the authors of *Out of Many*, endorse Dewey's perspective. "Creation comes from the impact of diversity," the American philosopher Horace Kallen wrote about the same time. We also endorse Kallen's vision of the American promise: "A democracy of nationalities, cooperating voluntarily and autonomously through common institutions, . . . a multiplicity in a unity, an orchestration of mankind." And now, let the music begin.

Out of Many

Reconstruction
1863–1877

Hale County, Alabama: From Slavery to Freedom in a Black Belt Community

On a bright Saturday morning in May 1867, 4,000 former slaves streamed into the town of Greensboro, bustling seat of Hale County in west-central Alabama. They came to hear speeches from two delegates to a recent freedmen's convention in Mobile and to find out about the political status of black people under the Reconstruction Act just passed by Congress. Tensions mounted in the days following this unprecedented gathering, as military authorities began supervising voter registration for elections to the upcoming constitutional convention that would rewrite the laws of Alabama. On June 13, John Orrick, a local white, confronted Alex Webb, a politically active freedman, on the streets of Greensboro. Webb had recently been appointed a voter registrar for the district. Orrick swore he would never be registered by a black man and shot Webb dead. Hundreds of armed and angry freedmen formed a posse to search for Orrick but failed to find him. Galvanized by Webb's murder, 500 local freedmen formed a chapter of the Union League, the Republican Party's organizational arm in the South. The chapter functioned as both a militia company and a forum to agitate for political rights.

Violent political encounters between black people and white people were common in southern communities in the wake of the Civil War. Communities

SOURCE: Theo. Kaufmann, "On to Liberty," 1867, Oil on canvas. The Metropolitan Museum of Art. Gift of Erving and Joyce Wolf, 1982 (1982.443.3) Photograph ©1982 The Metropolitan Museum of Art.

throughout the South struggled over the meaning of freedom in ways that reflected their particular circumstances. The 4 million freed people constituted roughly one-third of the total southern population, but the black–white ratio in individual communities varied enormously. In some places, the Union army had been a strong presence during the war, hastening the collapse of the slave system and encouraging experiments in free labor. Other areas had remained relatively untouched by the fighting. In some areas, small farms prevailed; in others, including Hale County, large plantations dominated economic and political life.

West-central Alabama had emerged as a fertile center of cotton production just two decades before the Civil War. There African Americans, as throughout the South's black belt, constituted more than three-quarters of the population. With the arrival of ➤

federal troops in the spring of 1865, African Americans in Hale County, like their counterparts elsewhere, began to challenge the traditional organization of plantation labor.

One owner, Henry Watson, found that his entire workforce had deserted him at the end of 1865. "I am in the midst of a large and fertile cotton growing country," Watson wrote to a partner. "Many plantations are entirely without labor, many plantations have insufficient labor, and upon none are the laborers doing their former accustomed work." Black women refused to work in the fields, preferring to stay home with their children and tend garden plots. Nor would male field hands do any work, such as caring for hogs, that did not directly increase their share of the cotton crop.

Above all, freed people wanted more autonomy. Overseers and owners grudgingly allowed them to work the land "in families," letting them choose their own supervisors and find their own provisions. The result was a shift from the gang labor characteristic of the antebellum period, in which large groups of slaves worked under the harsh and constant supervision of white overseers, to the sharecropping system, in which African American families worked small plots of land in exchange for a small share of the crop. This shift represented less of a victory for newly freed African Americans than a defeat for plantation owners, who resented even the limited economic independence it forced them to concede to their black workforce.

Only a small fraction—perhaps 15 percent—of African American families were fortunate enough to be able to buy land. The majority settled for some version of sharecropping, while others managed to rent land from owners, becoming tenant farmers. Still, planters throughout Hale County had to change the old routines of plantation labor. Local African Americans also organized politically. In 1866, Congress had passed the Civil Rights Act and sent the Fourteenth Amendment to the Constitution to the states for ratification; both promised full citizenship rights to former slaves. Hale County freedmen joined the Republican Party and local Union League chapters. They used their new political power to press for better labor contracts, demand

greater autonomy for the black workforce, and agitate for the more radical goal of land confiscation and redistribution. "The colored people are very anxious to get land of their own to live upon independently; and they want money to buy stock to make crops," reported one black Union League organizer. "The only way to get these necessaries is to give our votes to the [Republican] party." Two Hale County former slaves, Brister Reese and James K. Green, won election to the Alabama state legislature in 1869.

It was not long before these economic and political gains prompted a white counterattack. In the spring of 1868, the Ku Klux Klan—a secret organization devoted to terrorizing and intimidating African Americans and their white Republican allies—came to Hale County. Disguised in white sheets, armed with guns and whips, and making nighttime raids on horseback, Klansmen flogged, beat, and murdered freed people. They intimidated voters and silenced political activists. Planters used Klan terror to dissuade former slaves from leaving plantations or organizing for higher wages. With the passage of the Ku Klux Klan Act in 1871, the federal government cracked down on the Klan, breaking its power temporarily in parts of the former Confederacy. But no serious effort was made to stop Klan terror in the west Alabama black belt, and planters there succeeded in reestablishing much of their social and political control.

The events in Hale County illustrate the struggles that beset communities throughout the South during the Reconstruction era after the Civil War. The destruction of slavery and the Confederacy forced African Americans and white people to renegotiate their old roles. These community battles both shaped and were shaped by the victorious and newly expansive federal government in Washington. But the new arrangements of both political power sharing and the organization of labor had to be worked out within local communities. In the end, Reconstruction was only partially successful. Not until the "Second Reconstruction" of the twentieth-century civil rights movement would the descendants of Hale County's African Americans begin to enjoy the full fruits of freedom—and even then not without challenge.

Focus Questions

1. What were the competing political plans for reconstructing the defeated Confederacy?

2. How did African Americans negotiate the difficult transition from slavery to freedom?

3. What were the most important political and social legacies of Reconstruction in the southern states?

4. How did economic and political transformations in the North reflect another side of Reconstruction?

1863–1877

THE POLITICS OF RECONSTRUCTION

When General Robert E. Lee's men stacked their guns at Appomattox, the bloodiest war in American history ended. More than 600,000 soldiers had died during the four years of fighting, 360,000 Union and 260,000 Confederate. Another 275,000 Union and 190,000 Confederate troops had been wounded. Although President Abraham Lincoln insisted early on that the purpose of the war was to preserve the Union, by 1863 it had evolved as well into a struggle for African American liberation. Indeed, the political, economic, and moral issues posed by slavery were the root cause of the Civil War, and the war ultimately destroyed slavery, although not racism, once and for all.

The Civil War also settled the Constitutional crisis provoked by the secession of the Confederacy and its justification in appeals to states' rights. The name "United States" would from now on be understood as a singular rather than a plural noun, signaling an important change in the meaning of American nationality. The old notion of the United States as a voluntary union of sovereign states gave way to the new reality of a single nation, in which the federal government took precedence over the individual states. The key historical developments of the Reconstruction era revolved around precisely how the newly strengthened national government would define its relationship with the defeated Confederate states and the 4 million newly freed slaves.

THE DEFEATED SOUTH

The white South paid an extremely high price for secession, war, and defeat. In addition to the battlefield casualties, the Confederate states sustained deep material and psychological wounds. Much of the best agricultural land lay waste, including the rich fields of northern Virginia, the Shenandoah Valley, and large sections of Tennessee, Mississippi, Georgia, and South Carolina. Many towns and cities—including Richmond, Atlanta, and Columbia, South Carolina—were in ruins. By 1865, the South's most precious commodities, cotton and African American slaves, no longer were measures of wealth and prestige. Retreating Confederates destroyed most of the South's cotton to prevent its capture by federal troops. What remained was confiscated by Union agents as contraband of war. The former slaves, many of whom had fled to Union lines during the latter stages of the war, were determined to chart their own course in the reconstructed South as free men and women.

Emancipation proved the most bitter pill for white Southerners to swallow, especially the planter elite. Conquered and degraded, and in their view robbed of their slave property, white people responded by regarding African Americans, more than ever, as inferior to themselves. In the antebellum South, white skin had defined a social bond that transcended economic class. It gave even the lowliest poor white a badge of superiority over even the most skilled slave or prosperous free African American. Emancipation, however, forced white people to redefine their world. The specter of political power and social equality for African Americans made racial order the consuming passion of most white Southerners during the Reconstruction years. In fact, racism can be seen as one of the major forces driving Reconstruction and, ultimately, undermining it.

ABRAHAM LINCOLN'S PLAN

By late 1863, Union military victories had convinced President Lincoln of the need to fashion a plan for the

"Decorating the Graves of Rebel Soldiers," *Harper's Weekly,* August 17, 1867. After the Civil War, both Southerners and Northerners created public mourning ceremonies honoring fallen soldiers. Women led the memorial movement in the South that, by establishing cemeteries and erecting monuments, offered the first cultural expression of the Confederate tradition. This engraving depicts citizens of Richmond, Virginia, decorating thousands of Confederate graves with flowers at the Hollywood Memorial Cemetery on the James River. A local women's group raised enough funds to transfer over 16,000 Confederate dead from northern cemeteries for reburial in Richmond.

reconstruction of the South (see Chapter 16). Lincoln based his reconstruction program on bringing the seceded states back into the Union as quickly as possible. His Proclamation of Amnesty and Reconstruction of December 1863 offered "full pardon" and the restoration of property, not including slaves, to white Southerners willing to swear an oath of allegiance to the United States and its laws, including the Emancipation Proclamation. Prominent Confederate military and civil leaders were excluded from Lincoln's offer, though he indicated that he would freely pardon them.

The president also proposed that when the number of any Confederate state's voters who took the oath of allegiance reached 10 percent of the number who had voted in the election of 1860, this group could establish a state government that Lincoln would recognize as legitimate. Fundamental to this Ten Percent Plan was acceptance by the reconstructed governments of the abolition of slavery. Lincoln's plan was designed less as a blueprint for reconstruction than as a way to shorten the war and gain white people's support for emancipation.

Lincoln's amnesty proclamation angered those Republicans—known as Radical Republicans—who advocated not only equal rights for the freedmen but also a tougher stance toward the white South. In July 1864, Senator Benjamin F. Wade of Ohio and Congressman Henry W. Davis of Maryland, both Radicals, pro-

posed a harsher alternative to the Ten Percent Plan. The Wade–Davis bill required 50 percent of a seceding state's white male citizens to take a loyalty oath before elections could be held for a convention to rewrite the state's constitution. The Radical Republicans saw reconstruction as a chance to effect a fundamental transformation of southern society. They thus wanted to delay the process until war's end and to limit participation to a small number of southern Unionists. Lincoln viewed Reconstruction as part of the larger effort to win the war and abolish slavery. He wanted to weaken the Confederacy by creating new state governments that could win broad support from southern white people. The Wade–Davis bill threatened his efforts to build political consensus within the southern states. Lincoln, therefore, pocketvetoed the bill by refusing to sign it within ten days of the adjournment of Congress.

As Union armies occupied parts of the South, commanders improvised a variety of arrangements involving confiscated plantations and the African American labor force. For example, in 1862 General Benjamin F. Butler began a policy of transforming slaves on Louisiana sugar plantations into wage laborers under the close supervision of occupying federal troops. Butler's policy required slaves to remain on the estates of loyal planters, where they would receive wages according to a fixed schedule, as well as food and medical care for the aged and sick. Abandoned plantations would be leased to northern investors.

In January 1865, General William T. Sherman issued Special Field Order 15, setting aside the Sea Islands off the Georgia coast and a portion of the South Carolina lowcountry rice fields for the exclusive settlement of freed people. Each family would receive forty acres of land and the loan of mules from the army—the origin, perhaps, of the famous call for "forty acres and a mule" that would soon capture the imagination of African Americans throughout the South. Sherman's intent was not to revolutionize southern society but to relieve the demands placed on his army by the thousands of impoverished African Americans who followed his march to the sea. By the summer of 1865 some 40,000 freed people, eager to take advantage of the general's order, had been settled on 400,000 acres of "Sherman land."

Photography pioneer Timothy O'Sullivan took this portrait of a multigenerational African American family on the J. J. Smith plantation in Beaufort, South Carolina, in 1862. Many white plantation owners in the area had fled, allowing slaves like these to begin an early transition to freedom before the end of the Civil War.

Conflicts within the Republican Party prevented the development of a systematic land distribution program. Still, Lincoln and the Republican Congress supported other measures to aid the emancipated slaves. In March 1865 Congress established the Freedmen's Bureau. Along with providing food, clothing, and fuel to destitute former slaves, the bureau was charged with supervising and managing "all the abandoned lands in the South and the control of all subjects relating to refugees and freedmen." The act that established the bureau also stated that forty acres of abandoned or confiscated land could be leased to freed slaves or white Unionists, who would have an option to purchase after three years and "such title thereto as the United States can convey."

On the evening of April 14, 1865, while attending the theater in Washington, President Lincoln was shot by John Wilkes Booth and died of his wounds several hours later. At the time of his assassination, Lincoln's reconstruction policy remained unsettled and incomplete. In its broad outlines the president's plans had seemed to favor a speedy restoration of the southern states to the Union and a minimum of federal intervention in their affairs. But with his death the specifics of postwar Reconstruction had to be hammered out by a new president, Andrew Johnson of Tennessee, a man whose personality, political background, and racist leanings put him at odds with the Republican-controlled Congress.

ANDREW JOHNSON AND PRESIDENTIAL RECONSTRUCTION

Andrew Johnson, a Democrat and former slaveholder, was a most unlikely successor to the martyred Lincoln. By trade a tailor, educated by his wife, Johnson overcame his impoverished background and served as state legislator, governor, and U.S. senator. Throughout his career, Johnson had championed yeoman farmers and viewed the South's plantation aristocrats with contempt. He was the only southern member of the U.S. Senate to remain loyal to the Union, and he held the planter elite responsible for secession and defeat. In 1862, Lincoln appointed Johnson to the difficult post of military governor of Tennessee. There he successfully began wartime Reconstruction and cultivated Unionist support in the mountainous eastern districts of that state.

In 1864, the Republicans, in an appeal to northern and border state "War Democrats," nominated Johnson for vice president. But despite Johnson's success in Tennessee and in the 1864 campaign, many Radical Republicans distrusted him, and the hardscrabble Tennessean remained a political outsider in Republican circles. In the immediate aftermath of Lincoln's murder, however, Johnson appeared to side with those Radical Republicans who sought to treat the South as a conquered province. The new president hinted at indicting prominent Confederate officials for treason, disfranchising them, and confiscating their property. Such tough talk appealed to Radical Republicans. But support for Johnson quickly faded as the new president's policies unfolded. Johnson defined Reconstruction as the province of the executive, not the legislative branch, and he planned to restore the Union as quickly as possible. He blamed individual Southerners—the planter elite—rather than entire states for leading the South down the disastrous road to secession. In line with this philosophy, Johnson outlined mild terms for reentry to the Union.

In the spring of 1865, Johnson granted amnesty and pardon, including restoration of property rights except slaves, to all Confederates who pledged loyalty to the Union and support for emancipation. Fourteen classes of Southerners, mostly major Confederate officials and wealthy landowners, were excluded. But these men could apply individually for presidential pardons. (During his tenure Johnson pardoned roughly 90 percent of those who applied.) Significantly, Johnson instituted this plan while Congress was not in session.

By the fall of 1865, ten of the eleven Confederate states claimed to have met Johnson's requirements to reenter the Union. On December 6, 1865, in his first annual message to Congress, the president declared the "restoration" of the Union virtually complete. But a serious division within the federal government was taking shape, for the Congress was not about to allow the president free rein in determining the conditions of southern readmission.

Andrew Johnson used the term "restoration" rather than "reconstruction." A lifelong Democrat with ambitions to be elected president on his own in 1868, Johnson hoped to build a new political coalition composed of northern Democrats, conservative Republicans, and southern Unionists. Firmly committed to white supremacy, he opposed political rights for the freedmen. Johnson's open sympathy for his fellow white Southerners, his antiblack bias, and his determination to control the course of Reconstruction placed him on a collision course with the powerful Radical wing of the Republican Party.

FREE LABOR AND THE RADICAL REPUBLICAN VISION

Most Radicals were men whose careers had been shaped by the slavery controversy. One of the most effective rhetorical weapons used against slavery and its spread had been the ideal of a society based upon free labor. The model of free individuals, competing equally in the labor market and enjoying equal political rights, formed the core of this worldview. Equality of opportunity created a more fluid social structure where, as Abraham Lincoln had noted, "There is not of necessity any such thing as a free hired laborer being fixed in that condition."

Radicals now looked to reconstruct southern society along these same lines, backed by the power of the national government. They argued that once free labor, universal education, and equal rights were implanted in the South, that region would be able to share in the North's material wealth, progress, and social mobility. Representative George W. Julian of Indiana typified the Radical vision for the South. He called for elimination of the region's "large estates, widely scattered settlements, wasteful agriculture, popular ignorance, social degradation, the decline of manufactures, contempt for honest labor, and a pampered oligarchy." This process would allow Republicans to develop "small farms, thrifty tillage, free schools, social independence, flourishing manufactures and the arts, respect for honest labor, and equality of political rights."

In the Radicals' view, the power of the federal government would be central to the remaking of southern society, especially in guaranteeing civil rights and suffrage for freedmen. In the most far-reaching proposal, Representative Thaddeus Stevens of Pennsylvania called for the confiscation of 400 million acres belonging to the wealthiest 10 percent of Southerners to be redistributed to black and white yeomen and northern land buyers. "The whole fabric of Southern society must be changed," Stevens told

Pennsylvania Republicans in September 1865, "and never can it be done if this opportunity is lost. How can republican institutions, free schools, free churches, free social intercourse exist in a mingled community of nabobs and serfs?"

Northern Republicans were especially outraged by the stringent "black codes" passed by South Carolina, Mississippi, Louisiana, and other states. These were designed to restrict the freedom of the black labor force and keep freed people as close to slave status as possible. Laborers who left their jobs before contracts expired would forfeit wages already earned and be subject to arrest by any white citizen. Vagrancy, very broadly defined, was punishable by fines and involuntary plantation labor. Apprenticeship clauses obliged black children to work without pay for employers. Some states attempted to bar African Americans from land ownership. Other laws specifically denied African Americans equality with white people in civil rights, excluding them from juries and prohibiting interracial marriages.

The black codes underscored the unwillingness of white Southerners to accept freedom for African Americans. The Radicals, although not a majority of their party, were joined by moderate Republicans as growing numbers of Northerners grew suspicious of white southern intransigence and the denial of political rights to freedmen. When the Thirty-ninth Congress convened in December 1865, the large Republican majority prevented the seating of the white Southerners elected to Congress under President Johnson's provisional state governments. Republicans also established the Joint Committee on Reconstruction. After hearing extensive testimony from a broad range of witnesses, it concluded that not only were old Confederates back in power in the South but also that black codes and racial violence required increased protection for African Americans.

As a result, in the spring of 1866, Congress passed two important bills designed to aid African Americans. The landmark Civil Rights bill, which bestowed full citizenship on African Americans, overturned the 1857 *Dred Scott* decision and the black codes. It defined all persons born in the United States (except Indian peoples) as national citizens, and it enumerated various rights, including the rights to make and enforce contracts, to sue, to give evidence, and to buy and sell property. Under this bill, African Americans acquired "full and equal benefit of all laws and proceedings for the security of person and property as is enjoyed by white citizens."

Congress also voted to enlarge the scope of the Freedmen's Bureau, empowering it to build schools and pay teachers, and also to establish courts to prosecute those charged with depriving African Americans of their civil rights. The bureau achieved important, if limited, success in aiding African Americans. Bureau-run schools helped lay the foundation for southern public education.

"Office of the Freedmen's Bureau, Memphis, Tennessee," *Harper's Weekly*, June 2, 1866. Established by Congress in 1865, the Freedmen's Bureau provided economic, educational, and legal assistance to former slaves in the post–Civil War years. Bureau agents were often called on to settle disputes between black and white Southerners over wages, labor contracts, political rights, and violence. Although most southern whites only grudgingly acknowledged the bureau's legitimacy, freed people gained important legal and psychological support through testimony at public hearings like this one.

The bureau's network of courts allowed freed people to bring suits against white people in disputes involving violence, nonpayment of wages, or unfair division of crops. The very existence of courts hearing public testimony by African Americans provided an important psychological challenge to traditional notions of white racial domination.

But an angry President Johnson vetoed both of these bills. In opposing the Civil Rights bill, Johnson denounced the assertion of national power to protect African American civil rights, claiming it was a "stride toward centralization, and the concentration of all legislative powers in the national Government." But Johnson's intemperate attacks on the Radicals—he damned them as traitors unwilling to restore the Union—united moderate and Radical Republicans and they succeeded in overriding the vetoes. Congressional Republicans, led by the Radical faction, were now unified in challenging the president's power to direct Reconstruction and in using national authority to define and protect the rights of citizens.

In June 1866, fearful that the Civil Rights Act might be declared unconstitutional, and eager to settle the basis for the seating of southern representatives, Congress passed the Fourteenth Amendment. The amendment defined national citizenship to include former slaves ("all persons born or naturalized in the United States") and prohibited the states from violating the privileges of citizens without due process of law. It also empowered Congress to reduce the representation of any state that denied the suffrage to males over twenty-one. Republicans adopted the Fourteenth Amendment as their platform for the 1866 congressional elections and suggested that southern states would have to ratify it as a condition of readmission. President Johnson, meanwhile, took to the stump in August to support conservative Democratic and Republican candidates. His unrestrained speeches often degenerated into harangues, alienating many voters and aiding the Republican cause.

For their part, the Republicans skillfully portrayed Johnson and northern Democrats as disloyal and white Southerners as unregenerate. Republicans began an effective campaign tradition known as "waving the bloody shirt"—reminding northern voters of the hundreds of thousands of Yankee soldiers left dead or maimed by the war. In the November 1866 elections, the Republicans increased their majority in both the House and the Senate and gained control of all the northern states. The stage was now set for a battle between the president and Congress. Was it to be Johnson's "restoration" or Congressional Reconstruction?

CONGRESSIONAL RECONSTRUCTION AND THE IMPEACHMENT CRISIS

United against Johnson, moderate and Radical Republicans took control of Reconstruction early in 1867. In March, Congress passed the First Reconstruction Act over Johnson's veto. This act divided the South into five military districts subject to martial law. To achieve restoration, southern states were first required to call new constitutional conventions, elected by universal manhood suffrage. Once these states had drafted new constitutions, guaranteed African American voting rights, and ratified the Fourteenth Amendment, they were eligible for readmission to the Union. Supplementary legislation, also passed over the president's veto, invalidated the provisional governments established by Johnson, empowered

MAP EXPLORATION

To explore an interactive version of this map, go to
www.prenhall.com/faragher6/map17.1

MAP 17.1 Reconstruction of the South, 1866–77 Dates for the readmission of former Confederate states to the Union and the return of Democrats to power varied according to the specific political situations in those states.

the military to administer voter registration, and required an oath of loyalty to the United States (see Map 17.1).

Congress also passed several laws aimed at limiting Johnson's power. One of these, the Tenure of Office Act, stipulated that any officeholder appointed by the president with the Senate's advice and consent could not be removed until the Senate had approved a successor. In this way, congressional leaders could protect Republicans, such as Secretary of War Edwin M. Stanton, entrusted with implementing Congressional Reconstruction. In August 1867, with Congress adjourned, Johnson suspended Stanton and appointed General Ulysses S. Grant interim secretary of war. This move enabled the president to remove generals in the field that he judged to be too radical and replace them with men who were sympathetic to his own views. It also served as a challenge to the Tenure of Office Act. In January 1868, when the Senate overruled Stanton's suspension, Grant broke openly with Johnson and vacated the office. Stanton resumed his position and barricaded

himself in his office when Johnson attempted to remove him once again.

Outraged by Johnson's relentless obstructionism, and seizing upon his violation of the Tenure of Office Act as a pretext, moderate and Radical Republicans in the House of Representatives again joined forces and voted to impeach the president by a vote of 126 to 47 on February 24, 1868, charging him with eleven counts of high crimes and misdemeanors. To ensure the support of moderate Republicans, the articles of impeachment focused on violations of the Tenure of Office Act. The case against Johnson would have to be made on the basis of willful violation of the law. Left unstated were the Republicans' real reasons for wanting the president removed: Johnson's political views and his opposition to the Reconstruction Acts.

An influential group of moderate Senate Republicans feared the damage a conviction might do to the constitutional separation of powers. They also worried about the political and economic policies that might be pursued by Benjamin Wade, the president pro tem of the Senate and a leader of the Radical Republicans, who, because there was no vice president, would succeed to the presidency if Johnson were removed from office. Behind the scenes during his Senate trial, Johnson agreed to abide by the Reconstruction Acts. In May, the Senate voted 35 for conviction, 19 for acquittal—one vote shy of the two-thirds necessary for removal from office. Johnson's narrow acquittal established the precedent that only criminal actions by a president—not political disagreements—warranted removal from office.

THE ELECTION OF 1868

By the summer of 1868, seven former Confederate states (Alabama, Arkansas, Florida, Louisiana, North Carolina, South Carolina, and Tennessee) had ratified the revised constitutions, elected Republican governments, and ratified the Fourteenth Amendment. They had thereby earned readmission to the Union. Though Georgia, Mississippi, Texas, and Virginia still awaited readmission, the presidential election of 1868 offered some hope that the Civil War's legacy of sectional hate and racial tension might finally ease.

Republicans nominated Ulysses S. Grant, the North's foremost military hero. An Ohio native, Grant had graduated from West Point in 1843, served in the Mexican War, and resigned from the army in 1854. Unhappy in civilian life, Grant received a second chance during the Civil War. He rose quickly to become commander in the western theater, and he later destroyed Lee's army in Virginia. Although his armies suffered terrible losses, Grant enjoyed tremendous popularity after the war, especially when he broke with Johnson. Totally lacking in political experience, Grant admitted, after receiving the nomination, that he had been forced into it in spite of himself.

Significantly, at the very moment that the South was being forced to enfranchise former slaves as a prerequisite for readmission to the Union, the Republicans rejected a campaign plank endorsing black suffrage in the North. Their platform left "the question of suffrage in all the loyal States . . . to the people of those States." State referendums calling for black suffrage failed in eight northern states between 1865 and 1868, succeeding only in Iowa and Minnesota. The Democrats, determined to reverse Congressional Reconstruction, nominated Horatio Seymour, former governor of New York and a long-time foe of emancipation and supporter of states' rights.

The Ku Klux Klan, founded as a Tennessee social club in 1866, emerged as a potent instrument of terror (see the opening of this chapter). In Louisiana, Arkansas, Georgia, and South Carolina, the Klan threatened, whipped, and murdered black and white Republicans to prevent them from voting. This terrorism enabled the Democrats to carry Georgia and Louisiana, but it ultimately cost the Democrats votes in the North. In the final tally, Grant carried twenty-six of the thirty-four states for an electoral college victory of 214 to 80. But he received a popular majority of less than 53 percent, beating Seymour by only 306,000 votes. Significantly, more than 500,000 African American voters cast their ballots for Grant, demonstrating their overwhelming support for the Republican Party. The Republicans also retained large majorities in both houses of Congress.

In February 1869, Congress passed the Fifteenth Amendment, providing that "the right of citizens of the United States to vote shall not be denied or abridged on account of race, color, or previous condition of servitude." To enhance the chances of ratification, Congress required the four remaining unreconstructed states—Mississippi, Georgia, Texas, and Virginia—to ratify both the Fourteenth

The Fifteenth Amendment, ratified in 1870, stipulated that the right to vote could not be denied "on account of race, color, or previous condition of servitude." This illustration expressed the optimism and hopes of African Americans generated by this consitutional landmark aimed at protecting black political rights. Note the various political figures (Abraham Lincoln, John Brown, Frederick Douglass) and movements (abolitionism, black education) invoked here, providing a sense of how the amendment ended a long historical struggle.

and Fifteenth Amendments before readmission. They did so and rejoined the Union in early 1870. The Fifteenth Amendment was ratified in February 1870. In the narrow sense of simply readmitting the former Confederate states to the Union, Reconstruction was complete.

WOMAN SUFFRAGE AND RECONSTRUCTION

Many women's rights advocates had long been active in the abolitionist movement. The Fourteenth and Fifteenth Amendments, which granted citizenship and the vote to freedmen, both inspired and frustrated these activists. For example, Elizabeth Cady Stanton and Susan B. Anthony, two leaders with long involvement in both the antislavery and feminist movements, objected to the inclusion of the word "male" in the Fourteenth Amendment. "If that word 'male' be inserted," Stanton predicted in 1866, "it will take us a century at least to get it out."

Insisting that the causes of the African American vote and the women's vote were linked, Stanton, Anthony, and Lucy Stone founded the American Equal Rights Association in 1866. The group launched a series of lobbying and petition campaigns to remove racial and sexual restrictions on voting from state constitutions. Throughout the nation, the old abolitionist organizations and the Republican Party emphasized passage of the Fourteenth and Fifteenth Amendments and withdrew funds and support from the cause of woman suffrage. Disagreements over these amendments divided suffragists for decades.

The radical wing, led by Stanton and Anthony, opposed the Fifteenth Amendment, arguing that ratification would establish an "aristocracy of sex," enfranchising all men while leaving women without political privileges. They argued for a Sixteenth Amendment that would secure the vote for women. Other women's rights activists, including Lucy Stone and Frederick Douglass, asserted that "this hour belongs to the Negro." They feared a debate over woman suffrage at the national level would jeopardize passage of the two amendments.

By 1869 woman suffragists had split into two competing organizations: the moderate American Woman Suffrage Association (AWSA), which sought the support of men, and the more radical all-female National Woman Suffrage Association (NWSA). For the NWSA, the vote represented only one part of a broad spectrum of goals inherited from the Declaration of Sentiments manifesto adopted at the first women's rights convention held in 1848 at Seneca Falls, New York (see Chapter 13.)

Although women did not win the vote in this period, they did establish an independent suffrage movement that eventually drew millions of women into political life. The NWSA in particular demonstrated that self-government

Susan B. Anthony (1820–1906) and Elizabeth Cady Stanton (1815–1902), the two most influential leaders of the woman suffrage movement. As founders of the militant National Woman Suffrage Association, Stanton and Anthony established an independent woman suffrage movement with a broader spectrum of goals for women's rights and drew millions of women into public life during the late nineteenth century.

and democratic participation in the public sphere were crucial for women's emancipation. The failure of woman suffrage after the Civil War was less a result of factional fighting than of the larger defeat of Radical Reconstruction and the ideal of expanded citizenship.

THE MEANING OF FREEDOM

For nearly 4 million slaves, freedom arrived in various ways in different parts of the South. In many areas, slavery had collapsed long before Lee's surrender at Appomattox. In regions far removed from the presence of federal troops, African Americans did not learn of slavery's end until the spring of 1865. There were thousands of sharply contrasting stories, many of which revealed the need for freed slaves to confront their owners. One Virginia slave, hired out to another family during the war, had been working in the fields when a friend told her she was now

OVERVIEW | Reconstruction Amendments to the Constitution, 1865–1870

Amendment and Date Passed by Congress	Main Provisions	Ratification Process (3/4 of all States Including Ex-Confederate States Required)
13 (January 1865)	• Prohibited slavery in the United States	December 1865 (27 states, including 8 southern states)
14 (June 1866)	• Conferred national citizenship on all persons born or naturalized in the United States • Reduced state representation in Congress proportionally for any state disfranchising male citizens • Denied former Confederates the right to hold state or national office • Repudiated Confederate debt	July 1868 (after Congress made ratification a prerequisite for readmission of ex-Confederate states to the Union)
15 (February 1869)	• Prohibited denial of suffrage because of race, color, or previous condition of servitude	March 1870 (ratification required for readmission of Virginia, Texas, Mississippi, and Georgia)

free. "Is dat so?" she exclaimed. Dropping her hoe, she ran the seven miles to her old place, confronted her former mistress, and shouted, "I'se free! Yes, I'se free! Ain't got to work fo' you no mo'." But regardless of specific regional circumstances, the meaning of "freedom" would be contested for years to come. The deep desire for independence from white control formed the underlying aspiration of newly freed slaves. For their part, most southern white people sought to restrict the boundaries of that independence. As individuals and as members of communities transformed by emancipation, former slaves struggled to establish economic, political, and cultural autonomy. They built on the twin pillars of slave culture—the family and the church—to consolidate and expand African American institutions and thereby laid the foundation for the modern African American community.

MOVING ABOUT

The first impulse of many emancipated slaves was to test their freedom. The simplest, most obvious way to do this involved leaving home. Throughout the summer and fall of 1865, observers in the South noted enormous numbers of freed people on the move. One former slave squatting in an abandoned tent outside Selma, Alabama, explained his feeling to a northern journalist: "I's want to be free

man, cum when I please, and nobody say nuffin to me, nor order me roun'." When urged to stay on with the South Carolina family she had served for years as a cook, a slave woman replied firmly: "No, Miss, I must go. If I stay here I'll never know I am free."

Yet many who left their old neighborhoods returned soon afterward to seek work in the general vicinity or even on the plantation they had left. Many wanted to separate themselves from former owners, but not from familial ties and friendships. Others moved away altogether, seeking jobs in nearby towns and cities. Many former slaves left predominantly white counties, where they felt more vulnerable and isolated, for new lives in the relative comfort of predominantly black communities. In most southern states, there was a significant population shift toward black belt plantation counties and towns after the war. Many African Americans, attracted by schools, churches, and fraternal societies as well as the army, preferred the city. Between 1865 and 1870, the African American population of the South's ten largest cities doubled, while the white population increased by only 10 percent.

Disgruntled planters had difficulty accepting African American independence. During slavery, they had expected obedience, submission, and loyalty from African Americans. Now many could not understand why so many former slaves wanted to leave, despite urgent pleas to continue working at the old place. The deference and humility white people expected from African Americans could no longer be taken for granted. Indeed, many freed people went out of their way to reject the old subservience. Moving about freely was one way of doing this, as was refusing to tip one's hat to white people, ignoring former masters or mistresses in the streets, and refusing to step aside on sidewalks. When freed people staged parades, dances, and picnics to celebrate their new freedom, as they did, for example, when commemorating the Emancipation Proclamation, white people invariably condemned them angrily for "insolence," "outrageous spectacles," or "putting on airs."

THE AFRICAN AMERICAN FAMILY

Emancipation allowed freed people to strengthen family ties. For many former slaves, freedom meant the opportunity to find long-lost family members. To track down these relatives, freed people trekked to faraway places, put ads in newspapers, sought the help of Freedmen's Bureau agents, and questioned anyone who might have information about loved ones. Many thousands of family reunions, each with its own story, took place after the war. One North Carolina slave, who had seen his parents separated by sale, recalled many years later what for him had been the most significant aspect of freedom. "I has got thirteen great-gran' chilluns an' I know whar dey ever'one am. In slavery times dey'd have been on de block long time ago." Thousands of African American couples who had lived together under slavery streamed to military and civilian authorities and demanded to be legally married. By 1870, the two-parent household was the norm for a large majority of African Americans.

For many freed people, the attempt to find lost relatives dragged on for years. Searches often proved frustrating, exhausting, and ultimately disappointing. Some "reunions" ended painfully with the discovery that spouses had found new partners and started new families.

Emancipation brought changes to gender roles within the African American family as well. By serving in the Union army, African American men played a more direct role than women in the fight for freedom. In the political sphere, black men could now serve on juries, vote, and hold office; black women, like their white counterparts, could not. Freedmen's Bureau agents designated the husband as household head and established lower wage scales for women laborers. African American editors, preachers, and politicians regularly quoted the biblical injunction that wives submit to their husbands.

African American men asserted their male authority, denied under slavery, by insisting their wives work at home instead of in the fields. African American women generally wanted to devote more time than they had under slavery to caring for their children and to performing such domestic chores as cooking, sewing, gardening, and laundering. Yet African American women continued to work outside the home, engaging in seasonal field labor for wages or working a family's rented plot. Most rural black families barely eked out a living and, thus, the labor of every family member was essential to survival. The key difference from slave times was that African American families themselves, not white masters and overseers, decided when and where women and children worked.

AFRICAN AMERICAN CHURCHES AND SCHOOLS

The creation of separate African American churches proved the most lasting and important element of the energetic institution building that went on in postemancipation years. Before the Civil War, southern Protestant churches had relegated slaves and free African Americans to second-class membership. Black worshipers were required to sit in the back during services, they were denied any role in church governance, and they were excluded from Sunday schools. Even in larger cities, where all-black congregations sometimes built their own churches, the law required white pastors. In rural areas, slaves preferred their own preachers to local white ministers, who quoted Scripture to justify slavery and white supremacy. "That old white preachin' wasn't nothin'," former slave Nancy Williams recalled. "Old white preachers used to talk with their tongues without sayin' nothin', but Jesus told us slaves to talk with our hearts."

In communities around the South, African Americans now pooled their resources to buy land and build their own churches. Before these structures were completed, they might hold services in a railroad boxcar, where Atlanta's First Baptist Church began, or in an outdoor arbor, the original site of the First Baptist Church of Memphis. Churches became the center not only for religious life but also for many other activities that defined the African American community: schools, picnics, festivals, and political meetings. The church became the first social institution fully controlled by African Americans. In nearly every community, ministers, respected for their speaking and organizational skills, were among the most influential leaders. By 1877, the great majority of black Southerners had withdrawn from white-dominated churches. In South Carolina, for example, only a few hundred black Methodists attended biracial churches, down from over 40,000 in 1865. Black Baptist churches, with their decentralized and democratic structure and more emotional services, attracted the greatest number of freed people. By the end of Reconstruction, the vast majority of African American Christians belonged to black Baptist or Methodist churches.

An overflow congregation crowds into Richmond's First African Baptist Church in 1874. Despite their poverty, freed people struggled to save money, buy land, and erect new buildings as they organized hundreds of new black churches during Reconstruction. As the most important African American institution outside the family, the black church, in addition to tending to spiritual needs, played a key role in the educational and political life of the community.

education effort. Throughout the South in 1865 and 1866, African Americans raised money to build schoolhouses, buy supplies, and pay teachers. Black artisans donated labor for construction, and black families offered room and board to teachers.

LAND AND LABOR AFTER SLAVERY

Most newly emancipated African Americans aspired to quit the plantations and to make new lives for themselves. Leaving the plantation was not as simple as walking off. Some freed people did find jobs in railroad building, mining, ranching, or construction work. Others raised subsistence crops and tended vegetable gardens as squatters. White planters, however, tried to retain African Americans as permanent agricultural laborers. Restricting the employment of former slaves was an important goal of the black codes. For example, South Carolina legislation in 1865 provided that "no person of color shall pursue or practice the art, trade, or business of an artisan, mechanic, or shopkeeper, or any other trade employment, or business, besides that of husbandry, or that of a servant under contract for service or labor" without a special and costly permit.

The majority of African Americans hoped to become self-sufficient farmers. Many former slaves believed they were entitled to the land they had worked throughout their lives. General Oliver O. Howard, chief commissioner of the Freedmen's Bureau, observed that many "supposed that the Government [would] divide among them the lands of the conquered owners, and furnish them with all that might be necessary to begin life as an independent farmer." This perception was not merely a wishful fantasy. Frequent reference in the Congress and the press to the question of land distribution made the idea of "forty acres and a mule" not just a pipe dream but a matter of serious public debate. But by 1866, the federal government had already pulled back from the various wartime experiments involving the breaking up of large plantations and the leasing of small plots to individual families. President Johnson directed General Howard of the Freedmen's Bureau to evict tens of thousands of freed people settled on confiscated and abandoned land in southeastern Virginia, southern Louisiana, and the Georgia and South Carolina low country.

The rapid spread of schools reflected African Americans' thirst for self-improvement. Southern states had prohibited education for slaves. But many free black people managed to attend school, and a few slaves had been able to educate themselves. Still, over 90 percent of the South's adult African American population was illiterate in 1860. Access to education thus became a central part of the meaning of freedom. Freedmen's Bureau agents repeatedly expressed amazement at the number of makeshift classrooms organized by African Americans in rural areas. A bureau officer described these "wayside schools": "A negro riding on a loaded wagon, or sitting on a hack waiting for a train, or by the cabin door, is often seen, book in hand delving after the rudiments of knowledge. A group on the platform of a depot, after carefully conning an old spelling book, resolves itself into a class."

African American communities received important educational aid from outside organizations. By 1869, the Freedmen's Bureau was supervising nearly 3,000 schools serving over 150,000 students throughout the South. Over half of the roughly 3,300 teachers in these schools were African Americans, many of whom had been free before the Civil War. Other teachers included dedicated northern white women, volunteers sponsored by the American Missionary Association (AMA). The bureau and the AMA also assisted in the founding of several black colleges, including Tougaloo, Hampton, and Fisk, designed to train black teachers. Black self-help proved crucial to the

In communities throughout the South, freed people and their former masters negotiated new arrangements for

Finding my way Back
Javier

organizing agricultural labor. In Hale County, Alabama, for example, local black farm hands contracted to work on Henry Watson's plantation in 1866 deserted him when they angrily discovered that their small share of the crop left them in debt. Local Union League activists encouraged newly freed slaves to remain independent of white farmers, and political agitation for freedmen's rights encouraged them to push for better working conditions as well. Yet few owners would sell or even rent land to blacks. Watson, desperate for field hands, finally agreed to subdivide his plantation and rent it to freedmen, who would work under their own supervision without overseers. Black families left the old slave quarters and began building cabins scattered around the plantation. By 1868 Watson was convinced that black farmers made good tenants; like many other landowners, he grudgingly accepted greater independence for black families in exchange for a more stable labor force. By 1869, as one Hale County correspondent reported, "Many planters have turned their stock, teams, and every facility to farming, over to the negroes, and only require an amount of toll for the use of the land" (See Map 17.2).

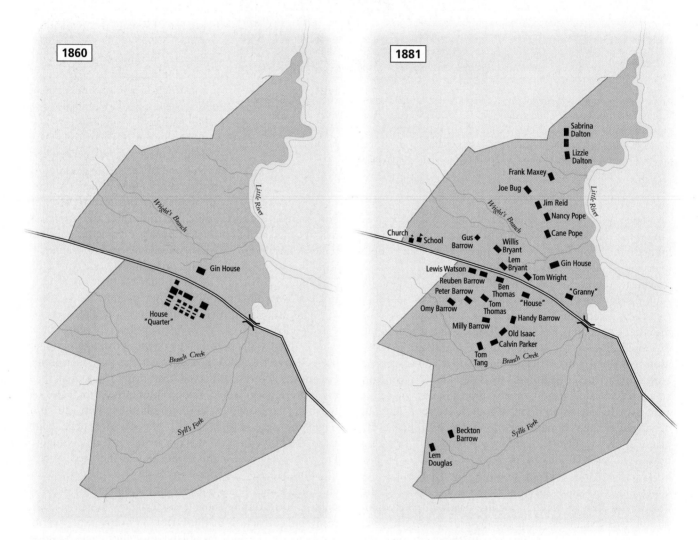

MAP 17.2 **The Barrow Plantation, Oglethorpe County, Georgia, 1860 and 1881 (approx. 2,000 acres)** These two maps, based on drawings from *Scribner's Monthly*, April 1881, show some of the changes brought by emancipation. In 1860, the plantation's entire black population lived in the communal slave quarters, right next to the white master's house. In 1881, black sharecropper and tenant families lived on individual plots, spread out across the land. The former slaves had also built their own school and church.

"The First Vote," *Harper's Weekly*, November 16, 1867, reflected the optimism felt by much of the northern public as former slaves began to vote for the first time. The caption noted that freedmen went to the ballot box "not with expressions of exultation or of defiance of their old masters and present opponents depicted on their countenances, but looking serious and solemn and determined."

By the late 1860s, sharecropping and tenant farming had emerged as the dominant form of working the land. Sharecropping represented a compromise between planters and former slaves. Under sharecropping arrangements that were usually very detailed, individual families contracted with landowners to be responsible for a specific plot. Large plantations were thus broken into family-sized farms. Generally, sharecropper families received one-third of the year's crop if the owner furnished implements, seed, and draft animals or one-half if they provided their own supplies. African Americans preferred sharecropping to gang labor, as it allowed families to set their own hours and tasks and offered freedom from white supervision and control. For planters, the system stabilized the workforce by requiring sharecroppers to remain until the harvest and to employ all family members. It also offered a way around the chronic shortage of cash and credit that plagued the postwar South. Freed people did not aspire to sharecropping. Owning land outright or tenant farming (renting land) were both more desirable. But though black sharecroppers clearly enjoyed more autonomy than in the past, the vast majority never achieved economic independence or land ownership. They remained a largely subordinate agricultural labor force.

THE ORIGINS OF AFRICAN AMERICAN POLITICS

Inclusion, rather than separation, was the objective of early African American political activity. The greatest political activity by African Americans occurred in areas occupied by Union forces during the war. In 1865 and 1866, African Americans throughout the South organized scores of mass meetings, parades, and petitions that demanded civil equality and the right to vote. In the cities, the growing web of churches and fraternal societies helped bolster early efforts at political organization.

Hundreds of African American delegates, selected by local meetings or churches, attended statewide political conventions held throughout the South in 1865 and 1866. Previously free African Americans, as well as black ministers, artisans, and veterans of the Union army, tended to dominate these proceedings, setting a pattern that would hold throughout Reconstruction. Convention debates sometimes reflected the tensions within African American communities, such as friction between poorer former slaves and better-off free black people, or between lighter- and darker-skinned African Americans. But most of these

SEEING HISTORY

Changing Images of Reconstruction

After the Civil War, northern journalists and illustrators went south to describe Reconstruction in action. They took a keen interest in how the newly freed slaves were reshaping local and national politics. A drawing by *Harper's Weekly* illustrator William L. Sheppard titled "Electioneering in the South" clearly approved of the freedmen's exercise of their new citizenship rights. "Does any man seriously doubt," the caption asked, "whether it is better for this vast population to be sinking deeper and deeper in ignorance and servility, or rising into general intelligence and self-respect? They can not be pariahs; they can not be peons; they must be slaves or citizens."

Thomas Nast was the nation's best-known political cartoonist during the 1860s and 1870s. During the Civil War he strongly supported the Union cause and the

aspirations of the newly freed slaves. But by 1876, like many Northerners originally sympathetic to guaranteeing blacks full political and civil rights, Nast had turned away from the early ideals of Reconstruction. Nast used grotesque racial caricature to depict southern African Americans and northern Irish immigrants as undeserving of the right to vote. The aftermath of the disputed 1876 presidential election included charges of widespread vote fraud from both Republicans and Democrats. Nast's view—published in *Harper's Weekly* in December 1876, while the election's outcome was still in doubt—reflected concerns among many middle-class Northerners that the nation's political system was tainted by the manipulation of "ignorant" voters in both the South and the North.

How does the portrayal of the larger African American community in "Electioneering in the South" reflect the political point being made?
What do the caricatures in "The Ignorant Vote" suggest about Reconstruction era ideas about the meaning of "whiteness"?

state gatherings concentrated on passing resolutions on issues that united all African Americans. The central concerns were suffrage and equality before the law.

The passage of the First Reconstruction Act in 1867 encouraged even more political activity among African Americans. The military started registering the South's electorate, ultimately enrolling approximately 735,000 black and 635,000 white voters in the ten unreconstructed states. Five states—Alabama, Florida, Louisiana, Mississippi, and South Carolina—had black electoral majorities. Fewer than half the registered white voters participated in the elections for state constitutional conventions in 1867 and 1868. In contrast, four-fifths of the registered black voters cast ballots in these elections. Much of this new African American political activism was channeled through local Union League chapters throughout the South. However, as the fate of Alex Webb in Hale County, Alabama, again makes clear, few whites welcomed this activism.

Begun during the war as a northern, largely white middle-class patriotic club, the Union League now became the political voice of the former slaves. Union League chapters brought together local African Americans, soldiers, and Freedmen's Bureau agents to demand the vote and an end to legal discrimination against African Americans. It brought out African American voters, instructed freedmen in the rights and duties of citizenship, and promoted Republican candidates. Not surprisingly, newly enfranchised freedmen voted Republican and formed the core of the Republican Party in the South. For most ordinary African Americans, politics was inseparable from economic issues, especially the land question. Grassroots political organizations frequently intervened in local disputes with planters over the terms of labor contracts. African American political groups closely followed the congressional debates over Reconstruction policy and agitated for land confiscation and distribution. Perhaps most important, politics was the only arena where black and white Southerners might engage each other on an equal basis.

SOUTHERN POLITICS AND SOCIETY

By the summer of 1868, when the South had returned to the Union, the majority of Republicans believed the task of Reconstruction to be finished. Ultimately, they put their faith in a political solution to the problems facing the vanquished South. That meant nurturing a viable two-party system in the southern states, where no Republican Party had ever existed. If that could be accomplished, Republicans and Democrats would compete for votes, offices, and influence, just as they did in northern states.

Most Republican congressmen were moderates, conceiving Reconstruction in limited terms. They rejected radical calls for confiscation and redistribution of land, as well as permanent military rule of the South. The Reconstruction Acts of 1867 and 1868 laid out the requirements for the readmission of southern states, along with the procedures for forming and electing new governments.

Yet over the next decade, the political structure created in the southern states proved too restricted and fragile to sustain itself. To most southern whites, the active participation of African Americans in politics seemed extremely dangerous. Federal troops were needed to protect Republican governments and their supporters from violent opposition. Congressional action to monitor southern elections and protect black voting rights became routine. Despite initial successes, southern Republicanism proved an unstable coalition of often conflicting elements, unable to sustain effective power for very long. By 1877, Democrats had regained political control of all the former Confederate states.

SOUTHERN REPUBLICANS

Three major groups composed the fledgling Republican coalition in the postwar South. African American voters made up a large majority of southern Republicans throughout the Reconstruction era. Yet African Americans outnumbered whites in only three southern states; Republicans would have to attract white support to win elections and sustain power.

A second group consisted of white Northerners, derisively called "carpetbaggers" by native white Southerners. Most carpetbaggers combined a desire for personal gain with a commitment to reform the "unprogressive" South by developing its material resources and introducing Yankee institutions, such as free labor and free public schools. Most were veterans of the Union army who stayed in the South after the war. Others included Freedmen's Bureau agents and businessmen who had invested capital in cotton plantations and other enterprises.

Carpetbaggers tended to be well educated and from the middle class. Albert Morgan, for example, was an army veteran from Ohio who settled in Mississippi after the war. When he and his brother failed at running a cotton plantation and sawmill, Morgan became active in Republican politics as a way to earn a living. He won election to the state constitutional convention, became a power in the state legislature, and risked his life to keep the Republican organization alive in the Mississippi Delta region. Although they made up a tiny percentage of the population, carpetbaggers played a disproportionately large role in southern politics. They won a large share of Reconstruction offices, particularly in Florida, South Carolina, and Louisiana and in areas with large African American constituencies.

The third major group of southern Republicans were the native whites pejoratively termed "scalawags." They had even more diverse backgrounds and motives than the northern-born Republicans. Some were prominent prewar Whigs who saw the Republican Party as their best chance to regain political influence. Others viewed the party as an agent of modernization and economic expansion. "Yankees and Yankee notions are just what we want in this country," argued Thomas Settle of North Carolina. "We want their capital to build factories and workshops. We want their intelligence, their energy and enterprise." Loyalists during the war and traditional enemies of the planter elite (most were small farmers), these white Southerners looked to the Republican Party for help in settling old scores and relief from debt and wartime devastation.

Southern Republicanism also reflected prewar political divisions. Its influence was greatest in those regions that had long resisted the political and economic power of the plantation elite. Thus, southern Republicans could dominate the mountainous areas of western North Carolina, eastern Tennessee, northern Georgia, and southwestern Virginia as much as Democrats controlled other areas. Yet few white Southerners identified with the political and economic aspirations of African Americans. Moderate elements more concerned with maintaining white control of the party, and encouraging economic investment in the region, outnumbered and defeated "confiscation radicals" who focused on obtaining land for African Americans.

RECONSTRUCTING THE STATES: A MIXED RECORD

With the old Confederate leaders barred from political participation, and with carpetbaggers and newly enfranchised African Americans representing many of the plantation districts, Republicans managed to dominate the ten southern constitutional conventions from 1867 to 1869. Most of these conventions produced constitutions that expanded democracy and the public role of the state. The new documents guaranteed the political and civil rights of African Americans, and they abolished property qualifications for officeholding and jury service as well as imprisonment for debt. They created the first state-funded systems of education in the South to be administered by state commissioners. The new constitutions also mandated establishment of orphanages, penitentiaries, and homes for the insane. In 1868, only three years after the end of the war, Republicans came to power in most of the southern states. By 1869, new constitutions had been ratified in all the old Confederate states. "These constitutions and governments," one South Carolina Democratic newspaper vowed bitterly, "will last just as long as the bayonets which ushered them into being, shall keep them in existence, and not one day longer."

Republican governments in the South faced a continual crisis of legitimacy that limited their ability to legislate change. They had to balance reform against the need to gain acceptance, especially by white Southerners. Their achievements were thus mixed. In the realm of race relations there was a clear thrust toward equal rights and against discrimination. Republican legislatures followed up the federal Civil Rights Act of 1866 with various antidiscrimination clauses in new constitutions and laws prescribing harsh penalties for civil rights violations. African Americans could now be employed in police forces and fire departments, serve on juries, school boards, and city councils, and they could hold public office at all levels of government.

Segregation, though, became the norm in public school systems. African American leaders often accepted segregation because they feared that insistence on integrated education would jeopardize funding for the new school systems. African Americans opposed constitutional language requiring racial segregation in schools; most African Americans were less interested in the abstract ideal of integrated education than in ensuring educational opportunities for their children and employment for African American teachers.

Segregation in railroad cars and other public places was more objectionable. By the early 1870s, as black influence and assertiveness grew, laws guaranteeing equal access to transportation and public accommodation were passed in many states. By and large, though, such civil rights laws were difficult to enforce in local communities.

In economic matters, Republican governments failed to fulfill African Americans' hopes of obtaining land. Few former slaves possessed the cash to buy land in the open market, and they looked to the state for help. Republicans tried to weaken the plantation system and promote black ownership by raising taxes on land. Yet even when state governments seized land for nonpayment of taxes, the property was never used to help create black homesteads.

Republican leaders envisioned promoting northern-style capitalist development—factories, large towns, and diversified agriculture—through state aid. Much Republican state lawmaking was devoted to encouraging railroad construction. Between 1868 and 1872 the southern railroad system was rebuilt and over 3,000 new miles of track added, an increase of almost 40 percent. But in spite of all the new laws, it proved impossible to attract significant amounts of northern and European investment capital. The obsession with railroads withdrew resources from education and other programs. As in the North, it also opened the doors to widespread corruption and bribery of public officials. Railroad failures eroded public confidence in the Republicans' ability to govern. The "gospel of prosperity" ultimately failed to modernize the economy or solidify the Republican Party in the South.

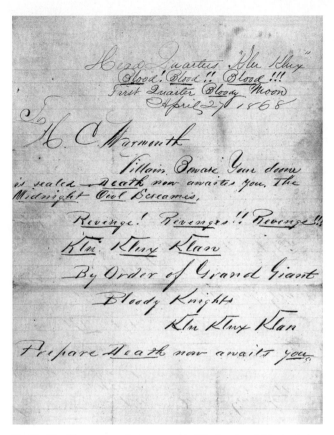

The Ku Klux Klan emerged as a potent political and social force during Reconstruction, terrorizing freed people and their white allies. An 1868 Klan warning threatens Louisiana governor Henry C. Warmoth with death. Warmoth, an Illinois-born "carpetbagger," was the state's first Republican governor. Two Alabama Klansmen, photographed in 1868, wear white hoods to hide their identities.

WHITE RESISTANCE AND "REDEMPTION"

The emergence of a Republican Party in the reconstructed South brought two parties, but not a two-party system, to the region. The opponents of Reconstruction, the Democrats, refused to acknowledge Republicans' right to participate in southern political life. In their view, the Republican Party, supported primarily by the votes of former slaves, was the partisan instrument of the northern Congress. Since Republicans controlled state governments, this denial of legitimacy meant, in effect, a rejection of state authority itself. In each state, Republicans were split between those who urged conciliation in an effort to gain white acceptance and those who emphasized consolidating the party under the protection of the military.

From its founding in 1868 through the early 1870s, the Ku Klux Klan fought an ongoing terrorist campaign against Reconstruction governments and local leaders. Although not centrally organized, the Klan was a powerful presence in nearly every southern state, producing the worst legacy of domestic terrorism in the nation's history. Just as the institution of slavery had depended on violence and the threat of violence, the Klan acted as a kind of guerrilla military force in the service of the Democratic Party, the planter class, and all those who sought the restoration of white supremacy. It employed a wide array of terror tactics: destroying ballot boxes, issuing death threats, the beating and murdering of politically active blacks and their white allies (see Communities in Conflict). Planters sometimes employed Klansmen to enforce labor discipline by driving African Americans off plantations to deprive them of their harvest share. Klansmen concentrated on attacking people and institutions associated with Radical Reconstruction and the challenge to white supremacy. Freedmen and their allies sometimes resisted the Klan. In Hale County, Alabama, Union Leaguers set up a warning system using buglers to signal the activities of Klan raiders. But violence and intimidation decimated Union League leadership in the countryside by 1869.

In October 1870, after Republicans carried Laurens County in South Carolina, bands of white people drove

The Ku Klux Klan in Alabama

During Reconstruction the Ku Klux Klan (KKK) claimed as many as 12,000 members in Alabama, or about one in every nine white male voters. The KKK enjoyed deep and widespread support from many whites, including women and children, who viewed the Klan as the protector of white supremacy and a weapon against the Republican Party. Democratic newspapers routinely printed favorable accounts of Klan activities, as well as pro-Klan advertisements, songs, and jokes—and threats directed at intended Klan victims. The following excerpt from a sympathetic newspaper report of Klan activities in the central Alabama town of Florence was published in the *Shelby County Guide* on December 3, 1868.

African Americans and their Republican allies, however, experienced the Klan as a terrorist organization responsible for murder, beatings, arson, and violent intimidation aimed at preventing African American political organizing and economic advancement. This view is vividly presented in a first-person account of Klan terror given by George Houston, an ex-slave and tailor, who had been elected to represent Sumter County in the Alabama state legislature. Houston had helped organize a Union League chapter and actively registered black voters. After local Klansmen wounded his son and broke down the door to his house, Houston grabbed his gun and shot back. In this testimony to a congressional committee investigating the KKK's terrorist campaign, he describes the immediate scene and the campaign to intimidate him.

How do the documents reveal profoundly different understandings of the consequences of freedom for African Americans?

What do the sources tell us about the connections between political dominance and economic power in the Reconstruction era South?

Movements of the Mystic Klan, from the *Shelby County Guide*, December 3, 1868

About a week ago Saturday night the Ku Klux came into town to regulate matters. They were here from eleven p.m. to three o'clock a.m. — five hundred in all. They shot one very bad Negro, putting six balls through his head. Many heard the noise, but did not know what was going on. They also hung three or four Negroes nearly dead, and whipped others severely in order to make them tell them about their nightly meetings, and what their object was in holding the same; also, as to who their leaders were. They made a clean breast of the whole matter, telling everything. The strongest thing about these Ku Klux was that they did not hesitate to unmask themselves when asked to do so; and out of the whole party none were identified. —Every one who saw them says their horses were more beautiful than, and far superior to, any in the country round about. They spoke but little but always to a purpose. They went to several stores and knocked; the doors were opened at once. They then called for rope, and at each place a coil was rolled out to them. They cut it in suitable length to hang a man with. No one asked for money and they offered none. They did not disturb any one else, nor did they take any thing except some few Enfield rifles which were found in possession of some very bad Negroes. —They called on the revenue officer and passed a few remarks with him. What transpired is not known, but it has made a great improvement in his conversation. The visitants advent has been productive of much good and benefit to the community, though all regret such steps should have to be resorted to, every one says "give us peace," and really I believe them to be truly sincere.

SOURCE: Alabama Department of History and Archives, http://www.alabamamoments.state.al.us/sec28ps.html

"They shot one very bad Negro . . .[T]hey also hung three or four . . . nearly dead. . . ."

"[I was] opposed to colored men being shot down like dogs."

George Houston's Testimony, Montgomery, October 17, 1871

Q: How many were there in the crowd that attacked your house?

A: I can't tell. It looked like a great many men. It was starlight and before day. There was a good deal of cursing after they got shot and broke down my door. The reason they were afraid to come in was, I think, because that shot was fired. They didn't come back.

Q: Did you notice whether they were disguised?

A: Only the one that I shot at. He looked like he was wrapped up in some white cloth; it looked so by starlight. That is all I could see.

Q: Had you any trouble with your neighbors?

A: Nothing more than some talk that I didn't like from some wealthy men of the county. One of them had come to me, and told me if I turned against them they would turn against me. They looked upon me as being the prominent Negro of the county. I know the men that told me that thing very well. It was in a dry goods store in that town.

Q: What did they want you to do?

A: They wanted me to deny what was called the Union League. They had understood I belonged to it. The reason they took a great fancy to me was, I was a tailor in that place. My master had learned me this trade on account of my health and crippleness when I was a slave. I had run a shop for sixteen years there. They came to me, and said I made my living off of them and not off of the damned niggers, and if I turned against them they would turn against me. I said my belonging to the Union League didn't do them any harm. They said, 'Yes, it does.' I said, 'It's only to teach our ignorant colored men.' This was our talk privately, and this was only a few months before I was shot. That is all I could assign for the cause of it, and taking the fact that the other colored men were shot down just before, and I was a representative of that county. There was a public meeting; we had made some public speeches, some white and some black men, and I told them I was opposed to this.

Q: Opposed to what?

A: Opposed to colored men being shot down like dogs, when I knew that the officers of the county could stop it. I told the sheriff that to his face. If they took exceptions to me on that account, that is all I can tell, for I was raised there, and they never could put a scratch of a pen against me before, and nothing else could they have taken from it except that I tried to hold up the men that had been shot down by violence; some at night, some by daylight; some were found in the stock pools with their guts cut out. All this came to my ears and the other men's ears.

Q: How many colored men were assassinated in that county?

A: I think eight or nine, before I was shot, were killed dead, according to the accounts of the white men and black men I got through the county. I stop at eight or nine, but I really think there were a few more.

Q: Is the bullet there now in the leg?

A: Yes sir; and it will stay there until God Almighty takes it out. I had a doctor fifteen minutes probing to get that out. The ball went through my child's flesh, too. My child had to go fifteen miles to his grandfather and I had to suffer and go off. I had to sacrifice my property. And yet I am a Republican, and I will die one. I say the Republican Party freed me, and I will die on top of it. I don't care who is pleased. I vote every time. I was register of my county, and my master sent in and lent me his pistols to carry around my waist when I was register, to protect myself against my enemies. I am a Republican today, and if the Republican Party can't do me any good, I will never turn against it. I can work in the cotton patch and work at my trade, and get along without any benefit from my party, and so I will stick to the Republican Party and die in it.

SOURCE: "Affairs in Insurrectionary States: Report and Minority Reviews, Alabama, vol. 2," *Senate Reports*, 42nd Congress, 2nd Session, vol. 2, pt. 9, no. 41.

150 African Americans from their homes and murdered thirteen white and black Republican activists. In March 1871, three African Americans were arrested in Meridian, Mississippi, for giving "incendiary" speeches. At their court hearing, Klansmen killed two of the defendants and the Republican judge, and thirty more African Americans were murdered in a day of rioting. The single bloodiest episode of Reconstruction era violence took place in Colfax, Louisiana, on Easter Sunday 1873. Nearly 100 African Americans were murdered after they failed to hold a besieged courthouse during a contested election.

Southern Republicans looked to Washington for help. In 1870 and 1871, Congress passed three Enforcement Acts designed to counter racial terrorism. These declared that interference with voting was a federal offense. The acts provided for federal supervision of voting and authorized the president to send the army and to suspend the writ of habeas corpus in districts declared to be in a state of insurrection. The most sweeping measure was the Ku Klux Klan Act of April 1871, which made the violent infringement of civil and political rights a federal crime punishable by the national government. Attorney General Amos T. Akerman prosecuted hundreds of Klansmen in North Carolina and Mississippi. In October 1871, President Grant sent federal troops to occupy nine South Carolina counties; they rounded up thousands of Klan members. By the election of 1872, the federal government's intervention had helped break the Klan and restore a semblance of law and order.

The Civil Rights Act of 1875 outlawed racial discrimination in theaters, hotels, railroads, and other public places. But the law proved more an assertion of principle than a direct federal intervention in southern affairs. Enforcement required African Americans to take their cases to the federal courts, a costly and time-consuming procedure.

As wartime idealism faded, northern Republicans became less inclined toward direct intervention in southern affairs. They had enough trouble retaining political control in the North. In 1874, the Democrats gained a majority in the House of Representatives for the first time since 1856. Key northern states also began to fall to the Democrats. Northern Republicans slowly abandoned the freedmen and their white allies in the South. Southern Democrats were also able to exploit a deepening fiscal crisis by blaming Republicans for excessive extension of public credit and the sharp increase in tax rates. Republican governments had indeed spent public money for new state school systems, orphanages, roads, and other internal improvements.

Gradually, conservative Democrats "redeemed" one state after another. Virginia and Tennessee led the way in 1869, North Carolina in 1870, Georgia in 1871, Texas in 1873, and Alabama and Arkansas in 1874. In Mississippi,

white conservatives employed violence and intimidation to wrest control in 1875 and "redeemed" the state the following year. Republican infighting in Louisiana in 1873 and 1874 led to a series of contested election results, including bloody clashes between black militia and armed whites, and finally to "redemption" by the Democrats in 1877. Once these states returned to Democratic rule, African Americans faced obstacles to voting, more stringent controls on plantation labor, and deep cuts in social services.

Several Supreme Court rulings involving the Fourteenth and Fifteenth Amendments effectively constrained federal protection of African American civil rights. In the so-called Slaughterhouse Cases of 1873, the Court issued its first ruling on the Fourteenth Amendment. The cases involved a Louisiana charter that gave a New Orleans meatpacking company a monopoly over the city's butchering business on the grounds of protecting public health. A rival group of butchers had sued, claiming the law violated the Fourteenth Amendment, which prohibited states from depriving any person of life, liberty, or property without due process of law. The Court held that the Fourteenth Amendment protected only the former slaves, not butchers, and that it protected only national citizenship rights, not the regulatory powers of states. It separated national citizenship from state citizenship and declared that most of the rights that Americans enjoyed on a daily basis—freedom of speech, fair trials, the right to sit on juries, protection from unreasonable searches, and the right to vote—were under the control of state law. The ruling in effect denied the original intent of the Fourteenth Amendment—to protect against state infringement of national citizenship rights as spelled out in the Bill of Rights.

Three other decisions curtailed federal protection of black civil rights. In *United States* v. *Reese* (1876) and *United States* v. *Cruikshank* (1876), the Court restricted congressional power to enforce the Ku Klux Klan Act. Future prosecution would depend on the states rather than on federal authorities. In these rulings, the Court held that the Fourteenth Amendment extended the federal power to protect civil rights only in cases involving discrimination by states; discrimination by individuals or groups was not covered. The Court also ruled that the Fifteenth Amendment did not guarantee a citizen's right to vote; it only barred certain specific grounds for denying suffrage—"race, color, or previous condition of servitude." This interpretation opened the door for southern states to disenfranchise African Americans for allegedly nonracial reasons. States back under Democratic control began to limit African American voting by passing laws restricting voter eligibility through poll taxes and property requirements.

Finally, in the 1883 Civil Rights Cases decision, the Court declared the Civil Rights Act of 1875 unconstitutional, holding that the Fourteenth Amendment gave Congress the power to outlaw discrimination by states but not by private individuals. The majority opinion held that black people must no longer "be the special favorite of the laws." Together, these Supreme Court decisions marked the end of federal attempts to protect African American rights until well into the next century.

KING COTTON: SHARECROPPERS, TENANTS, AND THE SOUTHERN ENVIRONMENT

The Republicans' vision of a "New South" remade along the lines of the northern economy failed to materialize. Instead, the South declined into the country's poorest agricultural region. Unlike midwestern and western farm towns burgeoning from trade in wheat, corn, and livestock, Southern communities found themselves almost entirely dependent on the price of one commodity. In the post–Civil War years, "King Cotton" expanded its realm, as greater numbers of small white farmers found themselves forced to switch from subsistence crops to growing cotton for the market (see Map 17.3).

A chronic shortage of capital and banking institutions made local merchants and planters the sole source of credit. They advanced loans and supplies to small owners, tenant farmers, and sharecroppers in exchange for a lien, or claim, on the year's cotton crop. They often charged extremely high interest rates on advances, while marking up the prices of the goods sold in their stores. Taking advantage of the

MAP EXPLORATION

To explore an interactive version of this map, go to **www.prenhall.com/faragher6/map17.3**

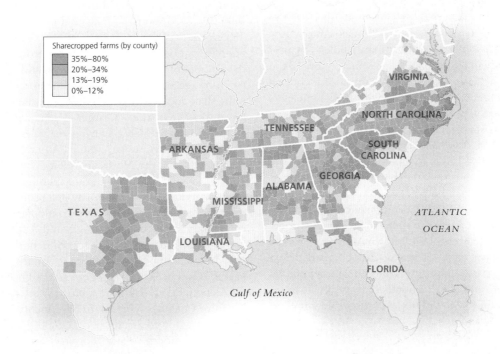

MAP 17.3 Southern Sharecropping and the Cotton Belt, 1880 The economic depression of the 1870s forced increasing numbers of southern farmers, both white and black, into sharecropping arrangements. Sharecropping was most pervasive in the cotton belt regions of South Carolina, Georgia, Alabama, Mississippi, and eastern Texas.

high illiteracy rates among poor Southerners, landlords and merchants easily altered their books to inflate the figures. At the end of the year, sharecroppers and tenants found themselves deep in debt to stores for seed, supplies, and clothing. Despite hard work and even bountiful harvests, few small farmers could escape from heavy debt. The spread of the "crop lien" system as the South's main form of agricultural credit forced more and more farmers into cotton growing.

The pent-up demand for cotton following the war brought high prices (as much as 43 cents per pound) through the late 1860s. But as the "crop lien" system spread, and as more and more farmers turned to cotton growing as the only way to obtain credit, expanding production depressed prices. Competition from new cotton centers in the world market, such as Egypt and India, accelerated the downward spiral. As cotton prices declined alarmingly, to roughly 11 cents per pound in 1875 to 5 cents by the early 1890s, per capita wealth in the South fell steadily, equaling only one-third that of the East, Midwest, or West by the 1890s. Small farmers caught up in a vicious cycle of low cotton prices, debt, and dwindling food crops found their old ideal of independence sacrificed to the cruel logic of the cotton market.

To obtain precious credit, most southern farmers, both black and white, found themselves forced to produce cotton for market and, thus, became enmeshed in the debt-ridden crop lien system. In traditional cotton producing areas, especially the black belt, landless farmers growing cotton had replaced slaves growing cotton. In the up-country and newer areas of cultivation, cotton-dominated commercial agriculture, with landless tenants and sharecroppers as the main workforce, had replaced the more diversified subsistence economy of the antebellum era. These patterns hardened throughout the late nineteenth century. By 1900, roughly half of the South's 2,620,000 farms were operated by tenants, who rented land, or sharecroppers, who pledged a portion of the crop to owners in exchange for some combination of work animals, seed, and tools. Over one-third of the white farmers and nearly three-quarters of the African American farmers in the cotton states were tenants or sharecroppers. Large parts of the southern landscape would remain defined by this system well into the twentieth century: small farms operated by families who did not own their land, mired in desperate poverty and debt.

RECONSTRUCTING THE NORTH

Abraham Lincoln liked to cite his own rise as proof of the superiority of the northern system of "free labor" over slavery. "There is no permanent class of hired laborers amongst us," Lincoln asserted. "Twenty-five years ago, I was a hired laborer. The hired laborer of yesterday, labors on his own account today; and will hire others to labor for him tomorrow. Advancement—improvement in condition—is the order of things in a society of equals." But the triumph of the North brought with it fundamental changes in the economy, labor relations, and politics that brought Lincoln's ideal vision into question. The spread of the factory system, the growth of large and powerful corporations, and the rapid expansion of capitalist enterprise all hastened the development of a large unskilled and routinized workforce. Rather than becoming independent producers, more and more workers found themselves consigned permanently to wage labor.

The old Republican ideal of a society bound by a harmony of interests had become overshadowed by a grimmer reality of class conflict. A violent national railroad strike in 1877 was broken only with the direct intervention of federal troops. That conflict struck many Americans as a turning point. Northern society, like the society of the South, appeared more hierarchical than equal.

THE AGE OF CAPITAL

In the decade following Appomattox, the North's economy continued the industrial boom begun during the Civil War. By 1873, America's industrial production had grown 75 percent over the 1865 level. By that time, too, the number of nonagricultural workers in the North had surpassed the number of farmers. Between 1860 and 1880, the number of wage earners in manufacturing and construction more than doubled, from 2 million to over 4 million. Only Great Britain boasted a larger manufacturing economy than the United States. During the same period, nearly 3 million immigrants arrived in America, almost all of whom settled in the North and West.

The railroad business both symbolized and advanced the new industrial order. Shortly before the Civil War, enthusiasm mounted for a transcontinental line. Private companies took on the huge and expensive job of construction, but the federal government funded the project, providing the largest subsidy in American history. The Pacific Railway Act of 1862 granted the Union Pacific and the Central Pacific rights to a broad swath of land extending from Omaha, Nebraska, to Sacramento, California. An 1864 act bestowed a subsidy of $15,000 per mile of track laid over smooth plains country and varying larger amounts up to $48,000 per mile in the foothills and mountains of the Far West. The Union Pacific employed gangs of Irish American and African American workers to lay track heading west from Omaha.

Meanwhile the Central Pacific, pushing east from California, had a tougher time finding workers, and began recruiting thousands of men from China. In 1868, the

Chinese immigrants, like these section gang workers, provided labor and skills critical to the successful completion of the first transcontinental railroad. This photo was taken in Promontory Point, Utah Territory, in 1869.

Senate ratified the Burlingame Treaty, giving Chinese the right to emigrate to the United States, while specifying that "nothing contained herein shall be held to confer naturalization." The right to work in America, in other words, did not bestow any right to citizenship. Some 12,000 Chinese laborers (about 90 percent of the workforce) bore the brunt of the difficult conditions in the Sierra Nevada where blizzards, landslides, and steep rock faces took an awful toll. Chinese workers earned a reputation for toughness and efficiency. "If we found we were in a hurry for a job of work," wrote one of the Central Pacific's superintendents, "it was better to put on Chinese at once." Working in baskets suspended by ropes, Chinese laborers chipped away at solid granite walls and became expert in the use of nitroglycerin for blasting through the mountains. But after completion of the transcontinental line threw thousands of Chinese railroad workers onto the California labor market, the open-door immigration pledge in the Burlingame Treaty would soon be eclipsed by a virulent tide of anti-Chinese agitation among western politicians and labor unions. In 1882, Congress passed the Chinese Exclusion Act, suspending any further Chinese immigration for ten years.

On May 10, 1869, Leland Stanford, the former governor of California and president of the Central Pacific Railroad, traveled to Promontory Point in Utah Territory to hammer a ceremonial golden spike, marking the finish of the first transcontinental line. Other railroads went up with less fanfare. The Southern Pacific, chartered by the state of California, stretched from San Francisco to Los Angeles, and on through Arizona and New Mexico to connections with New Orleans. The Atchison, Topeka, and Santa Fe reached the Pacific in 1887 by way of a southerly route across the Rocky Mountains. The Great Northern, one of the few lines financed by private capital, extended west from St. Paul, Minnesota, to Washington's Puget Sound.

Railroad corporations became America's first big businesses. Railroads required huge outlays of investment capital, and their growth increased the economic power of banks and investment houses centered in Wall Street. Bankers often gained seats on the boards of directors of railroad companies, and their access to capital sometimes gave them the real control of the corporations. By the early 1870s the Pennsylvania Railroad was the nation's largest single company with more than 20,000 employees. A new breed of aggressive entrepreneur sought to ease cutthroat competition by absorbing smaller companies and forming "pools" that set rates and divided the market. A small group of railroad executives, including Cornelius Vanderbilt, Jay Gould, Collis P. Huntington, and James J. Hill, amassed unheard-of fortunes. When he died in 1877, Vanderbilt left his son $100 million.

By comparison, a decent annual wage for working a six-day week was around $350.

Some of the nation's most prominent politicians routinely accepted railroad largesse. Republican senator William M. Stewart of Nevada, a member of the Committee on Pacific Railroads, received a gift of 50,000 acres of land from the Central Pacific for his services. The worst scandal of the Grant administration grew out of corruption involving railroad promotion. As a way of diverting funds for the building of the Union Pacific Railroad, an inner circle of Union Pacific stockholders created the dummy Crédit Mobilier construction company. In return for political favors, a group of prominent Republicans received stock in the company. When the scandal broke in 1872, it politically ruined Vice President Schuyler Colfax and led to the censure of two congressmen.

Other industries also boomed in this period, especially those engaged in extracting minerals and processing natural resources. Railroad growth stimulated expansion in the production of coal, iron, stone, and lumber, and these also received significant government aid. For example, under the National Mineral Act of 1866, mining companies received millions of acres of free public land. Oil refining enjoyed a huge expansion in the 1860s and 1870s. As with railroads, an early period of fierce competition soon gave way to concentration. By the late 1870s, John D. Rockefeller's Standard Oil Company controlled almost 90 percent of the nation's oil-refining capacity.

LIBERAL REPUBLICANS AND THE ELECTION OF 1872

With the rapid growth of large-scale, capital-intensive enterprises, Republicans increasingly identified with the interests of business rather than the rights of freedmen or the antebellum ideology of "free labor." The old Civil War–era Radical Republicans had declined in influence. State Republican parties now organized themselves around the spoils of federal patronage rather than grand causes such as preserving the Union or ending slavery. Despite the Crédit Mobilier affair, Republicans had no monopoly on political scandal. In 1871 New York City newspapers reported the shocking story of how Democratic Party boss William M. Tweed and his friends had systematically stolen tens of millions from the city treasury. The "Tweed Ring" had received enormous bribes and kickbacks from city contractors and businessmen. But to many, the scandal represented only the most extreme case of the routine corruption that now plagued American political life.

By the end of President Grant's first term, a large number of disaffected Republicans sought an alternative. The Liberal Republicans, as they called themselves, emphasized the doctrines of classical economics, stressing the law of supply and demand, free trade, defense of property rights, and individualism. They called for a return to limited government, arguing that bribery, scandal, and high taxes all flowed from excessive state interference in the economy.

Liberal Republicans were also suspicious of expanding democracy. They believed that politics ought to be the province of "the best men"—educated and well-to-do men like themselves, devoted to the "science of government." They proposed civil service reform as the best way to break the hold of party machines on patronage.

Although most Liberal Republicans had enthusiastically supported abolition, the Union cause, and equal rights for freedmen, they now opposed continued federal intervention in the South. The national government had done all it could for the former slaves; they must now take care of themselves. "Root, Hog, or Die" was the harsh advice offered by Horace Greeley, editor of the *New York Tribune*. In the spring of 1872 a diverse collection of Liberal Republicans nominated Greeley to run for president. A longtime foe of the Democratic Party, Greeley nonetheless won that party's presidential nomination as well. He made a new policy for the South the center of his campaign against Grant. All Americans, Greeley urged, must put the Civil War behind them and "clasp hands across the bloody chasm."

Grant easily defeated Greeley, carrying every state in the North and winning 56 percent of the popular vote. Most Republicans were not willing to abandon the regular party organization, and "waving the bloody shirt" was still a potent vote-getter. But the 1872 election accelerated the trend toward federal abandonment of African American citizenship rights. The Liberal Republicans quickly faded as an organized political force. But their ideas helped define a growing conservative consciousness among the northern public. Their agenda included retreat from the ideal of racial justice, hostility toward trade unions, suspicion of immigrant and working-class political power, celebration of competitive individualism, and opposition to government intervention in economic affairs.

THE DEPRESSION OF 1873

In the fall of 1873 the postwar boom came to an abrupt halt as a severe financial panic triggered a deep economic depression. The collapse resulted from commercial overexpansion, especially speculative investing in the nation's railroad system. By 1876 half the nation's railroads had defaulted on their bonds. Over the next two years more than 100 banks folded and 18,000 businesses shut their doors. The depression that began in 1873 lasted sixty-five

"The Tramp," *Harper's Weekly*, September 2, 1876. The depression that began in 1873 forced many thousands of unemployed workers to go "on the tramp" in search of jobs. Men wandered from town to town, walking or riding railroad cars, desperate for a chance to work for wages or simply for room and board. The "tramp" became a powerful symbol of the misery caused by industrial depression and, as in this drawing, an image that evoked fear and nervousness among the nation's middle class.

months—the longest economic contraction in the nation's history until then.

The human toll was enormous. As factories began to close across the nation, the unemployment rate soared to about 15 percent. In many cities the jobless rate was much higher; roughly one-quarter of New York City workers were unemployed in 1874. Many thousands of men took to the road in search of work, and the "tramp" emerged as a new and menacing figure on the social landscape. The Pennsylvania Bureau of Labor Statistics noted that never before had "so many of the working classes, skilled and unskilled been moving from place to place seeking employment that was not to be had." Farmers were also hard hit by the depression. Agricultural output continued to grow, but prices and land values fell sharply. As prices for their crops fell, farmers had a more difficult time repaying their fixed loan obligations; many sank deeper into debt.

Mass meetings of workers in New York and other cities issued calls to government officials to create jobs through public works. But these appeals were rejected. Indeed, many business leaders and political figures de-nounced even meager efforts at charity. They saw the depression as a natural, if painful, part of the business cycle, one that would allow only the strongest enterprises (and workers) to survive.

The depression of the 1870s prompted workers and farmers to question the old free-labor ideology that celebrated a harmony of interests in northern society. More people voiced anger at and distrust of large corporations that exercised great economic power from outside their communities

THE ELECTORAL CRISIS OF 1876

With the economy mired in depression, Democrats looked forward to capturing the White House in 1876. New scandals plaguing the Grant administration also weakened the Republican Party. In 1875, a conspiracy surfaced between distillers and U.S. revenue agents to cheat the government out of millions in tax revenues. The government secured indictments against more than 200 members of this "Whiskey Ring," including Orville E.

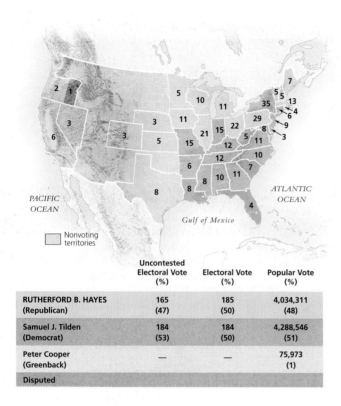

MAP 17.4 The Election of 1876 The presidential election of 1876 left the nation without a clear-cut winner.

PACIFIC OCEAN

ATLANTIC OCEAN

Gulf of Mexico

Nonvoting territories

	Uncontested Electoral Vote (%)	Electoral Vote (%)	Popular Vote (%)
RUTHERFORD B. HAYES (Republican)	165 (47)	185 (50)	4,034,311 (48)
Samuel J. Tilden (Democrat)	184 (53)	184 (50)	4,288,546 (51)
Peter Cooper (Greenback)	—	—	75,973 (1)
Disputed			

Babcock, Grant's private secretary. Though acquitted, thanks to Grant's intervention, Babcock resigned in disgrace. In 1876, Secretary of War William W. Belknap was impeached for receiving bribes for the sale of trading posts in Indian Territory, and he resigned to avoid conviction.

Democrats nominated Governor Samuel J. Tilden of New York, who brought impeccable reform credentials to his candidacy. In 1871 he had helped expose and prosecute the "Tweed Ring" in New York City. As governor he had toppled the "Canal Ring," a graft-ridden scheme involving inflated contracts for repairs on the Erie Canal. In their platform, the Democrats linked the issue of corruption to an attack on Reconstruction policies. They blamed the Republicans for instituting "a corrupt centralism."

Republican nominee Rutherford B. Hayes, governor of Ohio, also sought the high ground. As a lawyer in Cincinnati he had defended runaway slaves. Later he had distinguished himself as a general in the Union army. Hayes promised, if elected, to support an efficient civil service system, to vigorously prosecute officials who betrayed the public trust, and to introduce a system of free universal education.

On an election day marred by widespread vote fraud and violent intimidation, Tilden received 250,000 more popular votes than Hayes. But Republicans refused to concede victory, challenging the vote totals in the electoral college. Tilden garnered 184 uncontested electoral votes, one shy of the majority required to win, while Hayes received 165 (see Map 17.4). The problem centered on twenty disputed votes from Florida, Louisiana, South Carolina, and Oregon. In each of the three southern states two sets of electoral votes were returned. In Oregon, which Hayes had unquestionably carried, the Democratic governor nevertheless replaced a disputed Republican elector with a Democrat.

The crisis was unprecedented. In January 1877 Congress moved to settle the deadlock, establishing an Electoral Commission composed of five senators, five representatives, and five Supreme Court justices; eight were Republicans and seven were Democrats. The commission voted along strict partisan lines to award all the contested electoral votes to Hayes. Outraged by this decision, Democratic congressmen threatened a filibuster to block Hayes's inauguration. Violence and stalemate were avoided when Democrats and Republicans struck a compromise in February. In return for Hayes's ascendance to the presidency, the Republicans promised to appropriate more money for southern internal improvements, to appoint a Southerner to Hayes's cabinet, and to pursue a policy of noninterference ("home rule") in southern affairs.

Shortly after assuming office, Hayes ordered removal of the remaining federal troops in Louisiana and South Carolina. Without this military presence to sustain them, the Republican governors of those two states quickly lost power to Democrats. "Home rule" meant Republican abandonment of freed people, Radicals, carpetbaggers, and scalawags. It also effectively nullified the Fourteenth and Fifteenth Amendments and the Civil Rights Act of 1866. The Compromise of 1877 completed repudiation of the idea, born during the Civil War and pursued during Congressional Reconstruction, of a powerful federal government protecting the rights of all American citizens.

CHRONOLOGY

1865	Freedmen's Bureau established
	Abraham Lincoln assassinated
	Andrew Johnson begins Presidential Reconstruction
	Black codes begin to be enacted in southern states
	Thirteenth Amendment ratified
1866	Civil Rights Act passed
	Congress approves Fourteenth Amendment
	Ku Klux Klan founded
1867	Reconstruction Acts, passed over President Johnson's veto, begin Congressional Reconstruction
	Tenure of Office Act
	Southern states call constitutional conventions
1868	President Johnson impeached by the House but acquitted in Senate trial
	Fourteenth Amendment ratified
	Most Southern states readmitted to the Union
	Ulysses S. Grant elected president
1869	Congress approves Fifteenth Amendment
	Union Pacific and Central Pacific tracks meet at Promontory Point in Utah Territory
	Suffragists split into National Woman Suffrage Association and American Woman Suffrage Association
1870	Fifteenth Amendment ratified
1871	Ku Klux Klan Act passed
	"Tweed Ring" in New York City exposed
1872	Liberal Republicans break with Grant and Radicals, nominate Horace Greeley for president
	Crédit Mobilier scandal
	Grant reelected president
1873	Financial panic and beginning of economic depression
	Slaughterhouse Cases
1874	Democrats gain control of House for first time since 1856
1875	Civil Rights Act
1876	Disputed election between Samuel Tilden and Rutherford B. Hayes
1877	Electoral Commission elects Hayes president
	President Hayes dispatches federal troops to break Great Railroad Strike and withdraws last remaining federal troops from the South

CONCLUSION

Reconstruction succeeded in the limited political sense of reuniting a nation torn apart by the Civil War. The Radical Republican vision, emphasizing racial justice, equal civil and political rights guaranteed by the Fourteenth and Fifteenth Amendments, and a new southern economy organized around independent small farmers, never enjoyed the support of the majority of its party or the northern public. By 1877, the political force of these ideals was spent and the national retreat from them nearly complete.

The end of Reconstruction left the way open for the return of white domination in the South. The freed people's political and civil equality proved only temporary. It would take a "Second Reconstruction," the civil rights movement of the next century, to establish full black citizenship rights once and for all. The federal government's failure to pursue land reform left former slaves without the economic independence needed for full emancipation. Yet the newly autonomous black family, along with black-controlled churches, schools, and other social institutions, provided the foundations for the modern African American community. If the federal government was not yet fully committed to protecting equal rights in local communities, the Reconstruction Era at least pointed to how that goal might be achieved. Even as the federal government retreated from the defense of equal rights for black people, it took a more aggressive stance as the protector of business interests. The Hayes administration responded decisively to one of the worst outbreaks of class violence in American history by dispatching federal troops to several northern cities to break the Great Railroad Strike of 1877. In the aftermath of Reconstruction, the struggle between capital and labor had clearly replaced "the southern question" as the number one political issue of the day. "The overwhelming labor question has dwarfed all other questions into nothing," wrote an Ohio Republican. "We have home questions enough to occupy attention now."

— REVIEW QUESTIONS

1. How did various visions of a "reconstructed" South differ? How did these visions reflect the old political and social divisions that had led to the Civil War?

2. What key changes did emancipation make in the political and economic status of African Americans? Discuss the expansion of citizenship rights in the post–Civil War years. To what extent did women share in the gains made by African Americans?

3. What role did such institutions as the family, the church, the schools, and the political parties play in the African American transition to freedom?

4. How did white Southerners attempt to limit the freedom of former slaves? How did these efforts succeed, and how did they fail?

5. Evaluate the achievements and failures of Reconstruction governments in the southern states.

6. What were the crucial economic changes occurring in the North and South during the Reconstruction era?

— RECOMMENDED READING

David W. Blight, *Race and Reunion: The Civil War in American Memory* (2001). An elegantly written and deeply researched inquiry into how Americans "remembered" the Civil War in the half century after Appomattox, arguing that sectional reconciliation came at the cost of racial division.

Thomas J. Brown, ed., *Reconstructions: New Perspectives on the Postbellum United States* (2006). A wide-ranging collection of essays that explores Reconstruction from a broadly national perspective, including economic, political, and cultural impacts.

Jane Dailey, *Before Jim Crow: The Politics of Race in Postemancipation Virginia* (2000). A fine study that focuses on the tension between the drive to establish white supremacy and the struggle for biracial coalitions in post–Civil War Virginia politics.

Laura F. Edwards, *Gendered Strife & Confusion: The Political Culture of Reconstruction* (1997). An ambitious analysis of how gender ideologies played a key role in shaping the party politics and social relations of the Reconstruction era south.

Michael W. Fitzgerald, *The Union League Movement in the Deep South* (1989). Uses the Union League as a lens through which to examine race relations and the close connections between politics and economic change in the post–Civil War South.

Eric Foner, *Forever Free: The Story of Emancipation and Reconstruction* (2005). An excellent brief one-volume overview that condenses Foner's more comprehensive work on Reconstruction. It also includes several striking "visual essays" by Joshua Brown, documenting the changes in visual representations of African Americans in popular media of the era.

Eric Foner, *Reconstruction: America's Unfinished Revolution, 1863–1877* (1988). The most comprehensive and thoroughly researched overview of the Reconstruction era.

Steven Hahn, *A Nation Under Our Feet: Black Political Struggles in the Rural South from Slavery to the Great Migration* (2003). This Pulitzer Prize–winning history includes excellent chapters detailing the political activism of recently freed slaves and the violent resistance they encountered throughout the rural South.

Elizabeth Regosin, *Freedom's Promise: Ex-Slave Families and Citizenship in the Age of Emancipation* (2002). A thoughtful analysis of how freedmen and freedwomen asserted familial relationships as a means to claiming citizenship rights after emancipation, based on research into federal pension applications made by dependent survivors of Civil War soldiers.

Scott Reynolds Nelson, *Iron Confederacies: Southern Railways, Klan Violence, and Reconstruction* (1999). Pathbreaking analysis of how conservative southern and northern business interests rebuilt the South's railroad system and also achieved enormous political power within individual states.

Heather Cox Richardson, *West From Appomattox: The Reconstruction of America After the Civil War* (2007). A new interpretation of the era that both emphasizes post–Civil War change in the nation's West and large cities and locates the origins of current political divisions in the Reconstruction period.

For study resources for this chapter, go to **http://www.myhistorylab.com** and choose *Out of Many*. You will find a wealth of study and review material for this chapter, including pretests and posttests, customized study plan, key-term review flash cards, interactive map and document activities, and documents for analysis.

Conquest and Survival

The Trans–Mississippi West

1860–1900

The Oklahoma Land Rush

Indian Territory (Oklahoma)

Decades after the event, cowboy Evan G. Barnard vividly recalled the preparations made by settlers when Oklahoma territorial officials announced the biggest "land rush" in American history. "Thousands of people gathered along the border. . . . As the day for the race drew near, the settlers practiced running their horses and driving carts." Finally, the morning of April 22, 1889, arrived. "At ten o'clock people lined up . . . ready for the great race of their lives." Like many others, Barnard displayed his guns prominently on his hips, determined to discourage competitors from claiming the 160 acres of prime land that he intended to grab for himself.

Evan Barnard's story was one strand in the larger tale of the destruction and creation of communities in the trans–Mississippi West. In the 1830s, the federal government designated what was to become the state of Oklahoma as Indian Territory, reserved for the Five Civilized Tribes (Cherokees, Chickasaws, Choctaws, Creeks, and Seminoles) who had been forcibly removed from their eastern lands. All five tribes had reestablished themselves as sovereign republics in Indian Territory. The Cherokees and Choctaws became prosperous cotton growers. The Creeks managed large herds of hogs and cattle, and the Chickasaws grazed not only cattle but also sheep and goats on their open fields. The Five Tribes also ran sawmills, gristmills, and cotton gins. Indian merchants were soon dealing with other tribespeople as well as licensed white traders and even contracting with the federal government.

The Civil War, however, took a heavy toll on their success. Some tribes, slaveholders themselves, sided with the Confederacy; others with the Union. When the war ended, more than 10,000 people—nearly one-fifth of the population of Indian Territory—had died. To make matters worse, new treaties required the Five Civilized Tribes to cede the entire western half of the territory, including the former northern Indian territory of Nebraska and Kansas, for the resettlement of tribes from other regions.

Western Oklahoma thereby became home to thousands of newly displaced peoples, including the Pawnees, Peorias, Ottawas, Wyandots, and Miamis. Many small tribes readily took to farming and rebuilt their communities. But the nomadic, buffalo-hunting Kiowas, Cheyennes, Comanches, and Arapahoes did not settle so peacefully. They continued to traverse the plains until the U.S. Army finally forced them onto reservations. Eventually, more than 80,000 tribespeople were living on twenty-one separate reservations in western Oklahoma, all governed by agents appointed by the federal government. ➤

The opening of the unassigned far western district of Oklahoma, however, signaled the impending end of Indian sovereignty. Many non-Indians saw this almost 2-million-acre strip as a Promised Land, perfect for dividing into thousands of small farms. African Americans, many of whom were former slaves of Indian planters, appealed to the federal government for the right to stake claims there. Another group of would-be homesteaders, known as "Boomers," quickly tired of petitioning and invaded the district in 1880, only to be booted out by the Tenth Cavalry. Meanwhile, the railroads, seeing the potential for lucrative commerce, put constant pressure on the federal government to open No Man's Land for settlement. In 1889, the U.S. Congress finally gave in.

Cowboy Barnard was just one of thousands to pour into No Man's Land on April 22, 1889. Many homesteaders simply crossed the border from Kansas. Southerners, dispossessed by warfare and economic ruin in their own region, were also well represented. Market-minded settlers claimed the land nearest the railroads, and by nightfall of April 22, they had set up tent cities along the tracks. In a little over two months, after 6,000 homestead claims had been filed, the first sod houses appeared, sheltering growing communities of non-Indian farmers, ranchers, and other entrepreneurs.

Some Indian leaders petitioned the federal government for the right to resettle on new land distant from white settlers, but nothing came from their efforts.

Dramatic as it was, the land rush of 1889 was only one in a series of events that soon dispossessed Oklahoma's Indians of their remaining lands. First, the federal government broke up the estates held collectively by various tribes in western Oklahoma, assigning to individuals the standard 160-acre allotment and allowing non-Indian homesteaders to claim the rest. Then, in 1898, Congress passed the Curtis Act, which abolished tribal jurisdiction over all Indian Territory. Members of the former Indian nations were directed to dismantle their governments, abandon their estates, and join the ranks of other homesteaders (see Map 18.1). They nevertheless retained many of their tribal customs and managed to regain their sovereign status in 1977.

Later generations of Oklahomans often celebrated their historic ties to the Indian nations. At the formal ceremony marking statehood, just before the newly elected governor took the oath of office, a mock wedding ceremony united a tough and virile cowboy with a demure and submissive Indian maiden. By this time, in 1907, tribespeople were outnumbered in Oklahoma by ten to one.

By this time also, nearly one-quarter of the entire population of the United States lived west of the Mississippi River. Hundreds of new communities, supported primarily by cattle ranching, agriculture, mining, or other industries, had not only grown with the emerging national economy but also helped to shape it in the process. The newcomers had displaced communities that had formed centuries earlier. They also drastically transformed the physical landscape. Through their activities and the support of Easterners, the United States realized an ambition that John L. O'Sullivan had described in 1845 as the nation's "manifest destiny to overspread the continent" and remake it in a new image.

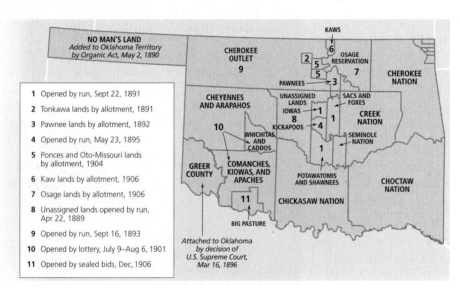

MAP 18.1 Oklahoma Territory Land openings to settlers came at different times, making new land available through various means.

SOURCE: From *Historical Atlas of Oklahoma*, 3rd edition, by John W. Morris, Charles R. Goins, and Edwin C. McReynolds. Copyright © 1965, 1976, 1986 by the University of Oklahoma Press, Norman. Reprinted by permission of the publisher. All rights reserved.

Focus Questions

1. What was the impact of U.S. western expansion on Indian societies?

2. In what ways was the post–Civil War West an "internal empire," and how did its development depend on the emergence of new technologies and new industries?

3. How can the history of the American West be told as the creation of new communities and the displacement of old communities?

4. How did agribusiness differ from forms of family farming?

5. What place did the West hold in the national imagination?

1860–1900

INDIAN PEOPLES UNDER SIEGE

The Indians living west of the Mississippi River keenly felt the pressure of the gradual incorporation of the West into the American nation. California became a state in 1850, Oregon in 1859. Congress consolidated the national domain in the next decades by granting territorial status to Utah, New Mexico, Washington, Dakota, Colorado, Nevada, Arizona, Idaho, Montana, and Wyoming. The purchase of Alaska in 1867 added an area twice the size of Texas and extended the nation beyond its contiguous borders so that it reached almost to Russia and the North Pole. The federal government made itself the custodian of all these thinly settled regions, with appointed white governors supervising the transition from territorial status to statehood.

A series of events brought large numbers of white settlers into these new states and territories: the discovery of gold in California in 1848, the opening of western lands to homesteaders in 1862, and the completion of the transcontinental railroad in 1869. With competition for the land and its resources escalating into violent skirmishes and small wars, federal officials became determined to end tribal rule and bring Indians into the American mainstream.

INDIAN TERRITORY

Before the European colonists reached the New World, various Indian tribes had occupied western lands for more than 20,000 years. Hundreds of tribes, totaling perhaps a million members, had adapted to such extreme climates as the desert aridity of present-day Utah and Nevada, the bitter cold of the northern Great Plains, and the seasonally heavy rain of the Pacific Northwest. Many cultivated maize (corn), foraged for wild plants, fished, or hunted game. Several tribes built cities with thousands of inhabitants and traded across thousands of miles of western territory.

Invasion by the English, Spanish, and other Europeans brought disease, religious conversion, and new patterns of commerce. But geographic isolation still gave many tribes a margin of survival unknown in the East. At the close of the Civil War, approximately 360,000 Indian peoples still lived in the trans–Mississippi West, the majority of them in the Great Plains.

The surviving tribes adapted to changing conditions. The Plains Indians learned to ride the horses and shoot the guns introduced by Spanish and British traders. The Pawnees migrated farther westward to evade encroaching non-Indian settlers, while the Sioux and the Comanches fought neighboring tribes to gain control of large stretches of the Great Plains. The southwestern Hopis and Zunis, conquered earlier by the Spanish, continued to trade with the Mexicans who lived near them. Some tribes took dramatic steps toward accommodation with white ways. Even before they were uprooted and moved across the Mississippi River, the Cherokees had learned English, converted to Christianity, established a constitutional republic, and become a nation of farmers.

Legally, the federal government had long regarded Indian tribes as autonomous nations residing within American boundaries and had negotiated numerous treaties with them over land rights and commerce. But pressured by land-hungry whites, several states had violated these federal treaties so often that the U.S. Congress passed the Indian Removal Act of 1830 (see Chapter 10), which provided funds to relocate all eastern tribes by force if necessary. The Cherokees challenged this legislation, and the Supreme Court ruled in their favor in *Cherokee Nation* v. *Georgia* (1831). Ignoring the Court's decision, President Andrew Jackson, known as a hardened Indian fighter, forced many tribes to cede their land and remove to Indian Territory. There, it was believed, they might live undisturbed by whites and gradually adjust to "civilized" ways. But soon, the onslaught of white settlers, railroad entrepreneurs, and prospectors rushing for gold pressured tribes to cede millions of their acres to the United States. In 1854, to open the Kansas and Nebraska Territories for white settlement, the federal government simply abolished the northern half of Indian Territory. As demand for resources and land accelerated, the entire plan for a permanent Indian Territory fell apart.

THE RESERVATION POLICY AND THE SLAUGHTER OF THE BUFFALO

As early as the 1840s, highly placed officials had outlined a plan to subdue the intensifying rivalry over natural resources and land. Under the terms of their proposal, individual tribes would agree to live within clearly defined zones—reservations. In exchange, the Bureau of Indian Affairs would provide guidance, while U.S. military forces ensured protection. This policy also reflected the vision of many "Friends of the Indian," educators and Protestant missionaries who aspired to "civilize the savages." By the end of the 1850s, eight western reservations had been established where Indian peoples were induced to speak English, take up farming, and convert to Christianity (see Map 18.2).

Several tribes signed treaties, although often under duress. High-handed officials, such as governor Isaac Stevens of Washington Territory, made no attempt at legitimate negotiations, choosing instead to intimidate or deceive the tribal chiefs into signing away their lands. State officials moved the Indians onto three reservations after their leaders signed away 45,000 square miles of tribal land. The Suquamish leader Seattle admitted defeat but warned the governor: "Your time of decay may be distant, but it will surely come."

Those tribes that moved to reservations often found federal policies inadequate to their needs. The Medicine Lodge Treaty of 1867 assigned reservations in existing Indian Territory to Comanches, Plains (Kiowa) Apaches, Kiowas, Cheyennes, and Arapahoes, bringing these tribes together with Sioux, Shoshones, and Bannocks. All told, more than 100,000 people found themselves competing intensely for survival. Over the next decade, a group of

Quakers appointed by President Ulysses S. Grant attempted to mediate differences among the tribes and to supply the starving peoples with food and seed. Corrupt officials of the Bureau of Indian Affairs routinely diverted funds for their own use and reduced food supplies, a policy promoting malnutrition, demoralization, and desperation. Meanwhile, white prospectors and miners continued to flood the Dakota Territory.

The nomadic tribes that hunted and gathered over large territories saw their freedom sharply curtailed. The Lakotas, or Western Sioux, a loose confederation of bands scattered across the northern Great Plains, were one of the largest and most adaptive of all Indian nations. Seizing buffalo-hunting territory from their rivals, the Pawnees and the Crows, the Sioux had learned to follow the herds on horseback. Buffalo meat and hides fed and clothed the Sioux and satisfied many of their other needs as well. Images of buffalo appeared in their religious symbols and ceremonial dress.

The mass slaughter of the buffalo brought this crisis to a peak. In earlier eras, vast herds of buffalo had literally darkened the western horizon. As gunpowder and the railroad moved west, the number of buffalo fell rapidly. Non-Indian traders avidly sought fur for coats, hide for leather, bones for fertilizer, and heads for trophies. New rifles, like the .50 caliber Sharps, could kill at 600 feet; one sharpshooter bragged of killing 3,000 buffalo. Army commanders encouraged the slaughter, accurately predicting that starvation would break tribal resistance to the reservation system. With their food sources practically destroyed, diseases such as smallpox and cholera (brought by fur traders) sweeping through their villages, and their way of life undermined, many Great Plains tribes, including many Sioux, concluded that they could only fight or die.

THE INDIAN WARS

In 1864, large-scale war erupted. Having decided to terminate all treaties with tribes in eastern Colorado, territorial governor John Evans encouraged a group of white civilians, the Colorado Volunteers, to stage raids through Cheyenne campgrounds. Seeking protection, Chief Black Kettle brought a band of 800 Cheyennes to a U.S. fort and received orders to set up camp at Sand Creek. Feeling secure in this arrangement, Black Kettle sent out most of his young warriors to hunt. Several weeks later, on November 29, 1864, the Colorado Volunteers and soldiers attacked. While Black Kettle held up a U.S. flag and a white truce banner, a disorderly group of 700 men, many of them drunk, slaughtered 105 Cheyenne women and children and 28 men. They mutilated the corpses and took scalps back to Denver to exhibit as trophies. Iron Teeth, who survived, remembered seeing a woman "crawling along on the ground, shot, scalped, crazy, but not yet dead." Months after the Sand Creek Massacre, bands of

MAP EXPLORATION

To explore an interactive version of this map, go to **www.prenhall.com/faragher6/map18.2**

MAP 18.2 Major Indian Battles and Indian Reservations,
1860–1900 As commercial routes and white populations passed through and occupied Indian lands, warfare inevitably erupted. The displacement of Indians to reservations opened access by farmers, ranchers, and investors to natural resources and to markets.

Cheyennes, Sioux, and Arapahoes were still retaliating, burning civilian outposts and sometimes killing whole families.

The Sioux played the most dramatic roles in the Indian Wars. In 1851, believing the U.S. government would recognize their own rights of conquest over other Indian tribes, the Sioux relinquished large tracts of land as a demonstration of good faith. But within a decade, a mass invasion of miners and the construction of military forts along the Bozeman Trail in Wyoming, the Sioux's principal buffalo range, threw the tribe's future into doubt. During the Great Sioux War of 1865–67, the Oglala Sioux warrior Red Cloud fought the U.S. Army to a stalemate

and forced the government to abandon its forts, which the Sioux then burned to the ground. The Treaty of Fort Laramie, signed in 1868, restored only a temporary peace to the region.

The Treaty of Fort Laramie granted the Sioux the right to occupy the Black Hills, or Paha Sapa, their sacred land, "as long as the grass shall grow," but the discovery of gold soon undermined this guarantee. White prospectors hurriedly invaded the territory. Directed to quash rumors of fabulous deposits of the precious metal, Lieutenant Colonel George Armstrong Custer organized a surveying expedition to the Black Hills during the summer of 1874, but, contrary to plan, the Civil War hero described rich veins of ore that

The Oglala Sioux spiritual leader, Chief Red Cloud, in an 1868 photograph. Here he is seen with (l. to r.) Red Dog, Little Wound, interpreter John Bridgeman (standing), (Red Cloud), American Horse, and Red Shirt. He ventured to Washington with this delegation to discuss with President Ulysses S. Grant the various provisions of the peace treaty, just signed, to end the violent conflict over the Bozeman Trail.

could be cheaply extracted. The U.S. Congress then pushed to purchase the territory for Americans. To protect their land, thousands of Sioux, Cheyenne, and Arapaho warriors moved into war camps during the summer of 1876 and prepared for battle (see Map 18.2).

After several months of skirmishes between the U.S. Army and Indian warriors, Lieutenant Colonel Custer decided to rush ahead to a site in Montana that was known to white soldiers as Little Bighorn and to Lakotas as Greasy Grass. This foolhardy move offered the allied Cheyenne and Sioux warriors a perfect opportunity to cut off Custer's logistical and military support. On June 25, 1876, Custer and his troops were wiped out by one of the largest Indian contingents ever assembled, an estimated 2,000 to 4,000 warriors.

"Custer's Last Stand" gave Indian-haters the emotional ammunition to whip up public excitement. After Custer's defeat, Sitting Bull reportedly said, "Now they will never let us rest." The U.S. Army tracked down the disbanded Indian contingents one by one and forced them to surrender. In February 1877, Sioux leadership in the Indian Wars ended.

Among the last to hold out against the reservation system were the Apaches in the Southwest. Most Apache bands had abided by the Medicine Lodge Treaty of 1867, but in 1874, some of the Apache bands, unable to tolerate the harsh conditions on the reservation, returned to their old ways of seizing territory and stealing cattle.

Pursued by the U.S. Army, the Apaches earned a reputation as intrepid warriors. Brilliant strategists like Geronimo and skilled horse-riding braves became legendary for lightning-swift raids against the white outposts in the rugged Arizona terrain. In 1874–75, the Kiowas and the Comanches, both powerful tribes, joined the Apaches in one of the bloodiest conflicts of the era, the Red River War. The U.S. Army ultimately prevailed, although less by military might than by denying Indians access to food. Small-scale warfare sputtered on until September 1886, when Geronimo, his band reduced to only thirty people, finally surrendered, thereby ending the Indian Wars.

THE NEZ PERCÉ

For generations, the Nez Percé had regarded themselves as good friends to white traders and settlers. Living in the plateau where Idaho, Washington, and Oregon now meet, they had saved the Lewis and Clark expedition from starvation in 1803. The Nez Percé had occasionally assisted American armies against hostile tribes, and many of them were converts to Christianity.

But the discovery of gold on Nez Percé territory in 1860 changed their relations with whites for the worse. Pressed by prospectors and mining companies, government officials demanded, in the treaty of 1863, that the Nez Percé cede 6 million acres, nine-tenths of their land, at less than ten cents per acre. Some of the Nez Percé leaders agreed to the terms of the treaty, which had been fraudulently signed on behalf of the entire tribe, but others refused. At first, federal officials listened to Nez Percé complaints against the treaty and decided to allow them to remain on their land. But responding to pressure from settlers and politicians, they almost immediately reversed their decision, ordering the Nez Percé, including Chief Joseph and his followers, to sell their land and to move onto a reservation.

Intending to comply, Chief Joseph's band set out from the Wallowa Valley with their livestock and all the possessions they could carry. Along the way, some young members of another Indian band traveling with them rode away from camp to avenge the death of one of their own by killing several white settlers. Hoping to explain the situation, a Nez Percé truce team approached U.S. troops.

Kiowa Preparing for a War Expedition, ca. 1887. This sketch on paper was made by an Indian artist, Silverhorn, who had himself taken part in the final revolt of the Kiowas in 1874. He later became a medicine man and then served as a private in the U.S. Cavalry at Fort Sill, Oklahoma Territory.

SOURCE: Silverhorn (Native American), "Kiowa Preparing for a War Expedition." From "Sketchbook," 1887. Graphite, ink and crayon on paper. Collection of the McNay Art Museum, Gift of Mrs. Terrell Bartlett.

THE INTERNAL EMPIRE

Since the time of Christopher Columbus, the Americas had inspired in Europeans visions of a land of incredible wealth, free for the taking. In the nineteenth century, the North American continent, stretching across sparsely populated territories toward the Pacific Ocean, revived this fantasy, especially as early reports conjured dreams of mountains of gold and silver. Determined to make their fortunes, be it from copper in Arizona, wheat in Montana, or oranges in California, numerous adventurers traveled west. As a group, they carried out the largest migration and greatest commercial expansion in American history.

But the settlers themselves also became the subjects of a huge "internal empire" whose financial, political, and industrial centers of power remained in the East. Only a small number of settlers actually struck it rich in the great extractive industries—mining, lumbering, ranching, and farming—that ruled the western economy. Meanwhile, older populations—Indian peoples, Hispanic peoples, and more recently settled communities like the Mormons—struggled to create places for themselves in this new expansionist order.

MINING TOWNS

The discovery of gold in California in 1848 attracted fortune seekers from across the United States, from Europe, and from as far away as Chile and China; just ten years later, approximately 35,000 Chinese men were working in western mines. Meanwhile, prospecting parties searching for the mother lode overran the territories, setting a pattern for intermittent rushes for gold, silver, and copper that extended from the Colorado mountains to the Arizona deserts, from California to Oregon and Washington, and from Alaska to the Black Hills of South Dakota. Mining camps and boomtowns soon dotted what had once been thinly settled regions and speeded the urban development of the West. The population of California alone jumped from 14,000 in 1848 to 223,856 just four years later. Mining soon brought the West into a vast global market for capital, commodities, and labor (see Map 18.3).

The troops opened fire, and the Indian riders fired back, killing one-third of the soldiers. Brilliantly outmaneuvering vengeful U.S. troops sent to intercept them, the 750 Nez Percé retreated for some 1,400 miles into Montana and Wyoming through mountains and prairies and across the Bitterroot Range. Over the three-and-a-half months of their journey, Nez Percé braves fought 2,000 regular U.S. troops and eighteen Indian auxiliary detachments in eighteen separate engagements and two major battles. U.S. troops finally trapped the Nez Percé in the Bear Paw Mountains of northern Montana, just thirty miles from the Canadian border. Suffering from hunger and cold, they surrendered.

Promised they would be returned to Oregon, the Nez Percé were sent instead to disease-ridden bottomland near Fort Leavenworth in Kansas, and then to Oklahoma. Arguing for the right of his people to return to their Oregon reservation, Joseph spoke eloquently, through an interpreter, to Congress in 1879: "Treat all men alike. Give them all the same law. Give them all an even chance to live and grow. All men were made by the same Great Spirit Chief." The last remnant of Joseph's band were deported under guard to a non–Nez Percé reservation in Washington, where Chief Joseph died in 1904 "of a broken heart," and where his descendants continue to live in exile to this day.

MAP EXPLORATION

To explore an interactive version of this map, go to **www.prenhall.com/faragher6/map18.3**

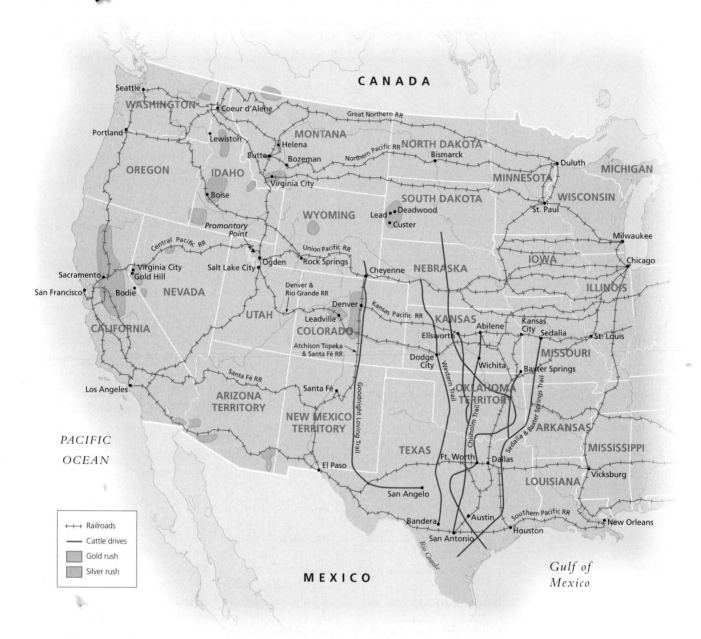

MAP 18.3 Railroad Routes, Cattle Trails, Gold and Silver Rushes, 1860–1900 By the end of the nineteenth century, the vast region of the West was crosscut by hundreds of lines of transportation and communication. The trade in precious metals and in cattle helped build a population almost constantly on the move, following the rushes for gold or the herds of cattle.

SOURCE: *Encyclopedia of American Social History.*

The mining industry quickly grew from its treasure-hunt origins into a grand corporate enterprise. The most successful mine owners bought out the smaller claims and built an entire industry around their stakes. They found investors to finance their expansion and used the borrowed capital to purchase the latest in extractive technology, such as new explosives, compressed-air or diamond-headed rotary drills, and wire cable. They gained access to timber to fortify their underground structures and water to feed the hydraulic pumps that washed down mountains. They built smelters to refine the crude ore into ingots and often financed railroads to transport the product to distant markets. By the end of the century, the Anaconda Copper Mining Company, which had mining interests throughout the West, had expanded into hydroelectricity to become one of the most powerful corporations in the nation.

The mining corporations laid the basis for a new economy as well as an interim government and established many of the region's first white settlements. Before the advent of railroads, ore had to be brought out of, and supplies brought into, mining areas by boats, wagons, and mules traveling hundreds of miles over rough territory. The railroad made transportation of supplies and products easier and faster. The shipping trade meanwhile grew into an important industry of its own, employing thousands of merchants, peddlers, and sailors. Gold Hill and nearby Virginia City, Nevada, began as a cluster of small mining camps and by the early 1860s became a thriving urban community of nearly 6,000 people. A decade later, the population had quadrupled, but it subsequently fell sharply as the mines gave out. Occasionally, ore veins lasted long enough—as in Butte, Montana, center of the copper-mining district—to create permanent cities.

The many boomtowns, known as "Helldorados," flourished, if only temporarily, as ethnically diverse communities. Men outnumbered women by as much as ten to one, and very few lived with families or stayed very long. The Chinese men, the sojourners who hoped to find riches in the "Gold Mountain" of America before returning home, clustered together and created their own institutions such as social clubs, temples, and fraternal societies known as tongs. Some miners lived unusually well, feasting on oysters trucked in at great expense. The town center was usually the saloon, where, as one observer complained, men "without the restraint of law, indifferent to public opinion, and unburdened by families, drink whenever they feel like it, whenever they have the money to pay for it, and whenever there is nothing else to do."

The western labor movement began in these camps, partly as a response to dangerous working conditions. In the hardrock mines of the 1870s, one of every thirty workers was disabled, one of eighty killed. Balladeers back in Ireland sang of Butte as the town "where the streets were paved with Irish bones." Miners began to organize in the 1860s, demanding good pay for dangerous and life-shortening work. By the end of the century, they had established the strongest unions in the West.

When mine owners' private armies "arrested" strikers or fought their unions with rifle fire, miners burned down the campsites, seized trains loaded with ore, and sabotaged company property. The miners' unions also helped to secure legislation mandating a maximum eight-hour day for certain jobs and workmen's compensation for injuries. Such laws were enacted in Idaho, Arizona, and New Mexico by the 1910s, long before similar laws in most Eastern states.

The unions fought hard, but they did so exclusively for the benefit of white workers. The native-born and the Irish and Cornish immigrants (from Cornwall, England) far outnumbered other groups before the turn of the

William Henry Jackson (1843–1942) was the first person to photograph the Yellowstone region in Wyoming Territory. Documenting the Grand Tetons, including the magnificent waterfalls and geysers, his images caught the public's attention and likewise helped to convince Congress to create the Yellowstone National Park in 1872. Jackson then joined up with the U.S. Geological Survey to photograph various sites in the Rocky Mountains. Here he captures "John, the Cook" baking slapjacks in a mining camp in 1874.

century, when Italians, Slavs, and Greeks began to replace them. Labor unions eventually admitted these new immigrants but refused Chinese, Mexican, Indian, and African American workers.

When prices and ore production fell sharply, not even unions could stop the owners from shutting down the mines and leaving ghost towns in their wake. Often they also left behind an environmental disaster. Hydraulic mining, which used water cannons to blast hillsides and expose gold deposits, drove tons of rock and earth into the rivers and canyons. By the late 1860s, California's rivers were clogged, producing floods that wiped out towns and farms. In 1893, Congress finally passed the Caminetti Act, giving the state the power to regulate the mines. (The act also created the Sacramento River Commission, which began to replace free-flowing rivers with canals and dams.) Underground mining continued unregulated, using up whole forests for timbers and filling the air with dangerous, sulfurous smoke.

MORMON SETTLEMENTS

Led by their new prophet, Brigham Young, the Mormons migrated in 1846–47 from the Midwest to the Great Salt Lake Basin to form an independent theocratic state called Deseret and to affirm the sanctity of plural marriage, or polygamy. By 1870, more than 87,000 Mormons lived in Utah Territory, creating relatively sizable communities complemented by satellite villages joined to communal farmlands and a common pasture. Relying on agricultural techniques learned from local Indian tribes, the Mormons built dams for irrigation and harvested a variety of crops from desert soil. Eventually, nearly 500 Mormon communities spread from Oregon to Idaho to northern Mexico (see Map 18.4).

As territorial rule tightened, the Mormons saw their unique way of life once again threatened. The newspapers and the courts repeatedly assailed the Mormons for the supposed sexual excesses of their system of plural marriage, condemning them as heathens and savages. Preceded by prohibitory federal laws enacted in 1862 and 1874, the Supreme Court finally ruled against polygamy in the 1879 case of *United States* v. *Reynolds,* which granted the freedom of belief but not the freedom of practice. In 1882, Congress passed the Edmunds Act, which effectively disenfranchised those who believed in or practiced polygamy and threatened them with fines and imprisonment. Equally devastating was the Edmunds-Tucker Act, passed five years later, which destroyed the temporal power of the Mormon Church by confiscating all assets over $50,000 and establishing a federal commission to oversee all elections in the territory. By the early 1890s, Mormon leaders officially renounced the practice of plural marriage.

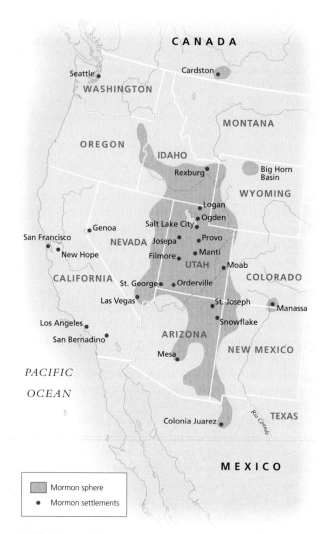

MAP 18.4 Mormon Cultural Diffusion, ca. 1883 Mormon settlements permeated many sparsely populated sections of Idaho, Nevada, Arizona, Wyoming, Colorado, and New Mexico. Built with church backing and the strong commitment of community members, they survived and even prospered in adverse climates.

SOURCE: *Mormon Cultural Diffusion, ca. 1883,* Donald W. Meinig, "The Geography of the American West, 1847–1964" from *The Annals of the Association of American Geographers* 55, no. 2, June 1965.

Although Brigham Young wed twenty-seven women and fathered fifty-six children, no more than 15 to 20 percent of Mormon families practiced polygamy and even then, two wives was the norm. Still, the "celestial" law of plural marriage had been central to the Mormons' messianic mission. Forced to give up the right to the practice, they gave up many other aspects of their distinctive communal life, including the common ownership of land. By the time Utah became a state in 1896, Mormon communities resembled in some ways the society that the original settlers had sought to escape. Nevertheless, they combined their religious cohesion with leadership in the expanding regional economy to become a major political force in the West.

MEXICAN BORDERLAND COMMUNITIES

The Treaty of Guadalupe Hidalgo, which ended the Mexican-American War in 1848, allowed the Hispanic people north of the Rio Grande to choose between immigrating to Mexico or staying in what was now the United States. But the new Mexican-American border, one of the longest unguarded boundaries in the world, did not sever communities that had been connected for centuries. What gradually emerged was an economically and socially interdependent zone, the Anglo-Hispanic borderlands linking the United States and Mexico.

Although under the treaty all Hispanics were formally guaranteed citizenship and the "free enjoyment of their liberty and property," local Anglos (as the Mexicans called white Americans) often violated these provisions and, through fraud or coercion, took control of the land. The Sante Fe Ring, a group of lawyers, politicians, and land speculators, stole millions of acres from the public domain and grabbed over 80 percent of the Mexicano landholdings in New Mexico alone. More often, Anglos used new federal laws to their own benefit.

For a time, Arizona and New Mexico seemed to hold out hope for a mutually beneficial interaction between Mexicanos and Anglos. A prosperous class of Hispanic landowners, with long-standing ties to Anglos through marriage, had established itself in cities like Albuquerque and Tucson, old Spanish towns that had been founded in the seventeenth and eighteenth centuries. Estevan Ochoa, merchant, philanthropist, and the only Mexican to serve as mayor of Tucson following the Gadsden Purchase in 1853, managed to build one of the largest business empires in the West. In Las Cruces, New Mexico, an exceptional family such as the wealthy Amadors could shop by mail from Bloomingdale's, travel to the World's Fair in Chicago, and send their children to English-language Catholic schools. Even the small and struggling Mexicano mid-

dle class could afford such modern conveniences as kitchen stoves and sewing machines. These Mexican elites, well integrated into the emerging national economy, continued to wield political power as ranchers, landlords, and real estate developers until the end of the century. They secured passage of bills for education in their regions and often served as superintendents of local schools. Several prominent merchants became territorial delegates to Congress.

But the majority of Mexicans who had lived in the mountains and deserts of the Southwest for well over two centuries were less prepared for these changes. Most had worked outside the commercial economy, farming and herding sheep for their own subsistence. Before 1848, they had few contacts with the outside world. With the Anglos came land closures as well as commercial expansion, prompted by railroad, mining, and timber industries. Many poor families found themselves crowded onto plots too small for subsistence farming. Many turned to seasonal labor on the new Anglo-owned commercial farms, where they became the first of many generations of poorly paid migratory workers. Other Mexicanos adapted by taking jobs on the railroad or in the mines. Meanwhile, their wives and daughters moved to the new towns and cities in such numbers that by the end of the century,

Mexican Americans in San Antonio continued to conduct their traditional market bazaar well after the incorporation of this region into the United States. Forced off the land and excluded from the better-paying jobs in the emerging regional economy, many Mexicanos, and especially women, sought to sell the products of their own handiwork for cash or for bartered food and clothing.

SOURCE: Thomas Allen, "Market Plaza," 1878–1879. Oil on canvas, 26 × 39 1/2. Witte Museum, San Antonio, Texas.

Mexicanos had become a predominantly urban population, dependent on wages for survival.

Women were quickly drawn into the expanding network of market and wage relations. They tried to make ends meet by selling produce from their backyard gardens; more often they worked as seamstresses or laundresses. Formerly at the center of a communal society, Mexicanas found themselves with fewer options in the cash economy. What wages they could now earn fell below even the low sums paid to their husbands, and women lost status within both the family and community.

Occasionally, Mexicanos organized to reverse these trends or at least to limit the damage done to their communities. In the 1880s, Las Gorras Blancas, a band of agrarian rebels in New Mexico, destroyed railroad ties and farm machinery and posted demands for justice on fences of the new Anglo farms and ranches. In 1890, Las Gorras turned from social banditry to political organization, forming *El Partido del Pueblo Unido* (The People's Party). Organized along similar lines, *El Alianzo Hispano-Americano* (The Hispanic-American Alliance) was formed "to protect and fight for the rights of Spanish Americans" through political action. *Mutualistes* (mutual aid societies) provided sickness and death benefits to Mexican families.

Despite many pressures, Mexicanos preserved much of their cultural heritage. Many persisted in older ways simply because they had few choices. In addition, the influx of new immigrants from Mexico helped to reinforce traditional cultural norms. Beginning in the late 1870s, the modernizing policies of Porfirio Diaz, the president of Mexico from 1876 to 1911, brought deteriorating living conditions to the masses of poor people and prompted a migration northward that accelerated through the first decades of the twentieth century. These newcomers revitalized old customs and rituals associated with family and religion. The Roman Catholic Church retained its influence in the community, and most Mexicans continued to turn to the church to baptize infants, to celebrate the feast days of their patron saints, to marry, and to bury the dead. Special saints like the Virgin of Guadalupe and distinctive holy days like the Day of the Dead survived, along with fiestas celebrating the change of seasons. Many communities continued to commemorate Mexican national holidays, such as *Cinco de Mayo* (the Fifth of May), marking the Mexican victory over French invaders in the battle of Puebla in 1862. Spanish language and Spanish place names continued to distinguish the Southwest.

THE OPEN RANGE

The slaughter of the buffalo made way for the cattle industry, one of the most profitable businesses in the West. Texas longhorns, introduced by the Spanish, numbered over 5 million at the close of the Civil War and represented a potentially plentiful supply of beef for eastern consumers. In the spring of 1866, entrepreneurs such as Joseph G. McCoy began to build a spectacular cattle market in the eastern part of Kansas, where the Kansas Pacific Railroad provided crucial transportation links to slaughtering and packing houses and commercial distributors in Kansas City, St. Louis, and Chicago.

Drovers pushed herd after herd north from Texas. Great profits were made on Texas steers bought for $7 to $9 a head and sold in Kansas for upward of $30. In 1880, nearly 2 million cattle were slaughtered in Chicago alone. For two decades, cattle represented the West's bonanza industry.

THE LONG DRIVES

The great cattle drives depended on the cowboy, a seasonal or migrant worker. After the Civil War, cowboys—one for every 300–500 head of cattle on the trail—rounded up herds of Texas cattle and drove them as much as 1,500 miles north to grazing ranches or to the stockyards where they were readied for shipping by rail to eastern markets. The boss supplied the horses, the cowboy his own bedroll, saddle, and spurs. The workday lasted from sunup to sundown, with short night shifts for guarding the cattle. Scurvy, a widespread ailment, could be traced to the basic chuckwagon menu of sowbelly, beans, and coffee, a diet bereft of fruits and vegetables. The cowboy worked without protection from rain or hail, and severe dust storms could cause temporary blindness.

In return for his labor, the cowboy received at the best of times about $30 per month. Wages were usually paid in one lump sum at the end of a drive, a policy that encouraged cowboys to spend their money quickly and recklessly in the booming cattle towns. In the 1880s, when wages began to fall along with the price of beef, cowboys fought back by stealing cattle or by forming unions. In 1883, many Texas cowboys struck for higher wages; nearly all Wyoming cowboys struck in 1886. Aided by the legendary camaraderie fostered in the otherwise desolate conditions of the long drive, cowboys, along with miners, were among the first western workers to organize against employers.

Like other parts of the West, the cattle range was ethnically diverse. Between one-fifth and one-third of all workers were Indian, Mexican, or African American. Indian cowboys worked mainly on the northern plains and in Indian Territory; the *vaqueros,* who had previously worked on the Mexican cattle *haciendas,* or huge estates, predominated in South Texas and California. African American cowboys worked primarily in Texas, where the range cattle industry was founded (see Seeing History).

Like the vaqueros, African American cowboys were highly skilled managers of cattle. Some were sons of former slaves who had been captured from the African territory of Gambia, where cattle raising was an age-old art. Unlike Mexicans, they earned wages comparable to those paid to Anglos and, especially during the early years, worked in integrated drover parties. By the 1880s, as the center of the cattle industry shifted to the more settled regions around the northern ranches, African Americans were forced out, and they turned to other kinds of work.

Very few women participated in the long drives. Sally Redus, wife of an early Texas cattleman, once accompanied her husband on the trip from Texas to Kansas. Carrying her baby on her lap, she most likely rode the enormous distance "sidesaddle," with both legs on one side of the horse. Most women stayed back at the ranch. Occasionally, a husband and wife worked as partners, sharing even the labor of wrangling cattle, and following her husband's death, a woman might take over altogether. Elizabeth Collins, for example, turned her husband's large ranch into an extraordinarily prosperous business, earning for herself the title "Cattle Queen of Montana." The majority of wives attended to domestic chores, caring for children and maintaining the household. Their daughters, however, often tagged along after their fathers and learned to love outdoor work. They were soon riding astride, "clothespin style," roping calves, branding cattle or cutting their ears to mark them, and castrating bulls. But not until 1901 did a woman dare to enter an official rodeo contest.

THE SPORTING LIFE

In cattle towns as well as mining camps, saloons, gambling establishments, and dance halls were regular features on the horizon. The hurdy-gurdy, a form of hand

SEEING HISTORY

The Legendary Cowboy: Nat Love, Deadwood Dick

Nat Love was born a slave in 1854 and spent his childhood on a plantation in Tennessee. In 1907 he published a short autobiography, *The Life and Adventures of Nat Love, Better Known in the Cattle Country as "Deadwood Dick,"* recounting his "unusually adventurous" life during the decades after emancipation. He worked as a cowboy, a ranch hand, an Indian fighter, and a rodeo performer. His most famous episode occurred in the boomtown of Deadwood, South Dakota, where in 1876 he won a cowboy tournament. It began with a roping contest, in which Love roped, saddled, and mounted a mustang in just nine minutes, winning the almost unbelievably large prize of $200. In the second part of this competition, a shooting contest, Love once again came out on top, hitting the bull's-eye in ten out of twelve shots. He boasted that the miners and gamblers who had gathered for the tournament were so awed that they called him "Deadwood Dick," a name he proudly claimed until his death in 1921.

That name became familiar to the many readers of Edward Wheeler's *Deadwood Dick* dime novels, and at least five of Love's contemporaries claimed to be that character. Wheeler published the first installment in this popular series in 1877 as *Deadwood Dick, the Prince of the Road, or, The Black Rider of the Black Hills.* It is said the Love's autobiography reads like a dime novel, packed with adventures that no historian has yet been able to authenticate.

The photograph illustrating Love's popular autobiography captures the standard image of the cowboy of the legendary Wild West—the chaps, firearm, and ammunition in the cartridge belt circling his waist, the tack on the floor (saddle, harness, rope), and the assertive body language. But in Love's case, the cowboy is a black man.

How does Nat Love fit into the legendary Wild West? How readily would you expect nineteenth-century readers of the *Deadwood Dick* dime novels to accept the hero's identity as a black man?
How does Nat Love's identity as an African American line up with the image of the heroic cowboy in modern American popular culture?

As early as 1879, the local newspaper described Leadville, Colorado, as a town that never sleeps: "The dancing houses and liquoring shops are never shut . . . . The streets are full of drunken carousers taking the town." This photograph of a typical saloon was taken shortly before the silver mining town reached its peak, with a population topping 60,000 in 1893. That year, the repeal of the Sherman Silver Act forced thousands of out-of-work miners to search for jobs elsewhere in the West.

organ, supplied raucous music for cowboys eager to spend their money and blow off steam after the long drive. Here they found dancing partners, often called hurdy-girls or hurdies. If they wanted to do more than dance, the cowboy and his partner could retreat to one of the small rooms for rent, which were often located at the rear of the building.

During the first cattle drive to Abilene in 1867, only a few women worked as prostitutes; but by the following spring, McCoy's assistant recalled, "they came in swarms, & as the weather was warm 4 or 5 girls could huddle together in a tent very comfortably." Although some women worked in trailside "hoghouses," the best-paid prostitutes congregated in the brothel districts. Most cattle towns boasted at least one bawdy house. Dodge City had two: one with white prostitutes for white patrons; another with black prostitutes for both white and black men. Although prostitution was illegal in most towns, the laws were rarely enforced until the end of the century, when reformers led campaigns to shut down the red-light districts. Until then, prostitution supplied these women with the largest source of employment outside the home.

Like the cowboys who bought their services, most prostitutes were unmarried and in their teens or twenties. Often fed up with underpaid jobs in dressmaking or domestic service, they found few alternatives to prostitution in the cattle towns, where the cost of food and lodg-

ing was notoriously high. Still, earnings in prostitution were slim, except during the cattle-shipping season when young men outnumbered women by as much as three to one. In the best of times, a fully employed Wichita prostitute might earn $30 per week, nearly two-thirds of which would go for room and board. Injury or even death from violent clients, addiction to narcotics such as cocaine or morphine, and venereal disease were workaday dangers.

FRONTIER VIOLENCE AND RANGE WARS

The combination of prostitution, gambling, and drinking discouraged the formation of stable communities. Personal violence was notoriously commonplace on the streets and in the barrooms of cattle towns and mining camps populated mainly by young, single men. Many western towns such as Wichita outlawed the carrying of handguns, but enforcement usually lagged. Local specialty shops and mail-order catalogues continued to sell weapons with little regulation. But contrary to popular belief, gunfights were relatively rare. Local police officers, such as Wyatt Earp and James "Wild Bill" Hickok, worked mainly to keep order among drunken cowboys.

After the Civil War, violent crime, assault, and robbery rose sharply throughout the United States. In the West, the most prevalent crimes were horse theft and cattle rustling, which peaked during the height of the open range period and then fell back by the 1890s. Death by legal hanging or illegal lynching—at "necktie parties" in which the victims were "jerked to Jesus"—was the usual sentence.

The "range wars" of the 1870s produced violent conflicts. By this time, both farmers and sheepherders were encroaching on the fields where cattle had once grazed freely. Sheep chew grass down to its roots, making it practically impossible to raise cattle on land they have grazed. Farmers meanwhile set about building fences to protect their domestic livestock and property. Great cattle barons fought back against farmers by ordering cowboys to cut the new barbed-wire fences.

The cattle barons helped to bring about their own demise, but they did not go down quietly. Eager for greater profits, and often backed by foreign capital, they overstocked their herds, and eventually the cattle began to deplete the limited supply of grass. Finally, during 1885–87, a combination of summer drought and winter blizzards killed 90 percent of the cattle in the northern Plains. Many ranchers went bankrupt. Along the way, they often took out their grievances against the former cowboys who had gathered small herds for themselves. They charged these small ranchers with cattle rustling, taking them to court or, in some cases, rounding up lynching parties. As one historian has written, violence was "not a mere sideshow" but "an intrinsic part of western society."

FARMING COMMUNITIES ON THE PLAINS

The vision of a huge fertile garden extending from the Appalachians to the Pacific Ocean had inspired Americans since the early days of the republic. But the first explorers who actually traveled through the Great Plains quashed this dream. "The Great Desert" was the name they gave to the region stretching west from Kansas and Nebraska, north to Montana and the Dakotas, and south again to Oklahoma and Texas. Few trees fended off the blazing sun of summer or promised a supply of lumber for homes and fences. The occasional river or stream flowed with "muddy gruel" rather than pure, sweet water. Economically, the entire region appeared as hopelessly barren as it was vast. It took massive improvements in both transportation and farm technology—as well as unrelenting advertising and promotional campaigns—to open the Great Plains to widescale agriculture.

THE HOMESTEAD ACT

The Homestead Act of 1862 offered the first incentive to prospective white farmers. This act granted a quarter section (160 acres) of the public domain free to any settler who lived on the land for at least five years and improved it; or a settler could buy the land for $1.25 per acre after only six months' residence. Restricting its provisions to household heads, the Homestead Act encouraged adventurous and hardworking unmarried women to file between 5 and 15 percent of the claims.

Homesteaders achieved their greatest success in the central and upper Midwest, where the soil was rich and weather relatively moderate. But those settlers lured to the Great Plains by descriptions of land "carpeted with soft grass—a sylvan paradise" found themselves locked in a fierce struggle with the harsh climate and arid soil.

The dream of a homestead nevertheless died hard. Five years after the passage of the Homestead Act, *New York Tribune* editor Horace Greeley still advised his readers to strike off "into the broad, free West" and "make yourself a farm from Uncle Sam's generous domain, you will crowd nobody, starve nobody, and . . . neither you nor your children need evermore beg for Something to Do." He was wrong. Although the Homestead Act did spark the largest migration in American history, only 10 percent of all farmers got their start under its terms, and nearly half of all homesteaders lost their claims.

Rather than filing a homestead claim with the federal government, most settlers acquired their land outright. State governments and land companies usually held the most valuable land near transportation and markets, and the majority of farmers were willing to pay a hefty price for those benefits. The big-time land speculators did even better, plucking choice locations at bargain prices and selling high. And the railroads, which received land grants from the federal government, did best, selling off the holdings near their routes at top dollar.

POPULATING THE PLAINS

The rapid settlement of the West could not have taken place without the railroad. Although the Homestead Act offered prospective farmers free land, it was the railroad that promoted settlement, brought people to their new homes, and carried crops and cattle to eastern markets. The railroads, therefore, wielded tremendous economic and political power. Their agents—reputed to know every cow in the district—made major decisions regarding territorial welfare. In designing routes and locating depots, railroad companies put whole communities "on the map," or left them behind.

Along with providing transportation links between the East and the West and potential markets as distant as Russia and China, the western railroads directly encouraged settlement. Unlike the railroads built before the Civil War, which followed the path of villages and towns, the western lines preceded settlement. Bringing people west became their top priority, and the railroad companies conducted aggressive promotional and marketing campaigns. Agents enticed Easterners and Europeans alike with long-term loans and free transportation by rail to distant points in the West. The Santa Fe Railroad sent agent C. B. Schmidt to Germany, where he managed to entice nearly 60,000 Germans to settle along the rail line. The railroads also sponsored land companies to sell parcels of their own huge allotments from the federal government. The National Land Company, founded in Chicago in 1869, alone organized sixteen colonies of mainly European immigrants in parts of Kansas and Colorado.

More than 2 million Europeans, many recruited by professional promoters, settled the Great Plains between 1870 and 1900. Some districts in Minnesota seemed to be virtual colonies of Sweden; others housed the largest number of Finns in the New World. Nebraska, whose population as early as 1870 was 25 percent foreign-born, concentrated Germans, Swedes, Danes, and Czechs. But Germans outnumbered all other immigrants by far. A smaller portion of European immigrants reached Kansas, still fewer the territories to the south where Indian and Hispanic peoples and African Americans remained the major ethnic populations.

Many immigrants found life on the Great Plains difficult but endurable. "Living in Nebraska," the locals joked, "is a lot like being hanged; the initial shock is a bit abrupt, but once you hang there for awhile you sort of get used to it." The German-speaking Russians who settled the Dakotas discovered soil similar to that of their homeland but weather that was even more severe. Having earlier

In 1887, Lizzie Chrisman filed the first homestead claim on Lieban Creek in Custer County, Nebraska. Joined by her three sisters, she is shown here standing in front of her sod cabin. "Soddies," as these small houses were called, were constructed of stacked layers of cut prairie turf, which were eventually fortified by a thick network of roots. The roofs, often supported by timber, were usually covered with more sod, straw, and small branches.

fled religious persecution in Germany for Russia, they brought with them heavy coats and the technique of using sun-dried bricks to build houses in areas where lumber was scarce. These immigrants often provided examples for other settlers less familiar with such harsh terrain.

Having traveled the huge distance with kin or members of their Old World villages, immigrants tended to form tight-knit communities on the Great Plains. Many married only within their own group. For example, only 3 percent of Norwegian men married women of a different ethnic background. Like many Mexicanos in the Southwest, several immigrant groups retained their languages well into the twentieth century, usually by sponsoring parochial school systems and publishing their own newspapers. A few groups closed their communities to outsiders. The Poles who migrated to central Nebraska in the 1880s, for example, formed an exclusive settlement; and the German Hutterites, who disavowed private property, lived in seclusion as much as possible in the Bon Homme colony of South Dakota, established in 1874.

Among the native-born settlers of the Great Plains, the largest number had migrated from states bordering the Mississippi River. Settling as individual families rather than as whole communities, they faced an exceptionally solitary life on the Great Plains. To stave off isolation, homesteaders sometimes built their homes on the adjoining corners of their homestead plots. Still, the prospect of doing better, which brought most homesteaders to the Great Plains in the first place, caused many families to keep seeking greener pastures. Mobility was so high that between one-third and one-half of all households pulled up stakes within a decade.

Communities eventually flourished in prosperous towns like Grand Island, Nebraska; Coffeyville, Kansas; and Fargo, North Dakota, that served the larger agricultural region. Built alongside the railroad, they grew into commercial centers, home to banking, medical, legal, and retail services. Town life fostered a special intimacy; even in the county graveyard, it was said, a town resident remained among neighbors. But closeness did not necessarily promote social equality or even friendship. A social hierarchy based on education (for the handful of doctors and lawyers) and, more important, investment property (held mainly by railroad agents and bankers) governed relationships between individuals and families. Reinforced by family ties and religious and ethnic differences, this hierarchy often persisted across generations.

WORK, DAWN TO DUSK

By the 1870s, the Great Plains, once the home of buffalo and Indian hunters, was becoming a vast farming region populated mainly by immigrants from Europe and white Americans from east of the Mississippi. In place of the first one-room shanties, sod houses, and log cabins stood substantial frame farmhouses, along with a variety of other buildings like barns, smokehouses, and stables. But the built environment took nothing away from the predominating vista—the expansive fields of grain. "You have no idea, Beulah," wrote a Dakota farmer to his wife, "of what [the wheat farms] are like until you see them. For mile after mile there is not a sign of a tree or stone and just as level as the floor of your house . . . . Wheat never looked better and it is nothing but wheat, wheat, wheat."

Most farm families survived, and prospered if they could, through hard work, often from dawn to dusk. Men's activities in the fields tended to be seasonal, with heavy work during planting and harvest. At other times, their labor centered on construction or repair of buildings and on taking care of livestock. Women's activities were usually far more routine, week in and week out: cooking and canning of seasonal fruit and vegetables, washing, ironing, churning cream for butter, and keeping chickens for their eggs. Women tended to the young children, and they might occasionally take in boarders, usually young men working temporarily in railroad construction. Many women complained about the ceaseless drudgery, especially when they watched their husbands invest in farm equipment rather than in domestic appliances. Others relished the challenge.

Milking the cows, hauling water, and running errands to neighboring farms could be done by the children, once they had reached the age of nine or so. The "one-room school," where all grades learned together, taught the basics of literacy and arithmetic that a future farmer or commercial employee would require.

The harsh climate and unyielding soil nevertheless forced all but the most reclusive families to seek out friends and neighbors. Many hands were needed to clear the land for cultivation or for roadbeds, to raise houses and barns, or to bring in a harvest before a threatening storm. Neighbors might agree to work together haying, harvesting, and threshing grain. A well-to-do farmer might "rent" his threshing machine in exchange for a small cash fee and, for instance, three days' labor. His wife might barter her garden produce for her neighbor's bread and milk or for help during childbirth or disability. Women often combined work and leisure in quilting bees and sewing circles, where they made friends while sharing scraps of material and technical information. Whole communities turned out for special events, such as the seasonal husking bees and apple bees, which were organized mainly by women.

Much of this informal barter, however, resulted from lack of cash rather than from a lasting desire to cooperate. When annual harvests were bountiful, even the farm woman's practice of bartering goods with neighbors and local merchants—butter and eggs in return for yard goods or seed—diminished sharply, replaced by cash transactions. Still, wheat production proved unsteady in the last half of the nineteenth century, and few farm families could remain wholly self-reliant.

For many farmers, the soil simply would not yield a livelihood, and they often owed more money than they took in. Start-up costs, including the purchase of land and equipment, put many farmers deep in debt to local creditors. Some lost their land altogether. By the turn of the century, more than one-third of all farmers in the United States were tenants on someone else's land.

The Garden of Eden was not to be found on the prairies or on the plains, no matter how hard the average farm family worked. Again and again, foreclosures wiped out the small landowner through dips in commodity prices, bad decisions, natural disasters, or illness. The swift growth of rural population soon ended. Although writers and orators alike continued to celebrate the family farm as the source of virtue and economic well-being, the hard reality of big money and political power told a far different story.

THE WORLD'S BREADBASKET

During the second half of the nineteenth century, commercial farms employed the most intensive and extensive methods of agricultural production in the world. Hardworking farmers brought huge numbers of acres under cultivation, while new technologies allowed them to achieve unprecedented levels of efficiency in the planting and harvesting of crops. As a result, farming became increasingly tied to international trade, and modern capitalism soon ruled western agriculture, as it did the mining and cattle industries.

NEW PRODUCTION TECHNOLOGIES

Only after the trees had been cleared and grasslands cut free of roots could the soil be prepared for planting. But as farmers on the Great Plains knew so well, the sod west of the Mississippi did not yield readily to cultivation and often broke the cast-iron plows typically used by eastern farmers. Farther west, some farmers resorted to drills to plant seeds for crops such as wheat and oats. Even in the best locations, where loamy, fertile ground had built up over centuries into eight or more inches of decayed vegetation, the preliminary breaking, or "busting," of the sod required hard labor. One man would guide a team of five or six oxen pulling a plow through the soil, while another regulated the depth of the cut, or furrow. But, as a North Dakota settler wrote to his wife back in Michigan, after the first crop, the soil became as "soft as can be, any team [of men and animals] can work it."

Agricultural productivity depended as much on new technology as on the farmers' hard labor. In 1837, John Deere had designed his famous "singing plow," which easily turned prairie grasses under and turned up even highly compacted soils. Around the same time, Cyrus McCormick's reaper began to be used for cutting grain; by the 1850s, his factories were turning out reapers in mass quantities. The harvester, invented in the 1870s, drew the cut stalks upward to a platform where two men could bind them into sheaves; by the 1880s, an automatic knotter tied them together. Drastically reducing the number of people traditionally required for this work, the harvester increased the pace many times over. The introduction of mechanized corn planters and mowing or raking machines for hay all but completed the technological arsenal (see Table 18.1).

In the 1890s, the U.S. commissioner of labor measured the impact of technology on farm productivity. Before the introduction of the wire binder in 1875, he reported, a farmer could not plant more than 8 acres of wheat if he were to harvest it successfully without help; by 1890, the same farmer could rely on his new machine to

This "thirty-three horse team harvester" was photographed at the turn of the century in Walla Walla, Washington. Binding the grain into sheaves before it could hit the ground, the "harvester" cut, threshed, and sacked wheat in one single motion.

handle 135 acres with relative ease and without risk of spoilage. The improvements in the last half of the century allowed an average farmer to produce up to ten times more than was possible with the old implements.

Scientific study of soil, grain, and climate conditions was another factor in the record output. Beginning in the mid-nineteenth century, federal and state governments added inducements to the growing body of expertise, scientific information, and hands-on advice. Through the Morrill Act of 1862, "land-grant" colleges acquired space for campuses in return for promising to institute agricultural programs. The Department of Agriculture, which attained cabinet-level status in 1889, and the Weather Bureau (transferred from the War Department in 1891) also made considerable contributions to farmers' knowledge. The federal Hatch Act of 1887, which created a series of state experimental stations, provided for basic agricultural research, especially in the areas of soil minerals and plant growth. Many states added their own agricultural stations, usually connected with state colleges and universities.

Nature nevertheless often reigned over technological innovation and seemed in places to take revenge against these early successes. West of the 98th meridian— a north–south line extending through western Oklahoma, central Kansas and Nebraska, and eastern Dakota—perennial dryness due to an annual rainfall of less than 20 inches constantly threatened to turn soil into dust and to break plows on the hardened ground. Summer heat burned out crops and ignited grass fires. Mountains of winter snows turned rivers into spring torrents that flooded fields; heavy fall rains washed crops away. Even good weather invited worms and flying insects to infest the crops. During the 1870s, grasshoppers in clouds a mile long ate everything organic, including tree bark and clothes.

After the Civil War, the veteran John Wesley Powell set off to explore much of the trans–Mississippi West and soon concluded that the shortage of water would remain a huge problem unless settlers worked together to plan irrigation projects. His *Report on the Lands of the Arid Region*, published in 1878, advised prospective farmers to settle near watersheds and to construct, where necessary, dams and canals. Congress ignored his suggestions, fearing that such planning would inhibit free enterprise.

PRODUCING FOR THE GLOBAL MARKET

Farming changed in important ways during the last third of the nineteenth century. Although the family remained the primary source of labor, farmers tended to put more emphasis on production for exchange rather than for home use. They continued to plant vegetable gardens and often kept fowl or livestock for the family's consumption but raised crops mainly for a market that stretched across the world.

Wheat farmers in particular prospered. With the world population increasing at a rapid rate, the international demand for wheat was enormous, and American farmers made huge profits from the sale of this crop. Wheat production ultimately served as a barometer of the

TABLE 18.1

Hand v. Machine Labor on the Farm, ca. 1880

Crop	Time Worked		Labor Cost	
	Hand	Machine	Hand	Machine
Wheat	61 hours	3 hours	$3.55	$0.66
Corn	39 hours	15 hours	3.62	1.51
Oats	66 hours	7 hours	3.73	1.07
Loose Hay	21 hours	4 hours	1.75	0.42
Baled Hay	35 hours	12 hours	3.06	1.29

agricultural economy in the West. Farmers in all corners of the region, from Nebraska to California, expanded or contracted their holdings and planned their crops according to the price of wheat.

The new machines and expanding market did not necessarily guarantee success. Land, draft animals, and equipment remained very expensive, and start-up costs could keep a family in debt for decades. A year of good returns often preceded a year of financial disaster. Weather conditions, international markets, and railroad and steamship shipping prices all proved equally unpredictable and heartless.

The new technology and scientific expertise favored the large, well-capitalized farmer over the small one. The majority of farmers with fewer resources expanded at more modest rates. Between 1880 and 1900, average farm size in the seven leading grain-growing states increased from 64.4 acres to more than 100 acres.

CALIFORNIA AGRIBUSINESS

The trend toward bonanza farming reached an apex in California, where farming as a business surpassed farming as a way of life. Bankers, railroad magnates, and other Anglos made rich by the gold rush took possession of the best farming land in the state. They introduced the latest technologies, built dams and canals, and invested huge amounts of capital, setting the pattern for the state's prosperous agribusiness. Farms of nearly 500 acres dominated the California landscape in 1870; by the turn of the century, two-thirds of the state's arable land was in 1,000-acre farms. As land reformer and social commentator Henry George noted, California was "not a country of farms but a country of plantations and estates."

This scale of production made California the national leader in wheat production by the mid-1880s. But it also succeeded dramatically with fruit and vegetables. Large- and medium-sized growers, shrewdly combined in cooperative marketing associations during the 1870s and 1880s, used the new refrigerator cars to ship produce in large quantities to the East and to Europe. By 1890, cherries, apricots, and oranges, packed in mountains of ice, made their way into homes across the United States.

California growers learned quickly that they could satisfy consumer appetites and even create new ones. Orange producers packed their products individually in tissue paper, a technique designed to convince eastern consumers that they were about to eat a luxury fruit. By the turn of the century, advertisers for the California Citrus Growers' Association described oranges as a necessity for good health, inventing the trademark "Sunkist" to be stamped on each orange. Meanwhile California's grape growing grew into a big business. Long considered inferior to French wines, California wines found a ready market at lower prices. Other grape growers made their fortunes in raisins. One company trademarked its raisins as "Sun Maid" and packaged them for schoolchildren in the famous "nickel" box.

By 1900, California had become the model for American agribusiness—not the home of self-sufficient homesteaders but the showcase of heavily capitalized farm factories that employed a huge tenant and migrant workforce, including many Chinese. After the mines gave out and work on the transcontinental railroad ended, thousands of Chinese helped to bring new lands under cultivation. Chinese tenant farmers specialized in labor-intensive crops, such as vegetables and fruits, and peddled their crops door-to-door or sold them in roadside stands. Others worked in packing and preserving in all the major agricultural regions of the state. However, the Chinese, like the majority of field hands, rarely rose to the ranks of agricultural entrepreneurs. By the turn of the century, amid intense legislative battles over land and irrigation rights, it was clear that the rich and powerful dominated California agribusiness.

This painting by the British-born artist Thomas Hill (1829–1908) depicts workers tending strawberry fields in the great agricultural valley of northern California. Chinese field hands, such as the two men shown here, supplied not only cheap labor but also invaluable knowledge of specialized fruit and vegetable crops.

SOURCE: Thomas Hill, "Irrigating at Strawberry Farm, Santa Clara," 1888. Courtesy of the Bancroft Library, University of California, Berkeley.

THE TOLL ON THE ENVIRONMENT

Viewing the land as a resource to command, the new inhabitants often looked past the existing flora and fauna toward a landscape remade strictly for commercial purposes. The changes they produced in some areas were nearly as cataclysmic as those that occurred during the Ice Age.

Farmers "improved" the land by introducing exotic plants and animals—that is, biological colonies indigenous to other regions and continents. Farmers also unintentionally introduced new varieties of weeds, insect pests, and rats. Surviving portions of older grasslands and meadows eventually could be found only alongside railroad tracks, in graveyards, or inside national parks.

Numerous species disappeared altogether or suffered drastic reduction. The grizzly bear, for example, an animal exclusive to the West, could once be found in large numbers from the Great Plains to California and throughout much of Alaska; by the early decades of the twentieth century, one nature writer estimated that only 800 survived, mostly in Yellowstone National Park. At the same time, the number of wolves declined from perhaps as many as 2 million to just 200,000. By the mid-1880s, no more than 5,000 buffalo survived in the entire United States, and little remained of the once vast herds but great heaps of bones sold for $7.50 per ton.

The slaughter of the buffalo had a dramatic impact, not only on the fate of the species, but also on the grasslands of the Great Plains. Overall, the biological diversity of the region had been drastically reduced. Having killed off the giant herds, ranchers and farmers quickly shifted to cattle and sheep production. Unlike the roaming buffalo, these livestock did not range widely and soon devoured the native grasses down to their roots. With the ground cover destroyed, the soil eroded and became barren. By the end of the century, huge dust storms swept across the plains.

In 1873, the U.S. Congress passed the Timber Culture Act, which allotted homesteaders an additional 160 acres of land in return for planting and cultivating 40 acres of trees. Because residence was not required, and because tree planting could not be assessed for at least thirteen years, speculators filed for several claims at once, then turned around and sold the land without having planted a single tree. Although some forests were restored, neither the weather nor the soil improved.

Large-scale commercial agriculture also took a heavy toll on inland waters. Before white settlement, rainfall had drained naturally into lakes and underground aquifers, and watering spots were abundant throughout the Great Plains. Farmers mechanically rerouted and dammed water to irrigate their crops, causing many bodies of water to disappear and the water table to drop significantly. In the 1870s, successful ranchers in California pressed for ever greater supplies of water and contracted Chinese work gangs to build the largest irrigation canal in the West. In 1887, the state of California formed irrigation districts, securing bond issues for the construction of canals, and other western states followed. But by the 1890s, irrigation had seemed to reach its limit without federal support. The Newlands or National Reclamation Act of 1902 added 1 million acres of irrigated land, and state irrigation districts added more than 10 million acres. Expensive to taxpayers, and ultimately benefiting corporate farmers rather than small landowners, these projects further diverted water and totally transformed the landscape.

Although western state politicians and federal officials debated water rights for decades, they rarely considered the impact of water policies on the environment. Lake Tulare in California's Central Valley, for example, had occupied up to 760 square miles. After farmers began to irrigate their land by tapping the rivers that fed Tulare, the lake shrank dramatically, covering a mere 36 square miles by the early twentieth century. Finally the lake, which had supported rich aquatic and avian life for thousands of years, disappeared entirely. The land left behind, now wholly dependent on irrigation, grew so alkaline in spots that it could no longer be used for agricultural purposes.

The need to maintain the water supply indirectly led to the creation of national forests and the Forest Service. Western farmers supported the General Land Revision Act of 1891, which gave the president the power to establish forest reserves to protect watersheds against the threats posed by lumbering, overgrazing, and forest fires. In the years that followed, President Benjamin Harrison established fifteen forest reserves exceeding 16 million acres, and President Grover Cleveland added more than 21 million acres. But only in 1897 did the secretary of the interior finally gain the authority to regulate the use of these reserves.

The Forest Management Act of 1897 and the National Reclamation Act of 1902 set the federal government on the path of large-scale regulatory activities. The Forest Service was established in 1905, and in 1907, forest reserves were transferred from the Department of the Interior to the Department of Agriculture. The federal government would now play an even larger role in economic development of the West, dealing mainly with corporate farmers and ranchers eager for improvements.

THE WESTERN LANDSCAPE

Throughout the nineteenth century, many Americans viewed western expansion as the nation's "manifest destiny," and just as many marveled at the region's natural and cultural wonders. The public east of the Mississippi craved stories about the West and visual images of its sweeping vistas. Artists and photographers built their reputations on what they saw and imagined. Scholars, from geologists and botanists to historians and anthropologists, toured the trans–Mississippi West in pursuit of new data. The region and its peoples came to represent what was both unique and magnificent about the American landscape.

NATURE'S MAJESTY

By the end of the century, scores of writers had described spectacular, breathtaking natural sites like the Grand Tetons and High Sierras, vast meadows of waving grasses and beautiful flowers, expansive canyons and rushing white rivers, and exquisite deserts covered with sagebrush or dotted with flowering cactus, stark yet enticing.

Moved by such evidence, the federal government began to set aside huge tracts of land as nature reserves. In 1864, Congress passed the Yosemite Act, which placed the spectacular cliffs and giant sequoias under the management of the State of California. Meanwhile, explorers returned to the East awestruck by the varied terrain of the Rocky Mountains, the largest mountain chain in North America, and described huge sky-high lakes, boiling mud, and spectacular waterfalls. In 1872, Congress named Yellowstone the first national park. Yosemite and Sequoia in California, Crater Lake in Oregon, Mount Rainier in Washington, and Glacier in Montana all became national parks between 1890 and 1910 (see Map 18.5).

Landscape painters, particularly the group that became known as the Rocky Mountain School, also piqued the public's interest in western scenery. In the 1860s, German-born Albert Bierstadt, equipped with a camera, traveled the Oregon Trail. Using his photographs as inspiration, Bierstadt painted mountains so wondrous that they seemed nearly surreal, projecting a divine aura behind the majesty of nature. His "earthscapes"—huge canvases with exacting details of animals and plants—thrilled viewers and sold for tens of thousands of dollars.

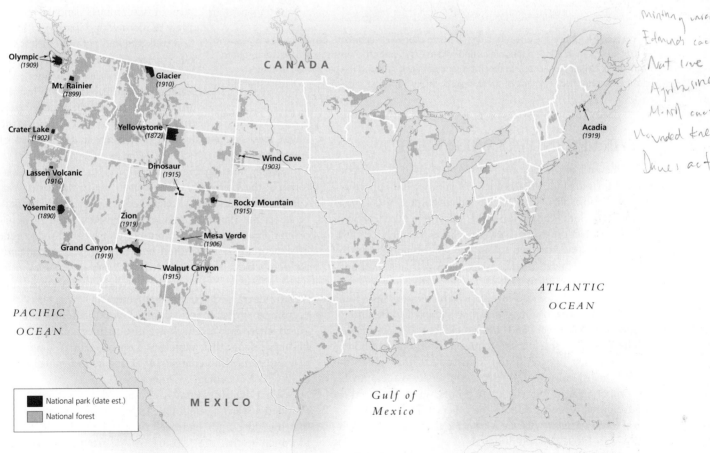

MAP 18.5 The Establishment of National Parks and Forests The
setting aside of land for national parks saved large districts of the West from early commercial development and industrial degradation, setting a precedent for the later establishment of additional parks in economically marginal, but scenic, territory. The West, home to the vast majority of park space, became a principal site of tourism by the end of the nineteenth century.

Albert Bierstadt became one of the first artists to capture on enormous canvases the vastness and rugged terrain of western mountains and wilderness. Many other artists joined Bierstadt to form the Rocky Mountain School. In time, the camera largely replaced the paintbrush, and most Americans formed an image of these majestic peaks from postcards and magazine illustrations.

THE LEGENDARY WILD WEST

By the end of the century, many Americans, rich and poor alike, imagined the West as a land of promise and opportunity and, above all, of excitement and adventure. Future president Theodore Roosevelt helped to promote this view. Soon after his election to the New York State Assembly in 1882, Roosevelt was horrified to see himself lampooned in the newspapers as a dandy and a weakling. A year later, after buying a ranch in North Dakota, he began to reconstruct his public image. He wrote three books recounting his adventures in the West, claiming that they had instilled in him not only personal bravery and "hardihood" but also self-reliance. The West, Roosevelt insisted, meant "vigorous manhood."

The first "westerns," the "dime novels" that sold in the 1860s in editions of 50,000 or more, reflected these myths. Competing against stories about pirates, wars, crime, and sea adventures, westerns outsold the others. Edward Zane Carroll Judson's *Buffalo Bill, the King of the Border Men,* first published in 1869, spawned hundreds of other novels, thousands of stories, and an entire magazine devoted to Buffalo Bill.

Cowman Joseph McCoy staged Wild West shows in St. Louis and Chicago, where Texas cowboys entertained prospective buyers by roping calves and breaking horses. Many cowboys played up this imaginary role, dressing and talking to match the stories told about them. The first professional photographers often made their living touring the West, setting up studios where cowboys and prostitutes posed in elaborate costumes.

The former Pony Express rider, army scout, and famed buffalo hunter William F. Cody hit upon the idea of an extravaganza that would bring the legendary West to those who could never experience it in person. "Buffalo Bill" Cody made sharpshooter Annie Oakley a star performer. Entrancing crowds with her stunning accuracy with pistol or rifle, Oakley shot dimes in midair and cigarettes from her husband's mouth. Cody also hired Sioux Indians and hundreds of cowboys to perform in mock stagecoach robberies and battles.

Cody's Wild West Show attracted masses of fairgoers at the World's Columbian Exposition, the spectacular celebration of the 400th anniversary of Columbus's landing in the New World held in Chicago in 1893. Less well attended but nonetheless significant was the annual meeting of the American Historical Association, the leading professional society of historians, and the presentation of an essay that one historian has deemed "the single most influential piece of writing in the history of American history."

At this meeting, Frederick Jackson Turner, a young historian at the University of Wisconsin, read a paper that, like Cody's Wild West Show, celebrated the West. "The Significance of the Frontier in American History" made a compelling argument that the continuous westward movement of settlement allowed Americans to develop new standards for democracy. Turner reasoned that each generation, in its move westward, mastered the "primitive conditions" and thereby developed a distinctive American character—"that coarseness and strength combined with acuteness and acquisitiveness; that practical inventive turn of mind, quick to find expedients; that masterful grasp of material things . . . that restless, nervous energy; that dominant individualism"—all of which encouraged democracy.

What became known as the "frontier thesis" also sounded a warning bell. The 1890 federal census revealed that the "free land" had been depleted, prompting Turner to conclude that the "closing" of the frontier marked the end of the formative period of American history. The "frontier thesis" lived on, although most historians no longer consider the frontier as the key to all American history. Many have pointed out that the concept of "the frontier" has meaning only to Euro-Americans and not to the tribal people who had occupied this land for centuries. Nevertheless, many of Turner's contemporaries found in his thesis the rationale for seeking new "frontiers" through overseas expansion.

Born Phoebe Ann Moses in 1860, Annie Oakley was a star attraction in Buffalo Bill's Wild West show. Dubbed "Little Sure Shot" by Chief Sitting Bull, Oakley traveled with Cody's show for seventeen years. This poster from 1901 advertises her sharp-shooting talents.

THE "AMERICAN PRIMITIVE"

New technologies of graphic reproduction encouraged painters and photographers to provide new images of the West, authentic as well as fabricated. A young German American artist, Charles Schreyvogel, saw Buffalo Bill's tent show in Buffalo and decided to make the West his life's work. His canvases depicted Indian warriors and U.S. cavalry fighting furiously but without blood and gore. Charles Russell, a genuine cowboy, painted the life he knew but also indulged in imaginary scenarios, producing paintings of buffalo hunts and first encounters between Indian peoples and white explorers.

Frederic Remington, the most famous of all the western artists, left Yale Art School to visit Montana in 1881, became a Kansas sheepherder and tavern owner, and then returned to painting. Inspired by newspaper stories of the army's campaign against the Apaches, he made himself into a war correspondent and captured vivid scenes of battle in his sketches. Painstakingly accurate in physical details, especially of horses, his paintings celebrated the "winning of the West" from the Indian peoples. By the turn of the century, Remington was the chief magazine illustrator of western history.

Remington joined hundreds of other painters and engravers in reproducing the most popular historic event:

Custer's Last Stand. Totally fictionalized by white artists to show a heroic Custer personally holding off advancing Indian warriors, these renditions dramatized the romance and tragedy of conquest. Indian artists recorded Custer's defeat in far less noble fashion.

Photographers often produced highly nuanced portraits of Indian peoples. Dozens of early photographers from the Bureau of American Ethnology captured the gaze of noble tribespeople or showed them hard at work digging clams or grinding corn. President Theodore Roosevelt praised Edward Sheriff Curtis for vividly conveying tribal virtue. Generations later, in the 1960s and 1970s, Curtis's photographs again captured the imagination of western enthusiasts, who were unaware or unconcerned that this sympathetic artist had often posed his subjects or retouched his photos to blur out any artifacts of white society.

Painters and photographers led the way for scholarly research on the various Indian societies. The early ethnographer and pioneer of fieldwork in anthropology Lewis Henry Morgan devoted his life to the study of Indian family or kinship patterns, mostly of eastern tribes such as the Iroquois, who adopted him into their Hawk Clan. In 1851, he published *League of the Ho-de-no-sau-nee, or Iroquois,* considered the first scientific account of an Indian tribe. A decade later, Morgan ventured into Cheyenne country to examine the naming patterns of this tribe. In his major work, *Ancient Society,* published in 1877, he posited a universal process of social evolution leading from savagery to barbarism to civilization.

One of the most influential interpreters of the cultures of living tribespeople was the pioneering ethnographer Alice Cunningham Fletcher. In 1879, Fletcher met Susette (Bright Eyes) La Flesche of the Omaha tribe, who was on a speaking tour to gain support for her people, primarily to prevent their removal from tribal lands. Fletcher, then forty-two years old, accompanied La Flesche to Nebraska, telling the Omahas that she had come "to learn, if you will let me, something about your tribal organization, social customs, tribal rites, traditions and songs. Also to see if I can help you in any way." After transcribing hundreds of songs, Fletcher became well known as an expert on Omaha music. She also promoted assimilation through the allotment of individual claims to 160-acre homesteads, eked out of tribal lands, and helped to draft the model legislation that was enacted by Congress as the Omaha Act of 1882. In 1885, Fletcher produced for the U.S. Senate a report titled *Indian Education and Civilization,* one of the first general statements on the status of Indian peoples. As a founder of the American Anthropological Society and president of the American Folklore Society, she encouraged further study of Indian societies.

While white settlers and the federal government continued to threaten the survival of tribal life, Indian lore became a major pursuit of scholars and amateurs alike. Adults and children delighted in turning up arrowheads. Fraternal organizations such as the Elks and Eagles borrowed tribal terminology. The Boy Scouts and Girl Scouts,

OVERVIEW | Major Indian Treaties and Legislation of the Late Nineteenth Century

1863	**Nez Percé Treaty**	Signed illegally on behalf of the entire tribe, in which the Nez Percé abandoned 6 million acres of land in return for a small reservation in northeastern Oregon. Led to Nez Percé wars, which ended in 1877 with the surrender of Chief Joseph.
1867	**Medicine Lodge Treaty**	Assigned reservations in existing Indian Territory to Comanches, Plains (Kiowa), Apaches, Kiowas, Cheyennes, and Arapahoes, bringing these tribes together with Sioux, Shoshones, Bannocks, and Navajos.
1868	**Treaty of Fort Laramie**	Successfully ended Red Cloud's war by evacuating federal troops from Sioux Territory along the Bozeman Trail; additionally granted Sioux ownership of the western half of South Dakota and rights to use Powder River country in Wyoming and Montana.
1871		Congress declares end to treaty system.
1887	**Dawes Severalty Act**	Divided communal tribal land, granting the right to petition for citizenship to those Indians who accepted the individual land allotment of 160 acres. Successfully undermined sovereignty.

the nation's premier youth organizations, used tribal lore to instill strength of character. And the U.S. Treasury stamped images of tribal chiefs and buffalo on the nation's most frequently used coins.

THE TRANSFORMATION OF INDIAN SOCIETIES

In 1871, the U.S. government formally ended the treaty system, eclipsing without completely abolishing the sovereignty of Indian nations. Still, the tribes persisted. Using a mixture of survival strategies from farming and trade to the leasing of reservation lands, they both adapted to changing conditions and maintained old traditions.

REFORM POLICY AND POLITICS

By 1880, many Indian tribes had been forcibly resettled on reservations, but very few had adapted to white ways. For decades, reformers, mainly from the Protestant churches, had lobbied Congress for a program of salvation through assimilation, and they looked to the Board of Indian Commissioners, created in 1869, to carry out this mission. The board often succeeded in mediating conflicts among the various tribes crowded onto reservations but made far less headway in converting them to Christianity or transforming them into prosperous farming communities.

The majority of Indian peoples lived in poverty and misery, deprived of their traditional means of survival and,

more often than not, subjected to fraud by corrupt government officials and private suppliers. Reformers who observed these conditions firsthand nevertheless remained unshaken in their belief that tribespeople must be raised out of the darkness of ignorance into the light of civilization. Some conceded, however, that the reservation system might not be the best means to this end.

Unlike most Americans, who saw the conquest of the West as a means to national glory, some reformers were genuinely outraged by the government's continuous violation of treaty obligations and the military enforcement of the reservation policy. One of the most influential was Helen Hunt Jackson, a noted poet and author of children's stories. In 1879, Jackson had attended a lecture in Hartford, Connecticut, by a chief of the Ponca tribe whose destitute people had been forced from their Dakota homeland. Heartstruck, Jackson lobbied former abolitionists such as Wendell Phillips to work for Indians' rights and she herself began to write against government policy. Her book-length exposé, *A Century of Dishonor*, published in 1881, detailed the plight of Indian peoples.

Jackson threw herself into the Indian Rights Association, an offshoot of the Women's National Indian Association (WNIA), which had been formed in 1874 to rally public support for a program of assimilation. The two organizations helped to place Protestant missionaries in the West to work to eradicate tribal customs as well as to convert Indian peoples to Christianity. According to the reformers' plans, men would now farm as well as hunt, while women would leave the fields to take care of home and children.

Likewise, all communal practices would be abandoned in favor of individually owned homesteads, where families could develop in the "American" manner and even celebrate proper holidays such as the Fourth of July. Children, hair trimmed short, would be placed in boarding schools where, removed from their parents' influence, they would shed traditional values and cultural practices. By 1882, the WNIA had gathered 100,000 signatures on petitions urging Congress to phase out the reservation system, to establish universal education for Indian children, and to award title to 160 acres to any Indian individual willing to work the land.

The Dawes Severalty Act, passed by Congress in 1887, incorporated many of these measures and established federal Indian policy for decades to come. The act allowed the president to distribute land, not to tribes, but to individuals legally "severed" from their tribes. The commissioner of Indian affairs rendered the popular interpretation that "tribal relations should be broken up, socialism destroyed and the family and autonomy of the individual substituted. The allotment of land in severalty, the establishment of local courts and police, the development of a personal sense of independence and the universal adoption of the English language are means to this end."

Those individuals who accepted the land allotment of 160 acres and agreed to allow the government to sell unallotted tribal lands (with some funds set aside for education) could petition to become citizens of the United States. A little over a decade after its enactment, many reformers believed that the Dawes Act had resolved the basis of the "Indian problem." Hollow Horn Bear, a Sioux chief, offered a different opinion, judging the Dawes Act to be "only another trick of the whites."

The celebrated artist Frederic Remington (1861–1909) produced this sketch of Oglala Sioux at the Pine Ridge Indian Reservation in South Dakota. Published in the popular magazine *Harper's Weekly,* Remington's depiction of the ghost dance of 1890 showed dancers in vividly patterned robes and shirts, some decorated with stars symbolizing the coming of a new age for the Indians.

SOURCE: Ogallala Sioux performing the Ghost Dance at the Pine Ridge Indian Agency, South Dakota. Illustration by Frederic Remington, 1890. The Granger Collection.

The Dawes Act successfully undermined tribal sovereignty but offered little compensation. Indian religions and sacred ceremonies were banned, the telling of legends and myths forbidden, and shaman and medicine men imprisoned or exiled for continuing their traditional practices. "Indian schools" forbade Indian languages, clothing styles, and even hair fashions (see Communities in Conflict).

These and other measures did little to integrate Indians into white society. Treated as savages, Indian children fled most white schools. Nor did adults receive much encouragement to become property holders. Government agencies allotted them inferior farmland, inadequate tools, and little training for agricultural self-sufficiency. Seeing scant advantage in assimilating, only a minority of adults dropped their tribal religion for Christianity or their communal ways for the accumulation of private property. Within the next forty years, the Indian peoples lost 60 percent of the reservation land remaining in 1887 and 66 percent of the land allotted to them as homesteaders. The tenets of the Dawes Act were not reversed until 1934. In that year, Congress passed the Indian Reorganization Act, which affirmed the integrity of Indian cultural institutions and returned some land to tribal ownership (see Chapter 24).

THE GHOST DANCE

After the passage of the Dawes Severalty Act, one more cycle of rebellion remained for the Sioux. In 1888, the Paiute prophet Wovoka, ill with scarlet fever, had a vision during a total eclipse of the sun. In his vision, the Creator told him that if the Indian peoples learned to love each other, they would be granted a special place in the afterlife. The Creator also gave him the Ghost Dance, which the prophet performed for others and soon spread throughout the tribe. The Sioux came to believe that when the day of judgment came, all Indian peoples who had ever lived would return to their lost world and white peoples would vanish from the earth. The chant sounded:

> *The whole world is coming.*
> *A nation is coming, a nation is coming.*
> *The Eagle has brought the message to the tribe.*
> *The father says so, the father says so.*
> *Over the whole earth they are coming.*
> *The buffalo are coming, the buffalo are coming.*
> *The Crow has brought the message to the tribe,*
> *The Father says so, the Father says so.*

Many white settlers and federal officials feared the Ghost Dancers, even though belief in a sudden divine judgment was common among Christians and Jews. Before the Civil War, Protestant groups such as the Millerites, who had renounced personal property and prepared themselves for the millennium, were tolerated by other Americans.

The Carlisle Indian Industrial School

Richard Henry Pratt (1840–1924) founded the Indian school in Carlisle, Pennsylvania, in 1879 with the approval of the Department of the Interior and the War Department. He had served in a volunteer regiment during the Civil War and then continued his military assignment in the Indian Territory, where he began to develop ideas of "civilizing" Native Americans. Before his first encounter he had anticipated meeting "atrocious aborigines," but he soon came to believe that, if given sufficient opportunities and guidance, Indian peoples could thrive and become equal citizens of the United States.

Pratt headed the Carlisle Indian School for twenty-five years, until he retired from military service in 1904. Together with his wife, Anna Mason Pratt, he supervised every aspect of the Indian children's life, including language, dress, and deportment. Sharing with many well-intentioned white re-

formers the conviction that Christianity provided the best moral guidance, the Pratts forbade the children to practice their native religion. Pratt's motto, "Kill the Indian, but save the man," aptly expressed his belief that the salvation of the Indians depended on the sacrifice of their culture.

Luther Standing Bear (1868–1939), the son of the Oglala Sioux chief Standing Bear, was born on the Sioux Pine Ridge reservation in South Dakota and educated at the Carlisle Indian School. He was a member of the first class to graduate. In 1898, he joined Buffalo Bill's Wild West Show as an interpreter and chaperon for Indian performers and also performed, along with his wife. In 1912, he moved on to the motion picture industry in California, where he became an actor and consultant on movies about Indians. He wrote several books about his experiences; an excerpt from one of them appears here.

Why did Richard Henry Pratt choose haircuts and new clothing as important measures in training Indian children for citizenship? How did Luther Standing Bear interpret this act?

Richard Henry Pratt Explains How He Made Indian Children "White."

Just before starting for the Indian Territory party, I employed a couple of barbers to cut the hair of the boys. This work was scarcely begun when I had to leave and the barbers were to finish the work under Mrs. Pratt's oversight. Upon my return Mrs. Pratt gave me this experience: The interpreter came to her saying all the boys had their hair cut except two of the older ones who refused to part with their long braids. She went at once to the room where the hair cutting was being done and asked these big boys why they refused to carry out the Captain's order. "Well," said one, "we were told we would have new clothes like the white men. We have none so we keep our long hair." "All right," said Mrs. Pratt, "the clothes will come later, and if you do not want to have your hair cut now, I must send away these barbers and then you must wait until the Captain returns." The spokesman relented and said that if she would stand by, he would let the man cut his hair, which she willingly did. The other, however, stubbornly held to his decision. Later that night she was aroused by a very discordant wailing, which grew in volume. Mrs. Pratt sent a boy for the interpreter. When the interpreter came, he gave the explanation that the young man who had refused to have his hair cut afterwards relented and did the job himself with a knife. He then said his people always wailed after cutting their hair, as it was an evidence of mourning, and he had come onto the parade ground to show his grief. His voice had awakened the girls, who joined with their shrill voices, then other boys joined and hence the commotion. . . .

There was a very considerable delay in the arrival of clothing, and when it finally came it was delivered under a Bureau

contract with one of our great American merchants. It was the shoddiest of shoddy clothing. As the price was insignificant, the worth was the same, but it illustrated the ill-considered system of buying the cheapest materials. Agent Miles stopped off on his way to Washington. I made a bundle of a cloth cap, through which I could push my finger, a coat out at the elbows and ripped, and trousers torn and worn out at the knees and seat, all in use less than a month . . .

We were scarcely underway when I received a letter from the Commissioner of Indian Affairs, enclosing a printed table of the per capita allowance of food for Indian schools. Experience in army service showed that children living on that ration would be hungry all the time . . . .

The next time I visited Washington, the Commissioner, Mr. Hayt, laughingly told me that he wanted me to see how that table came to be adopted by the Bureau and sent for the chief of the division in the Indian Office having the matter in charge. When he came in, the Commissioner said, "I want you to tell Captain Pratt how you came to make up that school food supply table." The man said: "We had a rational allowance considerably more liberal than that for several years, and as nobody complained about it I thought there could be a reduction."

"I accordingly made up that table and have been waiting for complaints." I said, "You did that, without investigating allowances at boarding schools for young people or making inquiries of people who know about such things, and pushed it on the Indians as the conclusion of this Bureau?" "Well," he said, "I knew no other way. No one complained and I thought it right to economize."

SOURCE: Richard Henry Pratt, *Battlefield and Classroom: Four Decades with the American Indian, 1867–1904,* edited and with an introduction by Robert M. Utley (Norman: University of Oklahoma Press, 2003), pp. 232–234.

"Kill the Indian,
but save the man."

". . . the 'civilizing' process began
with clothes. Never . . . could
we be civilized while wearing
the moccasin and blanket."

Luther Standing Bear Remembers Being Made "White."

. . . At the age of eleven years, ancestral life for me and my people was most abruptly ended without regard for our wishes, comforts, or rights in the matter. At once I was thrust into an alien world, into an environment as different from the one into which I had been born as it is possible to imagine, to remake myself, if I could into the likeness of the invader.

By 1879, my people were no longer free, but were subjects confined on reservations under the rule of agents. One day there came to the agency a party of white people from the East. Their presence aroused considerable excitement when it became known that these people were school teachers who wanted some Indian boys and girls to take away with them to train as were white boys and girls . . . .

I could think of no reason why white people wanted Indian boys and girls except to kill them, and not having the remotest idea of what a school was, I thought we were going East to die. ...In my decision to go, I gave up many things dear to the heart of a little Indian boy, and one of the things over which my child mind grieved was the thought of saying good-bye to my pony. I rode him as far as I could on the journey, which was to the Missouri River, where we took the boat. There we parted from our parents, and it was a heartbreaking scene, women and children weeping. Some of the children changed their minds and were unable to go on the boat, but for many who did go it was a final parting . . . .

At last at Carlisle the transforming, the "civilizing" process began. It began with clothes. Never, not matter what our philosophy or spiritual quality, could we be civilized while wearing the moccasin and blanket. The task before us was not only that of accepting new ideas and adopting new manners, but actual physical changes and discomfort had to be borne uncomplainingly until the body adjusted itself to new tastes and habits. Our accustomed dress was taken and replaced with clothing that felt cumbersome and awkward. Against trousers and handkerchiefs we had a distinct feeling—they were unsanitary and the trousers kept us from breathing well. High collars, stiff-bosomed shirts, and suspenders fully three inches in width were uncomfortable, while leather boots caused actual suffering. We longed to go barefoot, but were told that dew on the grass would give us colds. That was a new warning for us, for our mothers had never told us to beware of colds, and I remember as a child coming into the tipi with moccasins full of snow . . . . My niece once asked me what it was that I disliked the most during those first bewildering days, and I said, "red flannel." Not knowing what I meant, she laughed, but I still remember those horrid, sticky garments which we had to wear next to the skin, and I still squirm and itch when I think of them.

SOURCE: Luther Standing Bear, *Land of the Spotted Eagle* (Lincoln: University of Nebraska Press, 1933, reprinted 1978), pp. 230–234.

But after decades of Indian warfare, white Americans took the Ghost Dance as a warning of tribal retribution rather than a religious ceremony. As thousands of Sioux danced to exhaustion, local whites intolerantly demanded the practice be stopped. The U.S. Seventh Cavalry, led in part by survivors of the Battle of Little Bighorn, rushed to the Pine Ridge Reservation, and a group of the Sioux led by Big Foot, now fearing mass murder, moved into hiding in the Bad Lands of South Dakota. After a skirmish, the great leader Sitting Bull and his young son lay dead.

The Seventh Cavalry pursued the Sioux Ghost Dancers and 300 undernourished Sioux, freezing and without horses, to Wounded Knee Creek on the Pine Ridge Reservation. There, on December 29, 1890, while the peace-seeking Big Foot, who had personally raised a white flag of surrender, lay dying of pneumonia, they were surrounded by soldiers armed with automatic guns. The U.S. troops expected the Sioux to surrender their few remaining weapons, but an accidental gunshot from one deaf brave who misunderstood the command caused panic on both sides.

Within minutes, 200 Sioux had been cut down and dozens of soldiers wounded, mostly by their own cross fire. For two hours soldiers continued to shoot at anything that moved—mostly women and children straggling away. Many of the injured froze to death in the snow; others were transported in open wagons and finally laid out on beds of hay under Christmas decorations at the Pine Ridge Episcopal church. The massacre, which took place almost exactly 400 years after Columbus "discovered" the New World for Christian civilization, seemed to mark the final conquest of the continent's indigenous peoples.

ENDURANCE AND REJUVENATION

The most tenacious tribes were those occupying land rejected by white settlers or those distant from their new communities. Still, not even an insular, peaceful agricultural existence on semiarid, treeless terrain necessarily provide protection. Nor did a total willingness to peacefully accept white offers prevent attack.

The Pimas of Arizona, for instance, had a well-developed agricultural system adapted to a scarce supply of water, and they rarely warred with other tribes. After the arrival of white settlers, they integrated Christian symbolism into their religion, learned to speak English, and even fought with the U.S. cavalry against the Apaches. Still, the Pimas saw their lands stolen, their precious waterways diverted, and their families impoverished.

The similarly peaceful Yana tribes of California, hunters and gatherers rather than farmers, were even less fortunate. Suffering enslavement, prostitution, and multiple new diseases from white settlers, they faced near extinction within a generation. One Yana tribe, the Yahi, chose simply to disappear. For more than a decade, they lived in caves and avoided all contact with white settlers.

Many tribes found it difficult to survive in the proximity of white settlers. The Flatheads, for example, seemed to Indian commissioners in the Bitterroot region of Montana to be destined for quick assimilation. They had refused to join the Ghost Dance and had agreed to sell their rich tribal land and move to a new reservation. But while waiting to be moved, the dispossessed Flatheads nearly starved. When they finally reached the new reservation in October 1891, the remaining 250 Flatheads put on their finest war paint and whooped and galloped their horses, firing guns in the air in celebration. But disappointment and tragedy lay ahead. The federal government drastically reduced the size of the reservation, using a large part of it to provide a national reserve for buffalo. Only handfuls of Flatheads, mostly elderly, continued to live together in pockets of rural poverty.

A majority of tribes, especially smaller ones, sooner or later reached numbers too low to maintain their collective existence. Intermarriage, although widely condemned by the white community, drew many young people outside their Indian communities. Some tribal leaders also deliberately chose a path toward assimilation. The Quapaws, for example, formally disbanded in the aftermath of the Dawes Severalty Act. The minority that managed to prosper in white society as tradespeople or farmers abandoned their language, religious customs, and traditional ways of life. Later generations petitioned the federal government and regained tribal status, established ceremonial grounds and cultural centers (or bingo halls), and built up one of the most durable powwows in the state. Even so, much of the tribal lore that had underpinned distinct identity had simply vanished.

For those tribes who remained on reservations, the aggressively assimilationist policies of the Office of Indian Affairs (OIA) challenged their traditional ways. The Southern Ute, for example, at one time hunted, fished, and gathered throughout a huge region spanning the Rocky Mountains and the Great Basin. In 1848, they began to sign a series of treaties in accord with the reservation policy of the U.S. government. Twenty years later their territory had been reduced to approximately one-quarter of Colorado Territory, and in 1873, they had further relinquished about one-quarter of this land. After the passage of the Dawes Act, the U.S. government, pressured by white settlers, gave the tribe two choices: they could break up their communal land holdings and accept the 160 acres granted to the male heads of families, or they could maintain their tribal status and move to a reservation in Utah. The Utes divided over the issue, but a considerable number chose to live on reservations under the administration of the OIA.

Under the terms of the Dawes Act, Southern Ute men and women endured continuous challenges to their egalitarian practices. The OIA assumed, for example, that Ute men would represent the tribe in all official matters, a policy that forced Ute women to petition the U.S. government to recognize their rights and concerns. Similarly, Ute women struggled to hold on to their roles as producers within the subsistence family economy against the efforts of the OIA agents to train them for homemaking alone. In the 1880s, the OIA established a matrons program to teach Ute women to create a "civilizing" home, which included new lessons about sanitation, home furnishings, and health care. But even fifty years later, some Ute preferred to live at least part of the year in a teepee in a multigenerational family, rather than in a private residence designed for a single married couple and their children.

A small minority of tribes, grown skillful in adapting to dramatically changing circumstances, managed to persist and even grow. Never numbering more than a few thousand people, during the late eighteenth century the Cheyennes had found themselves caught geographically between aggressive tribes in the Great Lakes region and had migrated into the Missouri area, where they split into small village-sized communities. By the mid-nineteenth century, they had become expert horse traders on the Great Plains, well prepared to meet the massive influx of white settlers by shifting their location frequently. They avoided the worst of the pestilence that spread from the diseases white people carried and likewise survived widespread intermarriage with the Sioux in the 1860s and 1870s. Instructed to settle,

many Cheyenne took up elements of the Christian religion and became farmers, also without losing their tribal identity. Punished by revenge-hungry soldiers after the battle of Little Bighorn, their lands repeatedly taken away, they still held on. The Cheyennes were survivors.

The Navajos experienced an extraordinary renewal, largely because they built a life in territory considered worthless by whites. Having migrated to the Southwest from the northwestern part of the continent perhaps 700 years ago, the Diné ("the People"), as they called themselves, had already survived earlier invasions by the Spanish. In 1863, they had been conquered again through the cooperation of hostile tribes led by the famous Colonel Kit Carson. Their crops burned, their fruit trees destroyed, 8,000 Navajo were forced in the 300-mile "Long Walk" to the desolate Bosque Redondo reservation, where they nearly starved. Four years later, the Indian Bureau allowed the severely reduced tribe to return to a fraction of its former lands.

By 1880, the Navajos' population had returned to nearly what it had been before their conquest by white Americans. Quickly depleting the deer and antelope on their hemmed-in reservation, they had to rely on sheep

CHRONOLOGY

1848	Treaty of Guadalupe Hidalgo
1853	Gadsden Purchase
1862	Homestead Act makes free land available
	Morrill Act authorizes "land-grant" colleges
1865–67	Great Sioux War
1866	Texas cattle drives begin
1867	Medicine Lodge Treaty established reservation system
	Alaska purchased
1869	Board of Indian Commissioners created
	Buffalo Bill, the King of the Border Men sets off "Wild West" publishing craze
1870s	Grasshopper attacks on the Great Plains
1872	Yellowstone National Park created
1873	Timber Culture Act
1874–75	Sioux battles in Black Hills of Dakotas
	Red River War

1876	Custer's Last Stand
1877	Defeat of the Nez Percé
1878	John Wesley Powell published *Report on the Lands of the Arid Region*
1881	Helen Hunt Jackson, *A Century of Dishonor*
1882	Edmunds Act outlaws polygamy
1885–87	Droughts and severe winters cause the collapse of the cattle boom
1887	Dawes Severalty Act
1890	Sioux Ghost Dance movement
	Massacre of Lakota Sioux at Wounded Knee
	Census Bureau announces the end of the frontier line
1893	Frederick Jackson Turner presents his "frontier thesis"
1897	Forest Management Act gives the federal government authority over forest reserves

alone as a food reserve during years of bad crops. With their wool rugs and blankets much in demand in the East, the Navajos increasingly turned to crafts, eventually including silver jewelry as well as weaving, to survive. Although living on the economic margin, they persevered to become the largest Indian nation in the United States.

The nearby Hopis, like the Navajos, survived by stubbornly clinging to lands unwanted by white settlers, and by adapting to drastically changing conditions. A famous tribe of "desert people," the Hopis had lived for centuries in their cliff cities. Their highly developed theological beliefs, peaceful social system, sand paintings, and kachina dolls interested many educated and influential whites. The resulting publicity helped them gather the public supporters and financial resources needed to fend off further threats to their reservations.

Fortunate northwestern tribes remained relatively isolated from white settlers until the early twentieth century, although they had begun trading with white visitors centuries earlier. Northwestern peoples relied largely on salmon and other resources of the region's rivers and bays. In potlatch ceremonies, leaders redistributed tribal wealth and maintained their personal status and the status of their tribe by giving lavish gifts to invited guests. Northwestern peoples also made intricate wood carvings, including commemorative "totem" poles that recorded their history and identified their regional status. Northwestern peoples maintained their cultural integrity in part through connections with kin in Canada, as did southern tribes with kin in Mexico. In Canada and Mexico, native populations suffered less pressure from new populations and retained more tribal authority than in the United States.

Indian nations approached their nadir as the nineteenth century came to a close. The descendants of the great pre-Columbian civilizations had been conquered by foreigners, their population reduced to fewer than 250,000. Under the pressure of assimilation, the remaining tribespeople became known to non-Indians as "the vanishing Americans." It would take several generations before Indian sovereignty experienced a resurgence.

CONCLUSION

Amid the land rush of April 22, 1889, the town of Guthrie, Oklahoma, was built, contemporaries liked to brag, not in a day but in a single afternoon, its population leaping from a dozen or so to 10,000 by sundown. Throughout the territory, new communities formed almost as rapidly and often displaced old ones. Farms and ranches owned by white settlers soon spread out across the vast countryside that had earlier been Indian Territory. This spectacular development of Oklahoma was, however, but one chapter in the history of the trans–Mississippi West as an internal empire.

The West, rich in natural resources, soon served the nation in supplying ore and timber for its expanding industries and agricultural products for the growing urban populations. Envisioning the West as a cornucopia whose boundless treasures would offer themselves to the willing pioneer, most of the new residents failed to calculate the odds against their making a prosperous livelihood as miners, farmers, or petty merchants. Nor could they appreciate the long-term consequences of the violence they brought with them from the battlefields of the Civil War to the far reaches of the West.

The new settlers adapted their political and legal systems, as well as many of their economic and cultural institutions, to western circumstances. Ironically though, even after statehood, they would still be only distant representatives of an empire whose financial, political, and industrial centers remained in the Northeast. They were often frustrated by their isolation and enraged at the federal regulations that governed them and at the eastern investors and lawyers who seemed poised on all sides to rob them of the fruits of their labor. Embittered Westerners, along with Southerners, would form the core of a nationwide discontent that would soon threaten to uproot the American political system.

— REVIEW QUESTIONS —

1. Discuss the role of federal legislation in accelerating and shaping the course of westward expansion.

2. How did the incorporation of western territories into the United States affect Indian nations such as the Sioux or the Nez Percé? Discuss the causes and consequences of the Indian Wars. Discuss the significance of reservation policy and the Dawes Severalty Act for tribal life.

3. What were some of the major technological advances in mining and in agriculture that promoted the development of the western economy?

4. Describe the unique features of Mexicano communities in the Southwest before and after the mass immigration of Anglos. How did changes in the economy affect the patterns of labor and the status of women in these communities?

5. What role did the Homestead Act play in western expansion? How did farm families on the Great Plains divide chores among their members? What factors determined the likelihood of economic success or failure?

6. Describe the responses of artists, naturalists, and conservationists to the western landscape. How did their photographs, paintings, and stories shape perceptions of the West in the East?

RECOMMENDED READING

Jon Gjerde, *The Minds of the West: Ethnocultural Evolution in the Rural Middle West, 1830–1917* (1997). A combination cultural and economic history that weighs the importance of ethnicity in the shaping of American identities in the farming regions of the Middle West. Gjerde pays close attention to the religious institutions and systems of belief of European immigrants as the basis of community formation.

Robert V. Hine and John Mack Faragher, *The American West: A New Interpretive History* (2000). A sweeping, amply illustrated survey of western history with reference to recent scholarship. The authors emphasize Native Americans and include rich material on ethnicity, the environment, and the role of women.

John C. Hudson, *Making the Corn Belt: A Geographical History of Middle-Western Agriculture* (1994). An ecologically oriented study of corn growing that traces its development from Indians to Southerners moving westward.

Andrew C. Isenberg, *The Destruction of the Bison: An Environmental History, 1750–1920* (2000). A rich study of the forces behind the near-extinction of the bison, with special attention to the interplay among Indians, Euroamericans, and the environment of the Great Plains. Isenberg constructs a narrative that is as much cultural as economic in framing the problem.

Karl Jacoby, *Crimes Against Nature: Squatters, Poachers, Thieves, and the Hidden History of American Conservation* (2001). A complex analysis of the origins of national parks in the Adirondacks, Yellowstone, and the Grand Canyon. Rather than focusing on the individuals and groups that led the conservation of vast public lands, Jacoby switches perspective to focus on those who were dispossessed by the process.

Elizabeth Jameson and Susan Armitage, eds., *Writing the Range* (1997). A collection of essays on women in the West that presents an inclusive historical narrative based on the experiences of women of differing backgrounds, races, and ethnic groups.

Valerie Sherer Mathes and Richard Lowitt, *The Standing Bear Controversy: Prelude to Indian Reform* (2003). A fascinating account of the Ponca chief's efforts to bring attention to the injustices surrounding the forced removal of the Poncas from their tribal lands.

Katherine M. B. Osburn, *Southern Ute Women: Autonomy and Assimilation on the Reservation, 1887–1934* (1998). Presents a careful analysis of the impact of the Dawes Act on the role and status of women among the Southern Ute. Osburn acknowledges the changes brought by the Office of Indian Affairs programs on the reservations but emphasizes the resistance of the Ute and the retention of old ways.

Glenda Riley, *Building and Breaking Families in the American West* (1996). Essays covering the variety of cultures in the American West, organized topically to highlight courtship, marriage and intermarriage, and separation and divorce.

Thomas E. Sheridan, *Los Tucsonenses: The Mexican Community in Tucson, 1854–1941* (1986). A highly readable account of Mexican American communities in the Southwest. Sheridan shows how a midcentury accommodation of Anglos and Mexicanos faded with the absorption of the region into the national economy and with the steady displacement of the Mexicano community from its agricultural landholdings.

Louis S. Warren, *Buffalo Bill's America: William Cody and the Wild West Show* (2005). Deals with many of the legends Cody created about himself and his performers and relates his celebrity at the turn of the twentieth century to continuing forms of mass entertainment.

Liping Zhu, *A Chinaman's Chance: The Chinese on the Rocky Mountain Mining Frontier* (1997). Studies the mining communities of Chinese in the Boise Basin of Idaho. Zhu emphasizes the success the Chinese enjoyed not only as miners but also as merchants in the face of discriminatory practices and laws.

Production and Consumption in the Gilded Age

1865–1900

AMERICAN COMMUNITIES

Haymarket Square, Chicago, May 4, 1886

As rain approached the city, approximately 1,500 people gathered for a mass meeting in Haymarket Square to protest the brutality of the previous day, when Chicago police killed four strikers at the fiercely antiunion McCormick Reaper Works. The crowd listened peacefully as several speakers denounced the violence. Around 10:00 P.M., when the winds picked up, most headed for home, including the city's longtime mayor, Democrat Carter Harrison. According to newspaper reports, the crowd quickly dwindled to only 600 people. The final speaker, stone hauler Samuel Fielden, jumped up on the hay wagon that served as a make-shift stage and concluded on an ominous note. He warned that "war has been declared on us" and advised the crowd "to get hold of anything that will help you to resist the onslaught of the enemy and the usurper."

Within minutes, a column of 176 police marched down the street, pushing what remained of the crowd onto the wooden sidewalks and commanding them to disperse. Then, according to the city's leading newspaper, the *Tribune*, "something like a miniature rocket suddenly rose out of the crowd on the east sidewalk." The bomb exploded "with terrific force, shaking buildings on the street and creating havoc among the police." One policeman died immediately, provoking others to open fire into the scattering crowd. At the end of just a few minutes of chaos, seven policemen had received mortal wounds and as many as sixty more were injured,

CHAPTER 19

CHAPTER OUTLINE

many in their own cross fire. Several civilians were killed, and dozens were injured.

Those who attended the rally were mainly disgruntled workers, recent immigrants from central and eastern Europe who had come to Chicago to take advantage of the city's growing industries. Grateful for employment in the "city of smoke," they nevertheless balked at the pace of the newly mechanized production lines that sapped their life's blood and returned wages barely enough to support a family. At this moment, though, they were primarily determined to establish unions and a workday shorter than the customary ten or twelve hours.

Since early in the year, an eight-hour campaign had been sweeping the nation, with its center in Chicago. Workers and sympathetic consumers alike boycotted brands of beer, tobacco, bread, and other products made in longer-hour shops. They expressed their aspirations in their anthem, the "Eight-Hour Song." ➤

We want to feel the sunshine;
We want to smell the flowers;
We're sure God has willed it.
And we mean to have eight hours.

We're summoning our forces from
Shipyard, shop and mill;
Eight hours for work, eight hours for rest,
Eight hours for what we will.

With more than wages at stake, workers were joining unions and striking so often that the era became known as the "Great Upheaval." Their leaders responded to this upsurge by calling for a general strike across all industries on May 1, 1886.

A community of radical workers who had emigrated from Germany and settled in Chicago's near North Side made up the most militant contingent of the movement. They called themselves "revolutionary socialists," seeking a government of working people in place of politicians and corporate power. Writing in the *Arbeiter-Zeitung* (*Workers' Newspaper*), the local German-language newspaper, editor August Spies greeted May 1, hailed as "Emancipation Day," calling: "Workmen, let your watchword be: No compromise! Cowards to the Rear! Men to the front!"

On May Day, Spies renewed the cry of "eight for ten" and helped to lead the spectacular parade of 80,000 men, women, and children up Michigan Avenue, Chicago's main street. A Saturday, the day passed peacefully. However, when the workweek resumed on Monday, May 3, the deadly confrontation of strikers and police at the McCormick Reaper Works set the stage for virtual class warfare.

Feelings of animosity on all sides intensified. In the days following the tragedy at Haymarket Square, Chicago police arrested hundreds of working people, rounded up known leaders, and searched their homes and detained them without warrants. Meanwhile, newspapers denounced them as "enemy forces" and the "scum" of Europe. Sentiment swung sharply against immigrants. Many prominent citizens called for a ban on "foreign savages who might come to America with their dynamite bombs and anarchic purposes."

Ultimately, eight men were charged with incitement to murder. In the most celebrated trial of the nineteenth century, a jury of middle-class men pronounced all eight guilty despite the lack of evidence linking the defendants to the bombing. Three of the eight had not even been at Haymarket Square on the evening of May 4. The judge sentenced them to death by hanging.

At the other end of the social scale, the 1880s for middle- and upper-class Chicagoans was an era of unprecedented prosperity. Incorporated in 1837, the city now boasted a population of 200,000—second only to New York—and dozens of new mass industries and vibrant new classes of consumers. Thousands of large and small businesses produced goods ranging from ball bearings to baseballs to luxury passenger cars for travel by rail. Many of the workers in these industries, especially immigrants, could barely make ends meet. But thousands of better-off Chicagoans, foreign- and native-born alike, rushed to Marshall Field & Company to survey the ever-expanding range of goods in one of the finest department stores in the nation and a major source of pride for the city. If prices at Field's were beyond the capacity of their pocketbooks, aspiring consumers could turn to cheaper goods offered by Chicago-based Montgomery Ward, the nation's first large-scale mail-order business.

By the final decades of the nineteenth century, the nation's eyes were fixed on Chicago because the city was marking the steps being taken by the nation as a whole. If class differences sharpened and led to violence, the rise in living standards provided a different, more appealing focus. The city with the most technologically advanced industries in the world seemed to be leading the way—but to what?

THE RISE OF INDUSTRY, THE TRIUMPH OF BUSINESS

At the time of the Civil War, the typical American business firm was a small enterprise, owned and managed by a single family, and producing goods for a local or regional market. By the turn of the century, businesses depending on large-scale investments had organized as corporations and grown to unforeseen size. These mammoth firms could afford to mass-produce goods for national and even international markets. At the helm stood unimaginably wealthy men, powerful representatives of a new national business community, who led in the transformation of the United States from a rural to an urban industrial nation.

Focus Questions

1. What was the effect of the expansion in the production of both capital goods and consumer goods?

2. What were the sources of the new labor being recruited for factory work in Gilded Age America?

3. How did cities grow and change in the late nineteenth century?

4. How did the roles of middle-class men and women change during this period?

5. What accounts for the rise of a consumer society and how did various groups participate in its development?

1865–1900

MECHANIZATION TAKES COMMAND

The Centennial Exposition of 1876, held in Philadelphia, celebrated not so much the American Revolution 100 years earlier as the industrial and technological promise of the century to come. The visiting emperor of Brazil spoke into an unfamiliar device on display and gasped, "My God, it talks!" The telephone, patented that year by Alexander Graham Bell, signaled the rise of the United States to world leadership in industrial technology.

The year 1876 also marked the opening of Thomas Alva Edison's laboratory in Menlo Park, New Jersey, one of the first devoted to industrial research. Three years later, his team produced an incandescent lamp that burned for thirteen hours. By 1882, the Edison Electric Light Company had launched its service in New York City's financial district. Electricity revolutionized both urban life and industry.

The second industrial revolution (1871–1914) proceeded at a pace that was not only unprecedented but also previously unimaginable. In 1865, the annual production of goods was estimated at $2 billion; by 1900, it stood at $13 billion, transforming the United States from fourth to first in the world in terms of productivity. American industry had outstripped its European rivals, Germany and Great Britain, and manufactured one-third of the world's goods.

A major force behind economic growth was the vast transcontinental railroad, completed in 1869. The addition of three more major rail lines (the Southern Pacific; the Northern Pacific; and the Atchison, Topeka, and Santa Fe) in the early 1880s, and the Great Northern, a decade later, completed the most extensive transportation network in the world. As the nation's first big business and recipient of generous government subsidies, railroads linked cities in every state and served as a nationwide distributor of goods. Freight trains

In 1887, Thomas Alva Edison (1847–1931), shown here with the phonograph, moved his laboratory from Menlo Park to West Orange, New Jersey. Here he invented the alkaline storage battery, the phonograph, and the kinetoscope, the first machine to allow one person at a time to view motion pictures.

carried the bountiful natural resources, such as iron, coal, and minerals that supplied the raw materials for industry, as well as food and other commodities for the growing urban populations (see Map 19.1).

No factor was more important in promoting economic growth than the application of new technologies to increase the productivity of labor and the volume of goods. Machines, factory managers, and workers together created a system of continuous production by which more could be made—and faster—than anywhere else on earth. Higher productivity depended not only on machinery and technology but also on economies of scale and

speed, reorganization of factory labor and business management, and the unparalleled growth of a market for goods of all kinds.

New systems of mass production replaced wasteful and often chaotic practices and speeded up the delivery of finished goods. In the 1860s, meatpackers set up one of the earliest production lines. The process of converting livestock into meat began with a live animal. A chain around the hind leg whirled the body to an overhead rail, which carried it to slaughter—all in barely half a minute's time. Then hair and bristles were removed by a scraping machine, the carcass shifted to a conveyer belt

MAP EXPLORATION

To explore an interactive version of this map, go to **www.prenhall.com/faragher6/map19.1**

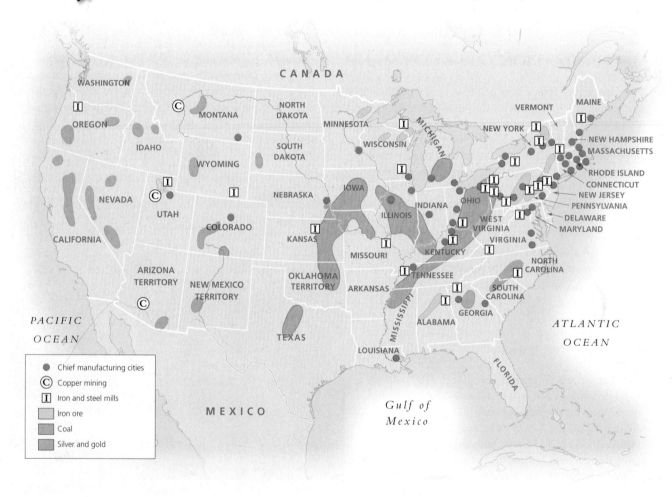

MAP 19.1 Patterns of Industry, 1900 Industrial manufacturing concentrated in the Northeast and Midwest, whereas the raw materials for production came mostly from other parts of the nation.

where the chest was split and the organs removed, and the body placed in a cooler. This "disassembly line" displaced patterns of hand labor that were centuries old.

Sometimes the invention of a single machine could instantly transform production, mechanizing every stage from processing the raw material to packaging the product. The cigarette-making machine, patented in 1881, shaped the tobacco, encased it in an endless paper tube, and snipped off the tube at cigarette-length intervals. This machine could produce more than 7,000 cigarettes per hour, replacing the worker who at best made 3,000 per day. After a few more improvements, fifteen machines could meet the total demand for American cigarettes. Within a generation, continuous production—the assembly line—became standard in most areas of manufacturing, revolutionizing the making of furniture, cloth, grain products, soap, and canned goods; the refining, distilling, and processing of animal and vegetable fats; and eventually, the manufacture of automobiles.

EXPANDING THE MARKET FOR GOODS

To distribute the growing volume of goods and to create a dependable market, businesses demanded new techniques of merchandising on a national and, in some cases, international scale. For generations, legions of sellers, or "drummers," had worked their routes, pushing goods, especially hardware and patent medicines, to individual buyers and local retail stores. After the Civil War, the appearance of mail-order houses, which accompanied the consolidation of the railroad lines and the expansion of the postal system, helped to get new products to consumers.

Growing directly out of these services, the successful Chicago-based mail-order houses drew rural and urban consumers into a common marketplace. Sears, Roebuck and Company and Montgomery Ward offered an enormous variety of goods, from shoes to buggies to gasoline stoves and cream separators. The mail-order catalogue also returned to rural folks the fruits of their own labor, now processed and packaged for easy use. The Sears catalogue offered Armour's summer sausage as well as Aunt Jemima's Pancake Flour and Queen Mary Scotch Oatmeal, both made of grains that came from the agricultural heartland. In turn, the purchases made by farm families through the Sears catalogue sent cash flowing into Chicago.

The chain store achieved similar economies of scale. By 1900, a half-dozen grocery chains had sprung up. The largest was A&P, originally named the Great Atlantic and Pacific Tea Company to celebrate the completion of the transcontinental railroad. Frank and Charles Woolworth offered inexpensive variety goods in five and-ten-cent stores. Other chains selling drugs, costume jewelry, shoes,

cigars, and furniture soon appeared, offering a greater selection of goods and lower prices than the small, independent stores.

Opening shortly after the Civil War, department stores began to take up much of the business formerly enjoyed by specialty shops, offering a spectrum of services that included restaurants, rest rooms, ticket agencies, nurseries, reading rooms, and post offices. Elegantly appointed with imported carpets, sweeping marble staircases, and crystal chandeliers, the department store raised retailing to new heights. By the close of the century, the names of Marshall Field of Chicago, Filene's of Boston, The Emporium of San Francisco, Wanamaker's of Philadelphia, and Macy's of New York had come to represent the splendors of those great cities as well as the apex of mass retailing.

The Marshall Field building constructed in Chicago's Loop between 1893 and 1915 came to occupy an entire block to reign as the world's largest department store. In addition to all kinds of fine goods, the retail store offered a host of personal amenities, such as lunch and tea rooms, travel agencies, hair salons, and even personal shoppers. The photograph here features its 6,000 square foot mosaic dome, which was surfaced with 1.6 million pieces of iridescent Tiffany art glass.

Advertising lured customers to the department stores, the chains, and the independent neighborhood stores. The advertising revolution began in 1869, when Francis Wayland Ayer founded the earliest advertising agency. Ayer's managed the accounts of such companies as Montgomery Ward, Wanamaker's Department Store, Singer Sewing Machines, and the National Biscuit Company. With the help of this new sales tool, gross revenues of retailers raced upward from $8 million in 1860 to $102 million in 1900.

INTEGRATION, COMBINATION, AND MERGER

The business community aspired to exercise greater control of the economy and to enlarge the commercial empire. From the source of raw materials to the organization of production, from the conditions of labor to the climate of public opinion, business leaders acted shrewdly. Economic cycles alternating between rapid growth and sharp decline also promoted the rise of big business. Major economic setbacks in 1873 and 1893 wiped out weaker competitors, allowing the strongest firms to rebound swiftly and to expand their sales and scale of operation during the recovery period.

Businesses grew in two distinct, if overlapping, ways. Through *vertical integration* a firm gained control of production at every step of the way—from raw materials through processing to the transporting and merchandising of the finished items. In 1899, the United Fruit Company began to build a network of wholesale houses in the United States, and within two years it had opened distribution centers in twenty-one major cities. Eventually, it controlled an elaborate system of Central American plantations and temperature-controlled shipping and storage facilities for its highly perishable bananas. The firm became one of the nation's largest corporations.

The second means of growth, *horizontal combination*, entailed gaining control of the market for a single product. The most famous case was the Standard Oil Company, founded by John D. Rockefeller in 1870. Operating out of Cleveland in a highly competitive but lucrative field, Rockefeller first secured preferential rates from railroads eager to ensure a steady supply of oil. He then convinced or coerced other local oil operators to sell their stock to him. The Standard Oil Trust, established in 1882, controlled over 90 percent of the nation's oil-refining industry (see Seeing History).

In 1890, Congress passed the Sherman Antitrust Act to restore competition by encouraging small business and outlawing "every . . . combination . . . in restraint of trade or commerce." Ironically, the courts interpreted the law in ways that inhibited the organization of trade unions (on the ground that they restricted the free flow of labor) and

actually helped the consolidation of business. More than 2,600 firms vanished between 1898 and 1902 alone. By 1910, the industrial giants that would dominate the American economy until the last half of the twentieth century—U.S. Rubber, Goodyear, American Smelting and Refining, Anaconda Copper, General Electric, Westinghouse, Nabisco, Swift and Company, Armour, International Harvester, Eastman Kodak, and American Can—had already formed.

THE GOSPEL OF WEALTH

Ninety percent of the nation's business leaders were Protestant, and the majority attended church services regularly. They attributed their personal achievement to hard work and perseverance and made these the principal tenets of a new faith that imbued the pursuit of wealth with old-time religious zeal.

One version of this "gospel of wealth" justified the ruthless behavior of the entrepreneurs who accumulated unprecedented wealth and power through shady deals and conspiracies. Speculator Jay Gould, known in the popular press as the "Worst Man in the World," wrung his fortune, it was widely believed, from the labor of others. He rose quickly from his modest origins through a series of unsavory financial maneuvers.

Speculation in railroads proved to be Gould's forte. He took over the Erie Railroad, paying off New York legislators to get the state to finance its expansion, and he acquired the U.S. Express Company by pressuring and tricking its stockholders. When threatened with arrest, Gould sold off his shares for $9 million and moved on to the Union Pacific, where he cut wages, precipitated strikes, and manipulated elections in the western and Plains states. Tired of being caricatured in the press as a great swindler, he bought the leading newspapers. At his death, one obituary described Jay Gould as "an incarnation of cupidity and sordidness," whose life symbolized "idolatrous homage [to] the golden calf."

Andrew Carnegie—the "Richest Man in the World"—offered a strikingly different model. A poor immigrant from Scotland, Carnegie spent his boyhood studying bookkeeping at night while working days in a textile mill. In 1852, he became the personal secretary of the superintendent of the Pennsylvania Railroad's Western division. He learned quickly and soon stepped into the superintendent's job. While improving passenger train service, he invested brilliantly to build funds for his next venture.

Carnegie built an empire in steel. A genius at vertical integration, he undercut his competitors by using the latest technology and designing his own system of cost analysis. By 1900, Carnegie managed the most efficient steel mills in the world, which accounted for one-third of the nation's output. When he sold out to J. P. Morgan's new United States Steel Corporation in 1901, his personal share of the proceeds came to $225 million.

Carnegie was well known as a civic leader. From one point of view, he was a factory despot who underpaid his employees and ruthlessly managed their working conditions. But to the patrons of the public libraries, art museums, concert halls, colleges, and universities that he funded, Carnegie appeared to be the single greatest philanthropist of the age. Late in his life, he outlined his personal philosophy in a popular essay, *The Gospel of Wealth* (1889), explaining that "there is no genuine, praiseworthy success in life if you are not honest, truthful, and fair-dealing." By the time he died, he had given away his massive personal fortune.

Whether following the rough road of Gould or the smooth path of Carnegie, the business community worked together to fashion the new conservative ideology of social Darwinism, which purportedly explained, and justified, why some Americans grew rich while others remained poor. Grafted on the biological theory of evolution propounded by the famed British naturalist Charles Darwin, social Darwinism raised the principle of the "survival of the fittest" as an ideal for modern society. In 1883, the Yale professor William Graham Sumner published an essay entitled *What Social Classes Owe to Each Other*, wherein he argued that only a few individuals were capable of putting aside selfish pleasures to produce the capital needed to drive the emerging industrial

SEEING HISTORY

The Standard Oil Company

John D. Rockefeller, who formed the Standard Oil Company in 1870, sought to control all aspects of the industry, from the transportation of crude oil to the marketing and distribution of the final products. By the end of the decade, after making shrewd deals with the railroads and underselling his rivals, he managed to control 90 percent of the oil-refining industry. To further consolidate his interests, in 1882 Rockefeller created the Standard Oil Trust, which, by integrating both vertically and horizontally, became a model for other corporations and an inspiration for critical commentary and antitrust legislation.

Rockefeller's best-known critic was Ida Tarbell. In 1904 she published *The History of the Standard Oil Company*, first in serial form in the popular *McClure's Magazine* and later as a book. Tarbell's muckraking exposé attracted a great deal of attention. But even more popular were political cartoons depicting Rockefeller's stranglehold on the entire oil industry. *Puck* magazine, which had been founded in 1871 by Joseph Keppler, an immigrant from Austria, held up Rockefeller and his company to ridicule. This cartoon, published in *Puck* in 1904, shows Standard Oil as a sinister octopus, wrapping its arms around the White House and Congress as well as workers and even the denizens of Wall Street. In 1911, in response to an antitrust suit, the Supreme Court ordered the company to break up. The modern corporations Exxon, Mobil, Chevron, Amoco, and Sohio (some of which have recently merged) all descended from Rockefeller's Standard Oil.

What does this cartoon tell us about Rockefeller's reputation at the turn of the twentieth century?
What does it suggest about Americans' feelings about the trusts?

This engraving of steel manufacturing at Andrew Carnegie's plant in 1886 features a Bessemer Converter, which converts molten pig iron into steel. The process was named after Sir Henry Bessemer of Sheffield, England, who first patented the process in 1855.

LABOR IN THE AGE OF BIG BUSINESS

Like the gospel of wealth, the "gospel of work" affirmed the dignity of hard work, the virtue of thrift, and the importance of individual initiative. But unlike business leaders, the philosophers of American working people did not believe in riches as the proof of work well done or in the lust for power as the driving force of progress. On the contrary, they contended that honesty and competence should be the badge of all morally responsible citizens.

Behind the "gospel of work" stood the reality of the rising industrial order, especially its new systems of production that were, in turn, enabled by new technologies. The impact of the new order on the lives of working people would be nothing less than revolutionary. Increasingly, Americans made their livelihoods by producing, not for their own subsistence, but exclusively for the market, and they earned wages in return for their labor. Big business thus found its mirror image in the labor movement spawned by the consolidation of the wage system.

THE WAGE SYSTEM

The accelerating growth of industry, especially the steady mechanization of production, dramatically changed employer–employee relations and created new categories of workers. Both in turn fostered competition among workers and created conditions often hazardous to health. In many occupations—meat processing, clothing and textile manufacturing, cigar making, and mining, for example—immigrants from Europe and Asia predominated by the end of the century.

For most craft workers, the new system destroyed long-standing practices and chipped away at their customary autonomy. Frederick Winslow Taylor, the pioneer of scientific management, explained that managers must "take all the important decisions . . . out of the hands of workmen." Teams of ironworkers, for example, had previously set the rules of production as well as their wages,

economy and, moreover, they were fully deserving of their great fortunes. In contrast, the vast majority, too lazy or profligate to rise above poverty, deserved their own miserable fates. To tamper with this "natural" order by establishing welfare programs to help the poor or redistributing wealth in any way would be hazardous to society. Meanwhile, the popular writer Horatio Alger produced a more temperate version of this credo. Publishing more than 100 rags-to-riches novels, he created heroes who manage to rise out of poverty by both hard work and luck and ultimately acquire, if not vast wealth, middle-class respectability and comfort.

while the company supplied equipment and raw materials. Once steel replaced iron, most companies gradually introduced a new system. Managers now constantly supervised workers, set the pace of production and rate of payment, and introduced new, faster machinery that made many skills obsolete. In the woodworking trades, highly skilled cabinetmakers, who for generations had brought their own tools to the factory, were largely replaced with "green hands"—immigrants, including many women—who with only minimal training and close supervision could operate new woodworking machines at cheaper rates of pay.

Not all trades conformed to this pattern. The garment industry, for example, grew at a very fast pace in New York, Boston, Chicago, Philadelphia, Cleveland, and St. Louis but retained older systems of labor along with the new. The highly mechanized factories employed hundreds of thousands of young immigrant women, while the outwork system, established well before the Civil War, contracted ever-larger numbers of families to work in their homes on sewing machines or by hand. Paid by the piece—a seam stitched, a collar turned, a button attached—workers in this "sweating" system labored faster and longer at home or in the factory to forestall a dip in wages.

Industrial expansion also offered new opportunities for women to work outside the home, and many young women fled the family farm for the factory. African American and immigrant women found employment in trades least affected by technological advances, such as domestic service. In contrast, English-speaking white women moved into the better-paying clerical and sales positions in the rapidly expanding business sector. After the typewriter and telephone came into widespread use in the 1890s, the number of women employed in office work rose even faster. At the turn of the century, 8.6 million women worked outside their homes—nearly triple the number in 1870.

By contrast, African American men found themselves excluded from many fields. In Cleveland, for example, the number of black carpenters declined after 1870, just as the volume of construction was rapidly increasing. African American men were also systematically driven from restaurant service and barred from newer trades such as boilermaking, plumbing, electrical work, and paperhanging, which European immigrants secured for themselves.

Discriminatory or exclusionary practices fell hardest on workers recruited earlier from China. From the 1860s on, many Chinese established laundries and restaurants in West Coast cities where they were viewed as potential competitors by both white workers and proprietors of small businesses. A potent and racist anti-Chinese movement organized to protest "cheap" Chinese labor and to demand a halt to Chinese immigration. By the 1870s white rioters were insistently calling for deportation measures and razing Chinese neighborhoods. In 1882, Congress passed the Chinese Exclusion Act, which restricted Chinese immigration by barring laborers, limited the civil rights of resident Chinese, and forbade their naturalization.

E PLURIBUS UNUM (EXCEPT THE CHINESE).

Thomas Nast (1840–1902), the most famous political cartoonist of the late nineteenth century, used his art to comment on pressing political issues, such as the plight of former slaves during Reconstruction, the evils of machine politics, and the rivalry between the national political parties. His drawings were made into wood engravings that were then printed in newspapers and popular magazines. In this cartoon, published in *Harper's Weekly*, April 1, 1882, Nast shows America welcoming all immigrants except Chinese.

For even the best-placed wage earners, the new workplace could be unhealthy, even dangerous. Meatpacking produced its own hazards—the dampness of the pickling room, the sharp blade of the slaughtering knife, and the noxious odors of the fertilizer department. Factory owners often failed to mark high-voltage wires, locked fire doors, and allowed the emission of toxic fumes. Extractive workers, such as coal and copper miners, labored in mineshafts where the air could suddenly turn poisonous and where cave-ins were possible and deadly. Moreover, machines ran faster in American factories than anywhere else in the world, and workers who could not keep up or suffered serious injury found themselves without a job.

Even under less hazardous conditions, workers complained about the tedium of performing repetitive tasks for many hours each day. Although federal employees had been granted the eight-hour day in 1868, most workers still toiled upward of ten to twelve hours. "Life in a factory," one textile operative grumbled, "is perhaps, with the

the art of excepting

exception of prison life, the most monotonous life a human being can live." Nor could glamour be found in the work of saleswomen in the elegant department stores. Clerks could not sit down, despite workdays as long as sixteen hours in the busy season, or hold "unnecessary conversations" with customers or other clerks. Despite these disadvantages, most women preferred sales and manufacturing jobs to domestic service, which required live-in servants to be on call seven days a week, enjoying at best an occasional afternoon off.

Moreover, steady employment was rare. Between 1866 and 1897, fourteen years of prosperity stood against seventeen years of hard times. The major depressions of 1873–79 and 1893–97 were the worst in the nation's history up to that time. Three "minor" recessions (1866–67, 1883–85, and 1890–91) did not seem insignificant to the millions who lost their jobs.

THE KNIGHTS OF LABOR

The Noble and Holy Order of the Knights of Labor, founded by a group of Philadelphia garment cutters in 1869, grew to become the largest labor organization in the nineteenth century. Led by Grand Master Workman Terence V. Powderly, the order sought to bring together wage earners, regardless of skill. The Knights endorsed a variety of reform measures—the restriction of child labor, a graduated income tax, more land set aside for homesteading, the abolition of contract labor, and monetary reform—to offset the power of the industrialists. They believed that the "producing classes," once freed from the grip of corporate monopoly and the curses of ignorance and alcohol, would transform the United States into a genuinely democratic society.

The Knights sought to overturn the wage system and, as an alternative, they promoted producers' cooperatives. In these factories, workers collectively made all decisions on prices charged for goods and shared all the profits. Local assemblies launched thousands of small co-ops, such as the Our Girls Co-operative Manufacturing Company, which was established by Chicago seamstresses in the 1880s. The Knights also ran small cooperative cigar shops and grocery stores, often housed in their own assembly buildings. Successful for a time, most cooperatives could not compete against the heavily capitalized enterprises and ultimately failed.

For women, the Knights of Labor created a special department within the organization "to investigate the abuses to which our sex is subjected by unscrupulous employers, to agitate the principles which our Order teaches of equal pay for equal work and the abolition of child labor." At the 1886 convention, delegates approved this plan, and Grand Master Powderly appointed knit-goods worker Leonora M. Barry general investigator. With perhaps 65,000 women members at its peak, the Knights ran daycare centers and occasionally even set up cooperative kitchens to reduce the drudgery of cooking.

The Knights reached their peak during the great campaign for a shorter workday. The organization grew from a few thousand in 1880 to nearly three-quarters of a million six years later. The Knights welcomed workers usually excluded by other unions. Nearly 3,000 women formed their own "ladies assemblies" or joined mixed locals. The Knights also organized African American workers—20,000 to 30,000 nationally—mainly in separate assemblies within the organization. Chinese workers, however, were barred from membership.

The Haymarket affair in Chicago, where the Knights were headquartered, virtually crushed the organization (see Communities in Conflict). Local employers' associations successfully pooled funds to rid their factories of troublesome organizers and announced that companies would no longer bargain with unions. The wage system had triumphed.

At the 1886 General Assembly of the Knights of Labor, which met in Richmond, Virginia, sixteen women attended as delegates. Elizabeth Rodgers, the first woman in Chicago to join the Knights and the first woman to serve as a master workman in a district assembly, attended with her two-week-old daughter. The convention established a Department of Women's Work and appointed Leonora M. Barry, a hosiery worker, as general investigator.

THE AMERICAN FEDERATION OF LABOR

The events of 1886 also signaled the rise of a very different kind of organization, the American Federation of Labor (AFL). Unlike the Knights, the AFL accepted the wage system. Following a strategy of "pure and simple unionism," the AFL sought recognition of its union status to bargain with employers for better working conditions, higher wages, and shorter hours. In return, it offered compliant firms the benefit of amenable day-to-day relations with the most highly skilled wage earners. Only if companies refused to bargain in good faith would union members resort to strikes.

The new federation, with twelve national unions and 140,000 affiliated members in 1886, rapidly pushed ahead of the rival Knights by organizing craft workers. AFL president Samuel Gompers disregarded unskilled workers, racial minorities, and immigrants, believing they were impossible to organize and even unworthy of membership. He also believed in the "family wage," a wage paid to a male household head that would keep women and children comfortable within the confines of domesticity. Women, Gompers insisted, did not belong in the factory, where they would serve only to lower wages. Under his leadership, the AFL advanced the interests of the "aristocrat of labor," the best-paid worker in the world.

Rank-and-file AFL members did not always share Gompers's opinions, and they often revived some of the best qualities of the Knights of Labor. They provided support to strikers, gathered votes for pro-labor political candidates, sponsored social activities, and published their own weekly newspapers.

Chicago's Central Labor Federation embodied the new spirit of the AFL. After the Haymarket tragedy, trade unionists worked more closely with urban reformers. Finding allies among women's clubs and church groups, within the state legislature, and even among some socially minded members of the business community, they cultivated an atmosphere of civic responsibility. The Illinois Factory Investigation Act of 1893 offered evidence of their hard work and patience: under its terms, unionists secured funds from the state legislature to monitor working conditions and, particularly, to improve the terrible conditions under which women and children worked in sweatshops.

Although the AFL represented only a small minority of working Americans—about 10 percent at the end of the century—local unions often played important roles in their communities. They may not have been able to slow the steady advance of mass production, which diminished the craft worker's autonomy and eliminated some of the most desirable jobs, but AFL members managed to make their presence felt. Local politicians courted their votes, and Labor Day, first celebrated in the 1880s, became a national holiday in 1894.

THE NEW SOUTH

"Fifteen years have gone over" since the Civil War, journalist Whitelaw Reid complained, yet the South "still sits crushed, wretched, busy displaying and bemoaning her wounds." Physically and financially devastated by the war, the South remained economically stagnant, its per capita wealth only 27 percent of that of the northeastern states. While a few urban centers moved very slowly into the era of modern industry, the countryside receded into greater isolation and poverty. The southern economy in general was held back by dependence on northern finance capital, continued reliance on cotton production, and the legacy of slavery.

AN INTERNAL COLONY

In the 1870s, a vocal and powerful new group of Southerners headed by Henry Woodfin Grady, editor of the *Atlanta Constitution*, insisted that the region enjoyed a great potential in its abundant natural resources of coal, iron, turpentine, tobacco, and lumber. Grady and his peers envisioned a "New South" where modern textile mills operated efficiently and profitably, close to the sources of raw goods, the expansive fields of cotton, and a plentiful and cheap supply of labor, unrestricted by unions or by legal limitations on the employment of children. Arguing against those planters who aspired to rejuvenate the agricultural economy based on the cultivation of a few staple crops, this group forcefully promoted industrial development and welcomed northern investors.

Northern investors secured huge concessions from southern state legislatures, including land, forest, and mineral rights and large tax exemptions. Exploiting the incentives, railroad companies laid more than 22,000 miles of new track, connecting the region to national markets and creating new cities. By 1890, a score of large railroad companies, centered mainly in New York, held more than half of all the track in the South.

Northerners also employed various means to protect their investments from southern competition. By the late 1870s, southern merchants, with help from foreign investors, had begun to run iron factories around Birmingham, Alabama. Southern iron production was soon encroaching on the northeastern market. To stave off this competition, Andrew Carnegie ordered the railroads to charge higher freight fees to Birmingham's iron producers. New York bankers later succeeded in expatriating Birmingham's profits through stock ownership in southern firms. After the turn of the century, U.S. Steel simply bought out the local merchants and took over much of Birmingham's production.

The production of cotton textiles followed a similar course. Powerful merchants and large landowners, realizing that they could make high profits by controlling the cotton crop from field to factory, promoted the vertical

Haymarket Square, Chicago, May 4, 1886

In the aftermath of the bombing at Haymarket Square, a grand jury was impaneled to hear evidence on the events that led to the death of the first policeman. The judge instructed the members of the grand jury to cast a large net and to look not only for the person who threw the bomb but also for those who had advised or incited him to do so. On June 5, 1886, the grand jury concluded that the bomb throwing resulted from a "deliberate conspiracy" and delivered its indictments.

August Spies, the editor of the *Arbeiter Zeitung*, was one of men indicted by the grand jury and put on trial. On August 20, 1886, he and the other alleged conspirators were found guilty and sentenced to death. Prior to his sentencing, on October 8 of that same year, Spies respectfully but defiantly addressed the court, refusing to beg for mercy. He was hanged on November 11, 1887.

Was August Spies tried and convicted for his crime or for his political beliefs?

June 5, 1886: The Chicago Grand Jury Indicts Anarchist Leaders for the Haymarket Bombing

To the Hon. Judge John G. Rogers: In presenting the bills of indictment which we have the honor herewith to submit, and what are known as the "Anarchist Cases," we deem it proper to accompany the same with a few words of explanation . . . . So far as we are informed, this is the first appearance of dynamite as a factor in the criminal annals of this state, and this is also the first organized conspiracy for the destruction of human life and the overthrow of law, in any part of this country, that has employed this new and dangerous agency. It is not surprising that the fatal and appalling success which has attended this first introduction should have inspired terror in this community.

We find the attack on the police on May 4 was the result of a deliberate conspiracy, the full details of which are now in the possession of the officers of the law, and will be brought out when the cases shall be reached in court. We find that this force of disorganizers had a very perfect force of organizers of its own, and that it was chiefly under the control of the coterie of men who were connected with the publication of their English and German newspaper organs, *The Alarm* and the *Arbeiter Zeitung*, the evidence has shown conclusively to us that these men were manipulating this agitation from base and selfish motives for the power and influence which it gave them, and for the money which they could make out of it; that the large majority of their followers were simply their dupes, and they have collected in this way large sums of money from those followers, and from the working men of this city. That their plan was to involve, so far as they could, not only the socialist and communist organizations, with whom they claim some kindred, but also the labor societies and trade unions, to the end that in the midst of the excitement they were creating they could not only rely upon them as a source of revenue, but also have them to fall back upon in the event of their finally being made amenable to the law . . . .

In conclusion, we desire, as citizens and as members of this Grand Jury, in this public way, to express our most grateful acknowledgment of the debt owing to the officers and men of the police force of Chicago.

SOURCE: From the transcript of the trial by the Grand Jury, as quoted in Fremont O. Bennett, *Politics and Politicians of Chicago, Cook County, and Illinois* (Chicago: Blakeley Printing Co., 1886), pp. 465–66.

---

integration of the cotton industry. The number of mills in the South grew from 161 in 1880 to 400 in 1900. Southern investors supplied large amounts of the capital for the industrial expansion and technological improvements. The latest machines ran the new mills, and the South boasted the first factory fully equipped with electricity. Production in the four leading cotton-manufacturing states—North Carolina, South Carolina, Georgia, and Alabama—skyrocketed, far outpacing the New England mills.

Recognizing the potential for great profit, northern manufacturers, including many New England mill owners, shifted their investments to the South. By the 1920s, northern investors held much of the South's wealth, including the major textile mills, but returned through employment or social services only a small share of the profits to the region's people.

Beyond iron or steel and textiles, southern industry remained largely extractive and, like the South itself, rural. Turpentine and lumbering businesses pushed ever farther

> "We find the attack on the police on May 4 was the result of a deliberate conspiracy, . . . these men were manipulating this agitation from base and selfish motives for the power and influence which it gave them, . . ."

> "You, in your blindness, think you can stop the tidal wave of civilization and human emancipation . . . . you are the real revolutionists. You and you alone are the conspirators and destructionists!"

October 8, 1886: August Spies Refuses to Plead for Mercy

Your honor: . . . By simply designating the defendants as "Anarchists," and picturing them as a newly discovered tribe or species of cannibals, and by inventing shocking and horrifying stories of dark conspiracies said to be planned by them, these good Christians zealously sought to keep the naked fact from the working people and other righteous parties, namely: That in the evening of May 4, 200 armed men, under the command of a notorious ruffian, attacked a meeting of peaceable citizens. With what intention? With the intention of murdering them, or as many of them as they could. I refer to the testimony given by two of our witnesses. The wageworkers of this city began to object to being fleeced too much—they began to say some very true things, but these were highly disagreeable to their patrician class; they put forth—well, some very modest demands. They thought eight hours hard toil a day for scarcely two hours' pay was enough. This lawless rabble had to be silenced! . . .

You want to "stamp out the conspirators"—the "agitators"—Ah, stamp out every factory lord who has grown wealthy upon the unpaid labor of his employees. Stamp out every landlord who has amassed fortunes from the rent of the overburdened workingmen and farmers. Stamp out every machine that is revolutionizing industry and agriculture, that intensifies the production, ruins the producer, that increases the national wealth, while the creator of all these things stands amidst them, tantalized with hunger! Stamp out the railroads, the telegraph, the telephone, steam and yourselves—for everything breathes the revolutionary spirit.

You, gentlemen, are the revolutionists! You rebel against the effects of social conditions which have tossed you, by the fair hand of Fortune, into a magnificent paradise. Without inquiring, you imagine that no one else has a right in that place. You insist that you are the chosen ones, the sole proprietors. The forces that tossed you into the paradise, the industrial forces, are still at work. They are growing more active and intense from day to day. Their tendency is to elevate all mankind to the same level, to have all humanity share in the paradise you now monopolize.

You, in your blindness, think you can stop the tidal wave of civilization and human emancipation by placing a few policemen, a few gatling [sic] guns,[*] and some regiments of militia on the shore—you think you can frighten the rising waves back into the unfathomable depths, when they have arisen, by erecting a few gallows in the perspective. You, who oppose the natural course of things, you are the real revolutionists. You and you alone are the conspirators and destructionists!.

SOURCE: *The Famous Speeches of the Eight Chicago Anarchists* (Chicago: L.E. Parsons, 1910).

*Designed by Richard J. Gatling in 1861, a Gatling gun is an early version of the machine gun.

---

into diminishing pine forests, the sawmills and distilleries moving with them. Toward the end of the century, fruit canning and sugar refining flourished. For the most part, southern enterprises mainly produced raw materials for consumption or use in the North, thereby perpetuating the economic imbalance between the sections.

The governing role of capital investments from outside the region reinforced long-standing relationships. Even rapid industrialization—in iron, railroads, and textiles—did not carry the same consequences achieved in the North. The rise of the New South reinforced, rather than diminished, the region's status as the nation's internal colony.

SOUTHERN LABOR

The advance of southern industry did little to improve the working lives of most African Americans, who made up more than one-third of the region's population. Although the majority continued to work in agriculture, large

The processing of raw tobacco employed thousands of African American women, who sorted, stripped, stemmed, and hung tobacco leaves as part of the redrying process. After mechanization was introduced, white women took jobs as cigarette rollers, but black women kept the worst, most monotonous jobs in the tobacco factories. The women shown in this photograph are stemming tobacco in a Virginia factory while their white male supervisor oversees their labor.

numbers found jobs in industries such as the railroad. In booming cities like Atlanta, they even gained skilled positions as bricklayers, carpenters, and painters. For the most part, however, African Americans were limited to unskilled, low-paying jobs. In the textile mills and cigarette factories, which employed both black and white workers, the workforce was rigidly segregated. African Americans were assigned mainly to janitorial jobs and rarely worked alongside the white workers who tended the machines. Nearly all African American women who earned wages did so as household workers; girls as young as ten worked as domestics or as nurses for white children.

Most trade unions refused membership to black workers. Locals of the all-white carpenters' union maintained a segregation policy so absolute that if too few members were available for a job, the union would send for out-of-town white workers rather than employ local members of the black carpenters' union. In an Atlanta mill in 1897, 1,400 white women operatives went on strike when the company proposed to hire two black spinners.

Only at rare moments did southern workers unite across racial lines. In the 1880s, the Knights of Labor briefly organized both black and white workers. But when white politicians and local newspapers began to raise the specter of black domination, the Knights were forced to retreat. Across the region their assemblies collapsed. Other unions remained the exclusive preserve of white skilled workers.

Wages throughout the South were low for both black and white workers. Southern textile workers' wages were barely half those of New Englanders. In the 1880s, when investors enjoyed profits ranging from 30 percent to 75 percent, southern mill workers earned as little as twelve cents per hour. Black men earned at or below the poverty line of $300 per year, while black women rarely earned more than $120 and white women about $220 annually. The poorest paid workers were children, the mainstay of southern mill labor.

As industry expanded throughout the nation, so too did the number of children earning wages. This was especially so in the South. In 1896, only one in twenty Massachusetts mill workers was younger than sixteen, but one in four North Carolina cotton mill operatives was that age or younger. Traditions rooted in the agricultural economy reinforced the practice of using the labor of all family members, even the very young. Seasonal labor, such as picking crops or grinding sugarcane, put families on the move, making formal education all but impossible. Not until well into the twentieth century did compulsory school attendance laws effectively restrict child labor in the South.

A system of convict labor also thrived in the South. Bituminous coal mines and public work projects of all kinds, especially in remote areas, employed disciplinary methods and created living and working conditions reminiscent of slavery. African Americans constituted up to 90 percent of the convict workforce. Transported and housed like animals—chained together by day and confined in portable cages at night—these workers suffered high mortality rates. White politicians expressed pride in what they called the "good roads movement"—the chief use of convict labor—as proof of regional progress.

THE TRANSFORMATION OF PIEDMONT COMMUNITIES

The impact of modern industry was nowhere greater than in the Piedmont, the region extending from southern Virginia and the central Carolinas into northern Alabama and Georgia. After 1870, long-established farms and plantations gave way to railroad tracks, textile factories, numerous mill villages, and a few sizable cities. By the turn of the century, five Piedmont towns had populations over 10,000. Even more dramatic was the swelling number of small towns with populations between 1,000 and 5,000—from fourteen in 1870 to fifty-two in 1900. Once the South's backcountry, the Piedmont now surpassed New England in the production of yarn and cloth to stand first in the world.

Rural poverty and the appeal of a new life encouraged many farm families to strike out for a mill town. Those with the least access to land and credit—mainly widows and their children and single women—were the first to go into the mills. Then families sent their children. Some families worked in the mills on a seasonal basis, between planting and harvesting. But as the agricultural crisis deepened, more and more people abandoned the countryside entirely for what they called "public work."

A typical mill community was made up of rows of single-family houses, a small school, several churches, a company-owned store, and the home of the superintendent, who governed everyone's affairs. The manager of the King Cotton Mill in Burlington, North Carolina, not only kept the company's accounts in order, purchased raw material, and sold the finished yarn, but also even bought Christmas presents for the workers' children. It was not unknown for a superintendent to prowl the neighborhood to see which families burned their lanterns past nine o'clock at night and, finding a violator, to knock on the door and tell the offenders to go to bed. Millworkers frequently complained that they had no private life at all. A federal report published shortly after the turn of the century concluded that "all the affairs of the village and the conditions of living of all the people are regulated entirely by the mill company. Practically speaking, the company owns everything and controls everything, and to a large extent controls everybody in the mill village."

Mill superintendents also relied on schoolteachers and clergy to set the tone of community life. They hired and paid the salaries of Baptist and Methodist ministers to preach a faith encouraging workers to be thrifty, orderly, temperate, and hardworking. The schools, similarly subsidized by the company, reinforced the lesson of moral and social discipline required of industrial life and encouraged students to follow their parents into the mill. But it was mainly young children between six and eight years old who attended school. When more hands were needed in the mill, superintendents plucked out those youngsters and sent them to join their older brothers and sisters who were already at work.

Piedmont mill villages like Greenville, South Carolina, and Burlington, Charlotte, and Franklinville, North Carolina, nevertheless developed a cohesive character typical of isolated rural communities. The new residents maintained many aspects of their agricultural pasts, tilling small gardens and keeping chickens, pigs, and cows in their yards. Factory owners rarely paved roads or sidewalks or provided adequate sanitation. Mud, flies, and diseases such as typhoid fever flourished. Millworkers endured poverty and health hazards by strengthening community ties through intermarriage. Within a few generations, most of the village residents had, according to one study, "some connection to each other, however distant, by marriage," blood, or both. Even the men and women without families boarded in households where privacy was scarce and collective meals created a family-like atmosphere. Historians have called this complex of intimate economic, family, and community ties the customs of incorporation.

THE INDUSTRIAL CITY

Before the Civil War, manufacturing had centered in the countryside, in new factory towns such as Lowell, Massachusetts, and Troy, New York. By the end of the nineteenth century, 90 percent of all manufacturing took place in cities. The metropolis stood at the center of the growing industrial economy, a magnet drawing raw material, capital, and labor, and a key distribution point for manufactured goods throughout the nation and worldwide. The industrial city became the home of nearly 20 million immigrants, mainly the so-called "new immigrants" from southern and eastern Europe, who hoped to escape famine, political upheaval, or religious persecution in their homelands or simply make a better life for themselves and their families.

POPULATING THE CITY

The population of cities grew at double the rate of the nation's population as a whole. In 1860, only sixteen cities had more than 50,000 residents. By 1890, one-third of all Americans were city dwellers. Eleven cities claimed more than 250,000 people (see Table 19.1).

The nation's largest cities—New York, Chicago, Philadelphia, St. Louis, Boston, and Baltimore—achieved international fame for the size and diversity of their populations. Many of their new residents had migrated from rural communities within the United States. Between 1870 and 1910, an average of nearly 7,000 African Americans moved north each year, hoping to escape the poverty and oppression in the South and to find better-paying jobs. By the end of the century, nearly 80 percent of African Americans in the North lived in urban areas.

Immigrants and their children were the major source of urban population growth in the late nineteenth century. Most of those in the first wave of immigration, before the Civil War, had settled in the countryside. In contrast, in the last half of the nineteenth century, it was the industrial city that drew the so-called new immigrants, who came primarily from eastern and southern Europe. In 1880, San Francisco claimed the highest proportion of foreign born (45 percent), although not the largest number. By the turn of the century, Chicago had more Germans than all but a few German cities and more Poles than most Polish cities;

TABLE 19.1

A Growing Urban Population

	1870	1880	1890	1900
U.S. population	35,558,000	50,156,000	62,947,000	75,995,000
Urban population	9,902,000	14,130,000	22,106,000	30,160,000
Percent urban	25.7	28.2	35.1	39.7
Percent rural	74.3	71.8	64.9	60.3

Note that during each decade, the U.S. population as a whole grew between 20 and 30 percent. Figures in the table have been rounded to the nearest thousand.
SOURCE: Robert G. Barrows, "Urbanizing America," in Charles W. Calhoun, ed., *The Gilded Age* (Wilmington DE, 1996), 93, 95.

New York had more Italians than a handful of the largest Italian cities, and Boston had nearly as many Irish as Dublin. In almost every group except the Irish, men outnumbered women (see Map 19.2).

Like rural migrants, immigrants came to the American city to take advantage of the expanding opportunities for employment. While many hoped to build a new home in the land of plenty, many others intended to work hard, save money, and return to their families in the Old Country. In the 1880s, for example, nearly half of all Italian, Greek, and Serbian men returned to their native lands. Others could not return to their homelands or did not wish to. Jews, for instance, had emigrated to escape persecution in Russia and Russian-dominated Polish and Romanian lands. A Yiddish writer later called this generation the "Jews without Jewish memories . . . . They shook them off in the boat when they came across the seas. They emptied out their memories."

Of all groups, Jews had the most experience with urban life. Forbidden to own land in most parts of Europe and boxed into *shtetls* (villages), Jews had also formed thriving urban communities in Vilna, Berlin, London, and Vienna. Many had worked in garment manufacturing, in London's East End, for example, and followed a path to American cities like New York, Rochester, Philadelphia, or Chicago where the needle trades flourished.

Other groups, the majority coming from rural parts of Europe, sought out their kinfolk in American cities, where they could most easily find housing and employment. Bohemians settled largely in Chicago, Pittsburgh, and Cleveland. French Canadians, a relatively small group of a few hundred thousand, emigrated from Quebec and settled almost exclusively in New England and upper New York State. Finding work mainly in textile mills, they transformed smaller industrial cities like Woonsocket, Rhode Island, into French-speaking communities. Cubans, themselves often first- or second-generation immigrants from Spain, moved to Ybor City, a section of Tampa, Florida, to work in cigar factories. Still other groups tended toward cities dominated by fishing, shoemaking, or even glassblowing, a craft carried directly from the Old Country. Italians, the most numerous among the new immigrants, settled mainly in northeastern cities, laying railroad track, excavating subways, and erecting buildings.

Resettlement in an American city did not necessarily mark the end of the immigrants' travels. Newcomers, both native-born and immigrant, moved frequently from one neighborhood to another and from one city to another. As manufacturing advanced outward from the city center, working populations followed. American cities experienced a total population turnover three or four times during each decade of the last half of the century.

THE URBAN LANDSCAPE

Faced with a population explosion and an unprecedented building boom, the cities encouraged the creation of many beautiful and useful structures, including commercial offices, sumptuous homes, and efficient public services. At the same time, cities did little to improve the conditions of the majority of the population, who worked in dingy factories and lived in crowded tenements. Open space decreased as American cities grew.

American streets customarily followed a simple gridiron pattern. Builders leveled hills, filled ponds, and pulled down any farms or houses in the way. City officials usually lacked any master plan, save the idea of endless expansion. Factories often occupied the best sites, typically near waterways, where goods could be easily transported and chemical wastes dumped.

Built after the Civil War, the tenement was designed to maximize the use of space. A typical tenement sat on a lot 25 by 100 feet and rose to five stories. There were four families on each floor, each with three rooms. By 1890, New York's Lower East Side packed more than 700 people per acre into back-to-back buildings, producing one of the highest population densities in the world.

At the other end of the urban social scale, New York's Fifth Avenue, St. Paul's Summit Avenue, Chicago's Michigan Avenue, and San Francisco's Nob Hill fairly gleamed with new mansions and town houses. Commonwealth Avenue marked Boston's fashionable Back Bay district, built on a filled-in 450-acre tidal flat. State engineers planned this community, with its magnificent boulevard, uniform five-story brownstones, and back alleys designed for deliveries. Like wealthy neighborhoods in other cities, Back Bay also provided space for the city's magnificent

MAP EXPLORATION

To explore an interactive version of this map, go to **www.prenhall.com/faragher6/map19.2**

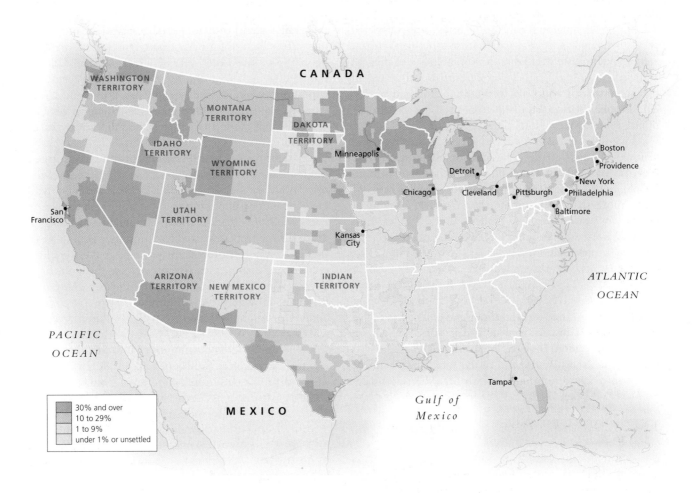

Legend:
- 30% and over
- 10 to 29%
- 1 to 9%
- under 1% or unsettled

MAP 19.2 Population of Foreign Birth by Region, 1880 European immigrants after the Civil War settled primarily in the industrial districts of the northern Midwest and parts of the Northeast. French Canadians continued to settle in Maine, Cubans in Florida, and Mexicans in the Southwest, where earlier immigrants had established thriving communities.

SOURCE: Clifford L. Lord and Elizabeth H. Lord, *Lord & Lord Historical Atlas of the United States* (New York: Holt, 1953).

public architecture: its stately public library, fine arts and science museums, and orchestra hall. Back Bay opened onto the Fenway Park system designed by the nation's premier landscape architect, Frederick Law Olmsted.

The industrial city established a new style of commercial and civic architecture. Using fireproof materials, expanded foundations, and internal metal construction, the era's talented architects focused on the factory and office building. Concentrating as many offices as possible in the downtown areas, they fashioned hundreds of buildings from steel, sometimes decorating them with elaborate wrought-iron facades. The office building could rise seven, ten, even twenty stories high, and with the invention of the safety elevator, people and goods could easily be moved vertically.

Architects played a key role in the late nineteenth-century City Beautiful movement. Influenced by American wealth and its enhanced role in the global economy, they turned to the monumental or imperial style common in European cities, laying grand concrete boulevards at enormous public cost. New sports amphitheaters spread pride in the city's accomplishments. New schools, courthouses, capitol buildings, hospitals, museums, and huge new art galleries, museums, and concert halls promoted urban excitement as well as cultural uplift. The imperial style also increased congestion and noise, making the city a more desirable place to visit than to live.

The city inspired other architectural marvels. Opened in 1883, the Brooklyn Bridge won wide acclaim as the most original American construction. Designed by John Roebling and his son Washington Roebling, the bridge was considered an aesthetic and practical wonder. Its soaring piers, elegant arches, and intricate steel cables convey an image of strength and elasticity, inspiring a belief among artists and writers in the potential of technology to unite function and beauty. The Brooklyn Bridge also helped to speed the transformation of rural townships into suburban communities.

Like the railroad, but on a smaller scale, streetcars and elevated railroads changed business dramatically, because they moved traffic of many different kinds—information, people, and goods—faster and farther than before. By 1895, more than 800 communities operated systems of electrically powered cars or trolleys. In 1902, New York opened its subway system, which would grow to become the largest in the nation.

THE CITY AND THE ENVIRONMENT

By making it possible for a great number of workers to live in communities distant from their place of employment, mass transportation allowed the metropolitan region to grow dramatically. By the end of the nineteenth century, suburban trains were bringing nearly 100,000 riders daily into the city of Chicago. Suburbs sprang up outside the major cities, offering many professional workers quiet residential retreats from the city's busy and increasingly polluted downtown.

Electric trolleys eliminated the tons of waste from horsecars that had for decades fouled city streets. But the new rail systems also increased congestion and created new safety hazards for pedestrians. During the 1890s, 600 people were killed each year by Chicago's trains. Elevated trains, designed to avoid these problems, placed entire communities under the shadow of noisy and rickety wooden platforms. Despite many technological advances, the quality of life in the nation's cities did not necessarily improve.

Modern water and sewer systems now constituted a hidden city of pipes and wires, mirroring the growth of the visible city above ground. These advances, which brought indoor plumbing to most homes, did not, however, eradicate serious environmental or health problems. Most cities continued to dump sewage into nearby bodies of water. Moreover, most municipal governments established separate clean-water systems through the use of reservoirs rather than outlawing upriver dumping by factories. Downriver communities began to complain about unendurable stench from the polluted rivers and streams.

The unrestricted burning of coal to fuel the railroads and to heat factories and homes after 1880 greatly intensified urban air pollution. Noise levels continued to rise in the most compacted living and industrial areas. Overcrowded conditions and inadequate sanitary facilities bred tuberculosis, smallpox, and scarlet fever, among other contagious diseases. Children's diseases like whooping cough and measles spread rapidly through poor neighborhoods. Only after the turn of the century, amid an intensive campaign against municipal corruption, did laws and administrative practices address the serious problems of public health (see Chapter 21).

Meanwhile, the distance between the city and the countryside narrowed. Naturalists had hoped for large open spaces—a buffer zone—to preserve farmland and wild areas, protect future water supplies, and diminish regional air pollution. But soon the industrial landscape invaded the countryside. Nearby rural lands not destined for private housing or commercial develop-

In his watercolor *The Bowery at Night*, painted in 1885, W. Louis Sonntag Jr. shows a New York City scene transformed by electric light. Electricity transformed the city in other ways as well, as seen in the electric streetcars and elevated railroad.

ment became sites for water treatment and sewage plants, garbage dumps, and graveyards—services essential to the city's growing population.

THE RISE OF CONSUMER SOCIETY

The growth of industry and the spread of cities promoted—and depended on—the consumption of mass-produced goods. During the final third of the nineteenth century, the standard of living climbed, although unevenly and erratically. Real wages (pay in relation to the cost of living) rose, fostering improvements in nutrition, clothing, and housing. Meanwhile, prices dropped. More and cheaper products came into the reach of all but the very poor. Food from the farms became more abundant and varied—grains for bread or beer; poultry, pork, and beef; fresh fruits and vegetables from California. Although many Americans continued to acknowledge the moral value of hard work, thrift, and self-sacrifice, the explosion of consumer goods and services promoted sweeping changes in behavior and beliefs, although in vastly and increasingly different ways.

"CONSPICUOUS CONSUMPTION"

Labeled the "Gilded Age" by humorist and social critic Mark Twain, the era following the Civil War favored the growth of a new business class that pursued both money and leisure and formed national networks to consolidate their power. Business leaders built diverse stock portfolios and often served simultaneously on the boards of several corporations. Similarly, they intertwined their interests by joining the same religious, charitable, athletic, and professional societies. Their wives and children vacationed together in the sumptuous new seashore and mountain resorts, while they themselves made deals in the exclusive social clubs and on the golf links of suburban country clubs. Just as Dun and Bradstreet ranked the leading corporations, the Social Register identified the 500 families that controlled most of the nation's wealth.

According to economist and social critic Thorstein Veblen, the rich had created a new style of "conspicuous consumption." The Chicago mansion of real estate tycoon Potter Palmer, for example, was constructed without exterior doorknobs. Not only could no one enter uninvited, but a visitor's calling card supposedly passed through the hands of twenty-seven servants before admittance was allowed. A vice president of the Chicago & Northwestern Railroad, Perry H. Smith, built his marble palace in the style of the Greek Renaissance. Its ebony staircase was trimmed in gold, its butler's pantry equipped with faucets not only for hot and cold water but also for iced champagne. The women who oversaw these elaborate households served as measures of their husbands' status, according to Veblen, by adorning themselves in jewels, furs, and dresses of the latest Paris design.

Conspicuous consumption reached new heights of extravagance. In New York, wealthy families hosted dinner parties for their dogs or pet monkeys, dressing the animals in fancy outfits for the occasion. Railroad magnate "Diamond Jim" Brady commonly enjoyed after-theater snacks at the city's "lobster palaces," where he consumed vast quantities of food—oysters for an appetizer, two soups, fish, a main dinner of beef and vegetables, punches and sherbet on the side, dessert, coffee, and quarts of orange juice.

Toward the end of the century, the wealthy added a dramatic public dimension to the "high life." New York's Waldorf-Astoria hotel, which opened in 1897, incorporated the grandeur of European royalty but with an important difference. Because rich Americans wanted to be watched, the elegantly appointed corridors and restaurants were visible to the public through huge windows. The New York rich also established a unique custom to welcome the New Year: they opened wide the curtains of their Fifth Avenue mansions so that passersby could marvel at the elegant decor.

The wealthy became the leading patrons of the arts as well as the chief procurers of art treasures from Europe and Asia. They provided the bulk of funds for the new symphonies, operas, and ballet companies, which soon rivaled those of Continental Europe. Nearly all major museums and art galleries, including the Boston Museum of Fine Arts, the Philadelphia Museum of Art, the Art Institute of Chicago, and the Metropolitan Museum of Art in New York, were founded during the last decades of the nineteenth century.

SELF-IMPROVEMENT AND THE MIDDLE CLASS

A new middle class, very different from its predecessor, formed during the last half of the century. The older middle class comprised the owners or superintendents of small businesses, doctors, lawyers, teachers, and ministers and their families. The new middle class included these professionals but also the growing number of salaried employees—the managers, technicians, clerks, and engineers who worked in the complex web of corporations and government. Long hours of labor earned their families a modest status and sufficient income to live securely in style and comfort.

By the end of the century, many middle-class families were nestled in suburban retreats far from the noise, filth, and dangers of the city. This peaceful domestic setting, with its manicured lawns and well-placed shrubs, afforded both privacy and rejuvenation as well as the separation of business from leisure and the breadwinner from his family for most of the day. Assisted by modern transportation

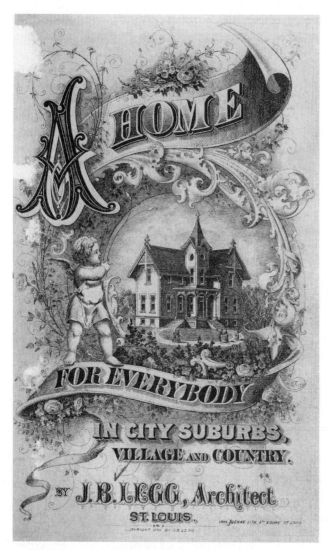

Taken from J. B. Legg's architecture book, this page illustrates the ideal suburban home. His book, published in 1876, was aimed at the prospering middle class.

systems, men often traveled one to two hours each day, five or six days a week, to their city offices and back again. Women and children stayed behind.

Middle-class women devoted a large part of their day to care of the home. They frequently employed one or two servants but relied increasingly on the many new appliances to get their work done. Improvements in the kitchen stove, such as the conversion from wood fuel to gas, saved a lot of time. Yet, simultaneously, with the widespread circulation of cookbooks and recipes in newspapers and magazines, as well as the availability of new foods, the preparation of meals became more complex and time-consuming. New devices such as the eggbeater speeded some familiar tasks, but the era's fancy culinary practices offset any gains in saving time. Similarly, the new carpet sweepers surpassed the broom in efficiency, but the fash-

ionable high-napped carpeting demanded more care. Thus, rather than diminishing with technological innovation, household work expanded to fill the time available.

By the end of the century, though, middle-class women had added shopping to their list of household chores. They took charge of the household budget and purchased an ever expanding range of machine-made goods, packaged foods, manufactured clothing, and personal luxuries. With the rise of department stores, which catered specifically to them, shopping combined work and pleasure and became a major pastime for women.

Almost exclusively white, Anglo-Saxon, and Protestant, the new middle class embraced "culture" not for purposes of conspicuous consumption but as a means of self-improvement. Whole families visited the new museums and art galleries. One of the most cherished institutions, the annual season of lectures at the Chautauqua campgrounds in upstate New York, brought thousands of families together in pursuit of knowledge of literature and the fine arts. The middle class also provided the bulk of patrons for the new public libraries.

Middle-class families applied the same standards to their leisure activities. What one sporting-goods entrepreneur rightly called the "gospel of exercise" involved men and women in calisthenics and outdoor activities, not so much for pleasure as for physical and mental discipline. Hiking was a favorite among both men and women and required entirely new outfits: for women, loose upper garments and skirts short enough to prevent dragging; for men, rugged outerwear and jaunty hats. Soon men and women began camping out, with almost enough amenities to recreate a middle-class home in the woods. Roller-skating and ice-skating, which became crazes shortly after the Civil War, took place in specially designed rinks in almost every major town. By the 1890s, the "safety" bicycle had also been marketed. It replaced the large-wheel variety, which was difficult to keep upright. A good-quality "bike" cost $100 and, like the piano, was a symbol of middle-class status. In 1895, Chicago hosted thirty-three cycle clubs comprising nearly 10,000 members.

Leisure became the special province of middle-class childhood. Removed from factories and shops and freed from many domestic chores, children enjoyed creative play and physical activity. The toy market boomed, and lower printing prices helped children's literature flourish. Uplifting classics such as *Little Women* and *Black Beauty* were popular.

LIFE IN THE STREETS

Immigrants often weighed the material abundance they found in the United States against their memories of the Old Country. One could "live better" here, but only by working much harder. In letters home, immigrants described the riches of the new country but warned friends

George Washington Carver (1864–1943), who had been born in slavery, had been invited by Booker T. Washington to direct agricultural research at the Tuskegee Institute in Alabama. A leader in development of agriculture in the New South, Carver promoted crop diversification to rejuvenate soil that was depleted by the continuous planting of cotton and encouraged the cultivation of alternative, high-protein crops such as peanuts and soybeans. He designed his programs in sustainable agriculture mainly for African American farmers and sharecroppers rather than for commercial purposes.

LEISURE AND PUBLIC SPACE

Most large cities set aside open land for leisure-time use by residents. New York's Central Park opened for ice-skating in 1858, providing a model for urban park systems across the United States. In 1869, planners in Chicago secured funds to create a citywide system comprising six interconnected large parks, and within a few years, Lincoln Park, on the city's north side, was attracting crowds of nearly 30,000 on Sundays. These parks were rolling expanses, cut across by streams and pathways and footbridges and set off by groves of trees, ornamental shrubs, and neat flower gardens. According to the designers' vision, the urban middle class might find here a respite from the stresses of modern life. To ensure this possibility, posted regulations forbade many activities, ranging from walking on the grass to gambling, picnicking, or ball playing without permission, to speeding in carriages.

The working classes had their own ideas about the use of parks and open land in their communities. Trapped in overcrowded tenements or congested neighborhoods, they wanted space for sports, picnics, and lovers' trysts. Young people openly defied ordinances that prohibited play on the grassy knolls, while their elders routinely voted against municipal bonds that did not include funds for more recreational space. Immigrant ward representatives on the Pittsburgh City Council, for instance, argued that band shells for classical music meant little to their constituents, while spaces suitable for sports meant much.

Eventually, most park administrators set aside some sections for playgrounds and athletic fields and others for public gardens and band shells. Yet intermittent conflicts erupted. The Worcester, Massachusetts, park system, for example, allowed sports leagues to schedule events but prohibited pickup games. This policy gave city officials more control over the use of the park for outdoor recreation but at the same time forced many ball-playing boys into the streets. When working-class parents protested, city officials responded by instituting programs of supervised play to the further dismay of the children.

Public drinking of alcoholic beverages, especially on Sunday, provoked similar disputes. "Blue laws," forbidding businesses to open on Sunday, were rigidly enforced when it came to neighborhood taverns, while large firms like the railroads enjoyed exemptions. Although civil leaders hoped to discourage Sunday drinking by sponsoring alternative events, such as free organ recitals and other concerts, many working people, especially beer-loving German immigrants, continued to treat Sunday as their one day of relaxation. In Chicago, when not riding the streetcars to the many beer gardens and taverns that thrived on the outskirts, Germans gathered in large numbers for picnics in the city's parks.

Toward the end of the century, many park administrators relaxed the rules and expanded the range of permitted activities. By this time, large numbers of the middle class had become sports enthusiasts and pressured municipal governments to turn meadowlands into tennis courts and golfing greens. In the 1890s, bicycling brought many women into the parks. Still, not all city residents enjoyed these facilities. Officials in St. Louis, for example, barred African Americans from the city's grand Forest Park and set aside the smaller Tandy Park for their use. After challenging this policy in court, African Americans won a few concessions, such as the right to picnic at any time in Forest Park and to use the golf course on Monday mornings.

NATIONAL PASTIMES

Toward the end of the century, the younger members of the urban middle class had begun to find common ground in lower-class pastimes, especially ragtime music. Introduced to many Northerners by the African American composer Scott Joplin at the Chicago World's Fair of 1893, "rag" quickly became the staple of entertainment in the new cabarets and nightclubs. Middle-class urban dwellers began to seek out ragtime bands and congregated in nightclubs and even on the rooftops of posh hotels to listen and dance and even to drink.

and relatives not to send weaklings, who would surely die of stress and strain amid the alien and intense commercialism of American society. Embittered German immigrants called their new land *Malhuerica*, "misfortune"; Jews called it *Ama Reka*, Hebrew for "without soul"; and Slavs referred to it as *Dollaryka*.

Many newcomers, having little choice about their place of residence, concentrated in urban districts marked off by racial or ethnic lines. In San Francisco, city ordinances prevented Chinese from operating laundries in most of the city's neighborhoods, and the city's schools excluded their children. In the 1880s, Chinese San Franciscans, representing 10 percent of the city's population, crowded into a dozen blocks of restaurants, shops, and small factories known as Chinatown. In Los Angeles and San Antonio, Mexicans lived in distinctive barrios. In most cities, African American families were similarly compelled to remain in the dingiest, most crime ridden, and dangerous sections of town.

The working-class home did not necessarily ensure privacy or offer protection from the dangers of the outside world. In the tenements, families often shared their rooms with other families or paying boarders. During the summer heat, adults, children, and boarders alike competed for a sleeping place on the fire escape or roof, and all year round, noise resounded through paper-thin walls. But so complex and varied were income levels and social customs that no single pattern emerged. Chicago's Slovaks, Lithuanians, and Poles, for example, frequently took in boarders, yet Bohemians rarely did. Neither did the skilled iron rollers who worked at the Carnegie Steel Company in Homestead, Pennsylvania. These well-paid craft workers often owned their own homes, boasting parlors and even imported Belgian carpets. At the other extreme, Italian immigrants, who considered themselves fortunate to get work with a shovel, usually lived in overcrowded rented apartments, just a paycheck away from eviction.

Whether it was a small cottage or a tenement flat, the working-class home involved women and children in routines of household labor without the aid of new mechanical devices. In addition to cooking and cleaning, women used their cramped domestic space for work that provided a small income. They gathered their children—and their husbands after a hard day's labor—to sew garments, wrap cigars, string beads, or paint vases for a contractor who paid them by the piece. And they cooked and cleaned for the boarders whose rent supplemented the family income.

Despite working people's slim resources, their combined buying power created new and important markets for consumer goods. Often they bought shoddy replicas of products sold to the middle class: cheaper canned goods, inferior cuts of meat, and partially spoiled fruit. Several leading clothing manufacturers specialized in inexpensive ready-to-wear items, usually copied from patterns designed for wealthier consumers but constructed hastily from flimsy materials. Patent medicines for ailments caused by working long periods in cramped conditions sold well in working-class communities, where money for doctors was scarce.

The close quarters of the urban neighborhood allowed immigrants to preserve many Old World customs. In immigrant communities such as Chicago's German North Side, Pittsburgh's Poletown, New York's Lower East Side, or San Francisco's Chinatown, people usually spoke their native language while visiting friends and relatives. The men might play cards while women and children gathered in the stairwell or on the front stoop to trade stories. In good weather, they walked and talked, an inexpensive pastime common in European cities. No organization was as important as the fraternal society, which sponsored social clubs and provided insurance benefits. Social organizations,

The intersection of Orchard and Hester Streets on New York's Lower East Side, photographed ca. 1905. Unlike the middle classes, who worked and played hidden away in offices and private homes, the Jewish lower-class immigrants who lived and worked in this neighborhood spent the greater part of their lives on the streets.

known as *huiguan*, were especially important in preserving clan and dialect among the largely male unmarried population of Chinese San Francisco. Immigrants also re-created Old World religious institutions such as the temple, church, or synagogue, or secular institutions such as German family-style saloons or Russian Jewish tearooms. Chinese theaters, in inexpensive daily and nightly performances, presented dramas depicting historical events or explicating moral teachings and thereby preserved much of Chinese native culture. Immigrants also replicated their native cuisine and married, baptized children, and buried their dead according to Old World customs.

In the cosmopolitan cities, immigrants, by being innovative entrepreneurs as well as the best customers, helped to shape the emerging popular culture. German immigrants, for example, created Tin Pan Alley, the center of the popular music industry. They also became the first promoters of ragtime, which found its way north from Storyville, the red-light district of New Orleans. Created by African American and Creole bands, ragtime captivated those teenage offspring of immigrants who rushed to the new dance halls.

When developers realized that "wholesome fun" for the masses could pay better than upper-class leisure or lower-class vice, in 1895 they decided to transform Coney Island into a magnificent seaside park filled with ingenious amusements such as water slides, mechanized horse races, carousels, roller coasters, and fun houses. On the rides or at the nearby beach, young men and women could easily meet apart from their parents, cast off their inhibitions, and enjoy a hug or kiss. Or they could simply stroll through the grounds, looking at exotic performers, enjoying make-believe trips to the Far East or even the moon, entranced by fantastic towers, columns, minarets, and lagoons lit up at night to resemble dreams rather than reality. At Coney Island or at Riverview, Chicago's oldest amusement park, located on the city's North Side, millions of working-class people enjoyed cheap thrills that offset the hardships of their working lives.

CULTURES IN CONFLICT, CULTURE IN COMMON

The new commercial entertainments gave Americans from various backgrounds more in common than they would otherwise have had. On New York's Lower East Side, for instance, theater blossomed with dramas that Broadway would adopt years later, while children dreamed of going "uptown" where the popular songs they heard on the streets were transcribed onto sheet music and sold in stores throughout the city. Even so, just as the changes in production fostered conflict in the forms of strikes and workers' protests, so too did the accompanying changes in the daily life of the community. Competing claims to the resources of the new urban, industrial society, such as public schools and urban parks, became more intense as the century moved to a close.

EDUCATION

Business and civic leaders realized that the welfare of society now depended on an educated population, one possessing the skills and knowledge required to keep both industry and government running. In the last three decades of the nineteenth century, the idea of universal free schooling, at least for white children, took hold. Kindergartens in particular flourished. St. Louis, Missouri, opened the first public school kindergarten in 1873, and by the turn of the century, more than 4,000 similar programs throughout the country enrolled children between the ages of three and seven.

Public high schools, which were rare before the Civil War, also increased in number, from 160 in 1870 to 6,000 by the end of the century. In Chicago alone, average daily attendance multiplied sixfold. Despite this spectacular growth, which was concentrated in urban industrial areas, as late as 1890 only 4 percent of children between the ages of fourteen and seventeen were enrolled in school, the majority of them girls planning to become teachers or office workers (See Figure 19.1) Most high schools

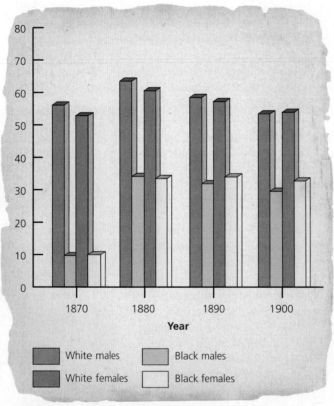

FIGURE 19.1 School Enrollment of 5- to 19-Year-Olds, 1870–1900
In the final decades of the nineteenth century, elementary and high school enrollments grew across the board but especially so for children of color and for girls.

SOURCE: U.S. Department of Commerce, Bureau of the Census, *Historical Statistics of the United States, Colonial Times to 1970.* U.S. Department of Education, Office of Educational Research and Improvement.

continued to serve mainly the middle class. In 1893, the National Education Association reaffirmed the major purpose of the nation's high schools as preparation for college, rather than for work in trades or industry, and endorsed a curriculum of rigorous training in the classics, such as Latin, Greek, and ancient history. The expected benefits of this kind of education rarely outweighed the immediate needs of working-class families who depended on their children's wages. At the end of the century, 50 percent of the children in Chicago between the ages of ten and twelve were working for wages.

Higher education also expanded along several lines. Agricultural colleges formed earlier in the century developed into institutes of technology and took their places alongside the prestigious liberal arts colleges. To extend learning to the "industrial classes," Representative Justin Morrill (R., Vermont) sponsored the Morrill Federal Land Grant Act of 1862, which funded a system of state colleges and universities for teaching agriculture and mechanics "without excluding other scientific and classic studies." Meanwhile, established private institutions like Harvard, Yale, Princeton, and Columbia grew with the help of huge endowments from business leaders. By 1900, sixty-three Catholic colleges were serving mainly the children of immigrants from Ireland and eastern and southern Europe. Still, as the overall number of colleges and universities grew from 563 in 1870 to nearly 1,000 by 1910, only 3 percent of the college-age population took advantage of these new opportunities. One of the most important developments occurred in the area of research and graduate studies, pioneered in this country in 1876 by the Johns Hopkins University. By the end of the century, several American universities, including Stanford University and the University of Chicago, offered advanced degrees in the arts and sciences.

This expansion benefited women, who previously had had little access to higher education. After the Civil War, a number of women's colleges were founded, beginning in 1865 with Vassar, which set the academic standard for the remainder of the century. Smith and Wellesley followed in 1875, Bryn Mawr in 1885. By the end of the century, 125 women's colleges offered a first-rate education comparable to that given to men at Harvard, Yale, or Princeton. Meanwhile, coeducation grew at an even faster rate; by 1890, 47 percent of the nation's colleges and universities admitted women. The proportion of women college students changed dramatically. Women constituted 21 percent of undergraduate enrollments in 1870, 32 percent in 1880, and 40 percent in 1910.

An even greater number of women enrolled in vocational courses. Normal schools, which offered one- or two-year programs for women who planned to become elementary school teachers, developed a collegiate character after the Civil War and had become accredited state teachers' colleges by the end of the century. Other

institutions, many founded by middle-class philanthropists, also prepared women for vocations. For example, the first training school for nurses opened in Boston in 1873, followed in 1879 by a diet kitchen that taught women to become cooks in the city's hospitals. Founded in 1877, the Women's Educational and Industrial Union offered a multitude of classes to Boston's wage-earning women, ranging from elementary French and German to drawing, watercolor, and oil and china paintings; to dressmaking and millinery, stenography and typing; as well a crafts less familiar to women, such as upholstering, cabinetmaking, and carpentry. In the early 1890s, when the entering class at a large women's college like Vassar still averaged less than 100, the Boston Women's Educational and Industrial Union reported that its staff of 83 served an estimated 1,500 clients per day. By that time, one of it most well-funded programs was a training school for domestic servants.

The leaders of the business community had also begun to promote manual training for working-class and immigrant boys. Trade unionists often opposed this development, preferring their own methods of apprenticeship to training programs they could not control. But local associations of merchants and manufacturers lobbied hard for "industrial education" and raised funds to supplement the public school budget. In 1884, the Chicago Manual Training School opened, teaching "shop work" along with a few academic subjects, and by 1895, all elementary and high schools in the city offered courses that trained boys for future jobs in industry and business.

The expansion of education did not benefit all Americans or benefit them all in the same way. Because African Americans were often excluded from colleges attended by white students, special colleges were founded shortly after the Civil War. All-black Atlanta and Fisk Universities both soon offered rigorous curricula in the liberal arts. Other institutions, such as Hampton, founded in 1868, specialized in vocational training, mainly in manual trades. Educator Booker T. Washington encouraged African Americans to resist "the craze for Greek and Latin learning" and to strive for practical instruction. In 1881, he founded the Tuskegee Institute in Alabama to provide industrial education and moral uplift. By the turn of the century, Tuskegee enrolled 1,400 men and women in more than thirty different vocational courses, including special cooking classes for homemakers and domestic servants. Black colleges, including Tuskegee, trained so many teachers that by the century's end the majority of black schools were staffed by African Americans.

The nation's educational system was becoming more inclusive and yet more differentiated. The majority of children attended school for several years or more. At the same time, students were tracked—by race, gender, and class—to fill particular roles in an industrial society.

Vaudeville, the most popular form of commercial entertainment since the 1880s, also bridged middle- and working-class tastes. Drawing on a variety-show tradition of singers, dancers, comedians, jugglers, and acrobats, who had entertained Americans since colonial days, "vaude" became a big business that made ethnic and racial stereotypes and the daily frustrations of city life into major topics of amusement. Vaudeville palaces—ten in New York, six in Philadelphia, five in Chicago, and at least one in every other large city—attracted huge, "respectable" crowds that sampled between twenty and thirty dramatic, musical, and comedy acts averaging fifteen minutes each. Sunday matinees were especially popular with women and children.

Sports, however, outdistanced all other commercial entertainments in appealing to all kinds of fans and managing to create a sense of national community. No doubt the most popular parks in the United States were the expanses of green surrounded by grandstands and marked by their unique diamond shape—the baseball fields. Baseball clubs formed in many cities, and shortly after the Civil War traveling teams with regular schedules made baseball a professional sport. The formation of the National League in 1876 encouraged other spectator sports, but for generations baseball remained the most popular.

Rowdy behavior gave the game a working-class ambience. Team owners, themselves often proprietors of local breweries, counted heavily on beer sales in the parks. Having to contend with hundreds of drunken fans, officials maintained order only with great difficulty. To attract more subdued middle-class fans, the National League raised admission prices, banned the sale of alcohol, and observed Sunday blue laws. Catering to a working-class audience, the American Association kept the price of admission low, sold liquor, and played ball on Sunday.

Baseball, like many other sports, soon became incorporated into the larger business economy. In Chicago, local merchants, such as Marshall Field, supported teams, and by the end of the 1860s there were more than fifty company-sponsored teams playing in the local leagues. By 1870, a Chicago Board of Trade team emerged as the city's first professional club, the White Stockings. Capitalized as a joint stock company, the White Stockings soon succeeded in recruiting a star pitcher from the Boston Red Stockings, Albert Spalding, who eventually became manager and then president of the team. Spalding also came to see baseball as a source of multiple profits. He procured the exclusive rights to manufacture the official ball and the rule book, while producing large varieties of other sporting equipment. Meanwhile, he built impressive baseball parks in Chicago, with seating for 10,000 and special private boxes above the grandstands for the wealthy.

Spalding's Base Ball Guide offered fans nothing less than "the official records of America's national game." The first issue came out in 1877 and by 1889 the publication grew to 180 pages packed with statistics, editorials by players, photographs, and overall assessments of teams in the major and minor leagues.

Spalding also succeeded in tightening the rules of participation in the sport. In 1879, he dictated the "reserve clause," which prevented players from negotiating a better deal and leaving the team that originally signed them. He encouraged his player-manager "Cap" Anson to forbid the White Stockings from playing against any team with an African American member. The firing of Moses "Fleet" Walker, an African American, from the Cincinnati Red Stockings in 1884 marked the first time the color line had been drawn in a major professional sport. Effectively excluded, African Americans organized their own traveling teams. In the 1920s, they formed the Negro Leagues, which produced some of the nation's finest ball players.

Players occasionally organized to regain control over their sport. They frequently complained about low wages and arbitrary rules, and like the Knights of Labor in the 1880s, they formed their own league, the Brotherhood of Professional Base Ball Players, with profits divided between participants and investors. This effort failed, partly because fans would not desert the established leagues, but mostly because successful baseball franchises demanded large quantities of capital. American sports had become big business.

As attendance continued to grow, the enthusiasm for baseball straddled major social divisions, bringing together Americans of many backgrounds, if only on a limited basis. By the end of the century, no section of the daily newspaper drew more readers than the sports pages. Although it interested relatively few women, sports news riveted the attention of men from all social classes. Loyalty to the "home team" helped to create an urban identity, while individual players became national heroes.

CHRONOLOGY

1862	Morrill Act authorizes "land-grant" colleges
1869	Knights of Labor founded
1870	Standard Oil founded
1873	Financial panic brings severe depression
1876	Baseball's National League founded
	Alexander Graham Bell patents the telephone
1879	Thomas Edison invents the incandescent bulb
	Depression ends
1881	Tuskegee Institute founded
1882	Peak of immigration to the United States (1.2 million) in the nineteenth century
	Chinese Exclusion Act passed
	Standard Oil Trust founded

1883	William Graham Sumner published the social Darwinist classic *What Social Classes Owe to Each Other*
1886	Campaigns for eight-hour workday peak
	Haymarket riot and massacre discredit the Knights of Labor
	American Federation of Labor founded
1889	Andrew Carnegie's *The Gospel of Wealth* recommends honesty and fair dealing
1890	Sherman Antitrust Act passed
1893	Stock market panic precipitates severe depression
1895	Coney Island opens
1901	U.S. Steel Corporation formed

CONCLUSION

By the end of the nineteenth century, industry and the growing cities had opened a new world for Americans. Fresh from Europe or from the native countryside, ordinary urban dwellers struggled to form communities of fellow newcomers through both work and leisure, in the factory, the neighborhood, the ballpark, and the public school. Meanwhile, their "betters," the wealthy and the new middle class, made and executed the decisions of industry and marketing, established the era's grand civic institutions, and set the tone for high fashion and art. Rich and poor alike shared many aspects of the new order. Yet inequality not only persisted but also increased and prompted new antagonisms.

The Haymarket tragedy highlighted the often strained relationships between Chicago's immigrant working population and civic leaders, precipitating violence, which included the public hanging of four of the eight men brought to trial, including August Spies. Although the new governor of Illinois, Peter Altgeld, pardoned the three who had their sentences commuted to life in prison, his attempt at amelioration did not signal a shift in the political climate. In the 1890s, hopes for a peaceful reconciliation of these tensions had worn thin, and the lure of overseas empire appeared as one of the few goals that held together a suffering and divided nation.

— REVIEW QUESTIONS —

1. Discuss the sources of economic growth in the decades after the Civil War. Historians often refer to this period as the era of the "second industrial revolution." Do you agree with this description?

2. Describe the impact of new technologies and new forms of production on the routines of industrial workers. How did these changes affect African American and women workers in particular? What role did trade unions play in this process?

3. Discuss the role of northern capital in the development of the New South. How did the rise of industry affect the lives of rural Southerners? Analyze these changes from the point of view of African Americans.

4. How did urban life change during the Gilded Age? How did economic development affect residential patterns? How did the middle class aspire to live during the Gilded Age? How did their lifestyles compare with those of working-class urbanites?

5. How did the American educational system change to prepare children for their adult roles in the new industrial economy?

6. How did the rise of organized sports and commercial amusements reflect and shape social divisions at the end of the century? Which groups were affected most (or least) by new leisure activities?

RECOMMENDED READING

Cindy S. Aron, *Working at Play: A History of Vacations in the United States* (1999). Covers the expansion of vacations from wealthy families to the middle class in the nineteenth century. Aron examines several types of settings, ranging from the grand summer hotels and posh resorts to camping vacations in the new national parks.

Sven Beckert, *The Monied Metropolis: New York City and the Consolidation of the American Bourgeoisie, 1850–1896* (2001). A highly informative study of the rise of the industrial elite, their business strategies, political advances, and engagements with consumer culture. This book examines the formation of a distinct social class and assesses the power it amassed during the Gilded Age.

William Cronon, *Nature's Metropolis: Chicago and the Great West* (1991). Analyzes the changing economic and political relationship between the city of Chicago and the surrounding countryside. Cronon demonstrates, through a variety of evidence, the tight interdependence of urban and rural regions.

Sarah Deutsch, *Women and the City: Gender, Space, and Power in Boston, 1870–1940* (2000). A close study of women's struggle to define the shape of the modern city and to ease the oppressive quality of spacial divisions along lines of gender, race, and class. Deutsch illustrates the efforts of women to exert their own principles of "moral geography" in shaping Boston's urban landscape.

Rebecca Edwards, *New Spirits: Americans in the Gilded Age, 1865–1905* (2006). A synthesis of recent scholarship with a thematic arrangement that takes the shape of an engaging essay. Edwards provides regional coverage and links domestic events—political, cultural, and social—to overseas expansion.

James Green, *Death in the Haymarket* (2006). Examines the Haymarket event within the context of changing class relations in Chicago and explores its significance as the first act of bombing for political purposes.

Tera W. Hunter, *To 'Joy My Freedom: Southern Black Women's Lives and Labors after the Civil War* (1997). A careful study of African American working women in the New South city of Atlanta. Hunter covers their various occupations in the modern urban economy without sacrificing attention to their pursuits of pleasure in the emerging world of mass entertainments and leisure.

William G. Roy, *Socializing Capital: The Rise of the Large Industrial Corporation in America* (1997). A sociologist, Roy examines key years in business history, 1898 to 1904, when companies shifted from private ownership by families to groups of investors and stockholders. He examines the rise of the corporation in relation to improvements in both technology and efficiency in production.

Susan Strasser, *Satisfaction Guaranteed: The Making of the American Mass Market* (1989). A clear and concise explanation of marketing and distribution during the rise of consumer society. Illustrated with examples of early advertising.

Alan Trachtenberg, *The Incorporation of America: Culture and Society in the Gilded Age*, Twenty-Fifth Anniversary ed. (2007). One of the best and most readable overviews of the post–Civil War era. Trachtenberg devotes great care to describing the rise of the corporation to the defining institution of national life and the reorientation of culture to reflect the new middle classes employed by the corporation.

Democracy and Empire
1870–1900

Oahu

The Annexation of Hawai'i

On January 17, 1891, Lili'uokalani succeeded her brother, King Kalakaua, to become the queen of Hawai'i. Raised a Christian and fluent in English, the fifty-two-year-old monarch was nevertheless intensely loyal to the Hawaiian people and to their language and customs. This allegiance—and her strong opposition to a movement to annex Hawai'i to the United States—brought her downfall. On January 17, 1893, the queen was deposed in a plot carried out by an American diplomat and his co-conspirators.

This event followed more than a half century of intense economic and diplomatic maneuvering by the United States and other nations. Both American and British missionaries, who had arrived in the 1820s to convert Hawaiians to Christianity, had bought up huge parcels of land, and they and their children—known as the *haole* to native Hawaiians—had grown into a large and powerful community of planters. The missionaries in turn encouraged American businesses to buy into the sugar plantations, and by 1875 U.S. corporations dominated the sugar trade. Within a year Hawaiian sugar was entering the United States duty free. Hawai'i was beginning to appear, in the opinion of Secretary of State James G. Blaine, to be "an outlying district of the state of California," and he pushed for formal annexation.

In 1888 American planters forced on the weak King Kalakaua a new constitution that severely limited his power and established wealth and property qualifications for voting. This so-called Bayonet Constitution, because it implied the use of U.S. arms to implement it, allowed noncitizens, Europeans as well as Americans, to vote

but denied the right of suffrage to poor native Hawaiians and the Chinese and Japanese who had come to work in the sugar fields.

In the name of democracy, the haole planters had secured a constitutional government that was closely allied to their economic interests—until King Kalakaua died in 1891. After ascending to the throne, Queen Lili'uokalani struck back. She decided she must empower native Hawaiians and limit the political influence of the haole elite and noncitizens.

The U.S.-led annexation forces first denounced the queen for attempting to abrogate the Bayonet Constitution and then welcomed Blaine's decision to send in U.S. troops to protect American lives and property. With no shots fired or documents signed, Lili'uokalani was deposed and a new provisional government installed. Sanford B. Dole, Honolulu-born son of Protestant missionaries, stepped in as the president of the new provisional government of Hawai'i, now a protectorate of the United States. ➤

Lili'uokalani immediately protested to President Grover Cleveland, explaining that she had yielded "to the superior force of the United States of America" only to avoid a serious armed confrontation and the loss of life. She called on President Cleveland to recognize her authority as "the constitutional sovereign of the Hawaiian Islands" and to reinstate her as queen. After investigating the situation, Cleveland agreed and ordered Lili'uokalani's reinstatement as queen. Ironically, Dole, who had been a major force for annexation, countered by refusing to recognize the right of the U.S. president "to interfere in our domestic affairs." On July 3, 1894, he proclaimed Hawai'i an independent republic, with himself retaining the office of president.

After Lili'uokalani's supporters attempted an unsuccessful military uprising in 1895, the deposed queen was arrested, tried by a military tribunal, and convicted of misprision of treason (having knowledge of treason but not informing the authorities). She was fined and sentenced to a five-year term in prison at hard labor, although Dole allowed her to serve a shorter sentence under "house arrest."

President Cleveland later declared privately that he was "ashamed of the whole affair" and stubbornly refused to listen to arguments for annexation. But he was powerless to stop the process before William McKinley succeeded him as president in 1896. Although more than a hundred members of Congress voted against annexation, an improper joint resolution passed to annex Hawai'i. In 1900, at McKinley's urging, Hawai'i became a territory. The people of Hawai'i were never consulted about this momentous change in their national identity.

Many Americans had long viewed Hawai'i as a stepping-stone to vast Asian markets, and by the 1890s they were determined to acquire the island nation in order to extend the reach of the United States beyond the continent. Business leaders, among others, reasoned that new foreign markets for goods might serve as a safety valve for domestic pressures. And this safety valve seemed much in need: the 1890s was turning out to be a decade of the most severe social conflict and economic crisis in American history. Domestic unrest increased pressures for overseas expansion. "American factories are making more than the American people can use; American soil is producing more than they can consume," declared Senator Albert J. Beveridge, Republican from Indiana. "[T]he trade of the world must and shall be ours." Others had different reasons for expanding the national boundaries, and a sizable number of Americans strongly opposed all such ventures. Nevertheless, the century closed on the heels of a war with Spain that won for the United States a swatch of new possessions that extended halfway around the world from Puerto Rico to the Philippines.

The path to empire was paved with major changes in government and the party system. As the 1890s culminated in the acquisition of new territories, it also witnessed a decisive realignment of the party system. Voters not only changed affiliations that had been in place since the Civil War but also waged significant challenges to the two-party system at the local, regional, and national levels. While Queen Lili'uokalani was trying to regain control of her government, a mass political movement was forming in the United States to revive the nation's own democratic impulse.

TOWARD A NATIONAL GOVERNING CLASS

The basic structure of government changed dramatically in the last quarter of the nineteenth century. Mirroring the fast-growing economy, public administration expanded at all levels—municipal, county, state, and federal—and took on greater responsibility for regulating society, especially market and property relations. Growing numbers of citizens for the first time looked to the government, from the local level upward, for public education, military veterans' pensions, and other social services. The leaders of the business community looked just as eagerly, and with far more influence, for protection of their property and sometimes for personal gain.

Reformers mobilized to rein in corruption and to promote both efficiency and professionalism in the multiplying structures of government. Meanwhile, some notable politicians acted to benefit directly, competing with one another for control of the new mechanisms of power. A lot was at stake. The expansion of government at home, particularly its increasing oversight of commerce, laid the foundation for economic and territorial expansion abroad.

THE GROWTH OF GOVERNMENT

Before the Civil War, local governments attended mainly to the promotion and regulation of trade and relied on private enterprise to supply vital services such as fire protection and water supplies. Cities gradually introduced professional police and firefighting forces and began to

Focus Questions

1. How did the growth of federal and state governments and the consolidation of the modern two-party system reshape the meaning of citizenship in the Gilded Age?

2. How and why did workers and farmers organize to participate in politics during this era?

3. In what ways did the election of 1896 represent a turning point in U.S. political history?

4. What explains the turn of the United States toward imperialist ventures in the late nineteenth century?

5. Why did the United States go to war with Spain in 1898 and with what results?

1870–1900

finance expanding school systems, public libraries, roads, and parks, an expansion requiring huge increases in local taxation. State governments grew in tandem, consolidating oversight of banking, transportation systems such as the railroads, and major enterprises such as the construction of dams and canals. By the end of the nineteenth century, city halls and state capitols had become beehives of activity.

At the national level, mobilization for the Civil War and Reconstruction had demanded an unprecedented degree of resources and their coordination, as both revenues and administrative bureaucracy grew quickly. At the end of Reconstruction, various aspects of federal government were trimmed at Congressional order, and the army was reduced to a fraction of its swollen size. Despite these particular reductions, the federal government as a whole continued to expand under the weight of new tasks and responsibilities. Federal revenues also skyrocketed, from $257 million in 1878 to $567 million in 1900. The administrative bureaucracy grew dramatically, from about 50,000 employees in 1871 to 100,000 only a decade later.

The modern apparatus of departments, bureaus, and cabinets took shape amid this upswing. The Department of the Interior, created in 1849, grew into the largest and most important federal office other than the Post Office. It consisted of some twenty agencies, including the Bureau of Indian Affairs and the U.S. Geological Survey. Through its authority, the federal government was the chief landowner of all the West. The Department of the Treasury, responsible for collecting federal taxes and customs as well as printing money and stamps, quadrupled its own size from 1873 to 1900, to nearly 25,000 employees. The Pension Office, pressured by a powerful veterans' lobby, the

Grand Army of the Republic, accounted for a quarter to a third of all federal expenditures.

Regulatory agencies sprung up: foremost among them was the Interstate Commerce Commission (ICC). The ICC was created in 1887 to bring order to the growing patchwork of state laws concerning railroads. The five-member commission appointed by the president approved freight and passenger rates set by the railroads. The ICC remained weak in the period, its rate-setting policies usually voided by the Supreme Court. But ICC commissioners could take public testimony on possible violations, examine company records, and generally oversee enforcement of the law. This set a precedent for future regulation of trade as well as for positive government, making rules for business while superseding state laws with federal power—that is, for the intervention of the federal government into the affairs of private enterprise.

THE MACHINERY OF POLITICS

Only gradually did Republicans and Democrats adapt to the demands of government expansion. The Republican Party continued to run on its Civil War record, pointing to its achievements in reuniting the nation and in passing new reform legislation. Democrats, by contrast, sought to reduce the influence of the federal government, slash expenditures, repeal legislation, and protect states' rights. While Republicans held on to their longtime constituencies, Democrats gathered support from southern white voters and immigrants newly naturalized in the North. But neither party commanded a clear majority of votes until the century drew to a close.

Presidents in the last quarter of the century—Rutherford B. Hayes (1877–81), James A. Garfield (1881), Chester A. Arthur (1881–85), Grover Cleveland (1885–89), Benjamin Harrison (1889–93), and Cleveland again (1893–97)—lacked luster. They customarily yielded power to Congress and the state legislatures. Only 1 percent of the popular vote separated the presidential candidates in three of five elections between 1876 and 1892. Congressional races were equally tight, less than two percentage points separating total votes for Democratic and Republican candidates in all but one election in the decade before 1888. Democrats usually held a majority in the House and Republicans a majority in the Senate. With neither party sufficiently strong to govern effectively, Congress passed little legislation before 1890.

One major political issue that separated the two parties was the tariff. First instituted in 1789 to raise revenue for the young republic, the tariff imposed a fee on imported goods, especially manufactured commodities. Soon its major purpose became the protection of the nation's "infant industries" from foreign competition. Manufacturing regions, especially the Northeast, favored a protective policy, while the southern and western agricultural regions opposed high tariffs as unfair to farmers and ranchers who had to pay the steep fees on imported necessities. Democrats, with a stronghold among southern voters, argued for sharp reductions in the tariff as a way to save the rural economy and to give a boost to workers. Republicans, who represented mainly business interests, raised tariffs to new levels on a wide array of goods during the Civil War and retained high tariffs as long as they held power. The so-called McKinley Tariff of 1890, introduced by Representative William McKinley (Rep. Ohio), further increased the tax rate on imported goods, including sugar from Hawai'i, thus provoking haole planters to push even more strongly for annexation to the United States and thereby avoid all tariffs on their products. Despite the importance of the tariff in setting apart Republicans and Democrats, the two political parties operated essentially as state or local organizations.

By the 1870s partisan politics had become a full-time occupation, with local officials usually running for office every two years. "We work through one campaign," quipped one candidate, "take a bath and start in on the next." Election paraphernalia—leaflets or pamphlets, banners, hats, flags, buttons, inscribed playing cards, or clay pipes featuring a likeness of a candidate's face or the party symbol—became a major expense for both parties. Partisans embraced the Democratic donkey or the Republican elephant as symbols of party fidelity. And voters did turn out. During the last quarter of the century, participation in presidential elections peaked at nearly 80 percent of those eligible to vote. Thousands, in fact, voted several times on any given election day; voters who had died, or had never lived, also miraculously cast ballots.

The rising costs of maintaining local organizations and orchestrating mammoth campaigns drove party leaders to seek ever-larger sources of revenue. Winners often seized and added to the "spoils" of office through an elaborate system of payoffs and patronage. Legislators who supported government subsidies for railroad corporations, for instance, commonly received stock in return and sometimes cash bribes. At the time, few politicians or business leaders regarded these practices as unethical.

At the local level, where a combination of ethnicity, race, and religion determined party loyalty, powerful bosses and political machines dominated both parties. Democrats William Marcy Tweed of New York's powerful political organization, Tammany Hall, and Michael "Hinky Dink" Kenna of Chicago, specialized in giving municipal jobs to loyal voters and holiday food baskets to their families. Hundreds of smaller political machines ruled cities and rural courthouses through a combination of "boodle" (bribe money) and personal favors. As Democrat George Plunkitt of New York once remarked, "Men ain't in politics for nothin'."

A large number of federal jobs, meanwhile, changed hands each time the presidency passed from one party to another. More than 50 percent of all federal jobs were patronage positions—nearly 56,000 in 1881—jobs that could be awarded to loyal supporters as part of the "spoils" of the "victor."

Upon taking office, President James Garfield encountered loyal Republicans "lying in wait" for him "like vultures for a wounded bison." His colleagues in Congress were no less besieged. Observers estimated that decisions about patronage filled one-third of their time. Garfield himself served as president for only four months before being mortally wounded by a disgruntled office seeker, an event that prompted his successor, Chester A. Arthur, to encourage reform of the civil service system.

THE SPOILS SYSTEM AND CIVIL SERVICE REFORM

As early as 1865, Republican representative Thomas A. Jenckes of Rhode Island proposed a bill for civil service reform, but the majority in Congress, fearing that such a measure would hamper candidates in their relentless pursuit of votes, refused to pass legislation. Finally, a group comprising mainly professors, newspaper editors, lawyers, and ministers organized the Civil Service Reform Association and enlisted Ohio Democratic senator George H. Pendleton to sponsor reform legislation.

In 1888, Grover Cleveland, with his running mate, Allen G. Thurman, led a spirited campaign for reelection to the presidency. Although he played up his strong record on civil service reform and tariff reduction, Cleveland, an incumbent, lost the election to his Republican challenger, Benjamin Harrison. Cleveland tallied the greatest number of popular votes, but Harrison easily won in the electoral college by a margin of 233 to 168. In this lithograph campaign poster, the Democratic ticket invokes the legacy of Thomas Jefferson and the patriotism of Uncle Sam.

In January 1883, a bipartisan congressional majority passed the Pendleton Civil Service Reform Act. This measure allowed the president to create, with Senate approval, a three-person commission to draw up a set of guidelines for executive and legislative appointments. The commission established a system of standards for various federal jobs and instituted "open, competitive examinations for testing the fitness of applicants for public service." The Pendleton Act also barred political candidates from funding their campaigns by assessing a "tax" on the salaries of holders of party-sponsored government jobs.

Although patronage did not disappear entirely, many departments of the federal government took on a professional character similar to that which doctors, lawyers, and scholars were imposing on their fields through regulatory societies such as the American Medical Association and the American Historical Association. At the same time, the federal judiciary began to act more aggressively to establish the parameters of government. With the Circuit Courts of Appeals Act of 1891, Congress granted the U.S. Supreme Court the right to review all cases at will. Despite these reforms, many observers still viewed government as a sinkhole of self-interest and corruption.

FARMERS AND WORKERS ORGANIZE THEIR COMMUNITIES

Farmers and workers began to build regional as well as national organizations to oppose, as a Nebraska newspaper put it, "the wealthy and powerful classes who want the control of government to plunder the people." Over the course of the last quarter of the nineteenth century, they gradually developed a distinctively radical agenda that spoke directly to the increasing power of elected officials and government. By the 1890s, farmers and workers had formed a mass movement that presented the most significant challenge to the two-party system since the Civil War— Populism—and pledged themselves to restore the reins of government to "the hands of the people."

THE GRANGE

In 1867, white farmers in the Midwest formed the Patrons of Husbandry for their own "social, intellectual, and moral improvement." Led by Oliver H. Kelley, this fraternal society resembled the secretive Masonic order. Whole families staffed a complex array of offices and engaged in mysterious rituals involving passwords, flags, songs, and costumes. In many farming communities, the headquarters of the local chapter, known as the Grange (a word for "farm"), became the main social center, the site of summer dinners and winter dances.

The Granger movement spread rapidly, especially in areas where farmers were experiencing their greatest hardships. Great Plains farmers barely survived the blizzards, grasshopper infestations, and droughts of the early 1870s. Meanwhile, farmers throughout the trans–Mississippi West and the South watched the prices for grains and cotton fall year by year in the face of growing competition from producers in Canada, Australia,

Argentina, Russia, and India (see Figure 20.1). The Patrons of Husbandry soon swelled to more than 1.5 million members.

Grangers blamed hard times on a band of "thieves in the night"—especially railroads and banks—that charged exorbitant fees for service. They fumed at American manufacturers, such as Cyrus McCormick, who sold farm equipment more cheaply in Europe than in the United States. They raged at the banks that charged high interest rates for the money farmers had to borrow to pay the steep prices for equipment and raw materials.

Grangers mounted their greatest assault on the railroad corporations. By bribing state legislators, railroads enjoyed a highly discriminatory rate policy, commonly

The symbols chosen by Grange artists represented their faith that all social value could be traced to honest labor and most of all to the work of the entire farm family. The hardworking American required only the enlightenment offered by the Grange to build a better community.

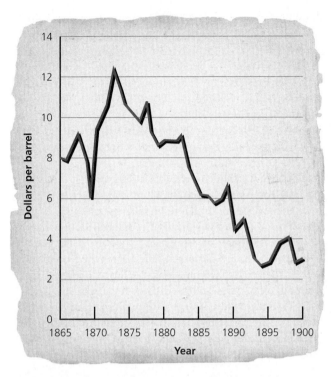

FIGURE 20.1 Falling Price of Wheat Flour, 1865–1900

The falling price of wheat was often offset by increased productivity, giving farmers a steady, if not higher, income. Nevertheless, in the short term farmers often carried more debt and faced greater risk, both factors in sparking the populists protest by the end of the century.

charging farmers more to ship their crops short distances than over long hauls. In 1874, several midwestern states responded to pressure and passed a series of so-called Granger laws establishing maximum shipping rates. Grangers also complained to their lawmakers about the price-fixing policies of grain wholesalers and operators of grain elevators. In 1873, the Illinois legislature passed a Warehouse Act establishing maximum rates for storing grains. Chicago firms challenged the legality of this measure, but in *Munn* v. *Illinois* (1877), the Supreme Court upheld the law, ruling that states had the power to regulate privately owned businesses like the railroads in the public interest.

Determined to buy less and produce more, Grangers created a vast array of cooperative enterprises for both the purchase of supplies and the marketing of crops. They established local grain elevators, set up retail stores, and even manufactured some of their own farm machinery. As early as 1872, the Iowa Grange claimed to control one-third of the grain elevators and warehouses in the state. In other states, Grangers ran banks as well as fraternal life and fire insurance companies.

The deepening depression of the late 1870s wiped out most of these cooperative programs, and Grange membership soon fell to 100,000. In the mid-1880s, the Supreme Court overturned most of the key legislation regulating railroads. Despite these setbacks, the Patrons of Husbandry had nonetheless effectively promoted the idea of an activist government with primary responsibility to its producer-citizens. This idea would remain at the heart of farmer-worker protest movements until the end of the century.

THE FARMERS' ALLIANCE #4

Agrarian unrest did not end with the downward turn of the Grange but instead moved south. In the 1880s, farmers organized in communities where both poverty and the crop-lien system prevailed. They adopted as their motto, "Equal Rights to All, Special Privileges to None."

In the South, the falling price of cotton underscored the need for action, and farmers readily translated their anger into intense loyalty to the one organization pledged to improve their lot. With more than 500 chapters in Texas alone, and cooperative stores complemented by the cooperative merchandising of crops, the Southern Farmers' Alliance became a viable alternative to the capitalist marketplace—if only temporarily.

The Northern Farmers' Alliance took shape in the Great Plains states, drawing on larger organizations in Minnesota, Nebraska, Iowa, Kansas, and the Dakota Territory. During 1886 and 1887, summer drought followed winter blizzards and ice storms, reducing wheat harvests by one-third on the plains. Locusts and cinch bugs ate much of the rest. As if this were not enough, prices for wheat on the world market fell sharply for what little remained.

In 1889, the regional organizations joined forces to create the National Farmers' Alliance and Industrial Union. Within a year the combined movement claimed 3 million white members. Excluded from the all-white chapters, the Colored Farmers' Alliance and Cooperative Union organized separately and quickly spread across the South; from its beginnings in Texas and Arkansas it grew to more than a million members.

Grangers had pushed legislation that would limit the salaries of public officials, provide public school students with books at little or no cost, establish a program of teacher certification, and widen the admissions policies of the new state colleges. But only rarely did they put up candidates for office. In comparison, the Farmers' Alliance had few reservations about entering electoral races. At the end of the 1880s, regional alliances put up candidates on platforms demanding state ownership of the railroads, a graduated income tax, lower tariffs, restriction of land ownership to citizens, and easier access to money through "the free and unlimited coinage of silver." By 1890, the alliances had won several local and state elections, gained control of the Nebraska legislature, and held the balance of power in Minnesota and South Dakota.

WORKERS SEARCH FOR POWER

Before the end of the century, more than 6 million workers would strike in industries ranging from New England textiles to southern tobacco factories to western mines. Some of the largest strikes were against the corporations targeted by farmers: the railroads. Although most of these strikes ended in failure, they revealed the readiness of workers to spell out their grievances in a direct and dramatic manner. They also suggested how strongly many townspeople, including merchants who depended on workers' wages, would support local strikes and turn them into community uprisings (see Map 20.1).

While the Farmers' Alliance put up candidates in the South and Plains states, workers launched labor parties in dozens of industrial towns and cities. In New York City, popular economist and land reformer Henry George, with the ardent support of the city's Central Labor Council, the Knights of Labor, and the Irish community, put himself forward in 1886 as candidate for mayor on the United Labor Party ticket. His best-selling book *Progress and Poverty* (1879) advocated a sweeping "single tax" on all property to generate enough revenue to allow all Americans to live in comfort. George called on "all honest citizens" to join in independent political action as "the only hope of exposing and breaking up the extortion and speculation by which a standing army of professional politicians corrupt the people whom they plunder."

Tammany Hall delivered many thousands of the ballots cast for George straight into the Hudson River. Nevertheless, George managed to finish a respectable second with 31 percent of the vote, running ahead of young patrician Theodore Roosevelt. Although his campaign ended in defeat, George had issued a stern warning to the entrenched politicians. Equally important, his impressive showing encouraged labor groups in other cities to form their own parties.

In the late 1880s, labor parties won seats on many city councils and state legislatures. The Milwaukee People's Party elected the mayor, a state senator, six assemblymen, and one member of Congress. In smaller industrial towns

MAP EXPLORATION

To explore an interactive version of this map, go to **www.prenhall.com/faragher6/map20.1**

MAP 20.1 Strikes by State, 1880 Most strikes after the Uprising of 1877 could be traced to organized trades, concentrated in the manufacturing districts of the Northeast and Midwest.

SOURCE: Carville Earle, *Geographical Inquiry and American Historical Problems* (Stanford, CA: Stanford University Press, 1992).

where workers outnumbered the middle classes, labor parties did especially well. Rochester, New Hampshire, with a population of only 7,000, workers, mainly shoemakers, elected a majority slate from city council to mayor.

The victories of local labor parties caught the attention of farmers, who began to weigh their prospects for a political alliance with discontented urban workers. For the 1888 presidential election, they formed a coalition to sponsor the Union Labor Party, which ran on a plank of government ownership of the railroads. The new party made no headway against the two-party system, polling little more than 1 percent of the vote. Still, the successes in local communities nurtured hopes for a viable political alliance of the "producing classes," rural as well as urban.

WOMEN BUILD ALLIANCES

Women activists helped build both the labor and agrarian protest movements while campaigning for their own rights as citizens.

The Grangers issued a charter to a local chapter only when women were well represented on its rolls, and in the 1870s, delegates to its conventions routinely gave speeches endorsing woman suffrage and even dress reform. In both the Northern and Southern Farmers' Alliances, women made up perhaps one-quarter of the membership, and several advanced through the ranks to become leading speakers and organizers. A Kansas newspaper editor claimed that orator Mary E. Lease "could recite the multiplication table and set a crowd hooting and harrahing at her will." Lease achieved lasting fame purportedly for advising farmers to raise less corn and more hell.

Women in both the Knights of Labor and the Farmers' Alliance found their greatest leader in Frances E. Willard, the most famous woman of the nineteenth century and a shrewd politician in her own right. Willard argued that women, who guarded their families' physical and spiritual welfare, could have only a beneficial impact on the world outside their homes. From 1878 until her death in 1897, she presided over the Woman's Christian Temperance Union (WCTU). Most numerous in the Midwest, WCTU members preached total abstinence from the consumption of alcohol but ultimately endorsed Willard's "do everything" agenda. By the 1880s, the most militant branches had joined the campaign for an activist government, demanding an overhaul of the prison system, the eradication of prostitution, changes in the age of consent, and even the elimination of the wage system. Willard went so far as to draw up plans for a new system of government whereby all offices, right up to the presidency, would be shared jointly by men and women. By 1890, she had mobilized nearly 200,000 paid members into the largest organization of women in the world.

Willard understood that for women to participate in politics they needed the right to vote. Under her leadership, the WCTU grew into the major force for woman suffrage, far surpassing the American Woman Suffrage Association and the National Woman Suffrage Association. By 1890, when the two rival suffrage associations merged to form the National American Woman Suffrage Association, the WCTU had already pushed the heart of the suffrage campaign into the Great Plains states and the West. In Iowa, Nebraska, Colorado, and especially Kansas, agitation for the right to vote provided a political bridge among women in the WCTU, Farmers' Alliance, Knights of Labor, and various local suffrage societies. The most active members—like Willard and Lease, who were both members of the Knights of Labor—affiliated with several organizations or, in some cases, with all.

The Great Uprising of 1877, which began as a strike of railroad workers, spread rapidly to communities along the railroad routes. Angry crowds defied the armed militia and the vigilantes hired to disperse them. In Philadelphia, for example, strikers set fire to the downtown, destroying many buildings before federal troops were brought in to stop them. More than a hundred people died before the strike ended, and the railroad corporations suffered a $10 million loss in property.

POPULISM AND THE PEOPLE'S PARTY

In December 1890, the Farmers' Alliance called a meeting at Ocala, Florida, to press for the creation of a national third party. This was a risky proposition because the Southern Alliance hoped to capture control of the Democratic Party, whereas many farmers in the Plains states voted Republican. In some areas, however, the Farmers' Alliance established its own parties, put up full slates of candidates for local elections, won majorities in state legislatures, and even sent a representative to Congress. Reviewing these successes, delegates at Ocala decided to push ahead and form a national party, and they appealed to other farm, labor, and reform organizations to join them.

In February 1892, 1,300 representatives from the Farmers' Alliance, the Knights of Labor, and the Colored Farmers' Alliance, among others, met in St. Louis under a broad banner that read: "We do not ask for sympathy or pity. We ask for justice." The new People's Party called for government ownership of railroads, banks, and telegraph lines, prohibition of large landholding companies, a graduated income tax, an eight-hour workday, and restriction of immigration. The most ambitious plan called for the national government to build local warehouses—"subtreasuries"—where farmers could store their crops until prices reached acceptable levels. A universal suffrage plank drafted by Frances Willard, who served on the platform committee, failed to pass. The People's Party convened again in Omaha in July 1892 and nominated James Baird Weaver of Iowa for president and, to please the South, the Confederate veteran James G. Field from Virginia for vice president.

The Populists, as supporters of the People's Party styled themselves, quickly became a major factor in American politics. Although Democrat Grover Cleveland regained the presidency in 1892 (he had previously served from 1885 to 1889), Populists scored a string of local victories. In Idaho, they elected three governors, ten representatives to Congress, and five senators. Despite poor showings among urban workers east of the Mississippi, Populists looked forward to the next round of state elections in 1894. But the great test would come with the presidential election in 1896.

THE CRISIS OF THE 1890s

Populist Ignatius Donnelly wrote in the preface to his pessimistic novel *Caesar's Column* (1891) that industrial society appears to be a "wretched failure" to "the great mass of mankind." On the road to disaster rather than to a truly democratic community, "the rich, as a rule, hate the poor; and the poor are coming to hate the rich . . . society divides itself into two hostile camps . . . They wait only for the drum beat and the trumpet to summon them to armed conflict."

A series of events in the 1890s shook the confidence of many citizens in the reigning political system. But nothing was more unsettling than the severe economic

Frances E. Willard (1839–1898) became a full-time activist for the national Woman's Christian Temperance Union (WCTU) in 1874. From 1879 until her death, she served as president, pushing the organization to expand its interests beyond temperance under the rubric of her "do-everything" policy. Under her leadership, the WCTU established 39 departments promoting a wide array of reform causes ranging from the establishment of free kindergartens to the prohibition of the manufacture of cigarettes.

depression that consumed the nation and lasted for five years. Many feared—while others hoped—that the entire political system would topple.

FINANCIAL COLLAPSE AND DEPRESSION

By the spring of 1893, the nation was drawn into a depression that had been plaguing European nations since the late 1880s. Their market for imported goods, including those manufactured in the United States, sharply contracted. Financial panic in England spread across the Atlantic, as British investors began to sell off their American stocks to obtain funds. Other factors—tight credit, falling agricultural prices, a weak banking system, and overexpansion, especially in railroad construction—all helped to bring about the collapse of the U.S. economy. In May and June a crash in the stock market sent waves of panic splashing over business and financial institutions across the country. In a few months, more than 150 banks went into receivership and hundreds more closed; nearly 200 railroads and more than 15,000 businesses also slipped into bankruptcy. Agricultural prices meanwhile continued to plummet until they reached new lows. The business boom of nearly two decades ended, and the entire economy ground to a halt. The new century arrived before prosperity returned.

In many cities, unemployment rates reached 25 percent; Samuel Gompers, head of the American Federation of Labor (AFL), estimated nationwide unemployment at 3 million. Few people starved but millions suffered. Inadequate diets prompted a rise in communicable diseases, such as tuberculosis and pellagra. Unable to buy food, clothes, or household items, families learned to survive with the barest minimum.

Tens of thousands "rode the rails" or went "on the tramp" to look for work, hoping that their luck might change in a new city or town. Some panhandled for the nickel that could buy a mug of beer and a free lunch at a saloon. By night they slept in parks. Vagrancy laws (enacted during the 1870s) forced many into prison. In New York City alone, with more than 20,000 homeless people, thousands ended up in jail. Newspapers warned against this "menace" and blamed the growing crime rates on the "dangerous classes."

As the depression deepened so did demands on the federal government for positive action. Populist Jacob Sechler Coxey decided to gather the masses of unemployed into a huge army and then to march to Washington, DC. Far in advance of the New Deal, Coxey proposed that Congress fund a public works program in order to give jobs to the unemployed. On Easter Sunday, 1894, Coxey left Massillon, Ohio, with several hundred followers. Meanwhile, brigades from across the country joined his "petition in boots." Although the marchers received a warm welcome from most communities along the way, U.S. Attorney General Richard C. Olney conspired with local officials to halt them. Only 600 men and women reached the nation's capital, where the police first clubbed and then arrested the leaders for trespassing on the grass. "Coxey's Army" quickly disbanded but not before voicing the public's expectation of federal responsibility for the welfare of its citizens, especially in times of crisis.

STRIKES: COEUR D'ALENE, HOMESTEAD, AND PULLMAN

Even before the onset of the depression, the conflict between labor and capital had escalated to the brink of civil war. In the 1890s, three major strikes dramatized the extent of collusion between the corporations and government. In each case, state or federal troops were deployed to crush the labor uprising, providing a vivid lesson to workers on the growing role of government in this era.

Wage cuts in the silver and lead mines of northern Idaho led to one of the most bitter conflicts of the decade. To put a brake on organized labor, mine owners had formed a "protective association," and in March 1892, they announced a wage cut throughout the Coeur d'Alene district.

After five weeks the main body of Coxey's Army reached Washington, DC, where on May 1, 1894, the leaders were immediately arrested for trespassing on government property. Fifty years later, on May 1, 1944, the ninety-year-old Coxey finally gave his speech advocating public works programs on the steps of the nation's capitol.

After the miners' union refused to accept the cut, the owners locked out all union members and brought in strikebreakers by the trainload. Unionists tried peaceful methods of protest. But after three months of stalemate, they loaded a railcar with explosives and blew up a mine. The governor proclaimed martial law and dispatched a combined state-federal force of about 1,500 troops, who broke the strike. Ore production resumed with "scab" labor, and by November, when the troops were withdrawn, the mine owners declared a victory. But the miners' union survived, and most members became active in the Populist Party, which at the next session of the Idaho legislature allied with Democrats to cut back all appropriations to the National Guard.

At Homestead, Pennsylvania, members of the Amalgamated Iron, Steel and Tin Workers, the most powerful union of the AFL, had carved out an admirable position for themselves in the Carnegie Steel Company. Well paid, proud of their skills, the unionists customarily directed their unskilled helpers without undue influence of company supervisors. But, determined to gain control over every stage of production, Carnegie and his chairman, Henry C. Frick, decided not only to lower wages but also to break the union.

In 1892, when Amalgamated's contract expired, Frick announced a drastic wage cut. He also ordered a wooden stockade built around the factory, with grooves for rifles and barbed wire on top. When Homestead's city government—the mayor and police chief were both union members—refused to assign police to disperse the strikers, Frick dispatched a barge carrying a private army armed to the teeth. Gunfire broke out and continued throughout the day. Finally, the governor stepped in and sent the Pennsylvania National Guard, 8,000 strong, to restore order, and Carnegie's factory reopened with strikebreakers doing the work.

After four months, the union was forced to concede a crushing defeat, not only for itself but, in effect, for all steelworkers as well. The Carnegie company reduced its workforce by 25 percent, lengthened the workday, and cut wages 25 percent for those who remained on the job. If the Amalgamated Iron, Steel and Tin Workers, known throughout the industry as the "aristocrats of labor," could be brought down, less-skilled workers could expect little from the corporate giants. Within a decade, every major steel company operated without union interference.

Pullman, Illinois, just south of Chicago, had been constructed as a model industrial community. Its creator and proprietor, George M. Pullman, had manufactured luxurious "sleeping cars" for railroads since 1881. He built his company as a self-contained community, with the factory at the center, surrounded by modern cottages, a library,

The popular magazine *Harper's Weekly* published this illustration of workers and their families protesting the use of a private security force at the Carnegie Steel Company in Homestead, Pennsylvania, in July 1892.

churches, parks, an independent water supply, even its own cemetery, but no saloons. The Pullman Palace Car Company deducted rent, library fees, and grocery bills from each worker's weekly wages. In good times, workers enjoyed a decent livelihood, although many resented Pullman's autocratic control of their daily affairs.

When times grew hard, the company cut wages by as much as one-half, in some cases down to less than $1 a day. Charges for food and rent remained unchanged. Furthermore, factory supervisors sought to make up for declining profits by driving workers to produce more. In May 1894, after Pullman fired members of a committee that had drawn up a list of grievances, workers voted to strike.

Pullman workers found their champion in Eugene V. Debs, who had recently formed the American Railway Union (ARU) in order to bring railroad workers across the vast continent into one organization. Debs, the architect of the ARU's victory over the Great Northern rail line just one month earlier, advised caution, but delegates to an ARU convention voted to support a nationwide boycott of all Pullman cars. This action soon turned into a sympathy strike by railroad workers across the country.

Compared to the Great Uprising of 1877, the orderly Pullman strike at first produced little violence. ARU officials urged strikers to ignore all provocations and hold their ground peacefully. But Richard C. Olney, a former railroad lawyer, used his current office as attorney general, claiming that the ARU was disrupting mail shipments (actually Debs had banned such interference), to issue a blanket injunction against the strike. On July 4, President Cleveland sent army units to Chicago, over the pro-labor Illinois governor John Peter Altgeld's objections. After a bitter confrontation that left thirteen people dead and more than fifty wounded, the army dispersed the strikers. For the next week, railroad workers in twenty-six other states resisted federal troops, and a dozen more people were killed. On July 17, the strike finally ended when federal marshals arrested Debs and other leaders.

Assailing the arrogance of class privilege that encouraged the government to use brute force against its citizens, Debs concluded that the labor movement could not regain its dignity without seizing the reigns of government. He came out of jail committed to the ideals of socialism, and in 1898 helped to form a political party dedicated to its principles.

THE SOCIAL GOSPEL

"What is socialism?" Debs once asked. "Merely Christianity in action. It recognizes the equality in men." During the 1890s, especially as hard times spread across the nation, a growing number of Protestant and Catholic clergy and lay theologians came close to sharing his perspective, noting a discrepancy between the ideals of Christianity and prevailing attitudes toward the poor.

Social gospel ministers called on the government to be more responsible toward its most impoverished and unprotected citizens. Supporting labor's right to organize and, if necessary, to strike, they petitioned government officials to regulate corporations and place a limit on profits. Washington Gladden, a Congregationalist minister, warned that if churches continued to ignore pressing social problems, they would devolve into institutions whose sole purpose was to preserve obscure rituals and superstitions. He addressed his most important book, *Applied Christianity* (1886), to the nation's business leaders, imploring them to return to Christ's teachings.

The depression of the 1890s produced an outpouring of similar treatises. The very popular *If Christ Came to Chicago* (1894), by British journalist W. T. Stead, forced readers to confront the "ugly sight" of a city with 200 millionaires and 200,000 unemployed men. It inspired Edward Everett Hale's *If Jesus Came to Boston* (1894), which similarly questioned social inequalities. The most famous tract, *In His Steps* (1896), by Methodist minister Charles M. Sheldon of Topeka, Kansas, urged middle-class readers to rethink their actions in the light of the simple question "What would Jesus do?"

Catholic clergy, doctrinally more inclined than Protestants to accept poverty as a natural condition, joined the social gospel movement in smaller numbers. But many of their parishioners, especially Polish and Irish Americans, allied with the labor movement, finding solace in Pope Leo XIII's encyclical *Rerum Novarum* (1891), which endorsed the right of workers to form trade unions.

Women guided the social gospel movement in their communities. Since the early part of the nineteenth century, middle-class women in northern cities had formed numerous voluntary associations to improve the conditions of the poor and destitute. They founded orphanages and hospitals and shelters for the homeless. After the Civil War, these enterprises, considered the heart of the woman's movement, expanded until the movement affected communities throughout the nation. In 1888, representatives from dozens upon dozens of individual societies met to form the National Council of Women and elect Frances Willard its first president.

In the midst of the depression, women activists were well placed to respond to the plight of the poor and dispossessed. In nearly every sizable city, groups of white women affiliated with various evangelical Protestant sects raised money to establish inexpensive residential hotels for working women, whose low wages rarely covered the price of safe, comfortable shelter. At the forefront of this movement was the Young Women's Christian Association (YWCA), which by 1900 had more than 600 local chapters. The "Y" sponsored a range of services for needy Christian women, ranging from homes for the elderly and for unmarried mothers to elaborate programs of vocational instruction and physical fitness. Meanwhile, Catholic laywomen and nuns served the poor women of their faith, operating numerous schools, hospitals, and orphanages.

Affiliated principally with the Baptist Church, African American women sponsored dozens of self-help programs and, in addition, emphasized the importance of education to racial uplift. Excluded by the whites-only policy of the YWCA in most localities, they organized their own chapters and branched out to form nurseries, orphanages, hospitals, and nursing homes. In Chicago, for example, African American women established the Phyllis Wheatley Home, which opened in 1908 to provide, in the founders' words, a "Christian influence" for the working women and college students who boarded there. Fannie Barrier Williams, a leader in racial uplift, acknowledged the importance of the churches as "the great preparatory schools in which the primary lessons of social order, mutual trustfulness and united effort have been taught."

POLITICS OF REFORM, POLITICS OF ORDER

The severe hardships of the 1890s, following a quarter century of popular unrest and economic uncertainty, led to a crisis in the two-party system. The presidential election of 1896, considered a turning point in American politics, marked both a dramatic realignment of voters and the centrality of economic issues. It also sanctioned the popular call for a stronger government, making the question of control vital to the nation's voters as well as the composition of the electorate. Ultimately, the election of 1896 brought to national office politicians who perceived a clear link between domestic problems and the expansion of markets overseas and were willing to act aggressively to implement this vision.

THE FREE SILVER ISSUE

Grover Cleveland owed his victory in 1892 over Republican incumbent Benjamin Harrison to the predictable votes of the Southern Democratic Party and to the unanticipated support of such northern states as Illinois and Wisconsin, whose German-born voters turned against the increasingly nativist Republicans. But when the economy collapsed the following year, Cleveland and the Democrats who controlled Congress faced a public demanding action. Convinced that the economic crisis was "largely the result of financial policy . . . embodied in unwise laws," the president called for a special session of Congress to reform the nation's currency.

For generations, reformers had advocated "soft" currency, that is, an increase in the money supply that would loosen credit. During the Civil War the federal government took decisive action, replacing state bank notes with a national paper currency popularly called "greenbacks" (from the color of the bills). Then in 1873 the Coinage Act tightened the money supply by eliminating silver from circulation, prompting farmers who depended on credit to call it "the Crime of '73." This measure actually had little real impact on the economy but opened the door to yet more tinkering.

The Sherman Silver Purchase Act of 1890 directed the Treasury to increase the amount of currency coined from silver mined in the West and also permitted the U.S. government to print paper currency backed by silver. In turn Westerners, who stood to benefit most from this reform, agreed to support the McKinley Tariff of 1890 which, by establishing the highest import duties yet on foreign goods, pleased the business community.

Following the crash of 1893, a desperate President Cleveland demanded the repeal of the Sherman Act, insisting that only the gold standard could pull the nation out of depression. By exerting intense pressure on congressional Democrats, Cleveland succeeded in October 1893, but not without ruining his chances for renomination. The midterm elections of 1894 brought the largest shift in congressional power in American history: the Republicans gained 117 seats, while the Democrats lost 113. The "Silver Democrats" of Cleveland's own party vowed revenge and began to look to the Populists, mainly Westerners and farmers who favored "free silver," that is, the unlimited coinage of silver. Republicans confidently began to prepare for the presidential election of 1896, warming to what they called the "battle of the standards."

POPULISM'S LAST CAMPAIGNS

Populists had been buoyed by the 1894 elections, which delivered to their candidates nearly 1.5 million votes—a gain of 42 percent over their 1892 totals. They made impressive inroads into several southern states and raised expectations west of the Mississippi. Still, even in the Midwest, where Populists doubled their vote, they managed to win less than 7 percent of the total, and, overall, they lost two seats in Congress.

As Populists prepared for the 1896 presidential campaign, they found themselves at a crossroad: what were they to do with the growing popularity of the Democratic candidate, William Jennings Bryan? A spellbinding orator, Bryan won a congressional seat in 1890. After seizing the Populist slogan "Equal Rights to All, Special Privilege to None," the thirty-six-year-old lawyer from Nebraska became a major contender for president of the United States.

Noting the surging interest in free silver, Bryan became its champion. For two years before the 1896 election, he wooed potential voters in a speaking tour that took him to every state in the nation. Pouring new life into his divided party, Bryan pushed Silver Democrats to the forefront.

At the 1896 party convention, Brian thrilled delegates with his evocation of agrarian ideals. "Burn down your cities and leave our farms," Bryan preached, "and your cities will spring up again as if by magic; but destroy our farms and the grass will grow in the streets of every city in the country." What became one of the most famous speeches in American political history closed on a yet more dramatic note. Spreading his arms to suggest the crucified Christ figure, he pledged to answer all demands for a gold standard by saying, "You shall not press down upon the brow of labor this crown of thorns, you shall not crucify mankind upon a cross of gold." The next day, Bryan carried the Democratic presidential nomination.

The Populists realized that by nominating Bryan the Democrats had stolen their thunder. They also feared that the growing emphasis on currency would overshadow their more important planks calling for government ownership of the nation's railroads and communications systems. As the date of their own convention approached, delegates divided over strategy: they could endorse Bryan and give up their independent status, or they could run an independent campaign and risk splitting the silver vote. In the end, Populists nominated Bryan for president and one of their own, Georgian Tom Watson, for vice president. Most of the state Democratic Party organizations, however, refused to put the "fusion" ticket on the ballot, and Bryan and his Democratic running mate Arthur Sewall simply ignored the Populist campaign.

THE REPUBLICAN TRIUMPH

After Cleveland's blunders, Republicans anticipated an easy victory in 1896, but Bryan's nomination, as party stalwart Mark Hanna warned, "changed everything." Luckily, they had their own handsome, knowledgeable, courteous, and ruthless candidate, Civil War veteran William McKinley.

The Republican campaign in terms of sheer expense and skill of coordination outdid all previous campaigns and established a precedent for future presidential elections. Hanna guided a strategy that raised up to $7 million and outspent Bryan more than ten to one. Using innumerable pamphlets, placards, hats, and parades, Republicans advertised their promise to "rebuild out of the ruins of the last four years the stately mansions of national happiness, prosperity and self-respect." McKinley even invited voters to his home, managing to attract as many as 750,000 people to his famous "Front Porch." In the campaign's final two weeks, organizers dispatched 1,400 speakers to spread the word. Fearful that the silver issue would divide their own ranks, Republicans stepped around it while emphasizing the tariff. Delivering a hard-hitting negative campaign, they consistently cast Bryan as a nay-sayer.

McKinley triumphed in the most important presidential election since Reconstruction. Bryan managed to win 46 percent of the popular vote but failed to carry the Midwest, West Coast, or Upper South (see Map 20.2). Moreover, the free silver campaign rebuffed traditionally Democratic urban voters who feared that soft money would bring higher prices. Many Catholics uncomfortable with Bryan's Protestant moral piety also deserted the Democrats. Finally, neither the reform-minded middle classes nor impoverished blue-collar workers were convinced that Bryan's grand reform vision really included them. The Populist following, disappointed and disillusioned, dwindled away.

Once in office, McKinley strengthened the executive branch and actively promoted a mixture of probusiness and expansionist measures. He supported the Dingley Tariff of 1897, which raised import duties to an all-time high. In 1897 McKinley also encouraged Congress to create the United States Industrial Commission, which would plan business regulation; in 1898, he promoted a bankruptcy act that eased the financial situation of small businesses; and he proposed the Erdman Act of the same year, which established a system of arbitration to avoid rail strikes. The Supreme Court ruled in concert with the president, finding eighteen railways in violation of antitrust laws, and granting states the right to regulate hours of labor under certain circumstances. In 1900, he settled the currency issue by overseeing the passage of the Gold Standard Act.

McKinley's triumph ended the popular challenge to the nation's governing system. With prosperity returning by the end of the century and nationalism rising swiftly, McKinley encouraged Americans to go for "a full dinner pail," the winning Republican slogan of the 1900 presidential campaign. With news of his second triumph, stock prices on Wall Street skyrocketed.

NATIVISM AND JIM CROW

Campaign rhetoric aside, McKinley and Bryan had differed only slightly on the major problems facing the nation in the

This Republican campaign poster of 1896 depicts William McKinley standing on sound money and promising a revival of prosperity. The depression of the 1890s shifted the electorate into the Republican column.

1890s. Neither Bryan, the reformer, nor McKinley, the prophet of prosperity, addressed the escalation of racism and nativism (anti-immigrant feeling) throughout the nation.

Toward the end of the century, many political observers noted, the nation's patriotic fervor took on a strongly nationalistic and antiforeign tone. Striking workers and their employers alike tended to blame "foreigners" for the hard times. Semisecret organizations such as the American Protective Association sprang up to defend American institutions. Fourth of July orators continued to celebrate freedom and liberty but more often boasted about the might and power of their nation.

In the South, local and state governments codified racist ideology by passing discriminatory and segregationist legislation, which became known as Jim Crow laws. The phrase, dating from the early decades of the nineteenth century, was made popular by a white minstrel in blackface who used the name "Jim Crow" to demean all African

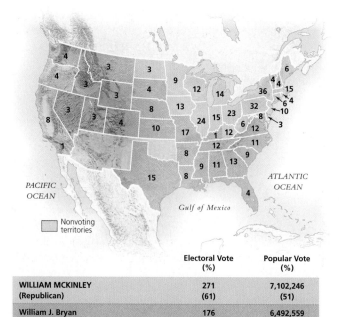

	Electoral Vote (%)	Popular Vote (%)
WILLIAM MCKINLEY (Republican)	271 (61)	7,102,246 (51)
William J. Bryan (Democrat)	176 (39)	6,492,559 (47)
Minor parties	—	315,398 (2)

MAP 20.2 Election of 1896 Democratic candidate William Jennings Bryan carried most of rural America but could not overcome Republican William McKinley's stronghold in the populous industrial states.

Americans. By the end of the century, "Jim Crow" referred to the customs of segregation that were becoming secured by legislation throughout the South. With nine of every ten black Americans living in this region, the significance of this development was sweeping.

"The supremacy of the white race of the South," New South promoter Henry W. Grady declared in 1887, "must be maintained forever . . . because the white race is the superior race." To secure their privileges, Grady and other white Southerners acted directly to impose firm standards of segregation and domination and to forestall any appearance of social equality. State after state in the South enacted new legislation to cover facilities such as restaurants, public transportation, and even drinking fountains. Signs "White Only" and "Colored" appeared over theaters, parks, rooming houses, and toilets. In banks, post offices, and stores, blacks were required to wait until all whites had been served, and special rules prohibited such common practices as trying on shoes or hats before purchasing them.

The United States Supreme Court upheld the new discriminatory legislation. Its decisions in the *Civil Rights Cases* (1883) overturned the Civil Rights Act of 1875; in *Plessy* v. *Ferguson* (1896), the Court upheld a Louisiana state law formally segregating railroad passenger cars on the basis of the "separate but equal" doctrine. The majority opinion, delivered by Justice Henry Billings Brown,

stated that political equality and social equality are distinct: "Legislation is powerless to eradicate racial instincts or to abolish distinctions based on physical differences. If one race be inferior to the other socially, the Constitution of the United States cannot put them on the same plane."

This ruling established the legal rationale for segregation, North as well as South, for the next fifty years. In *Cumming* v. *Richmond County Board of Education* (1899), the Court allowed separate schools for blacks and whites, even where facilities for African American children did not exist. This ruling reverberated in other parts of the country. For example, a year later, in 1900, the New Orleans school board decided to eliminate all schools for black children beyond the fifth grade, reasoning that African Americans needed only minimal education to fit them for menial jobs "to which they are best suited and seem ordained by the proper fitness of things."

Southern states enacted new literacy tests and property qualifications for voting, demanding proof of $300 to $500 in property and the ability to read and write. Loopholes permitted poor whites to vote even under these conditions, except where they threatened the Democratic Party's rule. "Grandfather clauses," invented in Louisiana, exempted from all restrictions those who had been entitled to vote on January 1, 1867, together with their sons and grandsons, a measure that effectively enfranchised whites while barring African Americans. In 1898, the Supreme Court ruled that poll taxes and literacy requirements enacted in order to prevent blacks (and some poor whites) from voting were a proper means of restricting the ballot to "qualified" voters. By this time, only 5 percent of the southern black electorate voted, and African Americans were barred from public office and jury service (see Figure 20.2).

Racial violence escalated. Race riots, which took the lives of hundreds of African Americans, broke out in small towns like Rosewood, Florida, and Phoenix, South Carolina, and in large cities like New Orleans and Tulsa. In November 1898, in Wilmington, North Carolina, where a dozen African Americans had ridden out the last waves of the Populist insurgency to win appointments to minor political offices, a group of white opponents organized to root them out and ultimately staged a violent coup, restoring white rule and forcing black leaders to leave town. "It come so," a black woman explained, "that we in this town is afraid of a white face." As many as 100 African Americans were killed in what came to be known as the Wilmington massacre.

Not only race riots but also thousands of lynchings took place. Between 1882 and the turn of the century, the number of lynchings usually exceeded 100 each year; 1892 produced a record 230 deaths (161 black, 69 white). Mobs often burned or dismembered victims in order to drag out their agony and entertain the crowd of onlookers. Announced in local newspapers, lynchings in the 1890s became public spectacles for entire white families, and railroads sometimes offered special excursion rates for travel to these events.

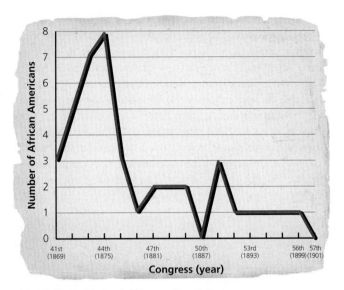

FIGURE 20.2 African American Representation in Congress, 1867–1900
Black men served in the U.S. Congress from 1870 until 1900. All were Republicans.

Antilynching became the one-woman crusade of Ida B. Wells, young editor of a black newspaper in Memphis. After three local black businessmen were lynched in 1892, Wells vigorously denounced the outrage, blaming the white business competitors of the victims. Her stand fanned the tempers of local whites, who destroyed her press and forced the outspoken editor to leave the city. She then launched an international movement against lynching, lecturing across the country and in Europe, demanding an end to the silence about this barbaric crime. Her work also inspired the growth of a black women's club movement. The National Association of Colored Women, founded in 1896, took up the antilynching cause and also fought to protect black women from sexual exploitation by white men.

Few white reformers rallied to defend African Americans. Even the National American Woman Suffrage Association, in an attempt to appease its southern members at its 1899 convention, voted down a resolution condemning racial segregation in public facilities. More than a few Americans had come to believe that their future welfare hinged on white supremacy, not only in their own country but across the globe as well.

THE PATH TO IMPERIALISM

Many Americans attributed the economic crisis of 1893–97 not simply to the collapse of the railroads and banks but also to basic structural problems: an overbuilt economy and an insufficient market for goods. Profits from total sales of manufactured and agricultural products had grown substan-tially over levels achieved in the 1880s, but output increased even more rapidly. Although the number of millionaires shot up from 500 in 1860 to more than 4,000 in 1892, the majority of Americans did not have enough money to buy a significant portion of what they produced. To find new markets for American goods, many Americans looked abroad.

ALL THE WORLD'S A FAIR

The World's Columbian Exposition, held in Chicago, commemorated the four hundredth anniversary of Columbus's landing and answered Congress's call for "an exhibition of the progress of civilization in the New World." On May Day 1893, less than two months after the nation's economy had collapsed, crowds began to flock to the fair, a complex of more than 400 buildings newly constructed in beaux arts design.

The section known as "The White City" celebrated the achievements of American business in the global economy. Agriculture Hall showcased the production of corn, wheat, and other crops and featured a gigantic globe encircled by samples of American-manufactured farm machinery. Another building housed a model of a canal cut across Nicaragua, suggesting the ease with which American traders might reach Asian markets if transport ships could travel directly from the Caribbean to the Pacific. One of the most popular exhibits, attracting 20,000 people a day, featured a mock ocean liner built to scale by the International Navigation Company, where fairgoers could imagine themselves as "tourists," sailing in luxury to distant parts of the world. The symbolism was evident: all eyes were on international trade as a marker of American prowess.

In contrast to the White City was the Midway, a strip nearly a mile long and more than 600 feet wide that offered entertainment. The new, spectacular Ferris wheel, designed to rival the Eiffel Tower of Paris, was the largest attraction. But the Midway also offered amusement in the form of "displays" of "uncivilized" people from foreign lands.

One enormous sideshow re-created Turkish bazaars and South Sea island huts. There were Javanese carpenters, Dahomean drummers, Egyptian swordsmen, and Hungarian Gypsies, as well as Eskimos, Syrians, Samoans, and Chinese. Hawai'ians were represented by a cyclorama of the Kilauea volcano, billed as the "Inferno of the Pacific" and guarded by the figure advertised as the "awful divinity" Pele, goddess of fire. Very popular was the World Congress of Beauty, parading "40 Ladies from 40 Nations" dressed in native costume. Another favorite attraction was "Little Egypt," who performed at the Persian Palace of Eros; her *danse du ventre* became better known as the hootchy-kootchy. According to the guidebook, all these peoples had come "from the nightsome North and the splendid South, from the wasty West and the effete East, bringing their manners, customs, dress, religions, legends, amusements, that we might know them better."

By celebrating the brilliance of American industry and simultaneously presenting the "uncivilized" people of the world as a source of exotic entertainment, the planners of the fair delivered a powerful message. Former abolitionist Frederick Douglass, who attended the fair on "Colored People's Day," recognized it immediately. He noted that the physical layout of the fair, by carefully grouping exhibits, sharply divided the United States and Europe from the rest of the world, namely, from the nations of Africa, Asia, and the Middle East. Douglass objected to the stark contrast setting off Anglo-Saxons from people of color, an opposi-

tion between "civilization" and "savagery." He and Ida B. Wells also objected to the exclusion of African Americans from representation among the exhibits at the White City. Wells boycotted the special day set aside for African Americans, while Douglass attended, using the occasion to deliver a speech upbraiding white Americans for their racism.

Also speaking at the fair was Frederick Jackson Turner, who read his famous essay, about the disappearance of the frontier. Having passed "from the task of filling up the vacant spaces of the continent," the young historian warned, the nation is now "thrown back upon itself."

SEEING HISTORY

The White Man's Burden

In 1899, the British poet Rudyard Kipling published "The White Man's Burden" in the American magazine *McClure's* with the subtitle "The United States and the Philippine Islands." Some interpreted the poem as an endorsement of the U.S. imperialist ventures in the Pacific; others read it as a cautionary note warning against taking on colonies. Those who favored expansion embraced the notion of the "white man's burden" as means to justify their position as a noble enterprise, that is, in "uplifting" those people of color who had not yet enjoyed the benefits of "civilization."

The concept even made its way into advertising for soap. In 1789, London soapmaster Andrew Pears began producing a distinctive oval bar of a transparent amber glycerin and marketing it as a luxury item under the name Pears Soap. He found a talented promoter in Thomas J. Barratt, considered a pioneer of modern advertising, who built an international market for the product. By the end of the nineteenth century, Pears Soap had achieved brand-name status among middle- and upper-class Americans.

Barratt's advertising presented Pears Soap as safe and beneficial but suitable only for discerning consumers. Among its many other advantages, Pears Soap promised a smooth, white complexion, underscoring this message by associating dark skins with "uncivilized" people. The man pictured in this ad is probably a colonial official. The advertisement appeared first in 1899 in *McClure's*—the same magazine in which Kipling's poetic exhortation was published.

The first step towards lightening
The White Man's Burden
is through teaching the virtues of cleanliness.

Pears' Soap

is a potent factor in brightening the dark corners of the earth as civilization advances, while amongst the cultured of all nations it holds the highest place—it is the ideal toilet soap.

Take up the White Man's burden—
Send forth the best ye breed—
Go bind your sons to exile
To serve your captives' need;
To wait in heavy harness,
On fluttered folk and wild—

Your new-caught, sullen peoples,
Half-devil and half-child.
Take up the White Man's burden—
In patience to abide,
To veil the threat of terror
And check the show of pride...

What did the readers of *McClure's* magazine understand as "the white man's burden"? How did this responsibility relate to the belief in a hierarchy of races and civilizations expressed in Kipling's poem?

His message was clear: if democracy were to survive, Americans required a new "frontier."

The Chicago World's Fair, which attracted 27 million visitors from all over the world, reassured Turner by marking the coming to age of the United States as a global power and by making a deliberate case for commercial expansion abroad. The exposition also gave material shape to prevalent ideas about the preeminence of American civilization as well as the superiority of the Anglo-Saxon race (see Seeing History).

THE "IMPERIALISM OF RIGHTEOUSNESS"

Social gospeler Josiah Strong, a Congregational minister who had begun his career hoping to "civilize" the Indians by converting them to Christianity, provided a prescient commentary in 1885. Linking economic and spiritual expansion, he advocated an "imperialism of righteousness." He identified white Americans, who, with "their genius for colonizing," as the best agents for "Christianizing" and "civilizing" the people of Africa and the Pacific and beyond. It was the white American, Strong argued, who had been "divinely commissioned to be . . . his brother's keeper."

The push for overseas expansion coincided with a major wave of religious evangelism and foreign missions. Early in the nineteenth century, Protestant missionaries, hoping to fulfill what they believed to be a divine command to carry God's message to all peoples and to win converts for their church, had focused on North America. Many disciples, like Josiah Strong himself, headed west and stationed themselves on Indian reservations. Others worked among the immigrant populations of the nation's growing cities. As early as the 1820s, however, a few missionaries had traveled to the Sandwich Islands (Hawai'i) in an effort to supplant the indigenous religion with Christianity. After the Civil War, the major evangelical Protestant denominations all sponsored missions directed at foreign lands.

By the 1890s, college campuses blazed with missionary excitement, and the intercollegiate Student Volunteers for Foreign Missions spread rapidly under the slogan "The Evangelicization of the World in This Generation." Magazines bristled with essays such as "The Anglo-Saxon and the World's Redemption." In 1863, there had been only 94 Methodist women missionaries in China; by 1902 the number had jumped to 783. By the turn of the century, some 23 American Protestant churches had established missions in China, the majority staffed by women.

Young Protestant women rushed to join foreign missionary societies. Since the early part of the nineteenth century, Protestant women had headed "cent" and "mite" societies, which gathered money to support overseas missionaries. By 1820, women were accompanying their minister husbands to distant parts to convert the "heathens" to Christianity. After the Civil War, in tandem with the expansion of higher educational opportunities, unmarried women petitioned church leaders to request their own missionary assignments. By 1900, the various Protestant denominations were supporting forty-one women's missionary boards; several years later more than 3 million women had enrolled in societies to support this work, together surpassing in size all other women's organizations in the United States. Women's foreign missions ranged from India and Africa to Syria, the Pacific Islands, and nearby Latin America.

By 1898, Protestants claimed to have made Christians of more than 80,000 Chinese, a tiny portion of the

By the end of the nineteenth century, women represented 60 percent of the American missionary force in foreign lands. This photograph shows two Methodist women using "back chairs," a traditional form of transportation, at Mount Omei in Szechwan, China.

population, but a significant stronghold for American interests in their nation. The missionaries did more than spread the gospel. They taught school, provided rudimentary medical care, offered vocational training programs, and sometimes encouraged young men and women to pursue a college education in preparation for careers in their homelands.

Outside the churches, the YMCA and YWCA, which had set up nondenominational missions for the working poor in many American cities, also embarked on a worldwide crusade to reach non-Christians. By the turn of the century, the YWCA had foreign branches in Ceylon (present-day Sri Lanka) and China. After foreign branches multiplied in the next decade, a close observer ironically suggested that the United States had three great occupying forces: the army, the navy, and the "Y." He was not far wrong.

Missionaries played an important role both in generating public interest in foreign lands and in preparing the way for American economic expansion. As Josiah Strong aptly put it, "Commerce follows the missionary."

THE QUEST FOR EMPIRE

Not only missionaries but also business and political leaders had set their sights on distant lands, which in turn meant new markets. In the 1860s, Secretary of State William Henry Seward, under Abraham Lincoln and then under Andrew Johnson, encouraged Americans to defer to "a political law—and when I say political law, I mean higher law, a law of Providence—that empire has [had], for the last three thousand years." Seward correctly predicted that foreign trade would play an increasingly important part in the American economy. Between 1870 and 1900, exports more than tripled, from about $400 million to over $1.5 billion, with textiles and agricultural products leading the way. But as European markets for American goods began to contract, business and political leaders, of necessity, looked more eagerly to Asia as well as to lands closer by.

Since the American Revolution, many Americans had regarded all nearby nations as falling naturally within their own territorial realm, destined to be acquired when opportunity allowed. Seward advanced these imperialist principles in 1867 by negotiating the purchase of Alaska (known at the time as Seward's Icebox) from Russia for $7.2 million, and he hoped someday to see the American flag flying over Canada and Mexico. Meanwhile, with European nations launched on their own imperialist missions in Asia and Africa, the United States increasingly viewed the Caribbean as an "American lake" and all of Latin America as a vast potential market for U.S. goods. The crisis of the 1890s transformed this long-standing desire into a perceived economic necessity. Unlike European imperialists, powerful Americans dreamed of empire

without large-scale permanent military occupation and costly colonial administration.

Americans focused their expansionist plans on the Western Hemisphere, determined to dislodge the dominant power, Great Britain. In 1867, when Canada became a self-governing dominion, American diplomats hoped to annex their northern neighbor, believing that Great Britain would gladly accede in order to concentrate its imperial interests in Asia. But Great Britain refused to give up Canada, and the United States backed away. Central and South America proved more accommodating to American designs (see Map 20.3).

Republican stalwart James G. Blaine, secretary of state under presidents Garfield and Harrison, determined to work out a Good Neighbor policy (a phrase coined by Henry Clay in 1820). Bilateral treaties with Mexico, Colombia, the British West Indies, El Salvador, and the Dominican Republic allowed American business to dominate local economies, importing their raw materials at low prices and flooding their local markets with goods manufactured in the United States. Often American investors simply took over the principal industries of these small nations, undercutting national business classes. The first Pan-American Conference, held in 1889–90, marked a turning point in hemispheric relations.

The Good Neighbor policy depended, Blaine knew, on peace and order in the Latin American states. As early as 1875, when revolt shook Venezuela, the Department of State warned European powers not to meddle. If popular uprisings proved too much for local officials, the U.S. Navy would intervene and return American allies to power.

In 1883, wishing to enforce treaties and protect overseas investments, Congress appropriated funds to build up American sea power and in 1884 established the Naval War College in Newport, Rhode Island, to train the officer corps. Beginning with ninety small ships, over one-third of them wooden, the navy grew quickly to include modern steel fighting ships. The hulls of these ships were painted a gleaming white, and the armada was known as the Great White Fleet. One of the most popular exhibits at the Chicago World's Fair featured full-sized models of the new armor-plated steel battleships. The force behind this build-up of the U.S. Navy was Captain Alfred Thayer Mahan, one of the first presidents of the Naval War College.

Mahan achieved international fame for outlining an imperialist strategy based on command of the seas. His book, *The Influence of Sea Power upon History, 1660–1873* (1890), helped to define foreign policy not only for the United States but also for Great Britain, Japan, and Germany by identifying sea power as the key to world dominance. For the United States to achieve global preeminence, he prescribed not only open markets but also the control of colonies. Viewing the U.S. Navy as the "handmaid of expansion," Mahan advocated the creation of bases in the Caribbean and the Pacific. In 1893, he came

MAP EXPLORATION

To explore an interactive version of this map, go to **www.prenhall.com/faragher6/map20.3**

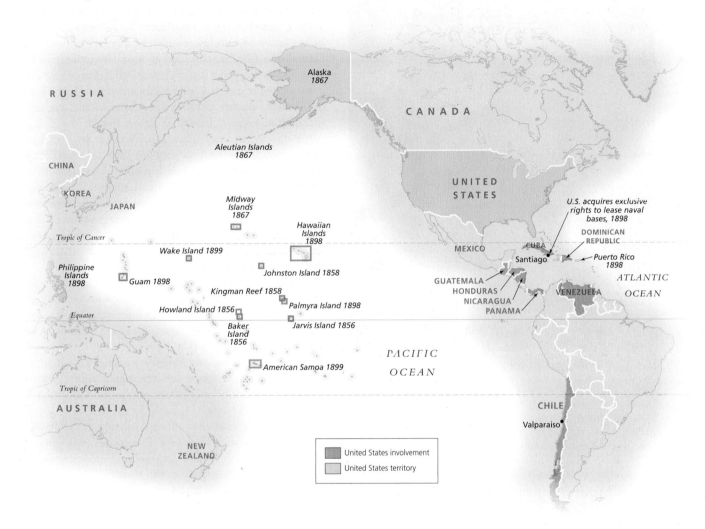

MAP 20.3 The American Domain, ca. 1900 The United States claimed numerous islands in the South Pacific and intervened repeatedly in Latin America to secure its own economic interests.

out for the annexation of Hawai'i, claiming the United States, with its continental border extending to the Pacific Ocean, was "the proper guardian for this most important position." The Hawai'ian archipelago, he insisted, held key strategic value as stepping-stone to Asia and beyond.

ONTO A GLOBAL STAGE

Influenced by Alfred Thayer Mahan, McKinley became an advocate of expansion as a means to make the United States first in international commerce and as a means to implement its humanitarian and democratic goals. He also hoped to achieve these ends peacefully. In taking office,

the new president specified: "We want no wars of conquest; we must avoid the temptation of territorial aggression." He was pleased, therefore, to grease the wheels for the annexation of Hawai'i and in June 1898 agreed with representatives from the Republic on a treaty of annexation. Soon, however, McKinley found himself embroiled in a war with Spain that would establish the United States as a strong player in global imperialism (see Map 20.4). McKinley had to admit: "Isolation is no longer possible or desirable." By the end of the century, the United States had joined Europe and Japan in the quest for empire and claimed territories spread out from the Caribbean Sea across the Pacific.

Brought to power with the assistance of American businessmen, Queen Lili'uokalani sought to limit outsider influence. American Marines, Christian missionaries, and sugar planters joined in 1893 to drive her from her throne. A century later, the U.S. government apologized to native Hawaiians for this illegal act.

A "SPLENDID LITTLE WAR" IN CUBA

Before the Civil War, Southerners pushed for the acquisition of Cuba, a possession of Spain, for the expansion of slavery into its sugar mills, tobacco plantations, and mines. After failing several times to buy the island outright, the United States settled for the continuation of the status quo and resolved to protect Spain's sovereignty over Cuba against the encroachment of other powers, including Cuba itself.

In the mid-1860s, a movement for independence began in Cuba when Spain, its empire in ruins, began to impose stiff taxes on the island. After a series of defeats, insurgents rallied in the 1890s under the nationalist leadership of José Martí. In May 1895 Spanish troops ambushed and killed Martí, turning him into a martyr and fanning the flames of rebellion. In February 1896 Spain appointed General Valeriano Weyler as governor and gave him full authority to crush the rebellion. Weyler instituted a policy *of reconcentrado,* forcing civilians from the countryside into concentration camps so they could not aid the rebels.

Thousands starved or died from the diseases that swept these crowded, dirty camps.

In the United States, the popular press whipped up support for the movement for *Cuba Libre,* circulating sensationalistic and even false stories of the atrocities that Weyler, "the butcher," perpetrated against the insurgents. Newspapers ran stories on mass executions in the "death camps" and featured drawings of emaciated children. This so-called "yellow journalism," practiced brilliantly by publishers Joseph Pulitzer and William Randolph Hearst, boosted circulation and simultaneously aroused sympathy for the Cubans and abundant patriotic fervor.

Public sympathy, again whipped up by the press, turned into frenzy on February 15, 1898, when an explosion ripped through the battleship USS *Maine,* stationed in Havana harbor to protect American interests. The newspapers ran banner headlines charging a Spanish conspiracy, although there was no proof. The impatient public, meanwhile, demanded revenge for the death of 266 American sailors. Within days, a new slogan appeared: "Remember the Maine! To Hell with Spain!"

Finally, on April 11, President McKinley asked Congress for a declaration of war against Spain. Yet Congress barely passed the war resolution on April 25, and only with the inclusion of an amendment by Senator Henry Teller (Rep., Colorado) that disclaimed "any disposition or intention to exercise sovereignty, jurisdiction or control over said island, except for the pacification thereof." McKinley called for volunteers, and by the end of April, the fighting had begun.

Ten weeks later the war was all but over. On land, Lieutenant Colonel Theodore Roosevelt—who boasted of killing Spaniards "like jackrabbits"—led his Rough Riders to victory. On July 3, the main Spanish fleet near Santiago Bay was destroyed; two weeks later Santiago itself surrendered, and the war drew to a close. Poorly trained and lacking supplies, less than 400 Americans died in battle. Disease and the inept treatment of the wounded created a medical disaster, spreading sickness and disease to more than 20,000 in the regiments. Roosevelt nevertheless felt invigorated by the conflict, agreeing with McKinley's Secretary of State John Hay that it had been a "splendid little war."

On August 12, at a small ceremony in McKinley's office marking Spain's surrender, the United States secured Cuba's independence from Spain, but not its own sovereignty. American businesses proceeded to tighten their hold on Cuban sugar plantations, while U.S. military forces oversaw the formation of a constitutional convention that made Cuba a protectorate of the United States. Under the Platt Amendment, sponsored by Republican senator Orville H. Platt of Connecticut in 1901, Cuba was required to provide land for American bases, including a navy base at Guantanomo Bay; to devote national revenues to pay back debts to the United States; to sign no treaty

MAP EXPLORATION

To explore an interactive version of this map, go to **www.prenhall.com/faragher6/map20.4**

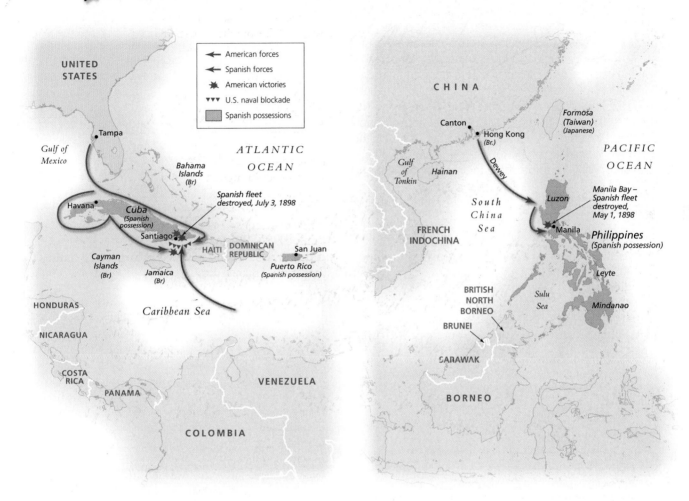

MAP 20.4 The Spanish–American War In two theaters of action, the United States used its naval power adeptly against a weak foe.

that would be detrimental to American interests; and to acknowledge the right of the United States to intervene at any time to protect its interests in Cuba. After the U.S. withdrawal of troops, the terms of the Platt Amendment were incorporated into the Cuban-American Treaty of 1903. This treaty, which remained in place until 1934, paved the way for American domination of the island's sugar industry and contributed to anti-American sentiment among Cuban nationalists.

WAR IN THE PHILIPPINES

The Philippines, another of Spain's colonies, seemed an especially attractive prospect, its 7,000 islands a natural way station to the markets of mainland Asia. In 1897, Assistant

Secretary of the Navy Theodore Roosevelt and President McKinley had discussed the merits of taking the Pacific colony in the event of war with Spain. At the first opportunity, McKinley acted to bring these islands into the U.S. strategic orbit. Shortly after Congress declared war on Spain, on May 4, the president dispatched 5,000 troops to occupy the Philippines. George Dewey, a Civil War veteran who commanded the American Asiatic Squadron, was ordered to "start offensive action." During the first week of the conflict, he demolished the Spanish fleet in Manila Bay through seven hours of unimpeded target practice. Once the war ended, McKinley refused to sign the armistice unless Spain relinquished all claims to its Pacific islands. When Spain conceded, McKinley quickly drew up plans for colonial administration. He pledged "to educate

Two Sides of Anti-Imperialism

Industrialist Andrew Carnegie (1835–1919) gave generously to help finance the Anti-Imperialist League from its formation until his death. He also served as a vice president of the league. His position on American expansion was complex, arising out of his opinion that some peoples were incapable of assimilation into a democratic society. For example, Carnegie reluctantly agreed with the annexation of Hawai'i, in part because the islands were only thinly settled and, therefore, could absorb more advanced "races," including American immigrants. Strongly opposed to acquiring the Philippines, he made an offer to President McKinley to purchase the islands from the United States, after which he would restore governance to the Filipinos. McKinley rejected this offer, ensuring Carnegie's alliance with the anti-imperialists. His statement was originally published in August 1898, when U.S. forces were invading the Philippines and Americans were debating what to do with the Spanish colonies.

The widow of a prominent businessman and throughout her life a committed reformer, Josephine Shaw Lowell (1843–1905) also opposed the Spanish-American War. Like Carnegie, she denounced the annexation of the Philippines and likewise was a leader of the Anti-Imperialist League, serving as a vice president from 1901 to 1905. Lowell wrote her impassioned protest after the outbreak of Filipino resistance against American rule but before the U.S. Army completed its bloody subjugation of the islands.

Are these two arguments contradictory or complementary?
Is there more to Carnegie's objection to imperialism than racism? And is Lowell correct in arguing
that some wars can be not only just but also morally elevating?

Andrew Carnegie, Anti-Imperialist: America Cannot Absorb Alien Populations (August 1898)

Is the Republic, the apostle of Triumphant Democracy, of the rule of the people, to abandon her political creed and endeavor to establish in other lands the rule of the foreigner over the people, Triumphant Despotism?

Is the Republic to remain one homogeneous whole, one united people, or to become a scattered and disjointed aggregate of widely separated and alien races?

Is she to continue the task of developing her vast continent until it holds a population as great as that of Europe, all Americans, or to abandon that destiny to annex, and to attempt to govern, other far distant parts of the world as outlying possessions, which can never be integral parts of the Republic? . . .

There are two kinds of national possessions, one colonies, the other dependencies. In the former we establish and reproduce our own race. Thus Britain has peopled Canada and Australia with English-speaking people, who have naturally adopted our ideas of self-government.

With dependencies it is otherwise. The most grievous burden which Britain has upon her shoulders is that of India, for there it is impossible for our race to grow. The child of English-speaking parents must be removed and reared in Britain. The British Indian official must have long respites in his native land. India means death to our race. The characteristic feature of a dependency is that the acquiring power cannot reproduce its own race there.

If we could establish colonies of Americans, and grow Americans in any part of the world now unpopulated and unclaimed by any of the great powers, and thus follow the example of Britain, heart and mind might tell us that we should have to think twice, yea, thrice, before deciding adversely. Even then our decision should be adverse; but there is at present no such question before us. What we have to face is the question whether we should embark upon the difficult and dangerous policy of undertaking the government of alien races in lands where it is impossible for our own race to be produced . . . .

I am no "Little" American, afraid of growth, either in population or territory, provided always that the new territory be American, and that it will produce Americans, and not foreign races bound in time to be false to the Republic in order to be true to themselves . . . . The Philippines have about seven and a half millions of people, composed of races bitterly hostile to one another, alien races, ignorant of our language and institutions. Americans cannot be grown there . . . .

SOURCE: Andrew Carnegie, "Distant Possessions: The Parting of the Ways," in *The Gospel of Wealth* (New York: Century Company, 1901), p. 151. Originally published in the *North American Review* (August. 1898).

"[T]he question [is] whether we should embark upon the difficult and dangerous policy of undertaking the government of alien races . . . ."

"[T]he United States, having obtained a foothold in a foreign country by professing friendship for the inhabitants, calls those inhabitants rebels because [they] resist the invasion . . . ."

Josephine Shaw Lowell, Anti-Imperialist: America Must Not Wage Unjust Wars (ca. 1900)

I cannot speak on this subject without making a distinction between different kinds of wars.

A war which requires personal sacrifice, a war which makes a whole people place patriotism and public duty above private comfort and ease, which forces men and women out of self-indulgence, devotion to material wealth—such a war does not as a whole cause moral deterioration but on the contrary, moral development in a nation.

Such a war was the Civil War in this country, forty years ago . . . .

The history of the introduction of the United States to the Philippine Islands is a disgraceful one . . . . In December, 1898 . . . the President of the United States proclaimed sovereignty over the Philippine Archipelago, this naturally aroused the anger of the Filipinos, who had been treasuring for six months or more the hope that the United States intended to help and protect their young republic against the attacks of other nations, and the feelings became more and more bitter, and finally culminated in a fight between the outposts of the two armies on February 4, 1899; and from that time, the United States devoted itself to the task of crushing out what was called the insurrection of the Filipinos.

That is, the United States, having obtained a foothold in a foreign country by professing friendship for the inhabitants, calls those inhabitants rebels because the people resist the invasion and try to defend their country. We direct our army to crush out all resistance. The Filipino people prefer death to subjugation, saying, as did Patrick Henry, the American patriot, "Give me liberty or give me death." Our unhappy army set to do such an un-American, such a wicked task, tried to obey orders, becomes gradually more and more cruel . . .

It is incredible that the American people should have been so ignorant and so careless in regard to the great wrong which has been done in their name; but now at last we are awakening, we are beginning to realize the facts . . . . I said, that the liberties of the United States are at stake equally with the liberties of the Filipino people, for it is inevitable that should we willingly become the tyrant of these helpless millions, should we turn our backs so completely upon the principles which have made this country a world power, molding and influencing the character of all governments of the world during the past hundred and twenty-five years, as to make it possible for us to do such a thing our moral deterioration is so rapid, our conscience must become so hardened in the process, our love of liberty so absolutely dead, that, we should become fit subjects for a tyranny ourselves.

SOURCE: "Moral Deterioration Following War," ca. 1900, reprinted in *The Philanthropic Work of Josephine Shaw Lowell: Containing a Biographical Sketch of Her Life,* collected by William Rhinelander Stewart (New York: Macmillan Co., 1911), pp. 466–470.

the Filipinos, and to uplift and civilize and Christianize them." But after centuries of Spanish rule, the majority of islanders—already Christians—were eager to create their own nation.

The Filipino rebels, like the Cubans, at first welcomed American troops and fought with them against Spain. But when the Spanish-American War ended and they perceived that American troops were not preparing to leave, the rebels, led by Emilio Aguinaldo, turned against their former allies and attacked the American base of operations in Manila in February 1899. Predicting a brief skirmish, American commanders seriously underestimated the population's capacity to endure great suffering for the sake of independence.

U.S. troops had provoked this conflict in various ways. Military leaders, the majority veterans of the Indian Wars, commonly described the natives as "gugus," and reported themselves, as one said, as "just itching to get at the niggers." While awaiting action, American soldiers repeatedly insulted or physically abused civilians, raped Filipino women, and otherwise whipped up resentment.

The resulting conflict took the form of modern guerrilla warfare, with brutalities on both sides. By the time the fighting slowed down in 1902, 4,300 American lives had been lost, and one of every five Filipinos had died in battle or from starvation or disease. On some of the Philippine islands, intermittent fighting lasted until 1935. In 1901, William Howard Taft headed a commission that established a special apparatus to rule in the Philippines; after 1905, the president appointed a Filipino governor general to maintain the provincial government. Meanwhile, Americans bought up the best land and invested heavily in the island's sugar economy.

The conquest of the Philippines, which remained a U.S. colony until 1946, evoked for its defenders the vision of empire. The Philippines joined Hawai'i as yet another stepping-stone for U.S. merchants en route to China. At the end of the Spanish-American War, the United States advanced its interests in the Caribbean to include Puerto Rico, ceded by Spain, and eventually the Virgin Islands of St. Thomas, St. John, and St. Croix, purchased from Denmark in 1917. The acquisition of Pacific territories, including Guam, marked the emergence of the United States as a global colonial power.

Once again, Josiah Strong proclaimed judgment over an era. His famous treatise *Expansion* (1900) roundly defended American overseas involvements by carefully distinguishing between freedom and independence. People could achieve freedom, he argued, only under the rule of law. And because white Americans had proven themselves superior in the realm of government, they could best bring "freedom" to nonwhite peoples by setting aside the ideal of national independence for a period of enforced guidance. Many began to wonder, however, whether the United States could become an empire without sacrificing its democratic spirit and to ask whether the subjugated people were really so fortunate under the rule of the United States (see Communities in Conflict).

CRITICS OF EMPIRE

No mass movement formed to forestall U.S. expansion, but distinguished figures like Mark Twain, Andrew Carnegie, William Jennings Bryan, and Harvard philosopher William James voiced their opposition strongly. To protest military action in the Philippines, a small group of prominent Bostonians organized the Anti-Imperialist League. They staged a mass meeting in June 1898 in historic Faneuil Hall, which had witnessed the birth of both the American Revolution and the antislavery movement. Those in attendance protested the "insane and wicked ambition which is driving the nation to ruin." Most supported American economic expansion but advocated free trade rather than political domination as the means to reach this goal. All strongly opposed the annexation of new territories, including Hawai'i.

"Uncle Sam Teaches the Art of Self-Government," editorial cartoon, 1898. Expressing a popular sentiment of the time, a newspaper cartoonist shows the rebels as raucous children who constantly fight among themselves and need to be brought into line by Uncle Sam. The Filipino leader, Emilio Aguinaldo, appears as a dunce for failing to learn properly from the teacher. The two major islands where no uprising took place, Puerto Rico and Hawai'i, appear as passive but exotically dressed women, ready to learn their lessons.

CHRONOLOGY

1867	Grange founded
	Secretary of State Seward negotiates the purchase of Alaska
1874	Granger laws begin to regulate railroad shipping rates
1877	Rutherford B. Hayes elected president
	Great Uprising of 1877
1879	Henry George publishes *Progress and Poverty*
1881	President James A. Garfield assassinated; Chester A. Arthur becomes president
1882	Chinese Exclusion Act
1883	Pendleton Act passed
1884	Grover Cleveland elected president
1887	Interstate Commerce Act creates the Interstate Commerce Commission
1888	Colored Farmers' Alliance formed
	Benjamin Harrison elected president
1889	National Farmers' Alliance formed
1890	Sherman Silver Purchase Act
	McKinley Tariff enacted
	National American Woman Suffrage Association formed
1892	Populist (People's) Party formed
	Coeur d'Alene miners' strike

	Homestead strike
	Ida B. Wells begins crusade against lynching
1893	Western Federation of Miners formed
	Financial panic and depression
	World's Columbian Exhibition opens in Chicago
1894	"Coxey's Army" marches on Washington, DC
	Pullman strike and boycott
1896	*Plessy* v. *Ferguson* upholds segregation
	William McKinley defeats William Jennings Bryan for president
1897	Dingley Tariff again raises import duties to an all-time high
1898	Eugene V. Debs helps found Social Democratic Party
	Hawai'i is annexed
	Spanish-American War begins
	Anti-Imperialist League formed
	Wilmington, North Carolina, massacre
1899	*Cumming* v. *Richmond County Board of Education* sanctions segregated education
	Guerrilla war begins in the Philippines
1900	Gold Standard Act
	Josiah Strong publishes *Expansion*

The *National Labor Standard* expressed its common hope that all those "who believe in the Republic against Empire should join." By 1899, the league claimed a half-million members. A few outspoken anti-imperialists, such as former Illinois governor John Peter Altgeld, openly toasted Filipino rebels as heroes. Morrison Swift, leader of the Coxey's Army contingent from Massachusetts, formed a Filipino Liberation Society and sent antiwar materials to American troops. Others, such as Samuel Gompers, a league vice president, felt no sympathy for conquered peoples and simply wanted to prevent colonized nonwhites from immigrating into the United States and "inundating" American labor.

Military leaders and staunch imperialists did not distinguish between racist and nonracist anti-imperialists. They called all dissenters "unhung traitors" and demanded their arrest. Newspaper editors accused universities of harboring antiwar professors, although college students as a group were enthusiastic supporters of the war.

Within the press, which overwhelmingly supported the Spanish-American War, the voices of opposition appeared primarily in African American and labor papers. The *Indianapolis Recorder* asked rhetorically in 1899, "Are the tender-hearted expansionists in the United States Congress really actuated by the desire to save the Filipinos from self-destruction or is it the worldly greed for gain?" The *Railroad Telegrapher* similarly commented, "The wonder of it all is that the working people are willing to lose blood and treasure in fighting another man's battle."

Most Americans put aside their doubts and welcomed the new era of imperialism. Untouched by the private tragedies of dead or wounded American soldiers and the mass destruction of civilian society in the Philippines, the vast majority could approve Theodore Roosevelt's defense of armed conflict: "No triumph of peace is quite so great as the supreme triumphs of war."

CONCLUSION

The conflicts marking the last quarter of the nineteenth century that pitted farmers, workers, and the proprietors of small businesses against powerful national interests had offered Americans an important moment of democratic promise. By the end of the century, however, the rural and working-class campaigns to retain a large degree of self-government in their communities had been defeated, their organizations destroyed, their autonomy eroded. The rise of a national governing class and its counterpart, the large bureaucratic state, established new rules of behavior, new sources of prestige, and new rewards for the most successful citizens.

But the nation would eventually pay a steep price for the failure of democratic reform. Regional antagonisms, nativist movements against the foreign-born, and above all deepening racial tensions blighted American society. As the new century opened, progressive reformers moved to correct flaws in government while accepting the framework of a corporate society and its overseas empire. So, too, did the majority of citizens who shared their president's pride in expansion.

William Jennings Bryan made another bid for the presidency in 1900 on a strong anti-imperialist platform and was roundly defeated by at the polls. The dream of Queen Lili'iokalani for an independent Hawai'i was likewise crushed, although a century after her overthrow, in 1993 President William Clinton signed a joint congressional resolution apologizing for the "alleged role the United States had played" in her deposing. But in 1900, Americans would find the widening divisions in their own society difficult—if not impossible—to overcome.

— REVIEW QUESTIONS —

1. Discuss some of the problems accompanying the expansion of government during the late nineteenth century. What role did political parties play in this process? Explain how a prominent reformer such as James Garfield might become a leading "machine" politician.

2. What were the major causes and consequences of the Populist movement of the 1880s and 1890s? Why did the election of 1896 prove so important to the future of American politics?

3. Discuss the role of women in both the Grange and the People's Party. What were their specific goals?

4. Discuss the causes and consequences of the financial crisis of the 1890s. How did various reformers and politicians respond to the event? What kinds of programs did they offer to restore the economy or reduce poverty?

5. How did the exclusion of African Americans affect the outcome of populism? Explain the rise of Jim Crow legislation in the South and discuss its impact on the status of African Americans.

6. Describe American foreign policy during the 1890s. Why did the United States intervene in Cuba and the Philippines? What were some of the leading arguments for and against overseas expansion?

RECOMMENDED READING

Steven Hahn, *A Nation Under Our Feet: Black Political Struggles in the Rural South from Slavery to the Great Migration* (2003). A sweeping history of African American politics with an eye on its influence in shaping the South and the nation in the last half of the nineteenth century. Hahn emphasizes the emergence of political communities and highlights the 1880s as a period of exceptional assertiveness on the part of southern African Americans.

Evelyn Brooks Higginbotham, *Righteous Discontent: The Women's Movement in the Black Baptist Church, 1880–1920* (1993). Documents the central role of women in shaping the theology and racial uplift programs of the National Baptist Convention, the largest denomination of African Americans at the end of the nineteenth century.

Matthew Frye Jacobson, *Barbarian Virtues: The United States Encounters Foreign Peoples at Home and Abroad, 1876–1917* (2000). Links the histories of immigration and empire-building to examine public discussions about foreign people, especially their "fitness" for self-government. Jacobson casts the search for markets as backdrop for cultural history.

Michael Kazin, *A Godly Hero: The Life of William Jennings Bryan* (2006). Makes a strong case for the relevance of Bryan to the history of American liberalism. Kazin explores the sources of Bryan's popularity among the nation's poor and working classes.

Walter LaFeber, *The New Empire: An Interpretation of American Expansion, 1860–1898* (1963, 1998). The best overview of U.S. imperial involvement in the late nineteenth century. LaFeber shows how overseas commitments grew out of the economic expansionist assumptions of American leaders and expanded continuously, if often chaotically, with the opportunities presented by the crises experienced by the older imperial powers.

Leon F. Litwack, *Trouble in Mind: Black Southerners in the Age of Jim Crow* (1998). An expansive social history of the first generation of African Americans born in freedom and surviving a period of extraordinary violent and repressive race relations in the South. Litwack examines the retrenchment of their political and civil rights but emphasizes their resourcefulness and resistance.

Eric T. L. Love, *Race over Empire and U.S. Imperialism, 1865–1900* (2004). An engaging narrative of expansion in the late nineteenth century and a keen analysis of the policies supporting and opposing annexation of territories and the assimilation of new populations.

Noenoe K. Silva, *Aloha Betrayed: Native Hawaiian Resistance to American Colonialism* (2004). Highlights the active role native Hawaiians played in the face of U.S. annexation pressures. Silva breaks ground by using Hawaiian-languages newspapers and sources.

John Lawrence Tone, *War and Genocide in Cuba, 1895–1898* (2006). Provides a new perspective on the Cuban rebellion from Spain and a careful study of Spanish policy in the hand of General Varleriano Weyler.

William Appleman Williams, *Empire as a Way of Life: An Essay on the Causes and Character of America's Present Predicament* (1982). A lucid general exploration of American views of empire. Williams shows that Americans allowed the idea of empire and, more generally, economic expansion to dominate their concept of democracy, especially in the last half of the nineteenth century.

myhistorylab
Where it's a good time to connect to the past!

For study resources for this chapter, go to **http://www.myhistorylab.com** and choose *Out of Many*. You will find a wealth of study and review material for this chapter, including pretests and posttests, customized study plan, key-term review flash cards, interactive map and document activities, and documents for analysis.

Urban America and the Progressive Era

1900–1917

New York City

The Henry Street Settlement House: Women Settlement House Workers Create a Community of Reform

A shy and frightened young girl appeared in the doorway of a weekly home-nursing class for women on Manhattan's Lower East Side. The teacher beckoned her to come forward. Tugging on the teacher's skirt, the girl pleaded in broken English for the teacher to come home with her. "Mother," "baby," "blood," she kept repeating. The teacher gathered up the sheets that were part of the interrupted lesson in bed making. The two hurried through narrow, garbage-strewn, foul-smelling streets, then groped their way up a pitch-dark, rickety staircase. They reached a cramped, two-room apartment, home to an immigrant family of seven and several boarders. There, in a vermin-infested bed, encrusted with dried blood, lay a mother and her newborn baby. The mother had been abandoned by a doctor because she could not afford his fee.

The teacher, Lillian Wald, was a twenty-five-year-old nurse at New York Hospital. Years later, she recalled this scene as her baptism by fire and the turning point in her life. Born in 1867, Wald had enjoyed a comfortable upbringing in a middle-class German Jewish family in Rochester. Despite her parents' objections, she had moved

to New York City to become a professional nurse. Resentful of the disdainful treatment nurses received from doctors, and horrified by the inhumane conditions at a juvenile asylum she worked in, Wald determined to find a way of caring for the sick in their neighborhoods and homes. With nursing school classmate Mary Brewster, Wald rented a fifth-floor walk-up apartment on the Lower East Side and established a visiting nurse service. The two provided professional care in the home to hundreds of families for a nominal fee of ten to twenty-five cents. They also offered each family they visited information on basic health care, sanitation, and disease prevention. In 1895, philanthropist Jacob Schiff generously donated a red brick Georgian house on Henry Street as a new base of operation. ➤

The Henry Street Settlement stood in the center of perhaps the most overcrowded neighborhood in the world, New York's Lower East Side. Roughly 500,000 people were packed into an area only as large as a midsized Kansas farm. Population density was about 500 per acre, roughly four times the figure for the rest of New York City, and far more concentrated than even the worst slums of London or Calcutta. A single city block might have as many as 3,000 residents. Home for most Lower East Siders was a small tenement apartment that might include paying boarders squeezed in alongside the immediate family. Residents were mostly recent immigrants from southern and eastern Europe: Jews, Italians, Germans, Greeks, Hungarians, Slavs. Men, women, and children toiled in the garment shops, small factories, retail stores, breweries, and warehouses to be found on nearly every street.

The Henry Street Settlement became a model for a new kind of reform community composed essentially of college-educated women who encouraged and supported one another in a wide variety of humanitarian, civic, and political activities. These included support for organized labor, campaigns for better sanitation and more parks, lobbying state legislatures for tougher laws regulating tenement construction and factory safety, and pushing for women's right to vote. Settlement house living arrangements closely resembled those in the dormitories of such new women's colleges as Smith, Wellesley, and Vassar. Like these colleges, the settlement house was an "experiment," but one designed, in settlement house pioneer Jane Addams's words, "to aid in the solution of the social and industrial problems which are engendered by the modern conditions of urban life." Unlike earlier moral reformers, who tried to impose their ideas from outside, settlement house residents lived in poor communities and worked for immediate improvements in the health and welfare of those communities. Yet, as Addams and others repeatedly stressed, the college-educated women were beneficiaries as well. The settlement house allowed them to preserve a collegial spirit, satisfy the desire for service, and apply their academic training.

With its combined moral and social appeal, the settlement house movement attracted many educated young women and grew rapidly. There were 6 settlement houses in the United States in 1891, some 74 in 1897, more than 200 by 1900, and more than 400 by 1910. Few women made settlement work a career, but those who did typically chose not to marry, and most lived together with female companions. As the movement flourished, settlement house residents called attention to the plight of the poor and fostered respect for different cultural heritages in countless articles and lectures. Leaders of the movement, including Jane Addams, Lillian Wald, and Florence Kelley, emerged as influential political figures during the progressive era.

The settlement house movement embodied the impulses toward social justice and civic engagement that were hallmarks of the progressive movement. But in a broader sense, the progressive era was defined by struggles over the true meaning of American democracy. If there was growing agreement that Americans needed to address the excesses of industrial growth and rapid urbanization, there was less consensus over precisely how. As progressive activism spread from reform communities like settlement houses, to city halls and statehouses, and finally to the national stage of the White House and Congress, Americans experimented with new approaches to urgent problems. How might the power of government be used to restrain corporate excess and improve the lives of children, industrial laborers, and others in need of protection? Could the machinery of democracy be reformed to make politics less corrupt and more responsive to the needs of ordinary citizens? Did the calls to social action mean that full citizenship rights be extended to African Americans, women, and new immigrants? What were the most effective ways to expose social problems and appeal to the public conscience?

During the first two decades of the twentieth century, millions of Americans identified themeselves as "progressives" and most, like Lillian Wald, were first drawn to causes and campaigns rooted in their local communities. But many soon saw that confronting the grim realities of an urban and industrial society required national and even global strategies for pursuing reform. It was no cliché for Wald to say, as she did on many occasions, "The whole world is my neighborhood." By the time America entered World War I in 1917, despite its contradictions, the progressive movement had reshaped the political and social landscape of the entire nation.

Focus Questions

1. What were the social and intellectual roots of progressive reform?

2. How did tensions between social justice and social control divide progressives?

3. How did the impact of new immigration transform American cities?

4. What new forms of activism emerged among the working class, women, and African Americans?

5. How did progressivism become a central force in national politics?

1900–1917

THE ORIGINS OF PROGRESSIVISM

Between the 1890s and World War I, a large and diverse number of Americans claimed the political label "progressive." Progressives could be found in all classes, regions, and races. They shared a fundamental belief that America needed a new social consciousness to cope with the problems brought on by the enormous rush of economic and social change in the post–Civil War decades. The devastating depression of the 1890s, the often bloody labor conflicts of that decade, and the Populist revolt caused many Americans to look for a stronger government response to economic and social ills. Yet progressivism was no unified movement with a single set of principles. It is best understood as a varied collection of reform communities, often fleeting, uniting citizens in a host of political, professional, and religious organizations, some of which were national in scope.

As a political movement, progressivism flowered in the soil of several key issues: ending political corruption, bringing more businesslike methods to governing, and offering a more compassionate legislative response to the excesses of industrialism. As a national movement, progressivism reached its peak in 1912, when the four major presidential candidates all ran on some version of a progressive platform. This last development was an important measure of the extent to which local reform movements, like the Henry Street Settlement, and new intellectual currents had captured the political imagination of the nation.

Some progressives focused on expanding state and federal regulation of private interests for the public welfare. Others viewed the rapid influx of new immigrants and the explosive growth of large cities as requiring more stringent social controls. Another variant emphasized eliminating corruption in the political system as the key to righting society's wrongs. In the South, progressivism was for white people only. Progressives could be forward-looking in their vision or nostalgic for a nineteenth-century world rapidly disappearing. Self-styled progressives often found themselves facing each other from opposite sides of an issue.

UNIFYING THEMES

Three basic attitudes underlay the various progressive crusades and movements. The first was anger over the excesses of industrial capitalism and urban growth. Unlike Populist era reformers, who were largely rural and small-town oriented, progressives focused their energies on the social and political ills experienced by Americans in factories or mines and in dreary city tenements or filthy streets. At the same time, progressives shared an essential optimism about the ability of citizens to improve social and economic conditions. They were reformers, not revolutionaries, who believed in using the democratic institutions available to them—the vote, the courts, the legislature—to address social problems. But if those political processes were found to be corrupt or undemocratic, they would have to be reformed as well. Second, progressives emphasized social cohesion and common bonds as a way of understanding how modern society and economics actually worked. They largely rejected the ideal of individualism that had informed nineteenth-century economic and political theory. For progressives, poverty and success hinged on more than simply individual character; the economy was more than merely a sum of individual calculations. Society's problems, in this view, were structural rather than simply the result of individual failures. Third, progressives believed in the need for citizens to intervene actively, both politically and morally, to improve social conditions. They looked to convert personal outrage into civic activism and to mobilize public opinion in new ways. Progressives thus called for expansion of the legislative and regulatory powers of the state. They moved away from the nineteenth-century celebration of minimal government as the surest way to allow all Americans to thrive.

Progressive rhetoric and methods drew on two distinct sources of inspiration. One was evangelical Protestantism, particularly the late nineteenth-century social gospel movement. Social gospelers rejected the idea of original sin as the cause of human suffering. They emphasized both the capacity and the duty of Christians to purge the world of poverty, inequality, and economic greed. Many progressive activists with roots in the evangelical tradition adapted the old emphasis on individual salvation into a new social activism more focused on finding the common good. A second strain of progressive thought looked to natural and social scientists to develop rational measures for improving the human condition. They believed that experts trained in statistical analysis, engineering, and the sciences could make government and industry more efficient and set new standards for personal behavior. Progressivism thus offered an uneasy combination of social justice and social control, a tension that would characterize American reform for the rest of the twentieth century.

NEW JOURNALISM: MUCKRAKING

Changes in journalism helped fuel a new reform consciousness by drawing the attention of millions to urban poverty, political corruption, the plight of industrial workers, and immoral business practices. As early as 1890, journalist Jacob Riis had shocked the nation with his landmark book *How the Other Half Lives*, a portrait of New York City's poor. Riis's book included a remarkable series of photographs he had taken in tenements, lodging houses, sweatshops, and saloons. These striking pictures, combined with Riis's analysis of slum housing patterns, had a powerful impact on a whole generation of urban reformers (see Seeing History).

Within a few years, magazine journalists had turned to uncovering the seamier side of American life. The key innovator was S. S. McClure, a young midwestern editor who in 1893, started America's first large-circulation magazine, *McClure's*. Charging only a dime for his monthly, McClure effectively combined popular fiction with articles on science, technology, travel, and recent history. He attracted a new readership among the urban

middle class through aggressive subscription and promotional campaigns, as well as newsstand sales. By the turn of the century, *McClure's* and several imitators—*Munsey's, Cosmopolitan, Collier's, Everybody's,* and the *Saturday Evening Post*—had circulations in the hundreds of thousands. Making extensive use of photographs and illustrations, these cheap upstarts soon far surpassed older, more staid and expensive magazines such as the *Atlantic Monthly* and *Harper's* in circulation.

In 1902, McClure began hiring talented reporters to write detailed accounts of the nation's social problems. Lincoln Steffens's series *The Shame of the Cities* (1903) revealed the widespread graft at the center of American urban politics. He showed how big-city bosses routinely worked hand in glove with businessmen seeking lucrative municipal contracts for gas, water, electricity, and mass transit. Ida Tarbell, in her *History of the Standard Oil Company* (1904), thoroughly documented how John D. Rockefeller ruthlessly squeezed out competitors with unfair business practices. Ray Stannard Baker wrote detailed portraits of life and labor in Pennsylvania coal towns.

McClure's and other magazines discovered that "exposure journalism" paid off handsomely in terms of increased circulation. The middle-class public responded to this new combination of factual reporting and moral exhortation. A series such as Steffens's fueled reform campaigns that swept individual communities. Between 1902 and 1908, magazines were full of articles exposing insurance scandals, patent medicine frauds, and stock market swindles. Upton Sinclair's 1906 novel *The Jungle*, a socialist tract set among Chicago packinghouse workers, exposed the filthy sanitation and abysmal working conditions in the stockyards and the meatpacking industry. In an effort to boost sales, Sinclair's publisher devoted an entire issue of a monthly magazine it owned, *World's Work*, to articles and photographs that substantiated Sinclair's devastating portrait.

Muckraking crusades could take many forms. In the 1890s the young African American newspaper editor Ida B. Wells set out to investigate an upsurge in lynchings around the city of Memphis. She paid special attention to the common white defense of lynching—that it was a necessary response to attempts by black men to rape white women. Her 1895 pamphlet *A Red Record* showed that the vast majority of black lynching victims had not even been accused of sexual transgression. Instead, Wells found that lynching was primarily a brutal device to eliminate African Americans who competed with white businesses or who had become too prosperous or powerful (see Chapter 20).

In 1906, David Graham Phillips, in a series for *Cosmopolitan* called "The Treason of the Senate," argued that many conservative U.S. senators were no more than mouthpieces for big business. President Theodore Roosevelt, upset by Phillips's attack on several of his friends and supporters, coined a new term when he angrily

SEEING HISTORY

Photographing Poverty in the Slums of New York

Jacob A. Riis was a twenty-year-old Danish immigrant when he arrived in New York City in 1870. After several years wandering the country as a casual laborer, he returned to New York and began a career as a reporter covering the police beat. By the early 1880s Riis found himself drawn to report on perhaps the most overwhelming and rapidly worsening problem in the city: the deteriorating conditions of tenement house life. As he accompanied city police and Board of Health employees in their inspections of sanitary conditions, Riis's reports on the tenement districts reflected a keen outrage and new sense of purpose. Part of the story could be reduced to staggering statistics. By 1880 more than 600,000 New Yorkers lived in 24,000 tenements, each of which housed anywhere from four to several score families. Overcrowding kept getting worse, as in one Mulberry Street tenement that housed nearly two hundred people in small apartments meant for twenty families. Thousands of buildings had terrible sanitary conditions, with seriously

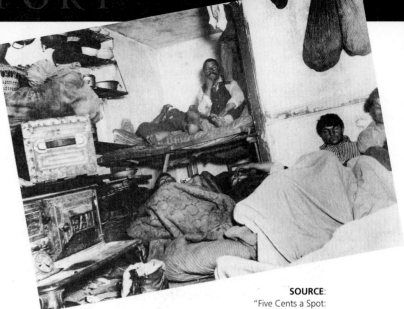

defective plumbing, and often no ventilation or sewer connections. "It was upon my midnight trips with the sanitary police," he recalled, "that the wish kept cropping up in me that there were some way of putting before the people what I saw there."

In 1888 Riis taught himself the rudiments of photography, using the new "flash powder" technology to take pictures where there was no natural light. He shot many of these photographs in the dead of the night, taking his subjects by surprise. Other photographs were carefully staged to ensure maximum emotional impact on the middle- and upper-class audience Riis was trying to reach. Riis converted his photographs into "lantern slides," which could be projected as large images before audiences. He spent two years touring the country, presenting an illustrated lecture called "The Other Half: How It Lives and Dies in New York" to churches and reform groups, appealing to the conscience and Christian sympathy of his listeners. Newspapers reviewed Riis's slide lecture as both an "entertainment" and a new philanthropic campaign. In 1890 he published his landmark book, *How the Other Half Lives: Studies Among the Tenements*, illustrated with his photographs. The use of photography would become a key element for reform crusades in the progressive era and beyond.

SOURCE: The Jacob A. Riis Collection 157, Museum of the City of New York.

Here are two Riis photographs, "Five Cents a Spot" and "Home of an Italian Ragpicker." What visual information does each communicate about tenement life? How do they differ in their depiction of New York City's immigrant poor? How do you imagine Riis set up the scene for each of these photographs?

Lewis Hine, one of the pioneers of social documentary photography, made this evocative 1908 portrait of "Mamie," a typical young spinner working at a cotton mill in Lancaster, South Carolina. The National Child Labor Committee hired Hine to help document, publicize, and curb the widespread employment of children in industrial occupations. "These pictures," Hine wrote, "speak for themselves and prove that the law is being violated."

SOURCE: Lewis Hine (American, 1874–1940), "A Carolina Spinner," 1908. Gelatin silver print, 4 3/4 × 7 in. Milwaukee Art Museum, Gift of the Sheldon M. Barnett Family. M1973.83.

denounced Phillips and his colleagues as "muckrakers" who "raked the mud of society and never looked up." Partly due to Roosevelt's outburst, the muckraking vogue began to wane. But muckraking had demonstrated the potential for mobilizing public opinion on a national scale.

INTELLECTUAL TRENDS PROMOTING REFORM

On a deeper level than muckraking, early twentieth-century thinkers challenged several of the core ideas in American intellectual life. Their new theories of education, law, economics, and society provided effective tools for reformers. The emergent fields of the social sciences—sociology, psychology, anthropology, and economics—emphasized observation of how people actually lived and behaved in their communities. Progressive reformers linked the systematic analysis of society and the individual characteristic of these new fields of inquiry to the project of improving the material conditions of Americans. Significantly, many of these intellectual currents transcended national boundaries. American progressives engaged in running dialogues with European counterparts who also contended with crafting effective and rational responses to the needs of overcrowded cities, impoverished industrial

workers, and unresponsive political systems. Jane Addams's original inspiration for the Hull House settlement in Chicago had come when she visited Toynbee Hall in London. Housing reformers in Glasgow and Manchester, as well as workmen's compensation reformers in Berlin, and old age insurance experts in Copenhagen provided important international forums for progressives here and around the world. Despite their national differences, progressives around the world searched for new ways to reinforce social bonds in the modern era.

Sociologist Lester Frank Ward, in his pioneering work *Dynamic Sociology* (1883), offered an important critique of social Darwinism, the orthodox theory that attributed social inequality to natural selection and the "survival of the fittest." Ward argued that the conservative social theorists responsible for social Darwinism, such as Herbert Spencer and William Graham Sumner, had wrongly applied evolutionary theory to human affairs. They had confused organic evolution with social evolution. Nature's method was genetic: unplanned, involuntary, automatic, and mechanical. By contrast, civilization had been built on successful human intervention in the natural processes of organic evolution. "Every implement or utensil," Ward argued, "every mechanical device, every object of design, skill, and labor, every artificial thing that serves a human purpose, is a triumph of mind over the physical forces of nature in ceaseless and aimless competition."

Philosopher John Dewey criticized the excessively rigid and formal approach to education found in most American schools. In books such as *The School and Society* (1899) and *Democracy and Education* (1916), Dewey advocated developing what he called "creative intelligence" in students, which could then be put to use in improving society. Schools ought to be "embryonic communities," miniatures of society, where children were encouraged to participate actively in different types of experiences. By cultivating imagination and openness to new experiences, schools could develop creativity and the habits required for systematic inquiry. Dewey's belief that education was the "fundamental method of social progress and reform" inspired generations of progressive educators.

At the University of Wisconsin, John R. Commons founded the new field of industrial relations and organized a state industrial commission that became a model for other states. Working closely with Governor Robert M. La Follette, Commons and his students helped draft pioneering laws in worker compensation and public utility regulation. Another Wisconsin faculty member, economist Richard Ely, argued that the state was "an educational and ethical agency whose positive aim is an indispensable condition of human progress." Ely believed the state must intervene directly to help solve public problems. He rejected the doctrine of laissez-faire as merely "a tool in the hands of the greedy." Like Commons, Ely worked with

Wisconsin lawmakers to apply his expertise in economics to reforming the state's labor laws.

Progressive legal theorists began challenging the conservative view of constitutional law that had dominated American courts. Since the 1870s, the Supreme Court had interpreted the Fourteenth Amendment (1868) as a guarantee of broad rights for corporations. That amendment, which prevented states from depriving "any person of life, liberty, or property, without due process of law," had been designed to protect the civil rights of African Americans against violations by the states. But the Court, led by Justice Stephen J. Field, used the due process clause to strike down state laws regulating business and labor conditions. The Supreme Court and state courts had thus made the Fourteenth Amendment a bulwark for big business and a foe of social welfare measures.

The most important dissenter from this view was Oliver Wendell Holmes Jr. A scholar and Massachusetts judge, Holmes believed the law had to take into account changing social conditions. And courts should take care not to invalidate social legislation enacted democratically. After his appointment to the Supreme Court in 1902, Holmes wrote a number of notable dissents to conservative court decisions overturning progressive legislation. Criticizing the majority opinion in *Lochner* v. *New York* (1905), in which the Court struck down a state law setting a ten-hour day for bakers, Holmes insisted that the Constitution "is not intended to embody a particular theory."

Before the late 1930s, Holmes's pragmatic views of the law seldom convinced a majority of the Court. But his views influenced a generation of lawyers who began practicing what came to be called sociological jurisprudence. In *Muller* v. *Oregon* (1908), the Court upheld an Oregon law limiting the maximum hours for working women, finding that the liberty of contract "is not absolute." Noting that "woman's physical structure and the performance of maternal functions place her at a disadvantage," the Court found that "the physical well-being of woman becomes an object of public interest and care." Louis Brandeis, the state's attorney, amassed statistical, sociological, and economic data, rather than traditional legal arguments, to support his arguments. The "Brandeis Brief" became a common strategy for lawyers defending the constitutionality of progressive legislation.

THE FEMALE DOMINION

In the 1890s, the settlement house movement had begun to provide an alternative to traditional concepts of private charity and humanitarian reform. Settlement workers found they could not transform their neighborhoods without confronting a host of broad social questions: chronic poverty, overcrowded tenement houses, child labor, industrial accidents, public health. They soon discovered the need to engage the political and cultural life of the larger community. As on Henry Street, college-educated, middle-class women were a key vanguard in the crusade for social justice.

Jane Addams founded one of the first settlement houses, Hull House, in Chicago in 1889, after years of struggling to find work and a social identity equal to her talents. A member of one of the first generations of American women to attend college, Addams was a graduate of Rockford College. Many educated women were dissatisfied with the life choices conventionally available to them: early marriage or the traditional female professions of teaching, nursing, and library work. Settlement work provided an attractive alternative. Hull House was located in a run-down slum area of Chicago. It had a day nursery, a dispensary for medicines and medical advice, a boardinghouse, an art gallery, and a music school. Addams often spoke of the "subjective necessity" of settlement houses. By this she meant that they gave young, educated women a way to satisfy their powerful desire to connect with the real world. "There is nothing after disease, indigence and guilt," she wrote, "so fatal to life itself as the want of a proper outlet for active faculties."

Lillian Wald attracted a dedicated group of nurses, educators, and reformers to live at the Henry Street Settlement. By 1909, Henry Street had more than forty residents, supported by the donations of well-to-do New Yorkers. Wald and her allies convinced the New York Board of Health to assign a nurse to every public school in the city. They

A portrait of the young Jane Addams, probably taken around the time she founded Hull House in Chicago, in 1889.

OVERVIEW | Currents of Progressivism

	Key Figures	Issues
Local Communities	Jane Addams, Lillian Wald, Florence Kelley, Frederic C. Howe, Samuel Jones	• Improving health, education, welfare in urban immigrant neighborhoods • Child labor, eight-hour day • Celebrating immigrant cultures • Reforming urban politics • Municipal ownership/regulation of utilities
State	Robert M. La Follette, Hiram Johnson, Al Smith	• Limiting power of railroads, other corporations • Improving civil service • Direct democracy • Applying academic scholarship to human needs
National	James K. Vardaman, Hoke Smith, Theodore Roosevelt, Woodrow Wilson	• Disfranchisement of African Americans • Trust-busting • Conservation and western development • National regulation of corporate and financial excesses • Reform of national banking
Intellectual/Cultural	Jacob Riis, Lincoln Steffens, Ida Tarbell, Upton Sinclair, S. S. McClure John Dewey, Louis Brandeis, Edwin A. Ross	• Muckraking • Education reform • Sociological jurisprudence • Empowering "ethical elite"

lobbied the board of education to create the first school lunch programs. They persuaded the city to set up municipal milk stations to ensure the purity of milk. Henry Street also pioneered tuberculosis treatment and prevention. Its leaders became powerful advocates for playground construction, improved street cleaning, and tougher housing inspection. The settlement's Neighborhood Playhouse became an internationally acclaimed center for innovative theater, music, and dance. Lillian Wald became a national figure—an outspoken advocate of child labor legislation and woman suffrage and a vigorous opponent of American involvement in World War I. She offered Henry Street as a meeting place to the National Negro Conference in 1909, out of which emerged the National Association for the Advancement of Colored People.

Social reformer Florence Kelley helped direct the support of the settlement house movement behind groundbreaking state and federal labor legislation. Arriving at Hull House in 1891, Kelley found what she described as a "colony of efficient and intelligent women." In 1893, she wrote a report detailing the dismal conditions in sweatshops and the effects of long hours on the women and children who worked in them. This report became the basis for landmark legislation in Illinois that limited women to an eight-hour workday, barred children under fourteen from working, and abolished tenement labor. Illinois governor John Peter Altgeld appointed Kelley as chief inspector for the new law. In 1895, Kelley published *Hull House Maps and Papers*, the first scientific study of urban poverty in America. Moving to the Henry Street Settlement in 1898, Kelley served as general secretary of the new National Consumers' League. With Lillian Wald, she established the New York Child Labor Committee and pushed for the creation of the U.S. Children's Bureau, established in 1912. Its director, the first woman to head a federal bureau, was Julia Lathrop, another alumna of Hull House.

New female-dominated occupations, such as social work, public health nursing, and home economics, allowed women to combine professional aspirations with the older traditions of moral reform, especially those centered on child welfare. The new professionalism, in turn, sustained reform commitments and a female dominion that simultaneously expanded the social welfare function of the state and increased women's public authority and influence.

Kelley, Addams, Wald, Lathrop, and their circle consciously used their power as women to reshape politics in the progressive era. Electoral politics and the state were historically male preserves, but female social progressives turned their gender into an advantage. Activists like Kelley used their influence in civil society to create new state powers in the service of social justice. "Women's place is Home," wrote reformer Rheta Childe Dorr, "but Home is not contained within the four walls of an individual home. Home is the community."

PROGRESSIVE POLITICS IN CITIES AND STATES

Progressive reformers poured much of their zeal and energy into local political battles. In cities and states across the nation, progressive politicians became a powerful force, often balancing the practical need for partisan support with nonpartisan appeals to the larger citizenry. Although their motives and achievements were mixed, progressives were united in their attacks on corruption in government, the need to reign in corporate power, and calls for more activist city and state governments.

THE URBAN MACHINE

By the turn of the century, Democratic Party machines, usually dominated by first- and second-generation Irish, controlled the political life of most large American cities. The keys to machine strength were disciplined organization and the delivery of essential services to both immigrant communities and business elites. The successful machine politician viewed his work as a business, and he accumulated his capital by serving people who needed assistance. For most urban dwellers, the city was a place of economic and social insecurity. Recent immigrants in particular faced frequent unemployment, sickness, and discrimination. In exchange for votes, machine politicians offered their constituents a variety of services. These included municipal jobs in the police and fire departments, work at city construction sites, intervention with legal problems, and food and coal during hard times.

For those who did business with the city—construction companies, road builders, realtors—staying on the machine's good side was simply another business expense. In exchange for valuable franchises and city contracts, businessmen routinely bribed machine politicians and contributed liberally to their campaign funds. George Washington Plunkitt, a stalwart

of New York's Tammany Hall machine, good-naturedly defended what he called "honest graft": making money from inside information on public improvements. "It's just like lookin' ahead in Wall Street or in the coffee or cotton market. . . . I seen my opportunities and I took 'em."

The machines usually had close ties to organized prostitution and gambling, as well as more legitimate commercial entertainments. Many machine figures began as saloonkeepers, and liquor dealers and beer brewers provided important financial support for "the organization." Vaudeville and burlesque theater, boxing, horse racing, and professional baseball were other urban enterprises with economic and political links to machines. Entertainment and spectacle made up a central element in the machine political style as well. Constituents looked forward to the colorful torchlight parades, free summer picnics, and riverboat excursions regularly sponsored by the machines.

On New York City's Lower East Side, where the Henry Street Settlement was located, Timothy D. "Big Tim" Sullivan embodied the popular machine style. Big Tim, who had risen from desperate poverty, remained enormously popular with his constituents until his death

Timothy D. "Big Tim" Sullivan, the popular and influential Democratic Party machine boss of the Bowery and Lower East Side districts of New York City, ca. 1901.

in 1913. Critics charged that Sullivan controlled the city's gambling and made money from prostitution. But his real fortune came through his investments in vaudeville and the early movie business. Sullivan, whose district included the largest number of immigrants and transients in the city, provided shoe giveaways and free Christmas dinners to thousands every winter. To help pay for these and other charitable activities, he informally taxed the saloons, theaters, and restaurants in the district.

In the early twentieth century, to expand their base of support, political machines in the Northeast began concentrating more on passing welfare legislation beneficial to working-class and immigrant constituencies. In this way, machine politicians often allied themselves with progressive reformers in state legislatures. In New York, for example, Tammany Hall figures such as Robert Wagner, Al Smith, and Big Tim Sullivan worked with middle-class progressive groups to pass child labor laws, factory safety regulations, worker compensation plans, and other efforts to make government more responsive to social needs. As Jewish and Catholic immigrants expanded in number and proportion in the city population, urban machines also began to champion cultural pluralism, opposing prohibition and immigration restrictions and defending the contributions made by new ethnic groups in the cities.

PROGRESSIVES AND URBAN REFORM

Political progressivism originated in the cities. It was both a challenge to the power of machine politics and a response to deteriorating urban conditions. City governments, especially in the Northeast and industrial Midwest, seemed hardly capable of providing the basic services needed to sustain large populations. For example, an impure water supply left Pittsburgh with one of the world's highest rates of death from typhoid, dysentery, and cholera. Most New York City neighborhoods rarely enjoyed street cleaning, and playgrounds were nonexistent. "The challenge of the city," Cleveland progressive Frederic C. Howe said in 1906, "has become one of decent human existence."

Reformers placed much of the blame for urban ills on the machines and looked for ways to restructure city government. The "good government" movement, led by the National Municipal League, fought to make city management a nonpartisan, even nonpolitical, process by bringing the administrative techniques of large corporations to cities. Reformers revised city charters in favor of stronger mayoral power and expanded use of appointed administrators and career civil servants. They drew up blueprints for model charters, ordinances, and zoning plans designed by experts trained in public administration.

Business and professional elites became the biggest boosters of structural reforms in urban government. In the summer of 1900, a hurricane in the Gulf of Mexico unleashed a tidal wave on Galveston, Texas. To cope with this disaster, leading businessmen convinced the state legislature to replace the mayor-council government with a small board of commissioners. Each commissioner was elected at large, and each was responsible for a different city department. Under this plan, voters could more easily identify and hold accountable those responsible for city services. The city commission, enjoying both policymaking and administrative powers, proved very effective in rebuilding Galveston. By 1917, nearly 500 cities, including Houston, Oakland, Kansas City, Denver, and Buffalo, had adopted the commission form of government. Another approach, the city manager plan, gained popularity in small and midsized cities. In this system, a city council appointed a professional, nonpartisan city manager to handle the day-to-day operations of the community.

Progressive politicians who focused on the human problems of the industrial city championed a different kind of reform, one based on changing policies rather than the political structure. In Cleveland, for example, wealthy businessman Thomas L. Johnson served as mayor from 1901 to 1909. He emphasized both efficiency and social welfare. His popular program included lower streetcar fares, public baths, milk and meat inspection, and an expanded park and playground system.

STATEHOUSE PROGRESSIVES

On the state level progressives focused on two major reform themes that sometimes coexisted uneasily. On the one hand they looked to make politics more open and accessible by pushing through procedural reforms. The *direct primary*, for example, promised to take the selection of electoral candidates out of the smoke-filled backrooms of party bosses and into the hands of party voters. In 1902 Oregon was the first state to adopt two other reforms: the *initiative*, the popular power to initiate legislation, and the *referendum*, the right to a popular vote on proposed legislation. Several states also adopted a related reform, the "Australian," or secret ballot, which took the mechanics of ballot printing and distribution from the parties and made it the responsibility of the government. California and other states also established the *recall*: the power to remove elected officials from office. And in 1913 the states and Congress ratified the Seventeenth Amendment, shifting the selection of U.S. senators from the state legislatures to direct election by voters. On the other hand, progressive activists sought to remove some decisions from the electoral process entirely. They believed that judgments about railroad regulations, improving a city's sewer system, or establishing tax rates might best be made by informed, unbiased experts appointed to boards and commissions charged with setting policy. Many progressive states became political laboratories for testing both more democratic procedures and a greater reliance on professional expertise.

In Wisconsin, Republican dissident Robert M. La Follette forged a coalition of angry farmers, small businessmen, and workers with his fiery attacks on railroads and other large corporations. Leader of the progressive faction of the state Republicans, "Fighting Bob" won three terms as governor (1900–06), then served as a U.S. senator until his death in 1925. As governor, he pushed through tougher corporate tax rates, a direct primary, an improved civil service code, and a railroad commission designed to regulate freight charges. La Follette used faculty experts at the University of Wisconsin to help research and write his bills. Other states began copying the "Wisconsin Idea," the application of academic scholarship and theory to the needs of the people. In practice, La Follette's railroad commission accomplished far less than progressive rhetoric claimed. It essentially represented special interests—commercial farmers and businessmen seeking reduced shipping rates. Ordinary consumers did not see lower passenger fares or reduced food prices. And as commissioners began to realize, the national reach of the railroads limited the effectiveness of state regulation.

In New York Theodore Roosevelt won the governor's race in 1898, propelled by his fame as a Spanish-American War hero. Although supported by the Republican Party machine, Roosevelt embraced the progressive view that the people's interest ought to be above partisan politics, and he used his personal popularity with voters to assert independence from party leaders. As governor he held frequent press conferences to communicate more directly with voters and gain support for progressive legislation. Roosevelt's administration strengthened the state's civil service system, set wage and hour standards for state employees, raised teachers' salaries, and placed a franchise tax on corporations controlling public utilities. Roosevelt also championed progressive conservation measures by expanding New York's forest preserves and reforming the fish and game service, thus anticipating his strong support of environmental regulation as president.

Western progressives displayed the greatest enthusiasm for institutional political reform. But they also targeted railroads, mining and timber companies, and public utilities for reform. Large corporations such as Pacific Gas and Electric and the Southern Pacific Railroad had amassed enormous wealth and political influence. They were able to corrupt state legislatures and charge consumers exorbitant rates. An alliance between middle-class progressives and working-class voters reflected growing disillusionment with the ideology of individualism that had helped pave the way for the rise of the big corporation. In California, attorney Hiram Johnson won a 1910 progressive campaign for governor on the slogan "Kick the Southern Pacific Railroad out of Politics." In addition to winning political reforms, Johnson also put through laws regulating utilities and child labor, mandating an eight-hour day for working women, and providing a state-worker compensation plan.

In the South, the Populist tradition of the 1880s and 1890s had been based in part on a biracial politics of protest. Based mostly in New South towns and cities, and with growing strength among educated professionals, small businessmen, and women's benevolent societies, southern progressives organized to control both greedy corporations and "unruly" citizens. Citizen groups, city boards of trade, and newspapers pressed reluctant legislators to use state power to regulate big business. Between 1905 and 1909, nearly every southern state moved to regulate railroads by mandating lower passenger and freight rates.

Southern progressives also directed their energies at the related problems of child labor and educational reform. In 1900, at least one-quarter of all southern cotton mill workers were between the ages of ten and sixteen, and many worked over sixty hours per week. Led by reform-minded ministers Edgar Gardner Murphy and Alexander McKelway and drawing on the activism of white club women, reformers attacked child labor by focusing on the welfare of children and their mothers and emphasizing the degradation of "Anglo Saxons." In 1903, Alabama and North Carolina enacted the first state child labor laws, setting twelve as a minimum age for employment. But the laws were weakened by many exemptions and no provisions for enforcement, as lawmakers also heard the loud complaints from parents and mill owners who resented the efforts of reformers to limit their choices.

But southern progressivism was for white people only. Indeed, southern progressives believed that the disenfranchisement of black voters and the creation of a legally segregated public sphere were necessary preconditions for political and social reform. With African Americans removed from political life, white southern progressives argued, the direct primary system of nominating candidates would give white voters more influence. Between 1890 and 1910, southern states passed a welter of statutes specifying poll taxes, literacy tests, and property qualifications with the explicit goal of preventing voting by blacks. This systematic disenfranchisement of African American voters stripped black communities of any political power. To prevent the disenfranchisement of poor white voters under these laws, states established so-called understanding and grandfather clauses. Election officials had discretionary power to decide whether an illiterate person could understand and reasonably interpret the Constitution when read to him. Unqualified white men were also registered if they could show that their grandfathers had voted.

Southern progressives also supported the push toward a fully segregated public sphere. Between 1900 and 1910, southern states strengthened Jim Crow laws requiring separation of races in restaurants, streetcars, beaches, and theaters. Schools were separate but hardly equal. A 1916 Bureau of Education study found that per capita expenditures for education in southern states averaged $10.32 a year for white children and $2.89 for black children. And African American teachers received far lower salaries than their white counterparts. Black taxpayers, in effect, subsidized improved schools for whites, even as they saw their own children's educational opportunities deteriorate. The legacy of southern progressivism was thus closely linked to the strengthening of the legal and institutional guarantees of white supremacy.

Contradictions in the progressive approach to political reform were not limited to the South. Undermining party control of voting and elections may have also weakened politicians' incentives to get out the vote. Greater reliance on city commissions and other experts meant less in the way of promised favors for voters, which may have also made voters less interested in elections. Tightening up on residency requirements and voter registration rules in the cities cut into turnout in immigrant and ethnic neighborhoods. The effort to make politics more open, nonpartisan, and voter friendly also led, ironically, to a decline in voter participation and interest around the country. Whereas in the 1890s voter participation in national elections was routinely close to 90 percent, by World War I that figure had fallen to barely 60 percent, where it would stay for most of the rest of the century.

SOCIAL CONTROL AND ITS LIMITS

Many middle- and upper-class Protestant progressives feared that immigrants and large cities threatened the stability of American democracy. They worried that alien cultural practices were disrupting what they viewed as traditional American morality. Edward A. Ross's landmark work *Social Control* (1901), a book whose title became a key phrase in progressive thought, argued that society needed an "ethical elite" of citizens "who have at heart the general welfare and know what kinds of conduct will promote this welfare." Progressives often believed they had a mission to frame laws and regulations for the "benefit" of immigrants, industrial workers, and African Americans. These efforts at social control usually required some form of coercion. This was the moralistic and frequently xenophobic side of progressivism, and it provided a powerful source of support for the regulation of drinking, prostitution, leisure activities, and schooling. Organizations devoted to social control constituted other versions of reform communities. But these attempts at moral reform met with mixed success amid the extraordinary cultural and ethnic diversity of America's cities.

THE PROHIBITION MOVEMENT

During the last two decades of the nineteenth century, the Woman's Christian Temperance Union (WCTU) had grown into a powerful mass organization. The WCTU appealed especially to women angered by men who used alcohol and then abused their wives and children. It directed most of its work toward ending the production, sale, and consumption of alcohol. But local WCTU chapters put their energy into nontemperance activities as well, including homeless shelters, Sunday schools, prison reform, child nurseries, and woman suffrage. The WCTU thus provided women with a political forum in which they could fuse their traditional moral posture as guardians of the home with broader public concerns. By 1911, the WCTU, with a quarter million members, was the largest women's organization in American history.

Other temperance groups had a narrower focus. The Anti-Saloon League, founded in 1893, began by organizing local-option campaigns in which rural counties and small towns banned liquor within their geographical limits. It drew much of its financial support from local businessmen, who saw a link between closing a community's saloons and increasing the productivity of workers. The league was a one-issue pressure group that played effectively on anti-urban and anti-immigrant prejudice. League lobbyists hammered away at the close connections among saloon culture, liquor dealers, brewers, and big-city political machines.

The battle to ban alcohol revealed deep ethnic and cultural divides within America's urban communities. Opponents of alcohol were generally "pietists," who viewed the world from a position of moral absolutism. These included native-born, middle-class Protestants associated with evangelical churches, along with some old-stock Protestant immigrant denominations. Opponents of prohibition were generally "ritualists" with less arbitrary notions of personal morality. These were largely new-stock, working-class Catholic and Jewish immigrants, along with some Protestants, such as German Lutherans (see Communities in Conflict).

THE SOCIAL EVIL

Many of the same reformers who battled the saloon and drinking also engaged in efforts to eradicate prostitution. Crusades against "the social evil" had appeared at intervals throughout the nineteenth century, but they reached a new level of intensity between 1895 and 1920. In part, this new sense of urgency stemmed from the sheer growth of cities and the greater visibility of prostitution in red-light districts and neighborhoods. Antiprostitution campaigns epitomized the diverse makeup and mixed motives of so much progressive reform. Male business and civic leaders joined forces with feminists, social workers, and clergy to eradicate "commercialized vice."

Between 1908 and 1914, exposés of the "white slave traffic" became a national sensation. Dozens of books, articles, and motion pictures alleged an international conspiracy to seduce and sell girls into prostitution. Most of these materials exaggerated the practices they attacked. They also made foreigners, especially Jews and southern Europeans, scapegoats for the sexual anxieties of native-born whites. In 1910, Congress passed legislation that permitted the deportation of foreign-born prostitutes or any foreigner convicted of procuring or employing them. That same year, the Mann Act made it a federal offense to transport women across state lines for "immoral purposes."

Reformers had trouble believing that any woman would freely choose to be a prostitute; such a choice was antithetical to conventional notions of female purity and sexuality. But for wage-earning women, prostitution was a rational choice in a world of limited opportunities. Maimie Pinzer, a prostitute, summed up her feelings in a letter to a wealthy female reformer: "I don't propose to get up at 6:30 to be at work at 8 and work in a close, stuffy room with people I despise, until dark, for $6 or $7 a week! When I could, just by phoning, spend an afternoon with some congenial person and in the end have more than a week's work could pay me." The antivice crusades succeeded in closing down many urban red-light districts and larger brothels, but these were replaced by the streetwalker and call girl, who were more vulnerable to harassment and control by policemen and pimps. Rather than eliminating prostitution, reform efforts transformed the organization of the sex trade.

THE REDEMPTION OF LEISURE

Progressives faced a thorny issue in the growing popularity of commercial entertainment. For large numbers of working-class adults and children, leisure meant time and money spent at vaudeville and burlesque theaters, amusement parks, dance halls, and motion picture houses. These competed with municipal parks, libraries, museums, YMCAs, and school recreation centers. For many cultural traditionalists, the flood of new urban commercial amusements posed a grave threat. As with prostitution, urban progressives sponsored a host of recreation and amusement surveys detailing the situation in their individual cities. One distinctively progressive response was the Playgrounds Movement. Los Angeles created the nation's first urban Department of Playgrounds in 1904, and proponents nationwide saw municipal playgrounds as a way to offer free, healthy, outdoor recreation for city kids.

"Commercialized leisure," warned Frederic C. Howe in 1914, "must be controlled by the community, if it is to become an agency of civilization rather than the reverse." By 1908, movies had become the most popular form of cheap entertainment in America. One survey estimated that 11,500 movie theaters attracted 5 million patrons each day. For five or ten cents, "nickelodeon" theaters offered programs that might include a slapstick comedy, a western, a travelogue, and a melodrama. Early movies were most popular in the tenement and immigrant districts of big cities and with children. As the films themselves became more sophisticated and as "movie palaces" began to replace cheap storefront theaters, the new medium attracted a large middle-class clientele as well.

Progressive reformers seized the chance to help regulate the new medium as a way of improving the commercial recreation of the urban poor. Movies held out the promise of an alternative to the older entertainment traditions, such as concert saloons and burlesque theater, that had been closely allied with machine politics and the vice economy. In 1909, New York City movie producers and exhibitors joined with the reform-minded People's Institute to establish the voluntary National Board of Censorship (NBC). Movie entrepreneurs, most of whom were themselves immigrants, sought to shed the stigma of the slums, attract more middle-class patronage, and increase profits. A revolving group of civic activists reviewed new movies, passing them, suggesting changes, or condemning them. Local censoring committees all over the nation subscribed to the board's weekly bulletin. They aimed at achieving what John Collier of the NBC called "the redemption of leisure." By 1914, the NBC was reviewing 95 percent of the nation's film output.

STANDARDIZING EDUCATION

Along with reading, writing, and mathematics, schools inculcated patriotism, piety, and respect for authority. Progressive educators looked to the public school primarily as an agent of "Americanization." Elwood Cubberley, a leading educational reformer, expressed the view that schools could be the vehicle by which immigrant children could break free of the parochial ethnic neighborhood. "Our task," he argued in *Changing Conceptions of Education* (1909), "is to break up these groups or settlements, to assimilate and amalgamate these people as a part of our American race, and to implant in their children, so far as can be done, the Anglo-Saxon conception of righteousness, law and order, and popular government."

The most important educational trends in these years were the expansion and bureaucratization of the nation's public school systems. In most cities, centralization served to consolidate the power of older urban elites who felt threatened by the large influx of immigrants. Children began school earlier and stayed there longer. Kindergartens spread rapidly in large cities. They presented, as one writer put it in 1903, "the earliest opportunity to catch the little Russian, the little Italian, the little German, Pole, Syrian, and the rest and begin to make good American citizens of them." By 1918, every state had some form of compulsory school attendance. High schools also multiplied, extending the school's influence beyond the traditional grammar school curriculum.

Debating Prohibition in Progressive-Era Ohio

Should the manufacture and sale of alcoholic beverages be made illegal? The State of Ohio had long been one of the most intense battlegrounds over this controversial issue. The Women's Christian Temperance Union had been founded in Cleveland in 1874, and the Anti-Saloon League was organized in Oberlin in 1893. Both groups quickly gained a national following. In 1909 the League established new national headquarters in Westerville, Ohio, a small city that strongly supported prohibition. But Ohio also had a large and well-organized brewery industry. Beer was by far the most popular alcoholic beverage among Americans, and the brewery industry was the most profitable sector of the alcohol business. German Americans dominated among brewers and maintained close ties to the large German American communities in cities like Cincinnati.

In 1908 the Anti-Saloon League and its allies succeeded in getting a law passed by the Ohio legislature granting counties a "local option" to ban the alcohol trade. As the "drys" set their sights on a statewide prohibition law, the brewers, working closely with German American community groups, organized a counterattack that featured lobbyists and a sophisticated propaganda campaign to mobilize the influence and votes of "wets." The brewers also tried to reform their industry by reducing the number of saloons and ensuring that saloonkeepers were citizens of "good character." With Ohioans closely divided between "wet" and "dry" views, both sides put an enormous amount of money into campaigns aimed at influencing public opinion. Well-financed interest group campaigns of this type were a distinctively new feature of progressive era politics. After losing statewide referendums in 1915 and 1917, the Anti-Saloon League spearheaded a narrow victory in 1918, finally achieving statewide prohibition in Ohio. National prohibition would follow in 1920 with the ratification of the Eighteenth Amendment to the Constitution.

Percy Andreae was a leading lobbyist for the brewery industry. James A. White was the head of the Ohio Anti-Saloon League and organizer of the Ohio Dry Federation, an umbrella group of prohibitionist forces. Here are their arguments.

What arguments does Andreae use to undermine the prohibitionist appeal, particularly with respect to religious belief? How does the Ohio Dry Federation make its case in this ad? Why do you think it emphasized this strategy over other prohibitionist objections to the alcohol trade?

Percy Andreae: "Behind the Mask of Prohibition" (1915)

I have met many active prohibitionists, both in this and in other countries, all of them thoroughly in earnest. In some instances I have found that their allegiance to the cause of prohibition took its origin in the fact that some near relative or friend had succumbed to over-indulgence in liquor. In one or two cases the man himself had been a victim of this weakness, and had come to the conclusion, firstly that every one else was constituted as he was, and, therefore, liable to the same danger; and secondly, that unless every one were prevented from drinking, he would not be secure from the temptation to do so himself.

This is one class of prohibitionists. The other, and by far the larger class, is made up of religious zealots, to whom prohibition is a word having at bottom a far wider application than that which is generally attributed to it. The liquor question, if there really is such a question per se, is merely put forth by them as a means to an end, an incidental factor in a fight which has for its object the supremacy of a certain form of religious faith. The belief of many of these people is that the Creator frowns upon enjoyment of any and every kind, and that he has merely endowed us with certain desires and capacities for pleasure in order to give us an opportunity to please Him by resisting them. They are, of course, perfectly entitled to this belief, though some of us may consider it eccentric and somewhat in the nature of a libel on the Almighty. But are they privileged to force that belief on all their fellow beings? That, in substance, is the question that is involved in the present-day prohibition movement. . . .

If there is any one who doubts the truth of this statement, let me put this to him: How many Roman Catholics are prohibitionists? How many Jews, the most temperate race on earth, are to be found in the ranks of prohibition? Or Lutherans? Or German Protestants generally? What is the proportion of Episcopalians to that of Methodists, Baptists and Presbyterians, and the like, in the active prohibition army? The answers to these questions will, I venture to say, prove conclusively the assertion that the fight for prohibition is synonymous with the fight of a certain religious sect, or group of religious sects, for the supremacy of its ideas.

"The liquor question . . . is merely put forth . . . as a means to an end, an incidental factor in a fight which has for its object the supremacy of a certain form of religious faith."

"Take away the smooth phrases and cunning twists of the Liquor Traffic's appeal For Permission to continue its career—get right down to naked truth and you will see that the liquor traffic is asking fathers of Ohio to 'give me your boys.'"

Temperance and self-control are convertible terms. Prohibition, or that which it implies, is the direct negation of the term self-control. In order to save the small percentage of men who are too weak to resist their animal desires, it aims to put chains on every man, the weak and the strong alike. And if this is proper in one respect, why not in all respects? Yet, what would one think of a proposition to keep all men locked up because a certain number have a propensity to steal? Theoretically, perhaps, all crime or vice could be stopped by chaining us all up as we chain up a wild animal, and only allowing us to take exercise under proper supervision and control. But while such a measure would check crime, it would not eliminate the criminal. . . .

Prohibition, though it must cause, and is already causing, incalculable damage, may never succeed in this country; but that which is behind it, as the catapults and the cannon were behind the battering rams in the battles of olden days, is certain to succeed unless timely measures of prevention are resorted to; and if it does succeed, we shall witness the enthronement of a monarch in this land of liberty compared with whose autocracy the autocracy of the Russian Czar is a mere trifle. The name of this monarch is Religious Intolerance.

SOURCE: Percy Andreae, *The Prohibition Movement in Its Broader Bearings upon Our Social, Commercial, and Religious Liberties* (1915); http://www.druglibrary.org/schaffer/alcohol.

Prohibitionist James A. White: "Give Me Your Boy" (1918)

Take away the "camouflage" with which the Liquor Traffic tries to disguise itself and [a] sinister figure . . . stands revealed.

Take away the smooth phrases and cunning twists of the Liquor Traffic's appeal For Permission to continue its career—get right down to naked truth and you will see that the liquor traffic is asking fathers of Ohio to "give me your boys."

WHAT WILL THE SALOON DO FOR THE BOYS?

Is its purpose to inspire them with greater ambitions; to teach them clean morals, to avoid bad habits, to become better men and citizens, better husbands and fathers?

You know the saloon does nothing FOR boys, but appalling harm TO them.

Its prosperity depends on the number of VICTIMS it entraps.

Men in the liquor traffic are not blind to its evils.

Many distillers will not allow THEIR OWN SON to drink intoxicants; many brewers forbid the use of intoxicants to their sons; many saloonists don't drink the stuff they sell; they won't hire drinking bartenders and they bar their sons from the saloons.

Still, they ask you to give YOUR son for the sake of the money they can make out of him. They ask you to approve temptation of your son to become a drunkard.

They ask you to vote MAKE DRUNKARDS out of thousands of Ohio's boys.

Are you with them? Are YOU for the Booze Huns or for the boys?

There can be no neutrality in this fight. Failure to vote "yes" on prohibition on November 5th is silent approval of the liquor traffic's record and misdeeds.

You must be either for the BEST INTERESTS of your state, your nation and humanity—or you must be for the ENEMY liquor traffic, which works AGAINST the best interest of the state, the nation and humanity.

Vote "Yes" for Prohibition November 5th

SOURCE: Ohio Dry Federation, 1918, http://ehistory.osu.edu/osu/sources.

Movies, by John Sloan, 1913, the most talented artist among the so-called Ashcan realist school of painting. Active in socialist and bohemian circles, Sloan served as art editor for *The Masses* magazine for several years. His work celebrated the vitality and diversity of urban working-class life and leisure, including the new commercial culture represented by the motion picture.

SOURCE: John Sloan, "Movies," 1913. Oil painting. The Toledo Museum of Art.

In 1890, only 4 percent of the nation's youth between fourteen and seventeen were enrolled in school; by 1930, the figure was 47 percent.

High schools reflected a growing belief that schools should be comprehensive, multifunctional institutions. In 1918, the National Education Association offered a report defining Cardinal Principles of Secondary Education. These included instruction in health, family life, citizenship, and ethical character. Academic programs prepared a small number of students for college. Vocational programs trained boys and girls for a niche in the new industrial order. Boys took shop courses in metal trades, carpentry, and machine tools. Girls learned typing,

bookkeeping, sewing, cooking, and home economics. The Smith-Hughes Act of 1917 provided federal grants to support these programs and set up a Federal Board for Vocational Education.

CHALLENGES TO PROGRESSIVISM

While most progressive reformers had roots in Protestantism and the middle-class professions, other Americans vigorously challenged their political vision. Organized workers often invoked progressive rhetoric and ideals but for quite different, sometimes radical, ends. The Industrial Revolution, which had begun transforming American life and labor in the nineteenth century, reached maturity in the early twentieth. In 1900, out of a total labor force of 28.5 million, 16 million people worked at industrial occupations and 11 million on farms. By 1920, in a labor force of nearly 42 million, almost 29 million were in industry, but farm labor had declined to 10.4 million. The world of the industrial worker included large manufacturing towns in New England; barren mining settlements in the West; primitive lumber and turpentine camps in the South; steelmaking and coal-mining cities in Pennsylvania and Ohio; and densely packed immigrant ghettos from New York to San Francisco, where workers toiled in garment-trade sweatshops.

All these industrial workers shared the need to sell their labor for wages in order to survive. At the same time, differences in skill, ethnicity, and race proved powerful barriers to efforts at organizing trade unions that could bargain for improved wages and working conditions. So, too, did the economic and political power of the large corporations that dominated much of American industry. Yet there were also small, closely knit groups of skilled workers, such as printers and brewers, who exercised real control over their lives and labors. And these years saw many labor struggles that created effective trade unions or laid the groundwork for others. Industrial workers also became a force in local and national politics, adding a chorus of insistent voices to the calls for social justice.

THE NEW GLOBAL IMMIGRATION

On the eve of World War I, close to 60 percent of the industrial labor force was foreign-born. Most of these workers were among the roughly 9 million new immigrants from southern and eastern Europe who arrived in the United States between 1900 and 1914. In the nineteenth century, much of the overseas migration had come from the industrial districts of northern and western Europe. English, Welsh, and German artisans had brought with them skills critical for emerging industries such as steelmaking and coal mining. Unlike their predecessors, nearly all the new Italian, Polish, Hungarian, Jewish, and Greek immigrants lacked industrial skills. They thus entered the bottom ranks of factories, mines, mills, and sweatshops.

Newly landed European immigrant families on the dock at Ellis Island in New York harbor, 1900.
Originally a black-and-white photograph, this image was later color tinted for reproduction as a postcard or book illustration.

These new immigrants had been driven from their European farms and towns by several forces, including the undermining of subsistence farming by commercial agriculture; a falling death rate that brought a shortage of land; and religious and political persecution. American corporations also sent agents to recruit cheap labor. Except for Jewish immigrants, a majority of whom fled virulent anti-Semitism in Russia and Russian Poland, most newcomers planned on earning a stake and then returning home. Hard times in America forced many back to Europe. In the depression year of 1908, for example, more Austro-Hungarians and Italians left than entered the United States (see Map 21.1).

The decision to migrate usually occurred through social networks—people linked by kinship, personal acquaintance, and work experience. These "chains," extending from places of origin to specific destinations in the United States, helped migrants cope with the considerable risks entailed by the long and difficult journey. A study conducted by the U.S. Immigration Commission in 1909 found that about 60 percent of the new immigrants had their passage arranged by immigrants already in America.

Immigrant communities used ethnicity as a collective resource for gaining employment in factories, mills, and mines. One Polish steelworker recalled how the process operated in the Pittsburgh mills: "Now if a Russian got his job in a shear department, he's looking for a buddy, a Russian buddy. He's not going to look for a Croatian buddy. And if he sees the boss looking for a man he says, 'Look, I have a good man,' and he's picking out his friends. A Ukrainian department, a Russian department, a Polish department. And it was a beautiful thing in a way." Such specialization of work by ethnic origin was quite common throughout America's industrial communities.

The low-paid, backbreaking work in basic industry became nearly the exclusive preserve of the new immigrants. In 1907, of the 14,359 common laborers employed at Pittsburgh's U.S. Steel mills, 11,694 were eastern Europeans. For twelve-hour days and seven-day weeks with two-thirds of these workers made less than $12.50 a week, with one-third less than $10.00. This was far less than the $15.00 that the Pittsburgh Associated Charities had estimated as the minimum for providing necessities for a

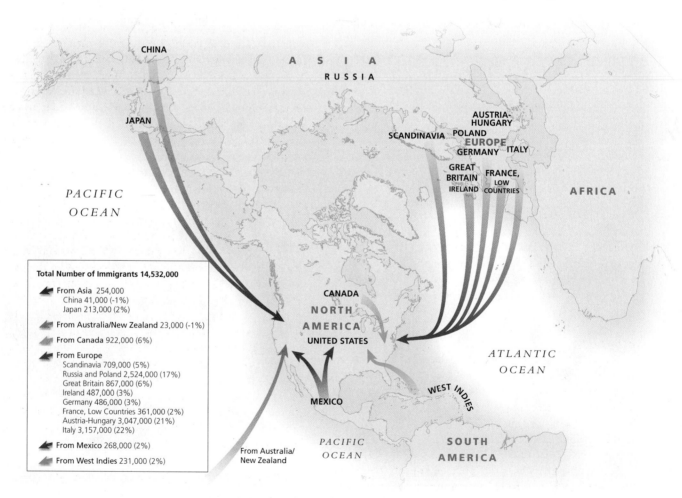

Total Number of Immigrants 14,532,000

From Asia 254,000
  China 41,000 (-1%)
  Japan 213,000 (2%)

From Australia/New Zealand 23,000 (-1%)

From Canada 922,000 (6%)

From Europe
  Scandinavia 709,000 (5%)
  Russia and Poland 2,524,000 (17%)
  Great Britain 867,000 (6%)
  Ireland 487,000 (3%)
  Germany 486,000 (3%)
  France, Low Countries 361,000 (2%)
  Austria-Hungary 3,047,000 (21%)
  Italy 3,157,000 (22%)

From Mexico 268,000 (2%)

From West Indies 231,000 (2%)

MAP 21.1 Immigration to the United States, 1901–20

family of five. Small wonder that the new immigration was disproportionately male. One-third of the immigrant steelworkers were single, and among married men who had been in the country less than five years, about two-thirds reported that their wives were still in Europe. Workers with families generally supplemented their incomes by taking in single men as boarders.

Not all of the new immigrants came from Europe, as hemispheric migration increased sharply as well. Over 300,000 French Canadians arrived in the United States between 1900 and 1930, settling mostly in New England. But the maturing continental railroad system had widened the choice of destinations to communities in upstate New York and Detroit, which had the largest number of French Canadian migrants outside of New England. The pull of jobs in New England's textile industry, along with its physical proximity, attracted male farmers and laborers unable to make a living in the rural districts of Quebec. Roughly one-third of female migrants were domestic servants looking for the higher pay and greater independence associated with factory labor. The significant French Canadian presence in communities such as Lowell, Holyoke, Manchester, Nashua, and Waterville often made them the largest single ethnic group. By 1918, for example, one-quarter of the Fall River, Massachusetts, population of 28,000 was French Canadian. French-language churches, newspapers, private schools, and mutual benefit societies reinforced the distinctive cultural milieu, and the presence of kin or fellow villagers facilitated the arrival of largely rural migrants into these new, highly industrialized, and urbanized settings.

Mexican immigration also grew in these years, providing a critical source of labor for the West's farms, railroads, and mines. Between 1900 and 1914, the number of people of Mexican descent living and working in the United States tripled, from roughly 100,000 to 300,000. Economic and political crises spurred tens of thousands of Mexico's rural and urban poor to emigrate north. Large numbers of seasonal agricultural workers regularly came up from Mexico to work in the expanding sugar beet industry and then returned. But a number of substantial resident Mexican communities also emerged in the early twentieth century.

Throughout Texas, California, New Mexico, Arizona, and Colorado, western cities developed *barrios*, distinct communities of Mexicans. Mexican immigrants attracted by jobs in the smelting industry made El Paso the most thoroughly Mexican city in the United States. In San Antonio, Mexicans worked at shelling pecans, becoming perhaps the most underpaid and exploited group of workers in the country. By 1910, San Antonio contained the largest number of Mexican immigrants of any city. In southern California, labor agents for railroads recruited Mexicans to work on building new interurban lines around Los Angeles.

Between 1898 and 1907, more than 80,000 Japanese entered the United States. The vast majority were young men working as contract laborers in the West, mainly in California. American law prevented Japanese immigrants (the *Issei*) from obtaining American citizenship because they were not white. This legal discrimination, along with informal exclusion from many occupations, forced the Japanese to create niches for themselves within local economies. Most Japanese settled near Los Angeles, where they established small communities centered around fishing, truck farming, and the flower and nursery business. In 1920, Japanese farmers produced 10 percent of the dollar volume of California agriculture on 1 percent of the farm acreage. By 1930, over 35,000 *Issei* and their children (the *Nisei*) lived in Los Angeles.

URBAN GHETTOS

In large cities, new immigrant communities took the form of densely packed ghettos. By 1920, immigrants and their children constituted almost 60 percent of the population of cities over 100,000. They were an even larger percentage in major industrial centers such as Chicago, Pittsburgh, Philadelphia, and New York. The sheer size and dynamism of these cities made the immigrant experience more complex than in smaller cities and more isolated communities. Workers in the urban garment trades toiled for low wages and suffered layoffs, unemployment, and poor health. But conditions in the small, labor-intensive shops of the clothing industry differed significantly from those in the large-scale, capital-intensive industries like steel.

New York City had become the center of both Jewish immigration and America's huge ready-to-wear clothing industry. The city's Jewish population was 1.4 million in 1915, almost 30 percent of its inhabitants. In small factories, lofts, and tenement apartments some 200,000 people, most of them Jews, some of them Italians, worked in the clothing trades. Most of the industry operated on the grueling piece-rate, or task, system, in which manufacturers and subcontractors paid individuals or teams of workers to complete a certain quota of labor within a specific time.

The garment industry was highly seasonal. A typical workweek was sixty hours with seventy common during the busy season. But there were long stretches of unemployment in slack times. Often forced to work in cramped, dirty, and badly lit rooms, garment workers strained under a system in which time equaled money. Morris Rosenfeld, a presser of men's clothing who wrote Yiddish poetry, captured the feeling:

> The tick of the clock is the boss in his anger
> The face of the clock has the eye of a foe
> The clock—I shudder—Dost hear how it draws me?
> It calls me "Machine" and it cries to me "Sew!"

In November 1909, two New York garment manufacturers responded to strikes by unskilled women workers by hiring thugs and prostitutes to beat up pickets. The strikers won the support of the Women's Trade Union League, a group of sympathetic female reformers that included Lillian Wald, Mary Dreier, and prominent society figures. The Uprising of the 20,000, as it became known, swept through the city's garment district. The strikers demanded union recognition, better wages, and safer and more sanitary conditions. They drew support from thousands of suffragists, trade unionists, and sympathetic middle-class women as well. Hundreds of strikers were arrested, and many were beaten by police. After three cold months on the picket line, the strikers returned to work without union recognition. But the International Ladies Garment Workers Union (ILGWU), founded in 1900, did gain strength and negotiated contracts with some of the city's shirtwaist makers. The strike was an important breakthrough in the drive to organize unskilled workers into industrial unions. It opened the doors to women's involvement in the labor movement and created new leaders, such as Clara Lemlich, Pauline Newman, and Rose Schneiderman.

On March 25, 1911, the issues raised by the strike took on new urgency when a fire raced through three floors of the Triangle Shirtwaist Company. As the flames spread, workers found themselves trapped by exit doors that had been locked from the outside. Fire escapes were too narrow and too weak to withstand the heat. Within half an hour, 146 people, mostly young Jewish women, had been killed by smoke or had leaped to their deaths. In the bitter aftermath, women progressives led by Florence Kelley and Frances Perkins of the National Consumers' League joined with Tammany Hall leaders Al Smith, Robert Wagner, and Big Tim Sullivan to create a New York State Factory Investigation Commission. Under Perkins's vigorous leadership, the commission conducted an unprecedented round of public hearings and on-site inspections, leading to a series of state laws that dramatically improved safety conditions and limited the hours for working women and children.

COMPANY TOWNS

Immigrant industrial workers and their families often established their communities in a company town, where a single large corporation was dominant. Cities such as Lawrence, Massachusetts; Gary, Indiana; and Butte, Montana, revolved around the industrial enterprises of Pacific Woolen, U.S. Steel, and Anaconda Copper. Workers had little or no influence over the economic and political institutions of these cities. In the more isolated company towns, residents often had no alternative but to buy their food, clothing, and supplies at company stores, usually for exorbitantly high prices. But they did maintain some community control in other ways. Family and kin networks, ethnic lodges, saloons, benefit societies, churches and synagogues, and musical groups affirmed traditional forms of community in a setting governed by individualism and private capital.

On the job, modern machinery and industrial discipline meant high rates of injury and death. In Gary, non-English-speaking immigrant steelworkers suffered twice the accident rate of English-speaking employees, who could better understand safety instructions and warnings. A 1910 study of work accidents revealed that nearly a fourth of all new steelworkers were killed or injured each year. Mutual aid associations, organized around ethnic groups, offered some protection through cheap insurance and death benefits.

In steel and coal towns, women not only maintained the household and raised the children, but they also boosted the family income by taking in boarders, sewing, and laundry. Many women also tended gardens and raised chickens, rabbits, and goats. Their produce and income helped reduce dependence on the company store. Working class women felt the burdens of housework more heavily than their middle-class sisters. Pump water, indoor plumbing, and sewage disposal were often available only on a pay-as-you-go basis. The daily drudgery endured by working-class women far outlasted the "man-killing" shift worked by the husband. Many women struggled with the effects of their husbands' excessive drinking and faced early widowhood.

New York City police set up this makeshift morgue to help identify victims of the disastrous Triangle Shirtwaist Company fire, March 25, 1911. Unable to open the locked doors of the sweatshop and desperate to escape from smoke and flames, many of the 146 who died had leaped eight stories to their death.

The adjustment for immigrant workers was not so much a process of assimilation as adaptation and resistance. Work habits and Old World cultural traditions did not always mesh with factory discipline or Taylor's "scientific management." A Polish wedding celebration might last three or four days. A drinking bout following a Sunday funeral might cause workers to celebrate "St. Monday" and not show up for work. Most immigrants were far more concerned with job security than with upward mobility. As new immigrants became less transient and more permanently settled in company towns, they increased their involvement in local politics and union activity.

The power of large corporations in the life of company towns was most evident among the mining communities of the West, as was violent labor conflict. The Colorado Fuel and Iron Company (CFI) employed roughly half of the 8,000 coal miners who labored in that state's mines. In mining towns such as Ludlow and Trinidad, the CFI thoroughly dominated the lives of miners and their families. "The miner," one union official observed, "is in this land owned by the corporation that owns the homes, that owns the boarding houses, that owns every single thing there is there . . . not only the mines, but all the grounds, all the buildings, all the places of recreation, as well as the school and church buildings." By the early twentieth century, new immigrants, such as Italians, Greeks, Slavs, and Mexicans, composed a majority of the population in these western mining communities.

In September 1913, the United Mine Workers led a strike in the Colorado coalfields, calling for improved safety, higher wages, and recognition of the union. Thousands of miners' families moved out of company housing and into makeshift tent colonies provided by the union. In October, Governor Elias Ammons ordered the Colorado National Guard into the tense strike region to keep order. The troops, supposedly neutral, proceeded to ally themselves with the mine operators. By spring, the strike had bankrupted the state, forcing the governor to remove most of the troops. The coal companies then brought in large numbers of private mine guards who were extremely hostile toward the strikers. On April 20, 1914, a combination of guardsmen and private guards surrounded the largest of the tent colonies at Ludlow, where more than a thousand mine families lived. A shot rang out (each side accused the other of firing), and a pitched battle ensued that lasted until the poorly armed miners ran out of ammunition. At dusk, the troops burned the tent village to the ground, routing the families and killing fourteen, eleven of them children. Enraged strikers attacked mines throughout southern Colorado in an armed rebellion that lasted ten days, until President Woodrow Wilson ordered the U.S. Army into the region. News of the Ludlow Massacre shocked millions and aroused widespread protests and demonstrations against the policies of Colorado Fuel and Iron and its owner, John D. Rockefeller Jr.

THE AFL: "UNIONS, PURE AND SIMPLE"

Following the depression of the 1890s, the American Federation of Labor (AFL) emerged as the strongest and most stable organization of workers. Samuel Gompers's strategy of recruiting skilled labor into unions organized by craft had paid off. Union membership climbed from under 500,000 in 1897 to 1.7 million by 1904. Most of this growth took place in AFL affiliates in coal mining, the building trades, transportation, and machine shops. The national unions—the United Mine Workers of America, the Brotherhood of Carpenters and Joiners, the International Association of Machinists—represented workers of specific occupations in collective bargaining. Trade autonomy and exclusive jurisdiction were the ruling principles within the AFL.

But the strength of craft organization also gave rise to weakness. In 1905, Gompers told a union gathering in Minneapolis that "caucasians" would not "let their standard of living be destroyed by negroes, Chinamen, Japs, or any others." Those "others" included the new immigrants from eastern and southern Europe, men and women, who labored in the steel mills and garment trades. Each trade looked mainly to the welfare of its own. Many explicitly barred women and African Americans from membership. There were some important exceptions. The United Mine Workers of America (UMWA) followed a more inclusive policy, recruiting both skilled underground pitmen and the unskilled aboveground workers. The UMWA even tried to recruit strikebreakers brought in by coal operators. With 260,000 members in 1904, the UMWA became the largest AFL affiliate.

AFL unions had a difficult time holding on to their gains. Economic slumps, technological changes, and aggressive counterattacks by employer organizations could be devastating. Trade associations using management-controlled efficiency drives fought union efforts to regulate output and shop practices. The National Association of Manufacturers (NAM), a group of smaller industrialists founded in 1903, launched an "open shop" campaign to eradicate unions altogether. "Open shop" was simply a new name for a workplace where unions were not allowed. Unfriendly judicial decisions also hurt organizing efforts. Not until the 1930s and New Deal legislation would unions be able to count on legislative and legal protections for collective bargaining and the right to strike.

THE IWW: "ONE BIG UNION"

Some workers developed more radical visions of labor organizing. In the harsh and isolated company towns of Idaho, Montana, and Colorado, miners suffered from low wages, poor food, and primitive sanitation, as well as injuries and death from frequent cave-ins and explosions. The Western Federation of Miners (WFM) had gained strength in the metal mining regions of the West by leading several strikes marred by violence. In 1899, during a strike in the silver mining district of Coeur d'Alene, Idaho, the Bunker Hill and Sullivan Mining Company had enraged the miners by hiring armed detectives and firing all union members. Desperate miners retaliated by destroying a company mill with dynamite. Idaho's governor declared martial law and obtained federal troops to enforce it. In a pattern that would become familiar in western labor relations, the soldiers served as strikebreakers, rounding up hundreds of miners and imprisoning them for months in makeshift bullpens.

In response to the brutal realities of labor organizing in the West, most WFM leaders embraced socialism and industrial unionism. In 1905, leaders of the WFM, the Socialist Party, and various radical groups gathered in Chicago to found the Industrial Workers of the World (IWW). The IWW charter proclaimed bluntly, "The working class and the employing class have nothing in common. . . . Between these two classes a struggle must go on until the workers of the world unite as a class, take possession of the earth and the machinery of production, and abolish the wage system."

William D. "Big Bill" Haywood, an imposing, one-eyed, hard-rock miner, emerged as the most influential and flamboyant spokesman for the IWW, or Wobblies, as they were called. Haywood, a charismatic speaker and effective organizer, regularly denounced the AFL for its conservative emphasis on organizing skilled workers by trade. He insisted that the IWW would exclude no one from its ranks. The Wobblies concentrated their efforts on miners, lumberjacks, sailors, "harvest stiffs," and other casual laborers.

The IWW briefly became a force among eastern industrial workers, tapping the rage and growing militance of the immigrants and unskilled. In 1909, an IWW-led steel strike at McKees Rocks, Pennsylvania, challenged the power of U.S. Steel. In the 1912 "Bread and Roses" strike in Lawrence, Massachusetts, IWW organizers turned a spontaneous walkout of textile workers into a successful struggle for union recognition. Wobbly leaders such as Haywood, Elizabeth Gurley Flynn, and Joseph Ettor used class-conscious rhetoric and multilingual appeals to forge unity among the ethnically diverse Lawrence workforce of 25,000.

The IWW failed to establish permanent organizations in the eastern cities, but it remained a force in the lumber camps, mines, and wheat fields of the West. In spite of its militant rhetoric, the IWW concerned itself with practical gains. "The final aim is revolution," said one Wobbly organizer, "but for the present let's see if we can get a bed to sleep in, water enough to take a bath in and decent food to eat." But when the United States entered World War I, the Justice Department used the IWW's anticapitalist rhetoric and antiwar stance to crush it.

REBELS IN BOHEMIA

During the 1910s, a small but influential community of painters, journalists, poets, social workers, lawyers, and political activists coalesced in the New York City neighborhood of Greenwich Village. These cultural radicals, nearly all of middle class background and hailing from provincial American towns, shared a deep sympathy toward the struggles of labor, a passion for modern art, and an openness to socialism and anarchism. But unlike most progressives, especially those from small towns and the nation's hinterlands, the "Village bohemians," particularly the women among them, challenged accepted middle-class morality and assumptions. They rejected the double standard of Victorian sexual morality, challenged traditional marriage and sex roles, advocated birth control, and experimented with homosexual relations. They became a powerful national symbol for rebellion and the merger of political and cultural radicalism.

The term "bohemian" referred to anyone who had artistic or intellectual aspirations and who lived with disregard for conventional rules of behavior. Other American cities, notably Chicago at the turn of the century, had supported bohemian communities. But the Village scene was unique, if fleeting. The neighborhood offered cheap rents, studio space, and good ethnic restaurants, and it was close to the exciting political and labor activism of Manhattan's Lower East Side. The worldview of the Village's bohemian community found expression in *The Masses*, a monthly magazine founded in 1911 by socialist critic Max Eastman, who was also its editor. "The broad purpose of *The Masses*," wrote John Reed, one of its leading writers, "is a social one—to everlastingly attack old systems, old morals, old prejudices—the whole weight of outworn thought that dead men have saddled upon us." Regular contributors included radical labor journalist Mary Heaton Vorse, artists John Sloan and George Bellows, and writers Floyd Dell and Sherwood Anderson.

For some, Greenwich Village offered a chance to experiment with sexual relationships or work arrangements. For others, it was an escape from small-town conformity, or a haven for like-minded artists and activists. Yet the Village bohemians were united in their search for a new sense of community. Intellectuals and artists, as well as workers, feeling alienated from the rest of society, sought shelter in the collective life and close-knit social relations of the Village community.

The Paterson, New Jersey, silk workers' strike of 1913 provided the most memorable fusion of bohemian sensibility and radical activism. After hearing Haywood speak about the strike at Mabel Dodge's apartment, John Reed offered to organize a pageant on the strikers' behalf at Madison Square Garden. The idea was to publicize the strike to the world and also raise money. The Villagers helped write a script, designed sets and scenery, and took care of publicity. A huge crowd watched more than a

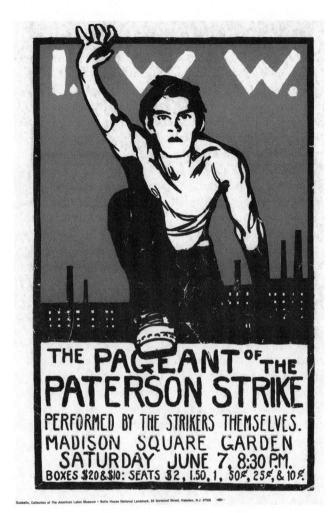

Publicity poster for the 1913 pageant, organized by John Reed and other Greenwich Village radicals, supporting the cause of striking silk workers in Paterson, New Jersey. This poster drew on aesthetic styles associated with the Industrial Workers of the World, typically including a heroic, larger-than-life image of a factory laborer.

thousand workers reenact the silk workers' strike, complete with picket line songs, a funeral, and speeches by IWW organizers. The spectacular production was an artistic triumph but a financial disaster. The Village bohemia lasted only a few years, a flame snuffed out by the chill political winds accompanying America's entry into World War I. Yet for decades, Greenwich Village remained a mecca for young men and women searching for alternatives to conventional ways of living.

WOMEN'S MOVEMENTS AND BLACK ACTIVISM

Like working-class radicals, politically engaged women and African American activists often found themselves at odds with more moderate and mainstream progressive reformers. They contested both gender and racial assumptions inherited from the nineteenth century. Some progressives supported the challenges in one or both of these spheres. They helped shape an agenda for social justice that would echo throughout the rest of the twentieth century. Women were at the forefront of several campaigns, such as the settlement house movement, prohibition, suffrage, and birth control. Millions of others took an active role in new women's associations that combined self-help and social mission. These organizations gave women a place in public life, increased their influence in civic affairs, and nurtured a new generation of female leaders.

In fighting racial discrimination, African Americans had a more difficult task. As racism gained ground in the political and cultural spheres, black progressives fought defensively to prevent the rights they had secured during Reconstruction from being further undermined. Still, they managed to produce leaders, ideas, and organizations that would have a long-range impact on American race relations.

THE NEW WOMAN

The settlement house movement discussed in the opening of this chapter was just one of the new avenues of opportunity opened to progressive-era women. A steady proliferation of women's organizations attracted growing numbers of educated, middle-class women. With more men working in offices, more children attending school, and family size declining, the middle-class home was emptier. At the same time, more middle-class women were graduating from high school and college. In 1870, only 1 percent of college-age Americans had attended college, about 20 percent of them women; by 1910, about 5 percent of college-age Americans attended college, but the proportion of women among them had doubled to 40 percent.

Single-sex clubs brought middle-class women into the public sphere by celebrating the distinctive strengths associated with women's culture: cooperation, uplift, service. The formation of the General Federation of Women's Clubs in 1890 brought together 200 local clubs representing 20,000 women. By 1900, the federation boasted 150,000 members, and by World War I, it claimed to represent over a million women. The women's club movement combined an earlier focus on self-improvement and intellectual pursuits with newer benevolent efforts on behalf of working women and children. The Buffalo Union, for example, sponsored art lectures for housewives and classes in typing, stenography, and bookkeeping for young working women. It also maintained a library, set up a "noon rest" downtown where women could eat lunch, and ran a school for training domestics.

For many middle-class women, the club movement provided a new kind of female-centered community. Club activity often led members to participate in other civic ventures, particularly "child-saving" reforms, such as child labor laws and mothers' pensions. Some took up the cause of working-class women, fighting for protective legislation and offering aid to trade unions. As wives and daughters of influential and well-off men in their communities, club women had access to funds and could generate support for projects they undertook.

Other women's associations made even more explicit efforts to bridge class lines between middle-class homemakers and working-class women. The National Consumers' League (NCL), started in 1898 by Maud Nathan and Josephine Lowell, sponsored a "white label" campaign in which manufacturers who met safety and sanitary standards could put NCL labels on their food and clothing. Under the dynamic leadership of Florence Kelley, the NCL took an even more aggressive stance by publicizing labor abuses in department stores and lobbying for maximum-hour and minimum-wage laws in state legislatures. In its efforts to protect home and housewife, worker and consumer, the NCL embodied the ideal of "social housekeeping."

BIRTH CONTROL

The phrase "birth control," coined by Margaret Sanger around 1913, described her campaign to provide contraceptive information and devices for women. Sanger had seen her own mother die at age forty-nine after bearing eleven children. In 1910, Sanger was a thirty-year-old nurse and housewife living with her husband and three children in a New York City suburb. Excited by a socialist lecture she had attended, she convinced her husband to move to the city, where she threw herself into the bohemian milieu. She became an organizer for the IWW, and in 1912, she wrote a series of articles on female sexuality for a socialist newspaper.

When postal officials confiscated the paper for violating obscenity laws, Sanger left for Europe to learn more about contraception. She returned to New York determined to challenge the obscenity statutes with her own magazine, the *Woman Rebel*. Sanger's journal celebrated female autonomy, including the right to sexual expression and control over one's body. When she distributed her pamphlet *Family Limitation*, postal inspectors confiscated copies and she found herself facing forty-five years in prison. In October 1914, she fled to Europe again. In her absence, anarchist agi-

tator Emma Goldman and many women in the Socialist Party took up the cause.

An older generation of feminists had advocated "voluntary motherhood," or the right to say no to a husband's sexual demands. The new birth control advocates embraced contraception as a way of advancing sexual freedom for middle-class women, as well as responding to the misery of those working-class women who bore numerous children while living in poverty. Sanger returned to the United States in October 1915. After the government dropped the obscenity charges, she embarked on a national speaking tour. In 1916, she again defied the law by opening a birth control clinic in a working-class neighborhood in Brooklyn and offering birth control information without a physician present. Arrested and jailed, she gained more publicity for her crusade. Within a few years, birth control leagues and clinics could be found in every major city and most large towns in the country.

RACISM AND ACCOMMODATION

At the turn of the century, four-fifths of the nation's 10 million African Americans still lived in the South, where most eked out a living working in agriculture. In the cities, most blacks were relegated to menial jobs, but a small African American middle class of entrepreneurs and professionals gained a foothold by selling services and products to the black community. They all confronted a racism that was growing in both intensity and influence in American politics and culture. White racism came in many variants and had evolved significantly since slavery days. The more virulent strains, influenced by Darwin's evolutionary theory,

A supportive crowd surrounds birth control pioneer Margaret Sanger and her sister, Ethel Byrne, as they leave the Court of Special Services in New York City in 1917. Police had recently closed Sanger's first birth control clinic in the immigrant neighborhood of Brownsville, New York, and Sanger herself had spent a month in jail.

held that blacks were a "degenerate" race, genetically predisposed to vice, crime, and disease and destined to lose the struggle for existence with whites. By portraying blacks as incapable of improvement, racial Darwinism justified a policy of repression and neglect toward African Americans.

African Americans also endured a deeply racist popular culture that made hateful stereotypes of black people a normal feature of political debate and everyday life. Benjamin Tillman, a U.S. senator from South Carolina, denounced the African American as "a fiend, a wild beast, seeking whom he may devour." Thomas Dixon's popular novel *The Clansman* (1905) described the typical African American as "half child, half animal, the sport of impulse, whim, and conceit . . . a being who, left to his will, roams at night and sleeps in the day, whose speech knows no word of love, whose passions, once aroused, are as the fury of a tiger." In northern cities "coon songs," based on gross caricatures of black life, were extremely popular in theaters and as sheet music. As in the antebellum minstrel shows, these songs reduced African Americans to creatures of pure appetite—for food, sex, alcohol, and violence.

Southern progressives articulated a more moderate racial philosophy. They also assumed the innate inferiority of blacks, but they believed that black progress was necessary to achieve the economic and political progress associated with a vision of the New South. Their solution to the "race problem" stressed paternalist uplift. Edgar Gardner Murphy, an Episcopal clergyman and leading Alabama progressive, held that African Americans need not be terrorized. The black man, Murphy asserted, "will accept in the white man's country the place assigned him by the white man, will do his work, not by stress of rivalry, but by genial cooperation with the white man's interests."

Amid this political and cultural climate, Booker T. Washington won recognition as the most influential black leader of the day. Born a slave in 1856, Washington was educated at Hampton Institute in Virginia, one of the first freedmen's schools devoted to industrial education. In 1881, he founded Tuskegee Institute, a black school in Alabama devoted to industrial and moral education. He became the leading spokesman for racial accommodation, urging blacks to focus on economic improvement and self-reliance, as opposed to political and civil rights. In an 1895 speech delivered at the Cotton States Exposition in Atlanta, Washington outlined the key themes of accommodationist philosophy. "Cast down your buckets where you are," Washington told black people, meaning they should focus on improving their vocational skills as industrial workers and farmers. "In all things that are purely social," he told attentive whites, "we can be as separate as the fingers, yet one as the hand in all things essential to mutual progress."

Washington's message won him the financial backing of leading white philanthropists and the respect of progressive whites. His widely read autobiography, *Up from Slavery* (1901), stands as a classic narrative of an American self-made man. Written with a shrewd eye toward cementing his support among white Americans, it stressed the importance of learning values such as frugality, cleanliness, and personal morality. But Washington also gained a large following among African Americans, especially those who aspired to business success. With the help of Andrew Carnegie, he founded the National Negro Business League to preach the virtue of black business development in black communities.

Washington also had a decisive influence on the flow of private funds to black schools in the South. Publicly he insisted that "agitation of questions of social equality is the extremest folly." But privately, Washington also spent money and worked behind the scenes trying to halt disfranchisement and segregation. He offered secret financial support, for example, for court cases that challenged Louisiana's grandfather clause, the exclusion of blacks from Alabama juries, and railroad segregation in Tennessee and Georgia.

RACIAL JUSTICE, THE NAACP, AND BLACK WOMEN'S ACTIVISM

Washington's focus on economic self-help remained deeply influential in African American communities long after his death in 1915. But alternative black voices challenged his racial philosophy while he lived. In the early 1900s, scholar and activist W. E. B. Du Bois created a significant alternative to Washington's leadership. A product of the black middle class, Du Bois had been educated at Fisk University and Harvard, where in 1895, he became the first African American to receive a Ph.D. His book *The Philadelphia Negro* (1899) was a pioneering work of social science that refuted racist stereotypes by, for example, discussing black contributions to that city's political life and describing the wide range of black business activity. In *The Souls of Black Folk* (1903), Du Bois declared prophetically that "the problem of the twentieth century is the problem of the color line." Through essays on black history, culture, education, and politics, Du Bois explored the concept of "double consciousness." Black people, he argued, would always feel the tension between an African heritage and their desire to assimilate as Americans. *Souls* represented the first effort to embrace African American culture as a source of collective black strength and something worth preserving.

Du Bois criticized Booker T. Washington's philosophy for its acceptance of "the alleged inferiority of the Negro." The black community, he argued, must fight for the right to vote, for civic equality, and for higher education for the "talented tenth" of their youth. In 1905, Du Bois and editor William Monroe Trotter brought together a group of educated black men to oppose Washington's conciliatory views. Discrimination they encountered in Buffalo, New York, prompted the men to move their meeting to Niagara Falls, Ontario. "Any discrimination based simply on race or color is barbarous," they declared. "Persistent manly agitation is the way to liberty." The Niagara movement protested legal segregation, the exclusion of blacks from labor unions, and the curtailment of voting and other civil rights.

The Niagara movement failed to generate much change. But in 1909, many of its members, led by Du Bois, attended a National Negro Conference held at the Henry Street Settlement in New York. The group included a number of white progressives sympathetic to the idea of challenging Washington's philosophy. A new interracial organization emerged from this conference, the National Association for the Advancement of Colored People. Du Bois, the only black officer of the original NAACP, founded and edited *The Crisis*, the influential NAACP monthly journal. For the next several decades, the NAACP would lead struggles to overturn legal and economic barriers to equal opportunity.

The disenfranchisement of black voters in the South severely curtailed African American political influence. In response, African American women created new strategies to challenge white supremacy and improve life in their communities. As Sallie Mial, a North Carolina Baptist home missionary, told her male brethren, "We have a

peculiar work to do. We can go where you cannot afford to go." Founded in 1900, the Women's Convention of the National Baptist Convention, the largest black denomination in the United States, offered African American women a new public space to pursue reform work and "racial uplift." They organized settlement houses and built playgrounds; they created daycare facilities and kindergartens; they campaigned for women's suffrage, temperance, and advances in public health. In effect, they transformed church missionary societies into quasi–social service agencies. Using the motto "Lifting as We Climb," the National Association of Colored Women Clubs by 1914 boasted 50,000 members in 1,000 clubs nationwide.

NATIONAL PROGRESSIVISM

The progressive impulse had begun at local levels and percolated up. Some state progressive leaders, such as Robert La Follette of Wisconsin and Hiram Johnson of California, achieved national influence as they pushed Progressive forces in both major political parties to take a more aggressive stance on the reform issues of the day. On the presidential level, both Republican Theodore Roosevelt and Democrat Woodrow Wilson laid claim to the progressive mantle—a good example of how on the national level, progressivism animated many perspectives. In their pursuit of reform agendas, both significantly reshaped the office of the president. As progressivism moved to Washington, nationally organized interest groups and public opinion began to rival the influence of the old political parties in shaping the political landscape.

THEODORE ROOSEVELT AND PRESIDENTIAL ACTIVISM

The assassination of William McKinley in 1901 made forty-two-year-old Theodore Roosevelt the youngest man to ever hold the office of president. Born to a wealthy New York family in 1858, Roosevelt overcame a sickly childhood through strenuous physical exercise and rugged outdoor living. After graduating from Harvard, he immediately threw himself into a career in the rough-and-tumble of New York politics. He won election to the state assembly, ran an unsuccessful campaign for mayor of New York, and served as president of the New York City Board of Police Commissioners. In New York Roosevelt was converted to progressivism by this friend Jacob Riis, the muckraking journalist, who took him on tours of the city's tenement districts. In 1897 Roosevelt went to Washington as assistant secretary of the navy, and during the Spanish-American War he won national fame as leader of the Rough Rider regiment in Cuba. Upon his return, he was elected governor of New York, and then in 1900, vice president. Roosevelt viewed the presidency as a "bully pulpit"—a

In July 1905, a group of African American leaders met in Niagara Falls, Ontario, to protest legal segregation and the denial of civil rights to the nation's black population. This portrait was taken against a studio backdrop of the falls. In 1909, the leader of the Niagara movement, W. E. B. Du Bois (second from right, middle row) founded and edited *The Crisis*, the influential monthly journal of the National Association for the Advancement of Colored People.

SOURCE: Photographs and Prints Division, Schomburg Center for Research in Black Culture, The New York Public Library, Astor, Lenox and Tilden Foundations.

platform from which he could exhort Americans to reform their society—and he aimed to make the most of it.

Roosevelt was a uniquely colorful figure, a shrewd publicist, and a creative politician. His three-year stint as a rancher in the Dakota Territory; his fondness for hunting and nature study; his passion for scholarship, which resulted in ten books before he became president—all these set "T. R." apart from most of his upper-class peers. Roosevelt preached the virtues of "the strenuous life," and he believed that educated and wealthy Americans had a special responsibility to serve, guide, and inspire those less fortunate. But he believed the nation was at a crossroads that required the national state to play a more active role in curbing the power of wealthy industrialists.

Roosevelt made key contributions to national progressivism and to changing the office of the president. He knew how to inspire and guide public opinion. He stimulated discussion and aroused curiosity like no one before him. In 1902, Roosevelt demonstrated his unique style of activism when he personally intervened in a bitter dispute in the anthracite coal industry. Using public calls for conciliation, a series of White House meetings, and private pressure on the mine owners, Roosevelt secured an arbitrated settlement that won better pay and working conditions for the miners but without recognition of their union. Roosevelt also pushed for efficient government as the solution to social problems. Unlike most nineteenth-century Republicans, who had largely ignored economic and social inequalities, Roosevelt frankly acknowledged them. Administrative agencies run by experts, he believed, could find rational solutions that would satisfy everyone.

TRUST-BUSTING AND REGULATION

One of the first issues Roosevelt faced was growing public concern with the rapid business consolidations taking place in the American economy. In 1902, he directed the Justice Department to begin a series of prosecutions under the Sherman Antitrust Act. The first target was the Northern Securities Company, a huge merger of transcontinental railroads brought about by financier J. P. Morgan. The deal would have created a giant holding company controlling nearly all the long-distance rail lines from Chicago to California. The Justice Department fought the case all the way through a hearing before the Supreme Court. In *Northern Securities* v. *United States* (1904), the Court held that the stock transactions constituted an illegal combination in restraint of interstate commerce.

This case established Roosevelt's reputation as a "trustbuster." During his two terms, the Justice Department filed forty-three cases under the Sherman Antitrust Act to restrain or dissolve business monopolies. These included actions against the so-called tobacco and beef trusts and the Standard Oil Company. Roosevelt viewed these suits as necessary to publicize the issue and assert the federal government's ultimate authority over big business.

But he did not really believe in the need to break up large corporations. "Trust-busting" might be good politics, but unlike many progressives, who were nostalgic for smaller companies and freer competition, Roosevelt accepted centralization as a fact of modern economic life. Indeed many of the legal cases against trusts were dropped after business executives met privately with Roosevelt in the White House. What was most important, in T. R.'s view, was to insist on the right and power of the federal government to reign in excessive corporate behavior.

After easily defeating Democrat Alton B. Parker in the 1904 election, Roosevelt felt more secure in pushing for regulatory legislation. In 1906, Roosevelt responded to public pressure for greater government intervention and, overcoming objections from a conservative Congress, signed three important measures into law. The Hepburn Act strengthened the Interstate Commerce Commission (ICC), established in 1887 as the first independent regulatory agency, by authorizing it to set maximum railroad rates and inspect financial records.

Two other laws passed in 1906 also expanded the regulatory power of the federal government. The battles surrounding these reforms demonstrate how progressive measures often attracted supporters with competing

This 1909 cartoon by Clifton Berryman depicts President Theodore Roosevelt slaying those trusts he considered "bad" for the public interest while restraining those whose business practices he considered "good" for the economy. The image also plays on T. R.'s well-publicized fondness for big-game hunting.

motives. The Pure Food and Drug Act established the Food and Drug Administration (FDA), which tested and approved drugs before they went on the market. The Meat Inspection Act (passed with help from the shocking publicity surrounding Upton Sinclair's muckraking novel, *The Jungle*) empowered the Department of Agriculture to inspect and label meat products. In both cases, supporters hailed the new laws as providing consumer protection against adulterated or fraudulently labeled food and drugs.

But regulatory legislation found advocates among American big business as well. Large meatpackers such as Swift and Armour strongly supported stricter federal regulation as a way to drive out smaller companies that could not meet tougher standards. The new laws also helped American packers compete more profitably in the European export market by giving their meat the official seal of federal inspectors. Large pharmaceutical manufacturers similarly supported new regulations that would eliminate competitors and patent medicine suppliers. Thus, these reforms won support from large corporate interests that viewed stronger federal regulation as a strategy for consolidating their economic power. Progressive-era expansion of the nation-state had its champions among—and benefits for—big business as well as American consumers.

THE BIRTH OF ENVIRONMENTALISM

As a naturalist and outdoorsman, Theodore Roosevelt also believed in the need for government regulation of the natural environment. He worried about the destruction of forests, prairies, streams, and the wilderness. The conservation of forest and water resources, he argued, was a national problem of vital import. In 1905, he created the U.S. Forest Service and named conservationist Gifford Pinchot to head it. Pinchot recruited a force of forest rangers to manage the reserves. By 1909, total timber and forest reserves had increased from 45 to 195 million acres, and more than 80 million acres of mineral lands had been withdrawn from public sale.

On the broad issue of managing America's natural resources, the Roosevelt administration took the middle ground between preservation and unrestricted commercial development. "Wilderness is waste," Pinchot was fond of saying, reflecting an essentially utilitarian vision that balanced the demands of business with wilderness conservation. But other voices championed a more radical vision of conservation, emphasizing the preservation of wilderness lands against the encroachment of commercial exploitation. The most influential and committed of these was John Muir, an essayist and founder of the modern environmentalist movement. Muir made a passionate and spiritual defense of the inherent value of the American wilderness. Wild country, he argued, had a mystical power to inspire and refresh. "Climb the mountains and get their good tidings," he advised. "Nature's peace will flow into you as the sunshine into the trees. The winds will blow their freshness into you, and the storms their energy, while cares will drop off like autumn leaves." Muir served as first president of the Sierra Club, founded in 1892 to preserve and protect the mountain regions of the West Coast as well as Yellowstone National Park in Wyoming, Montana, and Idaho.

A bitter, drawn-out struggle over new water sources for San Francisco revealed the deep conflicts between conservationists, represented by Pinchot, and preservationists, represented by Muir. After a devastating earthquake in 1906, San Francisco sought federal approval to dam and flood the spectacular Hetch Hetchy Valley, located 150 miles from the city in Yosemite National Park. The project promised to ease the city's chronic freshwater shortage and to generate hydroelectric power. Conservationists and their urban progressive allies argued that developing Hetch Hetchy would be a victory for the public good over greedy private developers, since the plan called for municipal control of the water supply. To John Muir and the Sierra Club, Hetch Hetchy was a "temple" threatened with destruction by the "devotees of ravaging

William Robinson Leigh painted this landscape, *Grand Canyon*, 1911, one of many western scenes he created. Like many contemporaries, Leigh expressed his frustration with trying to capture the sublime in nature: "It challenges man's utmost skill; it mocks and defies his puny efforts to grasp and perpetuate, through art, its inimitable grandeur."

SOURCE: Leigh, William Robinson (1866–1955), "Grand Canyon," 1911. Oil on canvas, 66″ × 99″. Collection of The Newark Museum, Newark, New Jersey, Gift of Henry Wallington Wack, 1930. Inv.: 30.203. © The Newark Museum / Art Resource, New York.

commercialism." Both sides lobbied furiously in Congress and wrote scores of articles in newspapers and magazines. Congress finally approved the reservoir plan in 1913; utility and public development triumphed over the preservation of nature. Although they lost the battle for Hetch Hetchy, the preservationists gained much ground in the larger campaign of alerting the nation to the dangers of a vanishing wilderness. They began to use their own utilitarian rationales, arguing that national parks would encourage economic growth through tourism and provide Americans with a healthy escape from urban and industrial areas. In 1916, the preservationists obtained their own bureaucracy in Washington with the creation of the National Park Service.

The Newlands Reclamation Act of 1902 represented another important victory for the conservation strategy of Roosevelt and Pinchot. With the goal of turning arid land into productive family farms through irrigation, the act established the Reclamation Bureau within the Department of the Interior and provided federal funding for dam and canal projects. But in practice, the bureau did more to encourage the growth of large-scale agribusiness and western cities than small farming. The Roosevelt Dam on Arizona's Salt River, along with the forty-mile Arizona Canal, helped develop the Phoenix area. The Imperial Dam on the Colorado River diverted water to California's Imperial and Coachella Valleys. The Newlands Act thus established a growing federal presence in managing water resources, the critical issue in twentieth-century western development.

REPUBLICAN SPLIT

By the end of his second term, Roosevelt had moved beyond the idea of regulation to push for the most far-reaching federal economic and social programs ever proposed. He saw the central problem as "how to exercise . . . responsible control over the business use of vast wealth." To that end, he proposed restrictions on the use of court injunctions against labor strikes, as well as an eight-hour day for federal employees, a worker compensation law, and federal income and inheritance taxes.

In 1908, Roosevelt kept his promise to retire after a second term. He chose Secretary of War William Howard Taft as his successor. Taft easily defeated Democrat William Jennings Bryan in the 1908 election. During Taft's presidency, the gulf between "insurgent" progressives and the "stand pat" wing split the Republican Party wide open. To some degree, the battles were as much over style as substance. Compared with Roosevelt, the reflective and judicious Taft brought a much more restrained concept of the presidency to the White House. He supported some progressive measures, including the constitutional amendment legalizing a graduated income tax (ratified in 1913), safety codes for mines and railroads, and the creation of a federal Children's Bureau (1912). But in a series of bitter political fights involving tariff, antitrust, and conservation policies, Taft alienated Roosevelt and many other progressives.

After returning from an African safari and a triumphant European tour in 1910, Roosevelt threw himself back into national politics. He directly challenged Taft for the Republican Party leadership. In a dozen bitter state presidential primaries (the first ever held), Taft and Roosevelt fought for the nomination. Although Roosevelt won most of these contests, the old guard still controlled the national convention, and renominated Taft in June 1912. Roosevelt's supporters stormed out, and in August, the new Progressive Party nominated Roosevelt and Hiram Johnson of California as its presidential ticket. Roosevelt's "New Nationalism" presented a vision of a strong federal government, led by an activist president, regulating and protecting the various interests in American society. The platform called for woman suffrage, the eight-hour day, prohibition of child labor, minimum-wage standards for working women, and stricter regulation of large corporations.

THE ELECTION OF 1912: A FOUR-WAY RACE

With the Republicans so badly divided, the Democrats sensed a chance for their first presidential victory in twenty years. They chose Governor Woodrow Wilson of New Jersey as their candidate. Although not nearly as well known nationally as Taft and Roosevelt, Wilson had built a strong reputation as a reformer. The son of a Virginia Presbyterian minister, Wilson spent most of his early career in academia. He studied law at the University of Virginia and then earned a Ph.D. in political science from Johns Hopkins. After teaching history and political science at several schools, he became president of Princeton University in 1902. In 1910, he won election as New Jersey's governor, running against the state Democratic machine. He won the Democratic nomination for president with the support of many of the party's progressives, including William Jennings Bryan.

Wilson declared himself and the Democratic Party to be the true progressives. Viewing Roosevelt rather than Taft as his main rival, Wilson contrasted his New Freedom campaign with Roosevelt's New Nationalism. Crafted largely by progressive lawyer Louis Brandeis, Wilson's platform was far more ambiguous than Roosevelt's. The New Freedom emphasized restoring conditions of free competition and equality of economic opportunity. Wilson did favor a variety of progressive reforms for workers, farmers, and consumers. But in sounding older, nineteenth-century Democratic themes of states' rights and small government, Wilson argued against allowing the federal government to become as large and paternalistic as Roosevelt advocated. "What this country needs above everything else," Wilson argued, "is a body of laws which will look after the men who are on the make rather than the men who are already made."

Socialist Party nominee Eugene V. Debs offered the fourth and most radical choice to voters. The Socialists had more than doubled their membership since 1908, to more than 100,000. On election days, Socialist strength was far

This political cartoon, drawn by Charles Jay Budd, appeared on the cover of *Harper's Weekly*, September 28, 1912. It employed the imagery of autumn county fairs to depict voters as unhappy with their three choices for president. Note that the artist did not include the fourth candidate, Socialist Eugene V. Debs, who was often ignored by more conservative publications such as *Harper's*.

greater than that, as the party's candidates attracted increasing numbers of voters. By 1912, more than a thousand Socialists held elective office in thirty-three states and 160 cities, including 56 mayors and one congressman. Geographically, Socialist strength had shifted to the trans–Mississippi South and West. The party's 1912 platform called for collective ownership of all large-scale industry and all means of transportation and communication. It demanded shorter working hours, an end to child labor, and the vote for women.

An inspiring orator who drew large and sympathetic crowds wherever he spoke, Debs proved especially popular in areas with strong labor movements and populist traditions. He wrapped his socialist message in an apocalyptic vision. Socialists would "abolish this monstrous system and the misery and crime which flow from it." Debs and the Socialists also took credit for pushing both Roosevelt and Wilson further toward the left. Both the Democratic and Progressive Party platforms contained proposals that had been considered extremely radical only ten years earlier.

In the end, the divisions in the Republican Party gave the election to Wilson (see Map 21.2). He won easily, polling 6.3 million votes to Roosevelt's 4.1 million. Taft came in third with 3.5 million. Eugene Debs won 900,000 votes, 6 percent of the total, for the strongest Socialist showing in American history. Even though he won with only 42 percent of the popular vote, Wilson swept the electoral college with 435 votes to Roosevelt's 88 and Taft's 8, giving him the largest electoral majority up to that time. In several respects, the election of 1912 was the first "modern" presidential race. It featured the first direct primaries, challenges to traditional party loyalties, an issue-oriented campaign, and a high degree of interest-group activity.

WOODROW WILSON'S FIRST TERM

As president, Wilson followed Roosevelt's lead in expanding the activist dimensions of the office. He became more responsive to pressure for a greater federal role in regulating business and the economy. This increase in direct lobbying—from hundreds of local and national reform groups, Washington-based organizations, and the new Progressive Party—was itself a new and defining feature of the

	Electoral Vote (%)	Popular Vote (%)
WOODROW WILSON (Democrat)	435 (82)	6,296,547 (42)
Theodore Roosevelt (Progressive)	88 (17)	4,118,571 (27)
William Taft (Republican)	8 (1)	3,486,720 (23)
Eugene Debs (Socialist)	—	900,672 (6)

MAP 21.2 The Election of 1912 The split within the Republican Party allowed Woodrow Wilson to become only the second Democrat since the Civil War to be elected president. Eugene Debs's vote was the highest ever polled by a Socialist candidate.

era's political life. With the help of a Democratic-controlled Congress, Wilson pushed through a significant battery of reform proposals.

The Underwood-Simmons Act of 1913 substantially reduced tariff duties on a variety of raw materials and manufactured goods, including wool, sugar, agricultural machinery, shoes, iron, and steel. Taking advantage of the newly ratified Sixteenth Amendment, which gave Congress the power to levy taxes on income, it also imposed the first graduated tax (up to 6 percent) on personal incomes. The Federal Reserve Act that same year restructured the nation's banking and currency system. It created twelve Federal Reserve Banks, regulated by a central board in Washington. Member banks were required to keep a portion of their cash reserves in the Federal Reserve Bank of their district. By raising or lowering the percentage of reserves required, "the Fed" could either discourage or encourage credit expansion by member banks. Varying the interest rate charged on loans and advances by Federal Reserve Banks to member banks also helped regulate both the quantity and cost of money circulating in the national economy, thus directly stimulating inflation or deflation. By giving central direction to banking and monetary policy, the Federal Reserve Board diminished the power of large private banks.

Wilson also supported the Clayton Antitrust Act of 1914, which replaced the old Sherman Act of 1890 as the nation's basic antitrust law. The Clayton Act reflected the growing political clout of the American Federation of Labor. It exempted unions from being construed as illegal combinations in restraint of trade, and it forbade federal courts from issuing injunctions against strikers. But Wilson adopted the view that permanent federal regulation was necessary for checking the abuses of big business. The Federal Trade Commission (FTC), established in 1914, sought to give the federal government the same sort of regulatory control over corporations that the ICC had over railroads. Wilson believed a permanent federal body like the FTC would provide a method for corporate oversight superior to the erratic and time-consuming process of legal trust-busting. Wilson's hope that the FTC would usher in an era of harmony between government and business recalled the aims of Roosevelt and his big business backers in 1912.

On social issues, Wilson proved more cautious in his first two years. His initial failure to support federal child labor legislation and rural credits to farmers angered many progressives. A Southerner, Wilson also issued an executive order that instituted legal segregation in federal employment, requiring African Americans to work separately from white employees in government offices around Washington, DC. As the reelection campaign of 1916 approached, Wilson worried about defections from the labor and social justice wings of his party. He proceeded to support a rural credits act providing government capital to federal farm banks, as well as federal aid to agricultural extension programs in schools. He also came out in favor of a worker compensation bill for federal employees, and he signed the landmark Keating-Owen Act, which banned children under fourteen from working in enterprises engaged in interstate commerce. Although it covered less than 10 percent of the nation's 2 million working children, the new law established a minimum standard of protection and put the power of federal authority behind the principle of regulating child labor. But by 1916, the dark cloud of war in Europe had already begun to cast its long shadow over progressive reform.

CONCLUSION

In her memoirs Lillian Wald summarized the growth of the Henry Street Settlement she had founded in 1895 as a home health and visiting nurse service on New York's Lower East Side. "Our experience in one small East Side section," she recalled in 1934, "a block perhaps, has led to a next contact, and a next, in widening circles, until our community relationships have come to include the city, the state, the national government, and the world at large." Much the same could be said of the progressive movement. What had begun as a series of interlocking, sometimes contradictory, reform initiatives had come to redefine Americans' relationship to government itself. Cities and state legislatures now routinely made active interventions to improve the lives of their citizens. Real advances had been made through a range of social legislation covering working conditions, child labor, minimum wages, and worker compensation. Social progressives, too, had discovered the power of organizing into extraparty lobbying groups, such as the National Consumers' League and the National American Woman Suffrage Association. But the national government had now become the focus of political power and reform energy. The president was now expected to provide leadership in policymaking, and new federal bureaucracies exerted more influence over the day-to-day lives of Americans.

Yet many progressive reforms had uneven or unintended consequences. The tensions between fighting for social justice and the urge toward social control remained unresolved. The emphasis on efficiency, uplift, and rational administration often collided with humane impulses to aid the poor, the immigrant, the slum dweller. The large majority of African Americans, blue-collar workers, and urban poor remained untouched by federal assistance programs. The drive for a more open and democratic political process, in particular, had the effect of excluding some people from voting while including others. For African Americans, progressivism largely meant disenfranchisement from voting altogether. Stricter election laws made it more difficult for third parties to get on the ballot. Voting itself steadily declined after 1916. Overall, party voting became a less important form of political participation. Interest-group activity, congressional and statehouse lobbying, and direct appeals to public opinion gained currency as ways of influencing government. Business groups and individual trade associations were among the most active groups pressing their demands on government. Political action often shifted from legislatures to the new administrative agencies and commissions created to deal with social and economic problems. Popular magazines and journals grew significantly in both number and circulation, becoming more influential in shaping and appealing to national public opinion. America's entry into World War I effectively drained the energy out of progressive reform. But the progessive movement, with all its contradictions and internal tensions, had profoundly changed the landscape of American political and social life.

CHRONOLOGY

1889	Jane Addams founds Hull House in Chicago
1890	Jacob Riis publishes *How the Other Half Lives*
1895	Booker T. Washington addresses Cotton States Exposition in Atlanta, emphasizing an accommodationist philosophy
	Lillian Wald establishes Henry Street Settlement in New York
1898	Florence Kelley becomes general secretary of the new National Consumers' League
1900	Robert M. La Follette is elected governor of Wisconsin
1901	Theodore Roosevelt succeeds the assassinated William McKinley as president
1903	Lincoln Steffens publishes *The Shame of the Cities*
1905	President Roosevelt creates U.S. Forest Service and names Gifford Pinchot head
	Industrial Workers of the World is founded in Chicago
1906	Upton Sinclair's *The Jungle* exposes conditions in the meatpacking industry
	Congress passes Pure Food and Drug Act and Meat Inspection Act and establishes Food and Drug Administration
1908	In *Muller* v. *Oregon* the Supreme Court upholds a state law limiting maximum hours for working women

1909	Uprising of 20,000 garment workers in New York City's garment industries helps organize unskilled workers into unions
	National Association for the Advancement of Colored People (NAACP) is founded
1911	Triangle Shirtwaist Company fire kills 146 garment workers in New York City
	Socialist critic Max Eastman begins publishing *The Masses*
1912	Democrat Woodrow Wilson wins presidency, defeating Republican William H. Taft, Progressive Theodore Roosevelt, and Socialist Eugene V. Debs
	"Bread and Roses" strike involves 25,000 textile workers in Lawrence, Massachusetts
	Margaret Sanger begins writing and speaking in support of birth control for women
1913	Sixteenth Amendment, legalizing a graduated income tax, is ratified
	Seventeenth Amendment, shifting the selection of U.S. senators to direct election by voters
1914	Clayton Antitrust Act exempts unions from being construed as illegal combinations in restraint of trade
	Federal Trade Commission is established
	Ludlow Massacre occurs
1916	National Park Service is established

— REVIEW QUESTIONS

1. Discuss the tensions within progressivism between the ideals of social justice and the urge for social control. What concrete achievements are associated with each wing of the movement? What were the driving forces behind them?

2. Describe the different manifestations of progressivism at the local, state, and national levels. To what extent did progressives redefine the role of the state in American politics?

3. How did workers use their own values and communities to restrain the power of large corporations during the progressive era?

4. How did the era's new immigration reshape America's cities and workplaces? What connections can you draw between the new immigrant experience and progressive era politics?

5. Analyze the progressive era from the perspective of African Americans. What political and social developments were most crucial, and what legacies did they leave?

6. How do the goals, methods, and language of progressives still find voice in contemporary America?

— RECOMMENDED READING

James Chace, *1912: Wilson, Roosevelt, Taft & Debs—The Election That Changed the Country* (2004). Narrative account of this pivotal presidential election that revolved around competing visions of progressivism.

Alan Dawley, *Struggles for Justice: Social Responsibility and the Liberal State* (1991). Offers an important interpretation of progressivism that focuses on how the working class and women pushed the state toward a more activist role in confronting social problems.

David von Drehle, *Triangle: The Fire That Changed America* (2003). Superb, deeply researched narrative of the disastrous Triangle Fire that re-creates the world of the victims and the reform movement that ensued.

Maureen Flanagan, *America Reformed: Progressives and Progressivisms, 1890s–1920s* (2007). An excellent new overview of progressive era achievements, including fine analysis of the contradictions within the movement.

Louise W. Knight, *Citizen: Jane Addams and the Struggle for Democracy* (2005). Beautifully written new biography of this key progressive figure, focusing on Addams's early life and the evolution of her political thought.

Michael McGerr, *A Fierce Discontent: The Rise and Fall of the Progressive Movement in America, 1870–1920* (2003). A new synthesis arguing that the heart of progressivism lay in the efforts of the urban middle class to reshape the behavior of both the poor and the wealthy.

Michael Perman, *Struggle for Mastery: Disfranchisement in the South, 1888–1908* (2001). A comprehensive, state-by-state overview of the campaigns to remove African Americans from the electoral process.

Daniel T. Rodgers, *Atlantic Crossings: Social Politics in a Progressive Age* (1998). A magisterial work of comparative history focusing on the transnational conversations that deeply influenced American progressive thinkers and reformers.

Christine Stansell, *American Moderns: Bohemian New York and the Creation of a New Century* (2000). Vividly written account that places radical politics and "New Women" at the center of the shaping of modernism.

myhistorylab™

Where it's a good time to connect to the past!

For study resources for this chapter, go to **http://www.myhistorylab.com** and choose *Out of Many*. You will find a wealth of study and review material for this chapter, including pretests and posttests, customized study plan, key-term review flash cards, interactive map and document activities, and documents for analysis.

A Global Power

The United States in the Era of the Great War

1901–1920

The American Expeditionary Force in France

At 5:30 A.M. on September 26, 1918, some 600,000 soldiers of the American Expeditionary Force (AEF) pulled themselves out of the mud and headed into the dense grey fog on a twenty-mile front between the Meuse River and the Argonne Forest in northern France. The biggest and costliest American operation of World War I had begun. In sheer size and scale, the Meuse-Argonne offensive dwarfed anything an American army had ever attempted. The number of American soldiers involved was more than the total of Union and Confederate soldiers who had fought at Gettysburg. American commander General John J. Pershing aimed to overwhelm the undermanned and dispirited German lines with massive numbers and swift movement and thereby force a German surrender. To be sure, elements of the AEF had seen action in several earlier battles, but in most of these engagements Americans had fought under British or French command. Pershing hoped to put a distinctively American stamp on ending the war with the Meuse-Argonne offensive.

But the individual infantryman had little time or use for grand strategy. Each man carried a rifle and bayonet, steel helmet, and gas mask, along with 250 rounds of ammunition. His two days of "iron rations" consisted of two cans of corned beef, six boxes of hard crackers, and a quart canteen of water. The American thrust quickly stalled as the Germans put up fierce resistance with well-placed machine gun nests and artillery batteries, spread out amidst a ghostly landscape littered with abandoned trenches, tangled barbed wire fences, water-filled craters, and dead and mangled bodies everywhere.

SOURCE: Thomas Derrick (20th CE), "American Troops in Southhampton Embarking for France," 1917. Imperial War Museum, London. Snark/Art Resource, NY.

The scene was nothing like the storybooks of war, recalled Lieutenant Maury Maverick. "There were no bugles, no flags, no drums, and as far as we knew, no heroes. . . . I have never read in any military history a description of the high explosives that break overhead. There is a great swishing scream, a smash-bang, and it seems to tear everything loose from you. The intensity of it simply enters your heart and brain and tears every nerve to pieces."

After America's entry into the European conflict in April 1917, millions of Americans traded their civilian clothes for a uniform, creating a new kind of community as soldiers in a modern mechanized army. The Wilson administration had acted swiftly to mobilize the nation's economy and civilian population. The Selective Service Act required the registration and classification for military service of all men between ages twenty-one and thirty-five, and by war's end in November 1918, some 24 million men had registered for the draft, and another 2 million had volunteered. The numbers were there, but the looming question remained: could the nation ➤

create a cohesive, efficient, and mass fighting force where none had existed before? The scale would be far greater than the Spanish-American conflict. And the nation's population was far more ethnically diverse than it had been at the time of the Civil War, America's only previous experience with mass mobilization of troops. In 1917 one out of five soldiers was born in another country and overall illiteracy rates ran as high as 25 percent. Nearly 400,000 African Americans would enter the armed forces, but they faced rigid segregation and deep prejudice against their fitness to fight.

Despite the extraordinary differences of region, class, education, and ethnicity, the "doughboys," as AEF members were affectionately called, shared a great deal of common experiences. For many, the journey to training camp represented their first substantial trip away from home. Many progressives saw the army as a field for continuing social reform and education. "The military tent where they all sleep side by side," Theodore Roosevelt predicted, "will rank next to the public schools among the great agents of democratization." In training camps, the War Department mounted a vigorous campaign against venereal disease, and the scientific discussions of sex to which recruits were subjected in lectures, pamphlets, and films were surely a first for the vast majority. Accepting military discipline was new to most as well, and it often rubbed against traditional American notions of freedom and independence. As members of the AEF shipped off for the front, they also carried with them vague and often romantic notions of what to expect on the battlefield. By the summer of 1918, when most American soldiers traveled to France, the carnage across Europe was no secret. Nor was the grim reality of death associated with machine guns, tanks, and trench warfare. But the blizzard of posters, films, war bond drives, and other propaganda activities coordinated by the Committee on Public Information (CPI) mostly avoided this side of war. Instead it emphasized appeals to patriotism, manhood, heroism, and the fight for democracy. And many doughboys carried to France images of war shaped by their grandfathers' stories about the Civil War or romantic accounts of medieval knights.

Their experiences in the Meuse-Argonne offensive brought them face-to-face with the very different reality of mass mechanized killing. Rather than the swift victory General Pershing had hoped for, the campaign turned into a slow, sometimes chaotic slog. American combat units measured their gains in yards as they found their advances blunted by tough German defenders. Between

September 25 and the Armistice ending the fighting on November 11, each day claimed an average of over 550 Americans dead, with a total of 26,000 Americans killed in the campaign. For many, the worst horror was artillery bombardment with unseen enemy guns lobbing high explosives that could instantly turn a group of men into unrecognizable piles of flesh. The men endured sleep deprivation, hunger, and lice, and they could never get dry. Behind the front, American inexperience with such a large-scale operation created enormous logistical problems. Huge traffic jams made it difficult to evacuate the wounded to hospitals and led to severe shortages of rations, water, and ammunition. Discipline frequently broke down with as many as 100,000 stragglers wandering in the rear areas, unable or unwilling to rejoin their units. Meanwhile, a lethal influenza outbreak, part of the worldwide pandemic that would claim over 20 million lives, swept through the AEF in France, afflicting 100,000 doughboys and killing about 10,000 troops.

Many AEF men would long remember their brief time in France as a life-changing high point of their lives, and for some it achieved a mythic significance. Revulsion at the horrors of warfare often coexisted with strong feelings of camaraderie, as expressed by one of the most celebrated doughboys, Sergeant Alvin York. A religious pacifist who had originally sought conscientious objector status, the Tennessee sharpshooter received the Medal of Honor for single-handedly eliminating an entire German machine gun battalion and taking 132 prisoners. War, York recalled, "turns you into a mad fightin' animal, but it also brings out something else, something I jes don't know how to describe, a sort of tenderness and love for the fellows fightin' with you."

America's emergence as a global power required mass mobilization of the armed forces and created a new community of veterans. In early 1919, encouraged by some senior officers, a group of AEF veterans founded the American Legion, "to preserve the memories and incidents of our association in the great war . . . to consecrate and sanctify our comradeship." American Legion halls soon became a familiar sight in communities across America. But the Legion had a political mission as well, one that would play out during the postwar "Red Scare." Legion leaders saw it as a way to counter radical ideas that might "infect" returning veterans, especially those who suffered from unemployment or had trouble readjusting to civilian life. It would commemorate the war, celebrate sacrifice, and honor the dead, all in the name of

Focus Questions

1. How and where did the United States expand its role on the international scene?

2. Why did the United States move from neutrality to participation in the Great War?

3. What methods and techniques did the federal government use to achieve wartime mobilization?

4. How did U.S. entry into the war alter the political landscape, especially with respect to dissent?

5. How can we explain Woodrow Wilson's failure to win the peace?

1901–1920

promoting "100 Per Cent Americanism" and fighting against "dangerous" socialists and other radical groups. As much a political lobby as a veterans' organization, the American Legion would extend the memory and life of the AEF community well into the twentieth century.

BECOMING A WORLD POWER

In the first years of the new century, the United States pursued a more vigorous and aggressive foreign policy than it had in the past. In addition to its newfound imperial presence in Asia, the United States marked out the Western Hemisphere—especially the Caribbean, Mexico, and Central America—as a site for establishing American hegemony. Presidents Theodore Roosevelt, William Howard Taft, and Woodrow Wilson all contributed to "progressive diplomacy," in which commercial expansion was backed by a growing military presence in the hemisphere. This policy reflected a view of world affairs that stressed the links between ensuring American commercial expansion and a foreign policy couched in terms of moralism, order, and a special, even God-given, role for the United States. By 1917, when the United States entered the Great War, the nation was just as complicit in building empire as were the European states and Japan.

ROOSEVELT: THE BIG STICK

Theodore Roosevelt left a strong imprint on the nation's foreign policy. Like many of his class and background, "T.R." took for granted the superiority of Protestant Anglo-American culture and the goal of spreading its values and influence. He believed that to maintain and increase its economic and political stature, America must be militarily strong. In 1900, Roosevelt summarized his activist views, declaring, "I have always been fond of the West African proverb, 'Speak softly and carry a big stick, you will go far.'"

Roosevelt brought the "big stick" approach to disputes in the Caribbean region. Since the 1880s, several British, French, and American companies had pursued plans for building a canal across the Isthmus of Panama, thereby connecting the Atlantic and Pacific Oceans. The canal was a top priority for Roosevelt, and he tried to negotiate a leasing agreement with Colombia, of which Panama was a province. But when the Colombian Senate rejected a final American offer in the fall of 1903, Roosevelt invented a new strategy. A combination of native forces and foreign promoters associated with the canal project plotted a revolt against Colombia. Roosevelt kept in touch with at least one leader of the revolt, Philippe Bunau-Varilla, an engineer and agent for the New Panama Canal Company, and the president let him know that U.S. warships were steaming toward Panama.

On November 3, 1903, just as the USS *Nashville* arrived in Colón harbor, the province of Panama declared itself independent of Colombia. The United States immediately recognized the new Republic of Panama. Less than two weeks later, Bunau-Varilla, serving as a minister from Panama, signed a treaty granting the United States full sovereignty in perpetuity over a ten-mile-wide canal zone. America guaranteed Panama's independence and agreed to pay it $10 million initially and an additional $250,000 a year for the canal zone. Years after the canal was completed, the U.S. Senate voted another $25 million to Colombia as compensation.

THE WORLD'S CONSTABLE.

This 1905 cartoon portraying President Theodore Roosevelt, "The World's Constable," appeared in *Judge* magazine. In depicting the president as a strong but benevolent policeman bringing order in a contentious world, the artist Louis Dalrymple drew on familiar imagery from Roosevelt's earlier days as a New York City police commissioner.

The Panama Canal was a triumph of modern engineering and gave the United States a tremendous strategic and commercial advantage in the Western Hemisphere. It took eight years to build and cost hundreds of poorly paid manual workers their lives. Several earlier attempts to build a canal in the region had failed. But with better equipment and a vigorous campaign against disease, the United States succeeded. In 1914, after $720 million in construction costs, the first merchant ships sailed through the canal.

"The inevitable effect of our building the Canal," wrote Secretary of State Elihu Root in 1905, "must be to require us to police the surrounding premises." Roosevelt agreed. He was especially concerned that European powers might step in if America did not. In 1903, Great Britain, Germany, and Italy had imposed a blockade on Venezuela in a dispute over debt payments owed to private investors. To prevent armed intervention by the Europeans, in 1904 Roosevelt proclaimed what became known as the Roosevelt Corollary to the Monroe Doctrine. "Chronic wrongdoing, or an impotence which results in a general loosening of the ties of civilized society," the statement read, justified "the exercise of an international police power" anywhere in the hemisphere. Roosevelt invoked the corollary to justify U.S. intervention in the region, beginning with the Dominican Republic in 1905. To counter the protests of European creditors (and the implied threat of armed intervention), the U.S. government assumed management of the Dominican debt and customs services. Roosevelt and later presidents cited the corollary to justify armed intervention in the internal affairs of Cuba, Haiti, Nicaragua, and Mexico.

With the outbreak of the Russo-Japanese War in 1904, Roosevelt worried about the future of the Open Door policy in Asia. (See Chapter 20.) A total victory by Russia or Japan could upset the balance of power in East Asia and threaten American business enterprises there. He became especially concerned after the Japanese scored a series of military victories over Russia and began to loom as a dominant power in East Asia. Roosevelt mediated a settlement of the Russo-Japanese War at Portsmouth, New

Hampshire, in 1905 (for which he was awarded the 1906 Nobel Peace Prize). In this settlement, Japan won recognition of its dominant position in Korea and consolidated its economic control over Manchuria. Yet repeated incidents of anti-Japanese racism in California kept American–Japanese relations strained. In 1906, for example, the San Francisco school board, responding to nativist fears of a "yellow peril," ordered the segregation of Japanese, Chinese, and Korean students. Japan angrily protested. In 1907, in the so-called Gentlemen's Agreement, Japan agreed not to issue passports to Japanese male laborers looking to emigrate to the United States, and Roosevelt promised to fight anti-Japanese discrimination. He then persuaded the San Francisco school board to exempt Japanese students from the segregation ordinance.

But Roosevelt did not want these conciliatory moves to be interpreted as weakness. He thus built up American naval strength in the Pacific, and in 1908, he sent battleships to visit Japan in a muscle-flexing display of sea power. In that same year, the two burgeoning Pacific powers reached a reconciliation. The Root-Takahira Agreement affirmed the "existing status quo" in Asia, mutual respect for territorial possessions in the Pacific, and the Open Door trade policy in China. From the Japanese perspective, the agreement recognized Japan's colonial dominance in Korea and southern Manchuria.

TAFT: DOLLAR DIPLOMACY

Roosevelt's successor, William Howard Taft, believed he could replace the militarism of the big stick with the more subtle and effective weapon of business investment. Taft and his secretary of state, corporate lawyer Philander C. Knox, followed a strategy (called "dollar diplomacy" by critics) in which they assumed that political influence would follow increased U.S. trade and investment. As Taft explained in 1910, he advocated "active intervention to secure for our merchandise and our capitalists opportunity for profitable investment."

Overall American investment in Central America grew rapidly, from $41 million in 1908 to $93 million by 1914. Most of this money went into railroad construction, mining, and plantations. The United Fruit Company alone owned about 160,000 acres of land in the Caribbean by 1913. But dollar diplomacy ended up requiring military support. The Taft administration sent the navy and the marines to intervene in political disputes in Honduras and Nicaragua, propping up factions pledged to protect American business interests. A contingent of U.S. Marines remained in Nicaragua until 1933. The economic and political structures of Honduras and Nicaragua were controlled by both the dollar and the bullet (see Map 22.1).

In China, Taft and Knox pressed for a greater share of the pie for U.S. investors. They gained a place for U.S. bankers in the European consortium, building the massive new Hu-kuang Railway in southern and central China.

But Knox blundered by attempting to "neutralize" the existing railroads in China. He tried to secure a huge international loan for the Chinese government that would allow it to buy up all the foreign railways and develop new ones. Both Russia and Japan, which had fought wars over their railroad interests in Manchuria, resisted this plan as a threat to the arrangements hammered out at Portsmouth with the help of Theodore Roosevelt. Knox's "neutralization" scheme, combined with U.S. support for the Chinese Nationalists in their 1911 revolt against the ruling Manchu dynasty, prompted Japan to sign a new friendship treaty with Russia. The Open Door to China was now effectively closed, and American relations with Japan began a slow deterioration that ended in war thirty years later.

WILSON: MORALISM AND INTERVENTION IN MEXICO

Right after he took office in 1913, President Woodrow Wilson observed that "it would be the irony of fate if my administration had to deal chiefly with foreign affairs." His political life up to then had centered on achieving progressive reforms in the domestic arena. As it turned out, Wilson had to face international crises from his first day in office. These were of a scope and complexity unprecedented in U.S. history. Wilson had no experience in diplomacy, but he brought to foreign affairs a set of fundamental principles that combined a moralist's faith in American democracy with a realist's understanding of the power of international commerce. He believed that American economic expansion, accompanied by democratic principles and Christianity, was a civilizing force in the world.

Wilson, like most corporate and political leaders of the day, emphasized foreign investments and industrial exports as the keys to the nation's prosperity. He believed that the United States, with its superior industrial efficiency, could achieve supremacy in world commerce if artificial barriers to free trade were removed. He championed and extended the Open Door principles of John Hay, advocating strong diplomatic and military measures "for making ourselves supreme in the world from an economic point of view." Wilson often couched his vision of a dynamic, expansive American capitalism in terms of a moral crusade. As he put it in a speech to a congress of salesmen, "[Since] you are Americans and are meant to carry liberty and justice and the principles of humanity wherever you go, go out and sell goods that will make the world more comfortable and more happy, and convert them to the principles of America." Yet he quickly found that the complex realities of power politics could interfere with moral vision.

Wilson's policies toward Mexico, which foreshadowed the problems he would encounter in World War I, best illustrate his difficulties. The 1911 Mexican Revolution had overthrown the brutally corrupt dictatorship of Porfirio Díaz, and popular leader Francisco Madero had won wide support by promising democracy and economic reform for

MAP EXPLORATION

To explore an interactive version of this map, go to **www.prenhall.com/faragher6/map22.1**

MAP 22.1 The United States in the Caribbean, 1865–1933 An overview of U.S. economic and military involvement in the Caribbean during the late nineteenth and early twentieth centuries. Victory in the Spanish-American War, the Panama Canal project, and rapid economic investment in Mexico and Cuba all contributed to a permanent and growing U.S. military presence in the region.

millions of landless peasants. But the U.S. business community was nervous about the future of its investments which, in the previous generation, had come to dominate the Mexican economy. By 1910, American companies owned over one-quarter—130 million acres—of Mexico's land, including over half of its coastlines and border areas. A handful of American mining companies had led the way in exploiting Mexican natural resources, using high capitalization, advanced technology, and sophisticated marketing networks to win control of roughly four-fifths of the gold, silver, and copper extracted from Mexican mines. Similar patterns

developed in the timber and petroleum sectors, and Mexican capitalists owned very little of the nation's export industries. Meanwhile, in Mexican industrial communities such as Tampico—transformed into an overcrowded and badly polluted boomtown by the expanding oil industry—virtually all Mexican workers were relegated to unskilled and badly paying jobs.

Wilson at first gave his blessing to the revolutionary movement, expressed regret over the Mexican-American War of 1846–48, and disavowed any interest in another war. But right before he took office, Wilson was stunned

we can have no sympathy with those who seek to seize the power of government to advance their own personal interests or ambition.

This 1914 political cartoon comments approvingly on the interventionist role adopted by the United States in Latin American countries. By depicting President Woodrow Wilson as a schoolteacher giving lessons to children, the image captures the paternalistic views that American policy makers held toward nations like Mexico, Venezuela, and Nicaragua.

by the ousting and murder of Madero by his chief lieutenant, General Victoriano Huerta. Other nations, including Great Britain and Japan, recognized the Huerta regime, but Wilson refused. He announced that the United States would support only governments that rested on the rule of law. An armed faction opposed to Huerta, known as the Constitutionalists and led by Venustiano Carranza, emerged in northern Mexico. Both sides rejected an effort by Wilson to broker a compromise between them. Carranza, an ardent nationalist, pressed for the right to buy U.S. arms, which he won in 1914. Wilson also isolated Huerta diplomatically by persuading the British to withdraw their support in exchange for American guarantees of English property interests in Mexico.

But Huerta stubbornly remained in power. In April 1914, Wilson used a minor insult to U.S. sailors in Tampico as an excuse to invade. American naval forces bombarded and then occupied Veracruz, the main port through which Huerta received arms shipments. Nineteen Americans and 126 Mexicans died in the battle, which brought the United States and Mexico close to war, and provoked anti-American demonstrations in Mexico and throughout

Latin America. Wilson accepted the offer of the ABC Powers—Argentina, Brazil, and Chile—to mediate the dispute. Huerta rejected a plan for him to step aside in favor of a provisional government. But then in August, Carranza managed to overthrow Huerta. Playing to nationalist sentiment, Carranza too denounced Wilson for his intervention.

As war loomed in Europe, Mexico's revolutionary politics continued to frustrate Wilson. For a brief period, Wilson threw his support behind Francisco "Pancho" Villa, Carranza's former ally, who now led a rebel army of his own in northern Mexico. But Carranza's forces dealt Villa a major setback in April 1915. In October, its attention focused on the war in Europe, the Wilson administration recognized Carranza as Mexico's de facto president. Meanwhile, Pancho Villa, feeling betrayed, turned on the United States and tried to provoke a crisis that might draw the United States into war with Mexico. In 1916, Villa led several raids in Mexico and across the border into the United States that killed a few dozen Americans. The man once viewed by Wilson as a fighter for democracy was now dismissed as a dangerous bandit.

In March 1916, enraged by Villa's defiance, Wilson dispatched General John J. Pershing and an army that eventually numbered 15,000 to capture him. For a year, Pershing's troops chased Villa in vain, penetrating 300 miles into Mexico. The invasion made Villa a symbol of national resistance in Mexico, and his army grew from 500 men to 10,000 by the end of 1916. Villa's effective hit-and-run guerrilla tactics kept the U.S. forces at bay. A frustrated General Pershing complained that he felt "just a little bit like a man looking for a needle in a haystack." He urged the U.S. government to occupy the northern Mexican state of Chihuahua and later called for the occupation of the entire country.

Skirmishes between American forces and Carranza's army brought the two nations to the brink of war again in June 1916. Although Wilson prepared a message to Congress asking permission for American troops to occupy all of northern Mexico, he never delivered it. There was fierce opposition to war with Mexico throughout the country. Perhaps more important, mounting tensions with Germany caused Wilson to hesitate. He told an aide that "Germany is anxious to have us at war with Mexico, so that our minds and our energies will be taken off the great war across the sea." Wilson thus accepted negotiations by a face-saving international commission.

Wilson's attempt to guide the course of Mexico's revolution and protect U.S. interests left a bitter legacy of suspicion and distrust in Mexico. It also suggested the limits of a foreign policy tied to a moral vision rooted in the idea of American exceptionalism. Militarism and imperialism, Wilson had believed, were hallmarks of the old European way. American liberal values—rooted in capitalist development, democracy, and free trade—were the wave of the future. Wilson believed the United States could lead the world in establishing a new international system based on peaceful commerce and political stability. In both the 1914 invasion and the 1916 punitive expedition, Wilson declared that he had no desire to interfere with Mexican sovereignty. But in both cases, that is exactly what he did. The United States, he argued, must actively use its enormous moral and material power to create the new order. That principle would soon engage America in Europe's bloodiest war and its most momentous revolution.

THE GREAT WAR

World War I, or the Great War, as it was originally called, took an enormous human toll on an entire generation of Europeans. The unprecedented slaughter on the battlefields of Verdun, Ypres, Gallipoli, and scores of other places appalled the combatant nations. At the war's start in August 1914, both sides had confidently predicted a quick victory. Instead, the killing dragged on for more than four years, and in the end, transformed the old power relations and political map of Europe. The United States entered the war reluctantly, and American forces played a supportive, rather than a central, role in the military outcome. Yet the wartime experience left a sharp imprint on the nation's economy, politics, and cultural life—one that would last into the next decades.

THE GUNS OF AUGUST

Only a complex and fragile system of alliances had kept the European powers at peace with each other since 1871. Two great competing camps had evolved by 1907: the Triple Alliance (also known as the Central Powers), which included Germany, Austria-Hungary, and Italy; and the Triple Entente (also known as the Allies), which included Great Britain, France, and Russia. At the heart of this division was the competition between Great Britain, long the world's dominant colonial and commercial power, and Germany, which had powerful aspirations for an empire of its own. The alliance system managed to keep small conflicts from escalating into larger ones for most of the late nineteenth and early twentieth centuries. But its inclusiveness was also its weakness: the alliance system threatened to entangle many nations in any war that did erupt. On June 28, 1914, Archduke Franz Ferdinand, heir to the throne of the unstable Austro-Hungarian Empire, was assassinated in Sarajevo, Bosnia. The archduke's killer was a Serbian nationalist who believed the Austro-Hungarian province of Bosnia ought to be annexed to neighboring Serbia. Germany gave Austria-Hungary a blank check to stamp out the Serbian threat, and the Serbians in turn asked Russia for help.

That summer both sides began mobilizing their armies, and by early August they had exchanged declarations of war. Germany invaded Belgium and prepared to move across the French border. At the beginning, most Europeans supported the war effort, believing there would be quick and glorious victories. Appeals to nationalist sentiment and glory overcame even the antiwar socialists, who had long fought to transcend national boundaries in their political work. But after the German armies were stopped at the River Marne in September, the war settled into a long, bloody stalemate. New and grimly efficient weapons, such as the machine gun and the tank, and the horrors of trench warfare, meant unprecedented casualties for all involved. In northern France, Poland, and on the Italian front, the fighting killed 5 million people over the next two and a half years. And Allied campaigns waged against German colonies in Africa and against the Ottoman Empire in the Middle East reflected the global nature of the war, as did the British and French dependence on colonial troops from India and Africa.

AMERICAN NEUTRALITY

The outbreak of war in Europe shocked Americans. President Wilson issued a formal proclamation of neutrality and urged citizens to be "impartial in thought as well as in action." In practice, powerful cultural, political, and economic factors made the impartiality advocated by Wilson impossible. The U.S. population included many ethnic groups with close emotional ties to the Old World. Out of a total population of 92 million in 1914, about one-third were "hyphenated" Americans, either foreign-born or having one or both parents who were immigrants. Strong support for the Central Powers could be found among the 8 million German-Americans, as well as the 4 million Irish-Americans, who shared their ancestral homeland's historical hatred of English rule. On the other side, many Americans were at least mildly pro-Allies due to cultural and language bonds with Great Britain and the tradition of Franco-American friendship.

Both sides bombarded the United States with vigorous propaganda campaigns. The British effectively exploited their bonds of language and heritage with Americans. Reports of looting, raping, and the killing of innocent civilians by German troops circulated widely in the press. Many of these atrocity stories were exaggerated, but verified German actions—the invasion of neutral Belgium, submarine attacks on merchant ships, and the razing of towns—lent them credibility. German propagandists blamed the war on Russian expansionism and France's desire to avenge its defeat by Germany in 1870–71. It is difficult to measure the impact of war propaganda on American public opinion. As a whole, though, it highlighted the terrible human costs of the war and, thus, strengthened the conviction that America should stay out of it.

Economic ties between the United States and the Allies were perhaps the greatest barrier to true neutrality. Early in the war, Britain imposed a blockade on all shipping to Germany. The United States, as a neutral country, might have insisted on the right of nonbelligerents to trade with both sides, as required by international law. But in practice, although Wilson protested the blockade, he wanted to avoid antagonizing Britain and disrupting trade between the United States and the Allies. Trade with Germany all but ended while trade with the Allies increased dramatically. As war orders poured in from Britain and France, the value of American trade with the Allies shot up from $824 million in 1914 to $3.2 billion in 1916. By 1917, loans to the Allies—primarily from private American banks—exceeded $2.5 billion, compared to loans to the Central Powers of only $27 million. As America's annual export trade jumped from $2 billion in 1913 to nearly $6 billion in 1916, the nation enjoyed a great economic boom and the United States became neutral in name only.

PREPAREDNESS AND PEACE

In February 1915, Germany declared the waters around the British Isles to be a war zone, a policy that it would enforce with unrestricted submarine warfare. All enemy shipping, despite the requirements of international law to the contrary, would be subject to surprise submarine attack. Neutral powers were warned that the problems of identification at sea put their ships at risk. The United States issued a sharp protest to this policy, calling it "an indefensible violation of neutral rights," and threatened to hold Germany accountable.

On May 7, 1915, a German U-boat sank the British liner *Lusitania* off the coast of Ireland. Among the 1,198

Patriotic marchers carry on over-sized American flag past spectators, as part of a "preparedness parade" in downtown Mobile Alabama, before American entry into World War I.

SOURCE: University of South Alabama Archives.

people who died were 128 American citizens. The *Lusitania* was, in fact, secretly carrying war materials, and passengers had been warned about a possible attack. Wilson nevertheless denounced the sinking as illegal and inhuman, and the American press loudly condemned the act as barbaric. An angry exchange of diplomatic notes led Secretary of State William Jennings Bryan to resign in protest against a policy he thought too warlike.

Tensions heated up again in March 1916 when a German U-boat torpedoed the *Sussex,* an unarmed French passenger ship, injuring four Americans. President Wilson threatened to break off diplomatic relations with Germany unless it abandoned its submarine warfare. He won a temporary diplomatic victory when Germany promised that all vessels would be visited prior to attack. But the crisis also prompted Wilson to begin preparing for war. The National Security League, active in large eastern cities and bankrolled by conservative banking and commercial interests, helped push for a bigger army and navy and, most important, a system of universal military training. In June 1916, Congress passed the National Defense Act, which more than doubled the size of the regular army to 220,000 and integrated the state National Guards under federal control. In August, Congress passed a bill that dramatically increased spending for new battleships, cruisers, and destroyers.

Not all Americans supported these preparations for battle, and opposition to military buildup found expression in scores of American communities. As early as August 29, 1914, 1,500 women clad in black had marched down New York's Fifth Avenue in the Woman's Peace Parade. Out of this gathering evolved the American Union against Militarism, which lobbied against the preparedness campaign and against intervention in Mexico. Antiwar feeling was especially strong in the South and Midwest.

A group of thirty to fifty House Democrats, led by majority leader Claude Kitchin of North Carolina, stubbornly opposed Wilson's military buildup. Jane Addams, Lillian D. Wald, and many other prominent progressive reformers spoke out for peace. A large reservoir of popular antiwar sentiment flowed through the culture in various ways. Movie director Thomas Ince won a huge audience for his 1916 film *Civilization,* which depicted Christ returning to reveal the horrors of war to world leaders. Two of the most popular songs of 1915 were "Don't Take My Darling Boy Away" and "I Didn't Raise My Boy to Be a Soldier."

Wilson acknowledged the active opposition to involvement in the war by adopting the winning slogan "He Kept Us Out of War" in the 1916 presidential campaign. He made a point of appealing to progressives of all kinds, stressing his support for the eight-hour day and his administration's efforts on behalf of farmers. The war-induced prosperity no doubt helped him to defeat conservative Republican Charles Evans.

SAFE FOR DEMOCRACY

By the end of January 1917, Germany's leaders had decided against a negotiated peace settlement, placing their hopes instead in a final decisive offensive against the Allies. On February 1, 1917, with the aim of breaking the British blockade, Germany declared unlimited submarine warfare, with no warnings, against all neutral and belligerent shipping. This strategy went far beyond the earlier, more limited use of the U-boat. The decision was made with full knowledge that it might bring America into the conflict. In effect, German leaders were gambling that they could destroy the ability of the Allies to fight before the United States would be able to effectively mobilize manpower and resources.

Wilson was indignant and disappointed. He still hoped for peace, but Germany had made it impossible for him to preserve his twin goals of U.S. neutrality and freedom of the seas. Reluctantly, Wilson broke off diplomatic relations with Germany and called on Congress to approve the arming of U.S. merchant ships. On March 1, the White House shocked the country when it made public a recently intercepted coded message, sent by German foreign secretary Arthur Zimmermann to the German ambassador in Mexico. The Zimmermann note proposed that an alliance be made between Germany and Mexico if the United States entered the war. Zimmermann suggested that Mexico take up arms against the United States and receive in return the "lost territory in New Mexico, Texas, and Arizona." The note caused a sensation and became a very effective propaganda tool for those who favored U.S. entry into the war. The specter of a German-Mexican alliance helped turn the tide of public opinion in the Southwest, where opposition to U.S. involvement in the war had been strong.

Revelation of the Zimmermann note stiffened Wilson's resolve. He issued an executive order in mid-March, authorizing the arming of all merchant ships and allowing them to shoot at submarines. In that month, German U-boats sank seven U.S. merchant ships, with a heavy death toll. Anti-German feeling increased, and thousands took part in prowar demonstrations in New York, Boston, Philadelphia, and other cities. Wilson finally called a special session of Congress to ask for a declaration of war.

On April 2, on a rainy night, before a packed and very quiet assembly, Wilson made his case. He reviewed the escalation of submarine warfare, which he called "warfare against mankind," and said that neutrality was no longer feasible or desirable. But the conflict was not merely about U.S. shipping rights, Wilson argued. He employed highly idealistic language to make the case for war, reflecting his deeply held belief that America had a special mission as the world's most enlightened and advanced nation:

It is a fearful thing to lead this great peaceful people into war, into the most terrible and disastrous of all wars, civilization itself seeming to be in the balance.

James Montgomery Flagg's Navy recruiting poster from 1918 combined appeals to patriotism, the opportunity to "make history," and traditional images depicting liberty as a woman.

But the right is more precious than peace, and we shall fight for the things which we have always carried nearest to our hearts—for democracy, for the right of those who submit to authority to have a voice in their own governments, for the rights and liberties of small nations, for a universal dominion of right by such a concert of free peoples as shall bring peace and safety to all nations and make the world itself at last free.

In effect, Wilson wrapped together American commercial and diplomatic interests in the language of universal principles like freedom of the seas and neutral rights. He expressed the realist ambition of making America a world power in terms of an absolute moral imperative. The Senate adopted the war resolution 82 to 6, the House 373 to 50. Wilson's eloquent speech won over not only the Congress, but also most of the press, and even his bitterest political critics, such as Theodore Roosevelt. Upper-class conservatives supported the language emphasizing national interest, while most progressives responded to the appeal of an idealistic mission. On April 6, President Wilson signed the declaration of war. All that remained was to win over the American public.

AMERICAN MOBILIZATION

The overall public response to Wilson's war message was enthusiastic. Most newspapers, religious leaders, state legislatures, and prominent public figures endorsed the call to arms. But the Wilson administration was less certain about the feelings of ordinary Americans and their willingness to fight in Europe. It therefore took immediate steps to win over public support for the war effort, to place a legal muzzle on antiwar dissenters, and to establish a universal military draft. War mobilization was, above all, a campaign to unify the country.

SELLING THE WAR

Just a week after signing the war declaration, Wilson created the Committee on Public Information (CPI) to organize public opinion. It was dominated by its civilian chairman, the journalist and reformer George Creel. He had become a personal friend of Wilson's while handling publicity for the 1916 Democratic campaign. Creel quickly transformed the CPI from its original function as coordinator of government news into a sophisticated and aggressive agency for promoting the war. To sell the war, Creel adapted techniques from the emerging field of public relations. He enlisted more than 150,000 people to work on a score of CPI committees. They produced more than 100 million pieces of literature—pamphlets, articles, books—that explained the causes and meaning of the war. Across the nation, a volunteer army of 75,000 "Four Minute Men" gave brief patriotic speeches before stage and movie shows. The CPI also created posters, slides, newspaper advertising, and films to promote the war. It called upon movie stars such as Charlie Chaplin, Mary Pickford, and Douglas Fairbanks to help sell war bonds at huge rallies. Famous journalists like the muckraker Ida Tarbell and well-known artists like Charles Dana Gibson were recruited. Many popular entertainers injected patriotic themes into their work as well, as when Broadway composer George M. Cohan wrote the rousing prowar anthem "Over There," sung by the great opera tenor Enrico Caruso (see Seeing History).

The CPI led an aggressively negative campaign against all things German. Posters and advertisements depicted the Germans as Huns, bestial monsters outside the civilized world. German music and literature, indeed the German language itself, were suspect and were banished from the concert halls, schools, and libraries of many communities. Many restaurants now offered "liberty cabbage" and "liberty steaks" instead of sauerkraut and hamburgers. The CPI also urged ethnic Americans to abandon their Old World ties, to become "unhyphenated Americans." The CPI's push for conformity would soon encourage thousands of local, sometimes violent, campaigns of harassment against German-Americans, radicals, and peace activists.

FADING OPPOSITION TO WAR

By defining the call to war as a great moral crusade, President Wilson was able to win over many Americans who had been reluctant to go to war. In particular, many liberals and progressives were attracted to the possibilities of war as a positive force for social change. Although some progressives—notably Senator Robert M. La Follette of Wisconsin—continued to oppose the war, many more identified with President Wilson's definition of the war as an idealistic crusade to defend democracy, spread liberal principles, and redeem European decadence and militarism. John Dewey, the influential philosopher, believed the war offered great "social possibilities" for promoting the public good through science and greater efficiency. He reflected a broad progressive shift from emphasizing the public interest to focusing on the national interest.

The writer and cultural critic Randolph Bourne was an important, if lonely, voice of dissent among intellectuals. A former student of Dewey's at Columbia University, Bourne wrote a series of antiwar essays warning of the disastrous consequences for reform movements of all kinds. He was particularly critical of "war intellectuals" such as Dewey, who were so eager to shift their energies to serving the war effort. "War is essentially the health of the State," Bourne wrote, and he accurately predicted sharp infringements on political and intellectual freedoms.

The Woman's Peace Party, founded in 1915 by feminists opposed to the preparedness campaign, dissolved. Most of its leading lights—Florence Kelley, Lillian D. Wald, and Carrie Chapman Catt—threw themselves into volunteer war work. Catt, leader of the huge National American Woman Suffrage Association (NAWSA), believed that supporting the war might help women win the right to vote. She joined the Women's Committee of the Council of National Defense and encouraged suffragists to mobilize women for war service of various kinds. A few lonely feminist voices, such as Jane Addams, continued steadfastly to oppose the war effort. But war work proved very popular among activist middle-class women. It gave them a leading role in their communities—selling bonds, coordinating food conservation drives, and working for hospitals and the Red Cross.

Selling War

The Committee on Public Information (CPI), chaired by the progressive Denver journalist George Creel, oversaw the crucial task of mobilizing public opinion for war. Creel employed the most sophisticated sales and public relations techniques of the day to get Americans behind the war effort. The CPI created a flood of pamphlets, billboards, and news articles; sent volunteer "Four Minute Men" to make hundreds of thousands of patriotic speeches in movie theaters between reels; sponsored government-funded feature films depicting life on the front lines; and staged celebrity-studded rallies to promote the sale of war bonds. CPI writers and artists worked closely with government agencies such as the Food Administration and the Selective Service, as well as private organizations like the YMCA and the Red Cross, in creating patriotic campaigns in support of the war. The Division of Pictorial Publicity, headed by the popular artist Charles Dana Gibson, churned out posters and illustrations designed to encourage military enlistment, food conservation, war bond buying, and contributions for overseas victims of war.

The posters generally defined the war as a clear struggle between good and evil, in which American democracy and freedom opposed German militarism and despotism. Yet artists used a wide range of visual themes to illustrate these stark contrasts. World War I posters drew upon traditional ideas about gender differences (men as soldiers, women as nurturers), but they also illustrated the new wartime expectations of women working outside the home in support of the war effort. Appeals to American patriotism cutting across lines of ethnic and religious difference were common, as was the demonizing of the German enemy. And just as the wartime economy blurred the boundaries between public and private enterprises, businesses adapted patriotic appeals to their own advertising.

Creel aptly titled the memoir of his war experience *How We Advertised America.* These three images illustrate the range of World War I propaganda posters.

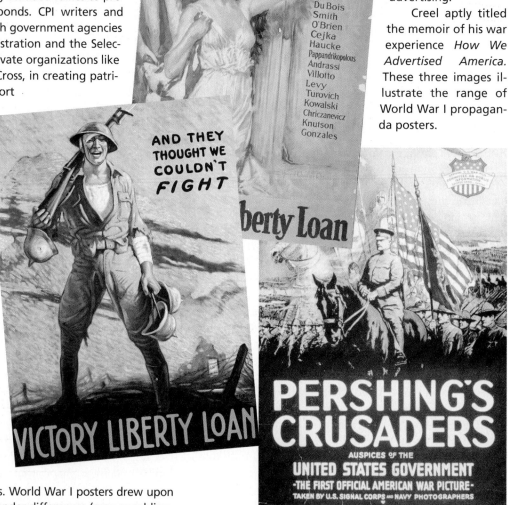

SOURCE: http://www.firstworldwar.com/posters/images

How would you contrast the different kind of patriotic appeals made by "Pershing's Crusaders" "Americans All," and "And They Thought We Couldn't Fight"? Which of these posters do you think makes the most compelling case for supporting the war? How do the artists portray gender differences as part of a visual strategy for winning the war?

"YOU'RE IN THE ARMY NOW"

The central military issue facing the administration was how to raise and deploy U.S. armed forces. When war was declared, there were only about 200,000 men in the army. Traditionally, the United States had relied on volunteer forces organized at the state level. But volunteer rates after April 6 were less than they had been for the Civil War or the Spanish-American War, reflecting the softness of prowar sentiment. The administration thus introduced the Selective Service Act, which provided for the registration and classification for military service of all men between ages twenty-one and thirty-five. To prevent the widespread opposition to the draft that had occurred during the Civil War, the new draft had no unpopular provision allowing draftees to buy their way out of service by paying for a substitute.

On June 5, 1917, nearly 10 million men registered for the draft. There was scattered organized resistance, but overall, registration records offered evidence of national support. A supplemental registration in August 1918 extended the age limits to eighteen and forty-five. By the end of the war, some 24 million men had registered. Of the 2.8 million men eventually called up for service, about 340,000, or 12 percent, failed to show up. Another 2 million Americans volunteered for the various armed services.

The vast, polyglot army posed unprecedented challenges of organization and control. But progressive elements within the administration also saw opportunities for pressing reform measures, especially for the one-fifth of U.S. soldiers born in another country. Army psychologists gave the new Stanford-Binet intelligence test to all recruits and were shocked to find illiteracy rates as high as 25 percent. The low test scores among recent immigrants and rural African Americans undoubtedly reflected the cultural biases embedded in the tests and a lack of proficiency in English for many test takers. After the war, intelligence testing became a standard feature of America's educational system.

The recruits themselves took a more lighthearted view, while singing the army's praises:

Oh, the army, the army, the democratic army,
They clothe you and feed you because the army needs you
Hash for breakfast, beans for dinner, stew for suppertime,
Thirty dollars every month, deducting twenty-nine.
Oh, the army, the army, the democratic army,
The Jews, the Wops, and the Dutch and Irish Cops,
They're all in the army now!

African American officers of the 367th Infantry Regiment, 77th Division, pose with a girl in France, 1918, Nicknamed the "Buffalos" a reference to the black "buffalo soldiers" who had served in the U.S. Army during the late nineteenth century campaigns against Indians, this was one of only two army units that commissioned African American officers.

RACISM IN THE MILITARY

But African Americans who served found severe limitations in the U.S. military. They were organized into totally segregated units, barred entirely from the marines and the Coast Guard, and largely relegated to working as cooks, laundrymen, stevedores, and the like in the army and navy. Thousands of black soldiers endured humiliating, sometimes violent treatment, particularly from southern white officers. African American servicemen faced hostility from white civilians as well, North and South, often being denied service in restaurants and admission to theaters near training camps. The ugliest incident occurred in Houston, Texas, in August 1917. Black infantrymen, incensed over continual insults and harassment by local whites, seized weapons from an armory and killed seventeen civilians. The army executed thirty black soldiers and imprisoned forty-one others for life, denying any of them a chance for appeal.

More than 200,000 African Americans eventually served in France, but only about one in five saw combat, as opposed to two out of three white soldiers. Black combat units served with distinction in various divisions of the French army. The French government awarded the Croix de Guerre to the all-black 369th U.S. Infantry regiment, and 171 officers and enlisted men were cited individually for exceptional bravery in action. African American soldiers by and large enjoyed a friendly reception from

French civilians as well. The contrast with their treatment at home would remain a sore point with these troops upon their return to the United States.

AMERICANS IN BATTLE

President Wilson appointed General John J. Pershing, recently returned from pursuing Pancho Villa in Mexico, as commander of the American Expeditionary Force (AEF). Pershing insisted that the AEF maintain its own identity, distinct from that of the French and British armies. He was also reluctant to send American troops into battle before they had received at least six months' training. The AEF's

combat role would be brief but intense: not until early 1918 did AEF units reach the front in large numbers; eight months later, the war was over (see Map 22.2).

Like Ulysses S. Grant, Pershing believed the object of war to be total destruction of the enemy's military power. He expressed contempt for the essentially defensive tactics of trench warfare pursued by both sides. But the brutal power of modern military technology had made trench warfare inevitable from 1914 to 1917. The awesome firepower of the machine gun and long-range artillery made the massed frontal confrontations of the Civil War era obsolete.

By the time the guns went silent on November 11, some 2 million men had served in the AEF. Overall

MAP 22.2 The Western Front, 1918 American units saw their first substantial action in late May, helping to stop the German offensive at the Battle of Cantigny. By September, more than 1 million American troops were fighting in a counteroffensive campaign at St. Mihiel, the largest single American engagement of the war.

60,000 Americans had died in battle with 206,000 wounded. Another 60,000 died from diseases, mainly influenza. These figures paled in comparison to the millions lost by the European nations. Yet the American contribution to winning the war was substantial, and both the Allies and the Germans attested to the bravery and enthusiasm that American soldiers displayed on the front. Still, the American impact in the Meuse-Argonne campaign was best understood not in terms of individual heroism or tactical brilliance. Rather, it was the prospect of facing seemingly unlimited quantities of American men and supplies that convinced the exhausted German army to surrender.

THE RUSSIAN REVOLUTION, THE FOURTEEN POINTS, AND ALLIED VICTORY

Since early 1917, the turmoil of the Russian Revolution had changed the climate of both foreign affairs and domestic politics. The repressive and corrupt regime of Czar Nicholas II had been overthrown in March 1917 by a coalition of forces demanding change. The new provisional government vowed to keep Russia in the fight against Germany. But the war had taken a terrible toll on Russian soldiers and civilians and had become very unpopular. The radical Bolsheviks, led by V. I. Lenin, gained a large following by promising "peace, land, and bread," and they began plotting to seize power. The Bolsheviks followed the teachings of German revolutionary Karl Marx, emphasizing the inevitability of class struggle and the replacement of capitalism by communism. In November 1917, the Bolsheviks took control of the Russian government.

Although sympathetic to the March revolution overthrowing the czar, President Wilson refused to recognize the authority of the Bolshevik regime. Bolshevism represented a threat to the liberal-capitalist values that Wilson believed to be the foundation of America's moral and material power. Thus, in January 1918 Wilson outlined American war aims, known as the Fourteen Points, in a speech before Congress. He wanted to counter a fierce Bolshevik campaign to discredit the war as a purely imperialist venture, their sensational publication of secret treaties that the czar had signed with the Allies, and their revelations about annexationist plans across Europe. In effect, Wilson's response to the Bolsheviks was the opening shot of the Soviet-American Cold War that would dominate so much of American domestic politics and foreign affairs for the remainder of the century.

As a blueprint for peace, the Fourteen Points contained three main elements. First, Wilson offered a series of specific proposals for setting postwar boundaries in Europe and creating new countries out of the collapsed Austro-Hungarian and Ottoman empires. The key idea here was the right of all peoples to "national self-determination."

Second, Wilson listed general principles for governing international conduct, including freedom of the seas, free trade, open covenants instead of secret treaties, reduced armaments, and mediation for competing colonial claims. Third, and most important, Wilson called for a League of Nations to help implement these principles and resolve future disputes. The Fourteen Points offered a plan for world order deeply rooted in the liberal progressivism long associated with Wilson. The plan reflected a faith in efficient government and the rule of law as means for solving international problems. It advocated a dynamic democratic capitalism as a middle ground between Old World autocracy and revolutionary socialism.

In March 1918, to the dismay of the Allies, the new Bolshevik government followed through on its promise and negotiated a separate peace with Germany, the Treaty of Brest-Litovsk. Russia was now lost as a military ally, and its defection made possible a massive shift of German troops to the western front. In the early spring of 1918, the Germans launched a major offensive that brought them within fifty miles of Paris. In early June, about 70,000 AEF soldiers helped the French stop the Germans in the battles of Château-Thierry and Belleau Wood. In July, Allied forces led by Marshal Ferdinand Foch of France began a counteroffensive designed to defeat Germany once and for all. American reinforcements began flooding the ports of Liverpool in England and Brest and Saint-Nazaire in France. The "doughboys" (a nickname for soldiers dating back to Civil War–era recruits who joined the army for the money) streamed in at a rate of over 250,000 a month. By September, General Pershing had more than a million Americans in his army.

In late September 1918, the AEF took over the southern part of a twenty-mile front in the Meuse-Argonne offensive. In seven weeks of fighting, most through terrible mud and rain, U.S. soldiers used more ammunition than the entire Union army had in the four years of the Civil War. The Germans, exhausted and badly outnumbered, began to fall back and look for a cease-fire. On November 11, 1918, the war ended with the signing of an armistice.

The massive influx of American troops and supplies no doubt hastened the end of the war. About two-thirds of the U.S. soldiers saw at least some fighting, but even they managed to avoid the horrors of the sustained trench warfare that had marked the earlier years of the war. For most Americans at the front, the war experience was a mixture of fear, exhaustion, and fatigue. Their time in France would remain a decisive moment in their lives. American casualty figures—120,000 dead and 200,000 wounded—awful as they were paled against the estimated casualties (killed and wounded) suffered by the European nations: 9 million for Russia, more than 6 million for Germany, nearly 5 million for France, and over 2 million each for Great Britain and Italy.

OVER HERE

In one sense, World War I can be understood as the ultimate progressive crusade: an opportunity to expand the powers of the federal government in order to win the war. Nearly all the reform energy of the previous two decades now turned toward that central goal. The federal government would play a larger role than ever in managing and regulating the wartime economy. Planning, efficiency, scientific analysis, and cooperation were key principles for government agencies and large volunteer organizations. Although much of the regulatory spirit was temporary, the war experience started some important and lasting organizational trends in American life.

ORGANIZING THE ECONOMY

In the summer of 1917, President Wilson established the War Industries Board (WIB) as a clearinghouse for industrial mobilization to support the war effort. Led by the successful Wall Street speculator Bernard M. Baruch, the WIB proved a major innovation in expanding the regulatory power of the federal government. Given broad authority over the conversion of industrial plants to wartime needs and the manufacture of war materials, the WIB had to balance price controls against war profits. Only by ensuring a fair rate of return on investment could it encourage stepped-up production.

The WIB eventually handled 3,000 contracts worth $14.5 billion with various businesses. Standardization of goods brought large savings and streamlined production. Baruch continually negotiated with business leaders, describing the system as "voluntary cooperation with the big stick in the cupboard." At first Elbert Gary of U.S. Steel refused to accept the government's price for steel, and Henry Ford balked at limiting private car production. But when Baruch warned that he would instruct the military to take over their plants, both industrialists backed down.

In August 1917, Congress passed the Food and Fuel Act, authorizing the president to regulate the production and distribution of the food and fuel necessary for the war effort. To lead the Food Administration (FA), Wilson appointed Herbert Hoover, a millionaire engineer who had already won fame for directing a program of war relief for Belgium. He became one of the best-known figures of the war administration. Hoover imposed price controls on certain agricultural commodities, such as sugar, pork, and wheat. These were purchased by the government and then sold to the public through licensed dealers. The FA also raised the purchase price of grain, so that farmers would increase production. But Hoover stopped short of imposing mandatory food rationing, preferring to rely on persuasion, high prices, and voluntary controls.

Hoover's success, like George Creel's at the CPI, depended on motivating hundreds of thousands of volunteers in thousands of American communities. The FA coordinated the work of local committees that distributed posters and leaflets urging people to save food, recycle scraps, and substitute for scarce produce. The FA directed patriotic appeals for "Wheatless Mondays, Meatless Tuesdays, and Porkless Thursdays." Hoover exhorted Americans to "go back to simple food, simple clothes, simple pleasures." He urged them to grow their own vegetables. These efforts resulted in a sharp cutback in the consumption of sugar and wheat as well as a boost in the supply of livestock. The resultant increase in food exports helped sustain the Allied war effort.

The enormous cost of fighting the war, about $33 billion, required unprecedentedly large expenditures for the federal government. The tax structure shifted dramatically as a result. Taxes on incomes and profits replaced excise and customs levies as the major source of revenue. The minimum income subject to the graduated federal income tax, in effect only since 1913, was lowered to $1,000 from $3,000, increasing the number of Americans who paid income tax from 437,000 in 1916 to 4,425,000 in 1918. Tax rates were as steep as 70 percent in the highest brackets.

FOOD WILL WIN THE WAR
You came here seeking Freedom
You must now help to preserve it
WHEAT is needed for the allies
Waste nothing

A Food Administration poster blended a call for conservation of wheat with an imaginative patriotic appeal for recent immigrants to support the war effort.

The bulk of war financing came from government borrowing, especially in the form of the popular Liberty Bonds sold to the American public. Bond drives became highly organized patriotic campaigns that ultimately raised a total of $23 billion for the war effort. The administration also used the new Federal Reserve Banks to expand the money supply, making borrowing easier. The federal debt jumped from $1 billion in 1915 to $20 billion in 1920.

THE GOVERNMENT–BUSINESS PARTNERSHIP

Overall, the war meant expansion and high profits for American business. Between 1916 and 1918, Ford Motor Company increased its workforce from 32,000 to 48,000, General Motors from 10,000 to 50,000. Total capital expenditure in U.S. manufacturing jumped from $600 million in 1915 to $2.5 billion in 1918. Corporate profits as a whole nearly tripled between 1914 and 1919, and many large businesses did much better than that. Annual prewar profits for U.S. Steel, for example, had averaged $76 million; in 1917, they were $478 million. The total value of farm produce rose from $9.8 billion in 1914 to $21.3 billion by 1918. Expanded farm acreage and increased investment in farm machinery led to a jump of 20 to 30 percent in overall farm production.

The most important and long-lasting economic legacy of the war was the organizational shift toward corporatism in American business. The wartime need for efficient management, manufacturing, and distribution could be met only by a greater reliance on the productive and marketing power of large corporations. Never before had business and the federal government cooperated so closely. Under war administrators like Baruch and Hoover, entire industries (such as radio manufacturing) and economic sectors (such as agriculture and energy) were organized, regulated, and subsidized. War agencies used both public and private power—legal authority and voluntarism—to hammer out and enforce agreements. Here was the genesis of the modern bureaucratic state.

Some Americans worried about the wartime trend toward a greater federal presence in their lives. As *The Saturday Evening Post* noted, "All this government activity will be called to account and reexamined in due time." Although many aspects of the government–business partnership proved temporary, some institutions and practices grew stronger in the postwar years. Among these were the Federal Reserve Board, the income tax system, the Chamber of Commerce, the Farm Bureau, and the growing horde of lobbying groups that pressed Washington for special interest legislation.

LABOR AND THE WAR

Organized labor's power and prestige, though by no means equal to those of business or government, clearly grew during the war. The expansion of the economy, combined with army mobilization and a decline in immigration from Europe, caused a growing wartime labor shortage. As the demand for workers intensified, the federal government was forced to recognize that labor, like any other resource or commodity, would have to be more carefully tended to than in peacetime. For the war's duration, working people generally enjoyed higher wages and a better standard of living. Trade unions, especially those affiliated with the American Federation of Labor (AFL), experienced a sharp rise in membership. In effect, the government took in labor as a junior partner in the mobilization of the economy.

Samuel Gompers, president of the AFL, emerged as the leading spokesman for the nation's trade union movement. An English immigrant and cigar maker by trade, Gompers had rejected the socialism of his youth for a philosophy of "business unionism." By stressing the concrete gains that workers could win through collective bargaining with employers, the AFL had reached a total membership of about 2 million in 1914. Virtually all its members were skilled white males, organized in highly selective crafts in the building trades, railroads, and coal mines.

Gompers pledged the AFL's patriotic support for the war effort, and in April 1918, President Wilson appointed him to the National War Labor Board (NWLB). During 1917, the nation had seen thousands of strikes involving more than a million workers. Wages were usually at issue, reflecting workers' concerns with spiraling inflation and higher prices. The NWLB, cochaired by labor attorney Frank Walsh and former president William H. Taft, acted as a kind of supreme court for labor, arbitrating disputes and working to prevent disruptions in production. The great majority of these interventions resulted in improved wages and reduced hours of work. Most important, the NWLB supported the right of workers to organize unions and furthered the acceptance of the eight-hour day for war workers—central aims of the labor movement. It also backed time-and-a-half pay for overtime, as well as the principle of equal pay for women workers. AFL unions gained more than a million new members during the war, and overall union membership rose from 2.7 million in 1914 to more than 5 million by 1920.

Yet the war also brought widespread use of federal troops under the War Department's new "public utilities" doctrine, under which any private business remotely connected to war production was defined as a public utility. An influx of federal troops poured into lumber camps, coal districts, mining towns, and rail junctions across the nation, as employers requested help in guarding against threatened strikes or alleged "sabotage" by militant workers. Wartime conditions often meant severe disruptions and discomfort for America's workers as well. Overcrowding, rapid workforce turnover, and high inflation rates were typical in war-boom communities. In Bridgeport, Connecticut, a center for small-arms manufacturing, the population grew by 50,000 in less than a year. In 1917, the number of families grew by 12,000, but available housing stock increased by only 6,000 units.

In the Southwest, the demand for wartime labor temporarily eased restrictions against the movement of Mexicans into the United States. The Immigration Act of 1917, requiring a literacy test and an $8 head tax, had cut Mexican immigration nearly in half, down to about 25,000 per year. But employers complained of severe shortages of workers. Farmers in Arizona's Salt River Valley and in southern California needed hands to harvest grain, alfalfa, cotton, and fruit. El Paso's mining and smelting industries, Texas's border ranches, and southern Arizona's railroads and copper mines insisted they depended on unskilled Mexican labor as well.

Responding to these protests, in June 1917, the Department of Labor suspended the immigration law for the duration of the war and negotiated an agreement with the Mexican government permitting some 35,000 Mexican contract laborers to enter the United States. Mexicans let in through this program had to demonstrate they had a job waiting before they could cross the border. They received identification cards and transportation to their place of work from American labor contractors. Pressure from southwestern employers kept the exemptions in force until 1921, well after the end of the war, demonstrating the growing importance of cheap Mexican labor to the region's economy.

If the war boosted the fortunes of the AFL, it also spelled the end for more radical elements of the U.S. labor movement. The Industrial Workers of the World (IWW), unlike the AFL, had concentrated on organizing unskilled workers into all-inclusive industrial unions. The Wobblies denounced capitalism as an unreformable system based on exploitation, and they opposed U.S. entry into the war. IWW leaders advised their members to refuse induction for "the capitalists' war." The IWW had grown in 1916 and 1917. It gained strength among workers in several areas crucial to the war effort: copper mining, lumbering, and wheat harvesting. In September 1917 the Wilson administration responded to appeals from western business leaders for a crackdown on the Wobblies. Justice Department agents, acting under the broad authority of the recently passed Espionage Act, swooped down on IWW offices in more than sixty towns and cities, arresting more than 300 people and confiscating files. The mass trials and convictions that followed broke the back of America's radical labor movement and marked the beginning of a powerful wave of political repression.

WOMEN AT WORK

For many of the 8 million women already in the labor force, the war meant a chance to switch from low-paying jobs, such as domestic service, to higher-paying industrial employment. About a million women workers joined the labor force for the first time. Of the estimated 9.4 million workers directly engaged in war work, some 2.25 million were women. Of these, 1.25 million worked in manufacturing. Female munitions plant workers, train engineers, drill press operators, streetcar conductors, and mail carriers became a common sight around the country. World War I also marked the first time that women were mobilized directly into the armed forces. Over 16,000 women served overseas with the AEF in France, where most worked as nurses, clerical workers, telephone operators, and canteen operators. Another

Women workers at the Midvale Steel and Ordnance Company in Pennsylvania, 1918. Wartime labor shortages created new opportunities for over 1 million women to take high-wage manufacturing jobs like the women shown here. The opportunities proved temporary, however, and with the war's end, nearly all of these women lost their jobs. By 1920, the number of women employed in manufacturing was lower than it had been in 1910.

12,000 women served stateside in the navy and U.S. Marine Corps, and tens of thousands of civilian women were employed in army offices and hospitals. But the war's impact on women was greatest in the broader civilian economy.

In response to the widened range of female employment, the Labor Department created the Women in Industry Service (WIS). Directed by Mary Van Kleeck, the service advised employers on using female labor and formulated general standards for the treatment of women workers. The WIS represented the first attempt by the federal government to take a practical stand on improving working conditions for women. Its standards included the eight-hour day, equal pay for equal work, a minimum wage, the prohibition of night work, and the provision of rest periods, meal breaks, and restroom facilities. These standards had no legal force, however, and WIS inspectors found that employers often flouted them. They were accepted nonetheless as goals by nearly every group concerned with improving the conditions of working women.

At war's end, women lost nearly all their defense-related jobs. Wartime women railroad workers, for example, were replaced by returning servicemen, through the application of laws meant to protect women from hazardous conditions. But the war accelerated female employment in fields already dominated by women. By 1920, more women who worked outside the home did so in white-collar occupations—as telephone operators, secretaries, and clerks, for example—than in manufacturing or domestic service. The new awareness of women's work led Congress to create the Women's Bureau in the Labor Department, which continued the WIS wartime program of education and investigation through the postwar years.

WOMAN SUFFRAGE

The presence of so many new women wageworkers, combined with the highly visible volunteer work of millions of middle-class women, helped finally to secure the vote for women. Volunteer war work—selling bonds, saving food, organizing benefits—was very popular among housewives and club women. These women played a key role in the success of the Food Administration, and the Women's Committee of the Council of National Defense included a variety of women's organizations.

Until World War I, the fight for woman suffrage had been waged largely within individual states. Western states and territories had led the way. Various forms of woman suffrage had become law in Wyoming in 1869, followed by Utah (1870), Colorado (1893), and Idaho (1896). Rocky Mountain and Pacific Coast states did not have the sharp ethnocultural divisions between Catholics and Protestants that hindered suffrage efforts in the East. For example, the close identification in the East between the suffrage and prohibition movements led many Catholic immigrants and German Lutherans to oppose the vote for women, because they feared it would lead to prohibition (see Map 22.3).

The U.S. entry into the war provided a unique opportunity for suffrage groups to shift their strategy to a national campaign for a constitutional amendment granting the vote to women. The most important of these groups was the National American Woman Suffrage Association (NAWSA). Before 1917, most American suffragists had opposed the war. Under the leadership of Carrie Chapman Catt, the NAWSA threw its support behind the war effort and doubled its membership to 2 million. Catt gambled that a strong show of patriotism would help clinch the century-old fight to win the vote for women. The NAWSA pursued a moderate policy of lobbying Congress for a constitutional amendment and calling for state referendums on woman suffrage.

At the same time, more militant suffragists, led by the young Quaker activist Alice Paul, injected new energy and more radical tactics into the movement. Dissatisfied with the NAWSA's conservative strategy of quiet lobbying and orderly demonstrations, Paul left the organization in 1916. She joined forces with western women voters to form the National Woman's Party. Borrowing from English suffragists, this party pursued a more aggressive and dramatic strategy of agitation. Paul and her supporters picketed the White House, publicly burned President Wilson's speeches, and condemned the president and the Democrats for failing to produce an amendment. In one demonstration, they chained themselves to the White House fence, and after their arrest, went on a hunger strike in jail. The militants generated a great deal of publicity and sympathy.

Although some in the NAWSA objected to these tactics, Paul's radical approach helped make the NAWSA position more acceptable to Wilson. Carrie Chapman Catt used the president's war rhetoric as an argument for granting the vote to women. The fight for democracy, she argued, must begin at home, and she urged passage of the woman suffrage amendment as a "war measure." She won Wilson's support, and in 1917, the president urged Congress to pass a woman suffrage amendment as "vital to the winning of the war." The House did so in January 1918 and a more reluctant Senate approved it in June 1919. Another year of hard work was spent convincing the state legislatures. In August 1920, Tennessee gave the final vote needed to ratify the Nineteenth Amendment to the Constitution, finally making woman suffrage legal nationwide.

PROHIBITION

Another reform effort closely associated with women's groups triumphed at the same time. The movement to eliminate alcohol from American life had attracted many Americans, especially women, since before the Civil War. Temperance advocates saw drinking as the source of many of the worst problems faced by the working class, including family violence, unemployment, and poverty. By the early twentieth century, the Woman's Christian Temperance Union, with a quarter-million members, had become the single largest women's organization in American history.

MAP EXPLORATION

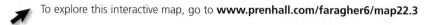

To explore this interactive map, go to **www.prenhall.com/faragher6/map22.3**

MAP 22.3 Woman Suffrage by State, 1869–1919 Dates for the enactment of woman suffrage in the individual states. Years before ratification of the Nineteenth Amendment in 1920, a number of western states had legislated full or partial voting rights for women. In 1917, Montana suffragist Jeannette Rankin became the first woman elected to Congress.

SOURCE: Barbara G. Shortridge, *Atlas of American Women* (New York: Macmillan, 1987).

The moral fervor that accompanied America's entry into the war provided a crucial boost to the cause. With so many breweries bearing German names, the movement benefited as well from the strong anti-German feeling of the war years. Outlawing beer and whiskey would also help to conserve precious grain, prohibitionists argued.

In 1917, a coalition of progressives and rural fundamentalists in Congress pushed through a constitutional amendment providing for a national ban on alcoholic drinks. The Eighteenth Amendment was ratified by the states in January 1919 and became the law of the land one year later. Although Prohibition would create a host of problems in the postwar years, especially as a stimulus for the growth of

organized crime, many Americans, particularly native Protestants, considered it a worthy moral reform.

PUBLIC HEALTH AND THE INFLUENZA PANDEMIC

Wartime mobilization brought deeper government involvement with public health issues, especially in the realm of sex hygiene, child welfare, and disease prevention. The rate of venereal disease among draftees was as high as 6 percent in some states, presenting a potential manpower problem for the army. In April 1917, the War Department mounted a vigorous campaign against venereal disease, which attracted the energies of progressive-era sex reformers—social hygienists and antivice crusaders. Under the direction of Raymond Fosdick and the Commission on Training Camp Activities, the military educated troops on the dangers of contracting syphilis and gonorrhea. Venereal disease rates for soldiers declined by more than 300 percent during the war. The Division of Venereal Diseases, created in the summer of 1918 as a branch of the U.S. Public Health Service, established clinics offering free medical treatment to infected persons.

The wartime boost to government health work continued into the postwar years. The Children's Bureau, created in 1912 as a part of the Labor Department, undertook a series of reports on special problems growing out of the war: the increase in employment of married women, the finding of day care for children of working mothers, and the growth of both child labor and delinquency. In 1918, Julia C. Lathrop, chief of the bureau, organized a "Children's Year" campaign designed to promote public protection of expectant mothers and infants and to enforce child labor laws. In 1917, Lathrop, who had come to the Children's Bureau from the settlement house movement, proposed a plan to institutionalize federal aid to the states for protection of mothers and children. Congress finally passed the Maternity and Infancy Act in 1921, appropriating over $1 million a year to be administered to the states by the Children's Bureau. In the postwar years, clinics for prenatal and obstetrical care grew out of these efforts and greatly reduced the rate of infant and maternal mortality and disease.

The disastrous influenza pandemic of 1918–19 offered the most serious challenge to national public health during the war years. It was part of a global scourge that originated in South China, then spread to the Philippines and moved across the United States, over to Europe, and then back with returning troops. Wartime conditions—large concentrations of people in military camps, on transport ships, and at the front—made its impact especially devastating. With no cure for the lethal combination of the "flu" and respiratory complications (mainly pneumonia), the pandemic killed over 21 million people worldwide. Few Americans paid attention to the disease until it swept through military camps and eastern cities in September 1918 and killed roughly 550,000 Americans in ten months. Most victims were young adults between the ages of twenty and forty. Professional groups such as the American Medical Association called for massive government appropriations to search for a cure. Congress did appropriate a million dollars to the Public Health Service to combat and suppress the epidemic, but it offered no money for research. The Public Health Service found itself overwhelmed by calls for doctors, nurses, and treatment facilities. Much of the care for the sick and dying came from Red Cross nurses and volunteers working in local communities across the nation. With a war on, and the nation focused on reports from the battlefront, even a public health crisis of this magnitude went relatively unnoticed.

REPRESSION AND REACTION

World War I exposed and intensified many of the deepest social tensions in American life. On the local level, vigilantes increasingly took the law into their own hands to punish those suspected of disloyalty. The push for national unity led the federal government to crack down on a wide spectrum of dissenters. The war inflamed racial hatred, and the worst race riots in the nation's history exploded in several cities. At war's end, a newly militant labor movement briefly asserted itself in mass strikes around the nation. Over all these developments loomed the 1917 Bolshevik Revolution in Russia. Radicals around the world had drawn inspiration from what looked like the first successful revolution against a capitalist state. Many conservatives worried that similar revolutions were imminent. From 1918 through 1920, the federal government directed a repressive antiradical campaign that had crucial implications for the nation's future.

A nurse takes a patient's pulse in the influenza ward at Walter Reed Hospital, Washington, DC, November 1, 1918. Intensified by the crowded conditions on the battlefield, in training camps, and on troop ships, the influenza pandemic killed over half a million Americans and some 21 million people worldwide.

The War at Home in Wisconsin

America's entry into World War I provoked deep concerns about the loyalties of "hyphenated" Americans, and socialists immediately came under suspicion for their vocal opposition to an "imperialist" war. Pressure to conform was especially strong in Wisconsin, where German-Americans constituted a large fraction of the population and socialists played a leading political role in many cities and towns. In Milwaukee, nearly half the 500,000 residents were of German descent, and the city had many German newspapers, theaters, clubs, and music societies. Milwaukee's Loyalty League successfully pressured the school board to ban the teaching of German and shut down German theaters and music halls.

Extralegal and legal sanctions against allegedly disloyal Americans reinforced each other. The news story reproduced here, dated April 1, 1918, from the *Ashland* (Wisconsin) *Daily Press,* under the headline "Professor of Northland Tarred and Feathered; Taken From Room By A Mob; Masked Men Take Him Half Mile From the City, Give Him a Coat of Tar and Feathers and Let Him Walk Back Home," describes a vigilante action. It was one among many directed against allegedly disloyal Americans during World War I. In the Revolutionary Era, American Patriots sometimes used this very painful and dangerous form of punishment on Loyalists.

Socialists were also sanctioned: Victor Berger, editor of the *Milwaukee Leader,* a self-described "spokesman for evolutionary socialism" and a vigorous opponent of the war, wrote this angry editorial on October 19, 1918. In October 1917, Postmaster General Albert S. Burleson had banned the *Leader* from the mails under authority of the recently passed Espionage Act, which allowed him to prevent the postal system from handling reading matter "advocating or urging treason, insurrection, or forcible resistance to any law of the United States." In February 1918 the federal government had indicted Berger and four other socialist leaders under the Espionage Act, and in December 1918 they were convicted of conspiracy to "willfully cause insubordination, disloyalty, and refusal of duty...by persistently dwelling upon the evils and horrors of war." Berger appealed his conviction and won election to Congress in 1918, but the House refused to seat him until 1923, when the Supreme Court finally overturned his conviction.

What does Professor Schimler's story tell us about local "vigilante justice" during World War I and its relationship to federal policies during the war?

How does Victor Berger appeal to American historical traditions as part of his editorial against wartime government censorship? How might those who favored that censorship try to refute Berger's arguments?

Professor E.A. Schimler Is Tarred and Feathered (April 1, 1918)

Professor E.A. Schimler, teacher of languages at Northland College, was taken from his room last night about midnight by nearly a dozen masked men, taken to a lonely spot about a half mile from the city, stripped of his clothing and given a substantial coat of tar and feathers.

After treating him to the coat of tar and feathers, the men in the party jumped into waiting automobiles and sped back to the city. They were very orderly. No one knew of the plot and it was carried out with such dispatch that hardly anyone in the city, except the parties interested, knew of the affair until everything was over.

Schimler, when left by the mob, found his undergarments and walked back to his boarding house. The police were then called and the police auto was sent at once to pick him up. He was taken to the city hall and later to the YMCA where he was given an opportunity to clean up.

When he arrived at the city hall, he was in such a condition that there was no question in any one's mind but that the mob were very liberal in the use of tar and also had on hand a lot of feathers.

Schimler could give absolutely no clue as to the parties who forcibly took him from his boarding house and the police have no clues to work on as they were not notified until the affair was all over. Chief of Police Blair stated that if the police had been called when the affair started that they would have prevented it and arrested the members of the mob. As they were not notified until the affair was all over and Schimler had time to walk back to the city, there was no way of apprehending them.

Schimler made claim to the police this morning that the mob not only treated him to a coat of tar and feathers but stole his coat and trousers and also his watch and other valuables from his person. He had not retired when the mob arrived at his boarding place but was sitting in his room, with his shoes off, reading.

"... the mob was very liberal in the use of tar and also had on hand a lot of feathers ..."

"Men with unrestricted power ... become wolves and tyrants."

Professor Schimler is an American citizen. He came to this country with his parents when he was fourteen years of age and received his education in this country, being a graduate of the Boys' Latin School of Boston and of Dartmouth College. After leaving college he taught school in this country and then went to Germany where he taught for six years, returning to this country in 1913. He taught school in Carlisle, Pennsylvania, and Chicago and came to Northland last September to teach the languages. The college authorities say that Professor Schimler has been a very efficient teacher and that there is absolutely no evidence that he was disloyal in words or actions.

Mayor Dennis called at the *Daily Press* office this afternoon and stated that the city authorities would do all in their power to apprehend the guilty parties and in furtherance of this objective will give a reward of $100 for information that will lead to the arrest and conviction of any of the members of the mob that tarred and feathered Professor Schimler.

SOURCE: Wisconsin Historical Society, http://www.wisconsinhistory.org

Victor Berger: "In the Land of the Free and the Home of the Brave" (October 19, 1918)

The following can not reach us by mail:
Money due on subscriptions.
Money for new subs.
Money for advertising.
Mail from our paid correspondents.
Mat and feature services.
Change of address and complaints.
Requests for advertising rates.
Mail from firms from which we buy material.
Price quotations.

But what's the use to go on? Any person with ordinary sense knows what the denial of the mail means to any concern, especially a newspaper. Since Oct. 3, 1917, when the mailing right of *The Leader* was revoked, we have LOST $70,000 IN SUBSCRIPTION MONEY AND $50,000 IN LOCAL AND NATIONAL ADVERTISING.

Now, mind you, no court has found us guilty of any crime. This tremendous loss of $120,000 was the result of the act of one man—the Postmaster General. The constitution says plainly: "No property shall be confiscated without due process of law." But a subjugated and "cowed congress" passed a law which violated, not only the constitution, but every principle of Americanism. This act gives to one man the power to ruin or confiscate the business of any citizen of this great democracy. This one man is prosecutor, judge, jury, and court of appeal. He may bankrupt the Standard Oil Company or the Steel Trust and snap his fingers at the sovereign people Of course, there is no danger that the Postmaster General will exercise his Royal Prerogative on the Steel Trust or any other profiteering concern. Plutocracy is safe, but democracy is being murdered.

No republic can live without the freedom of press and speech. No republic can live without opposition and opposition parties. "Government is not eloquence, but force," as George Washington said. And men with unrestricted power—as we have them in the national capital now—become wolves and tyrants. We are not whining. We are not cringing. We are not cowed. We will not cry "enough!" We will fight on until the prison door clinks behind us or until the noose tightens around our necks. More precious than the freedom of the few, dearer than life itself, is Liberty. Too many have died that "government of the people, by the people, and for the people" may not perish from this earth; too many great souls have breathed their last on fagot piles, amid dungeon walls and gallows ropes that Liberty may live. Go on, gentlemen, and do your worst! Someday a bruised and outraged people will rise in holy anger and cast you on the rubbish pile of history. Hiding behind the plea of making the "world safe for democracy" you are assassinating the freedom of the American people themselves. Go on! Do your damnedest and learn that all are not yet cowed "in the land of the free and the home of the brave."

SOURCE: http://www.marxisthistory.org

MUZZLING DISSENT: THE ESPIONAGE AND SEDITION ACTS

The Espionage Act of June 1917 became the government's key tool for the suppression of antiwar sentiment. It set severe penalties (up to twenty years' imprisonment and a $10,000 fine) for anyone found guilty of aiding the enemy, obstructing recruitment, or causing insubordination in the armed forces. The act also empowered the postmaster general to exclude from the mails any newspapers or magazines he thought treasonous. Within a year, the mailing rights of forty-five newpapers had been revoked. These included several anti-British and pro-Irish publications, as well as such leading journals of American socialism as the Kansas-based *Appeal to Reason,* which had enjoyed a prewar circulation of half a million, and *The Masses.*

To enforce the Espionage Act, the government had to increase its overall police and surveillance machinery. Civilian intelligence was coordinated by the newly created Bureau of Investigation in the Justice Department. This agency was reorganized after the war as the Federal Bureau of Investigation (FBI). In May 1918, the Sedition Act, an amendment to the Espionage Act, outlawed "any disloyal, profane, scurrilous, or abusive language intended to cause contempt, scorn, contumely, or disrepute" to the government, Constitution, or flag.

These acts became a convenient vehicle for striking out at socialists, pacifists, radical labor activists, and others who resisted the patriotic tide. The most celebrated prosecution came in June 1918, when federal agents arrested Eugene V. Debs in Canton, Ohio, after he gave a speech defending antiwar protesters. Sentenced to ten years in prison, Debs defiantly told the court: "I have been accused of having obstructed the war. I admit it. Gentlemen, I abhor war. I would oppose the war if I stood alone." Debs served thirty-two months in federal prison before being pardoned by President Warren G. Harding on Christmas Day 1921.

The Supreme Court upheld the constitutionality of the acts in several 1919 decisions. In *Schenck* v. *United States,* the Court unanimously agreed with Justice Oliver Wendell Holmes's claim that Congress could restrict speech if the words "are used in such circumstances and are of such a nature as to create a clear and present danger." The decision upheld the conviction of Charles Schenck for having mailed pamphlets urging potential army inductees to resist conscription. In *Debs* v. *United States,* the Court affirmed the guilt of Eugene V. Debs for his antiwar speech in Canton, even though he had not explicitly urged violation of the draft laws. Finally, in *Abrams* v. *United States,* the Court upheld Sedition Act convictions of four Russian immigrants who had printed pamphlets denouncing American military intervention in the Russian Revolution. The nation's highest court thus endorsed the severe wartime restrictions on free speech.

In many western communities local vigilantes used the superpatriotic mood to settle scores with labor organizers and radicals. In July 1917, for example, 2,000 armed vigilantes swept through the mining town of Bisbee, Arizona, acting on behalf of the Phelps-Dodge mining company and local businessmen. They wanted to break an IWW-led bitter strike that had crippled Bisbee's booming copper industry. The IWW's vocal opposition to the war made it vulnerable to charges of disloyalty. The vigilantes seized miners in their homes, on the street, and in restaurants and stores, delivering an ultimatum that any miner who refused to return to work would be deported. Some 1,400 miners refused to end their walkout; they were forced at gunpoint onto a freight train, which took them to Columbus, New Mexico, where they were dumped in the desert.

In thousands of other instances government repression and local vigilantes reinforced each other. The American Protective League, founded with the blessing of the Justice Department, mobilized 250,000 self-appointed "operatives" in more than 600 towns and cities. Members of the league, mostly businessmen, bankers, and former policemen, spied on their neighbors and staged a series of well-publicized "slacker" raids on antiwar protesters and draft evaders. Many communities, inspired by Committee on Public Information campaigns, sought to ban the teaching of the German language in their schools or the performance of German music in concert halls (see Communities in Conflict).

THE GREAT MIGRATION AND RACIAL TENSIONS

Economic opportunity brought on by war prosperity triggered a massive migration of rural black Southerners to northern cities. From 1914 to 1920, between 300,000 and 500,000 African Americans left the rural South for the North. Chicago's black population increased by 65,000, or 150 percent; Detroit's by 35,000, or 600 percent. Acute labor shortages led northern factory managers to recruit black migrants to the expanding industrial centers. The Pennsylvania Railroad alone drew 10,000 black workers from Florida and Georgia. Black workers eagerly left low-paying jobs as field hands and domestic servants for the chance at relatively high-paying work in meatpacking plants, shipyards, and steel mills (see Table 22.1).

Kinship and community networks were crucial in shaping what came to be called the Great Migration. They spread news about job openings, urban residential districts, and boardinghouses in northern cities. Black clubs, churches, and fraternal lodges in southern communities frequently sponsored the migration of their members, as well as return trips to the South. Single African American women often made the trip first, because they could more easily obtain steady work as maids, cooks, and laundresses.

TABLE 22.1

The Great Migration: Black Population Growth in Selected Northern Cities, 1910–20

Northern Cities	1910		1920		Percent Increase
	No.	Percent	No.	Percent	
New York	91,709	1.9%	152,467	2.7%	66.3%
Chicago	44,103	2.0	109,458	4.1	148.2
Philadelphia	84,459	5.5	134,229	7.4	58.9
Detroit	5,741	1.2	40,838	4.1	611.3
St. Louis	43,960	6.4	69,854	9.0	58.9
Cleveland	8,448	1.5	34,451	4.3	307.8
Pittsburgh	25,623	4.8	37,725	6.4	47.2
Cincinnati	19,739	5.4	30,079	7.5	53.2

SOURCE: U.S. Department of Commerce.

Relatively few African American men actually secured high-paying skilled jobs in industry or manufacturing. Most had to settle for such low-paying occupations as construction laborers, teamsters, janitors, or porters.

But rigid residential segregation of African Americans laid the foundation for the sprawling segregated ghettoes characteristic of twentieth-century northern cities. Shut out of white neighborhoods by a combination of custom and law (such as restrictive covenants forbidding homeowners to sell to non-whites), African American migrants found themselves forced to squeeze into less desirable and all-black neighborhoods. In 1920, for example, approximately 85 percent of Chicago's 110,000 black citizens lived within a narrow strip roughly three miles long and a quarter mile wide. The city's South Side ghetto—surrounded on all sides by railroad tracks—had been born.

The persistence of lynching and other racial violence in the South no doubt contributed to the Great Migration. But racial violence was not limited to the South. Two of the worst race riots in American history occurred as a result of tensions brought on by wartime migration. On July 2, 1917, in East St. Louis, Illinois, a ferocious mob of whites attacked African Americans, killing at least 200. Before this riot, some of the city's manufacturers had been steadily recruiting black labor as a way to keep local union demands down. Unions had refused to allow black workers as members, and politicians had cynically exploited white racism in appealing for votes. In Chicago, on July 27, 1919, antiblack rioting broke out on a Lake Michigan beach. For two weeks,

This southern African American family is shown arriving in Chicago around 1910. Black migrants to northern cities often faced overcrowding, inferior housing, and a high death rate from disease. But the chance to earn daily wages of $6 to $8 (the equivalent of a week's wages in much of the South), as well as the desire to escape persistent racial violence, kept the migrants coming.

white gangs hunted African Americans in the streets and burned hundreds out of their homes. Twenty-three African Americans and fifteen whites died, and more than 500 were injured. Yet in both East St. Louis and Chicago, local authorities held African Americans responsible for the violence.

African Americans had supported the war effort as faithfully as any group. In 1917, despite a segregated army and discrimination in defense industries, most African Americans thought the war might improve their lot. But black disillusionment with the war grew quickly, as did a newly militant spirit. A heightened sense of race consciousness and activism was evident among black veterans and the growing black communities of northern cities. Taking the lead in the fight against bigotry and injustice, the NAACP held a national conference in 1919 on lynching. It pledged to defend persecuted African Americans, publicize the horrors of lynch law, and seek federal legislation against "Judge Lynch." By 1919, membership in the NAACP had reached 60,000 and the circulation of its journal exceeded half a million.

LABOR STRIFE

The relative labor peace of 1917 and 1918 dissolved after the armistice. In 1919 alone more than 4 million American workers were involved in some 3,600 strikes. This unprecedented strike wave had several causes. Most of the modest wartime wage gains were wiped out by spiraling inflation and high prices for food, fuel, and housing. With the end of government controls on industry, many employers withdrew their recognition of unions. Difficult working conditions, such as the twelve-hour day in steel mills, were still routine in some industries.

Several of the postwar strikes received widespread national attention. They seemed to be more than simple economic conflicts, and they provoked deep fears about the larger social order. In February 1919, a strike in the shipyards of Seattle, Washington, over wages escalated into a general citywide strike involving 60,000 workers. The local press and Mayor Ole Hanson denounced the strikers as revolutionaries. Hanson effectively ended the strike by requesting federal troops to occupy the city. In September, Boston policemen went out on strike when the police commissioner rejected a citizens' commission study that recommended a pay raise. Massachusetts governor Calvin Coolidge called in the National Guard to restore order and won a national reputation by crushing the strike. The entire police force was fired.

The biggest strike took place in the steel industry and involved some 350,000 steelworkers. Centered in several midwestern cities, this epic struggle lasted from September 1919 to January 1920. The AFL had hoped to build on wartime gains in an industry that had successfully resisted unionization before the war. The major demands were

union recognition, the eight-hour day, and wage increases. The steel companies used black strikebreakers and armed guards to keep the mills running. Elbert Gary, president of U.S. Steel, directed a sophisticated propaganda campaign that branded the strikers as revolutionaries. Public opinion turned against the strike and condoned the use of state and federal troops to break it. The failed steel strike proved to be the era's most bitter and devastating defeat for organized labor.

AN UNEASY PEACE

The armistice of November 1918 ended the fighting on the battlefield, but the war continued at the peace conference. In the old royal palace of Versailles near Paris, delegates from twenty-seven countries spent five months hammering out a settlement. Yet neither Germany nor Russia was represented. The proceedings were dominated by leaders of the "Big Four": David Lloyd George (Great Britain), Georges Clemenceau (France), Vittorio Orlando (Italy), and Woodrow Wilson (United States). President Wilson saw the peace conference as a historic opportunity to project his domestic liberalism onto the world stage. But the stubborn realities of power politics would frustrate Wilson at Versailles and lead to his most crushing defeat at home.

PEACEMAKING AND THE SPECTER OF BOLSHEVISM

Even before November 1918, the Allies struggled with how to respond to the revolutionary developments in Russia. British and French leaders wanted to help counterrevolutionary forces overthrow the new Bolshevik regime, as well as reclaim military supplies originally sent for use against the Germans. They were fixated on the Bolshevik danger and the very real possibility of its appeal spreading throughout Central Europe. President Wilson refused to recognize the authority of the Bolshevik regime. Bolshevism represented a threat to the liberal-capitalist values that Wilson believed to be the foundation of America's moral and material power, and that provided the basis for the Fourteen Points. At the same time, however, Wilson at first resisted British and French pressure to intervene in Russia, citing his commitment to national self-determination and noninterference in other countries' internal affairs.

By August 1918, as the Russian political and military situation became increasingly chaotic, Wilson agreed to British and French plans for sending troops to Siberia and northern Russia. Meanwhile, Japan poured troops into Siberia and northern Manchuria in a bid to control the commercially important Chinese Eastern and Trans-Siberian railways. After the Wilson administration negotiated an agreement that placed these strategic railways under international control, the restoration and protection of the railways became the primary concern of American military forces in Russia. Wilson's idealistic support for self-determination had succumbed to the demands of international power politics. Eventually, some 15,000 American troops served in northern and eastern Russia, with some remaining until 1920. They stayed for two reasons: to counter Japanese influence and to avoid alienating the British and French, who opposed withdrawal.

The Allied armed intervention widened the gulf between Russia and the West. In March 1919, Russian Communists established the Third International, or Comintern. Their call for a worldwide revolution deepened Allied mistrust, and the Paris Peace Conference essentially ignored the new political reality posed by the Russian Revolution.

WILSON IN PARIS

Wilson arrived in Paris with the United States delegation in January 1919. He believed the Great War revealed the bankruptcy of diplomacy based on alliances and the "balance of power." He believed that peacemaking, based on the framework put forward in his Fourteen Points, meant an opportunity for America to lead the rest of the world toward a new vision of international relations. The most controversial element, both at home and abroad, would prove to be the League of Nations. The heart of the League Covenant, Article X, called for collective security as the ultimate method of keeping the peace: "The members of the League undertake to respect and preserve as against external aggression the territorial integrity and existing political independence of all Members." In the United States, Wilson's critics would focus on this provision as an unacceptable surrender of the nation's sovereignty and independence in foreign affairs.

Despite Wilson's devotion to "open covenants," much of the negotiating in Paris was in fact done in secret among the Big Four. The ideal of self-determination found limited expression. The independent states of Austria, Hungary, Poland, Yugoslavia, and Czechoslovakia were carved out of the homelands of the defeated Central Powers. But the Allies resisted Wilson's call for independence for the colonies of the defeated nations. A compromise mandate system of protectorates gave the French and British control of parts of the old German and Turkish empires in Africa and western Asia. Japan won control of former German colonies in China. Among those trying, but failing, to influence the treaty negotiations were the sixty-odd delegates to the first Pan African Congress, held in Paris at the same time as the peace talks. The group included Americans W. E. B. Du Bois and William Monroe Trotter as well as representatives from Africa and the West Indies. All were disappointed with the failure of the peace conference to grant self-determination to thousands of Africans living in former German colonies.

Another disappointment for Wilson came with the issue of war guilt. He had strongly opposed the extraction of harsh economic reparations from the Central Powers. But the French and British, with their awful war losses fresh in mind, insisted on making Germany pay. The final treaty contained a clause attributing the war to "the aggression of Germany," and a commission later set German war reparations at $33 billion. Bitter resentment in Germany over the punitive treaty helped sow the seeds for the Nazi rise to power in the 1930s.

The final treaty was signed on June 28, 1919, in the Hall of Mirrors at the Versailles palace. The Germans had no choice but to accept its harsh terms. President Wilson had been disappointed by the secret deals and the endless compromising of his ideals, no doubt underestimating the stubborn reality of power politics in the wake of Europe's most devastating war. He had nonetheless won a commitment to the League of Nations, the centerpiece of his plan, and he was confident that the American people would accept the treaty. The tougher fight would be with the Senate, where a two-thirds vote was needed for ratification.

Woodrow Wilson, Georges Clemenceau, and David Lloyd George are among the central figures depicted in John Christen Johansen's *Signing of the Treaty of Versailles.* But all the gathered statesmen appear dwarfed by their surroundings.

SOURCE: John Christen Johansen (1876–1964), "Signing of the Treaty of Versailles," 1919, oil on canvas, 249 cm × 224.5 cm (98-1/16 × 88-3/8"). Gift of an anonymous donor through Mrs. Elizabeth Rogerson, 1926. National Portrait Gallery, Smithsonian Institution, Washington, DC/Art Resource, New York.

THE TREATY FIGHT

Preoccupied with peace conference politics in Paris, Wilson had neglected politics at home. His troubles had actually started earlier. Republicans had captured both the House and the Senate in the 1918 elections. Wilson had then made a tactical error by including no prominent Republicans in the U.S. peace delegation. He therefore faced a variety of tough opponents to the treaty he brought home.

Wilson's most extreme enemies in the Senate were a group of about sixteen "irreconcilables" who were opposed to a treaty in any form. Some were isolationist progressives, such as Republicans Robert M. La Follette of Wisconsin and William Borah of Idaho, who opposed the League of Nations as steadfastly as they opposed American entry into the war. Others were racist xenophobes like Democrat James Reed of Missouri. He objected, he said, to submitting questions to a tribunal "on which a nigger from Liberia, a nigger from Honduras, a nigger from India, and an unlettered gentleman from Siam, each have votes equal to the great United States of America."

The less dogmatic, but more influential, opponents were led by Republican Henry Cabot Lodge of Massachusetts, powerful majority leader of the Senate. They had strong reservations about the League of Nations, especially the provisions for collective security in the event of a member nation's being attacked. Lodge argued that this provision impinged on congressional authority to declare war and placed unacceptable restraints on the nation's ability to pursue an independent foreign policy. Lodge proposed a series of amendments that would have weakened the League. But Wilson refused to compromise, motivated in part by the long-standing hatred he and Lodge felt toward each other.

In September, Wilson set out on a speaking tour across the country to drum up support for the League and the treaty. The crowds were large and responsive, but they did not change any votes in the Senate. The strain took its toll. On September 25, after speaking in Pueblo, Colorado, the sixty-three-year-old Wilson collapsed from exhaustion. His doctor canceled the rest of the trip. A week later, back in Washington, the president suffered a stroke that left him partially paralyzed. With Wilson badly incapacitated, his wife and his doctor exercised significant decision-making authority, and they reinforced his refusal to agree to any amendments on the Treaty and the League Covenant. In November, Lodge brought the treaty out of committee for a vote, having appended to it fourteen reservations—that is, recommended changes. A bedridden Wilson stubbornly refused to compromise and instructed Democrats to vote against the Lodge version of the treaty. On November 19, Democrats joined with the "irreconcilables" to defeat the amended treaty, 39 to 55.

Wilson refused to budge. In January, he urged Democrats to either stand by the original treaty or vote it down. The 1920 election, he warned, would be "a great and solemn referendum" on the whole issue. In the final vote, on March 19, 1920, twenty-one Democrats broke with the president and voted for the Lodge version, giving it a majority of 49 to 35. But this was seven votes short of the two-thirds needed for ratification. As a result, the United States never signed the Versailles Treaty, nor did it join the League of Nations. The absence of the United States weakened the League and made it more difficult for the organization to realize Wilson's dream of a peaceful community of nations.

THE RED SCARE

The revolutionary changes taking place in Russia became an important backdrop for domestic politics. In the United States, it became common to blame socialism, the IWW, trade unionism in general, and even racial disturbances on foreign radicals and alien ideologies. The accusation of Bolshevism became a powerful weapon for turning public opinion against strikers and political dissenters of all kinds. In truth, by 1919, the American radicals were already weakened and badly split. The Socialist Party had around 40,000 members. Two small Communist Parties, made up largely of immigrants, had a total of perhaps 70,000. In the spring of 1919, a few extremists mailed bombs to prominent business and political leaders. That June, simultaneous bombings in eight cities killed two people and damaged the residence of Attorney General A. Mitchell Palmer. With public alarm growing, state and federal officials began a coordinated campaign to root out subversives and their alleged Russian connections.

Palmer used the broad authority of the 1918 Alien Act, which enabled the government to deport any immigrant found to be a member of a revolutionary organization prior to or after coming to the United States. In a series of raids in late 1919, Justice Department agents in eleven cities arrested and roughed up several hundred members of the IWW and the Union of Russian Workers. Little evidence of revolutionary intent was found, but 249 people were deported, including prominent anarchists Emma Goldman and Alexander Berkman. In early 1920, some 6,000 people in thirty-three cities, including many U.S. citizens and non-Communists, were arrested and herded into prisons and bullpens. Again, no evidence of a grand plot was found, but another 600 aliens were deported. The Palmer raids had a ripple effect around the nation, encouraging other repressive measures against radicals. In New York, the state assembly refused to seat five duly elected Socialist Party members.

Palmer's popularity had waned by the spring of 1920, when it became clear that his predictions of revolutionary uprisings were wildly exaggerated. A report prepared by a group of distinguished lawyers questioned the legality of the attorney general's tactics. As part of the resistance to Palmer's policies, a group of progressive activists formed the American Civil Liberties Union (ACLU) in 1920. Its founders included Clarence Darrow, Felix Frankfurter, Jane Addams, Helen Keller, and John Dewey. For progressives dispirited by the wartime political repression, the ACLU offered a new political front stressing the militant defense of civil liberties jut when they seemed most fragile.

The Red Scare left an ugly legacy: wholesale violations of constitutional rights, deportations of hundreds of innocent people, fuel for the fires of nativism and intolerance. Business groups, such as the National Association of Manufacturers, found "Red-baiting" to be an effective tool in postwar efforts to keep unions out of their factories. Indeed, the government-sanctioned Red Scare reemerged later in the century as a powerful political force. In many communities local vigilantes invoked the threat of Bolshevism and used the superpatriotic mood to settle scores with labor organizers and radicals.

CHRONOLOGY

1903	United States obtains Panama Canal rights
1905	President Theodore Roosevelt mediates peace treaty between Japan and Russia at Portsmouth Conference
1908	Root-Takahira Agreement with Japan affirms status quo in Asia and Open Door policy in China
1911	Mexican Revolution begins
1914	U.S. forces invade Mexico
	Panama Canal opens
	World War I begins in Europe
	President Woodrow Wilson issues proclamation of neutrality
1915	Germany declares war zone around Great Britain
	German U-boat sinks *Lusitania*
1916	Pancho Villa raids New Mexico and is pursued by General Pershing
	Wilson is reelected
	National Defense Act establishes preparedness program
1917	February: Germany resumes unrestricted submarine warfare
	March: Zimmermann note, suggesting a German-Mexican alliance, shocks Americans

	April: United States declares war on the Central Powers
	May: Selective Service Act is passed
	June: Espionage Act is passed
	November: Bolshevik Revolution begins in Russia
1918	January: Wilson unveils Fourteen Points
	May: Sedition Act is passed
	June: U.S. troops begin to see action in France
	September: Influenza outbreaks among AEF troops in France
	November: Armistice ends war
1919	January: Eighteenth Amendment (Prohibition) is ratified
	Wilson serves as chief U.S. negotiator at Paris Peace Conference
	June: Versailles Treaty is signed in Paris
	July: Race riot breaks out in Chicago
	Steel strike begins in several midwestern cities
	November: Palmer raids begin
1920	March: Senate finally votes down Versailles Treaty and League of Nations
	August: Nineteenth Amendment (woman suffrage) is ratified
	November: Warren G. Harding is elected president

The Red Scare took its toll on the women's movement as well. Before the war, many suffragists and feminists had maintained ties and shared platforms with socialist and labor groups. The suffrage movement in particular had brought together women from very different class backgrounds and political perspectives. But the calls for "100 percent Americanism" during and after the war destroyed the fragile alliances that had made a group such as the National American Woman Suffrage Association so powerful. Hostility to radicalism marked the political climate of the 1920s, and this atmosphere narrowed the political spectrum for women activists.

THE ELECTION OF 1920

Woodrow Wilson had wanted the 1920 election to be a "solemn referendum" on the League of Nations and his conduct of the war. Ill and exhausted, Wilson did not run for reelection. A badly divided Democratic Party compromised on Governor James M. Cox of Ohio as its candidate. A proven vote-getter, Cox distanced himself from Wilson's policies, which had come under withering attack from many quarters.

The Republicans nominated Senator Warren G. Harding of Ohio. A political hack, the handsome and genial Harding had virtually no qualifications to be president, except that he looked like one. Harding's campaign was vague and ambiguous about the Versailles Treaty and almost everything else. He struck a chord with the electorate in calling for a retreat from Wilsonian idealism. "America's present need," he said, "is not heroics but healing; not nostrums but normalcy; not revolution but restoration."

The notion of a "return to normalcy" proved very attractive to voters exhausted by the war, inflation, big government, and social dislocation. Harding won the greatest landslide in history to that date, carrying every state outside the South and taking the popular vote by 16 million to 9 million. Republicans retained their majorities in the House and Senate as well. Socialist Eugene V. Debs, still a powerful symbol of the dream of radical social change, managed to poll 900,000 votes from jail. But the overall vote repudiated Wilson and the progressive movement. Americans seemed eager to pull back from moralism in public and international controversies. Yet many of the economic, social, and cultural changes wrought by the war would accelerate during the 1920s. In truth, there could never be a "return to normalcy."

CONCLUSION

The global impact of the Great War, including the United States' place in relation to the rest of the world, was profound. Although the casualties and social upheavals endured by the European powers might seem to dwarf the price paid by the United States, the war created economic, social, and political dislocations that helped reshape American life long after Armistice Day. The ability to raise and deploy the massive American Expeditionary Force overseas so quickly had proved decisive to ending the fighting. The government's direct intervention in every aspect of the wartime economy was unprecedented, and wartime production needs contributed to a "second industrial revolution" that transformed the economy in the decade following the war. Republican administrations invoked the wartime partnership between government and industry to justify an aggressive peacetime policy fostering cooperation between the state and business. Although the United States would not join the League of Nations, the war turned the United States into a major global force: the world's new leading creditor nation would now also take its place as a powerful commercial and industrial engine in the global economy.

Patriotic fervor and the exaggerated threat of Bolshevism were used to repress radicalism, organized labor, feminism, and the entire legacy of progressive reform. The wartime measure of national prohibition evolved into perhaps the most contentious social issue of peacetime. Sophisticated use of sales techniques, psychology, and propaganda during the war helped define the newly powerful advertising and public relations industries of the 1920s. The growing visibility of immigrants and African Americans, especially in the nation's cities, provoked a xenophobic and racist backlash in the politics of the 1920s. More than anything else, the desire for "normalcy" reflected the deep anxieties evoked by America's wartime experience.

REVIEW QUESTIONS

1. What central issues drew the United States deeper into international politics in the early years of the century? How did American presidents justify a more expansive role? What diplomatic and military policies did they exploit for these ends?

2. Compare the arguments for and against American participation in the Great War. Which Americans were most likely to support entry? Which were more likely to oppose it?

3. How did mobilizing for war change the economy and its relationship to government?

Which of these changes, if any, spilled over to the postwar years?

4. How did the war affect political life in the United States? What techniques were used to stifle dissent? What was the war's political legacy?

5. Analyze the impact of the war on American workers. How did the conflict affect the lives of African Americans and women?

6. What principles guided Woodrow Wilson's Fourteen Points? How would you explain the United States' failure to ratify the Treaty of Versailles?

RECOMMENDED READING

Alan Dawley, *Changing the World: American Progressives in War and Revolution* (2003). Thoughtful analysis that traces the interplay between progressive politics and America's involvement in the Great War.

James H. Hallas, *Doughboy War: The American Expeditionary Force in World War I* (2000). Excellent and wide-ranging account of the AEF told entirely from first-person accounts—letters, diaries, and interviews—of the doughboys themselves.

Robert Hannigan, *The New World Power: American Foreign Policy, 1898–1917* (2002). An ambitious analysis of how the American policy-making elite sought to impose political and economic order around the globe.

Paul L. Murphy, *World War I and the Origin of Civil Liberties* (1979). A good overview of the various civil liberties issues raised by the war and government efforts to suppress dissent.

Ronald Schaffer, *America in the Great War: The Rise of the War Welfare State* (1991). Excellent material on how the war transformed the relationship between business and government and spurred improved conditions for industrial workers.

Richard Slotkin, *Lost Battalions: The Great War and the Crisis of Nationality* (2006). A beautifully written and imaginative account of two AEF units: the African American 369th Infantry (the "Harlem Hellfighters") and the 77th Division (the "Melting Pot"). Slotkin explores the tensions inherent in the wartime mobilization that included large groups of citizens—in these cases blacks and immigrants—who were deemed inferior yet also promised the benefits of full citizenship rights.

Joe William Trotter Jr., ed., *The Great Migration in Historical Perspective* (1991). An excellent collection of essays examining the Great Migration, with special attention to issues of class and gender within the African American community.

Susan Zeiger, *In Uncle Sam's Service: Women Workers with the American Expeditionary Force, 1917–1919* (1999). The first in-depth study of American women's experiences with the armed forces overseas.

Robert H. Zieger, *America's Great War: World War I and the American Experience* (2000). The best recent one-volume synthesis on how the war transformed the United States and its role in the world.

The Twenties
1920–1929

AMERICAN COMMUNITIES

The Movie Audience and Hollywood: Mass Culture Creates a New National Community

Inside midtown Manhattan's magnificent new Roxy Theater, a sellout crowd eagerly settled in for opening night. Outside, thousands of fans cheered wildly at the arrival of movie stars such as Charlie Chaplin, Gloria Swanson, and Harold Lloyd. A squadron of smartly uniformed ushers guided patrons under a five-story-tall rotunda to some 6,200 velvet-covered seats. The audience marveled at the huge gold and rose-colored murals, classical statuary, plush carpeting, and Gothic-style windows. It was easy to believe newspaper reports that the theater had cost $10 million to build. Suddenly, light flooded the orchestra pit and 110 musicians began playing "The Star Spangled Banner." A troupe of 100 performers took the stage, dancing ballet numbers and singing old southern melodies such as "My Old Kentucky Home" and "Swanee River." Congratulatory telegrams from President Calvin Coolidge and other dignitaries flashed on the screen. Finally, the evening's feature presentation, *The Love of Sunya*, starring Gloria Swanson, began. Samuel L. "Roxy" Rothapfel, the theater's designer, had realized his grand dream—to build "the cathedral of the motion picture."

When Roxy's opened in March 1927, nearly 60 million Americans "worshiped" each week at movie theaters across the nation. The "movie palaces" of the 1920s were designed to transport patrons to exotic places and different times. As film pioneer Marcus Loew put it, "We sell tickets to theaters, not movies." Every large community boasted at least one opulent movie theater. Houston's Majestic was built to represent an ancient

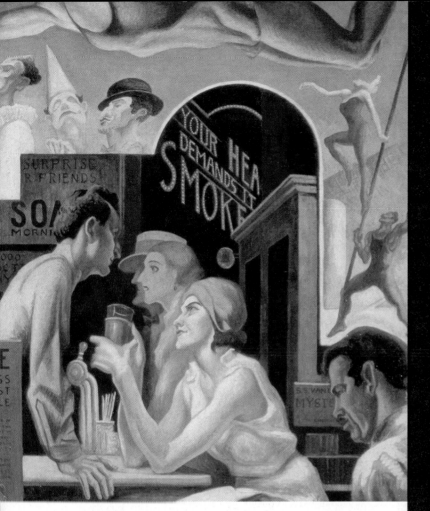

SOURCE: Thomas Hart Benton, "City Activities with Dance Hall" from "America Today," 1930. Distemper and egg tempera on gessoed linen with oil glaze 92 × 134 1/2 inches. Collection, AXA Financial, Inc., through its subsidiary, The Equitable Life Assurance Society of the U.S. © AXA Financial, Inc.

Italian garden; it had a ceiling made to look like an open sky, complete with stars and cloud formations. The Tivoli in Chicago featured French Renaissance decor; Grauman's Egyptian in Los Angeles recreated the look of a pharaoh's tomb; and Albuquerque's Kimo drew inspiration from Navajo art and religion.

The remarkable popularity of motion pictures, and later radio, forged a new kind of community. A huge national audience regularly went to the movies, and the same entertainment could be enjoyed anywhere in the country by just about everyone. People who may have had little in common in terms of ethnicity, background, or geographic location now found themselves part of a virtual community of movie fans. Hollywood films also achieved a global popularity that represented the cultural side of America's newfound influence in the world. American films, especially slapstick comedies, had begun appearing regularly in European theaters during the Great War, as producers took advantage of wartime dislocation ➤

to penetrate foreign markets. The Webb–Pomerene Act of 1918 proved a boon for the global expansion of Hollywood film, as it exempted export associations from antitrust laws, allowing them to form cartels, fix prices, and engage in other trade practices that would have been barred at home. Hollywood movies soon emerged as among the most widely circulated American commodities in the world, second only to Gillette razor blades and Ford automobiles. Producers found strong allies in the federal government, which touted the connections between the export of Hollywood movies and the growth of American trade around the world. "Trade follows the film," as one Commerce Department report put it, with movies supplying "an animated catalogue for ideas of dress, living, and comfort."

Hollywood's emergence might be thought of as part of a broader "second industrial revolution" that modernized industrial production and greatly expanded the availability of consumer goods in the postwar years. The studios concentrated on producing big-budget feature films designed for mass audiences, with the "star system" providing the industry's version of product branding. The economies of large-scale production allowed studios to sign popular actors to long-term contracts and invest heavily in their salaries and promotion. The stars themselves had to be willing to sacrifice their privacy in order to promote their "celebrity" status. Movie stars like Charlie Chaplin, Mary Pickford, Rudolph Valentino, Gloria Swanson, and Douglas Fairbanks became popular idols as much for their highly publicized private lives as for their roles on screen. Many accumulated great wealth, becoming the nation's experts on how to live well. They built luxurious mansions in a variety of architectural styles and outfitted them with swimming pools, tennis courts, golf courses, and lavish gardens. Americans embraced the culture of celebrity, voraciously consuming fan magazines, gossip columns, and news of the stars. Indeed during the 1920s there was a tight connection between celebrity and the rapid growth of new networks of mass culture—movies, radio, advertising, musical recordings, and big-time sports.

If the movies created a new kind of virtual community of fans in the 1920s, the town of Hollywood itself was also a new kind of American community. A suburb of Los Angeles that had barely existed in 1890, Hollywood was an alluring alternative to the East Coast cities where movies had been born. Its reliably sunny and dry climate was ideal for year-round filming. Its unique surroundings offered a perfect variety of scenic locations—mountains, desert, ocean—and downtown Los Angeles was only an hour away. Land was cheap and plentiful. And because Los Angeles was the leading nonunion, open-shop city in the country, so was labor. It lured the young and cosmopolitan with the promise of upward mobility and a new way of life.

Most of the top studio executives were Jewish immigrants from eastern and central Europe. In contrast to most Americans, who hailed from rural areas or small towns, more than half of Hollywood's writers, directors, editors, and actors were born in cities of over 100,000. Two-thirds of its performers were under thirty-five, and three-fourths of its actresses were under twenty-five. More than 90 percent of its writers (women made up one-third to one-half of this key group) had attended college or worked in journalism. Hollywood films celebrating the pleasures of leisure, consumption, and personal freedom redefined American cultural values in the 1920s. But the community that cranked them out was far from typically American.

Ordinary Americans found it easy to identify with movie stars despite their wealth and status. Unlike industrialists or politicians, stars had no social authority over large groups of employees or voters. They, too, had to answer to a boss, and most had risen from humble beginnings. But above all, Hollywood, like the movies it churned out, represented for millions of Americans new possibilities: freedom, material success, upward mobility, and the chance to remake one's very identity. By the end of the decade, the Hollywood "dream factory" had helped forge a national community whose collective aspirations and desires were increasingly defined by those possibilities, even if relatively few Americans realized them during the 1920s. And around the world, Hollywood movies became the preeminent version of the American way of life.

Of course, Hollywood films offered nothing near an accurate reflection of the complexities of American society. As American culture became increasingly defined by an urban-based mass media that claimed the entire nation for its audience, resentment toward and resistance against the new popular culture was widespread. Movies celebrated prosperity, new technologies, and expanded consumerism, but these were by no means shared equally among Americans in the decade following World War I. And while Hollywood films touted the promise of the modern, and the potential for people to remake themselves, tenacious belief in the old-fashioned verities of prewar America fueled some of the strongest political and cultural currents of the decade.

Focus Questions

1. How did the "second industrial revolution" transform the American economy?

2. What were the promises and limits of prosperity in the 1920s?

3. How and why did the Republican Party dominate 1920s' politics?

4. How did the new mass media reshape American culture?

5. Which Americans were less likely to share in postwar prosperity and why?

6. What political and cultural movements opposed modern cultural trends?

1920–1929

POSTWAR PROSPERITY AND ITS PRICE

Republican Warren G. Harding won the presidency in 1920, largely thanks to his nostalgic call for a "return to normalcy." But in the decade following the end of World War I, the American economy underwent profound structural changes that guaranteed life would never be "normal" again. The 1920s saw an enormous increase in the efficiency of production, a steady climb in real wages, a decline in the length of the average employee's workweek, and a boom in consumer-goods industries. Americans shared unevenly in the postwar prosperity, and by the end of the decade, certain basic weaknesses in the economy helped to bring on the worst depression in American history. Yet overall, the nation experienced crucial transformations in how it organized its business, earned its living, and enjoyed its leisure time.

THE SECOND INDUSTRIAL REVOLUTION

The prosperity of the 1920s rested on what historians have called the "second industrial revolution" in American manufacturing, in which technological innovations made it possible to increase industrial output without expanding the labor force. Electricity replaced steam as the main power source for industry in these years, making possible the replacement of older machinery with more efficient and flexible electric machinery. In 1914, only 30 percent of the nation's factories were electrified; by 1929, 70 percent relied on the electric motor rather than the steam engine.

Much of the newer, automatic machinery could be operated by unskilled and semiskilled workers, and it boosted the overall efficiency of American industry. Thus, in 1929, the average worker in manufacturing produced roughly three-quarters more per hour than he or she had in 1919. The machine industry itself, particularly the manufacture of electrical machinery, led in productivity gains, enjoying one of the fastest rates of expansion. It employed more workers than any other manufacturing sector—some 1.1 million in 1929—supplying not only a growing home market but 35 percent of the world market as well.

During the late nineteenth century, heavy industries such as machine tools, railroads, iron, and steel had pioneered mass-production techniques. These industries manufactured what economists call producer-durable goods. In the 1920s, modern mass-production techniques were increasingly applied to newer consumer-durable goods—automobiles, radios, washing machines, and telephones—permitting firms to make large profits while keeping prices affordable. Other consumer-based industries, such as canning, chemicals, synthetics, and plastics, began to change the everyday lives of millions of Americans. With more efficient management, greater mechanization, intensive product research, and ingenious sales and advertising methods, the consumer-based industries helped to nearly double industrial production in the 1920s.

The watchword for all this was efficiency, a virtue that progressives had emphasized in their prewar efforts to improve urban life and the mechanics of government itself. But efficiency was now an obsession for American businessmen, who thought it defined modernity as well.

American success in mechanization and the mass production of consumer goods evoked admiration and envy in much of the industrialized (and industrializing) world. Even in Russia, where the new government struggled to industrialize using a Marxist model of development, there was great admiration for American industrial efficiency and progress. Bolshevik leader V. I. Lenin coined the famous slogan, "Electrification plus Soviet Power equals Socialism."

THE MODERN CORPORATION

In the late nineteenth century, individual entrepreneurs such as John D. Rockefeller in oil and Andrew Carnegie in steel had provided a model for success. They maintained both corporate control (ownership) and business leadership (management) in their enterprises. In the 1920s, a managerial revolution increasingly divorced ownership of corporate stock from the everyday control of businesses (see Figure 23.1). The new corporate ideal was to be found in men such as Alfred P. Sloan of General Motors and Owen D. Young of the Radio Corporation of America. A growing class of salaried executives, plant managers, and engineers formed a new elite, who made corporate policy without themselves having a controlling interest in the companies they worked for. They stressed scientific management and the latest theories of behavioral psychology in their effort to make their workplaces more productive, stable, and profitable (see Figure 23.2). Modern managers also brought a more sophisticated understanding of global markets to their management. Exploiting overseas markets, especially in Europe, became a key element in corporate strategy, especially for car manufacturers, chemical

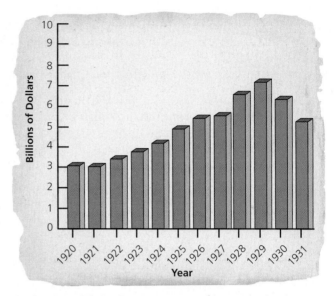

FIGURE 23.2 Consumer Debt, 1920–31
The expansion of consumer borrowing was a key component of the era's prosperity. These figures do not include mortgages or money borrowed to purchase stocks. They reveal the great increase in "installment buying" for such consumer durable goods as automobiles and household appliances.

companies, and businesses engaged in the new world of modern mass media.

During the 1920s, the most successful corporations were those that led in three key areas: the integration of production and distribution, product diversification, and the expansion of industrial research. Until the end of World War I, for example, the chemical manufacturer Du Pont had specialized in explosives such as gunpowder. After the war, Du Pont moved aggressively into the consumer market with a diverse array of products. The company created separate but integrated divisions that produced and distributed new fabrics (such as rayon), paints, dyes, and celluloid products (such as artificial sponges). The great electrical manufacturers—General Electric and Westinghouse—similarly transformed themselves after the war. Previously concentrating on lighting and power equipment, they now diversified into household appliances like radios, washing machines, and refrigerators. The chemical and electrical industries also led the way in industrial research, hiring personnel to develop new products and test their commercial viability.

By 1929, the 200 largest corporations owned nearly half the nation's corporate wealth—that is, physical plant, stock, and property. Half the total industrial income—revenue from sales of goods—was concentrated in 100 corporations. Oligopoly—the control of a market by a few large producers—became the norm. Four companies packed almost three-quarters of all American meat. Another four rolled nine out of every ten cigarettes. National chain grocery stores, clothing shops, and pharmacies began squeezing out local neighborhood businesses. One grocery chain alone, the Great Atlantic and

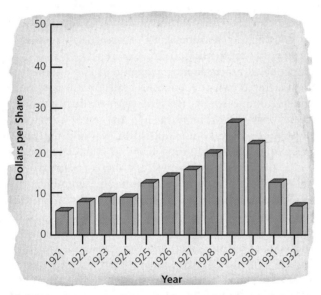

FIGURE 23.1 Stock Market Prices, 1921–32
Common stock prices rose steeply during the 1920s. Although only about 4 million Americans owned stocks during the period, "stock watching" became something of a national sport.

The A&P grocery chain expanded from 400 stores in 1912 to more than 15,000 by the end of the 1920s, making it a familiar sight in communities across America. A&P advertisements, like this one from 1927, emphasized cleanliness, order, and the availability of name-brand goods at discount prices.

Pacific Tea Company (A&P), accounted for 10 percent of all retail food sales in America. Its 15,000 stores sold a greater volume of goods than Ford Motor Company at its peak. A&P won out over thousands of older "mom and pop" grocery stores partly by selling its stores as "clean" and "modern," with no haggling over prices. These changes meant that Americans were increasingly members of national consumer communities, buying the same brands all over the country, as opposed to locally produced goods.

WELFARE CAPITALISM

The wartime gains made by organized labor, and the active sympathy shown to trade unions by government agencies such as the National War Labor Board (NWLB), troubled most corporate leaders. Shortly after the war's end, largely as a result of pressure from business leaders, the Wilson administration dismantled the NWLB and other mechanisms aimed at mediation of labor disputes. In contrast with Great Britain, where a broad social consensus now accepted the principle of state intervention in labor relations, American business and political parties pushed

for a retreat from government involvement. To challenge the power and appeal of trade unions and collective bargaining, large employers aggressively promoted a variety of new programs designed to improve worker well-being and morale while also fending off unionization. These schemes, collectively known as welfare capitalism, became a key part of corporate strategy in the 1920s.

Large corporations mounted an effective antiunion campaign in the early 1920s called "the American plan" as an alternative to trade unionism and the class antagonism associated with European labor relations. Backed by powerful business lobbies such as the National Association of Manufacturers and the Chamber of Commerce, campaign leaders called for the open shop, in which no employee would be compelled to join a union. In effect, an "open shop" meant that no known union member would be hired. If a union existed, nonmembers would still get whatever wages and rights the union had won—a policy that put organizers at a disadvantage in signing up new members.

The open shop undercut the gains won in a union shop, where new employees had to join an existing union, or a closed shop, where employers agreed to hire only union members. As alternatives, large employers such as U.S. Steel and International Harvester began setting up company unions. Their intent was to substitute largely symbolic employee representation in management conferences for the more confrontational process of collective bargaining. These management strategies contributed to a sharp decline in the ranks of organized labor. Total union membership dropped from about 5 million in 1920 to 3.5 million in 1926. A large proportion of the remaining union members were concentrated in the skilled crafts of the building and printing trades. A conservative and timid union leadership was also responsible for the trend. William Green, who became president of the American Federation of Labor after the death of Samuel Gompers in 1924, showed no real interest in getting unorganized workers, such as those in the growing mass-production industries of automobiles, steel, and electrical goods, into unions.

Another approach encouraged workers to acquire property through stock-purchase plans or, less frequently, home-ownership plans. By 1927, 800,000 employees had more than $1 billion invested in more than 300 companies. Other programs offered workers insurance policies covering accidents, illness, old age, and death. By 1928, some 6 million workers had group insurance coverage valued at $7.5 billion. Many plant managers and personnel departments consciously worked to improve safety conditions, provide medical services, and establish sports and recreation programs for workers. Employers hoped such measures would encourage workers to identify personally with the company and discourage complaints on the job. To some extent they succeeded. But welfare capitalism could not solve the chronic problems faced by industrial workers: seasonal unemployment, low wages, long hours, and unhealthy factory conditions. Indeed corporate policy reinforced economic insecurity for millions of workers and advanced growing income inequality. The failure of the 1920s' economy to distribute gains in productivity more equally would help set the stage for the Great Depression of the 1930s.

THE AUTO AGE

In their classic community study *Middletown* (1929), sociologists Robert and Helen Lynd noted the dramatic impact of the car on the social life of residents of Muncie, Indiana. "Why on earth do you need to study what's changing this country?" asked one lifelong Muncie resident in 1924. "I can tell you what's happening in just four letters: A-U-T-O!" This remark hardly seems much of an exaggeration today. No other single development could match the impact of the postwar automobile explosion on the way Americans worked, lived, and played. The auto industry offered the clearest example of the rise to prominence of consumer durables. During the 1920s, America made approximately 85 percent of all the world's passenger cars. By 1929, the motor vehicle industry was the most productive in the United States in terms of value. In that year, the industry added 4.8 million new cars to the more than 26 million—roughly one for every five people—already on American roads.

This extraordinary new industry had mushroomed in less than a generation. Its great pioneer, Henry Ford, had shown how the use of a continuous assembly line could drastically reduce the number of worker hours required to produce a single vehicle. Ford revolutionized the factory shop floor with new, custom-built machinery, such as the engine-boring drill press and the pneumatic wrench, and a more efficient layout. "Every piece of work in the shop moves," Ford boasted. "It may move on hooks or overhead chains, going to assembly in the exact order in which the parts are required; it may travel on a moving platform, or it may go by gravity, but the point is that there is no lifting or trucking of anything other than materials." In 1913, it took thirteen hours to produce one automobile. In 1914,

Finished automobiles roll off the moving assembly line at the Ford Motor Company, Highland Park, Michigan, ca. 1920. During the 1920s, Henry Ford achieved the status of folk hero, as his name became synonymous with the techniques of mass production. Ford cultivated a public image of himself as the heroic genius of the auto industry, greatly exaggerating his personal achievements.

at his sprawling new Highland Park assembly plant just outside Detroit, Ford's system finished one car every ninety minutes. By 1925, cars were rolling off his assembly line at the rate of one every ten seconds.

In 1914, Ford startled American industry by inaugurating a new wage scale: $5 for an eight-hour day. This was roughly double the going pay rate for industrial labor, along with a shorter workday as well. But in defying the conventional economic wisdom of the day, Ford acted less out of benevolence than out of shrewdness. He understood that workers were consumers as well as producers, and the new wage scale helped boost sales of Ford cars. It also reduced the high turnover rate in his labor force and increased worker efficiency. Roughly two-thirds of the labor force at Ford consisted of immigrants from southern and eastern Europe. By the early 1920s Ford also employed about 5,000 African Americans, more than any other large American corporation. Ford's mass-production system and economies of scale permitted him to progressively reduce the price of his cars, bringing them within the reach of millions of Americans. The famous Model T, thoroughly standardized and available only in black, cost just under $300 in 1924—about three months' wages for the best-paid factory workers.

By 1927, Ford had produced 15 million Model Ts. But by then, the company faced stiff competition from General Motors (GM), which had developed an effective new marketing strategy. Under the guidance of Alfred P. Sloan, GM organized into separate divisions, each of which appealed to a different market segment. Cadillac, for example, produced GM's most expensive car, which was targeted at the wealthy buyer; Chevrolet produced its least expensive model, which was targeted at working-class and lower-middle-class buyers. The GM business structure, along with its attempts to match production with demand through sophisticated market research and sales forecasting, became a widely copied model for other large American corporations. Both Ford and GM also pushed the idea of purchasing cars on credit, thus helping to make "installment buying" an underpinning of the new consumer culture.

The auto industry provided a large market for makers of steel, rubber, glass, and petroleum products. It stimulated public spending for good roads and extended the housing boom to new suburbs. Showrooms, repair shops, and gas stations appeared in thousands of communities. New small enterprises, from motels to billboard advertising to roadside diners, sprang up as motorists took to the highway. Automobiles widened the experience of millions of Americans. They made the exploration of the world outside the local community easier and more attractive. For some, the car merely reinforced old social patterns, making it easier for them to get to church on Sunday, for example, or visit neighbors. Others used their cars to go to new places, shop in nearby cities, or take vacations. The automobile made leisure, in the sense of getting away

from the routines of work and school, a more regular part of everyday life. It undoubtedly also changed the courtship practices of America's youth. Young people took advantage of the car to gain privacy and distance from their parents, and many had their first sexual experiences in automobiles.

CITIES AND SUBURBS

Cars also promoted urban and suburban growth. The federal census for 1920 was the first in American history in which the proportion of the population that lived in urban places (those with 2,500 or more people) exceeded

Until 1924, Henry Ford had disdained national advertising for his cars. But as General Motors gained a competitive edge by making yearly changes in style and technology, Ford was forced to pay more attention to advertising. This ad was directed at "Mrs. Consumer," combining appeals to female independence and motherly duties.

the proportion of the population living in rural areas. More revealing of urban growth was the steady increase in the number of big cities. In 1910, there were sixty cities with more than 100,000 inhabitants; in 1920, there were sixty-eight; and by 1930, there were ninety-two. During the 1920s, New York grew by 20 percent, to nearly 7 million, whereas Detroit, home of the auto industry, doubled its population, to nearly 2 million.

Cities promised business opportunity, good jobs, cultural richness, and personal freedom. They attracted millions of Americans, white and black, from small towns and farms, as well as immigrants from abroad. Immigrants were drawn to cities by the presence there of family and people of like background in already established ethnic communities. In a continuation of the Great Migration that began during World War I, roughly 1.5 million African Americans from the rural South migrated to cities in search of economic opportunities during the 1920s, doubling the black populations of New York, Chicago, Detroit, and Houston.

Houston offers a good example of how the automobile shaped an urban community. In 1910, it was a sleepy railroad town with a population of about 75,000 that served the Texas Gulf coast and interior. The enormous demand for gasoline and other petroleum products helped transform the city into a busy center for oil refining. Its population soared to 300,000 by the end of the 1920s. Abundant cheap land and the absence of zoning ordinances, combined with the availability of the automobile, pushed Houston to expand horizontally rather than vertically. It became the archetypal decentralized, low-density city, sprawling miles in each direction from downtown and thoroughly dependent upon automobiles and roads for its sense of community. Suburban communities grew at twice the rate of their core cities, also thanks largely to the automobile boom. Undeveloped land on the fringes of cities became valuable real estate. Grosse Pointe, near Detroit, and Elmwood Park, near Chicago, grew more than 700 percent in ten years. Long Island's Nassau County, just east of New York City, tripled in population. All the new "automobile suburbs" differed in important ways from earlier suburbs built along mass transit lines. The car allowed for a larger average lot size and, in turn, lower residential density.

THE STATE, THE ECONOMY, AND BUSINESS

Throughout the 1920s, a confident Republican Party dominated national politics, certain that it had ushered in a "new era" in American life. A new and closer relationship between the federal government and American business became the hallmark of Republican policy in both domestic and foreign affairs during the administrations of three successive Republican presidents: Warren Harding (1921–23), Calvin Coolidge (1923–29), and Herbert Hoover (1929–33). And Republicans never tired of claiming that the business–government partnership their policies promoted was responsible for the nation's economic prosperity.

HARDING AND COOLIDGE

Handsome, genial, and well-spoken, Warren Harding may have looked the part of a president—but acting like one was another matter. Harding was a product of small-town Marion, Ohio, and the machine politics in his native state. Republican Party officials had made a point of keeping Senator Harding, a compromise choice, as removed from the public eye as possible in the 1920 election. They correctly saw that active campaigning could only hurt their candidate by exposing his shallowness and intellectual weakness. Harding understood his own limitations. He sadly told one visitor to the White House shortly after taking office, "I knew that this job would be too much for me."

Harding surrounded himself with a close circle of friends, the "Ohio gang," delegating to them a great deal of administrative power. The president often conducted business as if he were in the relaxed, convivial, and masculine confines of a small-town saloon. In the summer of 1923, Harding began to get wind of the scandals for which his administration is best remembered. He wearily told his friend, Kansas journalist William Allen White: "This is a hell of a job! I have no trouble with my enemies. . . . But my damned friends, . . . White, they're the ones that keep me walking the floor nights."

Soon after Harding's death from a heart attack in 1923, a series of congressional investigations revealed a deep pattern of corruption. Attorney General Harry M. Daugherty had received bribes from violators of the Prohibition statutes. He had also failed to investigate graft in the Veterans Bureau, where Charles R. Forbes had pocketed a large chunk of the $250 million spent on hospitals and supplies. The worst affair was the Teapot Dome scandal involving Interior Secretary Albert Fall. Fall received hundreds of thousands of dollars in payoffs when he secretly leased navy oil reserves in Teapot Dome, Wyoming, and Elk Hills, California, to two private oil developers. He eventually became the first cabinet officer ever to go to jail.

But the Harding administration's legacy was not all scandal. Andrew Mellon, an influential Pittsburgh banker, served as secretary of the treasury under all three Republican presidents of the 1920s. One of the richest men in America, and a leading investor in the Aluminum Corporation of America and Gulf Oil, Mellon believed government ought to be run on the same conservative principles as a corporation. He was a leading voice for trimming the federal budget and cutting taxes on incomes, corporate profits, and inheritances. These cuts, he argued, would free up capital for new investment and, thus, promote general economic growth. Mellon's program sharply cut taxes for both higher-income brackets and for businesses. By 1926, a person with an income of a million a year paid less than a third of the income tax he or she had paid in 1921. Overall, Mellon's policies succeeded in rolling back much of the progressive taxation associated with Woodrow Wilson and the Great War.

When Calvin Coolidge succeeded to the presidency, he seemed to most people the temperamental opposite of Harding. Born and raised in rural Vermont, elected governor of Massachusetts, and coming to national prominence only through the 1919 Boston police strike (see Chapter 22), "Silent Cal" was the quintessential New England Yankee. Taciturn, genteel, and completely honest, Coolidge believed in the least amount of government possible. He spent only four hours a day at the office. His famous aphorism, "The business of America is business," perfectly captured the core philosophy of the Republican new era. He was in awe of wealthy men such as Andrew Mellon, and he thought them best suited to make society's key decisions.

Coolidge easily won election on his own in 1924. He benefited from the general prosperity and the contrast he provided with the disgraced Harding. Coolidge defeated little-known Democrat John W. Davis, the compromise choice of a party badly divided between its rural and urban wings. Also running was Progressive Party candidate Robert M. La Follette of Wisconsin, who mounted a reform campaign that attacked economic monopolies and called for government ownership of utilities. In his full term, Coolidge showed most interest in reducing federal spending, lowering taxes, and blocking congressional initiatives. He saw his primary function as clearing the way for American businessmen. They, after all, were the agents of the era's unprecedented prosperity.

HERBERT HOOVER AND THE "ASSOCIATIVE STATE"

The most influential figure of the Republican new era was Herbert Hoover, who as secretary of commerce dominated the cabinets of Harding and Coolidge before becoming president himself in 1929. A successful engineer, administrator, and politician, Hoover had earned an enviable reputation as wartime head of the U.S. Food Administration and director general of relief for Europe. He effectively embodied the belief that enlightened business, encouraged and informed by the government, would act in the public interest. In this sense Hoover maintained an essentially progressive outlook. But in the modern industrial age, Hoover believed, the government needed only to advise private citizens' groups about what national or international polices to pursue. "Reactionaries and radicals," he wrote in *American Individualism* (1922), "would assume that all reform and human advance must come through government. They have forgotten that progress must come from the steady lift of the individual and that the measure of national idealism and progress is the quality of idealism in the individual."

Hoover thus fused a faith in old-fashioned individualism with a strong commitment to the progressive possibilities offered by efficiency and rationality. Unlike an earlier generation of Republicans, Hoover wanted not just to create a favorable climate for business but also to actively assist the business community. He spoke of creating an "associative state," in which the government would encourage voluntary cooperation among corporations, consumers, workers, farmers, and small businessmen. This became the central occupation of the Department of Commerce under Hoover's leadership. The Bureau of Standards became one of the nation's leading research centers, setting engineering standards for key American industries such as machine tools and automobiles. The bureau also helped standardize the styles, sizes, and designs of many consumer products, such as canned goods and refrigerators.

Hoover actively encouraged the creation and expansion of national trade associations. By 1929, there were about 2,000 of them. At industrial conferences called by the Commerce Department, government officials explained the advantages of mutual cooperation in figuring prices and costs and then publishing the information. The idea was to improve efficiency by reducing competition. To some, this practice violated the spirit of antitrust laws, but in the 1920s, the Justice Department's Antitrust Division took a very lax view of its responsibility. In addition, the Supreme Court consistently upheld the legality of trade associations. The government thus provided an ideal climate for the concentration of corporate wealth and power.

The trend toward large corporate trusts and holding companies had been well under way since the late nineteenth century, but it accelerated in the 1920s. By 1929, the 200 largest American corporations owned almost half the total corporate wealth and about a fifth of the total national wealth. Concentration was particularly strong in manufacturing, retailing, mining, banking, and utilities. The number of vertical combinations—large, integrated firms that controlled the raw materials, manufacturing processes, and distribution networks for their products—also increased. Vertical integration became common not only in older industries but in the automobile, electrical, radio, motion picture, and other new industries as well.

WAR DEBTS, REPARATIONS, KEEPING THE PEACE

Rejection of the Treaty of Versailles and the League of Nations did not mean disengagement from the rest of the globe. The United States emerged from World War I as the strongest economic power in the world. The war transformed it from the world's leading debtor nation to its most important creditor. European governments owed the U.S. government about $10 billion in 1919. In the private sector, the war ushered in an era of expanding American investment abroad. As late as 1914, foreign investments in the United States were about $3 billion more than the total of American capital invested abroad. By 1919, that situation was reversed: America had $3 billion more invested abroad than foreigners had invested in the United States. By 1929, the surplus was $8 billion. New York replaced London as the center of international finance and capital markets. Yet America's postwar policies included a great contradiction: protectionism. The rest of the world owed the United States billions of dollars, but high tariffs on both farm products and manufactured goods made it much more difficult for debtor nations to repay by selling exports.

During the 1920s, war debts and reparations were the single most divisive issue in international economics. In France and Great Britain, which both owed the United States large amounts in war loans, many concluded that the Uncle Sam who had offered assistance during wartime was really a loan shark in disguise. In turn, many Americans viewed Europeans as ungrateful debtors. As President Coolidge acidly remarked, "They hired the money, didn't they?" In 1922, the U.S. Foreign Debt Commission negotiated an agreement with the debtor nations that called for them to repay $11.5 billion over a sixty-two-year period. But by the late 1920s, the European financial situation had become so desperate that the United States agreed to cancel a large part of these debts. Continued insistence by the United States that the Europeans pay at least a portion of the debt fed anti-American feeling in Europe and isolationism at home.

The Germans believed that war reparations, set at $33 billion by the Treaty of Versailles, not only unfairly punished the losers of the conflict but, by saddling their civilian economies with such massive debt, also deprived them of the very means to repay. In 1924, Herbert Hoover and Chicago banker Charles Dawes worked out a plan to aid the recovery of the German economy. The Dawes Plan reduced Germany's debt, stretched out the repayment period, and arranged for American bankers to lend funds to Germany. These measures helped stabilize Germany's currency and allowed it to make reparations payments to France and Great Britain. The Allies, in turn, were better able to pay their war debts to the United States.

In addition to the Dawes Plan and the American role in naval disarmament, the United States joined the league-sponsored World Court in 1926 and was represented at numerous league conferences. In 1928, with great fanfare, the United States and sixty-two other nations signed the Pact of Paris (better known as the Kellogg-Briand Pact, for the U.S. Secretary of State Frank B. Kellogg and French Foreign Minister Aristide Briand who initiated it), which grandly and naively renounced war in principle. Peace groups, such as the Woman's Peace Party and the Quaker-based Fellowship of Reconciliation, hailed the pact for formally outlawing war. But critics charged that the Kellogg-Briand Pact was essentially meaningless, since it lacked powers of enforcement and relied solely on the moral force of world opinion. Within weeks of its ratification, the U.S. Congress had appropriated $250 million for new battleships.

GLOBAL COMMERCE AND U.S. FOREIGN POLICY

Throughout the 1920s, Secretary of State Charles Evans Hughes and other Republican leaders pursued policies designed to expand American economic activity abroad. They understood that capitalist economies must be dynamic; they must expand their markets if they were to thrive. The focus must be on friendly nations and investments that would help foreign citizens to buy American goods. Toward this end, Republican leaders urged close cooperation between bankers and the government as a strategy for expanding American investment and economic influence abroad. They insisted that investment capital not be spent on U.S. enemies, such as the new Soviet Union, or on nonproductive enterprises such as munitions and weapons. Throughout the 1920s, investment bankers routinely submitted loan projects to Hughes and Secretary of Commerce Hoover for informal approval, thus reinforcing the close ties between business investment and foreign policy.

American oil, autos, farm machinery, and electrical equipment supplied a growing world market. Much of this expansion took place through the establishment of branch plants overseas by American companies. America's overall direct investment abroad increased from $3.8 billion in 1919 to $7.5 billion in 1929. Leading the American domination of the world market were General Electric, Ford, and Monsanto Chemical. American oil companies, with the support of the State Department, also challenged Great Britain's dominance in the oil fields of the Middle East and Latin America, forming powerful cartels with English firms.

The strategy of maximum freedom for private enterprise, backed by limited government advice and assistance, significantly boosted the power and profits of American overseas investors. But in Central and Latin America, in particular, aggressive U.S. investment also fostered chronically underdeveloped economies, dependent on a few staple crops (sugar, coffee, cocoa, bananas) grown for export. American investments in Latin America more than doubled between 1924 and 1929, from $1.5 billion to over $3.5 billion. A large part of this money went to taking over vital mineral resources, such as Chile's copper and Venezuela's oil. The growing wealth and power of U.S. companies made it more difficult for these nations to grow their own food or diversify their economies. U.S. economic dominance in the hemisphere also hampered the growth of democratic politics by favoring autocratic, military regimes that could be counted on to protect U.S. investments.

WEAKENED AGRICULTURE, AILING INDUSTRIES

Amid prosperity and progress, there were large pockets of the country that lagged behind. Advances in real income and improvements in the standard of living for workers and farmers were uneven at best. In 1920, some 32 million Americans still lived on farms, out of a total population of 106 million. Yet during the 1920s the farm sector failed to share in the general prosperity. The years 1914–19 had been a kind of golden age for the nation's farmers. Increased wartime demand, along with the devastation of much of European agriculture, had led to record-high prices for many crops. In addition, the wartime Food Administration had encouraged a great increase in agricultural production. But with the war's end, American farmers began to suffer from a chronic worldwide surplus of such farm staples as cotton, hogs, and corn.

In the South, farmers' dependency on "King Cotton" deepened, as the region lagged farther behind the rest of the nation in both agricultural diversity and standard of living. Cotton acreage expanded, as large and heavily mechanized farms opened up new land in Oklahoma, west Texas, and the Mississippi-Yazoo delta. But in most of the South, from North Carolina to east Texas, small one- and two-mule cotton farms, most under 50 acres, still dominated the countryside. While editors, state officials, and reformers preached the need for greater variety of crops, southern farmers actually raised less corn and livestock by the end of the decade. With few large urban centers and inadequate transportation, even those southern farmers who had access to capital found it extremely difficult to find reliable markets for vegetables, fruit, poultry, or dairy products. The average southern farm had land and buildings worth $3,525; for northern farms, the figure was $11,029. The number of white tenant farmers increased by 200,000 during the 1920s, while black tenantry declined slightly as a result of the Great Migration. Some 700,000 southern farmers, roughly half white and half black, still labored as sharecroppers. Modern conveniences such as electricity, indoor plumbing, automobiles, and phono-

graphs remained far beyond the reach of the great majority of southern farmers. Widespread rural poverty, poor diet, little access to capital—the world of southern agriculture had changed very little since the days of the Populist revolt in the 1890s.

The most important initiatives for federal farm relief were the McNary-Haugen bills, a series of complicated measures designed to prop up and stabilize farm prices. The basic idea, borrowed from the old Populist proposals of the 1890s, was for the government to purchase farm surpluses and either store them until prices rose or sell them on the world market. But President Calvin Coolidge viewed these measures as unwarranted federal interference in the economy and vetoed the McNary-Haugen Farm Relief bill of 1927 when it finally passed Congress. American farmers hoping to export produce abroad also suffered from the high tariffs imposed by European countries trying to protect their own devastated economies. Hard-pressed farmers would not benefit from government relief until the New Deal programs implemented in response to the Great Depression in the 1930s.

To be sure, some farmers thrived. Improved transportation and chain supermarkets allowed for a wider and more regular distribution of such foods as oranges, lemons, and fresh green vegetables. Citrus, dairy, and truck farmers in particular profited from the growing importance of national markets. Wheat production jumped more than 300 percent during the 1920s. Across the plains of Kansas, Nebraska, Colorado, Oklahoma, and Texas, wheat farmers brought the methods of industrial capitalism to the land. They hitched disc plows and combined harvester-threshers to gasoline-powered tractors, tearing up millions of acres of grassland to create a vast wheat factory. With prices averaging above $1 per bushel over the decade, mechanized farming created a new class of large-scale wheat entrepreneurs on the plains. Ida Watkins, "the Wheat Queen" of Haskell County, Kansas, made a profit of $75,000 from her 2,000 acres in 1926. Hickman Price needed twenty-five combines to harvest the wheat on his Plainview, Texas, farm—34,500 acres stretching over fifty-four square miles. But when the disastrous dust storms of the 1930s rolled across the grassless plains, the long-range environmental impact of destroying so much native vegetation became evident.

Overall, per capita farm income remained well below what it had been in 1919, and the gap between farm and nonfarm income widened. By 1929, the average income per person on farms was $223, compared with $870 for nonfarm workers. By the end of the decade, hundreds of thousands had quit farming altogether for jobs in mills and factories. And fewer farmers owned their land. In 1930, 42 percent of all farmers were tenants, compared with 37 percent in 1919.

Large sectors of American industry also failed to share in the decade's general prosperity. As oil and natural gas gained in importance, America's coal mines became a less important source of energy. A combination of shrinking demand, new mining technology, and a series of losing strikes reduced the coal labor force by one-quarter. The United Mine Workers, perhaps the strongest AFL union in 1920, with 500,000 members, had shrunk to 75,000 by 1928. Economic hardship was widespread in many mining communities dependent on coal, particularly Appalachia and the southern Midwest. And those miners who did work earned lower hourly wages.

In textiles, shrinking demand and overcapacity (too many factories) were chronic problems. The women's fashions of the 1920s generally required less material than had earlier fashions, and competition from synthetic fibers such as rayon depressed demand for cotton textiles. To improve profit margins, textile manufacturers in New England and other parts of the Northeast began a long-range shift of operations to the South, where nonunion shops and substandard wages became the rule. Between 1923 and 1933, 40 percent of New England's textile factories closed, and nearly 100,000 of the 190,000 workers employed there lost their jobs. Older New England manufacturing centers such as Lawrence, Lowell, Nashua, Manchester, and Fall River were hard hit by this shift. The center of the American textile industry shifted permanently to the Piedmont region of North and South Carolina. By 1933, factories there employed nearly 70 percent of the workers in the industry.

THE NEW MASS CULTURE

New communications media reshaped American culture in the 1920s, and much of the new mass culture was exported to the rest of the economically developed world. The phrase "Roaring Twenties" captures the explosion of image- and sound-making machinery that came to dominate so much of American life. Movies, radio, new kinds of journalism, the recording industry, and a more sophisticated advertising industry were deeply connected with the new culture of consumption. They also encouraged the parallel emergence of celebrity as a defining element in modern life. As technologies of mass impression, the media established national standards and norms for much of our culture—habit, dress, language, sounds, social behavior. For millions of Americans, the new media radically altered the rhythms of everyday life and redefined what it meant to be "normal." Cultural traditionalists both in America and abroad found these new norms deeply disturbing, and the 1920s saw powerful collisions between newer and older values. To be sure, most working-class families had only limited access to the world of mass consumption—and many had only limited interest in it. But the new mass culture helped redefine the ideal of "the good life" and made the images, if not the substance, of it available to a national community.

MOVIE-MADE AMERICA

The early movie industry, centered in New York and a few other big cities, had made moviegoing a regular habit for millions of Americans, especially immigrants and the working class. They flocked to cheap, storefront theaters, called nickelodeons, to watch short Westerns, slapstick comedies, melodramas, and travelogues. By 1914, there were about 18,000 "movie houses" showing motion pictures, with more than 7 million daily admissions and $300 million in annual receipts. With the shift of the industry westward to Hollywood, movies entered a new phase of business expansion.

Large studios such as Paramount, Fox, Metro-Goldwyn-Mayer (MGM), Universal, and Warner Brothers dominated the business with longer and more expensively produced movies—feature films. These companies were founded and controlled by immigrants from Europe, all of whom had a talent for discovering and exploiting changes in popular tastes. Adolph Zukor, the Hungarian-born head of Paramount, had been a furrier in New York City. Warsaw-born Samuel Goldwyn, a founder of MGM, had been a glove salesman. William Fox, of Fox Pictures, began as a garment cutter in Brooklyn. Most of the immigrant moguls had started in the business by buying or managing small movie theaters before beginning to produce films.

Each studio combined the three functions of production, distribution, and exhibition, and each controlled hundreds of movie theaters around the country. The era of silent films ended when Warner Brothers scored a huge hit in 1927 with *The Jazz Singer*, starring Al Jolson, which successfully introduced sound. New genres—musicals, gangster films, and screwball comedies—soon became popular. To maintain their hold on European markets, the major studios established production facilities abroad that used foreign actors for the "dubbing" of American films into other languages. The higher costs associated with "talkies" also increased the studios' reliance on Wall Street investors and banks for working capital.

At the heart of Hollywood's success was the star system and the accompanying cult of celebrity, both of which help define American popular culture to this day (see Seeing History). Stars became vital to the fantasy lives of millions of fans. For many in the audience, there was only a vague line separating the on-screen and off-screen adventures of the stars. Studio publicity, fan magazines, and gossip columns reinforced this ambiguity. Film idols, with their mansions, cars, parties, and private escapades, became the national experts on leisure and consumption. Their movies generally emphasized sexual themes and celebrated

Creating Celebrity

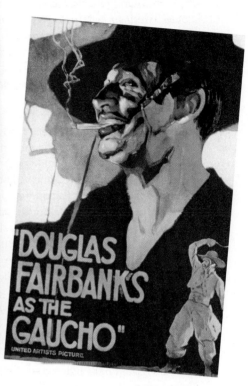

A common definition for "celebrity" is one who is famous for being famous. Although politics, the arts, science, and the military have produced famous people for centuries, the celebrity is a twentieth-century phenomenon, one closely linked to the emergence of modern forms of mass media. In the 1920s Hollywood's "star system," along with tabloid newspapers and the new profession of public relations, created the modern celebrity. Film producers were at first wary of identifying screen actors by name, but they soon discovered that promoting popular leading actors would boost the box office for their movies. The use of "close-ups" in movies and the fact that screen images were literally larger than life distinguished the images of film actors from, say, stage performers or opera singers.

Fans identified with their favorites in contradictory ways. Stars like Charlie Chaplin and Mary Pickford were like royalty, somehow beyond the realm of ordinary mortals. Yet audiences were also curious about the stars' private lives. Film studios took advantage of this curiosity by carefully controlling the public image of their stars through press releases, planted stories in newspapers, and carefully managed interviews and public appearances. Theda Bara, for example, one of the biggest female stars of the 1920s, was best known for her "vamp" roles depicting sexually aggressive and exotic women. According to the publicity from Fox Pictures, she was of Egyptian background, offspring of "a sheik and a princess, given in mystic marriage to the Sphinx, fought over by nomadic tribesmen, clairvoyant, and insatiably lustful." In truth, Theodosia Goodman was born and raised in Cincinnati, daughter of middle-class Jewish parents who had become a stage actress after two years of college. By the 1920s film stars were essentially studio owned and operated commodities, requiring enormous capital investment. And the new media universe of newspapers, magazines, radio, movies, and advertising was held together by the public fascination with, and the commercial power of, celebrities.

What visual themes strike you as most powerful in the accompanying images? How do they compare—in contrasts and parallels—to celebrity images of today? Why do you think male stars such as Valentino and Fairbanks were so often portrayed as exotic foreigners? How did these posters convey a more open and accepting attitude toward sexuality?

youth, athleticism, and the liberating power of consumer goods. Young Americans in particular looked to movies to learn how to dress, wear their hair, talk, or kiss. One researcher looking into the impact of moviegoing on young people asked several to keep "motion picture diaries." "Upon going to my first dance I asked the hairdresser to fix my hair like Greta Garbo's," wrote one eighteen-year-old college student. "In speaking on graduation day I did my best to finish with the swaying-like curtsy which Pola Negri taught me from the screen."

But many Americans, particularly in rural areas and small towns, worried about Hollywood's impact on traditional sexual morality. They attacked the permissiveness associated with Hollywood life, and many states created censorship boards to screen movies before allowing them to be shown in theaters. To counter growing calls for government censorship, Hollywood's studios came up with a plan to censor themselves. In 1922, they hired Will Hays to head the Motion Picture Producers and Distributors of America. Hays was just what the immigrant moguls needed. An Indiana Republican, elder in the Presbyterian Church, and former postmaster general under President Harding, he personified midwestern Protestant respectability. As the movie industry's czar, Hays lobbied against censorship laws, wrote pamphlets defending the movie business, and began setting guidelines for what could and could not be depicted on the screen. He insisted that movies be treated like any other industrial enterprise, for he understood the relationship between Hollywood's success and the growth of the nation's consumer culture.

RADIO BROADCASTING

In the fall of 1920, Westinghouse executive Harry P. Davis noticed that amateur broadcasts from the garage of an employee had attracted attention in the local Pittsburgh press. A department store advertised radio sets capable of picking up these "wireless concerts." Davis converted this amateur station to a stronger one at the Westinghouse main plant. Beginning with the presidential election returns that November, station KDKA offered regular nightly broadcasts that were probably heard by only a few hundred people. Radio broadcasting, begun as a service for selling cheap radio sets left over from World War I, would soon sweep the nation.

Before KDKA, wireless technology had been of interest only to the military, the telephone industry, and a few thousand "ham" (amateur) operators who enjoyed communicating with each other. The "radio mania" of the early 1920s was a response to the new possibilities offered by broadcasting. By 1923, nearly 600 stations had been licensed by the Department of Commerce, and about 600,000 Americans had bought radios. Early programs included live popular music, the playing of phonograph records, talks by college professors, church services, and news and weather reports. For millions of Americans, especially in rural areas and small towns, radio provided a new and exciting link to the larger national community of consumption.

Who would pay for radio programs? In the early 1920s, owners and operators of radio stations included radio equipment manufacturers, newspapers, department stores, state universities, cities, ethnic societies, labor unions, and churches. But by the end of the decade, commercial (or "toll") broadcasting emerged as the answer. The dominant corporations in the industry—General Electric, Westinghouse, Radio Corporation of America (RCA), and American Telephone and Telegraph (AT&T)—settled on the idea that advertisers would foot the bill for radio. Millions of listeners might be the consumers of radio shows, but sponsors were to be the customers. Only the sponsors and their advertising agencies enjoyed a direct relationship with broadcasters. Sponsors advertised directly or indirectly to the mass audience through such shows as the *Eveready Hour*, the *Ipana Troubadours*, and the *Taystee Loafers*. AT&T leased its nationwide system of telephone wires to allow the linking of many stations into powerful radio networks, such as the National Broadcasting Company (NBC) in 1926 and the Columbia Broadcasting System (CBS) in 1928. The rise of network radio squeezed out many of the stations and programs aimed at ethnic communities or broadcast in languages other than English, thus promoting a more homogenized culture.

NBC and CBS led the way in creating popular radio programs that relied heavily on older cultural forms. The variety show, hosted by vaudeville comedians, became network radio's first important format. Radio's first truly national hit, *The Amos 'n' Andy Show* (1928), was a direct descendant of nineteenth-century "blackface" minstrel entertainment. Radio did more than any previous medium to publicize and commercialize once isolated forms of American music such as country-and-western, blues, and jazz. Broadcasts of baseball and college football games proved especially popular. In 1930, some 600 stations were broadcasting to more than 12 million homes with radios, or roughly 40 percent of American families. By that time, all the elements that characterize the present American system of broadcasting—regular daily programming paid for and produced by commercial advertisers, national networks carrying shows across the nation, and mass ownership of receiver sets in American homes—were in place.

Radio broadcasting created a national community of listeners, just as motion pictures created one of viewers. And like movies it also transcended national boundaries. Broadcasting had a powerful hemispheric impact. In both Canada and Mexico, governments established national broadcasting systems to bolster cultural and political nationalism. Yet

American shows—and advertising—continued to dominate Canadian airwaves. Large private Mexican radio stations were often started in partnership with American corporations such as RCA, as a way to create demand for receiving sets. Language barriers limited the direct impact of U.S. broadcasts, but American advertisers became the backbone of commercial radio in Mexico. Radio broadcasting thus significantly amplified the influence of American commercialism throughout the hemisphere.

NEW FORMS OF JOURNALISM

A new kind of newspaper, the tabloid, became popular in the postwar years. The *New York Daily News*, founded in 1919 by Joseph M. Patterson, was the first to develop the tabloid style. Its folded-in-half page size made it convenient to read on buses or subways. The *Daily News* devoted much of its space to photographs and other illustrations. With a terse, lively reporting style that emphasized sex, scandal, and sports, *Daily News* circulation reached 400,000 in 1922 and 1.3 million by 1929.

This success spawned a host of imitators in New York and elsewhere. New papers like the *Chicago Times* and the *Los Angeles Daily News* brought the tabloid style to cities across America, while some older papers, such as the *Denver Rocky Mountain News*, adopted the new format. The circulation of existing dailies was little affected. Tabloids had instead discovered an audience of millions who had never read newspapers before. Most of these new readers were poorly educated working-class city dwellers, many of whom were immigrants or children of immigrants.

The tabloid's most popular new feature was the gossip column, invented by Walter Winchell, an obscure former vaudevillian who began writing his column "Your Broadway and Mine" for the *New York Daily Graphic* in 1924. Winchell described the secret lives of public figures with a distinctive, rapid-fire, slangy style that made the reader feel like an insider. He chronicled the connections among high society, show business stars, powerful politicians, and the underworld. By the end of the decade, scores of newspapers "syndicated" Winchell's column, making him the most widely read—and imitated—journalist in America.

Journalism followed the larger economic trend toward consolidation and merger. Newspaper chains like Hearst, Gannett, and Scripps-Howard flourished during the 1920s. One journalist lamented this standardization in 1930: "When one travels through the country on a Sunday on a fast train and buys Sunday papers, one finds the same 'comics,' the same Sunday magazines, the same special 'features' in almost all of them and, of course, in most of them precisely the same Associated Press news." There was a sizable increase in the number of these chains and in the percentage of total daily circulation that was chain-owned. By the early 1930s, the Hearst organization alone controlled twenty-six dailies in eighteen cities, accounting for 14 percent of the nation's newspaper circulation. One of every four Sunday papers sold in America was owned by the Hearst group.

ADVERTISING MODERNITY

A thriving advertising industry both reflected and encouraged the growing importance of consumer goods in American life. Previously, advertising had been confined mostly to staid newspapers and magazines and offered little more than basic product information. The most creative advertising was usually for dubious products, such as patent medicines. The successful efforts of the government's Committee on Public Information, set up to "sell" World War I to Americans, suggested that new techniques using modern communication media could convince people to buy a wide range of goods and services. As a profession, advertising reached a higher level of respectability, sophistication, and economic power in American life during the 1920s.

A 1919 advertisement for Lucky Strike cigarettes featured the image of actress Billie Burke. Paid celebrity endorsements for consumer goods became a common practice in the post WWI years. Tobacco companies were among the most aggressive purveyors of this new advertising strategy.

The larger ad agencies moved toward a more scientific approach by sponsoring market research and welcoming the language of psychology to their profession. Indeed psychology's growing prestige as a field in the 1920s was reflected throughout the world of mass culture. Behavioral psychologists like John B. Watson argued that all human behavior could be shaped (or manipulated) by careful study and application of stimulus and response. Watson left his post at Harvard for an executive position at the J. Walter Thompson advertising agency. The writings of Viennese psychoanalyst Sigmund Freud, especially his emphasis on the irrational in human behavior and the power of the sex drive, were widely popularized in American magazines and universities. Advertisers began focusing on the needs, desires, and anxieties of the consumer, rather than on the qualities of the product. "There are certain things that most people believe," noted one ad agency executive in 1927. "The moment your copy is linked to one of those beliefs, more than half your battle is won."

Ad agencies and their clients invested extraordinary amounts of time, energy, and money trying to discover and, to some extent, shape those beliefs. Leading agencies such as Lord and Thomas in Chicago and J. Walter Thompson in New York combined knowledge gained from market research and consumer surveys with carefully prepared ad copy and graphics to sell their clients' wares.

High-powered ad campaigns made new products like Fleischmann's Yeast, Kleenex, and Listerine household words across the country. Above all, advertising celebrated consumption itself as a positive good. In this sense, the new advertising ethic was a therapeutic one, promising that products would contribute to the buyer's physical, psychic, or emotional well-being.

THE PHONOGRAPH AND THE RECORDING INDUSTRY

Like radio and movies, the phonograph came into its own in the 1920s as a popular entertainment medium. Originally marketed in the 1890s, early phonographs used wax cylinders that could both record and replay. But the sound quality was poor, and the cylinders were difficult to handle. The convenient permanently grooved disc recordings introduced around World War I were eagerly snapped up by the public, even though the discs could not be used to make recordings at home. The success of records transformed the popular music business, displacing both cylinders and sheet music as the major source of music in the home. They led to a decline as well in self-produced music, as families were no longer dependent upon the piano in the parlor to make music.

Dance crazes such as the fox trot, tango, and grizzly bear, done to complex ragtime and Latin rhythms, boosted the record business tremendously. Dixieland jazz, which recorded well, also captured the public's fancy in the early 1920s, and records provided the music for new popular dances like the Charleston and the black bottom. In 1921, more than 200 companies produced some 2 million records, and annual record sales exceeded $100 million.

Record sales declined toward the end of the decade, due to competition from radio. But in a broader cultural sense, records continued to transform American popular culture. Record companies discovered lucrative regional and ethnic markets for country music, which appealed primarily to white Southerners, and blues and jazz, which appealed primarily to African Americans. Country musicians like the Carter Family and Jimmie Rodgers, and blues singers like Blind Lemon Jefferson

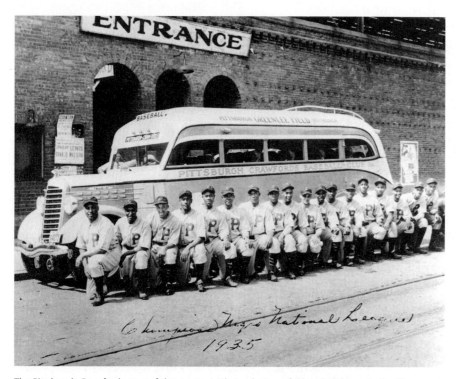

The Pittsburgh Crawfords, one of the most popular and successful baseball teams in the Negro National League, organized in 1920. Excluded from major league baseball by a "whites only" policy, black ballplayers played to enthusiastic crowds of African Americans from the 1920s through the 1940s. The "Negro leagues" declined after major league baseball finally integrated in 1947.

and Ma Rainey and Bessie Smith, had their performances put on records for the first time. Their records sold mainly in specialized "hillbilly" and "race" markets. Yet they were also played over the radio, and millions of Americans began to hear musical styles and performers who had previously been isolated from the general population. Jazz records by such African American artists as Louis Armstrong and Duke Ellington found a wide audience overseas as well, and jazz emerged as a uniquely American cultural form with broad appeal around the globe. The combination of records and radio started an extraordinary cross-fertilization of American musical styles that continues to this day.

SPORTS AND CELEBRITY

During the 1920s, spectator sports enjoyed an unprecedented growth in popularity and profitability. As radio, newspapers, magazines, and newsreels exhaustively documented their exploits, athletes took their place alongside movie stars in defining a new culture of celebrity. Bigtime sports, like the movies, entered a new corporate phase. Yet it was the athletes themselves, performing extraordinary feats on the field and transcending their often humble origins, who attracted millions of new fans. The image of the modern athlete—rich, famous, glamorous,

and often a rebel against social convention—came into its own during the decade.

Major league baseball had more fans than any other sport, and its greatest star, George Herman "Babe" Ruth, embodied the new celebrity athlete. Aided by the new "live ball," Ruth's prodigious home run hitting completely changed baseball strategy and attracted legions of new fans to the sport. Ruth was a larger-than-life character off the field as well. In New York, media capital of the nation, newspapers and magazines chronicled his enormous appetites—for food, whiskey, expensive cars, and big-city nightlife. He hobnobbed with politicians, movie stars, and gangsters, and he regularly visited sick children in hospitals. Ruth became the first athlete avidly sought after by manufacturers for celebrity endorsement of their products. As one of the most photographed individuals of the era, Ruth's round, beaming face became a familiar image around the world. In 1930, at the onset of the Great Depression, when a reporter told him that his $80,000 salary was more than President Herbert Hoover's, the Babe replied good-naturedly, "Well, I had a better year than he did."

Ruth's impact helped the game recover from the serious public relations disaster of the "Black Sox" scandal. In 1919, eight members of the poorly paid Chicago White Sox had become involved in a scheme to "throw" the World Series in exchange for large sums of money from gamblers.

Babe Ruth, baseball's biggest star, shakes hands with President Warren G. Harding at the Opening Day of the brand new Yankee Stadium, Bronx, New York, April 4, 1923. The new celebrity culture of the 1920s routinely brought together public figures from the worlds of politics, sports, show business, and even organized crime.

Although they were acquitted in the courts, baseball commissioner Judge Kenesaw Mountain Landis, looking to remove any taint of gambling from the sport, banned the accused players for life. Landis's actions won universal acclaim, but doubts about the integrity of the "national pastime" lingered.

Baseball attendance exploded during the 1920s, reaching a one-year total of 10 million in 1929. The attendance boom prompted urban newspapers to increase their baseball coverage, and the larger dailies featured separate sports sections. The best sportswriters, such as Grantland Rice, Heywood Broun, and Ring Lardner, brought a poetic sensibility to descriptions of the games and their stars. William K. Wrigley, owner of the Chicago Cubs, discovered that by letting local radio stations broadcast his team's games, the club could win new fans, especially among housewives.

Among those excluded from major league baseball were African Americans, who had been banned from the game by an 1890s "gentleman's agreement" among owners. During the 1920s, black baseball players and entrepreneurs developed a world of their own, with several professional and semiprofessional leagues catering to expanding African American communities in cities. The largest of these was the Negro National League, organized in 1920 by Andrew "Rube" Foster. Black ballclubs also played exhibitions against, and frequently defeated, teams of white major leaguers. African Americans had their own baseball heroes, such as Josh Gibson and Satchel Paige, who no doubt would have been stars in the major leagues if not for racial exclusion.

The new media configuration of the 1920s created heroes in other sports as well. Radio broadcasts and increased journalistic coverage made college football a big-time sport, as millions followed the exploits of star players such as Illinois's Harold E. "Red" Grange and Stanford's Ernie Nevers. Teams like Notre Dame, located in sleepy South Bend, Indiana, but coached by the colorful Knute Rockne, could gain a wide national following. The center of college football shifted from the old elite schools of the Ivy League to the big universities of the Midwest and Pacific Coast, where most of the players were now second-generation Irish, Italians, and Slavs. Athletes like boxers Jack Dempsey and Gene Tunney, tennis players Bill Tilden and Helen Wills, golfer Bobby Jones, and swimmers Gertrude Ederle and Johnny Weissmuller became household names who brought legions of new fans to their sports.

A NEW MORALITY?

Movie stars, radio personalities, sports heroes, and popular musicians became the elite figures in a new culture of celebrity defined by the mass media. They were the model for achievement in the new age. Great events and abstract issues were made real through movie close-ups, radio interviews, and tabloid photos. The new media relentlessly created and disseminated images that are still familiar today: Babe Ruth trotting around the bases after hitting a home run; the wild celebrations that greeted Charles Lindbergh after he completed the first solo transatlantic airplane flight in 1927; the smiling gangster Al Capone, bantering with reporters who transformed his criminal exploits into important news events.

But images do not tell the whole story. Consider one of the most enduring images of the "Roaring Twenties," the flapper. She was usually portrayed on screen, in novels, and in the press as a young, sexually aggressive woman with bobbed hair, rouged cheeks, and short skirt. She loved to dance to jazz music, enjoyed smoking cigarettes, and drank bootleg liquor in cabarets and dance halls. She could also be competitive, assertive, and a good pal. As writer Zelda Fitzgerald put it in 1924: "I think a woman gets more happiness out of being gay, light-hearted, unconventional, mistress of her own fate. . . . I want [my daughter] to be a flapper, because flappers are brave and gay and beautiful."

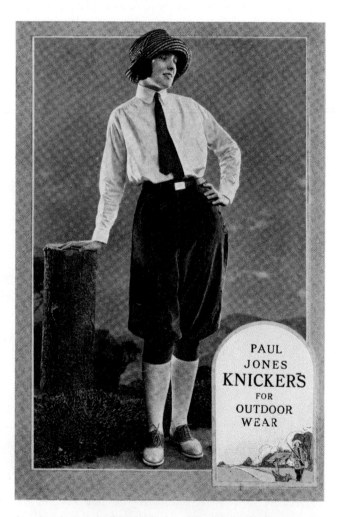

PAUL
JONES
KNICKERS
FOR
OUTDOOR
WEAR

A woman in a man's shirt and necktie wears a pair of Paul Jones knickers in this 1922 advertisement. Her boyish, almost androgynous look reflects one way that notions of the "new woman" intersected with the worlds of fashion and advertising.

Was the flapper a genuine representative of the 1920s? Did she embody the "new morality" that was so widely discussed and chronicled in the media of the day? The flapper certainly did exist, but she was neither as new nor as widespread a phenomenon as the image would suggest. The delight in sensuality, personal pleasure, and rhythmically complex dance and music had long been key elements of subcultures on the fringes of middle-class society: bohemian enclaves, communities of political radicals, African American ghettos, working-class dance halls. In the 1920s, these activities became normative for a growing number of white middle-class Americans, including women. Jazz, sexual experimentation, heavy makeup, and cigarette smoking spread to college campuses.

Several sources, most of them rooted in earlier years, can be found for the increased sexual openness of the 1920s. Troops in the armed forces during World War I had been exposed to government-sponsored sex education. New psychological and social theories like those of Havelock Ellis, Ellen Key, and Sigmund Freud stressed the central role of sexuality in human experience, maintaining that sex is a positive, healthy impulse that, if repressed, could damage mental and emotional health. The pioneering efforts of Margaret Sanger in educating women about birth control had begun before World War I (see Chapter 21). In the 1920s, Sanger campaigned vigorously—through her journal *Birth Control Review*, in books, and on speaking tours—to make contraception freely available to all women.

Sociological surveys also suggested that genuine changes in sexual behavior began in the prewar years among both married and single women. Katherine Bement Davis's pioneering study of 2,200 middle-class women, carried out in 1918 and published in 1929, revealed that most used contraceptives and described sexual relations in positive terms. A 1938 survey of 777 middle-class females found that among those born between 1890 and 1900, 74 percent were virgins before marriage; for those born after 1910, the figure dropped to 32 percent. Women born after the turn of the century were twice as likely to have had premarital sex as those born before 1900. The critical change took place in the generation that came of age in the late teens and early twenties. By the 1920s, male and female "morals" were becoming more alike.

The emergence of homosexual subcultures also reflected the newly permissive atmosphere of the postwar years. Although such subcultures had been a part of big city life since at least the 1890s, they had been largely confined to working-class saloons associated with the urban underworld. By the 1920s, the word "homosexual" had gained currency as a scientific term for describing romantic love between women or between men, and middle-class enclaves of self-identified homosexuals took root in cities like New York, Chicago, and San Francisco. Often organized around speakeasies, private clubs, tearooms, and masquerade balls, this more public homosexual world thrived in bohemian neighborhoods such as New York's Greenwich Village and in the interracial nightclubs of Harlem. These venues also attracted heterosexual tourists and those looking to experiment with their sexuality, as well as homosexuals, for whom they served as important social centers. But if these enclaves provided some sense of community and safety for homosexuals, the repressive shadow of the larger culture was never far away. Psychologists of the era, with Freud in the lead, condemned "perversion" as a mental illness and counseled the need for a "cure."

MODERNITY AND TRADITIONALISM

One measure of the profound cultural changes of the 1920s was the hostility and opposition expressed toward them by large sectors of the American public. Deep and persistent tensions, with ethnic, racial, and geographical overtones, characterized much of the decade's politics. The postwar Red Scare had given strength to the forces of antiradicalism in politics and traditionalism in culture. Resentments over the growing power of urban culture, on full display in Hollywood movies, modern advertising, and over the airwaves, were very strong in rural and small-town America. The big city, in this view, stood for all that was alien, corrupt, and immoral in the country's life. Several trends and mass movements reflected this anger and the longing for a less complicated past.

PROHIBITION

The Eighteenth Amendment, banning the manufacture, sale, and transportation of alcoholic beverages, took effect in January 1920. Prohibition was the culmination of a long campaign that associated drinking with the degradation of working-class family life and the worst evils of urban politics. Supporters, a coalition of women's temperance groups, middle-class progressives, and rural Protestants, hailed the new law as "a noble experiment." But it became clear rather quickly that enforcing the new law would be extremely difficult. The Volstead Act of 1919 established a federal Prohibition Bureau to enforce the Eighteenth Amendment. Yet the bureau was severely understaffed with only about 1,500 agents to police the entire country.

The public demand for alcohol, especially in the big cities, led to widespread lawbreaking. Drinking was such a routine part of life for so many Americans that bootlegging quickly became a big business. Illegal stills and breweries, as well as liquor smuggled in from Canada, supplied the needs of those Americans who continued to drink. Nearly every town and city had at least one "speakeasy," where people could drink and enjoy music and other entertainment. Local law enforcement personnel, especially in the cities, were easily bribed to overlook these illegal establishments. By the early 1920s, many eastern states no longer made even a token effort at enforcing the law.

But because liquor continued to be illegal, Prohibition gave an enormous boost to violent organized crime. The profits to be made in the illegal liquor trade dwarfed the traditional sources of criminal income—gambling, prostitution, and robbery. The pattern of organized crime in the 1920s closely resembled the larger trends in American business: smaller operations gave way to larger and more complex combinations. Successful organized crime figures, like Chicago's Al "Scarface" Capone, became celebrities in their own right and received heavy coverage in the mass media. Capone himself shrewdly used the rhetoric of the Republican new era to defend himself: "Everybody calls me a racketeer. I call myself a businessman. When I sell liquor it's bootlegging. When my patrons serve it on a silver tray on Lake Shore Drive, it's hospitality."

Organized crime, based on its huge profits from liquor, also made significant inroads into legitimate businesses, labor unions, and city government, especially in large cities. By the time Congress and the states ratified the Twenty-First Amendment in 1933, repealing Prohibition, organized crime was a permanent feature of American life. Prohibition did, in fact, significantly reduce per capita consumption of alcohol. In 1910, annual per capita consumption stood at 2.6 gallons; in 1934, the figure was less than a gallon. Yet among young people, especially college students, the excitement associated with speakeasies and lawbreaking contributed to increase drinking during Prohibition.

IMMIGRATION RESTRICTION

Sentiment for restricting immigration, growing since the late nineteenth century, reached its peak immediately after World War I. Barriers against Asian immigrants were already in place with the Chinese Exclusion Act of 1882 and the so-called Gentleman's Agreement with Japan in 1907. The movement to curb European immigration reflected the growing preponderance after 1890 of "new immigrants"—those from southern and eastern Europe—over the immigrants from northern and western Europe, who had predominated before 1890. Between 1891 and 1920, roughly 10.5 million immigrants arrived from southern and eastern Europe. This was nearly twice as many as arrived during the same years from northern and western Europe (see Figure 23.3).

The "new immigrants" were mostly Catholic and Jewish, and they were darker-skinned than the "old immigrants." To many old-stock Americans, they seemed more exotic, more foreign, and less willing and able to assimilate the nation's political and cultural values. They were also relatively poorer, more physically isolated in the nation's cities, and less politically strong than earlier immigrants. In the 1890s, the anti-Catholic American Protective Associa-

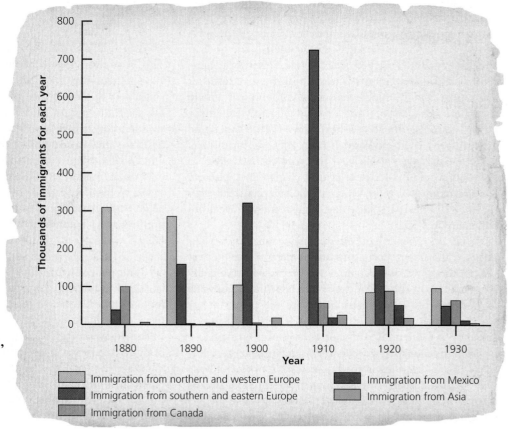

**FIGURE 23.3
Immigration Trends to the United States by Continent/Region, 1880–1930**

SOURCE: Adapted from Historical Statistics of the United States, Millenial Edition (NY: Cambridge University Press, 2006).

tion called for a curb on immigration, and by exploiting the economic depression of that decade, it reached a membership of 2.5 million. In 1894, a group of prominent Harvard graduates, including Senator Henry Cabot Lodge (Rep., Massachusetts) and John Fiske, founded the Immigration Restriction League, providing an influential forum for the fears of the nation's elite. The league used newer scientific arguments, based on a flawed application of Darwinian evolutionary theory and genetics, to support its call for immigration restriction. The new immigration, Lodge argued, "is bringing to the country people whom it is very difficult to assimilate and who do not promise well for the standard of civilization in the United States."

Theories of scientific racism, which had become more popular in the early 1900s, reinforced anti-immigrant bias. The most influential statement of racial hierarchy was Madison Grant's *The Passing of the Great Race* (1916), which distorted genetic theory to argue that America was committing "race suicide." According to Grant, inferior Alpine, Mediterranean, and Jewish stock threatened to extinguish the superior Nordic race that had made America great. Eugenicists, who enjoyed considerable vogue in those years, held that heredity determined almost all of a person's capacities and that genetic inferiority predisposed people to crime and poverty. Such pseudoscientific thinking sought to explain historical and social development solely as a function of "racial" differences.

Against this background, the war and its aftermath provided the final push for the restriction of European immigration. The "100 percent American" fervor of the war years fueled nativist passions. So did the Red Scare of 1919–20, which linked foreigners with Bolshevism and radicalism of all kinds in the popular mind. The postwar depression coincided with the resumption of massive immigration, bringing much hostile comment on the relationship between rising unemployment and the new influx of foreigners. The American Federation of Labor proposed stopping all immigration for two years. Sensational press coverage of organized crime figures, many of them Italian or Jewish, also played a part.

In 1921, Congress passed the Immigration Act, setting a maximum of 357,000 new immigrants each year. Quotas limited annual immigration from any European country to 3 percent of the number of its natives counted in the 1910 U.S. census. But restrictionists complained that the new law still allowed too many southern and eastern Europeans in, especially since the northern and western Europeans did not fill their quotas. The Reed-Johnson National Origins Act of 1924 revised the quotas to 2 percent of the number of foreign-born counted for each nationality in the census for 1890, when far fewer southern or eastern Europeans were present in the United States. The maximum total allowed each year was also cut to 164,000. A *Los Angeles Times* headline expressed both the fundamental premise and flawed science of the new law: "Nordic Victory Is Seen in Drastic Restrictions."

The 1924 National Origins Act in effect limited immigration to white Europeans eligible for immigration by country of origin (nationality), while it divided the rest of the world into "five colored races" (black, mulatto, Chinese, and Indian) who were ineligible for immigration. These new restrictions dovetailed with two recent Supreme Court decisions, *Ozawa* v. *U.S.* (1922) and *U.S.* v. *Thind* (1923), in which the Court held that Japanese and Asian Indians were unassimilable aliens and racially ineligible for U.S. citizenship. By the 1920s, American law had thus created the peculiar new racial category of "Asian" and codified the principle of racial exclusion in immigration and naturalization law.

THE KU KLUX KLAN

If immigration restriction was resurgent nativism's most significant legislative expression, a revived Ku Klux Klan (KKK) was its most effective mass movement. The original Klan had been formed in the Reconstruction South as an instrument of white racial terror against newly freed slaves (see Chapter 17). It had died out in the 1870s. The new Klan, born in Stone Mountain, Georgia, in 1915, was inspired by D. W. Griffith's racist spectacle *The Birth of a Nation*, a film released in that year depicting the original KKK as a heroic organization. The new Klan patterned itself on the secret rituals and antiblack hostility of its predecessor and, until 1920, it was limited to a few local chapters in Georgia and Alabama.

When Hiram W. Evans, a dentist from Dallas, became imperial wizard of the Klan in 1922, he transformed the organization. Evans hired professional fundraisers and publicists and directed an effective recruiting scheme that paid a commission to sponsors of new members. The Klan advocated "100 percent Americanism" and "the faithful maintenance of White Supremacy." It staunchly supported the enforcement of Prohibition, and it attacked birth control and Darwinism. The new Klan made a special target of the Roman Catholic Church, labeling it a hostile and dangerous alien power. In a 1926 magazine piece titled "The Klan's Fight for Americanism," Evans alleged that the Church's claims to full authority in temporal as well as spiritual matters "make it impossible for it as a church, or for its members if they obey it, to cooperate in a free democracy in which Church and State have been separated."

The new Klan presented itself as the righteous defender of the embattled traditional values of small-town Protestant America. But ironically, to build its membership rolls, it relied heavily on the publicity, public relations, and business techniques associated with modern urban culture. By 1924, the new Klan counted more than 3 million members across the country. Its slogan, "Native, White, Protestant Supremacy," proved especially attractive in the Midwest and South, including many cities. Klansmen boycotted businesses, threatened families, and sometimes resorted to violence—public whippings, arson, and

Women members of the Ku Klux Klan in New Castle, Indiana, August 1, 1923. The revived Klan was a powerful presence in scores of American communities during the early 1920s, especially among native-born white Protestants, who feared cultural and political change. In addition to preaching "100 percent Americanism," local Klan chapters also served a social function for members and their families.

lynching—against their chosen enemies. The Klan's targets sometimes included white Protestants accused of sexual promiscuity, blasphemy, or drunkenness, but most victims were African Americans, Catholics, and Jews. Support for Prohibition enforcement probably united Klansmen more than any single issue.

On another level, the Klan was a popular social movement, a defensive bastion against forces of modernity. Many members were more attracted by the Klan's spectacular social events and its efforts to reinvigorate community life than by its attacks on those considered outsiders. Perhaps a half million women joined the Women of the Ku Klux Klan, and women constituted nearly half of the Klan membership in some states. Klanswomen drew on family and community traditions, such as church suppers, kin reunions, and gossip campaigns, to defend themselves and their families against what they saw as corruption and immorality. One northern Indiana Klanswoman recalled, "Store owners, teachers, farmers . . . the good people, all belonged to the Klan. They were going to clean up the government, and they were going to improve the school books that were loaded with Catholicism." The Klan's power was strong in many communities precisely because it fit so comfortably into the everyday life of white Protestants.

At its height, the Klan also became a powerful force in Democratic Party politics, and it had a strong presence among delegates to the 1924 Democratic National Convention. The Klan began to fade in 1925, when its Indiana leader, Grand Dragon David C. Stephenson, became involved in a sordid personal affair. With one of its most famous leaders disgraced and in jail, the new Klan began to lose members and influence.

FUNDAMENTALISM IN RELIGION

Paralleling political nativism in the 1920s was the growth of religious fundamentalism. In many eastern Protestant churches, congregations focused less on religious practice and worship than on progressive social and reform activities in the larger community. By the early 1920s, a fundamentalist revival had developed in reaction to these tendencies, particularly in the South and Midwest. The fundamentalists emphasized a literal reading of the Bible, and they rejected the tenets of modern science as inconsistent with the revealed word of God. Fundamentalist publications and Bible colleges flourished, particularly among southern Baptists.

One special target of the fundamentalists was the theory of evolution, first set forth by Charles Darwin in his landmark work *The Origin of Species* (1859). Using fossil evidence, evolutionary theory suggested that, over time, many species had become extinct and that new ones had emerged through the process of natural selection. These ideas directly contradicted the account of one fixed creation in the Book of Genesis. Although most Protestant clergymen had long since found ways of blending the scientific theory with their theology, fundamentalists launched an attack on the teaching of Darwinism in schools and universities. By 1925, five southern state legislatures had passed laws restricting the teaching of evolution.

A young biology teacher, John T. Scopes, deliberately broke the Tennessee law prohibiting the teaching of Darwinism in 1925, in order to challenge it in court. The resulting trial that summer in Dayton, a small town near Chattanooga, drew international attention to the controversy. Scopes's defense team included attorneys from the American Civil Liberties Union and Clarence Darrow, the most famous trial lawyer in America. The prosecution was led by William Jennings Bryan, the old Democratic standard-bearer who had thrown himself into the fundamentalist and antievolutionist cause. Held in a circus atmosphere in sweltering heat, the trial attracted thousands of reporters and partisans to Dayton and was broadcast across the nation by the radio (see Communities in Conflict).

The Scopes "monkey trial"—so called because fundamentalists trivialized Darwin's theory into a claim that humans were descended from monkeys—became one of the most publicized and definitive moments of the decade. The real drama was the confrontation between Darrow and Bryan. Darrow, denied by the judge the right to call scientists to testify for the defense, put the "Great Commoner," Bryan, himself, on the stand as an expert witness on the Bible. Bryan delighted his supporters with a staunch defense of biblical literalism. But he also drew scorn from many of the assembled journalists, including cosmopolitan types such as H. L. Mencken of the *Baltimore Sun*, who ridiculed Bryan's simplistic faith. Scopes's guilt was never in question. The jury convicted him quickly, although the verdict was later thrown out on a technicality. Bryan died a week after the trial; his epitaph read simply, "He kept the Faith." The struggle over the teaching of evolution continued in an uneasy stalemate; state statutes were not repealed, but prosecutions for teaching evolution ceased. Fundamentalism, a religious creed and a cultural defense against the uncertainties of modern life, continued to have a strong appeal for millions of Americans.

PROMISES POSTPONED

The prosperity of the 1920s was unevenly distributed and enjoyed across America. Older progressive reform movements that had pointed out inequities faltered in the conservative political climate. But the new era did inspire a range of critics deeply troubled by unfulfilled promises in American life. Feminists sought to redefine their movement in the wake of the suffrage victory. Mexican immigration to the United States shot up, and in the burgeoning Mexican American communities of the Southwest and Midwest, economic and social conditions were very

difficult. African Americans, bitterly disappointed by their treatment during and after the Great War, turned to new political and cultural strategies. Many American intellectuals found themselves deeply alienated from the temper and direction of modern American society.

FEMINISM IN TRANSITION

The achievement of the suffrage removed the central issue that had given cohesion to the disparate forces of female reform activism. In addition, female activists of all persuasions found themselves swimming against a national tide of hostility to political idealism. During the 1920s, the women's movement split into two main wings over a fundamental disagreement about female identity. Should activists stress women's differences from men—their vulnerability and the double burden of work and family—and continue to press for protective legislation, such as laws that limited the length of the workweek for women? Or should they emphasize the ways that women were like men—sharing similar aspirations—and push for full legal and civil equality?

In 1920, the National American Woman Suffrage Association reorganized itself as the League of Women Voters. The league represented the historical mainstream of the suffrage movement, those who believed that the vote for women would bring a nurturing sensibility and a reform vision to American politics. This view was rooted in politicized domesticity, the notion that women had a special role to play in bettering society: improving conditions for working women, abolishing child labor, humanizing prisons and mental hospitals, and serving the urban poor. Most league members continued working in a variety of reform organizations, and the league itself concentrated on educating the new female electorate, encouraging women to run for office, and supporting laws for the protection of women and children.

A newer, smaller, and more militant group was the National Woman's Party (NWP), founded in 1916 by militant suffragist Alice Paul. The NWP downplayed the significance of suffrage and argued that women were still subordinate to men in every facet of life. The NWP opposed protective legislation for women, claiming that such laws reinforced sex stereotyping and prevented women from competing with men in many fields. Largely representing the interests of professional and business women, the NWP focused on passage of a brief Equal Rights Amendment (ERA) to the Constitution, introduced in Congress in 1923: "Men and women shall have equal rights throughout the United States and every place subject to its jurisdiction."

Many of the older generation of women reformers opposed the ERA as elitist, arguing that far more women benefited from protective laws than were injured by them. Mary Anderson, director of the Women's Bureau in the Department of Labor, argued that "women who are wage earners, with one job in the factory and another in the home, have little time and energy left to carry on the fight

The Scopes Trial in Dayton, Tennessee

The 1925 trial of John T. Scopes, a Tennessee high school science teacher arrested for teaching evolution, captured national attention. Scopes's guilt was never challenged, even by his defense team; the state's antievolution statute itself was on trial. Tennessee's case was argued by William Jennings Bryan, the aging stalwart of Populism, three-time Democratic presidential nominee, and hero to the growing legion of rural and small-town evangelical Christians. The defense, financed by the American Civil Liberties Union, was led by Chicago attorney Clarence Darrow, a labor and criminal defense lawyer long associated with radical causes and a religious skeptic.

The most electrifying moment of the trial came when Darrow put Bryan on the stand as an expert witness on the Bible. Although the judge expunged the testimony from the record, the wide press coverage proved embarrassing to Bryan and perhaps unfairly cemented his reputation as an antimodern rube. Bryan's criticism of Darwinian theory was in fact more sophisticated than his critics acknowledged. Bryan in particular objected to the use of evolutionary doctrine as scientific justification for social Darwinism, such as when eugenicists argued for selectively breeding human beings. After Bryan's testimony, Darrow, wanting to have the last word, asked the judge to instruct the jury to bring in a guilty verdict, thus making closing arguments unnecessary. The first excerpt is from the closing argument Bryan never had a chance to give. When he died three days after the trial, H. L. Mencken, the reporter for the *Baltimore Sun* and Bryan's most caustic critic, wrote a final assessment of "The Great Commoner," from which the second document is excerpted.

The clash between Bryan and Mencken embodied many of the profound cultural tensions that defined the 1920s. Today's conflicts over the teaching of "creationism" and "intelligent design," disputes over the authority of state and local boards to set curricula or choose textbooks, and the relevance of First Amendment protections in schools all echo the sharp clashes heard in 1925.

How does Bryan link his critique of science and scientific thinking to recent world events?
Why, in Bryan's view, does public school education require a Christian component?
From Mencken's perspective, how did Bryan exploit evangelical Christianity for political purposes?
Do you think his view has merit?

William Jennings Bryan's Undelivered Speech to the Jury

Science is a magnificent force, but it is not a teacher of morals. It can perfect machinery, but it adds no moral restraints to protect society from the misuse of the machine. It can also build gigantic intellectual ships, but it constructs no moral rudders for the control of storm tossed human vessels. It not only fails to supply the spiritual element needed but some of its unproven hypotheses rob the ship of its compass and thus endanger its cargo. In war, science has proven itself an evil genius; it has made war more terrible than it ever was before. Man used to be content to slaughter his fellowmen on a single plane—the earth's surface. Science has taught him to go down into the water and shoot up from below and to go up into the clouds and shoot down from above, thus making the battlefield three times as bloody as it was before; but science does not teach brotherly love. Science has made war so hellish that civilization was about to commit suicide; and now we are told that newly discovered instruments of destruction will make the cruelties of the late war seem trivial in comparison with the cruelties of wars that may come in the future. If civilization is to be saved from the wreckage threatened by intelligence not consecrated by love, it must be saved by the moral code of the meek and lowly Nazarene. His teachings, and His teachings, alone, can solve the problems that vex the heart and perplex the world. . . .

It is for the jury to determine whether this attack upon the Christian religion shall be permitted in the public schools of Tennessee by teachers employed by the state and paid out of the public treasury. This case is no longer local, the defendant ceases to play an important part. The case has assumed the proportions of a battle-royal between unbelief that attempts to speak through so-called science and the defenders of the Christian faith, speaking through the legislators of Tennessee. It is again a choice between God and Baal; it is also a renewal of the issue in Pilate's court. . . .

Again force and love meet face to face, and the question, "What shall I do with Jesus?" must be answered. A bloody, brutal doctrine—Evolution—demands, as the rabble did nineteen hundred years ago, that He be crucified. That cannot be the answer of this jury representing a Christian state and sworn to uphold the laws of Tennessee. Your answer will be heard throughout the world; it is eagerly awaited by a praying multitude. If the law is nullified, there will be rejoicing wherever God is repudiated, the savior scoffed at and the

> "The case has [become] a battle-royal between unbelief . . . and the defenders of the Christian faith . . . ."

> "The hatred in the old man's burning eyes was not for the enemies of God; it was for the enemies of Bryan."

Bible ridiculed. Every unbeliever of every kind and degree will be happy. If, on the other hand, the law is upheld and the religion of the school children protected, millions of Christians will call you blessed and, with hearts full of gratitude to God, will sing again that grand old song of triumph: "Faith of our fathers, living still, In spite of dungeon, fire and sword; O how our hearts beat high with joy Whene'er we hear that glorious word—Faith of our fathers—Holy faith; We will be true to thee till death!"

SOURCE: *Bryan's Last Speech: Undelivered Speech to the Jury in the Scopes Trial.* Oklahoma City: Sunlight Publishing Society, 1925. http://www.law.umkc.edu/faculty/projects/ftrials/scopes/scopes.htm

H. L. Mencken in the *Baltimore Evening Sun* (July 27, 1925)

One day it dawned on me that Bryan, after all, was an evangelical Christian only by sort of afterthought—that his career in this world, and the glories thereof, had actually come to an end before he ever began whooping for Genesis. So I came to this conclusion: that what really moved him was a lust for revenge. The men of the cities had destroyed him and made a mock of him; now he would lead the yokels against them. Various facts clicked into the theory, and I hold it still. The hatred in the old man's burning eyes was not for the enemies of God; it was for the enemies of Bryan.

Thus he fought his last fight, eager only for blood. It quickly became frenzied and preposterous, and after that pathetic. All sense departed from him. He bit right and left, like a dog with rabies. He descended to demagogy so dreadful that his very associates blushed. His one yearning was to keep his yokels heated up—to lead his forlorn mob against the foe. That foe, alas, refused to be alarmed. It insisted upon seeing the battle as a comedy. Even Darrow, who knew better, occasionally yielded to the prevailing spirit. Finally, he lured poor Bryan into a folly almost incredible.

I allude to his astounding argument against the notion that man is a mammal. I am glad I heard it, for otherwise I'd never believe it. There stood the man who had been thrice a candidate for the Presidency of the Republic—and once, I believe, elected—there he stood in the glare of the world, uttering stuff that a boy of eight would laugh at! The artful Darrow led him on: he repeated it, ranted for it, bellowed it in his cracked voice. A tragedy, indeed! He came into life a hero, a Galahad, in bright and shining armor. Now he was passing out a pathetic fool.

But what of his life? Did he accomplish any useful thing? Was he, in his day, of any dignity as a man, and of any value to his fellow-men? I doubt it. Bryan, at his best, was simply a magnificent job-seeker. The issues that he bawled about usually meant nothing to him. He was ready to abandon them whenever he could make votes by doing so, and to take up new ones at a moment's notice. For years he evaded Prohibition as dangerous; then he embraced it as profitable. At the Democratic National Convention last year he was on both sides, and distrusted by both. In his last great battle there was only a baleful and ridiculous malignancy. If he was pathetic, he was also disgusting.

Bryan was a vulgar and common man, a cad undiluted. He was ignorant, bigoted, self-seeking, blatant and dishonest. His career brought him into contact with the first men of his time; he preferred the company of rustic ignoramuses. It was hard to believe, watching him at Dayton, that he had traveled, that he had been received in civilized societies, that he had been a high officer of state. He seemed only a poor clod like those around him, deluded by a childish theology, full of an almost pathological hatred of all learning, all human dignity, all beauty, all fine and noble things. He was a peasant come home to the dung-pile. Imagine a gentleman, and you have imagined everything that he was not.

SOURCE: http://www.etsu.edu/cas/history/docs/menckenken.htm

to better their economic status. They need the help of other women and they need labor laws." ERA supporters countered that maximum-hours laws or laws prohibiting women from night work prevented women from getting many lucrative jobs. M. Carey Thomas, president of Bryn Mawr College, defended the ERA with language reminiscent of laissez-faire: "How much better by one blow to do away with discriminating against women in work, salaries, promotion and opportunities to compete with men in a fair field with no favour on either side!"

But most women's groups did not think there was a "fair field." Positions solidified. The League of Women Voters, the National Consumers' League, and the Women's Trade Union League opposed the ERA. ERA supporters generally stressed individualism, competition, and the abstract language of "equality" and "rights." ERA opponents emphasized the grim reality of industrial exploitation and the concentration of women workers in low-paying jobs in which they did not compete directly with men. ERA advocates dreamed of the labor market as it might be, one in which women might have the widest opportunity. Anti-ERA forces looked at the labor market as it was, insisting it was more important to protect women from existing exploitation. The NWP campaign failed to get the ERA passed by Congress, but the debates it sparked would be echoed during the feminist movement of the 1970s, when the ERA became a central political goal of a resurgent feminism.

A small number of professional women made real gains in the fields of real estate, banking, and journalism. The press regularly announced new "firsts" for women, such as Amelia Earhart's 1928 airplane flight across the Atlantic. Anne O'Hare McCormick won recognition as the "first lady of American journalism" for her reporting and editorial columns in the *New York Times*. In 1900, less than 18 percent of employed women worked in clerical, managerial, sales, and professional areas. By 1930, the number was 44 percent. But studies showed that most of these women were clustered in the low-paying areas of typing, stenography, bookkeeping, cashiering, and sales clerking. Men still dominated in the higher-paid and managerial white-collar occupations.

The most significant, if limited, victory for feminist reformers was the 1921 Sheppard-Towner Act, which established the first federally funded health care program, providing matching funds for states to set up prenatal and child health care centers. These centers also provided public health nurses for house calls. Although hailed as a genuine reform breakthrough, especially for women in rural and isolated communities, the act aroused much opposition. Many Republicans, including President Harding, had supported it as a way to curry favor with newly enfranchised women voters. But their support faded when it became clear that there was little "gender gap" in voting patterns. The NWP disliked Sheppard-Towner for its assumption that all women were mothers. Birth control advocates such as Margaret Sanger complained that contraception was not part of the program. The American Medical Association (AMA)

objected to government-sponsored health care and to nurses who functioned outside the supervision of physicians. By 1929, largely as a result of intense AMA lobbying, Congress cut off funds for the program.

MEXICAN IMMIGRATION

While immigration restriction sharply cut the flow of new arrivals from Europe, the 1920s also brought a dramatic influx of Mexicans to the United States. Mexican immigration, which was not included in the immigration laws of 1921 and 1924, had picked up substantially after the outbreak of the Mexican Revolution in 1911, when politically inspired violence and economic hardships provided incentives to cross the border to *El Norte*. According to the U.S. Immigration Service, an estimated 459,000 Mexicans entered the United States between 1921 and 1930, more than double the number for the previous decade. The official count no doubt underrepresented the true numbers of immigrants from Mexico. Many Mexicans shunned the main border crossings at El Paso, Texas; Nogales, Arizona; and Calexico, California, and thus avoided paying the $8 head tax and $10 visa fee (see Figure 23.4).

The primary pull was the tremendous agricultural expansion occurring in the American Southwest. Irrigation and large-scale agribusiness had begun transforming California's Imperial and San Joaquin Valleys from arid desert into lucrative fruit and vegetable fields. Cotton pickers were needed in the vast plantations of Lower Rio Grande Valley in Texas and the Salt River Valley in Arizona. The sugar beet fields of Michigan, Minnesota, and Col-

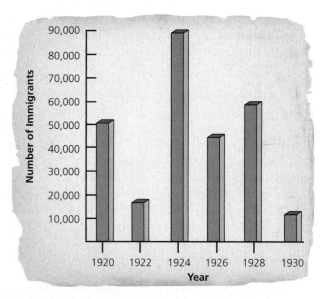

FIGURE 23.4 Mexican Immigration to the United States in the 1920s

Many Mexican migrants avoided official border crossing stations so they would not have to pay visa fees. Thus, these official figures probably underestimated the true size of the decade's Mexican migration. As the economy contracted with the onset of the Great Depression, immigration from Mexico dropped off sharply.

orado attracted many Mexican farm workers. American industry had also begun recruiting Mexican workers, first to fill wartime needs and later to fill the gap left by the decline in European immigration.

The new Mexican immigration appeared more permanent than previous waves—that is, more and more newcomers stayed—and, like other immigrants, settled in cities. This was partly the unintended consequence of new policies designed to make immigration more difficult. As the Border Patrol (established in 1924) made border crossing more difficult (through head taxes, visa fees, literacy tests, and document checks), what had once been a two-way process for many Mexicans became a one-way migration. Permanent communities of Mexicans in the United States grew rapidly. By 1930, San Antonio's Mexican community accounted for roughly 80,000 people out of a total population of a quarter million. Around 100,000 Mexicans lived in central and east Los Angeles, including 55,000 who attended city schools. Substantial Mexican communities also flourished in midwestern cities such as Chicago, Detroit, Kansas City, and Gary. Many of the immigrants alternated between agricultural and factory jobs, depending on the seasonal availability of work. Mexican women often worked in the fields alongside their husbands. They also had jobs as domestics and seamstresses, or took in laundry and boarders.

Racism and local patterns of residential segregation confined most Mexicans to barrios. Housing conditions were generally poor, particularly for recent arrivals, who were forced to live in rude shacks without running water or electricity. Disease and infant mortality rates were much higher than average, and most Mexicans worked at low-paying, unskilled jobs and received inadequate health care. Legal restrictions passed by states and cities made it difficult for Mexicans to enter teaching, legal, and other professions. Mexicans were routinely banned from local public works projects as well. Many felt a deep ambivalence about applying for American citizenship. Loyalty to the Old Country was strong, and many cherished dreams of returning to live out their days in Mexico.

Nativist efforts to limit Mexican immigration were thwarted by the lobbying of powerful agribusiness interests. The Los Angeles Chamber of Commerce typically employed racist stereotyping in arguing to keep the borders open. Mexicans, it claimed, were naturally suited for agriculture, "due to their crouching and bending habits, . . . while the white is physically unable to adapt himself to them."

Mutual aid societies—*mutualistas*—became key social and political institutions in the Mexican communities of the Southwest and Midwest. They provided death benefits and widows' pensions for members and also served as

Mexican workers gathered outside a San Antonio labor bureau in 1924. These employment agencies contracted Mexicans to work for Texas farmers, railroads, and construction companies. Note the three Anglo men in front (wearing suits and ties), who probably owned and operated this agency. During the 1920s, San Antonio's Mexican population doubled from roughly 40,000 to over 80,000, making it the second largest *colonia* in *El Norte* after Los Angeles.

centers of resistance to civil rights violations and discrimination. In 1928, the Federation of Mexican Workers Unions formed in response to a large farm labor strike in the Imperial Valley of California. A group of middle-class Mexican professionals in Texas organized the League of United Latin American Citizens (LULAC) in 1929. The founding of these organizations marked only the beginnings of a long struggle to bring economic, social, and racial equality to Mexican Americans.

THE "NEW NEGRO"

The Great Migration spurred by World War I showed no signs of letting up during the 1920s, and African American communities in northern cities grew rapidly. By far the largest and most influential of these communities was New York City's Harlem. Previously a residential suburb, Harlem began attracting middle-class African Americans in the prewar years. After the war, heavy black migration from the South and the Caribbean encouraged real estate speculators and landlords to remake Harlem as an exclusively black neighborhood. Between 1920 and 1930, some 120,000 new black arrivals settled in Harlem, giving it a black population of roughly 200,000 (see Map 23.1).

Harlem emerged as the demographic and cultural capital of black America, but its appeal transcended national borders, as mass migration from the Caribbean helped reshape the community. Between 1900 and 1930, some 300,000 West Indians emigrated to the United States, roughly half of whom settled in New York City. By the late 1920s, about one-quarter of Harlem's population had been born in Jamaica, Barbados, Trinidad, the Bahamas, and other parts of the Caribbean. Some of the leading cultural, business, and political figures of the era— poet Claude McKay, newspaper publisher P. M. H. Savory, labor organizer Hubert Harrison, black nationalist Marcus Garvey—had roots in the West Indies. Most black Caribbean migrants came from societies where class differences mattered more than racial ones, and many refused to accept racial bigotry without protest. A large number also carried with them entrepreneurial experience that contributed to their success in running small businesses. Intraracial tensions and resentment between American-born blacks and an increasingly visible West Indian population was one reflection of Harlem's transformation into a hemispheric center for black people.

Harlem was also headquarters to Marcus Garvey's Universal Negro Improvement Association. An ambitious

MAP EXPLORATION

To explore an interactive version of this map, go to **www.prenhall.com/faragher6/map23.1**

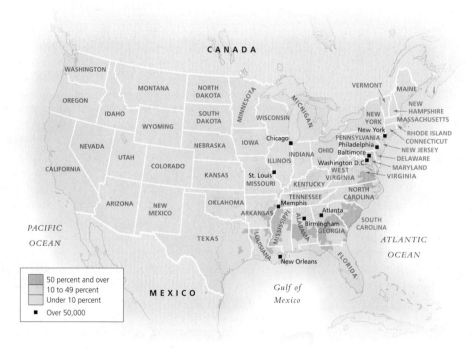

MAP 23.1 Black Population, 1920 Although the Great Migration had drawn hundreds of thousands of African Americans to the urban North, the southern states of the former Confederacy still remained the center of the African American population in 1920.

Jamaican immigrant who had moved to Harlem in 1916, Garvey created a mass movement that stressed black economic self-determination and unity among the black communities of the United States, the Caribbean, and Africa. With colorful parades and rallies and a central message affirming pride in black identity, Garvey attracted as many as a million members worldwide. Garvey's best-publicized project was the Black Star Line, a black-owned and -operated fleet of ships that would link people of African descent around the world. But insufficient capital and serious financial mismanagement resulted in the spectacular failure of the enterprise. In 1923, Garvey was found guilty of mail fraud in his fundraising efforts; he later went to jail and was subsequently deported to England. Despite the disgrace, Harlem's largest newspaper, the *Amsterdam News*, explained Garvey's continuing appeal to African Americans: "In a world where black is despised, he taught them that black is beautiful. He taught them to admire and praise black things and black people."

The demand for housing in this restricted geographical area led to skyrocketing rents, but most Harlemites held low-wage jobs. This combination produced extremely overcrowded apartments, unsanitary conditions, and the rapid deterioration of housing stock. Disease and death rates were abnormally high. Harlem was well on its way to becoming a slum. Yet Harlem also boasted a large middle-class population and supported a wide array of churches, theaters, newspapers and journals, and black-owned businesses. It became a mecca, as poet and essayist James Weldon Johnson wrote, for "the curious, the adventurous, the enterprising, the ambitious, and the talented of the entire Negro world." Poet Langston Hughes expressed the excitement of arriving in the community in 1921: "I can never put on paper the thrill of the underground ride to Harlem. I went up the steps and out into the bright September sunlight. Harlem! I stood there, dropped my bags, took a deep breath and felt happy again."

Harlem became the political and intellectual center for what writer Alain Locke called the "New Negro." Locke was referring to a new spirit in the work of black writers and intellectuals, an optimistic faith that encouraged African Americans to develop and celebrate their distinctive culture, firmly rooted in the history, folk culture, and experiences of African American people. This faith was the common denominator uniting the disparate figures associated with the Harlem Renaissance. The assertion of cultural independence resonated in the poetry of Langston Hughes and Claude McKay, the novels of Zora Neale Hurston and Jessie Fauset, the essays of Countee Cullen and James Weldon Johnson, the acting of Paul Robeson, and the blues singing of Bessie Smith. Most would agree with Johnson when he wrote in 1927 that "nothing can go farther to destroy race prejudice than the recognition of the Negro as a creator and contributor to American civilization."

There was a political side to the "New Negro" as well. The newly militant spirit that black veterans had brought home from World War I matured and found a variety of expressions in the Harlem of the 1920s. New leaders and movements began to appear alongside established organizations like the National Association for the Advancement of Colored People. A. Philip Randolph began a long career as a labor leader, socialist, and civil rights activist in these years, editing the *Messenger* and organizing the Brotherhood of Sleeping Car Porters.

Through the new mass media of radio and phonograph records, millions of Americans now listened and danced to a distinctively African American music, as jazz began to enter the cultural mainstream. Jazz found wildly enthusiastic fans in European capitals like Berlin and Paris, and noted classical composers such as Maurice Ravel and Igor Stravinsky treated it as a serious art form. The best jazz bands of the day, led by artists such as Duke Ellington, Fletcher Henderson, Cab Calloway, and Louis Armstrong, often had their performances broadcast live from such Harlem venues as the Cotton Club and Small's Paradise. Yet these clubs themselves were rigidly segregated. Black dancers, singers, and musicians provided the entertainment, but no African Americans were allowed in the audience. Chronicled in novels and newspapers, Harlem became a potent symbol to white America of the ultimate good time. Yet the average Harlemite never saw the inside of a nightclub. For the vast majority of Harlem residents, working menial jobs for low wages and forced to pay high rents, the day-to-day reality was depressingly different.

ALIENATED INTELLECTUALS

War, Prohibition, growing corporate power, and the deep currents of cultural intolerance troubled many intellectuals in the 1920s. Some felt so alienated from the United States that they left to live abroad. In the early 1920s, Gertrude Stein, an American expatriate writer living in Paris, told the young novelist Ernest Hemingway: "All of you young people who served in the war, you are a lost generation." The phrase "a lost generation" was widely adopted as a label for American writers, artists, and intellectuals of the postwar era. Yet it is difficult to generalize about so diverse a community. For one thing, living abroad attracted only a handful of American writers. Alienation and disillusion with American life were prominent subjects in the literature and thought of the 1920s, but artists and thinkers developed these themes in very different ways.

The mass slaughter of World War I provoked revulsion and a deep cynicism about the heroic and moralistic portrayal of war so popular in the nineteenth century. Novelists Ernest Hemingway and John Dos Passos, who both served at the front as ambulance drivers, depicted the war and its aftermath in world-weary and unsentimental tones. The search for personal moral codes that would allow one to endure life with dignity and authenticity was at the center of Hemingway's fiction. In the taut, spare language of *The Sun Also Rises* (1926) and *A Farewell to Arms* (1929), he questioned idealism, abstractions, and large meanings. As Jake Barnes, the wounded war hero of *The Sun Also Rises* explained, "I did not care what it was all about. All I wanted to know was how to live it."

Hemingway and F. Scott Fitzgerald were the most influential novelists of the era. Fitzgerald joined the army during World War I but did not serve overseas. His work celebrated the youthful vitality of the "Jazz Age" (a phrase he coined) but was also deeply distrustful of the promises of American prosperity and politics. His first novel, *This Side of Paradise* (1920), won a wide readership around the country with its exuberant portrait of a "new generation," "dedicated more than the last to the fear of poverty and the worship of success; grown up to find all Gods dead, all wars fought, all faiths in man shaken." Fitzgerald's finest work, *The Great Gatsby* (1925), written in the south of France, depicted the glamorous parties of the wealthy, while evoking the tragic limits of material success.

At home, many American writers engaged in sharp attacks on small-town America and what they viewed as its provincial values. Essayist H. L. Mencken, caustic editor of the *American Mercury*, heaped scorn on fundamentalists, Prohibition, and nativists, while ridiculing what he called the "American booboisie." Mencken understood the power of the small town and despaired of reforming politics. "Our laws," he wrote, "are invented, in the main, by frauds and fanatics, and put upon the statute books by poltroons and scoundrels." Fiction writers also skewered small-town America, achieving commercial and critical success in the process. Sherwood Anderson's *Winesburg, Ohio* (1919) offered a spare, laconic, pessimistic, yet compassionate, view of middle America. He had a lasting influence on younger novelists of the 1920s.

The most popular and acclaimed writer of the time was novelist Sinclair Lewis. In a series of novels satirizing small-town life, such as *Main Street* (1920) and especially *Babbitt* (1922), Lewis affectionately mocked his characters. His treatment of the central character in *Babbitt*—George Babbitt of Zenith—also had a strong element of self-mockery, for Lewis could offer no alternative set of values to Babbitt's crass self-promotion, hunger for success, and craving for social acceptance. In 1930, Lewis became the first American author to win the Nobel Prize for literature.

In the aftermath of the postwar Red Scare, American radicalism found itself on the defensive throughout the 1920s. But one *cause célèbre* did attract a great deal of support from intellectuals. In 1921, two Italian American immigrants, Nicola Sacco and Bartolomeo Vanzetti, were tried and convicted for murder in the course of robbing a shoe factory in South Braintree, Massachusetts. Neither Sacco, a shoemaker, nor Vanzetti, a fish peddler, had criminal records, but both had long been active in militant anarchist circles, labor organizing, and antiwar agitation. Their trial took place amidst an intense atmosphere of nativist and antiradical feeling, and both the judge and prosecuting attorney engaged in clearly prejudicial conduct toward the defendants. A six-year struggle to save Sacco and Vanzetti following the trial failed, despite attracting support from a broad range of liberal intellectuals, including Harvard law professor and future Supreme Court justice Felix Frankfurter. The two men were finally executed in 1927, and for many years, their case would remain a powerful symbol of how the criminal justice system could be tainted by political bias and anti-immigrant fervor.

Another side of intellectual alienation was expressed by writers critical of industrial progress and the new mass culture. The most important of these was a group of poets and scholars centered in Vanderbilt University in Nashville, Tennessee, collectively known as the Fugitives. They included Allen Tate, John Crowe Ransom, Donald Davidson, and Robert Penn Warren, all of whom invoked traditional authority, respect for the past, and older agrarian ways as ideals to live by. The Fugitives attacked industrialism and materialism as modern-day ills. Self-conscious Southerners, they looked to the antebellum plantation-based society as a model for a community based on benevolence toward dependents (such as black people and women) and respect for the land. Their book of essays, *I'll Take My Stand* (1930), was a collective manifesto of their ideas.

Not all intellectuals, of course, were critics of modern trends. Some, like the philosopher John Dewey, retained much of the prewar optimism and belief in progress. But many others, such as Walter Lippmann and Joseph Wood Krutch, articulated a profound uneasiness with the limits of material growth. In his 1929 book *A Preface to Morals*, the urbane and sophisticated Lippmann expressed doubts about the moral health of the nation. Modern science and technological advances could not address more cosmic questions of belief. The erosion of old religious faiths and moral standards, along with the triumph of the new mass culture, had left many people with nothing to believe in.

THE ELECTION OF 1928

The presidential election of 1928 served as a kind of national referendum on the Republican new era. It also revealed just how important ethnic and cultural differences had become in defining American politics. The contest reflected many of the deepest tensions and conflicts in American society in the 1920s: native-born versus immigrant; Protestant versus Catholic; Prohibition versus legal drinking; small-town life versus the cosmopolitan city; fundamentalism versus modernism; traditional sources of culture versus the new mass media (see Map 23.2).

The 1928 campaign featured two politicians who represented profoundly different sides of American life. Al Smith, the Democratic nominee for president, was a pure product of New York City's Lower East Side. Smith came from a background that included Irish, German, and Italian ancestry, and he was raised as a Roman Catholic. He rose through the political ranks of New York's Tammany Hall machine. A personable man with a deep sympathy for poor and working-class people, Smith served four terms as governor of New York, pushing through an array of laws reforming factory conditions, housing, and welfare programs. Two of his closest advisers were the progressives Frances Perkins and Belle Moskowitz. Smith thus fused older-style machine politics with the newer reform emphasis on state intervention to solve social problems.

Herbert Hoover easily won the Republican nomination after Calvin Coolidge announced he would not run for reelection. Hoover epitomized the successful and forward-looking American. An engineer and self-made millionaire, he offered a unique combination of experience in humanitarian war relief, administrative efficiency, and probusiness policies. Above all, Hoover stood for a commitment to voluntarism and individualism as the best method for advancing the public welfare. He was one of the best-known men in America and promised to continue the Republican control of national politics.

Smith himself quickly became the central issue of the campaign. His sharp New York accent, jarring to many Americans who heard it over the radio, marked him clearly as a man of the city. So did his brown derby and fashionable suits, as well as his promise to work for the repeal of Prohibition. As the first Roman Catholic nominee of a major party, Smith also drew a torrent of anti-Catholic bigotry, especially in the South and Midwest. Nativists and Ku Klux Klanners shamelessly exploited old anti-Catholic prejudices and intimidated participants in Democratic election rallies. But Smith was also attacked from more respectable quarters. Bishop James Cannon, head of the Southern Methodist

	Electoral Vote (%)	Popular Vote (%)
HERBERT HOOVER (Republican)	444 (82)	21,391,993 (58.2)
Alfred E. Smith (Democrat)	87 (17)	15,016,169 (40.9)
Norman Thomas (Socialist)	—	267,835 (0.7)
Other parties (Socialist Labor, Prohibition)	—	62,890 (0.2)

MAP 23.2 The Election of 1928 Although Al Smith managed to carry the nation's twelve largest cities, Herbert Hoover's victory in 1928 was one of the largest popular and electoral landslides in the nation's history.

Clifford K. Berryman's 1928 political cartoon interpreted that year's presidential contest along sectional lines. It depicted the two major presidential contenders as each setting off to campaign in the regions where their support was weakest. For Democrat Al Smith, that meant the West, and for Republican Herbert Hoover, the East.

CHRONOLOGY

1920 Prohibition takes effect

Warren G. Harding is elected president

Station KDKA in Pittsburgh goes on the air

Census reports that urban population is greater than rural population for the first time

1921 First immigration quotas are established by Congress

Sheppard-Towner Act establishes first federally funded health care program

1923 Equal Rights Amendment is first introduced in Congress

Harding dies in office; Calvin Coolidge becomes president

1924 Ku Klux Klan is at height of its influence

Dawes Plan for war reparations stabilizes European economies

Reed-Johnson Immigration Act tightens quotas established in 1921

1925 Scopes trial pits religious fundamentalism against modernity

F. Scott Fitzgerald publishes *The Great Gatsby*

1926 National Broadcasting Company establishes first national radio network

1927 McNary-Haugen Farm Relief bill finally passed by Congress but is vetoed by President Coolidge as unwarranted federal interference in the economy

Warner Brothers produces *The Jazz Singer*, the first feature-length motion picture with sound

Charles Lindbergh makes first solo flight across the Atlantic Ocean

1928 Kellogg-Briand Pact renounces war

Herbert Hoover defeats Al Smith for the presidency

1929 Robert and Helen Lynd publish their classic community study, *Middletown*

Episcopal Church, insisted that "no subject of the Pope" should be permitted to occupy the White House. For his part, Smith ran a largely conservative race. He appointed John Raskob, a Republican vice president of General Motors, to manage his campaign and tried to outdo Hoover in his praise for business. He avoided economic issues such as the unevenness of the prosperity, the plight of farmers, or the growing unemployment. Democrats remained regionally divided over Prohibition, Smith's religion, and the widening split between rural and urban values. Hoover did not have to do much, other than take credit for the continued prosperity.

Hoover polled 21 million votes to Smith's 15 million, and swept the electoral college 444 to 87, including New York State. Even the Solid South, reliably Democratic since the Civil War, gave five states to Hoover—a clear reflection of the ethnocultural split in the party. Yet the election offered important clues to the future of the Democrats. Smith ran better in the big cities of the North and East than any Democrat in modern times. He outpolled Hoover in the aggregate vote of the nation's twelve largest cities and carried six of them, thus pointing the way to the Democrats' future dominance with urban, northeastern, and ethnic voters.

CONCLUSION

America's big cities, if not dominant politically, now defined the nation's cultural and economic life as never before. With Hollywood movies leading the way, the new mass media brought cosmopolitan entertainment and values to the remotest small communities. The culture of celebrity knew no geographic boundaries. New consumer durable goods associated with mass-production techniques—automobiles, radios, telephones, household appliances—were manufactured largely in cities. The advertising and public relations companies that sang their praises were also distinctly urban enterprises. Even with the curtailing of European immigration, big cities attracted a kaleidoscopic variety of migrants: white people from small towns and farms, African Americans from the rural South, Mexicans from across the border, and intellectuals and professionals looking to make their mark.

Many Americans, of course, remained deeply suspicious of postwar cultural and economic trends. Yet the partisans of Prohibition, members of the Ku Klux Klan, and religious fundamentalists usually found themselves on the defensive against what they viewed as alien cultural and economic forces centered in the cities. Large sectors of the population did not share in the era's prosperity. But the large numbers who did—or at least had a taste of good times—ensured Republican political dominance throughout the decade. Thus, America in the 1920s balanced dizzying change in the cultural and economic realms with conservative politics. The reform crusades that attracted millions during the progressive era were a distant memory. Political activism was no match for the new pleasures promised by technology and prosperity.

— REVIEW QUESTIONS

1. Describe the impact of the "second industrial revolution" on American business, workers, and consumers. Which technological and economic changes had the biggest impact on American society?

2. Analyze the uneven distribution of the 1920s' economic prosperity. Which Americans gained the most, and which were largely left out?

3. How did an expanding mass culture change the contours of everyday life in the decade following World War I? What role did new technologies of mass communication play in shaping these changes? What connections can you draw between the "culture of consumption" then and today?

4. What were the key policies and goals articulated by Republican political leaders of the 1920s? How did they apply these to both domestic and foreign affairs?

5. How did some Americans resist the rapid changes taking place in the post–World War I world? What cultural and political strategies did they employ?

6. Discuss the 1928 election as a mirror of the divisions in American society.

— RECOMMENDED READING

Roger Daniels, *Guarding the Golden Door: American Immigration Policy and Immigrants Since 1882* (2002). A comprehensive overview by a pioneering scholar in the field, with special emphasis on how racism and ethnocentrism have shaped American immigration policy.

Victoria De Grazia, *Irresistible Empire: America's Advance through Twentieth Century Europe* (2005). A sophisticated analysis of how and why American commercial culture made such strong inroads into postwar Europe.

Lynn Dumenil, *The Modern Temper: America in the 1920s* (1995). An excellent synthesis of recent scholarship, which emphasizes the ambivalence that many Americans felt toward the emergence of modern society.

David J. Goldberg, *Discontented America: The United States in the 1920s* (1999). Focuses on Americans' continuing discomfort with racial, ethnic, religious, and class differences during the decade.

Desmond King, *Making Americans: Immigration, Race, and the Origins of Diverse Democracy* (2000). Fine analysis of the shift of U.S. immigration policies in the 1920s, with special attention to the influence of eugenics, and the long-term consequences of the new restrictive legislation.

Charles L. Ponce de Leon, *Self Exposure: Human Interest Journalism and the Emergence of Celebrity in America, 1890–1940* (2002). A thoughtful cultural history that explores the intersection of new mass media, journalism, and the American fascination with celebrity.

Susan Smulyan, *Selling Radio: The Commercialization of American Broadcasting, 1920–1934* (1994). The best analysis of the rise of commercial radio broadcasting in the 1920s.

Joshua Zeitz, *Flapper* (2006). A lively and well-researched new account of "the flapper" phenomenon, with emphasis on how a wide variety of women contributed to new cultural images for females.

myhistorylab™
Where it's a good time to connect to the past!

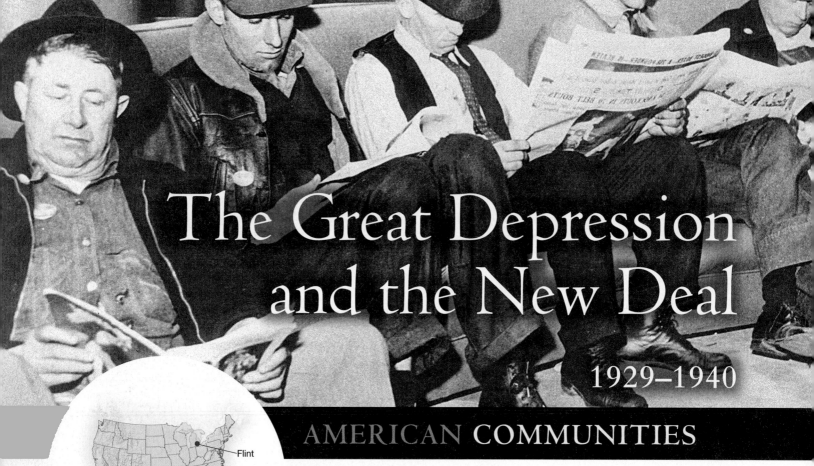

The Great Depression and the New Deal

1929–1940

Sit-Down Strike at Flint: Automobile Workers Organize a New Union

In the gloomy evening of February 11, 1937, 400 tired, unshaven, but very happy strikers marched out of the sprawling automobile factory known as Fisher Body Number 1 in Flint, Michigan. Most carried American flags and small bundles of clothing. A makeshift banner on top of the plant announced "Victory Is Ours." A wildly cheering parade line of a thousand supporters greeted the strikers at the gates. Shouting with joy, honking horns, and singing songs, the celebrants marched to two other factories to greet other emerging strikers. After forty-four days, the great Flint sit-down strike was over.

Flint was the heart of production for General Motors, the largest corporation in the world. In 1936, GM's net profits had reached $285 million, and its total assets were $1.5 billion. Originally a center for lumbering and then carriage making, Flint had boomed with the auto industry during the 1920s. Thousands of migrants streamed into the city, attracted by assembly-line jobs averaging about $30 a week. By 1930, Flint's population had grown to about 150,000 people, 80 percent of whom depended on work at General Motors. A severe housing shortage made living conditions difficult. Parts of the city resembled a mining camp, with workers living in tar-paper shacks, tents, and even railroad cars.

The Great Depression hit Flint very hard. Employment at GM fell from a 1929 high of 56,000 to fewer than 17,000 in 1932. As late as 1938, close to half the city's families were receiving some kind of emergency relief. By that time, as in thousands of other American communities, Flint's private and county relief agencies had been

overwhelmed by the needs of the unemployed and their families. Two new national agencies based in Washington, DC, the Federal Emergency Relief Administration and the Works Progress Administration, had replaced local sources of aid during the economic crisis. These New Deal programs embodied a new federal approach to providing relief and employment to American communities unable to cope with the enormity of mass unemployment.

The United Automobile Workers (UAW) came to Flint in 1936, seeking to organize GM workers into one industrial union. The previous year, Congress had passed the National Labor Relations Act (also known as the Wagner Act), which made union organizing easier by guaranteeing the right of workers to join unions and bargain collectively. The act established the National Labor Relations Board to oversee union elections and prohibit illegal antiunion activities by employers. But the obstacles to labor organizing were still enormous. ➤

Unemployment was high, and GM had maintained a vigorous antiunion policy for years. By the fall of 1936, the UAW had signed up only a thousand members. The key moment came with the seizure of two Flint GM plants by a few hundred auto workers on December 30, 1936. The idea was to stay in the factories until strikers could achieve a collective bargaining agreement with General Motors. "We don't aim to keep the plants or try to run them," explained one sit-downer to a reporter, "but we want to see that nobody takes our jobs. We don't think we're breaking the law, or at least we don't think we're doing anything really bad."

A new and daring tactic—the sit-down strike— gained popularity among American industrial workers during the 1930s. In 1936, there were 48 sit-downs involving nearly 90,000 workers, and in 1937 some 400,000 workers participated in 477 sit-down strikes. Sit-downs expressed the militant exuberance of the rank and file. As one union song of the day put it:

> *When they tie the can to a union man,*
> *Sit down! Sit down!*
> *When they give him the sack they'll take him back,*
> *Sit down! Sit down!*
> *When the speed up comes, just twiddle your thumbs,*
> *Sit down! Sit down!*
> *When the boss won't talk don't take a walk,*
> *Sit down! Sit down!*

The Flint strikers carefully organized themselves into what one historian called "the sit-down community." Each plant elected a strike committee and appointed its own police chief and sanitary engineer. No alcohol was allowed, and strikers were careful not to destroy company property. Committees were organized for food preparation, recreation, sanitation, education, and contact with the outside. A Women's Emergency Brigade—the strikers' wives, mothers, and daughters—provided crucial support preparing food and maintaining militant picket lines.

As the strike continued through January, support in Flint and around the nation grew. Overall production in the GM empire dropped from 53,000 vehicles per week to 1,500. Reporters and union supporters flocked to the plants. On January 11, in the so-called Battle of Running Bulls, strikers and their supporters clashed violently with Flint police and private GM guards. Michigan governor Frank Murphy, sympathetic to the strikers, brought in the National Guard to protect them. He refused to enforce an injunction obtained by GM to evict the strikers. In the face of determined unity by the sit-downers, GM gave in and recognized the UAW as the exclusive bargaining agent in all sixty of its factories.

The strike was perhaps the most important in American labor history, sparking a huge growth in union membership in the automobile and other mass-production industries. Out of the tight-knit, temporary community of the sit-down strike emerged a looser yet more permanent kind of community: a powerful, nationwide trade union of automobile workers. The UAW struggled successfully to win recognition and collective bargaining rights from other carmakers, such as Chrysler and Ford. The national UAW, like other new unions in the mass-production industries, was composed of locals around the country. The permanent community of unionized auto workers won significant improvements in wages, working conditions, and benefits. Locals also became influential in the political and social lives of their larger communities— industrial cities such as Flint, Detroit, and Toledo.

More broadly, the Flint sit-down embodied the new political and economic dynamics of Depression-era America. Workers, farmers, and consumers hard hit by the worst economic catastrophe in U.S. history called for a more activist federal government to relieve suffering and offer greater economic security for Americans. In response, a rejuvenated Democratic Party, led by President Franklin D. Roosevelt and in solid control of Congress, created the New Deal, an ambitious collection of measures designed to promote relief, recovery, and reform. With the 1935 National Labor Relations Act, the New Deal encouraged labor organizing by legally assuring the right to union membership for the first time in American history. A newly militant and aggressive labor movement in turn became a critical component of the "New Deal coalition" that kept Democrats in power. Organized labor provided crucial support for many of the social welfare initiatives associated with the New Deal throughout the 1930s and beyond: federal relief, a Social Security system, public works projects, new standards regulating minimum wages and maximum hours, and Washington-based efforts to improve the nation's housing. By the late 1930s, conservative resistance would limit the scope of New Deal reforms. But in communities around the nation labor unions inspired by the Flint sit-down reached unprecedented levels of popularity and influence in economic and political life. Nationally, they would remain a crucial component of the New Deal political coalition, and a key power broker in the Democratic Party, for decades to come.

Focus Questions

1. What were the causes of the Great Depression, and what were its consequences?

2. How did Hoover and Congress respond to the Great Depression?

3. What was the First New Deal, and how did it differ from the Second New Deal?

4. How did the New Deal expand the scope of the federal government in the South and West?

5. How did the Great Depression affect American cultural life during the 1930s?

6. What were the limits of the New Deal's reforms, and what legacy did they leave?

1929–1940

HARD TIMES

No twentieth-century event more profoundly affected American life than the Great Depression—the worst economic crisis in American history. Statistics tell only part of the story of a slumping economy, mass unemployment, and swelling relief rolls. Even today, the emotional and psychological toll of these years has left what one writer called an "invisible scar" on the lives and memories of millions of American families.

UNDERLYING WEAKNESSES OF THE 1920s' ECONOMY

It would be oversimple to say that the 1929 stock market collapse "caused" the Great Depression. Signs of deep economic weakness had already begun to surface amid the general prosperity of the 1920s. First, workers and consumers received too small a share of the enormous increases in labor productivity. Between 1923 and 1929, manufacturing output per worker-hour increased by 32 percent, while wages rose only 8 percent. Gains in wages and salaries were extremely uneven. While workers in newer industries such as automobiles and electrical manufacturing enjoyed pay increases, those in textiles and coal mining watched their wages fall. Moreover, the rise in productivity itself had encouraged overproduction in many industries, and the farm sector had never been able to regain the prosperity of the World War I years (see Chapter 23).

To be sure, Americans overall in the 1920s had more money to spend on cars, telephones, radios, washing machines, canned goods, and other consumer goods. Child labor was in decline, and more Americans than ever now graduated from high school. But economic insecurity was a brutal fact of life for millions of families, especially in rural communities. Most industrial workers endured regular bouts of unemployment and seasonal layoffs. The two-day weekend and paid vacations were largely unknown. Eighty percent of the nation's families had no savings at all, and an old age spent in poverty was far more likely for the average worker than "retirement." The most important weakness in the economy was the extremely unequal distribution of income, yielding the greatest concentration of wealth in the nation's history (see Table 24.1).

THE BULL MARKET AND THE CRASH

Stock trading in the late 1920s captured the imagination of the broad American public. The stock market resembled a sporting arena, millions following stock prices as avidly as the exploits of Babe Ruth or Jack Dempsey. Business leaders and economists as much as told Americans that it was their duty to buy stocks. John J. Raskob, chairman of the board of General Motors, wrote an article for the *Ladies' Home Journal* titled "Everybody Ought to Be Rich." A person who saved $15 each month and invested it in good common stocks would, he claimed, have $80,000 within twenty years.

During the bull market of the 1920s, stock prices increased at roughly twice the rate of industrial production. By the end of the decade, stocks that had been bought mainly on the basis of their earning power, which was passed on to stockholders in the form of dividends, now came to be purchased only for the resale value after their prices rose. In 1928 alone, for example, the price of Radio Corporation of America stock shot up from $85 per share to $420; Chrysler stock more than doubled, from $63 to $132.

TABLE 24.1

Distribution of Total Family Income Among Various Segments of the Population, 1929–44 (in Percentages)

Year	Poorest Fifth	Second Poorest Fifth	Middle Fifth	Second Wealthiest Fifth	Wealthiest Fifth	Wealthiest 5 Percent
1929		12.5	13.8	19.3	54.4	30.0
1935–36	4.1	9.2	14.1	20.9	51.7	26.5
1941	4.1	9.5	15.3	22.3	48.8	24.0
1944	4.9	10.9	16.2	22.2	45.8	20.7

SOURCE: Adapted from U.S. Bureau of the Census, *Historical Statistics of the United States, Colonial Times to 1970*, Bicentennial Edition (Washington, DC: U.S. Government Printing Office, 1975), 301.

Yet only about 3 million Americans—out of a total population of 120 million—owned any stocks at all. Many of these stock buyers had been lured into the market through easy-credit margin accounts, which allowed investors to purchase stocks with a small down payment (as low as 10 percent), borrowing the rest from a broker and using the shares as collateral on the loan. Just as installment plans had stimulated the automobile and other industries, "buying on the margin" brought new customers to the stock market. Investment trusts, similar to today's mutual funds, attracted many new investors with promises of high returns. Corporations found that lending excess capital to stockbrokers was more profitable than investing in new technologies. All these factors fed an expansive and optimistic atmosphere on Wall Street.

Although often portrayed as a one- or two-day catastrophe, the Wall Street crash of 1929 was actually a steep slide. The bull market peaked in early September, and prices drifted downward. Once expectations of an endless boom began to melt, the market had to decline. On Monday, October 28, the Dow lost 38 points—13 percent of its value. The next day—"Black Tuesday," October 29—the bottom fell out. Over 16 million shares, more than double the previous record, were traded as panic selling took hold. For many stocks, no buyers were available at any price.

The situation worsened. The market's fragile foundation of credit, based on the margin debt, quickly crumbled. Many investors with margin accounts had to sell when stock values fell. Since the shares themselves represented the security for their loans, more money had to be put up to cover the loans when prices declined. By mid-November, about $30 billion in the market price of stocks had been wiped out. Half the value of the stocks listed in *The New York Times* index was lost in ten weeks.

The nation's political and economic leaders downplayed all this. At the end of 1929, hardly anyone was predicting that a decade-long depression would follow. But the stock market crash undermined the confidence, investment, and spending of businesses and the well-to-do. Manufacturers cut produc-

tion and began laying off workers, which brought further declines in consumer spending, and so another round of production cutbacks ensued. A spurt of consumer spending might have checked this downward spiral, but consumers had less to spend as industries laid off workers and reduced work hours. With a shrinking market for products, businesses feared to expand. A large proportion of the nation's banking funds had been tied to the speculative bubble. Many banks began to fail as anxious depositors withdrew their funds, which were uninsured, costing thousands of families all their savings. And an 86 percent plunge in agricultural prices between 1929 and 1933, compared to a decline in agricultural production of only 6 percent, brought terrible suffering to America's farmers.

Rollin Kirby's 1929 cartoon depicts an individual investor losing his money as he clings to a bear running down Wall Street. The bear symbolizes an atmosphere of panic selling and heavy losses, the opposite of a "bull" market in which investor confidence spurs buying and faith in the future.

MASS UNEMPLOYMENT

At a time when unemployment insurance did not exist and public relief was completely inadequate, the loss of a job could mean economic catastrophe for workers and their families. Massive unemployment across America became the most powerful sign of a deepening depression. In 1930, the Department of Labor estimated that roughly 9 percent of the labor force was out of work. By 1933, 12.6 million workers—over one-quarter of the labor force—were without jobs. (Other sources put the figure that year above 16 million, or nearly one out of every three workers.) No statistics tells us how long people were unemployed or how many Americans found only part-time work.

Many Americans, raised believing that they were responsible for their own fate, blamed themselves for their failure to find work. Journalists and social workers noted the common feelings of shame and guilt expressed by the unemployed. One jobless Houston woman told a relief caseworker, "I'm just no good, I guess. I've given up ever amounting to anything. It's no use." A West Virginia man wrote his senator to complain, "My children have not got no shoes and clothing to go to school with, and we haven't got enough bed clothes to keep us warm." One despondent Pennsylvania man asked a state relief agency, "Can you be so kind as to advise me as to which would be the most human way to dispose of my self and family, as this is about the only thing that I see left to do."

Unemployment upset the psychological balance in many families by undermining the traditional authority of the male breadwinner. Women, because their labor was cheaper than men's, found it easier to keep jobs. Female clerks, secretaries, maids, and waitresses earned much less than male factory workers, but their jobs were more likely to survive hard times. Pressures on those lucky enough to have a job increased as well. Anna Novak, a Chicago meat packer, recalled the degrading harassment at the hands of foremen: "You could get along swell if you let the boss slap you on the behind and feel you up. God, I hate that stuff, you don't know!" Men responded in a variety of ways to unemployment. Some withdrew emotionally; others became angry or took to drinking. A few committed suicide. In 1934, one Chicago social worker summed up the strains she found in families: "Fathers feel they have lost their prestige in the home; there is much nagging, mothers nag at the fathers, parents nag at the children. Children of working age who earn meager salaries find it hard to turn over all their earnings and deny themselves even the greatest necessities and as a result leave home." Fear of unemployment and a deep desire for security marked the Depression generation.

HOOVER'S FAILURE

The enormity of the Great Depression overwhelmed traditional—and meager—sources of relief. In most communities across America, these sources were a patchwork

Dorothea Lange captured the lonely despair of unemployment in *White Angel Breadline, San Francisco, 1933*. During the 1920s, Lange had specialized in taking portraits of wealthy families, but by 1932, she could no longer stand the contradiction between her portrait business and "what was going on in the street." She said of this photograph: "There are moments such as these when time stands still and all you can do is hold your breath and hope it will wait for you."

SOURCE: Dorothea Lange, "White Angel Breadline, San Francisco, 1933." Copyright the Dorothea Lange Collection, The Oakland Museum of California, City of Oakland. Gift of Paul S. Taylor.

of private agencies and local government units, such as towns, cities, or counties. They simply lacked the money, resources, and staff to deal with the worsening situation. In large urban centers like Detroit and Chicago, unemployment approached 50 percent by 1932. Smaller communities could not cope either. For 1932, one West Virginia coal-mining county with 1,500 unemployed miners had only $9,000 to meet relief needs.

There was great irony, even tragedy, in President Hoover's failure to respond to human suffering. During World War I he had effectively administered Belgian war relief abroad and won wide praise for his leadership of the Food Administration at home. As a leader of the progressive wing of the Republican Party, Hoover had long championed a kind of cooperative individualism that relied upon public-spirited citizens. Although he felt real personal anguish over the hardships people suffered, he

Isaac Soyer's *Employment Agency*, a 1937 oil painting, offered one of the decade's most sensitive efforts at depicting the anxiety and sense of isolation felt by millions of depression-era job hunters.

SOURCE: Isaac Soyer, "Employment Agency," 1937. Oil on canvas, 34 1/2" × 45". Whitney Museum of American Art.

lacked the political skill to demonstrate his compassion in public. Failing to face the facts of the depression, Hoover worried more about undermining individual initiative than providing actual relief for victims. He ignored all mounting evidence to the contrary when he claimed, in his 1931 State of the Union Address, "Our people are providing against distress from unemployment in true American fashion by magnificent response to public appeal and by action of the local governments."

Hoover's plan for recovery centered on restoring business confidence. His administration's most important institutional response to the depression was the Reconstruction Finance Corporation (RFC), established in early 1932 and based on the War Finance Corporation of the World War I years. The RFC was designed to make government credit available to ailing banks, railroads, insurance companies, and other businesses, thereby stimulating economic activity. The key assumption here was that the problem was one of supply (for businesses) rather than demand (from consumers). But given the public's low purchasing power, most businesses were not interested in obtaining loans for expansion. Worried about undermining "the initiative and enterprise of the American people," Hoover resisted growing calls from Congress and local communities for a greater federal role in relief efforts or public works projects. The RFC managed to save numerous banks and other businesses from going under, but its ap-

proach did not hasten recovery. And Hoover was loath to use the RFC to make direct grants to states, cities, or individuals. In July 1932, congressional Democrats pushed through the Emergency Relief Act, which authorized the RFC to lend $300 million to states that had exhausted their own relief funds. Hoover grudgingly signed the bill, but less than $30 million had actually been given out by the end of 1933.

Two other federal actions—in each case, the opposite of what should have been done—worsened the situation. First, the Federal Reserve, whose policies of low interest rates and easy credit in the late 1920s had helped fuel the speculative boom in stock buying, now tightened credit sharply. That caused interest rates to spike, putting heavy pressure on the nation's banking system, especially the smaller banks on which farmers, merchants, and local businessmen relied. Without any state or federal insurance, more than 5,000 rural banks and ethnic-group-oriented savings and loans institutions failed between 1929 and 1932, and more than 9 million depositors lost their savings. Second, in 1930 Congress passed (and Hoover signed) the Smoot-Hawley Tariff, raising import duties to their highest levels in American history. Supporters, including the president, claimed that this would protect American farmers from global competition and raise farm prices. But as other nations responded by raising their own tariffs world trade declined steeply, exacerbating the economic collapse.

A GLOBAL CRISIS AND THE ELECTION OF 1932

By 1931 the depression had spread not only across the United States but also throughout the world, a sign of how interdependent the global economy had become. The immediate problem was the highly unstable system of international finance. The 1919 peace settlement had saddled Germany with $33 billion in war reparations, owed largely to Great Britain and France. The United States had loaned money to the British and French during the war, and American banks had loaned large sums to Germany in the 1920s. Germany used these loans to pay reparations to the British and French, who in turn used these reparations to repay their American debts. The 1929 stock market crash put an end to American loans for Germany, thus removing a critical link in the international cash flow. When Germany then defaulted on its reparations, Great Britain and France in turn stopped paying what they owed to this country. As German banks collapsed and unemployment swelled, nervous European investors sold their American stocks, depressing the stock market even further. Great Britain and several other European nations also abandoned the gold standard and devalued (lowered) their currency relative to the dollar. This made American goods more difficult to sell abroad, further dampening production at home. With many nations also raising their tariffs to protect national industries, international trade slowed to a crawl. The total volume of global trade declined from about $36 billion in 1929 to roughly $12 billion by 1932. American banks, badly hurt by both domestic depositors clamoring for their money and the foreign withdrawal of capital, began failing in record numbers. In 1931 alone, 2,294 U.S. banks failed, double the number that had collapsed in 1930.

By 1932 the desperate mood of many Americans was finding expression in direct, sometimes violent, protests that were widely covered in the press. On March 7, communist organizers led a march of several thousand Detroit auto workers and unemployed in Dearborn. Ford-controlled police fired tear gas and bullets, killing four demonstrators and seriously wounding fifty others. Desperate farmers in Iowa organized the Farmers' Holiday Association, aimed at raising prices by refusing to sell produce. In August, some 1,500 farmers dumped milk and other perishables into ditches.

The spring of 1932 also saw the "Bonus Army" begin descending on Washington, DC. This protest took its name from Congress's promise in 1924 to pay every veteran of World War I a $1,000 bonus—in the form of a bond that would not mature until 1945. The veterans who were gathering in Washington demanded immediate payment of the bonus in cash. By summer, they and their families numbered around 20,000 strong and were camping out all over the capital city. The House passed a bill for immediate payment, but when the Senate refused to agree, most of the downcast veterans left. At the end of July, U.S. Army troops, led by Chief of Staff General Douglas MacArthur, forcibly evicted the remaining 2,000 veterans. The spectacle of these unarmed and unemployed men, the heroes of 1918, being driven off by bayonets and bullets, provided the most disturbing evidence yet of the failure of Hoover's administration.

In 1932, Democrats nominated Franklin D. Roosevelt, governor of New York, for the presidency. Roosevelt's acceptance speech stressed the need for reconstructing the nation's economy. "I pledge you, I pledge myself," he said, "to a new deal for the American people." Roosevelt's plans for recovery were vague and contradictory. He frequently attacked Hoover for reckless and extravagant spending and accused him of concentrating too much power in Washington, but he also spoke of the need for government to meet "the problem of underconsumption" and to help in "distributing wealth and products more equitably." Above

MAP EXPLORATION

To explore an interactive version of this map, go to
www.prenhall.com/faragher6/map24.1

	Electoral Vote (%)	Popular Vote (%)
FRANKLIN D. ROOSEVELT (Democrat)	472 (89)	22,809,638 (57)
Herbert Hoover (Republican)	59 (11)	15,758,901 (40)
Minor parties	—	1,153,306 (3)

MAP 24.1 The Election of 1932 Democrats owed their overwhelming victory in 1932 to the popular identification of the depression with the Hoover administration. Roosevelt's popular vote was about the same as Hoover's in 1928, and FDR's electoral college margin was even greater.

all, Roosevelt stressed, "the country demands bold, persistent experimentation." Hoover bitterly condemned Roosevelt's ideas as a "radical departure" from the American way of life. But with the depression growing worse every day, probably any Democrat would have defeated Hoover. The Democratic victory was overwhelming. Roosevelt carried forty-two states, taking the electoral college 472 to 59 and the popular vote by about 23 million to 16 million. Democrats won big majorities in both the House and the Senate. The stage was set for FDR's "new deal" (see Map 24.1).

FDR AND THE FIRST NEW DEAL

No twentieth-century president had a greater impact on American life and politics than Franklin Delano Roosevelt (FDR). To a large degree, the New Deal was a product of his astute political skills and the sheer force of his personality. The only president ever elected to four terms, FDR would loom as the dominant personality in American political life through twelve years of depression and global war. Roosevelt's leadership also inaugurated a forty-year-long period of Democratic dominance of the nation's political life.

FDR THE MAN

Franklin Delano Roosevelt was born in 1882 in Dutchess County, New York, where he grew up an only child, secure and confident, on his family's vast estate. Roosevelt's education at private school, Harvard, and Columbia Law School reinforced his aristocratic family's sense of civic duty. In 1905, he married his distant cousin, Anna Eleanor Roosevelt, a niece of President Theodore Roosevelt. He was elected as a Democrat to the New York State Senate in 1910, served as assistant secretary of the navy from 1913 to 1920, and was nominated for vice president by the Democrats in the losing 1920 campaign.

In the summer of 1921, Roosevelt was stricken with polio; he was never to walk again without support. His illness proved the turning point in his life. The wealthy aristocrat, for whom everything had come relatively easily, now personally understood the meaning of struggle and hardship. "Once I spent two years lying in bed trying to move my big toe," he recalled. "After that anything else seems easy."

Elected governor of New York in 1928, Roosevelt served two terms and won a national reputation for reform. As governor, he instituted unemployment insurance, strengthened child labor laws, enacted tax relief for farmers, and provided pensions for the old. As the depression hit the state, he slowly increased public works.

"THE ONLY THING WE HAVE TO FEAR": RESTORING CONFIDENCE

In the first days of his administration, Roosevelt conveyed a sense of optimism and activism that helped restore the badly shaken confidence of the nation. "First of all," he told Americans in his Inaugural Address on March 4, 1933, "let me assert my firm belief that the only thing we have to fear is fear itself." The very next day, as people lined up to pull savings out of failing banks and hoarded cash under their mattresses, he issued an executive order calling for a four-day "bank holiday" to stop the collapse of the country's financial system.

The new Congress was not scheduled to convene until the end of 1933, but Roosevelt convened a special session to deal with the banking crisis, unemployment aid, and farm relief. On March 12, he broadcast his first "fireside chat" to explain the steps he had taken to meet the financial emergency. These radio broadcasts became a standard part of Roosevelt's political technique, and they

This *New Yorker* magazine cover depicted an ebullient Franklin D. Roosevelt riding to his 1933 inauguration in the company of a glum Herbert Hoover. This drawing typified many mass media images of the day, contrasting the different moods and temperaments of the new president and the defeated incumbent.

proved enormously successful. They gave courage to ordinary Americans and communicated a genuine sense of compassion from the White House.

Congress immediately passed the Emergency Banking Act, which gave the president broad discretionary powers over all banking transactions and foreign exchange. It authorized healthy banks to reopen only under licenses from the Treasury Department and provided for greater federal authority in managing the affairs of failed banks. By the middle of March, about half the country's banks, holding about 90 percent of the nation's deposits, were open for business again. Banks began to attract new deposits from people who had been holding back their money. The bank crisis had passed.

Roosevelt assembled a group of key advisers, the "brains trust," to counsel him in the White House. They gave conflicting advice. Some advocated fiscal conservatism to restore confidence in the dollar; others pushed for central planning to manage the economy. But the "brain trusters" shared a basic belief in expert-directed government–business cooperation. Structural economic reform, they argued, must accept the modern reality of large corporate enterprise based on mass production and distribution.

THE HUNDRED DAYS

From March to June 1933—"the Hundred Days"—FDR pushed through Congress an extraordinary amount of depression-fighting legislation. Roosevelt's enormous political skill—as a power broker, as a coalition builder, and as a communicator with the American public—was crucial. What came to be called the New Deal was no unified program to end the depression but rather an improvised series of reform and relief measures, some of which completely contradicted each other. Still, all the New Deal programs were united by the fundamental goals of relief, reform, and recovery.

Five measures were particularly important and innovative. The Civilian Conservation Corps (CCC), established in March as an unemployment relief effort, provided work for jobless young men in protecting and conserving the nation's natural resources. Road construction, reforestation, flood control, and national park improvements were some of the major projects performed in work camps across the country. CCC workers received room and board and $30 each month, up to $25 of which had to be sent home to dependents. By the time the program was phased out in 1942, more than 2.5 million youths had worked in some 1,500 CCC camps.

In May, Congress authorized $500 million for the Federal Emergency Relief Administration (FERA). Half the money went as direct relief to the states; the rest was distributed on the basis of a dollar of federal aid for every three dollars of state and local funds spent for relief. This system of outright federal grants differed significantly from Hoover's loans-only approach. Establishment of work relief projects, however, was left to state and local governments. To direct this massive undertaking, FDR tapped Harry Hopkins, a streetwise former New York City social worker driven by a deep moral passion to help the less fortunate and an impatience with bureaucracy. Hopkins would emerge as the key figure administering New Deal relief programs.

The Agricultural Adjustment Administration (AAA) was set up to provide immediate relief to the nation's farmers. The AAA established a new federal role in agricultural planning and price setting. It established parity prices for basic farm commodities, including corn, wheat, hogs, cotton, rice, and dairy products. The concept of parity pricing was based on the purchasing power that farmers had enjoyed during the prosperous years of 1909 to 1914. That period now became the benchmark for setting

A recruitment poster represents the Civilian Conservation Corps (CCC) as much more than simply an emergency relief measure, stressing character building and the opportunity for self-improvement. By the time the CCC expired in 1942, it had become one of the most popular of all the New Deal programs.

"floor"—that is, minimum—prices for farm commodities. The AAA also incorporated the principle of subsidy, whereby farmers received benefit payments in return for reducing acreage or otherwise cutting production where surpluses existed. New taxes on food processing were to pay for these programs.

The AAA raised total farm income and was especially successful in pushing up the prices of wheat, cotton, and corn. But it had some troubling side effects. Landlords often failed to share their AAA payments with tenant farmers, and they frequently used benefits to buy tractors and other equipment that displaced sharecroppers. Many Americans were disturbed, too, by the sight of surplus crops, livestock, and milk being destroyed while millions went hungry.

The Tennessee Valley Authority (TVA) proved to be one of the most unique and controversial projects of the New Deal era. The TVA, an independent public corporation, built dams and power plants, produced cheap fertilizer for farmers, and, most significantly, for the first time brought low-cost electricity to thousands of people in six southern states. Denounced by some as a dangerous step toward socialism, the TVA stood for decades as a model of how careful government planning could dramatically improve the social and economic welfare of an underdeveloped region.

On the very last of the Hundred Days, Congress passed the National Industrial Recovery Act, the closest attempt yet at a systematic plan for economic recovery. In theory, each industry would be self-governed by a code hammered out by representatives of business, labor, and consumers. Once approved by the National Recovery Administration (NRA) in Washington, the codes would have the force of law. In practice, almost all the National Recovery Administration codes were written by the largest firms in any given industry; labor and consumers got short shrift. The sheer administrative complexities involved with code writing and compliance made a great many people unhappy with the NRA's operation.

Finally, the Public Works Administration (PWA), led by Secretary of the Interior Harold Ickes, authorized $3.3 billion for the construction of roads, public buildings, and other projects. The idea was to provide jobs and, through increased consumer spending, stimulate the economy. "Priming the pump," this strategy was called, borrowing a phrase from what an old-time farmer had to do to get his well pump going. Eventually the PWA spent over $4.2 billion building roads, schools, post offices, bridges, courthouses, and other public buildings, which in thousands of communities today remain tangible reminders of the New Deal era.

During the Hundred Days and the months immediately following, Congress passed other legislation that would have important long-range effects. The Glass-Steagall Act created the Federal Deposit Insurance Corporation (FDIC), which provided protection to individual depositors by guaranteeing accounts of up to $5,000 in case of bank failure. Congress also established the Securities and Exchange Commission (SEC) to regulate stock exchanges and brokers, require full financial disclosures, and curb the speculative practices that had contributed to the 1929 crash. The 1934 National Housing Act, aimed at stimulating residential construction and making home financing more affordable, set up the Federal Housing Administration (FHA). The FHA insured loans made by banks and other private lenders for home building and home buying.

OVERVIEW | Key Legislation of the First New Deal ("Hundred Days," March 9–June 16, 1933)

Legislation	Purpose
Emergency Banking Relief Act	Enlarged federal authority over private banks
	Government loans to private banks
Civilian Conservation Corps	Unemployment relief
	Conservation of natural resources
Federal Emergency Relief Administration	Direct federal money for relief, funneled through state and local governments
Agricultural Adjustment Administration	Federal farm aid based on parity pricing and subsidy
Tennessee Valley Authority	Economic development and cheap electricity for Tennessee Valley
National Industrial Recovery Act	Self-regulating industrial codes to revive economic activity
Public Works Administration	Federal public works projects to increase employment and consumer spending

ROOSEVELT'S CRITICS, RIGHT AND LEFT

From the beginning, the New Deal had loud and powerful critics on the right who complained bitterly that FDR had overstepped the traditional boundaries of government action. From the left came angry cries that Roosevelt had not done nearly enough.

Pro-Republican newspapers and the American Liberty League, a group of conservative businessmen organized in 1934, vehemently attacked the administration for what they considered its attack on property rights, the growing welfare state, and the alleged decline of personal liberty. Dominated by wealthy Du Pont and General Motors executives, the Liberty League attracted support from conservative Democrats including Al Smith, the 1928 presidential candidate, who declared the New Deal "socialistic." But in the 1934 election, Democrats crushed their right-wing critics and—countering the losses that incumbent parties usually suffer at midterm—increased their majorities in both houses of Congress.

Father Charles E. Coughlin, a Catholic priest in suburban Detroit with a huge national radio audience of 40 million listeners, at first supported the New Deal—but by 1934, frustrated by his limited influence on the president, "the radio priest" began attacking FDR in passionate broadcasts that also denounced Wall Street, international bankers, Jews, and "plutocratic capitalism." Roosevelt, he charged, wanted dictatorial powers, and New Deal policies were part of a communist conspiracy.

More troublesome for Roosevelt were the vocal and popular movements on the left. These found the New Deal too timid. In California, the well-known novelist and socialist Upton Sinclair entered the 1934 Democratic primary for governor by running on a program he called EPIC ("End Poverty in California"). He proposed a monthly pension of $50 for all poor people over age sixty and championed a government-run system of "production for use" (rather than profit) workshops for the unemployed. Sinclair shocked local and national Democrats by winning the primary easily. He lost a close general election only because the Republican candidate received heavy financial and tactical support from wealthy Hollywood studio executives and frightened regular Democrats.

Another Californian, Francis E. Townsend, a retired dentist, won a large following among senior citizens with his Old Age Revolving Pension plan. He called for payments of $200 per month to all people over sixty, provided all the money was spent within thirty days. The pensions would be financed by a national 2 percent tax on commercial transactions. This plan managed to attract a nationwide following of more than 3 million by 1936.

Huey Long, Louisiana's flamboyant backcountry orator, posed the greatest potential threat to Roosevelt's leadership. Long had captured Louisiana's governorship in 1928 by attacking the state's entrenched oil industry and calling for a radical redistribution of wealth. In office, he significantly improved public education, roads, medical care, and other public services, winning the loyalty of the state's poor farmers and industrial workers. Elected to the U.S. Senate in 1930, Long came to Washington with national ambitions. He at first supported Roosevelt, but in 1934, his own presidential ambitions and his impatience with the pace of New Deal measures led to a break with FDR.

Long organized the Share Our Wealth Society. Its purpose, he thundered, "was to break up the swollen fortunes of America and to spread the wealth among all our people." Limiting the size of large fortunes, Long promised, would mean a homestead worth $5,000 and a $2,500 annual income for everyone. Although Long's economics were fuzzy, his "Every Man a King" slogan touched a deep popular nerve. A secret poll in the summer of 1935 stunned the Democratic National Committee by showing that Long might attract 3 or 4 million votes for president. Only his assassination that September by a political enemy of his corrupt political machine prevented Long's third-party candidacy, which might have proved disastrous for FDR.

A newly militant labor movement also loomed as a force to be reckoned with. Unemployed Councils, organized largely by the Communist Party in industrial cities, held marches and rallies demanding public works projects and relief payments. Section 7a of the National Industrial Recovery Act required that workers be allowed to bargain collectively with employers through representatives of their own choosing. Although this provision of the NIRA was not enforced, it did help raise expectations and sparked union organizing. Almost 1.5 million workers took part in some 1,800 strikes in 1934.

But employers resisted unionization, often with violence and the help of local and state police. In Minneapolis that year, a local of the International Brotherhood of Teamsters won a bloody strike against the combined opposition of the union's own national officials, vehemently antiunion employers, and a brutal city police force. Also in 1934, a San Francisco general strike in support of striking members of the International Longshoremen's Association (ILA) effectively shut down the city. Employer use of strikebreakers and violent intimidation prompted an outpouring of support for the ILA from the city's working class, as well as from many shopkeepers and middle-class professionals.

LEFT TURN AND THE SECOND NEW DEAL

The popularity of Coughlin, Sinclair, Townsend, and Long suggested Roosevelt might be losing electoral support among workers, farmers, the aged, and the unemployed. In addition, FDR had to contend with a conservative Supreme Court that did not share the public's enthusiasm for the New Deal. In May 1935, in *Schecter* v. *United States*, the Court found the NRA unconstitutional in its entirety. In early 1936, ruling in *Butler* v. *United States*, the Court invalidated the AAA, declaring it an unconstitutional attempt at regulating agriculture. The Court was composed mostly of Republican appointees, six of them over seventy. Looking toward the 1936 election and eager for a popular mandate, Roosevelt and his closest advisers responded by turning left and offering new social-reform programs. These programs had three major goals: strengthening the national commitment to creating jobs; providing security against old age, unemployment, and illness; and improving housing conditions and cleaning slums. What came to be called "the Second Hundred Days," marked the high point of progressive lawmaking in the New Deal.

THE SECOND HUNDRED DAYS

In April 1935 the administration pushed through Congress the Emergency Relief Appropriation Act, which allocated $5 billion for large-scale public works programs for the jobless. New Deal economists argued that each government dollar spent had a multiplier effect, pumping two or three dollars into the depressed gross domestic product. Over the next seven years, the WPA, under Harry Hopkins's leadership, oversaw the employment of more than 8 million Americans on a vast array of construction projects: roads, bridges, dams, airports, and sewers. Among the most innovative WPA programs were community

service projects that employed thousands of jobless artists, musicians, actors, and writers.

The landmark Social Security Act of 1935 provided for old-age pensions and unemployment insurance. A payroll tax on workers and their employers created a fund from which retirees received monthly pensions after age sixty-five. Payment size depended on how much employees and their employers contributed. The act's unemployment compensation plan established a minimum weekly payment and a minimum number of weeks during which those who lost jobs could collect. The old-age pensions were quite small at first, as little as $10 a month. And no one could collect unemployment who had not first lost a job. But the law, which has subsequently been amended many times, established the crucial principle of federal responsibility for America's most vulnerable citizens.

In July 1935, Congress passed the National Labor Relations Act, often called the Wagner Act for its chief sponsor, Democratic senator Robert F. Wagner of New York. For the first time, the federal government guaranteed the right of American workers to join, or form, independent labor unions and to bargain collectively for improved wages, benefits, and working conditions. The National Labor Relations Board would conduct secret-ballot elections in shops and factories to determine which union, if any, workers desired as their sole bargaining agent. The law also defined and prohibited unfair labor practices by employers, including firing workers for union activity. The Wagner Act, described as "the Magna Carta for labor," quickly proved a boon to union growth, especially in previously unorganized industries such as automobiles, steel, and textiles.

OVERVIEW | Key Legislation of the Second New Deal (1935–38)

Legislation	Purpose
Emergency Relief Appropriations Act (1935)	Large-scale public works program for the jobless (includes Works Progress Administration)
Social Security Act (1935)	Federal old-age pensions and unemployment insurance
National Labor Relations Act (1935)	Federal guarantee of right to organize trade unions and collective bargaining
Resettlement Administration (1935)	Relocation of poor rural families
	Reforestation and soil erosion projects
National Housing Act (1937)	Federal funding for public housing and slum clearance
Fair Labor Standards Act (1938)	Federal minimum wage and maximum hours

Finally, the Resettlement Administration (RA) produced one of the most utopian New Deal programs, designed to create new kinds of model communities. Established by executive order, and led by key brain truster Rexford G. Tugwell, the RA helped destitute farm families relocate to more productive areas. It granted loans for purchasing land and equipment, and it directed reforestation and soil erosion projects, particularly in the hard-hit Southwest. Due to lack of funds and poor administration, however, only about 1 percent of the projected 500,000 families were actually moved. Tugwell, one of the New Deal's most ardent believers in central planning, was more successful in his efforts at creating model greenbelt communities, combining the best of urban and rural environments. As suburbs, a few of these communities still thrive.

LABOR'S UPSURGE: RISE OF THE CIO

The Wagner Act greatly facilitated union organizing and galvanized the moribund labor movement. In 1932, only 2.8 million workers were union members, a half-million fewer than in 1929 and more than 2 million fewer than in 1920. Yet by 1942, unions claimed more than 10.5 million members, nearly a third of the total nonagricultural work force. This remarkable turnaround was one of the key events of the depression era. The growth in the size and power of the labor movement permanently changed the work lives and economic status of millions, as well as the national and local political landscapes.

At the core of this growth was a series of dramatic successes in the organization of workers in large-scale, mass-production industries such as automobiles, steel, rubber,

Photographer Milton Brooks won the first Pulitzer Prize for photography with this 1941 image for the *Detroit News*. He captured a violent labor confrontation in front of the Ford Motor Company's River Rouge plant, as private armed guards, employed by Ford, assault and beat organizers for the United Automobile Workers.

electrical goods, and textiles. The conservative, craft-oriented unions that dominated the American Federation of Labor (AFL) had largely ignored workers in these industries. At the 1935 AFL convention, a group of more militant union officials led by John L. Lewis (of the United Mine Workers) and Sidney Hillman (of the Amalgamated Clothing Workers) formed the Committee for Industrial Organization (CIO) and set about organizing mass-production workers by industry—regardless of a worker's level of skill. They differed from nearly all old-line AFL unions by calling for the inclusion of black and women workers.

The gruff son of a Welsh miner, Lewis was articulate, ruthless, and very ambitious. He saw the new legal protection given by the Wagner Act as a historic opportunity. Lewis knew that establishing permanent unions in the mass-production industries would be a bruising battle. He committed the substantial resources of the United Mine Workers to a series of organizing drives, focusing first on the steel and auto industries. Many CIO organizers were communists or radicals of other kinds, and their dedication, commitment, and willingness to work within disciplined organizations proved invaluable in the often dangerous task of creating industrial unions. Militant rank-and-file unionists were often ahead of Lewis and other CIO leaders. The sit-down strike—refusing to work but staying in the factory to prevent "scab" workers from taking over—emerged as a popular tactic among rubber and auto workers. (Sit-down strikes were declared illegal after World War II and are still banned.)

After the dramatic breakthrough in a 1937 sit-down strike against General Motors at Flint, Michigan, membership in CIO unions grew rapidly. In eight months, membership in the United Automobile Workers (UAW) alone soared from 88,000 to 400,000. CIO victories in the steel, rubber, and electrical industries followed, but often at a very high cost. One bloody example of the perils of union organizing was the 1937 Memorial Day Massacre in Chicago. In a field near the struck Republic Steel Mill in South Chicago, police fired into a crowd of union supporters, killing ten workers and wounding scores more.

In 1938, CIO unions, now boasting nearly 4 million members, withdrew from the AFL and reorganized themselves as the Congress of Industrial Organizations. For the first time ever, the labor movement had gained a permanent place in the nation's mass-production industries. Organized labor took its place as a key power broker in Roosevelt's New Deal and the national Democratic Party. Frances Perkins, FDR's secretary of labor and the nation's first woman cabinet member, captured the close relationship between the new unionism and the New Deal: "Programs long thought of as merely labor welfare, such as shorter hours, higher wages, and a voice in the terms of conditions of work, are really essential economic factors for recovery."

THE NEW DEAL COALITION AT HIGH TIDE

Both major political parties looked forward to the 1936 elections as a national referendum, and the campaign itself was exciting and hard fought. The Republicans nominated Governor Alfred M. Landon of Kansas, who had gained attention by surviving the Democratic landslide of 1934. An easygoing, colorless man, Landon emphasized a nostalgic appeal to traditional American values. His campaign served as a lightning rod for all those, including many conservative Democrats, who were dissatisfied with Roosevelt and the direction he had taken.

Roosevelt attacked the "economic royalists" who denied that government "could do anything to protect the citizen in his right to work and his right to live." At the same time, FDR was careful to distance himself from radicalism. "It was this administration," he declared, "which saved the system of private profit and free enterprise after it had been dragged to the brink of ruin." Huge and enthusiastic crowds greeted Roosevelt, especially in large cities. Still, the vast majority of the nation's newspapers endorsed Landon. And a widely touted "scientific" poll by the *Literary Digest* forecast a Republican victory in November.

Election day erased all doubts: Roosevelt carried every state but Maine and Vermont, polling 61 percent of the popular vote. Democrats increased their substantial majorities in the House and Senate as well. The *Literary Digest*, it turned out, had polled only people with addresses in telephone directories and car registration records, thus omitting poorer Americans who had no telephones or cars—and who supported Roosevelt. In 1936, the Democrats drew millions of new voters into the political process, and at the same time, forged a new coalition of voters that would dominate national politics for two generations.

This "New Deal coalition," as it came to be known, included white Southern Democrats, ethnics who supported big-city political machines, unionized workers (including those being organized by the CIO), and many depression-hit farmers. Black voters in the North and West, long affiliated with the Republicans as "the party of Lincoln," went Democratic in record numbers. (Of course, blacks were largely barred from voting in the South.) The Great Depression was by no means over. But the New Deal's active response to the nation's misery, particularly its bold initiatives in 1935, had obviously struck a powerful chord with the American electorate. Roosevelt was especially popular among first- and second-generation immigrants of Catholic and Jewish descent, and the New Deal drew enthusiastic support from millions who had never bothered with politics. As one Slovak worker in Chicago's stockyards put it, "Our people did not know anything about the government until the depression years. In my neighborhood, I don't remember anyone voting." The severity of the Great Depression had overwhelmed the ethnically based support networks—mutual benefit societies, immigrant banks, and religious charities—that had traditionally helped so many to survive hard times. Popular federal programs like Social Security, the WPA, and Home Owners Loan Corporation mortgages changed the consciousness of a generation of the ethnic working class. In exchange for their votes, they now looked to the state—especially the federal government—for relief, protection, and help in achieving the American dream.

THE NEW DEAL IN THE SOUTH AND WEST

The New Deal had its profoundest impact in the South and the West. Federal farm programs moved southern agriculture away from its longtime dependence upon sharecropping and tenant farming and helped reorganize it around new patterns of wage labor and agribusiness. New Deal dam building and power projects introduced electricity to millions of rural Southerners, transforming their lives. Per capita, Westerners received more from the federal government for welfare, work relief, and loans than did people in any other section of the country. New Deal programs reshaped western agriculture, created new sources of water and energy, and changed Indian policy. From Great Plains farming communities to Pacific Coast cities, federal subsidy and management became an integral part of western life. In the process, the New Deal helped propel both the South and the West into the modern era and laid the groundwork for the postwar "Sunbelt."

MODERNIZING SOUTHERN FARMING AND LANDHOLDING

In 1930, less than half of all southern farmers owned their own land; over three-quarters of the region's African American farmers and nearly half its white farmers were sharecroppers or tenants. Few of these earned any cash income at all; those who did averaged about $100 annually. The continued dominance of a few crops—mainly cotton and tobacco—had only intensified the depression by glutting the market and keeping crop prices at rock bottom. The Agricultural Adjustment Administration succeeded in boosting prices by paying farmers to "plow under"—take their land out of production. But particularly in the South, these federal subsidies went overwhelmingly to large landowners, who controlled local county committees charged with administering AAA programs.

Most planters did not share these payments with sharecroppers and tenants, and individual protest was usually futile. One Louisiana tenant farmer who dared ask his landlord if his AAA payment had arrived was told, "I had better move before he killed me. And he gave me 24 hours to be gone off the farm." The Southern Tenant Farmers Union (STFU), founded in 1934, fought both landlords and AAA policies. Active in six southern states and composed of about thirty thousand tenant farmers (over half of them black), the STFU protested evictions, called strikes to raise farm labor wages, and challenged landlords to give tenants their fair share of subsidy payments. The STFU drew national attention to the plight of sharecroppers and tenant farmers, but it failed to influence national farm policy.

New Deal policies helped destroy the old sharecropping and tenant system largely by helping landowners prosper. Those farmers who had access to government funds were able to diversify their crops, consolidate holdings, and work their land more efficiently with laborsaving machinery, such as tractors and mechanical harvesters. Mechanized farming and government-subsidized reductions of cultivated land cut the demand for labor and increased evictions. Uprooted tenants, sharecroppers, and day laborers found themselves on the road in search of work; many thousands migrated to cities and towns.

No New Deal initiative had more impact on southern communities than electrification. In the early 1930s, only about 3 percent of rural Southerners had access to electric power and, hence, to household appliances and farm machinery. The Tennessee Valley Authority and the Rural Electrification Administration (REA) helped millions of southern households move into the modern era by making electricity available for the first time. The TVA became a powerful symbol of how public investment and government planning could significantly improve the lives of ordinary Americans. It built sixteen dams across some 800 miles of the Tennessee River basin, bringing flood control and electric power to hundreds of thousands of families in seven southern states. It also significantly reduced consumer electric rates in many cities and towns by providing a cheaper alternative to private utilities. Pursuing a regional planning approach that cut across state lines, the TVA also created landscaped parks, rural libraries, and better school systems. By 1944, the TVA was the largest power producer in the United States. If rural life was still harsh, electrification allowed farm families to enjoy radio, electric lights, and other conveniences that other Americans had long taken for granted.

AN ENVIRONMENTAL DISASTER: THE DUST BOWL

An ecological and economic catastrophe of unprecedented proportions struck the southern Great Plains in the mid-1930s. The region had suffered several drought years in the early 1930s. Such dry spells occurred regularly, in roughly twenty-year cycles. But this time, the parched earth became swept up in violent dust storms, the likes of which had never been seen before. The dust storms were largely the consequence of years of stripping the landscape of its natural vegetation. During World War I, wheat brought record-high prices on the world market, and for the next twenty years Great Plains farmers turned the region into a vast wheat factory.

The wide flatlands of the Great Plains were especially suited to mechanized farming, and gasoline-powered tractors, disc plows, and harvester-thresher combines increased productivity enormously. Back in 1830, it had taken some fifty-eight hours of labor to bring an acre of wheat to the granary; in much of the Great Plains a hundred years later, it required less than three hours. As wheat prices fell in the 1920s, farmers broke still more land to make up the difference with increased production. Great Plains farmers had created an ecological time bomb that exploded when drought returned in the early 1930s. With native grasses destroyed to grow wheat, there was nothing left to prevent soil erosion. Dust storms blew away tens of millions of acres of rich topsoil, and thousands of farm families left the region. Those who stayed suffered calamitous economic and psychological losses. The hardest-hit regions were western Kansas, eastern Colorado, western Oklahoma, the Texas Panhandle, and eastern New Mexico—an area that a Denver journalist named the "Dust Bowl" (see Map 24.2).

—MAP EXPLORATION—

To explore an interactive version of this map, go to
www.prenhall.com/faragher6/map24.2

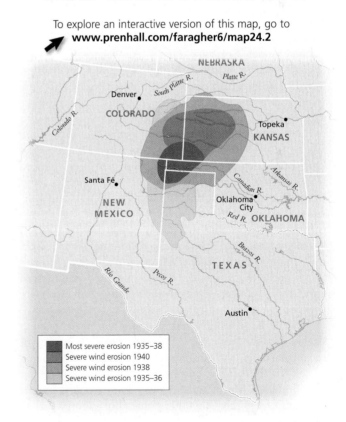

MAP 24.2 The Dust Bowl, 1935–40 This map shows the extent of the Dust Bowl in the southern Great Plains. Federal programs designed to improve soil conservation, water management, and farming practices could not prevent a mass exodus of hundreds of thousands out of the Great Plains.

Black blizzards of dust a mile and a half high rolled across the landscape, darkening the sky and whipping the earth into great drifts that settled over hundreds of miles. Dust storms made it difficult for humans and livestock to breathe, and destroyed crops and trees over vast areas. "Dust pneumonia" and other respiratory infections afflicted thousands, and many travelers found themselves stranded in automobiles and trains unable to move.

In most Great Plains counties, from one-fifth to one-third of the families applied for relief; in the hardest-hit communities, as many as 90 percent of the families received direct government aid. Several federal agencies intervened directly to relieve the distress. Many thousands of Great Plains farm families were given direct emergency relief by the Resettlement Administration. Other federal assistance included crop and seed loans, moratoriums on loan payments, and temporary WPA jobs. The AAA paid wheat farmers millions of dollars not to grow what they could not sell and encouraged the diversion of acreage from soil-depleting crops like wheat to soil-enriching crops such as sorghum.

The federal government also pursued longer-range policies designed to alter land-use patterns, reverse soil erosion, and restore grasslands. The Department of Agriculture, under Secretary Henry A. Wallace, sought to change farming practices through the Soil Conservation Service (SCS), which conducted research into controlling wind and water erosion, set up demonstration projects, and offered technical assistance, supplies, and equipment to farmers engaged in conservation work on farms and ranches. By 1940, the acreage subject to blowing in the Dust Bowl area of the southern plains had been reduced from roughly 50 million acres to less than 4 million acres. In the face of the Dust Bowl disaster, New Deal farm policies had restricted market forces in agriculture. But the return of regular rainfall and the outbreak of World War II led many farmers to abandon the techniques that the SCS had taught them to accept. Wheat farming expanded and farms grew, as farmers once again pursued commercial agriculture with little concern for its long-term effects on the land.

While large landowners and ranchers were reaping sizable benefits from New Deal programs, thousands of tenant farmers and sharecropper families were being forced off the land in cotton-growing regions of Texas, Oklahoma, Missouri, and Arkansas. They became part of a stream of roughly 300,000 people, disparagingly called "Okies," who migrated to California in the 1930s. California migrants included victims of the Dust Bowl, but the majority were blue-collar workers and small businessmen hoping to improve their economic lot. California suffered from the depression along with the rest of the nation, but it still offered more jobs, higher wages, and higher relief payments than the southern plains.

Years of Dust. This 1936 poster by the artist and photographer Ben Shahn, served to publicize the work of Resettlement Administration, which offered aid to destitute farm families hit hard by the Dust Bowl. Shahn's stark imagery here was typical of the documentary aesthetic associated with the Depression-era art and photography.

Most Okies could find work only as poorly paid agricultural laborers in the fertile San Joaquin and Imperial Valley districts, facing scorn as "poor white trash" while they struggled to create communities amid the squalor of migrant labor camps (see Communities in Conflict). Only the outbreak of World War II and the pressing demand for labor allowed migrants to improve their situation significantly.

Mexican farm laborers faced stiff competition from Dust Bowl refugees. By the mid-1930s, they no longer dominated California's agricultural workforce. In 1936, an estimated 85 to 90 percent of the state's migratory workers were white Americans, as compared to less than 20 percent before the depression. Mexican farm worker families who managed to stay employed in California, Texas, and Colorado saw their wages plummet.

MAP EXPLORATION

To explore an interactive version of this map, go to **www.prenhall.com/faragher6/map24.3**

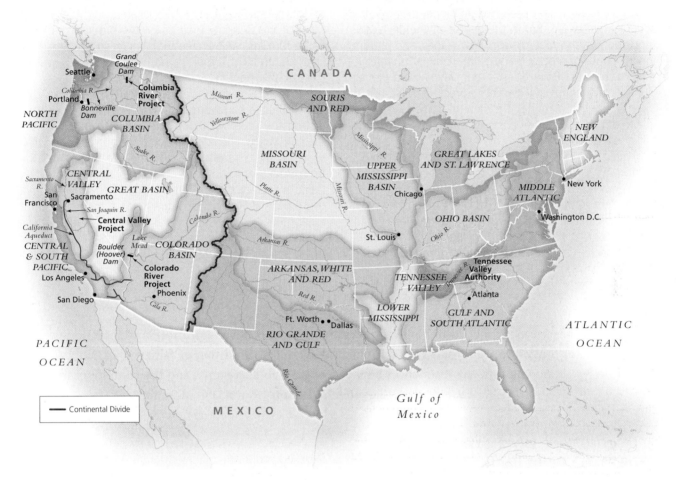

MAP 24.3 The New Deal and Water This map illustrates U.S. drainage areas and the major large-scale water projects begun or completed by federal agencies in them during the New Deal. By providing irrigation, cheap power, flood control, and recreation areas, these public works had a historically unprecedented impact on America's western communities.

Southwestern communities, responding to racial hostility from unemployed whites and looking for ways to reduce their welfare burden, campaigned to deport Mexicans and Mexican Americans. Employers, private charities, and the Immigration and Naturalization Service joined in this effort. Authorities made little effort to distinguish citizens from aliens; most of the children they deported had been born in the United States and, hence, were citizens. Los Angeles County had the most aggressive campaign, using boxcars to ship out more than 13,000 Mexicans between 1931 and 1934. The hostile climate convinced thousands more to leave voluntarily. Approximately one-third of Los Angeles's 150,000 Mexican and Mexican American residents left the city in the early 1930s.

WATER POLICY

The New Deal ushered in the era of large-scale water projects, designed to provide irrigation and cheap power and to prevent floods. The long-range impact of these undertakings on western life was enormous. The key government agency in this realm was the Bureau of Reclamation of the Department of the Interior, established in 1902. The bureau's original responsibility had been to construct dams and irrigation works and thereby to encourage the growth of small farms throughout the arid regions of the West. Until the late 1920s, its efforts had been of little consequence. But its fortunes changed when its focus shifted to building huge multipurpose dams designed to control entire river systems (see Map 24.3).

Californians Face the Influx of "Dust Bowl" Migrants

During the 1930s between 300,000 and 400,000 Americans left Oklahoma, Texas, Arkansas, and Missouri for a new life in California. Like westward pioneers of old they sought a better life. But in the depths of the depression most found a shortage of work, low wages, and housing in tent camps or shacks. Many of these migrants were victims of the Dust Bowl disaster, but others were depression-hit town and city dwellers attracted by stories of opportunity in California. The new migration was most visible in rich agricultural areas, such as the San Joaquin Valley, about 100 miles from Los Angeles.

The state was largely hostile to poor newcomers. California's 1933 Indigent Act made it a crime to bring people with no visible means of support into the state, and dozens were prosecuted for helping relatives move to California. In 1936 the Los Angeles police department set up a border patrol, known as the "Bum Blockade," to turn back "undesirables" trying to enter the city limits. But the plight of the migrants also received widespread publicity and support in works like John Steinbeck's 1939 novel, *The Grapes of Wrath*, the evocative photographs of Dorothea Lange, and the reporting of journalists like Carey McWilliams and Paul Taylor. Most of this publicity focused on the problems faced by white families, who increasingly replaced the Mexicans, Filipinos, and single males who had traditionally worked the seasonal harvest.

A feature piece in the *Los Angeles Times* on July 21, 1937, offers a harrowing but sympathetic account of life among the roughly 50,000 migrant workers in the San Joaquin Valley. The focus is on the poor conditions endured by the migrants, as well as where they have come from. The opposing excerpt reflects the views of the California Citizens' Association, one of several conservative groups that saw the migrants as a growing peril to California's economy and social stability. In 1941, after a challenge to the Indigent Act by the American Civil Liberties Union, the U.S. Supreme Court ruled in *Edwards* v. *California* that states had no power to restrict migration by poor people or any other American citizens.

How do these two accounts differ in their perceptions of who the migrants are and their motives for coming to California? How do they understand the meaning of "citizenship"? Do you find any resonances between these two documents and the contemporary debates over "illegal immigration" to the United States?

Los Angeles Times, July 21, 1937: "Squatter Army Wages Grim Battle for Life"

Human squalor—a picture of approximately 50,000 persons driven to California by dust storms, drought, ill health and debts—awaits the visitor looking beyond the roadside today in the San Joaquin Valley. A new chapter in American history is being written here. A battle for life, for food, health, homes and security is being waged by these hordes of transient indigents.

Within an hour the skeptic must admit he has seen disease, privation, filth and threats of epidemics. But he also must admit that he is seeing a fight for a home similar to that of the pioneers in the South and Middle West in the last century. These people are not hoboes. They are not tramps. They are not foreigners. They are men destroyed financially in the Middle West and Southwest. Many are the cotton belt "white trash" but they are Americans.

Whether one visits the Federal Resettlement Administration's camps at Shafter and Arvin or the huddles of migrant indigents beside the roads throughout Kern county, one almost is struck dumb with sympathy. Ranchers have provided eighty-six camps, ranging in size from a few dirty tents and tin shacks to the seventy-one bunkhouses, tents, trailer houses, railroad box and refrigerator cars on the Digiorgio farms near Alvin. The Digiorgio layout includes separate quarters for Americans, Filipinos, and Mexicans. But most camps throughout the county are populated by white Americans.

There is no starvation—yet. Despite Works Progress Administration, State Relief Administration, and Kern County Welfare Department rules to care first for permanent residents, these transients do occasionally receive financial aid and hospitalization. But funds are almost totally lacking to aid them adequately. The men pick fruit and chop cotton. They earn an average of $2.75 to $3 a day. But they work, at the

"These people are not hoboes. They are not tramps."

"We don't need relief chiselers from other States."

most, only half the days of the year. They must follow the crops throughout the San Joaquin Valley, and meantime their wives and children are falling prey to disease. Most camps have no baths, no showers, poor plumbing.

San Joaquin Valley growers welcome the indigents. Some have even advertised in the Southwestern States, inviting them, the workers say. As M.W. Skelton, Kern county welfare and county relief administration director, explains: "The growers prefer the migratory workers to permanent residents. The relief client may feel that if he doesn't like his job he can go back on the dole. The out-of-State workers must stay on the job."

What will happen next winter? Everyone is afraid to answer. Relief officials pray for Federal funds. Ranchers want more adequate camps. Police hope a crime wave will not break out. But no one can predict without a prayer.

SOURCE: Ray Zeman, "Squatter Army Wages Grim Battle for Life," *Los Angeles Times*, July 21, 1937.

Thomas McManus, California Citizens' Associations: California "Indigents Peril"

The Federal government is responsible for hundreds of thousands of indigents coming to this State. They stay here a year—then they are citizens, adding their burden of relief to the State. The State Relief Administration relief fund is near exhaustion. If this keeps up it will break down entirely the security of citizens of this State.

It has been necessary for manufacturers and employers of the State to meet this influx. The result has been a breaking down of our wage standards. These indigents are willing to work for from one-third to one-sixth of the wage scale throughout the State—anything to get food and anything to stay here long enough to gain citizenship in the State.

We've kept the wage scales high here. As a result, indigents can come here, get on WPA, and make more than they ever made in their lives in their home sectors. Our wage scales in WPA are two or three times as large as they are where these people come from.

It is up to us to defend our legitimate California people—we can care for them with old age pensions and relief, but certainly we can't take care of the indigents of other states.

Our program is to save California jobs for Californians—if the Federal government is going to spend moneys for them let them spend where they live and keep them there. We have plenty of native youth in this State growing up who need the jobs there are here—we don't need relief chiselers from other States coming here chiseling the jobs of Californians.

SOURCE: Speech by Thomas McManus, Secretary, California Citizens' Association, *Los Angeles Times*, August 24, 1938.

The first of these projects was Boulder Dam (later re-named Hoover Dam). The dam, actually begun during the Hoover administration, was designed to harness the Colorado River, the wildest and most isolated of the major western rivers. Its planned benefits included preventing floods, irrigating California's Imperial Valley, supplying domestic water for southern California, and generating cheap electricity for Los Angeles and southern Arizona. Hoover, however, had opposed the public power aspect of the project, arguing that the government ought not compete with private utility companies. Most Westerners, however, believed cheap public power was critical for development. Roosevelt's support for government-sponsored power projects was a significant factor in his carrying the western states in 1932 and subsequent election years.

Boulder Dam was completed in 1935 with the help of funds from the Public Works Administration. Its total cost was $114 million, to be offset by the sale of its hydroelectric power. Los Angeles and neighboring cities built a 259-mile aqueduct, costing $220 million, to channel water to their growing populations. Lake Mead, created by construction of the dam, became the world's largest artificial lake, extending 115 miles up the canyon and providing a popular new recreation area. The dam's irrigation water helped make the Imperial Valley, covering over 500,000 acres, one of the most productive agricultural districts in the world.

The success of Boulder Dam transformed the Bureau of Reclamation into a major federal agency commanding huge resources. In 1938, it completed the All-American Canal—an 80-mile channel connecting the Colorado River to the Imperial Valley and with a 130-mile branch to the Coachella Valley. This opened up more than a million acres of desert land to the cultivation of citrus fruits, melons, vegetables, and cotton. Irrigation districts receiving water promised to repay, without interest, the cost of the canal over a forty-year period.

In 1935, the bureau launched the giant Central Valley Project (CVP) in California's 500-mile-long interior watershed, designed to bring water from the Sacramento River in the north down to the arid San Joaquin Valley in the south. Costing $2.3 billion, the project was not completed until 1947. The CVP stored water and transferred it to the drier southern regions of the state. It also provided electricity, flood control, and municipal water. The federal government, local municipalities, and buyers of electric power paid most of the cost, and the project hugely benefited large-scale farmers in California's vast central valley.

The largest power and irrigation project of all was Grand Coulee Dam, northwest of Spokane, Washington. Completed in 1941, it was designed to convert the power of the Columbia River into cheap electricity and to irrigate previously uncultivated land, thereby stimulating economic development in the Pacific Northwest. Tens of thousands of workers built Grand Coulee, and the project pumped millions of dollars into the region's badly depressed economy.

Between 1933 and 1940, Washington State ranked first in per-capita federal expenditures. In the longer run, Grand Coulee provided the cheapest electricity in the United States and helped attract new manufacturing to a region previously dependent on the export of lumber and ore.

These technological marvels and the new economic development they stimulated were not without an environmental and human cost. Grand Coulee and smaller dams nearby reduced the Columbia River, long a potent symbol of the western wilderness, to a string of lakes. Spawning salmon could no longer run the river above the dam. In California, the federal guarantee of river water made a relative handful of large farmers fabulously wealthy. But tens of thousands of farm workers, mostly of Mexican descent, labored in the newly fertile fields for very low wages, and pesticides undermined their health. The Colorado River, its flow into the sea drastically diminished, began to build up salt deposits, making its water increasingly unfit for drinking or irrigation. Water pollution in the form of high salinity continues to plague the 2,000-mile river.

A NEW DEAL FOR INDIANS

The New Deal brought important changes and some limited improvements to the lives of Indians. In 1933, some 320,000 Indian people, belonging to about 200 tribes, lived on reservations, mostly in Oklahoma, Arizona, New Mexico, and South Dakota. Indians were the nation's poorest people with an infant mortality rate twice that of whites. Alcoholism, tuberculosis, and measles were at much higher rates on the reservation than off. Half of all those on reservations were landless. The Bureau of Indian Affairs (BIA) had a long history of corruption and mismanagement. For years it had tried to assimilate Indians through education, in the process routinely interfering with Indian religious and tribal customs.

In 1933, Roosevelt appointed John Collier to bring change to the BIA. Collier had deep roots in progressive-era social work in eastern big-city slums. During the 1920s, he had become passionately interested in—and sympathetic to—the Indians' plight after spending time in Taos, New Mexico. As the new BIA head, Collier pledged to "stop wronging the Indians and to rewrite the cruel and stupid laws that rob them and crush their family lives." Collier became the driving force behind the Indian Reorganization Act (IRA) of 1934. The IRA reversed the allotment provisions of the Dawes Severalty Act of 1887, which had weakened tribal sovereignty by shifting the distribution of land from tribes to individuals (see Chapter 18). The new legislation permitted the restoration of surplus reservation lands to tribal ownership, and it allocated funds to purchase additional lands and for economic development. At its heart, the IRA sought to restore tribal structures by making the tribes instruments of the federal government. Any tribe that ratified the IRA could then elect a tribal council that would enjoy federal recognition as the legal tribal government. Collier fought first to get the legislation through a reluctant Congress, uneasy with reversing the long-standing policy of Indian assimilation.

The more difficult battle involved winning approval by Indian peoples. Collier's efforts to win acceptance of the IRA met with mixed results on the reservations. Linguistic barriers made it nearly impossible for some tribes to fully assess the plan. In all, 181 tribes organized governments under the IRA, while 77 tribes rejected it.

Under Collier, the BIA became much more sensitive to Indian cultural and religious freedom. The number of Indian people employed by the BIA itself increased from a few hundred in 1933 to more than 4,600 in 1940. Collier trumpeted the principle of Indian political autonomy, a radical idea for the day. But in practice both the BIA and Congress regularly interfered with reservation governments, especially in money matters. For the long run, Collier's most important legacy was the reassertion of the status of Indian tribes as semisovereign nations. In 1934, a Department of the Interior lawyer, Nathan Margold, wrote a legal opinion that tribal governments retained all their original powers—their "internal sovereignty"—except when these were specifically limited by acts of Congress. Decades later, U.S. courts would uphold the Margold opinion, leading to a significant restoration of tribal rights and land to Indian peoples of the West.

THE LIMITS OF REFORM

In his second Inaugural Address, Roosevelt emphasized that much remained to be done to remedy the effects of the depression. Tens of millions of Americans were still denied the necessities for a decent life. "I see one third of a nation ill-housed, ill-clad, ill-nourished," the president said. With his stunning electoral victory, the future for further social reform seemed bright. Yet by 1937, the New Deal was in retreat. A rapid political turnaround over the next two years put continuing social reform efforts on the defensive.

COURT PACKING

After his landslide reelection, and still smarting from the Supreme Court having struck down the NRA and the AAA, Roosevelt wanted more friendly justices. In February 1937, he asked Congress to allow him to make new Supreme Court appointments whenever a justice failed to retire upon reaching age seventy. This would expand the Court from nine to a maximum of fifteen justices, the majority presumably sympathetic to the New Deal. Newspapers almost unanimously denounced FDR's "court-packing bill."

Even more damaging was the determined opposition from a congressional coalition of conservatives and outraged New Dealers. The president gamely fought on, disingenuously insisting that his purpose was simply to reduce the workload of elderly Supreme Court justices. But as the battle dragged on through the spring and summer, FDR's claims weakened. Then a conservative justice retired, permitting Roosevelt to make his first Court appointment. More important, several justices began voting for rather than against Roosevelt's law, so that the Court upheld the constitutionality of key measures from the second New Deal, including the Social Security Act and the National Labor Relations Act. At the end of August 1937, FDR backed off his court-packing scheme and accepted a compromise bill that reformed lower court procedures but left the Supreme Court untouched.

FDR lost the battle for his judiciary proposal, but he may have won the war for a more responsive Court. Still, the political price was very high. The Court fight badly weakened Roosevelt's relations with Congress. Many more conservative Democrats now felt free to oppose further New Deal measures.

THE WOMEN'S NETWORK

The New Deal brought a measurable, if temporary, increase in women's political influence. For those women associated with social reform, the New Deal opened up possibilities to effect change. A "women's network," linked by personal friendships and professional connections, made its presence felt in national politics and government. Most of the women in this network had deep roots in progressive era movements promoting suffrage, labor law reform, and welfare programs (see Chapter 21).

The center of the women's network, First Lady Eleanor Roosevelt, became a powerful political figure, using her prominence to fight for liberal causes. She revolutionized the role of the political wife by taking a position involving no institutional duties and turning it into a base for independent action. Privately, she enjoyed great influence with her husband, and behind the scenes she supported a wide network of women professionals and reformers whom she had come to know in the 1920s. As a strong supporter of protective labor legislation for women, she owed much to the social reform tradition of the women's movement. One of her first public acts as First Lady was to convene a White House Conference on the Emergency Needs of Women in November 1933. She helped Ellen Woodward, head of women's projects in the Federal Emergency Relief Administration (FERA), to find jobs for 100,000 women, ranging from nursery school teaching to sewing.

Eleanor Roosevelt worked vigorously for antilynching legislation, compulsory health insurance, and child-labor reform, and she fought racial discrimination in New Deal relief programs. She saw herself as the guardian of "human values" within the administration, a buffer between depression victims and government bureaucracy. She frequently testified before legislative committees, lobbied her husband privately and the Congress publicly, and wrote a widely syndicated newspaper column.

Mrs. Roosevelt's closest political ally was Molly Dewson. A longtime social worker and suffragist, Dewson wielded great political clout as director of the Women's Division of the national Democratic Party. Under her leadership, women for the first time played a central role in shaping the party platform and running election campaigns. Dewson proved a tireless organizer, traveling to cities and towns around the country and educating women about Democratic policies and candidates. Her success impressed the president, and he relied on her judgment in recommending political appointments. Dewson placed more than a hundred women in New Deal positions.

Perhaps Dewson's most important success came in persuading FDR to appoint Frances Perkins secretary of labor—the first woman cabinet member in U.S. history. A veteran activist for social welfare and reform, Perkins had served as FDR's industrial commissioner in New York before coming to Washington. As labor secretary, Perkins embodied the gains made by women in appointive offices. Her department was responsible for creating the Social Security Act and the Fair Labor Standards Act of 1938, both of which incorporated protective measures long advocated by women reformers. Perkins defined feminism as "the movement of women to participate in service to society." New Deal agencies opened up spaces for scores of women in the federal bureaucracy. These women were concentrated in Perkins's Labor Department, the FERA and WPA, and the Social Security Board. In addition, the social work profession, which remained roughly two-thirds female in the 1930s, grew enormously in response to the massive relief and welfare programs. In sum, although the 1930s saw no radical challenges to existing male and female roles, working-class women and professional women held their own and managed to make some gains.

During the Great Depression, most women continued to perform unpaid domestic labor, work that was not covered by the Social Security Act. A growing minority, however, also worked outside the home for wages and salaries. By 1940, 25.1 percent of the workforce was female. Hard times increased the ranks of married working women. But sexual stereotyping still routinely forced most women into low-paying, low-status jobs.

A NEW DEAL FOR MINORITIES?

Long near the bottom of the American economic ladder, African Americans suffered disproportionately in the Great Depression. The old saying among black workers that they were "last hired, first fired" was never truer than during times of high unemployment. Out-of-work whites coveted even traditional "Negro jobs"—domestic service, cooking, janitorial work, and elevator operating. One white clerk in Florida expressed a widely held view among white Southerners when he defended a lynch mob attack on a store with black employees: "A nigger hasn't got no right to have a job when there are white men who can do the work and are out of work."

Overall, the Roosevelt administration made little overt effort to combat the racism and segregation entrenched in American life. FDR was especially worried about offending the powerful Southern Democratic congressmen. And local administration of many federal programs meant that most early New Deal programs routinely accepted discrimination. The CCC established separate camps for African Americans. The NRA labor codes tolerated lower wages for black workers doing the same jobs as white workers. African Americans could not get jobs with the TVA. When local AAA committees in the South reduced acreage and production to boost prices, thousands of black sharecroppers and farm laborers were forced off the land. Racism was

First Lady Eleanor Roosevelt rides with miners in a flag-decorated car during a visit to the mining town of Bellaire, Ohio, in 1935. Mrs. Roosevelt was more outspoken than the president in championing the rights of labor and African Americans, and she actively used her prestige as First Lady in support of social justice causes.

also embedded in the entitlement provisions of the Social Security Act, which excluded domestics and casual laborers—whose ranks were disproportionately African American and Hispanic—from old-age insurance.

Yet some limited gains were made. Roosevelt issued an executive order in 1935 banning discrimination in WPA projects. In cities, the WPA enabled thousands of jobless African Americans to survive, at minimum wages of $12 a week. Between 15 and 20 percent of all WPA employees were black people, although African Americans made up less than 10 percent of the nation's population. The Public Works Administration, under Harold Ickes, constructed a number of integrated housing complexes and employed more than its fair share of black workers in construction.

FDR appointed several African Americans to second-level positions in his administration. This group became known as "the Black Cabinet." Mary McLeod Bethune, an educator who rose from a sharecropping background to found Bethune-Cookman College, proved a superb leader of the Office of Minority Affairs in the National Youth Administration. Her most successful programs substantially reduced black illiteracy. Harvard-trained Robert Weaver advised the president on economic affairs, and in 1966, became the first black cabinet member when he was appointed secretary of housing and urban development.

Hard times were equally trying for Mexican Americans. As the Great Depression drastically reduced the demand for their labor, they faced massive layoffs, deepening poverty, and deportation. During the 1930s, more than 400,000 Mexican nationals and their children returned to Mexico, often coerced by local officials unwilling to provide them with relief but happy to offer train fare to border towns. Many native-born Americans argued that deporting Mexicans could reduce unemployment for U.S. citizens. But these claims reflected deep racial prejudice, inflamed by the economic crisis. For those who stayed, the New Deal programs did little to help. The AAA benefited large growers, not laborers. Neither the National Labor Relations Act nor the Social Security Act made any provisions for farm laborers. The FERA and the WPA did, at first, provide relief and jobs to the needy, irrespective of citizenship status. But after 1937, the WPA eliminated aliens from eligibility, causing great hardship for thousands of Mexican families. By World War II, *colonias* would increasingly be dominated by the U.S.-born second generation. And since only citizens or aliens who had begun the process of naturalization were eligible for public works jobs, these programs motivated more Mexican immigrants to become U.S. citizens.

The New Deal made no explicit attempt to attack the deeply rooted patterns of racism and discrimination in American life. The entrenched power of white Southern Democrats in the Congress and the exclusion of black voters from southern politics made such an assault unthinkable. But there were occasional symbolic victories for racial equality. In 1939 the conservative Daughters of the American Revolution (DAR) refused to permit the world-renowned African American classical singer Marian Anderson to perform in the DAR's Washington hall. Eleanor Roosevelt and Interior Secretary Harold Ickes intervened to arrange for Anderson to perform on Easter Sunday at the Lincoln Memorial before an integrated audience of 75,000. More broadly, African Americans, especially in the cities, benefited from New Deal relief and work programs, even though this assistance was not color-blind. Black industrial workers made inroads into labor unions affiliated with the CIO. By 1936 an important political shift had begun: For the first time, a majority of black voters abandoned "the party of Lincoln" and voted Democratic. This was concrete evidence that African Americans supported the directions taken by FDR's New Deal. Black voters and hardened white segregationists would coexist uneasily as partners in the New Deal coalition, a tension that would strain the Democratic Party for decades to come.

THE ROOSEVELT RECESSION AND THE EBBING OF THE NEW DEAL

The nation's economy had improved significantly by 1937. Unemployment had declined to "only" 14 percent (9 million people), farm prices had improved to 1930 levels, and industrial production was slightly higher than the 1929 mark. Economic traditionalists, led by FDR's treasury secretary, called for reducing the federal deficit, which had grown to more than $4 billion in fiscal year 1936. Roosevelt, always uneasy about the growing national debt, called for large reductions in federal spending, and the Fed, worried about inflation, tightened credit policies.

This retrenchment caused a steep recession. The stock market plunged in August 1937, and industrial output and farm prices plummeted. Unemployment shot up alarmingly; by March 1938, it hovered around 20 percent, with more than 13 million people looking for work. As conditions worsened, Roosevelt began to blame the "new depression" on a "strike of capital"—on businessmen who refused to invest in order to make him look bad. In fact, the administration's own severe spending cutbacks and interest rate hikes were more responsible.

The blunt reality was that even after five years, the New Deal had not brought about economic recovery. Throughout 1937 and 1938, the administration drifted. Roosevelt received conflicting advice on the economy. Some advisers, suspicious of the reluctance of business to make new investments, urged a massive antitrust campaign against monopolies. Others urged a return to the strategy of "priming the economic pump" with more federal spending. Emergency spending bills in the spring of 1938 put new life into the WPA and the PWA. But Republican gains in the 1938 congressional elections made it harder than ever to get new reform measures through. Conservative Southern Democrats increasingly allied themselves with Republicans in a coalition that would dominate Congress until the mid-1960s.

There were a couple of important exceptions. The 1938 Fair Labor Standards Act established the first federal minimum wage (twenty-five cents an hour) and set a maximum workweek of forty-four hours for all employees engaged in interstate commerce. The National Housing Act of 1937, also known as the Wagner-Steagall Act, funded public housing construction and slum clearance and provided rent subsidies for low-income families. But by and large, by 1938, the reform whirlwind of the New Deal was over.

DEPRESSION-ERA CULTURE

The Great Depression profoundly affected American culture, as it did all other aspects of national life. Yet contradictory messages coexisted, sometimes within the same novel or movie. With American capitalism facing its worst crisis in history, radical expressions of protest and revolution became more frequent. But there were also strong celebrations of individualism, nostalgia for a simpler, rural past, and many attempts to define American core virtues. For a brief but significant moment, the federal government offered substantial—and unprecedented—support to artists and writers. In popular culture, Hollywood movies, network radio broadcasting, and big-band jazz achieved a central place in most Americans' everyday lives.

A NEW DEAL FOR THE ARTS

The depression hit America's writers, artists, and teachers just as hard as it did blue-collar workers. In 1935, the WPA allocated $300 million for the unemployed in these fields. Over the next four years, Federal Project No. 1, an umbrella agency covering writing, theater, music, and the visual arts, proved to be one of the most innovative and successful New Deal programs. "Federal One" offered work to desperate unemployed artists and intellectuals, enriched the cultural lives of millions, and left a substantial artistic and cultural legacy. Nearly all these works were informed by the "documentary impulse," a deep desire to record and communicate the experiences of ordinary Americans.

At its height, the Federal Writers Project employed 5,000 writers on a variety of programs. Most notably, it produced a popular (and still useful) series of state and city guidebooks. The 150-volume "Life in America" series included valuable oral histories of former slaves, studies of ethnic and Indian cultures, and pioneering collections of American songs and folk tales. Work on the Writers Project helped many American writers to survive, to hone their craft, and later to achieve prominence—among them Ralph Ellison, Richard Wright, Margaret Walker, John Cheever, Saul Bellow, and Zora Neale Hurston. Novelist Anzia Yezierska recalled a strong spirit of camaraderie among the writers: "Each morning I walked to the Project as light hearted as if I were going to a party." The Federal

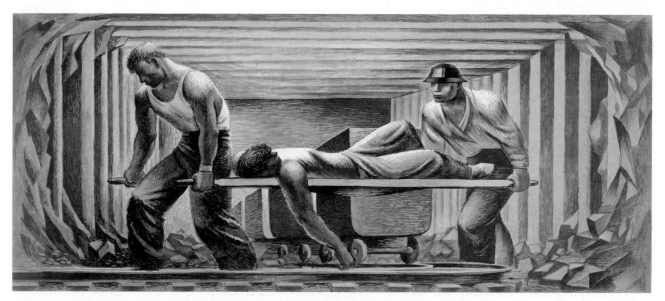

Fletcher Martin painted *Mine Rescue* (1939) in the Kellogg, Idaho, post office. The work was part of a Treasury Department program that employed unemployed artists to beautify government buildings. The mural was eventually removed under pressure from local citizens who worried that it might upset those who had lost loved ones in mine accidents.

SOURCE: Fletcher Martin (1904–1979), "Mine Rescue," 1939, mural study for Kellog, Idaho Post Office; tempera on panel, 15-3/4 x 36-1/2 in (40.0 x 92.7 cm). Copyright Smithsonian American Art Museum, Washington, DC/Art Resource, NY.

Theater Project (FTP) reached as many as 30 million Americans with its productions, expanding the audience for theater beyond the regular patrons of the commercial stage. Among its most successful productions were T. S. Eliot's *Murder in the Cathedral*, Maxwell Anderson's *Valley Forge*, and Orson Welles's version of *Macbeth* with an all-black cast. The parallel Federal Music Project, under Nikolai Sokoloff of the Cleveland Symphony Orchestra, employed 15,000 musicians and financed hundreds of thousands of low-priced public concerts by touring orchestras. The Composers' Forum Laboratory commissioned new works by important young American classical composers.

Among the struggling painters, later world famous, who received government assistance through the Federal Art Project (FAP) were Willem de Kooning, Jackson Pollock, and Louise Nevelson. The FAP employed painters and sculptors to teach studio skills and art history in schools, churches, and settlement houses. It also commissioned artists to paint hundreds of murals on the walls of post offices, meeting halls, courthouses, and other government buildings.

THE DOCUMENTARY IMPULSE

"You can right a lot of wrongs with 'pitiless publicity,'" Franklin Roosevelt once declared. Social change, he argued, "is a difficult thing in our civilization unless you have sentiment." During the 1930s, an enormous number of artists, novelists, journalists, photographers, and filmmakers tried to document the devastation wrought by the depression in American communities. They also depicted people's struggles to cope with, and reverse, hard times. Mainstream mass media, such as *Life* magazine with its photo essays or "March of Time" newsreels, also adapted this stance.

The "documentary impulse" became a prominent style in 1930s' cultural expression. The most direct and influential expression of the documentary style was the photograph. In 1935, Roy Stryker, chief of the Historical Section of the Resettlement Administration, gathered a remarkable group of photographers to help document the work of the agency. Stryker encouraged them to photograph whatever caught their interest, even if the pictures had no direct connection with RA projects. These photographers, including Dorothea Lange and Walker Evans, left the single most significant visual record of the Great Depression. They traveled through rural areas, small towns, and migrant labor camps, and they produced powerful images of despair and resignation, of hope and resilience. Stryker believed that the faces of the subjects were most memorable. "You could look at the people," he wrote, "and see fear and sadness and desperation. But you saw something else, too. A determination that not even the depression could kill. The photographers saw it—documented it" (see Seeing History).

That double vision, combining a frank portrayal of pain and suffering with a faith in the possibility of overcoming disaster, could be found in many other cultural works of the period. John Steinbeck's *Grapes of Wrath* (1939), soon made into an acclaimed film, sympathetically portrayed the hardships of Oklahoma Dust Bowl migrants on their way to California. "We ain't gonna die out," Ma Joad asserts near the end of the book. "People is goin' on—changing' a little, maybe, but goin' right on." A similar, if more personal, ending could be found in Margaret Mitchell's 1936 best seller *Gone with the Wind* (also one of the decade's most spectacular movies). Although Mitchell's romantic novel was set in the Civil War–era South and reinforced racial stereotypes, Americans identified with Scarlett O'Hara's determination to overcome the disaster of war.

Many writers interrupted their work to travel around the country and discover the thoughts and feelings of ordinary people. "With real events looming larger than any imagined happenings," novelist Elizabeth Noble wrote, "documentary films and still photographs, reportage and the like have taken the place once held by the grand invention." Writers also found a remarkable absence of bitterness and a great deal of faith. James Rorty, in *Where Life Is Better* (1936), was actually encouraged by his cross-country trip. "I had rediscovered for myself a most beautiful land, and a most vital, creative, and spiritually unsubdued people."

WAITING FOR LEFTY

For some, capitalism itself was responsible for the Great Depression. Relatively few Americans became communists or socialists in the 1930s (at its height, the Communist Party of the United States had perhaps 100,000 members), and many of these remained active for only a brief time. Yet Marxist analysis, with its emphasis on class conflict and the failures of capitalism, had a wide influence on thought and writing.

Some writers joined the Communist Party, seeing in the Soviet Union an alternative to an American system mired in exploitation, racial inequality, and human misery. Communist writers sought to radicalize art and literature and celebrated collective struggle rather than individual achievement. Granville Hicks, an editor of the radical magazine the *New Masses*, flatly declared: "If there is any other working interpretation of the apparent chaos than that which presents itself in terms of the class struggle, it has not been revealed."

A more common pattern for intellectuals, especially young ones, was brief flirtation with communism. Many African American writers, attracted by the Communist Party's militant opposition to lynching, job discrimination, and segregation, briefly joined the party or found their first supportive audiences there. These included

SEEING HISTORY

Documenting Hard Times in Black and White and Color

Many FSA photographs were published in newspapers and popular magazines as part of the agency's campaign to win public support for a greater federal role in building more migrant worker camps. Some of these photographs, such as those by Dorothea Lange and Walker Evans, have become among the most widely circulated images in the history of the medium. But even though Lange's "Migrant Mother" became a kind of universal symbol of suffering, its context and social-science origins have been lost. Her original caption simply read, "Destitute pea pickers in California. Mother of seven children. Age thirty-two."

In 1939 some FSA photographers began using new 35-mm Kodachrome film to make color slides. Unlike black-and-white prints, color slides were neither easily made nor reproducible in newspapers and magazines. Black-and-white images also seemed to offer a starker, more "realistic" documentation of poverty; many thought color photos too cheery. FSA photographers produced some 164,000 black-and-white images and only about 1,600 in color. But photographs like Russell Lee's remind us that people lived lives in color, even during the depression.

Between 1935 and 1942, photographers working for the Farm Security Administration (FSA) created a remarkable pictorial record of depression life. The photography project had a political goal as well: to prod New Deal agricultural policy into providing greater support for the poorest agricultural workers. The photographers thus took aim at social, economic, and racial inequalities within American agriculture. They worked under difficult conditions. On the road for months, they worked in harsh weather, often eating bad food and staying in primitive accommodations, trying to capture the lives of subjects suspicious of their motives. Their unexposed film had to be processed in Washington, so the photographers never knew what they had shot until they received prints weeks later.

How does Lee's portrait of the homesteader couple compare to Lange's portrait of the "Migrant Mother" as a document of rural life in the Great Depression? Are there differences beyond black and white and color?

Richard Wright, Ralph Ellison, and Langston Hughes. Playwrights and actors associated with New York's influential Group Theater were often part of the Communist Party orbit in those years. One production of the group, Clifford Odets's *Waiting for Lefty* (1935), depicted a union organizing drive. At the climax, someone yells that the organizer Lefty (for whom everyone has been waiting) has been killed by the police, and the audience joins the actors in shouting "Strike!" A commercial and political success, it offered perhaps the most celebrated example of radical, politically engaged art.

Left-wing influence reached its height after 1935 during the "Popular Front" period. Alarmed by the rise of fascism in Europe (see Chapter 25), communists around the world followed the Soviet line of aligning with liberals and other antifascists. Some 3,000 American men and women volunteered for the Communist Party–organized Abraham Lincoln Brigade, which fought in the Spanish Civil War on the republican side against the fascists led by Francisco Franco. The Lincolns' sense of commitment and sacrifice appealed to millions of Americans sympathetic to the republican cause. At home, the American Communist Party adopted the slogan "Communism is Twentieth-Century Americanism," and Communists proclaimed strong support of Roosevelt's New Deal (which before they had denounced). Their influence became especially strong within the labor movement as Communists and other radicals, known for their dedication and effectiveness, played a leading role in the difficult CIO unionizing drives in the auto, steel, and electrical industries. The radical presence was also strong within certain WPA arts projects. A decade later, many young idealists who came into the Communist Party orbit, no matter how briefly, would pay a heavy price.

RAISING SPIRITS: FILM, RADIO, AND THE SWING ERA

Despite the depression, the mass-culture industry expanded enormously during the 1930s. If mass culture offered little in the way of direct responses to the economic and social problems of the day, it nonetheless played a more integral role than ever in shaping the rhythms and desires of the nation's everyday life.

Toward the end of the 1920s, the coming of "talking pictures" helped make movies the most popular entertainment form of the day. More than 60 percent of Americans attended one of the nation's 20,000 movie houses each week, and millions followed the lives and careers of movie stars more avidly than ever. At the same time, the movie studios themselves, responding to pressure from the Roman Catholic Church and other advocates of traditional morality, instituted a more stringent Production Code in 1933. For the next three decades American filmmakers had to work within very narrow parameters of what was acceptable to depict on screen. The code required unambiguous depictions of good triumphing over evil and a straight-laced treatment of sex.

With so many movies being churned out by Hollywood studios for so many fans, it is difficult to generalize about the cultural impact of individual films. Gangster films did very well in the early depression years, depicting violent criminals brought to justice by society—but along the way, they gave audiences a vicarious exposure to the pleasures of wealth, power, and lawbreaking. Social disorder could also be treated comically, as in such classic Marx Brothers films as *Duck Soup* (1933) and *A Night at the Opera* (1935). Mae West's popular comedies made people laugh by cleverly subverting expectations about sex roles. West was an independent woman, not afraid of pleasure. When asked on screen (by Cary Grant), "Haven't you ever met a man who could make you happy?" she replied, "Sure, lots of times."

Most films were frankly "escapist." Movie musicals offered extravagant song-and-dance spectacles. "Screwball comedies" featured sophisticated, fast-paced humor and usually paired popular male and female stars, like Clark Gable and Claudette Colbert or Katharine Hepburn and Cary Grant. A few movies tried to offer a more "socially conscious" view of depression-era life. By and large, however, Hollywood avoided social or political controversy.

Some 1930s' filmmakers expressed highly personal visions of core American values. Two who succeeded in capturing both popular and critical acclaim were Walt Disney and Frank Capra. By the mid-1930s, Disney's animated cartoons (including Mickey Mouse) had become moral tales that preached following the rules. Capra's comedies idealized a small-town America, with close families and comfortable homes. Although Capra's films dealt with contemporary problems more than most, he seemed to suggest that most of the country's ills could be solved if only its leaders learned the old-fashioned values of "common people"—kindness, loyalty, and charity.

Radio broadcasting emerged as the most powerful medium of communication in the home, profoundly changing the rhythms and routines of everyday life. In 1930, roughly 12 million American homes (40 percent of the total) had radio sets; by the end of the decade, 90 percent had them. Advertisers dominated the structure and content of American radio, forming a powerful alliance with the two large networks, the National Broadcasting Company (NBC) and the Columbia Broadcasting System (CBS). The Federal Communications Commission, established in 1934, continued long-standing policies that favored commercial broadcasting over other arrangements, such as municipal or university programming.

Reginald Marsh, *Twenty Cent Movie*, 1936. Marsh documented the urban landscape of the 1930s with great empathy, capturing the city's contradictory mix of commercialism, optimism, energy, and degradation. The popularity of Hollywood films and their stars reached new heights during the Great Depression.

SOURCE: Reginald Marsh, "Twenty Cent Movie," 1936. Egg tempera on composition board. 40″ × 40″. Whitney Museum of American Art/Artists Rights Society, New York.

The depression actually helped radio expand. An influx of talent arrived from the weakened worlds of vaudeville, ethnic theater, and the recording industry. The well-financed networks offered an attractive outlet to advertisers seeking a national audience. Radio programming achieved a regularity and professionalism absent in the 1920s, making it much easier for a listener to identify a show with its sponsor. Much of network radio was based on older cultural forms. The variety show, hosted by comedians and singers, and based on the old vaudeville format, was the first important style. Its stars constantly plugged the sponsor's product. The use of an audible studio audience re-created the human interaction so necessary in vaudeville. The popular comedy show *Amos 'n' Andy* adapted the minstrel "blackface" tradition to the new medium. Its two white comedians used only their voices to invent a world of stereotyped African Americans for millions of listeners.

Daytime serials, dubbed "soap operas," dominated radio drama. Aimed at women working in the home, these serials alone constituted 60 percent of all daytime shows by 1940. Soaps revolved around strong, warm female characters who provided advice and strength to weak, indecisive friends and relatives. Action counted very little; the development of character and relationships was all-important. Thrillers such as *The Shadow* aired in the evening when whole families could listen; they emphasized crime and suspense and made clever use of music and sound effects.

Radio news arrived in the 1930s, showing the medium's potential for direct and immediate coverage of political events. Network news and commentary shows multiplied rapidly. Father Couglin's radio demagoguery for a while had a powerful political impact, and FDR always used the radio to great effect. Complex political and economic issues and the impending European crisis (see Chapter 25) fueled a news hunger among Americans. A 1939 survey found that 70 percent of Americans relied on the radio as their prime source of news. Yet commercial broadcasting, dominated by big sponsors and large radio manufacturers, failed to cover politically controversial events such as labor struggles.

One measure of radio's cultural impact was its role in popularizing jazz. Before the 1930s, jazz was heard largely among African Americans and a small coterie of white fans. Regular broadcasts of live performances exposed a broader public to the music. Bands led by black artists such as Duke Ellington and Count Basie began to enjoy reputations outside of traditional jazz centers like Chicago, Kansas City, and New York.

Benny Goodman became the key figure in the "swing era," largely through radio exposure. Goodman, a white, classically trained clarinetist, had been inspired by African American bandleaders who created big-band arrangements that combined harmonic call-and-response patterns with breaks for improvised solos. Goodman purchased a series of these arrangements, smoothing out the sound but keeping the strong dance beat. His band's late Saturday night broadcasts began to attract attention, and in 1935, at the Palomar Ballroom in Los Angeles, made the breakthrough that established his enormous popularity. When his band started playing, the young crowd, primed by radio broadcasts, roared its approval and began to dance wildly. Goodman's music was perfect for doing the jitterbug or lindy hop, dances borrowed from African American culture. As the "King of Swing," Goodman helped make big-band jazz a hit with millions of teenagers and young adults from all backgrounds. In the late 1930s, big-band music by artists like Goodman, Ellington, and Basie accounted for the majority of million-selling records.

CHRONOLOGY

1929	Stock market crash
1930	Democrats regain control of the House of Representatives
1932	Reconstruction Finance Corporation established to make government credit available
	"Bonus Army" marches on Washington
	Franklin D. Roosevelt elected president
1933	Roughly 13 million workers unemployed
	The "Hundred Days" legislation of the First New Deal
	Twenty-First Amendment repeals Prohibition (Eighteenth Amendment)
1934	Indian Reorganization Act repeals Dawes Severalty Act and reasserts the status of Indian tribes as semisovereign nations
	Growing popularity of Father Charles E. Coughlin and Huey Long, critics of Roosevelt
1935	Second New Deal
	Committee for Industrial Organization (CIO) established
	Dust storms turn the southern Great Plains into the Dust Bowl
	Boulder Dam completed
1936	Roosevelt defeats Alfred M. Landon in reelection landslide
	Sit-down strike begins at General Motors plants in Flint, Michigan
1937	General Motors recognizes United Automobile Workers
	Roosevelt's "Court-packing" plan causes controversy
	Memorial Day Massacre in Chicago demonstrates the perils of union organizing
	"Roosevelt recession" begins
1938	CIO unions withdraw from the American Federation of Labor to form the Congress of Industrial Organizations
	Fair Labor Standards Act establishes the first federal minimum wage

CONCLUSION

Far from being the radical program its conservative critics charged, the New Deal did little to alter fundamental property relations or the distribution of wealth. Indeed, most of its programs largely failed to help the most powerless groups in America—migrant workers, tenant farmers and sharecroppers, African Americans, and other minorities. But the New Deal profoundly changed many areas of American life. Overall, it radically increased the role of the federal government in American lives and communities, creating a new kind of liberalism defined by an activist state. Social Security, unemployment insurance, and federal relief programs established at least the framework for a welfare state. The FDIC and the SEC established important new federal rules protecting individuals from financial ruin and unregulated stock markets. For the first time in American history, the national government took responsibility for assisting its needy citizens. And also for the first time, the federal government guaranteed the rights of workers to join trade unions, and it set standards for minimum wages and maximum hours.

Western and southern communities in particular were transformed through federal intervention in water, power, and agricultural policies. In politics, the New Deal established the Democrats as the majority party. Some version of the Roosevelt New Deal coalition would dominate the nation's political life for another three decades.

The New Deal's efforts to end racial and gender discrimination were modest at best. Some of the more ambitious programs, such as subsidizing the arts or building model communities, enjoyed only brief success. Other reform proposals, such as national health insurance, never got off the ground. Conservative counterpressures, especially after 1937, limited what could be changed. Still, the New Deal did more than strengthen the presence of the national government in people's lives. It also fed expectations that the federal presence would intensify. Washington became a much greater center of economic regulation and political power, and the federal bureaucracy grew in size and influence. With the coming of World War II, the direct role of national government in shaping American communities would expand beyond the dreams of even the most ardent New Dealer.

— REVIEW QUESTIONS

1. What were the underlying causes of the Great Depression? What consequences did it have for ordinary Americans, and how did the Hoover administration attempt to deal with the crisis?

2. Analyze the key elements of Franklin D. Roosevelt's first New Deal program. To what degree did these succeed in getting the economy back on track and in providing relief to suffering Americans?

3. How did the so-called Second New Deal differ from the first? What political pressures did Roosevelt face that contributed to the new policies?

4. How did the New Deal reshape western communities and politics? What specific programs had the greatest impact in the region? How are these changes still visible today?

5. Evaluate the impact of the labor movement and radicalism on the 1930s. How did they influence American political and cultural life?

6. To what extent were the grim realities of the depression reflected in popular culture? To what degree were they absent?

7. Discuss the long- and short-range effects of the New Deal on American political and economic life. What were its key successes and failures? What legacies of New Deal–era policies and political struggles can you find in contemporary America?

— RECOMMENDED READING

Anthony J. Badger, *The New Deal: The Depression Years, 1933–1940* (1989). Very useful overview that emphasizes the limited nature of New Deal reforms.

Alan Brinkley, *The End of Reform: New Deal Liberalism in Recession and War* (1995). A sophisticated analysis of the political and economic limits faced by New Deal reformers from 1937 through World War II.

Lizabeth Cohen, *Making a New Deal: Industrial Workers in Chicago, 1919–1939* (1990). A brilliant study that demonstrates the transformation of immigrant and African American workers into key actors in the creation of the CIO, and in New Deal politics, and illuminates the complex relationship between ethnic cultures and mass culture.

Michael Denning, *The Cultural Front: The Laboring of American Culture in the Twentieth Century* (1997). A provocative reinterpretation of 1930s' culture, emphasizing the impact of the Popular Front and its lasting influence on American modernism and mass culture.

Ronald Edsforth, *The New Deal: America's Response to the Great Depression* (2000). A concise political history of the 1930s, offering an excellent synthesis of the massive secondary literature.

David M. Kennedy, *Freedom From Fear: The American People in Depression and War* (1999). An absorbing narrative account of the U.S. experience in depression and war.

Richard Lowitt, *The New Deal and the West* (1984). A comprehensive study of the New Deal's impact in the West, with special attention to water policy and agriculture.

Robert S. McElvaine, *The Great Depression: America, 1929–1941* (1984). The best one-volume overview of the Great Depression. It is especially strong on the origins and early years of the worst economic calamity in American history.

Jason Scott Smith, *Building New Deal Liberalism: The Political Economy of Public Works, 1935–1956* (2006). Argues for the centrality of public works programs such as the PWA and WPA for understanding how the New Deal transformed governmental priorities and remade the economy and landscape.

For study resources for this chapter, go to **http://www.myhistorylab.com** and choose *Out of Many*. You will find a wealth of study and review material for this chapter, including pretests and posttests, customized study plan, key-term review flash cards, interactive map and document activities, and documents for analysis.

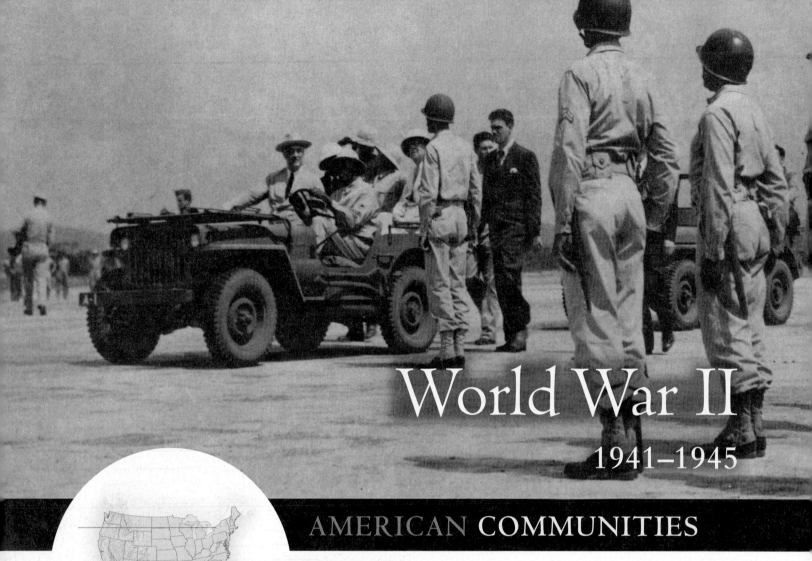

World War II
1941–1945

Los Alamos, New Mexico

On Monday, July 16, 1945, at 5:29:45 A.M., Mountain War Time, the first atomic bomb exploded in a brilliant flash visible in three states. Within just seven minutes, a huge, multicolored, bell-shaped cloud soared 38,000 feet into the atmosphere and threw back a blanket of smoke and soot to the earth below. The heat generated by the blast was four times the temperature at the center of the sun, and the light produced rivaled that of nearly twenty suns. Even ten miles away people felt a strong surge of heat. The giant fireball ripped a crater a half-mile wide in the ground, fusing the desert sand into glass. The shock wave blew out windows in houses more than 200 miles away. The blast killed every living creature—squirrels, rabbits, snakes, plants, and insects—within a mile and the smells of death lingered for nearly a month.

Very early that morning, Ruby Wilkening had driven to a nearby mountain ridge, where she joined several other women waiting for the blast. Wilkening worried about her husband, a physicist, who was already at the test site. No one knew exactly what to expect, not even the scientists who developed the bomb.

The Wilkenings were part of a unique community of scientists who had been marshaled for war. President Franklin D. Roosevelt, convinced by Albert Einstein and other physicists that the Nazis might successfully develop an atomic bomb, had inaugurated a small nuclear research program in 1939. Then, after the United States

entered World War II in 1941, the president released resources to create the Manhattan Project and placed it under the direction of the Army Corps of Engineers. By December 1942 a team headed by Italian-born Nobel Prize winner Enrico Fermi had produced the first chain reaction in uranium under the University of Chicago's football stadium. Now the mission was to build a new formidable weapon, the atomic bomb.

In March 1943, the government moved the key researchers and their families to Los Alamos, New Mexico, a remote and sparsely populated region of soaring peaks, ancient Indian ruins, modern Pueblos, and villages occupied by the descendants of the earliest Spanish settlers. Some families occupied a former boys' preparatory school until new houses could be built; others doubled up in rugged log cabins or at nearby ranches. Construction of new quarters proceeded slowly, causing nasty disputes between the "long-hairs" (scientists) and the "plumbers" (army engineers) in ➤

charge of the grounds. Despite the chaos, outstanding American and European scientists eagerly signed up. Most were young, with an average age of twenty-seven, and quite a few were recently married. Many couples began their families at Los Alamos, producing a total of nearly a thousand babies between 1943 and 1949.

The scientists and their families formed an exceptionally close-knit community, united by the need for secrecy and their shared antagonism toward their army guardians. The military atmosphere was oppressive. Homes and laboratories were cordoned off by barbed wire and guarded by military police. Everything, from linens to food packages, was stamped "Government Issue." The scientists were followed by security personnel whenever they left Los Alamos. Several scientists were reprimanded for discussing their work at home, although many of their wives worked forty-eight hours a week in the Technical Area. All outgoing mail was censored. Well-known scientists commonly worked under aliases—Fermi became "Eugene Farmer"—and code names were used for such terms as *atom, bomb*, and *uranium fission*. Los Alamos children were registered without surnames at nearby public schools. Even automobile accidents, weddings, and deaths went unreported. Only a group thoroughly committed to the war effort could accept such restrictions on personal liberty.

A profound urgency motivated the research team, which included refugees from Nazi Germany and Fascist Italy and a large proportion of Jews. The director of the project, California physicist J. Robert Oppenheimer, promoted a scientific élan that offset the military style of commanding general Leslie Groves. Just thirty-eight, slightly built, and deeply emotional, "Oppie" personified the idealism that helped the community of scientists overcome whatever moral reservations they held about placing such a potentially terrible weapon in the hands of the government.

In the Technical Area of Los Alamos, Oppenheimer directed research. At seven o'clock each workday morning, the siren dubbed "Oppie's Whistle" called the other scientists to their laboratories to wrestle with the theoretical and practical problems of building an atomic device. From May to November 1944, after the bomb had been designed, the key issue was testing it. Many scientists feared a test might fail, scattering the precious plutonium at the bomb's core and discrediting the entire project. Finally, with plutonium production increas-

ing, the Los Alamos team agreed to test "the gadget" at a site 160 miles away.

The unprecedented scientific mobilization at Los Alamos mirrored changes occurring throughout American society as the nation rallied behind the war effort. Sixteen million men and women left home for military service and nearly as many moved to take advantage of wartime jobs. In becoming what President Franklin Roosevelt called "a great arsenal of democracy," the American economy quickly and fully recovered from the Great Depression. Several states in the South and Southwest experienced huge surges in population. California alone grew by 2 million people, a large proportion from Mexico. Many broad social changes with roots in earlier times—the economic expansion of the West, the erosion of farm tenancy among black people in the South and white people in Appalachia, and the increasing employment of married women—accelerated during the war. The events of the war eroded old communities, created new ones like Los Alamos, and transformed nearly all aspects of American society.

The transition to wartime was, however, far from smooth. Suspecting Japanese Americans of disloyalty, President Roosevelt ordered the forced relocation of more than 112,000 men, women, and children to internment camps. Although African Americans won a promise of job equity in defense and government employment, hundreds of race riots broke out in the nation's cities. In Los Angeles, Mexican American youth, flaunting a new style of dress, provoked the ire of white sailors who proceeded to assault them, almost at random. And families of all kinds found themselves strained by wartime dislocations.

The United States nevertheless emerged from World War II far stronger than its European allies, who bore the brunt of the fighting. Indeed, the nation was now strong enough to claim a new role as the world's leading superpower.

THE COMING OF WORLD WAR II

The worldwide depression helped to undermine a political order that had been shaky since World War I. Political unrest spread across Europe and Asia as international trade dropped by as much as two-thirds and unemployment rose.

Focus Questions

1. How did World War II force the United States to adopt a more global outlook?

2. How did the government marshal the nation's resources to fight the war? What impact did this mobilization have on the federal bureaucracy and its relationship to business?

3. What major changes occurred in American society as a consequence of wartime mobilization?

4. What was the Allies' strategy for fighting the war in Europe?

5. What role did science and technology play in the Allied victory?

6. What strategy did the United States adopt in fighting Japan in the Pacific?

7. How did the American government and military leaders respond to the Holocaust, and what knowledge did the American people have of the Nazi genocide?

8. What were the factors behind the decision to deploy the atomic bomb against Japan?

1941–1945

Demagogues played on national and racial hatreds, fueled by old resentments and current despair, and offered solutions in the form of territorial expansion by military conquest.

Preoccupied with restoring the domestic economy, President Franklin D. Roosevelt had no specific plan to deal with growing conflict elsewhere in the world. Moreover, the majority of Americans strongly opposed foreign entanglements. But as debate over diplomatic policy heated up, terrifying events overseas pulled the nation steadily toward war.

THE SHADOWS OF WAR ACROSS THE GLOBE

Two major threats to peace gathered force in the 1930s in East Asia and in Central Europe. In Japan, devastated by the depression, military leaders decided that imperialism would make their nation the richest in the world, and in 1931 the army seized Manchuria from China. When the League of Nations objected, Japan simply quit the league. A full-scale Japanese invasion of China proper followed in 1937, and the world watched in horror the Rape of Nanking (today, Nanjing)—the destruction of what was then China's capital and the slaughter of as many as 300,000 Chinese men, women, and children. Within a year, Japan controlled most of coastal China.

In Europe, fanatical and tyrannical fascist leaders were taking power—first in Italy and later in Germany. "We have buried the putrid corpse of liberty," boasted Italy's Fascist dictator Benito Mussolini in the 1920s. In Germany, nationalist resentment over the Treaty of Versailles fueled Adolf Hitler's National Socialist (Nazi) movement with its racist doctrine of "Aryan" supremacy that condemned nonwhites and Jews as "degenerate races." In January 1933, by political intrigue, Hitler became chancellor. He posed as the last bastion against Communism and had the backing of German industrialists but only about one-third of the voters. With his brown-shirted storm troopers ruling the streets, Hitler quickly destroyed opposition parties and made himself absolute dictator. Renouncing the disarmament provisions imposed by the Versailles peace treaty, he began to rebuild Germany's armed forces. No European powers opposed him.

Soon enough, Mussolini and Hitler began to act on their imperial visions. In 1935 Italy conquered Ethiopia and turned the African nation into a colony. In 1936 Hitler sent 35,000 troops to occupy the formerly demilitarized Rhineland region. In the Spanish Civil War that broke out later that year, Italy and Germany both supported General Francisco Franco's fascist rebels against the democratic republican regime. In November, Germany and Italy forged an alliance, the Rome–Berlin Axis.

Hitler was now nearly ready to put into operation his plan to secure *Lebensraum*—living space for the "Aryan" population—through territorial expansion. In 1938 he annexed Austria and then turned his attention to Czechoslovakia, the one remaining democracy in Central Europe, which Britain and France had pledged to assist. War seemed imminent. But Britain and France surprised the world by agreeing, at Munich on September 30, 1938, to allow Germany to annex the Sudetenland—the German-speaking parts of Czechoslovakia. "Appeasement," this was called: Hitler pledged that he would make no more territorial demands. But within six months, in March 1939, Germany seized the rest of the country.

By then, much of the world was aware of the horror of Hitler's racist regime. On the night of November 9, 1938, Nazi storm troopers rounded up Jews, beating them mercilessly and murdering an untold number. From the smashed windows of Jewish shops and burned synagogues, this attack came to be known as *Kristallnacht*, the "Night of Broken Glass." The Nazi government expropriated Jewish property and excluded Jews from all but the most menial jobs. Pressured by Hitler, his allies Hungary and Italy also enacted laws curtailing the civil rights of Jews.

On September 27, 1938, Germany, Italy, and Japan signed the anti-Communist Tripartite Pact and pledged to "stand by and co-operate with one another" for the next ten years.

ISOLATIONISM

World War I had left a legacy of strong isolationist yearnings in the United States. Senseless slaughter might be a centuries-old way of life in Europe, many Americans reasoned, but not for the United States, which, as George Washington and Thomas Jefferson had advised, should shun "entangling alliances." College students, seeing themselves as future cannon fodder, organized an antiwar movement. In 1937, nearly 70 percent of Americans responding to a Gallup poll agreed that U.S. involvement in World War I had been a mistake.

Antiwar sentiment won strong support in Congress. In 1934, a committee headed by Republican senator Gerald P. Nye of North Dakota charged weapons manufacturers with driving the United States into World War I to make windfall profits. (Many in fact many did.) In 1935, Congress passed the first of five Neutrality Acts to deter entanglements in future foreign wars. It required the president to embargo the sale and shipment of munitions to all belligerents.

Isolationism spanned the political spectrum. In 1938 socialist Norman Thomas gathered leading liberals and trade unionists into the Keep America Out of War Congress; the communist-influenced American League against War and Fascism claimed more than 1 million members. In 1940 the arch-conservative Committee to Defend America First formed to oppose U.S. intervention. Some America Firsters were openly anti-Semitic and championed the Nazis as "anti-Communists." Chaired by top Sears executive Robert E. Wood, the America First Committee quickly gained attention because its members included movie stars Robert Young and Lillian Gish, automobile manufacturer Henry Ford, and Charles A. Lindbergh, the hero of the 1927 solo flight across the Atlantic. America First soon had more than 450 chapters and claimed more than 850,000 members.

ROOSEVELT READIES FOR WAR

FDR's instincts were to stand with other threatened democracies, but he knew that the American public was strongly isolationist. In October 1937 he had called for international cooperation to "quarantine the aggressors." But two-thirds of Congress opposed economic sanctions as a "back door to war." Forced to draw back, Roosevelt nevertheless won from Congress $1 billion to enlarge the navy. Another less stringent Neutrality Act in 1939 permitted wartime arms sales to Great Britain, France, and China.

War broke out in Europe in the fall of 1939. In August, Germany and the Soviet Union, hitherto mortal enemies, stunned the world by signing a nonaggression pact. A week later, on September 1, Hitler invaded Poland. Within days, Poland's allies, Great Britain and France, declared war on Germany. On September 17, Soviet troops invaded Poland too. Warsaw capitulated, and Hitler and Stalin divided Poland between them. Fighting slowed to a near halt as French and German troops did not even exchange fire. Soviet forces, however, attacked Finland and seized the tiny Baltic republics.

Hitler began a crushing offensive against Western Europe in April 1940. In a *blitzkrieg* (lightning war), fast-moving columns of German tanks supported by air power struck first at Denmark and Norway and soon thereafter conquered Holland, Belgium, and Luxembourg. More than 338,000 British troops had to escape across the English Channel. Hitler's army, joined at the last minute by the Italians, then easily overran France in June 1940. When Britain refused to surrender, Hitler launched the Battle of Britain. Nazi bombers pounded cities while U-boats tried to cut off incoming supplies.

The American public desperately hoped to stay out of the war, but they also agreed with Roosevelt that the nation's security depended on both a strong defense and Hitler's defeat. Invoking the Neutrality Act of 1939, which permitted the sale of arms to Britain, France, and China, the president affirmed his position: "All aid to the Allies short of war." In May 1940, when France collapsed, he began to transfer surplus U.S. warships and equipment to Britain, in exchange for West Indies naval bases. In September, while the Battle of Britain raged, Roosevelt and Congress enacted the nation's first peacetime military draft, which sent 1.4 million young men to army training camps by July 1941.

FDR could not yet admit the inevitability of U.S. involvement—especially during an election year. His popularity had dropped with the 1937 "Roosevelt recession," and the Republicans had nominated a popular former Democrat turned anti–New Dealer, Wendell L. Willkie, from Indiana. Although isolationists who hated Roosevelt flocked to the folksy yet successful Wall Street industrialist, Wilkie pushed away many potential voters by supporting aid to Britain and rearming America and by waging a campaign enlivened primarily by his slurs on the Roosevelt family. When FDR promised voters not to "send your boys to any foreign wars," he clinched an unprecedented third term.

Reelected, Roosevelt moved more aggressively to aid hard-pressed Great Britain. In his annual message to Congress in early 1941, he proposed a bill allowing the president to sell, exchange, or lease arms to any country whose defense he judged vital to U.S. security. Passed in March 1941, the Lend-Lease Act made Great Britain the first beneficiary of massive aid. Congress also authorized the merchant marine to sail fully armed while conveying Lend-Lease supplies directly to Britain.

In August 1941 Roosevelt met on a warship off Newfoundland with Winston Churchill, the embattled British prime minister. Roosevelt evaded Churchill's pleas to enter the war—he knew that Congress and the American public still hoped to stay out—but the two leaders declared common goals for the postwar world in what was called the Atlantic Charter, a lofty proclamation calling for all peoples to live in freedom from fear, want, and tyranny.

The European war now widened. Having conquered the Balkans, Hitler broke the Nazi–Soviet Pact and in June 1941 invaded the Soviet Union. Roosevelt sent Lend-Lease supplies to the Soviets and ordered U.S. warships to "sink on sight" any lurking German submarines. The result was an undeclared and unpublicized naval war between the United States and Nazi Germany on the North Atlantic.

PEARL HARBOR

While throughout 1940 and 1941 Americans watched with dread the widening European struggle, war also escalated in East Asia. Anticipating trouble in the Pacific, in May 1940 Roosevelt transferred the Pacific fleet from its California bases to a forward position at Pearl Harbor in Hawai'i. Less than five months later, Japan formally joined Germany and Italy as a full Axis ally.

Both the United States and Japan were playing for time. Roosevelt wanted to bank resources to fight Germany (the greater danger, he thought); Japan's leaders gambled that America's preoccupation with Europe might allow them to conquer all Southeast Asia, including France's Indochinese colonies (today, Vietnam, Cambodia, and Laos), British outposts like Hong Kong and Singapore, and the oil-rich Dutch East Indies (today, Indonesia). Lacking petroleum, Japan was desperate to obtain a reliable source for oil; without that, its navy and huge land army in China could not fight. When Japan occupied French Indochina in July 1941, Roosevelt moved from economic sanctions, which had been in place for several months, to freezing Japanese assets in the United States and cutting off its oil supplies.

War with Japan now looked likely. The Japanese military decided to hit the Americans with a knock-out blow that would give them time to seize Southeast Asia and the western Pacific; the United States, they hoped, would be too shaken to fight back. But American intelligence had broken the Japanese secret diplomatic code, and the president knew that Japan was preparing to strike somewhere, most likely the Philippines. By the end of November, all American Pacific forces were put on high alert.

On December 7, 1941, Japanese attack planes devastated the U.S. fleet stationed at Pearl Harbor, on the Hawaiian island of Oahu. This photograph shows the explosion of the USS *Shaw*, a drydocked destroyer, during the second wave of Japanese attack. The "sneak" attack on Pearl Harbor became a symbol of Japanese treachery and the necessity for U.S. revenge.

Early on Sunday morning, December 7, 1941, carrier-borne Japanese bombers struck the Pacific fleet at Pearl Harbor. Americans were caught completely off guard. No one expected such a skillful attack. Within two hours, Japanese pilots destroyed nearly 200 American planes and badly damaged the fleet; more than 2,400 Americans were killed and nearly 1,200 wounded. (Fortunately, the U.S. carriers were spared, being out to sea on the morning of the attack.) That same day, Japan bombed U.S. bases on the Philippines, Guam, and Wake Island and attacked the British fleet and colonies in East Asia.

On December 8, declaring the attack on Pearl Harbor a day that "will live in infamy," Roosevelt asked Congress for a declaration of war against Japan. With only one dissenting vote—by pacifist Jeannette Rankin of Montana, who had voted against U.S. entry into World War I in 1917—Congress agreed. The United States did not declare war on Germany; it was Hitler who made that fateful decision when he ordered his puppet Reichstag on December 11 to proclaim war against "half Judaized and the half Negrified" America. Mussolini chimed in. World War II had now begun for Americans.

On the day after the attack on Pearl Harbor, President Franklin D. Roosevelt addressed a joint session of Congress and asked for an immediate declaration of war against Japan. The resolution passed with one dissenting vote, and the United States entered World War II.

THE GREAT ARSENAL OF DEMOCRACY

As early as 1938, the American economy had begun to benefit from sales to the British and French when those countries started rearming. In 1940, Roosevelt told Americans in a radio "fireside chat" that the nation must become a "great arsenal of democracy," and by the time the United States entered the war the U.S. economy had already geared up for military purposes. After Pearl Harbor, the federal government poured unprecedented energy and money into wartime production and assigned a huge army of experts to manage it. During the next three years, the economic machinery that had failed during the 1930s was running at full speed. Defense spending would spark the greatest economic boom in the history of any nation. Suddenly, it seemed, the Great Depression ended.

MOBILIZING FOR WAR

A few days after the United States declared war, Congress passed the War Powers Act, establishing a precedent for executive authority that would endure long after the war's end. Under the new law, the president could reorganize the federal government and create new agencies, censor all news and information and abridge civil liberties, seize foreign-owned property, and even award government contracts without competitive bidding.

Roosevelt promptly used his authority to create special wartime agencies. At the top of his agenda was a massive reorientation and management of the economy, and to do that an alphabet soup of new agencies appeared. For example, the Supply Priorities and Allocation Board (SPAB) oversaw the use of scarce materials and resources vital to the war, adjusting domestic consumption to military needs, even ending it for some products such as automobiles. The Office of Price Administration (OPA) used price controls to check inflation. The National War Labor Board (NWLB) mediated labor–management disputes. The War Manpower Commission (WMC) directed the mobilization of military and civilian services. And the Office of War Mobilization (OWM) coordinated operations among all these new agencies.

Several new agencies took on the responsibility of creating propaganda to promote a war that was being fought 3,000 miles away. Although Pearl Harbor brought an outpouring of rage against Japan and ended all talk of isolationism, the government nevertheless fanned patriotic fires and tried to shape public opinion. In June 1942 the president created the Office of War Information (OWI) to engage the press, radio, and film industry in selling the war to the American people, as well as to publish leaflets for the armed services and to flood enemy ranks with subversive propaganda.

Domestic propaganda also fueled the selling of war bonds. Secretary of the Treasury Henry Morgenthau Jr., not only encouraged Americans to buy government bonds to finance the war but also planned the campaign "to use *bonds* to sell the war, rather than *vice versa*." Buying bonds would "mean bullets in the bellies of Hitler's hordes!" Discovering through market research that Americans felt more antagonism toward Japan than Germany, Morgenthau directed his staff to use more negative stereotypes of the Japanese in their advertising copy. Polls showed, however, that most depression-stung Americans bought war bonds—$185.7 billion by war's end—mainly to invest safely, to counter inflation, and to save for postwar purchases.

The federal government also sponsored various measures to prevent subversion. The Federal Bureau of Investigation (FBI) was busy, its appropriations rising from $6 million to $16 million in just two years. The attorney general authorized wiretapping in cases of espionage or sabotage, but the FBI also used it extensively—and illegally—for domestic surveillance. The Joint Chiefs of Staff created the Office of Strategic Services (OSS) to assess enemy military strength, gather intelligence, and conduct foreign espionage. Its head, Colonel William Donovan, envisioned the OSS as an "adjunct to military strategy" and engaged leading social scientists to plot psychological warfare.

In mid-1942 Roosevelt established an agency that would prove vital to the Allied victory and change the way science was conducted in the United States. The Office of Scientific Research and Development (OSRD) brought together government, business, and scientific leaders to coordinate military research. It developed better radar and early warning systems, more effective medicines and pesticides, and improved weapons. Although its work was mostly secret, its head, Vannever Bush, became famous as "the man who may win or lose the war." He was also closely involved with the Manhattan Project, which developed the atomic bomb.

With the creation of these new agencies, the size of the federal government increased many times over its New Deal level. It cost about $250 million a day to fight the war, and the government spent twice as much during the war as it had during its entire history up to then. The number of federal employees nearly quadrupled, from a little over 1 million in 1940 to nearly 4 million by the war's end.

The New Deal itself, however, withered away. "Dr. New Deal" had been replaced by "Dr. Win the War," said Roosevelt in 1942. With the depression over and chronic unemployment giving way to acute labor shortages, FDR's administration directed all its resources toward securing the planes, ships, guns, and food—and the war workers—required for victory. Moreover, the 1942 elections weakened the New Deal coalition by unseating many liberal Democrats while sending fifty-five new and mostly conservative Republicans to Congress. Republicans now quashed proposals to extend the social programs instituted during the 1930s, including the WPA and the CCC. One of the hallmarks of the New Deal, the Farm Security Administration, managed to hang on but only after severe cuts to its budget, as was the case with the Rural Electrification Administration, which the private power companies despised. One by one, New Deal agencies vanished.

ORGANIZING THE WAR ECONOMY

Victory, many experts agreed, would ultimately depend less on military prowess and superior strategy than on the ability of the United States to outproduce its enemies. The nation enjoyed incomparable advantages: freedom from bombing and invasions, a huge industrial base, abundant natural resources, and a civilian population large enough to swell both its labor force and its armed forces. But first the entire civilian economy had to be both expanded and transformed for the production of arms and other military supplies.

Even before Pearl Harbor, by the summer of 1941, the federal government was pouring vast sums into defense production. Six months after the attack, allocations topped $100 billion for equipment and supplies, which exceeded what American firms had produced in all previous wars. Facing war orders too large to fill, American industries were primed for all-out production. Once-idled factories operated around-the-clock, seven days a week.

With better equipment and more motivation, American workers proved twice as productive as the Germans, five times as productive as the Japanese. No wonder the actual volume of industrial output expanded at the fastest rate in American history. Military production alone grew from 2 percent of the 1939 gross national product (GNP) to 40 percent of the 1943 GNP. "Something is happening," announced *Time* magazine, "that Adolf Hitler does not understand . . . it is the miracle of production."

Defense production transformed entire regions. The impact was strongest in the West—the major staging area for the war in the Pacific—where the federal government spent nearly $40 billion for military and industrial expansion. California got 10 percent of all federal funds, and by 1944 Los Angeles was the nation's second largest manufacturing center, only slightly behind Detroit. The South benefited from having 60 of the army's 100 new military camps, and its textile factories hummed: the army alone required nearly 520 million pairs of socks and 230 million pairs of pants. Much of the South's sharecropping and tenant-farming population—already thinned by New Deal economic policies (see Chapter 24)—migrated into well-paid urban industrial jobs, and unprecedented profits poured into southern businesses.

Across the nation, the rural population decreased by almost 20 percent, and American farmers could not keep up with the rising international—or even the domestic—demand for milk, potatoes, fruits, and sugar. The Department of Agriculture reached its goals only in areas such as livestock production, thanks to skyrocketing wholesale meat prices. The war speeded the development of large-scale and mechanized crop production, including the first widespread use of chemical fertilizers and pesticides. By 1945 farm income had doubled, but thousands of small farms had disappeared.

Much like large-scale commercial agriculture, many big businesses did well during the war. Military contracts allowed huge profits. The government provided low-interest loans and even direct subsidies for the expansion of facilities, with generous tax write-offs for retooling. The 100 largest corporations, which manufactured 30 percent of all goods in 1940, garnered 70 percent of all war and civilian contracts and the bulk of war profits. On the other hand, many small businesses closed.

NEW WORKERS

The wartime economy required an unprecedented number of new workers. The *bracero* program, negotiated by the United States and Mexico in 1942, brought more than 200,000 Mexicans into the United States for short-term employment, mainly as farm and railroad workers. Sioux and Navajos were hired in large numbers to build ordnance depots and military training centers. African Americans secured in just four years a greater variety of jobs than in the seven decades since the outbreak of the Civil War. They joined white workers in defense industries—in iron and steel plants, shipyards and aircraft factories, and numerous government agencies. The number of black workers rose from 2.9 million to 3.8 million.

The war most dramatically altered the wage-earning patterns of women. The female labor force grew by more than 50 percent, reaching 19.5 million in 1945. The rate of growth proved especially high for white women over thirty-five, and for the first time married women became the majority of female wage earners. The employment rate changed comparatively little for African American women; fully 90 percent had been in the labor force in 1940. However, many black women left domestic service for higher-paying industrial jobs.

Neither government nor industry rushed to recruit women. Well into the summer of 1942 the Department of War advised businesses to hold back from hiring women "until all available male labor in the area had first been employed." Likewise, neither government nor industry expected women to stay in their jobs when the war ended. "Rosie, the Riveter" appeared in posters and advertisements as the model female citizen, but only "for the duration" (see Seeing History). In Washington, DC, women bus drivers were given badges to wear on their uniforms that read: "I am taking the place of a man who went to war."

For the most part, recruiters used conventional gender stereotypes to make wartime jobs appealing to women. Posters and informational films depicted women's new industrial jobs as simple variations of domestic tasks. Where once housewives sewed curtains for their kitchens, they now produced silk parachutes. Their skill with a vacuum cleaner easily translated into riveting on huge ships. "Instead of cutting a cake," one male-narrated newsreel explained, "this woman [factory worker] cuts the pattern of aircraft parts."

Facing a shortage of workers and increased production demands, the War Manpower Commission and the Office of War Information conducted a campaign to recruit women into the labor force. Women were encouraged to "take a job for your husband/son/brother" and to "keep the world safe for your children." Higher wages also enticed many women to take jobs in factories. In this photograph, women are shown packaging powdered milk.

Compared to the Great Depression, when married women were barred from many jobs, World War II opened up new fields. The number of women automobile workers jumped from 29,000 to 200,000, that of women electrical workers from 100,000 to 374,000. Polled near the end of the war, 75 percent of women workers said they wanted to keep working, preferably at the same jobs.

Although the war generated 17 million new jobs, the economic gains were not evenly distributed. Wages increased by as much as 50 percent, but never as fast as profits or prices. This widely reported disparity produced one of the most turbulent periods in American labor history (see Table 25.1). More workers went on strike in 1941, before the United States entered the war, than in any previous year except 1919. A militant union drive at Ford Motor Company's enormous River Rouge plant made the United Auto Workers (UAW) one of the most powerful labor organizations in the world. Total union membership increased from 10.5 million to 14.7 million, with the women's share alone rising from 11 to 23 percent. Unions also enrolled 1,250,000 African Americans, twice the prewar number.

Once the United States entered the war, the major unions patriotically agreed to no-strike pledges for the

SEEING HISTORY

Norman Rockwell's "Rosie, the Riveter"

During his long career as an artist-illustrator, Norman Rockwell published forty-seven covers of the popular family magazine *The Saturday Evening Post*, all venerating various aspects of American life. "Rosie, the Riveter" appeared on the magazine's cover May 29, 1943, and virtually enshrined women's contribution to the war effort.

The *Post* donated the original painting to the U.S. Treasury Department, which took "Rosie" on a national tour to get Americans to buy war bonds.

Now an iconic image, Rosie was modeled on a real-life woman, a telephone operator in Vermont. Rockwell took advantage of his artistic license by making Rosie older and more muscular than his slight nineteen-year-old model—who was quite surprised when she finally saw the portrait! There is no doubt, though, that Rockwell captured the spirit of wartime patriotism. The self-confident Rosie takes obvious pride in her work, keeping her riveter on her ample lap even during lunchtime. A halo encircles her head, the American flag waves in the background. To seal the message, Rockwell shows Rosie crushing Hitler's autobiography, *Mein Kampf*, under her penny loafer.

In calling attention to Rosie's impressive biceps, Rockwell nevertheless attended to the small details that assure viewers that his defense worker has lost none of her femininity. Like most other women in the 1940s, she wears lipstick and rouge and polishes her nails. She also keeps a lace hanky and compact in the pocket of her overalls and wears a necklace—albeit of merit buttons—around her neck. Moreover, Rockwell does not show Rosie riveting but instead eating a ham sandwich that she undoubtedly made at home.

Rockwell's painting, beloved during World War II, became even more popular with the rise of the women's liberation movement in the late 1960s and remains to this day an emblem of women's strength and determination. In May 2002, Sotheby's auctioned the original canvas for more than $4.9 million.

In what ways does Rockwell's painting convey ideals related to gender roles during the war?

TABLE 25.1

Strikes and Lockouts in the United States, 1940–45

Year	Number of Strikes	Number of Workers Involved	Number of Man-Days Idle	Percent of Total Employed
1940	2,508	576,988	6,700,872	2.3
1941	4,288	2,362,620	23,047,556	8.4
1942	2,968	839,961	4,182,557	2.8
1943	3,752	1,981,279	13,500,529	6.9
1944	4,956	2,115,637	8,721,079	7.0
1945	4,750	3,467,000	38,025,000	12.2

Despite "no-strike" pledges, workers staged wildcat strikes in the war years. Union leaders negotiated shorter hours, higher wages, and seniority rules and helped to build union membership to a new height. When the war ended, nearly 30 percent of all nonagricultural workers were union members.

SOURCE: "Work Stoppages Caused by Labor–Management Disputes in 1945," *Monthly Labor Review*, May 1946, p. 720; and Martin Glaberman, *War Time Strikes* (Detroit: Bewick, 1980), p. 36.

duration. Nevertheless, rank-and-file union members sporadically staged illegal "wildcat" strikes. The most dramatic, a walkout of more than a half-million coal miners in 1943 led by the rambunctious John L. Lewis, withstood the attacks of the government and the press. Roosevelt repeatedly ordered the mines seized, only to find, as Lewis retorted, that coal could not be mined with bayonets. The Democratic-majority Congress passed the first federal antistrike bill, giving the president power to penalize or even draft strikers. And yet the strikes reached a level greater than in any other four-year period in American history.

THE HOME FRONT

Alone among the major combatants, the homelands of the United States and Canada were neither invaded nor bombed, except for remote Pearl Harbor. On the U.S. mainland, most civilians—unless they had loved ones serving in the armed forces or relocated to distant parts—experienced the war mainly in terms of inconveniences: rationing, long workdays, and a sharp increase in income taxes. Nevertheless, Americans were not immune to the social upheavals that accompany war. Alongside an upsurge of patriotism and faith in what later became known as "the good war" ran deep conflicts on the home front. Families were disrupted, and racial and ethnic hostilities flared repeatedly and sometimes violently.

FAMILIES IN WARTIME

"Economic conditions were ripe for a rush to the altar," quipped one social scientist. Men and women rushed into marriage, despite (or maybe because of) wartime uncertainties. The wartime boom sent personal incomes surging, allowing many young couples to set up separate

households for the first time since the depression struck. The prospect of wartime separation pushed other couples into marriage. The Census Bureau estimated that between 1940 and 1943 at least a million more people married than would have been expected to do so without the war. The marriage rate peaked in 1946—but by then divorces were also setting records.

Housing shortages were acute and rents were high. With apartments scarce, taxi drivers (for an extra fee) became up-to-the-minute guides to vacances. Landlords were free to discriminate against families with children—and, even more so, against racial minorities.

Wartime wages made many Americans eager to stock up on consumer goods, including a few luxuries, but they soon discovered that even supplying a household was difficult. Shopping had to be squeezed in between long work hours. Rationing required extra planning for purchasing meat, cheese, sugar, milk, coffee, gasoline, and shoes, and such staples were often in short supply. One homemaker said she and her friends referred to butter as "twenty-four karat gold." Illegal black markets flourished despite the high prices charged for scarce or rationed goods.

Many women found it nearly impossible to manage both a demanding job and a household. This dual responsibility contributed to high turnover and absentee rates in factories. Caring for small children became a major problem. Wartime employment or military service often separated husbands and wives, leaving children in the care of only one parent. Even when families stayed together, both adults often worked long hours, sometimes on different shifts. Although the War Manpower Commission estimated that as many as 2 million children needed some form of child care, federally funded day-care centers served less than 10 percent of defense workers' children. In most communities, the limited facilities sponsored by industry

Students at Officers' Training School at Northwestern University, who were not allowed to marry until they were commissioned as ensigns, apply for marriage licenses in Chicago, August 20, 1943, shortly before graduation. These young couples helped the marriage rate skyrocket during World War II.

or municipal governments could not keep up with the growing number of "latchkey" children.

Juvenile delinquency rose. With employers relaxing minimum age requirements, many teenagers—too young for the draft—quit school for high-wage factory jobs. Runaways drifted from city to city, finding temporary work at wartime plants or military installations. Urban gangs spawned brawling, prostitution, and automobile thefts for joy rides. To curb this trend, the U.S. Office of Education and the Children's Bureau sponsored a back-to-school campaign and appealed to employers to hire only older workers.

Public health improved greatly. Forced to forgo medical care during the Great Depression, many Americans spent large portions of their wartime paychecks on doctors, dentists, and prescription drugs. Some families ate lots of healthy fresh vegetables raised in their backyard "victory gardens." Even more important were the medical benefits provided to the more than 16 million men inducted into the armed forces and their dependents. Nationally, incidences of such communicable diseases as typhoid fever, tuberculosis, and diphtheria dropped considerably, the infant

death rate fell by more than a third, and life expectancy increased by three years. The death rate in 1942, excluding battle deaths, was the lowest in the nation's history. In the South and Southwest, however, racism and poverty combined to halt or even reverse these trends. These regions continued to have the nation's highest infant and maternal mortality rates.

THE INTERNMENT OF JAPANESE AMERICANS

No families suffered more from wartime dislocations than Japanese Americans who were interned for the duration. After Pearl Harbor, military officials feared an invasion of the mainland and suspected Japanese Americans of secret disloyalty. On December 8, 1941, the federal government froze the financial assets of those born in Japan, called Issei, who had been barred from U.S. citizenship. Meanwhile, in the name of national defense, a coalition of politicians, patriotic organizations, business groups, and military officials called for the removal of all Americans of Japanese descent from Pacific coastal areas. Although a State Department intelligence

More than 110,000 Japanese Americans were interned during World War II, some for up to four years. This photograph, taken in May 1942 by Dorothea Lange (1895–1965), the famed photographer of depression-era migrant families, shows young boys waiting in the baggage-inspection line at the Assembly Center in Turlock, California.

report certified their loyalty, Japanese Americans—two-thirds of them American-born citizens—became the largest ethnic group singled out for legal sanctions.

Charges of sedition against the Japanese unleashed deep racial prejudices. Headlines freely blared the word *Jap*, while political cartoonists and the popular culture employed blatant racial stereotypes. "The very fact that no sabotage has taken place to date," an army report suggested, with twisted logic, "is a disturbing and confirming indication that action will be taken."

On February 19, 1942, Roosevelt signed Executive Order 9066, which banned more than 120,000 Japanese American men, women, and children from designated military areas, mainly in California, but also in Oregon, Washington, and southern Arizona. The army prepared for forced evacuation, rounding up and removing Japanese Americans from communities where they had lived and worked, sometimes for generations.

During the spring of 1942, Japanese American families received one week's notice to close up their businesses and homes. Told to bring only what they could carry, they were then transported to one of the ten internment camps managed by the War Relocation Authority. The guarded camps were located as far away as Arkansas, although the majority had been set up in the remote desert areas of

Utah, Colorado, Idaho, Arizona, Wyoming, and California. Karl G. Yoneda described his quarters at Manzanar in northern California:

> There were no lights, stoves, or window panes. My two cousins and I, together with seven others, were crowded into a 25 × 30 foot room. We slept on army cots with our clothes on. The next morning we discovered that there were no toilets or washrooms. . . . We saw GIs manning machine guns in the watchtowers. The barbed wire fence which surrounded the camp was visible against the background of the snow-covered Sierra mountain range. "So this is the American-style concentration camp," someone remarked.

By August, virtually every West Coast resident with at least one Japanese grandparent had been interned.

The Japanese American Citizens League charged that "racial animosity," not military necessity, motivated the internment policy. Despite the protest of the American Civil Liberties Union and several church groups, the Supreme Court in *Korematsu* v. *United States* (1944) upheld the constitutionality of relocation on grounds of national security. By this time a program of gradual release was in place, although the last center did not close until March 1946. In protest, nearly six thousand Japanese Americans renounced their U.S. citizenship. Japanese Americans had lost homes and businesses valued at $500 million in what many historians judge as being the worst violation of American civil liberties during the war. Not until 1988 did Congress vote to award each of the 60,000 surviving victims reparations of $20,000 and a public apology.

"DOUBLE V": VICTORY AT HOME AND ABROAD

Throughout the war, African American activists conducted a "Double V" campaign, mobilizing not only for Allied victory but also for their own rights as citizens. "The army is about to take me to fight for democracy," one Detroit resident said, "but I would as leave fight for democracy right here." Black militants demanded, at a minimum, fair housing and equal employment opportunities, laying the foundation for the postwar civil rights movement.

Even before the United States entered the war, the foremost black labor leader—A. Philip Randolph, president of both the Brotherhood of Sleeping Car Porters and the National Negro Congress—began to mobilize against discrimination. At a planning meeting in Chicago a black woman proposed sending African Americans to Washington, DC, "from all over the country, in jalopies, in trains, and any way they can get there until we get some action from the White House." African Americans across the country began to prepare for a "great rally" of no less

This painting is by Horace Pippin, a self-taught African American artist who began painting as therapy for an injury suffered while serving with the U.S. Army's 369th Colored Infantry Regiment during World War I. It is one of a series drawn during World War II illustrating the contradiction between the principles of liberty and justice, for which Americans were fighting abroad, and the reality of racial prejudice at home.

SOURCE: Horace Pippin (1888–1946), "Mr. Prejudice", 1943. Oil on canvas, 18 × 14 inches. Philadelphia Museum of Art, Gift of Dr. and Mrs. Matthew T. Moore. Photo by Graydon Wood. 1984–108–1.

than 100,000 people at the Lincoln Memorial on the Fourth of July.

Eager to stop the March on Washington movement, Roosevelt met with Randolph, who proposed an executive order "making it mandatory that Negroes be permitted to work in [defense] plants." Randolph reviewed several drafts before approving the text that became, on June 25, 1941, Executive Order 8802, banning discrimination in defense industries and government. The president later appointed a Fair Employment Practices Committee to hear complaints and redress grievances. Randolph called off the march but remained determined to "shake up white America."

Other civil rights organizations formed during wartime to fight discrimination and Jim Crow, including segregation in the armed forces. The interracial Congress of Racial Equality (CORE), formed by pacifists in 1942, staged sit-ins at Chicago, Detroit, and Denver restaurants

that refused to serve African Americans. Membership in the NAACP, which fought discrimination in defense plants and the military, grew from 50,000 in 1940 to 450,000 in 1946. The Supreme Court ruling in *Smith* v. *Albright* (1944) "white primaries" used in southern states to exclude black voters was a major victory paving the way for future civil rights struggles.

Approximately 1.2 million African Americans left the rural South to take wartime jobs, and they faced not only serious housing shortages but also whites intent on keeping them out of their own jobs and neighborhoods. "Hate strikes" broke out in defense plants across the country when African Americans were hired or upgraded to "white" positions. In February 1942, when twenty black families attempted to move into new federally funded apartments adjacent to a Polish American community in Detroit, a mob of 700 armed white protesters halted the moving vans and burned a cross on the project's grounds. The police ignored the white rioters but arrested black youths. Finally, two months later, 1,000 state troopers supervised the move of these families into the Sojourner Truth Housing Project, named after the famous abolitionist and former slave.

Racial violence reached its wartime peak during the summer of 1943, when 274 conflicts broke out in nearly fifty cities. In Detroit, where the black population had grown by more than a third since the beginning of the war, twenty-five blacks and nine whites were killed and more than 700 were injured. The poet Langston Hughes, who supported U.S. involvement in the war, expressed the new militancy of many African Americans:

> *Looky here, America*
> *What you done done—*
> *Let things drift*
> *Until the riots come*
> *Yet you say we're fighting*
> *For democracy.*
> *Then why don't democracy*
> *Include me?*
> *I ask you this question*
> *Cause I want to know*
> *How long I got to fight*
> *BOTH HITLER—AND JIM CROW.*

ZOOT-SUIT RIOTS

On the night of June 4, 1943, sailors poured into nearly 200 cars and taxis to drive through the streets of East Los Angeles in search of Mexican Americans dressed in "zoot suits." The sailors assaulted their victims at random, even chasing one youth into a movie theater and stripping him of his clothes while the audience cheered. Riots broke out and continued for five days.

Two communities had collided with tragic results. The sailors had only recently been uprooted from their hometowns and regrouped under the strict discipline of boot camp. Stationed in southern California while awaiting deployment overseas, they came face-to-face with Mexican American teenagers wearing long-draped coats, pegged pants, pocket watches with oversized chains, and big floppy hats. To the sailors, the zoot suit was not just a flamboyant fashion. Unlike the uniform the young sailors wore, the zoot suit signaled defiance and a lack of patriotism.

The zoot-suiters, however, represented less than 10 percent of the Hispanic community's youth. More than 300,000 Mexican Americans were serving in the armed forces (a number representing a greater proportion of their draft-age population than other Americans), often in the most hazardous branches, as paratroops and Marines. Many others were employed in war industries in Los Angeles, which had become home to the nation's largest Mexican American community. For the first time, Mexican Americans were finding well-paying jobs, and like African Americans, they expected their government to protect them from discrimination.

Military and civilian authorities eventually contained the zoot-suit riots by ruling several sections of Los Angeles off-limits to military personnel, and the city council passed legislation making the wearing of a zoot suit in public a criminal offense. Many Mexican Americans expressed concern about their personal safety; some feared that after the government rounded up the Japanese they would be the next group sent to internment camps.

POPULAR CULTURE AND "THE GOOD WAR"

Global events shaped the lives of American civilians but appeared to touch them only indirectly in their everyday activities. Food shortages, long hours in the factories, and even fears for loved ones abroad did not take away all the pleasures of full employment and prosperity. With money in their pockets, Americans spent freely at vacation resorts, country clubs, racetracks, nightclubs, dance halls, and movie theaters. Sales of books skyrocketed, and spectator sports attracted huge and diverse audiences.

Despite the sharpening racial divisions of the neighborhood and the workplace, popular music crossed racial lines. Transplanted southern musicians, black and white, brought their regional styles to northern cities. Played on jukeboxes in bars, bus stations, and cafés, "country" and "rhythm & blues" not only won new audiences but also inspired musicians to crisscross old boundaries. Musicians of the war years "made them steel guitars cry and whine," Ray Charles recalled. They also paved the way musically for the emergence of rock and roll a decade later.

War themes pervaded popular music, meshing personal experiences with government directives to enshrine World War II as a "good war" that justified massive sacrifice. The plaintive "A Rainbow at Midnight" by country singer Ernest Tubb expressed the hope of a common "dogface" soldier looking beyond the misery and horror to the promise of a brighter tomorrow. "Till Then," recorded by the Mills Brothers, a harmonious black quartet, offered the prospect of a romantic reunion when "the world will be free." The era's best-known tune, Irving Berlin's "White Christmas," evoked a lyrical nostalgia of past celebrations with family and friends close by. On the lighter side, novelty artist Spike Jones made his name with the "razz" or "Bronx cheer," in "We're Going to Ffft in the Fuehrer's Face."

Hollywood mobilized, as one screenwriters group explained, "to build morale" and to "stimulate…initiative and responsibility." Combat films such as *Action in the North Atlantic* made heroes of ordinary Americans under fire, depicting GIs of different races and ethnicities discovering their common humanity. With military cooperation, wartime movies encouraged Americans to think well of all the Allies—including the Soviet Union. Several films, such as *Tender Comrade*, plugged pro-Soviet views that would be abruptly reversed in the postwar years. Other films such as the Oscar-winning *Since You Went Away* portrayed the loyalty and resilience of American families with servicemen stationed overseas. Hollywood aided the war effort in additional ways. Frank Capra directed the government-sponsored *Why We Fight*, a series of documentaries to explain the war's aims to soldiers. Meanwhile, movie stars led the war bond campaign, selling nearly $1 billion worth in 1942 alone.

The wartime spirit infected even the juvenile world of comics. The climbing sales of nickel "books" spawned a proliferation of patriotic superheroes such as the Green Lantern, Captain Marvel, and Wonder Woman. Even Bugs Bunny put on a uniform and fought sinister-looking enemies.

The fashion industry also did its part. Production of nylon stockings was halted because the material was needed for parachutes; to save cotton and woolen fabric for the production of uniforms, women's skirts were shortened, while the War Production Board encouraged cuffless "Victory Suits" for men. Executive Order M-217 restricted the colors of shoes manufactured during the war to "black, white, navy blue, and three shades of brown." For many civilians, including civil defense volunteers and Red Cross workers, wearing a uniform demonstrated patriotism, and padded shoulders and straight lines became popular among fashion-conscious men and women. Women employed in defense plants wore slacks, often for the first time in their lives.

Much of this war fervor was spontaneous, but the government did all it could to encourage self-sacrificing patriotism. The Office of War Information screened all popular music, movies, radio programs, and advertisements to ensure that everyone got the message: only the collective effort of all Americans could preserve democracy at home and save the world from fascism. Washington tried to make sure that the public saw the daily inconveniences and shortages of wartime, and above all the drafting of young men to serve and die abroad, as sacrifices essential to victory. And in the government's zeal to popularize sacrifice among the citizenry, no one was excluded and no action considered insignificant. The government even worried about war workers' casual conversations. People were told that snooping Nazi spies lurked everywhere; posters and advertisements warned "Loose Lips Sink Ships."

By the mid-1940s, popular culture had helped to shape a collective memory of World War II as "the good war," the standard by which the nation's subsequent wars would be judged. It also played an important part in bringing diverse and sometimes antagonistic communities together, not only in support of the war but also as steadfast consumers of mass entertainment.

MEN AND WOMEN IN UNIFORM

World War II mobilized 16.4 million Americans into the armed forces. Although only 34 percent of men who served in the army saw combat—the majority during the final year of the war—the experience had a powerful impact on nearly everyone. Whether working in the steno pool at Great Lakes Naval Training Center in northern Illinois or slogging through mud with rifle in hand in the Philippines, many men and women saw their lives reshaped in unpredictable ways. For those who survived, the war often proved to be the defining experience of their lives.

CREATING THE ARMED FORCES

Before the European war broke out in 1939, most of the 200,000 men in the U.S. armed forces patrolled the Mexican border or occupied colonial possessions, such as the Philippines. Neither the army nor the navy was prepared for the scale of combat World War II entailed. Only the U.S. Marine Corps, which had been planning since the 1920s to seize the western Pacific from Japan in the event of war, was ready to fight.

On October 16, 1940, National Registration Day, all men between twenty-one and thirty-six had to register for military service. After the United States entered the war, the draft age was lowered to eighteen, and local boards were instructed to choose the youngest first.

The draft law exempted those "who by religious training or belief" opposed war, including members of a traditional "peace church" such as Quakers, Mennonites,

and Seventh Day Adventists. Nonreligious objections to war in general or to World War II in particular were not acceptable About 25,000 conscientious objectors served in noncombatant roles in the military services; another 12,000 performed "alternative service." Approximately 6,000 objectors were jailed for refusing to register for the draft.

One-third of the men examined by the Selective Service were rejected. Surprising numbers were refused induction as physically unfit. For the first time, men were screened for "neuropsychiatric disorders or emotional problems," and approximately 1.6 million were rejected for that reason. At a time when only one American in four graduated from high school, many conscripts were turned away as functionally illiterate. Those who passed the screening tests joined the best-educated army in history: nearly half of white draftees had graduated from high school and 10 percent had attended college.

The officer corps, whose top ranks came from the Command and General Staff School at Fort Leavenworth, tended to be highly professional, politically conservative, and personally autocratic. General Douglas MacArthur, supreme commander in the Pacific, was said to admire the discipline of the German army and to disparage political democracy. General Dwight D. Eisenhower, however, who became the supreme commander of Allied forces in Europe, projected a new spirit. Distrusted by MacArthur and many of the older brass, Eisenhower appeared to his troops a model of leadership.

The democratic rhetoric of the war and the sudden massive expansion of the armed forces contributed to this transformation of the officer corps. A shortage of officers during World War I had prompted a huge expansion of the Reserve Officer Training Corps (ROTC) on campuses, but it still could not meet the demand. Racing to make up for the deficiency, Army Chief of Staff George Marshall opened schools for officer candidates. In 1942, in seventeen-week training periods, these schools produced more than 54,000 platoon leaders. Closer in sensibility to the civilian population, these new officers were the kind of leaders Eisenhower sought.

Most GIs (short for "government issue"), who formed the vast majority of draftees, had little or no contact with high-ranking officers and instead forged bonds with the men in their own combat units and with their company commanders. "Everyone wants someone to look up to when he's scared," one GI explained. Most of all, soldiers depended on the solidarity of the group and the loyalty of buddies to pull them through. Proud to serve in "the best-dressed, best-fed, best-equipped army in the world," the majority of these citizen-soldiers did not actually know why the world was at war. Antifascist zeal or democratic idealism, military leaders discovered, meant little to them. Most soldiers wanted foremost "to get the task done" and return soon to their families and communities.

WOMEN ENTER THE MILITARY

With the approach of World War II, Massachusetts Republican congresswoman Edith Nourse Rogers proposed legislation for the formation of a women's corps. The army instead drafted its own bill, which both Rogers and Eleanor Roosevelt supported, creating in May 1942 the Women's Army Auxiliary Corps (WAAC), later changed to Women's Army Corps (WAC). In 1942–43 other bills established a women's division of the navy (WAVES), the Women's Air Force Service Pilots, and the Marine Corps Women's Reserve.

Overall, more than 350,000 women served in World War II, two-thirds of them in the WACS and WAVES. As a group, they were better educated and more skilled—although paid less—than the average enlisted man. However, military policy prohibited women from supervising male workers, even in desk jobs.

Barred from combat, women were not necessarily protected from danger. Nurses accompanied troops into combat, treated men under fire, and dug their own foxholes. More than 1,000 women flew planes, although not in combat missions. Others worked as photographers and cryptoanalysts. But the vast majority remained far from battlefronts. Stationed mainly within the United States, most women worked in familiar jobs, serving in administration, communications, clerical, or health care facilities.

The WACS and WAVES were both subject to hostile commentary and bad publicity. The overwhelming majority of soldiers believed that most WACS were prostitutes; the War Department itself, fearing "immorality" among women in the armed forces, closely monitored their conduct and established much stricter rules for women than for men. The U.S. Marine Corps even used intelligence officers to ferret out suspected lesbians or women who showed "homosexual tendencies" (as opposed to homosexual acts), both causes for dishonorable discharge.

OLD PRACTICES AND NEW HORIZONS

The Selective Service Act, in response to the demands of African American leaders, specified that "there shall be no discrimination against any person on account of race or color." The draft brought hundreds of thousands of young black men into the army, and African Americans enlisted at a rate 60 percent above their proportion of the general population. By 1944, black soldiers represented 10 percent of the army's troops, and overall approximately 1 million African Americans served in the armed forces during World War II. The army, however, channeled black recruits into segregated, poorly equipped units, commanded by white officers. Secretary of War Henry Stimson refused to challenge this policy, saying that the army could not be "a sociological laboratory." The majority of African Americans served mainly in construction or stevedore work. Only toward the end of the war, when the shortage of infantry neared a crisis, were African Americans permitted to rise to combat status. The all-black 761st Tank Battalion, the first African American unit in combat, won a Medal of Honor after 183 days in action. And despite the very small number of African Americans admitted to the Air Force, the 99th Pursuit Squadron, trained at the new base in Tuskegee, Alabama, earned high marks in action against the feared German Luftwaffe. Even the Marine Corps and the Coast Guard agreed to end their historic exclusion of African Americans, although they recruited and promoted only a small number.

The ordinary black soldier, sailor, or Marine experienced few benefits from these late-in-the-war gains. They encountered discrimination everywhere. Even the blood

New recruits to the Women's Army Corps (WAC) pick up their clothing "issue" (allotment). These volunteers served in many capacities, from nursing men in combat to performing clerical and communication duties "stateside" (within the United States). Approximately 140,000 women served in the WACS during World War II.

banks kept blood segregated by race (although a black physician, Dr. Charles Drew, had invented the process for storing plasma). The year 1943 marked the peak of unrest, with violent confrontations between blacks and whites breaking out at military installations, especially in the South, where the majority of African American soldiers were stationed. Toward the end of the war, to improve morale among black servicemen the army relaxed its policy of segregation, mainly in recreational facilities.

The army also grouped Japanese Americans into segregated units, sending most to fight far from the Pacific Theater. Better educated than the average soldier, many Nisei soldiers who knew Japanese served stateside as interpreters and translators. When the army decided to create a Nisei regiment, more than 10,000 volunteers stepped forward, although only one in five was accepted. The Nisei 442nd fought heroically in Italy and France and became the most decorated regiment in the war.

Despite segregation, the armed forces ultimately pulled Americans of all varieties out of their separate communities. Many Jews and other second-generation European immigrants, for example, described their military stint as an "Americanizing" experience. For the first time in their lives, many Indian peoples left reservations as approximately 25,000 served in the armed forces. In the Pacific war, Navajo "code talkers" used their native language (a complex, unwritten language unknown to the Japanese) to transmit information from the front lines and also improved their English in special classes. For many African Americans, military service provided a bridge to postwar civil rights agitation.

Many homosexuals also discovered a wider world in the service. Despite rules barring them from the military, most slipped through at the induction centers. Moreover, the emotional pressures of wartime, especially the fear of death, encouraged close friendships, and homosexuals in the military often found more room than in civilian life to express their sexual orientation openly. In army canteens, when there were no women present, even straight men often danced with one another. In civilian settings, such behavior would have brought ridicule or even arrest.

Most veterans looked back on World War II, with all its dangers and discomforts, as the greatest experience they ever knew. As *The New Republic* predicted in 1943, they met other Americans from every part of the country and recognized for the first time in their lives "the bigness and wholeness of the United States." "Hughie was a Georgia cracker, so he knew something about moonshine," remembered one soldier. Another fondly recalled "this fellow from Wisconsin we called 'Moose.'" The army itself promoted these expectations of new experience. *Twenty-Seven Soldiers* (1944), a government-produced film for the troops, showed Allied soldiers of several nationalities all working together in harmony.

The Marines recruited more than 400 Navajos to serve as code talkers by communicating in their own language. Deployed mainly to the Pacific Theater, they used radio and telegraph to transmit quickly vital information about battlefield activities, including troop movements. This photograph, taken in December 1943, shows Corporal Henry Bake, Jr., and Private First Class George H. Kirk operating a portable radio unit in a jungle clearing near the front lines.

THE MEDICAL CORPS

The chance of being killed in combat was surprisingly small, estimated at less than 1 in 50, but the risk of injury was much higher. By the time the war ended, the army reported 949,000 casualties, including 175,000 killed in action. Although the European Theater produced the most casualties, the Pacific held grave dangers beyond enemy fire. For soldiers in humid jungles, malaria, typhus, diarrhea, or dengue fever posed the most common threat to their lives. For the 25th Infantry Division, which landed in Guadalcanal in 1943, the malaria-carrying mosquito proved an even more deadly enemy than the Japanese.

The prolonged stress of combat also took a toll in "battle fatigue"—the official army term for combat stress and what would today be called posttraumatic stress. Despite rigorous screening, more than 1 million soldiers suffered at one time or another from debilitating psychiatric symptoms, and the number of men discharged for neuropsychiatric reasons was 2.5 times greater than in previous wars. The cause, psychiatrists concluded, was not individual weakness but long stints in the front lines. In France, for example, where soldiers spent up to 200 days in the field without a break from fighting, thousands cracked, occasionally wounding themselves in order to be sent home. In 1944 the army concluded that eight months in combat was the maximum. When replacements were available, it instituted a rotation system to relieve exhausted soldiers.

In basic training soldiers received first-aid instruction, and they went into battle with bandages to treat minor wounds. For anything more serious, however, they needed physicians and medics. Army Medical Corps doctors went to the front lines. There, in makeshift tent hospitals, these physicians advanced surgical techniques and used new "wonder drugs" such as penicillin to save many wounded soldiers who in earlier wars would have died. Of the soldiers who underwent emergency field surgery, more than 85 percent survived. Overall, less than 4 percent of all soldiers who received medical care died of their injuries. Much of the success in treatment came from the use of blood plasma, which reduced the often lethal effect of shock from severe bleeding. By 1945, the American Red Cross Blood Bank, formed four years earlier, had collected more than 13 million units of blood from volunteers, converted most of it into dried plasma, and made it readily available throughout the European Theater.

Grateful for the care of skilled surgeons, many soldiers nevertheless named medics the true heroes of the battlefront. Thirty to forty medics, many of them commissioned officers (COs), were attached to each infantry battalion, and under fire they gave emergency first aid and transported the wounded to the aid station and, if necessary, the field hospital.

In the military hospitals, American nurses gave the bulk of care to recovering soldiers. Before World War II, the Army Nurse Corps, created in 1901, was scarcely a military organization; its recruits earned neither military pay nor held rank. To overcome the short supply of nurses, Congress extended military rank to nurses in 1944, although only for the duration plus six months. In 1945 Congress came close to passing a bill to draft nurses. Like medics, army nurses went first to training centers in the United States, learning how to dig foxholes and dodge bullets before being sent overseas. By 1945, approximately 56,000 women, including 500 African American women, were on active duty in the Army Nurse Corps, staffing medical facilities in every theater of the war.

THE WORLD AT WAR

The Allies remained on the defensive almost until the end of 1942. During this time, from the Atlantic to deep in Russia, Hitler and his allies controlled most of continental Europe and continued to pound Great Britain from the air. A German army also swept across North Africa and almost took the Suez Canal from the British.

In the Pacific and East Asia the situation was just as dire. Just two hours after the attack on Pearl Harbor, Japanese planes struck the main U.S. airbase in the Philippines and demolished half the warplanes commanded by General Douglas MacArthur. Japanese troops soon conquered the entire Philippines. MacArthur retreated to the Bataan Peninsula and then fled by submarine to Australia. When his stranded troops on Bataan finally surrendered, they were subjected to a horrific "death march" into POW camps; where they would face abuse, disease, and starvation until liberated. The Japanese easily overran Britain's Southeast Asian colonies, the Dutch East Indies, and the entire western Pacific. Although China officially joined the Allies, Japanese forces on the Chinese mainland remained on the offensive. Roosevelt called the news "all bad," and his military advisers predicted a long fight to victory (see Map 25.1).

But the Allies enjoyed several important advantages: America's vast natural resources and a skilled workforce with sufficient reserves to accelerate the production of weapons and ammunitions; the determination of millions of antifascists throughout Europe and Asia; and the capacity of the Soviet people to endure immense losses. Slowly at first, but then with quickening speed, these advantages came into play.

SOVIETS HALT NAZI DRIVE

The weapons and tactics of World War II differed radically from those of World War I. Unlike that conflict, which was fought with poison gas and machine-gun fire by armies largely immobilized in trenches, World War II was a war of offensive maneuvers punctuated by surprise attacks. Its chief weapons—tanks and planes on land and aircraft carriers and submarines at sea—combined mobility and concentrated firepower. Also of major importance were artillery and explosives, which according to some estimates accounted for more than 30 percent of casualties. Major improvements in communication systems, mainly two-way radio transmission and radiotelephony that permitted commanders to stay in contact with division leaders, played a decisive role throughout the war.

From the beginning of the European war in 1939, Hitler had used these methods to seize the advantage, purposefully striking terror among stricken populations of Western Europe as he routed opposing armies. The Royal Air Force, however, fought the Luftwaffe to a standstill in the Battle of Britain, frustrating Hitler's hopes of invading England. By the spring of 1941, he had turned his attention eastward, planning to conquer the Soviet Union. But he had to delay the invasion to rescue Mussolini, whose weak army faced defeat in North Africa and Greece. Not until June 22, 1941, six weeks behind schedule, did Hitler invade the Soviet Union.

Hitler's forces initially devastated the Red Army, killing or capturing nearly 3 million soldiers and leaving thousands to die from exposure or starvation. But the brutality of the Nazis—from the beginning they intended to kill all the Jews and reduce the Russian population to slave laborers—kindled a desperate civilian resistance. The German army in Russia found its supply lines overextended and the brutal Russian winter just beginning, while Stalin was able to send every available resource to his troops concentrated just outside Moscow. The Red Army launched a

MAP EXPLORATION

To explore an interactive version of this map, go to **www.prenhall.com/faragher6/map25.1**

Legend:
- Axis powers before World War II
- Maximum area of Axis control, Nov 1942
- Allies
- Neutral nations
- Allied troop movements
- Major battles/Allied victories

ICELAND

ATLANTIC OCEAN

Finnish territory annexed by Soviet Union

SWEDEN   FINLAND

NORWAY

SOVIET UNION

NORTHERN IRELAND

North Sea

ESTONIA

Leningrad (besieged Sept 1941–Jan 19, 1943)

REPUBLIC OF IRELAND   GREAT BRITAIN

DENMARK   LATVIA   • Moscow

LITHUANIA

London •   NETH.   Berlin (surrendered May 2, 1945)   *East Prussia (Germany)*

Stalingrad (besieged Aug 1942–Jan 31, 1943)

D-Day June 6, 1944   Paris (liberated Aug 1944)   BELGIUM   • Warsaw

• Dresden   POLAND

Normandy   GERMANY

Battle of the Bulge Dec 16, 1944–Jan 31, 1945

FRANCE   *Rhine R.*   SLOVAKIA   *Ruthenia*   *Ukraine*

SWITZ.   AUSTRIA   HUNGARY   *Territory annexed by Hungary*

Vichy France (occupied Nov 1942)   ROMANIA   • Yalta

PORTUGAL   YUGOSLAVIA   *Black Sea*

SPAIN   ITALY   BULGARIA

Rome (liberated June 1944)   *Albania (Italy)*   TURKEY

GREECE

• Athens

SPANISH MOROCCO   *Mediterranean Sea*   *Rhodes (Italy)*   *Cyprus (British)*   SYRIA   IRAQ

MOROCCO   ALGERIA   *Crete (Greece)*   LEBANON

Kasserine Pass Feb 14–22, 1943   TUNISIA   *Palestine (British)*   TRANSJORDAN

French North Africa (Vichy France) (joined Allies Nov. 1942)   **El Alamein** Oct 23–Nov 5, 1942   SAUDI ARABIA

Libya (Italy)   EGYPT   *Red Sea*

MAP 25.1 The War in Europe The Allies remained on the defensive during the first years of the war, but by 1943 the British and Americans, with an almost endless supply of resources, had turned the tide.

massive counterattack, catching the frostbitten German troops off guard and driving them to retreat. For the first time, the Nazi war machine had suffered a major setback.

Hitler, however, remained stubbornly fixed on conquering Russia and then, with great resources at his disposal, turning on Britain and even the United States. In 1942, German troops had a new objective: occupying the rich oil fields of the Caucasus. But at Stalingrad (now Volgograd), a major Soviet industrial city on the Volga River, Hitler met his nemesis. In the battle for that city alone, the Soviets suffered more casualties than Americans did during the entire war. House-to-house fighting and a massive Red Army counterattack inflicted an even greater toll on the Nazis. Hitler ordered to his troops to die rather than surrender. But in February 1943 the German Sixth Army, reduced to 100,000 starving men and overpowered by Soviet weaponry, at last gave up. Years later, only a handful would return from Soviet prison camps.

Already in retreat but plotting one last desperate attempt to halt the Red Army, the Germans threw most of their remaining armored vehicles into action at Kursk in July 1943. The clash quickly spiraled into the greatest tank battle in history, involving more than 2 million troops and 6,000 tanks. After another stunning defeat, the Germans had decisively lost the initiative. Their only option was to delay the advance of the Red Army toward their own homeland.

Meanwhile, the Soviet Union had begun to recover from its early losses, even as tens of millions of its people remained homeless and near starvation. Assisted by Lend-Lease, by 1942 the Soviets were outproducing Germany in many types of weapons and other supplies. Nazi officers and German civilians alike began to doubt that Hitler could win.

Soviet victories had turned the tide; the Soviet Union, not the Western Allies, bore by far the heaviest burden in stopping what had once seemed an unstoppable Nazi advance. The American and British people were grateful for this immense Soviet contribution (the full extent of which they did not know at the time), and the British and American governments found themselves under enormous pressure from Stalin to open a second front in the west. But to do so required complex strategic planning and the assembling of immense material and human resources.

PLANNING AND INITIATING THE ALLIED OFFENSIVE

Despite the huge territories that Nazi Germany and Japan controlled in 1942, the Axis momentum was flagging. After Stalingrad, Hitler lost ground. In the Pacific that summer, Japan's plans to invade Hawai'i and Australia were stopped by the U.S. Navy. In the course of 1942 as well, American shipbuilding began to outpace the punishment Nazi U-boats could inflict on Allied shipping; that advance kept open the vital Lend-Lease supply lanes to Britain and Russia, while submarine-hunting destroyers greatly reduced the German undersea threat. The United States far outstripped Germany in building landing craft and amphibious vehicles, two of the most important innovations of the war. Now outnumbered by the Allies, the German Luftwaffe was increasingly limited to defensive action.

Against this backdrop, Roosevelt, Churchill, and their generals hammered out a strategy to defeat the Axis. They saw Japan as the lesser threat—one that for the moment should be contained rather than attacked all-out (although MacArthur, the U.S. Navy, and the American public all clamored for a "Japan-first" strategy of avenging Pearl Harbor). Germany, Roosevelt and Churchill agreed, must be beaten first, which meant eventually invading Europe and fighting Hitler's Reich from the west, while the Red Army advanced from the east.

But the Allies disagreed about where to attack Germany. Remembering the terrible bloodletting on the western front during World War I, the British dreaded another long, stalemated struggle in France. Churchill and his generals wanted to strike through what he called "Europe's soft under-belly," the Mediterranean. The American generals retorted that only a direct, though meticulously prepared, assault through France would bring down Nazi Germany.

In the end, Roosevelt and Churchill compromised: they would first send smaller armies into the Mediterranean, while gathering a huge Anglo-American invasion army in Britain. This strategy was set in motion in late 1942. On October 23–24, near El Alamein in the desert of western Egypt, the British Eighth Army halted a major offensive by the German Afrika Korps, headed by the famed "Desert Fox," General Erwin Rommel. Although suffering heavy losses, British forces destroyed the Italian North African Army and much of the Afrika Korps. Then, in November, American troops for the first time went into action in the European Theater by joining the British in Operation Torch, an invasion of Morocco and Algeria. While at the eastern end the British drove Rommel back from El Alamein, from the west, a mostly American army, still inexperienced and mistake-prone, forced the Germans out of Tunisia. In six months, North Africa was cleared of Axis troops.

In January 1943, while the fighting raged in North Africa, Roosevelt and Churchill met at Casablanca in Morocco and announced that they would accept nothing less than the unconditional surrender of their enemies. There would be no negotiations with Hitler and Mussolini. Roosevelt's supporters hailed the policy as a clear statement of goals, a promise to the world that the scourge of fascism would be completely banished. Stalin, who did not attend, criticized the policy, predicting that it would only increase enemy determination to fight to the end. Western critics charged that the demand for total capitulation would prolong the war and swell the casualty list.

Allied aerial bombing was increasing the pressure on Germany. Some U.S. leaders believed that the B-17 Flying Fortress, "the mightiest bomber ever built," could win the war from the air without any western troops having to fight their way into Europe. The U.S. Army Air Corps (predecessor of the Air Force) described the B-17 as a "humane" weapon, capable of hitting specific military targets while sparing civilians. That claim was nonsense. Especially when weather or darkness required bombardiers to sight with radar, they could not distinguish between industrial, military, and civilian targets, and even with the best available targeting, bombs might land anywhere within a nearly two-mile radius. More often, bomber crews, who suffered awful losses from ground-based antiaircraft fire, just wanted to dump their bombs fast and get away safely. American pilots preferred to bomb during daylight, while the British bombed at night, when they could see nothing at all of their blacked-out targets. Bombing missions over the Rhineland and the Ruhr did take out many German factories, while also costing tens of thousands of civilian lives, but the Germans successfully relocated many industrial plants to the countryside.

Determined to break German resistance, the Royal Air Force redirected its main attack away from military targets to cities, fuel dumps, and transportation lines. Indiscriminate bombing practically leveled the great city of Hamburg, killing between 60,000 and 100,000 people and destroying 300,000 buildings. Sixty other cities were hit hard, leaving 20 percent of Germany's total residential area in ruins. Americans joined in the very worst air raid of the war—650,000 incendiary bombs dropped on Dresden in 1945 destroying 8 square miles and killing perhaps 135,000 civilians (no one knows for sure, for the city sheltered uncounted refugees). Dresden, famous for its architecture and art galleries, had no military value. This was terror bombing. Hitler had started it, but the Allies more than repaid in kind.

Though the air war disappointed those who saw in it the means of a bloodless—to the attackers—victory, the Allied strategic air offensive did weaken the German economy and did terrorize (but also enrage) German civilians. Moreover, in trying to defend German cities and factories, the Luftwaffe sacrificed most of its remaining fighter planes and aircraft fuel. When the Allies finally invaded Western Europe in the summer of 1944, they would enjoy total air superiority.

THE ALLIED INVASION OF EUROPE

In the summer of 1943, the Allies continued their Mediterranean offensive by attacking southern Italy. On July 10, British and American troops stormed Sicily and by mid-August conquered the island. King Vittorio Emmanuel fired Mussolini, calling him "the most despised man in Italy." After Allied troops landed near Naples, Italy surrendered to the Western Allies on September 8. But Hitler sent new divisions into northern and central Italy, stalling the Allied campaign. Almost until the end of the European war, a large Allied army was still bogged down on Italy's rugged terrain, battling a much smaller German force.

All across occupied Europe, resistance to the Nazis spread. Jews walled off in the Nazi-built Warsaw ghetto, realizing that they were marked for extermination, revolted in the summer of 1943 and fought to the death.

As part of the air war on Germany, Allied bombers launched a devastating attack on Dresden, a major economic center, in February 1945. Of the civilians who died, most from burns or smoke inhalation during the firestorm, a large number were women and children, refugees from the eastern front. The city was left in ruins.

Scattered revolts followed in the Nazi labor camps, where military prisoners of war and civilians were being worked on starvation rations. Underground fighters, known as partisans, resisted the Nazis from Norway to Greece and from Poland to France. Untrained and lightly armed, men, women, and children risked their lives to distribute antifascist propaganda, committed sabotage, rescued downed Allied bomber crews, and killed Nazi collaborators. They smuggled food and weapons to clandestine resistance groups and prepared the way for the offensive that, in shortwave radio broadcasts, the Allies promised.

Allied preparations for that offensive were thorough and time-consuming. As a huge American army gathered and trained in Britain, Churchill's objections to invading France gradually wore down, while Stalin ceaselessly demanded a second front. (To him, the stalled invasion of Italy was no substitute.) By early 1944, Anglo-American plans were being readied for Operation Overlord, a campaign to retake the Continent with a decisive counterattack through France. General Dwight D. Eisenhower, who was put in command, displayed great skill not only in strategizing but also in dealing with contentious British, Americans, and the prickly Free French leader, General Charles de Gaulle.

D-Day—the start of the Allied invasion—finally came on June 6, 1944. Much depended on surprise and even the right mix of tides, moonlight, and clear weather. After receiving a forecast of a short break in storms that otherwise might have doomed the operation, "Ike" made the coura-

geous decision: "Go." Under heavy German machine-gun and mortar fire, wave after wave of American, British, Canadian, and Free French troops hit the Normandy beaches, the tides swelling with the dead and the wounded. Some 2,500 men died in the initial assault, many before they could fire a shot. Although the Germans responded slowly—they expected the invasion near Calais and at first thought Normandy a feint—at Omaha Beach they had prepared their defense almost perfectly, and the Americans who landed there had a particularly difficult time gaining a toehold. Within days, though, more than 175,000 Allied troops and 20,000 vehicles were battling the Germans—the largest landing operation in history. Over the next six weeks, nearly 1 million more Allied soldiers came ashore. But not until mid-July did this invasion army finally break out of Normandy and drive into the French interior.

All eyes now turned to Paris. Allied bombers pounded roads, bridges, rail lines, and factories that were producing German munitions all around the French capital. As demoralized German soldiers retreated, hoping only to survive, the French Resistance unfurled the French flag at impromptu demonstrations on Bastille Day, July 14. On August 10, railway workers staged one of the first successful strikes against Nazi occupiers, and three days later the Paris police defected to the Resistance, which distributed leaflets proclaiming that "the hour of liberation has come." With Free French and Allied troops, de Gaulle entered Paris on August 25 and announced a reconstituted French Republic. Belgium also fell swiftly to the liberators. But Allied troops had only reached a resting place between bloody battles, their supply lines stretched thin and German resistance stiffening.

THE HIGH COST OF EUROPEAN VICTORY

By September 1944 Allied commanders were searching for a way to end the war quickly. Missing a spectacular chance to move through largely undefended territory and on to Berlin, they turned north instead, intending to strike through the Netherlands into Germany's industrial heartland. Faulty intelligence reports overlooked a well-armed German division at the Dutch town of Arnhem, waiting to cut Allied paratroops to pieces. The Germans captured 6,000 Americans.

That winter, making a final, desperate effort to break the Allied momentum, Hitler sent his last reserves, a quarter-million men, against American lines in Belgium's dense Ardennes forest. In this so-called Battle of the Bulge, the Germans surprised the

D-Day landing, June 6, 1944, marked the greatest amphibious maneuver in military history. Troop ships ferried Allied soldiers from England to Normandy beaches. Within a month, nearly 1 million men had assembled in France, ready to retake western and central Europe from German forces.

Americans, driving them fifty miles back before literally running out of gas. This last effort—the bloodiest single campaign Americans had fought since Gettysburg—exhausted the German capacity for counterattack. After Christmas Day 1944, the Germans had to retreat into their own territory.

The end approached. In March 1945, discovery of a single intact bridge across the Rhine allowed the Allies to roll into the heart of Germany, taking the heavily industrialized Ruhr Valley.

By now, Soviet offenses were crushing the German army in the east. The Red Army had reached Warsaw in the midsummer of 1944 but then stood by while the anti-Russian Polish resistance rose up—only to be destroyed (along with most of the city) by the Nazis. While that tragedy unfolded, the Soviets occupied the Balkans and battled the Germans in Hungary. Only in January 1945 did the Red Army sweep across Poland and by April besiege Berlin, where Hitler had holed up.

The defense of Germany, now hopeless, had fallen into the hands of teenagers, terrified elderly men, and a few desperate Nazis.

THE WAR IN ASIA AND THE PACIFIC

Six months after Pearl Harbor, the United States began regaining naval superiority in the central Pacific. The Americans had been supremely lucky that their aircraft carriers were out at sea during the Pearl Harbor attack; that luck was spectacularly demonstrated in the great naval battle of the Coral Sea on May 7–8, 1942, in which carrier-based American aircraft blocked a Japanese thrust at Australia. A month later, on June 4, the Japanese fleet converged on Midway Island, an outpost vital to American communications and to the defense of Hawai'i. And there the Americans had another lucky break, for intelligence officers had broken the Japanese codes and thus knew when and where the attack would fall. Still separated by hundreds of miles of open sea, the Japanese and American carrier fleets clashed at long distance. Descending from the clouds, American warplanes sank four Japanese carriers and destroyed hundreds of planes, ending Japan's offensive threat to Hawai'i and the West Coast. These two battles signaled an historic shift in naval warfare: now aircraft carriers, not huge battleships, would rule the waves.

Even so, Japan controlled a vast arc of the western Pacific. That perimeter stretched from the outermost Aleutians (off Alaska) to northern New Guinea and the Solomon Islands (off Australia). Japan also dominated all of coastal China and the European colonies of Southeast Asia: Indochina, Malaya, present-day Indonesia, and Burma (see Map 25.2). In much of East Asia (except China), nationalistic and anticolonial sentiment played into Japanese hands at first. With only 200,000 troops,

Japan easily overran Southeast Asia because so few people in the British, French, and Dutch colonies would fight for their imperial masters. Japan installed puppet governments in Burma and the Philippines, and independent Thailand became a Japanese ally. But the new Japanese empire proved terrifyingly cruel. Local nationalists from Indochina to the Philippines turned against the Japanese, forming guerrilla bands that harassed the invaders. In China, Japan's huge land army bogged down fighting both the Nationalist forces of Chiang Kai-shek and the Communist People's Liberation Army led by Mao Zedong.

Thus, in mid-1942 the war for the Pacific was still only beginning. Pulling back their offensive operations, the Japanese concentrated their remaining forces. Their commanders calculated that bitter fighting, with high casualties on both sides, would wear down the American military and public. The U.S. command, divided between MacArthur in the southwest Pacific and Admiral Chester Nimitz in the central Pacific, developed a strategy to strangle the Japanese import-dependent economy and to "island-hop" from one strategic outpost to another, closing in on the home islands.

In the Solomons and New Guinea, American and Australian ground troops began the counterattack. On Guadalcanal in the Solomons, American Marines struck at one Japanese stronghold, and during a six-month struggle endured tropical diseases, dangerous parasites, food and ammunition shortages, and very high casualty rates against Japanese defenders who fought to the death and were reduced to eating roots and berries. Amid these horrors, the vaunted American logistical system was not always effective: a week before Christmas, a shipment of winter coats arrived! Finally, with strong supply lines secured by a string of costly naval battles, in February 1943 the Americans finally prevailed, proving that they could defeat Japanese forces in brutal jungle combat.

For the next two years, the U.S. Navy and Marine Corps opened a path to Japan, capturing a series of important Pacific atolls but bypassing others, helplessly stranding well-armed Japanese defenders. Tarawa in the Gilbert Islands was first of these assaults in November 1943; it cost more than 1,000 Marine lives. In June 1944, simultaneously with the Normandy landings, the U.S. Navy inflicted crippling losses on the Japanese fleet in the Battle of the Philippine Sea. Then in August 1944 the Americans took Guam, Saipan, and Tinian in the Mariana Islands, for the first time bringing the Japanese home islands within bomber range. And in October of that year, MacArthur led an American force of 250,000 to retake the Philippines. Trying to hold the islands, practically all that remained of the Japanese navy threw itself at the Americans in the Battle of Leyte Gulf, the largest naval battle in history. The Japanese lost eighteen capital ships, leaving the United States in control of the Pacific. While

MAP EXPLORATION

To explore an interactive version of this map, go to **www.prenhall.com/faragher6/map25.2**

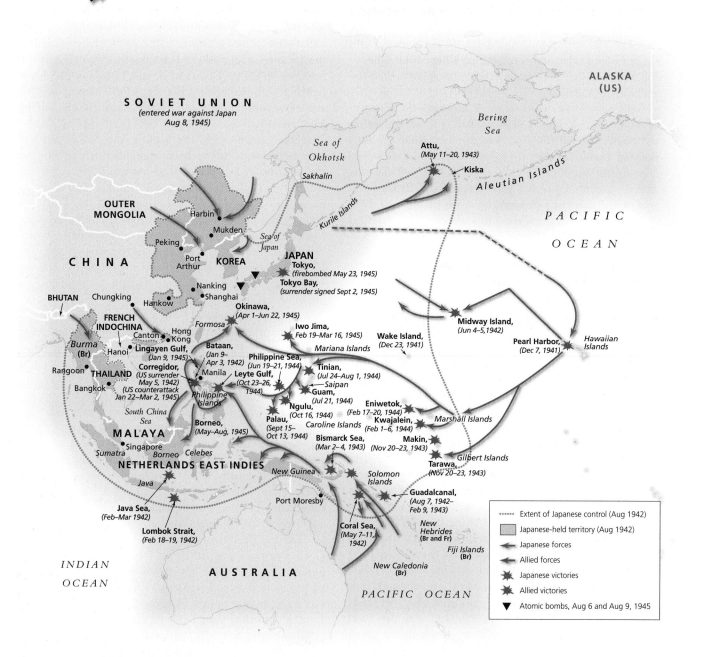

MAP 25.2 War in the Pacific Across an ocean battlefield utterly unlike the European Theater, Allies battled Japanese troops near their homeland.

MacArthur mopped up operations in the Philippines—at a cost of 100,000 Filipino lives and leaving Manila devastated—the small but strategically important island of Iwo Jima, south of Japan, fell. Here too, the American death toll was high; casualties were estimated at nearly 27,000.

Even bloodier was the struggle for Okinawa, an island 350 miles southwest of the Japanese home islands and the site of vital airbases. The invasion—the largest American amphibious operation in the Pacific war—began on Easter Sunday, April 1, 1945. Waves of Japanese *kamikaze* ("divine wind") pilots, flying suicide missions with a 500-pound bomb and only enough fuel for a one-way flight, met the Marines on the beaches. The U.S. troops who survived this onslaught used flame-throwers, each with 300 gallons of napalm, to incinerate dug-in Japanese defenders. On Okinawa, more Americans died or were wounded than at Normandy. But at the end of June, when the ghastly struggle ended, 140,000 Japanese were dead, including 42,000 civilians.

The war was now over in Europe, and the Allies could concentrate on Japan alone. Tokyo and other Japanese cities were targeted by B-17s and new B-29s flying from Guam with devastating results. Massive fire bombings burned thousands of civilians alive in their mostly wooden or bamboo houses, and hundreds of thousands were left homeless. Meanwhile U.S. submarines cut the home islands off from supplies on the East Asian mainland.

Japan could not hold out forever. Without a navy or air force, critically important oil, tin, rubber, and grain could not be transported to maintain its soldiers or feed its people. Great Britain and particularly the United States, however, pressed for a quick and unconditional surrender. They had special reasons to hurry. Earlier they had sought a commitment from the Soviet Union to invade Japan, but now they looked beyond the war, determined to prevent the Red Army from taking any Japanese-held territories. These calculations, as well as chilling forecasts of the bloody cost of invading and subjugating the home islands, set the stage for unleashing the top-secret weapon that American scientists had been building: the atomic bomb (see Communities in Conflict).

THE LAST STAGES OF WAR

From the attack on Pearl Harbor until mid-1943, Roosevelt and his advisers had focused on military strategy rather than on postwar plans. But once the defeat of Nazi Germany appeared in sight, high government officials began to consider long-range objectives. Roosevelt wanted both to crush the Axis powers and to establish a system of collective security to prevent another world war. He knew he could not succeed without the cooperation of the other key leaders, Stalin and Churchill.

In 1944 and early 1945, these "Big Three" met several times to hammer out the shape of the postwar world. Although none of these nations expected to reach a final agreement, neither did they anticipate how quickly they would confront momentous global events, including the obvious fact that the only thing holding the "Grand Alliance" together was the mission of destroying the Axis.

THE HOLOCAUST

Another fact also became clear, at least to the American public, as the European war entered its final stages: the full horror of Nazi atrocities. As part of a comprehensive plan for achieving Aryan superiority and the "final solution of the Jewish question," Hitler had ordered the extermination of "racial enemies" and others deemed undesirable, including mentally retarded and crippled German children and adults. The toll included some 6 million Jews, 250,000 Romany (Gypsies), 60,000 homosexuals, members of other "inferior races" (such as Slavs), and indeed anyone else deemed an enemy of the German Reich and its "master race." Beginning in 1933, but accelerating from 1941 onward, the Nazis murdered millions of people in Germany and all the European nations they conquered. Gruesome "medical experiments" were also performed on Jews and Soviet prisoners of war (POWs).

These policies had begun at the outset of the Hitler regime in 1933, and at the beginning of 1942 the Nazis initiated mass murder in death camps like Auschwitz in Poland. Very soon, word was leaking out of occupied Europe of what the Nazis were doing. But throughout almost the entire war, the U.S. government released little information about what came to be known as the Holocaust. Although liberal magazines such as *The Nation* and small committees of intellectuals tried to call attention to what was happening in the Nazi camps, major news media like the *New York Times* and *Time* magazine treated reports of genocide as minor news items. As late as 1943, only 43 percent of Americans polled believed that Hitler was systematically murdering European Jews.

Leaders of the American Jewish community, however, were better informed than the general population, and since the mid-1930s they had been petitioning the government to suspend immigration quotas that barred significant numbers of German Jews from taking refuge in the United States. Backed by public opinion (fixated on foreigners threatening American jobs), Roosevelt and

On Deploying the Atomic Bomb

Although the scientists employed in the Manhattan Project embraced their assignment with fervor, they nevertheless thought deep and hard about the moral ramifications of their work. After the first test of the atomic bomb revealed its horrifying power, they began to discuss among themselves the necessary criteria for using a weapon of such deadly force. By May 1945, under Robert Oppenheimer's leadership, a "target committee" had outlined a list of conditions necessary to deploy the "gadget" (a code name for the atomic bomb) against Japan. A month later, small groups of scientists working on the Manhattan Project at the University of Chicago began to appeal to government officials, advising supreme caution in considering the use of the atomic bomb. They acknowledged "the military advantages and the saving of American lives" that deployment against Japan might bring, but warned that such gain "may be outweighed by the ensuing loss of confidence and wave of horror and repulsion, sweeping over the rest of the world, and perhaps dividing even the public opinion at home." They also recommended that, rather than immediately deploying the bomb, the United States invite nations to witness a demonstration on a barren island or desert. Oppenheimer and Fermi, however, both disagreed and held firm to the letter of their assignment: to produce the bomb for military use. In secret correspondence, which is now declassified, two of the top scientists of the Manhattan Project map the opposing positions.

Leo Szilard (1898–1964), a Hungarian-born scientist, is said to have conceived of the idea of nuclear chain reaction, the process that in uranium provides the power for nuclear energy. In a letter to President Truman in July 1945, he warns against using the atomic bomb against Japan. The physicist Edward Teller (1908–2003), also Hungarian-born, worked closely with Fermi and Oppenheimer at Los Alamos. After the war, he promoted the development of a "super bomb," the hydrogen bomb, and ultimately convinced President Truman to fund the project as a bulwark against the Soviet Union. In his letter, he replies to Szilard's request.

What arguments did the scientists pose for and against the deployment of the atomic bomb?

July 3, 1945: A Petition to the President of the United States

Discoveries of which the people of the United States are not aware may affect the welfare of this nation in the near future. The liberation of atomic power which has been achieved places atomic bombs in the hands of the Army. It places in your hands, as Commander-in-Chief, the fateful decision whether or not to sanction the use of such bombs in the present phase of the war against Japan.

We, the undersigned scientists, have been working in the field of atomic power for a number of years. Until recently we have had to reckon with the possibility that the United States might be attacked by atomic bombs during this war and that her only defense might lie in a counterattack by the same means. Today with this danger averted we feel impelled to say what follows:

The war has to be brought speedily to a successful conclusion and the destruction of Japanese cities by means of atomic bombs may very well be an effective method of warfare. We feel, however, that such an attack on Japan could not be justified in the present circumstances. We believe that the United States ought not to resort to the use of atomic bombs in the present phase of the war, at least not unless the terms which will be imposed upon Japan after the war are publicly announced and subsequently Japan is given an opportunity to surrender.

If such public announcement gave assurance to the Japanese that they could look forward to a life devoted to peaceful pursuits in their homeland and if Japan still refused to surrender, our nation would then be faced with a situation which might require a re-examination of her position with respect to the use of atomic bombs in the war.

Atomic bombs are primarily a means for the ruthless annihilation of cities. Once they were introduced as an instrument of war it would be difficult to resist for long the temptation of putting them to such use.

The last few years show a marked tendency toward increasing ruthlessness. At present our Air Forces, striking at the Japanese cities, are using the same methods of warfare which were condemned by American public opinion only a few years ago when applied by the Germans to the cities of England. Our use of atomic bombs in this war would carry the world a long way further on this path of ruthlessness.

Atomic power will provide the nations with new means of destruction. The atomic bombs at our disposal represent only the first step in this direction and there is almost no limit to the destructive power which will become available in the

> "Atomic bombs are primarily a means for the ruthless annihilation of cities."

> "The more decisive a weapon is the more surely it will be used. . . ."

course of this development. Thus a nation which sets the precedent of using these newly liberated forces of nature for purposes of destruction may have to bear the responsibility of opening the door to an era of devastation on an unimaginable scale.

In view of the foregoing, we, the undersigned, respectfully petition that you exercise your power as Commander-in-Chief to rule that the United States shall not, in the present phase of the war, resort to the use of atomic bombs.

Leo Szilard and 58 co-signers

SOURCE: Szilard to Frank Oppenheimer, July 23, 1945, Robert Oppenheimer Papers, Library of Congress, Washington, D.C.

Teller's Response to Szilard

Dear Szilard:

Since our discussion I have spent some time thinking about your objections to an immediate military use of the weapon we may produce. I decided to do nothing; I should like to tell you my reasons.

First of all let me say that I have no hope of clearing my conscience. The things we are working on are so terrible that no amount of protesting or fiddling with politics will save our souls.

This much is true: I have not worked on the project for a very selfish reason and I have gotten mucsh (sic) more trouble than pleasure out of it. I worked because the problems interested me and I should have felt it a great restraint not to go ahead. I can not claim that I simply worked to do my duty. A sense of duty could keep me out of such work. It could not get me into the present kind of activity against my inclinations. If you should succeed in convincing me that your moral objections are valid, I should quit working. I hardly think that I should start protesting.

But I am not really convinced of your objections. I do not feel that there is any chance to outlaw any one weapon. If we have a slim chance of survival, it lies in the possibility to get rid of wars. The more decisive a weapon is the more surely it will be used in any real conflict and no agreements will help.

Our only hope is in getting the facts of our results before the people. This might help to convince everybody that the next war would be fatal. For this purpose actual combat use might even be the best thing.

And this brings me to the main point. The accident that we worked out this dreadful thing should not give us the responsibility of having a voice in how it is to be used. This responsibility must in the end be shifted to the people as a whole and that can be done only by making the facts known. This is the only cause for which I feel entitled in doing something: the necessity of lifting the secrecy at least as far as the broad issues of our work are concerned. My understanding is that this will be done as soon as the military situation permits it.

All this may seem to you quite wrong. I should be glad if you showed this letter to Eugene and to Franck who seem to agree with you rather than with me. I should like to have the advice of all of you whether you think it is a crime to continue to work. But I feel that I should do the wrong thing if I tried to say how to tie the little toe of the ghost to the bottle from which we just helped it to escape.

With best regards.

Yours,

E. Teller

SOURCE: Atomicarchive.com

Belsen Camp: The Compound for Women, painted by American artist Leslie Cole, depicts Belsen as the Allied troops found it when they invaded Germany in 1945.

SOURCE: Leslie Cole, "Belsen Camp: The Compound for Women". Imperial War Museum, London.

THE YALTA CONFERENCE

Roosevelt was elected to a fourth term in November 1944, defeating the moderately liberal Republican governor of New York, Thomas E. Dewey. Many loyal Democrats looked forward to a revival of the New Deal after the war was won. Elected with FDR was a new vice president, a middle-of-the-road Missouri senator named Harry S Truman, who replaced ultraliberal Henry Wallace. Unknown to the public, however, Roosevelt was now exhausted and gravely ill—though, as was his habit, he kept his vice president totally uninformed of his plans and of the most important wartime secrets.

In early 1945, with the end of the war in sight, Allied leaders began to reassess their goals. The Atlantic Charter of 1941 had stated noble objectives for the world after the defeat of fascism: national self-determination, no territorial aggrandizement, equal access of all peoples to raw materials and collaboration for the improvement of economic opportunities, freedom of the seas, disarmament, and "freedom from fear and want." Now, four years later, Roosevelt realized that neither Great Britain nor the Soviet Union intended to abide by any code of conduct that compromised their national security or conflicted with their economic interests. Stalin and Churchill soon reached a new agreement, one projecting their respective spheres of influence in Eastern Europe.

In early February 1945, Roosevelt held still another wartime meeting with Churchill and Stalin, this time at Yalta, a Crimean resort on the Black Sea. Seeking his partners' cooperation, the president recognized that prospects for postwar peace also depended on compromise. Although diplomats avoided the touchy phrase "spheres of influence," it was clear that this opportunistic principle guided all negotiations. Neither the United States nor Great Britain raised serious objections to Stalin's demand to retain the Baltic states and eastern Poland—booty from the time of the Nazi–Soviet pact—and to create an East European "buffer zone" protecting Russia against future German aggression. In return, Churchill insisted on restoring the British Empire in Asia, and the United States hoped to retain captured Pacific islands from which Japanese military resurgence could be checked. Roosevelt hoped to ease the harshness of these imperialistic goals by

Congress refused. Even after the United States entered the war, the president maintained that the liberation of European Jews and other oppressed peoples depended on a speedy and total Allied victory. Not until January 1944 did Roosevelt agree to change government policy. At that time, Secretary of the Treasury Henry Morgenthau, himself Jewish, reported to the president on "one of the greatest crimes in history, the slaughter of the Jewish people in Europe," and suggested that anti-Semitism in the State Department had stalled the development of an aggressive plan of action. Within a week, in part to avoid scandal, Roosevelt issued an executive order creating the War Refugee Board. However, when American Jews pleaded for bombing rail lines leading to the notorious death camp at Auschwitz, in occupied Poland, both Roosevelt and the War Department refused. Attempts to rescue civilians—such was the government's unshaken position—would divert resources from military operations.

The extent of Nazi depravity was finally revealed to Americans when Allied troops invaded Germany and began liberating the Nazi camps. Touring Ohrdruf concentration camp in April 1945, Eisenhower found barracks crowded with corpses and crematories still reeking of burned flesh. "I want every American unit not actually in the front lines to see this place," Eisenhower ordered. "We are told that the American soldier does not know what he is fighting for. Now, at least, he will know what he is fighting against."

creating a global peacekeeping organization, the United Nations, and by using promises of postwar American economic aid to persuade Stalin to behave with restraint in countries, like Poland, that the Red Army was liberating and occupying.

The biggest and most controversial item on the agenda at Yalta was the Soviet entry into the Pacific war, which Roosevelt believed necessary for a timely Allied victory. After driving a hard bargain involving Soviet rights to territory in China, Stalin agreed to declare war against Japan within three months of Germany's surrender. Roosevelt told Congress that the Yalta meeting had been a "great success," proof that the wartime alliance remained intact. Privately, however, the president concluded that the outcome of the conference revealed that the Atlantic Charter had been nothing more than "a beautiful idea."

The death of Franklin Roosevelt of a massive stroke on April 12, 1945, cast a dark shadow over all hopes for long-term, peaceful solutions to global problems. The president did not live to learn of Hitler's suicide in his Berlin bunker on April 30, 1945, or the unconditional surrender of Germany one week later, on May 8. Millions of Americans and people in other democratic nations deeply mourned the passing of the great pragmatic idealist, just as new and still greater challenges were looming.

THE ATOMIC BOMB

Roosevelt's death made Allied cooperation even more difficult. Harry Truman, an honest and plainspoken product of Kansas City machine politics, made a national reputation as a U.S. senator investigating wartime corruption, but he lacked foreign-policy experience and had none of FDR's finesse and prestige.

The wartime Big Three—now Stalin, Truman, and Churchill (the latter soon replaced as prime minister by Clement Atlee when the British voted in a Labour Party government)—held their final conference at Potsdam, just outside Berlin, from July 17 to August 2, 1945. The meeting lacked the spirited give-and-take of the conferences in which Roosevelt and Churchill had participated. A huge agenda of thorny issues confronted the victorious leaders: the future of defeated and occupied Germany and other former Axis powers, the Soviet occupation of Eastern Europe, reparations and economic aid to rebuild a shattered Europe, and crucial details about organizing the new United Nations, on which the Americans set great store. The Big Three clashed sharply over most of these issues, but they held fast in demanding the unconditional surrender of reeling but still defiant Japan.

It was while wrangling with Stalin at Potsdam that Truman learned a closely guarded secret: that on July 16 the United States had successfully tested an atomic bomb in New Mexico. As a senator and as vice president, Truman had not been informed of the existence of the Manhattan Project; he first heard about it upon Roosevelt's death. Until the moment of the test, Truman had been pressing Stalin to make good his Yalta promise to enter the Pacific war three months after Germany's surrender—a deadline that would fall on August 8. The president was eager to get Soviet participation in what everyone said would be a horrendously bloody U.S. invasion of Japan, and indeed he did extract Stalin's promise to attack Japan on schedule. But then Secretary of War Stimson received a cable: "Babies satisfactorily born." Truman and his advisers concluded that Soviet assistance was no longer needed to end the war.

On August 3, 1945, Japan announced its refusal to surrender. Its military leaders still demanded a fight to the death, and Japanese civilian politicians wanted Allied guarantees that the emperor, considered sacred, would keep his throne. This response the Americans deemed unsatisfactory: they still demanded unconditional surrender, preferably before the Red Army moved against Japan. Three days later, the B-29 bomber nicknamed *Enola Gay* dropped the five-ton uranium bomb that destroyed the Japanese city of Hiroshima. Instantly, some 40,000 people died; in the following weeks, 100,000 more perished from radiation poisoning or burns. By 1950, the death toll reached 200,000.

"This is not war, this is not even murder; this is pure nihilism . . . a crime against God which strikes at the very basis of moral existence." So wrote the Japanese *Nippon Times*. In the United States, several leading religious publications echoed this view. The *Christian Century* judged the use of the bomb as a "moral earthquake" that by comparison made the long-denounced use of poison gas by Germany in World War I utterly insignificant. Albert Einstein, whose physics provided the foundation for the Manhattan Project (but in which he had taken no part), said that the atomic bomb had changed everything—except the nature of man.

Americans first heard of the atomic bomb on August 7, when the news reported the destruction and death it had brought to Hiroshima. But fears about the implications of the awesome new weapon were overwhelmed by an outpouring of relief: Japan surrendered—still not unconditionally—on August 14, several days after a second nuclear bomb destroyed Nagasaki, killing another 73,000. (On schedule between these cataclysmic events, the Soviet army invaded Japanese-occupied Manchuria.)

Allied insistence on unconditional surrender and the decision to atom-bomb Japan remain two of the most controversial political and moral questions about the conduct of World War II. Although Truman insisted in his memoirs (written years later) that he gave the order so as to save "a half a million American lives" in ground combat, no such official estimate exists. An intelligence document of April 30, 1946, stated that "the dropping of the bomb was the pretext seized upon by all [American] leaders as the reason for ending the war, but [even if the bomb had not been used] the Japanese would have capitulated upon the entry of Russia into the war." There is no question, however, that the use of nuclear weapons did strengthen U.S. policymakers' hand. It certainly did force caution upon Stalin, soon to emerge as America's primary adversary. Truman and his advisers knew that their nation's atomic monopoly would not last, but they hoped that in the meantime the United States could play the leading role in building the postwar world.

CHRONOLOGY

1931   September: Japan occupies Manchuria

1933   March: Adolf Hitler seizes power

March: Adolf Hitler seizes power

May: Japan quits League of Nations

1935   October: Italy invades Ethiopia

1935–1937 Neutrality Acts authorize the president to block the sale of munitions to belligerent nations

1936   July: Spanish Civil War begins

1937   August: Japan invades China

October: Franklin D. Roosevelt calls for international cooperation against aggression

1938   March: Germany annexes Austria

September: Munich Agreement lets Germany annex Sudetenland of Czechoslovakia

November: *Kristallnacht*, Nazis attack Jews and destroy Jewish property

1939   March: Germany annexes remainder of Czechoslovakia

August: Germany and the Soviet Union sign nonaggression pact

September: Germany invades Poland; World War II begins

November: Soviet Union invades Finland

1940   April–June: Germany's *bliztkrieg* sweeps over Western Europe

September: Germany, Italy, and Japan—the Axis powers—conclude a military alliance

First peacetime military draft in American history

November: Roosevelt defeats Wendall Willkie and is elected to an unprecedented third term

1941   March: Lend-Lease Act extends aid to Great Britain

May: German troops secure the Balkans

A. Philip Randolph plans March on Washington movement for July

June: Germany invades Soviet Union

Fair Employment Practices Committee formed

August: The United States and Great Britain agree to the Atlantic Charter

December: Japanese attack Pearl Harbor; United States enters the war

1942   January: War mobilization begins

February: Executive order mandates internment of Japanese Americans

May–June: Battles of Coral Sea and Midway give the United States naval superiority in the Pacific

August: Manhattan Project begins

November: United States stages amphibious landing in North Africa; Operation Torch begins

1943   January: Casablanca Conference announces unconditional surrender policy

February: Soviet victory over Germans at Stalingrad

April–May: Coal miners strike

May: German Afrika Korps troops surrender in Tunis

July: Allied invasion of Italy

Summer: Race riots break out in nearly fifty cities

1944   June–August: Operation Overlord and liberation of Paris

November: Roosevelt elected to fourth term, defeating Thomas E. Dewey

1945   February: Yalta Conference renews American-Soviet alliance

February–June: United States captures Iwo Jima and Okinawa in Pacific

April: Roosevelt dies in office; Harry Truman becomes president

May: Germany surrenders

July–August: Potsdam Conference

August: United States drops atomic bombs on Hiroshima and Nagasaki; Japan surrenders

CONCLUSION

The new tactics and weapons of World War II, such as massive air raids and the atomic bomb produced by the Los Alamos scientists, made warfare incomparably more deadly than before to both military and civilian populations. Between 40 and 50 million people died in World War II— four times the number in World War I—and half the casualties were women and children. More than 405,000 Americans died, and more than 670,000 were wounded. Although slight compared to the casualties suffered by other Allied nations—more than 20 million Soviets died during the war—the human cost of World War II for Americans was second only to that of the Civil War.

Coming at the end of two decades of resolutions to avoid military entanglements, the war pushed the nation's leaders to the center of global politics and into risky military and political alliances that would not outlive the war. The United States emerged the strongest nation in the world, but in a world where the prospects for lasting peace appeared increasingly remote. If World War II raised the nation's international commitments to a new height, its impact on ordinary Americans was not so easy to gauge. Many new communities formed as Americans migrated in mass numbers to new regions that were booming as a result of the wartime economy. Enjoying a rare moment of full employment, many workers new to well-paying industrial jobs anticipated further advances against discrimination. Exuberant at the Allies' victory over fascism and the return of the troops, the majority were optimistic as they looked ahead.

— REVIEW QUESTIONS —

1. How did President Franklin D. Roosevelt ready the nation for war?

2. What role did the federal government, business, and labor play in gearing up the economy for wartime production?

3. How did the war affect the lives of American women?

4. Discuss the causes and consequences of the Japanese American internment program.

5. Describe the role of popular culture in promoting the war effort at home.

6. How did military service affect the lives of those who served in World War II?

7. What were the main points of Allied military strategy in both Europe and Asia?

8. How successful were diplomatic efforts in ending the war and in establishing the terms of peace?

— RECOMMENDED READING —

Philip D. Beidler, *The Good War's Greatest Hits: World War II and American Remembering* (1998). Examines the popular culture produced about World War II, such as movies, photographs, cartoons, and books, to show how these sources created a lasting image of World War II as the "good war."

Kenneth S. Davis, *FDR, the War President, 1940–1943* (2000). The fifth volume in Davis's biography of Franklin D. Roosevelt, this massive text examines the president's frenetic efforts to create a coherent policy for American involvement in World War II.

Laura Hein and Mark Selden, eds., *Living With the Bomb: American and Japanese Cultural Conflict in the Nuclear Age* (1997). Essays dealing with the ambiguous legacy of the atomic bomb in both the United States and Japan. Reviews the "official story" of the bomb as the symbol of U.S. triumph in the "good war" in light of the growing number of dissenting voices and the impact of both views on memorials and museum exhibits.

John W. Jeffries, *Wartime America: The World War II Homefront* (1996). Provides a useful synthesis of scholarship and assesses the major differences in the interpretations of leading historians.

Linda Gordon and Gary Y. Okihiro, *Impounded: Dorothea Lange and the Censored Images of Japanese Internment* (2006). An anthology of 100 images from the relocation camps by the famed WPA photographer. Gordon and Okihiro provide essays discussing the production of the photographs and the impact of internment on the Japanese American community.

David M. Kennedy, *The American People in World War II* (1999). The second volume in Kennedy's Pulitzer Prize–winning *Freedom from Fear*, this book examines U.S. strategy to win the war from the perspective of the nation's leader as well as its citizens. The narrative interweaves overseas military events and home front experiences.

Gerald F. Linderman, *The World within War: America's Combat Experience in World War II* (1997). Emphasizes the less glamorous aspects of war, mainly the strains placed on the combat soldiers on the front lines. Linderman examines in especially close detail the grim experiences of army infantrymen and the marine riflemen who fought in the Pacific campaign and provides a nuanced analysis of their complex responses to the horror of war.

Katrina R. Mason, *Children of Los Alamos: An Oral History of the Town Where the Atomic Age Began* (1995). Recollections of those who spent their childhood in Los Alamos. They describe their affection for the geographical setting as well as sense of safety growing up in a community so well protected. They also comment on the ethnic diversity of those who populated the town and on the pride they took in their parents' contribution to building the bomb and ending the war.

Neil R. McMillen, ed., *Remaking Dixie: The Impact of World War II on the American South* (1997). A collection of essays on the impact of World War II on the South that pay special attention to the experiences of African Americans and women. Several authors question the degree to which southern society was transformed by wartime mobilization.

Eduardo Obregón Pagán, *Murder at the Sleepy Lagoon: Zoot Suits, Race, and Riot in Wartime L.A.* (2003). Examines the 1942 murder trial of seventeen young Chicanos for an alleged gang slaying and the zoot-suit riots that followed just several months later. Pagán provides a rich portrait of urban culture as well as race relations as the setting for the murder and court trial.

Emily Rosenberg, *A Date Which Will Live: Pearl Harbor in American Memory* (2004). Examines the circulation of memories of Pearl Habor in American life and the media's role in shaping them. Rosenberg includes the impact of the fiftieth anniversary commemorations of Pearl Harbor.

Mark A. Stoler, *Allies in War; Britain and America Against the Axis Powers, 1940–1945* (2005). A compact overview of wartime military strategy and diplomatic missions. Stoler provides a useful synthesis of new scholarship on the war.

Ronald Takaki, *Double Victory: A Multicultural History of America in World War II* (2000). A history of the war years told from the perspective of ethnically diverse Americans. Takaki examines the tension between the "good war" and the treatment of people of color and the response to the Holocaust.

Kenneth William Townsend, *World War II and the American Indian* (2000). A close study of the policies developed by the Bureau of Indian Affairs to bring American Indians into the war effort.

Emily Yellin, *Our Mothers' War: American Women at Home and at the Front During World War II* (2004). Makes a convincing case, based on a wealth of primary courses, that the war greatly changed the expectations for many American women.

For study resources for this chapter, go to **http://www.myhistorylab.com** and choose *Out of Many*. You will find a wealth of study and review material for this chapter, including pretests and posttests, customized study plan, key-term review flash cards, interactive map and document activities, and documents for analysis.

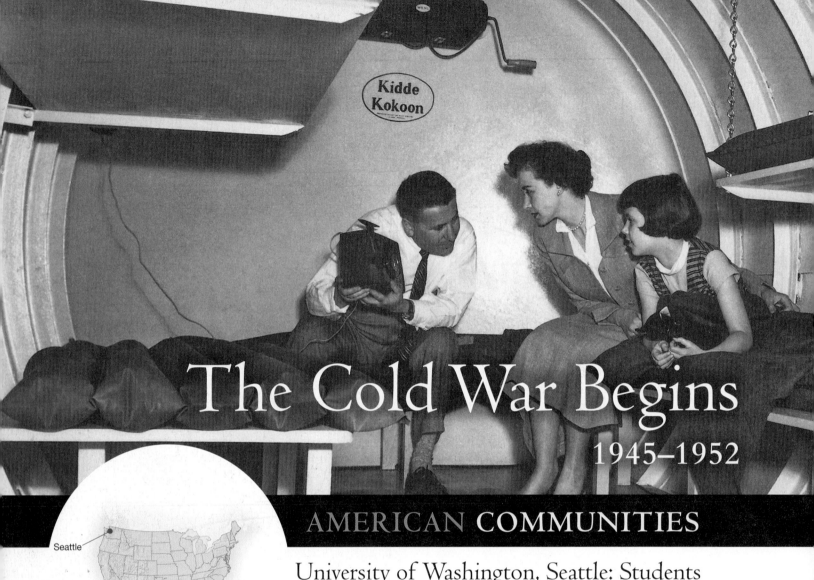

The Cold War Begins
1945–1952

Seattle

University of Washington, Seattle: Students and Faculty Face the Cold War

In May 1948, a philosophy professor at the University of Washington in Seattle answered a knock on his office door. Two state legislators, members of the state's Committee on Un-American Activities, entered. "Our information," they charged, "puts you in the center of a Communist conspiracy."

The accused professor, Melvin Rader, had never been a Communist. A self-described liberal, Rader drew fire because he had joined several organizations supported by Communists. During the 1930s, alarmed by the rise of fascism, Rader had become a prominent political activist in his community. At one point he served as president of the University of Washington Teacher's Union, which had formed during the upsurge of labor organizing during the New Deal. When invited to join the Communist Party, Rader bluntly refused. "The experience of teaching social philosophy had clarified my concepts of freedom and democracy," he later explained. "I was an American in search of a way—but it was not the Communist way."

Despite this disavowal, Rader was caught up in a second Red Scare—the first had been that of 1919–20 (see Chapter 22)—that curtailed free speech and political activity on campuses throughout the United States. At some universities, such as

Yale, the FBI set up camp with the consent of the college administration, spying on students and faculty, screening the credentials of job or scholarship applicants, and enticing students to report on friends or roommates. The University of Washington administration turned down the Physics Department's recommendation to hire J. Robert Oppenheimer, the famed atomic scientist and former director of Los Alamos Scientific Laboratory who had become a vocal opponent of the arms race.

Although one state legislator claimed that "not less than 150 members" of the University of Washington faculty were subversives, the state's Committee on Un-American Activities turned up just six Communist Party members. These six were hauled before the university's Faculty Committee on Tenure and Academic Freedom, charged with violations ranging from ➤

neglect of duty to failing to inform the university administration of their party membership. Three were ultimately dismissed, while the other three were placed on probation.

What had provoked this paranoia? Instead of peace in the wake of World War II, "Cold War"—tense, icy relations but no outright fighting—prevailed between the United States and the Soviet Union. Uneasy wartime allies, the two superpowers now viewed each other as archenemies, and nearly all other nations lined up with one or the other. Within the United States, the Cold War demanded pledges of absolute loyalty from citizens in every institution, from universities to unions and from the media to government itself.

Without the Cold War, this era might have marked one of the most fruitful in the history of higher education. The Servicemen's Readjustment Act, popularly known as the G.I. Bill of Rights, passed by Congress in 1944, offered stipends covering tuition and living expenses to veterans attending vocational schools or college. By the 1947–48 academic year, the federal government was subsidizing nearly half of all male college students. Between 1945 and 1950, 2.3 million students benefited from the G.I. Bill, at a cost of more than $10 billion.

At the University of Washington the student population in 1946 had grown by 50 percent over its prewar peak of 10,000, and veterans represented two-thirds of the student body. A quickly expanded faculty taught into the evening to use classroom space efficiently. Meanwhile, the state legislature pumped in funds for the construction of new buildings, including dormitories and prefabricated units for married students.

The Cold War squelched much of that. FBI director J. Edgar Hoover testified that the college campuses were centers of "red propaganda," full of teachers "tearing down respect for agencies of government, belittling tradition and moral custom and . . . creating doubts in the validity of the American way of life." Due to "Communistic" teachers and "Communist-line textbooks," a senator wailed, thousands of parents sent "their sons and daughters to college as good Americans," only to see them return home "four years later as wild-eyed radicals."

These extravagant charges were far from true. The overwhelming majority of college graduates in the late 1940s and 1950s were conservative and conformist. Nevertheless, several states, including Washington, enacted or revived loyalty-security programs, obligating all state employees to swear in writing their loyalty to the United States and to disclaim membership in any subversive organization. Nationwide, approximately 200 "radical" faculty members were dismissed outright and many others were denied tenure. Thousands of students simply left school, dropped out of organizations, or changed friends after "visits" from FBI agents or interviews with administrators. The main effect on campus was the restraint of free speech generally and fear of criticizing U.S. racial, military, or diplomatic policies in particular.

This tense, gloomy mood reversed the wave of optimism that had swept through America only a few years earlier. V-J Day had escalated into two days of wild celebrations, ticker-tape parades, spontaneous dancing, and kisses for returning G.I.s. Americans, living in the richest and most powerful nation in the world, finally seemed to have gained the peace they had fought for and sacrificed to win. But peace proved fragile and elusive.

GLOBAL INSECURITIES AT WAR'S END

The war that had engulfed the world from 1939 to 1945 created an international interdependence that no country could ignore. Legendary African American folksinger Leadbelly added fresh lyrics to an old spiritual: "We're in the same boat, brother. . . . And if you shake one end you're going to rock the other." Never before, not even at the end of World War I, had hopes been so strong for a genuine "community of nations." But, as a 1945 opinion poll indicated, most Americans believed that prospects for a durable peace rested to a large degree on one factor: Soviet–American harmony.

FINANCING THE FUTURE

In 1941 Henry Luce, the publisher of *Time, Life,* and *Fortune* magazines, forecast the dawn of "the American Century." During the darkest days of World War II, he wrote that Americans must "accept wholeheartedly our duty and our opportunity as the most powerful and vital nation in the world and in consequence to assert upon the world the full impact of our influence, for such means as

Focus Questions

1. What steps did the Allies take to promote growth in the postwar global economy?

2. How did the Truman Doctrine shape U.S. postwar foreign policy?

3. How did the "Fair Deal" differ from the "New Deal"?

4. What contributed to the rise of McCarthyism?

5. What were the most important trends in the 1950s?

6. What issues were at the center of the election of 1952?

1945–1952

we see fit." Immediately after the bombing of Hiroshima, President Truman pronounced the United States "the most powerful nation in the world—the most powerful nation, perhaps, in all history."

Americans had good reason to be confident about their prospects for setting the terms of reconstruction. Unlike Great Britain, France, and the Soviet Union, the United States had not only escaped the ravages of the war but had actually prospered. By June 1945, the capital assets of manufacturing had increased 65 percent over prewar levels to equal in value approximately half the entire world's goods and services.

Yet many Americans recognized that massive wartime government spending, not the New Deal, had ended the nightmare of the Great Depression. A stark question loomed: What would happen when wartime production slowed and millions of troops returned home to claim jobs?

"We need markets—big markets—in which to buy and sell," answered Assistant Secretary of State for Economic Affairs Will Clayton. Just to maintain the current level of growth, the United States needed to export—to a war-ravaged world—a staggering $14 billion in goods and services. During the war, many business leaders had looked to the Soviet Union as a future customer. With that prospect vanishing, with potential Eastern European markets threatened, and with the enormous European colonies closed to American enterprise, U.S. business and government leaders decided to integrate Western Europe, Latin America, and Asia into an international economy open to American trade and investment.

During the final stages of the war, President Roosevelt's advisers laid plans to establish U.S. primacy in the postwar global economy. In July 1944, representatives from forty-four Allied nations met at Bretton Woods, New Hampshire, and established the International Bank for Reconstruction and Development (the World Bank) and the International Monetary Fund (IMF). These institutions were expected to help rebuild war-torn Europe and Asia. By stabilizing exchange rates to permit the expansion of international trade, the IMF would deter currency conflicts and trade wars, two maladies of the 1930s that were blamed for the political instability and national rivalries leading to World War II. The United States was the principal supplier of funds for the IMF and the World Bank (more than $7 billion to each) and thus, by determining the allocation of loans, could unilaterally reshape the global economy.

The Soviet Union participated at Bretton Woods but refused to ratify the agreements. From Stalin's perspective, the United States intended to rebuild the world economy along capitalist lines; accepting World Bank and IMF aid would, he believed, make the Soviet Union an economic colony of the capitalist West. By spurning this aid, the Soviet Union economically isolated itself and its East European satellites.

THE DIVISION OF EUROPE

In the Atlantic Charter of 1941, the United States and Great Britain proclaimed the right of all nations to self-determination and renounced claims to new territories as spoils of war. Before the war ended, though, Churchill and Roosevelt violated the charter by dividing Europe into spheres of influence (see Chapter 25 and Map 26.1).

For Roosevelt, that strategy had seemed compatible with ensuring world peace. FDR balanced his internationalist idealism with a belief that the United States was entitled to extraordinary influence in Latin America and the Philippines and that other great powers might have similar privileges or responsibilities elsewhere. Roosevelt also recognized the diplomatic consequences of the brutal ground war that had been fought largely on Soviet territory: the Soviet Union's nonnegotiable demand for security along its western border. He hoped that American economic aid and the United Nations would serve, respectively, as carrot and stick in moderating Soviet domination in Eastern Europe.

From the earliest days of fighting Hitler, the Soviet Union was intent on reestablishing its 1941 borders. At the Potsdam Conference in July 1945, Stalin not only regained but also extended his territory, annexing eastern Poland with Western approval and the little Baltic nations without it. Soviet influence quickly became paramount in all East European countries that the Red Army had occupied. The question remained: Did Stalin aim to bring all of Europe into the Communist domain?

At the Potsdam Conference, when the wartime allies began to plan Germany's future, that question loomed over all deliberations. They decided to divide the conquered nation into four occupation zones, each temporarily ruled by one of the Allied nations. But they could not agree on long-term plans. Having borne the brunt of German aggression, France and the Soviet Union both opposed reunification. Stalin, moreover, demanded heavy reparations and a limit on postwar German reindustrialization. Although Roosevelt had appeared to agree with the Soviets, after FDR's death Truman shared Churchill's hope of rebuilding Germany into a powerful counterweight to the Soviet Union and a strong market for U.S. and British exports.

After the war, continuing disagreements about the future of Germany darkened hopes for Soviet-American cooperation. By July 1946, Americans had begun to withhold reparations due to the Soviets from their occupation zone and began to grant amnesty to some former Nazis. Then, in December, the Americans and British merged their zones and invited France and the Soviet Union to join. France agreed; Stalin, fearing a resurgence of a united Germany, refused.

The United States and the Soviet Union were now at loggerheads. Twice in the twentieth century, Germany had invaded Russia, and the Soviet Union interpreted any moves toward German reunification as menacing. For their part, American policymakers, assuming Stalin to be aggressively expansionist, envisioned a united Germany as a bulwark against further Soviet encroachments.

THE UNITED NATIONS AND HOPES FOR COLLECTIVE SECURITY

In 1944 at the Dumbarton Oaks Conference in Washington, and again in April 1945 at San Francisco, the Allies worked to shape the United Nations (UN) as a world organization that would arbitrate disputes among member nations and stop aggressors, by force if necessary.

The terms of membership, however, limited the UN's ability to mediate disputes. Although all fifty nations that signed the UN charter voted in the General Assembly, only five (the United States, Great Britain, the Soviet Union, France, and China) served permanently on the Security Council, which had the "primary responsibility for the maintenance of international peace and security," and each had absolute veto power over the Council's decisions.

The UN achieved its greatest success with its humanitarian programs. Its relief agency gave war-torn European and Asian countries billions of dollars for medical supplies, food, and clothing. The UN also dedicated itself to protecting human rights, and the high principles enunciated by its 1948 Universal Declaration of Human Rights owed much to lobbying by Eleanor Roosevelt, one of the first delegates from the United States.

On other issues, however, the UN operated strictly along lines dictated by the emerging Cold War. The Western nations allied with the United States held the balance of power and controlled the admission of new members. For example, when in 1949 the Communists won the Chinese civil war (discussed later), the Western powers would block the new People's Republic from claiming China's UN seat, held by the defeated Nationalists on Taiwan. East–West polarization made negotiated settlements virtually impossible.

THE POLICY OF CONTAINMENT

In March 1946, in a speech delivered in Fulton, Missouri, Winston Churchill spoke to the end of wartime cooperation. With President Truman at his side, the former British

MAP EXPLORATION

To explore an interactive version of this map, go to **www.prenhall.com/faragher6/map26.1**

MAP 26.1 Divided Europe During the Cold War, Europe was divided into opposing military alliances, the North American Treaty Organization (NATO) and the Warsaw Pact (Communist bloc).

Appointed to the UN delegation by President Harry Truman in 1946, Eleanor Roosevelt (1884–1962) pressured the organization to adopt the Declaration of Human Rights in 1948. In this photograph, taken in 1946, the former First Lady is exchanging ideas with Warren Austin, also a delegate to the United Nations.

dealing with the Soviet Union, sent an 8,000-word "long telegram" from Moscow to the State Department, insisting that Soviet fanaticism made cooperation impossible. The Soviet Union intended to extend its realm not by military means alone, he explained, but by "subversion" within "free" nations. Tough-minded realism, not idealistic hopes, should govern America's relations with the Soviet Union. In the long run, Kennan predicted, the Soviet system would collapse from within, but until that happened the West should pursue a policy of containment.

A perceived crisis in the Mediterranean marked the turning point. On February 21, 1947, amid a civil war in Greece, Great Britain informed the U.S. State Department that it could no longer afford to prop up the anti-Communist government there and announced its intention to withdraw all aid. Without U.S. intervention, Truman concluded, Greece, Turkey, and perhaps the entire oil-rich Middle East would fall under Soviet control. But, warned an influential Republican senator, Congress would not act unless president "scare[d] hell out of the American people."

On March 12, 1947, the president made his case in a speech to Congress. Never naming the Soviet Union, he appealed for all-out resistance to a "certain ideology" wherever it appeared in the world. The preservation of peace and the freedom of all Americans depended, the president insisted, on containing communism.

Congress approved $400 million to aid Greece and Turkey, which helped conservative forces in those countries crush left-wing rebels. By dramatically opposing communism, Truman somewhat buoyed his sagging popularity and helped generate popular support for an anti-communist crusade at home and abroad.

The significance of what became known as the Truman Doctrine far outlasted events in the Mediterranean: the United States had declared its right to intervene to save other nations from communism. In advocating containment of the Soviet Union, Kennan called for political and economic, not military, countermeasures. But Truman and his advisers were willing to consider military responses too. It was now the responsibility of the United States, the White House insisted, to safeguard what was coming to be called the Free World by any means necessary. They had fused anticommunism and internationalism into a strong foreign policy.

prime minister solemnly intoned: "An iron curtain has descended across the [European] continent." He called directly upon the United States, standing "at this time at the pinnacle of world power," to recognize its "awe-inspiring accountability to the future" and, in alliance with Great Britain, act vigorously to stop Soviet expansion.

Although Truman at first responded cautiously to Churchill's warning, his administration ultimately rose to the challenge. As a policy uniting military, economic, and diplomatic strategies, the "containment" of communism had a powerful ideological dimension—an "us versus them" division of the world into "freedom" and "slavery."

THE TRUMAN DOCTRINE

Many Americans believed that Franklin D. Roosevelt, had he lived, could have smoothed tensions between the Soviet Union and the United States. His successor sorely lacked FDR's diplomatic talent and experience. More comfortable with machine politicians than with polished New Dealers, Truman liked to talk tough and act defiantly. "I'm tired of babying the Soviets," he snapped.

Truman's distrust of the Soviet Union was not always consistent; during the first years after the war, at times he also attempted to be conciliatory. But among U.S. policymakers an anti-Soviet consensus was growing, fed by perceptions that Stalin was taking a hard line. In February 1946, George F. Kennan, the nation's premier diplomat in

OVERVIEW | Major Cold War Policies

Date	Policy	Provisions
1947	Truman Doctrine	Pledged the United States to the containment of communism in Europe and elsewhere. The doctrine was the foundation of Truman's foreign policy. It impelled the United States to support any nation whose stability was threatened by communism or the Soviet Union.
1947	Federal Employees Loyalty and Security Program	Established by Executive Order 9835, this barred Communists and fascists from federal employment and outlined procedures for investigating current and prospective federal employees.
1947	Marshall Plan	U.S. program to aid war-torn Europe, also known as the European Recovery Program. The Marshall Plan was a cornerstone in the U.S. use of economic policy to contain communism.
1947	National Security Act	Established Department of Defense (to coordinate the three armed services), the National Security Council (to advise the president on security issues), and the Central Intelligence Agency (to gather and evaluate intelligence data).
1948	Smith-Mundt Act	Launched an overseas campaign of anti-Communist propaganda.
1949	North Atlantic Treaty Organization (NATO)	A military alliance of twelve nations formed to deter possible aggression of the Soviet Union against Western Europe.
1950	NSC-68	National Security Council Paper calling for an expanded and aggressive U.S. defense policy, including greater military spending and higher taxes.
1950	Internal Security Act (also known as the McCarran Act and the Subversive Activities Control Act)	Legislation providing for the registration of all Communist and totalitarian groups and authorizing the arrest of suspect persons during a national emergency.
1951	Psychological Strategy Board created	Created to coordinate anti–Communist propaganda campaigns.
1952	Immigration and Nationality Act (also known as McCarran Walter Immigration Act)	Reaffirmed the national origins quota system but tightened immigration controls, barring homosexuals and people considered subversive from entering the United States.

THE MARSHALL PLAN

The Truman Doctrine complemented the European Recovery Program, commonly known as the Marshall Plan. Introduced in a commencement speech at Harvard University on June 5, 1947, by Secretary of State George C. Marshall, the plan sought to reduce "hunger, poverty, desperation, and chaos" and to restore "the confidence of the European people in the economic future of their own countries and of Europe as a whole." Indirectly, the Marshall Plan aimed to turn back left-wing Socialist and Communist bids for votes in Western Europe. Not least, of all the plan was also designed to boost the U.S. economy by securing a European market for American goods.

Considered by many historians the most successful postwar U.S. diplomatic venture, the Marshall Plan improved the climate for a viable capitalist economy in Western Europe and, in effect, brought aid recipients into bilateral agreements with the United States. In addition, the United States and seventeen Western European nations ratified the tariff-cutting General Agreement on Tariffs and Trade pact opening all to U.S. trade and investment. (Today, GATT has been renamed the World Trade Organization, or WTO.)

The Marshall Plan was costly to Americans. In its initial year it accounted for 12 percent of the federal budget. But much of that aid was American-made goods, produced by American workers. In the European nations covered by the plan, industrial production increased by 35 percent between 1947 and 1952, living standards improved, and American consumer goods and the American lifestyle became familiar.

As Truman later acknowledged, the Marshall Plan and the Truman Doctrine were "two halves of the same walnut." The Marshall Plan drove a deeper wedge between the United States and the Soviet Union. Although invited to participate, Stalin denounced the plan for what it was—an American scheme to rebuild Germany and incorporate it into an anti-Soviet bloc. Soon after the announcement of the Marshall Plan, the Soviet Union tightened its grip in Eastern Europe. In February 1948, as the U.S. Congress formally approved by the Marshall Plan, a Soviet-supported coup d'état established a communist government in Czechoslovakia.

THE BERLIN CRISIS AND THE FORMATION OF NATO

Within a year of the start of the Marshall Plan, the United States and Britain moved closer to the goal of economically integrating their occupation zones in Germany into the western sphere of influence. A common currency was established for these zones. Stalin reacted on June 24, 1948, by halting all traffic to the western occupation zones of Berlin, deep within Soviet-occupied eastern Germany (see Map 26.1).

The Berlin blockade created both a crisis and an opportunity for the Truman administration. With help from the Royal Air Force, the United States began an unprecedented around-the-clock airlift. "Operation Vittles" delivered nearly 2 million tons of supplies (including food and coal) to West Berliners. Stalin finally lifted the blockade in May 1949, clearing the way for the western powers to merge their occupation zones into a single nation, the Federal Republic of Germany. The Soviet Union countered by turning its zone into the communist-dominated German Democratic Republic.

The Berlin Crisis had made a U.S.-led military alliance against the Soviet Union attractive to noncommunist Western Europeans. In April 1949 ten European nations, Canada, and the United States formed the North Atlantic Treaty Organization (NATO), a mutual-defense pact in which "an armed attack against one or more of them . . . shall be considered an attack against them all." NATO complemented the Marshall Plan, strengthening economic ties among the member nations. It also deepened divisions between Eastern and Western Europe, making a permanent military mobilization on both sides almost inevitable.

Global implications flowed from the forging of the North Atlantic alliance. Several Western European allies ruled valuable but restive colonial empires. During the war, FDR had urged British and French leaders to start dismantling their empires, a suggestion welcomed neither by Churchill nor by France's Charles de Gaulle. In 1947, a financially strapped Britain granted independence to India and Pakistan, and under U.S. pressure the Dutch gave up Indonesia in 1949, but the French were determined to regain Indochina, lost to Japan before Pearl Harbor (see Chapter 25). Cold War anticommunism now trumped traditional American anticolonialism. Because the most important fighter against France's attempt to reconquer Indochina was Vietnamese communist Ho Chi Minh, Truman decided that France deserved American support and helped persuade France to join NATO. The first seeds had been planted of what would eventually become an American commitment to fight communism in Vietnam.

The Truman administration took Latin America for granted and was satisfied when the right-wing dictators ruling much of that region proclaimed themselves staunchly anticommunist. But Latin Americans complained that the United States' preoccupation with rebuilding Western Europe was depriving them of American investment capital desperately needed for economic development. The most positive gesture that the United States made toward Latin opinion was designating Puerto Rico a self-governing "commonwealth" in 1952. A rising Puerto Rican independence movement—extremist members of which attempted to assassinate Truman in 1950—prompted this move to make U.S. sovereignty over the island look less colonialist.

Located deep within communist East Germany, West Berlin was suddenly cut off from the West when Josef Stalin blockaded all surface traffic in an attempt to take over the war-torn city. Between June 1948 and May 1949, British and U.S. pilots made 272,000 flights, dropping food and fuel to civilians. The Berlin airlift successfully foiled the blockade, and the Soviet Union reopened access on May 12, 1949.

Beneath the surface, though, trouble was brewing for the United States throughout the hemisphere.

Congress in 1949 approved $1.3 billion in military aid to anticommunist allies in Europe and Asia, which involved building U.S. bases and deploying American troops abroad. Critics, such as isolationist Senator Robert A. Taft, warned that the United States could not afford to police all Europe—let alone the world—without sidetracking domestic priorities and undercutting the UN. But polls revealed strong support for Truman's tough anti-Soviet stance.

Between 1947 and 1949, the Truman administration had defined the policies that would shape the Cold War for decades to come. The Truman Doctrine explained the ideological basis of containment, not just in Europe but also around the globe; the Marshall Plan put into place its economic underpinnings in Western Europe; and NATO created the mechanisms for military defense. When NATO extended membership to a rearmed West Germany in May 1955, the Soviet Union responded by creating a counterpart, the Warsaw Pact, including East Germany.

ATOMIC DIPLOMACY

The containment policy depended on the ability of the United States to back its commitments through military force, and Truman invested his faith in the U.S. monopoly of atomic weapons. After 1945, the United States began to build an atomic stockpile and to conduct tests on remote Pacific islands. By 1950, as a scientific adviser subsequently observed, the United States "had a stockpile capable of somewhat more than reproducing World War II in a single day."

Despite warnings to the contrary by leading scientists, U.S. military analysts estimated it would take the Soviet Union three to ten years to produce an atomic bomb. In August 1949, the Soviet Union proved them wrong by testing its own atomic bomb. "There is only one thing worse than one nation having the atomic bomb," Nobel Prize–winning scientist Harold C. Urey said, "that's two nations having it."

The arms race that scientists had feared since 1945 was now under way. By the early 1950s, both the United

States and the Soviet Union were testing hydrogen bombs a thousand times more powerful than the weapons dropped on Hiroshima and Nagasaki in 1945. By the late 1950s, stockpiles of nuclear bombs were being supplemented by nuclear-armed missiles.

The United States and the Soviet Union were now firmly locked into the Cold War. The nuclear arms race risked global catastrophe, diverted economic resources, and fed public fears of impending doom. Despite the Allied victory in World War II, the world had again divided into hostile camps.

COLD WAR LIBERALISM

Truman's personality suited the confrontational mood of the early Cold War. He linked the Soviet threat abroad to the need for a strong presidency at home. Pressed to establish his own political identity, "Give 'em Hell" Harry cast himself as a fierce fighter against all challengers, yet loyal to Roosevelt's legacy.

Truman wanted to enlarge the New Deal but settled on a modest domestic agenda to promote social welfare

and an anti-isolationist, anti-Communist foreign policy. Fatefully, during his administration domestic and foreign policy became increasingly entangled. Out of that entanglement emerged a distinctive brand of liberalism—Cold War liberalism.

"TO ERR IS TRUMAN"

Within a year of assuming office, Harry Truman's poll ratings were among the lowest of any twentieth-century president. The responsibilities of reestablishing peacetime conditions seemed to overwhelm the new president. "To err is Truman," critics sneered.

The task of reconverting from a wartime to a peacetime economy was enormous. Truman faced millions of restless would-be consumers tired of rationing and eager to spend their wartime savings on shiny cars, new furniture, choice cuts of meat, and stylish clothing. The demand for consumer items rapidly outran supply, fueling inflation and a huge black market.

In 1945 and 1946, the country appeared ready to explode. While homemakers protested rising prices by boycotting neighborhood stores, industrial workers struck

Police and strikers confront each other in Los Angeles during one of many postwar strikes in 1946. Employers wanted to cut wages, and workers refused to give up the higher living standard achieved during the war.

in unprecedented numbers. Employers, fearing a rapid decline to depression-level profits, determined to slash wages; workers wanted a bigger cut of the huge war profits they had heard about. With nearly 4.6 million workers on picket lines, the new president was alarmed. In May 1946, Truman proposed to draft striking railroad workers. The usually conservative Senate killed this plan.

Congress defeated most of Truman's proposals to revive the New Deal. One week after Japan's surrender, the president introduced a twenty-one-point program that included greater unemployment compensation, higher minimum wages, and housing assistance. Later he added national health insurance and atomic-energy legislation. Congress rejected most of these bills and passed the Employment Act of 1946 but only with substantial modification. The act created the Council of Economic Advisers, a panel of three experts who would counsel the president and formulate policies for maintaining employment, production, and purchasing power. But no funding mechanisms guaranteed the full employment to which the government committed itself. "Had enough?" Republicans, anticipating victory in the midterm elections, asked voters that simple question. The voters had. They gave Republicans majorities in both houses of Congress and many state capitols. Symbolically repudiating FDR, Republican-dominated state legislatures ratified the Twenty-Second Amendment, limiting future presidents to two terms.

The Republicans, dominant in Congress for the first time since 1931, mounted a counterattack on the New Deal, beginning with organized labor. Unions had peaked in size and prestige; membership topped 15 million and encompassed nearly 40 percent of all wage earners. Claiming that "Big Labor" had gone too far, the Eightieth Congress aimed at abolishing many practices legalized by the Wagner Act of 1935 (see Chapter 24). The resultant Taft-Hartley Act of 1947, passed over Truman's veto, outlawed the closed shop, the secondary boycott, and the use of union dues for political activities; mandated an eighty-day cooling-off period in the case of strikes affecting "national safety or health"; and required all union officials to swear that they were not Communists—a Cold War mandate abridging First Amendment freedoms. Truman himself would later invoke the act against strikers.

THE 1948 ELECTION

Harry Truman had considered some of Roosevelt's advisers "crackpots and the lunatic fringe." By 1946 he forced out many of the remaining social planners who had staffed the Washington bureaus for more than a decade, including one of the best-loved New Dealers, Secretary of Interior Harold Ickes. Truman also fired Roosevelt's secretary of commerce and former vice president, Henry Wallace, for advocating a more conciliatory policy toward the Soviet Union.

Wallace, refusing to fade away, vowed to run against Truman for president. He pledged to expand New Deal programs by moving boldly to establish full employment, racial equality, and stronger unions. He also promised peace with the Soviet Union. As the 1948 election neared, Wallace appeared a viable candidate on the new Progressive Party ticket.

Truman shrewdly repositioned himself. He deflated Wallace by branding him a tool of the Communists (who in fact were part of a coalition of ex–New Dealers who encouraged Wallace to run). Truman also attacked the conservative congressional Republicans, proposing federal funds for education, housing, and medical insurance. Summoning Congress back for a special session after the summertime political conventions of 1948, he dared it to enact the Republican platform—and when it predictably failed—lambasted the "do-nothing Congress."

Wallace and the Republican nominee, New York governor Thomas E. Dewey, had taken strong leads on civil rights, but Truman outflanked them. In July 1948 he issued executive decrees desegregating the armed forces and banning discrimination in the federal civil service. In response, some 300 southern delegates bolted from the Democratic National Convention and named a States' Rights ("Dixiecrat") ticket, headed by the staunchly segregationist governor of South Carolina, J. Strom Thurmond. With the South looking as good as lost, with Wallace threatening to siphon off left-leaning Democrats, and with soothing Dewey heading the Republicans, Truman appeared doomed.

But "Give 'em Hell Harry's" vigorous campaign slowly revived the New Deal coalition. Fear of Republicans who had passed Taft-Hartley won back the bulk of organized labor, and Truman's decision in May 1948 immediately to recognize the new State of Israel kept many liberal Jews loyally Democratic. The success of the Berlin airlift buoyed the president's popularity, and by Election Day growing anti-Communist sentiment among liberals was limiting the Wallace vote to the extreme left. Meanwhile Dewey, who in 1944 had run a hard-hitting but unsuccessful campaign against Roosevelt, this time tried to coast to victory by appearing bland and "presidential."

Polls predicted a Dewey victory—but the pollsters stopped taking samples several weeks before Election Day and so missed a late Democratic surge. Truman won the popular vote by a 5 percent margin, trouncing Dewey 303 to 189 in electoral votes. Democrats regained majorities in both houses of Congress. But Truman had hit the apex of his popularity. A long downhill slide was about to begin (see Map 26.2).

—MAP EXPLORATION—

To explore an interactive version of this map, go to
www.prenhall.com/faragher6/map26.2

	Electoral Vote (%)	Popular Vote (%)
HARRY S. TRUMAN (Democrat)	303 (57)	24,105,812 (49.5)
Thomas E. Dewey (Republican)	189 (36)	21,970,065 (45.1)
Strom Thurmond (States' Rights)	39 (7)	1,169,063 (2.4)
Henry A. Wallace (Progressive)	—	1,157,172 (2.4)
Other candidates (Socialist, Prohibition, Socialist Labor, Socialist Workers)	—	272,713 (0.6)

MAP 26.2 The Election of 1948 Harry Truman holds up a copy of the *Chicago Daily Tribune* with headlines confidently and mistakenly predicting the victory of his opponent, Thomas E. Dewey. An initially unpopular candidate, Truman made a whistle-stop tour of the country by train to win 49.5 percent of the popular vote to Dewey's 45.1 percent.

THE FAIR DEAL

"Every segment of our population and every individual has a right," Truman announced in January 1949, "to expect from our Government a fair deal." Democratic congressional majorities would, he hoped, translate campaign promises into laws and expand the New Deal. But a powerful bloc of conservative southern Democrats and midwestern Republicans turned back his domestic agenda.

Truman broke little new ground. The National Housing Act of 1949 provided federally funded low-income housing. Congress also raised the minimum wage (from 40 to 75 cents per hour) and brought an additional 10 million people under Social Security coverage. Otherwise Truman made no headway. He and congressional liberals introduced a variety of bills to weaken southern racism, including a federal antilynching law, outlawing poll taxes, and banning discrimination in interstate transportation. Southern-led filibusters killed them all, while conservative-dominated congressional committees bottled up his initiatives for national health insurance, federal aid to education, and a repeal or modification of Taft-Hartley.

Truman's greatest domestic achievement was to articulate the basic principles of Cold War liberalism, which would remain the northern Democratic agenda for decades to come. Toning down visionary New Deal rhetoric about economic equality and reapportioning wealth and power, Truman's Fair Deal promoted bread-and-butter issues and economic growth. His administration insisted, therefore, on an ambitious program of expanded foreign trade, while relying on the federal government to encourage higher productivity. Equally important, Truman reshaped liberalism by making anticommunism a key element in both foreign policy and domestic affairs.

THE COLD WAR AT HOME

"Communists . . . are everywhere—in factories, offices, butcher shops, on street corners, in private businesses," Attorney General J. Howard McGrath warned in 1949. "At this very moment [they are] busy at work—undermining your government, plotting to destroy the liberties of every citizen, and feverishly trying, in whatever way they can, to aid the Soviet Union." FBI director J. Edgar Hoover spoke darkly of "the diabolic machinations of sinister figures engaged in un-American activities." Republican senator Joseph R. McCarthy claimed to have in his personal possession a list of Communists serving secretly in government agencies.

All global powers engage in espionage, and the Soviet Union, like the United States, placed intelligence-gathering agents in foreign governments. However, subversion by American-bred Communists was relatively insignificant. By the late 1940s the Communist Party, U.S.A., formed in 1919 and at the peak of its influence in the 1930s, was steadily losing ground. By this time, anticommunism held center stage in domestic politics. The federal government, with help from the media, led the crusade, using the threat of communism to reorder its operation and to quell dissent. Seeking absolute security, Americans permitted a greater concentration of power in government and, while promising to lead the Free World, allowed many of their own rights to be circumscribed.

THE NATIONAL SECURITY ACT OF 1947

The imperative of national security destroyed old-fashioned isolation, forcing the United States into unprecedented alliances such as NATO and global leadership. "If we falter in our leadership," Truman warned, "we may endanger the peace of the world—and we shall surely endanger the welfare of this nation." Such responsibility required massive resources. Truman, therefore, demanded a substantial increase in the size of the federal government in both military forces and surveillance agencies. Security measures designed to keep the nation in a steady state of preparedness, readily justified during wartime, were now extended indefinitely into the very uneasy peacetime.

The sweeping National Security Act, passed by Congress in July 1947, established the Department of Defense and the National Security Council (NSC) to administer and coordinate defense policies and advise the president. The Department of Defense combined the old War and Navy Departments, bringing the Army, the Navy, and the new Air Force under a single cabinet-level secretary. Ties between the armed forces and the State Department grew closer as retired military officers routinely filled positions in the State Department and diplomatic corps; the highest-ranking World War II soldier, Five-Star General George C. Marshall, became secretary of state. The act also created the National Security Resources Board (NSRB) to coordinate plans throughout the government "in the event of war" and, for the first time in American history, to maintain military preparedness in peacetime.

The Department of Defense and the NSRB became the principal sponsor of scientific research during the first ten years of the Cold War. It was commonly recognized at the time that World War II had been the "physicists' war." Scientists had built the ultimate weapon, the atom bomb, and achieved major advances in military navigation and detection, strategic targeting, and communication. The National Science Foundation was created in 1950 for education and research, although the Office of Naval Research conducted basic research and development on a much larger budget. Federal agencies tied to military projects supplied well over 90 percent of the funding for research in the physical sciences, much of it in major universities.

Published in 1947, this full-color comic book appeared as one of many sensationalistic illustrations of the threat of the "commie menace" to Americans at home. Approximately 4 million copies of *Is This Tomorrow?* were printed, the majority distributed to church groups or sold for ten cents a copy.

The Central Intelligence Agency (CIA) was another product of the National Security Act. With roots in the wartime Office of Strategic Services (OSS), the new CIA became a permanent operation devoted to collecting political, military, and economic information for security purposes throughout the world. (It was barred from domestic intelligence gathering: that was the domain of its rival, the FBI.) Although information about the CIA was classified—that is, kept secret from both Congress and the public—historians have estimated that the agency soon dwarfed the State Department in number of employees and size of budget.

The national-security state required a huge workforce. Before World War II, approximately 900,000 civilians worked for the federal government, about 10 percent of them in security work; by the beginning of the Cold War, nearly 4 million people were on the government's payroll, 75 percent of them in national-security agencies. The Pentagon, which had opened in 1943 as the world's largest office building, housed the Joint Chiefs of Staff and 35,000 military personnel.

National security absorbed increasingly large portions of the nation's resources. By the end of Truman's second term, defense allocations accounted for 10 percent of GNP, directly or indirectly employed hundreds of thousands of well-paid workers, and subsidized some of the nation's most profitable corporations. This vast financial outlay created the rationale for permanent, large-scale military spending and powerfully stimulated economic growth.

THE LOYALTY-SECURITY PROGRAM

National security required increased surveillance at home. Within two weeks of proclaiming the Truman Doctrine, the president signed Executive Order 9835 on March 21, 1947, establishing a civilian loyalty program for all federal employees. The new Federal Employees Loyalty and Security Program, directed at members of the Communist Party—as well as fascists and anyone guilty of "sympathetic association" with either—in effect established a political test for federal employment. It also outlined procedures for investigating current and prospective federal employees. The loyalty review boards often asked employees about their opinions of the Soviet Union, the Marshall Plan, or NATO and whether they would report fellow workers if they found out they were Communists. Any employee could be dismissed merely on "reasonable grounds," including guilt by association (that is, knowing or being related to a "subversive" person), rather than on proof of disloyalty. Later amendments added homosexuals as potential security risks on grounds that they might succumb to enemy blackmail.

Many state and municipal governments enacted loyalty programs and required public employees, including teachers at all levels, to sign loyalty oaths. In all, some 6.6 million people underwent loyalty and security checks. An estimated 500 government workers were fired, and perhaps as many as 6,000 more chose to resign. Numerous private employers and labor unions also instituted loyalty programs.

Attorney General Tom C. Clark aided this effort by publishing a list of hundreds of potentially subversive organizations selected by criteria so vague that any views "hostile or inimical to the American form of government" (as Clark's assistants noted in a memo) could make an organization liable for investigation and prosecution. There was no right of appeal for organizations so listed. The famous "Attorney General's List" effectively outlawed many political and social organizations, stigmatizing hundreds of thousands of individuals who had done nothing illegal. Church associations, civil rights organizations, musical groups, and even summer camps appeared on the list. Fraternal and social institutions, especially popular among aging Eastern European immigrants, were among the largest organizations destroyed. New York State, for example, legally dismantled the International Workers' Order, which had provided insurance to nearly 200,000 immigrants and their families. Only a handful of organizations had the funds to challenge legally "being on the List"; most simply closed their doors.

In 1950 Congress overrode the president's veto to pass a bill that Truman called "the greatest danger to freedom of press, speech, and assembly since the Sedition Act of 1798." The Internal Security (or McCarran) Act required Communist organizations to register with the Subversive Activities Control Board—if they did not register, they were prosecuted—and authorized the arrest of suspect persons during a national emergency. The Immigration and Nationality Act, also sponsored by Republican senator Pat McCarran of Nevada and adopted in 1952, again over Truman's veto, barred people deemed "subversive" or "homosexual" from becoming citizens or even visiting the United States. It also empowered the attorney general to deport immigrants who were members of Communist organizations, even if they had become citizens. Challenged repeatedly on constitutional grounds, the Subversive Activities Control Board remained in place until 1973, when it was terminated.

THE SECOND RED SCARE

Ultraconservative Democratic congressman Martin Dies of Texas, who had chaired a congressional committee on "un-American activities" since 1938, told reporters in 1944 that "Hollywood is the greatest source of revenue in this nation for the Communists and other subversive groups." Renamed and made a permanent standing committee in 1945, the House Committee on Un-American Activities (HUAC) had the power to subpoena witnesses and to compel them to answer all questions or face contempt of Congress charges. In well-publicized hearings held in Hollywood in October 1947, the mother of actress Ginger Rogers defended her daughter by saying that she had been duped into appearing in the 1943 pro-Soviet wartime film *Tender Comrade* and "had been forced" to read the subversive line "Share and share alike, that's democracy." HUAC encouraged such testimony by other "friendly witnesses," including actors Ronald Reagan and Gary Cooper. The committee intimidated many others, who feared loss of their careers, into naming former friends and co-workers in order to be cleared for future work in Hollywood.

A small but prominent minority refused to cooperate with HUAC. By claiming the freedoms of speech and association guaranteed by the First and Sixth Amendments, they became known as "unfriendly witnesses," and a handful served prison sentences for refusing to "name names."

Hollywood studios would not employ any writer, director, or actor who refused to cooperate with HUAC. The resulting blacklist remained in effect until the 1960s and limited the production of films dealing with "controversial" social or political issues. Meanwhile the privately published *Red Channels: The Report of Communist Influence in Radio and Television* (1950) persuaded advertisers to cancel their accounts with many programs considered friendly to the Soviet Union, the UN, or liberal causes.

The labor movement also became a victim of this second Red Scare. Like the Hollywood film industry, a sizable portion of its leaders and members had affiliated with the Communist Party or supported liberal causes in the 1930s, and they emerged from their wartime experiences even more deeply committed to social justice. The Food, Tobacco, Agricultural, and Allied Workers-Congress of Industrial Organizations (FTA-CIO) organized a postwar campaign against discriminatory practices within southern industry and allied with local civil rights activists to spearhead a major organizing drive. In 1947 the R.J. Reynolds Tobacco Company struck back by characterizing union organizers and supporters as Moscow's pawns. A year later, CIO president Philip Murray decided to rid his organization of all Communists. Soon, eleven unions representing more than a million workers were expelled. This "purge" succeeded in eliminating Communist influence and with it the commitment to industrial democracy that had buoyed the CIO since the 1930s.

SPY CASES

In August 1948, *Time* magazine editor Whittaker Chambers appeared before HUAC to name Alger Hiss as a fellow Communist in the Washington underground during the 1930s. Hiss, then president of the prestigious Carnegie Endowment for International Peace and a former member of FDR's State Department, denied the charges and sued his accuser for slander. Chambers then revealed his trump card, a cache of films of secret documents hidden in and then retrieved from a hollowed-out pumpkin on his Maryland farm. He claimed that Hiss had passed them to him for transmission to the Soviet Union. Republican representative Richard Nixon of California described these "Pumpkin Papers" as proof of "the most serious series of treasonable activities . . . in the history of America." The statute of limitations for espionage having run out, a federal grand jury in January 1950 convicted Hiss of perjury for denying he knew Chambers. He received a five-year prison term. Hiss was released two years later proclaiming his innocence, a position he held throughout his life. Historians remain divided on the question of his spying.

Many Democrats, including Truman, dismissed the allegations against Hiss—conveniently publicized at the start of the 1948 election campaign—as a Republican slander. Nevertheless, the highly publicized allegations against Hiss hurt the Democrats, suggesting that FDR and Truman had allowed Communists to infiltrate the federal government.

The most dramatic spy case of the era involved Julius Rosenberg, a former government engineer, and his wife Ethel, who were accused of conveying atomic secrets to Soviet agents during World War II. The government had only a weak case against Ethel but hoped that her conviction would "break" her husband, forcing him to name other spies. The Rosenberg case depended on testimony of alleged accomplices, some of them secretly coached by the FBI. Although the Rosenbergs maintained their innocence to the end, in March 1951 a jury found them both guilty. The American press showed them no sympathy, but the death sentence drew large protest demonstrations in the United States and abroad. Albert Einstein, Pope Pius XII, and the president of France, among many prominent figures, all pleaded for clemency. Julius and Ethel Rosenberg died in the electric chair on June 19, 1953. Documents declassified in the 1990s provided evidence of Julius (but not Ethel) Rosenberg's guilt.

McCARTHYISM

In a sensational Lincoln Day speech to the Republican Women's Club of Wheeling, West Virginia, on February 9, 1950, Republican senator Joseph R. McCarthy of Wisconsin announced that the United States had been sold out by the "traitorous actions" of men holding important positions in the federal government. These acted as part of a conspiracy, he charged, of 205 card-carrying Communists in the State Department (see Communities in Conflict).

McCarthy refused to reveal names because, in reality, he had none. Nevertheless, a few days later, after a drinking bout, he told persistent reporters: "I'm not going to tell you anything. I just want you to know I've got a pailful [of dirt] . . . and I'm going to use it where it does the most good." Although investigations uncovered not a single Communist in the State Department, McCarthy launched a flamboyant offensive against New Deal Democrats and the Truman administration for failing to defend the nation's security. He gave his name to the era: McCarthyism.

Behind the blitz of publicity, the previously obscure junior senator from Wisconsin had struck a chord. Communism seemed to many Americans to be much more than a military threat—nothing less than a demonic force undermining all basic values. It compelled patriots to prepare Americans even for atomic warfare: "Better Dead Than Red."

Civil rights organizations faced the worst persecution since the 1920s. But attacks on women's organizations

Congress and the Red Scare

Joseph McCarthy, the junior Republican senator from Wisconsin, stepped onto the national stage by pushing the Second Red Scare into the highest levels of government. On February 9, 1950, at a Lincoln's Day celebration in Wheeling, West Virginia, he took aim at President Truman's foreign policy. He charged Secretary of State Dean Acheson with harboring at least 205 "traitorous" Communists within his department. Two days later McCarthy sent a letter to the president, revising downward the number of Communists employed by the State Department to fifty-seven. He nevertheless demanded a full investigation and predicted that hundreds more would turn up. He warned the president not to stall, for failure to act would "label the Democratic Party as being the bedfellow of international communism." He would give versions of his Wheeling speech, excerpted here, on many later occasions, never tiring of Red-baiting the Democrats. One of the first critics to challenge McCarthy was Senator Margaret Chase Smith, a member of his own party. Smith (1897–1995) had served eight years in the House of Representatives before being elected to the Senate in 1948. She was the first woman elected to serve in both houses of Congress. On June 1, 1950, Smith read to the Senate a "Declaration of Conscience," which she had composed. She reviled the leaders of both parties for "lack of effective leadership," deplored the atmosphere of suspicion, and strongly denounced the mudslinging anti-Communist campaign. Six additional Republican senators signed her Declaration, although Smith and her allies refused to endorse a report later prepared by Democrats that defended the State Department against McCarthy's "fraudulent" charges.

What is the basis of Joseph McCarthy's charges, and why is he targeting the State Department? What is the basis of Margaret Chase Smith's response to McCarthy, and why is she criticizing a fellow Republican?

Senator Joseph McCarthy Charges That Communists Riddle the State Department, Wheeling, West Virginia (February 9, 1950)

Today we are engaged in a final, all-out battle between communistic atheism and Christianity. The modern champions of communism have selected this as the time, and ladies and gentlemen, the chips are down—they are truly down. . . .

Ladies and gentlemen, can there be anyone tonight who is so blind as to say that the war is not on? Can there be anyone who fails to realize that the Communist world has said the time is now? . . . that this is the time for the show-down between the democratic Christian world and the communistic atheistic world? . . .

As one of our outstanding historical figures once said, "When a great democracy is destroyed, it will not be from enemies from without, but rather because of enemies from within."
. . .

The reason why we find ourselves in a position of impotency is not because our only powerful potential enemy has sent men to invade our shores . . . but rather because of the traitorous actions of those who have been treated so well by this Nation. It has not been the less fortunate, or members of minority groups who have been traitorous to this Nation, but rather those who have had all the benefits that the wealthiest Nation on earth has had to offer . . . the finest homes, the finest college education and the finest jobs in government we can give.

This is glaringly true in the State Department. There the bright young men who are born with silver spoons in their mouths are the ones who have been most traitorous. . . . I have here in my hand a list of 205 . . . a list of names that were made known to the Secretary of State as being members of the Communist Party and who nevertheless are still working and shaping policy in the State Department. . . .

As you know, very recently the Secretary of State proclaimed his loyalty to a man guilty of what has always been considered as the most abominable of all crimes—being a traitor to the people who gave him a position of great trust—high treason. . . .

He has lighted the spark which is resulting in a moral uprising and will end only when the whole sorry mess of twisted, warped thinkers are swept from the national scene so that we may have a new birth of honesty and decency in government.

SOURCE: Joseph McCarthy, "Speech at Wheeling, West Virginia, 9 February 1950." In Michael P. Johnson, ed. *Reading the American Past*, Vol. II (Boston: Bedford Books, 1998), 191–195 (but also the speech is on several websites and freely available there).

"Today we are engaged in a final, all-out battle between communistic atheism and Christianity."

"I am not proud of the way in which the Senate has been made a publicity platform for irresponsible sensationalism."

Senator Margaret Chase Smith Announces Her Declaration of Conscience (June 1, 1950)

Mr. President, I would like to speak briefly and simply about a serious national condition. It is a national feeling of fear and frustration that could result in national suicide and the end of everything that we Americans hold dear. . . .

I speak as a Republican. I speak as a woman. I speak as a United States Senator. I speak as an American. . . .

I think that it is high time for the United States Senate and its Members to do some soul searching—for us to weigh our consciences—on the manner in which we are performing our duty to the people of America; on the manner in which we are using or abusing our individual powers and privileges.

I think that it is high time that we remembered that we have sworn to uphold and defend the Constitution. I think that it is high time that we remembered that the Constitution, as amended, speaks not only of the freedom of speech, but also of trial by jury instead of trial by accusation.

Whether it be a criminal prosecution in court or a character prosecution in the Senate, there is little practical distinction when the life of a person has been ruined.

Those of us who shout the loudest about Americanism in making character assassinations are all too frequently those who, by our own words and acts, ignore some of the basic principles of Americanism—

The right to criticize;

The right to hold unpopular beliefs;

The right to protest;

The right of independent thought.

The exercise of these rights should not cost one single American citizen his reputation or his right to a livelihood nor should he be in danger of losing his reputation or livelihood merely because he happens to know someone who holds unpopular beliefs. Who of us doesn't? Otherwise none of us could call our souls our own. Otherwise thought control would have set in.

The American people are sick and tired of being afraid to speak their minds lest they be politically smeared as "Communists" or "Fascists" by their opponents. Freedom of speech is not what it used to be in America. It has been so abused by some that it is not exercised by others. . . .

As a woman, I wonder how the mothers, wives, sisters, and daughters feel about the way in which members of their families have been politically mangled in Senate debate—and I use the word "debate" advisedly.

As a United States Senator, I am not proud of the way in which the Senate has been made a publicity platform for irresponsible sensationalism. . . .

I don't like the way the Senate has been made a rendezvous for vilification, for selfish political gain at the sacrifice of individual reputations and national unity. I am not proud of the way we smear outsiders from the floor of the Senate and hide behind the cloak of congressional immunity and still place ourselves beyond criticism on the floor of the Senate. . . .

SOURCE: Margaret Chase Smith (1972) *Declaration of Conscience*. (William C. Lewis, Jr., ed) Garden City NY: Doubleday & Company, Inc) (also on Website American Rhetoric: Top 100 Speeches).

The tables turned on Senator Joseph McCarthy (1908–57) after he instigated an investigation of the U.S. Army for harboring Communists. A special congressional committee then investigated McCarthy for attempting to make the Army grant special privileges to his staff aide, Private David Schine. During the televised hearings, Senator McCarthy discredited himself. In December 1954, the Senate voted to censure him, thus robbing him of his power. He died three years later.

and homosexuals, which cloaked deep fears about changing sexual mores, took a huge toll. Aided by FBI reports, the federal government fired up to sixty homosexuals per month in the early 1950s. Dishonorable discharges from the U.S. armed forces for homosexuality, an administrative procedure without appeal, also increased dramatically. A prominent liberal historian, Arthur Schlesinger Jr. suggested that critics of Cold War policies were not "real" men or, perhaps, "real" women either.

Joseph McCarthy and his fellow Red-hunters eventually burned themselves out. During nationally televised congressional hearings in 1954, not only did McCarthy fail to prove his wild charges of Communist infiltration of the Army but also in the glare of television appeared deranged. Cowed for four years, the Senate finally censured him for "conduct unbecoming a member." After the media lost interest in him, McCarthy succumbed to alcoholism. He died just three years later.

COLD WAR CULTURE

As the Truman Doctrine revealed, the Cold War did not necessarily mean military confrontation. Nor was it defined exclusively by a quest for economic supremacy. The Cold War embodied the struggle of one "way of life" against another. It was, in short, a contest of values. The president therefore, pledged the United States to "contain" communism within the parameters of the Soviet Union and its satellites and simultaneously called for fortifications at home. If Americans were to rebuild the world based on their own values, they must rededicate themselves to defending their birthright: freedom and democracy.

Edward Hopper (1882–1967) was the most well-known realist painter in the United States at midcentury. Many of his paintings portray the starkness and often the loneliness of American life, with cityscapes depicting empty streets or all-night restaurants where the few patrons sit at a distance from each other. This painting, owned by the Metropolitan Museum of Art in New York, expresses the mood of alienation associated with Cold War culture.

SOURCE: Edward Hopper (1882–1967), "Office in a Small City," 1953. Oil on canvas, H. 28 in. W. 40 in. Signed (lower left) Edward Hopper. The Metropolitan Museum of Art, George A. Hearn Fund, 1953. (53.183).

AN ANXIOUS MOOD

"We have about 50 percent of the world's wealth," Kennan noted in 1948, "but only 3.6 percent of its population." However, many Americans feared an economic backslide. If wartime production had ended the hardships of the Great Depression, how would the economy fare in peacetime? No one could say. Peace itself seemed precarious.

Anxieties surfaced as major themes in popular culture. *The Best Years of Our Lives* (1946), one of the most acclaimed Hollywood films of the era and winner of nine Academy Awards, showed three fictional veterans trying to readjust to civilian life. The former soldiers found that dreams of reunion with family and loved ones, which had sustained them through years of fighting, now seemed hollow. In some cases, their wives and children had become so self-reliant that the men had no clear function in the household; in other cases, the prospect for employment appeared dim. One veteran who had lost both arms was shunned by almost everyone. The feeling of community shared with wartime buddies dissipated, leaving only profound loneliness in a crass, selfish society.

The genre of *film noir* (French for "black film") deepened this postwar moodiness into a pessimistic aesthetic. American movies like *Out of the Past, Detour,* and *They Live by Night* told stories of relentless fate and ruthless betrayal. Their protagonists were loners running from a bad past, falsely accused of transgressions, or trapped into committing crimes. The high-contrast lighting of these black-and-white films accentuated the difficulty of distinguishing friend from foe.

Serious literature vividly captured a sense of anxious alienation. Playwright Arthur Miller in *Death of a Salesman* (1949) sketched an exacting portrait of self-destructive individualism. Willy Loman, the play's hero, is obsessively devoted to his career in sales but is nevertheless a miserable failure. Worse, he taught his sons to excel in personal presentation and style—the very methods prescribed by standard American success manuals—making them both shallow and materialistic. J. D. Salinger's novel *Catcher in the Rye* (1951) explored the mental anguish of a teenage boy estranged by his parents' psychological distance and materialism. The novel was (and remains) very controversial: conservatives accused Salinger of encouraging disrespect for adults as "phonies," while for many young people he precisely articulated their alienation.

Cold War anxiety manifested itself in a flurry of unidentified flying object (UFO) sightings. Thousands of Americans imagined that a Communist-like invasion from outer space was already under way or hoped that superior creatures might arrive to show the way to world peace. The U.S. Air Force discounted "flying saucer" reports, but dozens of private researchers and faddists claimed to have been contacted by aliens. Hollywood fed these beliefs. In *The Invasion of the Body Snatchers* (1956), for example, a small town is captured by aliens who take over the minds of its inhabitants when they fall asleep, a subtle warning against apathy toward the threat of communist "subversion" (see Seeing History).

THE FAMILY AS BULWARK

Postwar prosperity helped to strengthen the ideal of domesticity, although many Americans interpreted their rush toward marriage and parenthood, as one writer put it, as a "defense—an impregnable bulwark" against the era's anxieties.

Young couples were marrying younger and producing more children than at any time in the past century. The Census Bureau predicted that the "baby boom" would be temporary. To everyone's surprise, the birthrate continued to grow at a record pace, peaking at more than 118 per 1,000 women in 1957 (see Figure 26.1).

The new families who enjoyed postwar prosperity inaugurated a spending spree of trailblazing proportions.

SEEING HISTORY

The Hollywood Film *Invasion, U.S.A*

Invasion, U.S.A. was the first of the genre of Red-scare films to do well at the box office. Shot in just seven days and released by Columbia Pictures in 1952, the film opens by depicting a group of well-off Americans, drinking casually in a New York bar and showing no particular concern about the imminent threat to their nation. Suddenly, they hear the news of horrific attacks by The Enemy. After atomic bombs fall and The Enemy approaches the nation's capital, they have all learned a potent lesson about complacency and begin to renounce their selfish ways. The group disperses, each character now understanding that freedom carries with it the price of vigilance.

The Enemy is never named, but Slavic accents and references to the "People's Government" that takes over Manhattan strongly suggest that the evildoers are Russian Communists.

The poster builds on the foundation of fear. Studio publicists also advised local movie theaters to promote the movie along the same line: "Dress a young man in full paratroop regalia and have him walk through the principal streets of town in advance of playdate with a sign on his back reading HERE'S HOW IT WOULD HAPPEN IF IT HAPPENED NOW! SEE COLUMBIA PICTURES' *INVASION, U.S.A.* AT THE STATE THEATER FRIDAY!" The studio also suggested that blasts by air raid sirens and the use of local Civil Defense workers would be good choices to advertise the film. Despite these fear-provoking messages, one reviewer pointed out that poor production quality–stock footages from World War II—and stilted dialogue unintentionally made *Invasion, U.S.A,* the first film to make audiences laugh at the atomic bomb.

**How did Hollywood and other forms of mass media help to shape
Cold War culture in the late 1940s and early 1950s?**

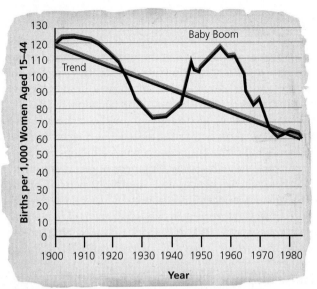

FIGURE 26.1   U.S. Birthrate, 1930–80

The bulge of the "baby boom," a leading demographic factor in the postwar economy, stands out for this fifty-year period.

SOURCE: National Archives and Records Administration.

"The year 1946," trumpeted *Life* magazine, "finds the U.S. on the threshold of marvels, ranging from runless stockings and shineless serge suits to jet-propelled airplanes that will flash across the country in just a little less than the speed of sound." By the time Truman left office, two-thirds of all American households claimed at least one television set.

These two trends—the baby boom and high rates of consumer spending—encouraged a major change in the middle-class family. Having worked during World War II, often in occupations traditionally closed to them, many women wished to continue in full-time employment. Reconversion to peacetime production forced the majority from their factory positions, but most women quickly returned, taking jobs at a faster rate than men and providing half the total growth of the labor force. By 1952, 2 million

more wives worked than during the war. Gone, however, were the high-paying unionized jobs in manufacturing. Instead, most women found low-wage jobs in the expanding service sector: clerical work, health care and education, and restaurant, hotel, and retail services. Older women whose children were grown might work because they had come to value a job for its own sake. Younger women often worked out of "economic necessity" that is, to maintain a middle-class standard of living that now required more than one income. Indeed, mothers of young children were the most likely to be employed (see Table 26.1).

Even though most women sought employment primarily to support their families, they ran up against popular opinion and expert advice urging them to go home. Polls registered resounding disapproval—by 86 percent of those surveyed—of a married woman working if jobs were scarce and her husband could support her. Noting that most Soviet women worked outside the home, many commentators appealed for a return to an imaginary "traditional" American family where men alone were breadwinners and women were exclusively homemakers.

This campaign began on a shrill note. Ferdinand Lundberg and Marynia Farnham, in their best-selling *Modern Woman: The Lost Sex* (1947), attributed the "super-jittery age in which we live" to women's abandonment of the home to pursue careers. To counter this danger, they proposed federally funded psychotherapy to readjust women to their housewifely roles and cash subsidies to encourage them to bear more children.

Articles in popular magazines, television shows, and high-profile experts chimed in with similar messages. In the first edition of his *Baby and Child Care* (1946), the child-rearing advice manual that soon outsold the Bible, Dr. Benjamin Spock advised women to devote themselves full time, if financially possible, to their maternal responsibilities.

Patterns of women's higher education reflected this conservative trend. Having made slight gains during World

TABLE 26.1

Distribution of Total Personal Income Among Various Segments of the Population, 1947–70 (in Percentages)*

Year	Poorest Fifth	Second Poorest Fifth	Middle Fifth	Second Wealthiest Fifth	Wealthiest Fifth	Wealthiest 5 Percent
1947	3.5	10.6	16.7	23.6	45.6	18.7
1950	3.1	10.5	17.3	24.1	45.0	18.2
1960	3.2	10.6	17.6	24.7	44.0	17.0
1970	3.6	10.3	17.2	24.7	44.1	16.9

Despite the general prosperity of the postwar era, the distribution of income remained essentially unchanged.

*Monetary income only.

SOURCE: Adapted from U.S. Bureau of the Census, *Historical Statistics of the United States, Colonial Times to 1970*, Bicentennial ed. (Washington, DC: U.S. Government Printing Office, 1975), p. 292.

This photograph, taken in 1955, presents an ideal image of domestic life for American women during the Cold War. This young mother sits with her three small children in a well-equipped kitchen that depicts the high standard of living that symbolized the "American way of life."

War II, when college-age men were serving in the armed forces or working in war industries, women lost ground after the G.I. Bill created a huge upsurge in male enrollment. Women represented 40 percent of all college graduates in 1940 but only 25 percent a decade later.

With a growing number of middle-class women working to help support their families, these Cold War policies and prescriptions clashed. As early as 1947, a worried *Life* magazine ran a thirteen-page feature, "American Woman's Dilemma." How could women comfortably take part in a world beyond the home and at the same time heed the advice of FBI director J. Edgar Hoover, who exhorted the nation's women to fight "the twin enemies of freedom—crime and communism" by fulfilling their "natural" role as "homemakers and mothers"?

MILITARY-INDUSTRIAL COMMUNITIES IN THE AMERICAN WEST

All regions of the United States felt the impact of the Cold War, but none so directly as the West. World War II defense spending had stimulated the western economy and encouraged a mass westward migration of people eager to find wartime jobs. Following the war, many cities successfully converted to peacetime production; Los Angeles, for example, attracted one-eighth of all new business in the nation during the late 1940s. It was the Cold War, however, that by reviving defense funding gave the western economy its most important boost. The Department of Defense and private businesses generated billions of dollars for military research and development of various kinds.

So much defense money—nearly 10 percent of the entire military budget—was poured by the federal government into California that the state's rate of economic growth between 1949 and 1952 outpaced that of the nation as a whole; nearly 40 percent came from aircraft manufacturing alone. Ten years later, an estimated one-third of all Los Angeles workers were employed by defense industries, particularly aerospace, and the absolute number of defense workers far exceeded those of the peak production years in World War II. The concentration of defense workers was even greater in the Los Angeles suburbs. Orange Country, for example, grew quickly during the Cold War to become a major producer of communication equipment. The Bay Area also benefited economically from defense spending, and cities such as San Jose began their rise as home to the nation's budding high-technology industry.

The Cold War pumped new life into communities that had grown up during World War II. Hanford, Washington, and Los Alamos, New Mexico, both centers of the Manhattan Project, employed more people in the construction of the Cold War nuclear arsenal than in the development of the atom bomb. Once-rural Los Alamos mushroomed so fast that thirty years later its population density was second only in New Mexico to metropolitan Albuquerque. New communities accompanied the growth of the U.S. military bases and training camps in the West. Many of these installations, as well as hospitals and supply depots, not only survived but also expanded during the transition from the actual warfare of World War II to the threatened warfare of the Cold War. Between 1950 and 1953, approximately twenty western bases were reopened. California became at least a temporary home to more military personnel than any other state, and Texas was not far behind. The availability of public lands with areas of sparse population made western states especially attractive to military planners designing such dangerous and secretive installations as the White Sands Missile Range in the New Mexican desert.

Local politicians, real estate agents, and merchants usually welcomed these developments as sources of revenue and employment. There were, however, heavy costs for speedy and unplanned federally induced growth. To accommodate the new populations, the government poured money into new highway systems but did little for public transportation. Uncontrolled sprawl, traffic congestion, air pollution, and strains on limited water and energy resources all grew with the military-industrial communities in the West. For those populations living near nuclear testing grounds, environmental degradation complemented the ultimate threat to their own physical well-being: over the next forty years, cancer rates soared.

ZEAL FOR DEMOCRACY

World War II revitalized patriotism by rallying Americans to define themselves and their institutions against foreign fascism. Pledging allegiance to the flag with hand over heart, for example, gained new symbolic meaning as schoolchildren were directed to avoid saluting, a gesture now perceived as disturbingly similar to Nazi "Heil Hitler" rituals.

Following the massive and spontaneous V-J Day celebrations, Americans began to retreat from public displays of patriotism, but soon new organizations, like the Freedoms Foundation of Valley Forge and the American Heritage Foundation, were joining such stalwarts as the American Legion and the Chamber of Commerce in scolding about "national apathy."

In Mosinee, Wisconsin, for example, the American Legion used political theater to inculcate the American way, orchestrating an imaginary Communist coup in the small community. In 1950, on May Day (the traditional left-wing holiday) "Communist agents," followed by more than sixty reporters, forced the mayor and the chief of police from their homes and announced that the Council of People's Commissars had taken over the local government. Roadblocks were put up to prevent residents from escaping to "free" territory. The restaurants served only Soviet fare: black bread, potato soup, and coffee. The local *Mosinee Times* printed a special edition on pink stock under its new "Red Star" masthead. Citizens discovered that all private property had been confiscated and all constitutional rights annulled. Every adult was required "to contribute to the State four extra hours of labor without compensation." That evening, after a full day of Communist indoctrination, the residents rallied in "Red Square" and declared an end to "Communist rule," then raised the American flag and headed home singing "God Bless America." The national media all covered Mosinee's "Day under Communism."

Meanwhile, Attorney General Tom Clark, supported by Truman, by private donors, and by the American Heritage Foundation, was putting on the nation's rails the "Freedom Train." Carrying copies of the Bill of Rights and the Constitution, the Freedom Train traveled to cities across the land. Local citizens got aboard to view various patriotic displays at the average rate of 8,500 people per day.

Patriotic messages also permeated public education. Following guidelines set down by the Truman administration,

teachers were to "strengthen national security through education," designing their lesson plans to illustrate the superiority of the American democratic system over Soviet communism. In 1947 the federal Office of Education launched a "Zeal for Democracy" program for implementation by school boards nationwide. The program veered toward propaganda, announcing its intention to "promote and strengthen democratic thinking and practice, just as the schools of totalitarian states have so effectively promoted the ideals of their respective cultures." Meanwhile, in a national civil defense program, schoolchildren learned to "duck" under their desks and "cover" their heads in the event of a surprise Soviet nuclear attack.

Voices of protest were raised. The black poet Langston Hughes expressed his skepticism in verse, writing that he hoped the Freedom Train would carry no Jim Crow car. (In some southern towns, however, viewing the Freedom Train was segregated.) A brave minority of scholars protested infringements on academic freedom by refusing to sign loyalty oaths and by writing books pointing out the potential dangers of aggressively nationalistic foreign and domestic policies. But the chilling atmosphere, such as the political climate pervading the University of Washington, made many individuals reluctant to express contrary opinions or ideas.

STALEMATE FOR THE DEMOCRATS

With Cold War tensions festering in Europe, neither the United States nor the Soviet Union would have predicted that events in Asia would bring them to the brink of a new world war. Yet in China, the most populous land on earth, Communists completed their seizure of power in late 1949. A few months later, in June 1950, Communist armies threatened to conquer all of Korea.

Truman sent American forces to conduct a "police action" in Korea, which within a few years absorbed more than 1.8 million U.S. troops with no victory in sight. For Truman, the "loss" of China and the Korean stalemate proved political suicide, ending the twenty-year Democratic lock on the presidency and the greatest era of reform in U.S. history.

DEMOCRATIZING JAPAN AND "LOSING" CHINA

At the close of World War II, the United States acted deliberately to secure Japan firmly within its sphere of influence. General Douglas MacArthur directed an interim Japanese government in a modest reconstruction program that included land reform, creation of independent trade unions, abolition of contract marriages, granting of woman suffrage, sweeping demilitarization, and eventually a constitutional democracy that renounced war and barred Communists from all posts. American leaders worked to rebuild the nation's economy along capitalist lines and integrate Japan, like West Germany, into an anti-Soviet bloc. Japan also housed huge U.S. military bases, placing U.S. troops and weapons on the doorstep of the Soviet Union's Asian rim.

China could not be handled so easily. After years of civil war, the pro–Western Nationalist government of Jiang Jeishi (Chiang Kai-shek) collapsed. Since World War II, the United States had been aiding Jiang's unpopular and corrupt regime, while warning him that without major reforms and a coalition with his political opponents, the Nationalists were heading for defeat. Jiang refused any concessions, and in the late 1940s the Truman administration cut off virtually all aid and then watched as Nationalist troops surrendered to the Communists, led by Mao Zedong. Mao's Communists had the support of the Chinese countryside, where 85 percent of the population lived. Abandoning the entire mainland, the defeated Nationalists fled to the island of Taiwan. On October 1, 1949, Mao proclaimed the People's Republic of China, and in February 1950 the Soviet Union and the People's Republic of China signed an alliance.

China's "fall" to communism set off an uproar in the United States. The Asia First wing of the Republican Party, which saw the Far East rather than Europe as the primary target of U.S. trade and investment, blamed Truman for the "loss" of China. The president's adversaries, pointing to the growing menace of "international communism," called the Democrats the "party of treason."

THE KOREAN WAR

At the end of World War II, the Allies had divided the Korean peninsula, surrendered by Japan, at the 38th Parallel. Although all Koreans hoped to reunite their nation under an independent government, the line between North and South hardened. While the United States backed the unpopular southern government of Syngman Rhee (the Republic of Korea), the Soviet Union sponsored a rival government in North Korea under Communist Kim Il-Sung (see Map 26.3).

On June 25, 1950, the U.S. State Department received a cablegram reporting an invasion of South Korea by the Communist North. "If we are tough enough now," President Truman pledged, "if we stand up to them like we did in Greece three years ago, they won't take any next steps." While the Soviet Union apparently regarded the invasion as Kim's affair, China supported and perhaps incited Kim to invade South Korea. Truman sought the Security Council's approval to send troops to defend South Korea under the UN's collective-security provisions. With the Soviet delegate (who could have cast a veto) unaccountably absent, the Security Council agreed. Two-thirds of Americans polled approved the president's decision to send troops under the command of General MacArthur.

Military events seemed at first to justify the president's decision. Seoul, the capital of South Korea, fell to North Korean troops within weeks, and Communist forces pushed south, occupying most of the peninsula. The situation appeared grim until Truman authorized MacArthur to carry out an amphibious landing at Inchon, near Seoul, on September 15, 1950. With tactical brilliance and good fortune, the general's campaign not only halted the Communist drive but also sent the North Koreans fleeing. By October, UN troops had retaken South Korea.

Basking in victory, the Truman administration could not resist the temptation to expand its war aims. Too prove that Democrats were not "soft on communism," the president decided to roll back the Communists beyond the 38th Parallel, uniting Korea as a showcase for democracy. China, not yet directly involved in the war, warned that crossing that dividing line would threaten its national security. Truman flew to Wake Island in the Pacific on October 15 to confer with MacArthur, who assured him of a speedy victory.

MacArthur had sorely miscalculated. Chinese troops massed along the Yalu River, the border between Korea and China. As the UN forces approached the Yalu, suddenly and without air support a Chinese "human wave" attack began. MacArthur, who had foolishly divided his forces, suffered a crushing defeat. The Chinese drove the UN troops back into South Korea, where they regrouped south of the 38th Parallel. Finally, by the summer of 1951 a stalemate had been reached very near the old dividing line. Then, for the next eighteen months, negotiations for an armistice dragged out amid heavy fighting.

MacArthur tried to convince Truman to prepare for a new invasion of Communist territory. Encouraged by strong support at home, and defying the American tradition of civilian control over the military, MacArthur publicly criticized the president's policy, calling for bombing supply lines in China and blockading the Chinese coast. Such actions would certainly have led to a Chinese-American war. Finally, on April 10, 1951, Truman fired MacArthur for insubordination.

THE PRICE OF NATIONAL SECURITY

The Korean conflict had profound implications for the use of executive power. By unilaterally instituting a peacetime draft in 1948 and in 1950 ordering American troops into Korea without a declaration of war, Truman had bypassed congressional authority. Republican Senator Robert Taft called the president's actions "evidence of an 'imperial presidency'" that was guilty of "a complete usurpation" of checks and balances. For a while, Truman sidestepped such criticisms and their constitutional implications by declaring a national emergency and by carefully referring to the military deployment not as a U.S. "war" but as a UN-sanctioned "police action."

MAP EXPLORATION

To explore an interactive version of this map, go to **www.prenhall.com/faragher6/map26.3**

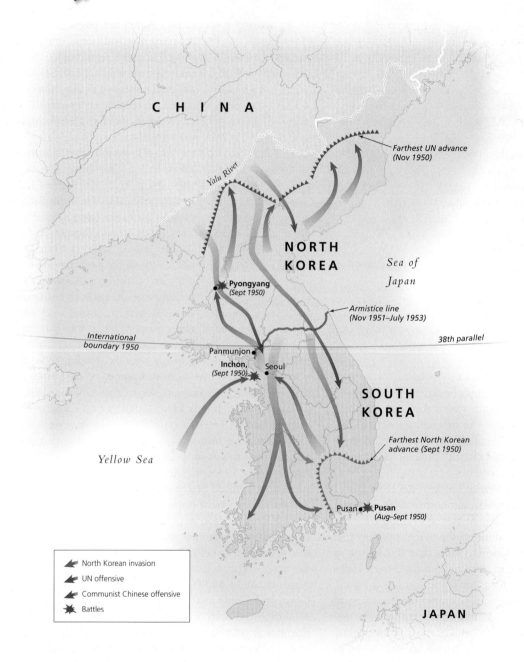

MAP 26.3 The Korean War The intensity of battles underscored the strategic importance of Korea in the Cold War.

The president was acting at the prompting of National Security Council Paper 68 (NSC-68), a sweeping declaration of Cold War policy. This lengthy document was submitted to Truman by the National Security Council in April 1950. NSC-68 declared it necessary and expedient not only to repel Communist influence wherever it appeared but also to "foster the seeds of destruction within the Soviet Union." The document defined the struggle between the United States and the Soviet Union as "permanent" and the era one of "total war."

By midcentury, General Douglas MacArthur (1880–1964) had earned a reputation as one of the most flamboyant and controversial American generals. This photograph, taken in September 1950, shows him during his finest hour as commander of the UN troops during the Korean War. He is observing the shelling of enemy forces shortly before he led a brilliant and successful amphibious landing at the Inchon peninsula. Nearly 1.8 million Americans served in Korea.

American citizens, it declared, must be willing to sacrifice— "to give up some of the benefits which they have come to associate with their freedom"—to defend their way of life. NSC-68 articulated the intellectual and psychological rationale behind U.S. national security policies for the next forty years.

Initially hesitant, after the outbreak of the Korean war Truman accepted the policies outlined in NSC-68 and agreed to a rapid and permanent military buildup. By the time the Korean conflict subsided, the defense budget had quadrupled, from $13.5 billion to more than $52 billion in 1953. The U.S. Army had grown to 3.6 million—six times its size at the beginning of the "police action." At the same time, the federal government accelerated development of both conventional and nonconventional weapons. Its nuclear stockpile now included "Super," the thermonuclear hydrogen (or "H") bomb, first tested at full scale in November 1952. NCS-68 also proposed expensive "large-scale covert operations" for the "liberation" of Communist-dominated countries, particularly in Eastern Europe.

The Korean war also provided the rationale to expand anti-Communist propaganda. At the end of World War II, Truman had taken steps to transform the Office of War Information into a peacetime program with a much smaller budget. But by 1948 Congress was ready to pass with bipartisan support the Smith-Mundt Act, designed "to promote the better understanding of the United States among the peoples of the world and to strengthen cooperative international relations." Within a year, Congress doubled the budget for such programming, granting $3 million to revive the Voice of America, the shortwave international radio program that had been established in 1942. The new legislation also funded films, print media, cultural exchange programs, and exhibitions, and it created a foundation to disseminate anti-Communist propaganda throughout the world.

By 1951 a massive "Campaign of Truth" was reaching 93 nations, and the Voice of America was broadcasting anti-Communist programming in 45 languages. Project Troy, which was initially designed by professors from Harvard and MIT, aimed to penetrate the iron curtain by using balloons to drop leaflets and cheap American goods, such as playing cards and plastic chess sets. Army pilots joined the effort, showering leaflets on North Korean troops reading "ENJOY LIFE and plenty of cigarettes away from the war by coming over to the UN side. Escape. Save your life." In his annual message to Congress that year, President Truman requested $115 million to fund these programs but, as the war in Korea bogged down, he managed to get only $85 million. In the end, the Korean conflict did nothing to roll back communism, and it cost the United States approximately $100 billion, inaugurating an era of huge federal budget deficits.

In Korea, peace negotiations and fighting proceeded in tandem until the summer of 1953, when a settlement was reached returning North and South Korea to almost the same territory each had held at the start of the war. Approximately 54,000 Americans died in Korea; North Korea and China lost well over 2 million. The UN troops had employed both "carpet bombing" (an intense, destructive attack on a small area) and napalm (jellied gasoline bombs), destroying most of the housing and food supplies in both North and South Korea. True to patterns of modern warfare that emerged during World War II, the majority of civilians killed were women and children. Nearly a million Koreans were left homeless.

The Korean conflict enlarged the geographical range of the Cold War to include East Asia. "Red China" and the United States would be implacable enemies for the next twenty years. Moreover, Korea did much to establish an ominous tradition of "unwinnable" conflicts that left many Americans skeptical of official policy.

In retrospect, many Americans recognized that Truman, in fighting communism in Korea, had pledged the United States to defend a corrupt dictatorship. Decades later, the Korean war inspired the dark comedy *M★A★S★H*, adapted for television from the film written by Hollywood screenwriter Ring Lardner Jr., an "unfriendly witness" before HUAC, who was jailed during the Korean war for contempt of Congress. As late as 1990, members of Congress were still debating the terms of a Korean war memorial. "It ended on a sad note for Americans," one historian has concluded, "and the war and its memories drifted off into a void."

"I LIKE IKE": THE ELECTION OF 1952

Korea dominated the election campaign of 1952. Truman's popularity had wavered continually since he took office in 1945, but it sank to an all-time low in the early 1950s shortly after he fired MacArthur. Thousands of letters and telegrams poured into Congress demanding Truman's impeachment, while MacArthur returned home to a hero's welcome. More than 7 million cheered him in New York City alone.

The case against Truman widened. The Asia First lobby argued that if in the late 1940s the president had aggressively turned back communism in China, there would have been no "limited war" in Korea. Large-scale corruption came to light in Truman's administration, with several agencies allegedly dealing in 5 percent kickbacks on government contracts. Business and organized labor complained about Korean war price and wage freezes. A late 1951 Gallup poll showed the president's approval rating at 23 percent. In March 1952, Truman announced he would not run for reelection, even though he was constitutionally permitted another term.

Accepting political defeat and disgrace, Truman endorsed the uncharismatic governor of Illinois, Adlai E. Stevenson Jr. Admired for his eloquence, wit, honesty, and intelligence, Stevenson offered no solutions to the conflict in Korea, the accelerating arms race, or the Cold War generally. Accepting the Democratic nomination, he candidly admitted that "the ordeal of the twentieth century is far from over."

The Republicans made the most of the Democrats' dilemma. Without proposing any sweeping answers of their own, they zeroed in on "K_1C_2"—Korea, Communism, and Corruption. When opinion polls showed retired General Dwight D. Eisenhower with an "unprecedented" 64 percent approval rating, they found in "Ike" the perfect candidate.

Eisenhower styled himself the voice of "modern Republicanism." He wisely avoided the negative impressions made in 1948 by Dewey, who had seemed as aggressive as Truman abroad and bent on repealing the New Deal at home. Eisenhower knew better: voters wanted peace and a limited welfare state. He called New Deal reforms "a solid floor that keeps all of us from falling into the pit of disaster," and without going into specifics promised "an early and honorable" peace in Korea. Whenever he was tempted to address questions of finance or the economy, his advisers warned him: "The chief reason that people want to vote for you is because they think you have more ability to keep us out of another war."

Richard Nixon, Eisenhower's vice presidential candidate, meanwhile waged a relentless and defamatory attack on "Adlai the Appeaser." Joe McCarthy chortled that with club in hand he might be able to make "a good American" of Stevenson. A month before the election, McCarthy went on network television with his requisite "exhibits"

On December 23, 1952, Republican vice-presidential candidate Richard M. Nixon appeared on national television to defend himself against charges that he had taken illegal campaign contributions. This photograph shows him with one of those gifts, a black-and-white spotted cocker spaniel. He said: "And our little girl Tricia, the six year old, named it 'Checkers.' And you know, the kids, like all kids, love the dog, and I just want to say this, right now, that regardless of what they say about it, we're gonna keep it." This speech, which was simulcast on radio, won the hearts of many voters.

and "documents," purportedly showing that the Democratic presidential candidate had promoted communism at home and abroad. These outrageous charges kept the Stevenson campaign off balance.

The Republican campaign was itself not scandal-free: Nixon was caught accepting personal gifts from wealthy benefactors. On national television, he pathetically described his wife Pat's "good Republican cloth coat" and their struggling life but then contritely admitted to indeed accepting one gift: a puppy named Checkers that his little daughters loved and that he refused to give back. "The Poor Richard Show," as critics called this masterfully maudlin "Checkers Speech," defused the scandal without answering the most important charges. And it underscored how important television was becoming in molding voters' perceptions.

Soaring above the scandal, Eisenhower inspired voters as the peace candidate. Ten days before the election he dramatically announced: "I shall go to Korea." Eisenhower carried 55 percent of the vote and thirty-nine states, bringing an unusually large harvest of voters in normally Democratic areas, such as the South, and in New York, Chicago, Boston, and Cleveland. Riding his coattails, the Republicans regained narrow control of Congress. The New Deal coalition—ethnic minorities, northern blacks, unionized workers, liberals, Catholics, Jews, and white southern conservatives—no longer commanded a majority.

CHRONOLOGY

1941	Henry Luce forecasts the dawn of "the American Century"
1944	G.I. Bill of Rights benefits World War II veterans
	International Monetary Fund and World Bank founded
1945	Franklin D. Roosevelt dies in office; Harry S. Truman becomes president
	United Nations charter signed
	World War II ends
	Strike wave begins
	Truman proposes program of economic reforms
1946	Employment Act creates Council of Economic Advisers
	Churchill's Iron Curtain speech
	Atomic Energy Act establishes Atomic Energy Commission
	Republicans win control of Congress
	Benjamin Spock publishes *Baby and Child Care*
1947	Truman Doctrine announced; Congress appropriates $400 million in aid for Greece and Turkey

	Federal Employees Loyalty and Security Program established and attorney general's list of subversive organizations authorized
	Marshall Plan announced
	Taft-Hartley Act restricts union activities
	National Security Act establishes Department of Defense, the National Security Council, and the Central Intelligence Agency
	House Un-American Activities Committee hearings in Hollywood
1948	Smith-Mundt Act passed by Congress
	Ferdinand Lundberg and Marynia Farnham publish *Modern Woman: The Lost Sex*
	State of Israel founded; immediately recognized by the United States
	Berlin blockade begins
	Henry Wallace nominated for president on Progressive Party ticket
	Truman announces peacetime draft and desegregates U.S. armed forces and civil service

Truman elected president, defeating Dewey, Wallace, and Thurmond; Democrats sweep both houses of Congress

1949   Truman announces Fair Deal

North Atlantic Treaty Organization (NATO) created

Communists, led by Mao Zedong, take power in China

Berlin blockade ends

Soviet Union detonates atomic bomb

1950   Alger Hiss convicted of perjury

Senator Joseph McCarthy begins anti-Communist crusade

Soviet Union and the People's Republic of China sign an alliance

Adoption of NSC-68 consolidates presidential war powers

Korean war begins

Internal Security (McCarran) Act requires registration of Communist organizations and arrest of Communists during national emergencies

1951   Truman dismisses General Douglas MacArthur

Psychological Strategy Board created

Armistice talks begin in Korea

1952   Immigration and Nationality Act retains quota system, lifts ban on immigration of Asian and Pacific peoples, but bans "subversives" and homosexuals

United States detonates first hydrogen bomb

Dwight D. Eisenhower wins presidency, defeating Adlai Stevenson; Richard Nixon becomes vice president

1953   Julius and Ethel Rosenberg executed for atomic espionage

Armistice ends fighting in Korea

1954   Army-McCarthy hearings end, discrediting McCarthy

1955   Warsaw Pact created

CONCLUSION

In his farewell address, in January 1953, Harry Truman reflected: "I suppose that history will remember my term in office as the years when the 'cold war' began to overshadow our lives. I have hardly had a day in office that has not been dominated by this all-embracing struggle."

The election of Dwight Eisenhower helped to diminish the intensity of this dour mood without actually bringing a halt to the conflict. The new president pledged himself to liberate the world from communism by peaceful means rather than force. "Our aim is more subtle," he announced during his campaign, "more pervasive, more complete. We are trying to get the world, by peaceful means, to believe the truth. . . ." Increasing the budget of the CIA, Eisenhower took the Cold War out of the public eye by relying to a far greater extent than Truman on psychological warfare and covert operations.

"The Eisenhower Movement," wrote journalist Walter Lippmann, was a "mission in American politics" to restore a sense of community among the American people. In a larger sense, many of the issues of the immediate post–World War II years seemed to have been settled or put off for a distant future. The international boundaries of communism were frozen with the Chinese Revolution, the Berlin Crisis, and now the Korean war. Meanwhile, at home Cold War defense spending had become a permanent part of the national budget, an undeniable drain on tax revenues but an important element in the government contribution to economic prosperity. If the nuclear arms race remained a cause for anxiety, joined by more personal worries about the changing patterns of family life, a sense of relative security nevertheless spread. Prospects for world peace had dimmed, but the worst nightmares of the 1940s had eased as well.

— REVIEW QUESTIONS

1. Discuss the origins of the Cold War and the sources of growing tensions between the United States and the Soviet Union at the close of World War II.

2. Describe the basic elements of President Harry Truman's policy of containment. How did the threat of atomic warfare affect this policy?

3. Compare the presidencies of Franklin D. Roosevelt and Harry S. Truman, both Democrats.

4. Describe the impact of McCarthyism on American political life. How did the anti-Communist campaigns affect the media? What were the sources of Senator Joseph McCarthy's popularity? What brought about his downfall?

5. How did the Cold War shape mid-twentieth-century American culture?

6. Discuss the role of the United States in Korea in the decade after World War II. How did the Korean war affect the 1952 presidential election?

7. Why did Dwight D. Eisenhower win the 1952 presidential election?

— RECOMMENDED READING

Mark S. Byrnes, *The Truman Years, 1945–1953* (2000). A concise history of the Truman administration and its role at the moment when the United States became the dominant economic power in the world. Byrnes covers this transformation with particular attention to the way the president helped to shape a view of the world that presented the United States and the Soviet Union as permanent enemies in a struggle for domination. Includes a set of twenty-one key documents and a detailed chronology of events.

Kevin J. Fernlund, ed., *The Cold War American West, 1945–1989* (1998). Ten essays illustrating the impact of the Cold War on the region of the United States that housed the bulk of military bases, airfields, nuclear testing grounds, and toxic waste dumps. Presenting a variety of interpretations, the contributors ask a common question: Was the West transformed or deformed by the policies of the growing national security state?

John Fousek, *To Lead the Free World: American Nationalism and the Cultural Roots of the Cold War* (2000). Examines the "public culture" of the Cold War through an innovative study of various responses to the official doctrines and declarations of the Truman administration. Fousek pays special attention to the publications of major civil rights organizations and the two largest labor unions of the period and argues that "a broad public consensus" supported Truman's nationalistic foreign policy.

Richard M. Fried, *The Russians Are Coming! The Russians Are Coming!: Pageantry and Patriotism in Cold-War America* (1998). Examines through vivid examples the creation of the fear of communism and its translation into patriotic zeal. Fried takes as his thesis that rallying the public to "fight" the Cold War required as much organization and energy as mobilizing Americans to defend the home front during World War II.

David Halberstam, *The Coldest Winter: America and the Korean War* (2007). The journalist David Halberstam conducted dozens of interviews with veterans to create a huge history of the Korean War that looks ahead to future U.S involvement in Southeast Asia and the Middle East.

David K. Johnson, *The Lavender Scare: The Cold War Persecution of Gays and Lesbians in the Federal Government* (2004). Goes beyond McCarthy and the persecution of Communists to examine the role of the national-security state in purging homosexuals from positions in federal government. Johnson also covers the gay subculture of Washington, DC, which grew with the expansion of government during the New Deal and World War II.

Elaine Tyler May, *Homeward Bound: American Families in the Cold War Era* (1988). A lively account of the effects on family life and women's roles of the national mood of "containment." May argues that government policy became part of a popular culture that solidified the Cold War era's "feminine mystique."

Robert J. McMahon, *The Cold War: A Very Short Introduction* (2003). A compact history of the Cold War that emphasizes its global dimensions. McMahon traces its origins to the devastation of World War II and ends with the unification of Germany in 1990.

Ellen Schrecker, *The Age of McCarthyism: A Brief History with Documents,* 2nd ed. (2002). A useful collection of primary sources on internal security and anticommunism by one of the foremost scholars of the field.

Naoko Shibusawa, *America's Geisha Ally: Reimagining the Japanese Enemy* (2006). With ample reference to American popular culture, this book examines the way the United States transformed Japan from a hated enemy into a bulwark against communism during the Cold War.

Judith E. Smith, *Visions of Belonging: Family Stories, Popular Culture, and Postwar Democracy, 1940–1960* (2004). Creatively uses literature, drama, and film to examine the ways public life and private experience were reshaped in the aftermath of World War II.

Stanley Weintraub, *MacArthur's War: Korea and the Undoing of an American Hero* (2000). Tells the story of the downfall of the commander of U.S. forces in the Far East, who was "senior to everyone but God" in the military services. The author additionally offers a detailed description of the horror and ruin accompanying the brutal ground war in Korea.

myhistorylab™
Where it's a good time to connect to the past!

For study resources for this chapter, go to **http://www.myhistorylab.com** and choose *Out of Many*. You will find a wealth of study and review material for this chapter, including pretests and posttests, customized study plan, key-term review flash cards, interactive map and document activities, and documents for analysis.

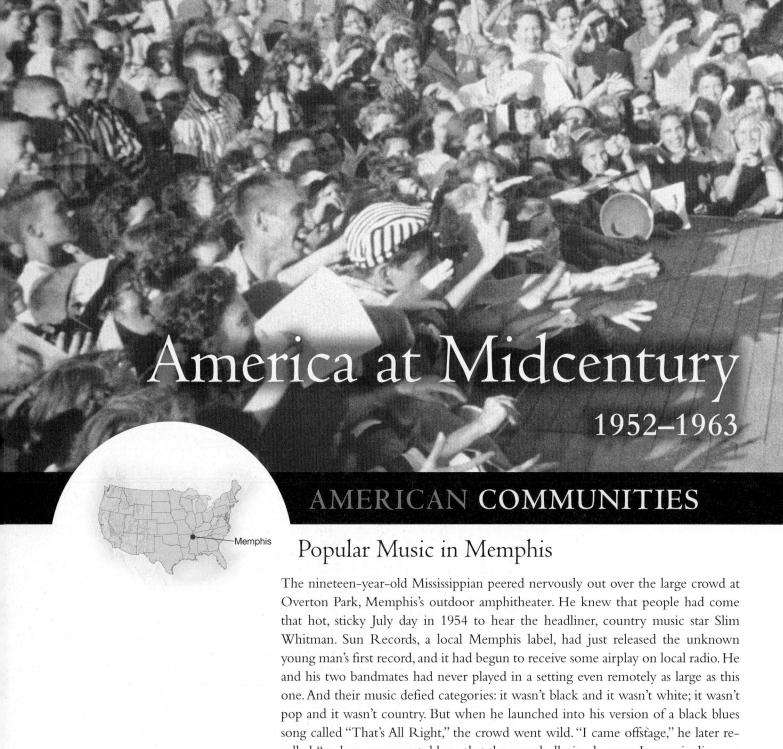

America at Midcentury

1952–1963

Popular Music in Memphis

The nineteen-year-old Mississippian peered nervously out over the large crowd at Overton Park, Memphis's outdoor amphitheater. He knew that people had come that hot, sticky July day in 1954 to hear the headliner, country music star Slim Whitman. Sun Records, a local Memphis label, had just released the unknown young man's first record, and it had begun to receive some airplay on local radio. He and his two bandmates had never played in a setting even remotely as large as this one. And their music defied categories: it wasn't black and it wasn't white; it wasn't pop and it wasn't country. But when he launched into his version of a black blues song called "That's All Right," the crowd went wild. "I came offstage," he later recalled, "and my manager told me that they was hollering because I was wiggling my legs. I went back out for an encore, and I did a little more, and the more I did, the wilder they went." Elvis Presley had arrived.

Elvis combined a hard-driving, rhythmic approach to blues and country music with a riveting performance style; as much as anyone he defined the new music known as rock 'n' roll. An unprecedented cultural phenomenon, rock 'n' roll was made largely for and by teenagers. In communities all over America, rock 'n' roll brought teens together around jukeboxes, at sock hops, in cars, and at private parties. It also demonstrated the enormous consumer power of an emerging youth culture. Postwar teenagers would constitute the most affluent generation of young people in

American history. Their ability and eagerness to buy records, phonograph players, transistor radios, clothing, makeup, and even cars forced business and advertisers to recognize a new teen market. Their buying power helped define the affluent society of the postwar era.

Elvis Presley's life and career also personified many of the themes and tensions of postwar American life. Elvis was born in Tupelo, Mississippi, in 1935, but like many thousands of other poor rural whites the Presley family moved to Memphis in 1949. Elvis's father found work in a munitions plant. The Presleys were poor enough to qualify for an apartment in Lauderdale Courts, a Memphis public housing project built during the New Deal. Located halfway between St. Louis and New Orleans on the Mississippi River, Memphis enjoyed healthy growth during World War II, with lumber mills, furniture factories, and chemical manufacturing supplementing the cotton market as sources of jobs and prosperity. Memphis also boasted a remarkable ➤

diversity of popular theater and music, including a large opera house, numerous brass bands, vaudeville and burlesque, minstrel shows, jug bands, and blues clubs. And like the rest of the South, Memphis was a legally segregated city; whites and blacks lived, went to school, and worked apart. But music—in live clubs and on the radio—was an important means of breaking through the barriers of racial segregation.

As a boy, Elvis turned to music for emotional release and spiritual expression. He soaked up the wide range of musical styles available in Memphis. The all-white Assembly of God Church his family attended featured a renowned hundred-voice choir. Elvis and his friends went to marathon all-night "gospel singings" at Ellis Auditorium, where they enjoyed the tight harmonies and emotional style of white gospel quartets. Elvis also drew from the sounds he heard on Beale Street, the main black thoroughfare of Memphis and one of the nation's most influential centers of African American music. In the postwar years, local black rhythm and blues artists like B. B. King, Junior Parker, and Muddy Waters attracted legions of black and white fans with their emotional power and exciting showmanship. Elvis himself performed along with black contestants in amateur shows at Beale Street's Palace Theater. Nat D. Williams, a prominent black Memphis disc jockey and music promoter, recalled how black audiences responded to Elvis's unique style. "He had a way of singing the blues that was distinctive. He could sing 'em not necessarily like a Negro, but he didn't sing 'em altogether like a typical white musician. . . . Always he had that certain humanness about him that Negroes like to put in their songs." Elvis himself understood his debt to black music and black performers. "The colored folks," he told an interviewer in 1956, "been singing and playing it just like I'm doing now, man, for more years than I know. They played it like that in the shanties and in their juke joints and nobody paid it no mind until I goosed it up. I got it from them."

Dissatisfied with the cloying pop music of the day, white teenagers across the nation were increasingly turning to the rhythmic drive and emotional intensity of black rhythm and blues. They quickly adopted rock 'n' roll (the term had long been African American slang for dancing and sexual intercourse) as their music. But it was more than just music: it was also an attitude, a celebration of being young, and a sense of having something that adult authority could not understand or control. For millions of young people, rock 'n' roll was an expression of revolt against the conformity and blandness found in so many new postwar suburbs. When Sun Records sold Presley's contract to RCA Records in 1956, Elvis became an international star. Records like "Heartbreak Hotel," "Don't Be Cruel," and "Jailhouse Rock" shot to the top of the charts and blurred the old boundaries between pop, country, and rhythm and blues. His appearances on network television shows contributed to his enormous popularity and demonstrated the extraordinary power of this new medium of communication. Television helped Elvis attract legions of new fans despite—and partly because of—the uproar over his overtly sexual performance style.

Yet in early 1958, at the height of his popularity, Elvis was drafted into the U.S. Army for a two-year hitch. The peacetime draft was a grim reminder for millions of American young men of the Cold War anxieties that hovered over the economic prosperity of the era. Even the most famous entertainer in the world could not escape them. Elvis did most of his service in Germany, a critical site of American and Soviet confrontation between 1948 and the early 1960s.

By helping to accustom white teenagers to the style and sound of black artists, Elvis helped establish rock 'n' roll as an interracial phenomenon. The considerable adult opposition to rock 'n' roll revolved largely around fears of race mixing. To a remarkable degree the new music anticipated and contributed to the collapse of segregation, at least in the realm of popular culture. Institutional racism would continue to plague the music business—many black artists were routinely cheated out of royalties and severely underpaid—but the music of postwar Memphis at least pointed the way toward the exciting cultural possibilities that could emerge from breaking down the barriers of race. It also gave postwar American teenagers a newfound sense of community. In a broader sense, rock 'n' roll heralded a generational shift in American society. Just as Elvis's extraordinary popularity led the way for a new kind of music, in 1960 the nation elected John F. Kennedy, the youngest president in its history, and a leader who came to symbolize youthful idealism. His assassination cut short the promise of the new frontier, but not before young people had established a crucial new presence in the nation's economy, culture, and political life.

Focus Questions

1. How did the Eisenhower administration's foreign policy respond to Cold War challenges?

2. On what foundations did the nation's post–World War II prosperity rest?

3. What ideals did America's suburban life evoke, and how did those ideals correspond to suburban realities?

4. What explains the emergence of a distinct youth culture in 1950s' America?

5. What criticisms did television and the 1950s' mass culture evoke?

6. Who was John F. Kennedy, and why did his New Frontier seem so promising to many Americans?

1952–1963

UNDER THE COLD WAR'S SHADOW

By the time Dwight D. Eisenhower—universally called "Ike"—entered the White House in 1953, the confrontation with communism was already providing the framework for America's relations with the world. Eisenhower developed new strategies for the containment of what he called "international communism," including a greater reliance on nuclear deterrence and aggressively using the CIA for covert action. Yet Eisenhower also resolved to do everything possible to forestall an all-out nuclear conflict. Recognizing the limits of raw military power, he accepted a less than victorious end to the Korean conflict and avoided full military involvement in Indochina. Ironically, Eisenhower's promotion of high-tech strategic weaponry fostered what he called—disapprovingly—the military-industrial complex. By the time he left office in 1961, he felt compelled to warn the nation against excessive military spending. His Democratic successor, John F. Kennedy, would discover just how difficult it was to escape the Cold War framework in shaping American foreign policy.

THE EISENHOWER PRESIDENCY

Ike's landslide election victory in 1952 set the stage for the first full two-term Republican presidency since Ulysses S. Grant's presidency. Eisenhower's experience in foreign affairs had been one of his most attractive assets as a presidential candidate. His success as supreme commander of Allied forces in World War II owed as much to his diplomatic as to his military prowess. And as he had promised during his campaign, in December 1952 Eisenhower traveled to Korea just after his election and spent three days at the front. He returned home determined to end the fighting. The death of Soviet leader Joseph Stalin in March 1953, along with the exhaustion of Chinese and North Korean forces, created conditions favorable for a truce. In July 1953 a cease-fire agreement—not a peace settlement—brought the fighting to an uneasy end, freezing the division of North and South Korea near the 38th Parallel.

Eisenhower's success in ending the Korean fighting set the tone for his administration and increased his popularity. As president, Eisenhower kept up anticommunist Cold War rhetoric while persuading Americans to accept the East–West stalemate as a more or less permanent fact. At home, Ike became the reassuring symbol of moderation and stability in a nation worried by threats ranging from communism and nuclear war to a new depression.

A conservative vision of community lay at the core of Eisenhower's political philosophy. He saw America as a corporate commonwealth, similar to Herbert Hoover's "associative state" of a generation before (see Chapter 23). Eisenhower believed the industrial strife, high inflation, and fierce partisan politics of the Truman years could be corrected only through cooperation, self-restraint, and disinterested public service. As president, Eisenhower sought to limit New Deal trends that had expanded federal power, and he encouraged a voluntary, as opposed to a regulatory, government–business partnership. To him, social harmony and "the good life" at home were closely linked to maintaining a stable, American-led international order abroad.

Consciously, Eisenhower adopted an evasive speaking style in public, including his press conferences, but in private and in writing he could be very incisive. He was fond of the phrase "middle of the road." As he told reporters, "I feel pretty good when I'm attacked from both sides. It makes me more certain I'm on the right track." Intellectuals and liberals found it easy to satirize Eisenhower for his "blandness," his vagueness, and his often contradictory pronouncements. (These were usually deliberate attempts to confuse both domestic critics and Cold War opponents.) The majority of the American public agreed with Eisenhower's seemingly easygoing approach. He kept the conservative and liberal wings of his party united and appealed to many Democrats and independents.

In running his White House staff and his administration, Eisenhower adapted the staff system with which he had effectively managed unwieldy Allied forces during World War II. His "hidden hand presidency" relied on letting the states and corporate interests guide domestic policy and the economy. He appointed nine businessmen—three with ties to General Motors—to his first cabinet. Former GM chief Charles Wilson, his secretary of defense, epitomized the administration's economic views when he famously told Congress, "What was good for our country was good for General Motors, and vice versa." He appointed men congenial to the corporate interests they were supposed to regulate to the Federal Trade Commission, the Federal Communications Commission, and the Federal Power Commission. Forty billion dollars' worth of disputed offshore oil lands were transferred from the federal government to the Gulf states under the Submerged Lands Act of 1953, whose passage Eisenhower secured. This enhanced the presence of state governments and private companies in the oil business—and cost the Treasury billions in lost revenues.

At the same time, Eisenhower accepted the New Deal legacy of greater federal responsibility for social welfare. He rejected conservative Republican appeals to dismantle Social Security. His administration agreed to a modest expansion of Social Security and unemployment insurance and small increases in the minimum wage. Ike also created the Department of Health, Education and Welfare, appointing as its head the second woman in history to hold a cabinet position, Oveta Culp Hobby. In agriculture, Eisenhower continued to sustain farm prices—and the interests of agribusiness—by means of New Deal–style parity payments. Between 1952 and 1960, federal spending on agriculture jumped from about $1 billion to $7 billion, and government storage facilities bulged with surpluses.

Eisenhower, a fiscal conservative in Hoover's mold, hesitated to use fiscal policy (government spending) to pump up the economy when it twice went into recession: after the Korean war and again in 1958. In that year, though unemployment hit 7.5 percent, the administration refused to cut taxes or increase spending. Eisenhower feared inflation more than unemployment or poverty—and indeed, by the time he left office he could boast that on his watch the average family's real wages (that is, factoring in inflation) had risen by 20 percent. With low inflation and steady, if modest, growth, the Eisenhower years were prosperous for most Americans. Long after he retired from public life, Ike liked to remember his major achievement as "an atmosphere of greater serenity and mutual confidence." Yet for minorities, the working poor, many old people, and Americans trapped in economically depressed areas, chronic poverty festered.

Presidential contender Dwight D. Eisenhower hosts a group of Republican National Committee women at his campaign headquarters in 1952. Ike's status as America's biggest war hero, along with his genial public persona, made him an extremely popular candidate with voters across party lines.

THE "NEW LOOK" IN FOREIGN AFFAIRS

The death of Joseph Stalin in 1953, just two months after Eisenhower's inauguration, brought an internal power struggle in the Soviet Union. It also opened up the prospects for a thaw in the Cold War, giving Eisenhower hope for peaceful coexistence between the two superpowers. Although Eisenhower recognized that the United States was engaged in a long-term struggle with the Soviet Union, he feared that permanent Cold War mobilization might overburden the American economy and create a "garrison state." He therefore pursued a high-tech, capital-intensive defense policy that emphasized America's qualitative advantage in strategic weaponry and sought cuts in the military budget. As a percentage of the federal budget, military spending fell from 66 percent to 49 percent during Eisenhower's two terms. Much of this saving was gained through increased reliance on nuclear weapons and long-range delivery systems, which were relatively cheaper than conventional forces.

Secretary of State John Foster Dulles gave shape to the "new look" in American foreign policy in the 1950s. A devout Presbyterian lawyer, Dulles had been involved in diplomacy since World War I. He brought to the job a strong sense of righteousness, an almost missionary belief in America's responsibility to preserve the Free World from godless, immoral communism. Dulles called not simply for "containing" communism but for a "rollback." The key would be greater reliance on America's nuclear superiority. As part of a new strategic doctrine, Dulles emphasized the capacity of the Strategic Air Command to inflict devastating destruction with thermonuclear H-bombs. This would be "massive retaliation . . . at times and places of our own choosing" to deter Soviet aggression. This policy especially appealed to conservative Republicans, frustrated by the UN rules of engagement calling only for conventional arms during the Korean war.

But the limits of a policy based on nuclear strategy became painfully clear when American leaders faced tense situations that offered no clear way to intervene without provoking full-scale war. When East Berliners rebelled against Communist rule in June 1953, Cold War hard-liners thought they saw the long-awaited moment for rollback. American agents had encouraged rebellion in East Berlin with implied promises of American support. It never came, and Soviet tanks crushed the uprising. But precisely how could the United States have responded? Bitter public sentiment about the still unresolved Korean conflict merged with Eisenhower's sense of restraint; in the end, the United States did nothing except protest angrily. On a greater scale, U.S. leaders faced the same dilemma in 1956 when Hungary revolted against Communist rule. The United States opened its gates to thousands of Hungarian refugees, but despite desperate appeals on the rebel radio it refused to intervene against Soviet tanks and troops. Eisenhower recognized that the Soviets would defend not just their own borders, but also their domination of Eastern Europe, by all-out war if necessary.

Nikita Khrushchev, who had emerged as Stalin's successor, in 1955 withdrew Soviet troops from eastern Austria in a conciliatory gesture. This first real rollback had been achieved by negotiation and a spirit of common hope, not by threats or force. In 1958 Khrushchev, probing American intentions and hoping to redirect the Soviet economy toward the production of more consumer goods, unilaterally suspended nuclear testing. Khrushchev made a twelve-day trip to America in 1959, visiting an Iowa farm, touring Hollywood, and conferring with Eisenhower at Camp David, the presidential retreat in Maryland. If nothing else, such "summit" diplomacy offered a psychological thaw in the Cold War. In early 1960 Khrushchev called for another summit in Paris, to discuss German reunification and nuclear disarmament. Eisenhower prepared for a friendship tour of the Soviet Union.

Soviet Premier Nikita Khrushchev enjoys a bite to eat during his tour of an Iowa farm in 1959. A colorful, earthy, and erratic man, Khrushchev loomed as the most visible human symbol of the Soviet Union for Americans. On this trip he called for Soviet–American friendship, yet he also boasted "We will bury you.".

All that collapsed in May 1960. The Soviets shot down an American U-2 spy plane gathering intelligence on nuclear facilities. Secret American surveillance and probes of Soviet air defenses had been going on for years—justified in American officials' eyes by Moscow's refusal to allow international inspections as part of any disarmament agreement. A deeply embarrassed Eisenhower at first denied the existence of U-2 flights, but then the Soviets produced the American pilot, who readily confessed. The summit collapsed when Eisenhower refused Khrushchev's demands for an apology and an end to spy flights. The U-2 incident demonstrated the limits of personal diplomacy in resolving the deep structural rivalry between the superpowers.

Eisenhower often provided a moderating voice on issues of defense spending and missile development. The Soviet Union's dramatic launch of *Sputnik,* the first Earth-orbiting satellite, in October 1957 upset Americans' precarious sense of security. This demonstration of Soviet technological prowess raised fears about Russian ability to deploy thermonuclear-tipped intercontinental ballistic missiles (ICBMs) against American cities. Critics attacked the Eisenhower administration for failure to keep up with the enemy. Senator Stuart Symington, a Missouri Democrat, bluntly warned, "Unless our defense policies are promptly changed, the Soviets will move from superiority to supremacy." In addition to huge increases in defense spending, some panic-stricken pundits urged a massive program to build fallout shelters for the entire population in case of nuclear attack.

Eisenhower rejected these radical responses. He knew from U-2 evidence that the Soviet Union in fact trailed far behind the United States in ICBM development, but he kept this knowledge secret so as not to reveal to the Soviets the sources of American intelligence. Instead of panicking before *Sputnik,* he held to a doctrine of "sufficiency": maintaining enough military strength to survive any attack and enough nuclear capability to deliver a massive counterattack. Two measures did emerge from Congress with Eisenhower's support: creation of the National Aeronautics and Space Agency (NASA) to coordinate space exploration and missile development, and the National Defense Education Act, which funneled more federal aid into science and foreign-language education. A bipartisan majority in Congress also voted to increase the military budget by another $8 billion, accelerating the arms race and bloating the defense sector of the economy.

COVERT ACTION

A heavy reliance on covert CIA operations was the other side of Eisenhower's "New Look" defense policy of threatening massive retaliation on America's foreign enemies. He had been an enthusiastic supporter of covert operations during World War II, and during his presidency secret CIA-sponsored paramilitary operations became a key element of American foreign policy. With the American public wary of direct U.S. military interventions, the CIA promised a cheap, quick, and quiet way to depose hostile or unstable regimes, or to prop up conservative governments under siege by indigenous radicals, reformers, or revolutionaries.

Eisenhower's new CIA chief was Allen Dulles, John Foster's brother and an important figure in the OSS, the CIA's World War II precursor. Under Dulles's command, the CIA far exceeded its mandate to collect and analyze information. All over the world, thousands of covert agents carried out operations that included making large, secret payments to friendly political parties (such as conservative Christian Democrats in Italy and Latin America) or to foreign trade unions that opposed the Communist Party.

Independence movements by now were shaking the European colonial empires throughout Asia and Africa, just as in Latin America dislike of U.S. hegemony was surging. To the Eisenhower administration's alarm, the Soviet Union began winning influence in the "Third World," appealing to allegedly common anti-imperialist solidarity and by offering modest foreign aid. Communists played only small roles in most Third World independence movements. But widespread anti-Western feelings in these lands were fanned by publicity about America's racial problems and by resentment against foreign investors' control of natural resources, including oil and mineral wealth. But if emerging nations questioned U.S. regional security arrangements by opting for neutrality—or, worse, expropriated American property—the Eisenhower administration was apt to try covert countermeasures and military intervention.

GLOBAL INTERVENTIONS

In Iran in 1953 the CIA produced a swift, major victory. The popular Iranian prime minister, Mohammed Mossadegh, had nationalized Britain's Anglo-Iranian Oil Company, and the State Department worried that this might set a precedent throughout the oil-rich Middle East. Kermit Roosevelt, the CIA chief in Iran, organized and financed opposition to Mossadegh within the Iranian army and on the streets of Teheran. This CIA-sponsored movement drove Mossadegh from office and put in power an autocratic monarch (shah), Riza Pahlavi. The shah proved his loyalty to his American sponsors by renegotiating oil contracts, assuring American companies 40 percent of Iran's oil concessions. But U.S. identification with the shah's repressive regime in the long run created a groundswell of anti-Americanism among Iranians.

U.S. policy throughout the Middle East was complicated by the conflict between Israel and its Arab neighbors.

MAP EXPLORATION

To explore an interactive version of this map, go to **www.prenhall.com/faragher6/map27.1**

MAP 27.1 The United States in the Caribbean, 1948–66 U.S. military intervention and economic presence grew steadily in the Caribbean following World War II. After 1960, opposition to the Cuban Revolution dominated U.S. Caribbean policies.

Immediately after the United States and the Soviet Union recognized the newborn Jewish state in 1948, the Arab countries launched an all-out attack. Israel repulsed the attack, drove thousands of Palestinians from their homes, and seized territory considerably beyond the lines of the projected UN partition of Palestine into a Jewish and an Arab state. While the Arab world boycotted Israel economically and refused to recognize its right to exist, hundreds of thousands of Palestinians languished in squalid refugee camps. Eisenhower believed that Truman had been too hasty in encouraging Israel. Yet most Americans supported the new Jewish state as a refuge for a people the Nazis had tried to exterminate in the Holocaust.

Israel became a reliable U.S. ally in an unstable region. Arab nationalism continued to vex American policy-makers, culminating in the 1956 Suez Crisis. Egyptian president Gamal Abdel Nasser, a leading voice of Arab nationalism, dreamed of building the Aswan High Dam on the Nile to create more arable land and provide cheap electric power. To build the dam, he sought American and British economic aid. But negotiations broke down and Nasser turned to the Soviet Union for aid and announced he would nationalize the strategically vital—and British-controlled—Suez Canal. Eisenhower refused European appeals for help in forcibly returning the canal to the British. British, French, and Israeli forces then invaded Egypt in October 1956. The United States sponsored a UN cease-fire resolution demanding withdrawal of foreign forces. Yielding to this pressure and to Soviet threats, the British, French, and eventually Israeli forces withdrew. Eisenhower had won a major diplomatic battle through patience and pressure. But it brought no lasting peace to the troubled region. Arab nationalists continued to look primarily to the Soviet Union for support against Israel.

Guatemala saw the most publicized CIA intervention of the Eisenhower years (Map 27.1). In that impoverished Central American country—where 2 percent of the population held 72 percent of all farmland and the American-based United Fruit Company owned vast banana plantations—a fragile democracy took root in 1944. President Jácobo Arbenz Guzmán, elected in 1950, aggressively pursued land reform, encouraged the formation of trade unions, and tried to buy (at assessed value) enormous acreage that United Fruit owned but did not cultivate. The company demanded far more compensation for this land than Guatemala offered and, having powerful friends in the administration (CIA director Dulles had sat on United Fruit's board of directors), it began lobbying intensively for U.S. intervention, linking land-reform programs to international communism. The CIA spent $7 million training Guatemalan dissidents in neighboring Honduras.

U.S. intervention began when the Navy stopped Guatemala-bound ships and seized their cargoes, and on June 14, 1954, the U.S.-trained antigovernment force invaded from Honduras. Guatemalans resisted by seizing United Fruit buildings, but U.S. Air Force bombing gave the invaders cover. Guatemala appealed in vain to the United Nations for help, while Eisenhower publicly denied any knowledge of CIA involvement. A newly appointed Guatemalan leader, Carlos Castillo Armas, flew to the Guatemalan capital in a U.S. embassy plane. In the widespread terror that followed, unions were outlawed and thousands were arrested. United Fruit circulated photos of Guatemalans murdered by the invaders, mislabeling them "victims of communism." In 1957 Castillo Armas was assassinated, initiating a decades-long civil war between military factions and peasant guerrillas.

Vice President Nixon declared that the new Guatemalan government had earned "the overwhelming support of the Guatemalan people"—a boast belied by events in Guatemala and by the resentment that the United States aroused throughout Latin America. In 1958, while Nixon made a "goodwill" tour of the region, angry mobs stoned his limousine in Caracas, Venezuela. U.S. actions had in fact triggered an anti-American backlash.

The global anticommunist strategy that the Truman and Eisenhower administrations embraced led to American backing of France's desperate attempt to maintain its colonial empire in Indochina (see Chapter 26). From 1950 to 1954, the United States poured $2.6 billion in military aid (about three-quarters of the total French costs) and CIA assistance into the fight against the nationalist Vietminh movement, led by Communist Ho Chi Minh. When in March 1954 Vietminh forces surrounded 25,000 French troops at Dien Bien Phu, France pleaded for direct American intervention. Secretary of State Dulles and Vice President Nixon, among others, called for using tactical nuclear weapons and U.S. ground troops to rescue the French. But Eisenhower, remembering Korea, refused. "I can conceive of no greater tragedy," he said, "than for the United States to become engaged in all-out war in Indochina."

Still, Eisenhower feared that the loss of one country to communism would inevitably lead to the loss of others. "You have a row of dominoes set up," he said, "and you knock over the first one and what will happen to the last one is the certainty that it will go over quickly." This so-called domino theory meant that the "loss" of Vietnam would threaten other Southeast Asian nations (Laos, Thailand, and the Philippines) and perhaps even India and Australia. After the French surrender at Dien Bin Phu, an international conference in Geneva established a cease-fire and a "temporary" division into a communist northern state and a noncommunist southern state. National elections and reunification were promised in 1956. But the United States refused to sign the accord. Instead, the Eisenhower administration created the Southeast Asia Treaty Organization (SEATO), a NATO-like and U.S.-dominated security pact including the United States, Great Britain, France, Australia, New Zealand, Thailand, the Philippines, and Pakistan.

Ngo Dinh Diem, who quickly emerged as South Vietnam's president, was a former Japanese collaborator and a Catholic in a 90 percent Buddhist country. Supported by Eisenhower, Diem refused to permit the promised 1956 elections, knowing that the popular hero Ho Chi Minh would easily win. American economic and military aid, along with covert CIA activity, kept the increasingly isolated Diem in power. His corrupt and repressive policies alienated many peasants. By 1959, his Saigon regime faced a civil war against the thousands of peasants who were joining guerrilla bands to drive him out. Eisenhower's commitment of military advisers and economic aid to South Vietnam, based on Cold War assumptions, had laid the foundation for the Vietnam war of the 1960s.

THE AFFLUENT SOCIETY

With the title of his influential book *The Affluent Society* (1958), economist John Kenneth Galbraith labeled postwar America. Galbraith observed that American capitalism had worked "quite brilliantly" in the years since World War II. But Americans, he argued, needed to spend less on personal consumption and devote more public funds to schools, medical care, culture, and social services. For most Americans, however, strong economic growth was the defining fact of the postwar period, and a fierce desire for consumer goods and the "good life" permeated American culture. The deeply held popular belief in the right to a continuously expanding economy and a steadily rising standard of living—even against the backdrop of global Cold War anxieties—shaped American social and political life.

SUBSIDIZING PROSPERITY

During the Eisenhower years the federal government played a crucial role in subsidizing programs that helped millions of Americans achieve middle-class status. Federal aid helped people to buy homes, attend colleges and technical schools, and live in new suburbs. Much of this assistance expanded on programs begun during the New Deal and World War II. The Federal Housing Administration (FHA), established in 1934, extended the government's role in subsidizing the housing industry by insuring long-term mortgage loans to private lenders for home building. By putting "the full faith and credit" of the federal government behind residential mortgages, the FHA attracted new private capital into home building and revolutionized the industry. A typical FHA mortgage required less than 10 percent for a down payment and spread low-interest monthly payments over thirty years. In addition, homeowners benefited from the provision in the Internal Revenue Code (dating back to 1913) that allowed the deduction of all forms of interest payments from taxes. The mortgage interest deduction was the most important middle-class tax benefit for millions of postwar home buyers.

Yet FHA policies had long-range drawbacks. FHA insurance went overwhelmingly to new residential developments, FHA policy favored the construction of single-family projects while discouraging multiunit housing, refused loans to repair older structures and rental units, and required for any loan guarantee an "unbiased professional estimate" rating of the property, the prospective borrower, and the neighborhood. In practice, these estimates resulted in blatant discrimination against racially mixed communities. Bluntly, the FHA's Underwriting Manual warned: "If a neighborhood is to retain stability, it is necessary that properties shall continue to be occupied by the same social and racial classes." Thus, the FHA reinforced racial and income segregation.

Most suburbs were built as planned communities. One of the first, Levittown, opened in 1947 in Hempstead, Long Island, on 1,500 acres of former potato fields. Developer William Levitt, who described his firm as "the General Motors of the housing industry," was the first entrepreneur to bring mass-production techniques to home building. All building materials were precut and

A family poses before their Cape Cod style home in Levittown, New York, 1950. The photo, taken by *Life Magazine* photographer Bernard Hoffman, embodies the postwar domestic ideal of the white suburban family.

prefabricated at a central factory, then assembled on-site into houses by largely unskilled, nonunion labor. In this way Levitt put up hundreds of identical houses each week. Eventually, Levittown encompassed more than 17,000 houses and 82,000 people. Yet in 1960 not one of Levittown's residents was African American, and owners who rented out their homes were told to specify that their houses would not be "used or occupied by any person other than members of the Caucasian race." Levitt himself angrily rejected any criticism of his racial policies: "As a company our position is simply this: we can solve a housing problem, or we can try to solve a racial problem, but we cannot combine the two" (see Communities in Conflict).

The impact on American life of the 1944 Servicemen's Readjustment Act—the G.I. Bill of Rights—reached far beyond higher education (see Chapter 26). In addition to educational grants, the act gave returning veterans low-interest mortgages and business loans, thus subsidizing suburban growth as much as the postwar expansion of higher education. Through 1956, nearly 10 million veterans received G.I. Bill tuition and training benefits. Veterans Administration–insured loans totaled more than $50 billion and assisted millions of former G.I.s in starting businesses.

Another key boost to postwar growth, especially in suburbs, came from the National Interstate and Defense Highways Act of 1956. Significantly, the program was sold to the country partly as a civil defense measure (supposedly to

Integrating Levittown, Pennsylvania

The construction of mass-produced suburban communities represented a crucial shift in the lives of millions of postwar American families. The opportunity to own a new home—one that often came with brand-new appliances such as refrigerators and ranges—proved enormously attractive. The availability of low-cost mortgages through the Federal Housing Administration (FHA) and the Veterans Administration (VA) provided a key boost into the middle-class world of home ownership. Builder William J. Levitt spearheaded this explosive expansion of suburbia by developing cheap prefabricated construction and creating Levittown, New York (with 17,500 homes on Long Island) and Levittown, Pennsylvania (with 15,500 homes just north of Philadelphia).

Most of the new postwar suburbs were racially segregated by a combination of local law and longstanding custom. Leavitt was blunt about his belief in the business necessity for all-white communities. "As a Jew," he said, "I have no room in my mind or heart for racial prejudice. But I have come to know that if I sell to a Negro family, then 90 to 95 per cent of our white customers will not buy into the community. That is their attitude, not ours."

Levitt and other builders had no say over the resale of houses. In August 1957 William Myers, an African American veteran of World War II, purchased a home in Levittown, Pennsylvania. When he and his wife and three small children moved in, they sparked an angry and violent response from some of their neighbors. Unlike the Deep South, northern communities did not live under the rules of legal segregation. But the opposition to integration in places like Levittown revealed that racial prejudice was by no means limited to the South. In 1959 the New Jersey Appellate Court, considering a discrimination lawsuit brought by two African Americans, ruled that a third Levittown being built in that state could not bar African Americans from purchasing homes. But incidents like the one described here were fairly widespread in northern suburbs, and they foreshadowed the fierce political and legal battles over de facto segregation that would become an important element of the civil rights movement.

A news account describes the opposition faced by the Myers family as they moved into Levittown. A more in-depth feature on the incident includes a variety of views expressed by members of the community.

What underlying assumptions about race relations do you find among white opponents to the integration of Levittown, Pennsylvania?

How are economic arguments used to justify resistance to African Americans as neighbors?

"Police Rout 400 at Negro's Home" (August 20, 1957)

Levittown, Pa.—State troopers armed with riot clubs broke up a disorderly crowd of 400 persons who had gathered here tonight to protest the purchase of a house by a Negro family.

The crowd, mostly teenagers, started to assemble at 6 P.M. near the home of Mr. and Mrs. William Myers Jr., the first Negroes to purchase a dwelling in this development. The Negro family moved into its home today in the Dogwood Hollow section of the 15,500 house development.

Despite an order barring the Dogwood Hollow section from all but residents and persons with business in the neighborhood, more people filtered into the area and the crowd numbered 400 at 9 P.M. There were derisive shouts and someone threw a stone, which struck a state trooper. Lieutenant M. J. Wicker [in charge of the state police contingent] announced over a loud speaker in a police car: "I will not tolerate this. I'll give you ten minutes to move out and go back to your homes."

The crowd refused to move and ten minutes later the police moved toward them. When the police used their clubs, poking and swinging, the crowd ran toward Haines Road, a block away. One man stopped to fight but was subdued and arrested. Some of the young girls in the group cried and there were shouts of "Gestapo" and "Is this Communist Russia?" The crowd thinned and at 10:30 o'clock there were only 150 left.

The incident tonight was the latest of several protest meetings by the residents of the community. The meetings had been forbidden as illegal assemblages.

Mr. Myers, an equipment tester for a refrigeration concern in near-by Trenton, N.J. moved some furniture into the $11,000 house a week ago. The next evening, shortly after the Myerses had left, two windows in the living room were smashed by persons in a crowd of more than 300.

Gov. George M. Leader denounced the stone throwing and assigned the state police at the request of C. Leroy Murray, sheriff of Bucks County. Today, a newly formed citizens' group, the Levittown Betterment Committee, declared that it would continue to hold protest meetings in defiance of Mr. Murray's edict.

Earlier today, when the Myerses walked into their home carrying some suitcases, towels and other small articles, Mr. Myers said: "Now we're here to stay."

SOURCE: *New York Times*, August 20, 1957.

"Now we're
here to stay."

"Just say that I'm against it
and I don't like it."

Reactions: "When a Negro Family Moved into a White Community" (August 30, 1957)

What happens when a Negro family buys a home and moves into a Northern community that has always had an all white population? This sprawling development of 16,000 homes just north of Philadelphia is finding out the hard way. It is a story of a peaceful community suddenly turned upside down by racial tension and unaccustomed turbulence.

Up till now, Levittown—with 55,000 residents—has been a quiet place. It was built between 1951 and 1955 by William J. Levitt, a real estate developer who also built the community of the same name on Long Island, N.Y.

No Negroes had ever lived in Levittown until August. Then William Myers, Jr., and his wife moved here from neighboring Bloomsdale Gardens, a racially integrated housing development. They are Negroes, parents of three small children.

Citizens committees—one favoring racial segregation for Levittown and another in favor of racial integration—quickly sprang up. The Levittown Betterment Association, formed among the Myerses' new neighbors, announced as its purpose the removal of the Negro family from the community by peaceful means. The Citizens' Committee for Levittown, composed of church and civic groups and backed by Quaker churchmen, appealed for an end to the violence and acceptance of the Myerses.

Almost overnight, Levittown residents whose principal concerns had been their homes and gardens and the cost of living found themselves on opposite sides of the fence in a king-sized row. Lewis Wechsler, who lives in the house next door, expresses one viewpoint. Of the Myerses he says: "They have a right to live here the same as any other American." Mr. Wechsler, a machinist, works in a plant across the Delaware River in Trenton, N.J.

James McDaniel, who lives on nearby Dogwood Drive, is one who doesn't like what has happened. A steelworker, he came north from Tennessee, and works in the big Fairless plant of U.S. Steel north of here. "We don't like Negroes living in the neighborhood," says Mr. McDaniel. "One family maybe is all right, but after one moves in others come. You hear a lot of talk among Negroes over at the plant that if the Myers family stays they'll move here, too. We don't like it, but there's nothing we can do about it legally."

George Bessam, a bachelor, also has a job at Fairless. What are his feelings on the racial storm that has struck Levittown? "I really don't have any objections to colored people, but I don't think they ought to live in white neighborhoods," he says. "A lot of people moved into Levittown from Philadelphia and other places for just one reason—to get away from colored people in their old neighborhoods. Now they're up against this—colored people moving into Levittown, too. I just don't think it ought to happen. And I think all this police stuff is terrible—people getting hit over the head by police clubs when they're just trying to see that they get their rights," adds Mr. Bessam.

Champney Bernauer lives with his family in Levittown's Willowood section. He's a salesman, is against Negroes moving into the community. "I know how I feel about this thing," he says, "but you couldn't print what I would have to say. Just say that I'm against it and I don't like it. What anyone can do about it, I don't know."

On the opposite side of the fence are the civic groups like the Citizens' Committee for Levittown, headed by Rev. Ray Harwick of Levittown's Evangelical and Reformed Church of the Reformation. "An overwhelming majority of our neighbors," the committee reports, "have been calmly accepting the Myerses move, regardless of whether they personally support or oppose the Myerses decision."

On taking up residence in his new home, Mr. Myers is quoted as having said he would try to be "a good neighbor." After all the trouble began, he is reported to have decided to stay put "if at all possible" and to have voiced the hope that he would be allowed to bring up his children in the community. "Pressure can't be any greater than it is now," he reportedly said.

The Levittown Betterment Association, which opposes the settling of the Myerses in the community, has indicated that it would try to raise the money to buy out the Negro family.

Real estate men say privately that Negroes never will be allowed in Levittown in any numbers. They point out that this community is one of low and medium-priced homes occupied for the most part by young couples just getting a start as homeowners. Such people, it is held, are touchy about things like property values, which they believe will drop precipitously when Negroes move into a neighborhood.

SOURCE: *U.S. News & World Report*, August 30, 1957.

facilitate evacuating American cities in case of nuclear attack). It originally authorized $32 billion to build a national interstate highway system. By 1972 the program had become the single largest public works program in American history, laying out 41,000 miles of highway at a cost of $76 billion. New taxes on gasoline, oil, tires, buses, and trucks paid for the program; the money was held in a Highway Trust Fund separately from general revenue. Federal subsidies for interstate highway construction stimulated both the automobile industry and suburb building, while helping transform the American landscape with motels, fast-food outlets, and other businesses servicing road-tripping Americans. It also accelerated the decline of American mass transit and of older cities. By 1970, the nation possessed the world's best roads—and one of the world's worst public transportation systems.

Cold War jitters also prompted the federal government to launch new initiatives to aid education. The Soviet launch of the *Sputnik* satellite in the fall of 1957 dealt a body-blow to Americans' confidence in the superiority of their technology and education; officials, pundits, and educators alike worried that the country might be lagging behind the Soviets in training scientists and engineers. With bipartisan congressional support, the administration pledged to strengthen support for educating American students in mathematics, science, and technology. The National Defense Education Act (NDEA) of 1958 allocated $280 million in grants—tied to matching grants from the states—for state universities to upgrade their science facilities. The NDEA also created $300 million in low-interest loans for college students, who had to repay only half the amount if they went on to teach in elementary or secondary school after graduation. In addition, the NDEA provided fellowship support for graduate students planning to go into college and university teaching. The NDEA represented a new consensus on the importance of high-quality education to the national interest.

In a broader sense, the postwar economy floated on a sea of Cold War–justified military spending. At the height of the Korean war, defense expenditures swallowed up about half the federal budget, or 14 percent of GNP; after Korea, though military spending declined, by 1960 defense contracts still constituted about 10 percent of GNP. That spending provided an enormous boost to defense-industry employers like Boeing and Douglas Aircraft and created hundreds of thousands of new jobs. New military bases, along with the growing aviation industry, spurred enormous economic and population growth across communities in southern California, around Seattle and Charleston, and on New York's Long Island. Military spending, which many associated with high-paying jobs and prosperous communities, thus acquired enormous local political support and powerful patrons in Congress, all devoted to keeping federal contracts flowing into their districts.

SUBURBAN LIFE

For millions of Americans, the Great Depression and World War II had meant squeezing into cramped apartments or rundown houses, often sharing space with relatives and boarders. Suburban home owning was irresistibly alluring for them, especially when home builders threw into the deal new appliances—gas ranges, refrigerators, washers, and dryers. Unquestionably, suburban living meant a huge improvement in material conditions for many postwar American families, and the suburban boom strengthened the domestic ideal of the nuclear family as the model for American life. The image of the perfect suburban wife—efficient, patient, always charming—permeated television, movies, and magazines. Suburban domesticity was usually presented as women's only path to happiness and fulfillment.

That glowing image often masked a stifling existence defined by housework, child care, and boredom. In the late 1950s, Betty Friedan, a wife, mother, and journalist, began a systematic survey of her Smith College classmates. She found "a strange discrepancy between the reality of our lives as women and the image to which we were trying to conform." Extending her research, in 1963 Friedan published her landmark book *The Feminine Mystique,* which gave voice to the silent frustrations of suburban women and helped to launch a new feminist movement.

For millions of suburban families, only two incomes could yield the middle-class life. The expansion of the female labor force—from 17 million in 1946 to 22 million in 1958—was a central economic fact of the post–World War II years. By 1960, 40 percent of women were employed full-time or part-time, and 30 percent of married women looked to supplement the family income and ensure a solidly middle-class standard of living. Often the opportunity to move to a more fashionable neighborhood, to purchase a second car, or take a family vacation depended on a wife's second income (see Figure 27.1).

The powerful postwar rebirth of American religion was strongly associated with suburban living. In 1940, less than half the American population belonged to institutional churches; by the mid-1950s nearly three-quarters called themselves church members, and a church-building boom was part of the nation's suburban expansion. Best-selling religious authors like the Presbyterian pastor Norman Vincent Peale and the Roman Catholic bishop Fulton J. Sheen (who also appeared on TV) offered a shallow blend of spiritual reassurance and "the power of positive thinking," stressing individual solutions to problems and opposing social or political activism. Billy Graham's hugely popular "Crusades for Christ" brought the religious revival

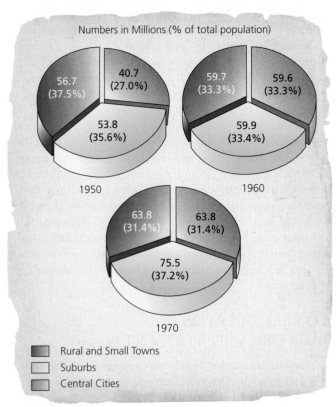

Numbers in Millions (% of total population)

FIGURE 27.1 The Growth of the
Suburbs, 1950–70

Suburban growth, at the expense of older inner cities, was one of
the key social trends in the twenty-five years following World War II.
By 1970, more Americans lived in suburbs than in either inner cities
or rural areas.

SOURCE: Adapted from U.S. Bureau of the Census, *Current Censuses,
1930–1970* (Washington, DC: U.S. Government Printing Office, 1975).

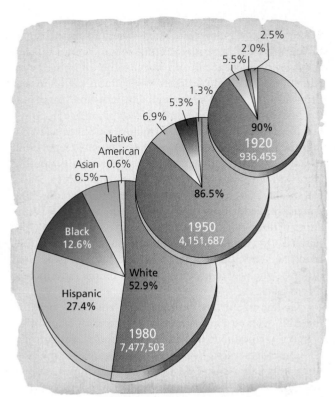

FIGURE 27.2 L.A. County Population
1920–80

to millions while warning of godless communism. Most popular religious writers emphasized the importance of belonging, of fitting in—an appeal that meshed perfectly with the conventional aspirations of suburban social life and with the ideal of family-centered domesticity.

California—so often the national trendsetter—came to embody postwar suburban life, centered on the automobile. Cars were a necessity for commuting to work. California led the nation in creating automobile-oriented facilities: motels ("motor hotels"), drive-in movies, drive-through fast-food eateries and banks, and parking-lot-encircled shopping malls. Around Los Angeles alone were more than 500 miles of highways. In Orange County, southeast of Los Angeles, the "centerless city" emerged as the dominant form of community. The experience of one woman resident there was typical: "I live in Garden Grove, work in Irvine, shop in Santa Ana, go to the dentist in Anaheim, my husband works in Long Beach, and I used to be the president of the League of Women Voters in Fullerton" (see Figure 27.2).

Contemporary journalists, novelists, and social scientists fed the popular image of suburban life as essentially dull, conformist, and peopled exclusively by the educated middle class. John Cheever, for example, won the National Book Award for *The Wapshot Chronicle* (1957), a novel set in fictional Remsen Park, "a community of four thousand identical homes." Yet these writers (who were largely urban by birth and residence) tended to obscure the real class and ethnic differences among and between different suburban communities. Many new suburbs had a distinctively blue-collar cast. Milpitas, California, for example, grew up around a Ford auto plant about fifty miles outside San Jose. Its residents were blue-collar assembly-line workers and their families, not the stereotypical salaried, college-educated, white-collar employees. Self-segregation and zoning ordinances gave some new suburbs distinctively Italian, Jewish, or Irish ethnic identities, similar to older urban neighborhoods. For millions of new suburbanites, architectural and psychological conformity was an acceptable price to pay for the comforts of home ownership, a small plot of land, and a sense of security and status.

ORGANIZED LABOR AND THE AFL-CIO

By the mid-1950s American trade unions reached an historic high point in their penetration of the labor market, reflecting enormous gains made during the organizing drives in core mass-production industries during the New Deal era and World War II. Whereas only one in eight nonagricultural workers were union members on the eve of the Great Depression, twenty-five years later the figure stood at one in three. Union influence in political life, especially within the Democratic Party, had also increased. Yet the Republican sweep to power in 1952 meant that for the first time in a generation organized labor was without an ally in the White House. New leaders in the nation's two major labor organizations, the American Federation of Labor (dominated by old-line construction and craft unions) and the Congress of Industrial Organizations (new unions in mass-production industry), now pushed for a merger of the two rival groups as the way to protect and build on the movement's recent gains.

George Meany, the brusque, cigar-chomping head of the AFL, seemed the epitome of the modern labor boss. Originally a plumber, he had worked his way through the AFL bureaucracy and had played a leading role on the National War Labor Board during World War II. An outspoken anticommunist, Meany pushed the AFL closer to the Democratic Party but took pride in never having been on a strike or a picket line. Unions, he believed, must focus on improving the economic well-being of their members. Meany's counterpart in the CIO was Walter Reuther, originally a tool-and-die maker in the auto shops of Detroit. Reuther had come to prominence as a leader of the United Automobile Workers during the tumultuous organizing drives of the 1930s and 1940s. Although he had moved away from his early socialist leanings, Reuther believed strongly that American unions ought to stand for something beyond the bread-and-butter needs of their members. His support of a broader social vision, including racial equality, aggressive union organizing, and expansion of the welfare state, reflected the more militant tradition of the CIO unions. Despite their differences, both Meany and Reuther believed a merger of their two organizations offered the best strategy for the labor movement. In 1955 the newly combined AFL-CIO brought some 12.5 million union members under one banner, with Meany as president and Reuther as director of the Industrial Union Department.

The merger marked the apex of trade union membership, and after 1955 its share of the labor market began a slow but steady decline. For millions of workers and their families in well-paying manufacturing jobs, union membership helped bring the trappings of middle-class prosperity: home ownership, higher education for children, travel, and a comfortable retirement. But the AFL-CIO showed little commitment to bringing unorganized workers into the fold. Scandals involving union corruption and racketeering hurt the labor movement's public image. In 1957 the AFL-CIO expelled its largest affiliate, the Inter-

national Brotherhood of Teamsters, because of its close ties to organized crime. In 1959, after highly publicized hearings into union corruption, Congress passed the Landrum-Griffin Act, which widened government control over union affairs and further restricted union use of picketing and secondary boycotts during strikes.

While union membership as a percentage of the total workforce declined, important growth did take place in new areas, reflecting a broader shift in the American workplace from manufacturing to service jobs. During the 1950s and 1960s, union membership among public sector employees, especially at the state and local levels, increased dramatically. Only 400,000 government workers belonged to unions in 1955. By the early 1970s the figure reached 4 million, as civil servants, postal employees, teachers, police, and firefighters joined unions for the first time.

LONELY CROWDS AND ORGANIZATION MEN

Perhaps the most ambitious and controversial critique of postwar suburban America was sociologist David Riesman's *The Lonely Crowd* (1950). Riesman argued that modern America had given birth to a new kind of character type, the "other-directed" man. Previously the nation had cultivated "inner-directed" people—self-reliant individualists who from early in life had internalized self-discipline and moral standards. By contrast, the "other-directed" person typical of the modern era was peer-oriented. Morality and ideals came from the overarching desire to conform. Americans, Riesman thought, were now less likely to take risks or act independently. Their thinking and habits had come to be determined by cues they received from the mass media.

Similarly, William H. Whyte's *Organization Man* (1956), a study of the Chicago suburb of Park Forest, offered a picture of people obsessed with fitting into their communities and jobs. In place of the old Protestant ethic of hard work, thrift, and competitive struggle, Whyte believed, middle-class suburbanites now strove mainly for a comfortable, secure niche in the system. They held to a new social ethic, he argued: "a belief in the group as the source of creativity; a belief in 'belongingness' as the ultimate need of the individual."

The most radical critic of postwar society, and the one with the most enduring influence, was Texas-reared sociologist C. Wright Mills. In *White Collar* (1951), Mills analyzed the job culture that typified life for middle-class salaried employees, office workers, and bureaucrats. "When white collar people get jobs," he wrote, "they sell not only their time and energy, but their personalities as well. They sell by the week or month their smiles and their kindly gestures, and they must practice the prompt repression of resentment and aggression." In *The Power*

A crowded commuter train in Philadelphia, ca. 1955. The rapid growth of suburbs in the postwar era made commuting to work, either by mass transit or auto, a routine part of life for millions of Americans.

Elite (1956), Mills argued that a small, interconnected group of corporate executives, military men, and political leaders had come to dominate American society. The arms race in particular, pursued in the name of Cold War policies, had given an unprecedented degree of power to what President Eisenhower later termed the military-industrial complex.

THE EXPANSION OF HIGHER EDUCATION

American higher education grew explosively after the war, creating the system of postsecondary training that still exists. This expansion both reflected and reinforced other postwar social trends. The number of students enrolled in colleges and universities climbed from 2.6 million in 1950 to 3.2 million in 1960, and then more than doubled—to 7.5 million—by 1970, as the baby boomers reached college age. Most of these new students attended greatly enlarged state university systems. Several factors contributed to this explosion. A variety of new federal programs, including the G.I. Bill and the National Defense Education Act, helped subsidize college education for millions of new students. Government spending on research and development in universities, especially for defense-related projects, promoted a postwar shift to graduate education and faculty research and away from traditional undergraduate teaching.

College students enjoyed a deferment from the draft, which normally faced young men soon after they finished high school. (If college graduates married and became fathers, or entered graduate or professional school, they could usually count on being deferred until they were past draft age, at twenty-six.) In this sense college marked an important class line in postwar America. Colleges and universities by and large accepted the values of postwar corporate culture. By the mid-1950s, 20 percent of all college graduates majored in business or similar fields.

A college degree was a gateway to the middle class. It became a requirement for a whole range of expanding white-collar occupations in banking, insurance, real estate, advertising and marketing, and corporate management in general. Most administrators accommodated large business interests, which were well represented on university boards of trustees. Universities themselves were increasingly run like businesses, with administrators adopting the language of input-output, cost effectiveness, and quality control.

HEALTH AND MEDICINE

Dramatic improvements in medical care allowed many Americans to enjoy longer and healthier lives. New antibiotics such as penicillin, the "wonder drug" of World War II, became widely available to the general population. Federal support for research continued after the war with the reorganization of the National Institutes of Health in 1948.

Perhaps the most celebrated achievement of postwar medicine was the victory over poliomyelitis. Between 1947 and 1951 this disease, which usually crippled those it did not kill, struck an average of 39,000 Americans every year. In 1952, 58,000 cases, most of them children, were reported. Frightened parents tried to keep children away from crowded swimming pools and other summer gathering places. In 1955 Jonas Salk pioneered the first effective vaccine against the disease, using a preparation of killed virus. A nationwide program of polio vaccination, later supplemented by the oral Sabin vaccine, virtually eliminated polio by the 1960s.

Yet access to "wonder drugs" and advanced medical techniques was not shared equally. More sophisticated treatments and expensive new hospital facilities sharply increased the costs of health care. Poor and many elderly Americans found themselves unable to afford modern medicine. Thousands of communities, especially in rural areas and small towns, lacked doctors or decent hospital facilities. Critics of the medical establishment charged that the proliferation of medical specialists and large hospital complexes had increased the number of unnecessary surgical operations, especially for women and children. The decline of the general practitioner—the family doctor—meant that fewer (and eventually no) physicians made house calls; for treatment, people went to hospital emergency rooms or outpatient clinics.

The American Medical Association (AMA), which certified medical schools, did nothing to increase the flow of new doctors. The number of physicians per 100,000 people actually declined between 1950 and 1960; doctors trained in other countries made up the shortfall. The AMA also lobbied hard against efforts to expand government responsibility for the public's health. Truman proposed national health insurance, to be run along the lines of Social Security, and Eisenhower had proposed a program that would offer government assistance to private health insurance companies. Both proposals were denounced as "socialized medicine" by the AMA. Until 1965, with the advent of Medicare (for the elderly) and Medicaid (for the poor)—both of which it also opposed—the AMA successfully fought any form of direct federal involvement in health care.

The growing prestige of science was not universally welcomed. In 1948 an Indiana University entomologist, Alfred Kinsey, published his landmark book on American sexuality, *Sexual Behavior in the Human Male,* followed five years later by *Sexual Behavior in the Human Female.* Based on personal interviews with thousands of subjects, Kinsey's books became best sellers—but offered a picture of American sexual behavior that many found shocking. He found, for example, that roughly half of American women had engaged in premarital sex and that some 10 percent of American men were homosexual. Overall Kinsey's work revealed that each new generation of young Americans was more sexually active than the preceding cohort, irrespective of class or gender. Many critics objected to what they saw as Kinsey's claim to objectivity and his reduction of sexual experience to statistics. Yet in the long run Kinsey's scientific approach helped to demystify sex and led to more openness about human sexuality.

YOUTH CULTURE

The term "teenager", describing someone between thirteen and nineteen, entered standard usage only at the end of World War II. According to the *Dictionary of American Slang,* the United States is the only country having a word for this age group and the only country to consider it "a separate entity whose influence, fads, and fashions are worthy of discussion apart from the adult world." During the fifteen years after World War II, unprecedented attention was paid to America's adolescents. Adults expressed deep fears about everything from teenage sexuality and juvenile delinquency to young people's driving habits, hairstyles, and choice of clothing. At the same time, advertisers and businesses pursued the disposable income of America's affluent youth with a vengeance. Teenagers often found themselves caught between their desire to carve out their own separate sphere and the pressure to become an adult as quickly as possible.

THE YOUTH MARKET

Birthrates had accelerated gradually during the late 1930s and more rapidly during the war years. The children born in those years had by the late 1950s grown into the original teenagers, the older siblings of the celebrated baby boomers of 1946–64. They came of age in a society that, compared with that of their parents and the rest of the world, was uniquely affluent. Converging, the demographic growth of teens and the postwar economic expansion created an explosive and profitable youth market. Manufacturers and advertisers rushed to cash in on the special needs and desires of young consumers: cosmetics, clothing, radios and phonographs, and cars.

The new power of the youth market was summarized by *Life* in 1959: "Counting only what is spent to satisfy their special teenage demands," the magazine reported, "the youngsters and their parents will shell out about $10 billion this year, a billion more than the total sales of GM." In addition, advertisers and market researchers found that teenagers often played a critical, if hard to measure, role as "secret persuaders" in a family's large purchase decisions. Specialized market research organizations, such as Eugene Gilbert & Company and Teen-Age Survey Incorporated, sprang up to serve business clients eager to attract teen consumers and instill brand loyalty. Throughout the 1950s and into the 1960s, teenagers had a major, sometimes dominant, voice in determining America's cultural fads.

To many parents, the emerging youth culture was a dangerous threat to their authority. One mother voiced this fear in a revealing, if slightly hysterical, letter to *Modern Teen* magazine:

> Don't you realize what you are doing? You are encouraging teenagers to write to each other, which keeps them from doing their school work and other chores. You are encouraging them to kiss and have physical contact before they're even engaged, which is morally wrong and you know it. You are encouraging them to have faith in the depraved individuals who make rock and roll records when it's common knowledge that ninety percent of these rock and roll singers are people with no morals or sense of values.

The special status of teenagers was also made apparent to the public by the increasing uniformity of public school education. In 1900, about one of every eight teenagers was in school; six out of eight were by the 1950s. Psychologists wrote guidebooks for parents, with titles like Dorothy Baruch's *How to Live with Your Teenager* (1953) and Paul Landis's *Understanding Teenagers* (1955). Social scientists stressed the importance of peer pressure for understanding teen behavior. Traditional sources of adult authority and socialization—the marketplace, schools, child-rearing manuals, the mass media—all reinforced the notion of teenagers as a special community, united by age, rank, and status.

"HAIL! HAIL! ROCK 'N' ROLL!"

The demands of the new teen market, combined with structural changes in the postwar American mass media, reshaped the nation's popular music. As television broadcasting rapidly replaced radio as the center of family entertainment, people began using radios in new ways. There was a rapid rise in the production of car radios and portable transistor radios as listeners increasingly tuned them in for diversion from or an accompaniment to other activities. By 1956, some 2,700 AM radio stations were on the air across the United States, with about 70 percent of their broadcast time devoted to record shows.

In the recording industry, change was in the air. Small independent record labels led the way in aggressively recording African American rhythm-and-blues artists. Atlantic Records, in New York, developed the most influential galaxy of artists, including Ray Charles, Ruth Brown, the Drifters, Joe Turner, LaVerne Baker, and the Clovers. Chess, in Chicago, had the blues-based, singer-songwriter-guitarists Chuck Berry and Bo Diddley, as well as the "doo-wop" group the Moonglows. In New Orleans, Imperial recorded the veteran pianist-singer Fats Domino, while Specialty unleashed on the world the outrageous Little Richard. On radio, over jukeboxes, and in record stores, all these African American artists "crossed over," adding millions of white teenagers to their solid base of black fans. In 1954 the music trade magazine *Billboard* noted a trend among white teenagers: "The present generation has not known the rhythmically exciting dance bands of the swing era. It therefore satisfies its hunger for 'music with a beat' in modern r&b (rhythm and blues) groups."

The older, more established record companies had largely ignored black music. They responded to the new trend with slick, toned-down "cover" versions of rhythm-and-blues originals by white pop singers. These were invariably pallid, artistically inferior imitations. (Compare Pat Boone's covers of Fats Domino's "Ain't That a Shame" or Little Richard's "Tutti Frutti" with the originals to hear how much was lost.)

But while African American artists began to enjoy newfound mass acceptance, there were limits to how closely white kids could identify with black performers. Racism, especially in so sexually charged an arena as musical performance, was a powerful force in American life. The major labels' superior promotional power, as well as institutional racism in the music business, ensured that white cover versions almost always outsold the black originals. But at live shows, white and black teenagers often listened and danced together to the music of African American performers. Some disc jockeys refused to play cover versions and attracted enthusiastic audiences of both black and white young people. Alan Freed, a white Cleveland DJ, popularized the term *rock 'n' roll* to describe the black rhythm and blues that he played on the air and promoted in live concerts before enthusiastic, racially mixed teen audiences.

The stage was thus set for the arrival of white rock 'n' roll artists who could exploit the new sounds and styles. As a rock 'n' roll performer and recording artist, Elvis Presley reinvented American popular music. His success challenged the old lines separating black music from white and pop from rhythm and blues or country. As a symbol of rebellious youth and as the embodiment of youthful sexuality, Elvis revitalized American popular culture. In his wake came a host of white rock 'n' rollers, many (like him) white Southerners: Jerry Lee Lewis, Buddy Holly, the Everly Brothers, Roy Orbison. But the

The marquee at the Paramount Theater, New York City, advertises Alan Freed's "Holiday of Stars" rock 'n' roll show, 1957. Freed promoted live shows featuring both white and African American performers, attracting enthusiastic mixed race audiences.

greatest songwriter and most influential guitarist to emerge from this first "golden age of rock 'n' roll" was Chuck Berry, an African American from St. Louis who worked part-time as a beautician and house painter. With humor, irony, and passion, Berry proved especially adept at capturing the teen spirit. He composed hits around the trials and tribulations of school ("School Days"), young love ("Memphis"), cars ("Maybellene"), and making it as a rock 'n' roller ("Johnny B. Goode"). As much as anyone, Berry created music that defined what it meant to be young in postwar America.

ALMOST GROWN

Teenage consumers remade into their own turf the landscape of popular music. The dollar value of annual record sales nearly tripled between 1954 and 1959, from $213 million to $603 million. New magazines aimed exclusively at teens flourished in the postwar years; *Modern Teen, Teen Digest,* and *Dig* were just a few. Most teen magazines, like rock 'n' roll music, focused on the rituals, pleasures, and sorrows surrounding teenage courtship. Paradoxically, behavior patterns among white middle-class teenagers in the 1950s and early 1960s exhibited a new kind of youth orientation and at the same time a more pronounced identification with adults.

While parents were worrying about the separate world inhabited by their teenage children, many teens seemed determined to become adults as quickly as possible. Postwar affluence multiplied the number of two-car families, making it easier for sixteen-year-olds to win driving privileges formerly reserved for eighteen-year-olds. Girls began dat-

ing, wearing brassieres and nylon stockings, and using cosmetics at an earlier age than before—twelve or thirteen rather than fifteen or sixteen. Several factors contributed to this trend, including a continuing decline in the age of menarche (first menstruation), the sharp drop in the age of marriage after World War II, and the precocious social climate of junior high schools (institutions that became widespread only after 1945). "Going steady," derived from the college custom of fraternity and sorority pinning, became commonplace among high schoolers. By the late 1950s, eighteen had become the most common age at which American females married.

Teenagers often felt torn between their identification with youth culture and pressures to assume adult responsibilities. Many young people juggled part-time jobs with school and very active social lives—a dilemma for which teen-oriented magazines, music, and movies routinely dispensed advice and sympathy. Rock 'n' roll offered the most sympathetic treatments of the conflicts teens experienced over work ("Summertime Blues"), parental authority ("Yakety Yak"), and the desire to look adult ("Sweet Little Sixteen").

DEVIANCE AND DELINQUENCY

Many adults blamed rock 'n' roll for the apparent decline of parental control over teens. Much of the opposition to rock 'n' roll, particularly in the South, played on long-standing racist fears of white females being attracted to black music and black performers. The undercurrent beneath all this opposition was a deep anxiety over the more open expression of sexual feelings by both performers and audiences.

Paralleling the rise of rock 'n' roll was a growing concern with an alleged increase in juvenile delinquency. An endless stream of magazine articles, books, and newspaper stories asserted that criminal behavior among the nation's young was chronic. Gang fights, drug and alcohol abuse, car theft, and sexual offenses drew the most attention. The U.S. Senate established a special subcommittee on juvenile delinquency. Highly publicized hearings in 1955 and 1956 convinced much of the public that youthful criminals were terrorizing the country. Although crime statistics do suggest an increase in juvenile crime during the 1950s, particularly in the suburbs, the public perception of the severity of the problem was surely exaggerated.

In retrospect, the juvenile delinquency controversy tells us more about anxieties over family life and the erosion of adult authority than about crime patterns. Teenagers seemed more defined by and loyal to their peer culture than to their parents. A great deal of their music, speech, dress, and style seemed alien and threatening. The growing importance of the mass media in defining youth culture brought efforts to regulate or censor media forms believed to cause juvenile delinquency. In 1954, for example, psychiatrist Fredric Wertham published *Seduction of the Innocent,* arguing that crime comic books incited youngsters to criminal acts. Mass culture, he believed, could overwhelm the traditional influences of family, school, and religion. He led a highly publicized crusade that forced the comic book industry to adopt a code strictly limiting the portrayal of violence and crime.

As reactions to two of the most influential "problem youth" movies of the postwar era indicate, teens and their parents frequently interpreted depictions of youthful deviance in the mass media in very different ways. In *The Wild One* (1954), Marlon Brando played the crude, moody leader of a vicious motorcycle gang. Most adults thought of the film as a critique of mindless gang violence, but many teenagers identified with the Brando character, who, when asked,

A 1950s' family watching *I Love Lucy,* one of the most popular situation comedies in the early days of television. Manufacturers designed and marketed TV sets as living room furniture and emphasized their role in fostering family togetherness.

"What are you rebelling against?" coolly replied, "Whattaya got?" In *Rebel Without a Cause* (1955), James Dean, Natalie Wood, and Sal Mineo played emotionally troubled youths in an affluent California suburb. The movie suggests that parents can cause delinquency when they fail to conform to conventional roles—Dean's father does housework wearing an apron, and his mother is domineering.

Elvis, Brando, and Dean (who died in a car crash at the height of his popularity) were probably the most popular and widely imitated teen idols of the era. For most parents, they were vaguely threatening figures whose sexual energy and lack of discipline placed them outside the bounds of middle-class respectability. For teens, however, they offered an irresistible combination of rough exterior and sensitive core. They embodied, as well, the contradiction of individual rebellion versus the attractions of a community defined by youth.

MASS CULTURE AND ITS DISCONTENTS

No mass medium ever achieved such power and popularity as rapidly as television. The basic technology for broadcasting visual images with sound had been developed by the late 1930s, but World War II and corporate competition postponed television's introduction to the public until 1946. By 1960, nearly nine in ten American families owned at least one set, which was turned on an average of more than five hours a day. Television reshaped leisure time and political life. It also helped create a new kind of national community defined by the buying and selling of consumer goods.

Dissident voices challenged the economic trends and cultural conformity of the postwar years. Academics, journalists, novelists, and poets offered a variety of works criticizing the overall direction of American life. These critics of what was dubbed "mass society" were troubled by the premium American culture put on conformity, status, and material consumption. Although a distinct minority, these critics were persistent. Many of their ideas and prescriptions would reverberate throughout the political and cultural upheavals of the 1960s and 1970s, and even into the "culture wars" of the 1980s and beyond.

TELEVISION: TUBE OF PLENTY

Television was a radical change from radio, and its development as a mass medium was quicker and less chaotic. The three main television networks—NBC, CBS, and ABC—grew directly from radio corporations. The networks led the industry from the start, rather than following individual stations, as radio had done. Nearly all TV stations were affiliated with one or more of the networks; only a handful of independent stations struggled for survival.

Television not only depended on advertising, but it also transformed the advertising industry. The television business, like radio, was based on the selling of time to advertisers who wanted to reach the mass audiences tuning into specific shows. Radio had offered entire shows produced by and for single sponsors, usually advertisers who wanted a close identification between their product and a star. But the higher costs of television production forced key changes. Sponsors left the production of programs to the networks, independent producers, and Hollywood studios.

Sponsors now bought scattered time slots for spot advertisements instead of bankrolling an entire show. Ad agencies switched their creative energy to producing slick thirty-second commercials rather than entertainment programs. A shift from broadcasting live shows to filming them opened up lucrative opportunities for reruns and exports. The total net revenue of the TV networks and their affiliated stations in 1947 was about $2 million; by 1957 it was nearly $1 billion. Advertisers spent $58 million on TV shows in 1949; ten years later the figure was almost $1.5 billion.

The staple of network radio, the comedy-variety show, was now produced with pictures. The first great national TV hit, *The Milton Berle Show*, followed this format when it premiered in 1948. Radio stars such as Jack Benny, Edgar Bergen, George Burns and Gracie Allen, and Eddie Cantor switched successfully to television. Boxing, wrestling, the roller derby, and other sporting events were also quite popular. For a brief time, original live drama flourished on writer-oriented shows such as *Goodyear Television Playhouse* and *Studio One*. In addition, early television featured an array of situation comedies with deep roots in radio and vaudeville.

Set largely among urban ethnic families, early shows like *I Remember Mama*, *The Goldbergs*, *The Life of Riley*, *Life with Luigi*, and *The Honeymooners* often featured working-class families struggling with the dilemmas posed by a consumer society. Most plots turned around comic tensions created and resolved by consumption: contemplating home ownership, going out on the town, moving to the suburbs, buying on credit, purchasing a new car. Generational discord and the loss of ethnic identity were also common themes. To some degree, these early shows mirrored and spoke to the real dilemmas facing families that had survived the Great Depression and World War II and were now finding their place in a prosperous consumer culture.

By the late 1950s, all the urban ethnic comedy shows were off the air. A new breed of situation comedies presented nonethnic white, affluent, and insular suburban middle-class families. Shows like *Father Knows Best*, *Leave It to Beaver*, *The Adventures of Ozzie and Harriet*, and *The Donna Reed Show* epitomized the ideal suburban American family of the day. Their plots focused on genial crises, usually brought on by children's mischief or wives' inability to cope with money matters, but patiently resolved by kindly fathers. Shows aimed explicitly at children, such as *Howdy Doody*, pulled kids into the television orbit at an early age. In retrospect, what is most striking about these shows is what is absent: virtually unrepresented were politics, social issues, cities, white ethnic groups, African Americans, and Latinos.

Television also demonstrated a unique ability to create overnight fads and crazes across the nation. Elvis Presley's 1956 appearances on several network television variety shows, including those hosted by Milton Berle and Ed Sullivan, catapulted him from regional success to international stardom. Successful television advertising campaigns made household names out of previously obscure products. A memorable example of TV's influence came in 1955 when Walt Disney produced a series of three one-hour shows on the life of frontier legend Davy Crockett. The tremendous success of the series instantly created a $300 million industry of Davy Crockett shirts, dolls, toys, and "coonskin" caps.

Fess Parker, the actor who starred as Davy Crockett in Walt Disney's popular television series, greets young fans at New York's Idlewild Airport in 1955. The series generated enormous sales of coonskin caps and other Crockett-inspired merchandise, demonstrating the extraordinary selling power of the new medium of television.

TELEVISION AND POLITICS

Prime-time entertainment shows carefully avoided any references to the political issues of the day. Network executives bowed to the conformist climate created by the Cold War. Any hint of political controversy could scare off sponsors, ever wary of public protest. Anti-Communist crusaders set themselves up as private watchdogs, warning of alleged subversive influence in the broadcasting industry. Television and advertising executives responded by effectively blacklisting many talented individuals.

As in Hollywood, the Cold War chill severely restricted the range of political discussion on television. Any honest treatment of the conflicts in American society threatened the consensus mentality at the heart of the television business. Even public affairs and documentary programs were largely devoid of substantial political debate. An important exception was journalist Edward R. Murrow's *See It Now* on CBS—but that show was off the air by 1955. Television news did not come into its own until 1963, with the beginning of half-hour nightly network newscasts. Only then did television's extraordinary power to rivet the nation's attention during a crisis become clear.

But some of the ways that TV would alter the nation's political life were already emerging in the 1950s. Television made Democratic senator Estes Kefauver of Tennessee a national political figure through live coverage of his 1951 Senate investigation into organized crime. In 1952, Republican vice presidential candidate Nixon's rambling, emotionally manipulative television appeal to voters—the famous "Checkers" speech (see Chapter 26)—saved his career.

The 1952 election brought the first use of TV political advertising for presidential candidates. The Republican Party hired a high-powered ad agency, Batten, Barton, Durstine & Osborn (BBD&O), to create a series of short, sophisticated advertisements touting Ike. The BBD&O campaign saturated TV with twenty-second Eisenhower spots for two weeks before Election Day. Ever since, television image-making has been the single most important element in American electoral politics. And TV could also destroy an image, as Joe McCarthy discovered in 1954, when his cruel bullying tactics got live national coverage during Senate hearings into alleged Communist influence in the Army. With some further help from Edward R. Murrow's documentary shows, his political collapse soon followed.

CULTURE CRITICS

The urge to denounce the mass media for degrading the quality of American life tended to unite radical and conservative critics. Thus, Marxist writer Dwight Macdonald sounded an old conservative warning when he described mass culture as "a parasite, a cancerous growth on High Culture." Society's most urgent problem, Macdonald claimed, was "a tepid, flaccid Middlebrow Culture that threatens to engulf everything in its spreading ooze."

Critics argued that the audiences for the mass media were atomized, anonymous, and detached. The media themselves had become omnipotent, capable of manipulating the attitudes and behavior of the isolated individuals in the mass. Many of these critics achieved great popularity themselves, suggesting that the public was deeply ambivalent about mass culture. One of the best-selling authors of the day was Vance Packard, whose 1957 exposé *The Hidden Persuaders* showed how advertisers exploited motivational research into the irrational side of human behavior. These critics undoubtedly overestimated

Jack Kerouac, founding voice of the Beat literary movement, in front of a neon-lit bar, ca. 1950. Kerouac's public readings, often to the accompaniment of live jazz music, created a performance atmosphere underlining the connections between his writing style and the rhythms and sensibility of contemporary jazz musicians.

the media's power. They ignored the preponderance of research suggesting that most people watched and responded to mass media in family, peer group, and other social settings. The critics also missed the genuine vitality and creative brilliance to be found within mass culture: African American music; the films of Nicholas Ray, Elia Kazan, and Howard Hawks; the experimental television of Ernie Kovacs; even the madcap satire of teen-oriented *Mad* magazine.

Some of the sharpest dissents from the cultural conformity of the day came from a group of writers known collectively as the Beats. Led by the novelist Jack Kerouac and the poet Allen Ginsberg, the Beats shared a distrust of the American virtues of progress, power, and material gain. The Beats sensibility celebrated spontaneity, friendship, jazz, open sexuality, drug use, and the outcasts of American society. Kerouac, born and raised in a working-class French Canadian family in Lowell, Massachusetts, coined the term *beat* in 1948. It meant for him "weariness with all the forms of the modern industrial state"—conformity, militarism, blind faith in technological progress. Kerouac's 1957 novel *On the Road,* chronicling the tumultuous adventures of Kerouac's circle of friends as they traveled by car back and forth across America, became the Beat manifesto.

Allen Ginsberg had grown up in New Jersey in an immigrant Jewish family. His father was a poet and teacher, and his mother had a history of mental problems. After being expelled from Columbia University, Ginsberg grew close to Kerouac and another writer, William Burroughs. At a 1955 poetry reading in San Francisco, Ginsberg read—actually, chanted—his epic poem *Howl* to a wildly enthusiastic audience. It began:

> *I saw the best minds of my generation destroyed*
> *by madness, starving hysterical naked,*
> *dragging themselves through the negro streets at dawn*
> *looking for an angry fix,*
> *angelheaded hipsters burning for the ancient heavenly*
> *connection*
> *to the starry dynamo in the machinery of night.*

Howl became one of the best-selling poetry books in the history of publishing, and it established Ginsberg as an important new voice in American literature.

Beat writers received a largely antagonistic, even virulent reception from the literary establishment, and the mass media soon trivialized them. A San Francisco journalist coined the word *beatnik,* which by the late 1950s had become popularly associated with scruffy, bearded men and promiscuous women, all dressed in black, sporting sunglasses and berets, and acting rebellious and alienated. But by challenging America's official culture, Beat writers foreshadowed the mass youth rebellion and counterculture of the 1960s.

THE COMING OF THE NEW FRONTIER

In personality, temperament, and public image, no one could have less resembled Dwight Eisenhower—or, for that matter, the beatniks—than John Fitzgerald Kennedy. The handsome son of a prominent, wealthy Irish American diplomat, husband of a fashionable, trendsetting heiress, forty-two-year-old JFK embodied youth, excitement, and sophistication. As only the second Catholic candidate for president—the first was Al Smith in 1928—Kennedy ran under the banner of his self-proclaimed "New Frontier." His liberalism inspired idealism and hope in millions of young people at home and abroad, and his presidency seemed to embody the call for a new sense of national purpose beyond simply enjoying affluence. In foreign affairs, Kennedy generally followed, and in some respects deepened, the Cold War precepts that dominated postwar policymaking. But by the time of his assassination in 1963, he may have been veering away from the hard-line anti-Communist ideology he had earlier embraced.

THE ELECTION OF 1960

John F. Kennedy's political career began in Massachusetts, which elected him to the House in 1946 and then the Senate in 1952. Kennedy won the Democratic nomination after a bruising series of primaries in which he defeated party stalwarts Hubert Humphrey of Minnesota and Lyndon B. Johnson of Texas. Vice President Richard M. Nixon, the Republican nominee, had faithfully served the Eisenhower administration for eight years and was far better known than his younger opponent. The Kennedy campaign stressed its candidate's youth and his war-hero image. During his World War II tour of duty in the Pacific, Kennedy had bravely rescued one of his crew after their PT boat had been sunk. Kennedy's supporters made much of his intellectual ability. JFK had won the Pulitzer Prize in 1957 for his book *Profiles in Courage,* which in fact had been written largely by his aides.

The 1960 election featured the first televised presidential debates. Political analysts have long argued over the impact of these four encounters but agree that they moved television to the center of presidential politics, making image and appearance more critical than ever. Nixon, just recovering from illness, looked nervous, and heat from studio lights made his makeup run and his jowls look unshaven. Kennedy benefited from a confident manner, telegenic good looks, and less propensity to sweat. Both candidates emphasized foreign policy. Nixon defended the Republican record and stressed his maturity and experience. Kennedy hammered away at the alleged—but non-existent—"missile gap" with the Soviet Union and promised executive leadership full of

Presidential candidates John F. Kennedy and Richard M. Nixon during the second of three televised debates held during the 1960 election campaign. Moderator Frank McGee sits at a desk upstage, facing a panel of newsmen. Eighty-five million viewers watched at least one of the first-ever televised debates, which both reflected and increased the power of television in the electoral process.

vigor. ("Vigah," he said in the Boston accent that became his trademark.)

Kennedy squeaked to victory in the closest election since 1884 (see Map 27.2). He won by a little more than 100,000 votes out of nearly 69 million cast. By solemnly promising to keep church and state separate, he had countered residual anti-Catholic prejudice among conservative Protestants and suspicious liberals. Still, he ran poorly in the South, but by overwhelmingly winning the Catholic vote he carried most of the Northeast and Midwest. Tiny though his margin of victory might be, Kennedy was a glorious winner. Surrounding himself with prestigious Ivy League academics, Hollywood movie stars, and talented artists and writers, he imbued the presidency with an aura of celebrity. The inauguration brought out a bevy of poets, musicians, and fashionably dressed politicians from around the world. The new administration promised to be exciting and stylish, a modern-day Camelot peopled by heroic young men and beautiful women. The new president's ringing inaugural address ("Ask not what your country can do for you—ask what you can do for your country") resonated through a whole generation of young Americans.

IKE'S WARNING: THE MILITARY-INDUSTRIAL COMPLEX

Just before Kennedy took office, President Eisenhower delivered a televised farewell address that included a stark and unexpected warning against what he called (coining a phrase) "the military-industrial complex." Throughout the 1950s, the small numbers of peace advocates in the United States had pointed to the ultimate illogic of Ike's "new look" in national-defense policy. Increasing reliance on nuclear weapons, they argued, did not strengthen national security—it threatened the entire planet with extinction. Peace advocates had demonstrated at military camps, nuclear-test sites, and missile-launching ranges, often getting arrested to make their point. Reports of radioactive fallout around the globe rallied a larger group of scientists and prominent intellectuals against further nuclear testing. In Europe, a Ban the Bomb movement gained a wide following; an American counterpart, the National Committee for a Sane Nuclear Policy (SANE), claimed 25,000 members by 1958. Small but well-publicized actions protesting civil defense drills by SANE and groups such as Women Strike for Peace took place in several big cities. They were precursors of a larger antiwar movement of the 1960s.

Eisenhower came to share some of the protesters' anxiety and doubts about the arms race, for he had found it difficult to rein in the "New Look" system he helped create. Frustrated—and disturbed by the incoming Democrats' demands for increased military spending to close the "missile gap"—he used his farewell address to express alarm at the growing influence of a large military and defense-industry establishment. "We annually spend on military security more than the net income of all United States

—MAP EXPLORATION—

To explore an interactive version of this map, go to
www.prenhall.com/faragher6/map27.2

	Electoral Vote (%)	Popular Vote (%)
JOHN F. KENNEDY (Democrat)	303 (56)	34,227,096 (49.7)
Richard M. Nixon (Republican)	219 (41)	34,108,546 (49.5)
Harry F. Byrd (Independent)	15 (3)	501,643 (0.7)

MAP 27.2 The Election of 1960 Kennedy's popular vote margin over Nixon was only a little over 100,000 votes, making this one of the closest elections in American history.

corporations," Eisenhower warned the country. "This conjunction of an immense military establishment and a large arms industry is new in the American experience. The total influence—economic, political, even spiritual—is felt in every city, every State house, every office of the Federal government. We recognize the imperative need for this development. Yet we must not fail to comprehend its grave implications. Our toil, resources and livelihood are all involved; so is the very structure of our society."

The old soldier understood better than most the dangers of raw military force, and in later years the sentiments behind this language would be adapted by critics of American foreign policy and budget priorities. Eisenhower's public posture of restraint and caution in foreign affairs accompanied an enormous expansion of American economic, diplomatic, and military strength. Yet the Eisenhower years also demonstrated the limits of power and intervention in a world that did not always conform to the simple dualistic assumptions of Cold War ideology.

NEW FRONTIER LIBERALISM

As president, John F. Kennedy promised to revive the liberal domestic agenda, stalled since Truman's presidency. His New Frontier advocated such liberal programs as medical care for the elderly, greater federal aid for education and public housing, raising Social Security benefits and the minimum wage, and various antipoverty measures. Yet the thin margin of his victory and stubborn opposition by conservative southern Democrats in Congress made it difficult to achieve these goals. Congress blocked the administration's attempt to extend Social Security and unemployment benefits to millions of uncovered workers. Congress also failed to enact administration proposals for aid to public schools, mass-transit subsidies, and medical insurance for retired workers over sixty-five.

There were a few New Frontier achievements: modest increases in the minimum wage (to $1.25 per hour), Social Security benefits, and $5 billion appropriated for public housing. The Manpower Retraining Act provided $435 million to train the unemployed. The Area Redevelopment Act provided federal funds for rural, depressed Appalachia. The Higher Education Act of 1963 offered aid to colleges for constructing buildings and upgrading libraries.

The Peace Corps was the New Frontier's best-publicized initiative sending thousands of mostly young men and women overseas for two-year stints to provide technical and educational assistance to underdeveloped Third World countries. Volunteers set up health care programs, helped villagers modernize farm technology, and taught English. As a force for change, the Peace Corps produced modest results, but it epitomized Kennedy's promise to provide opportunities for service for a new generation of idealistic young people.

Kennedy's Presidential Commission on the Status of Women, led by Eleanor Roosevelt, helped revive attention to women's rights issues. The commission's 1963 report was the most comprehensive study of women's lives ever produced by the federal government. It documented the ongoing discrimination faced by American women in the workplace and in the legal system, as well as the inadequacy of social services such as day care. It called for federally supported day-care programs, continuing education programs for women, and an end to sex bias in Social Security and unemployment benefits. The commission also insisted that more women be appointed to policy-making positions in government. The Equal Pay Act of 1963, a direct result of the commission's work, mandated equal wages for men and women employed in industries engaged in interstate commerce. Kennedy also directed executive agencies to prohibit sex discrimination in hiring and promotion. The work of the commission contributed to a new generation of women's rights activism.

Kennedy took a more aggressive stance on stimulating economic growth and creating new jobs than had Eisenhower. The administration pushed lower business taxes through Congress, even at the cost of a higher federal deficit. The Revenue Act of 1962 encouraged new investment and plant renovation by easing tax depreciation schedules for business. Kennedy also gained approval for lower U.S. tariffs as a way to increase foreign trade. To help keep inflation down, he intervened in the steel industry in 1961 and 1962, pressuring labor to keep its wage demands low and management to curb price increases.

A wholly new realm of government spending also won Kennedy's enthusiastic backing: the space program. In panicky reaction to the Soviets' *Sputnik,* under Eisenhower the National Aeronautics and Space Administration (NASA) had been established. In 1961, driven by the Cold War motivation of avoiding "another *Sputnik*" and beating the Soviets in the race to the moon, Kennedy won approval for a greatly expanded space program. Dramatically, he announced the goal of landing an American on the moon by the end of the decade. NASA eventually spent $33 billion before reaching this objective in 1969. This program of manned space flight—the *Apollo* missions, with their science fiction aura—appealed to the public.

Kennedy's longest-lasting achievement as president may have been his strengthening of the executive branch itself. He insisted on direct presidential control of details that Eisenhower had left to advisers and appointees. Moreover, under Kennedy the White House staff assumed many of the decision-making and advisory functions previously held by cabinet members. This arrangement increased Kennedy's authority, since these appointees, unlike cabinet secretaries, escaped congressional oversight and confirmation proceedings. White House aides lacked independent constituencies; their power derived solely from their ties to the president. Kennedy's aides—"the best and the brightest," he called them—dominated policymaking. Kennedy intensified a pattern whereby American presidents increasingly operated through small groups of fiercely loyal aides, often in secret.

KENNEDY AND THE COLD WAR

During Kennedy's three years as president, his approach to foreign policy shifted from aggressive containment to efforts at easing U.S.–Soviet tensions. Certainly when he first entered office, Kennedy and his chief aides saw their main task as confronting the Communist threat. In his first State of the Union Address, Kennedy told Congress that America must seize the initiative in the Cold War. The nation must "move outside the home fortress, and . . . challenge the enemy in fields of our own choosing." To head the State Department, Kennedy chose Dean Rusk, a conservative former assistant to Truman's secretary of state, Dean Acheson. Secretary of Defense Robert McNamara, a Republican and Ford executive, was deter-

mined to streamline military procedures and weapons buying; he typified the technical, cost-efficient, hyper-rational approach to policymaking. Allen Dulles remained CIA chief. These and other high officials believed, with Kennedy, that Eisenhower had timidly accepted stalemate when the Cold War could have been won.

Between 1960 and 1962 defense appropriations increased by nearly a third, from $43 billion to $56 billion. JFK expanded Eisenhower's policy of covert operations, deploying the Army's elite Special Forces to supplement covert CIA operations against Third World guerrillas. These soldiers, fighting under the direct orders of the president, could provide "rapid response" to "brush-fire" conflicts where Soviet influence threatened American interests. The Special Forces, authorized by Kennedy to wear the green berets that gave them their unofficial name, reflected the president's desire to acquire greater flexibility, secrecy, and independence in the conduct of foreign policy.

But Southeast Asia showed the limits of advancing American interests with covert actions and Green Berets. In Laos, the United States had ignored the 1954 Geneva agreement and installed a friendly, CIA-backed military regime, but it could not defeat Soviet-supported Pathet Lao guerrillas. The president had to arrange with the Soviets to neutralize Laos. In neighboring South Vietnam, a more difficult situation developed when Communist Vietcong guerrillas launched an insurgency against the U.S.-supported Diem regime. Kennedy began sending hundreds of Green Berets and other military advisers to bolster Diem. In May 1961, in response to North Vietnamese aid to the Vietcong, Kennedy ordered a covert action against Ho Chi Minh's northern regime that included sabotage and intelligence gathering.

Kennedy's approach to Vietnam reflected an analysis of the situation in that country by two aides, General Maxwell Taylor and Walt Rostow, who saw things solely through Cold War spectacles. "The Communists are pursuing a clear and systematic strategy in Southeast Asia," Taylor and Rostow concluded, ignoring the inefficiency, corruption, and unpopularity of the Diem government. By 1963, with Diem's army unable to contain the Vietcong rebellion, Kennedy had sent nearly 16,000 support and combat troops to South Vietnam. By then, a wide spectrum of South Vietnamese society had joined the revolt against the hated Diem, including highly respected Buddhist monks and their students. Americans watched in horror as evening newscasts showed Buddhists burning themselves to death on the streets of Saigon—the ultimate protest against Diem's repressive rule. American press and television also reported the mounting casualty lists of U.S. forces in Vietnam. The South Vietnamese army, bloated by U.S. aid and weakened by corruption, continued to disintegrate. In the fall of 1963, American military officers and CIA operatives stood aside with approval as a group of Vietnamese generals toppled Diem, killing him and his top advisers. It was the first of many coups that racked the South Vietnamese government over the next few years.

In Latin America, where millions of impoverished peasants were forced to relocate to already overcrowded cities, various revolutionary movements were also gaining ground—and Kennedy looked for ways to forestall them. In 1961 he unveiled the "Alliance for Progress," a ten-year, $100 billion plan to spur economic development in Latin America. The United States committed $20 billion to the project with the Latin nations responsible for the rest. The main goals included greater industrial growth and agricultural productivity, a more equitable distribution of income, and improved health and housing.

Kennedy saw the Alliance for Progress as a Marshall Plan that would benefit Latin America's poor and middle classes. It did help raise growth rates in Latin American economies. But the expansion in export crops and in consumption by the tiny upper class did little to aid the poor or encourage democracy. The United States hesitated to challenge the dictators and extreme conservatives who were its staunchly anti-Communist allies. Thus, the alliance soon degenerated into just another foreign-aid program, incapable of generating genuine social change.

THE CUBAN REVOLUTION AND THE BAY OF PIGS

The direct impetus for the Alliance for Progress was the 1959 Cuban Revolution, which loomed over Latin America—inspiring the left and alarming the right. The U.S. economic domination of Cuba, beginning with the Spanish-American War (see Chapter 20), had continued through the 1950s. American-owned businesses controlled all of Cuba's oil production, 90 percent of its mines, and roughly half of its railroads and sugar and cattle industries. Havana, the island's capital, was an attractive tourist center for Americans, but U.S. crime syndicates shared control—with dictator Fulgencio Batista—of the island's lucrative gambling, prostitution, and drug trade. As a response, in the early 1950s a peasant-based revolutionary movement, led by a middle-class student named Fidel Castro, began gaining strength in the rural districts and mountains outside Havana.

On New Year's Day 1959, after years of guerrilla war, the rebels entered Havana and amid great public rejoicing seized power. For a brief time, Castro seemed a hero in North America as well. *The New York Times* had conducted sympathetic interviews with Castro in 1958, while he was still fighting in Cuba's mountains. The CIA and President Eisenhower shared none of this exuberance. Castro's land-reform program, involving the seizure of acreage from the tiny minority that controlled much of the fertile land, threatened to set an example for other Latin American countries. Although Castro had not yet joined the Cuban

Communist Party, he turned to the Soviet Union after the United States withdrew economic aid. He began to sell sugar to the Soviets and soon nationalized American-owned oil companies and other enterprises. Eisenhower established an economic boycott of Cuba in 1960 and then severed diplomatic relations.

Kennedy inherited from Eisenhower plans for a U.S. invasion of Cuba, including the secret arming and training of Cuban exiles. The CIA drafted the invasion plan, which was based on the assumption that a U.S.-led invasion would trigger a popular uprising and bring down Castro. Kennedy went along with the plan, but at the last moment decided not to supply Air Force cover for the invaders. On April 17, 1961, a ragtag army of 1,400 counterrevolutionaries led by CIA operatives landed at the Bay of Pigs on Cuba's southern coast. Castro's efficient and loyal army easily subdued them.

The debacle revealed that the CIA, blinded by Cold War assumptions, had failed to understand the Cuban Revolution. There was no popular uprising against Castro. An embarrassed Kennedy reluctantly took the blame for the disaster, and his administration was censured time and again by Third World delegates in the United Nations. American liberals criticized Kennedy for plotting Castro's overthrow, while conservatives blamed him for not supporting the invasion. Despite the failure, Kennedy remained committed to getting rid of Castro.

The botched invasion had strengthened "Fidel's" standing among the urban poor and peasants, already attracted by his programs of universal literacy and medical care. As Castro stifled internal opposition, many Cuban intellectuals and professionals fled to the United States. These middle-class émigrés would transform Miami from a retirement resort into a bustling entrepreneurial center, but the growing Cuban presence in electoral-vote-rich Florida also created a powerful lobby for rigid anti-Castro U.S. policies. Even before the end of Kennedy's administration, the CIA's support for anti-Castro operations included at least eight attempts to assassinate Fidel, and the U.S. economic embargo against Cuba continues to this day.

THE 1962 MISSILE CRISIS

The aftermath of the Bay of Pigs led to the Cold War's most serious superpower confrontation: the Cuban missile crisis of October 1962. Frightened by U.S. belligerency, Castro asked Soviet Premier Khrushchev for military help. Khrushchev responded in the summer of 1962 by shipping to Cuba a large amount of sophisticated weaponry, including intermediate-range nuclear missiles capable of hitting Washington, the Northeast, and the Midwest. In early October, American U-2 reconnaissance planes found camouflaged missile silos dotting the island. Several Kennedy aides and the Joint Chiefs of Staff demanded an immediate bombing of these missile sites, arguing that the Soviet move had decisively eroded the United States' strategic global advantage. The president and his advisers pondered their options in a series of tense meetings. Kennedy's aggressive attempts to exploit Cuba in the 1960 election and the Bay of Pigs disaster came back to haunt him: He worried that critics would accuse him of weakness in failing to stand up to the Soviets. Even some prominent Democrats, including Senator J. William Fulbright, chairman of the Senate Foreign Relations Committee, called for invading Cuba. What no one in the United States knew was that Khrushchev had already sent tactical nuclear weapons to Cuba and authorized the Soviet commander on the island to use them to repel an American invasion; that was revealed only in the 1990s. Invasion would have meant nuclear war.

Kennedy went on national television on October 22 to announce discovery of the missile sites. He publicly demanded the removal of all missiles and proclaimed a naval "quarantine" of offensive military equipment shipped to Cuba. (This was actually a blockade; Kennedy avoided the word because a blockade is an act of war.) Requesting an emergency meeting of the UN Security Council, he promised that any missiles launched from Cuba would bring "a full retaliatory response upon the Soviet Union." For a grim week, Americans wondered whether the long-dreaded nuclear Armageddon was imminent. Eyeball to eyeball, each superpower waited for the other to blink. On October 26 and 27 Khrushchev blinked, ordering twenty-five Soviet ships off their course to Cuba, thus avoiding a challenge to the U.S. Navy.

Khrushchev offered to remove the missiles in return for a pledge from the United States not to invade Cuba and later added a demand for removal of American weapons from Turkey, as close to the Soviet Union as Cuba is to the United States. Secretly, Kennedy assured Khrushchev that the United States would dismantle its obsolete missiles in Turkey. On November 20, after weeks of delicate negotiations, Kennedy announced the withdrawal of Soviet missiles and bombers from Cuba. He also pledged to respect Cuban sovereignty and promised not to invade the island.

The crisis had passed. The Soviets, determined not to be intimidated again, began the largest weapons buildup in their history. For his part Kennedy, perhaps chastened by this brush with nuclear disaster, made important gestures toward peaceful coexistence with the Soviets. In a June 1963 address at American University, Kennedy called for a rethinking of Cold War diplomacy. Both sides, he said, had been "caught up in a vicious and dangerous cycle in which suspicion on one side breeds suspicion on the other, and new weapons beget counterweapons."

Shortly after, Washington and Moscow set up a "hot line"—a direct phone connection to permit instant communication during times of crisis. More substantial was the Limited Nuclear Test-Ban Treaty, signed in August 1963 by the United States, the Soviet Union, and Great Britain. The treaty prohibited above-ground, outer-space, and underwater nuclear weapons tests, easing global anxieties about radioactive fallout. But underground testing continued to accelerate for years. The limited test ban was perhaps more symbolic than substantive, a psychological breakthrough in East–West relations after three particularly tense years.

By November 1963, the situation in South Vietnam was deteriorating; Diem's overthrow and murder in a U.S.-backed coup was symptomatic of U.S. failure to secure an anticommunist alternative to Ho Chi Minh's revolutionary movement. Kennedy understood this. There are some indications that he was thinking of cutting losses, perhaps after winning reelection in 1964; there are other signs that he was preparing to escalate the U.S. commitment. Most likely, he meant to keep all options open. But we will never know what he would have done about Vietnam.

President John F. Kennedy, sitting before a television camera in the Oval Office, delivers an address to the nation during the Cuban missile crisis in October 1962. Kennedy's presidency coincided with the emergence of television as the nation's dominant mass medium.

Televising a National Tragedy

The assassination of President John F. Kennedy on Friday, November 22, 1963, marked the emerging power of television as a medium capable of focusing the entire nation's attention on an extraordinary news event.

Kennedy had traveled to Texas on November 21 to shore up popularity in a state crucial to his reelection hopes for 1964. Only local stations covered the presidential arrival and motorcade. But once the president had been shot and declared dead, the networks cut into regu-

lar programming, combining live coverage with videotape from local stations. The hasty inauguration of Vice President Lyndon B. Johnson aboard *Air Force One* was not televised, but widespread dissemination of still photos showed Americans how the constitutional process of succession proceeded side by side with the personal grief of the president's widow, Jacqueline Kennedy.

The next day, Saturday, audiences watched television coverage of world leaders arriving in Washington for the presidential funeral. On Sunday NBC offered live coverage of the accused assassin, Lee Harvey Oswald, being transferred from police custody to the county jail. Millions were stunned to suddenly see Jack Ruby, a shadowy Dallas underworld figure, emerge from the crowd and shoot Oswald himself to death—the first nationally televised murder.

On Monday, November 25, virtually the entire nation watched Kennedy's televised funeral: the ceremony at the National Cathedral and the procession to Arlington Cemetery. The images of the Kennedy family, especially five-year-old Caroline and three-year-old John Jr. saluting, lent a quiet dignity amid deep mourning. Critic Marya Mannes wrote of the four days of television coverage: "This was not viewing. This was total involvement . . . I stayed before the set, knowing—as millions knew—that I must give myself over entirely to an appalling tragedy, and that to evade it was a treason of the spirit."

What strikes you as most powerful about these images from more than four decades ago? Can you think of any recent national events that have brought the nation together via television coverage? How has that coverage changed—or remained similar—in terms of both techniques and subjects covered?

THE ASSASSINATION OF PRESIDENT KENNEDY

The assassination of John F. Kennedy in Dallas on November 22, 1963, sent the entire nation into shock and mourning. Just forty-six years old and president for only three years, Kennedy quickly ascended to martyrdom in the nation's consciousness. Millions had identified his strengths—intelligence, optimism, wit, charm, coolness under fire—as those of American society. In life, Kennedy had helped put television at the center of American politics. Now in the aftermath of his death, television riveted a badly shocked nation. One day after the assassination, the president's accused killer, an obscure misfit named Lee Harvey Oswald, was himself gunned down before television cameras covering his arraignment in Dallas. Two days later, tens of millions watched the televised spectacle of Kennedy's funeral, trying to make sense of the brutal murder (see Seeing History). Although a special commission headed by Chief Justice Earl Warren found the killing to be the work of Oswald acting alone, many Americans doubted this conclusion. Kennedy's death gave rise to a host of conspiracy theories, none of which seems provable.

We will never know, of course, what Kennedy might have achieved in a second term. But in his 1,000 days as president, he demonstrated a capacity to change and grow in office. Having gone to the brink during the

CHRONOLOGY

1950	David Riesman publishes *The Lonely Crowd*
1952	Dwight D. Eisenhower is elected president, defeating Adlai Stevenson
1953	CIA installs Riza Shah Pahlavi as monarch of Iran
1954	Vietminh force French surrender at Dien Bien Phu
	CIA overthrows government of Jácobo Arbenz Guzmán in Guatemala
	United States explodes first hydrogen bomb
1955	Jonas Salk pioneers vaccine for polio
	James Dean stars in the movie *Rebel Without a Cause*
1956	Congress passes the National Interstate and Defense Highways Act
	Elvis Presley signs with RCA
	Eisenhower is reelected, defeating Stevenson a second time
	Allen Ginsberg publishes *Howl*
1957	Soviet Union launches *Sputnik*, first space-orbiting satellite
	Jack Kerouac publishes *On the Road*
1958	National Defense Education Act authorizes grants and loans to college students
1959	Nikita Khrushchev visits the United States
1960	Soviets shoot down U-2 spy plane and cancel planned summit meeting with Eisenhower
	John F. Kennedy is elected president, defeating Richard Nixon
	Almost 90 percent of American homes have television
1961	President Kennedy creates "Green Berets"
	Bay of Pigs invasion of Cuba fails
1962	Cuban missile crisis brings the world to the brink of a superpower confrontation
1963	Report by the Presidential Commission on the Status of Women documents ongoing discrimination
	Betty Friedan publishes *The Feminine Mystique*
	Limited Nuclear Test-Ban Treaty is signed
	President Kennedy is assassinated; Lyndon B. Johnson becomes president

missile crisis, he managed to launch new initiatives toward peaceful coexistence. At the time of his death, relations between the United States and the Soviet Union were more amicable than at any time since the end of World War II. Much of the domestic liberal agenda of the New Frontier would be finally implemented by Kennedy's successor, Lyndon B. Johnson, who dreamed of creating a Great Society.

CONCLUSION

America in 1963 still enjoyed its postwar economic boom. To be sure, millions of Americans, particularly African Americans and Latinos, did not share in the good times. But millions had managed to reach the middle class since the early 1950s. An expanding economy, cheap energy, government subsidies, and dominance in the global marketplace had made the "the good life" available to more Americans than ever. The postwar "American dream" promised home ownership, college education, secure employment at decent wages, affordable appliances, and the ability to travel—for one's children if not for one's self. The nation's public culture—its schools, mass media, politics, advertising—presented a powerful consensus based on the idea that the American dream was available to all who would work for it.

The presidential transition of 1961—from grandfatherly war hero Dwight Eisenhower to charismatic young war hero Jack Kennedy—symbolized for many a generational shift as well. By 1963, young people had more influence than ever before in shaping the nation's political life, its media images, and its burgeoning consumer culture. Kennedy himself inspired millions of young Americans to pursue public service and to express their idealism. But even by the time of Kennedy's death, the postwar consensus and the conditions that nurtured it were beginning to unravel.

— REVIEW QUESTIONS

1. How did Cold War politics and assumptions shape American foreign policy in these years? What were the key interventions the United States made in Europe and the Third World?

2. How did postwar economic prosperity change the lives of ordinary Americans? Which groups benefited most and which were largely excluded from "the affluent society"?

3. What role did federal programs play in expanding economic opportunities?

4. Analyze the origins of postwar youth culture. How was teenage life different in these years from previous eras? How did popular culture both reflect and distort the lives of American youth?

5. How did mass culture become even more central to American everyday life in the two decades following World War II? What problems did various cultural critics identify with this trend?

6. Evaluate the domestic and international policies associated with John F. Kennedy and the New Frontier. What continuities with Eisenhower-era politics do you find in the Kennedy administration? How did JFK break with past practices?

— RECOMMENDED READING

Glenn C. Altschuler, *All Shook Up: How Rock 'n' Roll Changed America* (2003). The best new social history of rock 'n' roll, with excellent coverage of the generational and racial controversies surrounding the new music.

James L. Baughman, *Same Time, Same Station: Creating American Television, 1948–1961* (2007). The best new account of the emergence of television as the nation's dominant mass medium with emphasis on the influence of advertising.

Lizabeth Cohen, *A Consumers' Republic: The Politics of Mass Consumption in Postwar America* (2003). An ambitious, deeply researched overview of how postwar Americans negotiated the tensions between expanding opportunities for consumption and traditional ideals of citizenship and political activism.

Gary Donaldson, *The First Modern Campaign: Kennedy, Nixon, and the Election of 1960* (2007). New and deeply researched analysis of the 1960 election as the template for our media-dominated politics.

Lawrence Freedman, *Kennedy's Wars: Berlin, Cuba, Laos, and Vietnam* (2000). A new analysis of JFK's foreign policy, emphasizing the context of Cold War liberalism.

Edward Humes, *Over Here: How the GI Bill Transformed the American Dream* (2006). Comprehensive history of this crucial postwar legislation, including its discriminatory impact on women and racial minorities.

Kenneth T. Jackson, *Crabgrass Frontier* (1985). The most comprehensive overview of the history of American suburbs. Jackson provides a broad historical context for understanding postwar suburbanization and offers an excellent analysis of the impact of government agencies such as the Federal Housing Administration.

David E. Kaiser, *American Tragedy: Kennedy, Johnson, and the Origins of the Vietnam War* (2000). The most detailed account yet of how the contradictions of Cold War thinking pushed policymakers in three administrations toward an unnecessary and unwinnable war.

Elaine Tyler May, *Homeward Bound: American Families in the Cold War* (1988). A thoughtful social history linking family life of the 1950s with the political shadow of the Cold War.

Grace Palladino, *Teenagers: An American History* (1996). A lively and witty narrative account of the emergence of teenagers as a new social class.

The Civil Rights Movement

1945–1966

The Montgomery Bus Boycott: An African American Community Challenges Segregation

On December 1, 1955, Rosa Parks, a seamstress and well-known activist in the African American community of Montgomery, Alabama, was taken from a bus, arrested, and jailed for refusing to give up her seat to a white passenger. Composing roughly half the city's 100,000 people, Montgomery's black community had long endured the humiliation of a strictly segregated bus system. Drivers could order a whole row of black passengers to stand for one white person. Black people had to pay their fares at the front of the bus, then step back outside and reenter through the rear door.

Protesting Mrs. Parks's arrest, more than 30,000 African Americans answered a hastily organized call to boycott the city's buses. On the day of the boycott, a steady stream of cars and pedestrians jammed the streets around Holt Street Baptist Church. By early evening a patient, orderly, and determined crowd of more than 5,000 African Americans packed the church and spilled over onto the sidewalks. Loudspeakers had to be set up for the thousands who could not squeeze inside. After a brief prayer and a reading from Scripture, all attention focused on the twenty-six-year-old minister, the Reverend Martin Luther King Jr., who rose to address the gathering. "We are here this evening," he began slowly, "for serious business. We are here in a general sense because first and foremost we are American citizens, and we are determined to apply our citizenship to the fullness of its means."

Sensing the crowd's expectant mood, Dr. King got down to specifics and described Mrs. Parks's arrest. As he quickened his cadence and drew shouts of encouragement, he seemed to gather strength and confidence from the crowd. "You know, my friends, there comes a time when people get tired of being trampled over by the iron feet of oppression. There comes a time, my friends, when people get tired of being flung across the abyss of humiliation, when they experience the bleakness of nagging despair."

Even before Dr. King concluded, it was clear to all that the bus boycott would continue for more than just a day. The minister laid out the key principles that would guide the boycott—nonviolence, Christian love, unity. His brief but stirring address created a powerful sense of communion. "If we are wrong, justice is a lie," he told the clapping and shouting throng. "And we are determined here in Montgomery to work and fight until justice runs down like water and righteousness like a mighty stream." ▶

Dr. King made his way out of the church amid waves of applause and rows of hands reaching out to touch him.

Dr. King's prophetic speech catapulted him into leadership of the Montgomery bus boycott—but he had not started what would become known simply as the Movement. When Rosa Parks was arrested, local activists with deep roots in the black protest tradition galvanized the community with the idea of a boycott. Mrs. Parks herself had served for twelve years as secretary of the local NAACP chapter. She was a committed opponent of segregation and was thoroughly respected in the city's African American community. E. D. Nixon, president of the Alabama NAACP and head of the local Brotherhood of Sleeping Car Porters union, saw Mrs. Parks's arrest as the right case on which to make a stand. It was Nixon who brought Montgomery's black ministers together on December 5 to coordinate an extended boycott of city buses. They formed the Montgomery Improvement Association (MIA) and chose Dr. King as their leader. Significantly, Mrs. Parks's lawyer was Clifford Durr, a white liberal with a history of representing black clients. His politically active wife Virginia, for whom Mrs. Parks worked as a seamstress, had been a longtime crusader against the poll tax, which prevented many blacks from voting. And two white ministers, Rev. Robert Graetz and Rev. Glenn Smiley, would offer important support to the MIA.

While Nixon organized black ministers, Jo Ann Robinson, an English teacher at Alabama State College, spread the word to the larger black community. Robinson led the Women's Political Council (WPC), an organization of black professional women founded in 1949. With her WPC allies, Robinson wrote, mimeographed, and distributed 50,000 copies of a leaflet telling the story of Mrs. Parks's arrest and urging all African Americans to stay off city buses on December 5. They did. Now the MIA faced the more difficult task of keeping the boycott going. Success depended on providing alternate transportation for the 30,000 to 40,000 maids, cooks, janitors, and other black working people who needed to get to work.

The MIA coordinated an elaborate system of car pools, using hundreds of private cars and volunteer drivers to provide as many as 20,000 rides each day. Many people walked. Local authorities, although shocked by the discipline and sense of purpose shown by Montgomery's African American community, refused to engage in serious negotiations. With the aid of the NAACP, the MIA brought suit in federal court against bus segregation in Montgomery. Police harassed boycotters with traffic tickets and arrests. White racists exploded bombs in the homes of Dr. King and E. D. Nixon. The days turned into weeks, then months, but still the boycott continued. All along, mass meetings in Montgomery's African American churches helped boost morale with singing, praying, and stories of individual sacrifice. The spontaneous remark of one elderly woman, refusing all suggestions that she drop out of the boycott on account of her age, became a classic refrain of the Movement: "My feets is tired, but my soul is rested."

The boycott reduced the bus company's revenues by two-thirds. In February 1956, city officials obtained indictments against King, Nixon, and 113 other boycotters under an old law forbidding hindrance to business without "just cause or legal excuse." A month later King went on trial. A growing contingent of newspaper reporters and TV crews from around the country watched as the judge found King guilty, fined him $1,000, and released him on bond pending appeal. But on June 4, a panel of three federal judges struck down Montgomery's bus segregation ordinances as unconstitutional. On November 13 the Supreme Court affirmed the district court ruling. After eleven hard months and against all odds, the boycotters had won.

The boycotters' victory inspired a new mass movement for African American civil rights. A series of local struggles to dismantle segregation—in the schools of Little Rock, the department stores of Atlanta, the lunch counters of Greensboro, the streets of Birmingham—would coalesce into a broad-based national movement at the center of American politics. By 1963, the massive March on Washington would win the endorsement of President John F. Kennedy, and his successor, Lyndon B. Johnson, would push through the landmark Civil Rights Act and Voting Rights Act.

The struggle to end legal segregation took root in scores of southern cities and towns. African American communities led these fights, developing a variety of tactics, leaders, and ideologies. With white allies, they engaged in direct-action protests such as boycotts, sit-ins, and mass civil disobedience, as well as strategic legal battles in state and federal courts. The Movement was not without its inner conflicts. Tensions between local campaigns and national civil rights organizations flared up regularly. Within African American communities, long-simmering distrust between the working classes and rural folk on the one hand and middle-class ministers, teachers, and business people on the other sometimes threatened to destroy

Focus Questions

1. What were the legal and political origins of the African American civil rights struggle?

2. What accounts for Martin Luther King's rise to leadership?

3. How did student protesters and direct action shape the civil rights struggle in the South?

4. How did the civil rights movement intersect with national politics in the 1950s and 1960s?

5. What did the Civil Rights Act of 1964 and Voting Rights Act of 1965 accomplish?

6. How did America's other minorities respond to the African American struggle for civil rights?

1945–1966

political unity. Generational conflicts pitted African American student activists against their elders. But overall, the civil rights movement created new social identities for African Americans, inspired a new "rights consciousness" among other minority groups, and profoundly changed American society.

ORIGINS OF THE MOVEMENT

The civil rights movement arose out of the aspirations and community strength of African Americans. Its deepest roots lay in the historic injustices of slavery, racism, and segregation. African Americans' experiences during and immediately after World War II laid the foundation for the civil rights struggle of the 1950s and 1960s.

CIVIL RIGHTS AFTER WORLD WAR II

Between 1939 and 1945, almost 1 million black men and women served in the armed forces. The discrepancy between fighting totalitarianism abroad while enduring segregation and racism in the military embittered many combat veterans and their families. Nearly 2 million African Americans worked in defense plants, and another 200,000 entered the federal civil service. Black union membership doubled, reaching more than 1.2 million. African American newspapers like the *Pittsburgh Courier* fought for the "Double V" campaign—victory over fascism abroad and over segregation

at home. But wartime stress on national unity largely muted political protests. With the war's end, African Americans and their white allies determined to push ahead for full political and social equality.

The wartime boom spurred a mass northward migration of nearly a million black Southerners. Forty-three northern and western cities saw their black population double during the 1940s. Although racial discrimination in housing and employment was by no means absent in northern cities, greater economic opportunities and political freedom continued to attract rural African Americans after the war. With the growth of African American communities in cities like New York, Chicago, and Detroit, black people gained significant influence in urban political machines. Within industrial unions such as the United Automobile Workers and the United Steel Workers, white and black workers learned the power of biracial unity in fighting for better wages and working conditions. Harlem's congressman, Adam Clayton Powell Jr., captured the new mood of 1945 when he wrote that black people were eager "to make the dream of America become flesh and blood, bread and butter, freedom and equality."

After the war, civil rights issues returned to the national political stage for the first time since Reconstruction. Black voters had already begun to switch their allegiance from the Republicans to the Democrats during the New Deal. A series of symbolic and substantive acts by the Truman administration solidified that shift. In 1946 Truman created a President's Committee on Civil Rights. Its 1947 report, *To Secure These Rights*, set out an ambitious program to end racial inequality: creating a permanent civil rights division in the Justice Department, protecting voting rights, passing antilynching legislation, and challenging laws that permitted segregated housing. Yet although he publicly endorsed nearly all these proposals, Truman introduced no legislation to make them law.

Truman and his advisers walked a political tightrope on civil rights. They understood that black voters in several key northern states would be pivotal in the 1948 election. At the same time, they worried about the loyalty of white southern Democrats adamantly opposed to changing the racial status quo. In July 1948, the president made his boldest move on behalf of civil rights, issuing an executive order ending segregation in the armed forces. Later that summer, when liberals forced the Democratic National Convention to adopt a strong civil rights plank, outraged southern delegates walked out and nominated Governor Strom Thurmond of South Carolina for president on a States' Rights ticket. Thurmond carried four southern states in the election. But with the help of more than 70 percent of the northern black vote, Truman barely managed to defeat Republican Thomas E. Dewey in November. The deep split over race issues would continue to wrack the national Democratic Party for a generation.

Electoral politics was not the only arena for civil rights work. During the war, membership in the National Association for the Advancement of Colored People had mushroomed from 50,000 to 500,000. Working- and middle-class urban black people provided the backbone of this new membership. The NAACP conducted voter registration drives and lobbied against discrimination in housing and employment. Its Legal Defense and Education Fund, vigorously led by special counsel Thurgood Marshall, mounted several significant legal challenges to segregation laws. In *Morgan* v. *Virginia* (1946), the Supreme Court used the interstate-commerce clause to declare segregation on interstate buses unconstitutional. Other Supreme Court decisions struck down all-white election primaries, racially restrictive housing covenants, and the exclusion of blacks from law and graduate schools.

The NAACP's legal work demonstrated the potential for using federal courts in attacking segregation. Courts were one place where black people, using the constitutional language of rights, could make forceful arguments that could not be voiced in Congress or at political conventions. But federal enforcement of court decisions was often lacking. In 1947 a group of black and white activists tested compliance with the *Morgan* decision by traveling on a bus through the Upper South. This "Freedom Ride" was cosponsored by the Christian pacifist group Fellowship of Reconciliation (FOR) and its recent offshoot, the Congress of Racial Equality (CORE), which was devoted to interracial, nonviolent direct action. In North Carolina, several riders were arrested and sentenced to thirty days on a chain gang for refusing to leave the bus.

Two symbolic "firsts" raised black expectations and inspired pride. In 1947 Jackie Robinson broke the color barrier in major league baseball, winning rookie-of-the-year honors with the Brooklyn Dodgers. Robinson's courage in the face of racist taunts from fans and players paved the way for the other black ballplayers who soon followed him into the big leagues. In 1950 United Nations diplomat Ralph Bunche won the Nobel Peace Prize for arranging the 1948 Arab-Israeli truce. Bunche, however, later declined an appointment as undersecretary of state because he did not want to subject his family to Washington, D.C.'s humiliating segregation laws.

Charlie Parker (alto sax) and Miles Davis (trumpet) with their group in 1947, at the Three Deuces Club in New York City. Parker and Davis were two creative leaders of the "bebop" movement of the 1940s. Working in northern cities, boppers reshaped jazz music and created a distinct language and style that were widely imitated by young people. They challenged older stereotypes of African American musicians by insisting that they be treated as serious artists.

Cultural change could have political implications as well. In the 1940s, African American musicians created a new form of jazz that revolutionized American music and asserted a militant black consciousness. Although black musicians had pioneered swing and earlier styles of jazz, white bandleaders and musicians had reaped most of the recognition and money. Black artists such as Charlie Parker, Dizzy Gillespie, Thelonius Monk, Bud Powell, and Miles Davis revolted against the standard big-band format of swing, preferring small groups and competitive jam sessions to express their musical visions. The new music, dubbed "bebop," demanded a much more sophisticated knowledge of harmony and melody and featured more complex rhythms and extended improvisation than did previous jazz styles. In urban black communities the "boppers" consciously created a music that, unlike swing, white popularizers found difficult to copy or sweeten. These black artists insisted on independence from the white-defined norms of show business. Serious about both their music and the way it was presented, they refused to cater to white stereotypes of grinning, easygoing black performers.

THE SEGREGATED SOUTH

In the postwar South, still home to over half the nation's 15 million African Americans, the racial situation had changed little since the Supreme Court sanctioned "separate but equal" segregation in *Plessy* v. *Ferguson* (see Chapter 20). In practice, segregation meant separate but unequal. A tight web of state and local ordinances enforced strict separation of the races in schools, restaurants, hotels, movie theaters, libraries, restrooms, hospitals, and even cemeteries, and the facilities for black people were consistently inferior to those for whites. There were no black policemen in the Deep South and only a handful of black lawyers.

In the late 1940s only about 10 percent of eligible southern black people voted, most of these in urban areas. A combination of legal and extralegal measures kept all but the most determined blacks disenfranchised. Poll taxes, all-white primaries, and discriminatory registration procedures reinforced the belief that voting was "the white man's business." African Americans who insisted on exercising their right to vote, especially in remote rural areas, faced physical violence—beatings, shootings, and lynchings. A former

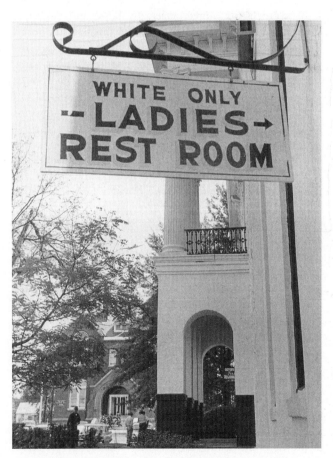

Signs designating "White" and "Colored" rest rooms, waiting rooms, entrances, benches, and even water fountains were a common sight in the segregated South. They were a constant reminder that legal separation of the races in public spaces was the law of the land.

president of the Alabama Bar Association expressed a commonly held view when he declared, "No Negro is good enough and no Negro will ever be good enough to participate in making the law under which the white people of Alabama have to live."

Outsiders often noted that despite Jim Crow laws (see Chapter 20), contact between blacks and whites was ironically close. The mass of black Southerners worked on white-owned farms or in white households. One black preacher neatly summarized the nation's regional differences this way: "In the South, they don't care how close you get as long as you don't get too big; in the North, they don't care how big you get as long as you don't get too close." The South's racial code forced African Americans to accept, at least outwardly, social conventions that reinforced their low standing with whites. A black person did not shake hands with a white person, or enter a white home through the front door, or address a white person except formally. In these circumstances, survival and self-respect depended to a great degree on patience and stoicism. Black people learned to endure humiliation by keeping their thoughts and feelings hidden from white people.

The consequences of violating the code could be fatal. In the summer of 1955 a fourteen-year-old African American boy from Chicago, unaccustomed to local "folkways," was visiting relatives near Money, Mississippi. Leaving a store with some friends, Till spoke in an informal tone to the white wife of the store owner. Several days later Till was kidnapped from his uncle's house in the middle of the night, and shortly thereafter his body was dragged out of the Tallahatchie River. Back in Chicago, Till's mother, Mamie Bradley, insisted on an open-casket funeral, and the photographs of his horribly mutilated body profoundly shocked African American readers of *Jet* magazine and other black publications around the country. No white publications carried these photos. Till's murderers were acquitted in a trial that attracted national attention and underlined the stark realities of southern segregation. It also reminded northern blacks that racist violence could touch their lives as well. In Mamie Bradley's words, "Two months ago I had a nice apartment in Chicago. I had a good job. I had a son. When something happened to the Negroes in the South I said, 'That's their business, not mine.' Now I know how wrong I was. The murder of my son has shown me that what happens to any of us, anywhere in the world, had better be the business of us all."

But broad demographic and economic changes were also remaking the postwar South. On the eve of World War II, more than 40 percent of Southerners lived on farms; two-thirds of its 35 million people resided in places with less than 2,500 inhabitants. During the 1950s, tens of thousands of nonagricultural jobs were created in factories, mills, and office buildings across the region. More and more national corporations, attracted by the region's cheaper labor costs, began establishing a southern presence, and the region's towns and cities competed to lure them. A more highly mechanized agriculture and rapid industrialization pushed more Southerners, black and white, into cities and suburbs. By 1960, roughly half of all Southerners inhabited metropolitan districts and only 15 percent lived on farms.

BROWN v. *BOARD OF EDUCATION*

Since the late 1930s, the NAACP had chipped away at the legal foundations of segregation. Rather than making a frontal assault on the *Plessy* separate-but-equal rule, civil rights attorneys launched a series of suits seeking complete equality in segregated facilities. Their strategy was to make segregation so prohibitively expensive that the South would be forced to dismantle it. In the 1939 case *Missouri* v. *ex rel. Gaines*, the Supreme Court ruled that the University of Missouri law school must either admit African Americans or build another, fully equal law school for them. NAACP lawyers pushed their arguments further, asserting that equality could not be measured simply by money or physical plant. In *McLaurin* v. *Oklahoma State Regents* (1950), the Court agreed with Thurgood Marshall's argument that regulations forcing a black law student to sit, eat, and study in areas apart from white students inevitably created a "badge of inferiority."

By 1951, Marshall had begun coordinating the NAACP's legal resources for a direct attack on the separate-but-equal doctrine, aiming to overturn *Plessy* and the constitutionality of segregation itself. For a test case, Marshall combined five lawsuits challenging segregation in public schools. One of these suits argued the case of Oliver Brown of Topeka, Kansas, who sought to overturn a state law permitting cities to maintain segregated schools. Topeka's ordinance, sanctioned by this law, forced Brown's eight-year-old daughter Linda to travel by bus to a black school even though she lived only three blocks from an all-white elementary school. The Supreme Court heard initial arguments on the cases, grouped together as *Brown* v. *Board of Education*, in December 1952. The *Brown* case offered an important reminder that segregation was not a purely southern phenomenon. Roughly 40 percent of America's 28 million schoolchildren attended legally segregated schools in the South and border states, while millions more were educated in northern communities where *de facto* segregation—created by housing patterns and school districting—was the norm.

In his argument before the Court, Thurgood Marshall argued that separate facilities, by definition, denied black people their full rights as American citizens. Marshall used sociological and psychological evidence that went beyond standard legal arguments. For example, he cited the research of African American psychologist Kenneth B. Clark, who had studied the self-esteem of black children in New York City and in segregated schools in the South. Using black and white dolls and asking the children which they preferred, Clark illustrated how black children educated in segregated schools developed a negative self-image. When Chief Justice Fred Vinson died suddenly in 1953, President Dwight Eisenhower appointed California Governor Earl Warren to fill the post. After hearing further arguments, the Court remained divided on the issue of overturning *Plessy*. Warren, eager for a unanimous decision, patiently worked at convincing two holdouts. Using his political skills to persuade and achieve compromise, Warren urged his colleagues to affirm a simple principle as the basis for the decision.

On May 17, 1954, Warren read aloud the Court's unanimous decision. "Does segregation of children in public schools solely on the basis of race . . . deprive the children of the minority group of equal educational opportunities?" The chief justice paused. "We believe that it does." Warren made a point of citing several of the psychological studies of segregation's effects. He ended by directly addressing the constitutional issue. Segregation deprived the plaintiffs of the equal protection of the laws guaranteed by the Fourteenth Amendment. "We conclude that in the field of public education the doctrine of 'separate but equal' has no place. Separate educational facilities are inherently unequal . . . Any language in *Plessy* v. *Ferguson* contrary to this finding is rejected."

African Americans and their liberal allies around the country hailed the decision and the legal genius of Thurgood Marshall. Marshall himself predicted that all segregated schools would be abolished within five years. Black newspapers were full of stories on the imminent dismantling of segregation. The *Chicago Defender* called the decision "a second emancipation proclamation." But the issue of enforcement soon dampened this enthusiasm. To gain a unanimous decision, Warren had to agree to let the Court delay for one year its ruling on how to implement desegregation. This second *Brown* ruling, handed down in May 1955, assigned responsibility for desegregation plans to local school boards. The Court left it to federal district judges to monitor compliance, requiring only that desegregation proceed "with all deliberate speed." Thus, although the Court had made a momentous and clear constitutional ruling, the need for compromise dictated gradual enforcement by unspecified means.

CRISIS IN LITTLE ROCK

Resistance to *Brown* took many forms. Most affected states passed laws transferring authority for pupil assignment to local school boards. This prevented the NAACP from bringing statewide suits against segregated school systems. Counties and towns created layers of administrative delays designed to stop implementation of *Brown*. Some school boards transferred public school property to new, all-white private "academies." State legislatures in Virginia, Alabama, Mississippi, and Georgia, resurrecting pre–Civil War doctrines, passed resolutions declaring their right to "interpose" themselves between the people and the federal government and to "nullify" federal laws. In 1956, 101 members of Congress from the former Confederate states signed the Southern Manifesto, urging their states to refuse compliance with desegregation. President Eisenhower declined to publicly endorse *Brown*, contributing to the southern resistance. "I don't believe you can change the hearts of men with laws or decisions," he said.

In Little Rock, Arkansas, the tense controversy over school integration became a test case of state versus federal power. A federal court ordered public schools to begin desegregation in September 1957, and the local school board made plans to comply. But Governor Orval Faubus, facing a tough reelection fight, decided to make a campaign issue out of defying the court order. He dispatched Arkansas National Guard troops to Central High School to prevent nine black students from entering. For three weeks, armed troops stood guard at the school. Screaming crowds, encouraged by Faubus, menaced the black students, beat up two black reporters, and chanted "Two, four, six, eight, we ain't going to integrate." Moderate whites opposed Faubus, fearing that his controversial tactics would make it harder to attract new businesses and investment capital to the city. Indeed Little Rock's industrial recruitment efforts declined with the integration crisis, suggesting to southern moderates that militant resistance to integration could be bad for business.

Four African American students walk swiftly past barricaded sidewalks as they integrate Central High School in Little Rock, Arkansas, in September 1957. Soldiers from the 101st Airborne Division, sent to Little Rock by President Eisenhower, protect the students during the tense racial confrontation.

SEEING

Civil Rights on the World Stage

As the civil rights struggle gained momentum through the late 1950s and early 1960s, it evolved from a regional effort aimed at ending southern segregation to a movement with national and ultimately international implications. The United States and the Soviet Union, locked in the Cold War, were both especially eager to win influence in the new Third World nations of Africa and Asia that emerged from the post–World War II collapse of European colonial empires. Because these nations were home to hundreds of millions of people of color, the increasingly tense racial conflicts in local American communities assumed global significance. Newspapers and magazines around the world began carrying dramatic photos of racist violence against the Freedom Riders in 1961 and of fire hoses and police dogs deployed against civil rights demonstrators in Birmingham in 1963. The Eisenhower and Kennedy administrations were acutely sensitive to the negative impact these images had on an American foreign policy that touted itself as the beacon of freedom around the world. They worried that Soviet propaganda would exploit the American racial crisis in the fierce competition to win allies in the Third World and at the United Nations.

— Хочешь учиться в университете? А читать умеешь?

Рисунок Л. САМОЙЛОВА

These two political cartoons illustrate the ongoing commentary that put the civil rights movement on the world stage. The *Oakland Tribune* published "Right into Their Hands," on September 11, 1957, during the integration crisis at Central High School in Little Rock, Arkansas. The cartoon published in the Soviet satirical magazine *Krokodil* on August 24, 1963, comments on the contemporary attempts to integrate American higher education. It depicts an African American student stopped by police from entering an American university, amid protest signs saying (in Russian) "Nigger Go Away," "Lynch Him," "We Want Segregation," and "Put the Colored on Their Knees."

What techniques did these cartoons share in their depiction of forces opposed to integration?
How does the *Oakland Tribune* cartoon seek to counter the kind of sentiments
evoked in the Soviet cartoon?

At first, Eisenhower tried to intervene quietly, gaining Faubus's assurance that he would protect the nine black children. But when Faubus suddenly withdrew his troops, leaving the black students at the mercy of the white mob, Eisenhower had to move. On September 24 he placed the Arkansas National Guard under federal command and ordered a thousand paratroopers of the 101st Airborne Division to Little Rock. The nine black students arrived in a U.S. Army car. With fixed bayonets, the soldiers protected the students as they finally integrated Central High School in Little Rock. Eisenhower, the veteran military commander, justified his actions on the basis of upholding federal authority and enforcing the law. He also defended his intervention as crucial to national prestige abroad, noting the propaganda victory Faubus was handing the Communist world (see Seeing History). "Our enemies," the president argued, "are gloating over this incident and using it everywhere to misrepresent our whole nation." But he neither endorsed desegregation nor offered the civil rights movement any meaningful support. Yet as the first president since Reconstruction to use armed federal troops in support of black rights, Eisenhower demonstrated that the federal government could, indeed, protect civil rights. Unfazed, Governor Faubus kept Little Rock high schools closed during the 1958–59 academic year to prevent what he called "violence and disorder."

NO EASY ROAD TO FREEDOM, 1957–62

The legal breakthrough represented by the *Brown* decision heartened opponents of segregation everywhere. Most important, *Brown* demonstrated the potential for using the federal court system as a weapon against discrimination and as a means of protecting the full rights of citizenship. Yet widespread opposition to *Brown* showed the limits of a strictly legal strategy. In Little Rock, the ugly face of white racism received wide media coverage and quickly sobered the more optimistic champions of integration. However welcome Eisenhower's intervention, his reluctance to endorse desegregation suggested that civil rights activists still could not rely on federal help. As the Montgomery bus boycott had proved, black communities would have to help themselves first.

MARTIN LUTHER KING JR. AND THE SCLC

When it ended with the Supreme Court decision in November 1956, the 381-day Montgomery bus boycott had made Martin Luther King Jr. a national figure. In January 1957 *Time* magazine put King on its cover. *The New York Times Magazine* published a detailed history of the bus boycott, stressing King's role. He was only the second African American ever to appear on NBC's *Meet the Press*. Speaking invitations poured in from universities and organizations around the country.

King himself was an extraordinary and complex man. Born in 1929 in Atlanta, he enjoyed a middle-class upbringing as the son of a prominent Baptist minister. After graduating from prestigious Morehouse College, an all-black school, King earned a divinity degree at Crozer Theological Seminary in Pennsylvania and a Ph.D. in theology from Boston University. In graduate school he was drawn to the Social Christianity of American theologian Walter Rauschenbusch, who insisted on connecting religious faith with struggles for social justice. Above all, King admired Mohandas Gandhi, a lawyer turned ascetic who had led a successful nonviolent resistance movement against British colonial rule in India. Gandhi taught his followers to confront authorities with a readiness to suffer in order to expose injustice and force those in power to end it. This tactic of nonviolent civil disobedience required discipline and sacrifice from its followers, who were sometimes called upon to lay their lives on the line against armed police and military forces. Crucially, King believed Gandhian nonviolence to be not merely a moral imperative but a potent political strategy that had "muzzled the guns of the British empire in India and freed more than three hundred and fifty million people from colonialism." A unique blend of traditional African American folk preacher and erudite intellectual, King used his passion and intelligence to help transform a community's pain into a powerful moral force for change.

In a December 1956 address celebrating the Montgomery bus boycott victory, King laid out six key lessons from the yearlong struggle: "(1) We have discovered that we can stick together for a common cause; (2) our leaders do not have to sell out; (3) threats and violence do not necessarily intimidate those who are sufficiently aroused and nonviolent; (4) our church is becoming militant, stressing a social gospel as well as a gospel of personal salvation; (5) we have gained a new sense of dignity and destiny; (6) we have discovered a new and powerful weapon—nonviolent resistance." Two northern pacifists, Bayard Rustin of the War Resisters' League and Glenn Smiley of the Fellowship of Reconciliation, helped deepen King's commitment to the Gandhian philosophy.

King recognized the need to exploit the momentum of the Montgomery movement. In early 1957, with the help of Rustin and others, he brought together nearly 100 black ministers to found the Southern Christian Leadership Conference (SCLC). The clergymen elected King president and his close friend, the Reverend Ralph Abernathy, treasurer. The SCLC called upon black people "to understand that nonviolence is not a symbol of weakness or cowardice, but as Jesus demonstrated, nonviolent resistance transforms weakness into strength and breeds courage in the face of danger."

But King and other black leaders also understood that the white South was no monolith. They believed white Southerners could be divided roughly into three groups: first, a tiny minority—often with legal training, social connections, and money—that might be counted on to help overthrow segregation; second, extreme segregationists who were willing and able to use violence and terror in defense of white supremacy; and third, a broad middle group who favored and benefited from segregation but were unwilling to take personal risks to prevent its destruction. In the battles to come, civil rights leaders made this nuanced view of the white South central to their larger political strategy. Extreme segregationists could be counted on to overreact, often violently, to civil rights campaigns, and thereby help to win sympathy and support for the cause. White moderates, especially in the business community, might be reluctant to initiate change, but they would try to distance themselves from the desperate violence of extremists and present themselves as pragmatic supporters of order and peace.

The SCLC gained support among black ministers, and King vigorously spread his message in speeches and writings. But the organization failed to generate the kind of mass, direct-action movement that had made history in Montgomery. Instead, the next great spark to light the fire of protest came from what seemed at the time a most unlikely source: black college students.

SIT-INS: GREENSBORO, NASHVILLE, ATLANTA

On Monday, February 1, 1960, four black freshmen from North Carolina Agricultural and Technical College in Greensboro sat down at the whites-only lunch counter in Woolworth's and politely ordered coffee and doughnuts. As the students had anticipated while planning the action in their dorm rooms, they were refused service. Although they could buy pencils or toothpaste, black people were not allowed to eat in Woolworth's. But the four students stayed at the counter until closing time. Word of their actions spread quickly, and the next day they returned with more than two dozen supporters. On the third day, students occupied sixty-three of the sixty-six lunch counter seats. By Thursday they had been joined by three white students from the Women's College of the University of North Carolina in Greensboro. Scores of sympathizers overflowed Woolworth's and started a sit-in down the street in S. H. Kress. On Friday, hundreds of black students and a few white sympathizers jammed the lunch counters.

The week's events made Greensboro national news. City officials, looking to end the protest, offered to negotiate in exchange for an end to demonstrations. But white business leaders and politicians proved unwilling to change the racial status quo, and the sit-ins resumed on April 1. In response to the April 21 arrest of forty-five students for trespassing, an outraged African American community organized a boycott of targeted stores that cut deeply into merchants' profits. Greensboro's leaders reluctantly gave in. On July 25, 1960, the first African American ate a meal at Woolworth's.

The Greensboro sit-in sent a shock wave throughout the South. During the next eighteen months, 70,000 people—most of them black students, a few of them white allies—participated in sit-ins against segregation in dozens of communities. More than 3,000 were arrested. African Americans had discovered a new form of direct-action protest, dignified and powerful, that white people could not ignore. The sit-in movement also transformed participants' self-image, empowering them psychologically and emotionally. Franklin McCain, one of the original four

The second day of the sit-in at the Greensboro, North Carolina, Woolworth lunch counter, February 2, 1960. From left: Joseph McNeil, Franklin McCain, Billy Smith, and Clarence Henderson. The Greensboro protest sparked a wave of sit-ins across the South, mostly by college students, demanding an end to segregation in restaurants and other public places.

Greensboro students, later recalled a great feeling of soul cleansing: "I probably felt better on that day than I've ever felt in my life. Seems like a lot of feelings of guilt or what-have-you suddenly left me, and I felt as though I had gained my manhood, so to speak, and not only gained it, but had developed quite a lot of respect for it."

In Nashville, Reverend James Lawson, a northern-born black minister, had led workshops in nonviolent resistance since 1958. Lawson had served a jail term as a conscientious objector during the Korean war and had become active in the Fellowship of Reconciliation. He had also spent three years as a missionary in India, where he had learned close up the Gandhian methods of promoting social change. Lawson gathered around him a group of deeply committed black students from Fisk and Vanderbilt universities and other Nashville colleges. The psychological pressures were enormous. To be successful, practitioners of nonviolent resistance had to learn and practice strict self-control needed to resist lashing back at the angry crowds that would abuse them. Young activists there talked not only of ending segregation but also of creating a "Beloved Community" based on Christian idealism and Gandhian principles.

In the spring of 1960, more than 150 Nashville students were arrested in disciplined sit-ins aimed at desegregating downtown lunch counters. Lawson, who preached the need for sacrifice in the cause of justice, found himself expelled from the divinity school at Vanderbilt. Lawson and other veterans of the Nashville sit-ins, such as John Lewis, Diane Nash, and Marion Barry, would go on to play influential roles in the national civil rights movement. The Nashville group developed rules of conduct that became a model for protesters elsewhere: "Don't strike back or curse if abused. . . . Show yourself courteous and friendly at all times. . . . Report all serious incidents to your leader in a polite manner. Remember love and nonviolence."

The most ambitious sit-in campaign unfolded in Atlanta, the South's largest and wealthiest city, home to the region's most powerful and prestigious black community. Students from Morehouse, Spelman, and the other all-black schools that made up Atlanta University took the lead. On March 15, 1960, 200 young black people staged a well-coordinated sit-in at restaurants in City Hall, the State Capitol, and other government offices. Police arrested and jailed seventy-six demonstrators that day, but the experience only strengthened the activists' resolve. Led by Julian Bond and Lonnie King, two Morehouse undergraduates, the students formed the Committee on an Appeal for Human Rights. We will "use every legal and nonviolent means at our disposal to secure full citizenship rights as members of this great democracy of ours," the students promised. Over the summer they planned a fall campaign of large-scale sit-ins at major Atlanta department stores and a boycott of downtown merchants. In October 1960 Martin Luther King Jr. and thirty-six students were arrested when they sat down in the all-white Magnolia Room

restaurant in Rich's Department Store. As in Greensboro and Montgomery, the larger African American community in Atlanta supported the continuing sit-ins, picketing, and boycotts. The campaign stretched on for months, and hundreds of protesters went to jail. The city's business leaders finally relented in September 1961, and desegregation came to Atlanta.

SNCC AND THE "BELOVED COMMUNITY"

The sit-in movement pumped new energy into the civil rights cause, creating a new generation of activists and leaders. Mass arrests, beatings, and vilification in the southern white press only strengthened the resolve of those in the Movement. Students also had to deal with the fears of their families, many of whom had made great sacrifices to send them to college. John Lewis, a seminary student in Nashville, remembered his mother in rural Alabama pleading with him to "get out of that mess, before you get hurt." Lewis wrote to his parents that he acted out of his Christian conscience: "My soul will not be satisfied until freedom, justice, and fair play become a reality for all people."

The new student militancy also caused discord within black communities. The authority of local African American elites had traditionally depended on their influence and cooperation with the white establishment. Black lawyers, schoolteachers, principals, and businessmen had to maintain regular and cordial relations with white judges, school boards, and politicians. Student calls for freedom disturbed many community leaders worried about upsetting traditional patronage networks. Some black college presidents, pressured by trustees and state legislators, sought to moderate or stop the Movement altogether. The president of Southern University in Baton Rouge, the nation's largest black college, suspended eighteen sit-in leaders in 1960 and forced the entire student body of 5,000 to reapply so that "agitators" could be screened out.

An April 1960 conference of 120 black student activists in Raleigh, North Carolina, underlined the generational and radical aspects of the new movement. The meeting had been called by Ella Baker, executive director of the SCLC, to help the students assess their experiences and plan future actions. Fifty-five at the time, Baker had for years played an important behind-the-scenes role in the civil rights cause, serving as a community organizer and field secretary for the NAACP before heading the staff of the SCLC. She understood the psychological importance of the students remaining independent of adult control. She counseled them to resist affiliating with any of the national civil rights organizations. Baker also encouraged the trend toward group-centered leadership among the students. She later commented that social movements needed "the development of people who are interested not in being leaders as much as in developing leadership among other people."

With Baker's encouragement, the conference voted to establish a new group, the Student Nonviolent Coordinating Committee (SNCC, pronounced "Snick"). The strong influence of the Nashville students, led by James Lawson, could be found in the SNCC statement of purpose:

> We affirm the philosophical or religious ideal of nonviolence as the foundation of our purpose, the presupposition of our faith, and the manner of our action. Nonviolence as it grows from Judaic-Christian tradition seeks a social order of justice permeated by love. Integration of human endeavor represents the crucial first step towards such a society.

In the fall of 1960 SNCC established an organizational structure, a set of principles, and a new style of civil rights protest. The emphasis was on fighting segregation through direct confrontation, mass action, and civil disobedience. SNCC field-workers initiated and supported local, community-based activity. Three-quarters of the first field-workers were less than twenty-two years old. Leadership was vested in a nonhierarchical Coordinating Committee, but local groups were free to determine their own direction. SNCC people distrusted bureaucracy and structure; they stressed spontaneity and improvisation. A small but dedicated group of young white Southerners, inspired by SNCC's idealism and activism, joined the cause. Groups such as the Southern Student Organizing Committee looked for ways to extend SNCC's radicalism to white communities. Over the next few years SNCC was at the forefront of nearly every major civil rights battle.

THE ELECTION OF 1960 AND CIVIL RIGHTS

The race issue was kept from center stage during the very close presidential campaign of 1960. As vice president, Richard Nixon had been a leading Republican voice for stronger civil rights legislation, whereas Democratic nominee Senator John F. Kennedy had played virtually no role in the 1950s' congressional battles over civil rights. But during the campaign, their roles reversed. Kennedy praised the sit-in movement as part of a revival of national reform spirit. "It is in the American tradition to stand up for one's rights," he declared, "even if the new way is to sit down." While the Republican platform contained a strong civil rights plank, Nixon, eager to court southern white voters, minimized his own identification with the Movement. Indeed, Republican conservatives such as Arizona senator Barry Goldwater and the activists grouped around the influential *National Review* magazine helped push the party toward "states rights" and away from the growing civil rights movement. By distancing Republicans from integration, they believed that the GOP might pick up southern electoral votes and plant seeds for a reborn conservative movement in the 1960s.

In October, Martin Luther King Jr. was jailed after leading a demonstration in Atlanta and faced the strong possibility of being sent to a notorious state prison, known for its harsh treatment of black inmates. Kennedy telephoned King's wife, Coretta Scott King, to reassure her and express his personal support. Senator Kennedy's brother and campaign manager Robert telephoned the judge in the case and angrily warned him that he had violated King's civil rights and endangered the national Democratic ticket. The judge released King soon afterward. News of this intervention did not gain wide attention in the white South, much to the relief of the Kennedys. The race was tight, and they knew they could not afford to alienate traditional white southern Democrats. But the Kennedy campaign effectively played up the story among black voters all over the country, using black churches as a grapevine. Kennedy won 70 percent of the black vote, which helped put him over the top in such critical states as Illinois, Texas, Michigan, and Pennsylvania and secure his narrow victory over Nixon. Many civil rights activists optimistically looked forward to a new president who would have to acknowledge his political debt to the black vote.

But the very closeness of his victory constrained Kennedy on race. Democrats had lost ground in the House and Senate, and Kennedy had to worry about alienating conservative Southern Democrats who chaired key congressional committees. Passage of major civil rights legislation would be virtually impossible. The new president told leaders such as Roy Wilkins of the NAACP that a strategy of "minimum legislation, maximum executive action" offered the best road to change. The president did appoint some forty African Americans to high federal positions, including Thurgood Marshall to a federal appellate court. He established a Committee on Equal Employment Opportunity, chaired by Vice President Lyndon B. Johnson, to fight discrimination in the federal civil service and in corporations that received government contracts.

Most significantly, the Kennedy administration sought to invigorate the Civil Rights Division of the Justice Department. That division had been created by the Civil Rights Act of 1957, which authorized the attorney general to seek court injunctions to protect people denied their right to vote. But the Eisenhower administration had made little use of this new power. Robert Kennedy, the new attorney general, began assembling a staff of brilliant and committed attorneys, headed by Washington lawyer Burke Marshall. Kennedy encouraged them to get out of Washington and into the field wherever racial troubles arose. In early 1961, when Louisiana school officials balked at a school desegregation order, Robert Kennedy warned them that he would ask the federal court to hold them in contempt. When Marshall started court proceedings, the state officials gave in.

The new, more aggressive mood at Justice could not solve the central political dilemma: how to move forward on civil rights without alienating southern Democrats. Pressure from the newly energized southern civil rights movement soon revealed the true difficulty of that problem. The movement would also provoke murderous outrage from white extremists determined to maintain the racial status quo (see Map 28.1).

FREEDOM RIDES

In the spring of 1961 James Farmer, national director of CORE, announced plans for an interracial Freedom Ride through the South. The goal was to test compliance with court orders banning segregation in interstate travel and terminal accommodations. CORE had just recently made Farmer its leader in an effort to revitalize the organization. One of the founders of CORE in 1942, Farmer had worked for various pacifist and socialist groups and served as program director for the NAACP. He designed the Freedom Ride to

induce a crisis, in the spirit of the sit-ins. "Our intention," Farmer declared, "was to provoke the southern authorities into arresting us and thereby prod the Justice Department into enforcing the law of the land." CORE received financial and tactical support from the SCLC and several NAACP branches. It also informed the Justice Department and the FBI of its plans but received no reply.

On May 4 seven blacks and six whites split into two interracial groups and left Washington on public buses bound for Alabama and Mississippi. At first the two buses encountered only isolated harassment and violence as they headed south. But when one bus entered Anniston, Alabama, on May 14, an angry mob surrounded it, smashing windows and slashing tires. Six miles out of town, the tires went flat. A firebomb tossed through a window forced the passengers out. The mob then beat the Freedom Riders with blackjacks, iron bars, and clubs, and the bus burst into flames. A caravan of cars organized

MAP EXPLORATION

To explore an interactive version of this map, go to **www.prenhall.com/faragher6/map28.1**

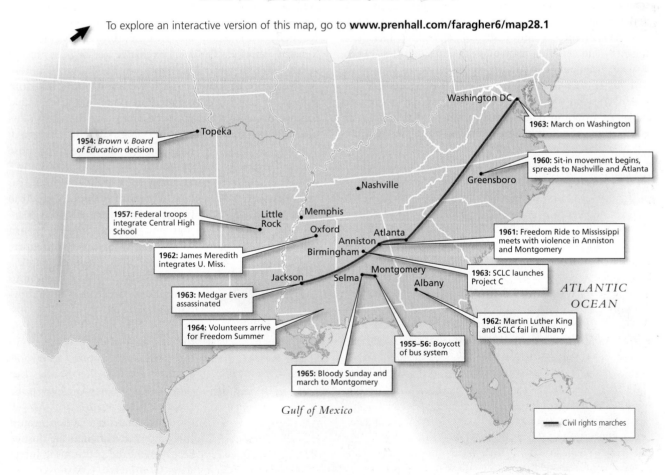

1954: *Brown v. Board of Education* decision

1957: Federal troops integrate Central High School

1962: James Meredith integrates U. Miss.

1963: Medgar Evers assassinated

1964: Volunteers arrive for Freedom Summer

1965: Bloody Sunday and march to Montgomery

1955–56: Boycott of bus system

1963: March on Washington

1960: Sit-in movement begins, spreads to Nashville and Atlanta

1961: Freedom Ride to Mississippi meets with violence in Anniston and Montgomery

1963: SCLC launches Project C

1962: Martin Luther King and SCLC fail in Albany

Topeka • Nashville • Little Rock • Memphis • Oxford • Atlanta • Anniston • Birmingham • Jackson • Selma • Montgomery • Albany • Greensboro • Washington DC

ATLANTIC OCEAN

Gulf of Mexico

— Civil rights marches

MAP 28.1 The Civil Rights Movement Key battlegrounds in the struggle for racial justice in communities across the South.

by the Birmingham office of the SCLC rescued the wounded. Another mob attacked the second bus in Anniston, leaving one Freedom Rider near death and permanently brain-damaged.

The violence escalated. In Birmingham, a mob of forty whites waited on the loading platform and attacked the bus that managed to get out of Anniston. Although police had been warned to expect trouble, they did nothing to stop the mob from beating the Freedom Riders with pipes and fists, nor did they make any arrests. FBI agents observed and took notes but did nothing. The remaining Freedom Riders decided to travel as a single group on the next lap, from Birmingham to Montgomery, but no bus would take them. Stranded and frightened, they reluctantly boarded a special flight to New Orleans arranged by the Justice Department. On May 17 the CORE-sponsored Freedom Ride disbanded.

That was not the end of the Freedom Rides. SNCC leaders in Atlanta and Nashville assembled a fresh group of volunteers to continue the trip. On May 20, twenty-one Freedom Riders left Birmingham for Montgomery. The bus station in the Alabama capital was eerily quiet and deserted as they pulled in. But when the passengers left the bus a mob of several hundred whites rushed them, yelling "Get those niggers!" and clubbing people to the ground. James Zwerg, a white Freedom Rider from the University of Wisconsin, had his spinal cord severed. John Lewis, veteran of the Nashville sit-in movement, suffered a brain concussion. As he lay in a pool of blood, a policeman handed him a state court injunction forbidding interracial travel in Alabama.

The mob indiscriminately beat journalists and clubbed John Siegenthaler, a Justice Department attorney sent to observe the scene. It took police more than an hour to halt the rioting. Montgomery's police commissioner later said, "We have no intention of standing guard for a bunch of troublemakers coming into our city."

The mob violence and the indifference of Alabama officials made the Freedom Ride first-page news around the country and throughout the world. Newspapers in Europe, Africa, and Asia denounced the hypocrisy of the federal government. The Kennedy administration, preparing for the president's first summit meeting with Soviet premier Nikita Khrushchev, saw the situation as a threat to the nation's global prestige. On May 21, an angry mob threatened to invade a support rally at Montgomery's First Baptist Church. A hastily assembled group of 400 U.S. marshals, sent by Robert Kennedy, barely managed to keep the peace. The attorney general called for a cooling-off period, but King, Farmer, and the SNCC leaders announced that the Freedom Ride would continue. A bandaged but spirited group of twenty-seven Freedom Riders prepared to leave Montgomery for Jackson, Mississippi, on May 24. To avoid further violence Robert Kennedy arranged a compromise through Mississippi's Senator James Eastland. In exchange for a guarantee of safe passage through Mississippi, the federal government promised not to interfere with the arrest of the Freedom Riders in Jackson. This Freedom Ride and several that followed thus escaped violence. But more than 300 people were arrested that summer in Jackson on charges of traveling "for the avowed purpose of inflaming public opinion." Sticking to a policy of "jail, no bail," Freedom Riders clogged the prison, where they endured beatings and intimidation by prison guards that went largely unreported in the press. Their jail experiences turned most of them into committed core leaders of the student movement.

The Freedom Rides exposed the ugly face of southern racism to the world and inspired grassroots activists around the South. But they also reinforced white resistance to desegregation and showed the limits of federal action against Jim Crow. Eventually the Justice Department did petition the Interstate Commerce Commission to issue clear rules prohibiting segregation on interstate carriers. At the end of 1962, CORE proclaimed victory in the battle against Jim

A Freedom Riders' bus burns after being firebombed in Anniston, Alabama, May 14, 1961. After setting the bus afire, whites attacked the passengers fleeing the smoke and flames. Violent scenes like this one received extensive publicity in the mass media and helped compel the Justice Department to enforce court rulings banning segregation on interstate bus lines.

Crow interstate travel. By creating a crisis, the Freedom Rides had forced the Kennedy administration to act. But they also revealed the unwillingness of the federal government to fully enforce the law of the land. The jailings and brutality experienced by Freedom Riders made clear to the civil rights community the limits of moral persuasion alone for effecting change.

THE ALBANY MOVEMENT: THE LIMITS OF PROTEST

Where the federal government chose not to enforce the constitutional rights of black people, segregationist forces tenaciously held their ground, especially in the more remote areas of the Deep South. One such place was Albany, a small city in southwest Georgia, where activists from SNCC, the NAACP, and other local groups formed a coalition known as the Albany Movement. For more than a year, beginning in October 1961, thousands of Albany's black citizens marched, sat in, and boycotted as part of a citywide campaign to integrate public facilities and win voting rights. More than a thousand people spent time in jail. In December, the arrival of Martin Luther King Jr. and the SCLC transformed Albany into a national symbol of the struggle.

But the gains at Albany proved minimal. Local SNCC workers opposed the more cautious approach of NAACP officials, even though the more established organization paid many of the campaign's expenses. King's arrival guaranteed national news coverage, but local activists worried that his presence might undermine the community focus and their own influence. Such infighting hurt the cause. Most important, Albany police chief Laurie Pritchett shrewdly deprived the movement of the kind of national sympathy won by the Freedom Riders. Pritchett filled the jails with black demonstrators, kept their mistreatment to a minimum, and prevented white mobs from running wild. King himself was twice arrested in the summer of 1962, but Albany officials quickly freed him to avoid negative publicity. The Kennedy administration kept clear of the developments in Albany, hoping to help the gubernatorial campaign of "moderate" Democrat Carl Sanders. By late 1962 the Albany movement had collapsed, and Pritchett proudly declared the city "as segregated as ever." One activist summed up the losing campaign: "We were naive enough to think we could fill up the jails. Pritchett was hep to the fact that we couldn't. We ran out of people before he ran out of jails." Albany showed that mass protest without violent white reaction and direct federal intervention could not end Jim Crow.

In contrast to the failure at Albany, a successful battle to integrate the University of Mississippi reinforced the importance of federal intervention for guaranteeing African American civil rights. In the fall of 1962 James Meredith, an Air Force veteran and a student at all-black Jackson State College, tried to register as the first black student at lily-white "Ole Miss." Defying a federal court order, Governor Ross Barnett personally blocked Meredith at the admissions office. When Barnett refused to assure Robert Kennedy that Meredith would be protected, the attorney general dispatched 500 federal marshals to the campus. Over the radio, Barnett encouraged resistance to the "oppressive power of the United States," and an enraged mob of several thousand whites, many of them armed, laid siege to the campus on September 30. A night of violence left two people dead and 160 marshals wounded, 28 from gunfire. President Kennedy ordered 5,000 Army troops onto the campus to stop the riot. A federal guard remained to protect Meredith, who graduated the following summer.

THE MOVEMENT AT HIGH TIDE, 1963–65

The tumultuous events of 1960–62 convinced civil rights strategists that segregation could not be dismantled merely through orderly protest and moral persuasion. Only comprehensive civil rights legislation, backed by federal power, could guarantee full citizenship rights for African Americans. To build the national consensus needed for new laws, civil rights activists looked for ways to gain broader support for their cause. By 1963, their sense of urgency had led them to plan dramatic confrontations that would expose the violence and terror routinely faced by southern blacks. With the whole country—indeed, the whole world—watching, the Movement reached the peak of its political and moral power.

BIRMINGHAM

At the end of 1962, King and his SCLC allies decided to launch a new campaign against segregation in Birmingham, Alabama. Having failed in Albany, King and his aides looked for a way to shore up his leadership and inject new momentum into the freedom struggle. They needed a major victory. Birmingham, the most segregated big city in America, had a deep history of racial violence. African Americans endured total segregation in schools, restaurants, city parks, and department store dressing rooms. Although black people constituted more than 40 percent of the city's population, fewer than 10,000 of Birmingham's 80,000 registered voters were black. The city's thriving steel industry relegated black workers to menial jobs.

Working closely with local civil rights groups led by the longtime Birmingham activist Reverend Fred Shuttlesworth, the SCLC carefully planned its campaign. The strategy was to fill the city jails with protesters, boycott downtown department stores, and enrage Public Safety Commissioner Eugene "Bull" Connor, a die-hard segregationist. In April, King arrived with a manifesto demanding an end to racist hiring practices and segregated public accommodations and the creation of a biracial committee to oversee desegregation. "Here in Birmingham," King told reporters, "we have reached the point of no return." Connor's police began jailing hundreds of demonstrators, including King himself, who defied a state court injunction against further protests. Held in solitary confinement for several days, King managed to write a response to a group of Birmingham clergy who had deplored the protests. King's "Letter from a Birmingham Jail" was soon widely reprinted and circulated as a pamphlet. It set out the key moral issues at stake, and scoffed at those who claimed the campaign was illegal and ill timed (see Communities in Conflict). After King's release on bail, the campaign intensified. The SCLC kept up the pressure by recruiting thousands of Birmingham's young students for a "children's crusade." In early May, Connor unleashed high-powered water cannons, billy clubs, and snarling police dogs to break up demonstrations. Millions of Americans reacted with horror to the violent scenes from Birmingham shown on national television. Many younger black people, especially from the city's poor and working-class districts, began to fight back, hurling bottles and bricks at police. On May 10, mediators from the Justice Department negotiated an uneasy truce. The SCLC agreed to an immediate end to the protests. In exchange, businesses would desegregate and begin hiring African Americans over the next three months, and a biracial city committee would oversee desegregation of public facilities.

King claimed the events in Birmingham represented "the most magnificent victory for justice we've ever seen in the Deep South." But white leaders such as Connor and Alabama's governor George Wallace denounced the agreement. A few days after the announcement, more than a thousand robed Ku Klux Klansmen burned a cross in a park on the outskirts of Birmingham. When bombs rocked SCLC headquarters and the home of King's brother, a Birmingham minister, enraged blacks took to the streets and pelted police and firefighters with stones and bottles. President Kennedy ordered 3,000 Army troops into the city and prepared to nationalize the Alabama National Guard. The violence receded, and white businesspeople and politicians began to carry out the agreed-upon pact. But in September a bomb killed four black girls in a Birmingham Baptist church, reminding the city and the world that racial harmony was still a long way off.

The Birmingham campaign and the other protests it sparked over the next seven months engaged more than 100,000 people and led to nearly 15,000 arrests. The civil rights community now drew support from millions of Americans, black and white, all inspired by the protesters and repelled by southern bigotry. At the same time, Birmingham changed the nature of black protest. The black unemployed and working poor who joined in the struggle brought a different perspective from that of the students, professionals, and members of the religious middle class who had dominated the Movement before Birmingham. They cared less about the philosophy of nonviolence and more about immediate gains in employment and housing and an end to police brutality.

JFK AND THE MARCH ON WASHINGTON

The growth of black activism and of white support convinced President Kennedy the moment had come to press for sweeping civil rights legislation. Continuing white resistance in the South also made clearer than ever the need for federal action. In June 1963, Governor Wallace threatened to personally block the admission of two black students to the University of Alabama. Only the deployment of National Guard troops, placed under federal control by the president, ensured the students' safety and their peaceful admission into the university.

It was a defining moment for Kennedy. Even more than for Eisenhower at Little Rock, the realities of international Cold War politics pushed Kennedy toward support for civil rights. On June 11 the president went on national television and offered his personal endorsement of the civil rights activism: "Today we are committed to a worldwide struggle to promote and protect the rights of all who wish to be free. And when Americans are sent to Vietnam or West Berlin, we do not ask for whites only. . . . Are we to say to the rest of the world, and much more importantly, to each other, that this is a land of the free except for Negroes?" Reviewing the racial situation, Kennedy told the nation: "We face . . . a moral crisis as a country and a people. It cannot be met by repressive police action. It cannot be left to increased demonstrations in the streets. It cannot be quieted by token moves or talk. It is a time to act in the Congress, in your state and local legislative body, and, above all, in all our daily lives." The next week Kennedy asked Congress for a broad law that would ensure voting rights, outlaw segregation in public facilities, and bolster federal authority to deny funds for discriminatory programs. Knowing they would face a stiff fight from congressional conservatives, administration officials began an intense lobbying effort in support of the law. After three years of fence sitting, Kennedy finally committed his office and his political future to the civil rights cause.

Movement leaders lauded the president's initiative. Yet they understood that racial hatred still haunted the nation. Only hours after Kennedy's television speech, a gunman murdered Medgar Evers, leader of the Mississippi NAACP, outside his home in Jackson, Mississippi. To pressure Congress and demonstrate the urgency of their cause, a broad coalition of civil rights groups planned a massive, nonviolent March on Washington. The idea had deep roots in black protest. A. Philip Randolph, head of the Brotherhood of Sleeping Car Porters, had originally proposed such a march in 1941 to protest discrimination against blacks in defense industries (see Chapter 25). Now, more than twenty years later, Randolph, along with his aide Bayard Rustin, revived the concept and convinced leaders of the major civil rights groups to support it.

The Kennedy administration originally opposed the march, fearing it would jeopardize support for the president's civil rights bill in Congress. But as plans for the rally solidified, Kennedy reluctantly gave his approval. Leaders from the SCLC, the NAACP, SNCC, the Urban League, and CORE—the leading organizations in the civil rights community—put aside their tactical differences to forge a broad consensus for the event. John Lewis, the young head of SNCC, who had endured numerous brutal assaults, planned a speech that denounced the Kennedys as hypocrites. Lewis's speech enraged Walter Reuther, the white liberal leader of the United Auto Workers union, which had helped finance the march. Reuther threatened to turn off the loudspeakers he was paying for, believing Lewis's speech would embarrass the Kennedys. At the last moment Randolph, the Movement's acknowledged elder statesman, convinced Lewis to tone down his remarks. "We've come this far," he implored. "For the sake of unity, change it."

On August 28, 1963, more than a quarter of a million people, including 50,000 whites, gathered at the Lincoln Memorial to rally for "jobs and freedom." Union members, students, teachers, clergy, professionals, musicians, actors—Americans from all walks of life joined the largest political assembly in the nation's history until then. The sight of all those people holding hands and singing "We Shall Overcome," led by white folksinger Joan Baez, would not be easily forgotten, either by participants or by millions of television viewers. At the end of a long, exhilarating day of speeches and freedom songs, Martin Luther King Jr. provided the emotional climax. Combining the democratic promise of the Declaration of Independence with the religious fervor of his Baptist heritage, King stirred the crowd and the nation with his dream for America:

> I have a dream today that one day this nation will rise up and live out the true meaning of its creed: "We hold these truths to be self-evident—that all men are created equal." . . . When we allow freedom to ring, when we let it ring from every village and every hamlet, from every state and every city, we will be able to speed up that day when all of God's children—black men and white men, Jews and Gentiles, Protestants and Catholics—will be able to join hands and sing in the words of the old Negro spiritual, "Free at last! Free at last! Thank God Almighty, we are free at last!"

The following year, at age 35, King received the Nobel Peace Prize, which both solidified his reputation as the premier voice of the Movement and added greatly to his stature within mainstream American culture. The award also demonstrated the truly global impact of the Movement he led.

LBJ AND THE CIVIL RIGHTS ACT OF 1964

An extraordinary demonstration of interracial unity, the March on Washington stood as the high-water mark in the struggle for civil rights. It buoyed the spirits of Movement leaders, as well as of liberals pushing the new civil rights bill through Congress. But the assassination of John F. Kennedy on November 22, 1963, in Dallas threw an ominous cloud over the whole nation and the civil rights movement in particular. In the Deep South, many ardent segregationists and ultraconservatives cheered the president's death because of his support for civil rights. Most African Americans probably shared the feelings of Coretta Scott King, who recalled her family's vigil: "We felt that President Kennedy had been a friend of the Cause and that with him as President we could continue to move forward. We watched and prayed for him."

Lyndon Baines Johnson (LBJ), Kennedy's successor, had never been much of a friend to civil rights. As a senator from Texas (1948–60, including six years as majority leader), Johnson had been one of the shrewdest and most powerful Democrats in Congress. Throughout the 1950s he had worked to obstruct the passage and enforcement of civil rights laws. But as vice president he had ably chaired Kennedy's working group on equal employment. Now, Johnson reassured a grieving nation, "the ideas and the ideals which [Kennedy] so nobly represented must and will be translated into effective action." Even so, civil rights activists looked upon Johnson warily as he took over the Oval Office.

As president, Johnson realized that he faced a new political reality, created by the civil rights movement. Eager to unite the Democratic Party and prove himself as a national leader, he seized on civil rights as a golden political opportunity. Throughout the early months of 1964, the new president let it be known publicly and privately that he would brook no compromise on civil rights. Johnson exploited all his skills as a political insider, cajoling, flattering, and threatening key members of the House and Senate. Working with the president, the fifteen-year-old Leadership Conference on Civil Rights coordinated a sophisticated lobbying effort in Congress. Groups such as the NAACP, the AFL-CIO, the National Council of Churches, and the American Jewish Congress made the case for a strong civil rights bill. The House passed the bill in February by a 290–130 vote. The more difficult fight would be in the Senate, where a southern filibuster promised to block or weaken the bill. But by June, Johnson's persistence paid off. The southern filibuster collapsed.

On July 2, 1964, Johnson signed the Civil Rights Act of 1964. Every major provision had survived intact. This landmark law represented the most significant civil rights legislation since Reconstruction. It prohibited discrimination in most places of public accommodation; it banned discrimination in employment on the basis of race, color, religion, sex,

Confrontation in Birmingham

The tumultuous civil rights demonstrations in Birmingham, Alabama, in the spring of 1963 attracted great attention around the country and throughout the world. Code-named "Project C"—for Confrontation—by organizers from the Southern Christian Leadership Conference, the campaign used mass picketing and civil disobedience to challenge segregation laws in the city. The response it evoked from Birmingham authorities—court injunctions, mass arrests (including many children), and fire hoses and police dogs to intimidate demonstrators—were precisely what Movement leaders had hoped for. The Birmingham demonstrations evoked enormous sympathy and support for the Movement, especially among northern whites appalled by the images they saw in newspapers and on television. It also spurred a profound debate on the nature, meaning, and morality of protest itself—especially protest that deliberately broke the law and invited mass arrests.

"A Call for Unity," was an open letter written by a group of eight Alabama clergymen from different faiths, published in the *Birmingham News* on April 12, 1963. These clergymen were deeply troubled by the SCLC campaign and criticized both the strategy and its leader, Rev. Martin Luther King Jr.; King himself had recently been jailed in Birmingham for defying a state court injunction against further protests. King read the "Call for Unity" while in prison and felt obliged to write a response, despite his difficult circumstances. "Begun on the margins of the newspaper in which the statement appeared while I was in jail," King later wrote, "the letter was continued on scraps of writing paper supplied by a friendly Negro trusty, and concluded on a pad my attorneys were eventually permitted to leave me." King's "Letter from a Birmingham Jail," excerpted here, eventually ran to more than six thousand words. It became one of the most widely quoted documents of the civil rights movement.

What specific criticisms does the "Call for Unity" make of Project C?
What alternative strategies does it put forth for addressing racial inequality in Birmingham?
How does Rev. King justify the breaking of the law as a political and moral tactic?

Birmingham Clergy Make "A Call for Unity" (April 12, 1963)

We the undersigned clergymen are among those who, in January, issued "an appeal for law and order and common sense," in dealing with racial problems in Alabama. We expressed understanding that honest convictions in racial matters could properly be pursued in the courts, but urged that decisions of those courts should in the meantime be peacefully obeyed.

Since that time there had been some evidence of increased forbearance and a willingness to face facts. Responsible citizens have undertaken to work on various problems which cause racial friction and unrest. In Birmingham, recent public events have given indication that we all have opportunity for a new constructive and realistic approach to racial problems.

However, we are now confronted by a series of demonstrations by some of our Negro citizens, directed and led in part by outsiders. We recognize the natural impatience of people who feel that their hopes are slow in being realized. But we are convinced that these demonstrations are unwise and untimely.

We agree rather with certain local Negro leadership which has called for honest and open negotiation of racial issues in our area. And we believe this kind of facing of issues can best be accomplished by citizens of our own metropolitan area, white and Negro, meeting with their knowledge and experience of the local situation. All of us need to face that responsibility and find proper channels for its accomplishment.

Just as we formerly pointed out that "hatred and violence have no sanction in our religious and political traditions," we also point out that such actions as incite to hatred and violence, however technically peaceful those actions may be, have not contributed to the resolution of our local problems. We do not believe that these days of new hope are days when extreme measures are justified in Birmingham.

We commend the community as a whole, and the local news media and law enforcement officials in particular, on the calm manner in which these demonstrations have been handled. We urge the public to continue to show restraint should the demonstrations continue, and the law enforcement officials to remain calm and continue to protect our city from violence.

We further strongly urge our own Negro community to withdraw support from these demonstrations, and to unite locally in working peacefully for a better Birmingham. When rights are consistently denied, a cause should be pressed in the courts and in negotiations among local leaders, and not in the streets. We appeal to both our white and Negro citizenry to observe the principles of law and order and common sense.

SOURCE: http://www.silvertorch.com.

"[S]uch actions as incite to hatred and violence, . . . have not contributed to the resolution of our local problems."

"Nonviolent direct action seeks . . . so to dramatize the issue that it can no longer be ignored."

Rev. Dr. Martin Luther King Jr. Responds: "Letter from a Birmingham Jail" (1963)

While confined here in the Birmingham city jail, I came across your recent statement calling my present activities "unwise and untimely." Seldom do I pause to answer criticism of my work and ideas. If I sought to answer all the criticisms that cross my desk, my secretaries would have little time for anything other than such correspondence in the course of the day, and I would have no time for constructive work. But since I feel that you are men of genuine good will and that your criticisms are sincerely set forth, I want to try to answer your statements in what I hope will be patient and reasonable terms.

You deplore the demonstrations taking place in Birmingham. But your statement, I am sorry to say, fails to express a similar concern for the conditions that brought about the demonstrations. I am sure that none of you would want to rest content with the superficial kind of social analysis that deals merely with effects and does not grapple with underlying causes. It is unfortunate that demonstrations are taking place in Birmingham, but it is even more unfortunate that the city's white power structure left the Negro community with no alternative.

In any nonviolent campaign there are four basic steps: collection of the facts to determine whether injustices exist; negotiation; self-purification; and direct action. We have gone through these steps in Birmingham. There can be no gainsaying the fact that racial injustice engulfs this community. Birmingham is probably the most thoroughly segregated city in the United States. Its ugly record of brutality is widely known. Negroes have experienced grossly unjust treatment in the courts. There have been more unsolved bombings of Negro homes and churches in Birmingham than in any other city in the nation. These are the hard, brutal facts of the case. On the basis of these conditions, Negro leaders sought to negotiate with the city fathers. But the latter consistently refused to engage in good-faith negotiation.

You may well ask: "Why direct action? Why sit-ins, marches and so forth? Isn't negotiation a better path?" You are

quite right in calling for negotiation. Indeed, this is the very purpose of direct action. Nonviolent direct action seeks to create such a crisis and foster such a tension that a community which has constantly refused to negotiate is forced to confront the issue. It seeks so to dramatize the issue that it can no longer be ignored. My citing the creation of tension as part of the work of the nonviolent-resister may sound rather shocking. But I must confess that I am not afraid of the word "tension." I have earnestly opposed violent tension, but there is a type of constructive, nonviolent tension which is necessary for growth. Just as Socrates felt that it was necessary to create a tension in the mind so that individuals could rise from the bondage of myths and half-truths to the unfettered realm of creative analysis and objective appraisal, we must see the need for nonviolent gadflies to create the kind of tension in society that will help men rise from the dark depths of prejudice and racism to the majestic heights of understanding and brotherhood.

The purpose of our direct-action program is to create a situation so crisis-packed that it will inevitably open the door to negotiation. I therefore concur with you in your call for negotiation. Too long has our beloved Southland been bogged down in a tragic effort to live in monologue rather than dialogue.

We know through painful experience that freedom is never voluntarily given by the oppressor; it must be demanded by the oppressed. Frankly, I have yet to engage in a direct-action campaign that was "well timed" in the view of those who have not suffered unduly from the disease of segregation. For years now I have heard the word "Wait!" It rings in the ear of every Negro with piercing familiarity. This "Wait" has almost always meant "Never." We must come to see, with one of our distinguished jurists, that "justice too long delayed is justice denied."

There comes a time when the cup of endurance runs over, and men are no longer willing to be plunged into the abyss of despair. I hope, sirs, you can understand our legitimate and unavoidable impatience.

SOURCE: http://www.nobelprizes.com/nobel/peace/MLK-jail.html.

OVERVIEW | Landmark Civil Rights Legislation, Supreme Court Decisions, and Executive Orders

Year	Decision, Law, or Executive Order	Significance
1939	*Missouri v. ex. rel. Gaines*	Required University of Missouri Law School either to admit African Americans or build another fully equal law school
1941	**Executive Order 8802 (by President Roosevelt)**	Banned racial discrimination in defense industry and government offices; established Fair Employment Practices Committee to investigate violations
1946	*Morgan v. Virginia*	Ruled that segregation on interstate buses violated federal law and created an "undue burden" on interstate commerce
1948	**Executive Order 9981 (by President Truman)**	Desegregated the U.S. armed forces
1950	*McLaurin v. Oklahoma State Regents*	Ruled that forcing an African American student to sit, eat, and study in segregated facilities was unconstitutional because it inevitably created a "badge of inferiority"
1950	*Sweatt v. Painter*	Ruled that an inferior law school created by the University of Texas to serve African Americans violated their right to equal protection and ordered Herman Sweatt to be admitted to University of Texas Law School
1954	*Brown v. Board of Education of Topeka I*	Declared "separate educational facilities are inherently unequal," thus overturning *Plessy v. Ferguson* (1896) and the "separate but equal" doctrine as it applied to public schools
1955	*Brown v. Board of Education of Topeka II*	Ordered school desegregation to begin with "all deliberate speed," but offered no timetable
1957	**Civil Rights Act**	Created Civil Rights Division within the Justice Department
1964	**Civil Rights Act**	Prohibited discrimination in employment and most places of public accommodation on basis of race, color, religion, sex, or national origin; outlawed bias in federally assisted programs; created Equal Employment Opportunity Commission
1965	**Voting Rights Act**	Authorized federal supervision of voter registration in states and counties where fewer than half of voting age residents were registered; outlawed literacy and other discriminatory tests in voter registration

or national origin; it outlawed bias in federally assisted programs; it authorized the Justice Department to institute suits to desegregate public schools and other facilities; and it provided technical and financial aid to communities desegregating their schools. The act also created the Equal Employment Opportunity Commission (EEOC) to investigate and litigate cases of job discrimination.

There were important unintended consequences of this landmark legislation as well. It gave legal foundation to affirmative action policies and to the assertion of equal

Part of the huge throng of marchers at the historic March on Washington for "jobs and freedom," August 28, 1963. The size of the crowd, the stirring oratory and song, and the live network television coverage produced one of the most memorable political demonstrations in the nation's history.

rights for women and nonblack minorities. The EEOC, for example, became an important site for contesting both gender and racial discrimination in the workplace, receiving over 100,000 complaints a year by the 1970s. And on a political level LBJ was perhaps more prescient than he realized when he commented after signing the bill that the Civil Rights Act "delivered the South to the Republican Party." It took real political courage for Johnson, a Southern Democrat, to support the legislation as vigorously as he did, for the new law did indeed initiate a long-term political realignment that would transform the South from a solidly Democratic region to a solidly Republican one.

MISSISSIPPI FREEDOM SUMMER

While Johnson and his liberal allies won the congressional battle for the new civil rights bill, activists in Mississippi mounted a far more radical and dangerous campaign than any yet attempted in the South. In the spring of 1964, a coalition of workers led by SNCC launched the Freedom Summer project, an ambitious effort to register black voters and directly challenge the iron rule of segregation. Mississippi stood as the toughest test for the civil rights movement. It was the nation's poorest state and by most statistical measures the most backward, and it had remained largely untouched by the freedom struggle. African Americans constituted 42 percent of the state's population, but fewer than 5 percent could vote. Median black family income was under $1,500 a year, roughly one-third that of white families. A small white-planter elite controlled most of the state's wealth, and a long tradition of terror against black people maintained the racial caste system.

Bob Moses of SNCC and Dennis of CORE planned Freedom Summer as a way of opening up this closed society. The project recruited over 900 volunteers, mostly white college students, to aid in voter registration, teach in "freedom schools," and help build a "Freedom Party" as an alternative to Mississippi's all-white Democratic Party. Organizers expected violence, which was precisely why they wanted white volunteers. Dave Dennis later explained their reasoning: "The death of a white college student would bring on more attention to what was going on than for a black college student getting it. That's cold, but that was also in another sense speaking the language of this country." Mississippi authorities prepared for the civil rights workers as if expecting a foreign army, beefing up state highway patrols and local police forces.

On June 21, while most project volunteers were still training in Ohio, three activists disappeared in Neshoba County, Mississippi, when they went to investigate the burning of a black church that was supposed to serve as a freedom school. Six weeks later, after a massive search belatedly ordered by President Johnson, FBI agents discovered the bodies of the three—northern white students Michael Schwerner and Andrew Goodman, and a local black activist, James Chaney—buried in an earthen dam. Goodman and Schwerner had been shot once; Chaney had been severely beaten before being shot three times. Over the summer, at least three other civil rights workers died violently. Project workers suffered 1,000 arrests, 80 beatings, 35 shooting incidents, and 30 bombings in homes, churches, and schools.

Within the project, simmering problems tested the ideal of the Beloved Community. Black veterans of SNCC resented the affluent white volunteers, many of whom had not come to terms with their own racial prejudices. White volunteers, staying only a short time in the state, often found it difficult to communicate in the southern communities with local African Americans, wary of breaking old codes of deference. Sexual tensions between black male and white female volunteers also strained relations. A number of both black and white women, led by Ruby Doris Robinson, Mary King, and Casey Hayden, began to raise the issue of women's equality as a companion goal to racial equality. The day-to-day reality of violent reprisals, police harassment, and constant fear took a hard toll on everyone.

The project did manage to rivet national attention on Mississippi racism, and it won enormous sympathy from northern liberals. Among their concrete accomplishments, the volunteers could point with pride to more than forty

Bob Moses of the Student Nonviolent Coordinating Committee was one of the driving forces behind the 1964 Freedom Summer Project. Here he instructs student volunteers gathered in Oxford, Ohio, before they leave for voter registration and other community organizing work in Mississippi. Moses, who had been working for voting rights in Mississippi since 1961, played a key role in persuading SNCC to accept white volunteers from the North.

freedom schools that brought classes in reading, arithmetic, politics, and African American history to thousands of black children. Some 60,000 black voters signed up to join the Mississippi Freedom Democratic Party (MFDP). In August 1964 the MFDP sent a slate of delegates to the Democratic National Convention looking to challenge the credentials of the all-white regular state delegation.

At the Democrats' Atlantic City convention, the idealism of Freedom Summer collided with the more cynical needs of the national Democratic Party. Concerned that Republicans might carry a number of southern states in November, Johnson opposed seating the MFDP because he wanted to avoid a divisive floor fight. But before the convention opened, MFDP leaders and sympathizers gave dramatic testimony detailing the racism and brutality in Mississippi politics. "Is this America," asked Fannie Lou Hamer, "the land of the free and the home of the brave, where we are threatened daily because we want to live as decent human beings?" Led by Senator Hubert Humphrey, whom LBJ had already picked as his running mate, Johnson's forces offered a compromise that would have given the MFDP two token seats on the floor. Bitter over what they saw as a betrayal, the MFDP delegates turned the offer down. Within SNCC, the defeat of the MFDP

intensified African American disillusionment with the Democratic Party and the liberal establishment.

MALCOLM X AND BLACK CONSCIOUSNESS

Frustrated with the limits of nonviolent protest and electoral politics, younger activists within SNCC found themselves increasingly drawn to the militant rhetoric and vision of Malcolm X, who since 1950 had been the preeminent spokesman for the black nationalist religious sect, the Nation of Islam (NOI). Founded in depression-era Detroit by Elijah Muhammad, the NOI, like the followers of black-nationalist leader Marcus Garvey in the 1920s (see Chapter 23), aspired to create a self-reliant, highly disciplined, and proud community—a separate "nation" for black people. Elijah Muhammad preached a message of racial solidarity and self-help, criticized crime and drug use, and castigated whites as "blue-eyed devils" responsible for the world's evil. During the 1950s the NOI (also called Black Muslims) successfully organized in northern black communities, appealing especially to criminals, drug addicts, and others on the margins of urban life. It operated restaurants, retail stores, and schools as models for black economic self-sufficiency.

The man known as Malcolm X had been born Malcolm Little in 1925 and raised in Lansing, Michigan. His father, a preacher and a follower of Marcus Garvey, was killed in a racist attack by local whites. In his youth, Malcolm led a life of petty crime, eventually serving a seven-year prison term for burglary. While in jail he educated himself and converted to the Nation of Islam. He took the surname "X" to symbolize his original African family name, lost through slavery. Emerging from jail in 1952, he became a dynamic organizer, editor, and speaker for the Nation of Islam. He spoke frequently on college campuses as well on the street corners of black neighborhoods like New York's Harlem. He encouraged his audiences to take pride in their African heritage and to consider armed self-defense rather than relying solely on nonviolence—in short, to break free of white domination "by any means necessary." Malcolm's fiery rhetoric frightened most whites who heard it and may have also given license to young African Americans who would soon resort to violent rebellion in the ghettoes of the urban North.

Malcolm ridiculed the integrationist goals of the civil rights movement. Black Muslims, he told audiences, do not want "to integrate into this corrupt society, but to separate from it, to a land of our own, where we can reform ourselves, lift up our moral standards, and try to be godly." In his best-selling *Autobiography of Malcolm X* (1965), he admitted that his position was extremist. "The black race here in North America is in extremely bad condition. You show me a black man who isn't an extremist," he argued, "and I'll show you one who needs psychiatric attention."

In 1964, troubled by Elijah Muhammad's personal scandals (he faced paternity suits brought by two young female employees) and eager to find a more politically effective approach to improving conditions for blacks, Malcolm X broke with the Nation of Islam. He made the pilgrimage to Mecca, the Muslim holy city, where he met Islamic peoples of all colors and underwent a "radical alteration in my whole outlook about 'white' men." He returned to the United States as El-Hajj Malik El-Shabazz, abandoned his black separatist views, and founded the Organization of Afro-American Unity. Malcolm now looked for common ground with the civil rights movement, addressing a Mississippi Freedom Democrats rally in Harlem and meeting with SNCC activists. He stressed the international links between the civil rights struggle in America and the problems facing emerging African nations. On February 21, 1965, Malcolm X was assassinated while giving a speech at Harlem's Audubon Ballroom. His assailants were members of a New Jersey branch of the NOI, possibly infiltrated by the FBI.

SNCC leader John Lewis thought Malcolm X had been the most effective voice "to articulate the aspirations, bitterness, and frustrations of the Negro people," forming "a living link between Africa and the civil rights movement in this country." In his death he became a martyr for the idea that soon became known as Black Power. As much as anyone, Malcolm X pointed the way to a new black consciousness that celebrated black history, black culture, African heritage, and black self-sufficiency.

Born Malcolm Little, Malcolm X (1925–65) took the name "X" as a symbol of the stolen identity of African slaves. He emerged in the early 1960s as the foremost advocate of racial unity and black nationalism. The Black Power movement, initiated in 1966 by SNCC members, was strongly influenced by Malcolm X.

SELMA AND THE VOTING RIGHTS ACT OF 1965

Lyndon Johnson won reelection in 1964 by a landslide, capturing 61 percent of the popular vote. Of the 6 million black people who voted in the election—2 million more than in 1960—an overwhelming 94 percent cast their ballots for Johnson. Republican candidate Barry Goldwater managed to carry only his home state of Arizona and five Deep South states, where fewer than 45 percent of eligible black people could vote. With Democrats in firm control of both the Senate and the House, civil rights leaders believed the time was ripe for further legislative gains. There had already been some progress toward guaranteeing voting rights with the 1964 ratification of the Twenty-Fourth Amendment to the Constitution, outlawing the poll tax or any other tax as a condition of voting. Such taxes had long been one of the methods used by southern states to discourage black voters. Now Johnson and his staff began drafting a tough voting rights bill in late 1964, partly with an eye toward countering Republican gains among Deep South whites with newly registered black Democratic voters (see Map 28.2).

Once again, Movement leaders decided to create a crisis that would arouse national indignation, pressure

Congress, and force federal action. King and his aides chose Selma, Alabama, as their target. Selma, a city of 27,000 some fifty miles west of Montgomery, had a notorious record of preventing black voting. Of the 15,000 eligible black voters in Selma's Dallas County, registered voters numbered only in the hundreds. In 1963, local activists had invited SNCC workers to aid voter registration efforts in the community. But they had met a violent reception from county sheriff Jim Clark. Sensing that Clark might be another Bull Connor, King arrived in Selma in January 1965, just after accepting the Nobel Peace Prize in Oslo. "We are not asking, we are demanding the ballot," he declared. King, the SCLC staff, and SNCC workers led daily marches on the Dallas County Courthouse, where hundreds of black citizens tried to get their names added to voter lists. By early February, Clark had imprisoned more than 3,000 protesters.

Despite the brutal beating of Reverend James Bevel, a key SCLC strategist, and the killing of Jimmy Lee Jackson, a young black demonstrator in nearby Marion, the SCLC failed to arouse the level of national indignation it sought. Consequently, in early March SCLC staffers called on

MAP EXPLORATION

To explore an interactive version of this map, go to **www.prenhall.com/faragher6/map28.2**

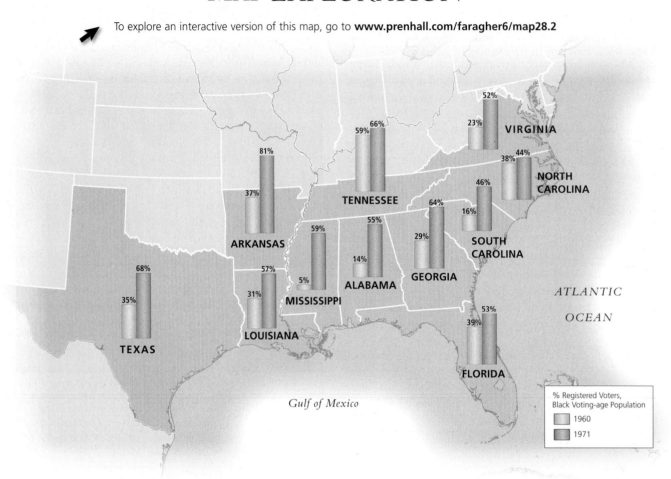

MAP 28.2 Impact of the Voting Rights Act of 1965 Voter registration among African Americans in the South increased significantly between 1960 and 1971.

black activists to march from Selma to Montgomery, where they planned to deliver a list of grievances to Governor Wallace. On Sunday, March 7, while King preached to his church in Atlanta, a group of 600 marchers crossed the Pettus Bridge on the Alabama River, on their way to Montgomery. A group of mounted, heavily armed county and state lawmen blocked their path and ordered them to turn back. When the marchers did not move, the lawmen attacked with billy clubs and tear gas, driving the protesters back over the bridge in a bloody rout. More than fifty marchers had to be treated in local hospitals.

The dramatic "Bloody Sunday" attack received extensive coverage on network television, prompting a national uproar. Demands for federal intervention poured into the White House from all over the country. King issued a public call for civil rights supporters to come to Selma for a second march on Montgomery. But a federal court tem-

porarily enjoined the SCLC from proceeding with the march. King found himself trapped. He reluctantly accepted a face-saving compromise: in return for a promise from Alabama authorities not to harm marchers, King would lead his followers across the Pettus Bridge, stop, pray briefly, and then turn back. This plan outraged the more militant SNCC activists and sharpened their distrust of King and the SCLC.

But just when it seemed the Selma movement might die, white racist violence revived it. A gang of white toughs attacked four white Unitarian ministers who had come to Selma to participate in the march. One of them, Reverend James J. Reeb of Boston, died of multiple skull fractures. His death brought new calls for federal action. On March 15, President Johnson delivered a televised address to a joint session of Congress to request passage of a voting rights bill. In a stirring speech, the president fused the political power of his office with the moral power of the movement. "Their cause must be our cause, too. Because it is not just Negroes, but really all of us who must overcome the crippling legacy of bigotry and injustice. And," he concluded firmly, quoting the Movement's hymn, "we shall overcome." Johnson also prevailed upon federal judge Frank Johnson to issue a ruling allowing the march to proceed, and he warned Governor Wallace not to interfere.

On March 21, Martin Luther King Jr. led more than 3,000 black and white marchers out of Selma on the road to Montgomery, where the bus boycott that marked the beginning of his involvement had occurred nine years before. Four days later they arrived at the Alabama statehouse. Their ranks had been swelled by more than 30,000 supporters, including hundreds of prominent politicians, entertainers, and black leaders. "I know some of you are asking today," King told the crowd, "'How long will it take?'" He went on in a rousing, rhythmic cadence:

> How long? Not long, because the arc of the moral universe is long but it bends toward justice. How long? Not long, because mine eyes have seen the glory of the coming of the Lord!

In August 1965 President Johnson signed the Voting Rights Act into law. It authorized federal supervision of registration in states and counties where fewer than half of voting-age residents were registered. It also outlawed literacy and other discriminatory tests that had been used to prevent blacks from registering to vote. Between 1964 and 1968, black registrants in Mississippi leaped from 7 percent to 59 percent of the statewide black population; in Alabama, from 24 percent to 57 percent. In those years the number of southern black voters grew from 1 million to 3.1 million. For the first time in their lives, black Southerners in hundreds of small towns and rural communities could enjoy full participation in American politics. Ten years after the Montgomery bus boycott, the civil rights movement had reached a peak of national influence and interracial unity.

Yet even amid this triumph, the growing mood of desperation among African Americans in northern ghettoes suggested the limits of the Movement and interracial unity. There had been a violent uprising in New York's Harlem in the summer of 1964 and a far more widespread and destructive rebellion in the Watts section of Los Angeles in August 1965 (see Chapter 29). These marked the first of the "long, hot summer" uprisings that would alienate many white citizens who had been sympathetic to the nonviolent civil rights struggle. They served notice as well that the growing frustration and alienation of northern blacks, increasingly defined by a militant turn to the rhetoric of "black power," could not be addressed with the same principles, tactics, and solutions that had made the southern civil rights movement successful.

CIVIL RIGHTS BEYOND BLACK AND WHITE

Other minorities as well had long been denied their civil rights. After World War II, Latinos, Indian peoples, and Asian Americans began making their own halting efforts to improve their political, legal, and economic status. They faced strong opposition from institutional racism and various economic interests that benefited from keeping these groups in a subordinate position. At the same time, the civil rights struggle helped spur a movement to reform immigration policies. The largely unintended consequences of the 1965 Immigration and Nationality Act would radically increase and reshape the flow of new immigrants into the United States.

MEXICAN AMERICANS AND MEXICAN IMMIGRANTS

The Mexican American community in the West and Southwest included both longtime U.S. citizens—who found white authorities nonetheless unwilling to recognize their rights—and noncitizen immigrants from Mexico. After World War II, several Mexican American political organizations sought to secure equal rights and equal opportunity for their community by stressing its American identity. The most important of these groups were the League of United Latin American Citizens (LULAC), launched in Texas in 1928, and the GI Forum, founded in Texas in 1948 by Mexican American veterans of World War II. Both emphasized learning English, assimilating into American society, improving education, and voting to gain political power. LULAC successfully pursued two important legal cases that anticipated *Brown* v. *Board of Education*. In *Mendez* v. *Westminster*, a 1947 California case, and in the 1948 *Delgado* case in Texas, the Supreme Court upheld lower-court rulings that declared segregation of Mexican Americans unconstitutional. Like *Brown*, these two decisions did not immediately end segregation, but they offered pathbreaking legal and psychological victories to Mexican American activists. LULAC won another significant legal battle in the 1954 *Hernandez* decision, in which the Supreme Court ended the exclusion of Mexican Americans from Texas jury lists.

Mexican migration to the United States increased dramatically during and after World War II. The *bracero* program, a cooperative effort between the U.S. and Mexican governments, brought some 300,000 Mexicans to the United States during the war as temporary agricultural and railroad workers. American agribusiness came to depend on Mexicans as a key source of cheap farm labor, and the program continued after the war. Most *braceros* endured harsh work, poor food, and substandard housing in migratory labor camps. Some migrated into the newly emerging *barrios*—Hispanic neighborhoods—in cities such as San Antonio, Los Angeles,

Delegates to the 1948 National Convention of the League of United Latin American Citizens met in Kingsville, Texas. After World War II, LULAC grew to about 15,000 members active in 200 local councils, mostly in Texas and California.

El Paso, and Denver. Many *braceros* and their children became American citizens, but most returned to Mexico. Another group of postwar Mexican immigrants were the *mojados*, or "wetbacks," so called because many swam the Rio Grande to enter the United States illegally.

This continued flow of immigrant workers into the Southwest heightened tensions within the Mexican American community. Both LULAC and the GI Forum contended that Mexican American civil rights activists needed to focus their efforts on American citizens of Mexican descent. Thus, they lobbied to end the *bracero* program and enforce stricter limits on immigration from Mexico to help maintain strict boundaries between Mexican American citizens and Mexican immigrants. Yet within Mexican American communities, where citizens and noncitizens shared language and work experience and made families together, this distinction had always been blurry. "I've been following the crops in California for about twelve years," one Mexican American farm worker noted in 1955, "and still don't know if I'm for or against the *braceros*. I guess that's because I first came to this country as a *bracero* myself in 1944, and know something about their problems."

In 1954, trying to curb the flow of undocumented immigrants from Mexico, the Eisenhower administration launched the massive "Operation Wetback." For three years, Immigration and Naturalization Service (INS) agents rounded up some 3.7 million allegedly undocumented migrants and sent them back over the border. INS agents made little effort to distinguish so-called illegals from *braceros* and Mexican American citizens. Many families were broken up, and thousands who had lived in the

United States for a decade or more found themselves deported. Many deportees were denied basic civil liberties, such as due process, and suffered physical abuse and intimidation. The breakup of families caused enormous resentment and anger, as did the contradictory policies of the federal government. As Ernesto Galarza, a leader of the National Agricultural Workers Union, put it, "while one agency of the United States government rounded up the illegal aliens and deported them to Mexico . . . another government agency was busily engaged in recruiting workers in Mexico to return them to U.S. farms."

The government campaign against aliens pushed LULAC, the GI Forum, and other activist groups to change their strategy in a critical way. The campaign to win full civil rights for American citizens of Mexican descent would increasingly be linked to improving the lives—and asserting the rights—of all Mexican immigrants, both documented and undocumented. If the government and the broader American public refused to distinguish between a Mexican national, a resident alien of the United States, a naturalized American citizen, or a native-born Spanish-speaking American, why should Mexican Americans cling to these distinctions? By the 1960s a new civil rights movement emerged, *la raza*, based on the shared ethnicity and historical experiences of the broader Mexican American community.

PUERTO RICANS

The United States seized Puerto Rico in 1898, during the final stages of the Spanish-American War. The Jones Act of 1917 made the island an unincorporated territory of the

United States and granted U.S. citizenship to all Puerto Ricans. Over the next several decades, Puerto Rico's economic base shifted from a diversified, subsistence-oriented agriculture to a single export crop—sugar. U.S. absentee owners dominated the sugar industry, claiming most of the island's arable land, previously tilled by small farmers growing crops for local consumption. Puerto Rico's sugar industry grew enormously profitable, but few island residents benefited from this expansion. By the 1930s, unemployment and poverty were widespread and the island was forced to import its foodstuffs.

Small communities of Puerto Rican migrants had begun to form in New York City during the 1920s. The largest was on the Upper East Side of Manhattan—*el barrio* in East Harlem. During World War II, labor shortages led the federal government to sponsor the recruitment of Puerto Rican workers for industrial jobs in New Jersey, Philadelphia, and Chicago. But the "great migration" took place from 1945 to 1964. During these two decades the number of Puerto Ricans living on the mainland jumped from less than 100,000 to roughly 1 million. Economic opportunity was the chief impetus for this migration, for the island suffered from high unemployment and low wages.

The advent of direct air service between Puerto Rico and New York in 1945 made the city easily accessible. The Puerto Rican community in East (or Spanish) Harlem mushroomed, and new communities in the South Bronx and Brooklyn began to emerge. By 1970 there were about 800,000 Puerto Ricans in New York—more than 10 percent of the city's population. New Puerto Rican communities also took root in Connecticut, Massachusetts, New Jersey, and the Midwest. Puerto Ricans frequently circulated between the island and the mainland, often returning home when economic conditions on the mainland were less favorable.

The experience of Puerto Rican migrants both resembled and differed from that of other immigrant groups in significant ways. Like Mexican immigrants, Puerto Ricans were foreign in language, culture, and experience, yet unlike Mexicans they entered the continental United States as citizens. Many Puerto Ricans were also black. Racial and ethnic discrimination came as a double shock, since Puerto Ricans, as citizens, came to America with a sense of entitlement. In New York, Puerto Ricans found themselves barred from most craft unions, excluded from certain neighborhoods, and forced to take jobs largely in the low-paying garment industry and service trades. Puerto Rican children were not well served by a public school system insensitive to language differences and too willing to track Spanish-speaking students into obsolete vocational programs.

By the early 1970s, Puerto Rican families were substantially poorer on average than the total U.S. population, and they had the lowest median income of any Latino group. The steep decline in manufacturing jobs and in the garment industry in New York during the 1960s and 1970s hit the Puerto Rican community especially hard. So did the city's fiscal crisis, which brought sharp cuts in funding for schools, health care, libraries, government jobs, and other public services traditionally available to immigrant groups. The structural shift in the U.S. economy away from manufacturing and toward service and high-technology jobs reinforced the Puerto Rican community's goal of improving educational opportunities for its members. The struggle to establish and improve bilingual education in schools became an important part of this effort. Most Puerto Ricans, especially those who had succeeded in school and achieved middle-class status, continued to identify strongly with their Puerto Rican heritage and Spanish language.

JAPANESE AMERICANS

The harsh relocation program of World War II devastated the Japanese American community on the West Coast (see Chapter 25). But the war against Nazism also helped weaken older notions of white superiority and racism. During the war, the state of California had aggressively enforced an alien land law by confiscating property declared illegally held by Japanese. In November 1946 a proposition supporting the law appeared on the state ballot. Thanks in part to a campaign by the Japanese American Citizens League (JACL) reminding voters of the wartime contributions of Nisei (second-generation Japanese American) soldiers, voters overwhelmingly rejected the referendum. One JACL leader hailed the vote as proof that "the people of California will not approve discriminatory and prejudiced treatment of persons of Japanese ancestry." Two years later the Supreme Court declared the law unconstitutional, calling it "nothing more than outright racial discrimination."

The 1952 Immigration and Nationality Act (see Chapter 26) removed the old ban against Japanese immigration and also made Issei (first-generation Japanese Americans) eligible for naturalized citizenship. Japanese Americans, who lobbied hard for the new law, greeted it with elation. "It gave the Japanese equality with all other immigrants," said JACL leader Harry Takagi, "and that was the principle we had been struggling for from the very beginning." By 1965 some 46,000 immigrant Japanese, most of them elderly Issei, had taken their citizenship oaths.

INDIAN PEOPLES

The postwar years also brought significant changes in the status and lives of Indian peoples. Congress reversed New Deal policies that had stressed Indian sovereignty and cultural independence. Responding to a variety of pressure groups, including mining and other economic interests wishing to exploit natural resources on reservations, Congress adopted a policy known as "termination," designed to cancel Indian treaties and terminate sovereignty rights.

In 1953, Congress passed House Concurrent Resolution 108, which allowed Congress to terminate a tribe as a political entity by passing legislation specific to that tribe. The leader of the termination forces, Senator Arthur Watkins of Utah, declared that the new law meant "the concept that the Indian people exist within the United States as independent nations has been rejected." Supporters of termination had varied motives, but the policy added up to the return of enforced assimilation for solving the "Indian problem."

Between 1954 and 1962, Congress passed twelve termination bills covering more than sixty tribes, nearly all in the West. Even when tribes consented to their own termination, they discovered that dissolution brought unforeseen problems. For example, members of the Klamaths of Oregon and the Paiutes of Utah received large cash payments from the division of tribal assets. But after these one-time payments were spent, members had to take poorly paid, unskilled jobs to survive. Many Indian peoples became dependent on state social services and slipped into poverty and alcoholism.

Along with termination, the federal government gave greater emphasis to a relocation program aimed at speeding up assimilation. The Bureau of Indian Affairs encouraged reservation Indians to relocate to cities, where they were provided with housing and jobs. For some, relocation meant assimilation, intermarriage with whites, and loss of tribal identity. Others, homesick and unable to adjust to an alien culture and place, either returned to reservations or wound up on the margins of city life. Still others regularly traveled back and forth. In some respects, this urban migration paralleled the larger postwar shift of rural peoples to cities and suburbs.

Indians increasingly came to see termination as a policy geared mainly to exploiting resources on Indian lands. By the early 1960s, a new movement was emerging to defend Indian sovereignty. The National Congress of American Indians (NCAI) condemned termination, calling for a review of federal policies and a return to self-determination. The NCAI led a political and educational campaign that challenged the goal of assimilation and created a new awareness among white people that Indians had the right to remain Indians. When the termination policy ended in the early 1960s, it had affected only about 3 percent of federally recognized Indian peoples.

Taking their cue from the civil rights movement, Indian activists used the court system to reassert sovereign rights. Indian and white liberal lawyers, many with experience in civil rights cases, worked through the Native American Rights Fund, which became a powerful force in western politics. A series of Supreme Court decisions, culminating in *United States* v. *Wheeler* (1978), reasserted the principle of "unique and limited" sovereignty. The Court recognized tribal independence except where limited by treaty or Congress.

The Indian population had been growing since the early years of the century, but most reservations had trouble making room for a new generation. Indians suffered increased rates of poverty, chronic unemployment, alcoholism, and poor health. The average Indian family in the early 1960s earned only one-third of the average family income in the United States. Those who remained in the cities usually became "ethnic Indians," identifying themselves more as simply "Indians" than as members of specific tribes. By the late 1960s, ethnic Indians had begun emphasizing civil rights over tribal rights, making common cause with African Americans and other minorities. The National Indian Youth Council (NIYC), founded in 1960, tried to unite the two causes of equality for individual Indians and special status for tribes. But the organization faced difficult contradictions between a common Indian identity, emphasizing Indians as a single ethnic group, and tribal identity, stressing the citizenship of Indians in separate nations.

REMAKING THE GOLDEN DOOR: THE IMMIGRATION AND NATIONALITY ACT OF 1965

The egalitarian political climate created by the civil rights movement nurtured efforts to modernize and reform the country's immigration policies. "Everywhere else in our national life, we have eliminated discrimination based on national origins," Attorney General Robert Kennedy told Congress in 1964. "Yet, this system is still the foundation of our immigration law." In 1965 Congress passed a new Immigration and Nationality Act, abolishing the national origins quotas that had been in place since the 1920s and substituting overall hemispheric limits: 120,000 visas annually for immigrants from the Western Hemisphere and 170,000 for those from the Eastern Hemisphere (with a 20,000 limit from any single country). The act was intended to redress the grievances of Eastern and Southern European ethnic groups who had been largely shut out since 1924. President Lyndon B. Johnson played down its importance. "It does not affect the lives of millions," he said when he signed the bill into law. "It will not reshape the structure of our daily lives, or really add importantly to our wealth or our power."

But the new law proved LBJ's prediction wrong. Exempted from numerical quotas were immigrants seeking family reunification with American citizens or resident aliens. In addition, preferences to those with specialized job skills and training, in fields like medicine and engineering, were extended to people from the nations of the Eastern Hemisphere. The high priority given family reunification created an unprecedented cycle of "chain immigration and sponsorship" of people seeking to join relatives already in the United States. As initial immigrants attained permanent resident or citizenship status, they would sponsor family members and relatives to come over. Once these family members and relatives arrived in the United States and became resident aliens or citizens, they in turn could sponsor their family members, and so on.

The consequences for Asian American communities in particular were profound. The number of Asian Americans soared from about 1 million in 1965 to 11 million by the end of the century. Immigrants from India and the Philippines included a high percentage of health care professionals, whereas many Chinese and Korean immigrants found work in professional and managerial occupations as well as their own small businesses. At the same time, low-skilled and impoverished Asians poured into the "Chinatowns" and "Koreatowns" of cities like New York and Los Angeles, taking jobs in restaurants, hotels, and garment manufacturing. Four times as many Asians settled in the United States in this period as in the entire previous history of the nation. This new wave also brought a strikingly different group of Asian immigrants to America. In 1960 the Asian American population was 52 percent Japanese, 27 percent Chinese, and 20 percent Filipino. In 1985, the composition had become 21 percent Chinese, 21 percent Filipino, 15 percent Japanese, 12 percent Vietnamese, 11 percent Korean, 10 percent Asian Indian, 4 percent Laotian, and 3 percent Cambodian.

The 1965 act also created conditions that increased undocumented immigration from Latin America. The new limits on Western Hemisphere migration, along with the simultaneous ending of the *bracero* program, tempted many thousands to enter the United States illegally. The Immigration and Naturalization Service arrested and deported 500,000 undocumented aliens each year in the decade following the act, most of them from Mexico, Central America, and the Caribbean. By the 1980s, more than 80 percent of all legal immigrants to the United States came from either Asia or Latin America; if one included illegal immigrants, the figure would surpass 90 percent.

CONCLUSION

The mass movement for civil rights was arguably the most important domestic event in twentieth-century American history. The struggle that began in Montgomery, Alabama, in December 1955 ultimately transformed race relations in thousands of American communities. By the early 1960s this community-based movement had placed civil rights at the very center of national political life. It achieved its greatest successes by invoking the Constitution—the supreme law of the land—to destroy legal segregation and win individual freedom for African Americans. The Civil Rights Act of 1964 and the Voting Rights Act of 1965 testified to the power of an African American and white liberal coalition. Yet the persistence of racism, poverty, and ghetto slums challenged a central assumption of liberalism: that equal protection of constitutional rights would give all Americans equal opportunities in life. By the mid-1960s, many black people had begun to question the core values of liberalism, the benefits of alliance with whites, and the philosophy of nonviolence. At the same time, a conservative white backlash against the gains made by African Americans further weakened the liberal political consensus.

In challenging the persistence of widespread poverty and institutional racism, the civil rights movement called for deep structural changes in American life. By 1967, Martin Luther King Jr. was articulating a broad and radical vision linking the struggle against racial injustice to other defects in American society. "The black revolution," he argued, "is much more than a struggle for the rights of Negroes. It is forcing America to face all its interrelated flaws—racism, poverty, militarism, and materialism. It is exposing evils that are deeply rooted in the whole structure of our society." Curing these ills would prove far more difficult than ending legal segregation.

A Korean couple working behind the counter of their newly opened restaurant in Los Angeles, ca. 2000. In the thirty-five years after the Immigration and Nationality Act of 1965, the city's Asian American population had grown to over 1.2 million, including the largest Korean community outside of Korea.

CHRONOLOGY

1941   Executive Order 8802 forbids racial discrimination in defense industries and government

1946   In *Morgan* v. *Virginia*, U.S. Supreme Court rules that segregation on interstate buses is unconstitutional

President Harry Truman creates the President's Committee on Civil Rights

1947   Jackie Robinson becomes the first African American on a major league baseball team

1948   President Truman issues executive order desegregating the armed forces

1954   In *Brown* v. *Board of Education*, Supreme Court rules segregated schools inherently unequal

1955   Supreme Court rules that school desegregation must proceed "with all deliberate speed"

Montgomery bus boycott begins

1956   Montgomery bus boycott ends in victory as the Supreme Court affirms a district court ruling that segregation on buses is unconstitutional

1957   Southern Christian Leadership Conference (SCLC) is founded

President Dwight Eisenhower sends in federal troops to protect African American students integrating Little Rock, Arkansas, high school

1960   Sit-in movement begins as four college students sit at a lunch counter in Greensboro, North Carolina, and ask to be served

Student Nonviolent Coordinating Committee (SNCC) founded

Board of Indian Commissioners is created

1961   Freedom Rides begin

1962   James Meredith integrates the University of Mississippi

The Albany movement fails to end segregation in Albany, Georgia

1963   SCLC initiates campaign to desegregate Birmingham, Alabama

Medgar Evers, leader of the Mississippi NAACP, is assassinated

March on Washington; Martin Luther King Jr. delivers his historic "I Have a Dream" speech

1964   Mississippi Freedom Summer project brings students to Mississippi to teach and register voters

President Johnson signs the Civil Rights Act of 1964

Civil rights workers Michael Schwerner, James Chaney, and Andrew Goodman are found buried in Philadelphia, Mississippi

Mississippi Freedom Democratic Party (MFDP) is denied seats at the 1964 Democratic Presidential Convention

1965   SCLC and SNCC begin voter registration campaign in Selma, Alabama

Malcolm X is assassinated

Civil rights marchers walk from Selma to Montgomery

Voting Rights Act of 1965 is signed into law

Immigration and Nationality Act

— REVIEW QUESTIONS

1. What were the key legal and political antecedents to the civil rights struggle in the 1940s and early 1950s? What organizations played the most central role? Which tactics continued to be used, and which were abandoned?

2. How did African American communities challenge legal segregation in the South? Compare the strategies of key organizations, such as the NAACP, SNCC, SCLC, and CORE.

3. Discuss the varieties of white resistance to the civil rights movement. Which were most effective in slowing the drive for equality?

4. Analyze the civil rights movement's complex relationship with the national Democratic Party between 1948 and 1964. How was the party transformed by its association with the movement? What political gains and losses did that association entail?

5. What legal and institutional impact did the movement have on American life? How did it change American culture and politics? Where did it fail?

6. What relationship did the African Americans who struggled for civil rights have with other American minorities? How—if at all—did these minorities benefit? Did they build their own versions of the movement?

— RECOMMENDED READING

Raymond Arsenault, *Freedom Riders: 1961 and the Struggle for Racial Justice* (2006). A new and definitive account of this pivotal moment in Movement history, Arsenault demonstrates how the Freedom Rides both galvanized national and international attention and inspired local activists around the South.

Thomas Borstelmann, *The Cold War and the Color Line: American Race Relations in the Global Arena* (2001). Analyzes how presidents from Harry S. Truman to George H. W. Bush have responded to the civil rights movement in the context of Cold War politics and the fight against colonialism and white supremacy in Africa.

Taylor Branch, *Parting the Waters: America in the King Years, 1954–1963* (1988); *Pillar of Fire: America in the King Years, 1963–1965* (1998). A deeply researched and monumental narrative history of the southern civil rights movement organized around the life and influence of Reverend Martin Luther King Jr.

Clayborne Carson et al., eds., *Reporting Civil Rights* (2003). A wide-ranging compilation of contemporary reportage on the movement and resistance to it.

Roger Daniels, *Guarding the Golden Door: American Immigration Policy and Immigrants Since 1882* (2004). A com-

prehensive history, including excellent coverage of the legislative and political battles behind post–World War II changes in immigration laws.

Mary L. Dudziak, *Cold War Civil Rights: Race and the Image of American Democracy* (2000). Excellent analysis of the connections between the struggle for racial equality in America and the nation's contest with communism abroad.

Aldon D. Morris, *The Origins of the Civil Rights Movement: Black Communities Organizing for Change* (1984). An important study combining history and social theory. Morris emphasizes the key role of ordinary black people, acting through their churches and other community organizations before 1960.

Howell Raines, *My Soul Is Rested: Movement Days in the Deep South Remembered* (1977). The best oral history of the civil rights movement, drawing from a wide range of participants and points of view. It is brilliantly edited by Raines, who covered the events as a journalist.

Jason Sokol, *There Goes My Everything: White Southerners in the Age of Civil Rights, 1945–1975* (2006). A sophisticated new study examining the range and complexity of white Southerners' encounters with the civil rights movement and the momentous changes it wrought.

myhistorylab
Where it's a good time to connect to the past!

For study resources for this chapter, go to **http://www.myhistorylab.com** and choose *Out of Many*. You will find a wealth of study and review material for this chapter, including pretests and posttests, customized study plan, key-term review flash cards, interactive map and document activities, and documents for analysis.

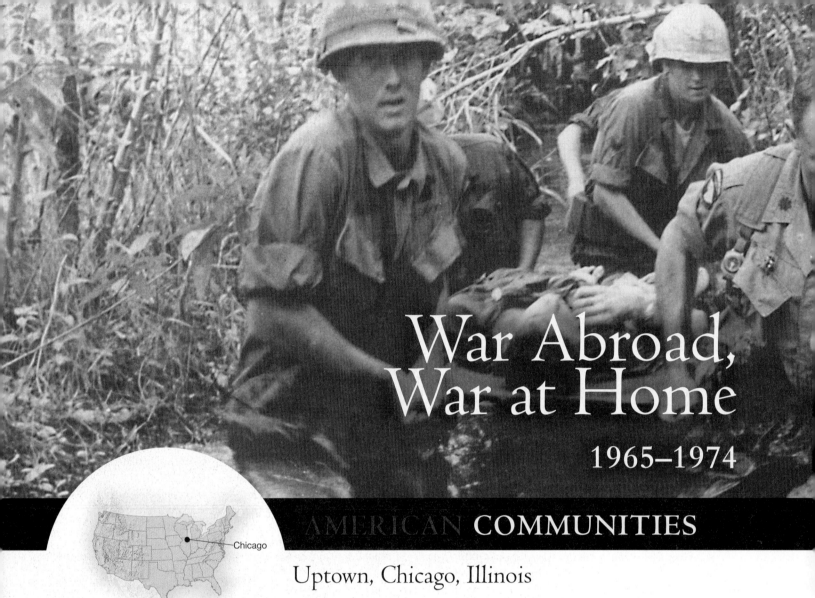

War Abroad, War at Home

1965–1974

Uptown, Chicago, Illinois

During the freedom summer of 1964, while teams of northern college students traveled south to join voter registration campaigns among African Americans, a small group moved to Chicago to help the city's poor people take control of their communities. They targeted a neighborhood known as Uptown, a one-mile-square section five miles north of the Loop, the city center. The residents, many transplanted from the poverty of the Appalachian South, lived in crowded tenements or in once elegant mansions now subdivided into tiny, run-down apartments. The student organizers hoped to mobilize the community "so as to demand an end to poverty and the construction of a decent social order."

With the assistance of the Packinghouse Workers union, the students formed Jobs or Income Now (JOIN), opened a storefront office, and invited local residents to work with them to demand jobs and better living conditions. They spent hours listening to people, drawing out their ideas, and helping them develop scores of programs. They campaigned against Mayor Richard Daley's policy of "police omnipresence" that had a fleet of squad cars and paddy wagons continually patrolling the neighborhood. They also helped establish new social clubs, a food-buying cooperative, a community theater, and a health clinic. Within a few years, Uptown street kids had formed the Young Patriots organization, put out a community newspaper, *Rising Up Angry*, and staffed free breakfast programs.

Chicago JOIN was one of ten similar projects sponsored by Students for a Democratic Society (SDS). Impatient with the nation's chronic poverty and Cold War politics, twenty-nine students from nine universities had met in June 1960 to form a new kind of campus-based political organization. SDS soon caught on with liberal students, encouraging them, as part of the nation's largest college population to date, to make their voices heard. By its peak in 1968, SDS had 350 chapters and between 60,000 and 100,000 members. Its principle of participatory democracy—with its promise to give people control over the decisions affecting their lives—appealed to a wider following of more than a million students.

In June 1962, in Port Huron, Michigan, SDS issued a declaration of principles, drafted mainly by graduate student Tom Hayden. "We are people . . . bred in at least modest comfort, housed now in universities," *The Port Huron Statement* opened, "looking uncomfortably ➤

to the world we inherit." Poverty and social injustice, it continued, were not the only problems. A deeper ailment plagued American society. Everyone, including middle-class students with few material wants, suffered from a sense of "loneliness, estrangement, and alienation." *The Port Huron Statement* defined SDS as a new kind of political movement that would bring people "out of isolation and into community" so that not just the poor but all Americans could overcome their feelings of "powerlessness [and hence] resignation before the enormity of events."

SDS began with a campaign to reform the university, especially to disentangle the financial ties between campus-based research programs and the military-industrial complex. SDS also sent small groups of students to live and organize in the poor communities of Boston, Louisville, Cleveland, and Newark as well as Chicago. Ultimately, none of these projects recruited large numbers of people. Protests against local government did little to combat unemployment, and campaigns for better garbage collection or more playgrounds rarely evolved into lasting movements. Nevertheless, organizers did succeed, to some degree, in realizing the goal specified in its slogan: "Let the People Decide." By late 1967, SDS prepared to leave JOIN in the hands of the people it had organized, which was its intention from the beginning.

Initially, even Lyndon Baines Johnson promoted civic participation. The Great Society, as the president called his domestic program, promised more than the abolition of poverty and racial inequality. In May 1964, at the University of Michigan, the president described his goal as a society "where every child can find knowledge to enrich his mind and to enlarge his talents," where "the city of man serves not only the needs of the body and the demands of commerce but the desire for beauty and the hunger for community."

By 1967 the Vietnam War had pushed aside such ambitions. If SDSers had once believed they could work with liberal Democrats like Johnson, they now interpreted social injustice at home as the inevitable consequence of the president's dangerous and destructive foreign policies. SDS threw its energies into building a movement against the war in Vietnam. President Johnson, meanwhile, pursued a foreign policy that would swallow up the funding for his own plans for a war on poverty and would precipitate a very different war at home, Americans against Americans. As hawks and doves lined up on opposite sides, the Vietnam War created a huge and enduring rift. SDS member Richard Flacks had warned that the nation had to "choose between devoting its resources and energies to maintaining military superiority and international hegemony or rechanneling those resources and energies to meeting the desperate needs of its people." Ultimately, even President Johnson himself understood that the "bitch of a war" in Asia ruined "the woman I really loved—the Great Society."

The dream of community did not vanish, but consensus became increasingly remote by the late 1960s. By this time, parents and children were at odds over values and aspirations, urban uprisings were rocking the nation, and political leaders were being struck down by assassins' bullets. New protest groups—Black Power, Women's Liberation, Gay Liberation, as well as Chicano, Native American, and Asian—were staking out a highly charged "politics of identity." Political conservatives managed to triumph in the election of Richard Nixon, who went on to disgrace the office. Meanwhile, the United States continued to fight—and eventually lost—the longest war in its history.

VIETNAM: AMERICA'S LONGEST WAR

The Vietnam War had its roots in the Truman Doctrine and its goal of containing communism (see Chapter 26). In 1954, after the Communist forces of Ho Chi Minh defeated the French colonialists and created a new government in the north, Vietnam emerged as a major zone of Cold War contention. President John Kennedy called it "the cornerstone of the Free World in Southeast Asia, the keystone in the arch, the finger in the dike," a barrier to the spread of communism throughout the region and perhaps the world. President Lyndon Johnson took office sounding the same note. With American security at stake, he insisted, Americans had little choice but to fight for "the principle for which our ancestors fought in the valleys of Pennsylvania."

Vietnam was not Valley Forge, however, and the United States ultimately paid a huge price for its determination to turn back communism in Indochina. More than 58,000 Americans died in an unwinnable overseas war that only deepened divisions at home.

JOHNSON'S WAR

Although President Kennedy had greatly increased the number of military advisers and Special Forces in South Vietnam (see Chapter 27), it was his successor, Lyndon B.

Focus Questions

1. Why did President Johnson escalate the war in Vietnam?

2. How did campus protests shape national political debate?

3. What were the goals of Johnson's Great Society?

4. What divided the Democratic Party in 1968?

5. How did Richard Nixon win the presidential election in 1968?

6. What is meant by the "politics of identity"?

1965–1974

Johnson, who made the decision to engage the United States in a major war there. At first, Johnson simply hoped to stay the course. Facing election in November 1964, he knew that a major military setback would cripple his campaign. But he was equally determined to avoid the fate of President Truman, who had been damaged politically after "losing" China to communism and producing a stalemate in Korea.

Throughout the winter and spring of 1964, as conditions worsened in South Vietnam, Johnson and his advisers quietly laid the groundwork for a sustained bombing campaign against North Vietnam. In early August, they found a pretext to set this plan in motion. The National Security Agency—decades later admitting to faulty intelligence—reported two attacks against U.S. destroyers by North Vietnamese patrol boats in the Gulf of Tonkin, off the coast of North Vietnam. Although the second alleged attack never took place, the report gave Johnson a reason to order retaliatory air strikes against bases in North Vietnam.

Johnson appealed to Congress to give him the authority "to take all necessary measures" and "all necessary steps" to defend U.S. armed forces and to protect Southeast Asia "against aggression or subversion." This Gulf of Tonkin resolution, secretly drafted six weeks before the alleged incident, passed the Senate on August 7 with only two dissenting votes and moved unanimously through the House. It served, in Undersecretary of State Nicholas Katzenbach's words, as the "functional equivalent" of a declaration of war.

Ironically, Johnson continued his presidential campaign in 1964 with a call for restraint in Vietnam. He assured voters that "we are not about to send American boys nine or ten thousand miles away from home to do what Asian boys ought to be doing for themselves." This strategy helped him win a landslide victory over conservative Republican Barry Goldwater of Arizona, who had proposed the deployment of "tactical" nuclear weapons in Vietnam.

With the election behind him, Johnson faced a hard decision. The limited bombing raids against North Vietnam had failed to slow Communist forces moving across the border into the South. Meanwhile, the government in Saigon, the capital city of South Vietnam, appeared near collapse. Faced with the prospect of a Communist victory, the president chose to escalate U.S. involvement in Vietnam.

DEEPER INTO THE QUAGMIRE

In early February 1965, Johnson found a rationale to justify massive bombing of the North. The Vietcong had fired at American soldiers at a military base at Pleiku in the central highlands of Vietnam, killing nine and wounding more than 100 Americans. Waving the list of casualties, the president rushed into an emergency meeting of the National Security Council to announce that the time had passed for keeping "our guns over the mantel and our shells in the cupboard." He ordered immediate reprisal bombing and one week later, on February 13, authorized Operation Rolling Thunder, a campaign of gradually intensifying air attacks.

Once Rolling Thunder began, President Johnson hesitated to speak frankly with the American public about his plan of action on the ground. Initially, he announced that only two battalions of marines were being assigned to Danang to defend the airfields where bombing runs began. But six weeks later, 50,000 U.S. combat troops were in Vietnam. By November 1965 the total topped 165,000, and more troops were on the way. But even after Johnson authorized a buildup to 431,000 troops in mid-1966, victory was still nowhere in sight.

The strategy pursued by the Johnson administration and implemented by General William Westmoreland—a war of attrition—was based on the premise that continuous use of heavy artillery and air power would eventually exhaust North Vietnam's resources. Meanwhile, U.S. ground forces would defeat the Vietcong in South Vietnam and thereby restore political stability to South Vietnam's pro-Western government. As Johnson once boasted, the strongest military power in the world surely could crush a Communist rebellion in a "pissant" country of peasants.

The massive bombing and ground combat created huge numbers of civilian casualties in Vietnam. The majority killed were women and children.

In practice, the United States wreaked havoc in South Vietnam, tearing apart its society and bringing ecological devastation to its land. Intending to eradicate the support network of the Vietcong, U.S. ground troops conducted search-and-destroy missions throughout the countryside. They attacked villagers and their homes. Seeking to ferret out Vietcong sympathizers, U.S. troops turned at any one time as many as 4 million people—approximately one-quarter of the population of South Vietnam—into refugees. By late 1968, the United States had dropped more than 3 million tons of bombs on Vietnam and eventually delivered more than three times the tonnage dropped by the Allies on all fronts during World War II. Using herbicides such as Agent Orange to defoliate forests, the United States also conducted the most destructive chemical warfare in history.

Several advisers urged the president to keep the American people informed about his decisions in Vietnam, even to declare a state of national emergency. But Johnson feared he would lose momentum on domestic reform, including his antipoverty programs, if he drew attention to foreign policy. Seeking to avoid "undue excitement in the Congress and in domestic public opinion," he held to a course of intentional deceit.

THE CREDIBILITY GAP

Johnson's popularity had surged at the time of the Gulf of Tonkin resolution, skyrocketing in one day from 42 to 72 percent, according to a Harris poll. But afterward it waned rapidly. Every night network television news tallied the soaring American body count, from 26 per week in 1965 to 180 in 1967. No president worked so hard to control the news media, but Johnson found himself badgered by reporters who accused him of creating a credibility gap.

During the early 1960s, network news had either ignored Vietnam or unquestioningly supported U.S. policy. Beginning with a CBS News report by Morley Safer in August 1965, however, the tenor changed. Although government officials described the U.S. operation in the South Vietnamese village Cam Ne as an attack on "fortified Vietcong bunkers," the *CBS Evening News* showed Marines setting fire to the thatched homes of civilians. President Johnson's sharp complaint to the CBS News director did little to staunch the criticism that surfaced in the wake of the report. And more unfavorable news commentary soon followed. By 1967, according to a noted media observer, "every subject tended to become Vietnam." The evening news programs reported on the varieties of American cluster bombs, which released up to 180,000 fiberglass shards, and showed the nightmarish effects of the defoliants used on South Vietnam's forests to uncover enemy strongholds. Such scenes of human suffering and devastation, now broadcast daily, ultimately weakened the administration's moral justification of U.S. involvement as a defense of freedom and democracy in South Vietnam.

The print media also became skeptical of Johnson's Vietnam policies. Harrison Salisbury, Pulitzer Prize–winning *New York Times* reporter, questioned the administration's claims of precision bombing in the North, charging that U.S. planes had struck the population center of Hanoi, capital of North Vietnam, and had intentionally destroyed villages in the South. As American military deaths climbed at the rate of more than 800 per month during the first half of 1967, newspaper coverage of the war focused yet more closely on such disturbing events.

The most vocal congressional critic of Johnson's war policy was Democratic Senator J. William Fulbright of Arkansas, who chaired the Senate Foreign Relations Committee and who had personally speeded the passage of the Gulf of Tonkin resolution. A strong supporter of the Cold War, Fulbright had nevertheless concluded that the war in Vietnam was both unwinnable and destructive to domestic reform. In 1967, in his best-selling *Arrogance of Power*, he proposed a negotiated withdrawal from a neutralized Southeast Asia. He also persuaded prominent Democrats to put aside their personal loyalty to Johnson and push through Congress a nonbinding resolution appealing to the United Nations to help negotiate an end to hostilities. Meanwhile, some of the nation's most trusted European allies called for restraint in Vietnam.

The impact of the war, which cost Americans $21 billion per year, was also felt by Americans at home. Johnson convinced Congress to levy a 10 percent surcharge on individual and corporate taxes. Later adjustments tapped the Social Security fund, heretofore safe from interference. Inflation raced upward, fed by spending on the war. Johnson replaced advisers who questioned his policy, but as casualties multiplied, more and more Americans began to mistrust his handling of the war.

A GENERATION IN CONFLICT

As the Vietnam war escalated, Americans from all walks of life protested U.S. involvement. But between 1965 and 1971, a peace movement took shape that had a distinctly generational character. At the forefront were the baby boomers who were just coming of age.

This so-called sixties generation, the largest generation in American history, was also the best educated. Nearly half of all young adults between the ages of 18 and 21 were enrolled in college. In 1965 there were 5 million college students; in 1973 the number had doubled to 10 million. Public universities made the largest gains; by 1970 eight had more than 30,000 students apiece.

At first a small minority, groups of college students began to combine protest against the war in Vietnam with a broader, penetrating critique of American society. Through music, dress, and even hairstyle, they expressed a deep estrangement from the values and aspirations of their parents' generation. As early as 1967, when opposition to the war began to swell, "flower children" were putting daisies in the rifle barrels of troops sent to quash campus protests, providing a seemingly innocent counterpoint to the grim news of slaughter abroad. Meanwhile, campus organizations such as SDS called upon college students to demand an immediate and unconditional withdrawal of U.S. troops from Vietnam.

"THE TIMES THEY ARE A-CHANGIN'"

The first sign of a new kind of protest was the free speech movement at the University of California at Berkeley. In the fall of 1964, civil rights activists returned to the 27,000-student campus from Freedom Summer in Mississippi and decided to picket Bay Area stores that practiced discrimination in hiring. When the university administration tried to stop them from setting up information booths on campus, eighteen groups objected, including the archconservative Students for Goldwater, claiming that their right to free speech had been abridged. The administration sent police to break up the protest rally and arrest participants. After university president Clark Kerr, under pressure from conservative regents, announced his intention to press charges against the free speech movement's leaders, a huge crowd gathered. Joining folk singer Joan Baez in singing "We Shall Overcome," nearly 1,000 people marched toward the university's administration building, where they planned to stage a sit-in until Kerr rescinded his order. The police moved in, detaining nearly 800 protestors in the largest mass arrest in California history.

Mario Savio, a Freedom Summer volunteer and philosophy student, explained that the free speech movement aspired to more than just the right to conduct political activity on campus. They wanted, in the phrase coined by SDS, participatory democracy. Across the country—and in many nations around the world—college students began to demand a say in their education. Brown University students, for example, demanded a revamp of the curriculum to eliminate all required courses and make grades optional. Students also spoke out against campus rules that treated students as children instead of as adults. After a string of campus protests, most large universities, including the University of California, relinquished *in loco parentis* (in the place of parents) policies and allowed students to live off-campus and to set their own hours.

Across the bay in San Francisco, other young adults staked out a new form of community—a counterculture. In 1967, the "Summer of Love," the population of the Haight-Ashbury district swelled by 75,000 as youthful adventurers from around the world gathered for a huge "be-in." Although the *San Francisco Chronicle* featured a headline reading "Mayor Warns Hippies to Stay Out of Town," masses of long-haired young men and women dressed in bell-bottoms and tie-dyed T-shirts congregated in "the Haight" to listen to music, take drugs, and "be" with each other. "If you're going to San Francisco," a popular rock group sang, "be sure to wear some flowers in your hair . . . you're going to meet some gentle people there." In the fall, the majority returned to their own communities, bringing with them the new hippie lifestyle.

The generational rebellion took many forms, including a revolution in sexual behavior that triggered countless quarrels between parents and their maturing sons and daughters. During the 1960s more teenagers experienced premarital sex—by the decade's end three-quarters of all college seniors had engaged in sexual intercourse—and far more talked about it openly than in previous eras. With birth control widely available, including the newly developed "pill," many young women were no longer deterred from sex by fear of pregnancy. "We've discarded the idea that the loss of virginity is related to degeneracy," one college student explained. "Premarital sex doesn't mean the downfall of society, at least not the kind of society that we're going to build." Many heterosexual couples chose to live together outside marriage, a practice few parents condoned. A much smaller but significant number formed communes—approximately 4,000 by 1970—where members could share housekeeping and child care as well as sexual partners.

Mood-altering drugs played a large part in this counterculture. Soon-to-be-former Harvard professor Timothy Leary urged young people to "turn on, tune in, drop out" and also advocated the mass production and distribution of LSD (lysergic acid diethylamide), which was not criminalized until 1968. Marijuana, illegal yet readily available, was often paired with rock music in a collective ritual of love and laughter. Singer Bob Dylan taunted adults with the lyrics of his hit single, "Everybody must get stoned."

Music played a large part in defining the counterculture. With the emergence of rock 'n' roll in the 1950s, popular music had begun to express a deliberate generational identity (see Chapter 27), a trend that gained international momentum with the emergence of the British rock group the Beatles in 1964. Folk music, popular on campuses since the early 1960s, served as a voice of protest. Many left-leaning students grew up with the social-conscious songs of Pete Seegar and now gravitated toward campus-based folk song clubs. Young people of all kinds flocked to concerts starring popular folk artists Peter, Paul, and Mary; Phil Ochs; Judy Collins; as well as Joan Baez. Folk singer Bob Dylan issued a warning to parents:

> *Your sons and your daughters*
> *are beyond your command*
> *Your old road is*
> *rapidly agin'.*
> *Please get out of the new one*
> *If you can't lend your hand*
> *For the times they are a-changin'.*

By 1965 Dylan himself had turned to the electric guitar and rock, which triumphed as the musical emblem of a generation worldwide.

At a farm near Woodstock, New York, more than 400,000 people gathered in August 1969 for a three-day rock concert celebrating the counterculture. Thousands took drugs while security officials and local police stood by, some stripped off their clothes to dance or swim, and a few even

The nationally acclaimed photographer Peter Simon was something of a hippie himself in the 1960s and took many photographs of the "alternative culture." Here he captures a group of hippies in the typically rural setting of back-to-the-land communes.

made love in the grass. "We were exhilarated," one reveler recalled. "We felt as though we were in liberated territory."

The Woodstock Nation, as the counterculture was mythologized, did not actually represent the sentiments of most young people. But its attitudes and styles, especially its efforts to create a new community, did speak for the large minority seeking a peaceful alternative to the intensifying climate of war. The slogan "Make Love, Not War" linked generational rebellion and opposition to the U.S. war in Vietnam.

FROM CAMPUS PROTEST TO MASS MOBILIZATION

Three weeks after the announcement of Operation Rolling Thunder in 1965, peace activists called for a daylong boycott of classes so that students and faculty might meet to discuss the war. At the University of Michigan in Ann Arbor, more than 3,000 students turned out. "Teach-ins" soon spread across the United States and to Europe and Japan. Meanwhile, SDS mobilized 20,000 people in an antiwar march on the nation's capital (see Communities in Conflict).

Students also protested against war-related research on their campuses. The expansion of higher education in the 1960s had depended largely on federally funded programs, including military research on counterinsurgency tactics and chemical weapons. Student protesters demanded an end to these programs and, receiving no response from university administrators, turned to civil disobedience. In October 1967, the Dow Chemical Company, manufacturers of napalm, a form of jellied gasoline that produces internal as well as external burns, sent job recruiters to the University of Wisconsin at Madison despite warnings that antiwar activists would try to disrupt interviews. A few hundred students sat-in at the building where the recruitment interviews were scheduled, and 2,000 onlookers gathered outside. Ordered by university administrators to disperse the crowd, the city's police broke glass doors, dragged students through the debris, and clubbed those who refused to move. Suddenly the campus erupted. Students chanted *Sieg Heil* at the police, who attempted to disperse them with tear gas and Mace. During the next three years, the momentum grew, and demonstrations took place on campuses in every region of the country.

Many student-led demonstrations merged opposition to the war with broader community issues. In 1968 at Columbia University, students protested the administration's plans to build a new gymnasium in a city park used by residents of neighboring Harlem. In the Southwest, Mexican American students opposed diverting tax revenues away from antipoverty and educational programs and toward military projects.

The peace movement spread well beyond the campus. In April 1967, a daylong antiwar rally in Manhattan's Central Park drew more than 300,000 people. Meanwhile, 60,000 protesters turned out in San Francisco. By summer, Vietnam Veterans Against the War had begun to organize returning soldiers and sailors, encouraging them to cast off the medals and ribbons they had won in battle.

The steadily increasing size of antiwar demonstrations provoked conservatives and prowar Democrats to take a stronger stand, some calling for the arrest of antiwar leaders on charges of treason. Secretary of State Dean Rusk, appearing on NBC's *Meet the Press*, declared that "authorities in Hanoi" might conclude, incorrectly, that the majority of Americans did not back their president. He predicted that "the net effect of these demonstrations will be to prolong the war, not to shorten it."

Many demonstrators themselves, concluding that peaceful protest alone had little impact on U.S. policy, decided to change tactics—"from protest to resistance"—and serve as moral witnesses. Despite a 1965 congressional act providing for a five-year jail term and a $10,000 fine for destroying a draft card, thousands of young men burned their draft cards. Approximately a half-million more refused induction. Two Jesuit priests, Daniel and Philip Berrigan, raided the draft board offices in Catonsville, Maryland, in May 1968 and poured homemade napalm over records. Other activists determined to "bring the war home" went beyond civil disobedience. An estimated 40,000 bombing incidents or bomb threats took place from January 1969 to April 1970; more than $21 million of property was damaged, and forty-three people were killed.

Parallel wars were now being fought, one between two systems of government in Vietnam, another between the American government and masses of its citizens. Those Americans sent to Vietnam were caught in between.

TEENAGE SOLDIERS

The average age of soldiers who fought in Vietnam hovered around nineteen. Until late 1969 the Selective Service System—the draft—gave deferments to college students and to workers in selected occupations while recruiting hard in poor communities by advertising the armed forces as a provider of vocational training and social mobility. Working-class young men, disproportionately African American and Latino, signed up in large numbers under these inducements. They also bore the brunt of combat. Whereas college graduates constituted only 12 percent of the 2.5 million men who served in Vietnam and 9 percent of those who were killed in combat, high school dropouts were the most likely to serve in Vietnam and by far the most likely to die there. The casualty rate for African Americans was approximately 30 percent higher than the overall death rate for U.S. forces in Southeast Asia. These disparities created a rupture that would last well past the end of the war.

The Prospects for Peace in Vietnam, April 1965

During the early months of 1965, President Johnson changed course in Vietnam by launching the "Rolling Thunder" campaign that sent massive bombing missions over North Vietnam and by introducing U.S. ground troops to fight the Vietcong in the South. In response, his opponents became yet more vocal in expressing their dissent. On college campuses, Students for a Democratic Society took the lead in organizing small, local demonstrations against the war and calling on peace activists throughout the United States to join a march in Washington on April 17 to protest the war.

In part to mollify critics of escalation, President Johnson decided to present the government of North Vietnam with an opportunity for "unconditional discussions" about a plan for peace. He also offered $1 billion in aid for a development project along the Mekong River, described by some in his administration as an extension of his Great Society policy abroad. He announced all this in a speech at the Johns Hopkins University on April 7, 1965, which was televised to 60 million viewers. Johnson's speech, called "Peace without Conquest," won approval from many Americans and briefly prompted optimism about prospects for peace.

But ten days later, the 20,000 to 25,000 peace activists who gathered in Washington, DC, were far from appeased by the president's offer. Paul Potter, the president of SDS and the final speaker at the rally, offered his own interpretation of the progress of the war and its significance for Americans. In his speech, titled "Naming the System," Potter directly answered Johnson's claims in the "Peace without Conquest" address. In speaking of "the system," the SDS president connected the injustices of war in Southeast Asia with the inequities borne by Americans in their own country. His speech inspired many to go home with renewed dedication to the peace movement and radical social change.

What are the main points of disagreement between President Johnson and Paul Potter?

In connecting the war to social injustices at home, what political or social challenges stand out in Potter's critique of "the system"?

President Lyndon Johnson Calls for "Peace without Conquest" (April 7, 1965)

Viet Nam is far away from this quiet campus. We have no territory there, nor do we seek any. The war is dirty and brutal and difficult. And some 400 young men, born into an America that is bursting with opportunity and promise, have ended their lives, on Viet-Nam's steaming soil.

Why must we take this painful road?

Why must this Nation hazard its ease, and its interest, and its power for the sake of a people so far away?

We fight because we must fight if we are to live in a world where every country can shape its own destiny. And only in such a world will our own freedom be finally secure. . . .

The first reality is that North Viet-Nam has attacked the independent nation of South Viet-Nam. Its object is total conquest.

Of course, some of the people of South Viet-Nam are participating in attack on their own government. But trained men and supplies, orders and arms, flow in a constant stream from north to south. . . .

Over this war and all Asia is another reality: the deepening shadow of Communist China. The rulers in Hanoi are urged on by Peking. This is a regime which has destroyed freedom in Tibet, which has attacked India, and has been condemned by the United Nations for aggression in Korea. . . .

Why are these realities our concern? Why are we in South Vietnam?

We are there because we have a promise to keep. Since 1954 every American President has offered support to the people of South Viet-Nam. We have helped to build, and we have helped to defend. Thus, over many years, we have made a national pledge to help South Viet-Nam defend its independence. And I intend to keep that promise . . .

We are also there to strengthen world order. Around the globe, from Berlin to Thailand, are people whose well-being rests, in part, on the belief that they can count on us if they are attacked. To leave Viet-Nam to its fate would shake the confidence of all these people in the value of an American commitment and in the value of America's word. The result would be increased unrest and instability, and even wider war.

We are also there because there are great stakes in the balance. Let no one think for a moment that retreat from Viet-Nam would bring an end to conflict. The battle would be renewed in one country and then another. The central lesson of our time is that the appetite of aggression is never satisfied. To withdraw from one battlefield means only to prepare for the next. We must say in Southeast Asia as we did in Europe in the words of the Bible: "Hitherto shalt thou come, but no further." . . .

Our objective is the independence of South Viet-Nam, and its freedom from attack. We want nothing for ourselves, only that the people of South Viet-Nam be allowed to guide their own country in their own way. We will do everything necessary to reach that objective. And we will do only what is absolutely necessary.

In recent months attacks on South Viet Nam were stepped up. Thus, it became necessary for us to increase our response and to make attacks by air. This is not a change of purpose. It is a change in which we believe that purpose requires . . .

These countries of Southeast Asia are homes for millions of impoverished people. Each day these people rise at dawn and

"Our objective is the independence of South VietNam, and its freedom from attack."

struggle through until the night to wrestle existence from the soil. They are often wracked by disease, plagued by hunger, and death comes at the early age of 40.

For our part I will ask the Congress to join in a billion dollar American investment in this effort as soon as it is underway.

The task is nothing less than to enrich the hopes and the existence of more than a hundred million people. And there is much to be done.

The vast Mekong River can provide food and water and power on a scale to dwarf even our own TVA. . . .

SOURCE: Public Papers of the Presidents of the United States: Lyndon B. Johnson, 1965, pp. 394–397, as excerpted in "The Wars for Viet Nam," Vassar College Web site.

SDS President Paul Potter, "Naming the System" (April 17, 1965)

Not even the President can say that this is a war to defend the freedom of the Vietnamese people. Perhaps what the President means when he speaks of freedom is the freedom of the American people. . . .

How much more of Mr. Johnson's freedom can we stand? How much freedom will be left in this country if there is a major war in Asia? By what weird logic can it be said that the freedom of one people can only be maintained by crushing another? . . .

What kind of system is it that allows good men to make those kinds of decisions? What kind of system is it that justifies the United States or any country seizing the destinies of the Vietnamese people and using them callously for its own purpose? What kind of system is it that disenfranchises people in the South, leaves millions upon millions of people throughout the country impoverished and excluded from the mainstream and promise of American society, that creates faceless and terrible bureaucracies and makes those the place where people spend their lives and do their work, that consistently puts material values before human values—and still persists in calling itself free and still persists in finding itself fit to police the world? What place is there for ordinary men in that system and how are they to control it, make it bend itself to their wills rather than bending them to its?

We must name that system. We must name it, describe it, analyze it, understand it and change it. For it is only when that system is changed and brought under control that there can be any hope for stopping the forces that create a war in Vietnam today or a murder in the South tomorrow or all the incalculable, innumerable more subtle atrocities that are worked on people all over—all the time.

"How much more of Mr. Johnson's freedom can we stand?"

How do you stop a war then? If the war has its roots deep in the institutions of American society, how do you stop it? Do you march to Washington? Is that enough? . . .

. . . If the people of this country are to end the war in Vietnam, and to change the institutions which create it, then the people of this country must create a massive social movement—and if that can be built around the issue of Vietnam then that is what we must do.

By a social movement I mean more than petitions or letters of protest, or tacit support of dissident Congressmen; I mean people who are willing to change their lives, who are willing to challenge the system, to take the problem of change seriously. By a social movement I mean an effort that is powerful enough to make the country understand that our problems are not in Vietnam, or China or Brazil or outer space or at the bottom of the ocean, but are here in the United States. What we must do is begin to build a democratic and humane society in which Vietnams are unthinkable, in which human life and initiative are precious. . . .

But that means that we build a movement that works not simply in Washington but in communities and with the problems that face people throughout the society. That means that we build a movement that understands Vietnam in all its horror as but a symptom of a deeper malaise, that we build a movement that makes possible the implementation of the values that would have prevented Vietnam, a movement based on the integrity of man and a belief in man's capacity to tolerate all the weird formulations of society that men may choose to strive for; a movement that will build on the new and creative forms of protest that are beginning to emerge, such as the teach-in, and extend their efforts and intensify them; that we will build a movement that will find ways to support the increasing numbers of young men who are unwilling to and will not fight in Vietnam; a movement that will not tolerate the escalation or prolongation of this war but will, if necessary, respond to the administration war effort with massive civil disobedience all over the country, that will wrench the country into a confrontation with the issues of the war; a movement that must of necessity reach out to all these people in Vietnam or elsewhere who are struggling to find decency and control for their lives.

For in a strange way the people of Vietnam and the people on this demonstration are united in much more than a common concern that the war be ended. In both countries there are people struggling to build a movement that has the power to change their condition. The system that frustrates these movements is the same. All our lives, our destinies, our very hopes to live, depend on our ability to overcome that system.

SOURCE: Web site of Students for a Democratic Society, Document Library.

On May 8, 1970, New York construction workers surged into Wall Street in Lower Manhattan, violently disrupting an antiwar rally and attacking the protesters with lead pipes and crowbars. Known as the "hard hat riots," the well-publicized event was followed later in the month by a march, 100,000 strong, of hard-hat workers unfurling American flags and chanting "All the way U.S.A."

Yet the soldiers were not entirely isolated from the changes affecting their generation. Many G.I.s smoked marijuana, listened to rock music, hung psychedelic posters in their barracks, and participated in the sexual revolution, but most condemned antiwar protest as the self-indulgent behavior of their privileged peers who did not have to fight. As the war dragged on, however, some soldiers showed their frustration. By 1971 many G.I.s were putting peace symbols on their combat helmets, joining antiwar demonstrations, and staging their own events such as "Armed Forces Day." Sometimes entire companies refused to carry out duty assignments or even to enter battle. A smaller number took revenge by "fragging" reckless commanding officers with grenades meant for the enemy. Some African American soldiers complained about fighting "a white man's war" and emblazoned their helmets with slogans like "No Gook Ever Called Me Nigger."

The war's course fed these feelings of disaffection. U.S. troops entering South Vietnam expected a warm welcome from the people whose homeland they had been sent to defend. Instead, they encountered anti-American demonstrations and placards with slogans like "End Foreign Dominance of Our Country." Moreover, despite their superior arms and air power, soldiers found themselves stumbling into booby traps as they chased an elusive guerrilla foe through deep, leech-infested swamps and dense jungles swarming with fire ants. They could never be sure who was friend and who was foe. Patently false U.S. government press releases that heralded glorious victories and extolled the gratitude of Vietnamese civilians deepened bitterness on the front lines.

Vietnam veterans returned to civilian life quietly and without fanfare, denied the glory earned by the combat veterans of previous wars. They reentered a society divided over the cause for which they had risked their lives. Tens of thousands suffered debilitating physical injuries. As many as 40 percent of the 8.6 million who served came back with drug dependencies or symptoms of posttraumatic stress disorder, haunted and depressed by troubling memories of atrocities. Moreover, finding and keeping a job proved to be particularly hard in the shrinking economy of the 1970s.

WARS ON POVERTY

During the early 1960s, the civil rights movement had spurred a new concern with poverty. What good was winning the right to sit at a lunch counter if one could not afford to buy a hamburger?

Hoping to build on Kennedy's legacy, President Johnson pledged to expand the antipoverty program that he had inherited. "That's my kind of program," he told his advisers. "It will help people. I want you to move full speed ahead on it." Over the next several years, he used the political momentum of the civil rights movement and the overwhelming Democratic majorities in the House and Senate to push through the most ambitious reform program since the New Deal. Ironically, violence at home as well as abroad ultimately undercut his aspiration to wage "an unconditional war on poverty" (see Figure 29.1 and 29.2).

African American Troops in Vietnam, 1970. Many black soldiers echoed the growing racial militancy in the United States and increasingly chose to spend their off-duty time apart from white soldiers.

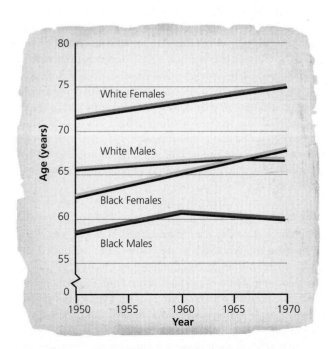

FIGURE 29.1 Comparative Figures on Life Expectancy at Birth by Race and Sex, 1950–70
Shifting mortality statistics suggested that the increased longevity of females increasingly cut across race lines but did not diminish the difference between white people and black people as a whole.

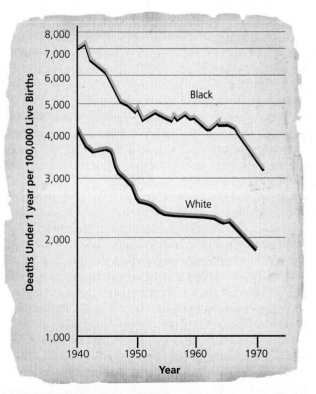

FIGURE 29.2 Comparative Figures on Infant Mortality by Race, 1940–70 The causes of infant mortality such as inadequate maternal diets, prenatal care, and medical services were all rooted in poverty, both rural and urban. Despite generally falling rates of infant mortality, nonwhite people continued to suffer the effects more than white people.

THE GREAT SOCIETY

The cornerstone of Johnson's plan for a Great Society was the Economic Opportunity Act, enacted in August 1964. The legislation established the Office of Economic Opportunity (OEO), which coordinated a network of community-based programs designed to help the poor help themselves by providing opportunities for education and employment. The results were mixed. The Job Corps provided vocational training mostly for urban black youth considered unemployable. Housed in dreary barracks-like camps far from home, trainees often found themselves learning factory skills that were already obsolete. The Neighborhood Youth Corps provided work for about 2 million young people aged sixteen to twenty-one, but nearly all the jobs were low paying and dead-end. Educational programs proved more successful. VISTA (Volunteers in Service to America), a kind of domestic Peace Corps, brought several thousand idealistic volunteers into poor communities for social service work.

The most innovative and controversial element of the OEO was the Community Action Program (CAP), which mandated "maximum feasible participation" of local residents. In theory, as the SDS organizers also believed, community action would empower the poor by giving them a direct say in mobilizing resources. What often resulted was a tug-of-war between local government officials and the poor over who should control funding and decision-making. Such was the case in Chicago, where Mayor Richard Daley complained that letting the poor head antipoverty programs was "like telling the fellow who cleans up [at the newspaper] to be the city editor."

More successful and popular were the so-called national-emphasis programs, designed in Washington and administered according to federal guidelines. The Legal Services Program, staffed by attorneys, helped millions of poor people in legal battles with housing authorities, welfare departments, police, and slumlords. Head Start and Follow Through reached more than 2 million poor children and significantly improved the long-range educational achievement of participants. Comprehensive Community Health Centers provided basic medical services to patients who could not afford to see doctors. Upward Bound helped low-income teenagers develop the skills and confidence needed for college. Birth control programs dispensed contraceptive supplies and information to hundreds of thousands of poor women (see Figure 29.3).

But the root cause of poverty lay in the unequal distribution of power as well as of income. The Johnson administration never committed itself to reallocating income or wealth. Spending on social welfare jumped from 7.7 percent of the GNP in 1960 to 16 percent in 1974. But roughly three-quarters of social welfare payments went to the nonpoor. The largest sums went to Medicare, established by Congress in 1965 to provide basic health care for the aged, and to expanded Social Security payments and unemployment compensation.

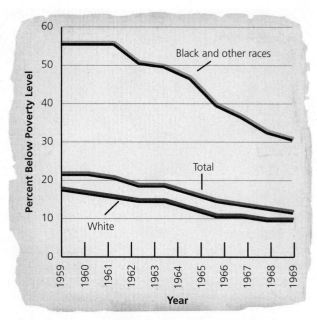

FIGURE 29.3 Percent of Population Below Poverty Level, by Race, 1959–69

NOTE: The poverty threshold for a nonfarm family of four was $3,743 in 1969 and $2,973 in 1959.

SOURCE: *Congressional Quarterly, Civil Rights: A Progress Report*, 1971, p. 46.

The Great Society became a forgotten dream. "More than five years after the passage of the Economic Opportunity Act," a 1970 study concluded, "the war on poverty has barely scratched the surface. Most poor people have had no contact with it, except perhaps to hear the promises of a better life to come." Having made the largest commitment to federal spending on social welfare since the New Deal, Johnson could take pride in the number of programs passed by Congress. At the same time, he had raised expectations higher than could be reached without a more drastic redistribution of economic and political power. Even in the short run, the president could not sustain the welfare programs and simultaneously fight a lengthy and expensive war abroad.

CRISIS IN THE CITIES

With funds for new construction limited during the Great Depression and World War II, and the postwar building boom taking place in the suburbs, the housing stock in the nation's cities declined. The Federal Housing Administration encouraged this trend by redlining poor urban neighborhoods (see Chapter 27). Slumlords took advantage of this situation, collecting high rents while allowing their properties to deteriorate. City officials meanwhile spearheaded civic revitalization programs that more often than not sliced up poor neighborhoods with new superhighways, demolished them to build new office complexes, or, as in Chicago's Uptown, favored residential developments for the middle class rather than for the poor. In 1968 a federal survey showed that 80 percent of

OVERVIEW   The Great Society

MAJOR LEGISLATION

CIVIL RIGHTS

Civil Rights Act of 1964, forbidding segregation in public accommodations and banning job discrimination

Voting Rights Act of 1965, ensuring minority voter registration in places where patterns of past discrimination existed

Immigration and Nationality Services Act of 1965, abolishing national-original quotas in immigration law

Civil Rights Act of 1968, banning discrimination in housing and extending constitutional protections to Native Americans on reservations

THE WAR ON POVERTY

Economic Opportunity Act of 1964, establishing the Office of Economic Opportunity to oversee such community-based antipoverty programs as the **Job Corps**, the **Neighborhood Youth Corps, VISTA**, the **Model Cities Program, Upward Bound**, the **Community Action Program**, and **Project Head Start**

EDUCATION

Elementary and Secondary Education Act of 1965, providing federal funds for programs to schools in low-income areas

Bilingual Education Act of 1968, providing federal aid to school districts with large numbers of children needing to learn English as a second language

HEALTH

Social Security Act of 1965, funding Medicare to help cover costs of health care for older Americans and Medicaid to provide funds for medical care of welfare recipients

CULTURE

National Foundation on the Arts and Humanities Act of 1965, creating the National Endowment for the Arts and the National Endowment for the Humanities

Public Broadcasting Act of 1967, chartering the Corporation for Public Broadcasting, which later established the Public Broadcasting Services (PBS) and National Public Radio (NPR)

TRANSPORTATION

Urban Mass Transportation Act of 1964, funding large-scale urban public and private rail projects

National Traffic and Motor Vehicle Safety Act of 1966, laying the foundation for the National Highway Traffic Safety Administration to effect policy to reduce traffic injuries and fatalities

Highway Safety Act of 1966, permitting the federal government to set standards for motor vehicles and highways

Department of Transportation, established in 1966

CONSUMER PROTECTION

Nine major enactments between 1965 and 1968, covering such areas as cigarette warning labels, motor safety, "fair packaging and labeling," child safety and flammable fabrics, meat and poultry packaging, "truth in lending," and radiation safety

ENVIRONMENT

Nine major enactments between 1964 and 1968, covering such areas as wilderness and endangered species protection, land and water conservation, solid waste disposal, air pollution, aircraft noise abatement, and historic preservation

National Environmental Policy Act of 1969, consolidating many of these gains, was passed in the first year of the Nixon administration

those displaced under these programs—dubbed "Negro removal" by former residents—were people of color.

Employment opportunities declined along with the housing stock. Nationwide, military spending for the Vietnam War brought the unemployment rate down from 6 percent, where it was in 1960, to 4 percent in 1966, where it remained until the end of the decade. Black unemployment, however, was nearly twice that of white unemployment. Moreover, the proportion working in the low-paying service sector continued to rise. In short, African Americans were steadily falling further behind whites.

Despite deteriorating conditions, millions of Americans continued to move to the cities, mainly African Americans from the Deep South, white people from the Appalachian Mountains, and Latinos from Puerto Rico.

By the mid-1960s, African Americans had become near majorities in the nation's decaying inner cities. Many had fled rural poverty only to find themselves earning minimum wages at best and living in miserable, racially segregated neighborhoods.

URBAN UPRISINGS

These conditions brought urban pressures to the boiling point. During the "long, hot summers" of 1964 to 1968, more than 100 urban uprisings rocked the nation. Unlike the race riots of the 1920s and 1940s, when angry whites assaulted blacks, masses of African Americans now took revenge for the white domination of their communities and specifically for police abuse (see Map 29.1).

MAP EXPLORATION

To explore an interactive version of this map, go to **www.prenhall.com/faragher6/map29.1**

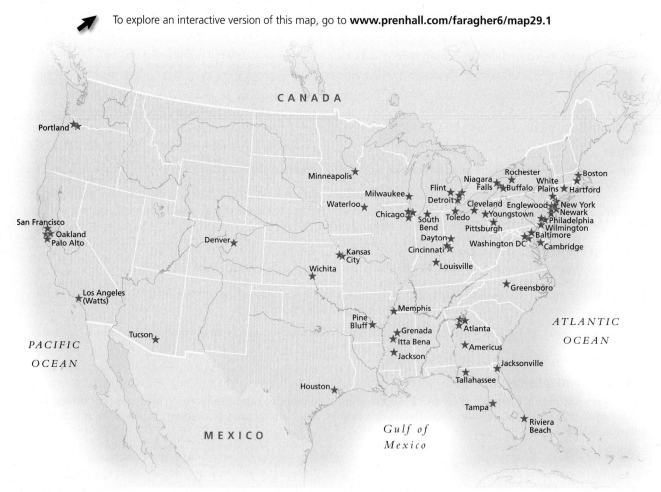

MAP 29.1 Urban Uprisings, 1965–1968 After World War II, urban uprisings precipitated by racial conflict increased in African American communities. In Watts in 1965 and in Detroit and Newark in 1967, rioters struck out at symbols of white control of their communities, such as white-owned businesses and residential properties.

The first major uprising erupted in August 1965 in the Watts section of Los Angeles. Here one in three men were unemployed, and the nearest hospital was twelve miles away. It took only a minor arrest to set off the uprising, which quickly spread outward for fifty miles. Throwing rocks and bottles through store windows, participants reportedly shouted, "This is for Selma! This is for Birmingham!" and "Burn, baby, burn!" Nearly 50,000 people turned out, and 20,000 National Guard troops were sent in. After six days, 34 people lay dead, 900 were injured, and 4,000 more had been arrested. The Los Angeles police chief blamed civil rights agitators, the mayor accused Communists, and both feigned ignorance when the media reported that white police assigned to "charcoal alley," their name for the Watts district, had customarily called their nightsticks "nigger knockers."

The following summer, large-scale uprisings occurred in San Francisco, Milwaukee, Dayton, and Cleveland. On July 12, 1967, in Newark, New Jersey, a city with severe housing shortages and the nation's highest black unemployment rate, the beating and arrest of a black taxi driver by a white police officer sparked the protest. Five days of looting and burning of buildings ended with 25 people dead. One week later Detroit police raided a bar and arrested the after-hours patrons. Army tanks and paratroopers were brought in to quell the disturbance, which lasted a week and left 34 people dead and 7,000 under arrest.

In July 1967 President Johnson created the National Advisory Commission on Civil Disorders to investigate the riots. Headed by Illinois Governor Otto Kerner, the eleven-member commission indicted "white racism" for creating an "explosive mixture" of poverty and police brutality. But the Johnson administration and Congress put aside the commission's warning that "our nation is moving toward two societies, one black, one white—separate and unequal" and disregarded its advice to direct funds into housing and jobs and to reduce segregation. By this time, the escalating costs of the Vietnam War left little federal money for antipoverty programs. Senator William Fulbright noted, "Each war feeds on the other, and, although the President assures us that we have the resources to win both wars, in fact we are not winning either of them."

1968: YEAR OF TURMOIL

The urban uprisings of the summer of 1967 marked the most drawn-out violence in the United States since the Civil War. But, rather than offering a respite, 1968 proved to be even more turbulent. The bloodiest and most destructive fighting of the Vietnam War resulted in a hopeless stalemate that soured most Americans on the conflict and undermined their faith in U.S. invincibility in world affairs. Disillusionment deepened in the spring when two of the most revered political leaders were struck down by assassins' bullets. Once again protesters and police clashed on the nation's campuses

and city streets, and millions of Americans asked what was wrong with their country.

But it was not just the United States that experienced 1968 as a year of turmoil. In May, hundreds of thousands of students and workers barricaded the streets of Paris in protest against their government. A sweeping series of liberal reforms in Czechoslovakia, known as the "Prague Spring," was followed in August by a massive invasion staged by Eastern-bloc countries. In October, an estimated 300 people were killed in the Tlatelolco section of Mexico City when government forces, using tanks and armored cars, broke up a student-led demonstration. And in China, Mao Zedong was deep into the "Cultural Revolution," a campaign to strengthen the Communist government against liberal reforms.

THE TET OFFENSIVE

On January 30, 1968, the North Vietnamese and their Vietcong allies launched the Tet Offensive (named for the Vietnamese lunar New Year holiday), stunning the U.S. military command in South Vietnam. The Vietcong pushed into the major cities and provincial capitals of the South, as far as the courtyard of the U.S. embassy in Saigon. U.S. troops ultimately halted the offensive, suffering comparatively modest casualties of 1,600 dead and 8,000 wounded. The North Vietnamese and Vietcong suffered more than 40,000 deaths, about one-fifth of their total forces. Civilian casualties ran to the hundreds of thousands. As many as 1 million South Vietnamese became refugees, their villages totally ruined (see Map 29.2).

The Tet Offensive, despite the U.S. success in stopping it, weakened the resolve of many Americans. News coverage—including scenes of U.S. personnel shooting from the embassy windows in Saigon—dismayed the nation. Television viewers saw the beautiful, ancient city of Hue devastated almost beyond recognition and heard a U.S. officer casually remark about a village in the Mekong Delta, "We had to destroy it, in order to save it."

The United States chalked up a major military victory but lost the war at home. For the first time, polls showed strong opposition to the war, 49 percent concluding that the entire operation in Vietnam was a mistake. Meanwhile, in Rome, Berlin, Paris, and London, huge crowds turned out to protest U.S. involvement in Vietnam. At home, sectors of the antiwar movement shifted from resistance to open rebellion.

President Johnson, facing the 1968 election campaign, watched his popularity plummet to an all-time low. On March 31 he announced he would not seek the Democratic Party's nomination. He also declared a bombing halt over North Vietnam and called Hanoi to peace talks, which began in Paris in May. Like Truman almost thirty years earlier, and despite his determination not to repeat that bit of history, Johnson had lost his presidency in Asia.

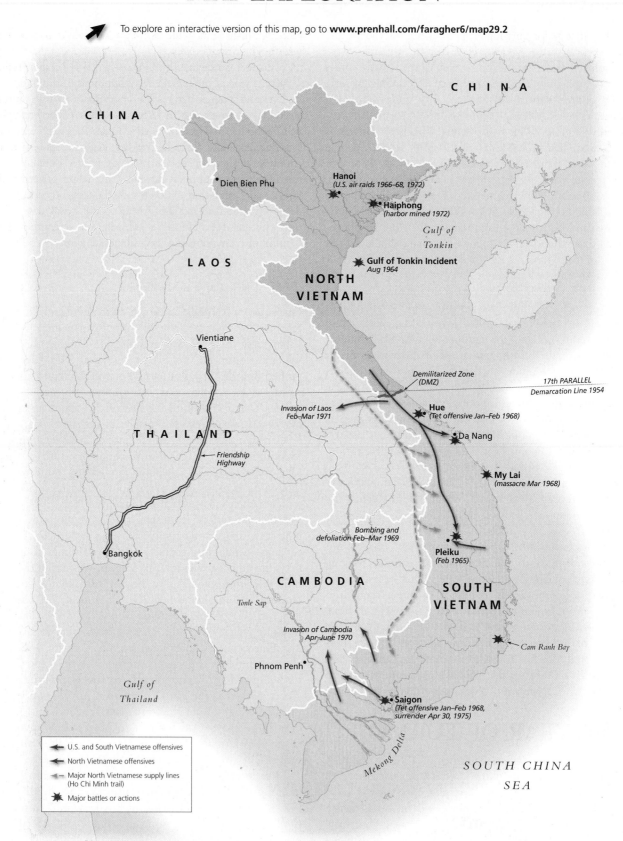

MAP 29.2 The Southeast Asian War The Indo-Chinese subcontinent, home to long-standing regional conflict, became the center of a prolonged war with the United States.

KING, THE WAR, AND THE ASSASSINATION

By 1968 the civil rights leadership stood firmly against the war, and Martin Luther King Jr. had reached a turning point in his life. The FBI had been harassing King, tapping his telephones and spreading malicious rumors about him. Despite these threats (Bureau Chief J. Edgar Hoover had sworn to "destroy the burrhead"), King abandoned his customary caution in criticizing U.S. policy in Vietnam. As early as 1965, he had connected domestic unrest with the war abroad, calling the U.S. government the "greatest purveyor of violence in the world today." He now became yet more outspoken in his opposition to the war, even if it meant losing the support of those liberal Democrats loyal to Johnson. King refused to compromise.

In the spring of 1968 King chose Memphis, Tennessee, home of striking sanitation workers, to launch a Poor People's Campaign for peace and justice. There he delivered, in what was to be his final speech, a message of hope. "I have a dream this afternoon that the brotherhood of man will become a reality," King told the crowd. "With this faith, I will go out and carve a tunnel of hope from a mountain of despair." The next evening, April 4, 1968, as he stood on the balcony of his motel, King was shot and killed.

Throughout the world crowds turned out to mourn King's death. Former SNCC leader Stokely Carmichael stormed, "When white America killed Dr. King, she declared war on us." Riots broke out in more than a hundred cities. Chicago Mayor Richard Daley ordered his police to shoot to kill. In Washington, DC, U.S. Army units set up machine guns outside the Capitol and the White House. King's dream of the nation as a "Beloved Community" died with him.

THE DEMOCRATS IN DISARRAY

The dramatic events of the first part of the year had a direct impact on the presidential campaign. For those liberals dissatisfied with Johnson's conduct of the war, and especially for African Americans suffering the loss of their greatest leader, Senator Robert F. Kennedy of New York emerged as the candidate of choice. Kennedy enjoyed a strong record on civil rights, and, like King, he had begun to interpret the war as a mirror of injustice at home. Kennedy insisted during the Tet Offensive that "our nation must be told the truth about this war, in all its terrible reality." On this promise he began to campaign for the Democratic nomination.

Ironically, Kennedy faced an opponent who agreed with him, Senator Eugene McCarthy of Minnesota. The race for the Democratic nomination positioned McCarthy, the witty philosopher, against Kennedy, the charismatic campaigner. McCarthy did well with liberal Democrats and white suburbanites. On college campuses his popularity with antiwar students was so great that his campaign became known as the "children's crusade." Kennedy reached out successfully to African Americans and Latinos and won all but the Oregon primary.

Kennedy appeared to be the Democratic Party's strongest candidate as June 4, the day of the California primary, dawned. But as the final tabulation of his victory came in just past midnight, Robert Kennedy was struck down by an assassin's bullet.

Vice President Hubert H. Humphrey, who had announced his candidacy in April, was now the sole Democrat with the credentials to succeed Johnson. He simultaneously courted Democrats who grimly supported the war and the King-Kennedy wing, which was sickened by it. He also skillfully cultivated the Democratic power brokers. Without entering a single state primary, he lined up delegates loyal to city bosses, labor leaders, and conservative southern Democrats. As the candidate least likely to rock the boat, he had secured his party's nomination well before delegates met in convention.

"THE WHOLE WORLD IS WATCHING!"

The events surrounding the Democratic convention in Chicago, August 21–26, demonstrated how deep the divisions within the United States had become. Mayor Richard Daley, still reeling from the riots following King's assassination, refused to issue parade permits to the antiwar activists, who had called for a massive demonstration at the convention center. According to later accounts, he sent hundreds of undercover police into the crowds to encourage rock throwing and generally to incite violence so that retaliation would appear necessary and reasonable.

Daley's strategy boomeranged when his officers staged what a presidential commission later termed a "police riot," randomly assaulting demonstrators, casual passersby, and the television crews broadcasting the events. Angered by the embarrassing publicity, Daley sent his agents to raid McCarthy's campaign headquarters where antiwar Democrats had gathered.

Inside the convention hall, a raging debate over a peace resolution underscored the depth of the division within the party. Representative Wayne Hays of Ohio lashed out at those who substituted "beards for brains . . . [and] pot [for] patriotism." When the resolution failed, McCarthy delegates put on black armbands and sang "We Shall Overcome." Later, as tear gas used against the demonstrators outside turned the amphitheater air acrid, the beaming Humphrey praised Mayor Daley and Johnson's conduct of the Vietnam War. When Senator Abraham Ribicoff of Connecticut protested the "Gestapo tactics" of the Chicago police, television cameras focused on Mayor Daley saying, "You Jew son of a bitch . . . , go home!" The crowd outside chanted, "The whole world is watching! The whole world is watching!" Indeed, through satellite transmission, it was.

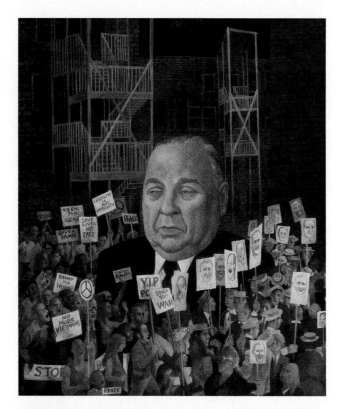

In 1968, Richard J. Daley had been elected mayor of Chicago four times and held power as a traditional city boss. In December of that year, the National Commission on Violence released a report that concluded that Chicago police, acting under Mayor Daley's orders, had been "unrestrained and indiscriminate" in their attacks on demonstrators at the National Democratic Convention held the previous August. In response, Mayor Daley brazenly announced a 22 percent salary increase for members of the city's police and fire personnel.

Protest had spread worldwide. Across the United States the antiwar movement picked up steam. In Paris, students and workers scrawled on building walls such humorous and half-serious slogans as "Be Realistic, Demand the Impossible!" In Prague, Czechoslovakia, students wearing blue jeans and singing Beatles songs threw rocks at Soviet tanks. Meanwhile, demonstrations in Japan, Italy, Ireland, Germany, and England all brought young people into the streets to demand democratic reforms in their own countries and an end to the U.S. war in Vietnam.

THE REPUBLICAN VICTORY

The Republicans stepped into the breech. Presidential contender Richard Nixon deftly built on voter hostility toward youthful protesters and the counterculture. He wooed a growing constituency that he later termed the "silent majority"—those Americans who worked, paid taxes, and did not demonstrate or picket, "people who are not haters, people who love their country." Recovering from election defeats for president in 1960 and California governor in 1962, Nixon claimed to be the one candidate

who could restore law and order. He chose as his running mate the governor of Maryland, Spiro T. Agnew, known for treating dissent as near treason (see Map 29.3).

After signing the landmark Civil Rights Act of 1964, President Johnson said privately, "I think we just delivered the South to the Republicans for a long time to come." Republican strategists moved quickly to make this prediction come true. They also recognized the growing electoral importance of the Sunbelt, where populations grew with the rise of high-tech industries and retirement communities. A powerful conservatism dominated this region, home to many military bases, defense plants, and an increasingly influential religious right. Although Johnson enjoyed a landslide victory in 1964, his conservative Republican rival, Barry Goldwater, had trumped him in several states in the Deep South. Nixon took advantage of this trend.

—MAP EXPLORATION—

To explore an interactive version of this map, go to
www.prenhall.com/faragher6/map29.3

	Electoral Vote (%)	Popular Vote (%)
RICHARD M. NIXON (Republican)	301 (56)	31,785,480 (43.4)
Hubert H. Humphrey (Democrat)	191 (36)	31,275,165 (42.7)
George C. Wallace (American Independent)	46 (8)	9,906,473 (13.5)
Other candidates (Dick Gregory, Socialist Labor; Fred Halstead and Paul Boutelle, Socialist Workers; Eugene McCarthy, Peace and Freedom; E. Harold Munn and Rolland E. Fisher, Prohibition)	—	221,134 (0.3)

MAP 29.3 The Election of 1968 Although the Republican Nixon-Agnew team won the popular vote by only a small margin, the Democrats lost in most of the northern states that had voted Democratic since the days of FDR. Segregationist Governor George Wallace of Alabama polled more than 9 million votes.

The 1968 campaign exposed the increasing conservatism of white voters even outside the South. The most dramatic example was the relative success of Alabama governor George Wallace's third-party bid for the presidency. Wallace took state office in 1963 promising white Alabamans "Segregation now! Segregation tomorrow! Segregation forever!" In 1968 he waged a national campaign around a conservative hate list that included school busing, antiwar demonstrations, and civil disorder. Wallace won five southern states and nearly 14 percent of the popular vote nationwide.

The Nixon-Agnew team squeaked to victory, capturing the popular vote by the slim margin of 43.6 percent to Democrat Hubert Humphrey and Maine senator Edmund Muskie's 42.7 percent but taking nearly all the West's electoral votes. Bitterly divided by the campaign, the Democrats would remain out of presidential contention for more than two decades, except when the Republicans suffered scandal and disgrace. The Republicans in 1968 had paved the way for the conservative ascendancy.

THE POLITICS OF IDENTITY

Richard Nixon campaigned promising to "bring Americans together again." But, if anything, the divisions among Americans, especially among the young, grew sharper during his presidency. The tragic events of 1968 brought whole sectors of the counterculture to political activism. With great media fanfare, gay liberation and women's liberation movements took shape while young Latinos, Asian Americans, and Indian peoples pressed their own claims. In different ways, these groups drew their own lessons from Black Power, the nationalist movement that formed in the wake of Malcolm X's death. Soon, "Brown Power," "Yellow Power," and "Red Power" became the slogans of movements constituted distinctly as new communities of protest.

BLACK POWER

Impatient with tactics based on voting rights and integration, many young activists spurned the civil disobedience of King's generation for direct action and militant self-defense. In 1966, Stokely Carmichael, who had helped turn SNCC into an all-black organization, began to advocate Black Power as a means for African Americans to take control of their own communities.

The Black Panther Party, founded in Oakland, California, in 1966 by Huey P. Newton and Bobby Seale, demanded "land, bread, housing, education, clothing, and justice." They adopted a paramilitary style—black leather jackets, shoes, and berets and firearms—that infuriated the authorities. Monitoring local police, a practice Panthers termed "patrolling the pigs," was their major activity. In several communities, volunteers also ran free breakfast programs for schoolchildren, established medical clinics, and conducted educational classes. Persecuted by police and the FBI—there were more than thirty raids on Panther offices in eleven states during 1968 and 1969—their leaders were arrested, prosecuted, and sentenced to long terms in jail that effectively destroyed the organization.

Black Power nevertheless continued to grow into a multifaceted movement. The Reverend Jesse Jackson, for example, rallied African Americans in Chicago to boycott the A&P supermarket chain until the firm hired 700 black workers. A dynamic speaker and skillful organizer, Jackson encouraged African Americans to support their own businesses and services. His program, Operation Breadbasket, spread beyond Chicago to fifteen other cities.

Cultural nationalism became the most enduring component of Black Power. In their popular book *Black Power* (1967), Stokely Carmichael and Charles V. Hamilton urged African Americans "to assert their own definitions, to reclaim their history, their culture; to create their own sense of community and togetherness." Thousands of college students responded by calling for more scholarships and for more classes on African American history and culture.

The war in Vietnam contributed to the growing racial militancy in the United States. African Americans served on the front lines in Vietnam in disproportionate numbers, and many came to view the conflict as a "white man's war."

At San Francisco State University, students, with help from the Black Panthers, demanded a black studies department. After a series of failed negotiations with the administration, a campus-wide strike called by black students in December 1968 shut down the university. Strikes for "Third World studies" soon broke out on other campuses, including the University of Wisconsin at Madison, where the National Guard was brought in to quell the protest.

Meanwhile, trendsetters put aside Western dress for African-style dashikis and hairdos, and black parents gave their children African names. Many well-known activists and artists such as Imamu Amiri Baraka (formerly LeRoi Jones), Muhammad Ali (formerly Cassius Clay), and Kwame Touré (formerly Stokely Carmichael) rejected their "slave names." The new holiday Kwanzaa followed Christmas as a weeklong celebration of African heritage and culture. This deepening sense of racial pride was summed up in the popular slogan "Black Is Beautiful."

SISTERHOOD IS POWERFUL

In 1966, Betty Friedan's best-selling *Feminine Mystique* (see Chapter 27) sparked the formation of the National Organization for Women (NOW), which pledged "to take action to bring women into full participation in the mainstream of American society now." Members campaigned for the enforcement of laws banning sex discrimination in work and in education, for maternity leaves, and for government funding of day-care centers. NOW also backed the Equal Rights Amendment, first introduced in Congress in 1923, and demanded the repeal of legislation that prohibited abortion or restricted birth control.

By the time Nixon took office, a different kind of movement had emerged: women's liberation. The women's liberation movement attracted young women who had been active in civil rights, SDS, and campus antiwar movements. Impatient with NOW's legislative agenda, angered by the sexism of male activists, these women organized separately under the slogan "Sisterhood Is Powerful."

The women's liberation movement issued a scathing critique of patriarchy—that is, the power of men to dominate all institutions, from the family to business and government to the protest movements themselves. Outraged and sometimes outrageous, one New York group created a lot of publicity for the movement by storming the 1968 Miss America Beauty Pageant in Atlantic City. They crowned a live sheep as queen and threw "implements of female torture" (bras, girdles, curlers, and copies of the *Ladies' Home Journal*) into a "freedom trash can."

The media focused on such audacious acts and brazen pronouncements, but the majority of activists were less flamboyant women simply trying to rise above the limitations imposed on them because of their gender. They met more often outside the limelight in consciousness-raising groups, where they examined the relationship between public events and

This is the Statue of Liberty as it appeared after nearly 100 women from various women's liberation groups demonstrated on the island, August 10, 1970. The demonstration was to show support for the proposed equal rights amendment which is currently before the Congress. Shortly after noon, park rangers made the women remove the banner from the base of the statue.

private lives. Here women shared their most intimate feelings toward men or other women and established the constituency for the movement's most important principle, expressed in the aphorism "The personal is political." Believing that no aspect of life lacked a political dimension, most emphatically including sexuality, consciousness-raising groups explored the power dynamics of the family and marriage as well as the workforce and government.

Women's liberation activism ranged widely. Some feminists staged sit-ins at *Newsweek* to protest demeaning media depictions of women. Others established health clinics, day-care centers, rape crisis centers, and shelters for women fleeing abusive husbands or lovers. The movement also had a significant educational impact. Feminist bookstores and publishing companies, such as the Feminist Press, reached out to eager readers. By the early 1970s, campus activists were demanding women's studies programs and women's centers. Like black studies, women's studies programs included traditional academic goals, such as the generation of new scholarship, but also encouraged personal change and self-esteem. Between 1970 and 1975, as many as 150 women's studies

OVERVIEW | Protest Movements of the 1960

Year	Organization/ Movement	Description
1962	**Students for a Democratic Society (SDS)**	Organization of college students that became the largest national organization of left-wing white students. Calling for "participatory democracy," SDS involved students in community-based campaigns against poverty and for citizens' control of neighborhoods. SDS played a prominent role in the campaign to end the war in Vietnam.
1964	**Free Speech Movement**	Formed at the University of California at Berkeley to protest the banning of on-campus political fundraising. Decried the bureaucratic character of the "multiuniversity" and advocated an expansion of student rights.
1965	**Anti–Vietnam War Movement**	Advocated grassroots opposition to U.S. involvement in Southeast Asia. By 1970 a national mobilization committee organized a demonstration of a half-million protesters in Washington, DC.
1965	La raza	A movement of Chicano youth to advance the cultural and political self-determination of Mexican Americans. La raza included the Brown Berets, which addressed community issues, and regional civil rights groups such as the Crusade for Social Justice, formed in 1965.
1966	**Black Power**	Militant movement that emerged from the civil rights campaigns to advocate independent institutions for African Americans and pride in black culture and African heritage. The idea of Black Power, a term coined by Stokely Carmichael, inspired the formation of the paramilitary Black Panthers.
1968	**American Indian Movement (AIM)**	Organization formed to advance the self-determination of Indian peoples and challenge the authority of the Bureau of Indian Affairs. Its most effective tactic was occupation. In February 1973, AIM insurgents protesting land and treaty violations occupied Wounded Knee, South Dakota, the location of an 1890 massacre, until the FBI and BIA agents drove them out.
1968	**Women's Liberation**	Movement of mainly young women that took shape following a protest at the Miss America Beauty Pageant. Impatient with the legislative reforms promoted by the National Organization for Women, founded in 1966, activists developed their own agenda shaped by the slogan "The Personal Is Political." Activities included the formation of "consciousness-raising" groups and the establishment of women's studies programs.
1968	Asian American Political Alliance (AAPA)	Formed at the University of California at Berkeley, the AAPA was one of the first pan-Asian political organizations to struggle against racial oppression. The AAPA encouraged Asian Americans to claim their own cultural identity and to protest the war against Asian peoples in Vietnam.
1969	**Gay Liberation**	Movement to protest discrimination against homosexuals and lesbians that emerged after the Stonewall Riots in New York City. Unlike earlier organizations such as the Mattachine Society, which focused on civil rights, gay liberationists sought to radically change American society and government, which they believed were corrupt.

programs were established; by 1980 nearly 30,000 women's studies courses were offered at colleges and universities throughout the United States. And the number of women in the workforce continued to increase (see Figure 29.4).

The women's liberation movement remained, however, a bastion of white middle-class women. The appeal to sisterhood did not unite women across race or class or even sexual orientation. Lesbians, who charged the early NOW leaders with homophobia, found large pockets of "heterosexism" in the women's liberation movement and broke off to form their own organizations. Although some African American women were outraged at Stokely Carmichael's infelicitous joke that "the only position for women in SNCC is prone," the majority remained wary of white women's appeals to sisterhood. African American women formed their own "womanist" movement to address their distinct cultural and political concerns. Similarly, by 1970 a Latina feminist movement addressed issues uniquely relevant to women of color in an Anglo-dominated society.

GAY LIBERATION

The gay community had been generations in the making but gained visibility only during World War II (see Chapter 25). In the mid-1950s, two pioneering homophile organizations, the Mattachine Society and the Daughters of Bilitis, campaigned against discrimination in employment, the armed forces, and all areas of social and cultural life. Other groups, such as the Society for Individual Rights, rooted themselves in New York's Greenwich Village, San Francisco's North Beach, and other centers of gay night life. But it was during the tumultuous late 1960s that a sizeable movement formed to encourage gays and lesbians to "come out": "Say It Loud, Gay Is Proud."

The major event prompting gays to organize followed repeated police raids of gay bars. On Friday, June 27, 1969, New York police raided the Stonewall Inn, a well-known gay bar in Greenwich Village, and provoked an uprising that lasted the entire night. The day after the Stonewall Riot, as it was called, "Gay Power" graffiti appeared throughout the neighborhood.

In New York City, the Gay Liberation Front (GLF) announced itself as "a revolutionary homosexual group of men and women formed with the realization that complete sexual liberation for all people cannot come about unless existing social institutions are abolished. We reject society's attempt to impose sexual roles and definitions of our nature. We are stepping outside these roles and simplistic myths. We are going to be who we are." Taking a stand against the war in Vietnam, the GLF quickly adopted the forms of public protest, such as street demonstrations and sit-ins, developed by civil rights activists and given new direction by antiwar protesters.

Changes in public opinion and policies followed. Several churches opened their doors to gay activists; the San Francisco–based Council on Religion and Homosexuality established a network for clergy sympathetic to gay and lesbian parishioners. In 1973 the American Psychiatric Association, which since World War II had viewed homosexuality as a treatable mental illness, reclassified it as a normal sexual orientation. Meanwhile, a slow process of decriminalization of homosexual acts between consenting adults began. In 1975 the U.S. Civil Service Commission ended its ban on the employment of homosexuals.

The gay liberation movement encouraged more than legal and institutional changes. "Gay Is Good" (like "Black Is

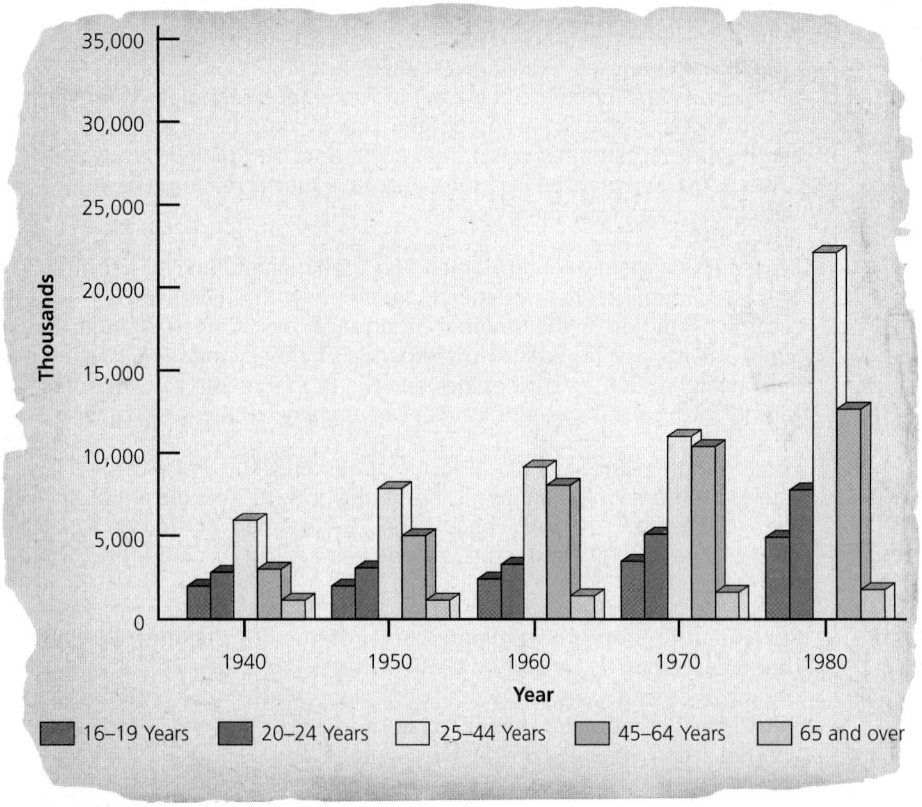

FIGURE 29.4 Women in the Workforce, 1940–80

SOURCE: U.S. Bureau of the Census.

Beautiful" and "Sisterhood Is Powerful") called to a large hidden minority to demand public acceptance of their sexual identity. In 1970, to commemorate the first anniversary of the Stonewall Riot, Gay Pride parades took place in at least eight American cities.

THE CHICANO REBELLION

To many Americans, the Chicano movement seemed to burst onto the scene in 1965, when the United Farm Workers (UFW), a union of mainly migrant workers, struck against grape growers of the San Joaquin Valley in California. By 1968, strike leaders Cesar Chavez and Dolores Huerta were heading a nationwide boycott of non-union-picked grapes and lettuce.

While Chavez emerged as a national hero, many young Mexican Americans spearheaded an urban-based movement based on identity politics, which Chavez himself rejected. They adopted the slang term *Chicano*, in preference to Mexican American, to express a militant ethnic nationalism. Chicano militants demanded not only their full civil rights but also recognition of their distinctive culture and history. Tracing their roots to the imperial Aztecs, they identified *la raza* (the race or people) as the source of a common language, religion, and heritage.

High school students were at the forefront of this new movement. In March 1968, the Brown Berets, a group modeled on the Black Panthers, helped to plan the "blow out" (walkout) that sent nearly 15,000 Chicano teenagers

Labor activist Cesar Chavez spearheaded the organization of Chicano agricultural workers into the United Farm Workers (UFW), the first successful union of migrant workers. In 1965, a strike of grape pickers in the fields around Delano, California, and a nationwide boycott of table grapes brought Chavez and the UFW into the media spotlight. Like Martin Luther King Jr., he advocated nonviolent methods for achieving justice and equality.

into the streets of East Los Angeles. The high school students demanded educational reform, including courses on the history, literature, art, and language of Mexican Americans. After the police arrested the protesters, students in San Antonio and Denver expressed their solidarity by conducting their own blow outs, holding placards reading "Teachers, Sí, Bigots, No!" Meanwhile, college students demanded Chicano studies programs. In 1969, a UC-Berkeley group staged a sit-in at the administrative offices, which one commentator called "the first important public appearance of something called Brown Power."

The larger Chicano movement found vivid expression in the performing and visual arts and in literature. *Teatro*, comprising film and drama, flourished as an exploration of the political dimensions of Mexican American society. One of the most popular and visible media was the mural, often inspired by art of Mexican masters such as Diego Rivera. Chicano muralists painted an estimated 1,500 murals on public buildings throughout their communities, from the exteriors of retail shops to freeway overpasses, even to large drainage pipes. Artistic expression found its way into music and dance. The rock group Los Lobos, for example, dedicated its first recorded album to the UFW. One of the most important writers to capture the excitement of the Chicano movement was Oscar Zeta Acosta, whose *Revolt of the Cockroach*, published in 1973, renders into fiction some of the major events of the era.

RED POWER

The phrase "Red Power," attributed to Vine Deloria Jr., commonly expressed a pan-Indian identity. At the forefront of this movement was the American Indian Movement (AIM). Founded in 1968, AIM represented mainly urban Indian communities. Like Black Panthers and Brown Berets, its young, militant leaders organized initially to monitor law enforcement practices. They soon built a network of urban centers, churches, and philanthropic organizations as well as the "powwow circuit" that publicized news of protest and educational activities across the country (see Map 29.4).

The movement's major catalyst was the occupation of the deserted federal prison on Alcatraz Island in San Francisco Bay. On November 20, 1969, a group of eighty-nine "Indians of All Tribes" claimed the island according to the terms of an 1868 Sioux treaty that gave Indians rights to unused federal property on Indian land. For the next nineteen months, around a hundred Indians, including about eighty UCLA students, occupied the island. Although the protestors ultimately failed to achieve their specific goals, which included a deed to the land and federal funding for a cultural center, they rallied the larger Indian community. With the occupation at Alcatraz, a participant testified, "we got back our worth, our pride, our dignity, our humanity."

Another series of dramatic events began in 1972, when AIM sponsored the "Trail of Broken Treaties" caravan.

MAP EXPLORATION

To explore an interactive version of this map, go to **www.prenhall.com/faragher6/map29.4**

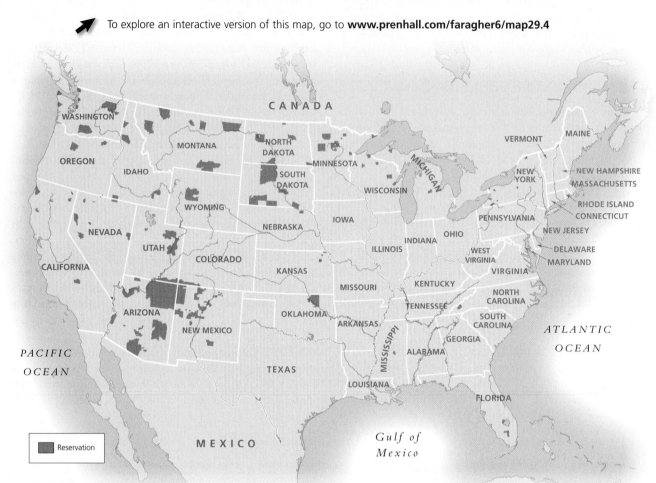

MAP 29.4 Major Indian Reservations, 1976 Although sizable areas, designated Indian reservations represented only a small portion of territory occupied in earlier times.

First they went to Washington, DC, where they staged a weeklong occupation of the Bureau of Indian Affairs. AIM insurgents then headed west, to the Pine Ridge Reservation, the site of the 1890 massacre at Wounded Knee, South Dakota. There in the spring of 1973 they demanded a restoration of treaty rights and began a siege that lasted ten weeks. Dozens of FBI agents with shoot-to-kill orders poured in, leaving two Indians dead and an unknown number of casualties on both sides.

The Red Power movement culminated in the "Longest Walk," a five-month march in 1978 from San Francisco to Washington, DC. Again, activists emphasized the history of the forced removal of Indians from their homelands and the U.S. government's repeated violation of treaty rights. By this time, several tribes had won in court, by legislation or by administrative fiat, small parts of what had been taken from them. The sacred Blue Lake was returned to Pueblo Indians in Taos, New Mexico, and a legal title to 40 million acres

(and compensation of almost $1 billion) was given to Alaskan natives. The Native American Rights Fund (NARF), established in 1971, gained thousands of acres in Atlantic coast states. But despite these victories, many tribal lands continued to suffer from industrial and government waste-dumping and other commercial uses. On reservations and in urban areas with heavy Indian concentrations, alcohol abuse and ill health remained serious problems.

The 1960s also marked the beginning of an "Indian Renaissance" in literature. Vine Deloria Jr.'s *Custer Died for Your Sins* (1969) reached numerous readers inside and outside Indian communities. A wide variety of Indian novelists, historians, and essayists, such as Pulitzer Prize–winning N. Scott Momaday and Leslie Silko, followed up these successes, and fiction and nonfiction works about Indian life and lore continued to attract a large audience. Inspired by these writers, many young Indians turned to their elders to learn tribal ways, including traditional dress and spiritual practices.

THE ASIAN AMERICAN MOVEMENT

In 1968 a groups of Chinese, Japanese, and Filipino students began to identify for the first time as Asian Americans. Students at San Francisco State University formed the Asian American Political Alliance (AAPA), while UC-Berkeley students mobilized to "express Asian American solidarity in a predominantly white society." Within a short time "Yellow Power" organizations spread throughout California and to the East Coast and Midwest.

These groups stood firmly against the Vietnam War, condemning it as a violation of the national sovereignty of the small Asian country. They also protested the racism directed against Southeast Asian peoples, particularly American soldiers' practice of referring to the enemy as "gooks." This racist epithet, first used to denigrate Filipinos during the Spanish-American War, implied that Asians were something less than human and therefore proper targets for slaughter. In response, Yellow Power activists proclaimed their solidarity with their "Asian brothers and sisters" in Vietnam.

Throughout 1968 and 1969 Asian American college students boycotted classes and demanded the establishment of ethnic studies programs. By 1973, major universities introduced courses on Asian American studies, and a few set up interdisciplinary departments. Meanwhile, artists, writers, documentary filmmakers, oral historians, and anthropologists worked to recover the Asian American past. Maxine Hong Kingston's *Woman Warrior: A Memoir of a Girlhood among Ghosts* (1976) became a major best seller.

Looking to the example of the Black Panthers, Yellow Power activists also took their struggle into the community. In 1968, a group presented the San Francisco municipal government with a list of grievances about conditions in Chinatown, particularly the poor housing and medical facilities, and organized a protest march down the neighborhood's main street. In 1977, activists led a community-wide struggle to save San Francisco's International Hotel, a low-income residential facility mainly for Filipino and Chinese men, which was ultimately leveled.

Community activists organized a variety of campaigns. The Redress and Reparations Movement, begun by Sansei (third-generation Japanese Americans), for example, encouraged children to ask their parents about their wartime internment experiences and prompted older civil rights organizations, such as the Japanese American Citizens League, to raise the issue of reparations. Trade unionists organized new Asian workers, mainly in service industries and garment trades. Other campaigns reflected the growing diversity of the Asian population. Filipinos, the fastest-growing group, demonstrated against the U.S.-backed Philippine dictator Ferdinand Marcos. Students from South Korea similarly denounced the repressive government in their homeland. Samoans publicized the damage caused by nuclear testing in the Pacific Islands. Ultimately, however, in blurring intergroup differences, the Asian American movement failed to reach the growing immigrant populations, especially the numerous Southeast Asians fleeing their devastated homeland.

Despite its shortcomings, the politics of identity would continue to grow through the next two decades of mainly conservative rule, broadening the content of literature, film, television, popular music, and even the curricula of the nation's schools. Collectively, the various movements pushed issues of race, gender, and sexual orientation to the forefront of American politics and simultaneously spotlighted the nation's cultural diversity as a major resource.

THE NIXON PRESIDENCY

Richard M. Nixon inherited not only an increasingly unpopular war but also a nation riven by internal discord. Without specifying his plans, he promised a "just and honorable peace" in Southeast Asia and the restoration of law and order at home. Yet, once in office, Nixon puzzled both friends and foes. He ordered unprecedented illegal government action against private citizens while agreeing with Congress to enhance several welfare programs and improve environmental protection. He widened and intensified the war in Vietnam, yet made stunning moves toward détente with the People's Republic of China. An architect of the Cold War in the 1950s, Nixon became the first president to foresee its end. Nixon worked hard in the White House, centralizing authority and reigning defiantly as an "Imperial President"—until he brought himself down.

DOMESTIC POLICY

Nixon deeply desired to restore order in American society. "We live in a deeply troubled and profoundly unsettled time," he noted. "Drugs, crime, campus revolts, racial discord, draft resistance—on every hand we find old standards violated, old values discarded." Despite his hostility to liberalism, however, Nixon had some surprises for conservatives. Determined to win reelection in 1972, he supported new Social Security benefits and subsidized housing for the poor and oversaw the creation of the Environmental Protection Agency and the Occupational Safety and Health Administration. Most notable was his support, under the guidance of Democratic adviser Daniel P. Moynihan, for the Family Assistance Plan, which proposed a minimal income for the poor in place of welfare benefits. Conservatives judged the plan too generous while liberals found it inadequate. Moreover, the plan was expensive. Bipartisan opposition ultimately killed the bill.

Nixon also embraced a policy of fiscal liberalism, even accepting the idea of deficit spending. Later that year he ordered the dollar's value to float against other currencies on the world market rather than being tied to a fixed value of gold, thereby ending the international monetary policy established at Bretton Woods that allowed U.S. domination of the rest of the capitalist world. His ninety-day freeze on wages, rents, and prices, designed to halt the inflation caused by the massive spending on the Vietnam War, also closely resembled Democratic policies. Finally, Nixon's support of "black capitalism"—adjustments or quotas favoring minority contractors in construction projects—created an explosive precedent for "set-aside" programs later blamed on liberals.

Yet, for the most part, Nixon remained committed to the "Southern Strategy" that brought him into office. He lined up with conservatives on most civil rights issues and thus enlarged his southern Republican base. He slowed school desegregation and rejected the busing programs required to achieve racial balance. His nominees to the Supreme Court were far more conservative than those appointed by Eisenhower. Warren E. Burger, who replaced Chief Justice Earl Warren, steered the Court away from the liberal direction it had taken since the 1950s.

One of the few unifying events of Nixon's administration was a distant result of President Kennedy's determination to outshine the Soviets in outer space (see Chapter 27). On July 21, 1969, the lunar module *Apollo 11* descended to the moon's Sea of Tranquility. As millions watched on television, astronauts Neil Armstrong and Buzz Aldrin stepped out to plant an American flag and to bear the message, "We came in peace for all mankind."

NIXON'S WAR

Nixon promised to bring "peace with honor." Yet, despite this pledge, the Vietnam War raged for four more years before a peace settlement was reached (see Figure 29.5).

Much of the responsibility for prolonging the war rested with Henry A. Kissinger, Nixon's national security adviser. A forceful personality, Kissinger insisted that the United States could not retain its global leadership by appearing weak to either allies or enemies. After centralizing foreign policymaking in the White House, Kissinger and Nixon together overpowered those State Department members who had concluded that the majority of Americans no longer supported the war (see Figure 29.6).

In public Nixon followed a policy of "Vietnamization." On May 14, 1969, he announced that the time was approaching "when the South Vietnamese . . . will be able to take over some of the fighting." During the next several months, he ordered the withdrawal of 60,000 U.S. troops. Hoping to placate public opinion, Nixon said he intended to "demonstrate to Hanoi that we were serious in seeking a diplomatic settlement." In private, Nixon mulled over the option of a "knockout blow" to the North Vietnamese.

On April 30, 1970, Nixon made one of the most controversial decisions of his presidency. Without seeking congressional approval, he ordered U.S. troops to invade the tiny nation of Cambodia. Nixon hoped in this way to end North Vietnamese infiltration into the South, but he also decided to live up to what he privately called his "wild man" or "mad bomber" reputation. The enemy would be unable to anticipate the location or severity of the next U.S. strike, Nixon reasoned, and would thus feel compelled to negotiate.

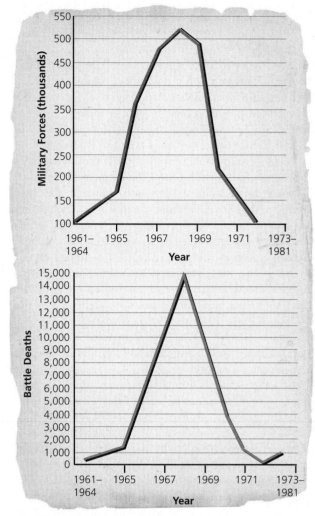

FIGURE 29.5 U.S. Military Forces in Vietnam and Casualties, 1961–81

The U.S. government estimated battle deaths between 1969 and 1973 for South Vietnamese troops at 107,504 and North Vietnamese and Vietcong at more than a half million. Although the United States suffered fewer deaths, the cost was enormous.

SOURCE: U.S. Department of Defense, *Selected Manpower Statistics*, annual and unpublished data; beginning 1981, National Archives and Records Service, "Combat Area Casualty File" (3-330-80-3).

Nixon could not have predicted what followed the invasion of Cambodia. The largest series of demonstrations and police–student confrontations in the nation's history erupted. At Kent State University in Ohio, twenty-eight National Guardsmen shot into an unarmed crowd of students, killing four and wounding nine. Ten days later, on May 14, at Jackson State University, a black school in Mississippi, state troopers entered a campus dormitory and began shooting wildly, killing two students and wounding twelve others. Huge demonstrations took place on fifty campuses, and thirty-seven college and university presidents signed a letter calling on the president to end the war.

A few weeks later the Senate adopted a bipartisan resolution outlawing the use of funds for U.S. military operations

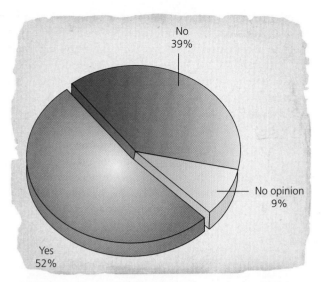

FIGURE 29.6 Public Opinion on the War in Vietnam

By 1969 Americans were sharply divided in their assessments of the progress of the war and peace negotiations. The American Institute of Public Opinion, founded in 1935 by George Gallup, charted a growing dissatisfaction with the war in Vietnam.

SOURCE: *The Gallup Poll: Public Opinion, 1935–74* (New York: Random House, 1974), p. 2189.

in Cambodia, starting July 1, 1970. Although the House rejected the resolution, Nixon saw the writing on the wall. He had planned to negotiate a simultaneous withdrawal of North Vietnamese and U.S. troops, but he could no longer afford to hold out for this condition.

The president did not accept defeat easily. In February 1971 Nixon directed the South Vietnamese army to invade Laos and cut supply lines, but the demoralized invading force suffered a quick and humiliating defeat. Faced with enemy occupation of more and more territory during a major offensive in April 1972, Nixon ordered the mining of North Vietnamese harbors and directed B-52s to conduct massively destructive bombing missions in Cambodia and North Vietnam (see Seeing History).

Nixon also sent Kissinger to Paris for secret negotiations with delegates from North Vietnam. They agreed to a cease-fire specifying the withdrawal of all U.S. troops and the return of all U.S. prisoners of war. Knowing these terms ensured defeat, South Vietnam's president refused to sign the agreement. On Christmas Day 1972, hoping for a better negotiating position, Nixon ordered one final wave of bomb attacks on North Vietnam's cities. To halt the bombing, the North Vietnamese resumed negotiations. But the terms of the Paris Peace Agreement, signed by North Vietnam and the United States in January 1973, differed little from the settlement Nixon could have procured in 1969. U.S. troops began to withdraw in March 1973.

In April 1975 the North Vietnamese took over Saigon, and the Communist-led Democratic Republic of Vietnam soon united the small nation. The war was finally over. It had cost the United States 58,000 lives and $150 billion. The nation had not only failed to achieve its stated war goal but also had lost an important post in Southeast Asia. Equally important, the United States proved it could not sustain the policy of containment introduced by President Truman.

While Nixon was maneuvering to bring about "peace with honor," the chilling crimes of war had already begun to haunt Americans. In 1971 the army court-martialed a young lieutenant, William L. Calley Jr., for the murder of "at least" twenty-two Vietnamese civilians during a 1968 search-and-destroy mission subsequently known as the My Lai Massacre. Calley's platoon had destroyed a village and slaughtered

On Monday, May 4, 1970, after a weekend of antiwar demonstrations against the invasion of Cambodia, Ohio National Guardsmen fired sixty-seven bullets into a crowd of students, killing four and wounding nine others on the campus of Kent State University. As news of the killings spread, students at hundreds of colleges and universities turned out in mass demonstrations to protest widening the war in Southeast Asia and the increasing violence on campus. Approximately 5 million students joined the national student strike, boycotting classes for the remainder of the week. As news of the Kent State "massacre" spread to Vietnam, some U.S. troops refused orders to invade Cambodia; others wore black armbands to demonstrate their solidarity with students at home.

more than 350 unarmed South Vietnamese, raping and beating many of the women before killing them. "My Lai was not an isolated incident," one veteran attested, but "only a minor step beyond the standard official United States policy in Indochina." The platoon commander at My Lai, Calley was first sentenced to life imprisonment before receiving a reduced term of ten years. The secretary of the army paroled Calley after three years of house arrest in his apartment.

PLAYING THE "CHINA CARD"

Apart from Vietnam, Nixon's foreign policy defied the expectations of liberals and conservatives alike. Actually, he followed traditions of previous Republican moderates such as Herbert Hoover and Dwight Eisenhower, who had so effectively "proved" their anticommunism that they could conciliate international foes without undermining their popularity at home. Nixon added a new page, however—a policy of détente that replaced U.S.–Soviet bipolarity with multilateral relations. Nixon could cultivate relations with the People's Republic of China, a rising world power more rigidly Communist than the Soviet Union, to form an alliance against the Soviet Union. And he could easily persuade the Soviet Union to cooperate on trade agreements, thus limiting the two nations' ruthless competition to control governments in Asia, the Middle East, and Africa. Opponents of the Vietnam War accused Nixon of double dealing, while conservatives howled at any com-

SEEING HISTORY

Kim Phuc, Fleeing a Napalm Attack near Trang Bang

In 1972, during the phase of the war termed "Vietnamization," South Vietnamese aircraft bombed the village of Trang Bang, about twenty-five miles from Saigon. They were attacking North Vietnamese and Vietcong fighters but mistakenly targeted a Buddhist pagoda. The incendiary bombs contained black, oily napalm that burned the villagers gathered there.

News photographer Nick Ut had been assigned to meet up with the South Vietnamese army at Trang Bang. "When we [the reporters] moved closer to the village we saw the first people running," he recalled in 1999. "I thought 'Oh my God' when I suddenly saw a woman with her left leg badly burned by napalm. Then came a woman carrying a baby, who died, then another woman carrying a small child with its skin coming off. When I took a picture of them I heard a child screaming and saw that young girl who had pulled off all her burning clothes. She yelled to her brother on her left. Just before the napalm was dropped soldiers [of the South Vietnamese Army] had yelled to the children to run but there wasn't enough time."

The Associated Press, which syndicates photographs to the media worldwide, at first refused to transmit the picture because of the nine-year-old girl's nudity but eventually concluded that the news value of the photograph was such that it could run provided no-close up of the girl be transmitted. Ut, who took the severely burned

girl to the hospital before delivering his film, won a Pulitzer Prize for the photograph.

In 1996, Phan Thi Kim Phuc, by then thirty-three, came to the United States, visited the Vietnam Veterans Memorial in Washington, DC, and resolved to form a foundation to help children victimized by war. She still wants the photograph to be seen: "Let the world see how horrible wars can be."

What does this photograph suggest about the role of the news media during the Vietnam war?
In focusing on civilians, what does Nick Ut's photograph suggest about the course of the war?

promise with Communist governments. But Nixon persisted in his plans, anticipating an end to the Cold War on American terms.

Playing the "China card" was the most dramatic of the president's moves. Early in his political career Nixon had avidly supported the archconservative China lobby. But as president he considered the People's Republic of China too important to be isolated by the West and too obviously hostile to the Soviet Union to be discounted as a potential ally.

"Ping-Pong diplomacy" began in April 1971, when the Chinese hosted a table tennis team from the United States. Henry Kissinger embarked on a secret mission a few months later. Finally, in February 1972, Richard and Pat Nixon flew to Beijing, where they were greeted by foreign minister Zhou Enlai and a band playing "The Star-Spangled Banner."

It was a momentous and surprising event, one that marked a new era in East-West diplomacy. Nixon claimed that he succeeded in bridging "16,000 miles and twenty-two years of hostility." The president's move successfully increased diplomatic pressure on the Soviet Union but simultaneously weakened the Nationalist Chinese government in Taiwan, which now slipped into virtual diplomatic obscurity.

Next the president went to Moscow to negotiate with Soviet leader Leonid Brezhnev, who was anxious about U.S. involvement with China and eager for economic assistance. Declaring, "There must be room in this world for two great nations with different systems to live together and work together," Nixon offered to sell $1 billion of grain to the Soviets. Winning the favor of American wheat farmers, this deal simultaneously relieved U.S. trade deficits and crop surpluses. Afterward, the Soviet leader became visibly more cautious about supporting revolutions in the third world. Nixon also completed negotiations of the Strategic Arms Limitation Treaty (SALT, known later as SALT I). A limited measure, SALT I represented the first success at strategic arms control since the start of the Cold War and a major public relations victory for the leaders of the two superpowers.

Nixon's last major diplomatic foray was far less effective. The president sent Kissinger on a two-year mission of "shuttle diplomacy" to mediate Israeli-Arab disputes, to ensure the continued flow of oil, and to increase lucrative U.S. arms sales to Arab countries. The Egyptians and Israelis agreed to a cease-fire in their October 1973 Yom Kippur War, but little progress toward peace in the area was achieved.

FOREIGN POLICY AS CONSPIRACY

Nixon's conduct of foreign policy offered early clues into his political character. Although he had welcomed the publicity surrounding his historic moves toward détente with the Soviet Union and normalized relations with China, Nixon generally handled the nation's foreign affairs behind closed doors. But as opposition to the Vietnam War mounted in Congress, he began to face hard questions about this practice. As early as 1970, Republicans as well as Democrats had condemned covert operations in foreign countries. In response, the president, the Department of State, and the CIA developed plans to tighten security even further. Nixon issued a tough mandate against all information leaks by government personnel, news specialists, or politicians.

At the time, apart from the highly publicized tour to China, Nixon revealed little about his policy for other parts of the globe. Unknown to most Americans, he accelerated the delivery of arms supplies to foreign dictators, including the shah of Iran, Ferdinand Marcos of the Philippines, and the white supremacist apartheid government in South Africa. His CIA assistants trained and aided SAVAK, the Iranian secret police force notorious for torturing political dissidents. They also stood behind the South African government in its effort to curtail the activities of the antiapartheid African National Congress. In Latin America, Nixon gave financial assistance and military aid to repressive regimes such as that of Anastasio Somoza of Nicaragua, notorious for its blatant corruption and repeated violations of human rights.

Still more controversial was Nixon's plan to overthrow the legally elected socialist government of Salvador Allende in Chile. With the assistance of nongovernment agencies, such as the AFL-CIO's American Institute for Free Labor Development, the CIA destabilized the regime by funding right-wing parties, launching demonstrations, and preparing the Chilean army for a coup. In September 1973, a military junta killed President Allende and captured, tortured, or murdered thousands of his supporters. Nixon and Kissinger warmly welcomed the new ruler, Augusto Pinochet, granting him financial assistance to restabilize the country.

Toward the end of Nixon's term, members of Congress who had been briefed on these policies began to break silence, and reports of clandestine operations flooded the media. Several former CIA agents issued anguished confessions of their activities in other countries. More troubling to Nixon, in spite of all his efforts the United States continued to lose ground as a superpower.

DIRTY TRICKS AND THE 1972 ELECTION

As Nixon approached the 1972 reelection campaign, he tightened his inner circle of White House staff who assisted him in withholding information from the public, discrediting critics, and engaging in assorted "dirty tricks." Staff members solicited illegal campaign contributions and laundered the money through Mexican bank accounts. They also formed a secret squad, "the plumbers," to halt the troublesome information leaks. This team, headed by former CIA agent E. Howard Hunt and former FBI agent G. Gordon Liddy, assisted in conspiracy at the highest levels of government.

Richard Nixon bid a final farewell to his White House staff as he left Washington, DC, on August 9, 1974. The first president to resign from office, Nixon had become so entangled in the Watergate scandal that his impeachment appeared certain. He was succeeded by Vice President Gerald Ford. After taking the oath of office later that day, President Ford remarked that the wounds of Watergate were "more painful and more poisonous than those of foreign wars."

The first person on the squad's "hit list" was Daniel Ellsberg, a former researcher with the Department of Defense, who in 1971 had turned over to the press secret documents outlining the history of U.S. involvement in Vietnam. The so-called Pentagon Papers exposed the role of presidents and military leaders in deceiving the public and Congress about the conduct of the United States in Southeast Asia. Nixon sought to bar publication by *The New York Times*, but the Supreme Court ruled in favor of the newspaper on the basis of the First Amendment. Within weeks, a complete version of the Pentagon Papers became a best-selling book, and in 1972 *The New York Times* won a Pulitzer Prize for the series of articles. Frustrated in his attempt to suppress the report, Nixon directed the Department of Justice to prosecute Ellsberg on charges of conspiracy, espionage, and theft. Meanwhile, Hunt and Liddy, seeking to discredit Ellsberg, broke into the office of his former psychiatrist. They found nothing that would make their target less heroic in the eyes of an increasingly skeptical public, and by 1973 the charges against Ellsberg were dropped after the Nixon administration itself stood guilty of misconduct.

At the same time, Nixon ran a skillful negative campaign charging George McGovern, his liberal Democratic opponent, with advocating "abortion, acid [LSD], and amnesty" for draft resisters and deserters. The Republicans also informed the news media that McGovern's running mate, Senator Thomas Eagleton, had earlier undergone electric shock therapy for depression, thus forcing his resignation from the Democratic team. Voter turnout fell to an all-time low, and McGovern lost every state but Massachusetts. (Later, when Nixon faced disgrace, bumper stickers appeared reading, "Don't Blame Me, I'm from Massachusetts.")

The Committee to Re-Elect the President (CREEP) enjoyed a huge war chest and spent a good portion on dirty tricks designed to divide the Democrats and discredit them in the eyes of the voting public. In the short run, they tallied a monumental success. Nixon presented himself as the candidate of "middle Americans," the Great Silent Majority, and won reelection by a landslide. More important in the long run, the Republicans captured the once solidly Democratic South and the majority of blue-collar, Catholic, and urban voters. As the carrier of conservatism, Nixon achieved the grandest moment of his long and complex political career. Nevertheless, even with this huge mandate from voters, the most audacious plan of his reelection committee—wiretapping the Democratic National Committee headquarters—ultimately backfired.

WATERGATE: NIXON'S DOWNFALL

On June 17, 1972, a security team had tripped up a group of intruders hired by CREEP to install listening devices in the Washington, DC, Watergate apartment and office complex where the Democrats were headquartered. The police arrested five men, who were later found guilty of conspiracy and burglary. Although Nixon disclaimed any knowledge of the plan, two *Washington Post* reporters, Bob Woodward and Carl Bernstein, followed a trail of evidence back to the nation's highest office.

Televised Senate hearings opened to public view more than a pattern of presidential wrongdoing: they showed an attempt to impede investigations of the Watergate case. Testifying before the committee, a former

CHRONOLOGY

1964   President Lyndon Johnson calls for "an unconditional war on poverty" in his state of the union address

Gulf of Tonkin resolution

The Economic Opportunity Act establishes the Office of Economic Opportunity

Free speech movement gets under way at University of California at Berkeley

Johnson defeats conservative Barry Goldwater for president

1965   President Johnson authorizes Operation Rolling Thunder, the bombing of North Vietnam

Teach-ins begin on college campuses

First major march on Washington for peace is organized

Watts uprising begins a wave of rebellions in black communities

1966   J. William Fulbright publishes *The Arrogance of Power*

Black Panther Party is formed

National Organization for Women (NOW) is formed

1967   Antiwar rally in New York City draws 300,000

Vietnam Veterans against the War is formed

Uprisings in Newark, Detroit, and other cities

Hippie "Summer of Love"

1968   U.S. ground troop levels in Vietnam number 500,000

Tet Offensive in Vietnam, followed by international protests against U.S. policies

Martin Luther King Jr. is assassinated; riots break out in more than 100 cities

Vietnam peace talks begin in Paris

Robert Kennedy is assassinated

Democratic National Convention, held in Chicago, nominates Hubert Humphrey; "police riot" against protesters

Richard Nixon elected president

American Indian Movement (AIM) founded

1969   Woodstock music festival marks the high tide of the counterculture

Stonewall Riot in Greenwich Village sparks the gay liberation movement

Apollo 11 lands on the moon

1970   U.S. incursion into Cambodia sparks campus demonstrations; students killed at Kent State and Jackson State universities

1971   Lieutenant William Calley Jr. court-martialed for My Lai Massacre

The New York Times starts publishing the Pentagon Papers

1972   Nixon visits China and Soviet Union

SALT I limits offensive intercontinental ballistic missiles

Intruders attempting to "bug" Democratic headquarters in the Watergate complex are arrested

Nixon is reelected in a landslide

Nixon orders Christmas Day bombing of North Vietnam

1973   Paris Peace Agreement ends war in Vietnam

FBI seizes Indian occupants of Wounded Knee, South Dakota

Watergate burglars tried; congressional hearings on Watergate

CIA destabilizes elected Chilean government, which is overthrown

Vice President Spiro T. Agnew resigns

1974   House Judiciary Committee adopts articles of impeachment against Nixon

Nixon resigns the presidency

Nixon aide revealed evidence of secret tape recordings of conversations held in the Oval Office. After special prosecutor Archibald Cox refused to allow Nixon to claim executive privilege and withhold the tapes, the president ordered Cox fired. This "Saturday Night Massacre," as it came to be called, further tarnished Nixon's reputation and swelled curiosity about the tapes. On June 24, 1974, the Supreme Court voted unanimously that Nixon had to release the tapes to a new special prosecutor, Leon Jaworski.

Although incomplete, the Watergate tapes proved damning. They documented Nixon's ravings against his enemies, including anti-Semitic and racist slurs, and his conniving efforts to harass private citizens through federal agencies. The tapes also proved that Nixon had not only known about plans to cover up the Watergate break-in but had in fact ordered it. The news media enjoyed a field day with the revelations of Nixon's role in a criminal conspiracy to obstruct justice. In July 1974, the House Judiciary Committee adopted three articles of impeachment, charging Nixon with obstructing justice, abusing the power of his office, and acting in contempt of Congress.

Charges of executive criminality had clouded the Nixon administration since his vice president left in disgrace. In 1972 Spiro Agnew admitted to accepting large kickbacks while serving as governor of Maryland. Pleading no contest to this and to charges of federal income tax evasion, Agnew resigned in October 1973. Gerald Ford, a moderate Republican representative from Michigan, replaced him and now stood in the wings while the president's drama unfolded.

A delegation from Congress, led by Senator Barry Goldwater, approached Nixon with the news that impeachment and conviction were certain. On August 8, 1974, in a speech underscoring his accomplishments and admitting only to "some errors in judgment," Nixon announced his intention to step down, becoming the first U.S. president to resign from office.

CONCLUSION

The resignations of Richard Nixon and Spiro Agnew did little to relieve the feeling of national exhaustion that followed the Vietnam War. U.S. troops pulled out of Vietnam in 1973 and the war officially ended in 1975, but bitterness lingered over the unprecedented—and, for many, humiliating—defeat. Moreover, confidence in the government's highest office was severely shaken. The passage of the War Powers Act in 1973, written to compel any future president to seek congressional approval for armed intervention abroad and passed over Nixon's veto, dramatized both the widespread suspicion of an "Imperial Presidency" and a yearning for peace. But the positive dream of community that had inspired Johnson, King, and a generation of student activists could not be revived. No other vision took its place.

In 1968 seven prominent antiwar protesters had been brought to trial for allegedly conspiring to disrupt the Democratic National Convention in Chicago. Just a few years later, the majority of Americans had concluded that presidents Johnson and Nixon had conspired to do far worse. They had intentionally deceived the public about the nature and fortunes of the war. This moral failure signaled a collapse at the center of the American political system. Since Dwight Eisenhower left office warning of the potential danger embedded in the "military-industrial complex," no president had survived the presidency with his honor intact. Watergate, then, appeared to cap the politics of the Cold War, its revelations only reinforcing futility and cynicism. The United States was left psychologically at war with itself.

REVIEW QUESTIONS

1. Discuss the events that led up to and contributed to U.S. involvement in Vietnam. How did U.S. involvement in the war affect domestic programs?

2. Discuss the reasons the protest movement against the Vietnam War started on college campuses. Describe how these movements were organized and how the opponents of the war differed from the supporters.

3. Discuss the programs sponsored by Johnson's plan for a Great Society. What was their impact on urban poverty in the late 1960s?

4. What was the impact of the assassinations of Martin Luther King Jr. and Robert Kennedy on the election of 1968? How were various communities affected?

5. How were the "politics of identity" movements different from earlier civil rights organizations? In what ways did the various movements resemble one another?

6. Why did Richard Nixon enjoy such a huge electoral victory in 1972? Discuss his foreign and domestic policies. What led to his sudden downfall?

— RECOMMENDED READING —

John A. Andrew III, *Lyndon Johnson and the Great Society* (1998). An assessment of the Great Society, with special emphasis on the two major issues of civil rights and poverty. Andrew discusses Johnson's aspirations and the obstacles that kept them out of reach.

Alexander Bloom, ed., *Long Time Gone: Sixties America Then and Now* (2001). Ten essays covering various aspects of the social and political movements of the 1960s. The authors draw out the meaning of the "sixties" for today and dispel commonplace myths by providing accurate information and a sound context for interpretation.

Winifred Breines, *The Trouble Between Us: An Uneasy History of White and Black Women in the Feminist Movement* (2006). Aims to explain the failure of feminists to create a racially integrated movement. The author deals equally with the experiences of both black and white women and uses a variety of sources, including oral histories, to document her case.

Robert Dallek, *Lyndon B. Johnson* (2005). A condensation of a two-volume study, Dallek's biography presents rich details of Johnson's life from his origins in Texas to his troubled years in the White House. The author does little to soften the image of Johnson and instead portrays him as both complex and flamboyant.

Jane F. Gerhard, *Desiring Revolution: Second-Wave Feminism and the Rewriting of American Sexual Thought, 1920–1982* (2001). Discusses the background of the feminist side of the sexual revolution with special attention to popular versions of Freud's theories. Gerhard discusses disagreements among feminists on the meaning and experience of sexual liberation.

Michael H. Hunt, *Lyndon Johnson's War: America's Cold War Crusade in Vietnam, 1945–1968* (1996). Tracks Johnson's decisions to wage all-out war in Vietnam. Hunt interprets Johnson's actions as consistent with the Cold War foreign policy that had prevailed since the Truman administration and its pledge to "contain" communism.

Maurice Isserman and Michael Kazin, *America Divided: The Civil War of the 1960s*, 3rd ed. (2007). A survey and astute analysis of the Vietnam War and its impact on domestic politics, with close scrutiny of the youth movements that rose in the late 1960s.

Rebecca E. Klatch, *A Generation Divided: The New Left, the New Right, and the 1960s* (1999). Compares and contrasts the respective roles of Students for a Democratic Society and the conservative Young Americans for Freedom on college campuses. Klatch, a sociologist, presents lengthy oral interviews with former student activists in both camps.

Joan Morrison and Robert K. Morrison, eds., *From Camelot to Kent State: The Sixties Experience in the Words of Those Who Lived It* (2001). A collection of fifty-nine oral histories with a range of people who lived through the 1960s. The volume includes stories of better-known activists, such as Eldridge Cleaver and Abbie Hoffman, as well as those who were soldiers in Vietnam or student activists. This edition also contains many photographs.

Laura Pulido, *Black, Brown, Yellow, and Left: Radical Activism in Los Angeles* (2006). A well-documented survey of activism in communities of color since the 1960s. Pulido examines the role of women in dealing within minority men within various organizations and movements.

Melvin Small, *AntiWarriors: The Vietnam War and the Battle for America's Hearts and Minds* (2002). A readable, succinct study of the groundswell of opposition to the war in Vietnam. Small covers many facets of the antiwar movement, ranging from hippies to Vietnam Veterans Against the War.

Anthony Summers, *The Arrogance of Power: The Secret World of Richard Nixon* (2000). A popular biography of Nixon's life from his early political career in California through his presidency. Summers drew on more than a thousand interviews, including those with Nixon's psychotherapist, to portray the former president's erratic behavior and mental instability during as well as before the disastrous Watergate affair.

myhistorylab™
Where it's a good time to connect to the past!

The Conservative Ascendancy
1974–1991

Grassroots Conservatism in Orange County, California

In 1962 Bee Gathright, a Brownie leader and mother of three young girls, invited her neighbors to her suburban Garden Grove home to hear a political talk by a man from the nearby Knott's Berry Farm Freedom Center. "This is when I discovered that I was a conservative," she later recalled. She feared that "the Communists were going to bury us, were going to take over the world . . . . " She convinced her skeptical husband Neil, an aerospace engineer, to share her new conviction. They soon joined the California Republican Assembly, a volunteer organization committed to electing conservatives to office. In 1964 the Gathrights' home served as a local headquarters for the presidential campaign of conservative Arizona Senator Barry Goldwater.

In Orange County in the 1960s and 1970s thousands of "kitchen table" activists like the Gathrights began a transformation of American conservatism and American politics that culminated in the presidential election of Ronald Reagan in 1980. Most of them were middle-class men and women, including large numbers of professionals and small business owners. Many, like the Gathrights, had moved to California to work in the burgeoning aerospace industry. Orange County's 800 square miles lie at the center of the southern California basin, and large lemon and orange groves dominated the economy until the 1940s. World War II and Cold War defense-related

spending accelerated the county's growth, creating thousands of new manufacturing jobs. A strong demand for housing spurred a construction boom and a roaring real estate market. By 1960, more than 700,000 people lived in Orange County, an increase of nearly 400 percent since 1940, and the population doubled again to top 2 million in the 1980s.

While Barry Goldwater's 1964 campaign ignited great enthusiasm in Orange County, his national defeat forced conservatives to consider ways to shed the "extremism" label. In 1966 they successfully backed the gubernatorial campaign of Ronald Reagan, a former Hollywood actor and New Deal liberal who had evolved in the 1950s into a prominent conservative and Republican Party activist. As governor, Reagan sought to limit state support for welfare and other social services, while expanding state power to enforce law and order. ➤

Reagan's success in California, as well as Richard Nixon's election as president in 1968, signaled an important new turn for American conservatives. They still championed anticommunism but no longer engaged in the loose talk about using nuclear weapons that had hurt Goldwater. They attacked "big government" but no longer spoke openly about repealing popular New Deal programs like Social Security. Instead, they focused on the "social issues" that increasingly troubled and mobilized Orange County's grassroots activists. Their concerns, largely defined by a "backlash" against the antiwar movement, counterculture, women's liberation, and urban uprisings, emphasized so-called family issues, in which opposition to sex education, obscenity, abortion rights, gay liberation, and the Equal Rights Amendment were all linked together. On the economic side, conservatives began to tap a deep well of resentment over rising property taxes and high inflation.

Two central themes of this new conservatism resonated with millions of Americans well beyond Orange County. One was the 1978 "revolt" of home owners that led to a sharp reduction in the property tax rate and soon spread to other states.

Orange County also helped form the second new force reshaping conservatism, "born-again" evangelical Christianity. Fundamentalist sects had long been associated with the rural poor of the South. But Orange County's religious revival featured educated professionals and middle-class suburbanites who turned to Christianity for spirituality and as a way to assert order amid rapid cultural and social change. "Born-again" Christians found community not only in Sunday services but also in a wide range of tightly organized activities: Bible study groups, summer retreats, "singles' fellowships," prayer breakfasts, and "Christian" consumer culture, which allowed people to simultaneously embrace faith, modern business techniques, and worldly goods. The political implications of the new evangelicalism soon became clear.

President Jimmy Carter, who took office in 1976, was a "born-again" Christian, and his successor, Ronald Reagan, raced to victory in 1980 with the strong backing of newly politicized Christian voters. For Bee Gathright, Reagan's victory vindicated her years of grassroots activism and set the nation on a conservative political course that led into the twenty-first century.

But unlike Carter, who advised Americans to accept limits, Reagan promised to not only restore but also enhance American global supremacy. As president, Reagan introduced a new economic program—"Reaganomics"—that reduced income taxes for wealthy Americans and at the same time increased federal spending for the largest military buildup in American history. Abolishing the Great Society antipoverty programs, he fostered the growth of a two-tiered society characterized by a disproportionate number of women and children filling the ranks of the nation's poor. Meanwhile, the increases in military spending complemented Reagan's foreign policy, which included a revival of Cold War patriotism, interventions in the Caribbean and Central America, and labeling the Soviet Union an "Evil Empire." However, it was Reagan's successor, George H. W. Bush, who presided during one of the most dramatic events of the era: the dissolution of the Soviet Union.

THE OVEREXTENDED SOCIETY

Postwar prosperity had effectively kept conservatives at bay from the Eisenhower years through the 1960s. Then, in the 1970s, economic growth ground to a halt and additionally presented Americans with an unfamiliar combination of skyrocketing prices and rising unemployment. Economists termed this novel condition "stagflation." By the mid-1970s, the unemployment rate had reached nearly 9 percent, its highest level since the Great Depression, and it remained close to 7 percent for most of the rest of the decade. Inflation, meanwhile, reached double digits.

The United States had come to an unhappy turning point in its economic history. Emerging from World War II as the world's most prosperous nation and retaining this status through the 1960s, the country suddenly found itself falling behind Western Europe and Japan. Meanwhile presidents Gerald Ford and Jimmy Carter promised little and, as far as many voters were concerned, delivered even less.

A TROUBLED ECONOMY

The most vivid sign of the troubled economy, the energy crisis, seemed to appear suddenly in the fall of 1973, although it had been decades in the making. The United States, which used about 70 percent of all oil produced in the world, had a sufficient domestic supply until the mid-1950s. But rising demand began to outstrip national reserves, and by 1973 the nation was importing one-third of its crude oil, mainly from the Middle East. On October 17,

Focus Questions

1. What explains the weakness in the U.S. economy in the 1970s?

2. What did Ford and Carter accomplish as presidents?

3. How successful was the environmentalist movement of the 1970s?

4. What are the factors behind the rise of the New Right?

5. How did the Iran hostage crisis affect the election of 1980?

6. What economic assumptions underlay "Reaganomics"?

7. Why did the gap between rich and poor grow in the 1980s?

8. How did the Cold War end?

1974–1991

members of the government-controlled Organization of Petroleum Exporting Countries (OPEC) announced an embargo on oil shipments to nations that had supported Israel in its war with Syria and Egypt, including the United States and its Western European allies (see Map 30.1).

President Nixon responded to the embargo by creating an "energy czar" and paving the way for the creation of the Department of Energy in 1977. He ordered a 10 percent reduction in air travel and appealed to Congress to lower speed limits on interstate highways to 55 miles per hour and to extend daylight-saving time into the winter months. But the impact of these measures was slight, and with the cost of gasoline, oil, and electricity up, many other prices also rose, from apartment rents and telephone bills to restaurant checks. Moreover, Americans became yet more dependent on Middle East oil supplies (see Figure 30.1).

Despite the drama of the oil crisis, the economic downturn had deeper roots in the failure of the United States to keep up with the rising industrial efficiency of other nations. Manufacturers from Asia, Latin America, and Europe now produced cheaper and better products, including automobiles, long considered the monopoly of Detroit. U.S. automakers, determined to reduce costs, turned to "outsourcing"—that is, making cars and trucks from parts cheaply produced abroad and imported into

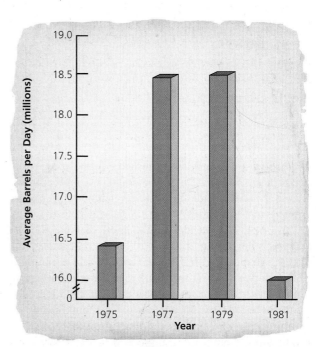

FIGURE 30.1 Decline of U.S. Oil Consumption, 1975–81
Boycotts causing shortages and high prices spurred the reduction in oil consumption. However, in the 1980s consumption once again began to rise to reach record highs.

SOURCE: Department of Energy, *Monthly Energy Review,* June 1982.

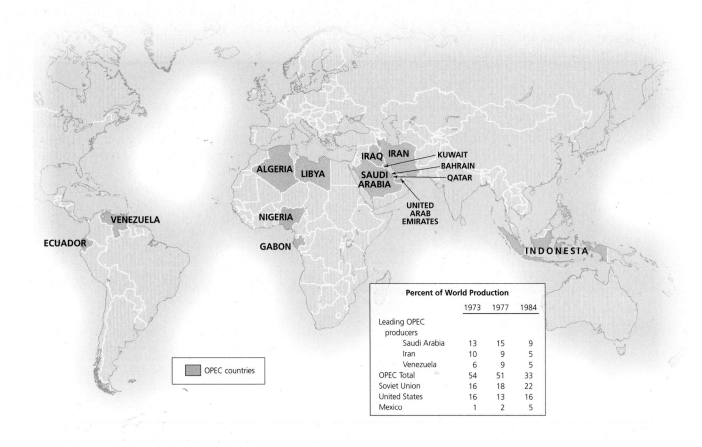

Percent of World Production			
	1973	1977	1984
Leading OPEC producers			
Saudi Arabia	13	15	9
Iran	10	9	5
Venezuela	6	9	5
OPEC Total	54	51	33
Soviet Union	16	18	22
United States	16	13	16
Mexico	1	2	5

OPEC countries

MAP 30.1 **World's Leading Oil Producers**

the United States as semifinished materials (which were subject to a lower tariff than finished goods). In high-tech electronics, the United States could scarcely compete against Japanese-made televisions, radios, tape players, cameras, and computers.

An AFL-CIO leader complained that the United States was becoming "a nation of hamburger stands . . . a country stripped of industrial capacity and meaningful work." Between 1970 and 1982 the AFL-CIO, since the early 1930s a leading source of support to the Democratic Party, lost nearly 30 percent of its membership (see Figure 30.2). The only real union growth took place among public employees, including teachers, civil service workers, and health professionals—all of them dependent on sagging public budgets.

Typical of hard times, an increasing number of women sought jobs to support their families. By 1980 more than half of all married women with children in their care were working outside the home. Yet despite their numerical

gains, women lost ground relative to men. In 1955 women earned 64 percent of the average wages paid to men; in 1980 they earned only 59 percent. The growing service economy accounted for this dip: women clustered in occupations where the lowest wages prevailed.

African American women made some gains. Through Title VII of the Civil Rights Act, which outlawed workplace discrimination by sex or race, and the establishment of the Equal Employment Opportunity Commission to enforce it, they managed to climb the lower levels of the job ladder. By 1980, northern black women's median earnings were about 95 percent of white women's earnings.

In contrast, Hispanic women, whose labor force participation leaped by 80 percent during the decade, were restricted to a very few occupations, mostly at or only slightly above the minimum wage. Puerto Ricans found jobs in the garment industry of the Northeast; Mexican Americans more typically worked as domestics or agricultural laborers in the Southwest.

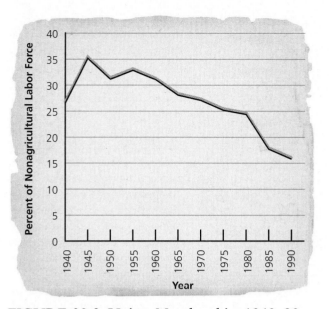

FIGURE 30.2 Union Membership, 1940–90
After reaching a peak during World War II, union membership steadily declined. In the 1980s, overseas production took an especially big toll on industrial unions.

SOURCE: Bureau of Labor Statistics, in Mary Kupiec et al., eds., *Encyclopedia of American Social History,* Vol. II. New York: Scribner's, 1993, p. 4188.

subsidies to agribusiness, California became the nation's most populous state; Texas moved to third, behind New York. Former farms and deserts were turned almost overnight into huge metropolitan areas ringed by new automobile-dependent suburbs. Phoenix grew from 664,000 in 1960 to 1,509,000 in 1980, Las Vegas from 127,000 to 463,000 (see Figure 30.3).

Much Sunbelt wealth tended to be temporary or sharply cyclical, producing a boom-and-bust economy. Corporate office buildings in cities such as Houston emptied almost as fast as they filled. Income was also distributed unevenly. Older Hispanic populations made only modest gains, while recent Mexican immigrants and Indian peoples suffered from a combination of low wages and poor public services. The Sunbelt states directed their tax and federal dollars to strengthening police forces, building roads or sanitation systems for the expanding suburbs, and creating budget surpluses, in contrast to eastern and midwestern states, which continued to spend significantly on public housing, education, and mass transit.

The "Snowbelt" (or "Rustbelt") states, longtime centers of voting strength for the Democratic Party, meanwhile suf-

SUNBELT/SNOWBELT COMMUNITIES

The problems of the economy did not fall equally on all regions, and the distinctive pattern of economic growth and decline mirrored changes in the nation's political tenor. The bastion of prosperity as well as the bulwark of political conservatism was the Sunbelt, which extended from Florida to Orange County, California. This region boasted a gross product greater than many nations and more cars, television sets, houses, and even miles of paved roads than the rest of the United States along with a growing number of Republicans.

Much of the Sunbelt's growth depended on a huge outlay of federal funds, including defense spending and the allocation of Social Security benefits. The number of residents over age sixty-five increased by 30 percent during the 1970s, reaching 26 million by 1980. Armed with retirement packages won decades earlier, huge "golden age" migrations created new communities in Florida, Arizona, and southern California. Immigrants from Latin America, the Caribbean, and Asia joined Americans fleeing the depressed Northeast to boost the region's population (see Map 30.2).

The Sunbelt witnessed a dramatic turnaround in demographic and economic trends. Southern cities reversed the century-long trend of out-migration among African Americans. The Southwest and West changed yet more dramatically. Aided by air conditioning, water diversions, public improvements, and large-scale development and

—MAP EXPLORATION—

To explore an interactive version of this map, go to
www.prenhall.com/faragher6/map30.2

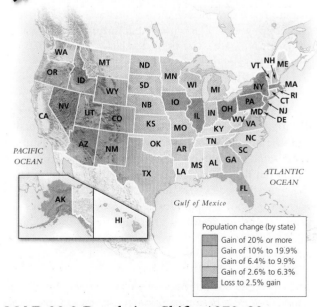

MAP 30.2 Population Shifts, 1970–80 Industrial decline in the Northeast coincided with an economic boom in the Sunbelt, encouraging millions of Americans to head for warmer climates and better jobs.

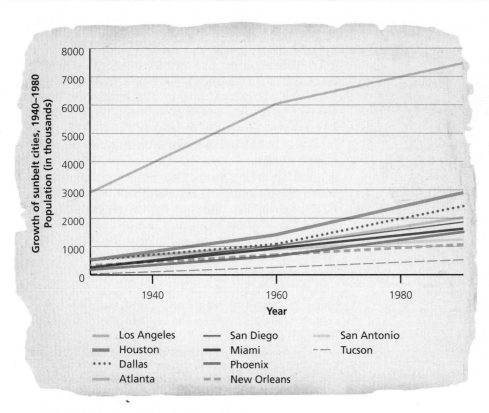

FIGURE 30.3 Growth of Sunbelt Cities, 1940–80
The old industrial cities in the Northeast and Midwest steadily lost population to the southern and western decentralized cities and their surrounding suburbs.

SOURCE: U.S. Bureau of the Census.

fered severe population losses accompanying the sharp decline of industry. Of the nineteen metropolitan areas that lost population during the 1970s, all were old manufacturing centers, topped by New York, Cleveland, Pittsburgh, Boston, Philadelphia, and Buffalo.

New York City offered a spectacular example of decline. A fiscal crisis in 1975 forced Democratic Mayor Abraham Beame to choose between wage freezes for public employees and devastating cuts and layoffs. Eventually, with the municipal government teetering on the brink of bankruptcy, he chose both. In response to cutbacks in mass transit and the deterioration of municipal services, a large sector of the middle class fled. At the same time, the proportion of poor people rose from 15 percent in 1969 to nearly 25 percent fourteen years later.

THE ENDANGERED ENVIRONMENT

The environmental downside of the post–World War II economic boom was becoming painfully evident. Cutting across nearly all population groups and regions, concern for the environment reached into conservative areas as far as the Deep South with warnings of the dangers of toxic wastes, the destruction of wetlands, and the ruin of fishing industries. Sometimes campaigns succeeded in blocking massive con-

struction projects, such as nuclear energy plants; more often they halted small-scale destruction of a natural habitat or historic urban district. One of the most dramatic campaigns took place in Love Canal, near Buffalo, New York, following the discovery of high rates of cancer and birth defects in the community. Here toxic wastes dumped by the Hooker Chemical Laboratory had oozed into basements and backyards, and in 1978 homemaker Lois Gibbs organized her neighbors to draw attention to the grim situation.

The environmentalist movement gained strength through long-standing organizations such as the Audubon Society, the Wilderness Society, and the Sierra Club, which swelled to 136 million members in 1972. New groups, such as the Environmental Defense Fund and Friends of the Earth, sprang up, most advocating the development of renewable energy sources such as solar power. Congress responded to pressure by passing scores of bills designed to protect endangered species, reduce pollution caused by automobile emissions, limit and ban the use of some pesticides, and control strip-mining practices. The Environmental Protection Agency (EPA), established in 1970, grew to become the federal government's largest regulatory agency, employing more than 10,000 people by the end of the decade (see Communities in Conflict).

Business-based groups fought back and sometimes found unexpected allies. City officials, both Democratic and Republican, generally avoided congressional mandates for reduction in air pollution by requesting lengthy extensions of deadlines for compliance. Top labor officials such as George Meany, president of the AFL-CIO, denounced "tree hugger" environmentalists as enemies of economic growth, and United Auto Workers lobbyists joined automakers in resisting compulsory gas mileage and tighter emissions controls in new models. Again and again, efforts at more environmentally attuned policies on energy met defeat. Environmentalists lost a key campaign with the approval of the Alaskan Pipeline, 800 miles of pipe often leaking into an endangered environment, connecting oil fields in Alaska's far north with refining facilities in the Lower 48. And despite the introduction of lead-free gasoline, the air in major metropolitan areas grew worse because automobile traffic increased.

The media attention given to Love Canal residents, who reported high incidents of birth defects and rates of cancer, led to the passage of a new federal law in 1980 regulating toxic waste disposal. This photograph shows one of the endangered children demonstrating during a neighborhood meeting.

"LEAN YEARS PRESIDENTS": FORD AND CARTER

Gerald R. Ford and Jimmy Carter presided over not only a depressed economy but also a nation of disillusioned citizens, many of them now wary of liberals and open to conservative appeals. The revelations of the Watergate break-in and Nixon's subsequent resignation as president had cast a pall over politics. Replacing Nixon in August 1974, Gerald Ford reassured the public that "our long national nightmare is over" but then quickly pardoned Nixon for all the federal crimes he may have committed. At the time, the pardon reinforced public cynicism toward government and Ford in particular. The midterm elections held later that year added fifty-two Democrats to the House and four to the Senate (see Map 30.3). To many Americans, Ford seemed a pleasant person of merely modest ability.

Ford immediately annoyed the conservatives in his ranks by choosing New York Governor Nelson Rocke-

feller, a well-known liberal, as his vice president. He then annoyed Rockefeller by directing him to head his "Whip Inflation Now" campaign, which almost everyone ridiculed for asking people to help curb inflation by wearing WIN lapel pins as reminders to hold back personal consumption. Even First Lady Betty Ford alienated conservative Republicans by breaking ranks to champion gun control, the Equal Rights Amendment, and abortion rights.

Ford banked on his incumbency for the 1976 election, dumped Rockefeller and welcomed Senator Robert Dole of Kansas as his running mate, but only narrowly won renomination after holding off a challenge from Ronald Reagan.

— MAP EXPLORATION —

To explore an interactive version of this map, go to
www.prenhall.com/faragher6/map30.3

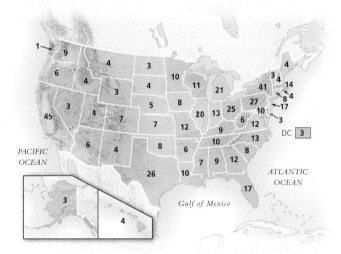

	Electoral Vote (%)	Popular Vote (%)
JIMMY CARTER (Democrat)	297 (55)	40,828,929 (50.1)
Gerald R. Ford (Republican)	240 (45)	39,148,940 (47.9)
Ronald Reagan	1	—
Other candidates (McCarthy, Independent, Libertarian)	—	1,575,459 (2.1)

MAP 30.3 The Election of 1976 Incumbent Gerald Ford could not prevail over the disgrace brought to the Republican Party by Richard Nixon. The lingering pall of the Watergate scandal, especially Ford's pardon of Nixon, worked to the advantage of Jimmy Carter, who campaigned as an outsider to national politics. Although Carter and his running mate Walter Mondale won by only a narrow margin, the Democrats gained control of both the White House and Congress.

Three Mile Island, Pennsylvania

On March 28, 1979, mechanical failures and judgment errors at the nuclear generating facility at Three Mile Island (TMI), near Harrisburg, Pennsylvania, caused the breakdown of the plant's cooling system and risked a catastrophic core meltdown. Although the company that ran the facility denied that there was any danger, nearly 150,000 horrified residents fled their homes. Quickly President Carter and First Lady Rosalynn Carter reassured the stricken community by visiting the site; ten days later, the Nuclear Regulatory Commission announced that any risk of explosion had passed. But what had seemed an isolated event had national repercussions. Elevated radioactivity was found in milk supplies several hundred miles away. Massive demonstrations against nuclear power culminated in a rally of more than 200,000 people in New York City.

The TMI accident climaxed a debate that had been building throughout the 1970s. The OPEC oil embargo and energy crisis had encouraged communities to explore nuclear energy. But just four years before the TMI accident, more than 2,300 scientists petitioned Congress and the president to warn against rapid expansion: The dangers were "altogether too great," and they advised a "drastic reduction" in the construction of nuclear power plants.

After TMI, many communities divided. Some citizens organized against funding nuclear power facilities; others endorsed plans for building new reactors. But of the ninety-six nuclear power plants under construction and the thirty more planned at the time of the TMI crisis, only a handful would ever be completed.

Events surrounding the accident suggested at least two possible positions. One side insisted that the harm caused by the release of radiation during the TMI accident had not yet surfaced. This was the position of Jane Lee, an assistant manager of a dairy farm 3.5 miles from TMI. In a 1980 interview, she discussed her long-standing opposition to nuclear power. Lee became an environmental activist, served the regional Environmental Quality Control Board, and opposed restarting Three Mile Island.

Others argued that the hazards had been exaggerated. After all, there had been neither a meltdown nor an explosion. Pennsylvania governor Richard Thornburgh twenty years later said: "I'm grateful that our prayers were answered and that the consensus view seems to be that there are no adverse long-term health or environmental consequences of the event." In his 2003 autobiography, Thornburgh spoke of the painful decisions that he had to face.

How do the events at Three Mile Island provide a context for examining the energy crisis of the 1970s? In view of today's fears of global warming, does the near-disaster at Three Mill Island take on new meaning?

Environmental Activist Jane Lee Opposes Nuclear Power (1980)

I'm on pretty firm ground when I say that I know, over and above the accident, that we have been exposed to more than our share of radiation because of the total incompetency of the people who are operating that plant. There is no question about it. The [government-sponsored] Kemmeny Commission report, if you read it, proves beyond a shadow of a doubt that the people who were operating the plants down there simply do not know what they're doing. And the same people are still operating them. They want to bring Unit 1 on line. During the accident they kept telling us there was nothing to worry about, that everything was under control, and all the time *nothing* was under control. Most people don't know we still have an ongoing accident at TMI . . . .

What I'm about to tell you is only the tip of the iceberg. Back in 1973 I began to log incidences of abortions, still births, birth defects and abnormalities in farm animals and livestock. At first I logged just what was happening here on this farm. Then as I began to get reports, I began to find out that it wasn't just this farm that was having problems—it was most of the farms in approximately a five-mile radius of TMI. . . .

The radiation is striking at the reproductive system, the area most vulnerable to radiation. . . .

For two weeks just after the accident, there wasn't a sign of a bird anywhere . . .

Anywhere. When the farmers go out to plow their fields, the birds usually hover all over the fields. It was the weirdest thing to plow the ground without a sign of a bird. There wasn't a sign of a bird! York County, where I live, is notorious for its starlings, but this year the starlings never showed up. Now, starlings don't just come like average birds. They come by the hundreds of thousands in wave after wave and cloud after cloud. In fact, we were saying that something was going to have to be done abut the starlings because they were so bad. But they never showed up this year. . . .

We have a housing development near here which sits up real high. When those plants were operating, many times I could see the steam go over the top and settle right on that development. There are pockets of women up there who are having miscarriages. There's been two suits filed already in the area against Met. Ed. The women had stillborns. We don't know yet how far-ranging this is because in the Hershey Medical Center the cancer department is so secret that nobody can go into there and get the statistics. . . .

A lot of people here are developing pneumonia. I'm really surprised at how many. These days, you don't hear of pneumonia like you used to. This is part and parcel of radiation, it destroys the immunity system. . . .

[After the accident] we had a metallic taste in our mouths. It tasted like, you know, like when you're a kid and you put money in your mouth? That's what it tasted like. And we all had it. . . .

"[Radiation] is affecting all of us."

[Radiation] is affecting all of us. The radioactive materials are going from the waste into our environment. They're coming back to us through the food chain. So it doesn't make any difference how close you live or how far away you live from a nuclear plant. We're all going to be affected. And in five years, if we continue with the operation of nuclear power plants, the people in this country are not going to be strong enough to go out and work on a job, much less defend their nation. That is a fact. We are not going to be strong enough because it is going to destroy the immunity system. And it will affect all of us. Every last one of us, I don't care where we live.

It isn't going to go away by pretending it doesn't exist. And the longer it's postponed the greater the danger is. Now that's my feeling. Somebody has to speak out. I went for three years with people making fun of me, telling me I was crazy and I didn't know what I was talking about. Now we all live in fear. All of us. I'm not alone anymore.

SOURCE: Robert Leppzer, *Voices from Three Mile Island: The People Speak Out* (Trumansburg, NY: The Crossing Press, 1980), pp. 21, 23, 37, 44, 45, 48, 50.

Pennsylvania Governor Richard Thornburgh Recalls the Three Mile Island Accident (2003)

It later became clear that, while some of the reactor fuel heated to the point of melting, a disastrous "meltdown" was never close to occurring. Detectable amounts of radiation escaped into our air, water and even milk, but these amounts were limited enough that their impact, if any, on public health remains debatable to this day. And a massive evacuation of the up to 200,000 people residing in the area, with its potential for panic, injury and even loss of life, would have been far more dangerous and damaging than was the accident itself. But at 7:50 on that March morning, we knew none of this. The thought of issuing a general evacuation order entered my mind immediately and never left during the days to follow. . . .

Our first task was to find out exactly what was happening. This was to prove far more difficult than any of us could have imagined. The utility (Metropolitan Edison), its parent company (General Public Utilities), state and federal regulators, and other groups and institutions issued increasingly contradictory assessments, telling the public either more or less than they knew of the accident and its consequences. Self-appointed experts exaggerated either the danger or the safety of the situation. The credibility of the utility, in particular, did not fare well. On that first day it sought to minimize the accident, assuring us, inaccurately, that "everything is under control" and that "all safety equipment functioned properly." When company technicians found that radiation levels in the surrounding area had climbed above normal, the company neglected to release that information to the public. It also vented some

"Self-appointed experts exaggerated either the danger or the safety of the situation."

radioactive steam into the air for two and one-half hours at midday on Wednesday, without informing us or the public.

Thus it fell to Lieutenant Governor Scranton. . . to tell the people of central Pennsylvania that "this situation is more complex than the company first led us to believe" and that there had indeed been a release of radioactivity. He stated that further discharges were possible, that we were "concerned," but that off-site radioactivity levels had been decreasing during the afternoon and there was no evidence that they had ever reached a danger point. . . .

Meanwhile, self-appointed experts and dubious eyewitnesses continued to feed us unsubstantiated stories about dead animals, along with exaggerated warnings and evacuation schemes. A poorly worded NRC [Nuclear Regulatory Commission] press release prompted a ridiculous tale, given currency by NBC's Tom Brokaw, of radiation so powerful that it was penetrating four feet of concrete and spreading up to sixteen miles from the plant. Signs popped up in grocery store windows in neighboring states proclaiming, "We don't sell Pennsylvania milk." Public faith in the experts and institutions involved was obviously beginning to erode. . . .

Shortly after noon on that third day of the crisis . . . I recommended that pregnant women and preschoolers leave the area within five miles of the plant until further notice, and that all schools within that zone be closed as well. I also ordered the opening of evacuation centers at various sites outside of the area to shelter those who had no place to go. "Current readings," I stated, "are no higher than they were yesterday [but] the continued presence of radioactivity in the area and the possibility of further emissions lead me to exercise the utmost of caution. . . ."

In general, reviews of our handling of TMI were favorable. . . . Syndicated columnists . . . noted the political implications, even saying, "Suddenly everyone is talking about how [Thornburgh] would make a marvelous candidate for vice president on the Republican ticket in 1980." There were, of course, critics as well, mostly focusing upon my unwillingness to order a "precautionary" evacuation in light of all the uncertainty. In time, I was to be labeled both "antinuke" (by the industry) and "pronuke" (by environmentalists) for various positions taken after the accident. On the theory that one should seek to please neither of these elements all of the time, I took these assessments to be a positive sign. In a May 1979 address to the American Society of Newspaper Editors, I called for "a middle ground between those who would abandon [nuclear power] and those who would expand it tomorrow. . . . The question is not yes or no, but how best we can use it and keep it under control. . . . [If] we can't prepare ourselves to control it, then we must prepare ourselves to do without it."

SOURCE: Dick Thornburgh, *Where the Evidence Leads: An Autobiography* (Pittsburgh: University of Pittsburgh Press, 2003), pp. 112, 113, 114–115, 117, 123–24.

Democrats chose Jimmy Carter, a former navy officer and governor of Georgia, who presented himself as a political outsider. When Carter told his mother he was running for president, she reportedly asked, "president of what?"

A born-again Christian and successful southern politician, Carter was the first Democratic presidential candidate since the 1930s who declined to call himself a liberal, offering instead personal integrity as his chief qualification for the nation's highest office. On domestic issues, he campaigned as a moderate. Counting on support from both conservative and southern voters who would ordinarily vote Republican, he defended existing entitlement programs while opposing Senator Edward Kennedy's call for comprehensive health coverage. He capitalized on Ford's unpopular Nixon pardon and, with his running mate Senator Walter Mondale of Minnesota, won with just over 50 percent of the popular vote and a 297-to-240 margin in the electoral college. Carter won more than 90 percent of the black vote, which provided his margin of victory in Pennsylvania, Ohio, and seven southern states. But apathy proved the next most important factor. A record 46.7 percent of eligible voters did not bother to cast ballots.

In office, Carter seemed to many observers enigmatic, even uninterested in the presidency, more conservative than liberal. His most successful innovation, deregulation of the airlines, brought lower fares for millions of passengers. But by freeing banks from congressional control, he inadvertently encouraged bad investments, outright fraud, and a round of disastrous bank failures. Inflation proved to be his worst enemy. As older Americans could recognize, half of all the inflation since 1940 had occurred in just ten years. Interest rates rose, driving mortgages out of reach for many would-be home buyers. Rents in many locations doubled, sales of automobiles and other consumer products slumped, and many small businesses went under. Tuition costs skyrocketed along with unemployment, and many young men and women who could neither afford to go to college nor find a job moved back home.

An outspoken fiscal conservative, Carter could not deliver on his promise to turn the economy around. By the time he left office in 1980, a majority of those polled agreed that "the people running the country don't really care what happens to you." He had managed to discredit the liberal tradition of the Democratic Party even while distancing himself from it, making his presidency the symbol of a larger political collapse.

THE LIMITS OF GLOBAL POWER

In April 1975 the North Vietnamese struck Saigon and easily captured the city as the South Vietnamese army, now without U.S. assistance, fell apart. All fighting stopped within a few weeks, and Saigon was renamed Ho Chi Minh City. Vietnam was reunited under a government dominated by Communists. For many Americans, this outcome underscored the futility of U.S. involvement in the Vietnam War; for others, it suggested the limits of the global power of the United States.

By the mid-1970s a new realism in U.S. diplomacy seemed to prevail. Presidents Ford and Carter, as well as their chief advisers, acknowledged that the cost of fighting the Vietnam War had been too high, speeding the decline of the United States as the world's reigning superpower. The realists shared with dissatisfied nationalists a single goal: "No More Vietnams."

DÉTENTE

The military defeat in Vietnam forced U.S. foreign policy makers to reassess priorities. The United States must continue to defend its "vital interests," declared Secretary of State Henry Kissinger, but must also recognize that "Soviet–American relations are not designed for tests of manhood." Both nations experienced a decline of power in world affairs. And both suffered from the already enormous and relentlessly escalating costs of their defense budgets.

Western European nations acted to nudge U.S. foreign policy away from its Cold War premises. In 1975, in Helsinki, Finland, representatives of thirty-five nations approved the national boundaries drawn in Eastern and Western Europe after World War II, and in return the Soviet Union agreed to enact a more liberal human rights policy, including the loosening of restrictions on the emigration of Soviet Jews. Recognizing that the Soviet Union no longer posed a military threat to their national sovereignty—if indeed it ever had—Western leaders also sought to strengthen economic relations between the two major blocs.

The Soviet Union joined the United States in moving toward détente. The signing of SALT I, the first Strategic Arms Limitation Treaty, during Nixon's administration, followed by the U.S. withdrawal from Vietnam, encouraged new negotiations on strategic arms control. In November 1974, Ford and Soviet leader Leonid Brezhnev met in Vladivostok to set the terms of SALT II, and President Carter secured the final agreement in 1979. However, the Senate refused to ratify the treaty when the Soviet Union invaded Afghanistan in December 1979.

FOREIGN POLICY AND "MORAL PRINCIPLES"

When he took office, President Carter presented his lack of experience in foreign affairs as an asset. "We've seen a loss of morality," he noted, "and we're ashamed." The "soul" of his policy would be an "absolute" commitment to human rights.

Carter condemned policies that allowed the United States to support "right-wing monarchs and military dictators" in the name of anticommunism. In 1976 a powerful human rights lobby pressured Congress to pass a bill that required the secretary of state to report annually on the status of human rights in all countries receiving U.S. aid and to cut off assistance to any country with a record of "gross violations." Carter's secretary of state, Cyrus R. Vance, and the assistant secretary for human rights and humanitarian affairs, Pat Derrian, worked to punish or at least to censure repressive military regimes in Brazil, Argentina, and Chile. For the first time, leading U.S. diplomats spoke out against the South African apartheid regime.

In line with this policy, Carter tried to reform operations at the CIA, particularly to halt intervention in the affairs of foreign governments. He appointed Admiral Stansfield Turner as director and ordered a purge of the "rogue elephants" who had pursued covert operations in Southeast Asia during the Vietnam War. "The CIA must operate within the law," Carter insisted. Under Turner, however, these reforms remained incomplete; they later proved temporary.

Carter seemed within reach of a historic triumph in the Middle East. Early in his administration, Carter met privately with Israeli prime minister Menachem Begin to encourage conciliation with Egypt. When negotiations between the two countries stalled in 1978, Carter brought Begin together with Egyptian president Anwar el-Sadat for a thirteen-day retreat at Camp David, Maryland.

The Camp David Accords, signed in September 1978, set the formal terms for peace in the region. Egypt became the first Arab country to recognize Israel's right to exist, as the two nations established mutual diplomatic relations for the first time since the founding of Israel in 1948. In return, Egypt regained control of the Sinai Peninsula, including important oil fields and airfields. In 1979 Begin and Sadat shared the Nobel Prize for Peace.

But disappointment lay ahead. Carter staked his hopes for regional peace on the final achievement of statehood, or at least political autonomy, for Palestinians in a portion of their former lands now occupied by the Israelis. The accords specified that Israel would eventually return to its approximate borders of 1967. However, although Begin agreed to dismantle some Israeli settlements in the Sinai, the Israeli government continued to sponsor more and more Jewish settlements, expropriating Palestinian holdings. The final status of the Palestinians remained in limbo, as did that of Jerusalem, which many Christians and Muslims felt should be an autonomous holy city. Meanwhile Sadat grew increasingly isolated within the Arab world. In 1981 he was assassinated by Egyptians allied with an Islamic Jihad organization.

Carter scored his biggest moral victory in foreign affairs by paving the way for Panama to assume the ownership, operation, and defense of the Panama Canal Zone. Negotiations with Panama had begun during Johnson's administration, following riots by Panamanians against U.S. territorial rule in their country. Carter pressured the Senate to ratify new treaties in 1978 (by a vote of 68 to 32) that would turn the Panama Canal over to Panama by the year 2000.

President Carter signs the Middle East Peace Treaty with Egyptian President Anwar Sadat and Israeli Prime Minister Menachem Begin, in Washington, DC, March 1979. President Carter had invited both leaders to Camp David, the presidential retreat in Maryland, where for two weeks he mediated between them on territorial rights to the West Bank and Gaza Strip. Considered Carter's greatest achievement in foreign policy, the negotiations, known as the Camp David Peace Accords, resulted in not only the historic peace treaty but also the Nobel Peace Prize for Begin and Sadat.

(MIS)HANDLING THE UNEXPECTED

Mired in problems inherited from his predecessors, Carter often found himself disoriented by contradictory advice. Secretary of State Cyrus Vance recommended well-planned negotiations to soothe Soviet–U.S. relations and resolve disagreements with Third World nations. But national security adviser Zbigniew Brzezinski, an anti-Communist Polish exile, interpreted events in even remote sections of Africa or South America as plays in a zero-sum game: wherever the United States lost influence, the Soviet Union gained, and vice versa. Despite Carter's commitment to human rights, he put aside his principles to stabilize repressive regimes in nations considered vital to U.S. interests, such as South Korea and the Philippines.

In 1979 the overthrow of the brutal Nicaraguan dictatorship of Anastasio Somoza, longtime U.S. ally, left Carter without a successor to support. When the new Sandinista revolutionary government pleaded for help, Congress turned down Carter's request for $75 million in aid to Nicaragua. Meanwhile, in El Salvador, the Carter administration continued to back a repressive government even after the assassination of Oscar Romero, a Catholic archbishop and opposition leader. Following the rape and murder of four American Catholic Church women, apparently by the ultraright Salvadoran armed forces trained in the United States, peace activists and other Americans pleaded with Carter to withhold further military aid.

The Soviet occupation of Afghanistan produced a major stalemate. In December 1979, 30,000 Soviet troops invaded their neighbor to put down a revolt by Islamic insurgents against the weakening Soviet-backed government. The invasion succeeded mainly in heating up the civil war, which the American press quickly labeled the "Russian Vietnam."

Noting that the Soviet occupation of Afghanistan posed "a grave threat to the free movement of Middle East oil," President Carter issued his own corollary to the Monroe Doctrine by affirming the right of the United States to use military force if necessary to protect its interests in the Persian Gulf. He backed up his increasingly hard-line policies by halting exports of grain and high technology to the Soviet Union, by supporting Afghan resistance against the Russians, and by canceling American participation in the 1980 Moscow Olympics. Carter also called for ever-larger increases in the military budget. The prospect of détente dried up.

THE IRAN HOSTAGE CRISIS

On November 4, 1979, Iranian fundamentalists seized the U.S. embassy in Tehran and held 52 American employees hostage for 444 days. This event made President Carter's previous problems seem small by comparison.

For decades, U.S. foreign policy in the Middle East had depended on a friendly government in Iran. After the

Iranians demonstrate outside the U.S. Embassy in Tehran, raising a poster with a caricature of President Carter. The Iran hostage crisis, which began November 8, 1979, when a mob of Iranians seized the U.S. embassy in Tehran, contributed to Carter's defeat at the polls the following year. Fifty-two embassy employees were held hostage for 444 days.

CIA had helped to overthrow the reformist, constitutional government and installed the Pahlavi royal family and the shah of Iran in 1953, millions of U.S. dollars had poured into the Iranian economy and the shah's armed forces. President Carter had toasted the shah for his "great leadership" and overlooked the rampant corruption in government and a well-organized opposition. But by early 1979, a revolution led by the Islamic leader Ayatollah Ruhollah Khomeini had overthrown the shah. After Carter had allowed the deposed Reza Shah Pahlavi to enter the United States for medical treatment, a group of Khomeini's followers retaliated, storming the U.S. embassy and taking the American staff as hostages.

Cyrus Vance assured Carter that only negotiations could free Americans. Caught up in a reelection campaign and lobbied by Brzezinski for decisive action, Carter ordered U.S. military forces to stage a nighttime helicopter rescue mission. But a sandstorm caused some of the aircraft to crash and burn, leaving eight Americans dead, their burned corpses displayed by the enraged Iranians. Short of an all-out attack, which surely would have resulted in the hostages' death, Carter had used up his options.

The political and economic fallout was heavy. Cyrus Vance resigned, the first secretary of state in sixty-five years to leave office over a political difference with the president. The price of oil rose by 60 percent. Carter had failed in the one area he had proclaimed central to the future of the United States: energy. He had also violated his own human rights policy, which was intended to be his distinctive mark on American foreign affairs.

THE NEW RIGHT

The failures in U.S. foreign policy, accompanied by the faltering economy, played a large part in mobilizing what one writer termed "the politics of resentment." Sizable numbers of white taxpayers begrudged the tax hikes required to fund the welfare programs that benefited minorities and provided expanded social services for the poor and, at the same time, slowed economic development. In 1978, the California "taxpayers' revolt," which cut property taxes, also sharply reduced government revenues for social programs and education. In other economically hard-pressed urban areas, white voters who resented the gains made by African Americans, Latinos, and women formed a powerful backlash movement against liberalism.

Old-style conservatives lined up behind these initiatives, as did the New Right. But what distinguished the New Right from the old was an emphasis on "moral values" and its populist character. One element in this coalition comprised conservative ideologues, some of them former Democrats who had become disenchanted with liberalism. By far the largest component, evangelical or born-again Protestants like the Gathrights organized to become a powerful political force.

NEOCONSERVATISM

By the mid-1970s, a new variation of conservatism appeared on the political landscape: neoconservatism. Unlike earlier conservatives, such as Barry Goldwater, who had allied with the Republican Party, the most prestigious leaders of this new movement had been liberal Democrats, some even socialists, in the preceding decades. The unsettling social movements of the 1960s had prompted them to turn against New Deal–style liberalism and the welfare state. They continued to believe in equal opportunity but forcefully rejected the goal of equality of outcome. "Neocons," as they were called, sought to repeal affirmative action programs and dismantle the antipoverty programs enacted during the Johnson administration.

The heart of the neoconservatism was, however, foreign policy. Angered over the failure to pursue victory in Vietnam, neoconservatives called for a stronger national defense against communism. They opposed Carter's move toward détente and accused the president of allowing Communists to advance in Third World countries. The Soviet occupation of Afghanistan, they charged, only underscored just how weak the United States had become in global affairs.

Neoconservatives played an important role in building the institutional foundation for the rightward turn in American politics. Richly funded by corporate donors, they established think tanks to engage scholars and intellectuals in policy-shaping discussions. The Heritage Foundation, founded by Coors in 1973, the American Enterprise Institute, the Hoover Institution, and the Scaife Foundations offered opportunities to individuals and institutions agreeable to their views. Wide access to the press, especially the *Wall Street Journal,* but also distinguished journals such as *Commentary* magazine and *The Public Interest* gave neoconservatives ample opportunities to express their views on both domestic and foreign policy.

The surge rightward gained intellectual respectability for neoconservatives and prepared the way for broader popular support. The American Conservative Union grew to 300,000 members by the end of the decade and played a vocal role in foreign policy.

THE RELIGIOUS RIGHT

Evangelical Protestants, more than 50 million Americans by the late 1970s, became the backbone of the new conservatism, serving as the chief fundraisers for key organizations such as the National Conservative Political Action Committee and recruiters for community-based organizations. The Religious Right typically endorsed neoconservative positions on foreign and domestic policy. They supported a balanced budget amendment to the Constitution, sought unsuccessfully to return prayer to the public schools, and endorsed the Supreme Court's approval of the death penalty in 1977. As grassroots activists, they provided the political muscle that carried Bee Gathright's conservatism from the margins to the center of the Republican Party.

Finding huge audiences among the growing evangelical and Pentecostal congregations, Protestant ministers took to the airwaves. Televangelists such as Pat Robertson, Jimmy Swaggart, and Jim and Tammy Bakker frequently mixed conservative politics with appeals for both prayer and money. Jerry Falwell's *Old-Time Gospel Hour* was broadcast weekly over 200 television stations and 300 radio stations. By the late 1970s more than 1,400 radio stations and 30 TV stations specialized in religious broadcasts that reached perhaps 20 million listeners weekly and became a major source of fundraising for conservative organizations and campaigns.

In 1979, the Reverend Jerry Falwell, a Bible Baptist, formed the Moral Majority following his U.S. tour to get evangelical Christians "saved, baptized, and registered" to vote. As a major political lobbying group, the Moral Majority, which claimed 2 to 3 million members, advocated tough laws against homosexuality and pornography and promoted a reduction of government services (especially welfare payments to single mothers) and increased spending for a stronger national defense. The Moral Majority also waged well-publicized campaigns against public school integration and especially the busing of schoolchildren.

THE PRO-FAMILY MOVEMENT

Most of all, the New Right embraced what they termed "traditional family values": defeating the Equal Rights Amendment (ERA) stood at the top of their political agenda. Approved by Congress in March 1972, nearly fifty years after its introduction (see Chapter 22), the ERA stated: "Equality of rights under the law shall not be denied or abridged by the United States or by any State on account of sex." Endorsed by both the Democratic and Republican parties, the amendment appeared likely to be ratified by the individual states. Nearly all mainstream women's organizations, including the Girl Scouts of America, endorsed the ERA. Even the AFL-CIO retracted its long-standing opposition and endorsed the amendment.

Cued by this groundswell of support in favor of the ERA, conservatives swung into action. Phyllis Schlafly, a self-described suburban housewife and popular lecturer, headed

the STOP-ERA campaign, describing the amendment's supporters as "a bunch of bitter women seeking a constitutional cure for their personal problems." While STOP-ERA was a loose coalition of local and state groups, the Eagle Forum, also founded by Schlafly, became a national organization functioning as the "alternative to women's lib." Under Schlafly's leadership, the New Right mounted large, expensive campaigns in each swing state and overwhelmed pro-ERA resources. Her supporters also built a strong, religious-based coalition, with southern Protestants, western Mormons, northeastern Catholics, and Orthodox Jews temporarily putting aside differences to join forces to defeat the amendment that they believed was "against God's plan."

Although thirty-five states had ratified the ERA by 1979, the amendment remained three votes short of passage. Despite a three-year extension, the ERA died in Congress in 1982, with 85 percent of the Democrats and only 30 percent of the Republicans voting in its favor.

Meanwhile, the anti-ERA campaign had grown into a comprehensive "pro-family" movement that placed abortion rights at the top of its political agenda. In 1973 the Supreme Court had ruled in *Roe v. Wade* that state laws decreeing abortion a crime during the first two trimesters of pregnancy constituted a violation of a woman's right to privacy. Opponents of *Roe* rallied for a constitutional amendment defining conception as the beginning of life and then argued that the "rights of the unborn" supersede a woman's right to control her own body. The Roman Catholic Church organized the first antiabortion demonstrations and sponsored the formation of the National Right to Life Committee, which claimed 11 million members by 1980.

Antiabortion groups, such as the Orange County Pro-Life Political Action Committee, founded in 1973, also rallied against sex education programs in public schools. They picketed Planned Parenthood counseling centers, intimidating potential clients. A small minority turned to more extreme actions and bombed dozens of abortion clinics.

THE 1980 ELECTION

Carter's reelection prospects appeared to rest on his conduct of international affairs. If he only could put his human rights policy on a firm ground, move toward lasting peace in the Middle East, strike a bargain with the Soviets on arms limitation, or—most of all—end the hostage crisis in Iran, he might restore voter confidence. If not, his presidency would end after a single term. Ultimately, his bid for renomination depended more on his incumbency than on his popularity. Democrats unenthusiastically endorsed Carter along with his running mate, Walter Mondale.

Christian televangelists Jim and Tammy Bakker hosted the popular "PTL Club" and capitalized on their success to build the PTL Network and "Heritage USA," which grew to become one of the largest and best attended theme parks in the United States. This photograph, taken in 1986, shows the couple shortly before reports of financial irregularities and a sex scandal forced Jim Bakker to resign his PTL ministry. They divorced in 1992 following Jim Bakker's conviction on federal charges of fraud and racketeering.

On the Republican side, former California governor Ronald Reagan had been building his campaign since his near nomination in 1976. Former CIA director and Texas oil executive George H. W. Bush, more moderate than Reagan, became the Republican candidate for vice president.

Reagan proudly assumed the conservative mantle, repeatedly asking voters, "Are you better off now than you were four years ago?" While Carter implored Americans to tighten their belts, Reagan assured them that "America's best days lay ahead." Although opponents questioned his competence, the attractive, soft-spoken actor shrugged off criticisms while spotlighting the many problems besetting the country.

The Republicans cruised to victory. Carter won only 41.2 percent of the popular vote to Reagan's 50.9 percent, 49 votes in the electoral college to Reagan's 489. Orange County gave the Reagan ticket a whopping 68 percent of the vote. The Republicans won control of the Senate for the first time since 1952 and with the largest majority since 1928. White working people, the traditional supporters of the Democratic Party, had defected to the Republicans in large numbers, although both women and African Americans voted for Reagan in far fewer numbers. And barely half of the eligible voters had turned out, bringing Ronald Reagan into office with a slim mandate of 25 percent. However, Reagan began on a high note: the Iranians released the American hostages on January 20, 1981, the day he took the oath of office (see Seeing History).

SEEING HISTORY

The Presidential Inauguration of Ronald Reagan

In 1977, Jimmy Carter held a "people's inaugural." He took the oath of office wearing a plain business suit and then walked hand in hand with his wife Rosalynn along the parade route.

On January 21, 1981, Ronald Reagan became the nation's fortieth president wearing a formal black coat, striped pants, and black shoes and accompanied First Lady Nancy Reagan down the parade route in a limousine.

Everything about Reagan's inauguration, including eight formal balls spread across four days of festivities, reflected what Nancy Reagan described as her aspiration to put the White House "symbolically back up on a hill in people's minds, to have stature and loftiness." The Reagans hired a public relations expert to ensure that every event was telecast. All the inaugural balls, concerts, and receptions, including the opening evening event (an $800,000 light show and concert on the steps of the Lincoln Memorial), were planned to entertain and astound at-home audiences. Festivities at the Washington, DC, balls were also beamed through a $2 million satellite hookup to "mini-balls" held simultaneously across the nation.

The press celebrated Nancy Reagan for restoring high style to the image of the First Lady. Whereas Rosalynn Carter had worn an old blue chiffon evening dress to the inaugural ball in 1977, Nancy Reagan chose a hand-beaded, crystal-studded gown designed by a leader in the fashion industry. Overall, her inaugural wardrobe was estimated to cost around $25,000. Unlike Rosalynn Carter, who appeared at the swearing-in ceremony in a modest cloth coat, Nancy Reagan chose a full-length mink.

Reagan's inauguration, touted by the press as the most expensive in U.S. history, showcased the theme the president-elect had chosen for his administration: "America—A New Beginning." Not the belt-tightening, "homespun ways" of the Carter presidency, noted one reporter, but an unabashed celebration of wealth would prevail.

Why did the newly elected President Reagan choose to celebrate wealth? What had happened in the United States between the mid-1970s and the beginning of the 1980s to make such a display of wealth and power acceptable to the public?

THE REAGAN REVOLUTION

No other twentieth-century president except Franklin D. Roosevelt left as deep a personal imprint on American politics as Ronald Reagan. Ironically, Reagan himself began his political life as an ardent New Deal Democrat who considered Roosevelt an inspirational leader. But by the time he entered the White House in 1981, shortly before his seventieth birthday, Reagan had rejected the activist welfare state legacy of the New Deal era. "In the present crisis . . . ," he declared, "government is not the solution to our problem, government is the problem." Reagan and his allies proceeded to reshape the political and social landscape of the nation along conservative lines (see Map 30.4).

—MAP EXPLORATION—

To explore an interactive version of this map, go to
www.prenhall.com/faragher6/map30.4

	Electoral Vote (%)	Popular Vote (%)
RONALD REAGAN (Republican)	489 (91)	43,201,220 (50.9)
Jimmy Carter (Democrat)	49 (9)	34,913,332 (41.2)
John B. Anderson (Independent)	—	5,581,379 (6.6)
Other candidates (Libertarian)	—	921,299 (1.1)

MAP 30.4 The Election of 1980 Ronald Reagan won a landslide victory over incumbent Jimmy Carter, who managed to carry only six states and the District of Columbia. Reagan attracted millions of traditionally Democratic voters to the Republican camp.

THE GREAT COMMUNICATOR

Even as he took office, most Americans knew Ronald Reagan mainly from his Hollywood movies and television appearances. Although never a big star, on screen he appeared tall, handsome, and affable. In later years, he credited his political success to his acting experience. He told one interviewer: "An actor knows two important things—to be honest in what he's doing and to be in touch with the audience. That's not bad advice for a politician either."

By midcentury, Reagan had emerged as one of the most prominent conservative politicians in the nation. While serving as president of the Screen Actors Guild from 1947 to 1952, he distanced himself from other New Deal Democrats by leading the anti-Communist forces in Hollywood. In 1954 he hosted a new national television program, *General Electric Theater,* and began a long stint as a national promoter for GE. In this role he repeatedly celebrated the achievements of corporate America and emphasized the dangers of excessive liberalism and radical trade unions.

Reagan switched his party affiliation and became a successful fundraiser and popular speaker for the California Republican Party. After playing a leading role in Barry Goldwater's 1964 presidential campaign, and with the financial backing of some wealthy conservatives, he won the 1966 race for California governor, securing 72 percent of the Orange County vote. He won reelection in 1970. As governor, Reagan cut the state welfare rolls, reduced the number of state employees, and funneled a large share of state tax revenues back to local governments. He vigorously attacked student protesters and black militants, thereby tapping into the conservative backlash against the 1960s' activism.

When Reagan entered the White House in January 1981, his supporters interpreted his election as a popular mandate for the conservatism that had been growing since Nixon took office. The "Reagan Revolution," they confidently predicted, would usher in a new age in American political life.

REAGANOMICS

Supply-side theory, dubbed "Reaganomics" by the media, dominated the Reagan administration's economic planning and helped redirect the American economy. Supply-side theorists urged a sharp break with the Keynesian policies that had prevailed since the New Deal era (see Chapter 24). During recessions, Keynesians traditionally favored moderate tax cuts and increases in government spending to stimulate the economy and reduce unemployment. By putting more money in people's pockets, they argued, greater consumer demand would lead to economic expansion.

By contrast, supply-siders called for simultaneous tax cuts and reductions in public spending. This combination—which Reagan himself described as simple "common sense"—would give private entrepreneurs and investors greater incentives to start businesses, take risks, invest capital,

Ronald Reagan, the fortieth president of the United States, was known for his ability to articulate broad principles of government in a clear fashion. The most popular president since Dwight Eisenhower, he built a strong coalition of supporters from long-term Republicans, disillusioned Democrats, and evangelical Protestants.

and thereby create new wealth and jobs. Whatever revenues were lost in lower tax rates would be offset by revenue from new economic growth. At the same time, spending cuts would keep the federal deficit under control and thereby keep interest rates down.

George Gilder, conservative author of the best-selling *Wealth and Poverty* (1981), summarized the supply-side view: "A successful economy depends on the proliferation of the rich." On the political level, supply-siders looked to reward the most loyal Republican constituencies: the affluent and the business community. At the same time, they hoped to reduce the flow of federal dollars to two core Democratic constituencies: the recipients and professional providers of health and welfare programs.

Reagan quickly won bipartisan approval for two key bills that culminated in the largest tax cut in the nation's history. The Economic Recovery Tax Act of 1981 brought across-the-board class cuts for corporations and individuals. The new legislation also reduced the maximum tax on all income from 70 percent to 50 percent, lowered the maximum capital gains tax—the tax paid on profitable investments—from 28 percent to 20 percent, and eliminated the distinction between earned and unearned income. This last measure proved a boon to the smallest although richest fraction of the population that derives most of its income from rent, dividends, and interest instead of from wages.

With the help of conservative southern and western Democrats in the House, the administration also pushed through a comprehensive program of spending cuts, awkwardly known as the Omnibus Reconciliation Act of 1981. This bill mandated huge cuts affecting more than 200 social and cultural programs. The hardest-hit areas included education, the environment, health, housing, urban aid, food stamps, research on synthetic fuels, and the arts. The conservative coalition in the House allowed only one vote on the entire package of spending cuts, a strategy that allowed conservatives to slash appropriations for a wide variety of domestic programs in one fell swoop.

While reducing spending on domestic programs, the Reagan administration greatly increased the defense budget, a trend already under way during Carter's final two years as president. Overall, the military buildup indicated a significant shift in federal budget priorities.

Meanwhile, the Reagan administration created a chilly atmosphere for organized labor. In the summer of 1981, some 13,000 federal employees, all members of the Professional Air Traffic Controllers Organization (PATCO), went on strike. The president retaliated by firing all the strikers, and a crash program started by the Federal Aviation Administration permanently replaced them. Conservative appointees to the National Labor Relations Board and the federal courts toughened their anti-union position. By 1990 fewer than 15 percent of American workers belonged to a labor union, the lowest proportion since before World War II.

Deregulation also served as a key element in Reaganomics. The president's appointments to head the Environmental Protection Agency, the Occupational Safety and Health Administration, and the Consumer Product Safety Commission abolished or weakened hundreds of rules governing environmental protection, workplace safety, and consumer protection, all to increase the efficiency and productivity of business. The deregulatory fever dominated cabinet departments as well. Secretary of the Interior James Watt opened up formerly protected wilderness areas and wetlands to private developers. Secretary of Transportation Andrew L. "Drew" Lewis Jr. eliminated regulations passed in the 1970s aimed at reducing air pollution and improving fuel efficiency in cars and trucks.

Following supply-side theory, the Reagan administration weakened the Justice Department's Antitrust Division, the Securities and Exchange Commission, and the Federal Home Loan Bank Board. Large corporations, Wall Street stock brokerages, investment banking houses, and the savings and loan industry were all allowed to operate with a much freer hand than ever before. The appointment of Alan Greenspan in 1983, to succeed Carter appointee Paul Volker, greatly encouraged trends toward speculation in market trading. By the late 1980s, the unfortunate consequences of this freedom would become apparent in a series of unprecedented scandals in the nation's financial and banking industries.

THE ELECTION OF 1984

Hoping to win back disgruntled voters, Democrats chose Carter's vice president, Walter Mondale, as their nominee. A former senator from Minnesota, Mondale had close ties with the party's liberal establishment but also the support of its more military-minded wing. At the Democratic National Convention, Mondale named New York Representative Geraldine Ferraro as his running mate, a first for women in American politics.

Opinion polls showed Mondale for a time running even with Reagan, but the president's enormous personal popularity, along with the booming economy, overwhelmed the Democratic ticket. While Mondale emphasized the growing deficit, called attention to Americans who were left out of prosperity, and promised to raise taxes, Reagan cruised above it all. He offered the voters a choice between a Democratic "government of pessimism, fear, and limits" or his own, based on "hope, confidence, and growth."

"It's morning again in America," Reagan's campaign ads promised, and in one of the biggest landslides in American history Reagan won 59 percent of the popular vote—nearly 75 percent in Orange County—and carried every state but Minnesota and the District of Columbia. A majority of blue-collar voters cast their ballots for the president, as did 54 percent of women, despite Ferraro's presence on the Democratic ticket. Even a quarter of all Democrats voted for Reagan.

RECESSION, RECOVERY, AND FISCAL CRISIS

Reagan's supply-side policies produced a mixed record but a highly favorable outcome for the wealthiest Americans. In 1982 a severe recession, the worst since the 1930s, gripped the nation. The official unemployment rate reached nearly 11 percent, or more than 11.5 million people. Another 3 million were out of work so long they no longer actively looked for jobs and, therefore, were not counted in official statistics. But by 1983 the economy recovered and headed into a long period of growth and expansion. Unemployment dropped to about 8 percent while inflation fell below 5 percent. The stock market boomed, pushing the Dow Jones industrial average from 776 in August 1982 to an all-time high of 2,722 in August 1987. The administration took credit for the turnaround, hailing the supply-side policies that had drastically cut

taxes and domestic spending. But critics pointed to other factors: the Federal Reserve Board's tight-money policies, an energy resource glut and a consequent sharp drop in energy prices, and the billions of dollars pumped into the economy for defense spending.

Few doubted, however, that the supply-side formula intensified a significant fiscal crisis. Although Reagan had promised to balance the federal budget, his policies had the opposite effect. The national debt tripled, growing from $914 billion in 1980 to over $2.7 trillion in 1989, more than the federal government had accumulated in its entire previous history. Expenditures for paying just the interest on the national debt reached 14 percent of the annual budget in 1988, double the percentage set aside for that purpose in 1974.

During the Reagan presidency the fiscal crisis became a structural problem with profound and long-lasting implications for the American economy. Big deficits kept interest rates high, as the government drove up the cost of borrowing the money it needed to pay its own bills. Foreign investors, attracted by high interest rates on government securities, pushed up the value of the dollar in relation to foreign currencies. The overvalued dollar made it difficult for foreigners to buy American products, while making overseas goods cheaper to American consumers. Basic American industries—steel, autos, textiles—thus found it difficult to compete abroad and at home. In 1980, the United States still enjoyed a trade surplus of $166 billion. By 1987 the nation was indebted to foreigners to the tune of $340 billion. Since World War I, the United States had been the world's leading creditor; in the mid-1980s it became its biggest debtor (see Figure 30.4).

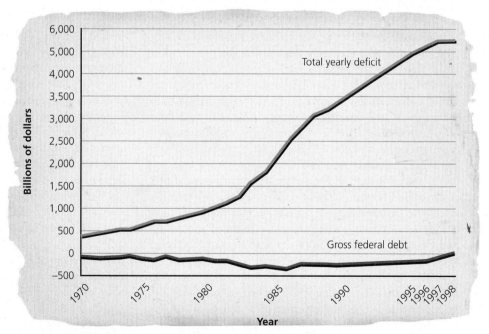

FIGURE 30.4 Federal Budget Deficit and National Debt, 1970–98
Tax cuts combined with huge increases in defense spending created a sharp increase in the budget deficit during the Republican administrations.

SOURCE: *Statistical abstract of the United States,* in Nash et al., *The American People,* 5th ed., p. 988.

Reaganomics also provided the backdrop for one of the biggest stock scandals in history. In late 1986, under investigation by the Securities and Exchange Commission (SEC), stock speculator Ivan Boesky admitted to using confidential information about upcoming corporate takeovers to trade stocks illegally. Just two years earlier the dapper Boesky boasted of making more than $100 million on just two deals. "Greed is all right," he told cheering business students in 1985. "Everybody should be a little bit greedy. . . . You shouldn't feel guilty." Once indicted, Boesky agreed to cooperate with SEC investigators and turned state's evidence to inform on several other operators.

On Wall Street, the bull market ended abruptly in the fall of 1987. After reaching its new high, the Dow Jones average of thirty leading industrial stocks began to slide downward and then crashed. On October 19, the Dow lost almost 23 percent of its value. The panic on the trading floors recalled the pandemonium set off by the 1929 stock market crash.

After the Dow Jones reached an all-time high at the end of August, stocks began to slide and then crashed. On October 19, 1987—"Black Monday"—traders at the New York Stock Exchange panicked, selling off stocks at such a rate that the market lost almost 23 percent of its value, marking the end of a five-year bull market. The market soon bounced back, and by September 1989 the Dow Jones had made up all its losses.

TABLE 30.1
Percentage Share of Aggregate Family Income, 1980–92

	1980	1992
Top 5 Percent	15.3%	17.6%
Highest Fifth	41.6	44.6
Fourth Fifth	24.3	24.0
Third Fifth	17.5	16.5
Second Fifth	11.6	10.5
Lowest Fifth	5.1	4.4

SOURCE: U.S. Bureau of the Census, *Current Population Reports: Consumer Incomes*, Series P-60, Nos. 167 and 184, 1990, 1993. U.S. federal data compiled by Ed Royce, Rollins College.

BEST OF TIMES, WORST OF TIMES

President Reagan set the tone for the era when he responded to a reporter's question asking him what was best about America. "What I want to see above all," Reagan replied, "is that this remains a country where someone can always get rich." The celebration of wealth, moneymaking, and entrepreneurship dominated much of popular culture, politics, and intellectual life in the 1980s, establishing a pattern that would persist into the twenty-first century.

Grimmer realities lay under the surface. Various data indicated that the nation was moving toward greater inequality, that the middle class was shrinking, and that poverty was on the rise. Analysts disagreed over the causes of these trends. However, after eight years of tax cuts, defense buildup, growing budget deficits, and record trade imbalances, many Americans feared that the future looked uncertain at best. Two of their most cherished beliefs—that life would improve for most people and their children, and that membership in the comfortable middle class was possible for all who worked for it—looked shaky by the end of the decade (see Table 30.1, 30.2, and 30.3).

TABLE 30.2
Share of Total Net Worth of American Families

	1983	1989
Richest 1 percent of families	31%	37%
Next richest 9 percent	35	31
Remaining 90 percent	33	32

SOURCE: *The New York Times*, April 21, 1992, from Federal Reserve Survey of Consumer Finances.

TABLE 30.3
Measures of Average Earnings, 1980–92 (In 1990 Dollars)

Year	Average Weekly Earnings	Average Hourly Earnings
1980	$373.81	$10.59
1985	363.30	10.41
1992	339.37	9.87

SOURCE: U.S. House of Representatives, Committee on Ways and Means, *Overview of Entitlement Programs* (Washington, DC: GPO, 1993), table 35, p. 557. U.S. federal data compiled by Ed Royce, Rollins College.

A TWO-TIERED SOCIETY

During the 1960s, despite the diversion of federal funds to military spending during the Vietnam War, President Johnson's Great Society brought a higher living standard to many Americans. By the time Carter took office in 1977, the sinking economy undercut these advances. Reagan's supply-side policies rescued the economy but widened the gap between rich and poor.

Affluent Americans made huge gains. In 1980 the top 5 percent of families earned 15.3 percent of the nation's total income; by 1992 their share had grown to 17.6 percent, an increase of 15 percent, with an average income of $156,000 a year. In 1980 the top 20 percent of families earned 41.6 percent of the nation's total; by 1992 their share had grown to 44.6 percent, an increase of about 7 percent, with an average income of $99,000 a year. In contrast, the bottom 40 percent of families had 16.7 percent of aggregate income in 1980; by 1992 their share had declined to 14.9 percent, a drop of nearly 2 percent, with an average income of about $16,500 a year.

The number and percentage of Americans in poverty grew at an alarming rate. The number of fully employed workers earning below poverty-level incomes increased by 50 percent. In 1979 the government classified about 26.1 million people as poor, 11.7 percent of the total population; by 1992 the number of poor had reached 36.9 million, or 14.5 percent of the population; and nearly 22 percent of all American children lived in poverty.

The gains for African Americans achieved by the civil rights movement steadily eroded. In 1954, the year of the *Brown* v. *Board of Education* decision, black families earned about 53 percent of the income of white families. This figure rose to 60 percent in 1969 and peaked at 62 percent in 1975. By 1979, black family income had fallen back to 57 percent and continued to slide during the next decade. By 1992, 33 percent of all African Americans lived in poverty, as did 29 percent of Hispanics (the rate was especially high among Puerto Ricans, yet low among Cuban Americans).

The majority of African Americans, six out of ten, lived in central cities with high unemployment rates, and the bleak prospects took a toll especially on the young. A black child was twice as likely as a white child to die before reaching the first birthday and four times more likely to be killed between the ages of one and four. Among black teenagers, the unemployment rate topped 40 percent; the few jobs available to them were among the lowest paid in the economy. Meanwhile, the high school dropout rate skyrocketed, and the number of serious crimes, such as burglary, car theft, and murder, perpetrated by children between the ages of ten and seventeen increased at an alarming rate.

Moreover, opportunities for advancement into the middle class were dwindling. By 1980 fewer black students attended integrated schools than in 1954, except in the South, where about half the black students did. The turnabout resulted in part from increasing opposition by white parents to court-ordered school busing, which had served since *Brown* v. *Board of Education* as the principal means of achieving racial balance in urban school systems. In 1975 a major clash between local white residents and black parents and their children occurred in Boston when a federally mandated busing plan was put into operation. During the 1980s the busing controversy nearly disappeared because federal judges hesitated to mandate such programs. But more important was the change in the racial composition of American cities. As a consequence of "white flight" to the suburbs, big-city school systems were serving mainly African American and Latino children, making the issue of integration moot (see Table 30.4, 30.5, and 30.6).

TABLE 30.4

Number of Poor, Rate of Poverty, and Poverty Line, 1979–92

	1979	1992
Millions of poor	26.1	36.9
Rate of poverty	11.7%	14.5%
Poverty line (family of four)	$7,412	$14,335

SOURCE: U.S. Bureau of the Census, *Current Population Reports: Consumer Income*, Series P-60, Nos. 161 and 185, 1988, 1993. U.S. federal data compiled by Ed Royce, Rollins College.

TABLE 30.5

Net New Job Creation by Wage Level, 1979–87

	Number of Net New Jobs Created	Percentage of Net New Jobs Created
Low-wage jobs (less than $11,611)	5,955,000	50.4%
Middle-wage jobs ($11,612 to $46,444)	4,448,000	31.7%
High-wage jobs ($46,445 and above)	1,405,000	11.9%

SOURCE: U.S. Senate, Committee on the Budget, *Wages of American Workers in the 1980s* (Washington, DC: U.S. Government Printing Office, 1988). U.S. federal data compiled by Ed Royce, Rollins College.

TABLE 30.6

Median Family Income and Ratio to White, by Race and Hispanic Origin, 1980–92 (in 1992 Dollars)

Year	All Races	White	Black	Hispanic
1980	$35,839	$37,341	$21,606 (58%)	$25,087 (67%)
1985	36,164	38,011	21,887 (58%)	25,596 (67%)
1992	36,812	38,909	21,161 (54%)	23,901 (61%)

SOURCE: U.S. Bureau of the Census, *Current Population Reports,* Series P-60, No. 184, 1993. U.S. federal data compiled by Ed Royce, Rollins College.

New legal rulings closed off important routes to employment in the professions. A 1978 U.S. Supreme Court decision dealt a sharp blow to affirmative action. To ensure acceptance of a minimum number of minority students, the University of California at Davis Medical School had established a quota system under affirmative action guidelines. In 1973 and 1974 the school denied admission to Allan Bakke, a white student. Bakke sued the university for "reverse discrimination," claiming his academic record was better than that of the sixteen minority students who were admitted. The U.S. Supreme Court handed down a five-to-four decision on June 18, 1978, stating that the use of an "explicit racial classification" in situations where no earlier discrimination had been demonstrated violated the equal protection clause of the Fourteenth Amendment. The Court ordered the University of California to admit Bakke to its medical school. During the 1980s, therefore, affirmative action programs could operate only when "a legacy of unequal treatment" could be proved.

THE FEMINIZATION OF POVERTY

While the gap between the rich and poor was growing to its widest point since 1945, the experience of poverty became the lot of primarily women and children. Throughout the era, women with young children continued to enter the labor force at a fast pace, but the majority found jobs that paid too little to support themselves and their children. It took the financial support of an adult male breadwinner to keep a family out of poverty.

The rising rate of divorce and desertion paralleled the increasing number of women and children in poverty. Most women usually lost ground following a divorce, which now affected nearly half of all new marriages. New no-fault divorce laws lowered or eradicated alimony, pushing even many middle-class women into poverty. Moreover, the majority of men defaulted on child-support payments within one year after separation. Whereas divorced men enjoyed a sizable increase in their standard of living, divorced women and their children suffered a formidable decline.

A sharp rise in teenage pregnancy reinforced this trend. By the end of the decade, nearly one in four babies was born to unmarried mothers. Many of these mothers were too young to have gained either the education or skills to secure jobs that paid enough to support themselves and their children. Even with Aid to Families with Dependent Children (AFDC) payments and food stamps, unemployed single mothers could rarely keep their families above the poverty line. By 1992, female-headed households, comprising 13.7 million people, accounted for 37 percent of the nation's poor. Among black women, the number of female-headed families increased in just one decade from 30 percent in 1970 to 47 percent in 1980. More than half of all black babies were now born to unmarried mothers. With few jobs for black men, especially for teenagers, the prospects for two-parent families were dim. But even in prosperous Orange County, by 1990 more than one in ten families was headed by a female householder with no husband present.

EPIDEMICS: DRUGS, AIDS, HOMELESSNESS

Drug addiction and drug trafficking took on frightening new dimensions in the early 1980s. Even the urban poor could afford the new arrival, "crack," a cheap, smokable, and highly addictive form of cocaine. As crack addiction spread, the drug trade assumed alarming new proportions both domestically and internationally. Crime rates rose dramatically, and over half the men arrested in the nation's largest cities tested positive for cocaine. The crack trade spawned a new generation of young drug dealers who were willing to risk jail and death for enormous profits. In city after city, drug wars over turf took the lives of dealers and innocents, both caught in the escalating violence.

In 1982, the Reagan administration declared a highly publicized "war on drugs," a multibillion-dollar paramilitary operation to halt drug trafficking. Critics charged that the war on drugs focused on supply from abroad when it needed to look at demand here at home. They urged more federal money for drug education, treatment, and rehabilitation, dismissing as insufficient First Lady Nancy Reagan's "Just Say No" campaign aimed at children. Drug addiction and drug use, they argued, were primarily health problems, not law enforcement issues.

In 1981 doctors in Los Angeles, San Francisco, and New York began encountering a puzzling new medical phenomenon. Young homosexual men were dying suddenly from

In May 1987, members of the Lesbian and Gay Community Services in downtown Manhattan organized ACT-UP. Protesting what they perceived to be the Reagan administration's mismanagement of the AIDS crisis, they used nonviolent direct action, which often took the form of dramatic acts of civil disobedience. ACT-UP grew to more than seventy chapters in the United States and around the world.

opportunistic infections such as pneumonia and cancer caused by a mysterious viral disease that damaged the body's immune system. Researchers at the Centers for Disease Control (CDC) in Atlanta called the new disease Acquired Immune Deficiency Syndrome (AIDS) and identified the means of transmission as the exchange of bodily fluids, such as semen and blood. Because full-blown AIDS might not appear for years after initial exposure to the virus, one could unknowingly infect others. Tests soon became available to determine whether one carried HIV, but there was no cure. Because the majority of early victims were homosexual men who acquired AIDS through sexual contact, many Americans perceived AIDS as a disease of homosexuals. But other victims became infected through intravenous drug use, blood transfusions, heterosexual transmission, or birth to AIDS-carrying mothers.

AIDS provoked fear, anguish, and anger. It also brought an upsurge of organization and political involvement. In city after city, the gay community responded to the AIDS crisis with energy and determination. Most gay men changed their sexual habits, practicing "safe sex" to lessen the chances of infection. The Reagan administration, playing to antigay prejudices, largely ignored the epidemic. One important exception was Surgeon General C. Everett Koop, who urged a comprehensive sex education program in the nation's schools.

Homelessness emerged as a chronic social problem during the 1980s. Often disoriented, shoeless, and forlorn, street people in growing numbers slept over heating grates, on subways, and in parks. Homeless people wandered city sidewalks panhandling and struggling to find scraps of food. In the early 1980s, the Department of Housing and Urban Development placed the number of the nation's homeless at between 250,000 and 350,000. But advocates for the homeless estimated that the number was as high as 3 million.

Who were the homeless? Analysts agreed that at least a third were mental patients who had been discharged from psychiatric hospitals amid the deinstitutionalization trend of the 1970s. Many more were alcoholics and drug addicts unable to hold jobs. But the ranks of the homeless also included female-headed families, battered women, Vietnam veterans, AIDS victims, and elderly people with no place to go. Some critics pointed to the decline in decent housing for poor people and the deterioration of the nation's health care system as the major causes.

TOWARD A NEW WORLD ORDER

Throughout his presidency, Reagan campaigned to restore American leadership in world affairs. He revived Cold War patriotism and championed U.S. interventionism in the Third World, especially in the Caribbean and Central America. His infusion of funds into national security programs had enormous consequences for the domestic economy as well as for America's position as a global power. Yet along with hard-line exhortations against the Soviet Union and international terrorism, the Reagan administration also pursued a less ideological, more pragmatic approach in key foreign policy decisions. Most important, sweeping and unanticipated internal changes within the Soviet Union made the entire Cold War framework of international affairs largely irrelevant by the late 1980s.

THE EVIL EMPIRE

In the early 1980s, the Reagan administration made vigorous anti-Communist rhetoric the centerpiece of its foreign policy. In a sharp turn from President Nixon's pursuit of détente and President Carter's focus on human rights, Reagan described the Soviet Union as "an evil empire . . . the focus of evil in the modern world."

Administration officials argued that during the 1970s the nation's military strength had fallen dangerously behind that of the Soviet Union. Critics disputed this assertion, pointing out that the Soviet advantage in intercontinental ballistic missiles (ICBMs) was offset by U.S. superiority in submarine-based forces and strategic aircraft. Polls showed that more than 70 percent of Americans favored not an escalation of the arms race but instead a nuclear freeze with the Soviet Union. In June 1982, three-quarters of a million people in the largest political rally in American history demonstrated in New York City for a halt to spending on and deployment of nuclear weapons. Nonetheless, the administration proceeded with plans to enlarge America's nuclear strike force.

In 1983 President Reagan introduced an unsettling new element into superpower relations when he presented his Strategic Defense Initiative (SDI), the plan for a space-based ballistic-missile defense system that journalists dubbed "Star Wars," after the popular Hollywood film series. This proposal for a five-year, $26 billion program promised to give the United States the capacity to shoot down incoming missiles with laser beams and homing rockets. As critics pointed out, this plan was unworkable, impossibly expensive, and likely to destabilize existing arms treaties. The Reagan administration pressed ahead, spending $17 billion in research before the president left office but without achieving any convincing results. The prospect of meaningful arms control dimmed in this atmosphere, and U.S.–Soviet relations deteriorated.

THE REAGAN DOCTRINE AND CENTRAL AMERICA

Declaring the "Vietnam syndrome" over, the president confidently reasserted America's right to intervene anywhere in the world to "roll back" communism by supplying overt and covert aid to anti-Communist resistance movements. The so-called Reagan Doctrine, shaped by conservative scholars affiliated with the Heritage Foundation, assumed that all political instability in the Third World resulted not from indigenous factors such as poverty or corruption but from the pernicious influence of the Soviet Union. It found its most important expression in Central America, where the United States hoped to reestablish its historical control over the Caribbean basin (see Map 30.5).

The Reagan administration believed that all problems throughout Central America stemmed from "Fidel Castro's Soviet directed, armed, and financed marauders" and required a military solution. Between 1980 and 1983 the United States poured more military aid into Central America than it had during the previous thirty years. In

October 1983, the administration directed U.S. Marines to invade Grenada, claiming that the tiny island had become a Cuban military base and, therefore, threatened the hemisphere. The easy triumph proved popular with most Grenadans and Americans. In the larger and more complicated nations of El Salvador and Nicaragua, this sort of unilateral military action proved politically and strategically more difficult to carry out.

In El Salvador, the Reagan administration continued to support the pro-American yet highly repressive regime, which received more U.S. economic assistance than any other Latin American country. By 1983 right-wing death squads had tortured and assassinated thousands of opposition leaders. The election in 1984 of centrist president José Napoleón Duarte failed to end the bloody civil war. Some 53,000 Salvadorans, more than one in every hundred, lost their lives in the conflict.

In Nicaragua, the Reagan administration claimed that the revolutionary Sandinista government posed "an unusual and extraordinary threat to the national security." U.S. officials accused the Sandinistas of shipping arms to antigovernment rebels in El Salvador. In December 1981, Reagan approved a CIA plan to arm and organize Nicaraguan exiles, known as Contras, to fight against the Sandinista government. As Reagan escalated this undeclared war, the aim became not merely the cutting of Nicaraguan aid to Salvadoran rebels but also the overthrow of the Sandinista regime itself.

In 1984 the CIA secretly mined Nicaraguan harbors. When Nicaragua won a judgment against the United States in the World Court over this violation of its sovereignty, the Reagan administration refused to recognize the court's jurisdiction in the case and ignored the verdict. Predictably, the U.S. covert war pushed the Sandinistas closer to Cuba and the Soviet bloc. Meanwhile, American grassroots opposition to Contra aid grew more vocal and widespread. A number of American communities set up sister-city projects offering humanitarian and technical assistance to Nicaraguan communities. Scores of American churches offered sanctuary to political refugees from Central America.

In 1984 Congress sought to rein in the covert war by passing the Boland Amendment, introduced by Democratic Representative Edward Boland of Massachusetts. It forbade government agencies from supporting "directly or indirectly military or paramilitary operations" in Nicaragua. Denied funding by Congress, President Reagan turned to the National Security Council (NSC) to find a way to keep the Contra war going. Between 1984 and 1986, the NSC staff secretly assisted the Contras, raising $37 million in aid from foreign countries and private contributors, creating the largest mercenary army in hemispheric history. In 1987 the revelation of this unconstitutional scheme exploded before the public as part of the Iran-Contra affair, the most damaging political scandal of the Reagan years.

MAP EXPLORATION

To explore an interactive version of this map, go to **www.prenhall.com/faragher6/map30.5**

Countries influenced by U.S.- Latin American activities

UNITED STATES

Gulf of Mexico

Thousands of Cubans come to U.S. Apr–Sept 1980

BAHAMAS

ATLANTIC OCEAN

CUBA

Virgin Islands (U.S.)   Virgin Islands (Br.)

JAMAICA

HAITI   DOMINICAN REPUBLIC

Puerto Rico (U.S.)

ANTIGUA and BARBUDA

Guadeloupe

ST. CHRISTOPHER-NEVIS   DOMINICA

Staging area for Nicaraguan anti-Sandinista rebels aided by U.S.

Pro–U.S. regime elected Nov 1980

Pro–Castro regime in power Mar 1979; U.S. forces land Oct 1983; Election held Dec 1984

Martinique

ST. LUCIA

MEXICO   BELIZE

Caribbean Sea

BARBADOS

GUATEMALA   HONDURAS

Sandinista rebels in power July 1979

GRENADA

ST. VINCENT AND THE GRENADINES

Continued guerrilla activity against rightist regimes

EL SALVADOR   NICARAGUA

Panama Canal Treaties, 1978: Canal Zone under Panamanian control, 1979 Canal under Panamanian control by 2000

TRINIDAD AND TOBAGO

Civil war begins, 1979

VENEZUELA

U.S. sends military advisors early 1981   COSTA RICA

PACIFIC OCEAN

PANAMA

GUYANA

COLOMBIA

BRAZIL

MAP 30.5 The United States in Central America, 1978–90 U.S. intervention in Central America reached a new level of intensity with the so-called Reagan Doctrine. The bulk of U.S. aid came in the form of military support for the government of El Salvador and the Contra rebels in Nicaragua.

THE MIDDLE EAST AND THE IRAN-CONTRA SCANDAL

In 1987 the revelations of what became known as the Iran-Contra scandal laid bare the continuing contradictions and difficulties of the U.S. role in world affairs. The scandal also revealed how overzealous and secretive government officials subverted the Constitution and compromised presidential authority under the guise of patriotism.

The threat of Middle Eastern terrorism, Reagan insisted, loomed as one of the most serious threats to U.S. national security. "Let terrorists beware," he declared, "our policy will be one of swift and effective retribution." Despite this warning, terrorist acts, including the seizing of

Western hostages and the bombing of commercial airplanes and cruise ships, continued to redefine the politics of the region. Many of these attacks were desperate attempts by small pro-Palestinian sects or Islamic extremists opposed to U.S. support of Israel. However, the Reagan administration insisted that behind international terrorism lay the sinister influence and money of the Soviet bloc, the Ayatollah Khomeini of Iran, and Libyan leader Muammar el-Qaddafi. In the spring of 1986 the president, eager to demonstrate his antiterrorist resolve, ordered the bombing of Tripoli in a failed effort to kill Qaddafi, whom he called "the mad dog of the Middle East."

As a fierce war between Iran and Iraq escalated, the administration tilted publicly toward Iraq to please the Arab

MAP EXPLORATION

To explore an interactive version of this map, go to **www.prenhall.com/faragher6/map30.6**

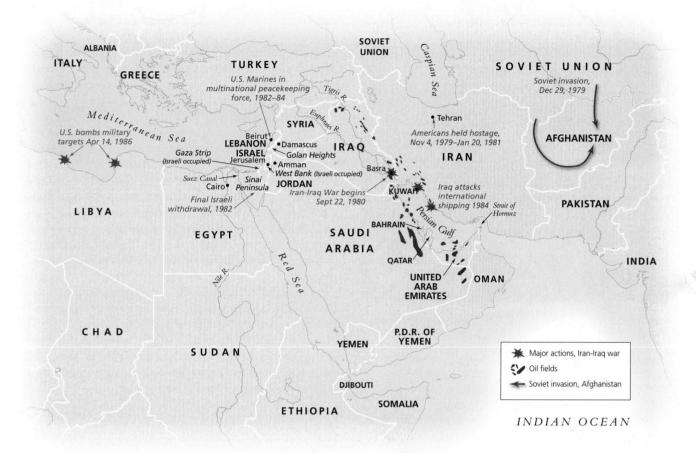

Legend:
- Major actions, Iran-Iraq war
- Oil fields
- Soviet invasion, Afghanistan

MAP 30.6 **The United States in the Middle East in the 1980s** The volatile combination of ancient religious and ethnic rivalries, oil, and emerging Islamic fundamentalism made peace and stability elusive in the Middle East.

states around the Persian Gulf. Iraq's dictator, Saddam Hussein, was treated as an ally and provided much sophisticated weaponry. But in 1986 Reagan's advisers changed course and began secret negotiations with the revolutionary Iranian government. They eventually offered to supply Iran with weapons for use against Iraq in exchange for help in securing the release of Americans who were being held hostage by radical Islamic groups in Lebanon (see Map 30.6).

Subsequent disclosures elevated the arms-for-hostages deal into a major scandal. Some of the money from the arms deal had been secretly diverted into covert aid for the Nicaraguan Contras. The American public soon learned the sordid details from investigative journalists and through televised congressional hearings held during the summer of 1987. In order to escape congressional oversight of the CIA, Reagan and CIA Director William Casey had essentially

turned the National Security Council, previously a policy-coordinating body, into an operational agency. Under the direction of National Security Advisers Robert McFarlane and later Admiral John Poindexter, the NSC had sold weapons and missiles to the Iranians, using Israel as a go-between. Millions of dollars from these sales were then given to the Contras in blatant and illegal disregard of the Boland Amendment.

In the televised congressional hearings, NSC staffer and Marine Lieutenant Colonel Oliver North emerged as the principal actor in what he euphemistically referred to as the "Enterprise." North defended his actions in the name of patriotism. Some Americans saw the dashing North as a hero; most were appalled by his and Poindexter's blithe admissions that they had lied to Congress, shredded evidence, and refused to keep the president fully informed in order to guarantee his "plausible deniability." A blue-ribbon commission

Lt. Col. Oliver North, who once described the scheme to sell arms to Iran to help the Contras as a "neat idea," is shown testifying in July 1987 before a joint Congressional committee formed to investigate the Iran-Contra affair.

concluded that Reagan himself "did not seem to be aware" of the policy or its consequences. But the report also offered a stunning portrait of a president who was at best confused and far removed from critical policy-making decisions.

Ultimately, the Iran-Contra investigation raised more questions than it answered. The full role of CIA Director Casey, who died in 1987, particularly his relationships with North and the president, remained murky. The role of Vice President George H. W. Bush remained mysterious as well. Both North and Poindexter were convicted of felonies, but higher courts overturned their convictions on technical grounds. Reagan held fast to his plea of ignorance. When pressed on what had happened, he repeatedly claimed, "I'm still trying to find out."

In December 1992, following his reelection defeat and six years after the scandal broke, President George H. W. Bush granted pardons to six key players in the Iran-Contra affair, making it unlikely that the truth about the arms-for-hostages affair would ever be known.

THE COLLAPSE OF COMMUNISM

Meanwhile, momentous political changes within the Soviet Union led ultimately to the end of the Cold War itself. Leonid Brezhnev, who had served as general secretary of the Soviet Communist Party since 1964, died in 1982. His successors, Yuri Andropov and Konstantin Chernenko, both died after brief terms. But in 1985 a reform-minded leader, Mikhail Gorbachev, took over as Soviet leader. Although a lifelong Communist, Gorbachev represented a new generation of disenchanted party members who wanted to end the Cold War.

Gorbachev and his advisers opened up political discussion and even encouraged critiques of the Soviet economy and political culture. The government released longtime dissidents from prison and took the first halting steps toward profit-based, private initiatives in the economy. This "new thinking" inspired an unprecedented wave of diverse, often critical perspectives in Soviet art, literature, journalism, and scholarship.

In Gorbachev's view, improving the economic performance of the Soviet system depended first on halting the arms race. Over 10 percent of the Soviet GNP went to defense spending, while the majority of its citizens could not find even the most basic consumer items in shops. Fully aware that the Soviet Union could not compete with Reagan's Star Wars program, Gorbachev took the lead to end the arms race with the United States. The historical ironies were stunning. Reagan had made militant anticommunism the centerpiece of his administration, but between 1985 and 1988 he had four separate summit meetings with the new Soviet leader. Culminating in a modest treaty allowing comprehensive, mutual, on-site inspections, the meetings also provided an important psychological breakthrough. At one of the summits a Soviet leader humorously announced, "We are going to do something terrible to you Americans—we are going to deprive you of an enemy."

Indeed, the reforms initiated by Gorbachev—and, more immediately, the failed Soviet war in Afghanistan—led to the dissolution of the Soviet Union and to the end of Communist rule throughout Eastern Europe. Beginning in June 1989, when Poland held its first free elections since the close of World War II in 1945, prodemocracy demonstrations forced out longtime Communist leaders in Hungary, Czechoslovakia, Bulgaria, and Romania. Most dramatic of all were the events in East Germany. The Berlin Wall, for thirty years the ultimate symbol of Cold War division, came down on November 9, 1989. Hundreds of thousands of East Germans immediately rushed into West Berlin, paving the way for German reunification the following year.

Political changes in the Soviet Union came more slowly, accompanied by such drastically reduced living standards that successful transition to a market economy and democratic political system was uncertain. In March 1989 the Soviet Union held its first open elections since 1917, and a new Congress of People's Deputies replaced the old Communist Party–dominated Supreme Soviet. In the next elections the following year, party officials in key Russian cities went down in defeat. In August 1991 party hard-liners made a final attempt to hold on to the old order and staged a coup, placing President Gorbachev under house arrest. The coup quickly failed, and meanwhile most of the fifteen republics had announced their withdrawal from the Soviet Union. On Christmas Day 1991 the weary and bitter presi-

In August 1961, the border between East and West Berlin was closed, and the Berlin Wall was built to divide the city into two sections. After twenty-eight years, on November 9, 1989, the government in East Germany lifted travel restrictions. This photograph shows demonstrators defiantly tearing down the Berlin Wall, which for three decades had embodied the political divisions of the Cold War.

dent of the Soviet Union recognized the new Commonwealth of Independent States and resigned.

The Soviet Union's dissolution marked the end of the great superpower rivalry that had shaped American foreign policy and domestic politics for nearly a half century. Reagan's successor, President George H. W. Bush, proclaimed the end of the Cold War as an event of "biblical proportions."

"A KINDER, GENTLER NATION"

Hoping to ride on Reagan's coattails during his 1988 presidential campaign, George Herbert Walker Bush also made a clear-cut pledge to voters: "Read my lips: no new taxes." He won the general election handily over Massachusetts governor George Dukakis with forty out of fifty states and 56 percent of the popular vote and concluded that, with such widespread support, he could set his own agenda. President Bush began to distance himself from Reagan, promising in his inaugural address to deliver a "kinder, gentler nation."

In international affairs, President Bush had prepared well to provide leadership in a dramatically changing world. Before serving as vice president, he held several major appointive offices that involved him directly in foreign policy—UN ambassador, envoy to China, and director of the CIA. However, as president, he soon found himself facing a host of problems complicated rather than resolved by the end of the Cold War. Somewhat belatedly, President Bush announced that it was "time to move beyond containment to a new policy for the 1990s" without specifying what that new policy would be. He also faced a Congress with a Democratic majority.

REAGAN'S SUCCESSOR: GEORGE H. W. BUSH

President Bush carried over several policies from the Reagan administration, such as the war on illegal drugs. He appointed William Bennett as the new "drug czar" and outlined a plan to increase funding for more police and prisons. He also fortified the border patrols in an attempt to stem the flow of drugs from Latin America. In December 1989, President Bush sent U.S. troops to Panama on a mission to capture General Manuel Noriega, an international drug dealer who at one time had been on the CIA payroll. Thousands of Panamanians died before Noriega was taken into custody and brought to the United States to stand trial on drug trafficking and racketeering charges. During the Bush presidency, the federal budget for drug control tripled.

As a self-proclaimed "compassionate" Republican, President Bush endorsed the Americans with Disabilities Act, which had been introduced during the Reagan administration and now passed through Congress. The act penalized employers who discriminated against qualified workers with disabilities and required employers and local governments to provide access to their facilities. Against the opposition of many business leaders, President Bush signed the bill in July 1990. Showing less compassion, he vetoed a family-leave bill that would have provided up to six months of unpaid leave to workers with new children or with family emergencies.

THE PERSIAN GULF WAR

President Bush soon saw that the end of the Cold War did not bring world peace but instead let loose a multitude of furies in the form of renewed nationalism, ethnic and religious conflict, and widening divisions between the world's rich and poor. Just as dramatically, as the old geopolitical order disappeared, ideological rivalry shifted to the Middle East and other areas in the world where Islamic militants had forcefully turned against the West.

On August 2, 1990, Iraqi troops swept into neighboring Kuwait and quickly seized control of its rich oil fields. The motives of Saddam Hussein, Iraq's military dictator, were mixed. Like most Iraqis, Hussein believed that oil-rich Kuwait was actually an ancient province of Iraq that had been illegally carved away by British imperial agents in the 1920s as part of the dismemberment of the Ottoman Empire. Control of Kuwait would give Saddam Hussein control of its huge oil reserves, as well as major Persian Gulf ports for his almost landlocked country. Just emerging from an exhausting and inconclusive eight-year war with Iran, Iraqis also bitterly resented Kuwait's production of oil beyond OPEC quotas, which had helped send the world price of oil plummeting from the highs of the 1970s and early 1980s.

The United States responded swiftly to news of the invasion. Its first concern was that Saddam Hussein might also attack Saudi Arabia, which the United States had defined as vital to its interests as far back as 1943. On August 15, President Bush ordered U.S. forces to Saudi Arabia and the Persian Gulf, calling the action Operation Desert Shield. The United States also led a broad coalition in the United Nations, including the Soviet Union, that condemned the Iraqi invasion of Kuwait and declared strict economic sanctions against Iraq if it did not withdraw.

In early November, President Bush announced a change in policy to what he called "an offensive military option." Administration officials now demonized Saddam Hussein as another Adolf Hitler. The UN sanctions failed to budge Hussein from Kuwait, and the drift to war now looked inevitable. In January 1991, Congress narrowly passed a joint resolution authorizing the president to use military force.

After a last-minute UN peace mission failed to break the deadlock, President Bush announced, on January 16, 1991, the start of Operation Desert Storm. U.S.-led air strikes began forty-two days of massive bombing of Iraqi positions in Kuwait, as well as Baghdad and other Iraqi cities. The ground war, which began on February 24, took only 100 hours to force Saddam Hussein's troops out of Kuwait. Hussein's vaunted military machine—the fourth largest army in the world—turned out to be surprisingly weak. U.S. forces lost only 184 dead, compared to nearly 100,000 Iraqi deaths, mostly from the bombing.

Victory in the Gulf War rekindled national pride, and many Americans declared the end of the "Vietnam syndrome." But for the 18 million people of Iraq, it produced the worst possible outcome. The ecological damage in the Gulf region was extensive and long-lasting. Oil fires burned out of control. Human rights groups reported an appalling death toll among civilians.

The limits of military power to solve complex political and economic disputes became clear in the aftermath of victory. The Persian Gulf War failed to dislodge Saddam Hussein, who remained in power despite CIA attempts to overthrow him and repeated bombings of Iraqi military positions. Iraqi Kurds, who had supported the U.S. invasion in hopes it would topple Saddam, faced violent reprisals, including gassing and chemical weapons, from the Iraqi army. Trade sanctions did little to weaken his rule, although the economic boycott, which brought increasing hardship to the civilian population, eventually divided the Western powers, leaving the United States and Great Britain isolated in their sanctions against Iraq.

The repercussions of the Gulf War were long-lasting. The leading U.S. ally in the region, the oil-rich kingdom of Saudi Arabia, had served as the launching pad for the invasion of Iraq, and following the war the Saudis had allowed the continuing presence of U.S. troops and weapons. This occupation of Saudi territory, which included Islamic holy sites, intensified the hatred of Americans among many Muslims and prompted appeals for revenge.

Among those actively opposed to the U.S. role in the region was Saudi millionaire Osama bin Laden, just a few years earlier a close ally of the United States during the Soviet invasion of Afghanistan. He now turned squarely against his former arms suppliers and CIA contacts. Using his own funds and a vast tribal network, bin Laden built his shadowy Al Qaeda organization, training small groups in terror tactics to be used against Western interests, particularly to force U.S. troops out of the Middle East.

THE ECONOMY AND THE ELECTION OF 1992

Politically, the Persian Gulf War marked the high point of Bush's popularity. His approval rating reached nearly 90 percent, higher than President Roosevelt's during World War II. Basking in his success, Bush proclaimed the United States the leader in the creation of a "new world order" that would be "freer from the threat of terror, stronger in the pursuit of justice, and more secure in the quest for peace, an era in which the nations of the world, East and West, North and South, can prosper and live in harmony."

However, it was the economy rather than foreign affairs that fueled the 1992 presidential election campaign. Republicans took credit for forcing the fall of communism and reviving America's military strength. But they had also promised to cut government spending and balance the budget. Just as Bush was about to take office in 1989, many of the nation's savings and loan institutions, which had been deregulated by Reagan, collapsed. Then, on Friday, October 13, 1989, the stock market took its worst nosedive since 1987, signaling a major recession. With the national debt reaching $4 trillion, the paradoxes of the Reagan-Bush years became readily apparent.

American consumers had been spending extravagantly, many falling deep into debt, and now, with the prospect of a recession, they pulled back. Real estate prices plummeted, unemployment hovered at 7 percent, and many businesses filed for bankruptcy. Eventually, Bush reneged on his campaign promise and worked with Democrats in Congress to raise taxes. By the end of 1991, the president's performance rating had dropped to just 51 percent.

As the 1992 campaign heated up, President Bush found himself facing a formidable opponent, William Jefferson Clinton. Personable, articulate, and highly intelligent, Bill Clinton won the Democratic nomination on the first ballot and chose Tennessee senator Albert Gore as his

CHRONOLOGY

1973   *Roe* v. *Wade* legalizes abortion

Arab embargo sparks oil crisis in the United States

1974   Richard Nixon resigns presidency; Gerald Ford takes office

President Ford pardons Nixon and introduces anti-inflation program

1975   Unemployment rate reaches nearly 9 percent

South Vietnamese government falls to communists

Antibusing protests break out in Boston

1976   Percentage of African Americans attending college peaks at 9.3 percent and begins a decline

Democrat Jimmy Carter defeats incumbent Gerald Ford in presidential election

1977   President Carter announces human rights as major tenet in foreign policy

1978   *Bakke* v. *University of California* decision places new limits on affirmative action programs

Camp David meeting sets terms for Middle East peace

California passes Proposition 13, cutting taxes and government social programs

1979   Three Mile Island nuclear accident threatens a meltdown

Nicaraguan Revolution overthrows Anastasio Somoza

Iranian fundamentalists seize the U.S. embassy in Tehran and hold U.S. citizens hostage for 444 days

Soviets invade Afghanistan

1980   Inflation reaches 13.5 percent

Republican Ronald Reagan defeats incumbent Jimmy Carter in presidential election

1981   Reagan administration initiates major cuts in taxes and domestic spending

Military buildup accelerates

AIDS is recognized and named

1982   Economic recession grips the nation

1983   Reagan announces the Strategic Defense Initiative, labeled "Star Wars" by the media

241 marines killed in Beirut terrorist bombing

1985   Mikhail Gorbachev initiates reforms in the Soviet Union

1986   Iran-Contra hearings before Congress reveal arms-for-hostages deal and funds secretly and illegally diverted to Nicaraguan rebels

1988   Republican George H. W. Bush defeats Michael Dukakis in presidential election

Communist authority collapses in Eastern Europe

1990   Iraqi invasion of Kuwait leads to massive U.S. military presence in the Persian Gulf

1991   Operation Desert Storm forces Iraq out of Kuwait

Soviet Union dissolves into Commonwealth of Independent States

1992   Democrat Bill Clinton defeats incumbent George H. W. Bush and independent candidate Ross Perot in the presidential election

running mate. In the Democrats' campaign headquarters a sign humorously reminded the staff: "It's the economy, stupid." Candidate Clinton promised economic leadership. While promising deficit reduction and a tax cut for the middle class, he also took advantage of Bush's betrayal of his own campaign promise not to raise taxes.

Clinton effectively adopted many of the conservative themes that proved so advantageous to Republicans over the past twelve years. He called for "responsibility" on the part of recipients of social programs and spoke of the importance of stable families, promised to be tough on crime and to reduce the bureaucracy, and stressed the need for encouraging private investment to create new jobs. Economic issues also fueled the independent campaign of Texas billionaire H. Ross Perot, who with his folksy East Texas twang argued that someone as successful in business as himself was better qualified to solve the nation's economic woes than Washington insiders.

At the polls in November, Orange County and the nation came in together, each giving Clinton 43 percent of the popular vote. He also carried thirty-two states. Although failing to carry a single state, Perot scored 19 percent of the popular vote. The newly elected Clinton interpreted Perot's relative success at the polls as a mandate to focus, as he put it, "like a laser beam on the economy."

CONCLUSION

The success of conservatives to halt and in some cases actually reverse key trends in American politics, from Franklin Roosevelt's New Deal to Lyndon Johnson's Great Society,

was made possible by the legacy of the Cold War and the trauma of defeat in Vietnam. But it also owed a great deal to a deepening anxiety about cultural changes and a growing pessimism about the ability of politicians to offer solutions, especially at the national level. Those community activists struggling to broaden the 1960s' protest movements into an updated, comprehensive reformism encompassing such issues as feminism, ecology, and affirmative action readily recognized that the liberal era had ended.

President Ronald Reagan, a charismatic figure who sometimes invented his own past and seemed to believe in it, offered remedies for a weary and nostalgic nation. By insisting that the rebellious 1960s had been a terrible mistake, lowering national self-confidence along with public morals and faith in the power of economic individualism, he successfully wedded the conservatism of Christian fundamentalists, many suburbanites, and Sunbelt voters with the more traditional conservatism of corporate leaders. In many respects, the Reagan administration actually continued and added ideological fervor to the downscaling of government services and upscaling of military spending already evident under President Jimmy Carter, while offering supporters the hope of a sweeping conservative revolution.

In the end, critics suggested, supporters of Ronald Reagan and Reaganism could not go back to the 1950s— just as the erstwhile rebels of the 1960s could not go back to their favorite era. Economically, conservatives achieved many of their goals, including widespread acceptance of sharper economic divisions within society and fewer restraints on corporations and investments. But socially and culturally, their grasp was much less secure.

— REVIEW QUESTIONS

1. Evaluate the significance of the major population shifts in the United States from the 1940s through the 1970s. What was their impact on local and national politics?

2. Discuss the connections between the energy crisis and the rise of the environmental movement.

3. Interpret the decline of liberalism and the rise of conservative political groups. How did these changes affect the outcome of presidential elections?

4. Was the Iran hostage crisis a turning point in American politics or only a thorn in Carter's

reelection campaign? How did the Iran-Contra scandal affect the Republicans?

5. Describe the central philosophical assumptions behind Reaganomics. What were the key policies by which it was implemented? To what extent were these policies a break with previous economic approaches?

6. Evaluate Reagan's foreign policy. How did it differ from Carter's approach to foreign affairs?

7. Analyze the key structural factors underlying recent changes in American economic and cultural life. Do you see any political solutions for the growth of poverty and inequality?

— RECOMMENDED READING

Lee Edwards, *The Conservative Revolution: The Movement That Remade America* (1999). Traces the rise of modern

political conservatism from its origins in Cold War anticommunism. A longtime conservative activist and writer, Edwards credits much of Reagan's success in office to the presence of a strong, vital, and grassroots conservative movement.

David Farber, *Taken Hostage: The Iran Hostage Crisis and America's First Encounter with Radical Islam* (2004). Examines the events of November 1979, emphasizing the larger context of a decade of uncertainty and anxiety. Farber also considers the meaning of Carter's hostage crisis for the larger war on terrorism at the turn of the century.

Frances FitzGerald, *Way Out There in the Blue: Reagan, Star Wars, and the End of the Cold War* (2000). A well-documented study of the conservative mood that made Star Wars both credible and popular among conservatives. FitzGerald provides a sweeping historical context for Star Wars with special attention given to the impact of the Cold War on traditional isolationism.

John Karaagac, *Between Promise and Policy: Ronald Reagan and Conservative Reformism* (2000). Assesses Reagan's major polities, such as increased funding for federal government and regulatory reform, in light of his professed conservative ideals. Karaagac argues that Reagan wielded ideology as a political weapon to gain support for his programs while acting pragmatically and with a good deal of flexibility on particular issues.

Melani McAlister, *Epic Encounters: Culture, Media, and U.S. Interests in the Middle East, 1945–2000* (2001). A close reading of American popular culture, including films, television news broadcasts, museum exhibits, and fiction, representing relationships between the Middle East and the United States. McAlister considers the importance of the abundance of oil and the Islamic religion of the Middle East as factors shaping U.S. foreign policy.

Lisa McGirr, *Suburban Warriors: The Origins of the New American Right* (2001). Traces the resurgence of American conservatism by analyzing issues that galvanized grassroots middle-class activism in southern California in the 1960s and 1970s.

Michael Schaller, *Right Turn: American Life in the Reagan-Bush Era, 1980–1992* (2007). A succinct overview of the rise of conservatism and its impact on national and foreign policies, with ample attention paid to major developments in American society and culture during the era.

Bruce J. Schulman, *The Seventies: The Great Shift in American Culture, Society, and Politics* (2001). Examines the move away from the public-spirited universalism that characterized the New Deal and civil rights movement toward the sovereignty of the free market and celebration of private life. With a geopolitical twist that emphasizes the increasing importance of the Sunbelt, Schulman argues that the conservative 1980s actually began a decade earlier.

Judith Stein, *Running Steel, Running America: Race, Economic Policy, and the Decline of Liberalism* (1998). Discusses the impact of the decline of the U.S. steel industry on its large African American labor force. Stein analyzes trade policy, especially under Carter, that benefited foreign steel producers and led to the closing of American plants.

Robert A. Strong, *Working in the World: Jimmy Carter and the Making of American Foreign Policy* (2000). A collection of nine case studies of international affairs covering Carter's presidency. Strong's goal is not to provide new insight into the central crises of the era but to open a window to the range of presidential responsibilities in the diplomatic arena.

Andrew Szasz, *EcoPopulism: Toxic Waste and the Movement for Environmental Justice* (1994). A careful analysis of a turning point in federal regulation of toxic waste. Szasz shows how the prevention of pollution, previously considered a local issue, through strengthened state and federal regulations became a national issue and a springboard for the environmental movement.

J. Samuel Walker, *Three Mile Island: A Nuclear Crisis in Historical Perspective* (2004). Sponsored by the United States Nuclear Regulatory Commission, this book provides a detailed description of the "accident" at Three Mile Island and a broad historical context, including the growth of commercial nuclear power and the emergence of forces in opposition to this source of energy.

Winifred D. Wandersee, *On the Move: American Women in the 1970s* (1988). A highly readable overview of the changes that brought American women into political life but also kept them at the margins of power. This study includes a close description of the National Organization for Women as well as media personalities, such as Jane Fonda, who gave feminism a public face.

Natasha Zaretsky, *No Direction Home: The American Family and the Fear of National Decline, 1868–1980* (2007). Studies the fears American faced in the aftermath of the Vietnam War, a sense of imperiled national identity fatefully linked to images of a family similarly endangered.

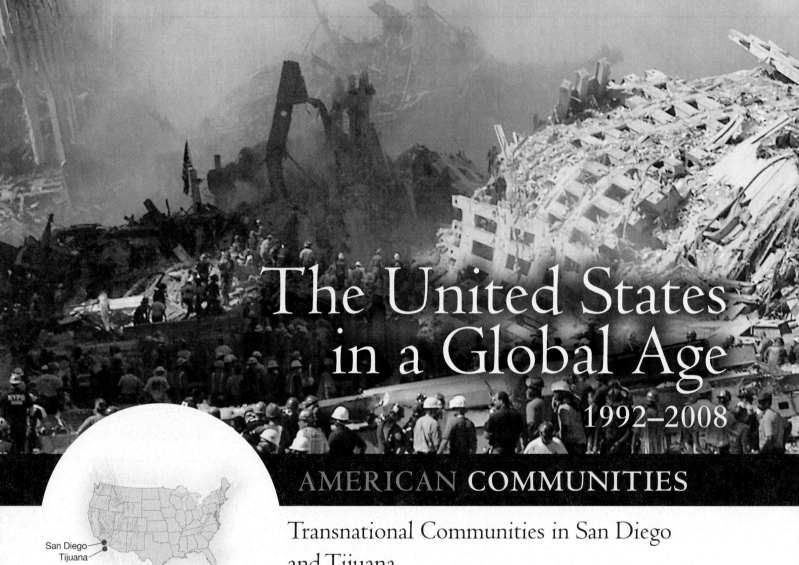

The United States in a Global Age
1992–2008

Transnational Communities in San Diego and Tijuana

As the new millennium began, Norma Ojeida crossed the U.S.-Mexico border on a daily basis, leaving for work in the morning and returning home at night. She held a position at a high-powered research institute in Rosarito, a suburb of the booming city of Tijuana in Baja, California, Mexico, and made her home in suburban San Diego, in the border community of Chula Vista, where nearly half the population was Hispanic. The second largest city in San Diego County was known locally as "Chulajuana" because it was just as much a suburb of Tijuana as of San Diego. Ojeida therefore had plenty of company in making the daily journey across the busiest border crossing in North America. Thousands of other affluent, educated professionals made the same trip southward, while a steady stream of 40,000 Mexicans left Tijuana to work on the U.S. side of the border.

Many of these "fonterizos" or "borderlanders" enjoyed some of the best of both nations. Often fluent in both Spanish and English, they could choose between upward mobility in Mexico and a rewarding life in San Diego County. Their children, growing up bilingual, often crossed the border to attend school or to go on dates. This transnational lifestyle, Ojeida explained, gave the residents of this growing region "the luxury of living where you want, working where you want, having the

identity you want," a luxury, however, that only a minority of residents on either side was fortunate enough to enjoy.

Tijuana, hardly more than a small, poor town of 60,000 in 1950, had depended on a lucrative tourist trade since at least 1919, when a transnational railroad connected it with San Diego. Since midcentury, Tijuana served as a mecca not only for a growing number of American tourists but also for Mexicans looking for better jobs. Poor people from distant regions of Mexico were migrating to the rich agricultural valleys and hills surrounding Tijuana, often to prepare themselves for *El Norte*, the trip north to the United States.

Meanwhile, San Diego, which grew from a Spanish mission and fishing village to a Navy boomtown during World War II, developed into a major center of defense-industry manufacturing and research. ➤

In the 1950s the aircraft industry dominated the local economy. Three decades later the city supported a thriving high-tech industry and the famed San Diego Zoo. Tourism, upscale retirement communities, and a major research branch of the University of California helped to make San Diego the second largest city in California and the seventh in the United States, with mainly Hispanics and Asians accounting for the major share of population growth since 1985.

For better or worse, the fates of these two border communities had become increasingly intertwined. In 1961, the Border Industrialization Program paved the way for a closer economic relationship between Tijuana and San Diego. The program fostered the creation of *maquiladoras*, assembly plants for such American-owned firms as Ford Motors and General Electric; in the 1990s, the adoption of the North American Free Trade Agreement (NAFTA) helped to secure these economic structures. By the end of the twentieth century Tijuana, the fourth largest city in Mexico and home to 1.5 million people, had become the only Mexican border city where the size of the middle class most nearly approached that of the impoverished population. Well-heeled shoppers from Tijuana were able to pour about $2.8 billion a year into the San Diego economy, $120 million from sales tax revenue alone.

San Diego and Tijuana, one of eight transnational metropolitan regions on the 2,000-mile U.S.-Mexico border, had come to share not only people but also problems that flout political boundaries. For example, unregulated growth on both sides of the border threatened ecological disaster, created bumper-to-bumper traffic on highways, and encouraged the kind of suburban sprawl that surrounded most large American cities. The Tijuana River, which flows into the San Diego Bay, by the 1990s was carrying 1.5 million gallons of untreated sewage per day, threatening to overwhelm the saltwater marsh that is home to some 370 species of birds and the estuaries that serve ocean fish and mammals. The virtually unregulated airborne pollution of the *maquiladoras* posed additional threats to the region. And the continuous cross-border traffic in goods and people caused substantial amounts of native vegetation to succumb to exotic weedy grasses.

By the end of the century, the Californian and Mexican governments began to catch up with problems festering for decades. A joint feasibility study was funded by the California legislature for the construction of an aqueduct to the Colorado River to bring more water into the region. Other plans included mass transit on the San Diego side and airport expansion on the Tijuana side to relieve congestion at San Diego's overtaxed international airport. To foster such projects and to bring them to the highest level of government, President Vicente Fox of Mexico created the Commission for Northern Border Affairs soon after he took office in December 2000, and he urged the new president of the United States, George W. Bush, to make the region a priority for Americans. The bright promise of the transnational San Diego/Tijuana community was held in check, however, by the dark shadows of world recession and environmental exhaustion that gathered in the first decade of the twenty-first century.

The governments of Mexico and the United States continued to explore scores of binational projects, while San Diego and Tijuana invested in a major border initiative to promote sustainable development and effective public health programs on both sides of the border. In 2006 the governors from the border states of the United States and Mexico met to affirm once again their "common values and … vision for the prosperity of the border region." It seemed clear to everyone that the accelerating diffusion of information technologies, such as television, film, and the Internet, continued to create sources of community where none had previously existed. But the key word of the new era, "globalization," held together many contradictory tendencies. For one, international terrorism offered dramatic and unwelcome proof that no part of the world was far removed—or safe—from the conflicts of any other part.

THE PRESIDENCY OF BILL CLINTON

During his campaign, Bill Clinton promised to bring a new kind of Democratic leadership to the presidency. Since 1985, he had been active in the Democratic Leadership Council (DLC), a group of Democrats serving in Congress or as governors who feared for the fate of their party after the Reagan Republicans won forty-nine of fifty states during the 1984 election. Responding to the conservative challenge, they sought to distance the Democratic Party even further from the liberal tradition established by Franklin D. Roosevelt and revived by Lyndon Johnson in the 1960s. They sought to recapture the blue-collar and white southern defectors "by redefining and reclaiming the political center."

Focus Questions

1. As a "New Democrat," what changes in public policy did Bill Clinton promote during his presidency?

2. What factors contributed to the economic boom of the 1990s?

3. What major demographic shifts were revealed by the 2000 Census?

4. How did the presidency of George W. Bush rekindle conservatism in the early years of the twenty-first century?

5. Is globalization a meaningful term and, if so, how did it affect U.S. policies at home and abroad?

6. How did the threat of global terrorism transform the American political landscape in the first decade of the twenty-first century?

1992–2008

Youthful and energetic, Clinton carried this mission to the White House. He presented a bold agenda that included balancing the federal budget, reforming welfare, reducing crime, promoting economic growth, and ensuring a strong national defense. Trimming the federal government and promoting free markets worldwide became hallmarks of his administration.

A "NEW DEMOCRAT" IN THE WHITE HOUSE

Despite his awesome powers of persuasion, President Clinton got off to a rocky start. As one of his first acts in office, he proposed to issue an executive order ending discrimination against homosexuals in the military and immediately ran into formidable opposition. He ultimately settled for a policy that satisfied virtually no one: "Don't ask, don't tell."

Clinton's biggest stumbling block during his first term was health care reform. Nearly 40 million Americans had no health insurance at all. Many simply could not afford it, and others were denied coverage by private insurers because of preexisting conditions ranging from cancer, cardiovascular disease, and diabetes to AIDS. For millions of others, health insurance was tied to the workplace and a loss or change of jobs threatened their coverage. National spending on health care skyrocketed from

roughly $200 billion in 1980 to more than $800 billion in 1992, constituting about one-seventh of the entire domestic economy.

Shortly after taking office, in a controversial move, President Clinton appointed First Lady Hillary Rodham Clinton, an accomplished attorney, to head a task force charged with preparing a sweeping legislative overhaul of health care. The task force sought a political middle ground between conservative approaches, which stressed fine-tuning the system by making private insurance available to all, and liberal approaches that would have the federal government guarantee health care as an entitlement for everyone. Ultimately, "Hillarycare" (as opponents branded it) proved to be an impossibly complicated compromise. Opposed by such powerful forces as the Chamber of Commerce, the National Association of Manufacturers, the Health Insurance Association of America, and most Republicans, the plan died in Congress in August, 1994, just as the midterm election campaign moved into its final phase.

In the 1994 midterm elections, Clinton's defeat on health care reform helped the Republicans gain control of both the House and Senate for the first time in forty years—a disaster of historic proportions for Clinton and the Democratic Party. Congress was now dominated by conservative Republicans led by the new House Speaker, Newt Gingrich of Georgia. With his scathing denunciations of big government and celebration of entrepreneurship, the formidable

Chief Justice William Rehnquist administers the oath of office to President William Jefferson Clinton on January 20, 1993. Daughter Chelsea and wife Hillary Rodham Clinton stand by his side. In his Inaugural Address as the nation's 42nd president, Clinton invited his fellow citizens to "celebrate the mystery of the American renewal" and to help him "revitalize our democracy."

polemicist Gingrich challenged Clinton's leadership by presenting his own set of proposals labeled the "Contract with America." The House did indeed pass much of the "Contract," including a large tax cut, an increase in military spending, cutbacks in federal regulatory power in the environment and at the workplace, a tough anticrime bill, and a sharp reduction in federal welfare programs.

The threat of presidential veto, however, as well as differences with the Senate, ultimately thwarted Gingrich's plans. In December 1995 the Republican-controlled Congress forced a shutdown of the federal government rather than accede to President Clinton's demand for changes in their proposed budget. The result was a public relations disaster for the Republicans. Gingrich's reputation plummeted.

Meanwhile, Clinton undercut the Republicans by adapting many of their proposals to his own. He endorsed the goal of a balanced federal budget and declared, in his January 1996 State of the Union message, that "the era of big government is over." Clinton opposed his own party's efforts to block a Republican plan to dismantle the federal welfare system in place since the New Deal and instead backed new legislation—the Welfare Reform Act—that abolished the sixty-year-old Aid to Families with Dependent Children program (AFDC). Poor mothers with dependent children would now have access to aid for only a limited period and only if they were preparing for or seeking work. After Congress passed the act in August 1996, Clinton held a public signing ceremony and declared "an end to welfare as we know it."

With such deft maneuvers, Clinton set the theme for his 1996 reelection campaign against Robert Dole of Kansas, the Republican majority leader of the Senate. By staking out the political center, the president won a resounding reelection victory in November 1996, confounding the predictions of the media pundits who had pronounced his political death. Dubbed "the comeback kid," Clinton won over 49 percent of the popular vote compared to Dole's 41 percent and carried thirty-three states (winning 70 percent of the electoral vote). But it was a victory without coattails: the Republicans retained control of both houses of Congress.

In his State of the Union address in 1997, Clinton backed yet further away from liberalism, promising a "new kind of government—not to solve all of our problems for us, but to give all our people the tools to make the most of their own lives." The era of big government may have ended, as the president proclaimed, but the era of divided government would continue.

THE "GLOBALIZATION" PRESIDENT

"Everything from the strength of our economy, to the safety of our cities, to the health of our people," Clinton declared, "depends on events not only within our border but half a world away." Following in the footsteps of his Democratic predecessor, Jimmy Carter, he insisted that U.S. foreign policy reflect "the moral principles most Americans share." Now that the Cold War had ended, the United States could replace the strategy of containment with humanitarian goals. But even more central to his vision was the goal of enlarging "the world's free community of market democracies" under the leadership of the United States. The editors of *Foreign Affairs* dubbed Clinton the "globalization" president.

These two principles drove Clinton's policy toward the People's Republic of China (PRC). During the spring of 1989, Chinese government forces had brutally attacked prodemocracy demonstrators in Beijing's Tiananmen Square, resulting in the death of some 3,000 protestors and the wounding of 10,000 more. President Bush had responded by imposing trade sanctions but only after Congress pressured him to do so. During the 1992 election campaign, Clinton criticized Bush for continuing "to coddle" China in light of such gross human rights violations. Then, after taking office, he modified his position and, looking for "hopeful seeds of change," recommended restoring Most Favored Nation (MFN) status with the PRC. Clinton acknowledged that serious human rights abuses continued, but he pointed out that China, the world's most populous nation, had the world's fastest growing economy—as well as a nuclear arsenal and veto in the Security Council of the UN. He defeated congressional opposition to detach human rights from MFN status and instead promoted free enterprise as a principal means to advance democracy in not only the PRC but also in other nations, such as Turkey, Saudi Arabia, and Indonesia.

After the 1994 midterm election gave Republicans control of the House of Representatives for the first time in forty years, the new Speaker, Newt Gingrich of Georgia, presented a list of legislative initiatives to be completed within the first one hundred days of the new session. On April 7, 1995, he appeared at a rally on Capitol Hill to celebrate the success of the Republicans' "Contract with America."

During his first term, President Clinton pushed through Congress two major trade agreements to expand markets and encourage "free trade," both building on the earlier efforts of the Reagan and Bush administrations. Approved in November 1993, the North American Free Trade Agreement (NAFTA) eased the international flow of goods, services, and investments among the United States, Mexico, and Canada by eliminating tariffs and other trade barriers. The second trade agreement, which led to the establishment of the World Trade Organization (WTO) in 1995, continued the GATT policy of keeping tariffs low on thousands of goods throughout the world and phased out many import quotas imposed by the United States and other industrialized nations—except in agriculture, where the United States and Europe maintained quotas to the detriment of the developing peasant-based Third World economies. The WTO would also mediate commercial disputes among 117 nations.

Critics and supporters argued over whether these trade agreements would encourage global competition, thereby boosting American export industries and creating new high-wage jobs for American workers, or simply erode the U.S. industrial base and accelerate environmental degradation. Cities on the U.S.-Mexico border, such as Tijuana and San Diego, were clear beneficiaries, but the downside was considerable. New *maquiladora* (factories and assembly plants) lacked pollution controls and spewed tons of toxic wastes into the air and groundwater. Despite the boost from NAFTA, the Mexican peso collapsed, and

only a $20 billion bailout of the Mexican economy directed by executive order from the White House on January 31, 1995, prevented a serious depression there.

On humanitarian grounds, Clinton's accomplishments fell far short of his lofty goals. During his first year in office, in October 1993, the United States took part in a UN mission to restore civil order in Somalia in East Africa. Eighteen ill-equipped American soldiers were killed in battle, while several thousand Somalian fighters and civilians died in the ill-fated attack. The president aborted the military mission and adopted a more cautious policy of intervention for humanitarian reasons.

In 1995, acting reluctantly, Clinton committed U.S. troops to a multinational effort in Bosnia where, following the collapse of communism and the dissolution of Yugoslavia, ethnic and religious rivalry among Serbs, Croats, and Muslims had erupted into a civil war. President Bush and his foreign policy advisers, seeing no threat to American interests, had opposed U.S. military intervention. But as reports of "ethnic cleansing"—forced removal and murder of Croats and Muslims by Bosnian Serbs—increased, and as the numbers of refugees grew, Clinton, with congressional support, joined NATO in bombing Serbian strongholds in Bosnia. After negotiating with Yugoslav president Slobodan Milosevic, on November 27 Clinton announced a peace accord that called for a federated, multiethnic state of Bosnia.

Clinton's worst foreign crisis erupted in the region of Kosovo, Yugoslavia, where intensifying clashes between Serbs and Albanians spread to neighboring Macedonia and to Albania itself. President Clinton once again tried to negotiate, but he failed to resolve the problems through diplomacy. After NATO authorized air strikes, he addressed Americans in March 1999, stating that U.S. armed forces had that day joined the attack on Serbian forces in Kosovo.

The so-called Clinton Doctrine, articulated in 1999 to justify the dispatch of U.S. troops to Yugoslavia, departed sharply from Cold War policies that sanctioned intervention primarily on the grounds of strategic interest and national security. In a later statement, Clinton insisted that "genocide is in and of itself a national interest where we should act." In 1998, he acknowledged that the United States, as part of the global community, must share the blame for failing to intervene in Rwanda in 1994, where a struggle for power led to genocide in the killing of up to 1 million Tutsis and moderate Hutu by Hutu extremists. This tragedy, Clinton now declared, represented "the most intensive slaughter in this blood-filled century we are about to leave." But at the time the Clinton administration had known about the genocide and had chosen not to act.

PRESIDING OVER THE BOOM

By any number of measures, Bill Clinton presided over one of the strongest and longest economic booms in American history. While economists, political analysts, and

U.S. Army Military Police stop and search vehicles for weapons and explosives at this checkpoint near Vitina, Kosovo in Yugoslavia, 1999. They were part of the NATO led international force sent to attack Serbian forces in Kosovo.

journalists argued over who deserved the credit, most Americans were content to enjoy the benefits apparent all around them. Between 1992 and 2000 the economy produced over 20 million new jobs, and by 2000 the unemployment rate fell below 4 percent, the lowest in more than thirty years. Despite fears of new inflation, prices remained low. A world glut of oil production kept energy prices down, while American corporations and workers found it difficult to raise prices or win wage increases in the face of stiffer global competition. With government spending down and economic growth increasing tax revenues, the largest federal budget deficit in American history (a quarter trillion dollars) became a surplus nearly as large by the time Clinton left office.

Perhaps the greatest boost to Clinton's second term as president came from the soaring stock market of the 1990s, with "tech stocks" leading the way. The record highs of the Bush years, when the Dow Jones index of thirty industrials approached 4,000, paled by comparison to the leap in 1999 when the Dow hit 10,000 in March and then peaked above 11,000 in May. The fastest growing sector of the market was NASDAQ, the acronym for National Association of Securities Dealers Automated Quotations, which was created in 1971 to report on the trading of domestic securities and was the prime trading venue for technology stocks. Throughout the decade, the market remained volatile, but profits were extraordinarily high.

Equally remarkable was the involvement of ordinary citizens "in the market." By the end of the century, Americans had 60 percent of their investments and savings in stocks, more than double the proportion in 1982. An estimated 78.7 million people held stocks, often through mutual funds or in retirement fund portfolios managed by their employers or unions.

The downside of the economic boom was nearly invisible. Productivity had risen sharply since the 1970s while labor costs had actually declined, hoisting profits to new levels. But critics observed that while a corporate official had earned around twenty or thirty times the pay of a blue-collar worker at the same company a few decades earlier, corporate executive income was more than two hundred times greater than that of a blue-collar employee. In the blue-collar sector, industrial jobs continued to disappear as factories closed or companies moved production of textiles, auto parts, and even electronics across borders or overseas. By the end of Clinton's second term, during the second half of 1999, the "dot-com" Internet-related stocks began to tumble, and economic analysts began to wonder if the business cycle had indeed been rendered obsolete.

HIGH CRIMES AND MISDEMEANORS

Questions of private and public morality dogged Bill Clinton's political career. During the 1992 election campaign, while intending to focus on the economy, he found himself offering explanations for past behavior, such as avoiding the draft during the Vietnam War and smoking—but "not inhaling," he claimed—marijuana during his college years. Once in office, he acted boldly on reproductive rights. Conservatives, including such religious groups as the Christian Coalition, the American Family Association, and the Traditional Values Coalition, as well as many Republicans, struck back.

During his second term as president, Clinton had to answer many questions about his moral conduct. Real estate deals involving both him and Hillary Rodham Clinton blew up into a scandal known as Whitewater. More predictive of troubles ahead, a former Arkansas state employee, Paula Jones, charged Clinton with sexual assault during his gubernatorial term. Attorney General Janet Reno, under extreme pressure from conservatives, appointed an independent counsel, former judge Kenneth Starr, to investigate allegations. But in the summer of 1998, Starr delivered to the House Judiciary Committee a report focusing on an extramarital affair that the president conducted with a young White House intern, Monica Lewinsky. Starr's report outlined several potential impeachable offenses, including false testimony under oath, witness tampering, and obstruction of justice, all allegedly committed by the president to keep his relationship with Lewinsky secret.

After agreeing to testify before a grand jury empanelled by Starr—a first for an American president—Clinton made an extraordinary television address to the nation. He defended his legal position and attacked the Starr inquiry as politically motivated. The Congress and the American people at large fiercely debated the nature of the charges against the president: Were they truly impeachable—"high crimes and misdemeanors" as the Constitution put it—or merely part of a partisan political effort to overturn the election of 1996? For only the third time in history, in October 1998, the House of Representatives voted to open an inquiry into possible grounds for impeachment.

Republicans hoping to reap a wholesale victory from the scandal in the midterm elections were bitterly disappointed. Contrary to predictions and traditions in off-term elections, the president's party added seats, trimming the Republican majority in the 105th Congress. Voters evidently had more on their minds than President Clinton's sex life. Higher than expected turnout from such core constituencies as union members and African Americans (especially in the South) contributed to the unexpectedly strong Democratic showing. The election also brought a shakeup in the Republican leadership. Newt Gingrich, under pressure from Republican colleagues angry about a campaign strategy that had narrowly focused on Clinton's impeachment problem, announced his resignation as Speaker of the House and from his seat in Congress. Ironically Gingrich, who had led the Republican resurgence in the 1990s, now appeared to be the first political victim of the Lewinsky scandal.

In the aftermath of the 1998 midterm election, most politicians and analysts, and indeed most Americans, believed the impeachment inquiry to be at a dead end. But the House Judiciary Committee voted to bring four articles of impeachment—charging President Clinton with perjury, obstruction of justice, witness tampering, and abuse of power—to the full House. But unlike the bipartisan case the Judiciary Committee brought against Richard Nixon in 1974 (see Chapter 29), this time the votes were strictly along party lines. On February 12, 1999, the Senate trial concluded with the president's acquittal. When Clinton left office, he enjoyed the highest approval rating—65 percent—of any president since Dwight Eisenhower.

CHANGING AMERICAN COMMUNITIES

During the Clinton administration, economists coined the phrase "the new economy" to underscore the increasing importance of globalization and corporate restructuring as well as the growing service sector, which included all those workers not directly involved in producing or processing a physical product: from highly paid lawyers, financial analysts, and software designers to poorly paid fast food employees. In 1965 an estimated 50 percent of all jobs were in the service sector; by 2000, the figure had grown to about 70 percent. The new economy depended on a global workforce, including the millions of immigrants, documented and undocumented, who were forming new communities throughout the United States.

SILICON VALLEY

The real and symbolic capital of the new economy was a thirty-by-ten-mile strip of Santa Clara County, California.

As late as 1960 this region was the major processor of fruits and vegetables in the world; forty years later one-third of the valley's workforce was employed by high-tech companies.

Dubbed "Silicon Valley" in 1971 after the material in semiconductor chips, the basic building block of modern microelectronics, the region flourished thanks to its unique combination of research facilities, investment capital, attractive environment, and a large pool of highly educated people. At first, military contracts predominated, but the consumer electronics revolution of the 1970s fueled an explosive new wave of growth. Silicon Valley firms gave birth to pocket calculators, video games, home computers, cordless telephones, digital watches, and almost every other new development in electronics. It became home to more than 1,700 high-tech firms that specialized in gathering, processing, or distributing information or in manufacturing information technology. Companies like Adobe, Cisco Systems, Hewlett-Packard, Apple, and Intel achieved enormous success and became household names. Silicon Valley boasted the greatest concentration of new wealth in the United States.

By the end of the twentieth century, Silicon Valley had become a continuous sprawl of two dozen cities between San Francisco and San Jose and the home and workplace of a diverse population. The managers and engineers, nearly all of whom were white males, had settled in affluent

Yi Li, a graduate student from Taiwan, uses a computer terminal at the New York Public Library to gain access to the Internet. By the 1990s banks of personal computers had become a familiar sight in American offices, businesses, schools, and libraries. Millions of Americans made connecting with the new world of cyberspace a part of their daily routines.

communities such as Palo Alto, Mountain View, and Sunnyvale. Manual workers on assembly lines and in low-paying service jobs clustered in San Jose and Gilroy. Most of these were immigrants or temporary workers—Mexican, Southeast Asian, Iranian, Vietnamese, Cambodian, and Filipino men and women who constituted a cheap, nonunionized labor pool with an extremely high turnover rate.

The prime example of the new economy, Silicon Valley was part of a global enterprise. Its firms were closely linked to the microelectronics industry of the greater Pacific Rim. The end of the Cold War and the accompanying decline in military spending in the United States forced high-tech firms in California into greater competition on the world market and especially against similar companies in Japan, Korea, China, and Malaysia. But many American companies protected themselves against such competition by owning and managing a large share of the plants in these countries.

By the end of Clinton's administration, the rate of growth showed signs of slowing, dramatized by the sharp plunge of technology stocks. In the aftermath of this burst of the so-called dot-com bubble in March 2000, entrepreneurs throughout the Pacific Rim found it more difficult to start successful new companies and to make the leap from a small, start-up company to a large corporation. By this time, scarcity in housing, traffic jams, and an inflated cost of living were already leading many companies and individuals to move out of the area.

AN ELECTRONIC CULTURE

The technological developments produced in Silicon Valley helped reconfigure cultural life in the United States and the world. Revolutions in computers and telecommunications merged telephones, televisions, computers, cable, and satellites into a global system of information exchange. The new technologies changed the way people worked, played, and conducted business and politics.

The twin arrivals of cable and the videocassette recorder (VCR) expanded and redefined the power of television. By the early 1990s pay cable services and VCRs had penetrated roughly two-thirds of American homes. Cable and satellite in the 1990s offered television viewers not just four or five channels but also scores of new programming choices, especially sports events and movies. Hollywood studios began releasing movies on videotape, and the rental and sale of movies for home viewing quickly outstripped ticket sales at theaters as the main profit source for filmmakers.

More than ever, television drove the key strategies and tactics defining American political life. Politicians and their advisers focused intently on a candidate's television image. Issues, positions, and debate all paled alongside the key question: How did it look on television? Fewer citizens voted or took an active role in campaigns, and most relied on television coverage to make their choices.

New digital technologies continued to reshape American culture into the early 2000s. Compact discs (CDs) and digital video discs (DVDs) emerged as the dominant media for popular music and movies, replacing tape-based technologies. Millions of Americans now used digital cameras to document their vacations and everyday lives. Digital telephones—"cell phones"—became a ubiquitous presence in the streets, malls, campuses, cars, and workplaces of American communities.

Perhaps no aspect of the electronic culture was more revolutionary than the creation of cyberspace, the conceptual region occupied by people linked through computers and communications networks. It began with ARPANET, the first computer network, which the Department of Defense developed in the early 1970s. Computer enthusiasts known as "hackers" created unexpected grassroots spinoffs from ARPANET, including electronic mail, computer conferencing, and computer bulletin board systems. In the mid-1980s, alongside the launch of Microsoft Word and Windows operating programs, the boom in cheap personal computers capable of linking individuals to the worldwide telecommunications network began a population explosion in cyberspace. By then, tens of thousands of researchers and scholars at universities and in private industry were linked to the Internet—the U.S. government–sponsored successor to ARPANET—through their institutions' computer centers. The establishment of the World Wide Web and easy-to-use browser software such as Netscape, introduced in 1994, made the "information highway" accessible to millions of Americans with few computer skills and created a popular communications medium with global dimensions.

By the beginning of the new century, the U.S. Census Bureau estimated that more than half of all households had at least one computer and more than 40 percent were connected to the Internet. Nearly 85 percent of classrooms in public schools were online. At work, Americans spent an average of 21 hours per week online. At home, they spent an average of 9.5 hours per week online, gaining access to the Web from independent service providers such as America Online and Earthlink. For a flat monthly fee users could play games, send electronic mail, discuss issues in public forums, and purchase a huge array of goods and services, ranging from books and airline tickets to automobiles and psychotherapy sessions.

These new information technologies gave birth to a media community that transcended national boundaries. During the 1980s, exports from Hollywood to the rest of the world doubled in value. The number of hours of television watched throughout the world nearly tripled: MTV was broadcast to an estimated 250 million households. By the mid-1990s there were more television sets in China than in the United States. Americans, however, owned a disproportionate share of the largest media corporations in the world, with Microsoft, Disney, and Time Warner in the lead. More than 40 percent of television programs in the world originated in the United States.

THE NEW IMMIGRANTS AND THEIR COMMUNITIES

The 2000 census showed that the nation's population during the 1990s grew by 32.7 million, a number greater than that of any other decade in U.S. history. Even the 1950s, which witnessed the post–World War II baby boom, could not compete against a decade marked by a huge number of immigrants and a birthrate that surpassed the death rate. In October 2006, the U.S. population hit 300 million.

The 2000 census confirmed what many Americans had observed over the previous decade in their communities and workplaces. The face of the nation was perceptibly changing and changing on a scale that compared to the first decades of the twentieth century, when immigration from Europe peaked. At the turn of the twenty-first century, more than a third of the nation's population growth came from the influx of new immigrants (see Figure 31.1). Although three-quarters of the newcomers joined many other Americans in flocking to the Sunbelt states, headed by California, Texas, and Florida, they also helped to reverse population loss in such major urban centers as New York and Chicago and slow the decline in Rustbelt cities like Cleveland, Detroit, and Milwaukee. And for the first time in any census, they played a major role in the population increase in all fifty states. Nationally, the percentage of Americans born outside the United States was 11.2 percent, its highest point since 1930; in California the percentage of foreign born approached 26 percent.

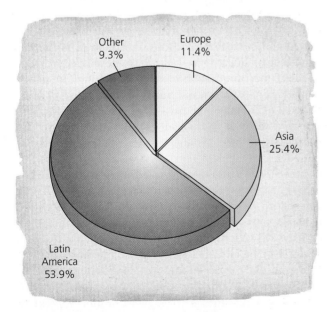

FIGURE 31.1 Continent of Birth for Immigrants, 1990–2000

By 2000, the number of foreign-born residents and their children—56 million according to the Census Bureau—had reached the highest level in U.S. history.

The Immigration Act of 1965, passed almost unnoticed in the context of the egalitarian political climate created by the civil rights movement, had revolutionary consequences, some of them unintended (see Chapter 28). The act abolished the discriminatory national origins quotas that had been in place since the 1920s. It also for the first time limited immigration from the Western Hemisphere, while giving preference to people from the nations of the Eastern Hemisphere who had specialized job skills and training. This provision created the conditions for Asian immigrants to become the fastest-growing ethnic group in the United States. But in setting limits on Western Hemisphere immigration, the 1965 act tempted many thousands of people from Latin America to enter the United States illegally.

By the mid-1980s, growing concern over "illegal aliens" had become a hotly debated political issue, particularly in the Southwest. The Immigration Reform and Control Act of 1986 marked a break with the past attempts to address this problem. Instead of mass deportation programs, the law strengthened the patrol along the border with Mexico and simultaneously offered an amnesty to all undocumented workers who had entered the country since 1982. Four years later, additional revisions of this act enlarged the quota of immigrants, once again giving priority to skilled and professional workers. Hispanics and Asians benefited from these changes in immigration law. Within the twenty fastest-growing cities, the number of Hispanics and Asians increased by approximately 70 percent. In 2006 millions of immigrants—both legal and undocumented—took to the streets in American cities to demand amnesty for so-called illegals and calling for reforms that would allow a clear and legal path to citizenship. These protests marked a new attempt to flex the political muscle of immigrant communities and served notice that anti-immigrant forces would not go unchallenged in the political arena.

Demographers predicted that Hispanics, who had grown from 22.4 million in 1990 to 35.3 million in 2000, according to census data, would replace African Americans as the nation's largest minority group by the middle of the twenty-first century. By 1990 Hispanics had already formed over a third of the population of New Mexico, a quarter of the population of Texas, and over 10 percent of the populations of California, Arizona, and Colorado. Nearly a million Mexican Americans lived in Los Angeles alone.

The 2000 census showed that Mexicans were the largest Hispanic group in the United States at 20.6 million, representing nearly 60 percent of the total Hispanic population. The boom of the U.S. economy in the 1990s provided a significant "pull" for these newcomers. But other factors encouraged many immigrants to make an often difficult and dangerous sojourn. First, a drop in worldwide oil prices followed by the deflation of the Mexican national currency dramatically lowered living standards in Mexico in the mid-1990s. NAFTA and the greater integration of the U.S. and Mexican economies brought new jobs but often with increasingly expensive living conditions. Tens and perhaps hundreds of thousands of Mexicans worked in the United States temporarily while planning a permanent move north—with or without legal documentation.

After settling across the border, most new Mexican Americans struggled in low-wage and often dangerous jobs such as meatpacking or construction, and they were more likely to die from workplace injuries than other workers. Through education and success in business, a significant number achieved middle-class status and wealth. But almost 20 percent of Mexican Americans lived below the poverty line. They tended to live in segregated neighborhoods and were less likely than non-Hispanic whites to have health insurance or to own their own homes.

In New York, the Puerto Rican–born population jumped from 100,000 in 1945 to roughly 1 million twenty years later. However, during the 1990s, this trend had begun to reverse, their numbers falling by 12 percent. The smaller but highly influential Cuban population declined even more, by 27 percent. Meanwhile, other Latin populations grew at an extraordinary rate. The Mexican-born population more than doubled, and Filipinos, who often speak Spanish as a first language, increased by 27 percent. Immigrants from the Dominican Republic, now second in population size only to Puerto Ricans, dominated sizable sections of Washington Heights and Brooklyn, while immigrants from various countries in Central and South America created new communities throughout the greater metropolitan region. In the five years since 2000, the Hispanic population of Staten Island increased by 31 percent.

The cultural implications for all Americans, not just New Yorkers, were far-reaching. Children born to the new immigrants of the 1980s and 1990s, despite increasing neighborhood segregation by race, played on the streets together, attended the same schools, and often married outside their racial group. In the 2000 census, 6.8 million Americans nationwide listed themselves as multiracial. Identities blurred as popular entertainment created new mixes of traditions and styles. "World beat" music (heavily influenced by "Afro-Pop"), *Alternalatino* (alternative Latin music—a mixture of salsa and merengue), Tjano, Reggae, and other music in fusion mixtures became as common to Manhattan or Los Angeles as to Mexico City or Rio. By the 1990s, the West

The sign at this 1996 vigil in Echo Park, Los Angeles, reads, "This fruit is the product of immigrants' labor." Members of the city's Latino community bless fruit baskets as they protest a state crackdown on illegal immigration and the increase of border patrol guards.

Indian carnival held annually in Brooklyn at the end of summer had become the most popular ethnic festival in greater New York City.

Although smaller in number than Hispanics, Asians were the fastest-growing racial group in the United States. With a steady flow of professionals and workers skilled in technology into their communities, Chinese Americans maintained their status as the largest Asian ethnicity in the United States. However, other groups grew at faster rates, particularly Indo Americans (from the subcontinent of India), whose numbers doubled during the 1990s to become the third-largest Asian group. Meanwhile Japanese Americans, once the largest and most influential members of the pan-Asian community, declined. Immigration from Japan had virtually ceased during the decade, while many young Japanese Americans married someone of a different race.

The 2000 census also revealed sharp divisions among Americans. Although the poverty rate had dropped to 11.3 percent of the population, near the lowest level ever recorded, more than 31 million people still lived in poverty. Five years later, average incomes had dipped further, and nearly half of all Americans earned less than $30,000. Moreover, the new economy had done little to close the gap between the highest and lowest income earners. Women as a group made few gains, earning 73 cents to each dollar earned by men. And with African Americans and Latinos continuing to earn, on average, far less than non-Hispanic whites, race relations benefited little from the economic boom of the 1990s.

A NEW AGE OF ANXIETY

Despite the prosperity of the 1990s, many Americans experienced an uneasiness that resembled the anxiety of the mid-twentieth century, when the world seemed on the brink of nuclear destruction. The Communist threat had expired along with the Cold War, but doubts and fears about the fate of their own society—and, indeed, the planet—had multiplied.

THE RACIAL DIVIDE

In the spring of 1992 an upheaval in Los Angeles offered the starkest evidence that racial tensions had not eased. Outrage over police brutality ignited the worst riot of the century. A year earlier, Rodney King, a black motorist, had been pulled from his vehicle and severely beaten by four white police officers. When, despite the graphic evidence of an amateur videotape of the incident, a jury acquitted the officers of all but one of eleven counts of assault, South Central Los Angeles erupted, with crowds looting and burning businesses throughout the community and into Koreatown. More than fifty people were killed, and 500 buildings were destroyed before L.A. police and National Guard troops restored order.

More than a quarter century after the uprising in Watts, the situation in South Central Los Angeles in 1992 seemed more desperate than ever to most African Americans. The poverty rate was 30.3 percent, more than twice the national average. The unemployment rate for adult black males hovered around 40 percent, and a quarter of the population was on welfare. Drug dealing and gang warfare had escalated, reflecting the sense of despair among young people.

The events in Los Angeles exposed the deep animosity among various groups—so much so that the observers referred to the event as a "multicultural riot." Almost 2,000 Korean businesses were destroyed, and Koreans angrily accused the police of making no effort to defend their stores. The division was sharpest, though, between whites and the minority populations. "We are all quite isolated in our own communities," a resident of Westwood, a mostly white upper middle-class neighborhood, explained. "We don't know and don't care about the problems in the inner cities. Driving to work every day most of us don't even know where South Central is—except many of us saw the fires from that direction when we were stuck in traffic."

The situation in Los Angeles was not unique. The 2000 census showed that segregation was on the rise, and not only in cities but also in their surrounding suburbs. For example, in the Atlanta region, which claimed the largest share of black suburbanites in the nation (26 percent), the percentage living separately from whites had increased from 52 percent in 1990 to nearly 60 percent by 2000. Similarly, in the nation's schools, the gains from the civil rights era diminished and, in some communities, disappeared altogether. A 2001 report showed that, despite the increasing racial and ethnic diversity of the nation's youth, segregation was more pronounced in grades K–12.

The publicity generated by Rodney King's arrest fed several major controversies concerning the U.S. criminal justice system. Racial disparities were evident, with ethnic and racial minorities accounting for approximately two-thirds of state prison inmates. In 2007, the Bureau of Justice estimated that 32 percent of African American men would enter a state or federal prison during their lifetimes.

Various civil liberties groups reviewed these statistics and concluded that African Americans were not necessarily more prone to criminal activity but were far more likely to be stopped, searched, arrested, convicted, and given harsher penalties than white Americans. Critics singled out the practice of "racial profiling" whereby police disproportionately stopped people of color as likely offenders. By 1999, "driving while black" had become a news item in all the major media, leading to the introduction of a bill into the U.S. Senate in 1999 to collect statistics on traffic stops.

THE CULTURE WARS

At the 1992 Republican National Convention, the conservative Patrick Buchanan gave the opening speech. "There is a religious war going on in our country for the soul of America," he declared. "It is a cultural war, as critical to the kind of nation we will one day be as was the Cold War itself." Other observers also noted that certain "hot-button" moral and social issues continued to outstrip ethnicity and socioeconomic class as the basic markers of political principle. Into the twenty-first century, politics focused on issues like reproductive rights and reproductive technology, homosexuality and gay rights, the curriculum in public schools, codes of speech and standards in the arts, gun control, and scientific developments such as cloning, genetic alteration, and fetal tissue research, and even the validity of Darwin's theory of evolution.

The growing racial and ethnic diversity of American society, as well as the expansion of rights for groups such as women and gays, had sparked a broad and controversial movement known as "multiculturalism." Unlike earlier descriptions of America as a "melting pot," new metaphors such as "salad bowl" or "mosaic" became popular expressions to call attention to the unique attributes and achievements of formerly marginal groups and recent immigrants. This celebration of diversity played a big part in Bill Clinton's campaign strategy, and he took a large share of votes by tailoring his appeals to specific groups. Like other Democrats, he won upward of 80 percent of black votes, but he secured more Latino and Asian American votes than any other candidate in American history. On college campuses, multiculturalism marked the high point of the curricular reform that had been ongoing since the late 1960s and early 1970s, when women's and ethnic studies programs were launched (see Chapter 29).

Reaching well beyond the academic world, the culture wars played out in immigration policy. In 1994, a California ballot initiative, Proposition 187, called for making all undocumented aliens ineligible for any social service, public schooling, and nonemergency medical care, and it required teachers and clinic doctors to report illegal immigrants to the police. Passed by a three-to-two margin, the new legislation was immediately challenged in the streets and in the courts. In 1998, after several years of legal wrangling, a federal judge ruled that Proposition 187 unconstitutionally usurped federal authority over immigration policy. In June 2001, the U.S. Supreme Court ruled that immigrants are entitled to the same protection by the Constitution as that afforded to citizens.

But the national debate over immigration policy, in which economic issues and racial fears were deeply entangled, continued unabated in California and elsewhere (see Communities in Conflict). As one Stanford law professor who had worked to overturn Proposition 187 put it: "Some people genuinely worry about the problem of too many immigrants in a stagnant economy. But for most, economics is a diversion. Underneath it is race."

The California ballot initiative Proposition 187 was designed to deny basic social services, including health and education, to undocumented immigrants. To express their opposition to the legislation, as many as 250,000 people took the streets in downtown Los Angeles. This photograph shows Grace Lee and a group of fellow students demonstrating in the Westwood section of the city shortly after voters approved the bill known as "the last gasp of White America in California" on November 8, 1994.

Similar controversies surrounded gay rights, particularly around a push for the legal recognition of civil unions and marriage for same-sex couples. In 1996, President Clinton responded to these challenges by signing the Defense of Marriage Act, which specified that gay couples would be ineligible for spousal benefits provided by federal law and that no state would be required to recognize such marriages even if legally recognized in another state.

The issue of same-sex marriage continued to evolve on the state level. In 2000, Vermont became the first state to recognize civil unions, allowing same-sex couples to receive many, although not all, of the legal benefits of marriage. Several other states passed versions of civil union or domestic partner laws. In 2004, Massachusetts became the first state in America to legally permit gay marriage. Meanwhile, seventeen states passed constitutional provisions defining marriage as a union of one man and one woman, while twenty-five others enacted legislative statutes with similar definitions. Gay marriage would continue as a powerful symbolic issue.

Nearly as volatile as a political issue was government financing of an area of scientific research of growing importance since the birth of the first test-tube baby in 1981—human embryonic stem cell research. Because these microscopic clusters of cells have the potential to grow into any tissue in the body, embryonic stem cells hold promise, scientists believe, for refurbishing or replacing damaged tissues or organs and, therefore, might prove useful in treating or perhaps even curing diseases such as diabetes, Parkinson's, and Alzheimer's. Religious conservatives opposed this research because it may involve the destruction of human embryos, usually derived from the excess products of *in vitro* fertilization processes and scheduled for disposal by fertility clinics. In 1995, in response to pressure from conservative groups such as the National Right to Life Committee, Congress enacted legislation banning the use of federal funds for research that involves the destruction of human embryos. However, in his last year in office, Clinton loosened the ban and thereby generated another round of controversy. Most Christian conservative groups remained firm in their opposition, agreeing with the United States Conference of Catholic Bishops, which insisted "that the government must not treat any living human being as research material, as a mere means for benefit to others."

THE FORCES OF FEAR

During the 1990s, anxiety about terrorism and random violence escalated. Within their own borders, Americans were actually far safer from terrorist attacks than the citizens of many other countries. Nevertheless, two events—the attack on the World Trade Center in 1993 and the destruction of the federal building in Oklahoma City in 1995—alerted Americans to danger at home and to U.S. interests abroad.

On February 26, 1993, a small group of Arab Islamist terrorists bombed the World Trade Center in New York City, killing six people and injuring more than a thousand others. Taken in retaliation for U.S. intervention in the Middle East, the attack was the most destructive act of terrorism committed within the United States to that time. It spurred the Antiterrorism and Effective Death Penalty Act of 1996, which greatly expanded the budget and powers of federal authorities to monitor likely terrorists. Despite increased surveillance, terrorists struck another lethal blow. On August 7, 1998, car bombings of U.S. embassies in Kenya and Tanzania injured more than 4,000 people and killed 220.

The bombing of the Alfred P. Murrah Federal Building in Oklahoma City raised an entirely different specter: terrorism by self-described patriotic Americans. The perpetrators represented the extremist wing of the New Right, the superpatriot movement, which included groups of people who set up "survivalist" encampments in rural areas and organized themselves into armed militias. Inspired by author William Pierce's *Turner Diaries* (1978), which predicted a revolt of "Aryans" against people of color and the federal government, the patriots found their martyrs in the Branch Davidians and their retribution in Oklahoma.

Two years earlier, on February 28, 1993, agents of the FBI and the Federal Bureau of Alcohol, Tobacco, and Firearms (ATF) had conducted a "search and arrest" operation against the Branch Davidians that turned deadly. Their object was David Koresh, the leader of the obscure religious sect who was suspected of stockpiling illegal firearms and ammunition. After a round of shots, which took the lives of four ATF agents and six Branch Davidians, Koresh's heavily armed followers barricaded themselves in their compound in Waco, Texas. Fifty-one days later, on April 19, government agents brought their siege to a fiery end. Nine Davidians managed to escape the flames engulfing their buildings, while seventy-six others, including twenty-one children, perished.

Choosing April 19, 1995, the anniversary of the federal raid at Waco, as their "Date of Doom," Timothy McVeigh and his accomplices took their revenge. Shortly after 9:00 A.M., a bomb went off in the federal office building in Oklahoma City, killing 168 people, including 19 children, and injuring more than 500 others. Picked up within hours of the bombing on a misdemeanor traffic violation, McVeigh was later indicted on eleven charges, including eight counts of first-degree murder. After a trial in federal court and demonstrations both for and against the death penalty, he was executed in June 2001.

Immediately after the Oklahoma City bombing, President Clinton declared a national day of mourning for the victims and their families. He addressed the nation, saying "Let us let our own children know that we will stand against the forces of fear. When there is talk of hatred, let us stand up and talk against it. When there is talk of violence, let us stand up and talk against it."

But terrorism continued, with many of the attacks politically or ideologically motivated. For example, medical clinics that provided abortion services to women became a prime target. Although the ratio of abortions to live pregnancies had been declining since 1979, antiabortion groups became more belligerent. Operation Rescue launched a well-publicized and illegal blockade of three abortion clinics in Wichita, Kansas, in September 1991. Although the "war in Wichita" ended peacefully after forty-six days, antiabortion protests became increasingly violent in its wake. Several medical providers were murdered outside their clinics.

Rescue workers carried an injured man from the rubble of the U.S. Embassy in Nairobi, Kenya. A terrorist bomb killed more than 100 people and injured more than 1,600 on August 8, 1998.

Illegal Immigrants and the Border Fence

In 2005 the House of Representatives initiated legislation to reform U.S. immigration policy, particularly to stem a flow of illegal immigrants now thought to have brought in 12 million people, more than half from Mexico. Opinions clashed, often along party lines, on proposals for amnesty programs, "guest worker" provisions, and the sanctioning and deportation of illegal migrants. One proposal proved especially divisive: a plan to construct a huge, high-tech, double-layered fence along the 2,000-mile U.S.-Mexico border, including powerful lighting, radar, cameras, and even unmanned aircraft. The Border Patrol would also be augmented by 1,500 new troops.

Politicians and experts on immigration reform heatedly debated these issues. The House ultimately passed the Border Protection, Antiterrorism, and Illegal Immigration Act of 2005, but the Senate initially refused to provide funding; only in September 2006 did the upper chamber vote $1.2 billion to construct a 700-mile fence, extending along just one-third of the 2,000-mile border separating the United States from Mexico. Senator Edward Kennedy (D-MA) voiced strong opposition, calling the new legislation "just a bumper sticker solution for a complex problem." Although most Republicans supported the measure, President Bush and some legislators feared that stringent measures would stem the flow of needed workers.

The most extreme opposition came from ultraconservatives, such as the superpatriotic organization Let Freedom Ring, which organized a petition and fundraising campaign to support construction of the entire fence. Meanwhile, a paramilitary anti-immigration group, the Minutemen, illegally started patrolling the border and constructing a 10-mile-long iron and steel fence. In response, the Mexican government garnered support from twenty-seven other nations to express "deep concern regarding the decision adopted by the United States of America to build and extend a wall on its border with Mexico, considering it to be a unilateral measure that goes against the spirit of understanding."

Bill Richardson, who served in Congress for seventeen years and is now governor of New Mexico, spoke for many Democrats in 2006, criticizing the proposed border fence and advocating comprehensive immigration reform that would address illegal immigration from Mexico. Richardson is of Hispanic American ancestry. Another viewpoint emerges in the statement of Jan C. Ting, a professor of law at Temple University and a former assistant commissioner of the U.S. Immigration and Naturalization Service, who in 2005 called for enhanced border security. Of Chinese American ancestry, Ting ran unsuccessfully for the U.S. Senate in Delaware.

How do the writers of these documents employ different perspectives on American history to help make their case? Do you find contrasting ideals of American patriotism and national interest here as well?

Governor Bill Richardson Urges Comprehensive Immigration Reform (December 7, 2006)

Today, there are over 11 million illegal immigrants in the United States. Most are law abiding, except for the fact that they have entered this country illegally. And almost all have come here to work—to build a better life for themselves and their families, just as previous generations of immigrants have done.

Eleven million people living in the shadows is a huge problem, and we need to address it intelligently and thoughtfully—and urgently. If Congress fails to do so, it will only get worse, and the demagoguery about it which we have heard so much of recently will only get louder.

As the California-born son of an American father and a Mexican mother, I have known immigrants all my life and I know why they come to America. And as Governor of New Mexico I have known the problem of illegal immigration all too well—we live with this issue every day in my state.

Like it or not, these people have become part of the fabric of our economy and our culture. They have broken the law to enter our country, but they are here—there are millions of them building and cleaning our homes and offices, picking and cooking our food, caring for our children. These men and women are here illegally,

but they work hard, pay taxes, and contribute to the communities they live in.

America needs to SOLVE this problem, not tear itself apart over it. . . .

Governors must promote public safety and ensure that all residents of the state—welcome or unwelcome, legally here or not—are productive, self-supporting, and law-abiding contributors to our community. But treating illegal immigrants like human beings won't make the problem go away. We also need to face up to the problem, and that begins with better border security.

Securing the border must come first—but we must understand that building a fence will not in any way accomplish that objective. No fence ever built has stopped history and this one wouldn't either. The Congress should abandon the fence, lock, stock, and barrel. It flies in the face of America as a symbol of freedom.

This is what we should do: immediately put enough National Guard troops at the border to keep it covered until we can secure it with Border Patrol officers. That should take no longer than three years. If it takes another year, let's do it.

Second, we must hire and train enough Border Guards to actually cover the entire border. I have spent a lot of time at the border and I know we cannot secure it with a fence, but we can secure it with enough trained Border Patrol officers. I propose doubling the number of Border Patrol agents from approximately 12 thousand to

"No fence ever built has stopped history and this one wouldn't either."

24 thousand. That would secure the border. And you could more than pay for it with the funding for the first segment of that ill-advised fence between Mexico and the United States. Real security, real results, at a fraction of the financial or political cost.

Third, we should give the Border Patrol the benefit of the best surveillance equipment available to our military. And, as suggested by Texas Congresswoman Sheila Jackson Lee, a leader on immigration issues, we should implement a system of "informant visas" and cash rewards for aliens who provide law enforcement with information on human traffickers and document forgers.

We should establish a "fraudulent documents task force" to constantly update law enforcement and border officials on the latest fraudulent documents being marketed for entry into the United States.

Finally, we have to work closely with the Mexican government. Illegal immigration is, at its root, primarily an economic problem: Mexicans need jobs and incomes, and Mexico benefits greatly from illegal immigration to the United States. It is a safety valve for their unemployed, and a major source of revenue in their economy, from the money illegal workers here send home.

Under present conditions, the Mexicans just don't have enough incentive to give us the help we need at the border. Mexico needs to do more to stem the flow. But if we create a reasonable guest worker program and provide a path to legalization for illegal immigrants already here . . . there is every reason to expect Mexico to do its part to create more jobs in Mexico and to help us with border security . . . .

SOURCE: Gov. Bill Richardson, "Speech on Comprehensive Immigration Reform at Georgetown University," Dec. 7, 2006. http://www.richardsonforpresident.com/issues/immigration

Republican Jan C. Ting Considers "Immigration, National Security, and the Need for a Border Fence" (2005)

[I]t is supremely ironic that four years after 9/11 our national borders remain open and uncontrolled, and our government seems unconcerned. The simple reality is that tonight, four years after 9/11, and every night of the year, thousands foreigners covertly enter the United States, and we have no idea who they are. Every night. Thousands. Who are they?

It's perhaps an overstatement to say we have no idea, because we do have some idea. We do catch some of them, and that provides us with a kind of sample of who is covertly crossing our borders into the U.S. in violation of our laws. But how big of a sample is it? The official estimate is that the Border Patrol catches 1 out of every 4 illegal border crossers, and this is typically the estimate public officials use in discussing the problem. Three get in for every one caught. But Border Patrol officers speaking off the record, and retired Border Patrol officials speaking for the record, say that the ratio of those getting in to those caught is much higher . . . .

"The fence is the essential element in any plan to limit illegal immigration. . . ."

Apprehensions along the southern border make up about 97–98% of the total apprehensions. Most of those apprehended near the southern border are Mexicans . . . .

Even though the number of Border Patrol apprehensions nationally and along the southern border has been fluctuating, the number of OTM's [Other Than Mexicans] apprehended near the southern border has been clearly and dramatically increasing from 28,598 in 2000 to 65,814 in 2004, despite a lower number of overall apprehensions in 2004. And we already have 100,142 OTM apprehensions for the first eight months of 2005. So the word is out to the rest of the world what the Mexicans have known for years. The border is wide open, and it's easy for anyone who wants to get into the United States covertly. . . .

Can it possibly be true that, although we can put a man on the moon, although we can put a rover on Mars and hit a comet in outer space with rockets, there's nothing we can do to stop people from walking across our borders into the United States? I think there's plenty that we could do if only we had the political will to do so. And I think it's remarkable that four years after 9/11 we still don't have the political will to do so. Are we not capable of building a fence like the one the Israelis have found effective in preventing terrorists from entering Israel? We can do it. We are in fact fortifying the westernmost 14 miles of our southern border. That leaves only 2,000 miles left on our southern border to go!

We can also put more people on the border fence, possibly using volunteers like the Minutemen, or using the U.S. military, positioning our bases near the borders where they can enhance national security, instead of by political considerations which put them in the districts of Congressional committee chairmen to help get them reelected. We can resume worksite raids to arrest illegal aliens. . . .

Our legal immigration system is appropriately the most generous in the world, admitting each year more legal permanent resident immigrants with a clear path to full citizenship than all the rest of the nations of the world combined. It is certainly possible to champion legal immigration while advocating restrictions on illegal immigration. Even those seeking reforms to our legal immigration system can see that addressing the problem of illegal immigration must come first to give legal immigration meaning. That effort begins with a fence.

The fence is the essential element in any plan to limit illegal immigration across our border. The southern border is the first priority because of the large numbers of illegal entrants compared to our northern border. But we have already had at least one terrorist enter from Canada, so we must also address northern border security once the southern border fence is complete. The fence is essential. . . . Without the fence to control illegal immigration, no reform of immigration is possible. Any reform will fail under the rising tide of illegal immigration and the dangers that accompany it.

SOURCE: Jan C. Ting "Immigration, National Security, and the Need for a Border Fence" Sept. 9, 2005. http://www.letfreedomringusa.com/Fileuploads/

In 1994, with the support of President Clinton, Congress enacted the Freedom of Access to Clinic Entrance Act, which provides protection to any abortion clinic requesting it. The number of violent incidents declined from the peak of thirty-two bombings, arsons, or attempted attacks in 1992 and twelve murders or attempted murders in 1994. After the turn of the century, the attacks continued to diminish but did not stop.

THE PRESIDENCY OF GEORGE W. BUSH AND THE WAR ON TERROR

At the beginning of the twenty-first century, citizens, politicians, and business and religious leaders had to rethink their basic assumptions about the American way of life. American society had become more stratified along lines of race and income. New immigrant groups, especially from Asia and Latin America, had changed the face of the nation's communities, schools, and workplaces. New media technologies had made cultural life more homogenized and caused the manipulation of image to become more crucial than ever to both politics and entertainment. The New Economy, service-oriented and high-tech, had fundamentally altered the way many Americans did business and earned a livelihood, and it depended not only on American consumers heavily burdened with debt but also on an expanding global market.

The end of the Cold War had reconfigured global politics, ending the bilateralism that had dominated international affairs since the end of World War II. The United States alone held fast to its superpower status, but this achievement did not necessarily make Americans more secure or safe. The old enemy, Soviet communism, was succeeded by more fanatic, less predictable foes. The September 11, 2001, attacks on the World Trade Center and other targets proved critical turning point for the Bush presidency as it looked to reconfigure American foreign policy and domestic politics around the strategy of a "war on terror." The Bush administration justified the American invasion of Iraq in 2003 largely as a necessary part of that strategy. The Iraq war defined the Bush presidency more than any other issue.

THE ELECTION OF 2000

After a relatively dull campaign season, the 2000 election played out as high drama. Voters went to the polls as usual on election day, watched as late-night television newscasters projected a victory for the Democratic candidate, Clinton's vice president Al Gore, and then woke up the next morning to learn that perhaps the winner was not the vice president but his Republican opponent, Governor George W. Bush of Texas, son of former president George H. W. Bush. It was clear that Gore and his running

mate, Connecticut Senator Joseph Lieberman, had won the popular vote, although by the closest margin since John F. Kennedy defeated Richard Nixon in 1961. In doubt was the number of votes in the electoral college. At 2:15 A.M., the pollsters who had projected Gore as the winner changed their minds. The cliffhanger in Florida had finally ended with the state's decisive twenty-five electoral votes earmarked for the Republicans. By morning Gore had called Bush to concede. *The New York Times*, however, ran a guarded headline "Bush Appears to Defeat Gore." Only a few hundred votes in Florida gave Bush the edge, and in cases where the margin is so narrow Florida law mandates a machine recount in all sixty-seven counties. Gore soon retracted his concession, putting voters into suspense until the middle of December, when the vice president finally ended his campaign (see Map 31.1).

Such a spectacular ending to the 2000 campaign could not have been foreseen from the primaries. As the son of a former president, George W. Bush had run a low-key campaign, calling himself a "compassionate conservative" who cared about the underdog and the nation's educational system. He nevertheless did not swerve from the Republican agenda that President Reagan had shaped: tax cuts, strong military defense, and the overhaul of Social Security and Medicare. He also promised relief from environmental regulations, new judicial appointments that would eventually limit reproductive rights, and

	Electoral Vote (%)	Popular Vote (%)
GEORGE W. BUSH (Republican)	271 (50.5)	50,456,169 (48.0)
Al Gore (Democrat)	266 (49.5)	50,996,116 (48.0)

MAP 31.1 The Election of 2000 The 2000 presidential election was the closest one in U.S. history and the first one to be decided by a decision of the Supreme Court.

the restoration of morality to public life. Albert Gore Jr., also the son of a prominent politician, carried the burden of association with Bill Clinton and waged an uphill battle. More notable was his running mate, Lieberman, the first Jewish candidate for vice president. Dick Cheney, who had served prominently in the senior Bush's administration, balanced the younger Bush's relative lack of experience in federal government. The emergence of consumer advocate Ralph Nader as Green Party candidate added spice to an often dull campaign.

The 2000 campaign played out as the first disputed presidential election since 1876, when Democrat Samuel J. Tilden, who won the popular vote, charged his Republican opponent, Rutherford B. Hayes, with fraudulent vote counting. A similar question of legitimacy hung over the 2000 election. After Florida completed its machine recount of votes, the Democrats requested a hand tally in selected counties where the ballots were in dispute. The Republicans responded by suing in the Miami district court to prohibit the manual recounting. Meanwhile Florida election officials, mainly Republicans, set November 14 as the date to certify the election results, thereby disallowing the returns on overseas ballots that might favor Al Gore. In turn, Democrats sued to extend the deadline. Eventually, appeals by both parties reached the Florida Supreme Court and finally the U.S. Supreme Court, which voted five to four along partisan lines to halt the counting. Time had run out, and on December 12 Gore conceded defeat, despite having received over 500,000 more votes than Bush. With less fanfare than usual, George W. Bush took the oath of office in January 2001.

A GLOBAL COMMUNITY?

On policies concerning the environment, Bush acted quickly and aggressively to defer or to overturn several key programs established under Clinton. In July 2001, the Environmental Protection Agency announced a delay in asking states to draft plans to protect some 21,000 waterways severely impaired by agricultural runoff. Meanwhile, Bush's advisers reconsidered proposals that would have prohibited the development of nearly one-third of the national forests.

No issue was so important or so controversial as climate change, a challenge that most scientists and world leaders agreed required international solutions. During the late 1970s, scientists presented data indicating that the earth was warming, causing polar ice caps to melt, oceans to rise, and ultimately marine life to die, and they pointed to the emission of "greenhouse gases," the by-products of the fossil fuels burned to run factories and automobiles, as the main cause. To curb this dangerous trend, the United States, the European Economic Community, and twenty-eight other countries had ratified the Montreal Protocol on Substances That Deplete the Ozone Layer of 1987, which established a timetable for phasing out the production of greenhouse gases by the end of the century. However, a few years later, in June 1992, at the first Earth Summit sponsored by the United Nations, the U.S. delegates took a more cautious approach, demanding that limits on greenhouse gas emissions be voluntary rather than mandatory. Although responsible for the production of more greenhouse gases than any other nation, nearly 25 percent of the total worldwide, the United States now refused to make a firm commitment.

The controversy came to a head four years later at the world summit on global warming held in Kyoto, Japan. In advance of the meetings, the major U.S. automakers advised President Clinton against signing any treaty. Meanwhile Senate Republicans secured a nonbinding resolution that specified that the terms of any treaty require developing nations, including China, India, and Mexico, to control their emissions as well. Clinton sent Gore to Kyoto to find a middle ground. In the end, the Kyoto Protocol outlined targets and timetables for the reduction of greenhouse gases and required the richer, industrialized countries to take the lead, specifying an average 5.2 percent reduction from 1990s' levels by 2012. Although the fifteen-member nations of the European Union endorsed the terms of the treaty, both Japan and the United States held out.

Shortly after taking office, President George W. Bush announced his opposition to the terms of the Kyoto Protocol, leaving 178 other countries to agree to mandatory reductions in greenhouse gases without the participation of the United States. Bush instead created a task force to conduct additional studies on the impact of human activity on climate change. Meanwhile, the U.S. Energy Information Administration released new data showing that carbon dioxide emissions had risen 3 percent in the United States during the previous year alone, one of the largest increases in recent times. In July 2001, 1,500 scientists affiliated with the UN Intergovernmental Panel on Climate Change, the leading authority on global warming, met in Amsterdam and confirmed, as a key member said, that "the problem of global change is real, and it is more serious than is currently perceived politically." The Kyoto treaty took effect in early 2005, but with the United States on the sidelines, its greatest value may prove mostly symbolic.

The changing climate was only one issue tied to globalization, a term used to characterize the belief that worldwide processes were causing national economies, cultures, and borders to melt away. Beginning in the 1970s, social scientists began to study and debate the degree to which people throughout the world were affected by events happening far from their homelands. The big questions concerning globalization centered on political economy. Now that communism has collapsed, they asked, would a steady expansion of free trade among nations create the basis for a global community?

There were many answers to this question. Some observers argued that the interpenetration of markets and cultural patterns—the enormous sales of Hollywood movies in China, for example—set the stage for other exchanges.

More than 5,000 activists gathered in Seattle in November 1999 to demonstrate against the meeting of the World Trade Organization. The event, which was marked by a violent clash with police and the arrest of dozens of protestors, marked the beginning of a movement for global economic justice.

Others argued that the global economy depended less on "interpenetration" than "domination" of the marketplace by the industrialized nations. Whereas physical occupation of territory defined the form of colonialism that prevailed before World War II, a new "colonialism" had come into existence since the 1960s that relied on a few multinational corporations controlling distant economies throughout the world. To back up this argument, they referred to a UN report that estimated that about 90 percent of the multinational corporations that did business worldwide were headquartered in the industrialized nations of North America, Europe, and Japan. Known collectively as the Triad, the consortium of these nations, home to only 15 percent of the world's population, produced nearly 75 percent of the world's goods by the late 1990s.

What made the current trend toward globalization distinctive was, therefore, not the rate of growth but the absolute volume and character of the exchange. Revenues from multinational corporations grew phenomenally at the end of the twentieth century. Because the member nations of the Triad were homes to the world's largest multinational corporations, they also reaped the largest share of the wealth. A UN annual human development report stated that "global inequalities in income and living standards have reached grotesque proportions." The report offered statistics showing that the gap in wealth between the upper 20 percent and the world's poorest people at the end of the nineteenth century was 30 to 1; by 1990 it reached 60 to 1; and by the end of the twentieth century it had widened to 74 to 1.

While many political observers and scholars predicted that globalization would bring both free markets and democracy to more and more of the world's people, others became increasingly skeptical. At the turn of the twenty-first century, an international protest movement emerged that targeted the most powerful organizations in the global economy, the World Trade Organization (WTO) and the International Monetary Fund (IMF), or World Bank. In November 1999, thousands of protestors converged in Seattle, Washington, site of the annual meeting of the WTO, only to be pushed back by local police. In response, the WTO formulated new procedures for its meetings, secreting delegates behind walls and banning demonstrations from the area near future sites. Nevertheless, confrontations continued, the most dramatic occurring at a meeting of delegates from the eight leading industrial nations in Genoa, Italy, in 2001, which resulted in the death of one protestor.

Experts on globalization could not agree if the trend toward a single international market challenged traditional notions of national sovereignty and laid the foundation for global democracy or if the post–Cold War world order was increasingly challenged by civil wars, ethnic and religious clashes, and the breakup of nation-states.

TERRORIST ATTACK ON AMERICA

On September 11, 2001, hijackers, armed only with knives and box cutters, crashed two jetliners into New York's World Trade Center towers, while a third jetliner slammed into the Pentagon in Virginia. A fourth plane, diverted from its terrorist mission by courageous passengers, hurtled to the ground near Pittsburgh. In all, 246 people perished in the four planes. At the sites of the attack, the damage was devastating. At the Pentagon, which had been built to withstand terrorist attacks, a huge explosion followed by fierce fires destroyed a large section of the defense complex. The death toll soon reached 184, including 59 people who had been on board the hijacked airliner. In New York City, the collapse of the twin towers, most likely caused by the intense fires propelled by the planes' jet fuel, killed 2,752 people, including hundreds of police and rescue workers who had run into the buildings to help. At the end of the day, the New York City Fire Department had lost 350 firefighters, nearly thirty times the number ever lost by the department in a single incident. The stark images of the second plane hitting the World Trade Center, the dramatic collapse of the buildings, and the fear on the faces of thousands fleeing the sites were replayed over and over again on televisions throughout the world (see Seeing History).

SEEING HISTORY

The 9/11 Attacks

The first plane hit at 8:48 A.M.; the second, at 9:03 A.M. Then, as millions of disbelieving television viewers watched, the 110-story Twin Towers collapsed. Already, many Americans were saying that they would forever remember where they were and what they were doing when they heard the news.

Journalists and ordinary Americans alike repeatedly invoked two twentieth-century catastrophes as parallels to 9/11: the Japanese attack at Pearl Harbor on December 7, 1941, and the assassination of John F. Kennedy on November 22, 1963. But neither disaster played out in real time over modern media.

The World Trade Center attack occurred virtually before the eyes of millions. Video cameras caught the image of the second plane hitting the South Tower, panic on the faces of those fleeing, smoke billowing from the towers, and their collapse. Reporters were soon pulling comments from traumatized survivors. The networks immediately preempted regular programming and allowed millions of horrified Americans to watch endless replays. Newscasters drew out the Pearl Harbor analogy as another "Day of Infamy." Within days, programmers edited the videotapes to enhance the drama—adding images of cell phones (to remind viewers of the final calls many of the victims made), overlaying images of the collapsing towers with an unfurling American flag, and piping in patriotic music. To enhance the emotional impact, they borrowed such cinematic techniques as slowing the pace and using jump cuts that fast-timed images of the burning towers with close-ups of anguished observers' faces.

Some seventy history-oriented institutions created an Internet site, 911history.net, to collect oral histories and artifacts. Said Diane Kresh of the Library of Congress, "The Internet has become for many the public commons, a place where they can come together and talk." But the searing pictures of the burning towers will likely remain the preeminent image for 9/11.

What role did the media play in shaping our understanding of the events of September 11, 2001? How does the ability of modern media to dramatize the horror and immediacy of such events enhance their "value" to terrorists launching attacks? In what ways did the 9/11 attacks facilitate the Bush administration's decision to go to war in Iraq?

While the media recalled Pearl Harbor, President Bush declared the deadly attacks an act of war and vowed to hunt down those responsible for the "evil, despicable acts of terror." Congress, with only one dissenting vote, granted him power to take whatever steps necessary. The Department of Justice began what it described as the largest and most intensive investigation ever conducted, and the president issued a blanket warning to all nations that harbor terrorists. Secretary of State Colin Powell stated clearly, "You're either with us or against us." For the first time ever, NATO invoked the mutual defense clause in its founding treaty, which in effect supported any U.S. military response.

Observers described Bush's response as the defining moment of his presidency, as it was for the lives of many Americans. Millions rushed to donate blood, and thousands traveled to New York to assist rescue efforts. Prayer vigils were held in churches, synagogues, mosques, public buildings, and parks, and flags were displayed on homes and cars. Millions of dollars were soon raised for the relief effort and to assist the families of those who perished.

Many businesses, especially those in the travel, entertainment, or hazardous materials industries, were closed in the days following the attack. The stock market, after a three-day pause, reopened to the worst week in the history of Wall Street since the Great Depression. Financial analysts declared that the already faltering economy had now certainly entered a recession.

Perhaps most dramatic was the unprecedented shutdown of all airports in the United States, stranding thousands around the world. Service returned several days later at greatly reduced levels and with enhanced security. But fear had chilled most Americans' spirit. In the face of a $15 billion bailout of the airline industry quickly passed by the Senate, they canceled vacations and applied for refunds for airline tickets already purchased. Two-thirds of those polled believed the worst might still come.

The day following the highly coordinated terrorist attack, President Bush identified the Saudi Arabian Osama bin Laden as the prime suspect. Administration officials linked the airline hijackers, all presumed to be Islamic fundamentalists, to his Al Qaeda network, which apparently had dispatched them to train at American flight schools. Bin Laden and Al Qaeda had based their operations in Afghanistan, where they enjoyed the protection of a government run by the Taliban, a radical Islamist group. The Taliban said its aim was to set up the world's most pure Islamic state, banning what they viewed as the corrupt influences of Western culture, such as movies, television, and the education of women. Although a communiqué from bin Laden denied involvement, U.S. intelligence sources insisted that only bin Laden had the resources to carry out such a sophisticated operation and sufficient motivation. In 1998, bin Laden had issued a decree that granted religious legitimacy to all efforts to expel the United States from the lands of Islam in the Middle East. His network of terrorist cells, which reportedly operated in sixty countries, had directed rage at what they believe to be the global arrogance of the United States—its accumulation of unprecedented wealth when poverty and hopelessness extended across the Middle East.

RESHAPING U.S. FOREIGN POLICY

The September 11 terrorist attacks transformed the presidency of George W. Bush and prompted dramatic changes in the conduct and goals of American foreign policy. At a memorial service for victims, Bush issued an ominous warning: "Our responsibility to history is already clear: to answer these attacks and rid the world of evil." And he outlined a new vision that would guide his policies. "From this day forward," the president announced, "any nation that continues to harbor or support terrorists will be regarded by the United States as a hostile regime." The first theater of the campaign against terror would be Afghanistan. With the support of a United Nations Security Council resolution, the United States delivered an ultimatum to the Taliban-dominated government of Afghanistan: hand over Osama bin Laden and other Al Qaeda leaders presumed to be responsible, and close all terrorist training camps immediately and unconditionally.

On October 7, after the Taliban had refused to comply, President Bush announced the beginning of Operation Enduring Freedom, a joint American–British military campaign aimed at capturing bin Laden and overthrowing the Taliban regime that had sheltered him. An aerial bombing campaign targeted Taliban and Al Qaeda forces, many of whom were Arab fighters from abroad. U.S. Special Forces launched a raid deep into the Taliban stronghold of Kandahar, in southeastern Afghanistan. A prerecorded videotape of Osama bin Laden, broadcast on Al-Jazeera, an Arabic satellite news channel, boasted that the United States would fail in Afghanistan just as the Soviet Union had twenty years earlier. Bin Laden called for a *jihad*, or holy war, of Muslims against the entire non-Muslim world. By mid-November American and British forces, joined by a loose coalition of anti-Taliban Afhgans known as the Northern Alliance, captured the capital city of Kabul.

Fierce fighting continued through December as U.S.-led coalition troops grew to a force of over 10,000. Intensive bombing routed the last remnants of Taliban and Al Qaeda forces from the mountain cave complex of Tora Bora. But bin Laden and much of the Al Qaeda leadership escaped into the tribal areas of Pakistan to the south and east. Despite a massive manhunt and the aid of Pakistan's government, American forces proved unable to capture bin Laden.

A grand council, or *loya jirga*, of Afghan factions and tribal leaders established an interim Afghan government in Kabul under the leadership of Hamid Karzai. In the fall of

2004 Karzai became the first democratically elected president of Afghanistan. But his power was limited largely to Kabul, and old problems stubbornly persisted. Warlords dominated much of the country, the Taliban remained a force in much of the countryside, and the illegal opium trade flourished. A Pentagon report examining the invasion of Afghanistan concluded that the Taliban's removal had given "warlordism, banditry, and opium production a new lease on life."

In his January 2002 State of the Union address President Bush expanded on his vision of a global war on terror. He argued that America now faced a grave and unprecedented danger not merely from Al Qaeda terrorists but also from nation-states seeking chemical, biological, or nuclear weapons of mass destruction. He denounced the regimes of North Korea, Iran, and Iraq as an "axis of evil, arming to threaten the peace of the world." America, the president promised, "will not permit the world's most dangerous regimes to threaten us with the world's most destructive weapons." The new focus on the threat of weapons of mass destruction formed a central part of a sweeping reformulation of American foreign policy. In the fall of 2002 the Bush administration released a new National Security Strategy Report that offered the most radical revision of American foreign policy since the Truman administration in the early days of the Cold War (see Chapter 26). It argued that "the struggle against global terrorism is different from any other war in our history," requiring the United States to "deter and defend against the threat before it is unleashed," acting preemptively and alone if necessary.

The war on terror had a domestic front as well. The partisan bitterness of the 2000 election largely dissolved amid post–9/11 calls for national unity, making it easier for the Bush administration to push new legislation through Congress. Signed into law in the fall of 2001, the USA Patriot Act gave federal officials greater authority to track and intercept communications for law-enforcement and intelligence-gathering purposes, new powers to curb foreign money laundering, and broader discretion in tightening borders against suspected foreign terrorists. It created new crimes and penalties against suspected domestic and international terrorists. In the months after the 9/11 attacks, over a thousand Muslims, some of them U.S. citizens, were arrested and detained, the largest such roundup since the Palmer Raids following World War I (see Chapter 22). Only a few of these suspects were actually charged with crimes related to terrorism. Although there were scattered legal and political protests against these secret detentions, Congress passed the USA Patriot Act II in 2003, further expanding the ability of law-enforcement and intelligence-gathering authorities to perform surveillance and authorize secret arrests.

The Bush administration also created a new cabinet-level Department of Homeland Security (DHS), consolidating twenty-two different domestic agencies to coordinate the nation's defense against military threats. Charged with guarding borders and airports, protecting critical infrastructure, and coordinating responses to future emergencies, the DHS represented the most ambitious reorganization of the federal government since the National Security Act of 1947. Its components included the Immigration and Naturalization Service, the U.S. Customs Service, the Secret Service, the Coast Guard, and the Federal Emergency Management Agency. Not surprisingly, combining so many huge federal bureaucracies into one effective whole proved quite difficult. Critics of the new department worried especially about the continued vulnerability of the nation's ports, rail system, chemical facilities, and nuclear plants to terrorist attacks.

Many questions remained unanswered about the events and circumstances surrounding the 9/11 attacks, particularly the multiple failures within the U.S. intelligence community. The Bush administration at first resisted efforts to mount a full-scale inquiry. But pressure from the families of 9/11 victims, as well as widespread calls for a bipartisan investigation, forced the administration to reverse its opposition, and in November 2002 Congress established the National Commission on Terrorist Attacks upon the United States. The panel of five Republicans and five Democrats worked for twenty months, interviewing more than 1,000 people, including members of the Clinton and Bush administrations, New York City emergency workers, and victims' families, in an effort to paint the most complete picture of what happened and why. In July 2004 it issued its final report—which became an instant best seller—concluding that the government "failed to protect the American people" because it did not understand the "gravity of the threat."

The report was especially damning on the bureaucratic rivalry between the CIA and FBI, which made it difficult to act despite clear evidence that "Islamist terrorists mean to kill Americans in high numbers." It noted that as late as August 2001 National Security Adviser Condoleeza Rice had ignored urgent warnings of impending Al Qaeda attacks brought directly to her by Richard Clarke, the president's counterterrorism chief. The report's recommendations included creation of a new post of national intelligence director, who could lead counterterrorism efforts and coordinate the disparate intelligence operations of the CIA, FBI, Homeland Security, and the Pentagon.

INVASION OF IRAQ

The new pledge to confront threats to security before they reached American shores became known as the Bush Doctrine, and its first major test was Iraq. Planning for a U.S.-led invasion and the overthrow of Saddam Hussein had actually begun in the first weeks after the September 11 attacks. President Bush himself had come to believe that "regime change" was necessary, and several major figures in his administration focused their attention on making the case to the nation and the world. Vice President Dick Cheney, Secretary of Defense Donald Rumsfeld, and his deputy secretary, Paul Wolfowitz, had all worked for Bush's father, President George H. W. Bush, and they viewed removal of Saddam as the unfinished business of the Persian Gulf War of 1991. Along with National Security Adviser Condoleeza Rice and a more reluctant Secretary of State Colin Powell, these aides began to plan for war in early 2002.

Proponents of war made three central claims that they repeated in various public speeches, testimony before Congress, and finally at the United Nations. First, Saddam Hussein must be removed by force because he possessed biological and chemical weapons that posed an imminent threat, and he was making serious efforts to develop nuclear weapons. A National Intelligence Estimate circulated in October 2002 seemed to provide evidence for this view. And advocates for war charged that UN weapons inspectors, active in Iraq throughout the 1990s, had failed to uncover large caches of weapons of mass destruction. Second, they argued that Saddam's intelligence services had

President George W. Bush announces the end of major combat operations in Iraq, May 1, 2003, speaking on the deck of the aircraft carrier USS *Abraham Lincoln*, anchored near San Diego. A banner proclaimed "Mission Accomplished," but American troops would continue to face stiff opposition and endure thousands of casualties battling Iraqi insurgents.

direct connections to the September 11 hijackers and had broader linkages with Al Qaeda operatives around the world. Third, toppling Saddam would make possible a democratic Iraq that could then stand as a beacon of political change throughout the Middle East and Muslim world. The majority of the Iraqi people, they asserted, would welcome and support an American campaign to oust the brutal dictator, ensuring a swift and fairly painless victory.

Throughout late 2002 and early 2003, as American military planners prepared for battle, significant opposition to war emerged at home and abroad. In the United States, many intelligence analysts and veteran diplomats expressed serious doubts about Bush administration claims regarding Saddam's weapons capabilities. They charged that Vice President Cheney and Secretary Rumsfeld had manipulated Pentagon intelligence estimates, selectively emphasizing data based on ideology rather than dispassionate analysis. Others doubted Saddam's links to Al Qaeda and argued that war with Iraq was a distraction from the hunt for bin Laden. Brent Scowcroft, former national security adviser for Bush's father, warned that an invasion of Iraq "could turn the whole region into a cauldron, and thus destroy the war on terrorism." A growing number of Americans questioned the assumption that removing Saddam would make America safer, and many worried that an invasion would likely boost the recruitment efforts of Al Qaeda and other terrorist organizations. Antiwar groups pointed to the large amounts of weapons of mass destruction that had already been identified and destroyed by UN inspectors before they had left Iraq in 1998. Why not let these inspections resume as an alternative to invasion? Millions of citizens began organizing against the push for war via Internet organizations such as MoveOn.org and in vigils and gatherings in their local communities.

Growing opposition to war helped impel the Bush administration to seek international support. In November 2002 the UN Security Council unanimously passed Resolution 1441 calling upon Iraq to fully disarm, provide a detailed account of its weapons programs, and to accept the return of UN weapons inspectors. The U.S. Senate and House of Representatives both voted to authorize the use of military action against Iraq should Saddam Hussein refuse to comply with UN resolutions. But although Iraq released voluminous records about its weapons programs as UN inspectors resumed their work, the United States concluded in December that the documents were inadequate and that Iraq was in "material breach" of Resolution 1441.

In February 2003 Secretary of State Powell made a detailed argument for war before the Security Council. Meanwhile, the antiwar movement went global on February 15 as millions of demonstrators turned out in the streets of over 300 cities, including 500,000 in New York, 2 million in London, and 1 million in Rome. This was the single largest expression of antiwar sentiment in history. At the UN, facing staunch opposition to war from France, Russia, and Germany, who argued for

MAP 31.2 Invasion in Iraq On March 20, 2003, American and British troops poured into Iraq from bases in Kuwait, crossing the Iraqi border to the east near Safwan. The American Third Infantry Division used armored bulldozers to create wide gaps in the Iraqi defensive line.

giving the UN inspection process more time, the United States withdrew its proposed resolution authorizing the use of force in Iraq (see Map 31.2).

Lacking UN approval, the Bush administration would invade Iraq with what it called a "coalition of the willing," with Great Britain as its major partner. On March 19 President Bush announced the beginning of war, claiming the United States "has the sovereign authority to use force in assuring its own national security." He also told Iraqis "the tyrant will soon be gone; the day of your liberation is near." Some 150,000 American troops based in Kuwait, along with a smaller British force, began a thrust toward Baghdad; and a "shock and awe" campaign of massive aerial bombing began on several major Iraqi cities. The American and British forces overwhelmed the regular Iraqi army fairly easily, suffering relatively light casualties. By early April they had secured Baghdad, Mosul, Basra, Kirkuk, and other major cities. Hundreds of journalists "embedded" with American combat units provided live television coverage of

various battles. On May 1, 2003, on the flight deck of the USS *Abraham Lincoln*, anchored off the San Diego coast, President Bush made a dramatic appearance before a cheering throng of American sailors and a live television audience. Standing beneath a large banner reading "Mission Accomplished," Bush announced the official end of combat operations. "In the battle of Iraq," the president declared, "the United States and our allies have prevailed."

But the purely military act of removing Saddam's regime from power proved far simpler than bringing peace and stability to Iraq. And rather than weaken terrorists, it instead strengthened a new generation of terror networks now drawn to do battle with American forces there. As the invasion turned into an occupation, the plight of ordinary Iraqis and American soldiers worsened quickly. In the summer of 2003 the Coalition Provisional Authority (CPA), led by Ambassador Paul Bremer, created the Governing Council to serve as an interim government for the new Iraq. But many parts of the country plunged into chaos amid widespread looting, killing, and near anarchy. Several decisions made by the CPA, including the disbanding of the Iraqi Army, contributed to the lawless climate. Millions of Iraqis found their electricity, water, and basic food supplies disrupted or unavailable.

As UN relief workers, journalists, and private American contractors poured into the country to help with reconstruction efforts, a violent campaign of suicide bombings, shootings, roadside ambushes, and kidnappings spread across Iraq. Insurgents began releasing videos of gruesome executions—often by beheading—of captured prisoners. In December 2003 the capture of Saddam Hussein, who had gone into hiding, proved a symbolic victory at best.

A coordinated, heavily armed, and well-financed resistance to the American occupation gained strength in early 2004. It included elements of Saddam's Baath party, foreign Islamist fighters, disaffected Sunni Muslims, and criminal gangs. Desperate poverty, widespread unemployment, deep anger toward the American occupiers, and hundreds of thousands of alienated former soldiers provided a continual supply of fresh recruits. The CPA was both unprepared and overwhelmed as it tried to wrestle with problems no one had even thought about, much less planned for. Tensions between major religious groups fueled the insurgency, as Sunni Muslims feared the loss of their traditional power to the majority Shiites. Badly stretched American forces, which included a high percentage of National Guard and Army Reserve units, were forced back into combat. In cities like Falluja and Najaf, a year after President Bush had confidently declared the fighting over, American troops engaged in the toughest fighting since the Vietnam War.

Troubling new questions about the decision to invade and the conduct of the war emerged. In early 2004 David Kay, the Bush administration's former chief weapons inspector, told Congress that any stockpiles of chemical or biological weapons Saddam might have possessed in the early 1990s had been destroyed by UN inspections and Iraq's own actions. Nor was there any nuclear weapons program. "It turns out," Kay testified, "we were all wrong, probably, in my judgment. And that is most disturbing."

In the spring of 2004, graphic images and descriptions of Iraqi detainees abused and tortured by American guards in the Abu Ghraib prison were broadcast around the world, inciting international outrage and protest. In public President Bush expressed "a deep disgust that those prisoners were treated the way they were treated." But White House memos revealed that the president's legal counsel Alberto Gonzales had urged Bush to declare the war on terror and the treatment of Al Qaeda and Taliban prisoners exempt from the provisions of the Geneva Convention.

U.S. Marines and Iraqi Special Forces conduct a security patrol in the war-torn city of Falluja, November 23, 2004. The brutal fighting there made it clear that defeating the Iraqi insurgency would be a tougher battle for American forces than the overthrow of Saddam Hussein's government.

This would reduce the threat of American officials being prosecuted for committing war crimes. In an angry open letter to President Bush a distinguished group of 130 American jurists, including twelve former federal judges, a former director of the FBI, and the heads of several human rights organizations, denounced these memos for seeking to "circumvent long established and universally acknowledged principles of law and common decency."

With American forces bogged down in the occupation and the resistance to it widening, American military commanders found themselves strapped for replacement troops. Tens of thousands of National Guard and Army Reserve soldiers were forced to stay in Iraq beyond their regular tour of duty, subject in effect to a "backdoor draft." By early 2005, over 1,500 Americans had been killed in Iraq and nearly 12,000 wounded, many of them severely. Estimates of Iraqi civilian casualties ranged as high as 100,000.

In July 2004 the Coalition Provisional Authority dissolved itself and formally transferred sovereignty to the interim Iraqi government. In January 2005 Iraq conducted its first national elections for an assembly charged with writing a new constitution by 2006. Amidst enormous media coverage, the Bush administration hailed the elections as a historic step toward democracy. Shiite Muslims, representing roughly 60 percent of the population, stood ready to replace the minority Sunni Muslims as the dominant political force. The Shiites themselves were divided into factions, including those with close ties to the Shiite rulers of neighboring Iran.

THE ELECTION OF 2004

President Bush launched his reelection bid determined to make national security and the war on terror the centerpieces of his campaign. With Iraq dominating the news, Bush described himself as a "wartime president" and appealed to patriotism and national unity. This strategy allowed him to largely ignore domestic issues, where his political strength was less certain. Bush promoted a sweeping tax cut in 2001 as the best way to jump-start the economy and create new jobs. The Economic Growth and Tax Relief Reconciliation Act squeaked through Congress with bipartisan support. It lowered tax rates and included a popular provision resulting in most Americans receiving a check in the mail from the IRS as "reconciliation" for paying too much in taxes.

Yet a small percentage of wealthy Americans benefited disproportionately from the cuts, which also expanded budget deficits as the government took in less money. While many Americans did see a decline in their income tax payments, many found that increases in local property taxes, school tuitions, and other fees continued to climb. Although by 2002 the economy was technically in recovery from the recession of 2000, economic growth and job creation were weak across most of the nation. And the historically unprecedented combination of fighting an expensive war abroad while lowering income and corporate taxes at home brought spiraling budget deficits that wiped out the surpluses of the Clinton years.

As the American dollar weakened against foreign currencies like the Euro and the Chinese *yuan*, a growing chorus of economists warned that high levels of American consumption and the superheated real estate markets in many U.S. cities made the economy increasingly vulnerable to the whims of foreign investors. If budget deficits continued to grow, foreign buyers of U.S. government securities might look elsewhere, with potentially devastating effects on the American economy.

Democrats, still smarting from the disputed 2000 election in which their nominee Al Gore had won the popular vote by over half a million, believed their chances for retaking the White House were strong. But the political aftermath of the September 11 attacks, the new focus on strengthening national security, and the invasion of Iraq forced attention away from the economic issues that had traditionally been their greatest source of voter appeal. In the early months of campaigning for the nomination, former Vermont Governor Howard Dean emerged as a surprising front-runner. Dean, looking to distinguish himself from more conservative Democrats, strongly opposed the invasion of Iraq and touted himself as representing "the Democratic wing of the Democratic Party." He energized antiwar sentiment and attracted large sums of money from Democrats through innovative use of the Internet. But once Democrats in primary states like Iowa and New Hampshire actually started voting, Dean stumbled badly and his campaign fizzled.

After winning in Iowa and New Hampshire, Senator John Kerry of Massachusetts quickly assumed the mantle of front-runner and captured the Democratic nomination. Kerry's life story helped him appeal to a broad cross section of the party. He had volunteered for naval combat duty in Vietnam, where he was wounded and highly decorated. When he returned home he became a leader in the Vietnam Veterans Against the War (VVAW) and in 1971 had made a memorable televised appearance before Congress criticizing U.S. policy. He had gone into state politics and won election to the Senate in 1984. His biography suggested he could bridge some of the deep Vietnam-era differences that still divided Americans. And his status as an authentic war hero would bolster Democrats' chances of appealing to voters' concerns about national security.

But after capturing the nomination, Kerry's campaign faltered. Republicans and their allies attacked his war record, claiming that his Purple Hearts and other medals had been undeserved. His patrician background, distant personality, and cool manner made it difficult for many voters to warm up to him. He could not articulate a clear vision or theme for his candidacy and the Republican campaign succeeded in painting him as a "flip flopper" who constantly changed his position on issues. Perhaps most damningly, Kerry was unable to communicate a clear position on the Iraq war. Along with many other Democrats he had voted to authorize the use of force, but he criticized President Bush's conduct of the war. Yet even when asked, in the late summer of 2004, whether he would have voted differently if he knew that there was no Iraqi weapons of mass destruction threat and no Iraqi link with the September 11 attacks, he refused to change his view.

President George W. Bush won reelection with 51 percent of the popular vote to Kerry's 48 percent, a 3-million-vote margin. He garnered 279 electoral votes to Kerry's 252, as Ohio, with 20 electoral votes, proved the key state. The results could be interpreted in a variety of ways. Bush polled the first popular vote majority in twenty years and the overall turnout of 60 percent was the highest since 1968. Republicans fielded a formidable grassroots get-out-the-vote operation, especially in small-town and rural America, where they appealed effectively to many voters on so-called "moral values" issues: opposition to gay marriage and abortion rights. Republicans also increased their majorities in both the House and the Senate. But Bush's victory margin was also the smallest for reelection in a century.

President Bush claimed his victory represented a victory for his Iraq war policy and promised to spend his hard-won "political capital" on the domestic front as well. In his State of the Union address delivered in February 2005, Bush defined his second-term agenda around two issues. On the foreign policy front, he hailed the recent Iraqi elections and promised to keep American forces there until Iraqis could provide their own security. Domestically, the president challenged Congress to "reinvent Social Security," as he called for a major overhaul of the New Deal–era social insurance program by emphasizing private investment accounts. Though not as close as the 2000 election, and without the disconnect between popular and electoral vote, few would dispute that the 2004 election revealed a nation that was as politically divided as any time since the Civil War.

HURRICANE KATRINA

In his second term, President Bush discovered that the "political capital" he had invoked in celebrating his narrow re-election victory would soon evaporate. As the Iraq war dragged into its third year, the post–9/11 political consensus largely dissolved as victory proved elusive and increasingly difficult to define. On the domestic front, his administration also endured a heated and prolonged controversy sparked by its response to one of the most cataclysmic events of the new century—Hurricane Katrina. In late August 2005, a tropical depression gained speed to become the third strongest hurricane to make landfall in the United States.

On August 25, Katrina made its way through Florida, killing six people, destroying homes, and uprooting trees before heading into the Gulf of Mexico. By the afternoon of the next day, Louisiana Governor Kathleen Babineaux Blanco declared a state of emergency for the state. Closely following the westward track of the storm, on August 27 Mayor Ray Nagin called for an evacuation of New Orleans, a city all below sea level, and opened the Superdome "as a refuge of last resort" for those without other resources. President Bush invoked the Stafford Disaster and Emergency Assistance Act, passed in 1887, which had created the Federal Emergency Management Agency (FEMA) as a mechanism to provide federal assistance to state and local governments in the case of disaster.

Hurricane Katrina made three landfalls in Louisiana, blowing houses off their foundations and submerging others. In New Orleans, several parishes were destroyed, including the Lower Ninth Ward, the home to an African American population already steeped in poverty. Canal levees failed, and by August 31, 80 percent of New Orleans was under water. The National Guard moved in, and the U.S. Navy relocated ships to support the relief efforts. President Bush, who had been vacationing at his ranch in Crawford, Texas, did not rush to the area but instead four days after the hurricane hit flew over in *Air Force One* on his early return to the White House. He declared a public health emergency for the entire Gulf Coast but predicted that, despite the enormous devastation, New Orleans would eventually recover from the costliest disaster in U.S. history.

Meanwhile, the rescue operations stalled amid bureaucratic mishaps. The American Red Cross, poised to set up a shelter in New Orleans, was told to wait while the National Guard handled the distribution of food and water. Conditions at the Superdome deteriorated to a point that newscasters described a reign of anarchy. Shortages of food, water, blankets, sanitary facilities, and medical supplies had put the lives of the 5,000 refugees at risk. Governor Blanco requested an additional 40,000 National Guard troops to quell the unrest, now spread across the city. Only slowly did FEMA relocate staff to the area and, worse, actually hampered private relief efforts. For example, FEMA officials turned away six trailer trucks of water dispatched by Wal-Mart. Television crews captured scenes

A U.S. Coast Guard helicopter rescues flood-stranded victims of Hurricane Katrina from their homes in New Orleans, September 2005. Images like this one received wide circulation in the news media, prompting criticism of the government's failures to offer more and swifter help to Katrina's victims.

of people stranded on rooftops, waiting rescue while the waters continued to rise, and bodies floating in the streets.

President Bush appeared perplexed by the situation. He excused FEMA's inept response by claiming that the disaster caught everyone off guard, although the National Weather Service had warned that Katrina could bring "human suffering incredible by modern standards." Everyone knew that the levees would not withstand a surge of water that a Category 5 hurricane would surely cause. Only on the sixth day after the hurricane did Bush visit the Gulf area, although even then he did not approach the people dislocated by the storm. Local officials kept up a steady barrage of complaints. Louisiana Senator Mary Landrieu characterized FEMA's response as "staggering incompetence." The press vilified President Bush, labeling his performance in the face of this disaster as "a national disgrace."

Much of the shame resulted from the way the unfolding of events underscored the race and class dimensions of the tragedy. The population of New Orleans, with a poverty rate of 23 percent, 76 percent higher than the national average, was nearly 68 percent African American, and more than a quarter of the black citizens of New Orleans lacked access to an automobile. When the mandatory evacuation order came, the majority of white residents drove away from the city, while many black residents had no choice but to board the special buses headed for the ill-equipped Superdome. When mainly black evacuees attempted to cross a bridge linking New Orleans with the suburb of Gretna, the white suburbanites turned them back at gunpoint. A news poll indicated that 60 percent of African Americans believed that race was a major factor in the government's slow and inefficient rescue efforts.

CHRONOLOGY

1981	MTV and CNN start broadcasting as cable channels
1986	Immigration Reform and Control Act addresses concerns about undocumented aliens
1987	Allan Bloom publishes *The Closing of the American Mind*
1988	George H. W. Bush is elected president
1989	Tiananmen Square demonstration in China
1990	Iraqi invasion of Kuwait leads to massive U.S. military presence in the Persian Gulf
1991	Operation Desert Storm forces Iraq out of Kuwait
	Operation Rescue launched in Wichita, Kansas
1992	Rodney King verdict sparks rioting in Los Angeles
	Bill Clinton is elected president
1993	Terrorist bombing of World Trade Center kills six people
	Federal agents conduct seige of Branch Davidian compound in Waco, Texas
	Clinton administration introduces comprehensive health care reform, but it fails to win passage in Congress
	Congress approves the North American Free Trade Agreement (NAFTA)
1994	Republicans win control of Senate and House for first time in forty years
	Congress approves the General Agreement on Tariffs and Trade (GATT)
	Congress passes the Comprehensive AIDS Revenue Emergency Act
	Congress passes Defense of Marriage Act
	California voters approve Proposition 187
1995	Bombing of Alfred P. Murrah Federal Building in Oklahoma City kills 168 people
1996	Congress passes Welfare Reform Act
	Congress enacts the Antiterrorism and Effective Death Penalty Act
	President Bill Clinton is reelected
1997	Kyoto Protocol endorsed by European Union but not United States
1998	U.S. embassies in Kenya and Tanzania bombed by terrorists
	House of Representatives votes to impeach President Clinton, but vote fails in Senate
1999	U.S. joins NATO forces in Kosovo
	Protesters disrupt meetings of the World Trade Organization in Seattle
2000	USS *Cole* bombed by terrorists
2001	George W. Bush becomes president after contested election
	Terrorists attack World Trade Center and Pentagon
	U.S. begins military campaign in Afghanistan
	Homeland Security Department established
	USA Patriot Act passed
2003	Invasion of Iraq and occupation
	USA Patriot Act II passed
2004	Release of *The 9/11 Commission Report*
	Reelection of George W. Bush
2005	Elections in Iraq
	Hurricane Katrina devastates New Orleans and the Gulf Coast

More than 1,600 people had died in New Orleans alone, and nearly a million had fled the greater region. In 2007 the population of New Orleans still hovered around 250,000, down from the nearly 485,000 who had lived inside the city limits at the time of the 2000 U.S. census. By 2007 business activity—especially tourism in the French Quarter district—had begun to revive, and the city managed to hold its annual Mardi Gras celebration, long a magnet for visitors from around the world. But the long range effects of Katrina loomed over the city's future. The devastating mental health problems associated with the catastrophe—the abrupt loss of loved ones and homes, the break-up of families, the sense of hopelessness and depression—were difficult to quantify but continued to plague tens of thousands of people. Two years after Katrina struck, the future of New Orleans—its housing, its economic base, and the world of its working class African American population—remained unclear at best.

DIVIDED GOVERNMENT, DIVIDED NATION

The Bush administration found itself on the defensive from attacks on its weak response to Hurricane Katrina. The president's plan to privatize Social Security also proved politically unpopular, as did rising gasoline prices. It also faced growing disillusionment with the Iraq War, the single issue that most clearly defined the Bush presidency. Thus, the 2006 elections loomed as a kind of referendum on the war itself.

The administration continued to defend the war as part of a broader, long-term struggle against global terrorism carried out by Islamic extremists. The president and other officials made analogies to World War II and other historic conflicts, but the differences were all too apparent. With no draft, no rationing, no war bond drives, and no war related taxes, there was little sense of shared sacrifice. The Iraq war remained a distant reality for the vast majority of Americans. Yet intensive television and press coverage kept the bloody stalemate front and center in the nation's consciousness. By the summer of 2007 the number of Americans killed in Iraq had climbed above 3,800. Over 27,000 more Americans had been wounded, with over half suffering such severe injuries as amputation and serious burns.

In Iraq itself the government of Prime Minister Nouri al-Maliki proved unable to provide basic security and services in Baghdad and many other areas of the country. The insurgency against the American occupation continued to spread, attracting elements of Al Qaeda, ex–Iraqi Army soldiers, foreign Islamic fighters, criminal gangs, and many Iraqi Sunnis fearful of the growing power of the Shiite majority. These groups were by no means united, as temporary alliances formed and dissolved depending on local conditions. The situation deteriorated further as heavily armed Shiite and Sunni militias escalated sectarian violence. Violent struggles between rival Shiite factions also destabilized Baghdad and contributed to a lawless atmosphere. Some 2 million Iraqis, including much of the nation's educated middle class and professionals, fled the country to nearby nations such as Syria, Jordan, and Egypt. Another 2 million Iraqis, forced to leave their neighborhoods and towns, found themselves refugees within their own country. American forces and their Iraqi Army allies could not establish order amid what looked more and more like a civil war.

The 2006 midterm elections in the United States brought a return of the divided government that had characterized the Clinton years. But this time, the parties and players were reversed. Democrats took control of both the House (233–202) and the Senate (51–49) for the first time since 1992. Nancy Pelosi (D-CA) became the first female Speaker of the House. A large number of Democrats had originally supported the invasion of Iraq, but many had since changed their minds and now believed that a military "victory" was both impossible and an illusion. Congress tried to reassert itself in the foreign policy arena by putting limits on the president's requests for war funding. But Democrats enjoyed only a narrow majority in Congress and were unable to override President Bush's vetoes. Thus, as the war dragged into its fifth year—longer than the United States' involvement in World War II—the government and the nation remained deeply divided over Iraq.

— REVIEW QUESTIONS —

1. How is the "new economy" different from the old economy? How has it reshaped American business and financial practices? Explain the relationship between the new economy and electronic media, such as the Internet and cable television.

2. Evaluate the presidency of Bill Clinton. Compare his domestic and foreign policies to those of the Republican presidents who preceded and followed him in office. What was the impact of the scandals that plagued his presidency?

3. Describe the major demographic trends revealed by the 2000 census. Identify the racial and ethnic groups with the greatest gains in population. How have various legislative acts since 1965 affected immigration to the United States? How have communities changed as a result of the influx of new immigrants?

4. The concept of globalization is highly controversial. Are borders between nations "melting away" as some scholars contend? How does this concept square with the description of the United States as the single superpower in the world? Does this concept apply primarily to economics, or is it useful for discussing issues related to culture, media, the environment, and population trends?

5. How has the "war on terror" differed from other wars in this century? How and why did the 9/11 attacks lead to fundamental changes in the conduct of U.S. foreign policy? What arguments for the American invasion of Iraq in 2003 do you find most and least persuasive?

— RECOMMENDED READING

William C. Berman, *From the Center to the Edge: The Politics and Policies of the Clinton Presidency* (2001). A highly readable assessment of Clinton's accomplishments as president. Although focusing on domestic issues, including the impact of Clinton's impeachment trial, Berman also considers major foreign policy developments in the context of globalization.

Douglas Brinkley, *The Great Deluge: Hurricane Katrina, New Orleans, and the Mississippi Gulf Coast* (2006). The first comprehensive narrative history of Hurricane Katrina, the government response, and the aftermath.

Richard Clarke, *Against All Enemies: Inside America's War on Terror* (2004). A critical look at the war on terror from a veteran diplomat and counterterrorism expert who argues that the invasion of Iraq will serve to strengthen Al Qaeda and allied groups.

Stephen Coll, *Ghost Wars: The Secret History of the CIA, Afghanistan, and Bin Laden from the Soviet Invasion to September 10, 2001* (2004). Deeply researched examination of the CIA's influence in Afghanistan and its support for Islamic fundamentalists resisting Soviet occupation.

Thomas Frank, *What's the Matter with Kansas? How Conservatives Won the Heart of America* (2004). A provocative look at how political conservatives have successfully recast themselves as the voice of populism and ordinary Americans over the last thirty years.

James Glanz and Eric Lipton, *City in the Sky: The Rise and Fall of the World Trade Center* (2003). A thorough investigation of the planning that gave birth to the two iconic towers in New York City and their destruction on September 11, 2001. Written by two journalists, this clear, detailed, and well-illustrated study poses hard questions about the collapse and recovery efforts.

National Commission on Terrorist Attacks upon the United States, *The 9/11 Commission Report* (2004). The best-selling final report of the independent bipartisan inquiry into the events surrounding the 9/11 attacks, including recommendations for reorganizing American intelligence to more effectively meet terrorist threats.

Todd S. Purdum, *A Time of Our Choosing: America's War in Iraq* (2004). An excellent narrative account of how the Bush administration made the decision to invade Iraq.

Thomas E. Ricks, *Fiasco: The American Military Adventure in Iraq* (2006). The first comprehensive and critical account of the American invasion of Iraq with a focus on lack of prewar planning for the occupation.

Sam Roberts, *Who We Are Now: The Changing Face of America in the Twenty-First Century* (2004). Using the 2000 census, Roberts focuses on the changes in American society that occurred between 1990 and 2000. He discusses population growth, the largest decadal increase in American history, as well as shifts in ethnic composition, family structure, and inequality.

Mary C. Waters and Reed Ueda, eds., *The New Americans: A Guide to Immigration since 1965* (2007). A team of interdisciplinary scholars provides an overview of the new immigrant populations since 1965.

Laurence Wright, *The Looming Tower: Al-Qaeda and the Road to 9/11* (2006). Pulitzer Prize–winning analysis of the origins, ideology, and operations of the group responsible for the 9/11 terrorist attacks.

THE DECLARATION OF INDEPENDENCE

When in the course of human events it becomes necessary for one people to dissolve the political bands which have connected them with another and to assume, among the powers of the earth, the separate and equal station to which the laws of nature and of nature's God entitle them, a decent respect to the opinions of mankind requires that they should declare the causes which impel them to the separation.

We hold these truths to be self-evident, that all men are created equal; that they are endowed by their Creator with certain unalienable rights; that among these are life, liberty, and the pursuit of happiness. That, to secure these rights, governments are instituted among men, deriving their just powers from the consent of the governed; that, whenever any form of government becomes destructive of these ends, it is the right of the people to alter or to abolish it, and to institute a new government, laying its foundation on such principles, and organizing its powers in such form, as to them shall seem most likely to effect their safety and happiness. Prudence, indeed, will dictate that governments long established should not be changed for light and transient causes; and, accordingly, all experience hath shown that mankind are more disposed to suffer, while evils are sufferable, than to right themselves by abolishing the forms to which they are accustomed. But when a long train of abuses and usurpations, pursuing invariably the same object, evinces a design to reduce them under absolute despotism, it is their right, it is their duty, to throw off such government and to provide new guards for their future security. Such has been the patient sufferance of these colonies, and such is now the necessity which constrains them to alter their former systems of government. The history of the present King of Great Britain is a history of repeated injuries and usurpations, all having, in direct object, the establishment of an absolute tyranny over these States. To prove this, let facts be submitted to a candid world:

He has refused his assent to laws the most wholesome and necessary for the public good.

He has forbidden his governors to pass laws of immediate and pressing importance, unless suspended in their operation till his assent should be obtained; and, when so suspended, he has utterly neglected to attend to them.

He has refused to pass other laws for the accommodation of large districts of people, unless those people would relinquish the right of representation in the legislature, a right inestimable to them and formidable to tyrants only.

He has called together legislative bodies at places unusual, uncomfortable, and distant from the depository of their public records, for the sole purpose of fatiguing them into compliance with his measures.

He has dissolved representative houses, repeatedly, for opposing, with manly firmness, his invasions on the rights of the people.

He has refused, for a long time after such dissolutions, to cause others to be elected; whereby the legislative powers, incapable of annihilation, have returned to the people at large for their exercise; the state remaining, in the meantime, exposed to all the danger of invasion from without and convulsions within.

He has endeavored to prevent the population of these States; for that purpose, obstructing the laws for naturalization of foreigners, refusing to pass others to encourage their migration hither, and raising the conditions of new appropriations of lands.

He has obstructed the administration of justice by refusing his assent to laws for establishing judiciary powers.

He has made judges dependent on his will alone for the tenure of their offices and the amount and payment of their salaries.

He has erected a multitude of new offices and sent hither swarms of officers to harass our people and eat out their substance.

He has kept among us, in time of peace, standing armies, without the consent of our legislatures.

He has affected to render the military independent of, and superior to, the civil power.

He has combined with others to subject us to a jurisdiction foreign to our Constitution and unacknowledged by our laws, giving his assent to their acts of pretended legislation—

For quartering large bodies of armed troops among us;

For protecting them by mock trial, from punishment for any murders which they should commit on the inhabitants of these States;

For cutting off our trade with all parts of the world;

For imposing taxes on us without our consent;

For depriving us, in many cases, of the benefit of trial by jury;

For transporting us beyond seas to be tried for pretended offences;

For abolishing the free system of English laws in a neighboring province, establishing therein an arbitrary government, and enlarging its boundaries, so as to render it at once an example and fit instrument for introducing the same absolute rule into these colonies;

For taking away our charters, abolishing our most valuable laws, and altering, fundamentally, the powers of our governments.

For suspending our own legislatures and declaring themselves invested with power to legislate for us in all cases whatsoever.

He has abdicated government here by declaring us out of his protection and waging war against us.

He has plundered our seas, ravaged our coasts, burnt our towns, and destroyed the lives of our people.

He is, at this time, transporting large armies of foreign mercenaries to complete the works of death, desolation, and tyranny already begun with circumstances of cruelty and perfidy scarcely paralleled in the most barbarous ages, and totally unworthy the head of a civilized nation.

He has constrained our fellow citizens, taken captive on the high seas, to bear arms against their country, to become the executioners of their friends and brethren, or to fall themselves by their hands.

He has excited domestic insurrections amongst us and has endeavored to bring on the inhabitants of our frontiers, the merciless Indian savages, whose known rule of warfare is an undistinguished destruction of all ages, sexes, and conditions.

In every stage of these oppressions, we have petitioned for redress in the most humble terms; our repeated petitions have been answered only by repeated injury. A prince whose character is thus marked by every act which may define a tyrant is unfit to be the ruler of a free people.

Nor have we been wanting in attention to our British brethren. We have warned them, from time to time, of attempts made by their legislature to extend an unwarrantable jurisdiction over us. We have reminded them of the circumstances of our emigration and settlement here. We have appealed to their native justice and magnanimity, and we have conjured them, by the ties of our common kindred, to disavow these usurpations, which would inevitably interrupt our connections and correspondence. They, too, have been deaf to the voice of justice and consanguinity. We must, therefore, acquiesce in the necessity which denounces our separation, and hold them, as we hold the rest of mankind, enemies in war, in peace, friends.

We, therefore, the representatives of the United States of America, in general Congress assembled, appealing to the Supreme Judge of the world for the rectitude of our intentions, do, in the name and by the authority of the good people of these colonies, solemnly publish and declare, that these united colonies are, and of right ought to be, free and independent states: that they are absolved from all allegiance to the British Crown, and that all political connection between them and the state of Great Britain is, and ought to be, totally dissolved; and that, as free and independent states, they have full power to levy war, conclude peace, contract alliances, establish commerce, and to do all other acts and things which independent states may of right do. And, for the support of this declaration, with a firm reliance on the protection of Divine Providence, we mutually pledge to each other our lives, our fortunes, and our sacred honor.

THE CONSTITUTION OF THE UNITED STATES OF AMERICA

We the people of the United States, in order to form a more perfect union, establish justice, insure domestic tranquillity, provide for the common defense, promote the general welfare, and secure the blessings of liberty to ourselves and our posterity, do ordain and establish this Constitution for the United States of America.

Article I

Section 1. All legislative powers herein granted shall be vested in a Congress of the United States, which shall consist of a Senate and House of Representatives.

Section 2. 1. The House of Representatives shall be composed of members chosen every second year by the people of the several States, and the electors in each State shall have the qualifications requisite for electors of the most numerous branch of the State legislature.

2. No person shall be a representative who shall not have attained to the age of twenty-five years, and been seven years a citizen of the United States, and who shall not, when elected, be an inhabitant of that State in which he shall be chosen.

3. Representatives and direct taxes[1] shall be apportioned among the several States which may be included within this Union, according to their respective numbers, which shall be determined by adding to the whole number of free persons, including those bound to service for a term of years, and excluding Indians not taxed, three fifths of all other persons.[2] The actual enumeration shall be made within three years after the first meeting of the Congress of the United States, and within every subsequent term of ten years, in such manner as they shall by law direct. The number of representatives shall not exceed one for every thirty thousand, but each State shall have at least one representative; and until such enumeration shall be made, the State of New Hampshire shall be entitled to choose three, Massachusetts eight, Rhode Island and Providence Plantations one, Connecticut five, New York six, New Jersey four, Pennsylvania eight, Delaware one, Maryland six, Virginia ten, North Carolina five, South Carolina five, and Georgia three.

4. When vacancies happen in the representation from any State, the executive authority thereof shall issue writs of election to fill such vacancies.

5. The House of Representatives shall choose their speaker and other officers; and shall have the sole power of impeachment.

Section 3. 1. The Senate of the United States shall be composed of two senators from each State, chosen by the legislature thereof,[3] for six years; and each senator shall have one vote.

---

[1]See the Sixteenth Amendment.

[2]See the Fourteenth Amendment.
[3]See the Seventeenth Amendment.

2. Immediately after they shall be assembled in consequence of the first election, they shall be divided as equally as may be into three classes. The seats of the senators of the first class shall be vacated at the expiration of the second year, of the second class at the expiration of the fourth year, and of the third class at the expiration of the sixth year, so that one third may be chosen every second year; and if vacancies happen by resignation, or otherwise, during the recess of the legislature of any State, the executive thereof may make temporary appointments until the next meeting of the legislature, which shall then fill such vacancies.[4]

3. No person shall be a senator who shall not have attained to the age of thirty years, and been nine years a citizen of the United States, and who shall not, when elected, be an inhabitant of that State for which he shall be chosen.

4. The Vice President of the United States shall be President of the Senate, but shall have no vote, unless they be equally divided.

5. The Senate shall choose their other officers, and also a president pro tempore, in the absence of the Vice President, or when he shall exercise the office of the President of the United States.

6. The Senate shall have the sole power to try all impeachments. When sitting for that purpose, they shall be on oath or affirmation. When the President of the United States is tried, the chief justice shall preside: and no person shall be convicted without the concurrence of two thirds of the members present.

7. Judgment in cases of impeachment shall not extend further than to removal from office, and disqualification to hold and enjoy any office of honor, trust or profit under the United States: but the party convicted shall nevertheless be liable and subject to indictment, trial, judgment and punishment, according to law.

Section 4. 1. The times, places, and manner of holding elections for senators and representatives, shall be prescribed in each State by the legislature thereof; but the Congress may at any time by law make or alter such regulations, except as to the places of choosing senators.

2. The Congress shall assemble at least once in every year, and such meeting shall be on the first Monday in December, unless they shall by law appoint a different day.

Section 5. 1. Each House shall be the judge of the elections, returns and qualifications of its own members, and a majority of each shall constitute a quorum to do business; but a smaller number may adjourn from day to day, and may be authorized to compel the attendance of absent members, in such manner, and under such penalties as each House may provide.

2. Each House may determine the rules of its proceedings, punish its members for disorderly behavior, and, with the concurrence of two thirds, expel a member.

3. Each House shall keep a journal of its proceedings, and from time to time publish the same, excepting such parts as may in their judgment require secrecy; and the yeas and nays of the members of either House on any question shall, at the desire of one fifth of those present, be entered on the journal.

4. Neither House, during the session of Congress, shall, without the consent of the other, adjourn for more than three days, nor to any other place than that in which the two Houses shall be sitting.

Section 6. 1. The senators and representatives shall receive a compensation for their services, to be ascertained by law, and paid out of the Treasury of the United States. They shall in all cases, except treason, felony, and breach of the peace, be privileged from arrest during their attendance at the session of their respective Houses, and in going to and returning from the same; and for any speech or debate in either House, they shall not be questioned in any other place.

2. No senator or representative shall, during the time for which he was elected, be appointed to any civil office under the authority of the United States, which shall have been created, or the emoluments whereof shall have been increased, during such time; and no person holding any office under the United States shall be a member of either House during his continuance in office.

Section 7. 1. All bills for raising revenue shall originate in the House of Representatives; but the Senate may propose or concur with amendments as on other bills.

2. Every bill which shall have passed the House of Representatives and the Senate, shall, before it become a law, be presented to the President of the United States; If he approves he shall sign it, but if not he shall return it, with his objections, to that House in which it shall have originated, who shall enter the objections at large on their journal, and proceed to reconsider it. If after such reconsideration two thirds of that House shall agree to pass the bill, it shall be sent, together with the objections, to the other House, by which it shall likewise be reconsidered, and if approved by two thirds of that House, it shall become a law. But in all such cases the votes of both Houses shall be determined by yeas and nays, and the names of the persons voting for and against the bill shall be entered on the journal of each House respectively. If any bill shall not be returned by the President within ten days (Sundays excepted) after it shall have been presented to him, the same shall be a law, in like manner as if he had signed it, unless the Congress by their adjournment prevent its return, in which case it shall not be a law.

3. Every order, resolution, or vote to which the concurrence of the Senate and the House of Representatives may be necessary (except on a question of adjournment) shall be presented to the President of the United States; and before the same shall take effect, shall be approved by him, or being disapproved by him, shall be repassed by two thirds of the Senate and House of Representatives, according to the rules and limitations prescribed in the case of a bill.

Section 8. 1. The Congress shall have the power to lay and collect taxes, duties, imposts, and excises, to pay the debts and provide for the common defense and general welfare of the United States; but all duties, imposts, and excises shall be uniform throughout the United States.

2. To borrow money on the credit of the United States;

---

[4]See the Seventeenth Amendment.

3. To regulate commerce with foreign nations, and among the several States, and with the Indian tribes;

4. To establish a uniform rule of naturalization, and uniform laws on the subject of bankruptcies throughout the United States;

5. To coin money, regulate the value thereof, and of foreign coin, and fix the standard of weights and measures;

6. To provide for the punishment of counterfeiting the securities and current coin of the United States;

7. To establish post offices and post roads;

8. To promote the progress of science and useful arts, by securing for limited times to authors and inventors the exclusive right to their respective writings and discoveries;

9. To constitute tribunals inferior to the Supreme Court;

10. To define and punish piracies and felonies committed on the high seas, and offenses against the law of nations;

11. To declare war, grant letters of marque and reprisal, and make rules concerning captures on land and water;

12. To raise and support armies, but no appropriation of money to that use shall be for a longer term than two years;

13. To provide and maintain a navy;

14. To make rules for the government and regulation of the land and naval forces;

15. To provide for calling forth the militia to execute the laws of the Union, suppress insurrections and repel invasions;

16. To provide for organizing, arming, and disciplining the militia, and for governing such part of them as may be employed in the service of the United States, reserving to the States respectively, the appointment of the officers, and the authority of training the militia according to the discipline prescribed by Congress;

17. To exercise exclusive legislation in all cases whatsoever, over such district (not exceeding ten miles square) as may, by cession of particular States, and the acceptance of Congress, become the seat of the government of the United States, and to exercise like authority over all places purchased by the consent of the legislature of the State in which the same shall be, for the erection of forts, magazines, arsenals, dockyards, and other needful buildings; and

18. To make all laws which shall be necessary and proper for carrying into execution the foregoing powers, and all other powers vested by this Constitution in the government of the United States, or any department or officer thereof.

Section 9. 1. The migration or importation of such persons as any of the States now existing shall think proper to admit, shall not be prohibited by the Congress prior to the year one thousand eight hundred and eight, but a tax or duty may be imposed on such importation, not exceeding ten dollars for each person.

2. The privilege of the writ of habeas corpus shall not be suspended, unless when in cases of rebellion or invasion the public safety may require it.

3. No bill of attainder or ex post facto law shall be passed.

4. No capitation, or other direct, tax shall be laid, unless in proportion to the census or enumeration hereinbefore directed to be taken.[5]

5. No tax or duty shall be laid on articles exported from any State.

6. No preference shall be given by any regulation of commerce or revenue to the ports of one State over those of another: nor shall vessels bound to, or from, one State be obliged to enter, clear, or pay duties in another.

7. No money shall be drawn from the treasury, but in consequence of appropriations made by law; and a regular statement and account of the receipts and expenditures of all public money shall be published from time to time.

8. No title of nobility shall be granted by the United States: and no person holding any office of profit or trust under them, shall, without the consent of the Congress, accept of any present, emolument, office, or title, of any kind whatever, from any king, prince, or foreign State.

Section 10. 1. No State shall enter into any treaty, alliance, or confederation; grant letters of marque and reprisal; coin money; emit bills of credit; make any thing but gold and silver coin a tender in payment of debts; pass any bill of attainder, ex post facto law, or law impairing the obligation of contracts, or grant, any title of nobility.

2. No State shall, without the consent of the Congress, lay any imposts or duties on imports or exports, except what may be absolutely necessary for executing its inspection laws: and the net produce of all duties and imposts laid by any State on imports or exports, shall be for the use of the treasury of the United States; and all such laws shall be subject to the revision and control of the Congress.

3. No State shall, without the consent of the Congress, lay any duty of tonnage, keep troops, or ships of war in time of peace, enter into any agreement or compact with another State, or with a foreign power, or engage in war, unless actually invaded, or in such imminent danger as will not admit of delay.

Article II

Section 1. 1. The executive power shall be vested in a President of the United States of America. He shall hold his office during the term of four years, and, together with the Vice President, chosen for the same term, be elected, as follows:

2. Each State shall appoint, in such manner as the legislature thereof may direct, a number of electors, equal to the whole number of senators and representatives to which the State may be entitled in the Congress: but no senator or representative, or person holding any office of trust or profit under the United States, shall be appointed an elector.

The electors shall meet in their respective States, and vote by ballot for two persons, of whom one at least shall not be an inhabitant of the same State with themselves. And they shall make a list of all the persons voted for, and of the

---

[5]See the Sixteenth Amendment.

number of votes for each; which list they shall sign and certify, and transmit sealed to the seat of the government of the United States, directed to the president of the Senate. The president of the Senate shall, in the presence of the Senate and House of Representatives, open all the certificates, and the votes shall then be counted. The person having the greatest number of votes shall be the President, if such number be a majority of the whole number of electors appointed; and if there be more than one who have such majority, and have an equal number of votes, then the House of Representatives shall immediately choose by ballot one of them for President; and if no person have a majority, then from the five highest on the list the said House shall in like manner choose the President. But in choosing the President, the votes shall be taken by States, the representation from each State having one vote; a quorum for this purpose shall consist of a member or members from two thirds of the States, and a majority of all the States shall be necessary to a choice. In every case after the choice of the President, the person having the greatest number of votes of the electors shall be the Vice President. But if there should remain two or more who have equal votes, the Senate shall choose from them by ballot the Vice President.[6]

3. The Congress may determine the time of choosing the electors, and the day on which they shall give their votes; which day shall be the same throughout the United States.

4. No person except a natural born citizen, or a citizen of the United States, at the time of the adoption of this Constitution, shall be eligible to the office of President; neither shall any person be eligible to the office who shall not have attained to the age of thirty-five years, and been fourteen years a resident within the United States.

5. In case of the removal of the President from office, or of his death, resignation, or inability to discharge the powers and duties of the said office, the same shall devolve on the Vice President, and the congress may by law provide for the case of removal, death, resignation or inability, both of the President and Vice President, declaring what officer shall then act as President, and such officer shall act accordingly until the disability be removed, or a President shall be elected.

6. The President shall, at stated times, receive for his services a compensation which shall neither be increased nor diminished during the period for which he shall have been elected, and he shall not receive within that period any other emolument from the United States, or any of them.

7. Before he enter on the execution of his office, he shall take the following oath or affirmation:—"I do solemnly swear (or affirm) that I will faithfully execute the office of President of the United States, and will to the best of my ability, preserve, protect and defend the Constitution of the United States."

Section 2. 1. The President shall be commander in chief of the army and navy of the United States, and of the militia of the several States, when called into the actual service of the United States; he may require the opinion in writing, of the principal officer in each of the executive departments, upon any subject relating to the duties of their respective offices, and he shall have power to grant reprieves and pardons for offenses against the United States, except in cases of impeachment.

2. He shall have power, by and with the advice and consent of the Senate, to make treaties, provided two thirds of the senators present concur; and he shall nominate, and by and with the advice and consent of the Senate, shall appoint ambassadors, other public ministers and consuls, judges of the Supreme Court, and all other officers of the United States, whose appointments are not herein otherwise provided for, and which shall be established by law; but the Congress may by law vest the appointment of such inferior officers, as they think proper, in the President alone, in the courts of laws, or in the heads of departments.

3. The President shall have power to fill up all vacancies that may happen during the recess of the Senate, by granting commissions which shall expire at the end of their next session.

Section 3. He shall from time to time give to the Congress information of the state of the Union, and recommend to their consideration such measures as he shall judge necessary and expedient; he may, on extraordinary occasions, convene both Houses, or either of them, and in case of disagreement between them with respect to the time of adjournment, he may adjourn them to such time as he shall think proper; he shall receive ambassadors and other public ministers; he shall take care that the laws be faithfully executed, and shall commission all the officers of the United States.

Section 4. The President, Vice President, and all civil officers of the United States, shall be removed from office on impeachment for, and conviction of, treason, bribery, or other high crimes and misdemeanors.

Article III

Section 1. The judicial power of the United States shall be vested in one Supreme Court, and in such inferior courts as the Congress may from time to time ordain and establish. The judges, both of the Supreme and inferior courts, shall hold their offices during good behavior, and shall, at stated times, receive for their services, a compensation, which shall not be diminished during their continuance in office.

Section 2. 1. The judicial power shall extend to all cases, in law and equity, arising under this Constitution, the laws of the United States, and treaties made, or which shall be made, under their authority;—to all cases of admiralty and maritime jurisdiction;—to controversies to which the United States shall be a party;[7]—to controversies between two or more States;—between a State and citizens of another State;—between citizens of different States;—between citizens of the same State claiming lands under grants of different States, and between a State, or the citizens thereof, and foreign States, citizens or subjects.

2. In all cases affecting ambassadors, other public ministers and consuls, and those in which a State shall be party, the Supreme Court shall have original jurisdiction.

---

[6]Superseded by the Twelfth Amendment.

[7]See the Eleventh Amendment.

In all the other cases before mentioned, the Supreme Court shall have appellate jurisdiction, both as to law and fact, with such exceptions, and under such regulations as the Congress shall make.

3. The trial of all crimes, except in cases of impeachment, shall be by jury; and such trial shall be held in the State where the said crimes shall have been committed; but when not committed within any State, the trial shall be such place or places as the congress may by law have directed.

Section 3. 1. Treason against the United States shall consist only in levying war against them, or in adhering to their enemies, giving them aid and comfort. No person shall be convicted of treason unless on the testimony of two witnesses to the same overt act, or on confession in open court.

2. The Congress shall have power to declare the punishment of treason, but no attainder of treason shall work corruption of blood, or forfeiture except during the life of the person attained.

Article IV

Section 1. Full faith and credit shall be given in each State to the public acts, records, and judicial proceedings of every other State. And the Congress may by general laws prescribe the manner in which such acts, records and proceedings shall be proved, and the effect thereof.

Section 2. 1. The citizens of each State shall be entitled to all privileges and immunities of citizens in the several States.[8]

2. A person charged in any State with treason, felony, or other crime, who shall flee from justice, and be found in another State, shall on demand of the executive authority of the State from which he fled, be delivered up to be removed to the State having jurisdiction of the crime.

3. No person held to service or labor in one State under the laws thereof, escaping into another, shall, in consequence of any law or regulation therein, be discharged from such service or labor, but shall be delivered up on claim of the party to whom such service or labor may be due.[9]

Section 3. 1. New States may be admitted by the Congress into this Union; but no new State shall be formed or erected within the jurisdiction of any other State, nor any State be formed by the junction of two or more States, or parts of States, without the consent of the legislatures of the States concerned as well as of the Congress.

2. The Congress shall have power to dispose of and make all needful rules and regulations respecting the territory or other property belonging to the United States; and nothing in this Constitution shall be so construed as to prejudice any claims of the United States, or of any particular State.

Section 4. The United States shall guarantee to every State in this Union a republican form of government, and shall protect each of them against invasion; and on application of the legislature, or of the executive (when the legislature cannot be convened) against domestic violence.

Article V

The Congress, whenever two thirds of both Houses shall deem it necessary, shall propose amendments to this Constitution, or, on the application of the legislatures of two thirds of the several States, shall call a convention for proposing amendments, which in either case shall be valid to all intents and purposes, as part of this Constitution, when ratified by the legislatures of three fourths of the several States, or by conventions in three fourths thereof, as the one or the other mode of ratification may be proposed by the Congress; Provided that no amendment which may be made prior to the year one thousand eight hundred and eight shall in any manner affect the first and fourth clauses in the ninth section of the first article; and that no State, without its consent, shall be deprived of its equal suffrage in the Senate.

Article VI

1. All debts contracted and engagements entered into, before the adoption of this Constitution, shall be as valid against the United States under this Constitution, as under the Confederation.[10]

2. This Constitution, and the laws of the United States which shall be made in pursuance thereof; and all treaties made, or which shall be made, under the authority of the United States, shall be the supreme law of the land; and the judges in every State shall be bound thereby, any thing in the Constitution or laws of any State to the contrary notwithstanding.

3. The senators and representatives before mentioned, and the members of the several State legislatures, and all executive and judicial officers, both of the United States and of the several States, shall be bound by oath or affirmation to support this Constitution; but no religious test shall ever be required as a qualification to any office or public trust under the United States.

Article VII

The ratification of the conventions of nine States shall be sufficient for the establishment of this Constitution between the States so ratifying the same.

Done in Convention by the unanimous consent of the States present the seventeenth day of September in the year of our Lord one thousand seven hundred and eighty-seven, and of the independence of the United States of America the twelfth. In witness whereof we have hereunto subscribed our names.

[Signatories' names omitted]

★ ★ ★

Articles in addition to, and amendment of, the Constitution of the United States of America, proposed by Congress, and ratified by the legislatures of the several States, pursuant to the fifth article of the original Constitution.

---

[8]See the Fourteenth Amendment, Sec. 1.
[9]See the Thirteenth Amendment.

[10]See the Fourteenth Amendment, Sec. 4.

Amendment I [First ten amendments ratified December 15, 1791]

Congress shall make no law respecting an establishment of religion, or prohibiting the free exercise thereof; or abridging the freedom of speech, or of the press; or the right of the people peaceably to assemble, and to petition the government for a redress of grievances.

Amendment II

A well regulated militia, being necessary to the security of a free State, the right of the people to keep and bear arms, shall not be infringed.

Amendment III

No soldier shall, in time of peace be quartered in any house, without the consent of the owner, nor in time of war, but in a manner to be prescribed by law.

Amendment IV

The right of the people to be secure in their persons, houses, papers, and effects, against unreasonable searches and seizures, shall not be violated, and no warrants shall issue, but upon probable cause, supported by oath or affirmation, and particularly describing the place to be searched, and the persons or things to be seized.

Amendment V

No person shall be held to answer for a capital or otherwise infamous crime, unless on a presentment or indictment of a grand jury, except in cases arising in the land or naval forces, or in the militia, when in actual service in time of war or public danger; nor shall any person be subject for the same offense to be twice put in jeopardy of life or limb; nor shall be compelled in any criminal case to be a witness against himself, nor be deprived of life, liberty, or property, without due process of law; nor shall private property be taken for public use, without just compensation.

Amendment VI

In all criminal prosecutions, the accused shall enjoy the right to a speedy and public trial, by an impartial jury of the State and district wherein the crime shall have been committed, which district shall have been previously ascertained by law, and to be informed of the nature and cause of the accusation; to be confronted with the witnesses against him; to have compulsory process for obtaining witnesses in his favor, and to have the assistance of counsel for his defense.

Amendment VII

In suits at common law, where the value in controversy shall exceed twenty dollars, the right of trial by jury shall be preserved, and no fact tried by a jury shall be otherwise reexamined in any court of the United States, than according to the rules of the common law.

Amendment VIII

Excessive bail shall not be required, nor excessive fines imposed, nor cruel and unusual punishments inflicted.

Amendment IX

The enumeration in the Constitution of certain rights shall not be construed to deny or disparage others retained by the people.

Amendment X

The powers not delegated to the United States by the Constitution, nor prohibited by it to the States, are reserved to the States respectively, or to the people.

Amendment XI [January 8, 1798]

The judicial power of the United States shall not be construed to extend to any suit in law or equity, commended or prosecuted against one of the United States by citizens of another State, or by citizens or subjects of any foreign State.

Amendment XII [September 25, 1804]

The electors shall meet in their respective States, and vote by ballot for President and Vice President, one of whom, at least, shall not be an inhabitant of the same State with themselves; they shall name in their ballots the person voted for as President, and in distinct ballots, the person voted for as Vice President, and they shall make distinct lists of all persons voted for as President and of all persons voted for as Vice President, and of the number of votes for each, which lists they shall sign and certify, and transmit sealed to the seat of the government of the United States, directed to the President of the Senate;—The President of the Senate shall, in the presence of the Senate and House of Representatives, open all the certificates and the votes shall then be counted;—The person having the greatest number of votes for President, shall be the President, if such number be a majority of the whole number of electors appointed; and if no person have such majority, then from the persons having the highest numbers not exceeding three on the list of those voted for as President, the House of Representatives shall choose immediately, by ballot, the President. But in choosing the President, the votes shall be taken by States, the representation from each State having one vote; a quorum for this purpose shall consist of a member or members from two thirds of the States, and a majority of all the States shall be necessary to a choice. And if the House of Representatives shall not choose a President whenever the right of choice shall devolve upon them, before the fourth day of March next following, then the Vice President shall act as President, as in the case of the death or other constitutional disability of the President. The person having the greatest number of votes as Vice President shall be the Vice President, if such number be a majority of the whole number of electors appointed, and if no person have a majority, then from the two highest numbers on the list, the Senate shall choose the Vice President; a quorum for the purpose shall consist of two thirds of the whole number of Senators, and a majority of the whole number shall be necessary to a choice. But no person constitutionally ineligible to the office of President shall be eligible to that of Vice President of the United States.

Amendment XIII [December 18, 1865]

Section 1. Neither slavery nor involuntary servitude, except as a punishment for crime whereof the party shall have been duly convicted, shall exist within the United States, or any place subject to their jurisdiction.

Section 2. Congress shall have power to enforce this article by appropriate legislation.

Amendment XIV [July 28, 1868]

Section 1. All persons born or naturalized in the United States, and subject to the jurisdiction thereof, are citizens of the United States and of the State wherein they reside. No State shall make or enforce any law which shall abridge the privileges or immunities of citizens of the United States; nor shall any State deprive any person of life, liberty, or property, without due process of law; nor deny to any person within its jurisdiction the equal protection of the laws.

Section 2. Representatives shall be apportioned among the several States according to their respective numbers, counting the whole number of persons in each State, excluding Indians not taxed. But when the right to vote at any election for the choice of electors for President and Vice President of the United States, representatives in Congress, the executive and judicial officers of a State, or the members of the legislature thereof, is denied to any of the male inhabitants of such State, being twenty-one years of age, and citizens of the United States, or in any way abridged, except for participating in rebellion, or other crime, the basis of representation there shall be reduced in the proportion which the number of such male citizens shall bear to the whole number of male citizens twenty-one years of age in such State.

Section 3. No person shall be a senator or representative in Congress, or elector of President and Vice President, or hold any office, civil or military, under the United States, or under any State, who having previously taken an oath, as a member of Congress, or as an officer of the United States, or as a member of any State legislature, or as an executive or judicial officer of any State, to support the Constitution of the United States, shall have engaged in insurrection or rebellion against the same, or given aid or comfort to the enemies thereof. But Congress may by a vote of two thirds of each House, remove such disability.

Section 4. The validity of the public debt of the United States, authorized by law, including debts incurred for payment of pensions and bounties for services in suppressing insurrection or rebellion; shall not be questioned. But neither the United States nor any State shall assume or pay any debt or obligation incurred in aid of insurrection or rebellion against the United States, or any claim for the loss or emancipation of any slave; but all such debts, obligations, and claims shall be held illegal and void.

Section 5. The Congress shall have the power to enforce, by appropriate legislation, the provisions of this article.

Amendment XV [March 30, 1870]

Section 1. The right of citizens of the United States to vote shall not be denied or abridged by the United States or by any State on account of race, color, or previous condition of servitude.

Section 2. The Congress shall have power to enforce this article by appropriate legislation.

Amendment XVI [February 25, 1913]

The Congress shall have power to lay and collect taxes on incomes, from whatever source derived, without apportionment among the several States, and without regard to any census or enumeration.

Amendment XVII [May 31, 1913]

The Senate of the United States shall be composed of two senators from each State, elected by the people thereof, for six years; and each senator shall have one vote. The electors in each State shall have the qualifications requisite for electors of the most numerous branch of the State legislature.

When vacancies happen in the representation of any State in the Senate, the executive authority of such State shall issue writs of election to fill such vacancies: Provided, That the legislature of any State may empower the executive thereof to make temporary appointments until the people fill the vacancies by election as the legislature may direct.

This amendment shall not be so construed as to affect the election or term of any senator chosen before it becomes valid as part of the Constitution.

Amendment XVIII[11] [January 29, 1919]

After one year from the ratification of this article, the manufacture, sale, or transportation of intoxicating liquors within, the importation thereof into, or the exportation thereof from the United States and all territory subject to the jurisdiction thereof for beverage purposes is thereby prohibited.

The Congress and the several States shall have concurrent power to enforce this article by appropriate legislation.

This article shall be inoperative unless it shall have been ratified as an amendment to the Constitution by the legislatures of the several States, as provided in the constitution, within seven years from the date of the submission hereof to the States by Congress.

Amendment XIX [August 26, 1920]

The right of citizens of the United States to vote shall not be denied or abridged by the United States or by any State on account of sex.

Congress shall have the power to enforce this article by appropriate legislation.

---

[11]Repealed by the Twenty-first Amendment.

Amendment XX [January 23, 1933]

Section 1. The terms of the President and Vice President shall end at noon on the 20th day of January and the terms of Senators and Representatives at noon on the 3d day of January, of the years in which such terms would have ended if this article had not been ratified; and the terms of their successors shall then begin.

Section 2. The Congress shall assemble at least once in every year, and such meeting shall begin at noon on the 3d day of January, unless they shall by law appoint a different day.

Section 3. If, at the time fixed for the beginning of the term of President, the President-elect shall have died, the Vice President-elect shall become President. If a President shall not have been chosen before the time fixed for the beginning of his term, or if the President-elect shall have failed to qualify, then the Vice President-elect shall act as President until a President shall have qualified; and the Congress may by law provide for the case wherein neither a President-elect nor a Vice President-elect shall have qualified, declaring who shall then act as President, or the manner in which one who is to act shall be selected, and such person shall act accordingly until a President or Vice President shall have qualified.

Section 4. The Congress may by law provide for the case of the death of any of the persons from whom, the House of Representatives may choose a President whenever the right of choice shall have devolved upon them, and for the case of the death of any of the persons from whom the Senate may choose a Vice President whenever the right of choice shall have devolved upon them.

Section 5. Sections 1 and 2 shall take effect on the 15th day of October following the ratification of this article.

Section 6. This article shall be inoperative unless it shall have been ratified as an amendment to the Constitution by the legislatures of three-fourths of the several States within seven years from the date of its submission.

Amendment XXI [December 5, 1933]

Section 1. The Eighteenth Article of amendment to the Constitution of the United States is hereby repealed.

Section 2. The transportation or importation into any State, Territory, or possession of the United States for delivery or use therein of intoxicating liquors in violation of the laws thereof, is hereby prohibited.

Section 3. This article shall be inoperative unless it shall have been ratified as an amendment to the Constitution by conventions in the several States, as provided in the Constitution, within seven years from the date of the submission thereof to the States by the Congress.

Amendment XXII [March 1, 1951]

No person shall be elected to the office of the President more than twice, and no person who has held the office of President, or acted as President, for more than two years of a term to which some other person was elected President shall be elected to the office of the President more than once.

But this article shall not apply to any person holding the office of President when this article was proposed by the Congress, and shall not prevent any person who may be holding the office of President, or acting as President, during the term within which this article becomes operative from holding the office of President or acting as President during the remainder of such term.

This article shall be inoperative unless it shall have been ratified as an amendment to the Constitution by the legislatures of three-fourths of the several States within seven years from the date of its submission to the States by the Congress.

Amendment XXIII [March 29, 1961]

Section 1. The District constituting the seat of Government of the United States shall appoint in such manner as the Congress may direct.

A number of electors of President and Vice President equal to the whole number of Senators and Representatives in Congress to which the District would be entitled if it were a State, but in no event more than the least populous State; they shall be in addition to those appointed by the States, but they shall be considered, for the purposes of the election of President and Vice President, to be electors appointed by a State; and they shall meet in the District and perform such duties as provided by the twelfth article of amendment.

Section 2. The Congress shall have power to enforce this article by appropriate legislation.

Amendment XXIV [January 23, 1964]

Section 1. The right of citizens of the United States to vote in any primary or other election for President or Vice President, for electors for President or Vice President, or for Senator or Representative in Congress, shall not be denied or abridged by the United States or any State by reason of failure to pay any poll tax or other tax.

Section 2. The Congress shall have power to enforce this article by appropriate legislation.

Amendment XXV [February 10, 1967]

Section 1. In case of the removal of the President from office or of his death or resignation, the Vice President shall become President.

Section 2. Whenever there is a vacancy in the office of the Vice President, the President shall nominate a Vice President who shall take office upon confirmation by a majority of both Houses of Congress.

Section 3. Whenever the President transmits to the President pro tempore of the Senate and the Speaker of the House of Representatives his written declaration that he is unable to discharge the powers and duties of his office, and until he transmits to them a written declaration to the contrary, such powers and duties shall be discharged by the Vice President as Acting President.

Section 4. Whenever the Vice President and a majority of either the principal officers of the executive departments or of such other body as Congress may by law provide, transmit to the President pro tempore of the Senate and the Speaker of the House of Representatives their written declaration that the President is unable to discharge the powers and duties of his office, the Vice President shall immediately assume the powers and duties of the office as Acting President.

Thereafter, when the President transmits to the President pro tempore of the Senate and the Speaker of the House of Representatives his written declaration that no inability exists, he shall resume the powers and duties of his office unless the Vice President and a majority of either the principal officers of the executive departments or of such other body as Congress may by law provide, transmit within four days to the President pro tempore of the Senate and the Speaker of the House of Representatives their written declaration that the President is unable to discharge the powers and duties of his office. Thereupon Congress shall decide the issue, assembling within forty-eight hours for that purpose if not in session. If the Congress, within twenty-one days after receipt of the latter written declaration, or, if Congress is not in session, within twenty-one days after Congress is required to assemble, determines by two-thirds vote of both Houses that the President is unable to discharge the powers and duties of his office, the Vice President shall continue to discharge the same as Acting President; otherwise, the President shall resume the powers and duties of his office.

Amendment XXVI [June 30, 1971]

Section 1. The right of citizens of the United States who are eighteen years of age or older to vote shall not be denied or abridged by the United States or by any State on account of age.

Section 2. The Congress shall have power to enforce this article by appropriate legislation.

Amendment XXVII[12] [May 7, 1992]

No law, varying the compensation for services of the Senators and Representatives, shall take effect until an election of Representatives shall have intervened.

---

[12]James Madison proposed this amendment in 1789 together with the ten amendments that were adopted as the Bill of Rights, but it failed to win ratification at the time. Congress, however, had set no deadline for its ratification, and over the years—particularly in the 1980s and 1990s—many states voted to add it to the Constitution. With the ratification of Michigan in 1992 it passed the threshold of 3/4ths of the states required for adoption, but because the process took more than 200 years, its validity remains in doubt.

PRESIDENTS AND VICE PRESIDENTS

1. George Washington (1789)
   John Adams (1789)

2. John Adams (1797)
   Thomas Jefferson (1797)

3. Thomas Jefferson (1801)
   Aaron Burr (1801)
   George Clinton (1805)

4. James Madison (1809)
   George Clinton (1809)
   Elbridge Gerry (1813)

5. James Monroe (1817)
   Daniel D. Thompkins (1817)

6. John Quincy Adams (1825)
   John C. Calhoun (1825)

7. Andrew Jackson (1829)
   John C. Calhoun (1829)
   Martin Van Buren (1833)

8. Martin Van Buren (1837)
   Richard M. Johnson (1837)

9. William H. Harrison (1841)
   John Tyler (1841)

10. John Tyler (1841)

11. James K. Polk (1845)
    George M. Dallas (1845)

12. Zachary Taylor (1849)
    Millard Fillmore (1849)

13. Millard Fillmore (1850)

14. Franklin Pierce (1853)
    William R. King (1853)

15. James Buchanan (1857)
    John C. Breckinridge (1857)

16. Abraham Lincoln (1861)
    Hannibal Hamlin (1861)
    Andrew Johnson (1865)

17. Andrew Johnson (1865)

18. Ulysses S. Grant (1869)
    Schuyler Colfax (1869)
    Henry Wilson (1873)

19. Rutherford B. Hayes (1877)
    William A. Wheeler (1877)

20. James A. Garfield (1881)
    Chester A. Arthur (1881)

21. Chester A. Arthur (1881)

22. Grover Cleveland (1885)
    T. A. Hendricks (1885)

23. Benjamin Harrison (1889)
    Levi P. Morgan (1889)

24. Grover Cleveland (1893)
    Adlai E. Stevenson (1893)

25. William McKinley (1897)
    Garret A. Hobart (1897)
    Theodore Roosevelt (1901)

26. Theodore Roosevelt (1901)
    Charles Fairbanks (1905)

27. William H. Taft (1909)
    James S. Sherman (1909)

28. Woodrow Wilson (1913)
    Thomas R. Marshall (1913)

29. Warren G. Harding (1921)
    Calvin Coolidge (1921)

30. Calvin Coolidge (1923)
    Charles G. Dawes (1925)

31. Herbert C. Hoover (1929)
    Charles Curtis (1929)

32. Franklin D. Roosevelt (1933)
    John Nance Garner (1933)
    Henry A. Wallace (1941)
    Harry S Truman (1945)

33. Harry S Truman (1945)
    Alben W. Barkley (1949)

34. Dwight D. Eisenhower (1953)
    Richard M. Nixon (1953)

35. John F. Kennedy (1961)
    Lyndon B. Johnson (1961)

36. Lyndon B. Johnson (1963)
    Hubert H. Humphrey (1965)

37. Richard M. Nixon (1969)
    Spiro T. Agnew (1969)
    Gerald R. Ford (1973)

38. Gerald R. Ford (1974)
    Nelson A. Rockefeller (1974)

39. James E. Carter Jr. (1977)
    Walter F. Mondale (1977)

40. Ronald W. Reagan (1981)
    George H. W. Bush (1981)

41. George H. W. Bush (1989)
    James D. Quayle III (1989)

42. William J. Clinton (1993)
    Albert Gore (1993)

43. George W. Bush (2001)
    Richard Cheney (2001)

PRESIDENTIAL ELECTIONS

Year	Number of States	Candidates	Party	Popular Vote*	Electoral Vote[†]	Percentage of Popular Vote*
1789	11	GEORGE WASHINGTON	No party designations		69	
		John Adams			34	
		Other Candidates			35	
1792	15	GEORGE WASHINGTON	No party designations		132	
		John Adams			77	
		George Clinton			50	
		Other Candidates			5	
1796	16	JOHN ADAMS	Federalist		71	
		Thomas Jefferson	Democratic-Republican		68	
		Thomas Pinckney	Federalist		59	
		Aaron Burr	Democratic-Republican		30	
		Other Candidates			48	
1800	16	THOMAS JEFFERSON	Democratic-Republican		73	
		Aaron Burr	Democratic-Republican		73	
		John Adams	Federalist		65	
		Charles C. Pinckney	Federalist		64	
		John Jay	Federalist		1	
1804	17	THOMAS JEFFERSON	Democratic-Republican		162	
		Charles C. Pinckney	Federalist		14	
1808	17	JAMES MADISON	Democratic-Republican		122	
		Charles C. Pinckney	Federalist		47	
		George Clinton	Democratic-Republican		6	
1812	18	JAMES MADISON	Democratic-Republican		128	
		DeWitt Clinton	Federalist		89	
1816	19	JAMES MONROE	Democratic-Republican		183	
		Rufus King	Federalist		34	
1820	24	JAMES MONROE	Democratic-Republican		231	
		John Quincy Adams	Independent-Republican		1	
1824	24	JOHN QUINCY ADAMS	Democratic-Republican	108,740	84	30.5
		Andrew Jackson	Democratic-Republican	153,544	99	43.1
		William H. Crawford	Democratic-Republican	46,618	41	13.1
		Henry Clay	Democratic-Republican	47,136	37	13.2
1828	24	ANDREW JACKSON	Democrat	647,286	178	56.0
		John Quincy Adams	National-Republican	508,064	83	44.0
1832	24	ANDREW JACKSON	Democrat	687,502	219	55.0
		Henry Clay	National-Republican	530,189	49	42.4
		William Wirt	Anti-Masonic	33,108	7	
		John Floyd	National-Republican		11	2.6

*Percentage of popular vote given for any election year may not total 100 percent because candidates receiving less than 1 percent of the popular vote have been omitted.

[†]Prior to the passage of the Twelfth Amendment in 1904, the electoral college voted for two presidential candidates; the runner-up became Vice-President. Data from *Historical Statistics of the United States, Colonial Times to 1957* (1961), pp. 682–683, and *The World Almanac.*

PRESIDENTIAL ELECTIONS (continued)

Year	Number of States	Candidates	Party	Popular Vote	Electoral Vote	Percentage of Popular Vote
1836	26	MARTIN VAN BUREN	Democrat	765,483	170	50.9
		William H. Harrison	Whig		73	
		Hugh L. White	Whig		26	
		Daniel Webster	Whig	739,795	14	49.1
		W. P. Mangum	Whig		11	
1840	26	WILLIAM H. HARRISON	Whig	1,274,624	234	53.1
		Martin Van Buren	Democrat	1,127,781	60	46.9
1844	26	JAMES K. POLK	Democrat	1,338,464	170	49.6
		Henry Clay	Whig	1,300,097	105	48.1
		James G. Birney	Liberty	62,300		2.3
1848	30	ZACHARY TAYLOR	Whig	1,360,967	163	47.4
		Lewis Cass	Democrat	1,222,342	127	42.5
		Martin Van Buren	Free-Soil	291,263		10.1
1852	31	FRANKLIN PIERCE	Democrat	1,601,117	254	50.9
		Winfield Scott	Whig	1,385,453	42	44.1
		John P. Hale	Free-Soil	155,825		5.0
1856	31	JAMES BUCHANAN	Democrat	1,832,955	174	45.3
		John C. Frémont	Republican	1,339,932	114	33.1
		Millard Fillmore	American ("Know Nothing")	871,731	8	21.6
1860	33	ABRAHAM LINCOLN	Republican	1,865,593	180	39.8
		Stephen A. Douglas	Democrat	1,382,713	12	29.5
		John C. Breckinridge	Democrat	848,356	72	18.1
		John Bell	Constitutional Union	592,906	39	12.6
1864	36	ABRAHAM LINCOLN	Republican	2,206,938	212	55.0
		George B. McClellan	Democrat	1,803,787	21	45.0
1868	37	ULYSSES S. GRANT	Republican	3,013,421	214	52.7
		Horatio Seymour	Democrat	2,706,829	80	47.3
1872	37	ULYSSES S. GRANT	Republican	3,596,745	286	55.6
		Horace Greeley	Democrat	2,843,446		★43.9
1876	38	RUTHERFORD B. HAYES	Republican	4,036,572	185	48.0
		Samuel J. Tilden	Democrat	4,284,020	184	51.0
1880	38	JAMES A. GARFIELD	Republican	4,453,295	214	48.5
		Winfield S. Hancock	Democrat	4,414,082	155	48.1
		James B. Weaver	Greenback-Labor	308,578		3.4
1884	38	GROVER CLEVELAND	Democrat	4,879,507	219	48.5
		James G. Blaine	Republican	4,850,293	182	48.2
		Benjamin F. Butler	Greenback-Labor	175,370		1.8
		John P. St. John	Prohibition	150,369		1.5

★Because of the death of Greeley, Democratic electors scattered their votes.

PRESIDENTIAL ELECTIONS (continued)

Year	Number of States	Candidates	Party	Popular Vote	Electoral Vote	Percentage of Popular Vote
1888	38	BENJAMIN HARRISON	Republican	5,447,129	233	47.9
		Grover Cleveland	Democrat	5,537,857	168	48.6
		Clinton B. Fisk	Prohibition	249,506		2.2
		Anson J. Streeter	Union Labor	146,935		1.3
1892	44	GROVER CLEVELAND	Democrat	5,555,426	277	46.1
		Benjamin Harrison	Republican	5,182,690	145	43.0
		James B. Weaver	People's	1,029,846	22	8.5
		John Bidwell	Prohibition	264,133		2.2
1896	45	WILLIAM MCKINLEY	Republican	7,102,246	271	51.1
		William J. Bryan	Democrat	6,492,559	176	47.7
1900	45	WILLIAM MCKINLEY	Republican	7,218,491	292	51.7
		William J. Bryan	Democrat; Populist	6,356,734	155	45.5
		John C. Woolley	Prohibition	208,914		1.5
1904	45	THEODORE ROOSEVELT	Republican	7,628,461	336	57.4
		Alton B. Parker	Democrat	5,084,223	140	37.6
		Eugene V. Debs	Socialist	402,283		3.0
		Silas C. Swallow	Prohibition	258,536		1.9
1908	46	WILLIAM H. TAFT	Republican	7,675,320	321	51.6
		William J. Bryan	Democrat	6,412,294	162	43.1
		Eugene V. Debs	Socialist	420,793		2.8
		Eugene W. Chafin	Prohibition	253,840		1.7
1912	48	WOODROW WILSON	Democrat	6,296,547	435	41.9
		Theodore Roosevelt	Progressive	4,118,571	88	27.4
		William H. Taft	Republican	3,486,720	8	23.2
		Eugene V. Debs	Socialist	900,672		6.0
		Eugene W. Chafin	Prohibition	206,275		1.4
1916	48	WOODROW WILSON	Democrat	9,127,695	277	49.4
		Charles E. Hughes	Republican	8,533,507	254	46.2
		A. L. Benson	Socialist	585,113		3.2
		J. Frank Hanly	Prohibition	220,506		1.2
1920	48	WARREN G. HARDING	Republican	16,143,407	404	60.4
		James M. Cox	Democrat	9,130,328	127	34.2
		Eugene V. Debs	Socialist	919,799		3.4
		P. P. Christensen	Farmer-Labor	265,411		1.0
1924	48	CALVIN COOLIDGE	Republican	15,718,211	382	54.0
		John W. Davis	Democrat	8,385,283	136	28.8
		Robert M. La Follette	Progressive	4,831,289	13	16.6
1928	48	HERBERT C. HOOVER	Republican	21,391,993	444	58.2
		Alfred E. Smith	Democrat	15,016,169	87	40.9
1932	48	FRANKLIN D. ROOSEVELT	Democrat	22,809,638	472	57.4
		Herbert C. Hoover	Republican	15,758,901	59	39.7
		Norman Thomas	Socialist	881,951		2.2

PRESIDENTIAL ELECTIONS (continued)

Year	Number of States	Candidates	Party	Popular Vote	Electoral Vote	Percentage of Popular Vote
1936	48	FRANKLIN D. ROOSEVELT	Democrat	27,752,869	523	60.8
		Alfred M. Landon	Republican	16,674,665	8	36.5
		William Lemke	Union	882,479		1.9
1940	48	FRANKLIN D. ROOSEVELT	Democrat	27,307,819	449	54.8
		Wendell L. Willkie	Republican	22,321,018	82	44.8
1944	48	FRANKLIN D. ROOSEVELT	Democrat	25,606,585	432	53.5
		Thomas E. Dewey	Republican	22,014,745	99	46.0
1948	48	HARRY S TRUMAN	Democrat	24,105,812	303	49.5
		Thomas E. Dewey	Republican	21,970,065	189	45.1
		J. Strom Thurmond	States' Rights	1,169,063	39	2.4
		Henry A. Wallace	Progressive	1,157,172		2.4
1952	48	DWIGHT D. EISENHOWER	Republican	33,936,234	442	55.1
		Adlai E. Stevenson	Democrat	27,314,992	89	44.4
1956	48	DWIGHT D. EISENHOWER	Republican	35,590,472	457 ★	57.6
		Adlai E. Stevenson	Democrat	26,022,752	73	42.1
1960	50	JOHN F. KENNEDY	Democrat	34,227,096	303 †	49.9
		Richard M. Nixon	Republican	34,108,546	219	49.6
1964	50	LYNDON B. JOHNSON	Democrat	42,676,220	486	61.3
		Barry M. Goldwater	Republican	26,860,314	52	38.5
1968	50	RICHARD M. NIXON	Republican	31,785,480	301	43.4
		Hubert H. Humphrey	Democrat	31,275,165	191	42.7
		George C. Wallace	American Independent	9,906,473	46	13.5
1972	50	RICHARD M. NIXON‡	Republican	47,165,234	520	60.6
		George S. McGovern	Democrat	29,168,110	17	37.5
1976	50	JAMES E. CARTER JR.	Democrat	40,828,929	297	50.1
		Gerald R. Ford	Republican	39,148,940	240	47.9
		Eugene McCarthy	Independent	739,256		
1980	50	RONALD W. REAGAN	Republican	43,201,220	489	50.9
		James E. Carter Jr.	Democrat	34,913,332	49	41.2
		John B. Anderson	Independent	5,581,379		
1984	50	RONALD W. REAGAN	Republican	53,428,357	525	59.0
		Walter F. Mondale	Democrat	36,930,923	13	41.0
1988	50	GEORGE H. W. BUSH	Republican	48,901,046	426	53.4
		Michael Dukakis	Democrat	41,809,030	111	45.6
1992	50	WILLIAM J. CLINTON	Democrat	43,728,275	370	43.2
		George H. W. Bush	Republican	38,167,416	168	37.7
		H. Ross Perot	United We Stand, America	19,237,247		19.0

★Walter B. Jones received 1 electoral vote.

†Harry F. Byrd received 15 electoral votes.

‡Resigned August 9, 1974: Vice President Gerald R. Ford became President.

PRESIDENTIAL ELECTIONS (continued)

Year	Number of States	Candidates	Party	Popular Vote	Electoral Vote	Percentage of Popular Vote
1996	50	WILLIAM J. CLINTON	Democrat	45,590,703	379	49.0
		Robert Dole	Republican	37,816,307	159	41.0
		H. Ross Perot	Reform	7,874,283		8.0
2000	50	GEORGE W. BUSH	Republican	50,459,624	271	47.9
		Albert Gore	Democrat	51,003,328	266	49.4
		Ralph Nader	Green	2,882,985	0	2.7
2004	50	GEORGE W. BUSH	Republican	59,117,523	286	51.1
		John Kerry	Democrat	55,557,584	252	48.0
		Ralph Nader	Green	405,623	0	0.3

ADMISSION OF STATES INTO THE UNION

	State	Date of Admission		State	Date of Admission
1.	Delaware	December 7, 1787	26.	Michigan	January 26, 1837
2.	Pennsylvania	December 12, 1787	27.	Florida	March 3, 1845
3.	New Jersey	December 18, 1787	28.	Texas	December 29, 1845
4.	Georgia	January 2, 1788	29.	Iowa	December 28, 1846
5.	Connecticut	January 9, 1788	30.	Wisconsin	May 29, 1848
6.	Massachusetts	February 6, 1788	31.	California	September 9, 1850
7.	Maryland	April 28, 1788	32.	Minnesota	May 11, 1858
8.	South Carolina	May 23, 1788	33.	Oregon	February 14, 1859
9.	New Hampshire	June 21, 1788	34.	Kansas	January 29, 1861
10.	Virginia	June 25, 1788	35.	West Virginia	June 20, 1863
11.	New York	July 26, 1788	36.	Nevada	October 31, 1864
12.	North Carolina	November 21, 1789	37.	Nebraska	March 1, 1867
13.	Rhode Island	May 29, 1790	38.	Colorado	August 1, 1876
14.	Vermont	March 4, 1791	39.	North Dakota	November 2, 1889
15.	Kentucky	June 1, 1792	40.	South Dakota	November 2, 1889
16.	Tennessee	June 1, 1796	41.	Montana	November 8, 1889
17.	Ohio	March 1, 1803	42.	Washington	November 11, 1889
18.	Louisiana	April 30, 1812	43.	Idaho	July 3, 1890
19.	Indiana	December 11, 1816	44.	Wyoming	July 10, 1890
20.	Mississippi	December 10, 1817	45.	Utah	January 4, 1896
21.	Illinois	December 3, 1818	46.	Oklahoma	November 16, 1907
22.	Alabama	December 14, 1819	47.	New Mexico	January 6, 1912
23.	Maine	March 15, 1820	48.	Arizona	February 14, 1912
24.	Missouri	August 10, 1821	49.	Alaska	January 3, 1959
25.	Arkansas	June 15, 1836	50.	Hawaii	August 21, 1959

DEMOGRAPHICS OF THE UNITED STATES

POPULATION GROWTH

Year	Population	Percent Increase
1630	4,600	
1640	26,600	478.3
1650	50,400	90.8
1660	75,100	49.0
1670	111,900	49.0
1680	151,500	35.4
1690	210,400	38.9
1700	250,900	19.2
1710	331,700	32.2
1720	466,200	40.5
1730	629,400	35.0
1740	905,600	43.9
1750	1,170,800	29.3
1760	1,593,600	36.1
1770	2,148,100	34.8
1780	2,780,400	29.4
1790	3,929,214	41.3
1800	5,308,483	35.1
1810	7,239,881	36.4
1820	9,638,453	33.1
1830	12,866,020	33.5
1840	17,069,453	32.7
1850	23,191,876	35.9
1860	31,443,321	35.6
1870	39,818,449	26.6
1880	50,155,783	26.0
1890	62,947,714	25.5
1900	75,994,575	20.7
1910	91,972,266	21.0
1920	105,710,620	14.9
1930	122,775,046	16.1
1940	131,669,275	7.2
1950	150,697,361	14.5
1960	179,323,175	18.5
1970	203,302,031	13.4
1980	226,542,199	11.4
1990	248,718,301	9.8
2000	281,421,906	13.1

Source: *Historical Statistics of the United States* (1975); *Statistical Abstract of the United States* (2001).

Note: Figures for 1630–1780 include British colonies within limits of present United States only; Native American population included only in 1930 and thereafter.

WORKFORCE

Year	Total Number Workers (1000s)	Farmers as % of Total	Women as % of Total	% Workers in Unions
1810	2,330	84	(NA)	(NA)
1840	5,660	75	(NA)	(NA)
1860	11,110	53	(NA)	(NA)
1870	12,506	53	15	(NA)
1880	17,392	52	15	(NA)
1890	23,318	43	17	(NA)
1900	29,073	40	18	3
1910	38,167	31	21	6
1920	41,614	26	21	12
1930	48,830	22	22	7
1940	53,011	17	24	27
1950	59,643	12	28	25
1960	69,877	8	32	26
1970	82,049	4	37	25
1980	106,940	3	43	23
1990	125,840	3	45	16
2000	140,863	2	47	12

Source: *Historical Statistics of the United States* (1975); *Statistical Abstract of the United States* (2001).

VITAL STATISTICS
(in thousands)

Year	Births	Deaths	Marriages	Divorces
1800	55	(NA)	(NA)	(NA)
1810	54.3	(NA)	(NA)	(NA)
1820	55.2	(NA)	(NA)	(NA)
1830	51.4	(NA)	(NA)	(NA)
1840	51.8	(NA)	(NA)	(NA)
1850	43.3	(NA)	(NA)	(NA)
1860	44.3	(NA)	(NA)	(NA)
1870	38.3	(NA)	9.6 (1867)	0.3 (1867)
1880	39.8	(NA)	9.1 (1875)	0.3 (1875)
1890	31.5	(NA)	9.0	0.5
1900	32.3	17.2	9.3	0.7
1910	30.1	14.7	10.3	0.9
1920	27.7	13.0	12.0	1.6
1930	21.3	11.3	9.2	1.6
1940	19.4	10.8	12.1	2.0
1950	24.1	9.6	11.1	2.6
1960	23.7	9.5	8.5	2.2
1970	18.4	9.5	10.6	3.5
1980	15.9	8.8	10.6	5.2
1990	16.7	8.6	9.8	4.7
1997	14.6	8.6	8.9	4.3

Source: *Historical Statistics of the United States* (1975); *Statistical Abstract of the United States* (1999). Population Estimates Program, Population Division, U.S. Census Bureau, January 2001.

RACIAL COMPOSITION OF THE POPULATION
(in thousands)

Year	White	Black	Indian	Hispanic	Asian
1790	3,172	757	(NA)	(NA)	(NA)
1800	4,306	1,002	(NA)	(NA)	(NA)
1820	7,867	1,772	(NA)	(NA)	(NA)
1840	14,196	2,874	(NA)	(NA)	(NA)
1860	26,923	4,442	(NA)	(NA)	(NA)
1880	43,403	6,581	(NA)	(NA)	(NA)
1900	66,809	8,834	(NA)	(NA)	(NA)
1910	81,732	9,828	(NA)	(NA)	(NA)
1920	94,821	10,463	(NA)	(NA)	(NA)
1930	110,287	11,891	(NA)	(NA)	(NA)
1940	118,215	12,866	(NA)	(NA)	(NA)
1950	134,942	15,042	(NA)	(NA)	(NA)
1960	158,832	18,872	(NA)	(NA)	(NA)
1970	178,098	22,581	(NA)	(NA)	(NA)
1980	194,713	26,683	1,420	14,609	3,729
1990	208,727	30,511	2,065	22,372	2,462
2000	211,461	34,658	2,476	35,306	10,642

Source: U.S. Bureau of the Census, *U.S. Census of Population: 1940*, vol. II, part 1, and vol. IV, part 1; 1950, vol. II, part 1; 1960, vol. I, part 1; 1970, vol. I, part B; and *Current Population Reports*, P25–1095 and P25–1104; *Statistical Abstract of the United States* (2001).

IMMIGRATION, BY ORIGIN
(in thousands)

Period	Europe	Americas	Asia
1820–30	106	12	—
1831–40	496	33	—
1841–50	1,597	62	—
1851–60	2,453	75	42
1861–70	2,065	167	65
1871–80	2,272	404	70
1881–90	4,735	427	70
1891–1900	3,555	39	75
1901–10	8,065	362	324
1911–20	4,322	1,144	247
1921–30	2,463	1,517	112
1931–40	348	160	16
1941–50	621	355	32
1951–60	1,326	997	150
1961–70	1,123	1,716	590
1971–80	800	1,983	1,588
1981–90	762	3,616	2,738
1991–2000	1,100	3,800	2,200

Source: *Historical Statistics of the United States* (1975); *Statistical Abstract of the United States* (1991); Population Estimates Program, Population Division, U.S. Census Bureau, April 2001.

BIBLIOGRAPHY

CHAPTER 1

Settling the Continent

Larry D. Agenbroad, et al., eds., *Megafauna and Man* (1990)

John Bierhorst, ed., *The Red Swan: Myths and Tales of the American Indians* (1976)

Robson Bonnichsen and Karen L. Turnmire, *Ice Age People of North America: Environments, Origins, and Adaptations* (1999)

Michael H. Crawford, *The Origins of Native Americans: Evidence from Anthropological Genetics* (1998)

Tom D. Dillehay, *The Settling of the Americas: A New Prehistory* (2000)

E. James Dixon, *Bones, Boats, and Bison: Archaeology and the First Colonization of Western North America* (2000)

Richard Erdoes and Alfonso Ortiz, eds., *American Indian Myths and Legends* (1984)

Guy Gibbon, *Archaeology of Prehistoric Native America: An Encyclopedia* (1998)

Lee Eldridge Huddleston, *Origins of the American Indians: European Concepts, 1492–1729* (1967)

George Kubler, *Esthetic Recognition of Ancient Amerindian Art* (1991)

Hanns J. Prem, *The Ancient Americas: A Brief History and Guide to Research* (1997)

Heather Anne Pringle, *In Search of Ancient North America: An Archaeological Journey to Forgotten Cultures* (1996)

Richard F. Townsend, ed., *The Ancient Americas: Art from Sacred Landscapes* (1992)

Frederick Hadleigh West, ed., *American Beginnings: The Prehistory and Palaeoecology of Beringia* (1996)

New Ways of Living on the Land

Kenneth M. Ames and Herbert D. G. Mascher, *Peoples of the Northwest Coast: Their Archaeology and Prehistory* (2000)

Leonard W. Blake and Hugh C. Cutler, *Plants from the Past* (2001)

David S. Brose, et al., *Ancient Art of the American Woodland Indians* (1985)

Thomas E. Emerson, et al., eds. *Late Woodland Societies: Tradition and Transformation Across the Midcontinent* (2000)

Richard I. Ford, ed., *Prehistoric Food Production in North America* (1985)

Sarah W. Neusius, *Foraging, Collecting, and Harvesting: Archaic Period Subsistence and Settlement in the Eastern Woodlands* (1986)

James L. Phillips and James A. Brown, eds., *Archaic Hunters and Gatherers in the American Midwest* (1983)

Richard H. Steckel and Jerome C. Rose, *The Backbone of History: Health and Nutrition in the Western Hemisphere* (2002)

The Development of Farming

Frances R. Berdan, *The Aztecs of Central Mexico* (1982)

David S. Brose and N'omi Greber, eds., *Hopewell Archaeology* (1979)

David Carrasco, et al., eds., *Mesoamerica's Classic Heritage: From Teotihuacan to the Aztecs* (2000)

William S. Dancey and Paul J Pacheco, eds., *Ohio Hopewell Community Organization* (1997)

Emil W. Haury, *The Hohokam* (1976)

Ted Hirschfield, *Middle Mississippians: Encounters with the Prehistoric Amerindians* (1996)

Rosemary Joyce, *Gender and Power in Prehispanic Mesoamerica* (2000)

William F. Keegan, ed., *Emergent Horticultural Economies of the Eastern Woodlands* (1987)

R. Barry Lewis and Charles Stout, eds., *Mississippian Towns and Sacred Spaces* (1998)

George R. Milner, *The Cahokia Chiefdom: The Archaeology of a Mississippian Society* (1998)

Warren King Moorehead, *The Cahokia Mounds* (2000)

Barker H. Morrow and V. B. Price, eds., *Anasazi Architecture and American Design* (1997)

Timothy R. Pauketat and Thomas E. Emerson, eds., *Cahokia: Domination and Ideology in the Mississippian World* (1997)

Stephen Plog, *Ancient Peoples of the American Southwest* (1998)

Paul F. Reed, ed., *Foundations of Anasazi Culture: The Basketmaker-Pueblo Transition* (2000)

Bruce D. Smith, *The Mississippian Emergence* (1990)

David E. Stuart, *Anasazi America: Seventeen Centuries on the Road from Center Place* (2000)

Christy G. Turner, *Man Corn: Cannibalism and Violence in the Prehistoric American Southwest* (2000)

W. H. Wills, *Early Prehistoric Agriculture* (1988)

Biloine W. Young and Melvin L. Fowler, *Cahokia, The Great Native American Metropolis* (2000)

Cultural Regions of North America on the Eve of Colonization

Michael A. Adler, ed., *The Prehistoric Pueblo World, A.D. 1150–1350* (1996)

Kenneth M. Ames and Herbert D. G. Mascher, *Peoples of the Northwest Coast: Their Archaeology and Prehistory* (2000)

Elizabeth M. Brunfiel and John W. Fox, *Factional Competition and Political Development in the New World* (1993)

Catherine M. Cameron, *Hopi Dwellings: Architecture at Oryi* (1999)

Lyle Campbell and Marianne Mithun, eds., *The Languages of Native America* (1979)

Paul H. Carlson, *The Plains Indians* (1999)

James Taylor Carson, *Searching for the Bright Path: The Mississippi Choctaws from Prehistory to Removal* (1999)

May Castleberry, *The New World's Old World: Photographic Views of Ancient America* (2003)

Cheryl Claassen and Rosemary A. Joyce, eds., *Women in Prehistory: North America and Mesoamerica* (1997)

Olive P. Dickason, *Canada's First Nations: A History of Founding Peoples* (1992)

Michelle Hegmon, ed., *The Archaeology of Regional Interaction: Religion, Warfare, and Exchange Across the American Southwest* (1999)

June Helm, *The People of Denendah: Ethnohistory of the Indians of Canada's Northwest Territories* (2000)

David LaVere, *The Caddo Chiefdoms: Caddo Economics and Politics, 700–1835* (1998)

Steven A. LeBlanc, *Prehistoric Warfare in the American Southwest* (1999)

Stephen H. Lekson, *The Chaco Meridian: Centers of Political Power in the Ancient Southwest* (1999)

Jill E. Neitzel, ed., *Great Towns and Regional Politics: In the Prehistoric American Southwest and Southeast* (1999)

Mallory McCane O'Connor, *Lost Cities of the Ancient Southeast* (1995)

Alfonso Ortiz, ed., *New Perspectives on the Pueblos* (1972)

Howard S. Russell, *Indian New England Before the Mayflower* (1980)

Frank G. Speck, *Penobscot Man* (1940)

Bruce Trigger, *The Children of Aataentsic: A History of the Huron People to 1660* (1976)

CHAPTER 2

The Expansion of Europe

James M. Blaut, *1492: The Debate on Colonialism, Eurocentrism, and History* (1992)

Fernand Braudel, *The Mediterranean and the Mediterranean World in the Age of Philip II* (1972)

Carol Cipolla, *Before the Industrial Revolution: European Society and Economy, 1100–1700* (1976)

Patrick Collinson, *The Religion of Protestants: The Church in English Society, 1559–1625* (1982)

Andre Gunder Frank, *World Accumulation, 1492–1789* (1978)

Giancarlo Masini and Iacopo Gari, *How Florence Invented America: Vespucci, Verranzano, and Mazzei and Their Contribution to the Conception of the New World* (1998)

Douglass North, *The Rise of the Western World: A New Economic History* (1973)

José Casas Pardo, ed., *Economic Effects of the European Expansion, 1492–1824* (1992)

J. H. Parry, *The Age of Reconnaissance* (1963)

———, *Europe and a Wider World: The Establishment of the European Hegemony: Trade and Expansion in the Age of the Renaissance* (1966)

Geoffrey Vaughn Scannell, *The First Imperial Age: European Overseas Expansion c. 1400–1715* (1989)

The Spanish in the Americas

Fredi Chiapelli, ed., *First Images of America: The Impact of the New World on the Old* (1976)

Kathleen Deagan and José María Cruxent, *Columbus's Outpost among the Taínos: Spain and America at La Isabela, 1493–1498* (2002)

Henry F. Dobyns, *Their Number Become Thinned: Native American Population Dynamics in Eastern North America* (1983)

J. H. Elliott, *The Old World and the New, 1492–14921* (1970)

Anthony Grafton, *New Worlds, Ancient Texts: The Power of Tradition and the Shock of Discovery* (1992)

John H. Hann, *A History of the Timucua Indians and Missions* (1996)

Hugh Honour, *New Golden Land: European Images of America from the Discoveries to the Present Time* (1975)

Charles Hudson and Carmen Chaves Tesser, eds., *The Forgotten Centuries: Indians and Europeans in the American South, 1521–1704* (1994)

René Jara and Nicholas Spadaccini, eds., *Amerindian Images and the Legacy of Columbus* (1992)

Elizabeth A. H. John, *Storms Brewed in Other Men's Worlds: The Confrontation of Indians, Spanish, and French in the Southwest, 1540–1795* (1975)

James Lang, *Conquest and Commerce: Spain and England in the Americas* (1975)

James Lockhart and Stuart B. Schwartz, *Early Latin America: A History of Colonial Spanish America and Brazil* (1983)

Albert Mauncy, *Sixteenth-Century St. Augustine: The People and Their Homes* (1997)

Jerald T. Milanich, *Laboring in the Fields of the Lord: Spanish Missions and Southeastern Indians* (1999)

Jerald T. Milanich and Charles Hudson, *Hernando de Soto and the Indians of Florida* (1993)

James Howlett O'Donnell III, *Southeastern Frontiers: Europeans, Africans, and American Indians, 1513–1840: A Critical Bibliography* (1982)

Edmundo O'Gorman, *The Invention of America: An Inquiry into the Historical Nature of the New World and the Meaning of its History* (1961)

Stuart B. Schwartz, *Victors and Vanquished: Spanish and Nahua Views of the Conquest of Mexico* (2000)

David M. Traboulay, *Columbus and Las Casas: The Conquest and Christianization of America, 1492–1566* (1994)

Northern Explorations and Encounters

Alfred Goldsworthy Bailey, *The Conflict of European and Eastern Algonkian Cultures, 1504–1700* (1969)

Peter T. Bradley, *British Maritime Enterprise in the New World: From the Late Fifteenth to the Mid-Eighteenth Century* (1999)

Carl Bridenbaugh, *Vexed and Troubled Englishmen, 1590–1642* (1968)

Susan Danforth, *Encountering the New World, 1493–1800* (1991)

Philip J. Deloria and Neal Salisbury, eds., *A Companion to American Indian History* (2002)

G. R. Elton, *England under the Tudors* (1974)

C. H. George and Katherine George, *The Protestant Mind of the English Reformation* (1961)

John Guy, *Tudor England* (1988)

R. J. Knecht, *The French Civil Wars, 1562–1598* (2000)

Karen Ordahl Kupperman, *Indians and English: Facing Off in Early America* (2000)

Peter Laslett, *The World We Have Lost* (1965)

Anthony McFarlane, *The British in the Americas, 1480–1815* (1994)

Lee Miller, *Roanoke: Solving the Mystery of England's Lost Colony* (2000)

James S. Pritchard, *In Search of Empire: The French in the Americas, 1670–1730* (2004)

David B. Quinn, *North America from Earliest Discovery to First Settlements* (1977)

———, *The Roanoke Voyages, 1584–1590*, 2 vols. (1955)

Bernard W. Sheehan, *Savagism and Civility: Indians and Englishmen in Colonial Virginia* (1980)

Russell Thornton, *American Indian Holocaust and Survival* (1987)

Margo Todd, ed., *Reformation to Revolution: Politics and Religion in Early Modern England* (1995)

Marcel Trudel, *The Beginnings of New France, 1524–1663* (1973)

Keith Wrightson, *English Society, 1580–1680* (1982)

Biography

Miles H. Davidson, *Columbus Then and Now: A Life Reexamined* (1997)

David A. Howard, *Conquistador in Chains: Cabeza de Vaca and the Indians of the Americas* (1997)

Harry Kelsey, *Sir Francis Drake: The Queen's Pirate* (1998)

Carole Levin, *The Heart and Stomach of a King: Elizabeth I and the Politics of Sex and Power* (1994)

Richard Lee Marks, *Cortés: The Great Adventurer and the Fate of Aztec Mexico* (1993)

James McDermott, *Martin Frobisher: Elizabethan Privateer* (2001)

P. E. Russell, *Prince Henry the Navigator: A Life* (2000)

David Starkey, *Elizabeth: The Struggle for the Throne* (2000)

Henry Raup Wagner, *The Life and Writings of Bartolomé de las Casas* (1967)

CHAPTER 3

Spain and Its Competitors in North America

Gary Clayton Anderson, *The Indian Southwest, 1580–1830: Ethnogenesis and Reinvention* (1999)

James Axtell, *The Invasion Within: The Contest of Culture in Colonial North America* (1985)

Denys Delâge, *Bitter Feast: Amerindians and Europeans in Northeastern North America, 1600–64* (1993)

W. J. Eccles, *The Canadian Frontier, 1534–1760* (1983)

Carl J. Ekberg, *French Roots in the Illinois Country: The Mississippi Frontier in Colonial Times* (1998)

Eric Hinderaker and Peter C. Mancall, *At the Edge of Empire: The Backcountry in British North America* (2003)

J. R. Jones, *The Anglo–Dutch Wars of the Seventeenth Century* (1996)

Cathy D. Matson, *Merchants and Empire: Trading in Colonial New York* (1998)

Peter Moogk, *La Nouvelle France: The Making of French Canada, a Cultural History* (2000)

Daniel Paul, *We Were Not the Savages: A Mi'kmaq Perspective on the Collision Between European and Native American Civilizations* (2000)

Oliver Rink, *Holland on the Hudson: An Economic and Social History of Dutch New York* (1986)

Sylvia Van Kirk, *Many Tender Ties: Women in Fur-Trade Society in Western Canada, 1670–1870* (1999)

England in the Chesapeake

Edward L. Bond, *Damned Souls in a Tobacco Colony: Religion in Seventeenth-Century Virginia* (2000)

Kathleen M. Brown, *Good Wives, Nasty Wenches, and Anxious Patriarchs: Gender, Race, and Power in Colonial Virginia* (1996)

Wesley F. Craven, *White, Red, and Black: The Seventeenth Century Virginian* (1971)

April Lee Hatfield, *Atlantic Virginia: Intercolonial Relations in the Seventeenth Century* (2004)

Ronald Hoffman, *Princes of Ireland, Planters of Maryland: A Carroll Saga, 1500–1782* (2000)

Karen Ordahl Kupperman, *Settling with the Indians: The Meeting of English and Indian Cultures in America, 1580–1640* (1980)

Gloria L. Main, *Tobacco Colony: Life in Early Maryland, 1650–1720* (1982)

Michael Leroy Oberg, *Dominion and Civility: English Imperialism and Native America, 1585–1685* (1999)

The New England Colonies

David Grayson Allen, *In English Ways: The Movement of Societies and the Transferal of English Local Law and Custom* (1981)

Bernard Bailyn, *The New England Merchants in the Seventeenth Century* (1955)

Carl Bridenbaugh, *Fat Mutton and Liberty of Conscience: Society in Rhode Island, 1636–1690* (1974)

Joyce E. Chaplin, *Subject Matter: Technology, the Body, and Science on the Anglo–American Frontier, 1500–1676* (2001)

David Cressy, *Coming Over: Migration and Communication between England and New England in the Seventeenth Century* (1987)

William Cronon, *Changes in the Land: Indians, Colonists, and the Ecology of New England* (1983)

John Demos, *A Little Commonwealth: Family Life in Plymouth Colony* (1970)

David D. Hall, ed., *Puritans in the New World: A Critical Anthology* (2004)

Timothy Hall, *Separating Church and State: Roger Williams and Religious Liberty* (1998)

Francis Jennings, *The Invasion of America: Indians, Colonialism, and the Cant of Conquest* (1975)

Benjamin W. Labaree, *America and the Sea: A Maritime History* (1998)

Amy Scrager Lang, *Prophetic Women: Anne Hutchinson and the Problem of Dissent in the Literature of New England* (1987)

Elizabeth Reis, *Damned Women: Sinners and Witches in Puritan New England* (1997)

The Restoration Colonies

Wesley F. Craven, *The Southern Colonies in the Seventeenth Century, 1607–1689* (1949)

Michael Kammen, *Colonial New York: A History* (1975)

Sung Bok Kim, *Landlord and Tenant in Colonial New York: Manorial Society, 1664–1775* (1978)

H. T. Merrens, *Colonial North Carolina* (1964)

Donna Merwick, *Death of a Notary: Conquest and Change in Colonial New York* (1999)

Gary B. Nash, *Quakers and Politics: Pennsylvania, 1681–1726* (1968)

M. Eugene Sirmans, *Colonial South Carolina: A Political History, 1663–1763* (1966)

Jack M. Sosin, *English America and the Restoration Monarchy of Charles II: Transatlantic Politics, Commerce, and Kinship* (1980)

Conflict and War

Thomas J. Archdeacon, *New York City, 1664–1710* (1976)

Paul Boyer and Stephen Nissenbaum, *Salem Possessed* (1974)

Colin G. Calloway, ed., *After King Philip's War: Presence and Persistence in Indian New England* (1997)

Guy Chet, *Conquering the American Wilderness: The Triumph of European Warfare in the Colonial Northeast* (2003)

Eveline Cruickshanks, *The Glorious Revolution* (2000)

James D. Drake, *King Philip's War: Civil War in New England, 1675–1676* (1999)

Ramón A. Gutiérrez, *When Jesus Came, the Corn Mothers Went Away: Marriage, Sexuality, and Power in New Mexico, 1500–1846* (1991)

Richard R. Johnson, *Adjustment to Empire: The New England Colonies, 1675–1715* (1981)

D. W. Jordan, *Maryland's Revolution of Government, 1689–1692* (1974)

Carol F. Karlsen, *The Devil in the Shape of a Woman: Witchcraft in Colonial New England* (1987)

Karen Ordahl Kupperman, *Indians and English: Facing Off in Early America* (2000)

Almon Wheeler Lauber, *Indian Slavery in Colonial Times within the Present Limits of the United States* (1913)

Jill Lepore, *The Name of War: King Philip's War and the Origins of American Identity* (1998)

David S. Lovejoy, *The Glorious Revolution in America* (1972)

Nancy Shoemaker, *A Strange Likeness: Becoming Red and White in Eighteenth-Century North America* (2004)

Wilcomb E. Washburn, *The Governor and the Rebel: A History of Bacon's Rebellion in Virginia* (1957)

Stephen S. Webb, *1676: The End of American Independence* (1980)

Biography

Mary K. Geiter, *Willlam Penn* (2000)

J. A. Leo Lemay, *The American Dream of Captain John Smith* (1991)

Edmund S. Morgan, *Puritan Dilemma: The Story of John Winthrop* (1958)

Ann Sanford, *Anne Bradstreet, the Worldly Puritan* (1974)

Marc Simmons, *The Last Conquistador: Juan de Oñate and the Settling of the Far Southwest* (1991)

Robert S. Tilton, *Pocahontas: The Evolution of an American Narrative* (1994)

Alvin Gardner Weeks, *Massasoit of the Pokanokets* (1919)

Selma R. Williams, *Divine Rebel: The Life of Anne Marbury Hutchinson* (1981)

CHAPTER 4

The African Slave Trade

Jay Coughtry, *The Notorious Triangle: Rhode Island and the African Slave Trade, 1799–1807* (1981)

Philip D. Curtin, *Economic Change in Precolonial Africa: Senegambia in the Era of the Slave Trade* (1975)

Basil Davidson, *The African Slave Trade* (1980)

Benedict G. Der, *The Slave Trade in Northern Ghana* (1998)

Elizabeth Donnan, ed., *Documents Illustrative of the History of the Slave Trade to America,* 4 vols. (1930–35)

David Eltis, et al., eds., *Slavery in the Development of the Americas* (2004)

Eli Faber, *Jews, Slaves, and the Slave Trade: Setting the Record Straight* (1998)

Philip Gould, *Barbaric Traffic: Commerce and Antislavery in the Eighteenth-Century Atlantic World* (2003)

Robert W. Harms, *The Diligent: A Voyage through the Worlds of the Slave Trade* (2001)

J. E. Inikori, *Forced Migration: The Impact of the Export Slave Trade on African Societies* (1982)

Robert W. July, *A History of the African People* (1992)

Herbert S. Klein, *The Middle Passage: Comparative Studies in the Atlantic Slave Trade* (1978)

Robin Law, *The Slave Coast of West Africa, 1550–1750: The Impact of the Atlantic Slave Trade on an African Society* (1991)

Paul E. Lovejoy, ed., *Africans in Bondage: Studies in Slavery and the Slave Trade* (1986)

Daniel P. Mannix and Malcolm Crowley, *Black Cargoes: A History of the Atlantic Slave Trade* (1962)

David Northrup, ed., *The Atlantic Slave Trade* (1994)

J. A. Rawley, *The Transatlantic Slave Trade* (1981)

Edward Reynolds, *Stand the Storm: A History of the Atlantic Slave Trade* (1985)

A. C. de C. M. Saunders, *A Social History of Black Slaves and Freemen in Portugal, 1441–1555* (1982)

Randy J. Sparks, *Two Princes of Calabar: An Eighteenth-Century Atlantic Odyssey* (2004)

Jon Vogt, *Portuguese Rule on the Gold Coast, 1469–1682* (1979)

James Walvin, *Making the Black Atlantic: Britain and the African Diaspora* (2000)

The Development of North American Slave Societies

L. R. Bailey, *Indian Slave Trade in the Southwest: A Study of Slave-Taking and the Traffic in Indian Captives* (1966)

Ira Berlin, *Generations of Captivity: A History of African-American Slaves* (2003)

T. H. Breen and Stephen Innes, *"Myne Owne Ground": Race and Freedom on Virginia's Eastern Shore* (1980)

Verner W. Crane, *The Southern Frontier, 1670–1732* (1929)

Richard S. Dunn, *Sugar and Slaves: The Rise of the Planter Class in the English West Indies, 1624–1713* (1972)

David Eltis, *The Rise of African Slavery in the Americas* (2000)

Sharla M. Fett, *Working Cures: Healing, Health, and Power on Southern Slave Plantations* (2002)

Laura Foner and Eugene D. Genovese, eds., *Slavery in the New World: A Reader in Comparative History* (1969)

Allan Gallay, *The Indian Slave Trade: The Rise of the English Empire in the American South, 1670–1717* (2002)

Graham Russell Hodges, *Root and Branch: African Americans in New York and East Jersey, 1613–1863* (1999)

Thomas N. Ingersoll, *Mammon and Manon in Early New Orleans: The First Slave Society in the Deep South, 1718–1819* (1999)

Charles Joyner, *Down by the Riverside: A South Carolina Slave Community* (1984)

Alan Kulikoff, *Tobacco and Slaves: The Development of Southern Cultures in the Chesapeake, 1680–1800* (1986)

Jane Landers, *Black Society in Spanish Florida* (1999)

Daniel Littlefield, *Rice and Slaves: Ethnicity and the Slave Trade in Colonial South Carolina* (1981)

Paul E. Lovejoy, *Transformations in Slavery: A History of Slavery in Africa* (1983)

Edgar J. McManus, *Black Bondage in the North* (1973)

Gary B. Nash, *Red, White, and Black: The Peoples of Early North America* (1992)

Julia Floyd Smith, *Slavery and Rice Culture in Low Country Georgia, 1750–1860* (1985)

Peter H. Wood, *Black Majority: Negroes in Colonial South Carolina from 1670 through the Stone Rebellion* (1974)

African to African American

John B. Boles, *Black Southerners, 1619–1869* (1984)

Alex Bontemps, *The Punished Self: Surviving Slavery in the Colonial South* (2001)

Sylviane A. Diouf, *Servants of Allah: African Muslims Enslaved in the Americas* (1998)

John Hope Franklin and Loren Schweniger, *Runaway Slaves: Rebels in the Plantation* (1999)

Michael Gomez, *Exchanging Our Country Marks: The Transformation of African Identities in the Colonial and Antebellum South* (1998)

Annette Gordon-Reed, *Thomas Jefferson and Sally Hemings: An American Controversy* (1997)

Herbert G. Gutman, *The Black Family in Slavery and Freedom, 1750–1925* (1976)

Joseph E. Harris, ed., *Global Dimensions of the African Diaspora* (1982)

Gerald W. Mullin, *Flight and Rebellion: Slave Resistance in Eighteenth-Century Virginia* (1972)

Orlando Patterson, *Slavery and Social Death: A Comparative Study* (1982)

Mark M. Smith, *Mastered by the Clock: Time, Slavery, and Freedom in the American South* (1997)

Sterling Stuckey, *Slave Culture: Nationalist Theory and the Foundations of Black America* (1987)

V. B. Thompson, *The Making of the African Diaspora in the Americas, 1441–1900* (1984)

Slavery and Empire

Joyce O. Appleby, *Economic Thought and Ideology in Seventeenth-Century England* (1978)

Heather Cateau and S. H. H. Carrington, eds., *Capitalism and Slavery Fifty Years Later: Eric Eustace Williams—A Reassessment of the Man and His Work* (2000)

Eugene Genovese and Elizabeth Fox-Genovese, *Fruits of Merchant Capital: Slavery and Bourgeois Property in the Rise and Expansion of Capitalism* (1983)

E. J. Hobsbawn, *Industry and Empire: The Making of Modern English Society, 1750 to the Present Day* (1968)

Michael Kammen, *Empire and Interest: The American Colonies and the Politics of Mercantilism* (1970)

John J. McCusker and Russell R. Menard, *The Economy of British America, 1607–1787* (1985)

Barbara L. Solow, ed., *Slavery and the Rise of the Atlantic System* (1991)

Eric Williams, *Capitalism and Slavery* (1944)

Slavery and Freedom

David Brion Davis, *The Problem of Slavery in Western Culture* (1966)

Carl N. Degler, *Neither Black nor White: Slavery and Race Relations in Brazil and the United States* (1971)

Edmund S. Morgan, *American Slavery, American Freedom: The Ordeal of Colonial Virginia* (1975)

Joel Williamson, *New People: Miscegenation and Mulattoes in the United States* (1980)

Biography

Philip D. Curtin, ed., *Africa Remembered: Narratives of West Africans from the Era of the Slave Trade* (1967)

Paul Edwards, ed., *The Interesting Narrative of the Life of Olaudah Equiano, or Gustavus Vassa, the African, written by himself* (1987)

James B. Hedges, *The Browns of Providence Plantation* (1952)

Kenneth A. Lockridge, *The Diary and Life of William Byrd II of Virginia, 1674–1744* (1987)

Phinizy Spalding, *Oglethorpe in America* (1977)

CHAPTER 5

North American Regions

Patricia Albers and Beatrice Medicine, eds., *The Hidden Half: Studies of Plains Indian Women* (1983)

Carole Blackburn, *Harvest of Souls: The Jesuit Missions and Colonialism in North America, 1632–1650* (2000)

Richard L. Bushman, *From Puritan to Yankee: Character and the Social Order in Connecticut, 1690–1765* (1967)

David Bussiert and Steven G. Reinhardt, eds., *Creolization in the Americas* (2000)

Edward D. Castillo, ed., *Native American Perspectives on the Hispanic Colonization of Alta California* (1992)

Andrew R. L. Cayton and Frederika J. Teute, eds., *Contact Points: American Frontiers from the Mohawk Valley to the Mississippi, 1750–1830* (1998)

Cornelia Hughes Dayton, *Women before the Bar: Gender, Law, and Society in Connecticut, 1639–1789* (1995)

Brian Leigh Dunnigan, *Frontier Metropolis: Picturing Early Detroit, 1701–1838* (2001)

John C. Ewers, *The Horse in Blackfoot Indian Culture* (1955)

David Hackett Fischer and James C. Kelly, *Bound Away: Virginia and the Westward Movement* (2000)

Joseph W. Glass, *The Pennsylvania Culture Region: A View from the Barn* (1986)

Robert F. Heizer, *The Destruction of California Indians* (1974)

Donald A. Hutslar, *The Architecture of Migration: Log Construction in the Ohio Country, 1750–1850* (1986)

Christine Leigh Hyrman, *Commerce and Culture: The Maritime Communities of Colonial Massachusetts* (1984)

Rhys Isaac, *Worlds of Experience: Communities in Colonial Virginia* (1987)

Robert H. Jackson, *Indian Population Decline: The Missions of Northwestern New Spain, 1687–1840* (1994)

———, *From Savages to Subjects: Missions in the History of the American Southwest* (2000)

Francis Jennings, *The Ambiguous Iroquois Empire* (1984)

Terry G. Jordan and Matti Kaups, *The American Backwoods Frontier: An Ethnic and Ecological Interpretation* (1988)

Lyle Kohler, *A Search for Power: "The Weaker Sex" in Seventeenth-Century New England, 1650–1750* (1982)

James T. Lemon, *The Best Poor Man's Country: A Geographical Study of Early Southeastern Pennsylvania* (1972)

Kenneth Lockridge, *Literacy in Colonial New England* (1974)

James H. Merrell, *The Indians' New World: Catawbas and Their Neighbors from European Contact through the Era of Removal* (1989)

———, *Into the American Woods: Negotiators on the Pennsylvania Frontier* (1999)

Jane T. Merritt, *At the Crossroads: Indians and Empires on a Mid-Atlantic Frontier, 1700–1763* (2003)

Gary B. Nash, *The Urban Crucible* (1979)

Jacqueline Peterson and Jennifer S. H. Brown, eds., *The New Peoples: Being and Becoming Métis in North America* (1985)

Daniel K. Richter, *The Ordeal of the Longhouse: The Peoples of the Iroquois League in the Era of European Colonization* (1992)

Darrett B. Rutman and Anita H. Rutman, *A Place in Time: Middlesex County, Virginia, 1650–1750* (1984)

Marylynn Salmon, *Women and the Law of Property in Early America* (1986)

Sally Schwartz, *A Mixed Multitude: The Struggle for Toleration in Colonial Pennsylvania* (1987)

William S. Simmons, *Spirit of the New England Tribes: Indian History and Folklore, 1620–1984* (1986)

Daniel Blake Smith, *Inside the Great House: Planter Family Life in Eighteenth-Century Chesapeake Society* (1980)

Laurel T. Ulrich, *Good Wives: Image and Reality in the Lives of Women in Northern New England, 1650–1750* (1982)

Daniel H. Usner Jr., *Indians, Settlers, and Slaves in a Frontier Exchange Economy: The Lower Mississippi Valley before 1783* (1992)

Diverging Social and Political Patterns

James E. Block, *Nation of Agents: The American Path to a Modern Self and Society* (2002)

Bernard Bailyn, *The Peopling of British North America: An Introduction* (1986)

Bruce C. Daniels, ed., *Power and Status: Essays on Officeholding in Colonial America* (1986)

Robert J. Dinkin, *Voting in Provincial America: A Study of Elections in the Thirteen Colonies, 1680–1776* (1977)

A. Roger Ekirch, *Bound for America: The Transportation of British Convicts to the Colonies, 1718–1775* (1987)

Carla Gardina Pestana and Sharon V. Salinger, eds., *Inequality in Early America* (1999)

Thomas L. Purvis, *Proprietors, Patronage, and Paper Money: Legislative Politics in New Jersey, 1703–1776* (1986)

Sharon V. Salinger, *"To Serve Well and Faithfully": Labor and Indentured Servants in Pennsylvania, 1682–1800* (1987)

The Cultural Transformation of British North America

Linda Baumgarten, *What Clothes Reveal: The Language of Clothing in Colonial and Federal America: The Colonial Williamsburg Collection* (2002)

Patricia U. Bonomi, *Under the Cope of Heaven: Religion, Society, and Politics in Colonial America* (1986)

Henry Steele Commager, *The Empire of Reason: How Europe Imagined and America Realized the Enlightenment* (1977)

Patricia Crain, *The Story of A: The Alphabetization of America from "The New England Primer" to "The Scarlet Letter"* (2000)

John Demos, *Circles and Lines: The Shape of Life in Early America* (2004)

Nancy Isenberg and Andrew Burstein, eds., *Mortal Remains: Death in Early America* (2003)

Ned C. Landsman, *From Colonials to Provincials: American Thought and Culture, 1680–1760* (1997)

Jackson Turner Main, *The Social Structure of Revolutionary America* (1965)

Barbara B. Oberg and Harry S. Stout, eds., *Benjamin Franklin, Jonathan Edwards, and the Representation of American Culture* (1993)

Mark A. Peterson, *The Price of Redemption: The Spiritual Economy of Puritan New England* (1997)

Nina Reid-Mahoney, *Philadelphia's Enlightenment, 1740–1800: Kingdom of Christ, Empire of Reason* (2001)

Frank Shuffelton, ed., *The American Enlightenment* (1993)

Biography

Verner W. Crane, *Benjamin Franklin and a Rising People* (1952)

Harry Kelsey, *Juan Rodriguez Cabrillo* (1986)

Gerald R. McDermott, *Jonathan Edwards Confronts the Gods* (2000)

Robert Middlekauff, *The Mathers: Three Generations of Puritan Intellectuals, 1596–1728* (1999)

Martin J. Morgado, *Junípero Serra's Legacy* (1987)

Harry S. Stout, *The Divine Dramatist: George Whitefield and the Rise of Modern Evangelicalism* (1991)

Laurel Ulrich, *A Midwife's Tale: The Life of Martha Ballard, Based on Her Diary, 1785–1812* (1990)

CHAPTER 6

The Seven Years' War in America

Fred Anderson, *A People's Army: Massachusetts Soldiers and Society in the Seven Years' War* (1984)

Frank W. Brecher, *Losing a Continent: France's North American Policy, 1753–1763* (1998)

Gregory Evans Dowd, *War Under Heaven: Pontiac, the Indian Nations, and the British Empire* (2002)

Sylvia R. Frey, *The British Soldier in America: A Social History of Military Life in the Colonial Period* (1981)

Dougles E. Leach, *Roots of Conflict: British Armed Forces and Colonial Americans, 1677–1763* (1986)

Richard Middleton, *The Bells of Victory: The Pitt–Newcastle Ministry and the Conduct of the Seven Years' War, 1757–1762* (1985)

Robert C. Newbold, *The Albany Congress and Plan of Union of 1754* (1955)

William Pencak, *War, Politics, and Revolution in Provincial Massachusetts* (1981)

Tom Pocock, *Battle for Empire: The Very First World War, 1756–63* (1998)

Alan Rogers, *Empire and Liberty* (1974)

David Curtis Skaggs and Larry L. Nelson, eds., *The Sixty Years' War for the Great Lakes, 1754–1814* (2001)

Noel T. St. John Williams, *Redcoats along the Hudson* (1997)

Richard White, *The Middle Ground: Indians, Empires, and Republics in the Great Lakes Region, 1650–1815* (1991)

Imperial Crisis in British North America

Stuart Andrews, *The Rediscovery of America: Transatlantic Crosscurrents in an Age of Revolution* (1998)

Thomas C. Barrow, *Trade and Empire: The British Customs Service in Colonial America* (1967)

Don Cook, *The Long Fuse: How England Lost the American Colonies, 1760–1785* (1995)

Theodore Draper, *A Struggle for Power: The American Revolution* (1996)

Marc Egnal, *A Mighty Empire: The Origins of the American Revolution* (1988)

Eliga H. Gould, *The Persistence of Empire: British Political Culture in the Age of the American Revolution* (2000)

Woody Holton, *Forced Founders: Indians, Debtors, Slaves, and the Making of the American Revolution in Virginia* (1999)

Alice Hanson Jones, *The Wealth of a Nation to Be* (1980)

John J. McCusker, *Rum and the American Revolution* (1989)

Philip James McFarland, *The Brave Bostonians: Hutchinson, Quincy, Franklin, and the Coming of the American Revolution* (1998)

J. G. A. Pocock, *The Machiavellian Moment: Florentine Political Thought and the Atlantic Republican Tradition* (1975)

William Lowell Putnam, *John Peter Zenger and the Fundamental Freedom* (1997)

Caroline Robbins, *The Eighteenth-Century Commonwealthman* (1959)

Arthur M. Schlesinger, *The Colonial Merchants and the American Revolution* (1917)

John W. Tyler, *Smugglers and Patriots: Boston Merchants and the Advent of the American Revolution* (1986)

Carl Ubbelohde, *The Vice-Admiralty Courts and the American Revolution* (1960)

Kathleen Wilson, *Island Race: Englishness, Empire, and Gender in the Eighteenth Century* (2003)

From Resistance to Rebellion

David Ammerman, *In the Common Cause: American Response to the Coercive Acts of 1774* (1974)

T. H. Breen, *Tobacco Culture: The Mentality of the Great Tidewater Planters on the Eve of Revolution* (1985)

Richard D. Brown, *Revolutionary Politics in Massachusetts: The Boston Committee of Correspondence and the Towns, 1772–1774* (1970)

Richard L. Bushman, *King and People in Provincial Massachusetts* (1985)

H. Trevor Colbourn, *The Lamp of Experience: Whig History and the Intellectual Origins of the American Revolution* (1965)

Light Townsend Cummins, *Spanish Observers and the American Revolution, 1775–1783* (1991)

Derek Davis, *Religion and the Continental Congress, 1774–1789: Contributions to Original Intent* (2000)

Bernard Donoughue, *British Politics and the American Revolution: The Path to War, 1773–1775* (1964)

Gregory T. Edgar, *Reluctant Break with Britain: From Stamp Act to Bunker Hill* (1997)

Jack P. Greene, *Understanding the American Revolution: Issues and Actors* (1995)

Benjamin W. Labaree, *The Boston Tea Party* (1974)

Pauline Maier, *From Resistance to Rebellion* (1972)

Edmund S. Morgan, *The Birth of the Republic, 1763–1789* (1956)

Ray Raphael, *First American Revolution: Before Lexington and Concord* (2002)

Jackson O'Shaughnessy, *An Empire Divided: The American Revolution and the British Caribbean* (2000)

John Shy, *Toward Lexington: The Role of the British Army in the Coming of the American Revolution* (1965)

Peter David Garner Thomas, *Tea Party to Independence: The Third Phase of the American Revolution, 1773–1776* (1991)

Morton White, *The Philosophy of the American Revolution* (1978)

Gary Wills, *Inventing America* (1978)

Biography

Bernard Bailyn, *The Ordeal of Thomas Hutchinson* (1974)

Della Gray Barthelmas, *The Signers of the Declaration of Independence* (1997)

Richard R. Beeman, *Patrick Henry: A Biography* (1974)

Jeremy Black, *Pitt the Elder* (1992)

John Brooke, *King George III* (1974)

John E. Ferling, *The Loyalist Mind: Joseph Galloway and the American Revolution* (1977)

————, *Setting the World Ablaze: Washington, Adams, and Jefferson and the American Revolution* (2000)

William M. Fowler, Jr., *The Baron of Beacon Hill: A Biography of John Hancock* (1979)

————, *Samuel Adams: Radical Puritan* (1997)

Rhys Isaac, *Landon Carter's Uneasy Kingdom: Revolution and Rebellion on a Virginia Plantation* (2004)

David A. McCants, *Patrick Henry, the Orator* (1990)

Colin Nicolson, *"Infamas Govener" Francis Bernard and the Origins of the American Revolution* (2001)

Peter Shaw, *The Character of John Adams* (1976)

Peter D. G. Thomas, *Lord North* (1974)

Andrew S. Walmsley, *Thomas Hutchinson and the Origins of the American Revolution* (1999)

Gordon S. Wood, *Americanization of Benjamin Franklin* (2004)

CHAPTER 7

The War for Independence

Ian Barnes, *The Historical Atlas of the American Revolution* (2000)

Ira Berlin and Ronald Hoffman, eds., *Slavery and Freedom in the Age of the American Revolution* (1983)

Wayne Bodle, *Valley Forge Winter: Civilians and Soldiers in War* (2002)

T. H. Breen, *Marketplace of Revolution: How Consumer Politics Shaped American Independence* (2004)

Charles E. Claghorn, *Women Patriots of the American Revolution* (1991)

Stephen Conway, *British Isles and the War of American Independence* (2000)

Lawrence D. Cress, *Citizens in Arms: The Army and the Militia in American Society to the War of 1812* (1982)

Paul Finkleman, ed., *Slavery, Revolutionary America, and the New Nation* (1989)

William M. Fowler Jr., *Rebels Under Sail: The American Navy During the Revolution* (1976)

Francis Fox, *Sweet Land of Liberty: The Ordeal of the American Revolution in Northampton County, Pennsylvania* (2000)

Barbara Graymont, *The Iroquois in the American Revolution* (1972)

Leslie Hall, *Land and Allegiance in Revolutionary Georgia* (2001)

David C. Hendrickson, *Peace Pact: The Lost World of the American Founding* (2003)

Ronald Hoffman and Peter J. Albert, eds., *Arms and Independence: The Military Character of the American Revolution* (1984)

————, *Women in the Age of the American Revolution* (1989)

Ronald Hoffman and Thad W. Tate, eds., *An Uncivil War: The Southern Backcountry during the American Revolution* (1985)

Francis Jennings, *The Creation of America: Through Revolution to Empire* (2000)

Mark E. Kann, *A Republic of Men: The American Founders, Gendered Language, and Patriarchial Politics* (1998)

Cynthia A. Kierner, *Southern Women in Revolution, 1776–1800* (1998)

Arthur S. Lefkowitz, *The Long Retreat: The Calamitous American Defense of New Jersey, 1776* (1999)

Paul C. Nagel, *The Adams Women: Abigail and Louise Adams, Their Sisters and Daughters* (1987)

Gary B. Nash, *Race and Revolution* (1990)

Mary Beth Norton, *The British Americans: The Loyalist Exiles in England, 1774–1789* (1972)

James O'Donnell, *Southern Indians in the American Revolution* (1973)

Andrew Jackson O'Shaughnessy, *An Empire Divided: The American Revolution and the British Caribbean* (2000)

Howard W. Peckham, *The Toll of Independence: Engagements and Battle Casualties of the American Revolution* (1974)

Elizabeth Perkins, *Border Life: Experience and Memory in the Revolutionary Ohio Valley* (1998)

Benjamin Quarles, *The Negro in the American Revolution*, rev. ed. (1996)

David Lee Russell, *The American Revolution in the Southern Colonies* (2000)

James W. St. G. Walker, *The Black Loyalists* (1976)

Anthony F. C. Wallace, *The Death and Rebirth of the Seneca* (1970)

Alfred F. Young, ed., *The American Revolution: Explorations in American Radicalism* (1976)

The United States in Congress Assembled

Joyce Appleby, *Inheriting the Revolution: The First Generation of Americans* (2000)

Richard Beeman, et al., eds., *Beyond Confederation: Origins of the Constitution and American National Identity* (1987)

E. Wayne Carp, *To Starve the Army at Pleasure: Continental Army Administration and American Political Culture, 1774–1783* (1984)

E. J. Ferguson, *The Power of the Purse: A History of American Public Finance, 1776–1790* (1960)

Calvin C. Jillson, *Congressional Dynamics: Structure, Coordination, and Choice in the First American Congress, 1774–1789* (1994)

Jackson Turner Main, *Political Parties before the Constitution* (1973)

Jack N. Rakove, *The Beginnings of National Politics: An Interpretive History of the Continental Congress* (1979)

Gerald Sourzh, *Benjamin Franklin and American Foreign Policy* (1969)

Gordon S. Wood, *The Creation of the American Republic, 1776–1787* (1969)

Revolutionary Politics in the States

Willi Paul Adams, *The First American Constitutions: Republican Ideology and the Making of the State Constitutions* (1980)

Roger H. Brown, *Redeeming the Republic: Federalists, Taxation, and the Origins of the Constitution* (1993)

Donald S. Lutz, *Popular Consent and Popular Control: Whig Political Theory in the Early State Constitutions* (1980)

Jackson Turner Main, *The Sovereign States, 1775–1789* (1973)

Biography

William Howard Adams, *Gouverneur Morris: An Independent Life* (2003)

Silvio A. Bedini, *The Life of Benjamin Banneker* (1972)

Patricia Cleary, *Elizabeth Murray: A Woman's Pursuit of Independence in Eighteenth-Century America* (2000)

John Mack Faragher, *Daniel Boone: The Life and Legend of an American Pioneer* (1992)

Douglas Southall Freeman, *George Washington*, 7 vols. (1948–57)

Lowell Hayes Harrison, *George Rogers Clark and the War in the West* (1976)

John W. Hartmann, *The American Partisan: Henry Lee and the Struggle for Independence, 1776–1780* (2000)

Isabel Thompson Kelsay, *Joseph Brant, 1743–1807: Man of Two Worlds* (1984)

James Kirby Martin, *Benedict Arnold, Revolutionary Hero* (1997)

Gregory D. Massey, *John Laurens and the American Revolution* (2000)

William Henry Robinson, *Phillis Wheatley and Her Writings* (1984)

Susan Burgess Shenstone, *So Obstinately Loyal: James Moody, 1744–1809* (2000)

Henry Wiencek, *Imperfect God: George Washington, His Slaves, and the Creation of America* (2003)

Alfred F. Young, *Masquerade: The Life and Times of Deborah Sampson, Continental Soldier* (2004)

Rosemarie Zagarri, *A Woman's Dilemma: Mercy Otis Warren and the American Revolution* (1995)

CHAPTER 8

The Crisis of the 1780s

Roger H. Brown, *Redeeming the Republic: Federalists, Taxation, and the Origin of the Constitution* (1993)

Keith L. Dougherty, *Collective Action Under the Articles of Confederation* (2001)

Ronald Hoffman and Peter J. Albert, eds., *Sovereign States in an Age of Uncertainty* (1982)

Robert A. Gross, eds., *In Debt to Shays: The Bicentennial of an Agrarian Rebellion* (1993)

Merrill Jensen, *The New Nation: A History of the United States during the Confederation, 1781–1789* (1950)

Leonard L. Richards, *Shay's Rebellion: The American Revolution's Final Battle* (2002)

David Szatmary, *Shay's Rebellion: The Making of an Agrarian Insurrection* (1980)

The New Constitution

Douglass Adair, *Fame and the Founding Fathers*, ed. Trevor Colbourn (1974)

Bernard Bailyn, *To Begin the World Anew: The Genius and Ambiguities of the American Founders* (2003)

Charles A. Beard, *An Economic Interpretation of the Constitution of the United States* (1913)

Saul Cornell, *The Other Founders: Anti-Federalism and the Dissenting Tradition in America, 1788–1828* (1999)

Robert A. Dahl, *How Democratic Is the American Constitution?* (2003)

Max Farrand, ed., *Records of the Federal Convention of 1787*, 4 vols. (1911–37)

Paul Finkelman, *Slavery and the Founders: Race and Liberty in the Age of Jefferson* (2001)

John P. Kaminski and Gaspare J. Saladino, eds., *The Documentary History of the Ratification of the Constitution* (1982)

Mark E. Kann, *A Republic of Men: The American Founders, Gendered Language, and Patriarchal Politics* (1998)

Leonard W. Levy, *Origins of the Bill of Rights* (1999)

James H. Read, *Power Versus Liberty: Madison, Hamilton, Wilson, and Jefferson* (2000)

Gary Rosen, *American Compact: James Madison and the Problem of Founding* (1999)

Herbert J. Storing, ed., *The Complete Anti-Federalist*, 7 vols. (1981)

The New Nation

Kenneth R. Bowling and Donald R. Kennon, eds., *Neither Separate Nor Equal: Congress in the 1790s* (2000)

Collin G. Calloway, *Crown and Calumet: British-Indian Relations, 1783–1815* (1987)

Noble E. Cunningham, *Jefferson vs. Hamilton: Confrontations That Shaped a Nation* (2000)

Wilbur Edel, *Kekionga! The Worst Defeat in the History of the U.S. Army* (1997)

James Horn et al., eds., *Revolution of 1800: Democracy, Race, and the New Republic* (2002)

Edward S. Kaplan, *The Bank of the United States and the American Economy* (1999)

Peter McNamara, *Political Economy and Statesmanship: Smith, Hamilton, and the Foundation of the Commercial Republic* (1998)

Mark J. Rozell, et al., eds., *George Washington and the Origins of the American Presidency* (2000)

Garrett Ward Sheldon, *The Political Philosophy of James Madison* (2001)

Wiley Sword, *President Washington's Indian War: The Struggle for the Old Northwest, 1790–1795* (1985)

Garry Wills, *Negro President: Jefferson and the Slave Power* (2003)

Federalists and Jeffersonian Republicans

Doron Ben-Atar and Barbara B. Oberg, eds., *Federalists Reconsidered* (1998)

Alexander De Conde, *The Quasi-War: Politics and Diplomacy of the Undeclared War with France, 1797–1801* (1966)

Andrew Lenner, *The Federal Principle in American Politics, 1790–1833* (2001)

Forrest McDonald, *States' Rights and the Union: Imperium in Imperio, 1776–1876* (2000)

Michael A. Palmer, *Stoddert's War: Naval Operations During the Quasi-War with France, 1798–1801* (2000)

Andrew W. Robertson, *The Language of Democracy: Political Rhetoric in the United States and Britain, 1790–1900* (1995)

James Roger Sharp, *American Politics in the Early Republic: The New Nation in Crisis* (1993)

David Waldstreicher, *In the Midst of Perpetual Fetes: The Making of American Nationalism, 1776–1820* (1997)

"The Rising Glory of America"

R. A. Burchell, ed., *The End of Anglo–America: Historical Essays in the Study of Cultural Divergence* (1991)

Andrew Burstein, *Sentimental Democracy: The Evolution of America's Romantic Self-Image* (1999)

Ellen Fernandez-Sacco, *Spectacular Masculinities: The Museums of Peale, Baker, and Bowen in the Early Republic* (1998)

Linda Kerber, *Women of the Republic: Intellect and Ideology in Revolutionary America* (1980)

Biography

Gay Wilson Allen, *St. John de Crèvecoeur: The Life of an American Farmer* (1987)

Aleine Austin, *Matthew Lyon, "New Man" of the Democratic Revolution, 1749–1822* (1981)

Lance Banning, *The Sacred Fire of Liberty: James Madison and the Founding of the Federal Republic* (1995)

R. B. Bernstein, *Thomas Jefferson* (2003)

Richard Brookhiser, *Alexander Hamilton, American* (1999)

Harvey Lewis Carter, *The Life and Times of Little Turtle: First Sagamore of the Wabash* (1987)

Helen A. Cooper, *John Trumbull: The Hand and Spirit of a Painter* (1982)

John Patrick Diggins, *John Adams* (2003)

Dorinda Evans, *The Genius of Gilbert Stuart* (1999)

Roger G. Kennedy, *Burr, Hamilton, and Jefferson: A Study in Character* (2000)

David McCullough, *John Adams* (2001)

David Micklethwait, *Noah Webster and the American Dictionary* (2000)

Jules David Prown, *John Singleton Copley* (1966)

William M. S. Rasmussen and Robert S. Tilton, *George Washington: The Man Behind the Myths* (1999)

Sheila L. Skemp, *Judith Sargent Murray: A Brief Biography with Documents* (1998)

K. Alan Synder, *Defining Noah Webster: Mind and Morals in the Early Republic* (1990)

Harlow G. Unger, *Noah Webster: The Life and Times of an American Patriot* (1998)

Mason Locke Weems, *The Life of Washington,* ed. Marcus Cunliffe (1962)

CHAPTER 9

North American Communities from Coast to Coast

James Gibson, *Imperial Russia in Frontier America* (1976)

Marcel Giraud, *A History of French Louisiana, 1698–1715* (1974)

Barbara Sweetland Smith and Redmond Barnett, eds., *Russian America* (1990)

David Weber, *The Spanish Frontier in North America* (1993)

The National Economy

W. Eliot Brownlee, *Dynamics of Ascent: A History of the American Economy* (1979)

Stuart Bruchey, *The Roots of American Economic Growth, 1607–1861* (1965)

Curtis P. Nettels, *The Emergence of a National Economy, 1775–1815* (1962)

Douglass C. North, *The Economic Growth of the United States, 1790–1860* (1966)

The Jefferson Presidency

Henry Adams, *The United States in 1800* (1955)

Robert Lowry Clinton, *Marbury v. Madison and Judicial Review* (1989)

Noble E. Cunningham, *The Jeffersonian Republicans and Power: Party Operations, 1801–1809* (1963)

George Drago, *Jefferson's Louisiana: Politics and the Clash of Legal Traditions* (1975)

James Horn, Jan Ellen Lewis, and Peter S. Onuf, eds., *The Revolution of 1800: Democracy, Race and the New Republic* (2002)

Frank Lambert, *The Barbary Wars* (2005)

Larry E. Morris, *The Fate of the Corps: What Became of the Lewis and Clark Explorers After the Expedition* (2004)

Peter S. Onuf., *Jefferson's Empire* (2000)

Burton Spivak, *Jefferson's English Crisis: Commerce, Embargo, and the Republican Revolution* (1979)

Robert W. Tucker and David Hendrickson, *Empire of Liberty: The Statecraft of Thomas Jefferson* (1990)

G. Edward White, *The Marshall Court and Cultural Change, 1815–1835,* abridged ed. (1991)

James S. Young, *The Washington Community, 1800–1828* (1966)

Renewed Imperial Rivalry in North America

Henry Warner Bowden, *American Indians and Christian Missions: Studies in Cultural Conflict* (1981)

Gregory Evans Dowd, *A Spirited Resistance: The North American Indian Struggle for Unity, 1745–1815*

Donald Hickey, *The War of 1812: A Forgotten Conflict* (1989)

Reginald Horsman, *Expansion and American Indian Policy, 1783–1812* (1967)

Drew R. McCoy, *The Last of the Fathers: James Madison and the Republican Legacy* (1989)

Francis Paul Prucha, *The Great Father: The United States Government and the American Indians,* 2 vols. (1984)

Ian W. Toll, *Six Frigates: The Epic History of the Founding of the U.S. Navy* (2006)

Defining the Boundaries

John Boles, *Religion in Antebellum Kentucky* (1976)

Andrew Cayton, *The Frontier Republic: Ideology and Politics in the Ohio Country, 1789–1812* (1986)

———, *Frontier Indiana* (1996)

George Dangerfield, *The Era of Good Feelings* (1952)

Anita Shafer Goodstein, *Nashville, 1780–1860: From Frontier to City* (1989)

Christine Leigh Heyrman, *Southern Cross: The Beginnings of the Bible Belt* (1997)

Walter LaFeber, ed., *John Quincy Adams and the American Continental Empire* (1965)

Malcolm J. Rohrbough, *The Land Office Business* (1968)

———, *The Trans-Appalachian Frontier: Peoples, Societies, and Institutions, 1775–1850* (1978)

C. Edward Skeen, *1816: America Rising* (2003)

Richard Slotkin, *Regeneration Through Violence: The Mythology of the American Frontier* (1973)

Richard C. Wade, *The Urban Frontier: The Rise of Western Cities, 1790–1850* (1973)

CHAPTER 10

King Cotton and Southern Expansion

Bruce Levine, *Half Slave and Half Free: The Roots of Civil War* (1992)

Daniel S. Dupre, *Transforming the Cotton Frontier, Madison County, Alabama, 1800–1840* (1997)

Robert W. Fogel and Stanley Engerman, *Time on the Cross: The Economics of American Negro Slavery* (1974)

Robert Gudmestad, *A Troublesome Commerce: The Transformation of the Interstate Slave Trade* (2002)

Joseph P. Reidy, *From Slavery to Agrarian Capitalism in the Cotton Plantation South: Central Georgia, 1800–1880* (1992)

Adam Rothman, *Slave Country: American Expansion and the Origins of the Deep South* (2005)

Michael Tadman, *Speculators and Slaves: Masters, Traders, and Slaves in the South* (1989)

Gavin Wright, *The Political Economy of the Cotton South: Households, Markets, and Wealth in the Nineteenth Century* (1978)

Slavery and African American Communities

Ira Berlin and Philip D. Morgan, eds., *Cultivation and Culture: Labor and the Shaping of Slave Life in the Americas* (1993)

John Blassingame, *The Slave Community,* rev. ed. (1979)

Thomas C. Buchanan, *Black Life on the Mississippi: Slaves, Free Blacks, and the Western Steamboat World* (2004)

Stephanie Camp, *Closer to Freedom: Enslaved Women and Everyday Resistance in the Plantation South* (2004)

Randolph B. Campbell, *An Empire for Slavery: The Peculiar Institution in Texas, 1821–1865* (1989)

Charles B. Dew, *Bond of Iron: Master and Slave at Buffalo Forge* (1994)

Douglas Egerton, *Gabriel's Rebellion: The Virginia Slave Conspiracies of 1800 and 1802* (1993)

Barbara Field, *Slavery on the Middle Ground: Maryland during the Nineteenth Century* (1985)

Eugene D. Genovese, *From Rebellion to Revolution: Afro-American Slave Revolts in the Making of the Modern World* (1979)

Jean M. Humez, *Harriet Tubman: The Life and Life Stories* (2003)

Walter Johnson, *Soul By Soul: Inside the Antebellum Slave Market* (1999)

Charles Joyner, *Down by the Riverside: A South Carolina Slave Community* (1984)

Lawrence W. Levine, *Black Culture and Black Consciousness: Afro-American Folk Thought from Slavery to Freedom* (1977)

Ann Patton Malone, *Sweet Chariot: Slave Family and Household Structure in Nineteenth-Century Louisiana* (1992)

Dylan Penningroth, *The Claims of Kinfolk: African American Property and Community in the Nineteenth Century South* (2003)

Albert Raboteau, *Slave Religion: The "Invisible Institution" in the Antebellum South* (1978)

Marie Jenkins Schwartz, *Birthing a Slave: Motherhood and Medicine in the Antebellum South* (2006)

Kenneth Stampp, *The Peculiar Institution* (1956)

Brenda Stevenson, *Life in Black and White: Family and Community in the Slave South* (1996)

Sterling Stuckey, *Slave Culture: Nationalist Theory and the Foundation of Black America* (1987)

Richard C. Wade, *Slavery in the Cities: The South 1820–1860* (1964)

Deborah Gray White, *Arn't I a Woman?* (1985)

Yeomen, Planters, and the Defense of Slavery

David T. Bailey, *Shadow on the Church: Southwestern Evangelical Religion and the Issue of Slavery, 1783–1860* (1985)

Charles C. Bolton, *Poor Whites of the Antebellum South: Tenants and Laborers in Central North and Northern Mississippi* (1994)

F. N. Boney, *Southerners All* (1990)

Bill Cecil-Fronsman, *Common White: Class and Culture in Antebellum North Carolina* (1992)

William J. Cooper, *The South and the Politics of Slavery, 1829–1856* (1978)

Clement Eaton, *The Freedom of Thought Struggle in the Old South* (1964)

Drew Gilpin Faust, ed., *The Ideology of Slavery: Proslavery Thought in the Antebellum South, 1830–1860* (1981)

———, *James Henry Hammond and the Old South* (1982)

Lacy K. Ford, Jr., *Origins of Southern Radicalism: The South Carolina Upcountry, 1800–1860* (1988)

Elizabeth Fox-Genovese, *Within the Plantation Household* (1988)

Jean Friedman, *The Enclosed Garden: Women and Community in the Evangelical South, 1830–1900* (1985)

J. William Harris, *Plain Folk and Gentry in a Slave Society: White Liberty and Black Slavery in Augusta's Hinterlands* (1985)

Christopher Morris, *Becoming Southern: The Evolution of a Way of Life, Warren County and Vicksburg, Mississippi, 1770–1860* (1995)

Joshua Rothman, *Notorious in the Neighborhood: Sex and Families Across the Color Line in Virginia, 1787–1861* (2003)

Michael Wayne, *Death of an Overseer* (2001)

Jonathan Daniel Wells, *The Origins of the Southern Middle Class, 1800–1861* (2004)

Bertram Wyatt-Brown, *Southern Honor: Ethics and Behavior in the Old South* (1982)

Jeffrey Robert Young, *Domesticating Slavery: The Master Class in Georgia and South Carolina, 1670–1837* (1999)

CHAPTER 11

The New Democratic Politics and Jackson Presidency

Glenn C. Altschuler and Stuart M. Blumin, *Rude Republic: Americans and Their Politics in the Nineteenth Century* (2000)

William L. Anderson, *Cherokee Removal: Before and After* (1991)

Steven C. Bullock, *Revolutionary Brotherhood: Freemasonry and the Transformation of the American Social Order, 1730–1840* (1996)

Donald B. Cole, *The Presidency of Andrew Jackson* (2003)

John Ehle, *Trail of Tears* (1988)

Ronald P. Formisano, *The Transformation of Political Culture: Massachusetts Parties, 1790s–1840s* (1983)

William W. Freehling, *Prelude to Civil War* (1966)

John Lauritz Larson, *Internal Improvement: National Public Works and the Promise of Popular Government in the Early United States* (2001)

Lucy Maddox, *Removals: Nineteenth-Century American Literature and the Politics of Indian Affairs* (1991)

Reeve Huston, *Land and Freedom: Rural Society, Popular Protest, and Party Politics in Antebellum New York* (2000)

Arthur M. Schlesinger Jr., *The Age of Jackson* (1945)

John Ward, *Andrew Jackson: Symbol for an Age* (1955)

Chilton Williamson, *American Suffrage: From Property to Democracy, 1760–1860* (1960)

The Rise of the Whigs and the Second American Party System

Michael Holt, *The Rise and Fall of the American Whig Party* (1999)

Daniel W. Howe, *The Political Culture of the American Whigs* (1980)

Lawrence F. Kohl, *The Politics of Individualism: Parties and the American Character in the Jacksonian Era* (1989)

Richard P. McCormick, *The Second American Party System: Party Formation in the Jacksonian Era* (1966)

Joel H. Sibley, *The Partisan Imperative: The Dynamics of American Politics before the Civil War* (1985)

American Arts and Letters

Richard D. Brown, *Knowledge Is Power: The Diffusion of Information in Early America, 1700–1865* (1989)

Cathy N. Davidson, *Revolution and the Word: The Rise of the Novel in America* (1986)

Nathan O. Hatch, *The Democratization of American Christianity* (1989)

Jean V. Matthews, *Toward a New Society: American Thought and Culture, 1800–1830* (1991)

Barbara Novak, *Nature and Culture: American Landscape Painting 1825–1875* (1982)

Kenneth Silverman, *Lightening Man: The Accursed Life of Samuel F. B. Morse* (2003)

Gwendolyn Wright, *Building the Dream: A Social History of Housing in America* (1981)

CHAPTER 12

The Transportation Revolution

Clarence Danhof, *Changes in Agriculture: The Northern United States, 1820–1870* (1969)

E. M. Dodd, *American Business Corporations until 1860* (1954)

Albert Fishlow, *American Railroads and the Transformation of the Ante-Bellum Economy* (1965)

Paul W. Gates, *The Farmer's Age: Agriculture. 1815–1860* (1966)

John Denis Haeger, *The Investment Frontier: New York Businessmen and the Economic Development of the Old Northwest* (1981)

Oscar Handlin and Mary Handlin, *Commonwealth: A Study of the Role of Government in the American Economy: Massachusetts, 1774–1861* (1947)

Morton J. Horwitz, *The Transformation of American Law, 1780–1860* (1977)

Karl Raitz, ed., *The National Road* (1995)

Ronald E. Shaw, *Canals for a Nation: The Canal Era in the United States, 1790–1860* (1990)

Peter Way, *Common Labour: Workers and the Digging of North American Canals, 1780–1860* (1993)

The Market Revolution

Ian R. Bartky, *Selling the True Time: Nineteenth-Century Timekeeping in America* (2000)

Martin Bruegel, *Farm, Shop, Landing: The Rise of a Market Society in the Hudson Valley, 1780–1860* (2002)

Thomas C. Cochran, *Frontiers of Change: Early Industrialism in America* (1981)

Robert F. Dalzell Jr., *Enterprising Elite: The Boston Associates and the World They Made* (1987)

Thomas Dublin, *Women at Work: The Transformation of Work and Community in Lowell, Massachusetts, 1826–1860* (1979)

———, *Transforming Women's Work: New England Lives in the Industrial Revolution* (1994)

David J. Jeremy, *Transatlantic Industrial Revolution: The Diffusion of Textile Technology between Britain and America* (1981)

Paul Johnson, *A Shopkeeper's Millennium: Society and Revivals in Rochester, New York, 1815–1837* (1978)

Bruce Laurie, *Artisans into Workers: Labor in Nineteenth-Century America* (1989)

Walter Licht, *Industrializing America: The Nineteenth Century* (1995)

Merritt R. Smith, *Harpers Ferry Armory and the New Technology* (1977)

Melvyn Stokes and Stephen Conway, eds., *The Market Revolution in America: Social, Political and Religious Expressions 1800–1880* (1996)

Barbara Tucker, *Samuel Slater and the Origins of the American Textile Industry, 1790–1860* (1984)

From Artisan to Worker

Mary H. Blewett, *Men, Women, and Work: Class, Gender, and Protest in the New England Shoe Industry, 1780–1910* (1988)

Paul G. Faler, *Mechanics and Manufacturers in the Early Industrial Revolution: Lynn, Massachusetts* (1981)

Michael H. Glickstein, *Concepts of Free Labor in Antebellum America* (1991)

Joan M. Jensen, *Loosening the Bonds: Mid-Atlantic Farm Women, 1750–1850* (1986)

Bruce Laurie, *Working People of Philadelphia, 1800–1850* (1980)

W. J. Rorabaugh, *The Craft Apprentice: From Franklin to the Machine Age in America* (1986)

A New Social Order

Stuart M. Blumin, *The Emergence of the Middle Class: Social Experience in the American City* (1989)

Jeanne Boydston, *Home and Work* (1990)

Janet Farrell Brodie, *Contraception and Abortion in Nineteenth-Century America* (1994)

Nancy E. Cott, *The Bonds of Womanhood: "Woman's Sphere" in New England, 1780–1835* (1977)

Anthony F. C. Wallace, *Rockdale: The Growth of an American Village in the Early Industrial Revolution* (1977)

Middle-Class Culture

Barbara A. Bardes and Suzanne Gossett, *Declarations of Independence: Women and Political Power in Nineteenth-Century American Fiction* (1990)

Karen Halttunen, *Confidence Men and Painted Women: A Study of Middle-Class Culture in America* (1982)

John F. Kasson, *Rudeness and Civility: Manners in Nineteenth-Century America* (1990)

Walter Benn Michaels and Donald E. Pease, eds., *The American Renaissance Reconsidered* (1985)

Lewis Perry, *Intellectual Life in America* (1984)

Ann Rose, *Transcendentalism as a Social Movement* (1981)

Richard Teichgraeber III, *Sublime Thoughts/Penny Wisdom: Situating Emerson and Thoreau in the American Market* (1995)

Jane Tompkins, *Sensational Designs: The Cultural World of American Fiction, 1790–1860* (1986)

Steven J. Ross, *Workers on the Edge: Work, Leisure and Politics in Industrializing Cincinnati, 1788–1890* (1985). Studies the growth of wage labor in a major western city.

CHAPTER 13

Immigration and Ethnicity

Oscar Handlin, *The Uprooted* (1951; 2nd ed. 1973)

Noel Ignatiev, *How the Irish Became White* (1995)

Kerby A. Miller, *Emigrants and Exiles: Ireland and the Irish Exodus to North America* (1985)

Stanley Nadel, *Little Germany: Ethnicity, Religion, and Class in New York City, 1845–1880* (1990)

Dennis P. Ryan, *Beyond the Ballot Box: A Social History of the Boston Irish, 1845–1917* (1989)

Urban America

Oliver E. Allen, *The Tiger: The Rise and Fall of Tammany Hall* (1995)

W. Jeffrey Bolster, *Black Jacks: African American Seamen in the Age of Sail* (1997)

Amy Bridges, *A City in the Republic: Antebellum New York and the Origins of Machine Politics* (1984)

John Duffy, *The Sanitarians* (1990)

Paul A. Gilje, *The Road to Mobocracy: Popular Disorder in New York City, 1763–1834* (1987)

Herbert G. Gutman, *Work, Culture, and Society in Industrializing America: Essays in American Working-Class History* (1976)

James Oliver Horton, *Free People of Color: Inside the African American Community* (1993)

Gerard T. Koeppel, *Water for Gotham* (2000)

W. T. Lhaman Jr., *Jump Jim Crow* (2003)

Gary B. Nash, *Forging Freedom: Philadelphia's Black Community, 1720–1840* (1988)

Benjamin Reiss, *The Showman and the Slave: Race, Death and Memory in Barnum's America* (2001)

Charles E. Rosenberg, *The Cholera Years* (1962)

Dennis C. Rousey, *Policing the Southern City, New Orleans 1805–1889* (1997)

Sam Bass Warner, *The Private City: Philadelphia in Three Periods of Its Growth* (1968)

Religion, Reform, and Utopianism

Arthur Bestor, *Backwoods Utopias* (1950)

Richard Lyman Bushman, *Joseph Smith: Rough Stone Rolling* (2006)

Lawrence Cremin, *American Education: The National Experience, 1783–1861*

Whitney R. Cross, *The Burned-Over District: The Social and Intellectual History of Enthusiastic Religion in Western New York, 1800–1850* (1950)

Barbara Epstein, *The Politics of Domesticity: Women, Evangelism, and Temperance in Nineteenth Century America* (1981)

Lori D. Ginzberg, *Women and the Work of Benevolence: Morality, Politics, and Class in the Nineteenth-Century United States* (1990)

Carl F. Kaestle, *Pillars of the Republic: Common Schools and American Society, 1780–1860* (1983)

W. J. Rorabaugh, *The Alcoholic Republic: An American Tradition* (1979)

David Rothman, *The Discovery of the Asylum: Social Order and Disorder in the New Republic* (1971)

Abolitionism

Eric Burin, *Slavery and the Peculiar Solution: A History of the American Colonization Society* (2005)

David Brion Davis, *The Problem of Slavery in the Age of Revolution, 1770–1823* (1975)

Frederick Douglass, *The Narrative of the Life of Frederick Douglass, An American Slave* (1845)

Peter P. Hinks, *To Awaken My Afflicted Brethren: David Walker and the Problem of Antebellum Slave Resistance* (1997)

Howard Jones, *Mutiny on the* Amistad (1987)

Jean Fagan Yellin, *Women and Sisters: The Antislavery Feminists in American Culture* (1989)

Women's Rights

Ellen C. DuBois, *Feminism and Suffrage: The Emergence of an Independent Women's Movement in America, 1848–1869* (1978)

Gerda Lerner, *The Grimké Sisters from South Carolina: Pioneers for Women's Rights and Abolition* (1967)

Nancy Lusignan Schultz, *Fire and Roses* (2000)

Kathryn Sklar, *Catharine Beecher: A Study in American Domesticity* (1973)

Sandra S. Weber, *Special History Study, Women's Rights National Historical Park, Seneca Falls, New York* (1985)

CHAPTER 14

Exploration and Expansion

Jennifer S. H. Brown, *Strangers in Blood: Fur Trade Company Families in Indian Country* (1980)

William H. Goetzmann, *Army Exploration in the American West, 1803–1863* (1959)

William H. Goetzmann and William N. Goetzmann, *The West of the Imagination* (1986)

Norman A. Graebner, *Empire on the Pacific: A Study in American Continental Expansion* (1955)

LeRoy R. Hafen, ed., *The Mountain Men and the Fur Trade of the Far West*, 10 vols. (1968–72)

Sam W. Haynes, *James Polk and the Expansionist Impulse,* (1997)

Thomas R. Hietala, *Manifest Design: Anxious Aggrandizement in Late Jacksonian America* (1985)

Reginald Horsman, *Race and Manifest Destiny* (1981)

Theodore J. Karaminski, *Fur Trade and Exploration: Opening of the Far Northwest, 1821–1852* (1983)

Patricia Nelson Limerick, *The Legacy of Conquest: The Unbroken Past of the Unbroken West* (1987)

Frederick Merk, *Manifest Destiny and Mission in American History: A Reinterpretation* (1963)

———, *History of the Westward Movement* (1978)

Dale Morgan, *Jedediah Smith and the Opening of the West* (1982)

Peter Nabakov, ed., *Native American Testimony: An Anthology of Indian and White Relations* (1978)

James P. Ronda, *Astoria and Empire* (1990)

Charles G. Sellers, *James K. Polk: Jacksonian, 1795–1843* (1957)

———, *James K. Polk: Continentalist, 1843–1846* (1966)

Henry Nash Smith, *Virgin Land: The American West as Symbol and Myth* (1950)

Edward H. Spicer, *Cycles of Conquest: The Impact of Spain, Mexico, and the United States on the Indians of the Southwest, 1533–1960* (1981)

Robert A. Trennert, *Alternative to Extinction: Federal Indian Policy and the Beginnings of the Reservation System, 1846–1851* (1975)

Sylvia Van Kirk, *"Many Tender Ties": Women in Fur Trade Society in Western Canada, 1670–1870* (1980)

Albert K. Weinberg, *Manifest Destiny: A Study of Nationalist Expansionism in American History* (1957)

Peter Booth Wiley with Korogi Ichiro, *Yankees in the Land of the Gods: Commodore Perry and the Opening of Japan* (1990)

David J. Wishart, *The Fur Trade of the American West, 1807–1840: A Geographic Synthesis* (1979)

California and Oregon

John W. Caughey, *The California Gold Rush* (1975)

Malcolm Clark Jr., *Eden Seekers: The Settlement of Oregon, 1818–1862* (1981)

Douglas H. Daniels, *Pioneer Urbanites: A Social and Cultural History of Black San Francisco* (1980)

James R. Gibson, *Farming the Frontier: The Agricultural Opening of Oregon Country, 1786–1846* (1985)

Ramon Gutierrez and Richard J. Orsi, *Contested Eden: California before the Gold Rush* (1998)

Albert L. Hurtado, *Indian Survival on the California Frontier* (1988)

Julie Roy Jeffrey, *Frontier Women: Civilizing The West? 1840–1860* (1998)

———, *Converting the West: A Biography of Narcissa Whitman* (1991)

Marquis James, *The Raven: The Story of Sam Houston* (1929)

David Johnson, *Founding the Far West: California, Oregon, and Nevada, 1840–1890* (1992)

Alvin Josephy, *The Nez Percé and the Opening of the Northwest* (1965)

Rodman W. Paul, *California Gold: The Beginning of Mining in the Far West* (1974)

Leonard Pitt, *The Decline of the Californios: A Social History of the Spanish-Speaking Californians, 1846–1890* (1966)

James J. Rawls, *Indians of California: The Changing Image* (1984)

Brian Roberts, *American Alchemy: The California Gold Rush and Middle-Class Culture* (2000)

Malcolm Rohrbough, *Days of Gold: The California Gold Rush and the American Nation* (2001)

Kevin Starr, *Americans and the California Dream, 1850–1915* (1973)

———, and Richard J. Orsei., eds., *Rooted in Barbarous Soil: People, Culture and Community in Gold Rush California* (2000)

John I. Unruh Jr., *The Plains Across: Overland Emigrants and the Trans–Mississippi West, 1840–1860* (1979)

Texas and the Mexican–American War

K. Jack Bauer, *The Mexican War, 1846–1848* (1974)

William C. Binkley, *The Texas Revolution* (1952)

Gene M. Brack, *Mexico Views Manifest Destiny* (1976)

Holly Beachley Brear, *Inherit the Alamo: Myth and Ritual at an American Shrine* (1995)

Donald E. Chipman, *Spanish Texas, 1519–1821* (1992)

Seymour Conner and Odie Faulk, *North America Divided: The Mexican War, 1846–1848* (1971)

Arnoldo De León, *They Called Them Greasers: Anglo Attitudes toward Mexicans in Texas, 1821–1900* (1983)

———, *The Tejano Community 1836–1900* (1982)

John S. D. Eisenhower, *So Far from God: The U.S. War with Mexico 1846–1848* (1989)

Neil Harlow, *California Conquered: War and Peace on the Pacific, 1846–1850* (1982)

Timothy J. Henderson, *A Glorious Defeat: Mexico and Its War with the United States* (2007)

Ernest McPherson Lander Jr., *Reluctant Imperialist: Calhoun, South Carolina, and the Mexican War* (1980)

Timothy Matovina, *Tejano Religion and Ethnicity: San Antonio, 1921–1860* (1995)

Frederick Merk, *Slavery and the Annexation of Texas* (1972)

David Montejano, *Anglos and Mexicans in the Making of Texas, 1836–1986* (1987)

Stanley Noyes, *Los Comanches: The Horse People, 1751–1845* (1994)

David Pletcher, *The Diplomacy of Annexation: Texas, Oregon, and the Mexican War* (1973)

Andreas V. Reichstein, *Rise of the Lone Star: The Making of Texas* (1989)

Susan Scholwer, *Alamo Images: Changing Perceptions of a Texas Experience* (1985)

John H. Schroeder, *Mr. Polk's War: American Opposition and Dissent, 1846–1848* (1971)

Otis A. Singletary, *The Mexican War* (1960)

Jésus F. de la Teja, *San Antonio de Béxar: A Community on New Spain's Northern Frontier* (1995)

The Politics of Manifest Destiny

Chaplain W. Morrison, *Democratic Politics and Sectionalism: The Wilmot Proviso Controversy* (1967)

Michael Morrison, *Slavery and the American West: The Eclipse of Manifest Destiny and the Coming of the Civil War* (1997)

Joseph G. Raybeck, *Free Soil: The Election of 1848* (1970)

Joel H. Sibley, *The Shrine of Party: Congressional Voting Behavior, 1841–1852* (1967)

———, *Storm Over Texas: The Annexation Controversy and the Road to Civil War* (2005)

CHAPTER 15

The Crisis over Slavery

Richard H. Abbott, *Cotton and Capital: Boston Businessmen and Antislavery Reform, 1854–1868* (1991)

Gary Collison, *Shadrach Minkins: From Fugitive Slave to Citizen* (1997)

W. Ehrlich, *They Have No Rights: Dred Scott's Struggle for Freedom* (1979)

C. C. Goen, *Broken Churches, Broken Nation* (1985)

Thomas F. Grossett, *Uncle Tom's Cabin and American Culture* (1985)

William Lee Miller, *Arguing About Slavery: The Great Battle in the United States Congress* (1996)

H. Craig Miner and William E. Unrau, *The End of Indian Kansas* (1978)

Stephen Oates, *To Purge This Land with Blood: A Biography of John Brown* (1970)

Leonard L. Richards, *The Slave Power: The Free North and Southern Domination, 1780–1860* (2000)

Anne C. Rose, *Voices of the Marketplace: American Thought and Culture, 1830–1860* (1995)

J. Rossbach, *Ambivalent Conspirators: John Brown, the Secret Six and a Theory of Black Political Violence* (1982)

Thomas P. Slaughter, *Bloody Dawn: The Christiana Riots and Racial Violence in the Antebellum North* (1991)

Albert Von Frank, *The Trials of Anthony Burns: Freedom and Slavery in Emerson's Boston* (1998)

Edward L. Widmer, *Young America: The Flowering of Democracy in New York City* (1999)

Gerald W. Wolff, *The Kansas-Nebraska Bill: Party, Section, and the Coming of the Civil War* (1977)

Bertram Wyatt-Brown, *Yankee Saints and Southern Sinners* (1985)

The Crisis of the National Party System

Tyler Anbinder, *Nativism and Slavery: The Northern Know-Nothings and the Politics of the 1850s* (1992)

J. H. Baker, *Affairs of Party: The Political Culture of Northern Democrats in the Mid-Nineteenth Century* (1983)

Robert F. Engs and Randall M. Miller, eds., *The Birth of the Grand Old Party* (2002)

Ronald Formisano, *The Birth of Mass Political Parties: Michigan, 1827–1861* (1971)

William E. Gienapp, *The Origins of the Republican Party, 1852–1856* (1987)

Michael Holt, *The Political Crisis of the 1850s* (1978)

Robert W. Johannsen, *The Lincoln-Douglas Debates* (1965)

John Mayfield, *Rehearsal for Republicanism: Free Soil and the Politics of Antislavery* (1980)

The South Secedes

William. L. Barney, *The Road to Secession* (1972)

Charles H. Brown, *Agents of Manifest Destiny: The Lives and Times of the Filibusters* (1980)

Steven A. Channing, *Crisis of Fear: Secession in South Carolina* (1970)

William J. Cooper, *The South and the Politics of Slavery* (1978)

Avery O. Craven, *The Growth of Southern Nationalism 1848–1861* (1953)

William W. Freehling, *The Road to Disunion, Vol. I : Secessionists at Bay, 1776–1854* (1991)

———, *The Road to Disunion, Vol II: Secessionists Triumphant* (2007)

Michael P. Johnson, *Secession and Conservatism in the Lower South: The Social and Ideological Bases of Secession in Georgia, 1860–1861* (1983)

Robert E. May, *The Southern Dream of a Caribbean Empire, 1854–1861* (1973)

John McCardell, *The Idea of a Southern Nation: Southern Nationalists and Southern Nationalism, 1830–1861* (1979)

K. M. Stampp, *And the War Came: The North and the Secession Crisis 1860–1861* (1950)

Joe A. Stout, *The Liberators: Filibustering Expeditions into Mexico, 1848–1862, and the Last Thrust of Manifest Destiny* (1973)

Ronald L. Takaki, *A Proslavery Crusade: The Agitation to Reopen the African Slave Trade* (1971)

J. Mills Thornton, *Politics and Power in a Slavery Society* (1978)

Eric H. Walter, *The Fire-Eaters* (1992)

CHAPTER 16

The Lincoln Presidency and the Northern Home Front

Jeanie Attie, *Patriotic Toil: Northern Women and the American Civil War* (1998)

Richard Franklin Bensel, *Yankee Leviathan: The Origins of Central State Authority in America, 1859–1877* (1991)

Joan Cashin, *The War Was You and Me: Civilians in the American Civil War* (2002)

George M. Frederickson, *The Inner Civil War: Northern Intellectuals and the Crisis of the Union* (1965)

J. Matthew Gallman, *The North Fights the Civil War: The Home Front* (1994)

Doris Kearns Goodwin, *Team of Rivals: The Political Genius of Abraham Lincoln* (2005)

Frank L. Klement, *The Limits of Dissent: Clement L. Vallandigham and the Civil War* (1970)

Ernest A. McKay, *The Civil War and New York City* (1990)

James M. McPherson, *Abraham Lincoln and the Second American Revolution* (1990)

Mark E. Neely, *The Fate of Liberty: Abraham Lincoln and Civil Liberties* (1991)

Thomas H. O'Connor, *Civil War Boston: Homefront and Battlefield* (1997)

Phillip Shaw Paludan, *The Presidency of Abraham Lincoln* (1994)

———, *"A People's Contest": The Union at War, 1861–1865* (1988)

Heather Cox Richardson, *The Greatest Nation of the Earth: Republican Economic Policies during the Civil War* (1997)

Anne C. Rose, *Victorian America and the Civil War* (1992)

Joel Sibley, *A Respectable Minority: The Democratic Party in the Civil War Era, 1860–1868* (1977)

Lyde Cullen Sizer, *The Political Work of Northern Women Writers and the Civil War* (2000)

Jennifer L. Weber, *Copperheads: The Rise and Fall of Lincoln's Opponents in the North* (2006)

Bell I. Wiley, *The Life of Johnny Reb* (1943)

———, *The Life of Billy Yank* (1952)

The Death of Slavery

Ira Berlin et al. eds., *Freedom, A Documentary History of Emancipation, 1861–1867,* Series 1, Volume I: *The Destruction of Slavery* (1985)

———, eds., *Freedom, A Documentary History of Emancipation, 1861–1867,* Series 1, Volume II: *The Wartime Genesis of Free Labor: The Upper South* (1993)

———, eds. *Freedom, A Documentary History of Emancipation, 1861–1867,* Series 1, Volume III: *The Wartime Genesis of Free Labor: The Lower South* (1990)

———, eds. *Freedom, A Documentary History of Emancipation, 1861–1867,* Series 2: *The Black Military Experience* (1988)

John Hope Franklin, *The Emancipation Proclamation* (1963)

Willie Lee Rose, *Rehearsal for Reconstruction: The Port Royal Experiment* (1964)

The Confederacy and the Southern Home Front

Steven V. Ash, *When the Yankees Came: Conflict and Chaos in the Occupied South 1861–1865* (1995)

William Blair, *Virginia's Private War: Feeding Body and Soul in the Confederacy, 1861–1865* (1998)

Joan Cashin, *First Lady of the Confederacy: Varina Davis's Civil War* (2006)

Daniel W. Crofts, *Reluctant Confederates: Upper South Unionists in the Secession Crisis* (1989)

William C. Davis, *"A Government of Our Own": The Making of the Confederacy* (1994)

Wayne K. Durrill, *War of Another Kind: A Southern Community in the Great Rebellion* (1990)

Laura F. Edwards, *Scarlett Doesn't Live Here Anymore: Southern Women in the Civil War Era* (2000)

Drew Gilpin Faust, *The Creation of Confederate Nationalism* (1988)

———, *The Confederate Republic: A Revolution against Politics* (1994)

William W. Freehling, *The South vs. The South: How Anti-Confederate Southerners Shaped the Course of the Civil War.*

James L. Roark, *Masters without Slaves: Southern Planters in the Civil War and Reconstruction* (1978)

William Rogers, *Confederate Home Front: Montgomery during the Civil War* (1999)

Jonathan Dean Sarris, *A Separate Civil War: Communities in Conflict in the Mountain South* (2006)

Daniel E. Sutherland, *Seasons of War: The Ordeal of a Confederate Community 1861–1865* (1995)

LeeAnn Whites, *The Civil War as a Crisis in Gender: Augusta, Georgia, 1860–1890* (1995)

David Williams, Teresa Crisp Williams, and David Carlson, *Plain Folk in a Rich Man's War: Class and Dissent in Confederate Georgia* (2002)

The Fighting

Michael Barton, *Good Men: The Character of Civil War Soldiers* (1981)

Ken Burns, *The Civil War* (1990)

Bruce Catton, *A Stillness at Appomattox* (1953)

David Eocher, *The Longest Night* (2001)

Shelby Foote, *The Civil War: A Narrative,* 3 vols. (1958–1974)

Joseph T. Glatthaar, *Forged in Battle: The Civil War Alliance of Black Soldiers and White Officers* (1990)

———, *The March to the Sea and Beyond: Sherman's Troops in the Savannah and Carolinas Campaign* (1985)

Mark Grimsley, *The Hard Hand of War: Union Policy toward Southern Civilians, 1861–1865* (1995)

Edward Hagerman, *The American Civil War and the Origins of Modern Warfare* (1988)

Alvin Josephy, *The Civil War in the West* (1992)

Bruce Levine, *Confederate Emancipation: Southern Plans to Free and Arm Slaves during the Civil War* (2006)

Gerald F. Linderman, *Embattled Courage: The Experience of Combat in the American Civil War* (1987)

Edwin S. Redkey, ed., *A Grand Army of Black Men: Letters from African-American Soldiers in the Union Army, 1861–1865* (1992)

Charles Royster, *The Destructive War: William Tecumseh Sherman, Stonewall Jackson, and the Americans* (1991)

John David Smith, ed., *Black Soldiers in Blue: African American Troops in the Civil War Era* (2002)

CHAPTER 17

The Politics of Reconstruction

Richard H. Abbott, *The Republican Party and the South, 1855–1877* (1986)

Herman Belz, *Emancipation and Equal Rights* (1978)

Michael Les Benedict, *A Compromise of Principle: Congressional Republicans and Reconstruction* (1974)

———, *The Impeachment and Trial of Andrew Johnson* (1973)

Michael Kent Curtis, *No State Shall Abridge: The Fourteenth Amendment and the Bill of Rights* (1990)

Ellen Carol DuBois, *Feminism and Suffrage* (1978)

Eric Foner, *Politics and Ideology in the Age of the Civil War* (1980)

William C. Harris, *With Charity for All: Lincoln and the Restoration of the Union* (1997)

Robert Kaczorowski, *The Politics of Judicial Interpretation: The Federal Courts, Department of Justice, and Civil Rights, 1866–1876* (1985)

James McPherson, *Ordeal by Fire: The Civil War and Reconstruction* (1982)

Michael Perman, *Emancipation and Reconstruction, 1862–1879* (1987)

Brooks D. Simpson, *The Reconstruction Presidents* (1998)

Kenneth M. Stampp, *The Era of Reconstruction, 1865–1877* (1965)

The Meaning of Freedom

Ira Berlin et al., eds., *Freedom: A Documentary History*, 3 vols. (1985–1991)

Paul A Cimbala and Randall M. Miller, eds., *The Freedmen's Bureau and Reconstruction.* (1999)

W. E. B. DuBois, *Black Reconstruction* (1935)

Carol Faulkner, *Women's Radical Reconstruction: The Freedmen's Aid Movement* (2004)

Barbara J. Fields, *Slavery and Freedom on the Middle Ground* (1985)

Eric Foner, *Freedom's Lawmakers: A Directory of Black Officeholders during Reconstruction* (1996)

Noralee Frankel, *Freedom's Women: Black Women and Families in Civil War Era Mississippi* (1999)

Herbert G. Gutman, *The Black Family in Slavery and Freedom* (1976)

Sharon Ann Holt, *Making Freedom Pay: North Carolina Freedpeople Working for Themselves, 1865–1900* (2000)

Thomas Holt, *Black over White: Negro Political Leadership in South Carolina during Reconstruction* (1977)

Leon Litwack, *Been in the Storm So Long: The Aftermath of Slavery* (1975)

Lynda J. Morgan, *Emancipation in Virginia's Tobacco Belt* (1992)

Nell Irvin Painter, *Exodusters* (1977)

Howard N. Rabinowitz, *Race Relations in the Urban South, 1865–1890* (1978)

Roger L. Ransom and Richard Sutch, *One Kind of Freedom: The Economic Consequences of Emancipation* (1977)

Edward Royce, *The Origins of Southern Sharecropping* (1993)

Leslie A. Schwalm, *A Hard Fight for We: Women's Transition from Slavery to Freedom in South Carolina* (1997)

Southern Politics and Society

James A. Baggett, *The Scalawags: Southern Dissenters in the Civil War and Reconstruction* (2003)

Nancy Bercaw, *Gendered Freedoms: Race, Rights, and the Politics of the Household in the Delta, 1861–1875* (2003)

Pamela Brandwein, *Reconstructing Reconstruction: The Supreme Court and the Production of Historical Truth* (1999)

Charles W. Calhoun, *Conceiving a New Republic: The Republican Party and the Southern Question, 1869–1900* (2006)

Dan T. Carter, *When the War Was Over: The Failure of Self Reconstruction in the South, 1865–1877* (1985)

Richard N. Current, *Those Terrible Carpetbaggers* (1988)

Stephen Hahn, *The Roots of Southern Populism* (1983)

Sally McMillen, *To Raise Up the South: Sunday Schools in Black and White Churches, 1865–1915* (2001)

Scott Reynolds Nelson, *Iron Confederacies: Southern Railroads, Klan Violence, and Reconstruction* (1999)

Michael S. Perman, *The Road to Redemption: Southern Politics, 1868–1979* (1984)

Daniel W. Stowell, *Rebuilding Zion: The Religious Reconstruction of the South, 1863–1877* (1998)

Allen W. Trelease, *White Terror: The Ku Klux Klan Conspiracy and Southern Reconstruction* (1971)

Richard Valelly, *The Two Reconstructions: The Struggle for Black Enfranchisement* (2004)

Jonathan M. Wiener, *Social Origins of the New South* (1978)

Reconstructing the North

Stephen Buechler, *The Transformation of the Woman Suffrage Movement* (1986)

Morton Keller, *Affairs of State* (1977)

David Montgomery, *Beyond Equality: Labor and the Radical Republicans, 1862–1872* (1967)

Keith I. Polakoff, *The Politics of Inertia: The Election of 1876 and the End of Reconstruction* (1973)

Heather Cox Richardson, *The Death of Reconstruction: Race, Labor, and Politics in the Post Civil War North, 1865–1901* (2001)

Amy Dru Stanley, *From Bondage to Contract: Wage Labor, Marriage, and the Market in the Age of Slave Emancipation* (1998)

Mark W. Summers, *Railroads, Reconstruction, and the Gospel of Prosperity* (1984)

———, *The Era of Good Stealings* (1993)

Xi Wang, *The Trial of Democracy: Black Suffrage and Northern Republicans, 1860–1910* (1997)

C. Vann Woodward, *Reunion and Reaction: The Compromise of 1877 and the End of Reconstruction* (1956)

Biography

Kenneth D. Ackerman, *Boss Tweed* (2005)

David Donald, *Charles Sumner and the Rights of Man* (1970)

Russell Duncan, *Freedom's Shore: Tunis Campbell and the Georgia Freedmen* (1986)

Stephen Kantrowitz, *Ben Tillman and the Reconstruction of White Supremacy* (2000)

William S. McFeely, *Frederick Douglass* (1989)

———, *Grant: A Biography* (1981)

———, *Yankee Stepfather: General O. O. Howard and the Freedmen* (1968)

Hans L. Trefousse, *Andrew Johnson* (1989)

———, *Thaddeus Stevens: Nineteenth Century Egalitarian* (1997)

CHAPTER 18

Indian Peoples and Indian–White Relations

David Wallace Adams, *Education for Extinction: American Indians and the Boarding School Experience, 1875–1928* (1995)

Ian Frazier, *Great Plains* (2001)

Lisbeth Haas, *Conquests and Historical Identities in California, 1769–1936* (1995)

Shelley Bowen Hatfield, *Chasing Shadows: Indians along the United States–Mexico Border, 1876–1911* (1998)

Frederick E. Hoxie, *A Final Promise: The Campaign to Assimilate the Indians, 1880–1920* (1984, 2001)

Albert L. Hurtado, *Indian Survival on the California Frontier* (1988)

Patricia Nelson Limerick, *The Legacy of Conquest: The Unbroken Past of the American West* (1987)

John D. McDermott, *A Guide to the Indian Wars of the West* (1998)

Valerie Sherer Mathes and Richard Lowitt, *The Standing Bear Controversy: Prelude to Indian Reform* (2003)

Devon Abbott Mihesuah, *Cultivating the Rosebuds: The Education of Women at the Cherokee Female Seminary, 1851–1909* (1993)

Theda Perdue, ed., *Sifters: Native American Women's Lives* (2001)

Catherine Price, *The Oglala People, 1841–1879* (1996)

Glenda Riley, *Women and Indians on the Frontier, 1825–1915* (1984)

Clifford E. Trafzer, Jean A. Keller, and Lorene Sisquoc, *Boarding School Blues: Revisiting American Indian Educational Experiences* (2006)

Elliott West, *The Way to the West: Essays on the Central Plains* (1995)

Richard White, *The Roots of Dependency: Subsistence, Environment, and Social Change among the Choctaws, Pawnees, and Navajos* (1983)

Murray R. Wickett, *Contested Territory: Whites, Native Americans, and African Americans in Oklahoma, 1865–1907* (2000)

Internal Empire

Armando C. Alonzo, *Tejano Legacy: Rancheros and Settlers in South Texas, 1734–1900* (1998)

Susan Armitage and Elizabeth Jameson, eds., *The Women's West* (1987)

Susan Armitage, Ruth B. Moynihan, and Christiane Fischer Dichamp, eds., *So Much to Be Done: Women Settlers on the Mining and Ranching Frontier* (1990)

Arnoldo De Leon, *Racial Frontiers: Africans, Chinese, and Mexicans in Western America, 1848–1890* (2002)

Sarah Deutsch, *No Separate Refuge: Culture, Class and Gender on an Anglo-Hispanic Frontier in the American Southwest, 1880–1940* (1987)

David M. Emmons, *The Butte Irish: Class and Ethnicity in an American Mining Town, 1875–1925* (1989)

Sarah Barringer Gordon, *The Mormon Question: Polygamy and Constitutional Conflict in Nineteenth-Century America* (2002)

David Igler, *Industrial Cowboys: Miller & Lux and the Transformation of the Far West, 1850–1920* (2001)

Eugene P. Moehring, *Urbanism and Empire in the Far West, 1840–1890* (2004)

Douglas Monroy, *Thrown among Strangers: The Making of Mexican Culture in Frontier California* (1990)

Katherine G. Morrissey, *Mental Territories: Mapping the Inland Empire* (1997)

Gunter Peck, *Reinventing Free Labor: Padrones and Immigrant Workers in the North American West, 1880–1930* (2000)

William G. Robbins, *Colony and Empire: The Capitalist Transformation of the American West* (1994)

Quintard Taylor, *In Search of the Racial Frontier: African Americans in the American West, 1528–1990* (1998)

Sally Zanjani, *A Mine of Her Own: Women Prospectors in the American West, 1850–1950* (1997)

Ranching and Farming

Allan G. Bogue, *From Prairie to Corn Belt: Farming on the Illinois and Iowa Prairies in the Nineteenth Century* (1963)

Sucheng Chan, *This Bitter-Sweet Soil: The Chinese in California Agriculture, 1860–1910* (1986)

Philip Durham and Everett L. Jones, *The Negro Cowboys* (1965)

Mark Fiege, *Irrigated Eden: the Making of an Agricultural Landscape in the American West* (1999)

Dee Garceau, *The Important Things of Life: Women, Work, and Family in Sweetwater County, Wyoming, 1880–1929* (1997)

C. Robert Haywood, *Victorian West: Class and Culture in Kansas Cattle Towns* (1991)

Stan Hoig, *The Oklahoma Land Rush of 1889* (1984)

Lawrence Jelinek, *Harvest Empire: A History of California Agriculture*, 2nd ed. (1982)

Frederick C. Luebke, ed., *European Immigrants in the American West: Community Histories* (1998)

Pamela Riney-Kehrberg, *Childhood on the Farm: Work, Play, and Coming of Age in the Midwest* (2005)

David Vaught, *Cultivating California: Growers, Specialty Crops, and Labor, 1875–1920* (1999)

Paul I. Wellman, *The Trampling Herd: The Story of the Cattle Range in America* (1939, 1988)

Donald E. Worcester, *The Chisholm Trail* (1980)

The Western Landscape

Alfred L. Bush and Lee Clark Mitchell, *The Photograph and the American Indian* (1994)

William Cronon, George Miles, and Jay Gitlin, eds., *Under an Open Sky: Rethinking America's Western Past* (1992)

Mick Gidley, *Edward S. Curtis and the North American Indian, Incorporated* (1998)

William H. Goetzmann and William N. Goetzmann, *The West of the Imagination* (1986)

Joy S. Kasson, *Buffalo Bill's Wild West: Celebrity, Memory, and Popular History* (2000)

Chris J. Magoc, *Yellowstone: The Creation and Selling of an American Landscape, 1870–1903* (1999)

Walter Nugent and Martin Ridge, eds., *The American West: The Reader* (1999)

Paige Raibmon, *Authentic Indians: Episodes of Encounter from the Late-Nineteenth-Century Northwest Coast* (2005)

Paul Reddin, *Wild West Shows* (1999)

Martha A. Sandweiss, *Print the Legend: Photography and the American West* (2002)

Richard Slotkin, *Gunfighter Nation: The Myth of the Frontier in 20th-Century America* (1992)

Mark David Spence, *Dispossessing the Wilderness: Indian Removal and the Making of the National Parks* (1999)

Richard White, *"It's Your Misfortune and None of My Own": A History of the American West* (1991)

Richard White and Patricia Nelson Limerick, *The Frontier in American Culture* (1994)

Donald Worster, *An Unsettled Country: Changing Landscapes of the American West* (1994)

David M. Wrobel, *Promised Lands: Promotion, Memory, and the Creation of the American West* (2002)

Biography

Matthew Baigell, *Albert Bierstadt* (1981)

Louise Barnett, *Touched by Fire: The Life, Death, and Mythic Afterlife of George Armstrong Custer* (1996)

Robert W. Larson, *Red Cloud: Warrior-Statesman of the Lakota Sioux* (1997)

James D. McLaird, *Calamity Jane* (2005)

Joan T. Mark, *A Stranger in Her Native Land: Alice Fletcher and the American Indians* (1988)

Joseph M. Marshall, *The Journey of Crazy Horse* (2004)

Sara R. Massey, ed., *Black Cowboys of Texas* (2000)

Valerie Mathes, *Helen Hunt Jackson and Her Indian Reform Legacy* (1990)

Elinore Pruitt Stewart, *Letters of a Woman Homesteader* (1914, 1989)

Edwin R. Sweeney, *Cochise, Chiricahua Apache Chief* (1991)

Jerry D. Thompson, ed., *Juan Cortina and the Texas-Mexico Frontier, 1859–1877* (1994)

Benson Tong, *Susan La Flesche Picotte, M.D.: Omaha Indian Leader and Reformer* (1999)

Robert M. Utley, *The Lance and the Shield: The Life and Times of Sitting Bull* (1993)

Donald Worster, *A River Running West: The Life of John Wesley Powell* (2001)

Sally Zanjani, *Sarah Winnemucca* (2001)

CHAPTER 19

Science, Technology, and Industry

Alfred D. Chandler Jr., *The Visible Hand: The Managerial Revolution in American Business* (1977)

David A. Hounshell, *From the American System to Mass Production, 1800–1932* (1984)

Walter Licht, *Industrializing America: The Nineteenth Century* (1995)

A. J. Millard, *Edison and the Business of Innovation* (1990)

David F. Noble, *America by Design: Science, Technology and the Rise of Corporate Capitalism* (1977)

William S. Pretzer, ed., *Working at Inventing: Thomas A. Edison and the Menlo Park Experience* (2001)

Leonard S. Reich, *The Making of American Industrial Research: Science and Business at G.E. and Bell, 1876–1926* (1985)

Business and the Economy

Jack Beatty, *Age of Betrayal: The Triumph of Money in America, 1865–1900* (2007)

Wendy Gamber, *The Female Economy: The Millinery and Dressmaking Trades, 1860–1930* (1997)

Pamela Walker Laird, *Advertising Progress: American Business and the Rise of Consumer Marketing* (1998)

Naomi R. Lamoreaux, *The Great Merger Movement in American Business, 1895–1904* (1985)

Daniel Nelson, *Managers and Workers: Origins of the Factory System in the United States, 1880–1920* (1975)

Sarah Lyons Watts, *Order against Chaos: Business Culture and Labor Ideology in America, 1800–1915* (1991)

Olivier Zunz, *Making America Corporate, 1870–1920* (1990)

Working Class and Labor

Eric Arnesen, *Waterfront Workers of New Orleans: Race, Class, and Politics, 1863–1923* (1991)

James R. Barrett, *Work and Community in the Jungle* (1987)

John Bodnar, *Immigration and Industrialization: Ethnicity in an American Mill Town* (1977)

Ileen A. Devault, *United Apart: Gender and the Rise of Craft Unionism* (2004)

Lisa M. Fine, *The Souls of the Skyscraper: Female Clerical Workers in Chicago, 1870–1930* (1990)

Herbert G. Gutman, *Work, Culture and Society in Industrializing America: Essays in American Working-Class and Social History* (1977)

David M. Katzman, *Seven Days a Week: Women and Domestic Service in Industrializing America* (1978)

Joanne Meyerowitz, *Women Adrift: Industrial Wage Earners in Chicago, 1880–1930* (1988)

David Montgomery, *The Fall of the House of Labor: The Workplace, the State, and American Labor Activism, 1865–1925* (1987)

Daniel T. Rodgers, *The Work Ethic in Industrial America, 1850–1920* (1978)

Dave Roediger and Franklin Rosemont, eds., *Haymarket Scrapbook* (1986)

Roy Rosenzweig, *Eight Hours for What We Will: Workers and Leisure in an Industrial City, 1870–1920* (1983)

Robert E. Weir, *Beyond Labor's Veil: The Culture of the Knights of Labor* (1996)

The Industrial City

Robert M. Fogelson, *Bouregeois Nightmares: Suburbia 1870–1930* (2005)

John S. Garner, ed., *The Midwest in American Architecture* (1991)

Dolores Hayden, *The Grand Domestic Revolution: A History of Feminist Designs for American Homes, Neighborhoods, and Cities* (1981)

Scott Molloy, *Trolley Wars: Streetcar Workers on the Line* (1996)

Christopher Robert Reed, *Black Chicago's First Century*: Vol. 1: 1833–1900 (2005)

Mark H. Rose, *Cities of Light and Heat: Domesticating Gas and Electricity in Urban America* (1995)

Carl Smith, *Urban Disorder and the Shape of Belief: The Great Chicago Fire, the Haymarket Bomb, and the Model Town of Pullman* (1995)

John R. Stilgoe, *Borderland: Origins of the American Suburb, 1820–1939* (1988)

The New South

Edward L. Ayers, *The Promise of the New South* (1992)

Don Doyle, *New Men, New Cities, New South* (1990)

Jacquelyn Dowd Hall, et al., *Like a Family: The Making of a Southern Cotton Mill World* (1987, 2000)

Gerald D. Jaynes, *Branches without Roots: Genesis of the Black Working Class in the American South, 1862–1882* (1986)

Lawrence H. Larsen, *The Rise of the Urban South* (1985)

Cathy McHugh, *Mill Family: The Labor System in the Southern Textile Industry, 1880–1915* (1988)

Karin A. Shapiro, *A New South Rebellion: The Battle Against Convict Labor in the Tennessee Coalfields, 1871–1896* (1998)

Rise of Consumer Society

Elaine S. Abelson, *When Ladies Go A-Thieving* (1989)

Stuart Blumin, *The Emergence of the Middle Class* (1989)

Joshua Brown, *Beyond the Lines: Pictorial Reporting, Everyday Life, and the Crisis of Gilded Age America* (2003)

Sarah Burns, *Inventing the Modern Artist: Art and Culture in Gilded Age America* (1996)

Yong Chen, *Chinese San Francisco, 1850–1943* (2000)

Priscilla Ferguson Clement, *Growing Pains: Children in the Industrial Age, 1850–1890* (1997)

Steven Conn, *Museums and American Intellectual Life, 1876–1926* (1998)

Perry Duis, *Challenging Chicago: Coping with Everyday Life, 1837–1920* (1998)

Robert M. Fogelson, *Bourgeois Nightmares: Suburbia, 1870–1930* (2005)

Warren Goldstein, *Playing for Keeps: A History of Early Baseball* (1989)

Katherine C. Grier, *Culture and Comfort: Parlor Making and Middle-Class Identity, 1850–1930* (1988, 1997)

Judy Hilkey, *Character Is Capital: Success Manuals and Manhood in Gilded Age America* (1997)

John F. Kasson, *Amusing the Millions: Coney Island at the Turn of the Century* (1978)

Lawrence W. Levine, *Highbrow/Lowbrow: The Emergence of Cultural Hierarchy in America* (1988)

Patricia Marks, *Bicycles, Bangs, and Bloomers: The New Woman in the Popular Press* (1990)

Steven A. Riess, *City Games: The Evolution of American Urban Society and the Rise of Sports* (1989)

Roy Rosenzweig and Elizabeth Blackmar, *The Park and the People: A History of Central Park* (1992)

Leigh Eric Schmidt, *Consumer Rites: The Buying and Selling of American Holidays* (1995)

Biography

David Cannadine, *Mellon: An American Life* (2006)

Ron Chernow, *Titan: The Life of John D. Rockefeller, Sr.* (1998)

Bruce J. Evensen, *God's Man for the Gilded Age: D. L. Moody and the Rise of Modern Mass Evangelism* (2003)

Helen Lefkowitz Horowitz, *The Power and Passion of M. Carey Thomas* (1994)

Paul Israel, *Edison: A Life of Invention* (1998)

J. Paul Jeffers, *Diamond Jim Brady* (2001)

David Nasaw, *Andrew Carnegie* (2006)

Craig Phelan, *Grand Master Workman: Terence Powderly and the Knights of Labor* (2000)

Jean Strouse, *Morgan: American Financier* (1999)

Robert C. Twombly, *Louis Sullivan* (1986)

Michael Zuckerman, *Almost Chosen People: Oblique Biographies in the American Grain* (1993)

CHAPTER 20

The Nation and Politics

Paula C. Baker, *The Moral Frameworks of Public Life: Gender, Politics and the State in Rural New York, 1870–1930* (1991)

Jack Beatty, *Age of Betrayal: The Triumph of Money in America, 1865–1900* (2007)

Michael Lewis Goldberg, *An Army of Women: Gender and Politics in Gilded Age Kansas* (1997)

J. William Harris, *Deep Souths: Delta, Piedmont, and Sea Island Society in the Age of Segregation* (2001)

Erika Lee, *At America's Gates: Chinese Immigration during the Exclusion Era, 1882–1943* (2003)

Gwendolyn Mink, *Old Labor and New Immigrants in American Political Development* (1986)

Nell Irvin Painter, *Standing at Armageddon: The United States, 1877–1919* (1987)

Douglas Steeples and David O. Whitten, *Democracy in Desperation: The Depression of 1893* (1998)

Mark. W. Summers, *Party Games: Getting, Keeping, and Using Power in Gilded Age Politics* (2004)

Brook Thomas, Plessy *v.* Ferguson: *A Brief History with Documents* (1997)

David Traxel, *1898: The Birth of the American Century* (1998)

C. Vann Woodward, *The Strange Career of Jim Crow,* 3rd rev. ed. (1974)

Populism

Peter Argersinger, *The Limits of Agrarian Radicalism: Western Populism and American Politics* (1995)

Lawrence Goodwyn, *Democratic Promise: The Populist Moment in America* (1976)

Steven Hahn, *The Roots of Southern Populism* (1983)

Michael Kazin, *The Populist Persuasion: An American History* (1995, rev. ed., 1998)

Robert C. McMath, *American Populism: A Social History* (1993)

Scott G. McNall, *The Road to Rebellion: Class Formation and Kansas Populism 1865–1900* (1988)

Norman Pollack, *The Humane Economy: Populism, Capitalism and Democracy* (1990)

Protest and Reform Movements

Ruth Bordin, *Woman and Temperance: The Quest for Power and Liberty, 1873–1900* (1981)

Kathleen Ann Clark, *Defining Moments: African American Commemoration and Political Culture in the South, 1863–1913* (2005)

Susan Curtis, *A Consuming Faith: The Social Gospel and Modern American Culture* (1991)

William D. Harpine, *From the Front Porch to the Front Page: McKinley and Bryan in the 1896 Presidential Campaign* (2005)

Paul Krause, *The Battle for Homestead, 1880–1892* (1992)

Ralph E. Luker, *The Social Gospel in Black and White* (1991)

Alison M. Parker, *Purifying America: Women, Cultural Reform, and Pro-Censorship Activism, 1873–1933* (1997)

Gretchen Ritter, *Goldbugs and Greenbacks: The Antimonopoly Tradition and the Politics of Finance in America, 1865–1896* (1997)

Richard Schneirov, Shelton Stromquist, and Nick Salvatore, eds., *The Pullman Strike and the Crisis of the 1890s: Essays on Labor and Politics* (1999)

Carlos A. Schwantes, *Coxey's Army* (1985)

Gary Scott Smith, *The Search for Social Salvation: Social Christianity and America, 1880–1925* (2000)

David O. Stowell, *Streets, Railroads, and the Great Strike of 1877* (1999)

Imperialism and Empire

Tunde Adeleke, *Unafrican Americans: Nineteenth-Century Black Nationalists and the Civilizing Mission* (1998)

Nupur Chaudhuri and Margaret Strobel, eds., *Western Women and Imperialism* (1992)

Willard B. Gatewood, Jr., *Black Americans and the White Man's Burden* (1975)

Patricia Hill, *The World Their Household: The American Women's Foreign Mission Movement and Cultural Transformation, 1870–1920* (1985)

Amy Kaplan and Donald E. Pease, eds., *Cultures of United States Imperialism* (1993)

Paul A. Kramer, *The Blood of Government: Race, Empire, the United States, and the Philippines* (2007)

Paul T. McCartney, *Power and Progress: American National Identity, the War of 1898, and the Rise of American Imperialism* (2006)

Emily S. Rosenberg, *Spreading the American Dream: American Economic and Cultural Expansion, 1890–1945* (1982)

Robert W. Rydell, *All the World's a Fair: Vision of Empire at the American International Expositions, 1876–1916* (1984)

Anders Stephanson, *Manifest Destiny: American Expansion and the Empire of Right* (1995)

Spanish–American War and the Philippines

Virginia M. Bouvier, ed., *Whose America? The War of 1898 and the Battles to Define the Nation* (2001)

Kenneth E. Hendrickson, *The Spanish-American War* (2003)

Kristin L. Hoganson, *Fighting for American Manhood: How Gender Politics Provoked the Spanish-American and Philippine-American Wars* (1998)

Paul A. Kramer, *The Blood of Government: Race, Empire, the United States, and the Philippines* (2006)

Brian McAllister Linn, *The Philippine War, 1899–1902* (2000)

Stuart Creighton Miller, *"Benevolent Assimilation": The American Conquest of the Philippines, 1899–1903* (1982)

Ivan Musicant, *Empire By Default: The Spanish-American War and the Dawn of the American Century* (1998)

Louis A. Perez, Jr., *The War of 1898: The United States and Cuba in History and Historiography* (1998)

Harvey Rosenfeld, *Diary of a Dirty Little War: The Spanish-American War of 1898* (2000)

Thomas David Schoonover, *Uncle Sam's War of 1898 and the Origins of Globalism* (2003)

Angel Smith and Emma Davila-Cox, eds., *The Crisis of 1898: Colonial Redistribution and Nationalist Mobilization* (1999)

John Lawrence Tone, *War and Genocide in Cuba, 1895–1898* (2006)

Biography

Ruth Bordin, *Frances Willard: A Biography* (1986)

Mari Jo Buhle, Paul Buhle, and Harvey J. Kaye, eds., *The American Radical* (1995)

Edward P. Crapol, *James G. Blaine: Architect of Empire* (2000)

Bruce J. Evensen, *God's Man for the Gilded Age: D. L. Moody and the Rise of Modern Mass Evangelism* (2003)

Jane Taylor Nelsen, *A Prairie Populist: The Memoirs of Luna Kellie* (1992)

Allan Peskin, *Garfield: A Biography* (1978)

Ben Procter, *William Randolph Hearst: The Early Years, 1863–1910* (1998)

Nick Salvatore, *Eugene V. Debs* (1982)

Peggy Samuels and Harold Samuels, *Teddy Roosevelt at San Juan: The Making of a President* (1997)

Patricia A. Schechter, *Ida B. Wells-Barnett and American Reform, 1880–1930* (2001)

C. Van Woodward, *Tom Watson* (1963)

CHAPTER 21

The Origins of Progressivism

Walter M. Brasch, *Forerunners of Revolution: Muckrakers and the American Social Conscience* (1990)

Mina Carson, *Settlement Folk: Social Thought and the American Settlement Movement, 1885–1930* (1990)

Nancy Cohen, *Reconstruction of American Liberalism, 1865–1914* (2002)

Leon Fink, *Progressive Intellectuals and the Dilemmas of Democratic Commitment* (1997)

Richard Hofstadter, *The Age of Reform: From Bryan to FDR* (1955)

James T. Kloppenberg, *Uncertain Victory: Social Democracy and Progressivism in European and American Thought, 1870–1920* (1986)

Richard McCormick, *The Party Period and Public Policy* (1986)

Steven L. Piott, *American Reformers, 1870–1920: Progressivism in Word and Deed* (2006)

Robert Wiebe, *The Search for Order, 1877–1920* (1967)

Progressive Politics in Cities and States

John D. Buenker, *Urban Liberalism and Progressive Reform* (1973)

Robert D. Johnston, *The Radical Middle Class: Populist Democracy and the Question of Capitalism in Progressive Era Portland, Oregon* (2003)

William A. Link, *The Paradox of Southern Progressivism, 1880–1930* (1992)

John L. Recchiuti, *Civic Engagement: Social Science and Progressive Era Reform in New York City* (2007)

Social Control and Its Limits

Paul M. Boyer, *Urban Masses and Moral Order in America, 1820–1920* (1978)

Eldon J. Eisenach, *The Lost Promise of Progressivism* (1994)

Randy D. McBee, *Dance Hall Days: Intimacy and Leisure among Working-Class Immigrants in the United States* (2000)

Ruth Rosen, *The Lost Sisterhood: Prostitutes in America, 1900–1918* (1982)

Andrea Tone, *The Business of Benevolence: Industrial Paternalism in Progressive America* (1997)

Challenges to Progressivism: Working-Class Communities and Protest

John Bodnar, *The Transplanted* (1985)

Susan A. Glenn, *Daughters of the Shtetl: Life and Labor in the Immigrant Generation* (1990)

James R. Green, *The World of the Worker: Labor in Twentieth-Century America* (1980)

Alice Kessler-Harris, *Out to Work: A History of Wage-Earning Women in the United States* (1982)

David Montgomery, *The Fall of the House of Labor* (1987)

Kathy Peiss, *Cheap Amusements: Working Women and Leisure in Turn-of-the-Century New York* (1986)

Roy Rosenzweig, *Eight Hours for What We Will* (1983)

Shelton Stromquist, *Reinventing the People: The Progressive Movement, the Class Problem, and the Origins of Modern Liberalism* (2006)

Ronald Takaki, *Strangers from a Different Shore: A History of Asian Americans* (1989)

Women's Movements and Black Activism

Paula Baker, *The Moral Frameworks of Public Life* (1991)

Mari Jo Buhle, *Women and American Socialism* (1983)

Rebecca Edwards, *Angels in the Machinery: Gender in American Party Politics from the Civil War to the Progressive Era* (1997)

Linda Gordon, *Woman's Body, Woman's Right: A Social History of Birth Control* (1976)

Molly Ladd-Taylor, *Mother Work: Women, Child Welfare, and the State, 1890–1930* (1994)

Elizabeth Sanders, *Roots of Reform: Farmers, Workers, and the American State, 1877–1917* (1999)

David W. Southern, *The Progressive Era and Race: Reaction and Reform, 1900–1917* (2005)

Michael R. West, *The Education of Booker T. Washington* (2006)

National Progressivism

Kendrick A. Clements, *The Presidency of Woodrow Wilson* (1992)

John M. Cooper Jr., *The Warrior and the Priest: Theodore Roosevelt and Woodrow Wilson* (1983)

Lewis L. Gould, *The Presidency of Theodore Roosevelt* (1991)

Robert Harrison, *Congress, Progressive Reform, and the New American State* (2004)

Morton Keller, *Regulating a New Society: Public Policy and Social Change in America, 1900–1930* (1994)

David Traxel, *Crusader Nation: The United States in Peace and the Great War, 1898–1920* (2006)

Biography

Ellen Chesler, *Woman of Valor: Margaret Sanger and the Birth Control Movement in America* (1992)

Louis R. Harlan, *Booker T. Washington: Wizard of Tuskegee, 1901–1915* (1983)

J. Joseph Huthmacher, *Senator Robert F. Wagner and the Rise of Urban Liberalism* (1971)

Stephen Kantrowitz, *Ben Tillman and the Reconstruction of White Supremacy* (2000)

David Levering Lewis, *W.E.B. DuBois: Biography of a Race, 1868–1919* (1993)

Nick Salvatore, *Eugene V. Debs: Citizen and Socialist* (1982)

Patricia A. Schechter, *Ida B. Wells-Barnett and American Reform, 1880–1930* (2001)

Kathryn Kish Sklar, *Florence Kelley and the Nation's Work* (1995)

Bernard A. Weisberger, *The LaFollettes of Wisconsin* (1994)

Robert Westbrook, *John Dewey and American Democracy* (1991)

CHAPTER 22

Becoming a World Power

Richard H. Collin, *Theodore Roosevelt's Caribbean* (1990)

John M. Hart, *Empire and Revolution: The Americans in Mexico since the Civil War* (2002)

Walter LaFeber, *The Panama Canal* (1978)

Lester E. Langley, *The Banana Wars: An Inner History of American Empire, 1900–1934* (1983)

Mary A. Renda, *Taking Haiti: Military Occupation and the Culture of U.S. Imperialism, 1915–1940* (2001)

William Tilchin and Charles E. Neu, eds., *Artists of Power: Theodore Roosevelt, Woodrow Wilson, and Their Enduring Impact on U.S. Foreign Policy* (2006)

The Great War

Lloyd E. Ambrosius, *Woodrow Wilson and the American Diplomatic Tradition* (1987)

Paul Fussell, *The Great War and Modern Memory* (1973)

Martin Gilbert, *The First World War: A Complete History* (1994)

James Joll, *The Origins of the First World War* (1984)

American Mobilization

A. E. Barbeau and Florette Henri, *The Unknown Soldiers: Black American Troops in World War I* (1974)

Carol R. Byerly, *Fever of War: The Influenza Epidemic in the U.S. Army during World War I* (2005)

John W. Chambers, *To Raise an Army: The Draft in Modern America* (1987)

Nancy Gentile Ford, *Americans All! Foreign Born Soldiers in World War I* (2001)

Jeanette Keith, *Rich Man's War, Poor Man's Fight: Race, Class, and Power in the Rural South during the First World War* (2004)

Gerald E. Shenk, *"Work or Fight": Race, Gender, and the Draft in World War I* (2006)

Robert W. Tucker, *Woodrow Wilson and the Great War* (2007)

Stephen Vaughn, *Holding Fast the Inner Lines: Democracy, Nationalism, and the Committee on Public Information* (1980)

Over Here

Allen J. Brandt, *No Magic Bullet: A Social History of Venereal Disease in the United States since 1880* (1985)

Leslie M. DeBauche, *Reel Patriotism: The Movies and World War I* (1997)

Frances R. Early, *A World Without War: How U.S. Feminists and Pacifists Resisted World War I* (1997)

Margaret Mary Finnegan, *Selling Suffrage: Consumer Culture and Votes for Women* (1999)

Maureen Greenwald, *Women, War, and Work* (1980)

Ellis W. Hawley, *The Great War and the Search for Modern Order*, 2nd ed. (1992)

Jeffrey Haydu, *Making American Industries Safe for Democracy* (1997)

David M. Kennedy, *Over Here* (1980)

Barbara Steinson, *American Women's Activism in World War I* (1982)

Neil A. Wynn, *From Progressivism to Prosperity: World War I and American Society* (1986)

Repression and Reaction

James P. Grossman, *Land of Hope: Chicago, Black Southerners, and the Great Migration* (1989)

Frederick C. Luebke, *Bonds of Loyalty: German Americans and World War I* (1974)

Regin Schmidt, *Red Scare: The FBI and the Origins of Anticommunism in the United States, 1919–1943* (2000)

Mark Robert Schneider, *"We Return Fighting": The Civil Rights Movement in the Jazz Age* (2002)

An Uneasy Peace

Dana Frank, *Purchasing Power: Consumer Organizing, Gender, and the Seattle Labor Movement, 1919–1929* (1994)

Lloyd Gardner, *Safe for Democracy: The Anglo-American Response to Revolution, 1913–1923* (1984)

Robert D. Johnson, *The Peace Progressives and American Foreign Relations* (1995)

Carol Wilcox Melton, *Between War and Peace: Woodrow Wilson and the American Expeditionary Force in Siberia, 1918–1921* (2002)

Richard Polenberg, *Fighting Faiths: The Abrams Case, the Supreme Court, and Free Speech* (1987)

Daniel D. Stid, *The President As Statesman: Woodrow Wilson and the Constitution* (1998)

Biography

H. W. Brands, *Woodrow Wilson* (2003)

Ellen Carol DuBois, *Harriot Stanton Blatch and the Winning of Woman Suffrage* (1997)

Godfrey Hodgson, *Woodrow Wilson's Right Hand: The Life of Colonel Edward M. House* (2006)

Patricia O'Toole, *When Trumpets Call: Theodore Roosevelt after the White House* (2005)

Jacqueline van Voris, *Carrie Chapman Catt* (1987)

Warren Zimmerman, *First Great Triumph: How Five Americans Made Their Country a World Power* (2002)

CHAPTER 23

Postwar Prosperity and Its Price

David Brody, *Workers in Industrial America* (1980)

Gilbert C. Fite, *Cotton Fields No More: Southern Agriculture, 1865–1980* (1984)

Ellis W. Hawley, *The Great War and the Search for Modern Order* (1979)

Kenneth T. Jackson, *Crabgrass Frontier* (1985)

William Leuchtenberg, *The Perils of Prosperity, 1914–1932* (1958)

Clay McShane, *Down the Asphalt Path* (1994)

Gwendolyn Wright, *Building the American Dream* (1981)

Gerald Zahavi, *Workers, Managers, and Welfare Capitalism* (1988)

The New Mass Culture

Beth A. Bailey, *From Front Porch to Back Seat: Courtship in Twentieth-Century America* (1988)

Douglas B. Craig, *Fireside Politics: Radio and Political Culture in the United States, 1920–1940* (2000)

Daniel J. Czitrom, *Media and the American Mind* (1982)

John D'Emilio and Estelle B. Freedman, *Intimate Matters: A History of Sexuality in America* (1988)

Susan J. Douglas, *Listening In: Radio and the American Imagination* (1999)

Pamela Walker Laird, *Advertising Progress: American Business and the Rise of Consumer Marketing* (1998)

Jackson Lears, *Fables of Abundance: A Cultural History of Advertising in America* (1994)

Roland Marchand, *Advertising the American Dream: Making Way for Modernity, 1920–1940* (1985)

Steven J. Ross, *Working Class Hollywood: Silent Film and the Shaping of Class in America* (1998)

Robert Sklar, *Movie Made America,* rev. ed. (1995)

Resistance to Modernity

Katherine M. Blee, *Women and the Klan: Racism and Gender in the 1920s* (1991)

John Higham, *Strangers in the Land: Patterns of American Nativism, 1860–1925* (1955)

Edward J. Larson, *Summer of the Gods: The Scopes Trial and America's Continuing Debate over Science* (1997)

Mae M. Ngai, *Impossible Subjects: Illegal Aliens and the Making of Modern America* (2004)

Thomas R. Pegram, *Battling Demon Rum: The Struggle for a Dry America, 1800–1933* (1998)

Daniel J. Tichenor, *Dividing Lines: Immigration Control in America* (2002)

The State, the Economy, and Business

Kendrick A. Clements, *Hoover, Conservation, and Consumerism: Engineering the Good Life* (2000)

Warren I. Cohen, *Empire without Tears* (1987)

Louis Galambos and Joseph Pratt, *The Rise of the Corporate Commonwealth* (1988)

John Earl Haynes, ed., *Calvin Coolidge and the Coolidge Era* (1998)

Roland Marchand, *Creating the Corporate Soul: The Rise of Public Relations and Corporate Imagery in American Big Business* (1998)

Charles L. Mee, *The Ohio Gang: The World of Warren G. Harding* (1981)

Emily S. Rosenberg, *Spreading the American Dream* (1982)

Promises Postponed

Nancy F. Cott, *The Grounding of American Feminism* (1987)

Ann Douglas, *Terrible Honesty: Mongrel Manhattan in the 1920s* (1995)

Nathan I. Huggins, *Harlem Renaissance* (1971)

Cary D. Mintz, *Black Culture and the Harlem Renaissance* (1988)

Kathy H. Ogren, *The Jazz Revolution: Twenties America and the Meaning of Jazz* (1989)

George J. Sanchez, *Becoming Mexican American* (1993)

Mark Robert Schneider, *"We Return Fighting": The Civil Rights Movement in the Jazz Age* (2002)

Judith Stein, *The World of Marcus Garvey* (1985)

Biography

Edith L. Blumhofer, *Aimee Semple McPherson* (1993)

David Burner, *Herbert Hoover: The Public Life* (1979)

Robert Creamer, *Babe: The Legend Comes to Life* (1975)

Neal Gabler, *Winchell: Gossip, Power, and the Culture of Celebrity* (1994)

Fred Hobson, *Mencken: A Life* (1994)

David Levering Lewis, *W. E. B. DuBois: The Fight for Equality and the American Century, 1919–1963* (2000)

David Nasaw, *The Chief: The Life of William Randolph Hearst* (2000)

Arnold Rampersad, *The Life of Langston Hughes,* 2 vols. (1986–1988)

Robert A. Slayton, *Empire Statesman: The Rise and Redemption of Al Smith* (2001)

CHAPTER 24

Hard Times

Michael A. Bernstein, *The Great Depression* (1987)

Michael D. Bordo, et al., eds., *The Defining Moment: The Great Depression and the American Economy in the Twentieth Century* (1998)

John A. Garraty, *The Great Depression* (1986)

Robert S. McElvaine, ed., *Down and Out in the Great Depression* (1983)

Janet Poppendieck, *Breadlines Knee-Deep in Wheat* (1986)

Jeff Singleton, *The American Dole: Unemployment Relief and the Welfare State in the Great Depression* (2000)

Studs Terkel, *Hard Times* (1970)

T.H. Watkins, *The Hungry Years: A Narrative History of the Great Depression in America* (1999)

Elmos Wicker, *The Banking Panics of the Great Depression* (1996)

FDR and the First New Deal

Jonathan Alter, *The Defining Moment: FDR's Hundred Days and the Triumph of Hope* (2006)

Paul K. Conkin, *The New Deal,* 2nd ed. (1975)

Steve Fraser and Gary Gerstle, eds., *The Rise and Fall of the New Deal Order* (1988)

R. Alan Lawson, *A Commonwealth of Hope: The New Deal Responds to Crisis* (2006)

William Leuchtenberg, *The FDR Years* (1995)

George McJimsey, *The Presidency of Franklin Delano Roosevelt* (2000)

James S. Olson, *Saving Capitalism* (1988)

Albert U. Romasco, *The Politics of Recovery: Roosevelt's New Deal* (1983)

Elliot Rosen, *Roosevelt, the Great Depression, and the Economics of Recovery* (2005)

Theodore M. Saloutos, *The American Farmer and the New Deal* (1982)

Left Turn and the Second New Deal

Kristi Andersen, *The Creation of a Democratic Majority, 1928–1936* (1979)

Irving Bernstein, *The Turbulent Years: A History of the American Worker, 1933–1941* (1970)

John Braeman et al., eds., *The New Deal: The State and Local Levels* (1975)

Alan Brinkley, *Voices of Protest: Huey Long, Father Coughlin, and the New Deal* (1982)

Peter Friedlander, *The Emergence of a UAW Local* (1975)

Gary Gerstle, *Working Class Americanism* (1989)

Kenneth J. Heineman, *A Catholic New Deal: Religion and Reform in Depression Pittsburgh* (1999)

Robin D. G. Kelley, *Hammer and Hoe: Alabama Communists during the Great Depression* (1990)

Joseph P. Lash, *Dealers and Dreamers* (1988)

Roy Lubove, *The Struggle for Social Security* (1968)

Robert H. Zieger, *The CIO, 1935–1955* (1995)

The New Deal and the West

James M. Gregory, *American Exodus: The Dust Bowl Migration and Okie Culture in California* (1989)

Norris Hundley Jr., *The Great Thirst: California and Water, 1770s–1990s* (1992)

Laurence Kelly, *The Assault on Assimilation: John Collier and the Origins of Indian Policy Reform, 1920–1954* (1983)

Sarah T. Phillips, *This Land, This Nation: Conservation, Rural America, and the New Deal* (2007)

Vicki Ruiz, *Cannery Women/Cannery Lives: Mexican Women, Unionization, and the California Food Processing Industry, 1930–1950* (1987)

Charles J. Shindo, *Dust Bowl Migrants in the American Imagination* (1997)

Kevin Starr, *Endangered Dreams: The Great Depression in California* (1996)

Graham D. Taylor, *The New Deal and American Indian Tribalism* (1980)

Donald Worster, *Dust Bowl* (1979)

Depression-Era Culture

Thomas P. Doherty, *Pre-Code Hollywood: Sex, Immorality, and Insurrection in American Cinema, 1930–1934* (1999)

Lewis A. Erenberg, *Swingin' the Dream: Big Band Jazz and the Rebirth of American Culture* (1998)

Vivian Gornick, *The Romance of American Communism* (1976)

Harvey Klehr, *The Heyday of American Communism* (1984)

Anthony W. Lee, *Painting on the Left* (1999)

Bruce Lenthall, *Radio's America: The Great Depression and the Rise of Modern Mass Culture* (2007)

J. Fred MacDonald, *Don't Touch That Dial* (1979)

Richard McKinzie, *The New Deal for Artists* (1973)

Barbara Melosh, *Engendering Culture: Manhood and Womanhood in New Deal Public Art and Theater* (1991)

David P. Peeler, *Hope among Us Yet* (1987)

Richard H. Pells, *Radical Visions and American Dreams: Culture and Social Thought in the Depression Years* (1973)

Thomas Schatz, *The Genius of the System: Hollywood Filmmaking in the Studio Era* (1988)

William Stott, *Documentary Expression and Thirties America* (1973)

William H. Young and Nancy K. Young, *The Great Depression in America: A Cultural Encyclopedia* (2007)

The Limits of Reform

Francisco E. Balderrama, *Decade of Betrayal: Mexican Repatriation in the 1930s* (1995)

Suzanne Mettler, *Dividing Citizens: Gender and Federalism in New Deal Public Works* (1998)

Mark Naison, *Communists in Harlem during the Depression* (1983)

James T. Patterson, *Congressional Conservatism and the New Deal* (1967)

Mary Poole, *The Segregated Origins of Social Security* (2006)

Robert Shogan, *Backlash: The Killing of the New Deal* (2006)

Landon R.Y. Storrs, *Civilizing Capitalism: The National Consumers' League, Women's Activism, and Labor Standards in the New Deal Era* (2000)

Patricia Sullivan, *Days of Hope: Race and Democracy in the New Deal Era* (1996)

Susan Ware, *Beyond Suffrage: Women in the New Deal* (1981)

———, *Partner and I: Molly Dewson, Feminism, and New Deal Politics* (1987)

Nancy J. Weiss, *Farewell to the Party of Lincoln: Black Politics in the Age of FDR* (1983)

G. Edward White, *The Constitution and the New Deal* (2000)

Robert L. Zangrando, *The NAACP Crusade against Lynching* (1980)

Biography

David Burner, *Herbert Hoover* (1978)

Blanche W. Cook, *Eleanor Roosevelt: A Life* (1992)

Steven Fraser, *Labor Will Rule: Sidney Hillman and the Rise of American Labor* (1991)

Dorothy Healey and Maurice Isserman, *California Red: A Life in the American Communist Party* (1990)

June Hopkins, *Harry Hopkins: Sudden Hero, Brash Reformer* (1999)

J. Joseph Huthmacher, *Robert F. Wagner and the Rise of Urban Liberalism* (1968)

Nelson Lichtenstein, *The Most Dangerous Man in Detroit: Walter Reuther and the Fate of American Labor* (1995)

Karen Becker Ohrn, *Dorothea Lange and the Documentary Tradition* (1980)

Naomi E. Pasachoff, *Frances Perkins: Champion of the New Deal* (1999)

Lois Scharf, *Eleanor Roosevelt* (1987)

Jean Edward Smith, *FDR* (2007)

Robert Zieger, *John L. Lewis* (1988)

CHAPTER 25

Coming of World War II

Justus D. Doenecke, *Storm on the Horizon: The Challenge to American Intervention, 1939–1941* (2000)

Akira Iriye, *The Origins of the Second World War in Asia and the Pacific* (1987)

Deborah Lipstadt, *Beyond Belief: The American Press and the Coming of the Holocaust, 1933–1945* (1986)

Emily Rosenberg, *A Date Which Will Live: Pearl Harbor in American Memory* (2004)

Geoffrey S. Smith, *To Save a Nation* (1992)

Robert B. Stinnett, *Day of Deceit: The Truth about FDR and Pearl Harbor* (2000)

Arsenal of Democracy and the Home Front

Karen Anderson, *Wartime Women* (1981)

Amy Bentley, *Eating for Victory: Food Rationing and the Politics of Domesticity* (1998)

Alison R. Bernstein, *American Indians and World War II* (1991)

Allan Berube, *Coming Out under Fire: The History of Gay Men and Women in World War II* (1990)

Dominic J. Capeci and Martha Wilkerson, *Layered Violence: The Detroit Rioters of 1943* (1991)

Paul D. Casdorph, *Let the Good Times Roll: Life at Home in America during World War II* (1989)

Charles D. Chamberlain, *Victory at Home: Manpower and Race in the American South during World War II* (2003)

Roger Daniels, *Concentration Camps USA: Japanese Americans and World War II* (1971)

Thomas Doherty, *Projections of War: Hollywood, American Culture and World War II* (1993)

Lewis A. Erenberg and Susan E. Hirsch, eds., *The War in American Culture: Society and Consciousness during World War II* (1996)

Sherna Berger Gluck, *Rosie the Riveter Revisited: Women, the War, and Social Change* (1987)

Rachel Waltner Goosen, *Women against the Good War: Conscientious Objection and Gender on the American Home Front, 1941–1947* (1997)

Maureen Honey, *Bitter Fruit: African American Women in World War II* (1999)

James J. Kimble, *Mobilizing the Home Front: War Bonds and Domestic Propaganda* (2006)

Andrew E. Kersten, *Labor's Home Front: The American Federation of Labor during World War II* (2006)

Paul A. C. Koistinen, *Arsenal of World War II: The Political Economy of American Warfare, 1940–1945* (2004)

Daniel Kryder, *Divided Arsenal: Race and the American State during World War II* (2000)

Roger W. Lotchin, *The Bad City in the Good War: San Francisco, Los Angeles, Oakland, and San Diego* (2003)

Franklin Odo, *No Sword to Bury: Japanese Americans in Hawai'i during World War II* (2004)

Gary Y. Okihiro, *Whispered Silences: Japanese Americans and World War II* (1996)

Greg Robinson, *By Order of the President: FDR and the Internment of Japanese Americans* (2001)

George H. Roeder, *The Censored War: American Visual Experience during World War II* (1993)

Lawrence R. Samuel, *Pledging Allegiance: American Identity and the Bond Drive of World War II* (1997)

Bartholomew H. Sparrow, *From the Outside In: World War II and the American State* (1996)

William M. Tuttle Jr., *"Daddy's Gone to War": The Second World War in the Lives of America's Children* (1993)

K. Scott Wong, *Americans First: Chinese Americans and the Second World War* (2005)

World at War

William H. Bartsch, *December 8, 1941: MacArthur's Pearl Harbor* (2003)

Alison Bernstein, *American Indians and World War II* (1991)

Conrad C. Crane, *Bombs, Cities, and Civilians* (1993)

John W. Dower, *War without Mercy* (1986)

Akira Iriye, *Power and Culture: The Japanese-American War, 1941–1945* (1981)

Lee Kennett, *G.I.: The American Soldier in World War II* (1987)

Eric Markusen and David Kopf, *The Holocaust and Strategic Bombing: Genocide and Total War in the Twentieth Century* (1995)

Peter Maslowski, *Armed with Cameras: The American Military Photographers of World War II* (1993)

Brenda L. Moore, *Serving Our Country: Japanese American Women in the Military during World War II* (2003)

Williamson Murray and Allan R. Millett, *A War to be Won: Fighting the Second World War* (2000)

Barbara Brooks Tomblin, *G.I. Nightingales: The Army Nurse Corps in World War II* (1996)

Edward W. Wood Jr., *Worshipping the Myths of World War II* (2006)

David S. Wyman, *The Abandonment of the Jews: America and the Holocaust, 1941–1945* (1984)

Last Stages of War

John D. Chappell, *Before the Bomb: How America Approached the End of the Pacific War* (1997)

David P. Colley, *Blood for Dignity: The Story of the First Integrated Combat Unit in the U.S. Army* (2003)

Paul Fussell, *The Boy's Crusade: The American Infantry in Northwestern Europe, 1944–1945* (2003)

Lloyd C. Gardner, *Spheres of Influence: The Great Powers Partition Europe, from Munich to Yalta* (1993)

J. Robert Moskin, *Mr. Truman's War: The Final Victories of World War II and the Birth of the Postwar World* (1996)

Peter Schrijvers, *The Crash of Ruin: American Combat Soldiers in Europe during World War II* (1998)

Michael S. Sherry, *The Rise of American Air Power* (1987)

Atomic Bomb

Gar Alperovitz, *The Decision to Use the Atomic Bomb and the Architecture of an American Myth* (1995)

Paul Boyer, *By the Bomb's Early Light: American Thought and Culture at the Dawn of the Atomic Age* (1985)

Peter Bacon Hales, *Atomic Spaces: Living on the Manhattan Project* (1997)

Ruth H. Howes, *Their Day in the Sun: Women of the Manhattan Project* (1999)

J. Samuel Walker, *Prompt and Utter Destruction: Truman and the Use of Atomic Bombs against Japan* (1997)

Eileen Welsome, *The Plutonium Files: America's Secret Medical Experiments in the Cold War* (1999)

Biography/Memoir

Mark M. Anderson, ed., *Hitler's Exiles: Personal Stories of the Flight from Nazi Germany to America* (1998)

Jeremy Bernstein, *Oppenheimer: Portrait of an Enigma* (2004)

Carlo D'Este, *Patton: A Genius for War* (1995)

Preston John Hubbard, *Apocalypse Undone: My Survival of Japanese Imprisonment during World War II* (1990)

Michael Korder, *Ike: An American Hero* (2007)

Paula F. Pfeffer, *A. Philip Randolph* (1990)

Robert Underhill, *FDR and Harry: Unparalleled Lives* (1996)

CHAPTER 26

Global Insecurities and the Policy of Containment

Christian G. Appy, ed., *Cold War Constructions: The Political Culture of United States Imperialism, 1945–1966* (2000)

H. W. Brands Jr., *The Devil We Knew: Americans and the Cold War* (1993)

Warren I. Cohen, *America in the Age of Soviet Power, 1945–1991* (1993)

John Gaddis, *The Cold War: A New History* (2006)

Walter Hixson, *Parting the Curtain: Propaganda, Culture, and the Cold War, 1945–1961* (1997)

Townsend Hoopes and Douglas Brinkley, *FDR and the Creation of the U.N.* (1997)

Walter LaFeber, *America, Russia, and the Cold War, 1945–1992,* 7th ed. (1993)

Arnold A. Offner, *Another Such Victory: President Truman and the Cold War* (2002)

Arch Puddington, *Broadcasting Freedom: The Cold War Triumph of Radio Free Europe and Radio Liberty* (2000)

Richard Rhodes, *Dark Sun: The Making of the Hydrogen Bomb* (1995)

David F. Rudgers, *Creating the Secret State: The Origins of the Central Intelligence Angency, 1943–1947* (2000)

Michael Schaller, *American Occupation of Japan: The Origins of the Cold War in Asia* (1985)

The Truman Presidency

Jonathan Bell, *The Liberal State on Trial: The Cold War and American Politics in the Truman Years* (2004)

Gary A. Donaldson, *Truman Defeats Dewey* (1999)

Michael R. Gardner, *Harry Truman and Civil Rights* (2002)

Zachary Karabell, *The Last Campaign: How Harry Truman Won the 1948 Election* (2000)

Robert David Johnson, *Congress and the Cold War* (2006)

Melvyn P. Leffler, *A Preponderance of Power: National Security, the Truman Administration, and the Cold War* (1992)

Steve Neal, ed., *HST: Memories of the Truman Years* (2003)

Sean J. Savage, *Truman and the Democratic Party* (1997)

Elizabeth Edwards Spalding, *The First Cold Warrior: Harry Truman, Containment, and the Remaking of Liberal Internationalism* (2006)

The Cold War at Home

Larrry Ceplair and Steven Englund, *The Inquisition in Hollywood: Politics in the Film Community, 1930–1960* (1980)

Robert W. Cherny, William Issel, Kieran Walsh Taylor, eds., *American Labor and the Cold War* (2004)

Noam Chomsky, ed., *The Cold War and the University: Toward an Intellectual History of the Postwar Years* (1997)

K. A. Cuordileone, *Manhood and American Political Culture in the Cold War* (2005)

Sigmund Diamond, *Compromised Campus: The Collaboration of Universities with the Intelligence Community, 1945–1995* (1992)

Andrew D. Grossman, *Neither Dead Nor Red: Civilian Defense and American Political Development during the Early Cold War* (2001)

Michael J. Hogan, *A Cross of Iron: Harry S Truman and the Origins of the National Security State, 1945–1954* (1998)

Michael Kackman, *Citizen Spy: Television, Espionage, and Cold War Culture* (2005)

Scott Lucas, *Freedom's War: The American Crusade against the Soviet Union* (1999)

Patrick McGilligan and Paul Buhle, *Tender Comrades: A Backstory of the Hollywood Blacklist* (1997)

Lisle A. Rose, *The Cold War Comes to Main Street: America in 1950* (1999)

Ellen Schrecker, *Many Are the Crimes: McCarthyism in America* (1998)

———, *No Ivory Tower: McCarthyism and the Universities* (1986)

Jeff Woods, *Black Struggle, Red Scare: Segregation and Anti-Communism in the South, 1948–1968* (2004)

Cold War Culture

Michael Barson, *"Better Dead Than Red!" A Nostalgic Look at the Golden Years of Russiaphobia, Red-Baiting, and Other Commie Madness* (1992)

Paul Buhle and Dave Wagner, *Radical Hollywood* (2002)

Michael L. Krenn, *Fall-out Shelters for the Human Spirit: American Art and the Cold War* (2005)

George Lipsitz, *A Rainbow at Midnight: Labor and Culture in the 1940s* (1994)

Lary May, ed., *Recasting America: Culture and Politics in the Age of the Cold War* (1989)

Elaine McClarnand and Steve Goodson, eds., *The Impact of the Cold War on American Popular Culture* (1999)

Julia L. Mickenberg, *Learning from the Left: Children's Literature, the Cold War, and Radical Politics in the United States* (2006)

John L. Rudolph, *Scientists in the Classroom: The Cold War Reconstruction of American Science Education* (2002)

David Seed, *American Science Fiction and the Cold War* (1999)

Joanne P. Sharp, *Condensing the Cold War:* Reader's Digest *and American Identity* (2000)

Jessica Wang, *American Science in an Age of Anxiety: Scientists, Anticommunism, and the Cold War* (1999)

Scott C. Zeman, ed. *Atomic Culture: How We Learned to Stop Worrying and Love the Bomb* (2004),

Korean War

Bevin Alexander, *Korea: The First War We Lost,* rev. ed., (2000)

William T. Bowers, William M. Hammond, George L. MacGarrigle, *Black Soldier, White Army: The 24th Infantry Regiment in Korea* (1996)

Albert E. Cowdrey, *The Medics' War* (1987)

Stephen Endicott and Edward Hagerman, *The United States and Biological Warfare: Secrets from the Early Cold War and Korea* (1998)

Paul G. Pierpaoli Jr., *Truman and Korea: The Political Culture of the Early Cold War* (1999)

Ron Robin, *The Making of the Cold War Enemy* (2001)

Stanley Sandler, *The Korean War: No Victors, No Vanquished* (1999)

Biography

Robert L. Beisner, *Dean Acheson: A Life in the Cold War* (2006)

Kai Bird and Margin J. Sherwin, *American Prometheus: The Triumph and Tragedy of J. Robert Oppenheimer* (2005)

Allida M. Black, *Casting Her Own Shadow: Eleanor Roosevelt and the Shaping of Postwar Liberalism* (1996)

John C. Culver, *American Dreamer: The Life and Times of Henry A. Wallace* (2000)

Martin Bauml Duberman, *Paul Robeson* (1988)

Curt Gentry, *J. Edgar Hoover: The Man and the Secrets* (1991)

Alonzo L. Hamby, *Man of the People: A Life of Harry S Truman* (1995)

Arthur Herman, *Joseph McCarthy: Reexamining the Life and Legacy of America's Most Hated Senator* (1999)

Robert M. Lichtman, *Deadly Farce: Harvey Matusow and the Informer System in the McCarthy Era* (2004)

George Lukacs, *George Kennan: A Study of Character* (2007)

David G. McCullough, *Truman* (1992)

Geoffrey Perret, *Old Soldiers Never Die: The Life of Douglas MacArthur* (1996)

CHAPTER 27

Under the Cold War's Shadow

James G. Blight and Peter Kornbluh, eds., *Politics of Illusion: The Bay of Pigs Invasion Reexamined* (1999)

Robert R. Bowie, *Waging Peace: How Eisenhower Shaped an Enduring Cold War Strategy* (1998)

James Carroll, *House of War: The Pentagon and the Disastrous Rise of American Power* (2006)

Nick Cullather, *Secret History: The CIA's Classified Account of its Operations in Guatemala, 1952–1954* (1999)

Paul Dickson, *Sputnik: The Shock of the Century* (2001)

Piero Gleijeses, *Shattered Hope: The Guatemalan Revolution and the United States, 1944–1954* (1991)

Zachary Karabell, *Architects of Intervention: The United States, the Third World, and the Cold War, 1946–1962* (1999)

Kathryn Statler and Andrew Johnson, eds., *The Eisenhower Administration, the Third World, and the Globalization of the Cold War* (2006)

Odd Arne Westad, *The Global Cold War: Third World Interventions and the Making of Our Times* (2005)

The Affluent Society

Roslayn Fraad Baxandall and Elizabeth Ewen, *Picture Windows: How the Suburbs Happened* (2000)

Stephanie Coontz, *The Way We Never Were* (1992)

John P. Diggins, *The Proud Decades: America in War and Peace, 1941–1960* (1988)

Benita Eisler, *Private Lives: Men and Women of the Fifties* (1986)

James T. Patterson, *Grand Expectations: Postwar America, 1945–1974* (1996)

Adam Ward Rome, *The Bulldozer in the Countryside: Suburban Sprawl and the Rise of American Environmentalism* (2001)

Stephen Wagner, *Eisenhower Republicanism: Pursuing the Middle Way* (2006)

Jessica Weiss, *To Have and to Hold: Marriage, the Baby Boom and Social Change* (2000)

Youth Culture

Wini Breines, *Young, White, and Miserable: Growing Up Female in the Fifties* (1992)

Thomas Doherty, *Teen Pics* (1994)

Marc Fisher, *Something in the Air: Radio, Rock, and the Revolution that Shaped a Generation* (2007)

Nelson George, *The Death of Rhythm and Blues* (1988)

James B. Gilbert, *A Cycle of Outrage: America's Reaction to the Juvenile Delinquent in the 1950s* (1986)

Jim Miller, *Flowers in the Dustbin: The Rise of Rock and Roll, 1947–1977* (1999)

Mass Culture and Its Discontents

Erik Barnouw, *Tube of Plenty* (1982)

Nancy E. Bernhard, *U.S. Television News and Cold War Propaganda, 1947–1960* (1999)

Joel Foreman, ed., *The Other Fifties: Interrogating Midcentury American Icons* (1997)

George Lipsitz, *Time Passages* (1990)

J. Fred MacDonald, *Television and the Red Menace* (1985)

David Marc, *Demographic Vistas: Television and American Culture* (1984)

Lynn Spigel, *Make Room for TV* (1992)

Stephen J. Whitfield, *The Culture of the Cold War* (1991)

The Coming of the New Frontier

Vincent Bugliosi, *Reclaiming History: The Assassination of President John F. Kennedy* (2007)

James N. Giglio, *The Presidency of John F. Kennedy* (2006)

Trumbull Higgins, *The Perfect Failure: Kennedy, Eisenhower, and the CIA at the Bay of Pigs* (1988)

Walter LaFeber, *Inevitable Revolutions* (1983)

Thomas G. Paterson, ed., *Kennedy's Quest for Victory* (1989)

Sheldon M. Stern, *Averting "The Final Failure": John F. Kennedy and the Secret Cuban Missile Crisis Meetings* (2003)

David Talbot, *Brothers: The Hidden History of the Kennedy Years* (2007)

Richard E. Welch Jr., *Response to Revolution: The United States and Cuba, 1959–1961* (1985)

Mark J. White, ed., *Kennedy: The New Frontier Revisited* (1998)

Garry Wills, *The Kennedy Imprisonment* (1983)

Biography

Chuck Berry, *Chuck Berry: The Autobiography* (1987)

Rick Coleman, *Blue Monday: Fats Domino and the Lost Dawn of Rock' n'Roll* (2007)

Robert Dallek, *An Unfinished Life: John F. Kennedy, 1917–1963* (2003)

Carol George, *God's Salesman: Norman Vincent Peale and the Power of Positive Thinking* (1993)

Peter Guralnick, *Last Train to Memphis: The Rise of Elvis Presley* (1994)

Daniel Horowitz, *Betty Friedan and the Making of the Feminine Mystique* (1998)

Bill Morgan, *I Celebrate Myself: The Somewhat Private Life of Allen Ginsberg* (2006)

Gerald Nicosia, *Memory Babe: A Critical Biography of Jack Kerouac* (1983)

Geoffrey Perret, *Eisenhower* (1999)

CHAPTER 28

Origins of the Movements

Michael R. Belknap, *Federal Law and Southern Order* (1987)

Scott DeVeaux, *The Birth of BeBop* (1998)

Grace Elizabeth Hale, *Making Whiteness: The Culture of Segregation in the South, 1890–1940* (1998)

Charles P. Henry, *Ralph Bunche: Model Negro or American Other* (1999)

Grace Williams O'Brien, *The Color of the Law: Race, Violence, and Justice in the Post–World War II South* (1999)

James T. Patterson, Brown *v.* Board of Education: *A Civil Rights Milestone and Its Troubled Legacy* (2001)

Bernard Schwartz, *The NAACP's Legal Strategy against Segregated Education* (1987)

Mark Tushnet, *Making Civil Rights Law: Thurgood Marshall and the Supreme Court, 1936–1961* (1994)

No Easy Road to Freedom, 1957–1962

Clayborne Carson, *In Struggle: SNCC and the Black Awakening of the 1960s* (1981)

William Chafe, *Civilities and Civil Rights: Greensboro, North Carolina, and the Black Struggle for Equality* (1980)

David Chappell, *A Stone of Hope: Prophetic and the Death of Jim Crow* (2004)

Constance Curry, et al., *Deep In Our Hearts: Nine White Women in the Freedom Movement* (2000)

John Dittmer, *Local People: The Struggle for Civil Rights in Mississippi* (1994)

James Farmer, *Lay Bare the Heart* (1985)

David J. Garrow, *The FBI and Martin Luther King, Jr.* (1983)

Cheryl L. Greenberg, ed., *A Circle of Trust: Remembering SNCC* (1998)

Charles M. Payne, *I've Got the Light of Freedom: The Organizing Tradition and the Mississippi Freedom Struggle* (1995)

Miles Wolff, *Lunch at the 5&10* (1990)

J. Mills Thornton, *Dividing Lines: Municipal Politics and the Struggle for Civil Rights in Montgomery, Birmingham, and Selma* (2002)

The Movement at High Tide, 1963–1965

Nick Bryant, *The Bystander: John F. Kennedy and the Struggle for Black Equality* (2006)

Seth Cagin and Philip Dray, *We Are Not Afraid* (1988)

Emilye Crosby, *A Little Taste of Freedom: The Black Freedom Struggle in Claiborne County, Mississippi* (2005)

Sara Evans, *Personal Politics: The Roots of Women's Liberation in the Civil Rights Movement and the New Left* (1979)

Henry Hampton and Steve Fayer, *Voices of Freedom: An Oral History of the Civil Rights Movement* (1990)

Peniel E. Joseph, *Waiting 'Til the Midnight Hour: A Narrative History of Black Power in America* (2006)

Doug McAdam, *Freedom Summer* (1988)

Diane McWhorter, *Carry Me Home: Birmingham, Alabama: The Climax of the Civil Rights Revolution* (2001)

Belinda Robnett, *How Long? How Long? African American Women in the Struggle for Civil Rights* (1997)

Renee C. Romano and Leigh Raiford, eds., *The Civil Rights Movement in American Memory* (2006)

Clive Webb, *Fight against Fear: Southern Jews and Black Civil Rights* (2001)

Robert Weisbrot, *Freedom Bound: A History of America's Civil Rights Movement* (1990)

Civil Rights Beyond Black and White

Thomas W. Conger, *The National Congress of American Indians* (1999)

Donald Fixico, *Termination and Relocation: Federal Indian Policy, 1945–1960* (1986)

Manuel G. Gonzalez, *Mexicanos: A History of Mexicans in the United States* (1999)

David G. Gutierrez, *Walls and Mirrors: Mexican Americans, Mexican Immigrants, and the Politics of Ethnicity* (1998)

Gabriel Haslip-Viera, et al., eds, *Boricuans in Gotham: Puerto Ricans and the Making of New York City* (2004)

Mae M. Ngai, *Impossible Subjects: Illegal Aliens and the Making of Modern America* (2004)

David Palumbo-Liu, *Asian Americans: Historical Crossings of a Racial Frontier* (1999)

Maria E. Perez y Gonzalez, *Puerto Ricans in the United States* (2000)

Kenneth R. Philp, *Termination Revisited: American Indians on the Trail to Self-Determination, 1933–1953* (1999)

Zaragosa Vargas, *Labor Rights Are Civil Rights: Mexican American Workers in Twentieth Century America* (2005)

Carmen Theresa Whalen, *From Puerto Rico to Philadelphia: Puerto Rican Workers and Postwar Economies* (2001)

Biography

Robert Dallek, *Flawed Giant: Lyndon B. Johnson and His Times, 1961–1973* (1998)

John D'Emilio, *Lost Prophet: The Life and Times of Bayard Rustin* (2003)

Michael Eric Dyson, *I May Not Get There With You: The True Martin Luther King, Jr.* (2000)

James Forman, *The Making of Black Revolutionaries* (1985)

David J. Garrow, *Bearing the Cross: Martin Luther King, Jr., and the Southern Christian Leadership Conference* (1986)

Chana Kai Lee, *For Freedom's Sake: The Life of Fannie Lou Hamer* (1999)

John Lewis, *Walking With the Wind: A Memoir of the Movement* (1998)

Barbara Ramsey, *Ella Baker and the Black Freedom Movement* (2003)

Jo Ann Gibson Robinson, *The Montgomery Bus Boycott and the Women Who Started It* (1987)

Malcolm X, with Alex Haley, *The Autobiography of Malcolm X* (1965)

CHAPTER 29

Vietnam: America's Longest War

David L. Anderson, *The Columbia Guide to the Vietnam War* (2002)

Christian G. Appy, *Working-Class War: American Combat Soldiers in Vietnam* (1993)

Larry Berman, *No Peace, No Honor: Nixon, Kissinger, and Betrayal in Vietnam* (2001)

Robert Buzzanco, *Vietnam and the Transformation of American Life* (1999)

Kenton J. Clymer, *The Vietnam War: Its History, Literature and Music* (1998)

Gerald J. DeGroot, *A Noble Cause? America and the Vietnam War* (1999)

Michael S. Foley, *Confronting the War Machine: Draft Resistance during the Vietnam War* (2003)

Herman Graham III, *The Brothers' War: Black Power, Manhood, and the Military Experience* (2003)

William M Hammond, *Reporting Vietnam: Media and Military at War* (1998)

George C. Herring, *America's Longest War: The United States and Vietnam, 1950–1975,* 3rd ed. (1996)

————, ed., *The Pentagon Papers,* abridged ed. (1993)

Andrew E. Hunt, *The Turning: A History of Vietnam Veterans Against the War* (1999)

David Kaiser, *American Tragedy: Kennedy, Johnson, and the Origins of the Vietnam War* (2000)

Jeffrey Kimball, *Nixon's Vietnam War* (1998)

Fredrik Logevall, *Choosing War: The Lost Chance for Peace and the Escalation of War in Vietnam* (1999)

Robert Mann, *A Grand Illusion: America's Descent into Vietnam* (2001)

James S. Olson and Randy Roberts, *My Lai: A Brief History with Documents* (1998)

Randy Shilts, *Conduct Unbecoming: Lesbians and Gays in the U.S. Military, Vietnam to the Persian Gulf* (1993)

Fred Turner, *Echoes of Combat: The Vietnam War in American Memory* (1996)

James E. Westheider, *Fighting on Two Fronts: African Americans and the Vietnam War* (1997)

Marilyn B. Young, *The Vietnam Wars, 1945–1990* (1991)

A Generation in Conflict

David Allyn, *Make Love, Not War: The Sexual Revolution, Unfettered History* (2000)

Beth Bailey, *Sex in the Heartland* (1999)

Alexander Bloom and Wini Breines, eds., *Takin' It to the Streets: A Sixties Reader* (1995)

Aniko Bodroghkozy, *Groove Tube: Sixties Television and the Youth Rebellion* (2001)

Peter Braunstein and Michael William Doyle, eds., *Imagine Nation: The American Counterculture of the 1960s and '70s* (2002)

Howard Brick, *Age of Contradiction: American Thought and Culture in the 1960s* (1998)

Paul Buhle and John McMillian, eds., *The New Left Revisited* (2003)

David Farber, *The Age of Great Dreams: America in the 1960s* (1994)

James J. Farrell, *The Spirit of the Sixties: The Making of Postwar Radicalism* (1997)

Jennifer Frost, *"An Interracial Movement of the Poor": Community Organizing and the New Left in the 1960s* (2001)

Maurice Isserman and Michael Kazin, *America Divided: The Civil War of the 1960s* (2000)

Robbie Lieberman, *Prairie Power: Voices of 1960s Midwestern Student Protest* (2004)

Paul Lyons, *New Left, New Right, and the Legacy of the Sixties* (1996)

Mark Hamilton Lytle, *America's Civil Wars: The Sixties Era from Elvis to the Fall of Richard Nixon* (2005)

John C. McWilliams, *The 1960s Cultural Revolution* (2000)

Sidney M. Milkis and Jerome M. Mileur, eds. *The Great Society and the High Tide of Liberalism* (2005)

Timothy Miller, *The 60s Communes: Hippies and Beyond* (1999)

Mark Oppenheimer, *Knocking on Heaven's Door: American Religion in the Age of Counterculture* (2003)

George Rising, *Clean for Gene: Eugene McCarthy's 1968 Presidential Campaign* (1997)

William L. Van Deburg, *New Day in Babylon: The Black Power Movement and American Culture, 1965–1975* (1992)

Mary Ann Wynkoop, *Dissent in the Heartland: The Sixties at Indiana University* (2002)

The Politics of Identity

Kathleen C. Berkeley, *The Women's Liberation Movement in America* (1999)

Winifred Breines, *The Trouble Between Us: An Uneasy History of White and Black Women in the Feminist Movement* (2006)

Dudley Clendinen and Adam Nagourney, *Out for Good: The Struggle to Build a Gay Rights Movement in America* (1999)

Rachel Blau De Plessis and Ann Snitow, *The Feminist Memoir Project: Voices from Women's Liberation* (1998)

Susan J. Douglas, *Where the Girls Are: Growing Up Female with the Mass Media* (1994)

Martin Duberman, *Stonewall* (1993)

Gerald Horne, *Fire This Time: The Watts Uprising and the 1960s* (1995)

Matthew Frye Jacobson, *Roots, Too: White Ethnic Revival in Post–Civil Rights America* (2006)

Blance Linden-Ward and Carol Hurd Green, *American Women in the 1960s* (1993)

Marguerite V. Marin, *Social Protest in an Urban Barrio: A Study of the Chicano Movement, 1966–1974* (1991)

George Mariscal, *Brown-eyed Children of the Sun: Lessons from the Chicano Movement, 1965–1975* (1991)

Peter Matthiessen, *In the Spirit of Crazy Horse* (1992)

Joane Nagel, *American Indian Ethnic Renewal: Red Power and the Resurgence of Identity and Culture* (1996)

Armando Navarro, *Mexican American Youth Organization: Avant-Garde of the Chicano Movement in Texas* (1995)

Jeffrey Ogbonna Green Ogbar, *Black Power: Radical Politics and African American Identity* (2005)

Ruth Rosen, *The World Split Open: How the Modern Women's Movement Changed America* (2000)

Kimberly Springer, *Living for the Revolution: Black Feminist Organizations, 1968–1980* (2005)

Joy Ann Williamson, *Black Power on Campus* (2003)

The Nixon Presidency and Watergate

Mary C. Brennan, *Turning Right in the Sixties: The Conservative Capture of the GOP* (1995)

Robert Dallek, *Nixon and Kissinger* (2007)

J. Brooks Flippen, *Nixon and the Environment* (2000)

Leonard Garment, *In Search of Deep Throat: The Greatest Political Mystery of Our Time* (2000)

Lewis L. Gould, *1968: The Election That Changed America* (1993)

Jussi Hanhimaki, *The Flawed Architect: Henry Kissinger and American Foreign Policy* (2004)

Dean J. Kotlowski, *Nixon's Civil Rights: Politics, Principle, and Policy* (2001)

Frank Kusch, *Battleground Chicago: The Police and the 1968 Democratic National Convention* (2004)

Margaret MacMillan, *Nixon and Mao: The Week That Changed the World* (2007)

Allen J. Matusow, *Nixon's Economy: Booms, Busts, Dollars and Votes* (1998)

Keith W. Olson, *Watergate: The Presidential Scandal that Shook America* (2003)

Richard Reeves, *President Nixon: Alone in the White House* (2001)

Biography

David L. Anderson, ed., *The Human Tradition in the Vietnam Era* (2000)

Avital H. Bloch and Lauri Umansky, eds., *Impossible to Hold: Women and Culture in the 1960s* (2005)

Elaine Brown, *A Taste of Power: A Black Woman's Story* (1992)

Jody Carlson, *George C. Wallace and the Politics of Powerlessness* (1981)

Robert Dallek, *Flawed Giant: Lyndon Johnson and His Times, 1961–1973* (1998)

Robert Dallek, *Nixon and Kissinger* (2007)

Adam Fortunate Eagle, *Heart of the Rock: The Indian Invasion of Alcatraz* (2002)

Robert Alan Goldberg, *Barry Goldwater* (1995)

Elliot Gorn, ed., *Muhammed Ali: The People's Champ* (1996)

Joan Hoff, *Nixon Reconsidered* (1994)

Daniel Horowitz, *Betty Friedan and the Making of the Feminine Mystique: The American Left, the Cold War, and Modern Feminism* (1998)

Maurice Isserman, *The Other American: The Life of Michael Harrington* (2000)

Joseph A. Palermo, *In His Own Right: The Political Odyssey of Senator Robert F. Kennedy* (2001)

Jonah Raskin, *For the Hell of It: The Life and Times of Abbie Hoffman* (1996)

Dominic Sandbrook, *Eugene McCarthy* (2004)

Kenneth S. Stern, *Loud Hawk: The United States versus the American Indian Movement* (1994)

Evan Thomas, *Robert Kennedy: His Life* (2000)

Jack Todd, *Desertion: In the Time of Vietnam* (2001)

Irwin Unger and Debi Unger, *LBJ: A Life* (1999)

CHAPTER 30

The Overextended Society

Edward D. Berkowitz, *Something Happened: A Political and Cultural Overview of the Seventies* (2006)

Michael A. Bernstein and David E. Adler, eds., *Understanding American Economic Decline* (1994)

W. Carl Biven, *Jimmy Carter's Economy: Policy in an Age of Limits* (2002)

Jefferson Cowie and Joseph Heathcott, eds., *Beyond the Ruins: The Meanings of Deindustrialization* (2003)

Claudia Goldin, *Understanding the Gender Gap: An Economic History of American Women* (1990)

Burton I. Kaufman, *The Arab Middle East and the United States: Inter-Arab Rivalry and Superpower Diplomacy* (1996)

Paul Krugman, *Peddling Prosperity: Economic Sense and Nonsense in the Age of Diminished Expectations* (1994)

Bonnie A. Osif, Anthony J. Baratta, and Thomas W. Conkling, *TMI 25 Years Later* (2004)

Bruce J. Schulman, *From Cotton Belt to Sunbelt* (1991)

Jon Teaford, *Cities of the Heartland: The Rise and Fall of the Industrial Midwest* (1993)

J. Samuel Walker, *Three Mile Island: A Nuclear Crisis in Historical Perspective* (2004)

Daniel Yergin, *The Prize: The Epic Quest for Oil, Money, and Power* (1990)

"Lean Year" Presidents

Gary M. Fink and Hugh Davis Graham, eds., *The Carter Presidency: Policy Choices in the Post–New Deal Era* (1998)

John Robert Greene, *The Presidency of Gerald R. Ford* (1995)

Yanek Mieczkowski, *Gerald Ford and the Challenges of the 1970s* (2005)

Gary Sick, *October Surprise: America's Hostages in Iran and the Election of Ronald Reagan* (1991)

The New Conservatism

William C. Berman, *America's Right Turn: From Nixon to Clinton* (1998)

Joel A. Carpenter, *Revive Us Again: The Reawakening of American Fundamentalism* (1997)

Dan T. Carter, *From George Wallace to Newt Gingrich: Race in the Conservative Counterrevolution, 1963–1994* (1996)

Joseph Crespino, *In Search of Another Country: Mississippi and the Conservative Counterrevolution* (2007)

Susan Faludi, *Backlash: The Undeclared War Against American Women* (1991)

Angela Howard and Sasha Ranae Adams Tarrant, eds., *Reaction to the Modern Women's Movement, 1963 to the present* (1997)

Kevin M. Kruse, *White Flight: Atlanta and the Making of Modern Conservatism* (2005)

Matthew D. Lassiter, *The Silent Majority: Suburban Politics in the Sunbelt South* (2005)

William Martin, *With God on Our Side: The Rise of the Religious Right in America* (1996)

Catherine E. Rymph, *Republic Women: Feminism and Conservatism from Suffrage through the Rise of the New Right* (2006)

Bryon E. Shafer and Richard Johnston, *The End of Southern Exceptionalism: Class, Race, and Partisan Change in the Postwar South* (2006)

Grass-Roots Politics

Henry F. Bedford, *Seabrook Station: Citizen Politics and Nuclear Power* (1990)

Nicholas Dagen Bloom, *Suburban Alchemy: 1960s New Towns and the Transformation of the American Dream* (2001)

Craig Cox, *Storefront Revolution: Food Co-ops and the Counterculture* (1994)

David Frum, *How We Got Here: The 70s, The Decade That Brought You Modern Life (For Better or Worse)* (2000)

Lois Gibbs, *Love Canal: The Story Continues* (1998)

Gerald Markowitz and David Rosner, *Deceit and Denial: The Deadly Politics of Industrial Pollution* (2002)

Donald G. Mathews and Jane S. De Hart, *Sex, Gender, and the Politics of ERA* (1990)

Stephen Paul Miller, *The Seventies Now: Culture as Surveillance* (1999)

Gordana Rabrenovic, *Community Builders: A Tale of Neighborhood Mobilization in Two Cities* (1996)

David Brian Robertson, ed., *Loss of Confidence: Politics and Policy in the 1970s* (1998)

Suzanne Staggenborg, *The Pro-Choice Movement: Organization and Activism in the Abortion Conflict* (1991)

Foreign Policy

David Farber, *Taken Hostage: The Iran Hostage Crisis and America's First Encounter with Radical Islam* (2006)

Beth A. Fischer, *The Reagan Reversal: Foreign Policy and the End of the Cold War* (1997)

Mark Gasiorowski, *U.S. Foreign Policy and the Shah* (1991)

Christopher Hemmer, *Which Lessons Matter? American Foreign Policy Decision Making in the Middle East, 1979–1987* (2000)

William M. LeoGrande, *Our Own Backyard: The United States in Central America, 1977–1992* (1998)

Timothy P. Maga, *The World of Jimmy Carter: U.S. Foreign Policy, 1977–1981* (1994)

Jack F. Matlock Jr., *Reagan and Gorbachev: How the Cold War Ended* (2004)

Morris H. Morley, *Washington, Somoza, and the Sandinistas: State and Regime in U.S. Policy toward Nicaragua, 1969–1981* (1994)

Bob Woodward, *Veil: The Secret Wars of the CIA* (1987)

The Reagan Revolution

Dean Baker, The United States since 1980 (2007)

Robert M. Collins, *More: The Politics of Economic Growth in Postwar America* (2000)

Matthew Dallek, *The Right Moment: Ronald Reagan's First Victory and the Decisive Turning Point in American Politics* (2000, 2004)

John Ehrman, *The Eighties: America in the Eighties* (2005)

Nicholas Laham, *Ronald Reagan and the Politics of Immigration Reform* (2000)

Kyle Longley, Jeremy Mayer, Michael Schaller, and John Sloan, *Deconstructing Reagan: Conservative Mythology and America's Fortieth President* (2007)

John W. Sloan, *The Reagan Effect: Economics and Presidential Leadership* (1999)

Gil Troy, *Morning in America: How Ronald Reagan Invented the 1980s* (2005)

Best of Times, Worst of Times

John-Manuel Andriote, *Victory Deferred: How AIDS Changed Gay Life in America* (1999)

James D. Cockcroft, *Outlaws in the Promised Land: Mexican Immigrant Workers and America's Future* (1986)

Robert M. Collins, *Transforming America: Politics and Culture During the Reagan Years* (2006)

Barbara Ehrenreich, *Fear of Falling: The Inner Life of the Middle Class* (1989)

Elizabeth Fee and Daniel M. Fox, eds., *AIDS: The Making of a Chronic Disease* (1992)

Jacqueline Jones, *The Dispossessed: America's Underclasses from the Civil War to the Present* (1992)

Michael B. Katz, ed., *The "Underclass" Debate* (1993)

Hilda Scott, *Working Your Way to the Bottom: The Feminization of Poverty* (1985)

Randy Shilts, *And the Band Played On: Politics, People, and the AIDS Epidemic* (1987)

Ruth Sidel, *Women and Children Last: The Plight of Poor Women in Affluent America* (1986)

Lenore J. Weitzman, *The Divorce Revolution: The Unexpected Social and Economic Consequences for Women and Children in America* (1985)

Richard White, *Rude Awakenings: What the Homeless Crisis Tells Us* (1992)

"A Kinder, Gentler Nation"

Meena Bose and Rosanna Perotti, eds., *From Cold War to New World Order: The Foreign Policy of George H. W. Bush* (2002)

Stephen F. Cohen, *Failed Crusade: America and the Tragedy of Post-Communist Russia* (2000)

John L. Gaddis, *The United States and the End of the Cold War* (1992)

David Halberstam, *War in a Time of Peace: Bush, Clinton, and the Generals* (2001)

William G. Hyland, *Clinton's World: Remaking American Foreign Policy* (1999)

Robert D. Kaplan, *The Coming Anarchy: Shattering the Dreams of the Post–Cold War* (2000)

Tomas W. Lippman, *Madeleine Albright and the New American Diplomacy* (2000)

Robert Litwak, *Rogue States and U.S. Foreign Policy: Containment after the Cold War* (2000)

David Mosler and Bob Catley, *Global America: Imposing Liberalism on a Recalcitrant World* (2000)

Micah L. Sifry and Christopher Cerf, eds., *The Gulf War Reader* (1991)

Jeff Wheelwright, *The Irritable Heart: The Medical Mystery of the Gulf War* (2001)

Biography

Peter G. Bourne, *Jimmy Carter: A Comprehensive Biography from Plains to Postpresidency* (1997)

Jimmy Carter, *Keeping Faith: Memoirs of a President* (1982, 1995)

Rosalynn Carter, *First Lady from Plains* (1984)

Adam Clymer, *Edward M. Kennedy: A Biography* (1999)

Donald T. Critchlow, *Phyllis Schlafly and Grassroots Conservatism* (2005)

Jim Cullen, *Born in the U.S.A.: Bruce Springsteen and the American Tradition* (1997, 2005)

John Patrick Diggins, *Ronald Reagan: Fate, Freedom, and the Making of History* (2007)

Betty Ford, with Chris Chase, *Betty, A Glad Awakening* (1987)

Marshall Frady, *Jesse: The Life and Pilgrimage of Jesse Jackson* (1996)

Ernest B. Furgurson, *The Hard Right: The Rise of Jesse Helms* (1986)

Steven M. Gillon, *The Democrats' Dilemma: Walter F. Mondale and the Legacy of Liberalism* (1992)

Kitty Kelley, *Nancy Reagan* (1991)

Linda J. Lear, *Rachel Carson* (1997)

Peter Meyer, *Defiant Patriot: The Life and Exploits of Lt. Colonel Oliver L. North* (1987)

Edmund Morris, *Dutch: A Memoir of Ronald Reagan* (1999)

William E. Pemberton, *Exit with Honor: The Life and Presidency of Ronald Reagan* (1997)

Ronald Reagan, *The Reagan Diaries* (2007)

Wilbur C. Rich, *Coleman Young and Detroit Politics* (1989)

Tom Wicker, *George Herbert Walker Bush* (2004)

CHAPTER 31

The Clinton Presidency

Lauren Berlant and Lisa Duggan, eds., *Our Monica, Ourselves: The Clinton Affair and the National Interest* (2001)

Sidney Blumenthal, *The Clinton Wars* (2003)

James Carville, *Stickin': The Case for Loyalty* (2000)

Nigel Hamilton, *Bill Clinton: Mastering the Presidency* (2007)

Richard A. Posner, *An Affair of State: The Investigation, Impeachment, and Trial of President Clinton* (1999)

Alvin Z. Rubinstein, Albina Shayevich, and Boris Zlotnikov, eds., *The Clinton Foreign Policy Reader: Presidential Speeches with Commentary* (2000)

Steven E. Schier, ed., *The Postmodern Presidency: Bill Clinton's Legacy in U.S. Politics* (2000)

Susan Schmidt and Michael Weisskopf, *Truth at Any Cost: Ken Starr and the Unmaking of Bill Clinton* (2000)

Hanes Walton Jr., *Reelection: William Jefferson Clinton as a Native-Son Presidential Candidate* (2000)

Alex Waddan, *Clinton's Legacy: A New Democrat in Governance* (2001)

Changing American Communities

David Brooks, *Bobos in Paradise: The New Upper Class and How They Got There* (2000)

Sara M. Evans, *Tidal Wave: How Women Changed America at Century's End* (2003)

Helen Hayes, *U.S. Immigration and the Undocumented: Ambivalent Lives, Furtive Lives* (2001)

Edward S. Herman and Robert W. McChesney, *The Global Media: The New Missionaries of Corporate Capitalism* (1997)

Denis Lynn Daly Heyck, ed., *Barrios and Borderlands: Cultures of Latinos and Latinas in the United States* (1994)

Bill Ong Hing, *Making and Remaking Asian America through Immigration Policy, 1850–1990* (1993)

Godfrey Hodgson, *More Equal Than Others: America from Nixon to the New Century* (2004)

Ted G. Lewis, *Microsoft Rising: . . . and Other Tales of Silicon Valley* (1999)

Neil Howe, *Millennials Rising: The Next Generation* (2000)

New York Times, *The Downsizing of America* (1996)

J. Eric Oliver, *Democracy in Suburbia* (2001)

Mae M. Ngai, *Impossible Subjects: Illegal Aliens and the Making of Modern America* (2005)

Howard Rheingold, *The Virtual Community* (1994)

Adam Ward Rome, *The Bulldozer in the Countryside: Suburban Sprawl and the Rise of American Environmentalism* (2001)

Reed Ueda, *Postwar Immigrant America* (1994)

Bernard P. Wong, *The Chinese in Silicon Valley: Globalization, Social Networks, and Ethnic identity* (2006)

A New Age of Anxiety

John D'Emilio, William B. Turner, Urbashi Vaid, eds., *Creating Damage: Sexuality, Public Politicy and Civil Rights* (2000)

Jewelle Taylor Gibbs, *Race and Justice: Rodney King and O. J. Simpson in a House Divided* (1996)

Anthony Giddens, *Runaway World* (1999)

Chester Hartman, ed., *Double Exposure: Poverty and Race in America* (1997)

Randall Kennedy, *Race, Crime, and the Law* (1997)

Lawrence Levine, *The Opening of the American Mind: Canons, Culture, and History* (1996)

Joanne Meyerowitz, ed. *History and September 11th* (2003)

Christian Parenti, *Lockdown America: Police and Prisons in the Age of Crisis* (1999)

Daniel R. Pinello, *America's Struggle for Same-Sex marriage* (2006)

David M. Reimers, *Unwelcome Strangers: American Identity and the Turn Against Immigration* (1998)

Roger Simon, *Divided We Stand: How Al Gore Beat George Bush and Lost the Presidency* (2001)

Robert C. Smith, *Racism in the Post–Civil Rights Era* (1995)

James D. Tabor and Eugene V. Gallagher, *Why Waco? Cults and the Battle for Religious Freedom in America* (1995)

Stuart A. Wright, *Patriots, Politics, and the Oklahoma City Bombing* (2007)

The Bush Presidency

Rajiv Chandrasekaran, *Imperial Life in the Emerald City: Inside Iraq's Green Zone* (2006)

Alexander Cockburn, Jeffrey St. Clair, and Alan Sekula, *Five Days That Shook the World: Seattle and Beyond* (2000)

William Crotty, ed., *A Defining Moment: The Presidential Election of 2004* (2005)

David Held, ed., *A Globalizing World? Culture, Economics, Politics* (2000)

Joshua Karliner, *The Corporate Planet: Ecology and Politics in the Age of Globalization* (1997)

Margaret Keck and Kathryn Sikkink, *Activists beyond Borders: Advocacy Networks in International Politics* (1998)

Michael T. Klare, *Blood and Oil: The Dangers and Consequences of America's Growing Dependecy (2004)*

Amory Starr, *Naming the Enemy: Anti-Corporate Movements Confront Globalization* (2000)

John D. Wirth, *Smelter Smoke in North America: The Politics of Transborder Pollution* (2000)

Biography

Barbara Bush, *Reflections: Life after the White House* (2003)

Bill Clinton, *My Life* (2004)

Karlene Faith, *Madonna, Brawdy & Soul* (1997)

Nigel Hamilton, *Bill Clinton: An American Journey* (2003)

Molly Ivins and Lou Dubose Shrub: *The Short but Happy Political Life of George W. Bush* (2000)

Joyce Milton, *The First Partner: Hillary Rodham Clinton* (1999)

Kevin Phillips, *American Dynasty* (2004)

Gerald L. Posner, *Citizen Perot: His Life and Times* (1996)

Richard A. Serrano, *One of Ours: Timothy McVeigh and the Oklahoma City Bombing* (1998)

Mel Steely, *The Gentleman from Georgia: The Biography of Newt Gingrich* (2000)

Tom Wicker, *George Herbert Walker Bush* (2004)

Text, Tables, Maps and Figures

Chapter 4   Figure 4.1: Reproduced from *The American Colonies: From Settlement to Independence* Copyright © R.C. Simmons 1976) by permission of PFD (www.pfd.co.uk) on behalf of Professor Richard Simmons. **Figure 4.2:** from TIME ON THE CROSS: THE ECONOMICS OF AMERICAN NEGRO SLAVERY by Robert William Fogel and Stanley L. Engerman. Copyright © 1974 by Robert William Fogel and Stanley L. Engerman. Used by permission of W.W. Norton & Company, Inc.

Chapter 5   Table 5.2: MAIN JACKSON, TURNER; *SOCIAL STRUCTURE OF REVOLUTIONARY AMERICA* © 1965 Princeton University Press, 1993 renewed PUP. Reprinted by permission of Princeton University Press.

Chapter 8   Figure 8.1: Used by permission of Courstesy, American Antiquarian Society.

Chapter 9   Figure 9.2: from AMERICA MOVES WEST 5/E edition by Riegel R. 1971. reprinted with permission of Wadsworth, a division of Thomson Learning: www.thomsonrights.com. Fax 800 730-2215.

Chapter 11   Figure 11.1: From RIGHT TO VOTE by ALEXANDER KEYSSAR. Reprinted by permission of BASIC BOOKS, a member of Perseus Books Group.

Chapter 12   Figure 12.1: Reprinted from Thomas Dublin: *Transforming Women's Work: New England Lives in the Industrial Revolution.* Copyright © 1994 by Thomas Dublin. Used by permission of the Publisher, Cornell University Press.

Chapter 13   Figure 13.1: Reprinted by permission of the estate of Robert Ernst. **Figure 13.2:** From THE ALCOHOLIC REPUBLIC: AN AMERICAN TRADITION by W.J. Rarabaugh, copyright © 1979 by Oxford University Press, Inc. Used by permission of Oxford University Press, Inc. **Map 13.2:** Reprinted from Whitney R. Cross, *The Burned-Over District: The Social and Intellectual History of Enthusiastic Religion in Western New York 1800–1850.* Copyright © 1950 by Cornell University. Used with permission of the publisher, Cornell University Press.

Chapter 14   Figure 14.1: From *The Plains Across: The Overland Emigrants and the Trans-Mississippi West, 1840–60.* Copyright 1979 by the Board of Trustees of the University of Illinois. Used with permission of the University of Illinois Press. **Map 14.7:** From *Historical Atlas of California,* by Warren A. Beck and Ynez D. Haase. Copyright © 1974 by The University of Oklahoma Press, Norman. Reprinted by permission of the publisher. All rights reserved.

Chapter 18   Page 507: Reprinted from *Land of the Spotted Eagle* by Luther Standing Bear by permission of University of Nebraska Press. Copyright, 1933 by Luther Standing Bear. Renewal copyright, 1960, by May Jones. **Map 18.1:** From *Historical Atlas of Oklahoma, 3rd edition,* by John W. Morris, Charles R. Goins and Edwin C. McReynolds. Copyright © 1965, 1976, 1986 by the University of Oklahoma Press, Norman. Reprinted by permission of the publisher. All rights reserved. **Map 18.4:** The Geography of the American West, 1847–1964', Donald W. Meinig from *ANNA: Annals of the*

Association of American Geographers, vol. 55, issue 2. Reprinted by permission of Blackwell Publishers. www.blackwell-synergy.com

Chapter 19   Table 19.1: From THE GILDED AGE edited by Charles W. Calhown. © 1996. Reprinted by permission of Rowman & Littlefield. **Map 19.2:** From *Historical Atlas of the United States,* 1st edition by LORD. © 1962. Reprinted with permission of Wadsworth, a division of Thomson Learning: www.thomsonrights.com. Fax: 800 730-2215.

Chapter 22   Map 22.3: From *ATLAS OF AMERICAN WOMEN,* by Barbara C. Shortridge.1987. Reprinted by permission of Thomson Learning: www.thomsonrights.com. Fax 800 730-2215.

Chapter 24   Page 688: Los Angeles Times.

Chapter 25   Page 715: From THE COLLECTED POEMS OF LANGSTON HUGHES by Langston Hughes, copyright © 1994 by The Estate of Langston Hughes. Used by permission of Alfred A. Knopf, a division of Random House, Inc. **Page 729:** From Atomicarchive.com. Used with permission.

Chapter 27   Page 778: Copyright © 1957 by The New York Times Co. Reprinted with permission. **Page 779:** Copyright 1957 U.S. News & World Report, L.P. Reprinted with permission. **Page 790:** Six lines from "HOWL" FROM COLLECTED POEMS 1947–1980 by Allen Ginsberg. Copyright © 1955 by Allen Ginsberg. Reprinted by permission of HarperCollins Publishers.

Chapter 28   Page 817: Reprinted by arrangement with the Estate of Martin Luther King Jr., c/o Writers House for the proprietor New York, NY. *Copyright 1963 Martin Luther King, Jr., copyright renewed 1991 Coretta Scott King.* **Page 818:** http://www.silvertorch.com/ **Page 819:** Reprinted by arrangement with the Estate of Martin Luther King Jr., c/o Writers House for the proprietor New York, NY. *Copyright 1963 Martin Luther King, Jr., copyright renewed 1991 Coretta Scott King.* **Page 825:** Reprinted by arrangement with the Estate of Martin Luther King Jr., c/o Writers House for the proprietor New York, NY. *Copyright 1965 Martin Luther King, Jr., copyright renewed 1991 Coretta Scott King.*

Chapter 29   Page 838: San Francisco, John Phillips © 1967 Universal MCA Music Publishing **Page 838:** Copyright © 1963 by Warner Bros. Inc. Copyright renewed 1991 Special Rider Music. All rights reserved. International copyright secured. Reprinted by permission. **Figure 29.6:** From THE GALLUP POLL, 1835–1971 by George Gallup, Copyright © 1972 by the American Institute of Public Opinion. Used by permission of Random House.

Chapter 30   Page 874: Robert Leppzer, *Voices from Three Mile Island: The People Speak Out* (Trumansburg, NY: The Crossing Press, 1980). **Page 875:** Excerpts from the textbook WHERE THE EVIDENCE LEADS: AN AUTOBIOGRAPHY, by Dick Thornburgh, © 2003. All rights controlled by the University of Pittsburgh Press, Pittsburgh, PA 15260. Used by permission of University of Pittsburgh Press. **Figure 30.2:** From Encyclopedia of American Social History (3 volumes) 1st edition by Peter W. Cayton and Mary Kupiec Williams (editors). 1993. reprinted with permission of Gale, a division of Thomson Learning: www.thomsonrights.com. Fax 800 730-2215.

Photos

Chapter 1 Chapter Opener: Cahokia Mounds State Historic Site, painting by Michael Hampshire. **Page 3:** James Chatters/James Chatters/Agence France Presse/Getty Images **Page 5:** ©Warren Morgan/CORBIS **Page 12 (top left):** David Muench/CORBIS-NY **Page 12 (bottom right):** Tony Linck/ SuperStock, Inc. **Page 14:** Bayerische Staatsbibliothek Munchen... Rar. 5k.

Chapter 2 Page 28: October, from Tres Riches Heures du Duc de Berry. Musee Conde, Chantilly/Bridgeman-Giraudon, Art Resource, NY **Page 31:** Beinecke Rare Book and Manuscript Library, Yale University **Page 32:** The Granger Collection **Page 34:** Photo Courtesy of the Edward E. Ayer Collection, The Newberry Library, Chicago **Page 35 (top):** Beinecke Rare Book and Manuscript Library, Yale University **Page 35 (bottom):** The Granger Collection **Page 42:** Olive and Arthur Kelsall/Nova Scotia Museum **Page 44:** John White (1570–93), "Woman and Child of Pomeiooc." Watercolor. British Museum, London. The Bridgeman Art Library International Ltd.

Chapter 3 Chapter Opener: Beinecke Rare Book and Manuscript Library, Yale University **Page 51:** Kevin Fleming/Corbis/Bettmann **Page 53:** Courtesy of the Library of Congress **Page 55:** From Samuel de Champlain, Les Voyages, Paris, 1613. Illustration opp. pg. 232. Rare Books Division, The New York Public Library, Astor Lenox and Tilden Foundations. The New York Public Library/Art Resource, NY **Page 56:** Getty Images Inc. - Hulton Archive Photos **Page 57 (top left):** Virginia Historical Society **Page 57 (bottom right):** The Granger Collection **Page 61:** Courtesy, American Antiquarian Society **Pages 62–63:** The Granger Collection, New York **Page 64:** Courtesy of The John Carter Brown Library, at Brown University. **Page 67 (bottom):** Courtesy of The Historical Society of Pennsylvania Collection, Atwater Kent Museum of Philadelphia. **Page 69:** Courtesy of the John Carter Brown Library at Brown University.

Chapter 4 Chapter Opener: Courtesy of the Library of Congress **Page 77:** Library of Congress **Page 78:** Beinecke Rare Book and Manuscript Library, Yale University **Page 81:** Bibliotheque de L'Arsenal, Paris, France/The Bridgeman Art Library **Page 83 (top left):** The Granger Collection, New York **Page 83 (bottom right):** The Granger Collection, New York **Pages 84–85:** Courtesy of the Library of Congress **Page 90:** Courtesy of the Massachusetts Historical Society, Boston. **Page 101:** Virginia Historical Society, Richmond, Virginia.

Chapter 5 Chapter Opener: MARK SEXTON/The Granger Collection **Page 110:** Laurie Platt Winfrey, Inc. **Page 111:** Jack W. Dykinga/Jack Dykinga Photography **Page 112:** EROS Data Center, U.S. Geological Survey **Page 117:** Beinecke Rare Book and Manuscript Library, Yale University **Page 119 (left):** The Granger Collection **Page 119 (right):** The Granger Collection **Page 123:** "Human Races (Las Castas)", 18th century, oil on canvas, 1.04 x 1.48 m. Museo Nacional del Virreinato, Tepotzotlan, Mexico. Schalkwijk/Art Resource, NY **Page 126:** Art Resource/The New York Public Library, Research Libraries **Pages 128–129:** Mary Evans Picture Library/Photo Researchers, Inc.

Chapter 6 Chapter Opener: The Granger Collection, New York **Page 142:** National Museum of the American Indian/Smithsonian Institution **Page 144:** Art Resource/The New York Public Library **Page 149:** Library of Congress **Page 150:** Library of Congress **Page 152:** © Christie's Images Inc. 2004 **Page 154:** National Archives and Records Administration **Page 155:** The New York Public Library, Prints Division, Stokes Collection **Page 158:** The Granger Collection **Page 159:** The Granger Collection **Pages 160–161:** Library of Congress.

Chapter 7 Chapter Opener: The Granger Collection **Page 167:** Anne S.K. Brown Military Collection, John Hay Library, Brown University **Page 169:** The Granger Collection **Page 173:** Gilbert Stuart, "The Mohawk Chief Joseph Brant," 1786. Oil on canvas, 30 x 25 in. Fenimore Art Museum, Cooperstown, New York **Page 178:** The Granger Collection, New York **Page 180:** Library of Congress **Page 183:** © CORBIS **Pages 184–185:** Library of Congress **Page 188:** Corbis/Bettmann **Page 189:** ©Bettmann/CORBIS.

Chapter 8 Chapter Opener: The Granger Collection **Page 197:** Print and Picture Collection, The Free Library of Philadelphia. **Pages 200–201:** Kenneth Garrett/National Geographic Image Collection **Page 203 (left):** Smithsonian Institution, NNC, Douglas Mudd. **Page 203 (right):** Smithsonian Institution, NNC, Douglas Mudd. **Page 204:** John Trumbull (1756–1843), "Portrait of Alexander Hamilton" (1755/57–1804), statesman, 1806, oil on canvas, 76.2 x 61 cm (20 x 24 in). Gift of Henry Cabot Lodge. National Portrait Gallery, Smithsonian Institution, Washington, DC/Art Resource, NY **Page 208:** Beinecke Rare Book and Manuscript Library, Yale University **Page 213:** The Granger Collection.

Chapter 9 Page 223: Illustration by Kittlitz, F. H. v. (Friedrich Heinrich von) in Litke, F. P. (Fedor Petrovich), Voyage autour du monde, exécuté par ordre de Sa Majesté l'empereur Nicolas 1er, sur la corvette le Séniavine, dans les années 1826, 1827, 1828. [Rare Book C0024] Alaska and Polar Regions Collections, Elmer E. Rasmuson Library, University of Alaska Fairbanks. **Page 225:** National Museum of American History, Smithsonian Institution, Photo No. 73–11287 **Page 227 (left):** Courtesy of the Library of Congress **Page 227 (right):** Library of Congress **Page 233 (left):** The Granger Collection, New York **Pages 234–235:** Library of Congress **Page 237:** Courtesy of the Bostonian Society/Old State House **Page 239:** The Granger Collection **Page 242 (top):** Courtesy of the Library of Congress **Page 242 (bottom):** Courtesy of the Library of Congress

Chapter 10 Chapter Opener: The Granger Collection, New York **Page 253:** Copyright © The Granger Collection, New York/The Granger Collection **Page 257 (top):** Library of Congress **Page 257 (bottom):** Culver Pictures, Inc. **Page 262 (top left):** Monticello/Thomas Jefferson Foundation, Inc. **Page 265 (top left):** The Granger Collection **Page 265 (bottom left):** Library of Congress **Page 266 (left):** American Numismatic Society of New York **Page 266 (right):** American Numismatic Society of New York **Page 267:** Carl G. von Iwonski, Block House, New Braunfels. Daughters of the Republic of Texas Library. Yanaguana Society Collection **Page 270:** Corbis/Bettmann **Page 271:** Courtesy of the Library of Congress **Pages 272–273:** Library of Congress

Chapter 11 Chapter Opener: Courtesy of the Library of Congress **Page 287:** Courtesy of the Library of Congress **Page 289:** Robert Cruikshank. "The President's Levee, or all Creation going to the White House. Courtesy of the Library of Congress **Page 290 (top left):** The Granger Collection, New York **Page 290 (bottom left):** The Granger Collection **Page 295:** Courtesy of the Library of Congress **Pages 296–297:** Courtesy of the Library of Congress **Page 299:** Library of Congress **Page 301:** Courtesy, American Antiquarian Society **Page 302:** Collection of the Boston Athenaeum.

Chapter 12 Page 311: The Granger Collection **Page 314:** Library of Congress **Page 317:** Chicago Historical Society **Page 319:** Lee Snider/Corbis/Bettmann **Page 321 (top):** James L. Amos/National Geographic Image Collection **Page 321 (bottom):** Joseph H. Bailey/National Geographic Image Collection **Page 323:** Courtesy American Antiquarian Society **Page 324:** Baker Library, Harvard Business School **Pages 326–327:** Print Collection, Miriam and Ira D. Wallach Division of Art, Prints and Photographs. The New York Public Library, Astor, Lenox and Tilden Foundations. **Page 330:** Library of Congress.

Chapter 25 Chapter Opener: Library of Congress **Page 707:** Navy Visual News Service **Page 708:** AP Wide World Photos **Page 710:** Harry_Todd/Getty Images Inc.-Hulton Archive Photos **Page 713:** © Bettmann/CORBIS **Page 714:** National Archives and Records Administration **Page 718:** National Archives and Records Administration **Page 719:** Stilpx/NARA National/National Archives and Records Administration **Page 723:** Fred Ramage/Getty Images Inc.-Hulton Archive Photos **Page 724:** Courtesy of the Library of Congress **Pages 728–729:** National Archives and Records Administration.

Chapter 26 Chapter Opener: Courtesy of the Library of Congress **Page 742:** UPI/Corbis/Bettmann **Page 745:** Corbis/Bettmann **Page 746:** AP Wide World Photos **Page 747:** ©Bettmann/CORBIS **Page 749:** Michael Barson/Michael Barson **Pages 752–753:** Getty Images Inc.-Hulton Archive Photos **Page 754:** Hank Walker/Getty Images/Time Life Pictures **Page 756:** Conelrad Collection **Page 758:** Harold M Lambert/Getty Images Inc.-Hulton Archive Photos **Page 762:** CORBIS- NY **Page 763:** AP Wide World Photos.

Chapter 27 Chapter Opener: Getty Images, Inc. **Page 772:** ©Bettmann/CORBIS **Page 773:** ©Bettmann/CORBIS **Page 777:** Bernard Hoffman/Bernard Hoffman/Life Magazine/©1950 TimePix **Pages 778–779:** Getty Images Inc.-Hulton Archive Photos **Page 783:** Getty Images, Inc. **Page 786:** Getty Images Inc.-Hulton Archive Photos **Page 787:** PPP/Popperfoto/Getty Images/Retrofile **Page 788:** Bettmann/Corbis/Bettmann **Page 789:** Globe Photos, Inc. **Page 791:** Bettmann/Corbis/Bettmann **Page 795:** Getty Images Inc.-Hulton Archive Photos **Page 796 (top left):** AP Wide World Photos **Page 796 (bottom left):** Robert Jackson/Dallas Morning News **Page 796 (top right):** Getty Images, Inc.

Chapter 28 Chapter Opener: Courtesy of the Library of Congress **Page 804:** Frank Driggs Collection **Page 805:** Corbis/Bettmann **Page 807:** Ed Clark/Getty Images/Time Life Pictures **Page 808 (left):** The Oakland Tribune **Page 808 (right):** Library of Congress **Page 810:** News & Record Library/John G. Moebes **Page 814:** Corbis/Bettmann **Pages 818–819:** © Bettmann/CORBIS All Rights Reserved **Page 821:** Black Star **Page 822:** Steve Schapiro/Black Star **Page 823:** Library of Congress **Page 826:** Benson Latin American Collection **Page 829:** Michael Newman/PhotoEdit Inc.

Chapter 29 Chapter Opener: SSG Paul Halverson/U.S. Army Photo **Page 836:** Jim Pickerell/Black Star **Page 838:** Peter Simon/Peter Simon **Pages 840–841:** Library of Congress **Page 842:** AP Wide World Photos **Page 843:** From "THE VIETNAM PHOTO BOOK" by Mark Jury. Copyright © 1971, 1986 by Mark Jury Preface copyright © 1986 by Bernard Edelman. Used by permission of Random House, Inc. **Page 850:** Library of Congress **Page 851:** Matt Herron/© 2001 Matt Herron c/o Mira.com **Page 852:** AP Wide World Photos **Page 855:** Paul Fusco/Magnum Photos, Inc. **Page 859:** Getty Images Inc.-Hulton Archive Photos **Page 860:** Nick Ut/AP Wide World Photos **Page 862:** CORBIS-NY.

Chapter 30 Chapter Opener: Owen Franken/Corbis/Bettmann **Page 873:** AP Wide World Photos **Pages 874–875:** Laimute E. Druskis/Pearson Education/PH College **Page 877:** Corbis/Bettmann **Page 878:** AP Wide World Photos **Page 880:** AP Wide World Photos **Page 881:** Dennis Brack/Black Star **Page 883:** Wally McNamee/CORBIS-NY **Page 885:** AP Wide World Photos **Page 888:** AP Wide World Photos **Page 892:** AP Wide World Photos **Page 893:** Robert Maass/CORBIS- NY.

Chapter 31 Chapter Opener: REUTERS/Pool/Beth Kaiser/Corbis/Reuters America LLC **Page 902:** Susan Walsh/AP Wide World Photos **Page 903:** AP Wide World Photos **Page 904:** Getty Images, Inc. **Page 905:** AP Wide World Photos **Page 908:** AP Wide World Photos **Page 910:** Chris Pizzello/AP Wide World Photos **Page 911:** Agence France Presse/Getty Images **Pages 912–913:** Marcio Jose Sanchez/AP Wide World Photos **Page 916:** AFP/Agence France Presse/Getty Images **Page 917:** Getty Images, Inc. **Page 920:** AP Wide World Photos **Page 922:** Reuters/Landov LLC **Page 924:** David J. Phillip/AP Wide World Photos.

INDEX

SINGLE PC LICENSE AGREEMENT AND LIMITED WARRANTY

READ THIS LICENSE CAREFULLY BEFORE OPENING THIS PACKAGE. BY OPENING THIS PACKAGE, YOU ARE AGREEING TO THE TERMS AND CONDITIONS OF THIS LICENSE. IF YOU DO NOT AGREE, DO NOT OPEN THE PACKAGE. PROMPTLY RETURN THE UNOPENED PACKAGE AND ALL ACCOMPANYING ITEMS TO THE PLACE YOU OBTAINED THEM.

1. GRANT OF LICENSE and OWNERSHIP: The enclosed computer programs <<and data>> ("Software") are licensed, not sold, to you by Pearson Education, Inc. publishing as Pearson Prentice Hall ("We" or the "Company") and in consideration of your purchase or adoption of the accompanying Company textbooks and/or other materials, and your agreement to these terms. We reserve any rights not granted to you. You own only the disk(s) but we and/or our licensors own the Software itself. This license allows you to use and display your copy of the Software on a single computer (i.e., with a single CPU) at a single location for academic use only, so long as you comply with the terms of this Agreement. You may make one copy for back up, or transfer your copy to another CPU, provided that the Software is usable on only one computer.

2. RESTRICTIONS: You may not transfer or distribute the Software or documentation to anyone else. Except for backup, you may not copy the documentation or the Software. You may not network the Software or otherwise use it on more than one computer or computer terminal at the same time. You may not reverse engineer, disassemble, decompile, modify, adapt, translate, or create derivative works based on the Software or the Documentation. You may be held legally responsible for any copying or copyright infringement that is caused by your failure to abide by the terms of these restrictions.

3. TERMINATION: This license is effective until terminated. This license will terminate automatically without notice from the Company if you fail to comply with any provisions or limitations of this license. Upon termination, you shall destroy the Documentation and all copies of the Software. All provisions of this Agreement as to limitation and disclaimer of warranties, limitation of liability, remedies or damages, and our ownership rights shall survive termination.

4. LIMITED WARRANTY AND DISCLAIMER OF WARRANTY: Company warrants that for a period of 60 days from the date you purchase this SOFTWARE (or purchase or adopt the accompanying textbook), the Software, when properly installed and used in accordance with the Documentation, will operate in substantial conformity with the description of the Software set forth in the Documentation, and that for a period of 30 days the disk(s) on which the Software is delivered shall be free from defects in materials and workmanship under normal use. The Company does not warrant that the Software will meet your requirements or that the operation of the Software will be uninterrupted or error-free. Your only remedy and the Company's only obligation under these limited warranties is, at the Company's option, return of the disk for a refund of any amounts paid for it by you or replacement of the disk. THIS LIMITED WARRANTY IS THE ONLY WARRANTY PROVIDED BY THE COMPANY AND ITS LICENSORS, AND THE COMPANY AND ITS LICENSORS DISCLAIM ALL OTHER WARRANTIES, EXPRESS OR IMPLIED, INCLUDING WITHOUT LIMITATION, THE IMPLIED WARRANTIES OF MERCHANTABILITY AND FITNESS FOR A PARTICULAR PURPOSE. THE COMPANY DOES NOT WARRANT, GUARANTEE OR MAKE ANY REPRESENTATION REGARDING THE ACCURACY, RELIABILITY, CURRENTNESS, USE, OR RESULTS OF USE, OF THE SOFTWARE.

5. LIMITATION OF REMEDIES AND DAMAGES: IN NO EVENT, SHALL THE COMPANY OR ITS EMPLOYEES, AGENTS, LICENSORS, OR CONTRACTORS BE LIABLE FOR ANY INCIDENTAL, INDIRECT, SPECIAL, OR CONSEQUENTIAL DAMAGES ARISING OUT OF OR IN CONNECTION WITH THIS LICENSE OR THE SOFTWARE, INCLUDING FOR LOSS OF USE, LOSS OF DATA, LOSS OF INCOME OR PROFIT, OR OTHER LOSSES, SUSTAINED AS A RESULT OF INJURY TO ANY PERSON, OR LOSS OF OR DAMAGE TO PROPERTY, OR CLAIMS OF THIRD PARTIES, EVEN IF THE COMPANY OR AN AUTHORIZED REPRESENTATIVE OF THE COMPANY HAS BEEN ADVISED OF THE POSSIBILITY OF SUCH DAMAGES. IN NO EVENT SHALL THE LIABILITY OF THE COMPANY FOR DAMAGES WITH RESPECT TO THE SOFTWARE EXCEED THE AMOUNTS ACTUALLY PAID BY YOU, IF ANY, FOR THE SOFTWARE OR THE ACCOMPANYING TEXTBOOK. BECAUSE SOME JURISDICTIONS DO NOT ALLOW THE LIMITATION OF LIABILITY IN CERTAIN CIRCUMSTANCES, THE ABOVE LIMITATIONS MAY NOT ALWAYS APPLY TO YOU.

6. GENERAL: THIS AGREEMENT SHALL BE CONSTRUED IN ACCORDANCE WITH THE LAWS OF THE UNITED STATES OF AMERICA AND THE STATE OF NEW YORK, APPLICABLE TO CONTRACTS MADE IN NEW YORK, EXCLUDING THE STATE'S LAWS AND POLICIES ON CONFLICTS OF LAW, AND SHALL BENEFIT THE COMPANY, ITS AFFILIATES, AND ASSIGNEES. THIS AGREEMENT IS THE COMPLETE AND EXCLUSIVE STATEMENT OF THE AGREEMENT BETWEEN YOU AND THE COMPANY AND SUPERSEDES ALL PROPOSALS OR PRIOR AGREEMENTS, ORAL, OR WRITTEN, AND ANY OTHER COMMUNICATIONS BETWEEN YOU AND THE COMPANY OR ANY REPRESENTATIVE OF THE COMPANY RELATING TO THE SUBJECT MATTER OF THIS AGREEMENT. If you are a U.S. Government user, this Software is licensed with "restricted rights" as set forth in subparagraphs (a)–(d) of the Commercial Computer-Restricted Rights clause at FAR 52.227-19 or in subparagraphs (c)(1)(ii) of the Rights in Technical Data and Computer Software clause at DFARS 252.227-7013, and similar clauses, as applicable.

Should you have any questions concerning this agreement or if you wish to contact the Company for any reason, please contact in writing: Legal Department, Prentice Hall, 1 Lake Street, Upper Saddle River, NJ 07450 or call Pearson Education Product Support at 1-800-677-6337.